Anonymous

Supplement to the Catalogue of the Public Library

of New South Wales, Sydney, Reference Department

Anonymous

Supplement to the Catalogue of the Public Library
of New South Wales, Sydney, Reference Department

ISBN/EAN: 9783337323615

Printed in Europe, USA, Canada, Australia, Japan

Cover: Foto ©ninafisch / pixelio.de

More available books at **www.hansebooks.com**

SUPPLEMENT

TO THE

CATALOGUE

OF THE

PUBLIC LIBRARY OF NEW SOUTH WALES, SYDNEY,

FOR THE YEARS

1893-95.

REFERENCE DEPARTMENT.

SYDNEY: WILLIAM APPLEGATE GULLICK, GOVERNMENT PRINTER.
1897.

SUPPLEMENTARY CATALOGUE—1893-95.

A

A.C. [*See* Essai de la Langue de Viti.] MK 1 R 48

A.M. [*See* Aynme-San.] J 4 U 14

A.R. [*See* Designs for Church Embroidery.] A 12 S 17†

AARON, Dr. E. Murray-. The Butterfly-hunters in the Caribbees. 8vo. New York, 1894. D 17 S 10

ABBEY, E. A. She stoops to conquer. Illustrated. [*See* Goldsmith, Oliver.] H 40 T 3‡

ABBOTT, Dr. Chas. C. The Birds about us. Illustrated. 8vo. Philad., 1895. A 27 S 22

ABBOTT, Rev. Dr. Edwin A. Latin prose through English Idiom: Rules and Exercises on Latin Prose Composition. 12mo. Lond., 1887. K 16 P 41

ABBOTT, Dr. Evelyn. Pericles and the Golden Age of Athens. 8vo. New York, 1892. B 27 Q 8

ABBOTT, John. Correspondence on the Claim of John Abbott to a Pension. 8vo. Hobart, 1862. MF 1 Q 35

ABDUR RAHMAN, Ameer of Afghanistan. [Life of]; by S. Wheeler. 12mo. Lond., 1895. C 22 P 8

A'BECKETT, Gilbert A. Quizziology of the British Drama. 12mo. Lond., 1846. H 4 P 39

A'BECKETT, Thos. T. The Legislative Council: its Past and Future, considered with reference to proposals for its reform. 8vo. Melb. 1874. MJ 3 Q 10

The Power of the Purse considered constitutionally. 8vo. Melb., 1867. MF 2 T 71

ABELARD. [*See* Compayré, G.] G 18 Q 6

ABER, Prof. Wm. M. The Oswego State Normal School. 8vo. New York, 1893. G 18 R 25

ABERCROMBIE, Dr. John. Inquiries concerning the Intellectual Powers and the Investigation of Truth. 14th ed. 12mo. Lond., 1855. G 7 U 31

Philosophy of the Moral Feelings. 8th ed. 12mo. Lond., 1849. G 9 V 23

Portrait of. [*See* Lowe, Dr. J.—Medical Missions.] G 3 P 25

ABERDEEN, Earl of. [Life of]; by the Hon. Sir A. Gordon. (Prime Ministers of Queen Victoria.) 8vo. Lond., 1893. C 13 P 28

ABNEY, Capt. Wm. de W. Colour Vision: being the Tyndall Lectures, 1894. Illustrated. 8vo. Lond., 1895. A 21 T 35

ABORIGINES in the British Colonies, Information respecting. 8vo. Lond., 1838. MG 1 R 77

Aborigines of Australia and Pacific Islands. Photographs. Fol. Sydney, 1895. MA 45‡

ABOUT, Edmond. Masonic Reform. 12mo. Melb. MJ 3 P 10

ABRAHAM, Felix. The New Era of the Goldmining Industry in the Witwatersrand [S. Africa]. Translated by H. C. Simonsen. With an authentic Map of the Fields. 8vo. Lond., 1894. A 24 S 12

ABÛ SÂLIH, the Armenian. Churches and Monasteries of Egypt and some neighbouring Countries. Translated by B. T. A. Evetts; with notes by A. J. Butler. Sm. 4to. Oxford, 1895. G 16 U 20

Another Copy, with Arabic Text. [*See* Anecdota Oxoniensia, Sem. ser., 7.] E

ACADÉMIE DES SCIENCES, Comptes Rendus Hebdomadaires des Séances. Tomes 114-119. 4to. Paris, 1892-94. E

ACADEMY OF NATURAL SCIENCES, PHILADELPHIA. Proceedings, 1892-1894. 8vo. Philad., 1893-1895. E

ACCLIMATISATION SOCIETY OF N.S.W. Annual Reports, 1864-1867. 8vo. Sydney, 1862-1868. MA 2 T 30

ACCLIMATISATION SOCIETY OF QUEENSLAND. Report for 1878. 8vo. Brisb., 1879. ME 5 Q

ACORN. The Future of Victoria. [*See* Victoria.] MF 2 P 47

ACTON, E. Hamilton. Physiology of Plants. [*See* Darwin, F.] A 20 Q 13

ACUÑA, R. A. Leyes Constitucionales. [*See* Ovalle, E. O.] F 7 U 17

ACWORTH, W. M. The State in relation to Railways. (A policy of Free Exchange.) 8vo. Lond., 1894. F 14 S 26

ADAM, G. Mercer. Sandow on Physical Training. [*See* Sandow, E.]   A 29 U 32

ADAMNAN, Abbot of Iona. Vita S. Columbae. Edited, with Notes and Glossary, by Dr. J. J. Fowler. [Latin Text.] 8vo. Oxford, 1894.   G 2 U 1

ADAMS, B. The Law of Civilization and Decay. 8vo. Lond., 1895.   F 11 U 21

ADAMS, Dr. Chas. K. Manual of Historical Literature, comprising brief Descriptions of the most important Histories in English, French, and German. 3rd ed. 8vo. New York, 1889.   K 19 R 10

ADAMS, Estelle Davenport. The Poets' Praise, from Homer to Swinburne. 8vo. Lond., 1894.   H 7 S 42

ADAMS, Francis W. L. The Australians: a social sketch. 8vo. Lond., 1893.*   MF 1 Q 40
A Child of the Age. 8vo. Lond., 1894.   MJ 3 Q 14
John Webb's End: Australian Bush Life. 12mo. Lond., 1891.   MJ 3 Q 41
The New Egypt: a Social Sketch. 12mo. Lond., 1893.   D 14 P 6
Songs of the Army of the Night. 12mo. Lond., 1894.   MH 1 U 58

ADAMS, Prof. George B. Civilization during the Middle Ages, especially in relation to Modern Civilization. 8vo. Lond., 1894.   B 25 R 4

ADAMS, Dr. Henry Carter. Taxation in the United States, 1789–1816. (Johns Hopkins University Studies, 2.) 8vo. Baltimore, 1884.   B 18 S 2

ADAMS, Dr. Herbert B. Account of E. A. Freeman's Visit to Baltimore. (Johns Hopkins University Studies, 1.) 8vo. Baltimore, 1882.   B 18 S 1
The Germanic Origin of New England Towns; with Notes on Co-operation in University Work. (Johns Hopkins University Studies, 1.) 8vo. Baltimore, 1882.   B 18 S 1
Maryland's Influence upon Land Cessions to the United States; with Minor Papers on George Washington's Interest in Western Lands, the Potomac Company, and a National University; Origin of the Baltimore and Ohio Railroad. (Johns Hopkins University Studies, 3.) 8vo. Baltimore, 1885.   B 18 S 3
Methods of Historical Study. (Johns Hopkins University Studies, 2.) 8vo. Baltimore, 1884.   B 18 S 2
Norman Constables in America. (Johns Hopkins University Studies, 1.) 8vo. Baltimore, 1883.   B 18 S 1
Notes on the Literature of Charities. (Johns Hopkins University Studies, 5.) 8vo. Baltimore, 1887.   B 18 S 5
Saxon Tithing-men in America. (Johns Hopkins University Studies, 1.) 8vo. Baltimore, 1883.   B 18 S 1
Seminary Libraries and University Extension. (Johns Hopkins University Studies, 5.) 8vo. Baltimore, 1887.   B 18 S 5

ADAMS, Dr. H. B., VINCENT, Dr. J. M., and SCAIFE, Dr. W. B. Seminary Notes on recent Historical Literature. (Johns Hopkins University Studies, 8.) 8vo. Baltimore, 1890.   B 18 S 8

——— and WOOD, Dr. Henry. Columbus and his Discovery of America. (Johns Hopkins University Studies, 10.) 8vo. Baltimore, 1892.   B 18 S 10

ADAMS, Capt. H. E. G. Korea. [*See* Cavendish, Capt. A. E. J.]   D 17 U 21

ADAMS, John. Sketch of. [*See* Thompson, R. W.—Recollections of Sixteen Presidents.]   C 18 T 21, 22
Sketch of. [*See* Wilson, J. G.—Presidents of the United States.]   C 2 V 30

ADAMS, John Quincy. Sketch of. [*See* Thompson, R. W.—Recollections of Sixteen Presidents.]   C 18 T 21, 22
Sketch of. [*See* Wilson, J. G.—Presidents of the United States.]   C 2 V 30

ADAMS, Philip F. Hand-book for Determination of the True Meridian by Observation of Circumpolar Stars at their greatest elongations. 4to. Sydney, 1876.   MA 9 P 31 †
Sending and Judging of Wine Samples in connection with the Competition for National Prizes. 8vo. Sydney, 1893.   MA 1 Q 73

ADAMS, Samuel, the Man of the Town Meeting. [*See* Hosmer, Prof. J. K.]   B 18 S 2

ADAMS, Sebastian C. Chronological Chart of Ancient, Modern, and Biblical History synchronized. Fol. Cincinnati (n.d.)   B 8 P 22 ‡

ADAMS, W. M. The House of the Hidden Places: a clue to the Creed of Early Egypt from Egyptian sources. 12mo. Lond., 1895.   G 2 U 7

ADAMSON, D. B. Improvements in the Construction of Curre's Di-electric Machine. (Trans. Roy. Soc., S. Australia, 6.) 8vo. Adelaide, 1883.   ME 1 S

ADAMSON, Prof. Robert. Fichte, Philosopher. [*See* Fichte, J. G.]   G 9 V 4

ADAMSON, T. Index to Acts of Parliament, Sessions 21–24, Vict., 1858–61. Sm. fol. Melb. (n.d.)   ME

ADAMSON, Wm. Australian Gardener: an Epitome of Horticulture for Victoria. 13th ed., revised by W. Elliott. 8vo. Melb., 1891.   MA 1 R 53

ADDISON, G. C. Digest of Criminal and Magistrates' Cases decided in New South Wales, 1840–94. Roy. 8vo. Sydney, 1895.   MF 3 R 58

ADDISON, Joseph. Cato: a Tragedy. [See London Stage, 2.] H 2 S 31
Essays, Moral and Humourous. 8vo. Edinb., 1839. J 8 V 8
Sir Roger de Coverley; with Notes and Illustrations. 8vo. Lond., 1850. J 4 Q 37
Ten Essays from The Spectator. [See Harlin, T.] MJ 2 T 28
——— and STEELE, Sir Richard. The Spectator: Selected Essays, with Notes by A. C. Ewald. 8vo. Lond., 1887. J 12 T 26

ADDRESS on ignorance of the Scriptures and of the power of God, the true cause of religious error. 8vo. Melb. (n.d.) MG 2 Q 23

ADDRESS on the Necessity of Free Inquiry and Plain Speaking. [See Religious Pamphlets, 1.] G 9 V 16

ADELAIDE OBSERVATORY. Meteorological Observations made under the direction of Sir Chas. Todd, 1876-90. Sm. fol. Adelaide, 1878-92. ME

ADELAIDE UNIVERSITY Calendars, 1893 and 1894. 8vo. Adelaide, 1893-94. ME

ADELER, Max. [See Clark, C. H.]

ADENEY, Prof. Walter F. Ezra, Nehemiah, and Esther [See Expositor's Bible.] G 19 R and S

ADLER, Dr. Hermann. Alternating Generations: a Biological Study of Oak Galls and Gall Flies. Translated and edited by C. R. Straton. Illustrated. 8vo. Oxford, 1894. A 27 Q 41

ADOLPHUS, F. Some Memories of Paris. 8vo. Edinb., 1895. B 26 R 16

ADVANCED BUILDING CONSTRUCTION: a Manual for Students; by the Author of "Notes on Building Construction." 12mo. Lond., 1892. A 19 P 3

ADVICE to the ladies of Great Britain: a New Court Ballad. Sm. fol. [d. and p. torn out.] H 39 Q 13 ‡

ADY, Mrs. Henry. (Julia Cartwright.) Jules Bastien Lepage. (Portfolio Monograph, 4.) Roy. 8vo. Lond., 1894. E
Madame: a Life of Henrietta, Daughter of Charles I. and Duchess of Orleans. 8vo. Lond., 1894. C 15 P 6

ADYE, Gen. Sir John. Recollections of a Military Life. 8vo. Lond., 1895. B 31 T 9

ÆSCHYLUS. Agamemnon. [Greek Text and Latin Notes.] 8vo. Cantabrig æ, 1818. H 10 S 11
Septem contra Thebas. [See Trollope, W.] H 3 S 37
Tragedies of. Translated by R. Potter. New ed. Lond., 1809. H 2 T 27
[See Westcott, Rt. Rev. B.F—Religious Thought in the West.] G 2 U 37

AFFLECK, T., & Co. The Border Post (Albury) Almanac for 1895. 12mo. Albury, 1895. ME ‡ Q

AGASSIZ, Alexander. Exploration of the Surface Fauna of the Gulf Stream. 4to. Camb., 1883. A 5 P 24 †
Bibliography of Echinodermata. [See Harvard University.—Bulletins of Museum of Comparative Zoology.] A 30 U 17
On the young stages of some Osseous Fishes. Parts 1 and 3. 8vo. (n.p.) 1877-82. A 30 U 22
The Development of Lepidosteus Part 1. 8vo. (n.p.) 1878. A 30 U 23
Report on Echinoidea. [See Thomson, Sir C. W., and Murray, Dr. J.—Voyage of H.M.S. Challenger.] A 6 †
——— and WHITMAN, C. O. Development of some Pelagic Fish Eggs. 8vo. (n.p.) 1884. A 30 U 25

AGASSIZ, Prof. Jean Louis Rodolphe. Contributions to the Natural History of the Acalephæ of North America. 4to. Boston, 1819. A 15 Q ‡ †
Part 1. On the naked-eyed Medusæ of the shores of Massachusetts, in their perfect state of development.
Part 2. On the Beroid Medusæ of the shores of Massachusetts, in their perfect state of development.
Plaster Casts of. [See Hutton, L.—Portraits in Plaster.] A 23 V 13

AGE, The. Sept., 1892—April, 1895. 16 vols. fol. Melb., 1892-95. HE

AGE ANNUAL, The: a Political and Statistical Register of Victoria, 1876, 1877, 1879, 1883, 1885, 1889, 1890, 1892-93. 9 vols. 8vo. Melb., 1877-93. ME

AGESILAUS. Life of. [See Plutarch.] MC 1 R 45

AGLEN, Rev. Anthony S. Selection from the Writings of Dean Stanley. 8vo. Lond., 1894. G 15 P 29

AGOGOS. [See Day, C. W.]

AGRICULTURAL GAZETTE OF NEW SOUTH WALES. Vols. 1-4. Roy. 8vo. Sydney, 1890-94. ME ‡ R

AGRICULTURAL SCIENCE [a Journal of General Agriculture]. Vols. 1-7. 8vo. New York, &c., 1887-93. E

AGRICULTURAL SOCIETY OF ENGLAND. [See Royal Agricultural Society.]

AGRICULTURAL SOCIETY OF N.S.W. [See Royal Agricultural Soc.]

AGRICULTURE. Essay on Present Condition and Future Prospects of Agriculture in New South Wales; by "A Farmer." 8vo. Sydney, 1878. MA 1 Q 71
Agriculture in South Australia; by the Special Reporter of The Leader. 8vo. Melb., 1874. MA 1 Q 72
Agriculture in New South Wales: an Essay. 8vo. Sydney, 1878. MA 1 Q 53

AIKMAN, Prof. C. M. Johnston's Agricultural Chemistry. [*See* Johnston, J. F. W.] A 18 R 30

AITCHISON, Sir Chas. [Life of] Lord Lawrence. (Rulers of India.) 8vo. Oxford, 1892. C 13 P 15

AITKIN, G. A. [Plays of] R. Steele. [*See* Steele, R.] H 3 P 49

A'KEMPIS, Thos. [*See* Kempis, T. à.]

AKENSIDE, Mark. Pleasures of the Imagination, and other Poems. Illustrated. 18mo. Lond., 1853. H 10 T 34

AKHURST, W. M. The Battle of Hastings; or, the Earl, the Duke, the Witch, the Why and the Wherefore: a Historical Burlesque. 12mo. Melb. (n.d.) MH 1 U 71

ALABAMA. Geological Map of, with explanatory Chart. Folded 8vo. Montgomery, 1894. A 22 V 5
Hand-book of. 8vo. Richmond, 1893. D 15 T 5

ALBERONI, J. M. Lettres intimes de, addressées au Comte I. Rocca. (Annales de l'Université de Lyon, 4.) Roy. 8vo. Paris, 1893. C 10 U 13

ALBERT, Prince Consort. Sketch of. [*See* Bagehot, W.—Biographical Studies.] C 22 P 10

ALBERT EDWARD, Prince of Wales. Marriage of, with Alexandra, Princess of Denmark. Fol. Lond. (n.d.) C G P 3 ‡

ALBERT, Dr. Maurice. Le culte de Castor et Pollux en Italie. 8vo. Paris, 1883. B 35 R 13

ALBINUS, Peter. Treatise of Foreign Languages and Unknown Islands. (Bibliotheca Curiosa.) 12mo. Edinb., 1884. J 18 Q 3

ALBUQUERQUE, Affonso de. [Life of]; by H. Morse Stephens. (Rulers of India.) 8vo. Oxford, 1892. C 13 P 12

ALCOCK, Peter C. The Ladies' Companion and Family Year-book for 1875-76. 8vo. Melb., 1875. ME 5 Q

ALCORN AGRICULTURAL AND MECHANICAL COLLEGE, near Rodney, Miss. Catalogue, 1892-1893. 8vo. Jackson, Miss., 1892. E

ALCOTT, Amos Bronson. His Life and Philosophy; by F. B. Sanborn and W. T. Harris. 2 vols. 8vo. Lond., 1893. C 13 P 26, 27

ALDEN, Prof. Edmund K. The World's Representative Assemblies of To-day: a Study in Comparative Legislation. (Johns Hopkins University Studies, 11.) 8vo. Baltimore, 1893. B 18 S 11

ALDEN, P. The University Settlement in relation to local administration. [*See* Knapp, J. M.—The Universities and the Social Problem.] F 8 U 22

ALDEN, Wm. L. Shooting Stars, as observed from the sixth column of the *Times*, 12mo, Melb., 1878. MJ 1 P 53

ALDRICH, C. First Biennial Report of the Historical Department of Iowa, 1893. 8vo. Des Moines, 1894. E

ALDRICH, Thos. B. A Chat with; with Portrait. [*See* Blathwayt, R.—Interviews.] J 10 U 34

ALEXANDER OF LYCOPOLIS. Writings of. [Ante-Nicene Christ. Lib., 14.] 8vo. Edinb., 1869. G 14 U 14

ALEXANDER III OF RUSSIA. [Life of]; by C. Lowe. 8vo. Lond., 1895. C 21 P 12

ALEXANDER, A. Healthful Exercises for Girls. 4th ed., illustrated. 12mo. Lond., 1893. G 18 R 4
Musical Drill for Infants. 5th ed., illustrated. 12mo. Lond., 1893. G 18 R 5
Musical Drill for use in Schools and Calisthenic Classes. Illustrated. 8vo. Lond., 1892. G 18 R 6
Modern Gymnastic Exercises. Illustrated. 2 vols. 8vo. Lond., 1890. G 18 R 7, 8
Physical Drill of All Nations. Illustrated. 2 vols. 8vo. Lond., 1894. G 18 R 9

ALEXANDER, Jas. The Unemployed Settled on the Land. 8vo. Sydney, 1884. MF 1 Q 36

ALEXANDER, W. F. [*See* Mendelssohn-Bartholdy, F.]

ALEXANDER, Rt. Rev. Wm. Primary Convictions. 8vo. Lond., 1893. G 14 S 10
Epistle of St. John. [*See* Expositor's Bible.] G 19 R 5

ALEXANDER LYCEUM, ST. PETERSBURG. Short Sketch of the History of. 8vo. St. Petersburg, 1893. G 18 R 20

ALEXANDRA, Princess of Denmark. Marriage of, with Albert Edward, Prince of Wales. Fol. Lond. (n.d.) C G P 3 ‡

ALFIERI, Count V. [*See* Elliot, Frances—Roman Gossip.] C 21 Q 10

ALGER, J. G. Glimpses of the French Revolution: Myths, Ideals, and Realities. 12mo. Lond., 1894. B 37 Q 2

ALGERIA. Statistique Générale de l'Algérie, 1885-90. 2 vols. fol. Alger, 1889-91. E
Exposé de la Situation Générale de l'Algérie, 1893-94. 2 vols. 8vo. Alger, 1893-94. E

ALISON, Rev. A. Essays on the Nature and Principles of Taste. 8vo. Lond., 1853. J 4 U 1

ALL AROUND THE WORLD. Illustrated Record of Voyages, Travels, and Adventures in all parts of the Globe. Illustrated. 2 vols. 4to. New York (n.d.) D 12 U 9, 10 †

ALL THE EARTH ROUND: a Nautical Poem; by "A Wanderer." 8vo. Lond., 1892. H 9 U 41

ALL THE WORLD. Monthly Record of the Work of the Salvation Army. No. 6, vol. 12. Roy. 8vo. Melb., 1893. ME

ALL THE YEAR ROUND: a weekly journal. 3rd series, vols. 8-13. 8vo. Lond., 1892-95. E

ALLAN, Dr. Wm. Strength of Beams under Transverse Loads. 2nd ed. [illustrated.] 18mo. New York, 1893. A 22 P 35

ALLARDYCE, W. L. Rotooma and the Rotoomans. (Geograph. Soc. of Australasia, Q. Branch, 1.) 8vo. Brisbane, 1886. ME 20 P

ALLDAY, J. L. Gossiping Guide to Birmingham. 16mo. Birm , 1893. D 18 P 9

ALLÈGRE, Dr. F. Etude sur la Déesse Grecque Tyché. 8vo. Paris, 1889. B 27 V 9

Mélanges Grecs. [*See* Cucuel, C.] J 7 U 44

ALLEN, A. G. [Life of] T. G. Wainewright, Poisoner, 1794-1852. (Lives of twelve Bad Men.) 8vo. Lond., 1894 C 18 T 9

ALLEN, Alfred H. Commercial Organic Analysis: A treatise on the properties, proximate analytical examination, and modes of assaying the various organic chemicals and products employed in the arts, manufactures, medicine, &c. 2nd edition. Vols. 1-3. 4 vols. 8vo. Lond., 1885-92. A 21 T 22-25

ALLEN, Chas. D. American Book-plates: a Guide to their Study with a Bibliography by Eben N. Howins. 8vo. Lond., 1895. J 8 U 6

ALLEN, Chas. Grant B. Grant Allen at Home: with Portrait. [*See* Blathwayt, R.—Interviews.] J 10 U 34

The Lower Slopes: Reminiscences of Excursions round the base of Helicon. 8vo. Lond., 1894. H 8 S 46

Science in Arcady. 8vo. Lond., 1892. A 17 T 31

ALLEN, Rev. L. The City, its Sins and Sorrows; or, the Dark-doing of Sydney: a lecture. 8vo. Sydney. 1873.* MG 1 Q 46

ALLEN, Edward Heron-. De Fidiculis Bibliographia: being an attempt towards a Bibliography of the Violin and all other Instruments played with a bow in ancient and modern times. 2 vols. sm. 4to. Lond., 1890-94 K 19 R 8, 9

Manual of Cheirosophy: being a Practical Hand-book of Cheirognomy and Cheiromancy. 6th ed., illustrated 12mo. Lond., 1892. A 24 R 20

Violin-making, as it was and is: being a Historical Theoretical, and Practical Treatise on the Science and Art of Violin-making. 2nd ed., illustrated. 8vo Lond., 1885. A 25 T 8

ALLEN, Sir Geo. W. Debate on the Prerogative of Pardon. [*See* Parkes, Sir H.] MF 4 Q 40

ALLEN, Dr. H. B. Report on Hospital Construction and Management. Sm. fol. Melb., 1891. MA 9 Q 19 †

ALLEN, J. W. [Life of] Simon Fraser, Lord Lovat, 1697-1747. (Lives of Twelve Bad Men.) 8vo. Lond., 1894. C 18 T 9

[Life of] E. Kelly, Bushranger. 1855-80. (Lives of Twelve Bad Men.) 8vo. Lond., 1894. C 18 T 9

ALLEN, John. [*See* Calvin, John.] G 19 Q 3, 4

ALLEN, John P. Practical Building Construction. 8vo. Lond., 1893. A 19 T 7

ALLEN, Thos. G., and SACHTLEBEN, Wm. L. Across Asia on a Bicycle. 8vo. Lond., 1895. D 17 Q 26

ALLEN'S NATURALIST'S LIBRARY. Marsupialia and Monotremata. [*See* Lydekker, R.] MA 3 U 1

ALLGEMEINE DEUTSCHE BIOGRAPHIE. Bände 34-38. 8vo. Leip., 1892-93. C 20 Q

ALLIBONE, Dr. Samuel A. Poetical Quotations from Chaucer to Tennyson. Roy. 8vo. Philad., 1892. H 4 V 13

ALLINGHAM, J. Till. Fortune's Frolic: a Farce. [*See* London Stage, 2.] H 2 S 34

ALLINSON, Edward P., and PENROSE, Boies. The City Government of Philadelphia. (Johns Hopkns University Studies, 5.) 8vo. Baltimore, 1887. B 18 S 5

Philadelphia, 1681-1887: a History of Municipal Development. (Johns Hopkins University Studies, extra vol. 2.) 8vo. Philad., 1897. B 18 T 2

ALLMAN, Prof. G. J. Hydroida. [*See* Thomson, Sir C. W., and Murray, Dr. J.—Voyage of H.M.S. *Challenger*—Zoölogy.] A 6 †

ALLSOP, P. C. Electric Bell Construction. Illustrated. 12mo. Lond , 1890. A 22 P 38

Practical Electric Bell-fitting. Illustrated. 12mo. Lond., 1892. A 22 P 40

Practical Electric-light Fitting, including the Phoenix Fire Office Rules. 8vo. Lond., 1892. A 21 Q 40

ALLSTON, Washington. Life and Letters of; by J. B. Flagg. 8vo. Lond., 1893. C 12 U 30

ALMANACH DE GOTHA. Annuaire Généalogique, Diplomatique et Statisque, 1893-95. 3 vols. 18mo. Gotha, 1893-94. E

ALTHAUS, Dr. Julius. The Value of Electrical Treatment. 8vo. Lond., 1895. A 33 S 10

ALTHORP, Lord. Sketch of. [*See* Bagehot, W.—Biographical Studies] C 22 P 13

AMANS, Dr. P. Essai sur le Vol des Insectes. 4to. Montpellier, 1883. A 5 P 17 †

AMERICA: a Journal for Americans. Vols.3-5. sm.fol. Chicago, 1896-01. E

AMERICAN AGRICULTURIST, The. Vols. 51-54. Sm. fol. New York, 1892-94. E

AMERICAN ANTIQUARIAN AND ORIENTAL JOURNAL. Vols. 14-16. 8vo. Chicago, 1892-94. E

AMERICAN ASSOCIATION OF STATE WEATHER SERVICES. Report of third annual meeting. 8vo. Wash., 1884. E

AMERICAN CATALOGUE, The Annual, 1892-94. Roy. 8vo. New York, 1893-95. E

AMERICAN FORESTRY ASSOCIATION. Proceedings. Vol. 10, 1891-93. 8vo. Wash., 1894. E

AMERICAN HISTORICAL ASSOCIATION. Report of, 1893. 8vo. Wash., 1894. E

AMERICAN HISTORY, Magazine of. [*See* Magazine.]

AMERICAN INSTITUTE OF MINING ENGINEERS. Transactions. Vols. 20-24. 8vo. New York, 1892-95. E

AMERICAN IRON AND STEEL ASSOCIATION. Directory of the Iron and Steel Works, to which is added a complete list of the Iron and Steel Works of Canada and Mexico. 12th ed. 8vo. Philad., 1894. E

AMERICAN JOURNAL OF ARCHÆOLOGY and of the History of the Fine Arts. Vols. 8-9. Roy. 8vo. Princeton, 1893-94. E

AMERICAN JOURNAL OF INSANITY. Vol. 51. 8vo. Chicago, 1894-95. E

AMERICAN JOURNAL OF SCIENCE, The. 3rd series. Vols. 43-48. 3 vols. 8vo. New Haven, 1892-94. E

AMERICAN LIBRARY ASSOCIATION. Catalog of 5,000 vols. selected by. [*See* United States—Bureau of Education.]

AMERICAN MAHOMET, The. [*See* Smith, Joseph.]

AMERICAN MUSEUM OF NATURAL HISTORY. Bulletin, 1. Museums. 8vo. New York, 1881. E

AMERICAN ORIENTAL SOCIETY. Proceedings at New Haven, October, 1881. 8vo. (n.p.) 1881. E

AMERICAN PHILOSOPHICAL SOCIETY. Proceedings. Vols. 1-10. 8vo. Philad., 1838-60. E

AMERICAN SOCIETY OF CIVIL ENGINEERS. Constitution and List of Members, 1895. 8vo. New York, 1895. E
Transactions, July to December, 1893. 2 vols. 8vo. New York, 1893. E

AMERICAN SOCIETY OF MECHANICAL ENGINEERS. Transactions. Vol. 14. 8vo. New York, 1893. E

AMÉRO, C. Aux Antipodes. [*See* Tissot, V.] MD 5 V 5)

AMES, John G. Comprehensive Index of the publications of the United States Government, 1889-93. 4to. Wash., 1894. K 15 P 2 †
Official Register of the United States, containing a list of the officers and employés in the Civil, Military, and Naval Service on the 1st July, 1893. Vol. 2. Post Office Department. Imp. 8vo. Wash., 1894. E

AMHERST, Wm. Pitt Amherst, Earl. Lord Amherst and the British advance eastwards to Burma; by Anne Thackeray Ritchie and R. Evans. (Rulers of India.) 12mo. Oxford, 1894. C 14 P 26

AMHERST STATE AGRICULTURAL EXPERIMENT STATION. Reports of the Board of Control, 1892-93. 8vo. Boston, 1893-94. E

AMICIS, Edmondo de. Holland. Translated by Helen Zimmern. Illustrated. 2 vols. 8vo. Philad., 1894. B 23 R 10, 11

AMUNÁTEGUI, Don Miguel L. Don Andres Bello y el codigo civil. 8vo. Santiago, 1885. F 11 U 8
Las princeras representaciones Dramáticas en Chile. Roy. 8vo. Santiago, 1888. H 5 U 36
La Alborada Poética en Chile despuéy del 18 de Setiembre de 1810. 8vo. Santiago, 1892. H 5 U 37
Vida de Don Andres Bello. 8vo. Santiago, 1882. C 21 T 7
Don J. J. de Mora, apuntes Biográficos. 8vo. Santiago, 1888. C 21 T 6
[Vida de] C. Henríquez. 2 vols. 8vo. Santiago, 1889. C 21 T 4, 5
Don M. J. Ramos. 8vo. Santiago, 1889. C 21 T 3
El Cabildo de Santiago desde 1573 hastá 1581. 3 vols. 8vo. Santiago, 1890-91. B 16 S 20-22
Salvador Sanfuentes, apuntes Biográficos. 8vo. Santiago, 1892. C 21 T 8
Amunátegui, 1828-88, por C. M. Vicuña. 8vo. Paris (n.d.) C 21 T 1

AN, L', deux Mille Quatre Cent Quarante. [*See* Mercier, L. S.] F 12 P 32

ANACREON. [Greek text.] With Thomas Stanley's Translation. Edited by A. H. Bullen. Sm. 4to. Lond., 1893. H 7 U 9
Odaria. 8vo. Lond., 1813. H 9 U 27
Works of. [*See* Fawkes, F.] H 9 U 28

ANCIENT FRATERNITY OF FREE AND ACCEPTED MASONS under the United Grand Lodge of New South Wales. Constitutions. 12mo. Sydney, 1889. MJ 1 P 33

ANDERSEN, Hans C. Story of my Life; and In Sweden. 12mo. Lond., 1852. C 17 P 7

ANDERSON, Dr. Alex. Life and Works of, the first American Wood Engraver; by F. M. Burr. Illustrated. Roy. 8vo. New York, 1893.   C 19 S 3

ANDERSON, D. Patent for improvements in contrivances for varying the guage of the wheels of rolling stock for rail and other permanent ways. (Roy. Soc., Vict., 19.) 8vo. Melb., 1883.   ME 1 P

ANDERSON, Edward L. Curb Snaffle, and Spur: a Method of Training Young Horses for the Cavalry Service, and for general use under the Saddle. Illustrated. 8vo. Edinb., 1894.   A 29 T 30

ANDERSON, Ernest, and SPRY, Frank P. Victorian Butterflies, and how to collect them. 8vo. Melb., 1893.   MA 3 S 15

ANDERSON, G. The Agnostic and other Poems. 8vo. Paisley, 1894.   H 9 U 15

ANDERSON, Henry Chas. Lennox. How to Increase the Percentage of Butter Fat in Milk. 8vo. Sydney, 1893.   MA 1 Q 68
Orchard Manures. 8vo. Sydney, 1890.   MA 1 Q 61
Dried Blood as a Manure. 8vo. Sydney, 1892.   MA 1 Q 61

ANDERSON, J. [See Great Brit. and Ireland. Col. Offi.] E

ANDERSON, J. Corbet. Catalogue of the Hartley Library. [See Hartley Library.]   K 7 U 33

ANDERSON, J. S. Australian History. 12mo. Sydney, 1894.   MB 1 P 43

ANDERSON, James. A Pocket Guide to the Watercure. 32mo. Sydney, 1868.   MA 2 P 84

ANDERSON, Prof. W. C. F. Atlas of Classical Antiquities. [See Schreiber, Th.]   B 7 R S †

ANDERSON, Dr. Wm. Interdependence of Abstract Science and Engineering. 8vo. Lond., 1893.   A 22 S 23

ANDERSON, Wm. J. La Mission Franco-Australienne; Cantiques choisis par le Missionaire. 18mo. Sydney, 1886.   MH 1 P 75

ANDRADE, David A. The Melbourne Riots, and how Harry Holdfast and his friends emancipated the workers. 8vo. Melb., 1892.   MJ 3 Q 12

ANDRÉ, George G. Rock Blasting. 8vo. Lond., 1878.   A 24 T 22

ANDREWS, C. M. The River Towns of Connecticut: a Study of Wethersfield, Hartford, and Windsor. (Johns Hopkins University Studies, 7.) 8vo. Baltimore, 1889.   B 18 S 7

ANDREWS, Clement W. Periodicals and Society Publications in the Libraries of the Massachusetts Institute of Technology. 8vo. Camb., Mass., 1893.   K 7 Q 30

ANDREWS, E. B. Outline of the Principles of History. [See Droysen, J. G.]   B 36 Q 9

ANDREWS, F. W. Notes on some rare Birds inhabiting South Australia. (Trans. Roy. Soc., S. Australia, 6.) 8vo. Adelaide, 1883.   ME 1 S
Notes on the Night Parrot. (Trans. Roy. Soc., S. Australia, 6.) 8vo. Adelaide, 1883.   ME 1 S

ANDREWS, M. P. Better Late than Never. [See London Stage, 3.]   H 2 S 35

ANDREWS, Mrs. T. R. A Glimpse of Hell. 8vo. Melb., 1895.   MG 2 R 32

ANDREWS, Wm. Bygone England Social Studies in its Historic Byways and Highways. 8vo. Lond., 1892.   B 5 T 42
Bygone Leicestershire. Edited by Wm. Andrews. 8vo. Leicester, 1892.   B 5 T 43
Bygone Warwickshire. Edited by Wm. Andrews. 8vo. Hull, 1893.   B 5 T 44

ANECDOTA OXONIENSIA. Aryan Series. Vol. 1, pt. 7. The Buddha-Karita of Asvaghosha. Edited by Prof. E. B. Cowell. [Sanskrit Text.] Sm. 4to. Oxford, 1893.   E
Classical Series. Vol. 1, part. 6. Collation with the Ancient Armenian Versions of the Greek Text of Aristotle's Categories, De Interpretatione, De Mundo, De Virtutibus ot Vitiis, and of Porphyry's Introduction. By F. C. Conybeare. Sm. 4to. Oxford, 1892.   E

Mediæval and Modern Series. Vol. 4, Part 8. Hibernica Minora: being a Fragment of an Old-Irish Treatise on the Psalter. Sm. 4to. Oxford, 1894.   E
Mediæval and Modern Series. Vol. 4, Part 9. The Elucidarium and other Tracts in Welsh [and Latin] from Llyvyr Agkyr Llandewivrevi, 1346. Sm. 4to. Oxford, 1894.   E
Mediæval and Modern Series. Vol. 4, Part 10. The Earliest Translation of the Old Testament into the Basque Language; by Pierre D'Urte. Sm. 4to. Oxford, 1894.   E
Semetic Series. Vol. 1, pt 5. The Palestinian Version of the Holy Scriptures. The Syriac Text with English Translation. Edited by G. H. Gwilliam. Sm. 4to. Oxford, 1893.   E
Semetic Series, part 7. The Churches and Monasteries of Egypt, and some neighbouring Countries; attributed to Abû Sâlih, the Armenian. Translated by B. T. A. Evetts; with Notes by A. J. Butler. [With Arabic Text.] Sm. 4to. Oxford, 1895.   E
Semetic Series, part 8. The Ethiopic version of the Hebrew Book of Jubilees. Edited from four manuscripts by R. H. Charles. Sm. 4to. Oxford, 1895.   E

ANGAS, J. H. On the Merino in South Australia. (Proc. Roy. Agricult. and Horticult. Soc., S. Australia, 1884.) 8vo. Adelaide, 1884.   ME 1 S

ANGEL, Henry. Practical Plane and Solid Geometry. 8vo. Lond., 1895.   A 23 R 15

ANIMAL VACCINATION : being Information supplied by the Government of Bombay to that of New South Wales on the subject of Animal Lymph and Vaccination. 8vo. Sydney, 1882.   MA 2 S 54

ANIMAL WORLD, The. Vols. 22, 23. Fol. Lond., 1892.   E

ANNALES DES MINES. Lois, Décrets, etc. 9th série. Tomes 1-3. 8vo. Paris, 1892-94.   E
Mémoires. 9th série. Tomes 3-7. 8vo. Paris, 1893-95.   E

ANNALS AND MAGAZINE OF NATURAL HISTORY, including Zoology, Botany, and Geology. 6th series, vols. 10-14. 8vo. Lond., 1892-94.   E

ANNANDALE, Dr. Chas. [*See* Popular Encyclopedia.]   K 4 T 11-24
Blackie's Modern Cyclopedia. [*See* Blackie's.]   K 7 T 11-18

ANNE, Queen of England. Historical Sketches of the Reign of; by Mrs. M. O. Oliphant. 8vo. Lond., 1894.   B 36 Q 6

ANNUAL AMERICAN CATALOGUE, The. [*See* American Catalogue.]

ANNUAL LITERARY INDEX, 1892-94. 3 vols. 8vo. New York, 1893-95.   E

ANNUAL REGISTER, The : A Review of Public Events, 1892-94. 3 vols. 8vo. Lond., 1893-95.   E

ANNUAL SUMMARIES, reprinted from *The Times.* [*See* Times, The.]   E

ANNUARIO GENERALE per la Viticoltura e la Enologia. 8vo. Roma, 1893.   E

ANSELM, Archbishop of Canterbury, 1093-1109. Sketch of. [*See* Fowler, Rev. M.—Notable Archbishops.]   C 13 V 12

ANSON, Sir Wm. R. Principles of the English Law of Contract and of Agency in its relation to Contract. 8th ed. 8vo. Oxford, 1895.   F 11 U 20

ANSON BROS. Settlement of Port Arthur (Penal Settlement), past and present. Photographed by Anson Bros. Fol. Hobart (n.d.)   MD 2 P 23 ‡

ANTANANARIVO ANNUAL : The Madagascar Magazine. Pt. 4 of vol. 4. 8vo. Antananarivo, 1892. E

ANTE-NICENE CHRISTIAN LIBRARY. Translation of the Writings of the Fathers down to A.D. 325. Edited by the Rev. Dr. A. Roberts and Dr. J. Donaldson. 24 vols. 8vo. Edinb., 1867-72.   G 14 U 1-24

ANTHONY, Rev. A. S. Lenâpé-English Dictionary. [*See* Brinton, Dr. D. G.]   J 10 U 32

ANTHROPOLOGICAL INSTITUTE OF GREAT BRITAIN AND IRELAND, Journal of. Vols. 22-24. 8vo. Lond., 1893-95.   E
Index to Publications of, 1843-91, by G. W. Bloxam 8vo. Lond., 1893.   E

ANTIPHON. Œuvres complètes de l'orateur Antiphon, [*See* Cucuel, C.—Mélanges Grecs.]   J 7 U 44

ANTIPODEAN, The : an Illustrated Annual. Edited by G. E. Evans and J. T. Ryan. 2nd ed. 8vo. Lond., 1893.   ME 1 U

ANTIPODES. [*See* Revelations of Common Sense.]   G 19 P 33

ANTIQUAIRES DU NORD, Société Royale des. [*See* Kongeligt Nordisk Oldskrift-Selskab.]

ANTIQUARIES OF LONDON, SOCIETY OF. [*See* Society of Antiquaries of London.]

ANTIQUARY, The. Vols. 25-28 and 30. Sm. 4to. Lond, 1892-94.   E

ANTONELLI, Cardinal. [*See* Elliott, Frances—Roman Gossip.]   C 21 Q 10

ANTROBUS, Rev. Frederick I. History of the Popes. [*See* Pastor, Dr. L.]   G 15 S 24, 25

APOCRYPHAL GOSPELS, &c. [*See* Bibles, &c.]   G 14 U 16

APOSTATE OF THE AGE reproving Sin ; by "A Protestant Watchman." 8vo. Melb., 1856.   MG 1 S 75

APOSTOLIC FATHERS, The. Writings of. Translated by Rev. Dr. Roberts, Dr. Donaldson, and Rev. F. Crombie. (Ante-Nicene Christ. Lib., 1.) 8vo. Edinb., 1867.   G 14 U 1

APOSTOLICAL CONSTITUTIONS, The. Edited by Dr. J. Donaldson. (Ante-Nicene Christ. Lib., 17.) 8vo. Edinb., 1870.   G 14 U 17

APPEARANCE IS AGAINST THEM : A Farce. [*See* London Stage, 4.]   H 2 S 36

APPLEGARTH, Dr. A. C. Quakers in Pennsylvania. (Johns Hopkins University Studies, 10.) 8vo. Baltimore, 1892.   B 18 S 10

APPLETON, D., & Co. Annual Cyclopædia and Register of Important Events of 1887-93. [Illustrated.] Vols. 12-14. Roy. 8vo. New York, 1891-94.   E
Cyclopædia of American Biography. Edited by J. G. Wilson and J. Fiske. [Illustrated.] 6 vols. imp. 8vo. New York, 1894.   C 16 U 1-6

APRÈS DE MANNEVILLETTE, J. B. N. D. d'. Neptune Oriental. Fol. Paris (n.d.)   D 8 P 23 ‡

APTHORP, Wm. F. Cyclopedia of Music and Musicians. [*See* Champlin, J. D.]   K 18 S 9-11

ARABIAN NIGHTS' ENTERTAINMENTS; or, the Thousand and One Nights. Translated by E. W. Lane. 3 vols. 8vo. Lond., 1850. J 5 S 32-34

Plain and literal translation of with Supplemental Nights. By Sir R. F. Burton. 16 vols. 8vo. Benares [Lond.] 1885-88. Libr.

One Hundred Illustrations to above, from paintings by S. L. Wood. 8vo. Lond. (n.d.) Libr.

ARAGO, Francs. History of my Youth. Translated by the Rev. Baden Powell. 12mo. Lond., 1855. C 17 P 16

ARAGO, Jacques E. V. Narrative of a Voyage Round the World in the *Uranie* and *Physicienne* Corvettes. 4to. Lond. 1823. MD 1 Q 39 †

ARAÚJO, O. Geografía Nacional, Fisica, Politica, y Corográfica. 8vo. Montevideo, 1892. D 15 T 23

ARBER, Edward. Transcript of the Registers of the Company of Stationers of London, 1554-1640 A.D. Vol. 5. Index. 4to. Birm., 1894. B 12 S 22 †

ARBOUSSET, Thos. Tahiti et les Iles adjacentes. 8vo. Paris, 1867. M B 1 P 46

ARCHÆOLOGIA. [*See* Society of Antiquaries of London.]

ARCHÆOLOGIA CAMBRENSIS. [*See* Cambrian Archæological Assoc.]

ARCHÆOLOGIA CANTIANA. [*See* Kent Archæological Soc.]

ARCHÆOLOGICAL INSTITUTE OF AMERICA. Papers. American Series, 4. Final Report of Investigations among the Indians of the South-western United States, 1880-85. Part 2; By A. F. Bandelier. 8vo. Camb., 1892. E

Papers. American Series, 5 Hemenway South-western Expedition. Contributions to the History of the South-western Portion of the United States, by A. F. Bandelier. 8vo. Camb., 1890. E

ARCHBOLD, W. A. J. [Life of] George Jeffreys, Unjust Judge, 1648-89. (Lives of Twelve Bad Men.) 8vo. Lond., 1894. C 18 T 9

ARCHELAUS. Works of. [Ante-Nicene Christ. Lib. 20.] 8vo. Edinb., 1871. G 14 U 20

ARCHER, T. A., and KINGSFORD, C. L. The Crusades: The Story of the Latin Kingdom of Jerusalem. 8vo. Lond., 1894. B 36 Q 6

ARCHER, Thos. Our Sovereign Lady Queen Victoria: Her Life and Jubilee. 4 vols. Sm. 4to. Lond., 1888. C 9 V 1-2

ARCHER, Wm. The Theatrical World, 1894. 8vo. Lond., 1895. H 9 U 21

ARCHER, Wm. H. Facts and Figures; or, Notes of Progress, Statistical and General. Sm. 4to. Melb., 1858. MF 1 U 23

Statistical Notes on the Progress of Victoria in relation to Agriculture and Live Stock, to March, 1863. 4to. Melb., 1863. MF 3 U 60

Victoria Patents and Patentees, 1854-66. 4to. Melb., 1868. ME

ARCHIBALD, J. Notes on the Ancient Wreck discovered near Warrnambool. (Roy. Geog. Soc. Australasia, Vic. Branch, 9.) 8vo. Melb., 1891. ME 20

Notes on the Antiquity of the Australian Aboriginal Race, founded upon the collection in the Warrnambool Public Museum. (Roy. Geog. Soc. Australasia, Vic. Branch, 11.) 8vo. Melb., 1894. ME 20

ARCHITECT AND CONTRACT REPORTER, The. Vols. 48-50. Sm. fol. Lond., 1892-93. E

ARCHITECTURAL PUBLICATION SOCIETY. Dictionary of Architecture, with illustrations. 11 vols. fol Lond., 1853-92. K 37 P 11-21 ‡

ARCHITECTURAL SOCIETIES OF THE COUNTIES OF LINCOLN, NOTTINGHAM, YORK, &c. Reports and Papers read, 1889-91. Vols. 20, 21. 8vo. Lincoln, 1890-93. E

ARCHIV FÜR MIKROSKOPISCHE ANATOMIE. Bände, 40-44. 8vc. Bonn, 1892-94. E

Namen — und Sachregister zu Bände 31-40. 8vo. Bonn, 1893. E

ARE CATHOLIC CLAIMS REASONABLE? 8vo. Melb., 1875. MJ 3 Q 16

ARENA, The. Vols. 10-12, 1894-95. 8vo. Boston, 1894-94. E

ARGENSOLA, Bartolome Leonardo de. Conquista de las Islas Malucas. Sm. fol. Madrid, 1609. D 39 Q 27 ‡

ARGENSON, Marquis d'. A Study in Criticism; being the Stanhope Essay, Oxford, 1893; by A. Ogle. 12mo. Lond., 1893. C 19 Q 16

ARGENTINE REPUBLIC. The Province of La Rioja: its Mines, Agriculture, and Stock-breeding. 12mo. Buenos Aires, 1895. A 18 P 23

Message of the President of the Republic on opening the Session of Congress, 1895. 8vo. Buenos Aires, 1895. F 3 V 14

ARGLES, T. E. [*See* Grey, Harold.]

ARGUS, The. July, 1895-June, 1890. 109 vols. fol. Melb., 1855-90. ME ‡

ARGYLL, George Douglas Campbell, Duke of. Irish Nationalism: an appeal to history. 8vo. Lond., 1893. B 29 Q 19

The Unseen Foundations of Society; an examination of the fallacies and failures of economic science due to neglected elements. 8vo. Lond., 1893. F 14 S 22

ARIAS, Rev. E. P. El Beato Sanz y Campañeros Mártires del Orden de Predicadores. 8vo. Bruxelles, 1893.
G 3 R 20

ARIOSTO, Lodovico. Orlando Furioso. Con note e dilucidazione grammaticali, da R. Zotti, ad uso degli Lingua Italiana. 4 vols. 12mo. Lond., 1814.
H 10 U 10-13

ARISTOPHANES. A Metrical Version of the Acharnians, the Knights and the Birds. With occasional comment by J. H. Frere. 3rd ed. 12mo. Lond., 1890.
H 9 U 23

Une Scène des "Grenouilles." [*See* Cucuel, Ch.]
J 7 U 44

Les Scolies du Manuscrit d'Aristophane à Ravenne. [*See* Martin, A.]
J 7 U 19

ARISTOTELES. Aristotle's Constitution of Athens: A revised Text, with notes, &c., by J. E. Sandys. 8vo. Lond., 1893.
F 4 P 23

Aristotle's Categories. [*See* Anecdota Oxoniensia.]

Aristotle's Theory of Poetry and Fine Art, with a Critical Text and a Translation of the Poetics, by Dr. S. H. Butcher. 8vo. Lond., 1895.
J 4 T 26

Politics of. [*See* Susemihl, Prof. F.]
F 7 R 30

ARKANSAS—*General.* Arkansas in 1892-93, from Census Returns 1890. 8vo. Little Rock, Arkansas, 1893.
D 15 V 18

Beskrivelse af Staten Arkansas. 8vo. St. Louis, 1893.
D 15 T 21

Description of the State of. (1 and 2.) 8vo. St. Louis, 1893.
D 15 T 21

Eine genaue und zuverlässige Schilderung des Staates Arkansas. 8vo. St. Louis, 1893.
D 15 T 21

Fort Smith; what it is, what it has, and what it offers. 8vo. Fort Smith, 1893.
D 15 T 21

Hand-book of. 8vo. Richmond, 1893.
D 15 T 5

Pine Bluff and Jefferson County, Arkansas, full Description. Imp. 8vo. (n.p.) 1893.
D 10 V 20

Something of interest to all: the South Land. 12mo. St. Louis, 1893.
D 15 P 11

Statistics and Information showing the Agricultural and Mineral Resources, the opportunities for successful Stock and Fruit Raising, Manufacturing, Mining, and Lumbering, &c. 8vo. (n.p.) 1893.
D 15 Q 23

[*See also* Pine Bluff Coloured Industrial Institute.]
G 18 R 30

ARKANSAS—SUPERINTENDENT OF PUBLIC INSTRUCTION. Report, 1891-92. 8vo. Little Rock, 1893.
E

ARKANSAS INDUSTRIAL UNIVERSITY. Catalogue, 1892-93. 8vo. Little Rock, 1892.
E

ARLOING, Dr. Saturnin, RODET, A., and COURMONT, J. Etude Expérimentale sur les Propriétés attribuées à la Tuberculine de M. Koch. (Annales de l'Université de Lyon, 6.) Roy. 8vo. Paris, 1892.
A 33 U 24

ARLOT, M. Complete Guide for Coach Painters. Translated from the French by A. A. Fesquet. 12mo. Philad., 1888.
A 25 Q 38

ARMATAGE, George. Every Man his own Cattle Doctor. 6th ed. 8vo. Lond., 1890.
A 18 T 18

The Sheep Doctor. Illustrated. 8vo. Lond., 1895.
A 30 R 13

ARMIT, W. E. Notes on the Philology of the Islands adjacent to the south-eastern extremity of New Guinea. (Proc. Roy. Soc., Queensland, 1.) 8vo. Brisbane, 1895.
ME 1 T

The Papuans. (Proc. Roy. Soc., Queensland, 2.) 8vo. Brisbane, 1886.
ME 1 T

ARMOUR, Philip D. Biographical Sketch of. [*See* Stoddard, Wm. O.—Men of Business.]
C 16 R 19

ARMSBY, Dr. Henry P. Manual of Cattle-feeding: a Treatise on the Laws of Animal Nutrition and the Chemistry of Feeding-stuffs in their application to the feeding of Farm Animals. 5th ed., illustrated. 12mo. New York, 1893.
A 18 R 30

———— and JENKINS, Dr. E. H. The Farmer's Annual Hand-book for 1883. 12mo. New York, 1883.
A 18 P 7

ARMSTRONG, Rev. Dr. Geo. Dodd. The two Books of Nature and Revelation collated. 8vo. New York, 1886.
G 10 P 24

ARMSTRONG, Robert. Chimneys for Furnaces and Steam Boilers. 3rd. ed. With an Appendix on the Theory of Chimney Draught, by F. E. Idell. 18mo. New York, 1894.
A 19 P 4

ARMSTRONG, W. [*See* Corroyer, E.]
A 19 R 2

ARMSTRONG, Walter. Thomas Gainsborough. (Portfolio Monograph, 9.) Roy. 8vo. Lond., 1894.
E

ARMSTRONG, Sir Wm. Portrait of. [*See* Johnson, R. W.—The Making of the Tyne.]
B 21 V 6

ARMY AND NAVY CALENDAR, 1891-94. 8vo. Lond., 1891-93.
E

ARMY AND NAVY MAGAZINE. [*See* United Service Magazine.]

ARNOBIUS. The Seven Books of Arnobius Adversus Gentes. Translated by Dr. A. H. Bryce and H. Campbell. (Ante-Nicene Christ. Lib., 19.) 8vo. Edinb., 1871.
G 14 U 19

ARNOLD, Sir Edwin. Adzuma; or, the Japanese Wife: a play in four acts. 8vo. Lond., 1893.
H 1 R 33

Pearls of the Faith; or, Islam's Rosary; being the Ninety-nine beautiful Names of Allah. 6th ed. 12mo. Lond., 1891.
H 9 Q 18

The Tenth Muse, and other Poems. 8vo. Lond., 1895.
H 9 U 26

ARNOLD, Rev. Frederick H. Sussex Tokens. [See Warren, J. L.] A 27 Q 43

ARNOLD, Matthew. A French Eton; or, Middle Class Education and the State. 12mo. Lond., 1864. G 18 P 15

God and the Bible: a Sequel to "Literature and Dogma." 12mo. Lond., 1884. G 0 V 20

Isaiah of Jerusalem, in the authorised English Version. 8vo. Lond., 1883. G 19 P 26

Mixed Essays. 2nd ed. 8vo Lond., 1880. J 11 T 25

St. Paul and Protestantism; with other Essays. 12mo. Lond., 1887. G 9 V 21

Arnold's Criticism. [See Burroughs, J.—Indoor Studies.] J 16 T 40

Sketch of the Work of. [See Dawson, W. J.—Makers of Modern English.] H 10 S 14

ARNOLD, Richard A. New South Wales Parliamentary Handbook. 8vo. Sydney, 1894. MF 2 T 53

ARNOLD, Robert Arthur. The Lords as Landlords. [See Subjects of the Day, 4.] F 7 U 29

ARNOLD, Samuel G. History of the State of Rhode Island, 1636-1700. 4th ed. 8vo. Providence, R.I., 1894. B 20 S 7, 8

ARNOLD, T. K [See Frädersdorff, Dr. J. W.] K 14 P 10

ARNOLD, Thomas. Sketch of; with Portrait. [See Bolton, Sarah K.—Famous Leaders.] C 17 P 27

ARNOLD, Mrs. William. [See Brentano, L.] F 5 Q 1

ARNOULD, Sir Joseph. On the Law of Marine Insurance. 6th ed.; by D. MacLachlan. 2 vols. roy. 8vo. Lond., 1887. F 6 V 28, 29

ARRIAN, Flavius. Anabasis of Alexander, and Indica, translated by Rev. E. J. Chinnock. 12mo. Lond., 1893. B 14 P 36

ARROWSMITH, Aaron. Chart of Rio de la Plata. Fol. Lond., 1798. MD 1 P 15 ‡

Chart of the Marquesas. Fol. Lond., 1798. MD 1 P 15 ‡

Chart of several Harbours in the S.E. part of Van Diemans Land. Fol. Lond., 1798. MD 1 P 15 ‡

Chart of the Southern Promontory of America from the Spanish Survey, 1789-95. Fol. Lond., 1802. MD 1 P 15 ‡

Plan of the River Oregon. Fol. Lond., 1798. MD 1 P 15 ‡

Reduced Chart of the Pacific Ocean. Fol. Lond., 1798. MD 1 P 15 ‡

Survey of the Harbour of Panama by the Sloops Descubierta and Atrivida, 1791. Fol. Lond., 1800. MD 1 P 15 ‡

ART JOURNAL, The, 1892-94. 3 vols. 4to. Lond., 1892-94. E

ART OF PREACHING; in imitation of Horace's Art of Poetry. Sm. fol. Lond. (n.d.) H 39 Q 13 ‡

ART OF PRESERVING THE FEET. Practical Instructions for the Prevention of Corns, Bunnions, &c.; by "An Experienced Chiropodist." 4th ed. 12mo. Lond., 1818. A 33 P 2

ART OF TEA BLENDING: a Hand-book for the Tea Trade. 12mo. Sydney, 1882. MA 3 U 6

ART OF WRITING FICTION. [Chapters by various writers on the different Styles of novel writers.] 8vo. Lond. (n.d.) J 6 S 42

ART, L', POUR TOUS. Tomes 31-33. Fol. Paris, 1892-94. E

ART SOCIETY OF NEW SOUTH WALES. Annual Reports, 1888 and 1889. 8vo. Sydney, 1888-89. ME 3 R

ARTHUR, Chester A. Sketch of. [See Wilson, J. G.—Presidents of the United States.] C 2 V 30

ARTHUR, Lieut.-Col. Sir G. [Papers relating to Van Diemen's Land.] Copy of a Despatch to Lord Glenelg, dated 29th Oct., 1836, together with its Enclosures, and any answer. Sm. fol. Lond., 1837. MF 1 U 24

ARTHUR, J. K. Kangaroo and Kauri: Sketches and Anecdotes of Australia and New Zealand. Illustrated. 8vo. Lond., 1894. MD 8 R 17

ARTHUR, Rev. Wm. The People's Day: an Appeal to the Rt. Hon. Lord Stanley against his advocacy of a French Sunday. 11th ed. 8vo. Lond., 1856. G 15 P 43

ARTHURLEIGH, The: issued quarterly by the senior pupils of Argyle School, Surry Hills. 8vo. Sydney, 1886-88. ME 15 Q

ASCHERSON, Prof. P. On the Propagation of Cymodocea Antarctica. (Trans. Roy. Soc. S. Australia, 5.) 8vo. Adelaide, 1882. ME 4 S

ASCLEPIAD, The: a Book of Original Research and Observation in the Science, Art, and Literature of Medicine, Preventive and Curative. Vol. 1, No 1. 8vo. Lond, 1884. E

ASHE, Rev. R. P. Chronicles of Uganda. Illustrated. 8vo. Lond., 1894. B 33 Q 1

ASHTON, J. A right merrie Christmasse: the Story of Christ-tide. 4to. Lond., 1855. B 15 P 4 †

ASHURST, Eliza A. Letters of a Traveller. [See Didevant, A. L. A.] C 17 F 22

ASIATIC QUARTERLY REVIEW. [See Imperial and Asiatic Quarterly Review]

Supplementary Catalogue—1893-95.

ASIATIC SOCIETY OF BENGAL. Journal. Vols. 60-62. 8vo. Calcutta, 1892-94. E
Rules of. 8vo. Calcutta, 1876. E

ASIATIC SOCIETY OF JAPAN. Transactions. Vol. 15, part 1. 8vo. Yokohama, 1887. E

ASPECTS OF MODERN STUDY; being University Extension Addresses. 8vo. Lond., 1894. G 18 Q 15

ASPLAND, Rev. R. Attempt to ascertain the import of the title Son of Man, commonly assumed by our Lord. 18mo. Lond., 1821. G 19 P 31

ASSOCIATED BANKS [VICTORIA]. Agreement between, to afford mutual support. 8vo. Melb., 1893. MF 2 T 55

ASSOCIATION FRANCAISE POUR L'AVANCEMENT DES SCIENCES. Comptes Rendus des 20°—22° Sessions. 6 vols. roy. 8vo. Paris, 1891-94. E

ASSOCIATION OF OFFICIAL AGRICULTURAL CHEMISTS. Proceedings of the eleventh annual convention, 1894. Edited by H. W. Wiley. 8vo. Wash., 1894. E

ASTLEY, Sir John D., "The Mate." Fifty Years of my Life in the World of Sport at Home and Abroad. 4th ed. 8vo. Lond., 1895. C 14 S 22

ASTLEY, Wm., "Price Warung." Tales of Australian Early Days. 12mo. Lond., 1894. MJ 3 P 1

ASTOR, John J. Biographical Sketch of. [See Stoddard, Wm. O.—Men of Business.] C 16 R 19

ASTRONOMY AND ASTRO-PHYSICS. Vol. 13, 1894. 8vo. Northfield, Minn., 1894. E

ASVAGHOSHA. The Buddha-Karita of. [See Anecdota Oxon.] E

ASYLUM FOR DESTITUTE CHILDREN, RANDWICK. Inquiry into alleged ill-treatment at. 8vo. Sydney, 1878. MA 2 Q 47

ATHA. [See Westbury, F. A.]

ATHENÆUM, The. Journal of Literature, Science, the Fine Arts, Music, and the Drama. July, 1892-Dec., 1894. 5 vols. 4to. Lond., 1894. E

ATHENAGORAS. Writings of. (Ante-Nicene Christ. Lib., 2.) 8vo. Edinb., 1867. G 14 U 2

ATKINS, John. Notes on the Mining Statute, 1865. 8vo. Melb., 1871. MF 1 R 51

ATKINS, T. De Courcy. The Kelt or Gael: his ethnography, geography, and philology. 8vo. Lond., 1892. A 18 T 31

ATKINSON, Dr. Edmund. Ganot's Physics. [See Ganot, Prof. A.] A 29 R 12

ATKINSON, Dr. Edward. The Distribution of Products; or, the Mechanism and the Metaphysics of Exchange. 5th ed. New York, 1892. F 8 U 28
Industrial Progress of the Nation. Roy. 8vo. New York, 1889. F 3 V 8
The Margin of Profits: how it is now divided. 8vo. New York, 1887. F 8 U 30
Taxation and Work: a series of Treatises on the Tariff and the Currency. 8vo. New York, 1892. F 8 U 24

ATKINSON, Prof. George F. Study of the Biology of Ferns by the Collodion Method. 8vo. New York, 1894. A 20 T 9

ATKINSON, J. J. Friction of Air in Mines. 18mo. New York, 1889. A 24 P 10
Practical Treatise on the Gases met with in Coal Mines. 3rd ed., to which is added the Action of Coal Dusts; by E. H. Williams, jun. 18mo. New York, 1886. A 24 P 12

ATKINSON, John James. Our Railways, and how they are managed; or, a Sequel to the Royal Commission Report on Railways. 8vo. Dunedin, 1881. MF 1 Q 39

ATKINSON, Dr. Philip. The Electric Transformation of Power and its application by the Electric Motor, including Electric Railway construction. 8vo. New York, 1893. A 21 R 12

ATKINSON, Wm. Small Hospitals. [See Worcester, Dr. A.] A 10 Q 4

ATLANTIC MONTHLY. Vol. 75. 8vo. Boston, 1895. E

ATTFIELD, Dr. John. Chemistry, General, Medical, and Pharmaceutical, including the Chemistry of the British Pharmacopœia. 15th ed. 8vo. Lond., 1893. A 21 R 6

ATWATER, Dr. Wilbur O. Methods and Results of Investigations on the Chemistry and Economy of Food. 8vo. Wash., 1895. A 30 U 34

ATWOOD, T. Portrait of. [See Gammage R. G.—Chartist Movement.] F 7 R 24

AUBERTIN, J. J. By Order of the Sun to Chile to see his Total Eclipse, April 16, 1893. Illustrated. 8vo. Lond., 1894. A 10 Q 22

AUBINEAU, L. History of the Little Sisters of The Poor. 12mo. Melb. (n.d.) MG 2 R 25

AUBREY, J. Carmina varia, being Miscellaneous Poems. 8vo. Dunedin (n.d.) MH 1 P 54

AUCKLAND, George Eden, Earl of. [Life of]; by Capt. L. J. Trotter. (Rulers of India.) 8vo. Oxford, 1893. C 13 P 10

AUDIFFRET-PASQUIER, Duc d'. [See Pasquier, Chancellor.]

AUDSLEY, Wm. J. and Geo. A. Polychromatic Decoration. Fol. Lond., 1882. A 6 U 2‡

AUFFRAY, Mrs. E., (Edith O'Gorman). The Escaped Nun: What she has been and what she is. 8vo. Melb. (n.d.) MG 2 Q 7

AUGUSTINE, Archbishop of Canterbury, 597-604. Sketch of. [*See* Fowler, Rev. M.—Notable Archbishops.] C 13 V 12
[Life of]; by Rev. F. L. Cutts. 8vo. Lond., 1895. G 2 U 10

AULDJO, J., F.R.S. Narrative of an Ascent to the Summit of Mont Blanc, 1827. 3rd ed. 12mo. Lond., 1856. D 20 Q 15

AURANGZIB. [Life of]; by S Lane-Poole. (Rulers of India.) 8vo. Oxford, 1893. C 13 P 11

AURELIUS ANTONINUS, Marcus. Marc-Aurèle et la Fin du Monde Antique. [*See* Renan, E.] G 12 U 22
Conférences d'Angleterre. Marc-Aurèle. [*See* Renan, E.] G 12 U 1
[Life of.] [*See* Farrar, Ven. F. W.—Seekers after God.] C 21 Q 6

AURIFERA. [*See* Victorian Miners' Manual] MA 2 P 33

AUSTEN, W. C. Roberts-. Introduction to the Study of Metallurgy. 3rd ed. 8vo. Lond, 1894. A 24 S 7

AUSTIN, Alfred. The Garden that I love. 8vo. Lond., 1894. A 32 R 24

AUSTIN, J. B. Mines of South Australia. 8vo. Adelaide, 1863. MA 2 Q 48

AUSTRALASIAN ASSOCIATION FOR THE ADVANCEMENT OF SCIENCE. Reports of the Fourth and Fifth Meetings. 8vo. Sydney, 1893-94. ME 18 S
Handbook of Sydney. [*See* Hamlet, W. M.] MA 1 P 73
Handbook of Hobart. [*See* Morton, A.] MA 1 P 72

AUSTRALASIAN BOARD OF MISSIONS. Reports, 1889 and 1894. 8vo. Sydney; 1889-04. ME 6 S

AUSTRALASIAN BUILDER AND CONTRACTOR'S NEWS, July, 1890-April, 1895. 17 vols. fol. Sydney, 1890-1895. ME

AUSTRALASIAN CONFERENCE OF CHARITY. Proceedings, 1890. 8vo. Melb., 1890. ME 6 S

AUSTRALASIAN CONGREGATIONAL YEARBOOK AND CALENDER, for 1868. 12mo. Melb., 1868. ME 5 Q

AUSTRALASIAN FEDERAL-PASTORAL DIRECTORY. List of Stockowners in the Colonies. 8vo. Sydney, 1895. ME 7 Q

AUSTRALASIAN FEDERATION CONFERENCE, 1890. Official Record of the Proceedings and Debates, held in the Parliament House, Melbourne. Fol. Sydney, 1890. MF 2 U 20

AUSTRALASIAN FEDERATION LEAGUE. Rules and Proposals of. 8vo. Sydney, 1894. MF 1 R 64
[List of Members and Rules.] 18mo. Sydney, 1894. MF 4 P 7

AUSTRALASIAN INSURANCE AND BANKING RECORD AND STATISTICAL REGISTER, The. Vols. 14-16. 4to. Melb., 1890-92. ME

AUSTRALASIAN MEDICAL GAZETTE, The. Vols. 1, 4, 8-13, 1881-94. 8 vols. sm. 4to. Sydney, 1881-94. ME 7 R

AUSTRALASIAN METHODIST CHURCH. Minutes of the South Australian Conferences, 1887-89. 4 vols. 8vo. Adelaide, 1887-89. ME 15 Q

AUSTRALASIAN MISSIONARY NEWS, April-Oct., 1888, and Jan-Dec , 1889. 2 vols. 8vo. Sydney, 1888-89. ME 6 R

AUSTRALASIAN PASTORALISTS' REVIEW. Vol. 1, March, 1891-Feb., 1892. Sm. fol. Melb., 1891-92. ME 19 T

AUSTRALASIAN SANITARY CONFERENCE OF SYDNEY, 1881. Report, Minutes of Proceedings, and Appendix. Sm. fol. Sydney, 1884. MA 1 P 32 †

AUSTRALASIAN SCIENTIFIC MAGAZINE, August-November, 1885. 8vo. Melb , 1885. ME 3 S

AUSTRALASIAN WESLEYAN METHODIST CHURCH. Minutes of the 3rd and 8th New South Wales and Queensland Annual Conferences, 1876, 1881. 2 vols. 8vo. Sydney, 1876-81. ME 15 Q
Minutes of the South Australian Conferences, 1887-88. 3 vols. 8vo. Adelaide, 1887-89. ME 15 Q
General Conference of the Australasian Wesleyan Methodist Church, 1894. 8vo. Adelaide, 1894. ME 15 Q
Minutes of the 11th Annual Conference, 1865. 12mo. Sydney, 1865. ME 15 Q

AUSTRALASIAN WESLEYAN METHODIST MISSIONARY SOCIETY. Report, 1857. 12mo. Sydney, 1857. ME 15 Q

AUSTRALIA. A true Picture of Australia: its Merits and Demerits. 8vo. Glasgow, 1839. MB 1 T 25

AUSTRALIAN, An. [*See* Golden Gates of Australia.] MD 7 T 61

AUSTRALIAN ALPS. Illustrated Guide to the Australian Alps and Buffalo Ranges. 8vo. Bright, Vict (n.d.) MD 8 P 15

AUSTRALIAN ART: a Monthly Magazine and Journal. January and February, 1888. 8vo. Sydney, 1888. ME 19 P

AUSTRALIAN BEE BULLETIN: a Monthly Journal devoted to Bee-keeping. Vol. 3, 1894-95. 8vo. Maitland, 1894-95. ME 9 P

14   *Supplementary Catalogue*—1893-95.

AUSTRALIAN BOARD OF MISSIONS. [*See* Australasian Board of Missions.]

AUSTRALIAN CHRISTMAS BOX, The: A Series of Stories. 8vo. Melb. (n.d.)   MJ 2 S 13

AUSTRALIAN CHRISTMAS CHIMES, for Old and Young. 4to. Melb. (n.d.)   MJ 1 V 9

AUSTRALIAN COLONIES GOVERNMENT BILL. Copy of a Letter from Mr. Coulson, upon the Bill. Sm. fol. Lond., 1850.   MF 1 U 25

AUSTRALIAN COLONIST, An. [*See* Victim of Circumstantial Evidence.]   MJ 1 R 43

AUSTRALIAN FEDERATION: a Review of Mr. Forster's Paper "Fallacies of Federation." 8vo. Sydney, 1877.   MF 1 Q 37

AUSTRALIAN FREE RELIGIOUS PRESS. Vol. 2, Feb., 1871, to Jan., 1872. (Pam.) 8vo. Sydney, 1872.   MG 1 Q 53

AUSTRALIAN HEALTH SOCIETY, MELBOURNE. Publications, 1880-81. 8vo. Melb., 1880-81. MA 3 S 33
   1. Hints about the prevention of Scarlet Fever.
   2. Pure Air and Ventilation.
   3. Rules for the prevention of Typhoid Fever.
   4. Under the Floor ; by Dr. F. M. Girdlestone.
   5. Rules for the Management of Infants.
   6. Notes on Diet ; by S. Gibbons.
   7. What kills our Babies ; by Dr. C. D. Hunter.
   8. Diseases which should be prevented ; by Dr. J. Jamieson.
   9. Summer Diseases—Ophthalmia ; by Dr. Rudall. Sunstroke ; by Dr. J. Jamieson.
   10. A Bad Smell ; by A. Sutherland.
   11. Preservation of the Teeth ; by Miss A. C. Moon.
   12. Infectious and Contagious Diseases of Children.
   13. Small-pox and Vaccination ; by Dr. J. P. Ryan.

AUSTRALIAN HOME COMPANION, The, and Band of Hope Journal. Vol. 4. 8vo. Sydney, 1859.   ME 3 R

AUSTRALIAN HOME JOURNAL: a Domestic Journal. Vol. 1, 1894. Sm. 4to. Sydney, 1894.   ME 19 R

AUSTRALIAN HOMŒOPATHIC PROGRESS, Aug., 1870–July, 1871. 8vo. Sydney, 1870-71. ME 15 Q

AUSTRALIAN HORTICULTURAL MAGAZINE AND GARDEN GUIDE, The. Edited by D. A. Crichton. Vols. 1 and 2. 8vo. Melb., 1878.   ME 3 S

AUSTRALIAN HOUSEWIVES' MANUAL, The: a book for beginners and people with small incomes ; by "An Old Housekeeper." 2nd ed. 12mo. Melb., 1885.   MA 3 P 60

AUSTRALIAN INDEPENDENT. Vol. 3, 1890. Sm. 4to. Sydney, 1890.   ME 21 T

AUSTRALIAN INDEPENDENT YEAR BOOK AND CALENDAR FOR 1893. 8vo. Sydney, 1893.   ME 3 R

AUSTRALIAN JOINT STOCK BANK. Circular to the shareholders, July, 1831. 8vo. Sydney, 1861.   MF 4 Q 31

Report of the Proceedings of the Shareholders of the Joint Stock Bank, 1861. 8vo. Sydney, 1861.   MF 4 Q 31

AUSTRALIAN JOURNAL, The: a Family Newspaper of Literature, Science, and the Arts. Vols. 10-29. 20 vols. 4to. Melb., 1875-94.   ME 3 V

AUSTRALIAN LLOYDS. Rules and Regulations. 8vo. Melb., 1864.   MF 1 R 47

AUSTRALIAN MAGAZINE OF CONTEMPORARY OPINION. Vol. 1, Nos. 1 and 2. July-Aug., 1886. Roy. 8vo. Melb., 1886.   ME 19 P

AUSTRALIAN MEDICAL JOURNAL, The. Edited under the superintendence of the Victoria Medical Society. 38 vols. 8vo. Melb., 1856-93.   ME 9 S-T

AUSTRALIAN MESSENGER, The, of the Sacred Heart: Organ of the Apostleship of Prayer. Conducted by the Jesuit Fathers. Vols. 4-8, 1890-94. 5 vols. 12mo. Sydney, 1890-94.   ME 15 P

AUSTALIAN MINING STANDARD, Jan., 1891–June, 1894. 7 vols. fol. Sydney, 1891-94.   ME

AUSTRALIAN MUSEUM. Act of Incorporation, By-laws, Rules and Regulations of. 8vo. Sydney, 1892.   MF 4 R 27

Catalogue of the Specimens of Natural History and Miscellaneous Curiosities. 8vo. Sydney, 1837.   MA 2 U 40

Catalogue of Marine Shells. [*See* Brazier, J.] MA 2 U 40

Catalogue of Australian Mammals. [*See* Ogilby, J. D.]   MA 2 U 44

Records of. Vols. 1 and 2. 8vo. Sydney, 1890-93.   ME 8 R

Reports, 1881-90, and 1893-94. 2 vols. Sm. fol. and 8vo. Sydney, 1882-91.   ME

AUSTRALIAN MUTUAL PROVIDENT SOCIETY. By-laws, confirmed and passed, 1867. 8vo. Sydney, 1867.   MF 1 Q 38

Forty-fourth Annual Report, with Schedules and Returns for the Colonial Governments. 4to. Sydney, 1893.   ME

New Tables, Regulations, and By-laws. 12mo. Sydney, 1874.   MF 4 P 32

Reports, 1859-95. Sm. fol. Sydney, 1859-95.   ME 7 Q

Report on the 6th Quinquennial Investigation. Sm. 4to. Sydney, 1879.   ME 7 Q

AUSTRALIAN PARLOR & CLUB-ROOM GAMES. 12mo. Melb., 1857.   MA 3 P 61

AUSTRALIAN PARTICULAR BAPTIST MAGAZINE. 8vo. Sydney, 1884-86.   ME 3 S

AUSTRALIAN PHOTOGRAPHIC JOURNAL, The. Vols. 1 and 2, 1892-93. Sm. 4to. Sydney, 1892-93.
   ME 18 R

AUSTRALIAN PLAIN COOKERY; by "A Practical Cook." 6th ed. 12mo. Melb. (n.d.)
   MA 3 P 62

AUSTRALIAN PRACTITIONER, The: a Quarterly Journal of Medical, Surgical, and Sanitary Science for the Australian Colonies. Nos. 1-4, October, 1877, to October, 1878. [*All published.*] 8vo. Sydney, 1877-78.
   ME 8 S

AUSTRALIAN PRIMITIVE METHODIST YEAR-BOOK, 1890. 12mo. Sydney, 1890.
   ME 4 U

AUSTRALIAN RELIGIOUS TRACT SOCIETY. Report for 1850. 8vo. Sydney, 1851.
   ME 6 S

AUSTRALIAN SPELLING BOOK, The. 32mo. Sydney, 1893.
   MK 1 P 56

AUSTRALIAN SPORTING CELEBRITIES. Edited by "Vigilant." 8vo. Melb., 1887.
   MC 1 T 21

AUSTRALIAN STAR, The. October, 1892-Dec., 1895. 13 vols. Fol. Sydney, 1892-95.
   ME

AUSTRALIAN STORIES in Prose and Verse. 8vo. Melb., 1892.
   MJ 3 R 9

AUSTRALIAN STUD BOOK, The; containing Pedigrees of Racehorses, &c. Vols. 1-4. Compiled by W. C. Yuille. 8vo. Melb., 1878-89.
   MA 3 W 1-4

AUSTRALIAN VIGNERON AND FRUIT-GROWERS' JOURNAL: a Monthly Paper in the interest of Australian Wine and Fruit-growers. Sm 4to. Sydney, 1890-91.
   ME 10 S

AUSTRALIAN WORKMAN, The, 1891. Fol. Sydney 1891.
   ME

AUSTRALISCHER VOLKS-KALENDER für das jahr 1874. 8vo. Tanunda, S. Aust., 1873.
   ME 4 R

AUTONNE, Dr. Léon. Sur la théorie des Equations différentielles du premier ordre et du premier degré. (Annales de l'Université de Lyon, 3.) 8vo. Paris, 1892.
   A 25 V 21

AUTORIELLO, Prof. Francesco. Corso Completo di Prospettiva Ragionata. Seconda edizione. Text, 8vo. Plates, fol. 2 vols. Napoli, 1889.
   A 23 U 17 and A 2 P 1-

AUVRAY, Lucien. Les Manuscrits de Dante des Bibliothèques de France. (Bibliothèque des Ecoles Françaises d'Athènes et de Rome, 56° Fascicule.) 8vo. Paris, 1892.
   K 19 S 4

AVELINE, Wm. T. Portrait of. [*See* Ramsay, Sir A. C.—Memoir of.]
   C 21 R 20

AVIS, John O. The Australian Melodist; or, Songs and Hymns for use at public meetings and private circles. 12mo. Sydney, 1894.
   MH 1 U 64

AYAME-SAN. A Japanese Romance of the 23rd year of Meiji (1890); by "A.M." Illustrated from photographs by W. K. Burton. 8vo. Lon., 1893.
   J 4 U 14

AYLING, John. Book of the Lifeboat. [*See* Dibdin, J. C.]
   F 14 T 33

AYLMER, Capt. Fenton. A Cruise in the Pacific. 2 vols. 8vo. Lond., 1860.
   MD 8 P 10, 11

B

B.V. [*See* Thomson, Jas.]

BABA, N. Organization of the Meteorological System in Japan. Imp. 8vo. Tokio, 1883.
   A 12 U 18 †

BABINGTON, W. D. Fallacies of Race Theories as applied to National Characteristics. 12mo. Lond., 1895.
   A 19 Q 6

BABO, Freiherr A. von, and MACH, E. Handbuch des Weinbaues und der Kellerwirthschaft. 2 vols. 8vo. Berlin, 1881-85.
   A 18 U 16, 17

BABYLONIAN AND ORIENTAL RECORD, The: a Monthly Magazine of the Antiquities of the East. Vols. 5-7. 8vo. Lond., 1891-94.
   E

BACHE, Dr. Alex. Dallas. Discussion of the Magnetic and Meteorological Observations made at the Girard College Observatory, Philadelphia, 1841-45. 4to. Wash., 1859.
   A 15 Q 9 †

Eulogy on; by Prof. J. Henry. 8vo. Wash., 1872.
   C 1 9 S 5

BACHE, Dr. Franklin. Dispensatory of the United States. [*See* Wood, Dr. G. B.]
   A 26 V 13

BACKHOUSE, Jas., and WALKER, G. W. Address to the Prisoner Population. 12mo. Sydney, 1837.
   MG 1 P 51

BACON, Alice Mabel. A Japanese Interior. 12mo. Lond., 1893.
   D 17 P 2

BACON, Francis, Baron Verulam. Works of; with a Life of the Author by B. Montague. 3 vols. roy. 8vo. Philad., 1841.
   J 9 V 26-28

Physical and Metaphysical Works of; by J. Devey. 12mo. Lond., 1853.
   G 2 V 32

Selections from Writings of. [*See* Grosart, A. B.]
   J 7 P 46

Essays; with Annotations by Archbishop Whately. 3rd ed. 8vo. Lond., 1857.
   J 6 T 3

Essays, Civil and Moral. 8vo. Lond., 1853.
   J 4 U 1

Essays, Moral, Economical, and Political; with the Life of the Author. 32mo. Lond., 1832.
   Libr.

BACON, Francis, Baron Verulam—*contd.*
The New Atlantis. [*See* More, Sir T.—Utopia.]
F 15 Q 7
Bacon the Poet: Indications of Bacon's Mind in the Shakespearean Poems. [*See* Royal Soc. of Lit., 2nd Series, 16.]
E
Francis Bacon: His Life and Philosophy; by Prof. John Nichol. (Philosophical Classics.) 2 vols. 8vo. Edinb., 1888-89.
G 9 V 11, 12
Francis Bacon of Verulam: Realistic Philosophy and its Age; by Kuno Fischer. Translated by John Oxenford. 8vo. Lond., 1857.
G 13 S 43
Lord Bacon: his Writings and Philosophy; by Dr. G. L. Craik. 12mo. Lond., 1860.
J 12 S 31
The First English Freethinker. [*See* Maxwell, Sir H.— Post Meridiana.]
J 7 S 11
Story of Lord Bacon's Life; by W. H. Dixon. 12mo. Lond., 1862.
C 17 P 11

BACON, Henry. The Salon. [*See* Paris Salon.]
E 1 R 57

BACON, Roger. The Famous Historic of Fryer Bacon. [*See* Bibliotheca Curiosa.]
J 18 Q 42

BADDELEY, Welbore St. Clair. Queen Joanna I of Naples, Sicily, and Jerusalem: an Essay on her Times. 8vo. Lond, 1893.
C 16 T 11

BADEAUX, J. B. Journal des Opérations de l'Armée Américaine, 1775-76. 8vo. Montreal, 1871.
B 24 T 20

BADHAM, Prof. Chas. Adhortatio ad Juventutem Academicam Sydneiensem. 8vo. Sydney, 1869.
MJ 2 S 34

BAEDEKER, Karl. London and its Environs: Handbook for Travellers. 8th ed., with Maps and Plans. 12mo. Lond., 1892.
D 12 P 13

BAGEHOT, Walter. Biographical Studies. 12mo. Lond., 1895.
C 22 P 10
Economic Studies. 8vo. Lond., 1895.
F 7 V 35
Estimates of some Englishmen and Scotchmen. Roy. 8vo. Lond., 1858.
J 10 V 32
Literary Studies. 3 vols. 8vo. Lond, 1895.
J O P 22-24

BAGENAL, Philip H. D. The Priest in Politics. 8vo. Lond., 1893.
F 6 S 30

BAGSHAW, J. S. An Outline of the Psalms. 2nd ed. 12mo. Sydney (n.d.)
MG 2 R 31

BAILEY, Frederick M. Botany abridged. 8vo. Brisbane, 1894.
MA 1 T 55
Companion for the Queensland Student of Plant Life. 8vo. Brisbane, 1893.
MA 1 T 55
Contributions to the Queensland Flora. (Proc. Roy. Soc., Queensland, 1.) 8vo. Brisbane, 1884. ME 1 T
Contributions to the Queensland Flora. Oct., 1890- Dec., 1893. 8vo. Brisbane, 1890-93. MA 1 T 55

BAILEY, Frederick M.—*contd.*
Description of *Acacia melaleucoides*. (Proc. Roy. Soc., Queensland, 5.) 8vo. Brisbane, 1888. ME 1 T
Description of a New Eucalypt. (Proc. Roy. Soc., Queensland, 10.) 8vo. Brisbane, 1893. ME 1 T
Handbook to the Ferns of Queensland. 12mo. Brisb., 1874.
MA 1 P 81
Notes for the Guidance of Amateur Fruit-growers. 8vo. Brisbane, 1895.
MA 1 T 55
Notes upon some Plant Specimens collected on the Diamantina. (Proc. Roy. Soc., Queensland, 8.) 8vo. Brisbane, 1892.
ME 1 T
Official Guide to the Museum of Economic Botany. 8vo. Brisb., 1891.
MA 1 T 55
Queensland Woods. 8vo. Brisbane, 1886. MA 2 V 64
Specimens of Blackall Range Plants. (Proc. Roy. Soc., Queensland, 8.) 8vo. Brisbane, 1892. ME 1 T

BAILEY, H. T. Industrial Drawing in the Public Schools of Massachusetts. 8vo. Boston, 1893.
G 18 R 30

BAILEY, Henry, "Bula N'Zau." Travel and Adventures in the Congo Free State, and its big Game Shooting. Illustrated. With Map. 8vo. Lond., 1894. D 14 S 18

BAILEY, Prof. Liberty Hyde. Annals of Horticulture in North America for 1893. 8vo. New York, 1894.
A 18 S 39
Apricot-growing in Western New York. 8vo. Ithaca, N.Y., 1894.
A 32 R 4
The Japanese Plums in North America. 8vo. Ithaca, N.Y., 1894.
A 32 R 3
Impressions of the Peach Industry in Western New York. 8vo. Ithaca, N.Y., 1894.
A 32 R5
Field Notes on Apple Culture. 12mo. New York, 1886.
A 18 Q 35

BAILEY, Vernon. The Pocket Gophers of the United States. 8vo. Wash., 1895.
A 30 T 17

BAILLIERE, F. F. Bailliere's South Australian Gazetteer and Road Guide. Compiled by R. P. Whitworth. 8vo. Adelaide, 1866.
MD 5 S 56
Another copy. 2nd ed. 8vo. Adelaide, 1869.
MD 5 S 57
Bailliere's Queensland Gazetteer and Road Guide. Compiled by R. P. Whitworth. 8vo. Brisb., 1876.
MD 5 S 55
Bailliere's Tasmanian Gazetteer and Road Guide. Compiled by R. P. Whitworth. 8vo. Hobart, 1877.
MD 5 S 54

BAILWARD, W. A. The Oxford House and the Organization of Charity. [*See* Knapp, J. M.—The Universities and the Social Problem.] F 8 U 22

BAIN, F. W. The English Monarchy and its Revolutions: a Study in Analytical Politics. 8vo. Lond., 1894.
B 21 U 13

BAINBRIDGE, Edwin. A Memoir; by T. Darlington. 12mo. Lond., 1887. MC 1 P 52

BAINES, Edward. History of the County Palatine and Duchy of Lancaster. New Edition, edited by J. Croston. Vol. 5. 4to. Manchester, 1893. B 23 V 12

BAINES, Thos. Greenhouse and Stove Plants, flowering and fine-leaved Palms, Ferns, and Lycopodiums. 8vo. Lond., 1885. A 4 Q 14

BAIRD, Prof. Spencer F. Smithsonian Institution Report, 1879. [See Smithsonian Institution.] E

BAKER, Chas. W. Monopolies and the People. 12mo. New York, 1890. F 8 U 3

BAKER, John G. Handbook of the Amaryllideæ, including the Alstræmerieæ and Agaveæ. 8vo. Lond., 1888. A 4 Q 13
Synopsis Filicum. [See Hocker, Sir W. J.] A 20 T 13

BAKER, M. N. Sewage Disposal in the U.S. [See Rafter, G. W.] A 22 V 18
Sewage Purification in America. 12mo. New York, 1893. A 22 P 24

BAKER, Sir Samuel. A Memoir; by J. D. Murray and A. S. White. 8vo. Lond., 1895. C 21 T 10

BAKER, Wm. S. Early Sketches of George Washington. 8vo. Philad., 1894. C 21 R 10

BALBIANI, G. Le Phylloxera du Chêne et le Phylloxera de la Vigne. 4to. Paris 1884. A 15 S 8 †

BALDWIN, Dr. Jas. Mark. Mental Development in the Child and the Race. Illustrated. 8vo. New York, 1895. G 14 S 20

BALDWIN, Wm. J. Hot Water Heating and Fitting; or, Warming Buildings by Hot Water. Illustrated. 8vo. Lond., 1892. A 22 T 15
Steam Heating for Buildings; or, Hints to Steam Fitters. 13th ed. 12mo. New York, 1893. A 22 Q 18

BALE, W. M. Further Notes on Australian Hydroids; with descriptions of some new species. (Proceedings Royal Society, Victoria, 6; new series.) 8vo. Melb., 1894. ME 1 P

BALFOUR, Rt. Hon. Arthur J. Essays and Addresses. 8vo. Edinb., 1873. J 4 Q 29
The Foundations of Belief; being Notes introductory to the study of Theology. 8vo. Lond., 1895. G 14 Q 30
Sketch of. [See Smalley, G. W.—Studies of Men.] C 19 R 20

BALFOUR, Henry. Evolution of Decorative Art. 12mo. Lond., 1893. A 23 Q 37

BALFOUR, Jas. The Political Situation: a Speech. 8vo. Melb., 1887. MJ 3 Q 15

BALFOUR, Jas. M. Durability of New Zealand Timber. [See Kirk, T.] MA 1 V 58

BALFOUR, Dr. John H. Phyto-Theology; or, Botanical Sketches intended to illustrate the works of God in the structure, functions, and general distribution of Plants. 12mo. Lond., 1851. A 20 P 21

BALFOUR, L. Geological Notes on Tasmania. [See Officer, L.] ME 1 P

BALL, Adm. Sir A. A Sailor's Fortune; by S. T. Coleridge. [Bound with Confessions of an Inquiring Spirit.] 18mo. Lond., 1886. J 7 P 47

BALL, Rev. Chas. Jas. Jeremiah. [See Expositor's Bible.] G 19 R and S

BALL, I. Warren. Handbook of Examination Papers in Arithmetic and Algebra, being questions at the Matriculation Examinations of Melbourne University, 1864-1874. 8vo. Melb., 1874. MA 2 P 43
Comprehensive Examinations on Geography. 8vo. Melb., 1883. MD 8 Q 28

BALL, J. Dyer. Things Chinese, being Notes on various subjects connected with China. 8vo. Lond., 1892 D 17 T 3

BALL, Sir Robert S. An Atlas of Astronomy. Sm. 4to. Lond., 1892. A 19 T 31
Dynamics and Modern Geometry: a new chapter in the Theory of Screws. (Trans. R.I. Academy—Cunningham Memoirs, 3.) 4to. Dublin, 1887. E
In Starry Realms. Illustrated. 8vo. London, 1893. A 19 S 20
In the High Heavens. Illustrated. 8vo. Lond., 1893. A 19 S 27
Starland: being Talks with Young People about the Wonders of the Heavens. 8vo. Illustrated. Lond., 1893. A 19 Q 29
The Story of the Sun. 8vo. Lond., 1893. A 19 T 19

BALLAN SELTERS WATER: Sketch of Mineral Springs and their uses, with references to the properties of 12mo. Melb. (n.d.) MA 2 P 39

BALLANTINE, Henry. On India's Frontier; or, Nepal, the Gurkhas' Mysterious Land. 12mo. New York, 1895. D 17 Q 25

BALLANTYNE, Archibald. Voltaire's Visit to England, 1726-29. 8vo. Lond., 1893. C 14 S 26

BALLANTYNE, Rev. Jas. Our Colony in 1880, Pictorial and Descriptive, with Map of Victoria. 12mo. Melb., 1880. MD 1 Q 41

BALLARAT. Visitor's Guide-book to. 12mo. Ballarat 1875. MD 5 Q 30

BALLARAT GENERAL CEMETERY. Reports, 1885, 1887-90, 1894. 6 vols. 8vo. Ballarat, 1885-94.
ME 15 Q
BALLARAT SCHOOL OF MINES. Reports, 1881-83, 1886-88, 1890. 7 vols. 8vo. Ballarat, 1881-90.
ME 15 Q
BALLARD, Harlan H. The World of Matter: a Guide to the Study of Chemistry and Mineralogy. Illustrated. 8vo. Chicago, 1892. A 21 R 11

BALLARD, Capt. V. V. Chart of the Moluccas and Eastern Islands. [See Moor, Lieut. H.] D 1 S 12 ‡

BALLET GIRL, The, her Theatrical and Domestic History. 12mo. Sydney, 1893. MJ 1 U 32

BALMFORTH, Ramsden. The New Reformation and its Relation to Moral and Social Problems. 12mo. Lond., 1893. G 7 U 10

BANCROFT, Hubert H. History of California, 1542-1890. 7 vols. 8vo. San Francisco, 1890.
B 17 T 19-25

BANCROFT, Dr. J. Diseases of Plants and Animals. (Divinity Hall Record.) 8vo. Brisb., 1879.
ME 15 Q
The Microscope in our Gardens. (Divinity Hall Record.) 8vo. Brisbane, 1879. ME 15 Q
Food of the Aborigines of Australia. (Proc. Roy. Soc., Queensland, 1.) 8vo. Brisbane, 1884. ME 1 T
Experiments with Indian Wheats in Queensland. (Proc. Roy. Soc., Queensland, 1.) 8vo. Brisb., 1885.
ME 1 T

BANCROFT, Dr. Thos. L. Distillation of Native Essential Oils from a commercial aspect. (Proc. Roy. Soc., Queensland, 7.) 8vo. Brisbane, 1891. ME 1 T
On Echinicoccus in a Wallaby. (Proc. Roy. Soc., Queensland, 7.) 8vo. Brisbane, 1891. ME 1 T
On Filariæ of Birds. (Proc. Roy. Soc., Queensland, 6.) 8vo. Brisbane, 1889. ME 1 T
Pharmacology of *Carissa ovata*, var. *stolonifera*, Bail. (Journal Roy. Soc., N.S.W., 28.) 8vo. Sydney, 1894.
ME 1 R
On the poisonous property of *Nicotiana suaveolens*. (Proc. Roy. Soc., Queensland, 4.) 8vo. Brisbane, 1887. ME 1 T
Preliminary Notes on some new Poisonous Plants. (Proc. Roy. Soc., Queensland, 8.) 8vo. Brisb., 1891.
ME 1 T
On Psoriasis in Horses. (Proc. Roy. Soc., Queensland, 8.) 8vo. Brisbane, 1892. ME 1 T
Strychnine, a useless remedy in snakebite. (Proc. Roy. Soc., Queensland, 8.) 8vo. Brisbane, 1891. ME 1 T
On the Whip-worm of the Rat's Liver. (Journal Roy. Soc. N.S.W., 27.) 8vo. Sydney, 1893. ME 1 R

BANDELIER, Adolph F. A. Indians of South-western United States. [See Archæological Institute of America.] E

BANK OF NEW SOUTH WALES. Continuation of Correspondence between the Government of New South Wales and. 8vo. Sydney, 1885. MF 3 P 32
Rules and Regulations for the Management of the Fidelity Guarantee and Provident Fund of. 8vo. Sydney, 1876. MF 1 R 54

BANKERS' INSTITUTE OF AUSTRALIA. Journal of, 1887-92. 4 vols. 8vo. Melb., 1887-92. ME 15 T

BANKS, George N. Across France in a Caravan; being some account of a Journey from Bordeaux to Genoa, 1889-90. 8vo. Edinb., 1892. D 18 S 7

BANKS, Sir Joseph. Photograph of. [See Photographs of New South Wales Scenery, 4.] MA 45 ‡

BANKS, S. H., & GILL, W. B. The Yellow Dwarf: an Extravaganza. 12mo. Sydney, 1872. MH 1 P 53

BANKS, W. J. The Australian Musical Album. Ob. 4to. Sydney, 1894. MA 8 P 7 †

BANNISTER, Saxe. Papers relating to the case of. Sm. fol. Lond., 1861-62. MF 3 U 5

BARACCHI, Pietro. Results of Observations with Kater's Invariable Pendulums, made at the Melbourne Observatory, June to September, 1893. (Proceedings of Royal Society, Victoria, 6; new series.) 8vo. Melb., 1894. ME 1 P

BARANTE, Amable G. P. Brugière, Baron de. Etudes Littéraires et Historiques. 2 vols. 12mo. Paris, 1859. B 37 P 4, 5
The Chieftains of Vendée. [See Bibliotheca Curiosa.]
J 18 Q 4 ‡

BARBAULD, Mrs. Anna L. Selections from the Spectator, Tatler, Guardian, and Freeholder. 2 vols. 12mo. Lond., 1819. J 12 T 24, 25

BARBER, Dr. Edwin A. The Pottery and Porcelain of the United States. Illustrated. Roy. 8vo. New York, 1893. A 23 V 10

BARBER, Dr. Henry. British Family Names: their Origin and Meaning; with Lists of Scandinavian, Frisian, Anglo-Saxon, and Norman Names. 8vo. Lond., 1894. K 15 P 36

BARBER, Thos. W. Repair and Maintenance of Machinery. Illustrated. 8vo. Lond., 1895.
A 22 S 11

BARBOSA, Ruy. Finanças e Politica de Republica [Brazil]. 8vo. Rio de Janeiro, 1892. F 9 T 17
Martial Law; its constitution, limits, and effects. Roy. 8vo. Rio de Janeiro, 1892. F 12 P 29

BARBOUR, A. J. Clara; a Romance of Rural Life; an Australian Poem. 8vo. Melb., 1888.* MH 1 P 60

BARCLAY, Robt. The Silver Question and the Gold Question. 4th ed. 12mo. Lond., 1894. F 7 V 28

BARDOT, G., POUZET, P., ot BRETON, A. Mélanges Carolingiens. 8vo. Paris, 1890. B 26 V 22

BARINE, Arvède. Bernardin de St. Pierre. (Great French Writers.) 8vo. Lond., 1893. C 19 Q 9

BARING-GOULD, Rev. Sabine. The Deserts of Southern France: an Introduction to the Limestone and Chalk Plateaux of Ancient Aquitaine. 2 vols. 8vo. Lond., 1894. A 24 U 30, 31
 Strange Survivals: Some Chapters in the History of Man. 8vo. Lond., 1892. B 14 Q 3
 The Tragedy of the Cæsars: a Study of the Characters of the Cæsars of the Julian and Claudian Houses. 2 vols. Roy. 8vo. Lond., 1892. B 30 V 11, 12

BARKER, D. W. Notes on the Storms of High South Latitudes. (Ray. Soc. of Vic, 19). 8vo. Melb., 1893. ME 1 P

BARKER, Edward H. Two Summers in Guyenne. Illustrated. 8vo. Lond., 1894. D 18 U 12
 Wanderings by Southern Waters, Eastern Aquitaine. 8vo. Lond., 1893. D 8 U 38

BARKER, Rt. Rev. Frederic. An Address delivered in St. James' School-room, Sydney, on Dec. 6th, 1864. 8vo. Sydney, 1865. MG 1 S 3
 Charge delivered to the Clergy of the Diocese of Sydney, Nov. 23, 1858, at the Primary Visitation. 8vo. Sydney, 1859. MG 1 S 2

BARKER, W. H. Gold-fields of Western Australia. With Map. 8vo. Lond., 1894. MA 3 T 22

BARLOW, Wm. The Local Courts Act; the Intercolonial Debts Act of South Australia, New South Wales, and Victoria; and the Abolition of Imprisonment for Debt Act; with notes. 8vo. Adelaide, 1890. MF 1 Q 42

BARNARD, Chas. Talks about the Soil. 18mo. Boston, 1896. A 18 P 4
 Talks about our useful Plants. 18mo. Boston, 1887. A 18 P 5

BARNARD, G. L. The Olive: its Present Condition in South Australia, Mode of Pruning, &c. (Proc. Roy. Agricult. and Horticult. Soc., S. Australia, 1882.) 8vo. Adelaide, 1882. ME 1 S

BARNARD, Major J. G. Rotary Motion, as applied to the Gyroscope 18mo. New York, 1887. A 25 P 32

BARNES, W. E. Fourth Book of Maccabees in Syriac. [See Bensly, Prof. R. L.] G 14 Q 32

BARNET, Nat. J. Mixed: a Holiday Dish of Tales, Sketches, Poems, and Pictures. Sm. 4to. Melb., 1889. MJ 2 S 42

BARNETT, Rev. Canon. Hospitalities. [See Knapp, J. M.—The Universities and the Social Problem.] F 8 U 22

BARNETT, S. and Henrietta. Practicable Socialism: Essays on Reform. 2nd ed. 8vo. Lond., 1894. F 14 R 24

BARRA, Eduardo de la. Elementos de Métrica Castellana. Roy. 8vo. Santiago, 1887. H 5 U 30
 Poesias. 2 vols. 8vo. Santiago, 1889. H 9 U 18, 19

BARRAS, Paul. Memoirs of. Edited by G. Duruy, and translated by C. E. Roche. Vols. 1 and 2. 8vo. Lond., 1895. C 21 T 15, 16

BARRETT, C. R. B. Somersetshire: Highways, Byways, and Waterways. Illustrated. 4to. Lond., 1894. D 18 V 12
 Surrey: Highways, Byways, and Waterways. Illustrated Sm. 4to. Lond., 1893. B 21 V 9
 The Trinity House of Deptford Strond. Sm. 4to. Lond., 1893. B 21 V 22

BARRETT, Charlotte. Diary and Letters of Mme. D'Arblay. 4 vols. 8vo. Lond. (n.d.) C 17 R 10-13

BARRETT, J. O. The Forest Tree Planter's Manual. 8vo. Minneapolis, 1894. A 32 R 20

BARRETT, J. W. Some Statistics showing the extent of the Damage done to Members of the Medical Profession by the Abuse of Alcohol. (Proceedings Royal Society, Victoria, 6; new series.) 8vo. Melb., 1894. ME 1 P

BARRETT, John P. Electricity at the Columbian Exposition. Roy. 8vo. Chicago, 1894. A 21 V 18

BARRETT, Lawrence. [Plaster Cast of.] [See Hutton, L.—Portraits in Plaster.] A 23 V 13

BARRIE, Jas. Matthew. Auld Licht Idylls. Illustrated by W. Hole. Roy. 8vo. Lond., 1895. J 2 U 26

BARRISTER, A. [See Stephen, J. F.]

BARRON, Rev. D. G. Court Book of Barony of Urie. [See Scottish History Soc., 12.] E

BARROS, João de, and COUTO, Diogo de. Asia. 9 vols. 12mo Lisboa, 1778. D 17 P 5-13

BARROWS, Rev. Dr. John Henry. The World's Parliament of Religions: an illustrated and popular story of the World's first Parliament of Religions, held in Chicago in connection with the Columbian Exposition of 1893. 2 vols. 8vo. Chicago, 1893. G 10 S 28, 29

BARRY, John W. Studies in Corsica, Sylvan and Social. 8vo. Lond., 1893. D 18 S 6

BARTHOLOMEW Anglicus. [See Steel, R.]

BARTHOLOMEW, John. Plan of Dublin, with Environs. 8vo. Lond. (n.d.) D 18 P 28
 Plans of Manchester and Liverpool. 12mo. Lond. (n.d.) D 12 P 14, 15

BARTLETT, John. New and complete Concordance or verbal Index to Words, Phrases, and Passages in the Dramatic Works of Shakespeare. 4to. Lond., 1894. K 17 S 21

BARTLETT, W. H. The Scenes and Antiquities of Ireland. Illustrated; with Historical and Descriptive Text. 2 vols. 4to. Lond. (n.d.) D 19 V 18, 19

BARTLEY, N. Gold Occurrence in Queensland. (Proc. Roy. Soc., Queensland, 4.) 8vo. Brisb., 1887. ME 1 T
The first Discovery of Gold in Queensland. (Proc. Roy. Soc. Queensland, 4.) 8vo. Brisbane, 1887. ME 1 T
The Mountains of Queensland. (Roy. Geogr. Soc. of Australasia, Q. Branch, 2.) 8vo. Brisbane, 1887. ME 20

BARTON, Chas. H. Outlines of Australian Physiography. 8vo. Maryborough (Q.), 1895. MA 3 U 18

BARTON, Edmund. Speeches delivered at a dinner given [in honour of the visit of the Earl of Roseberry], 1883. 8vo. Sydney, 1883. MF 3 T 57

BARUCHSON, A. Beetroot Sugar: being an abridgment of the pamphlet by A. Baruchson. 8vo. Hobart, 1868. MA 1 P 64

BARUS, Carl. Report on the Condensation of Atmospheric Moisture. 8vo. Wash., 1895. A 31 Q 3

BASCH & Co. Mineral Guide and Prospecters' Companion. 12mo. Sydney, 1872. MA 2 P 37

BASHKIRTSEFF, Marie. Journal of. Translated by Mathilde Blind. 8vo. Lond., 1890. C 22 P 1

BASILE, Giovanni Battista, Count of Torone. Il Pentamerone: or, the Tale of Tales; being a Translation by the late Sir Richard Burton, K.C.M.G., of Il Pentamerone; Overo lo cunto de li l'eccerillo, of Basile. 2 vols. 8vo. Lond., 1893. J 5 T 31, 32

BASIS of a New Reformation. [See Religious Pamphlets, 1.] G 9 V 16

BASS, G. [Chart of] Western Port on the South Coast of New South Wales, 1798. Fol. Lond., 1801. MD 1 P 15 ‡

BASSETT, J. S. Constitutional Beginnings of North Carolina, 1663-1729. (Johns Hopkins Univ. Studies, 12.) Roy. 8vo. Baltimore, 1894. B 18 S 12

BASSETT-SMITH, Dr. P. W. [See Smith, Dr. P. W. Bassett-.]

BASTABLE, Dr. C. F. Public Finance. 2ud ed. 8vo. Lond., 1895. F 11 U 15

BASTIAN, Adolf. Einiges aus Samoa und andern Inseln der Südsee. 8vo. Berlin, 1889. MD S Q 17
Samoa und andern Inseln der Südsee. 8vo. Berlin, 1889. MD 1 R 30

BASTIEN-LEPAGE, Jules. [Sketch of;] by Julia Cartwright. [See Portfolio, Monograph 4.] E

BATAILLON, E. Recherches Anatomiques et Expérimentales sur la Métamorphose des Amphibiens Anoures. (Annales de l'Université de Lyon, 2.) Roy. 8vo. Paris, 1891. A 27 V 18

BATCHELLOR, Albert S. Provincial, Town, and State Papers of New Hampshire. [See New Hampshire.] E

BATE, G. Spence. Crustacea Macrura. [See Thomson, Sir C. W., and Murray, Dr. J.—Voyage of H.M.S. Challenger.] A 6 †

BATE, John M. Silk Cultivation: Plain and Practical Directions for Planting the Mulberry, and Treatment of the Silkworm. 8vo. Sydney, 1864. MA 1 P 62

BATEMAN, Wm. The Colonist: a Work on the Past and Present Position of the Colony of New Zealand. 8vo. Christchurch, 1881. MB 1 T 26

BATES, Katherine Lee. The English Religious Drama. 12mo. New York, 1893. H 8 Q 46

BATES, Wm. The Maclise Portrait Gallery of Illustrious Literary Characters; with Memoirs. 8vo. Lond., 1883. C 17 R 21

BATESON, Wm. Materials for the Study of Variation treated with especial regard to Discontinuity in the Origin of Species. 8vo. Lond., 1894. A 27 U 12

BATH AND WEST AND SOUTHERN COUNTIES SOCIETY. Journal. 4th series. Vols. 1-5. 8vo. Lond., 1890-95. E

BATHGATE, John. New Zealand: its Resources and Prospects. 8vo. Lond., 1881. MD 8 R 34

BATHOENG, African Chief. Sketch of. [See Lloyd, Rev. E.—Three Great African Chiefs.] B 1 P 21

BATHURST, James. Atomic-Consciousness: an Explanation of Ghosts, Spiritualism, Witchcraft, Occult Phenomena, and all Supernormal Manifestations. 8vo. Whimple, 1892. G 16 T 37

BATHURSTIAN, The, 1882-93. 5 vols. 8vo. Bathurst, 1882-93. ME 15 Q

BATMAN, John, the Founder of Victoria; by James Bonwick. 12mo. Melb., 1867. MC 1 P 59

BATTELY, Rev. Dr. John. Antiquities of Richborough and Reculver. 12mo. Lond., 1774. B 35 P 24

BATTLE OF MORDIALLOC; or, How we Lost Australia. 12mo. Melb., 1888. MJ 1 Q 53

BATTLE OF THE YARRA, The; by "An Old Colonist." 12mo. Melb., 1883. MJ 1 P 60

BATTY, Beatrice. Forty-two years amongst the Indians and Eskimo; Pictures from the Life of Rt. Rev. J. Horden, first Bishop of Moosonee. 12mo. Lond., 1893. D 15 Q 20

BATTYE, Aubyn Trevor-. Ice-bound on Kolguev: a Chapter in the Exploration of Arctic Europe, to which is added a Record of the Natural History of the Island. Illustrated. 8vo. Lond., 1895. D 16 V 10

BAUCHE, P. Hemisphere Meridional. [See De L'Isle, G.] MD 8 P 28

BAUDRILLART, André. Les Divinités de la Victoire en Grèce et en Italie. 8vo. Paris, 1894. B 35 R 31

BAUMANN, Arthur A. Betterment: being the Law of Special Assessment for Benefits in America; with some Observations on its adoption by the London County Council. 12mo. Lond., 1893. F 14 Q 51
Betterment, Worsement, and Recoupment; with a Note on Betterment in America. 12mo. Lond., 1894.
F 5 Q 3

BAX, Ernest Belfort. German Society at the close of the Middle Ages. 8vo. Lond., 1894. B 27 R 8
The Problem of Reality, being outline suggestions for a philosophical reconstruction. 8vo. Lond., 1892.
G 7 U 23
Socialism. [See Morris, W.] F 14 Q 29

BAXTER, Jas. P. The Pioneers of New France in New England. Sm. 4to. Albany, N.Y., 1894. B 18 R 10

BAXTER, Mrs. Lucy E. "Leader Scott." Echoes of Old Florence; her Palaces and those who have lived in them. 12mo. Lond., 1894. B 30 P 8

BAYE, Joseph Baron de. Industrial Arts of the Anglo-Saxons. 4to. Lond., 1893. A 12 S 1 †

BAYLY, Capt. W. M. Infantry Attack Formations and Fire Disciplinc. (United Service Institution, N.S.W. 5.) 8vo. Sydney, 1894. ME

BAYNE, Emily. Truth and Trust. 12mo. Melb., 1880
MH 1 U 68

BAYNE, Dr. Peter. The Free Church of Scotland; her Origin, Founders, and Testimony. 8vo. Edinb., 1893. G 2 P 2½
Another Copy. 2nd ed. 8vo. Edinb., 1894. G 2 P 39

BAYNES, Thomas Spencer. Reminiscences of. [See Skelton, Dr. J.—Table-talk of Shirley.] C 19 V 10

BAZLEY, Thos. S. Index to the Geometric Chuck. 8vo. Lond., 1875. A 25 T 35

BEACH, Thos. Eugenia; or, Virtuous and Happy Life: a Poem. Sm. fol. Lond. 1737. H 39 Q 13 ‡

BEACH, Thos. [See Le Caron, Major H.]

BEACONSFIELD, Earl of. Church Policy: a Speech. 12mo. Lond., 1864. G 4 V 14
Reprint of Beaconsfield's "Vindication of the English Constitution"; with Introduction by F. A. Hyndman. 12mo. Lond. (n.d.) F 7 V 30
Plaster Cast of. [See Hutton, L.—Portraits in Plaster.]
A 23 V 13
Reminiscences of. [See Skelton, Dr. J.—Table-talk of Shirley.] C 19 V 10
Sketch of. [See Bagehot, W.—Biographical Studies.]
C 22 P 10

BEADLE, C. Cellulose. [See Cross, C. F.] A 20 S 17

BEADON, Robert J. Imperial Federation. 8vo. Hobart, 1888. MF 1 S 39

BEAL, Dr. Wm. Jas. Grasses of North America for Farmers and Students, comprising Chapters on their Physiology, Composition, Selection, Improving, Cultivation, Management of Grass Lands; also, Chapters on Clovers, Injurious Insects, and Fungi. [Illustrated.] 8vo. Lansing, 1887. A 10 T 18

BEALE, Thos. Wm. An Oriental Biographical Dictionary. New edition, by H. G. Keene. Roy. 8vo. Lord., 1894. C 18 T 2

BEAMAN, A. H. [Life of] Stambuloff. 8vo. Lond., 1895. C 22 P 11

BEAN Dr. Tarleton H. Fishes of Pennsylvania; with Descriptions of the Species, and Notes on their Common Names, Distribution, Rate of Growth, and Mode of Capture. Illustrated. 8vo. Harrisburg, Pa., 1893. A 30 U 12

BEAN W. Orchids. [See Watson, W.]
A 4 U 19 : A 20 S 10

BEANEY, Dr. James G. Diseases of the Hip-joint. 8vo. Melb., 1878. MA 2 S 57
History and Progress of Surgery: An Address. Sm. 4to. Melb., 1877. MA 2 S 58
Surgical Diagnosis: A Lecture. Sm. 4to. Melb., 1877.
MA 2 S 59
Spermatorrhœa in its Physiological, Medical, and Legal Aspects. 8vo. Melb., 1870. MA 3 S 34

BEAR, J. Over the Cliff: A Sensational Story. 12mo. Melb., 1886. MJ 1 P 66

BEAR J. M. The Coming Industry of Victoria: Viticulture. 8vo. Melb., 1894. MA 3 T 15

BEAR, Wm. E. A Study of Small Holdings. 12mo. Lond., 1893. F 14 Q 26

BEARD, J. T. The Ventilation of Mines. 12mo. New York, 1874. A 24 Q 28

BEASLEY, Benjamin. Stammering: its Treatment. 15th ed. 12mo. Birmingham, 1893. A 26 Q 18

BEASLEY, Henry. Book of Prescriptions. 18mo. Lond., 1892. A 26 P 13
The Pocket Formulary and Synopsis of the British and Foreign Pharmacopœias. 11th ed. 18mo. Lond., 1886. A 26 P 14

BEATON, Rev. Patrick. Creoles and Coolies; or, Five Years in Mauritius. 2nd ed. 12mo. Lond., 1859. D 14 P 13
Six Months in Reunion. 2 vols. 8vo. Lond., 1860. D 14 R 16, 17

BEATTIE, James. Poetical Works of. 18mo. Lond., 1830. H 10 T 28
Poetical Works of. 8vo. Lond., 1852. H 7 U 34

BEATTIE, Dr. Wm. Castles and Abbeys of England, from the National Records, Early Chronicles, and other Standard Authors. Illustrated. Imp. 8vo. Lond. (n.d.) B 15 P 9 †

BEATTY-KINGSTON, W. [See Kingston, W. Beatty-.]

BEATY-POWNALL, S. [See Pownall, S. Beaty-.]

BEAUDOUIN, Mondry. Etude du Dialecte Chyprioté Moderne et Médiéval. 8vo. Paris, 1884. J 7 U 31

BEAULIEU, A. Leroy-. The Empire of the Tzars and the Russians. Translated by Z. A. Ragozin; with Maps and Illustrations. 2 vols. 8vo. New York, 1893. B 31 T 5, 6

BEAUMONT, Francis, and FLETCHER, John. Works of: with an Introduction by G. Darley. 2 vols. 8vo. Lond., 1840. H 2 U 26, 27

BEAUMONT, Sir Harry. [See Spence, Joseph.]

BEAUTIFUL BRITAIN. The Scenery and Splendours of the United Kingdom: Views of our Stately Houses. Ob. imp. 8vo. Lond., 1894. A 8 Q 3 †

BECHARD, A. P. and E. L'Egypte et la Nubie: Grand Album, Monumental, Historique, Architectural. Fol. Paris, 1887. B 8 Q 15 ‡

BECK, Dr. M. Surgery. [See Erichsen, Sir J. E.] A 33 T 25, 26

BECKE, Louis. By Reef and Palm. 8vo. Lond., 1894. MJ 3 P 35

BECKER, Dr. Geo. F. Geology of the Quicksilver Deposits of the Pacific Slope; with an atlas. (U.S. Geol. Survey, 13.) 4to. Wash., 1888. E

BECKET, Thomas. Journal of a Voyage round the World in H.M.S. *Endeavour*, 1768-71. 12mo. Dublin, 1772. MD 1 P 34

BECKET, Thomas A', Archbishop of Canterbury, 1162-1171. Sketch of. [See Fowler, Rev. M.—Notable Archbishops.] C 13 V 12
Thomas of London before his Consecration; by L. B. Radford. (Camb. Hist. Essays, 7.) 8vo. Camb., 1894. C 18 P 18

BECKWOURTH, James P. Life and Adventures of James P. Beckwourth, Mountaineer, Scout, Pioneer, and Chief of the Crow Nations of Indians; by T. D. Bonner. 8vo. Lond., 1892. C 16 R 12

BEDDARD, Frank E. A Text-book of Zoögeography. 12mo. Camb., 1895. A 28 P 30
Isopoda. [See Thomson, Sir C. W., and Murray, Dr. J.—Voyage of H.M.S. *Challenger*.] A 6 †

BEDDOES, Thos. L. Letters of. Edited by E. Gosse. 12mo. Lond., 1894. C 19 P 5

BEDELL, Dr. Frederick, and CREHORE, Dr. Albert C. Alternating Currents. 8vo. New York, 1893. A 21 V 17

BEDFORD, C. T. Reminiscences of a Surveying Trip from Boulia to the South Australian Border. (Roy. Geograph. Soc. of Australasia, Q. Branch, 2.) 8vo. Brisbane, 1887. ME 20

BEDFORD, W. K. R. Malta and the Knights Hospitallers. (Portfolio Monograph, 2.) Roy. 8vo. Lond., 1894. E

BEDNALL, W. T. Description of, and Notes upon, the species of the *Murex* and *Typhus*, known and recorded as existing on the Coast of South Australia. (Trans. Roy. Soc., S. Australia, 8.) 8vo. Adelaide, 1886. ME 1 S
New Land-shell from Central Australia. (Trans. Roy. Soc., S. Australia, 18.) 8vo. Adelaide, 1894. ME 1 S

BEECHER, Rev. Henry Ward. The Vices; or, Lectures to Young Men. 12mo. Lond. (n.d.) G 9 V 36
Sketch of; with Portrait. [See Bolton, Sarah K.—Famous Leaders.] C 17 P 27

BEETHOVEN, Ludwig von. [Plaster cast of.] [See Hutton, L.—Portraits in Plaster.] A 23 V 13

BEETON, Samuel O. Dictionary of Universal Information. 8vo. Lond., 1861. K 5 U 21
Everybody's Lawyer: a Practical Compendium of the General Principles of English Jurisprudence. 9th ed. 8vo. Lond., 1891. F 7 V 3

BEG, Rev. Dr. Wazir. Reply to Archbishop Vaughan's first Advent Conference or Attack on the Protestant Church. 8vo. Sydney, 1876. MG 2 S 2

BEHNKE, Emil. The Mechanism of the Human Voice. 8th ed. 12mo. Lond. (n.d.) A 26 Q 19
Voice, Song, and Speech. [See Browne, L.]

BEHREND, Dr. Henry. The Communicability to Man of Diseases from Animals used as food. 8vo. Sydney, 1882. MA 1 U 55

BEHRENDT, P. Modern Fireproof and Waterproof Building Materials. (Roy. Soc., Vict., 20.) 8vo. Melb., 1884. ME 1 P

BEHRENS, Prof. H. Manual of Microchemical Analysis; with an introductory chapter by Prof. J. W. Judd. 8vo. Lond., 1894. A 21 P 26

BEHRS, C. A. Recollections of Count Leo Tolstoy. 8vo. Lond., 1893. C 16 R 16

BEILBY, J. Wood. Auriferous Drifts in Australasia ; or, the Cause and its Continuity of the Great Geological Convulsions, and the Theory of the Origin and Position of Auriferous Drifts ; by "Research." 8vo. Melb., 1868. MA 2 Q 54
Eureka : An Elucidation of Hysterics in Nature—the Problems of Science. Roy. 8vo. Melb., 1883. MA 2 Q 60
Reasons suggestive of Mining on Physical Principles for Gold and Coal. 12mo. Melb., 1875. MA 3 U 6

BELDING, L. Land Birds of the Pacific District. 8vo. San Francisco, 1890. A 30 U 15

BELGIUM. Abolition des Octrois Communaux en Belgique. 2 vols. imp. 8vo. Bruxelles, 1867. F 11 V 6, 7
Album des Dépenses et des Recettes faites par l'état sur le réseau des Voies Navigables de 1830 à 1880. Fol. Bruxelles (n.d.) A 13 P 20 ‡
Bibliographie de Belgique : Journal Officiel de la Librairie, 1875-78, 1881-84, 1886-93. 24 vols. 8vo. Bruxelles, 1876-93. E
Bibliothèque Royale de Belgique. Rapport, 1890-91. 8vo. Bruxelles, 1892. E
Commissions Royales d'Art et d'Archéologie. Bulletin, 1858-92, et parts 1-8, 1893. 6 vols. 8vo. Bruxelles, 1858-93. E
Documents Parlementaires relatifs à la Loi établissant la Libération Conditionnelle et les Condamnations Conditionnelles dans le Système Pénal. 8vo. Bruxelles, 1889. F 7 U 15
Fondations de Bourses d'Étude établies en Belgique. 7 vols. 4to. Bruxelles, 1889-90. G 12 W 1-6 †
Grands Concours du Gouvernement dits Concours de Rome : Règlement organique. 8vo. Anvers, 1891. A 23 S 11
Lois du 27 Nov., 1891, sur l Assistance Publique et sur l'Assistance Médicale Gratuite. Roy. 8vo. Bruxelles, 1893. F 6 T 25
Loi établissant la Libération Conditionnelle et Condamnations Conditionnelles dans le Système Pénal. 8vo. Bruxelles, 1888. F 8 U 36
Loi pour la Répression du Vagabondage et de la Mendicité. Roy. 8vo. Bruxelles, 1893. F 9 T 26
Ponts et Chaussées : Direction des Travaux Hydrauliques, service des Voies Navigables, Profils en long des Voies Navigables. Fol. Bruxelles, 1880. A 40 T 19 ‡
Recueil des Rapports des Secrétaires de Légation de Belgique, 1-8. 8 vols. 8vo. Bruxelles, 1872-93. E
Salaires et Budgets Ouvriers en Belgique au Mois d'Avril, 1891. 8vo. Bruxelles, 1892. E
Voies Navigables de la Belgique. Recueil de Renseignements. 2 vols. imp. 8vo. Bruxelles, 1880. F 11 V 3, 4
Voies Navigables. Règlement de Police, 1889. 8vo. Bruxelles, 1889. F 2 V 6

BELL, Alexander G. Sketch of. [*See* Hubert, P. G.—Inventors.] C 17 R 3

BELL, Alfred B. Oscar : a Romance of Australia and New Caledonia. 8vo. Brisbane, 1895. MJ 3 Q 35

BELL, Andrew. History of Canada. [*See* Garneau, F. X.] B 16 Q 38-40

BELL, Sir Chas. The Hand : its Mechanism and Vital Endowments as evincing Design. 5th ed., illustrated. 8vo Lond., 1852. A 26 R 5

BELL, Rev. Dr. Chas. D. Some of our English Poets. 8vo Lond., 1895. C 21 P 11

BELL, Clara. Horses and Dogs. [*See* Ecrelmau, O.] A 40 U 4 ‡

BELL, David C. and Alexander M. Bell's Standard Elocutionist. 8vo. Lond., 1892. J 4 R 1

BELL, Ernest. Hand-books of Athletic Sports. 8 vols. 12mo. Lond., 1890-93. A 29 P 21-28
1. Cricket, Lawn Tennis, Tennis, Rackets, Fives, Golf, Hockey.
2. Rowing and Sculling, Sailing, Swimming.
3. Boxing, Wrestling, Fencing, Broadsword, Singlestick.
4. Rugby Football, Association Football, Baseball, Rounders, Quoits, Bowls, Skittles, Curling.
5. Athletics, Cycling, Skating.
6. Practical Horsemanship.
7. Canoeing and Camping-out.
8. Gymnastics and Indian Clubs.

BELL, Sir Francis D. The Public Debt of Australasia : a Paper read before the Royal Colonial Institute, 21st November, 1882. 8vo. Lond., 1882. MJ 3 Q 16

BELL, Prof. Francis J. Collection of Crinoids from the Sahul Bank, North Australia—(*in* Journal of Linnean Society, London, 24.) E

BELL, Frederick A. Handbook of Practical Directions for Sugar-cane Planting, Sugar-making, and the Distillation of Rum. 8vo. Sydney, 1866. MA 1 P 80

BELL, Col. George W. Street-paving in Sydney. Roy. 8vo. Sydney, 1895. MA 3 R 40
The World to-morrow ; or, Great Federal Ideas. 8vo. Melb. (n.d.) MF 4 R 33

BELL, Horace. Railway Policy of India. [With Map of Indian Railway System.] 8vo. Lond., 1894. F 14 R 13

BELL, Dr. James. Analysis and Adulteration of Foods. 8vo. Lond., 1883. A 26 R 18
Part 2. Milk, Butter, Cheese, Cereal Food, Prepared Starches, &c.

BELL, John. Plan of Betsies Island [Tasmania]. Fol. (n.p.) 1830. MD 5 Q 16 ‡

BELL, Mrs. Nancy R. E. (N. D'Anvers). Contemporary German Art. [*See* Pietsch, N.] A 39 Q 18, 19 ‡
Discovery of Lakes Rudolf and Stefanic. [*See* Höhnel, Lieut. L. von.] D 14 V 11 12
Venezia. [*See* Perl, H.] D 42 Q 11 ‡

BELL, Mrs. Nancy R. E., and TRAILL, Henry D. The Capitals of the World. 2 vols. 4to. Lond., 1892.
D 9 V 11, 12

BELL, Robert. Ancient Poems, Ballads, and Songs of the Peasantry of England. 12mo. Lond., 1857.
H 10 T 15

Early Ballads. [*See* Early Ballads.] H 10 T 32
Poetical Works of Ben Jonson. [*See* Jonson, Ben.]
H 10 T 1
Poetical Works of E. Waller. [*See* Waller, E.]
H 10 T 22

BELL'S LIFE IN VICTORIA AND SPORTING CHRONICLE, 1857-59. Fol. Melb., 1857-59.
ME

BELLAMY, Edward. Looking Backward, 2000-1887. 12mo. Lond. (n.d.) F 7 V 16
A Talk with; with Portrait. [*See* Blathwayt, R.— Interviews.] J 10 U 31

BELLO, Andres. Don A. Bello y el codigo civil. [*See* Amunátegui, M. L.] F 11 U 8
Vida de; por M. L. Amunátegui. 8vo. Santiago, 1882.
C 21 T 7

BELLOC, M. A. Lives of E. and J. de Goncourt. [*See* Goncourt, E. and J. de.] C 21 R 3, 4

BELLOWS, Dr. Albert J. How not to be Sick. 8vo. Lond., 1869. A 12 Q 17

BELMORE, Somerset R. Lowry-Corry, Earl of. History of the Corry Family, of Castlecoole. 8vo. Lond., 1891. C 16 S 22

BEMIS, Dr. Edward W. Local Government in Michigan and the Northwest. (Johns Hopkins University Studies, 1.) 8vo. Baltimore, 1883. B 18 S 1
Coöperation in New England. (Johns Hopkins University Studies, 6.) 8vo. Baltimore, 1888. B 18 S 6
Coöperation in the Middle States. (Johns Hopkins University Studies, 6.) 8vo. Baltimore, 1888.
B 18 S 6
Local Government in the South and the Southwest. (Johns Hopkins University Studies, 11.) 8vo. Baltimore, 1893. B 18 S 11

BEMROSE, Wm. Fret-cutting and Perforated Carving. Illustrated. 14th ed. 4to. Lond. (n.d.) A 13 P 18 †

BENDER, Charles. Properties of Continuous Bridges. 18mo. New York, 1876. A 22 P 30

BENDIGO MINING REGISTRY; or, Guide to all the Bendigo Mines. 8vo. Sandhurst, 1883. MA 3 U 19

BENDIGO SCHOOL OF MINES. Reports, 1887 and 1890. 2 vols. 8vo. Sandhurst, 1887-90. ME 15 Q

BENDIGO WATER WORKS CO. Report, 1860. 8vo. Melb., 1860. ME 6 Q

BENECKE, E. F. M. Vergil in the Middle Ages. [*See* Comparetti, D.] J 12 R 3

BENECKE, Ida. Heine on Shakespeare. [*See* Heine, H.]
J 10 R 27

BENEDEN, P. J. Van. Descriptions des Ossements Fossiles des environs d'Anvers. [*See* Musée Royal d'Histoire Naturelle de Belgique, Annales du.] A 6 V & W ‡

BENEDIKT, Prof. Dr. R. Chemical Analysis of Oils, Fats, Waxes, and of the Commercial Products derived therefrom. Revised by Dr. J. Lewkowitsch. 8vo. Lond., 1895. A 21 U 3

BENEVOLENT SOCIETY OF NEW SOUTH WALES. Correspondence between the Colonial Government and the Benevolent Society of New South Wales, with regard to the recent changes in, and future management of, Asylums for the Destitute. 8vo. Sydney, 1803. MF 4 Q 83
Reports for 1878, 1887, and 1888. 8vo. Sydney, 1879-89. ME 6 S

BENHAM, Rev. Wm. [Life of] William Cowper. [*See* Masson, Prof. D.—In the Footsteps of the Poets.]
J G R 43

BENJAFIELD, Harry. The Blood and its Circulation. 12mo. Hobart, 1874. MA 2 P 47
The Eye. 12mo. Hobart, 1874. MA 2 P 47
Food and its Forces. 12mo. Hobart, 1874.
MA 2 P 47
How and Why do I Breathe. 12mo. Hobart, 1874.
MA 2 P 47
Lecture on the Human Voice. 8vo. Hobart, 1877.
MA 2 P 47
The Nervous System. 12mo. Hobart, 1874.
MA 2 P 47
Public Health. 12mo. Hobart, 1874. MA 2 P 47
Structure of the Human Body. 12mo. Hobart, 1874.
MA 2 P 47

BENJAMIN, Dr. Park. Modern Mechanism, exhibiting the latest progress in Machines, Motors, and the Transmission of Power. Roy. 8vo. Lond., 1892.
A 11 V 23

BENNETT, A. R. Telephone Systems of the Continent of Europe. Illustrated. 8vo. Lond., 1895. A 21 S 32

BENNETT, Mrs. Alfred. Vignettes of Travel. 8vo. Sydney, 1896. MD 5 S 52

BENNETT, C. W. Unforeshadowed Sequences: a Novel-Drama. 12mo. Ballarat (n.d.) MH 1 U 45

BENNETT, Chas. H. London People; sketched from Life. Sm. 4to. Lond., 1863. J 9 T 37

BENNETT, E. J. A few Thoughts on Natural Phenomena, Heat, Light, Electricity, Atmospheric Disturbances, Barometer, &c. (Roy. Geogr. Soc. of Australasia, Q. Branch, 2.) 8vo. Brisbane, 1887. ME 20

BENNETT, Elizabeth A. Triumph in Suffering: Memorial of, by T. Williams. 12mo. Ballarat, 1879.
MC 1 S 12

BENNETT, Dr. George. Acclimatisation: its Eminent Adaptation to Australia. 8vo. Melb., 1862.
MA 2 T 30
Miscellaneous Papers of. 8vo. Lond., 1827–72.
MA 2 T 30
Notes on Queensland. 4to. Sydney, 1873. MD 6 U 10
———, GIBSON, Andrew, and SHERWIN, Wm. Reports on Epidemic Catarrh or Influenza among Sheep. 12mo. Sydney, 1835. MA 1 P 47
BENNETT, James F. Account of South Australia. 8vo. Lond., 1843. MB 1 P 44
BENNETT, Joseph. Instrumentation and Orchestration. [See Berlioz, H.] A 23 V 12
BENNETT, Wm. C. [Biography of.] 8vo. Lond., 1890. MC 1 T 24
BENNETT, Prof. W. H. Chronicles. [See Expositor's Bible.] G 10 R and S
BENSLY, Prof. Robert L. Fourth Book of Maccabees and kindred documents in Syriac; with Introduction and Translations by W. E. Barnes. 8vo. Camb., 1895.
G 14 Q 32
———, HARRIS, J. R., and BURKITT, F. C. The four Gospels in Syriac. Transcribed from the Sinaitic Palimpsest. 4to Camb., 1894. G 6 V 24
BENSON, A. H. Prune, Growing, and Curing. 8vo. Sydney, 1892. MA 1 Q 62
How and when to spray for Codling Moth and Aphides on Fruit Trees. 8vo. Sydney, 1892. MA 1 Q 66
Principal Insect and Fungus Pests on Fruit and Fruit Trees in New South Wales, with a few Remedies. 8vo. Sydney, 1892. MA 1 Q 66
Paris Green as an Insecticide. 8vo. Sydney, 1892.
MA 1 Q 66
BENSON, Capt. L. Book of Remarkable Trials, 1700–1840. 8vo. Lond. (n.d.) F 7 V 31
BENT, Jas. Theodore. The Ruined Cities of Mashonaland; being a Record of Excavation and Exploration in 1891; with a chapter on the Orientation and Mensuration of the Temples, by R. M. W. Swan. 8vo. Lond., 1392. D 14 T 19
The Sacred City of the Ethiopians; being a Record of Travel and Research in Abyssinia in 1893. 8vo. Lond., 1893. D 14 T 5
BENTHAM, Jeremy. Letters to Lord Pelham, giving a comparative view of the System of Penal Colonization in New South Wales and the Home Penitentiary System. 8vo. Lond., 1802. MF 2 Q 22
Plea for the Constitution: Showing the enormities committed to the oppression of British Subjects in and by the the Design, Foundation, and Government of the penal Colony of New South Wales; including an inquiry into the Right of the Crown to legislate without Parliament in Trinidad, &c. 8vo. Lond., 1803. MF 2 Q 22
The Church of England Catechism examined. [See Religious Pamphlets, 3.] G 9 V 18
[Plaster Cast of.] [See Hutton, L.—Portraits in Plaster.]
A 23 V 13

BENTLEY, Arthur F. The Condition of the Western Farmer, as illustrated by the Economic History of a Nobraska Township. (Johns Hopkins University Studies, 11.) 8vo. Baltimore, 1893. B 18 S 11
BENTLEY, E. L. The Settler's Guide to New Zealand. 8vo. Lond., 1893. MF 2 Q 40
BENTLEY, Richard. Designs for six Poems by T. Gray. Fol. Lond., 1765. H 40 T 8 ‡
BENTLEY BALLADS, The: containing the choice Ballads, Songs, and Poems contributed to Bentley's Miscellany. 12mo. Lond., 1861. H 7 U 33
A Selection of the Choice Ballads, Songs, &c., contributed to Bentley's Miscellany. Edited by Dr. Doran. 12mo. Lond., 1858. H 7 U 32
BENTON, Thos. H. Sketch of. [See Brooks, N.—Statesmen.] C 16 R 20
BENVENUTO DA IMOLA. Dante. [See Vernon, Hon. W. W.] H 9 Q 5, 6
BENYOWSKY, Count de. The Memoirs and Travels of Mauritius Augustus, Count de Benyowsky, in Siberia, Kamenatka, Japan, the Liukiu Islands, and Formosa. 8vo. Lond., 1893. D 17 S 6
BERANGER, Pierre Jean de. Essay on. [See Bagehot, W.—Literary Studies.] J 9 P 23
BÉRARD. Victor. De l'Origine des Cultes Arcadiens. 8vo. Paris, 1894. B 27 V 10
BERDOE, Edward. The Origin and Growth of the Healing Art: A popular history of Medicine in all Ages and Countries. 8vo. Lond., 1893. A 13 Q 33
Browning Studies. [See Browning, Robert.] J 6 U 14
BERENSON, Bernhard. Lorenzo Lotto: an Essay in Art Criticism. 8vo. New York, 1895. C 21 R 12
The Venetian Painters of the Renaissance; with an Index to their Works. [List of Galleries in which they are to be found.] 8vo. New York, 1894.
A 23 Q 41
BERGER, Elie. Histoire de Blanche de Castille, Reine de France. 8vo. Paris, 1895. B 26 V 19
Notice sur divers Manuscrits de la Bibliothèque Vaticana: Richard le Poitevin. 8vo. Paris, 1879. J 7 U 35
BERGH, Dr. Rudolph. Marseinadæ; Nudibranchiata. [See Thomson, Sir C. W., and Murray, Dr. J.—Voyage of H.M.S. Challenger.] A 6 †
BERGROTH, Dr. E. Rhyncota of Australia. (Proc. Roy. Soc., Victoria, 7.) 8vo. Melb., 1895. ME 1 P
BERIGNY, Dr. T. Chaos and Order; or, the Orthodox Practice of Medicine unveiled versus the Medical Heresy. 8vo. Melb., 1858. MJ 3 Q 15

D

BERKELEY, Dr. George; by Prof A. C. Fraser. (Philosophical Classics.) 12mo. Edinb., 1884. G 9 V 3
Helps to Study of. [*See* Huxley, Prof. T.—Essays, 6.] J 11 P 40

BERLINER, Otto. Particulars of the various Duties performed through the General Mercantile Agency and Private Inquiry Office. 8vo. Sydney (n.d.) MF 2 Q 73

BERLIOZ, Hector. Treatise on Modern Instrumentation and Orchestration. Translated by Mary C. Clarke. New ed. by J. Bennett. Roy. 8vo. Lond. (n.d.) A 23 V 12
Sketch of. [*See* Heine, H.—Heine in Art and Letters.] J 11 T 39

BERNARD, St., of Clairvaux. The Times, the Man, and his Work; by Dr. R. S. Storrs. 8vo. Lond., 1892. C 15 P 14

BERNARD, Sir Chas. E. [*See* Campbell, Sir G.] C 15 P 16, 17

BERNARD, H. and M. Structure of Man. [*See* Wiedersheim, Dr. R.] A 33 U 20

BERNAYS, Dr. Adolphus. German Word-book. Sm. 4to. Lond., 1852. J 9 P 38
German Phrase-book. Sm. 4to. Lond., 1852. J 9 P 39

BERNAYS, Lewis A. Description of Exotic Fruits new to Queensland. (Proc. Roy. Soc., Queensland, 1.) 8vo. Brisb., 1884. ME 1 T
The Economic Aspects of Entomology. (Proc. Roy. Soc., Queensland, 1.) 8vo. Brisbane, 1885. ME 1 T
Guinea Grass, *Panicum maximum*: its History, Cultivation, and Value. (Proc. Roy. Soc., Queensland, 8.) 8vo. Brisbane, 1891. ME 1 T
Sechium Edule: its introduction into Queensland—Cultivation and Uses. (Proc. Roy. Soc., Queensland, 7.) 8vo. Brisbane, 1891. ME 1 T

BERNERS, Juliana. A Treatyse of Fysshynge wyth an Angle. [*See* Bibliotheca Curiosa.] J 18 Q 24

BERNERS, Lord. Chronicles of Froissart. [*See* Froissart, Sir J.] B 23 S 14

BERNSTEIN, A. Origin of the Legends of Abraham, Isaac, and Jacob. 12mo. Lond., 1871. G 2 V 36

BERNSTEIN, Edward. Ferdinand Lassalle as a Social Reformer. 8vo. Lond., 1893. C 13 P 32

BERRY, Duchess of. (Marie Caroline Ferdinande Louise de Bourbon.) The Duchess of Berry and the Court of Louis XVIII; by Imbert de Saint-Amand. 8vo. Lond., 1892. C 19 Q 12
The Duchess of Berry and the Court of Charles X; by Imbert de Saint-Amand. 8vo. Lond., 1893. C 19 Q 13
The Duchess of Berry and the Revolution of 1830; by Imbert de Saint-Amand. 8vo. Lond., 1893. C 19 Q 14

BERRY, Sir Graham. History of the Berry Ministry and how it made Victoria a fine country for the working-man. Sm. 4to. Melb., 1879. MJ 1 V 14

BERRY, Wm. Genealogia Antiqua; or Mythological and Classical Tables on Fabulous and Ancient History. 2nd ed. Fol. Lond., 1840. K 22 P 20‡

BERRYMAN, John R. Subject-index to Law Books in the Wisconsin State Library. [*See* Wisconsin State Library.] K 8 R 21

BERT, J. Chailley-. Colonisation of Indo-China. Translated from the French by A. B. Brabant. 8vo. Lond., 1894. F 14 R 31

BERTHELOT, Marcellin. Explosives and their Power; translated by C. N. Hake and William Macnab. 8vo. Lond., 1892. A 21 S 14

BERTHON, Capt. H. On the Potato Grub of Tasmania. 8vo. Hobart, 1855. MA 1 P 61

BERTILLON, Alphonse. L'Anthropométrie Judiciaire à Paris en 1889. Installations et Plans des locaux récents perfectionnements une expérience de Sociologie Bureaucratique. Avec Planches. Roy. 8vo. Lyon, 1890. F 4 R 21
Identification Anthropométrique. Instructions Signalétiques, et Album. Nouvelle édition. Roy. 8vo. Melun, 1893. F 4 R 20

BERTRAM, James. Some Memories of Books, Authors, and Events. 8vo. Lond., 1893. C 19 R 19

BERTRAND, A. Science et Psychologie de Maine de Biran. [*See* Maine de Biran, F. P. G.] G 16 U 37

BERTRAND, Alejandro. Memoria sobre las Cordilleras del Desierto de Atacama. 8vo. Santiago, 1885. D 15 V 19

BERTRAND DE BORN. Du Rôle Historique de, 1175–1200; par L. Clédat. 8vo. Paris, 1879. B 35 R 25

BESANT, Mrs. Annie. An Autobiography. 8vo. Lond., 1893. C 16 S 17

BESANT, Walter. An Interview with, on Fact and Fiction; with Portrait. [*See* Blathwayt, R.—Interviews.] J 10 V 34
Man-hunting in the Desert. [*See* Haynes, Capt. A. E.] D 14 V 14
Westminster. 8vo. Lond., 1895. D 18 T 21

BETCHE, Ernst. Flora of New South Wales. [*See* Moore, C.] MA 1 T 63

BETHAM-EDWARDS, M. [*See* Edwards, M. B.]

BETHANY COLLEGE, Bethany, West Virginia. Catalogue for 1893, 1894. 8vo. Bethany, 1893. E

BETHELL, Charles. The Colony of Queensland. 12mo. Lond., 1870. MD 3 P 47

BETTANY, George T. Germination of Seeds: a Lecture. (Inst. of Agricult., Lond.) 8vo. Lond., 1884.
A 18 R 28
History of Guy's Hospital. [See Wilks, Dr. S.]
C 15 P 12
Life of Charles Darwin. 12mo. Lond., 1887. C 17 P 9
Popular History of the Reformation and Modern Protestantism. Illustrated. 8vo. Lond., 1895. G 14 Q 33
Red, Brown, and Black Men of America and Australia, and their White Supplanters. Illustrated. 8vo. Lond, 1890.
MA 3 P 32

BEVAN, Dr. D. Practical Hygiene. [See Coplin, Dr. W. M. L.]
A 26 V 13

BEVAN, E. J. Cellulose. [See Cross, C. F.] A 20 S 17

BEVAN, Rev. Dr. Llewelyn I. Reply of the Churches to Rome and Canterbury. 8vo. Molb., 1895.
MG 2 Q 29

BEYER, Dr. O. W. Physiological Psychology. [See Ziehen, Dr. T.]
G 2 U 6

BIANCONI, F. Le Mexique à la portée des Industriels, des Capitalistes et des Travailleurs. 12mo. Paris, 1889.
F 7 V 17

BIBLES AND TESTAMENTS.
BASQUE. The Earliest Translation of the Old Testament into the Basque Language (a Fragment); by P. D'Urte. (Anecdota Oxoniensia.) Sm. 4to. Oxford, 1894.
F
ENGLISH. Annotated Paragraph Bible. New ed. Roy. 8vo. Lond. (n.d.)
G 13 V 32
Apocryphal Gospels, Acts, and Revelations. Translated by A. Walker. (Ante-Nicene Christ. Lib., 16.) 8vo. Edinb., 1870.
G 14 U 16
Expositor's Bible. [See Expositor's Bible.] G 10 R and S
The New Testament in an improved version. 8vo. Lond., 1808.
G 3 R 8
The New Testament: [with a Note by Lieut.-Col. O. D. Ainsworth, showing this book to have formerly been the property of Sir John Franklin.] 8vo. Camb., 1826.
G 3 R 1
FIJIAN. St. Luke, Acts, Thessalonians, and Epistle of St. James. 12mo. Melb (n.d.)
MG 2 R 40
GERMAN. Die Bibel, oder die ganze Heilige Schrift, alten und neuen Testaments. 8vo. Frankfurt am Main, 1841.
G 15 P 41
GREEK. Novum Testamentum. [Greek Text.] 2 vols. 32mo. Lugd. Batav., 1624.
G 9 U 19, 20
Novum Testamentum Græce. 2 vols. 8vo. Lond., 1796.
G 16 U 25, 26
The New Testament [in Greek]; with English Notes by the Rev. E. Valpy. 3 vols. 8vo. Lond., 1847.
G 3 R 5–7
Novum Testamentum Græce ad antiquissimos testes denuo recensuit apparatum criticum apposuit C. Tischendorf. 8vo. Lipsiæ, 1894. G 14 R 17

BIBLES AND TESTAMENTS—contd.
HEBREW. Biblia Hebraica ex recensione Aug. Hahnii cum Vulgata interpretatione Latina. 12mo. Lipsiæ, 1868.
G 9 V 28
PHONOGRAPHIC. The Holy Bible in easy reporting style of Phonography (Pitman's). 8vo. Lond., 1890.
G 2 S 31
PROVENÇAL. Le Nouveau Testament; traduit au XIII Siècle en Langue Prevençale suivi d'un Ritual Cathare. 8vo. Paris, 1888.
G 16 U 21
SYRIAC. The Four Gospels in Syriac. [See Bensly, Prof. R. L.]
G G V 24
Fourth Book of Maccabees. [See Bensly, Prof. R. L.]
G 14 Q 32
TURKISH. The Four Gospels. Sm. 4to. (n.p.n.d.)
G 1 R 29

BIBLIOGRAPHICA. Vol. 1. Sm. fol. Lond., 1895
J 15 Q 23 †

BIBLIOTECA NACIONAL, CHILE. [See Chili.]

BIBLIOTECA NACIONAL DO RIO DE JANEIRO. [See Brazil.]

BIBLIOTHECA ARCANA, seu Catalogus Librorum Penetralium. Sm. 4to. Lond., 1885. J 6 T 31

BIBLIOTHECA CURIOSA. 50 vols. 12mo. Edinb., 1883–88.
J 18 Q 1–50
Ballad Book; by C. K. Sharpe.
King Charles II's Escape from Worcester; by Charles I.
Origin of the Native Races of America; by H. Grotius and P. Albinus.
Counter Blast to Tobacco; by James I.
A North Countrie Garland; by J. Maidment.
History of Reynard the Fox.
Political Songs of England, from the Reign of John to Edward II; by T. Wright.
Miraculous Escape of the Young Chevalier from the Battle of Culloden.
King Haco's Expedition against Scotland, 1263. Translated by Rev. J. Johnstone.
New Book of Old Ballads. Edited by J. Maidment.
The Apology of George Brissot.
The Maner of the Tryumphe of Caleys and Buloyn.
Political Satires of the 17th Century; from the Writings of the Earl of Rochester.
The Pretty Gentleman; or, Softness of Manners vindicated.
Journey round my Room; by Count Xavier de Maistre
A Nocturnal Expedition round my Room; by Count Maistre.
The Ballad Book; by G. R. Kinloch.
Trial of Francis Ra-aillac for the Murder of Henry the Great.
A Treatyse of Fysshynge wyth an Angle; by Dame Juliana Berners.
Speech on American Affairs; by Governor Johnston, 1776.
Edward Webbe, chief Master Gunner; his Travailes, 1590.
Crito; or, a Dialogue on Beauty; by Sir H. Beaumont.
The Secrets of Angling; by J. Dennys.
Catalogue of the Publications of the Elzevier Presses.
The Mystery of Iniquity as it is now practised among the Jesuits; by Titus Oates, 1370.
A Commonwealth of Women; by Mr. D'Urfey.
Conspiracy of the Count de Fieschi against the Republick of Genoa, in the year 1547.
Chancellor's Voyage to Muscovy, 1550.
Magic Plants; by M. J. H. Heucher.
Treatise of Magic Incantations Translated by C. Pazig.
The Last Fight of the Revenge and the Death of Sir Richard Grenville.

BIBLIOTHECA CURIOSA—*contd.*
   The Hearse of the Rt. Hon. the Earl of Essex ; by Richard Vines.
   Love's Mistress ; or, the Queen's Masque ; by T. Heywood.
   Dissertation on the Druids ; by E. Pufendorff.
   The Famous Historie of Fryer Bacon.
   Conspiracy of the Normans against William the Bastard ; by the Abbé le Cointe.
   The Chieftains of Vendée ; by Baron de Barante.
   Thespis on Tryal ; or, the Moralitie of Players considered ; by J. Geier.
   A King's Mistress ; or, Charles VII and Agnes Sorel ; by B. H. R. Capefigue.
   Voyage to the Canaries, Cape Verd, and the Coast of Africa, under the command of M. Dancourt, 1682 ; by J. Le Maire.
   The Life and Times of Christopher Columbus ; by A. M. L. P. de Lamartine.
   Sketch of the Aldine Press at Venice ; by A. A. Renouard.
   Chronological History of New England, in the form of Annals ; by T. Prince.

BIBLIOTHECA OENOLOGICA. Zusammenstellung des gesamuten Weinliteratur des in-und Auslandes. 8vo. Heidelberg, 1875.   J 5 S 30

BIBLIOTHEQUE ROYALE DE BELGIQUE. [*See* Belgium.]

BICKELI, Dr. I. Bookbindings from the Hessian Historical Exhibition, illustrating the Art of Binding from the 15th–18th Centuries. Fol. Leipzig, 1893.   A 6 S 3 ‡

BICKERSTAFF, Isaac. The Hypocrite : a Comedy. [*See* London Stage, 1.]   H 2 S 33
  Lionel and Clarissa : an Opera. [*See* London Stage, 1.]   H 2 S 33
  Love in a Village : an Opera. [*See* London Stage, 1.]   H 2 S 33
  The Maid of the Mill : an Opera. [*See* London Stage, 1.]   H 2 S 33
  The Padlock : a Comic Opera. [*See* London Stage, 1.]   H 2 S 33
  The Recruiting Sergeant : a Musical Entertainment. [*See* London Stage, 3.]   H 2 S 35
  The Romp : a Comic Opera. [*See* London Stage, 4.]   H 2 S 36
  The Sultan ; or, a Peep into the Seraglio : a Farce. [*See* London Stage, 3.]   H 2 S 35

BICKERSTETH, Mary. Japan as we saw it. 8vo. Lond., 1893.   D 17 V 2

BICKERTON, Prof. Alexander Wm. Copies of Letters on Partial Impact. 8vo. Canterbury, N.Z., 1879.   MA 3 R 56
  The Immortality of the Cosmos : being an attempt to show that the theory of dissipation of energy is limited to finite portions of space. 8vo. Canterbury, N.Z., 1894.   MA 2 T 71
  New Story of the Stars. 12mo. Christchurch, N.Z., 1894.   MA 3 U 20
  Oversight in Croll's Method of lengthening the age of the Sun's heat. 8vo. Canterbury, N.Z., 1894.   MA 2 T 71

BICKERTON, Prof. Alexander Wm.—*contd.*
  Partial Impact, Paper No. 4—General Problem of Stellar Collision. 8vo. Christchurch, N.Z., 1879.   MA 3 R 56
  Reply to Critics on a New Story of the Stars. 12mo. Christchurch, N.Z., 1895.   MA 3 U 20
  Some recent evidence in favour of Impact. 8vo. Wellington, 1894.   MA 2 T 70
  Synoptic Statement of the Principles and Phenomena of Cosmic Impact. 8vo. Wellington, 1894.   MA 2 T 71

BICKHAM, George. The Universal Penman ; or, the Art of Writing. Fol. Lond., 1743.   G 40 T 15 ‡

BICKMORE, Albert S. Travels in the East Indian Archipelago. Illustrated. 8vo. Lond., 1868.   D 19 R 3

BIDDER, A. de. Catalogue des Bronzes de la Société Archéologique d'Athènes. 8vo. Paris, 1894.   K 8 R 25

BIDDULPH, C. E. Four Months in Persia, and a Visit to Trans-Caspia. 8vo. Lond., 1892.   D 10 V 3

BIEWEND, A. B. C. About Gymnastics in the Schools. 8vo. Milwaukee (n.d.)   G 18 R 35
  Nature of Gymnastics, and Gymnastics in School. 8vo. Milwaukee (n.d.)   G 18 R 35
  Teaching Gymnastics : a State Affair. 8vo. Milwaukee (n.d.)   G 18 R 35

BIGELOW, Capt. John. Principles of Strategy, illustrated mainly from American Campaigns. 2nd ed. Roy. 8vo. Philad., 1894.   A 29 V 24

BIGELOW, Poultney. The Borderland of Czar and Kaiser. Illustrated. 8vo. New York, 1895.   D 17 Q 23

BIGGE, I. A. S-. [*See* Hume, D.]   G 16 Q 41

BIGGS, C. H. W. Electrical Distribution. [*See* Kilgour, M. H.]   A 21 Q 39

BIGNOLD, Thos. F. Leviora : being the Rhymes [Indian Subjects] of a successful competitor. 8vo. Calcutta, 1888.   H 10 S 13

BILLINGS, Robt. Wm. The Infinity of Geometric Design exemplified. 4to. Lond. (n.d.)   A 12 T 15 †

BILLINGTON, Mary Frances. Woman in India. Illustrated. 8vo. Lond., 1895.   F 14 U 7

BINNEY, Rev. Dr. Thomas. Objections to Theatrical Amusements. 8vo. Melb., 1877.   MG 2 Q 20

BINNY, J. Criminal Prisons of London. [*See* Mayhew, H.]   F 6 V 20

BIOLLEY, Paul. Costa Rica and her Future. Translated from the French by C. Charles. With Map. 8vo. Wash., 1889.   D 12 T 16

BIOLOGISCHES CENTRALBLATT. Bände 12-15. Roy. 8vo. Leipzig, 1892-94. E

BION. Works of. [*See* Fawkes, F.] H 9 U 28

BIRCH, Samuel. The Adopted Child: a Musical Drama. [*See* London Stage, 1.] H 2 S 33

BIRD IN A GOLDEN CAGE, A; by "Cleofas." 18mo. Melb., 1867. MJ 3 P 8

BIRDS. [Colored plates of.] Fol. (n.p.n.d.) MA 2 P 31 ‡

Birds of Chili, New Guinea, and New Ireland. [Illustrations to accompany "Voyage de la *Coquille*," and " Historia de Chile."] Fol. (n.p.n.d.) MA 2 P 29

BIRDWOOD, Sir Geo. [*See* East India Co.] B 29 V 2

BIRDWOOD, Dr. George C. M. Industrial Arts of India. 2 vols. 8vo. Lond., 1880. A 23 R 36, 37

BIRKMYRE, Wm. Tin: its Chemistry and Commercial Value. 8vo. Melb., 1877. MA 2 Q 53

BIRKS, Rev. Thos. R. The Uncertainties of Modern Physical Science. 8vo. Lond., 1876. G 1 R 32

BIRMINGHAM, John. The Red Stars. (Trans. R.I. Academy—Cunningham Memoirs, 5.) 4to. Dublin, 1888. E

BIRMINGHAM MUSEUM AND ART GALLERY. Catalogue of Photographs of the Photographic Survey of Warwickshire. Sm. 4to. Birmingham, 1892. K 7 R 55

BIRRELL, Augustine. Essays about Men, Women, and Books. 12mo. Lond., 1894. C 19 P 2

BISHOP, A. English and Hawaiian Words and Phrases for the use of learners in both languages. 12mo Honolulu, 1854. MK 1 P 42

BISHOP, Maria C. Memoir of Mrs. Augustus Craven. (Pauline de la Ferronnays). 2 vols. 8vo. Lond., 1894. C 21 P 3, 4

BISMARCK-SCHÖNHAUSEN, Prince von. Prince Bismarck at Home. [*See* Kingston, W. Beatty-.— Men, Cities, and Events.] C 22 R 2

[Life of]; by C. Lowe. 12mo. Lond. 1895. C 21 P 17

Sketch of. [*See* Smalley, G. W.— Studies of Men.] C 19 R 20

BJÖRNSON, B. Account of [*See* Twoodie, Mrs. A.] D 18 T 15

BLACK, Adam and Chas. General Atlas of the World. Fol. Lond., 1895. D 8 P 25 ‡

Guide to the English Lakes. 12mo. Edinb., 1856. D 18 Q 13

BLACK, Alex., C.E. First Principles of Building. Illustrated. 8vo. Lond., 1894. A 19 Q 3

BLACK, Alex. Photography, Indoor and Out: a Book for Amateurs. 12mo. Boston. 1894. A 23 Q 45

BLACK, George. Labor in Politics. The New South Wales Labor Party; what it did and what it prevented. 2nd ed. 8vo. Sydney, 1893*. MF 2 R 48

BLACK, Helen C. Notable Women Authors of the Day. Biographical Sketches. 8vo. Glasgow, 1893. C 15 R 23

BLACK, J. The Mysteries of Revelation revealed. 8vo. West Maitland, 1883. MG 1 S 4

BLACK, Dr. J. W. Maryland's Attitude in the Struggle for Canada. (Johns Hopkins University Studies, 10.) 8vo. Baltimore, 1892. B 18 S 10

BLACK, Reginald. New South Wales Land Laws. 12mo. Sydney (n.d.) MF 4 P 13

BLACK, Robert. Horse-racing in England. 8vo. Lond., 1893. A 29 T 15

BLACK AND WHITE: a Weekly Illustrated Record and Review. Vols. 1-10. Fol. Lond., 1891-95. E

BLACKBURN, A. H., and STEVENS, James. Engineering Telegraph Code for the use of Engineers, Contractors, Manufacturers, Merchants, &c. 4to. Lond., 1892. K 9 S 11

BLACKBURN, Chas. F. Rambles in Books. 12mo. Lond., 1893. J 5 P 49

BLACKBURN, Henry. Academy Notes, 1875, 1877-81, 1893-95. 8 vols. 8vo. Lond., 1875-95. E

Academy Sketches, 1893-94. 2 vols. 8vo. Lond., 1893-94. E

Art of Illustration. Illustrated. Sm. 4to. Lond., 1894. A 23 U 19

Artistic Travel in Normandy, Brittany, the Pyrenees, Spain, and Algeria. 8vo. Lond., 1892. D 9 S 33

The New Gallery, 1893-95; a complete illustrated catalogue. 3 vols. 8vo. Lond., 1893-95. E

BLACKBURN, Rev. Thos. New Genera and Species of Australian Coleoptera. (Trans. Roy. Soc., S. Australia, 17, 18.) 8vo. Adelaide, 1895. ME 1 S

BLACKIE, Prof. John Stuart. A Biography; by Anna M. Stoddart. 2 vols. 8vo. Edinb., 1895. C 13 V 18, 19

Lyrical Poems. 8vo. Edinb., 1860. H 9 U 9

BLACKIE'S Modern Cyclopedia of Universal Information. Edited by Dr. C. Annandale. 8 vols. 8vo. Lond., 1889-90. K 7 T 11-18

BLACKLEY, Frank. Notes of Interest : "On Change." 4to. Sydney, 1880. MF 3 U 63

BLACKMAN, R. D. Dictionary of Foreign Phrases. [*See* Deacon, C. W.] K 12 Q 48

BLACKMAR, Dr. F. W. Spanish Colonization in the Southwest. (Johns Hopkins University Studies, 8.) 8vo. Baltimore, 1890. B 18 S 8

BLACKMORE, Edwin G. The Law of the Constitution of South Australia. Sm. 4to. Adelaide, 1894. MF 3 U 62

BLACKTOWN LAND CO. Memorandum and Articles of Association. 8vo. Sydney (u.d.) MF 4 R 85

BLACKWOOD'S EDINBURGH MAGAZINE. Vols. 152-156. 8vo. Edinb., 1892-94. E

BLADEN, Frank M. Growth of the Australasian Colonies and their present relation to the Mother Country. (Rosebery Prize Essay, 1885.) 8vo. Sydney, 1889. MB 2 R 40

History of New South Wales. [*See* New South Wales.] MB 2 S 33

BLADES, Wm. Books in Chains, and other Bibliographical Papers. 12mo. Lond., 1892. K 19 P 12

BLAIKIE, Rev. Dr. Wm. G. Joshua, and 1st and 2nd Samuel. [*See* Expositor's Bible.] G 19 R and S

BLAINE, Jas. G. Sketch of. [*See* Brooks, N.—Statesmen.] C 16 R 20

BLAIR, Edward T. Henry of Navarre and the Religious Wars. Roy. 8vo. Philad., 1895. B 26 V 14

BLAIR, Dr. John. Remarks on Diphtheria. 8vo. Melb., 1868. MA 1 V 73

The Chinese Specifics for Diphtheria. 8vo. Melb., 1874. MA 3 S 64

BLAKE, Hon. E. Address at the Convocation of the University of Toronto, 1892. Roy. 8vo. Toronto, 1892. G 18 S 6

BLAKE, Rev. G. L. Yachting. [*See* Sullivan, Sir E.] A 29 Q 40, 41

BLAKE, Wm. Works of; Poetic, Symbolical, and Critical: Edited by E. J. Ellis and W. B. Yeats. 3 vols. 8vo. Lond., 1893. J 4 U 11-13

Selections from the Writings of; with an Essay by L. Housman. 12mo. Lond., 1893. H 10 P 30

Wm. Blake, his Life, Character, and Genius; by A. T. Story. 12mo. Lond., 1893. C 14 P 12

BLANCHARD, Jas. T. Essays and Addresses on Educational and Social Subjects. 8vo. Melb., 1881. MG 1 R 73

BLANCHE OF CASTILLE, Queen of France. History of. [*See* Berger, Elie.] B 26 V 19

BLANCHE, John F. The Prince's Visit, and other Poems. 2nd ed. 8vo. Melb., 1881. MH 1 S 31

BLANCHÈRE, R. de la. Terracene: essai d'histoire locale. 8vo. Paris, 1884. B 35 R 17

BLANFORD, Henry F. Physical Explanation of the inequality of the two semidiurnal oscillations of Barometric Pressure. [*See* Journal of Asiatic Society, Bengal, vol. 45, part 2.] E

BLATHWAYT, Raymond. Interviews; with Portraits. 8vo. Lond., 1893. J 10 U 34

BLAVATSKY, Mme. Hélène Petrovna. The Theosophical Glossary. Roy. 8vo. Lond., 1892. G 2 T 27

The Secret Doctrine. 2 vols. roy. 8vo. Lond., 1888. G 16 U 5, 6

A Modern Priestess of Isis. [*See* Solovyoff, V. S.] G 2 U 12

Madame Blavatsky and her Theosophy. [*See* Lillie, A.] G 2 U 13

BLAXLAND, Gregory. Journal of a Tour of Discovery across the Blue Mountains in New South Wales. (*Reprint.*) 8vo. Edinb., 1893.* MD 5 Q 50

BLEASDALE, Rev. Dr. John Ignatius. Practical Education: its present condition on the Continent of Europe, and in Great Britain. 8vo. Melb., 1869. MJ 3 Q 15

BLENNERHASSETT, Lady. [Life of] Talleyrand. Translated from the German by F. Clark. 2 vols. 8vo. Lond., 1894. C 17 S 18, 19

BLENNERHASSETT, Rose, and SLEEMAN, Lucy. Adventures in Mashonaland. 8vo. Lond., 1893. D 14 S 7

BLESSINGTON, Marguerite Power, Countess of. Confessions of an Elderly Lady. 8vo. Paris, 1841. J 10 U 30

Confessions of an Elderly Gentleman. 8vo. Paris, 1841. J 10 S 30

BLEW, William C. A. Brighton and its Coaches. Roy. 8vo. Lond., 1894. B 24 V 16

BLIND, Mathilde. Journal of Marie Bashkirtseff. [*See* Bashkirtseff, Marie.] C 22 P 1

BLISS, W. D. P. Hand-book of Socialism. 8vo. Lond., 1895. F 8 U 47

BLISSARD, Rev. W. The Ethic of Usury and Interest: a Study in Inorganic Socialism. 8vo. Lond., 1892. F 14 Q 40

BLOCH, Prof. Gustave. Les origines du Sénat Romain; recherches sur la Formation et la Dissolution du Sénat Patricien. 8vo. Paris, 1883. F 1 R 10

BLOCKMAR, Dr. F. W. Federal and State Aid to Higher Education in the United States. 8vo. Wash., 1890. G 18 R 20

BLOCKX, Jacques. A Compendium of Painting. Translated by H. Gordon. 12mo. Lond., 1894. A 23 P 4

BLOOMFIELD, Capt. Harry. *The Sea Spray.* 8vo. Lond., 1875. MJ 3 Q 7

BLOOMFIELD, Robert. The Farmer's Boy. 8vo. Lond., 1857. H 9 U 7

BLOUET, Paul, "Max O'Rell." La Maison John Bull & Cie. les Grandes succursales: le Canada, l'Australie, la Nouvelle Zélande, l'Afrique du sud. 12mo. Paris, 1894. MD 7 T 57
John Bull & Co.: the Great Colonial Branches of the firm—Canada, Australia, New Zealand, and South Africa. 8vo. Lond., 1894. MD 7 T 58

BLOW, Susan E. Symbolic Education. 8vo. New York, 1894. G 18 P 13

BLOXAM, Chas. L. Chemistry, Inorganic and Organic. 8th ed., revised by Prof. J. M. Thomson and A. G. Bloxam. 8vo. Lond., 1895. A 21 U 4

BLOXAM, G. W. Index to Publications of the Anthropological Institute of Great Britain and Ireland. [See Anthropological Institute.] E

BLUMLER, M. F. History of Amulets. [See Collectanea Adamantæa.] J 18 R 27

BLUNDELL, Jas. J., & Co. Street Guide and Index to the Distance Map of Melbourne and Suburbs. 12mo. Melb. (n.d.) MD 1 P 35

BLUNT, T. P. The influence of Light on Bacteria. (Roy. Soc., Vict., 20.) 8vo. Melb., 1884. ME 1 P

BOADEN, Jas. Memoirs of Mrs. Siddons, interspersed with Anecdotes of Authors and Actors. 12mo. Lond., 1893. C 19 Q 2

BOARDING-OUT SYSTEM in Victoria, Extension of. Protest on behalf of the Abbotsford Convent Industrial School, with the Official Reply. 8vo. Melb., 1884. MF 2 Q 60

BOAS, Franz. Chinook Texts. 8vo. Wash., 1894. J 7 U 39

BOCCACCIO, Giovanni, as Man and Author; by J. A. Symonds. 8vo. Lond., 1895 C 18 T 18

BODDAM, Lieut.-Col. F. B. Harbour Defences. [See United Service Inst.]

BŒHME, Henry. Scriptural, Historical, and Experimental Facts. 8vo. Sydney (n.d.) MH 1 S 27

BOHEMIAN. [See Industrial Schools.] MF 1 P 73

BOITO, Arrigo. Sketch of. [See Streatfeild, R. A.— Masters of Italian Music.] C 22 P 13

BOLDREWOOD, Rolf. [See Browne, T. A.]

BOLINGBROKE, Henry St. John, Viscount. Sketch of. [See Bagehot, W.—Biographical Studies.] C 22 P 10

BOLLAND, Simpson. The Iron-founder: a comprehensive treatise on the Art of Moulding. 8vo. New York, 1892. A 25 R 6
The Iron-founder Supplement: a complete Illustrated Exposition of the Art of Casting in Iron. 8vo. New York, 1893. A 25 R 14

BOLLES, Frank. Harvard University: a brief Statement of what Harvard University is, how it may be entered, and how its Degrees may be obtained. 8vo. Camb., Mass., 1892. G 18 R 46
Students' Expenses, Harvard University. 8vo. Camb., Mass., 1893. G 18 R 47

BOLTON, Reginald. Motive Powers and their Practical Selection. 8vo. Lond., 1895. A 25 Q 21

BOLTON, Sarah Knowles. Famous Voyagers and Explorers. 8vo. Lond., 1893. C 18 P 10
Famous Leaders among Men. 12mo. New York, 1894. C 17 P 27

BONANZA. [See Gold-fields Reminiscences.] MA 3 S 58
BONAR, Rev. Dr. Andrew Alex. Diary and Letters. Transcribed and edited by his daughter, Marjory Bonar. 8vo. Lond., 1893. C 19 R 7
Reminiscences of; edited by his daughter. 8vo. Lond., 1895. C 19 R 21

BONAR, Marjory. [See Bonar, Rev. Dr. A. A.]

BONAVIA, Dr. E. The Flora of the Assyrian Monuments and its Outcomes. 8vo. Westminster, 1894. A 20 S 11
Studies in the Evolution of Animals. Illustrated. Sm. 4to. Lond., 1895. A 28 U 11

BOND, Chas. G. Cast Away, and other poems. 8vo. Sydney, 1893. MH 1 P 08

BONHAM, John M. Secularism: its Progress and its Morals. 8vo. New York, 1894. G 19 P 21

BONNAR, Thos. Biographical Sketch of G. M. Kemp. 8vo. Edinb., 1892. C 21 R 5

BONNARD, H. Report on the Amsterdam International Exhibition, 1883. Sm fol. Sydney, 1884. ME

BONNER, Hypatia Bradlaugh. Life and Works of Chas. Bradlaugh. 2 vols. 8vo. Lond., 1894. C 21 R 1, 2

BONNER, T. D. Life and Adventures of James P. Beckwourth, Mountaineer, Scout, Pioneer, and Chief of the Crow Nation of Indians. 8vo. Lond., 1892. C 16 R 12

BONNEY, Rev. Dr. Thos. Geo. Charles Lyell and Modern Geology. 12mo. Lond., 1895. C 19 V 9
The Story of our Planet. 8vo. Lond., 1893. A 24 U 20
[See Year-book of Science.] E

BONSAL, Stephen, junr. Morocco as it is, with an account of Sir C. Euan Smith's Mission to Fez. 8vo. Lond., 1893. D 14 P 9

BONWICK, James. Astronomy for Young Australians. 18mo. Melb., 1866. MA 1 P 83
Climate and Health in Australasia, to which is added a Chapter on the Land Laws of the Colony of New South Wales. 12mo. Lond., 1886. MA 3 U 2
Egyptian Belief and Modern Thought. 8vo. Lond., 1878. G 2 P 32
Geography for the Use of Australian Youth. 2nd ed. 18mo. Launceston, 1850. MD 1 P 37
Geography of Australia and New Zealand. 3rd ed. 18mo. Melb., 1855. MD 1 P 45
Irish Druids and Old Irish Religions. 8vo. Lond., 1864. G 16 R 47
[Life of] John Batman, the Founder of Victoria. 12mo. Melb., 1867. MC 1 P 59
Reader for Australian Youth. Part I. 12mo. Adelaide, 1852. MJ 1 Q 48
The Resources of Queensland. 8vo. Lond., 1883. MD 8 P 19
Western Victoria; its Geography, Geology, and Social Condition. 8vo. Geelong, 1858. MD 1 Q 42

BOOK OF COMMON PRAYER, The. [See Liturgies.] G 13 T 49

BOOK FOR THE FARM, A: or, Bones and Bone Dust; their use and application as a Manure. 8vo. Hobart, 1851. MA 1 P 63

BOOK OF ENGLISH SONGS, The. 8vo. Lond. (n.d.) H 9 U 8

BOOK OF MORMON, The. Translated by Joseph Smith, jun. 12mo. Lamoni, 1874. G 13 V 31

BOOK OF RIDDLES, The. 18mo. Lond., 1851. A 29 S 14

BOOK OF THE DEAD, The. Fac-simile of the Papyrus of Ani, in the British Museum. Fol. Lond., 1894. B 8 Q 14 ‡
Papyrus of Ani, &c. Egyptian Text, with Translation by Dr. E. A. W. Budge. 4to. Lond., 1895. B 8 Q 2 †
The Egyptian Book of the Dead. [See Davis, Dr. C. H. S.] G 37 Q 10‡

BOOKWORM, The: an Illustrated Treasury of Old-time Literature. Vols. 5-7. 8vo. Lond., 1892-94. E

BOORE, F. A. Description of the Exploration of the Aird River, New Guinea. (Roy. Geogr. Soc. of Australasia, Q. Branch, 3.) 8vo. Brisbane, 1888. ME 20

BOOSÉ, J. R. Crozet's Voyage. [See Crozet's.] MD 8 Q 43

BOOT, W. H. J. Trees, and how to Paint them in Water-colours. 2nd ed. Ob. 8vo. Lond., 1883. A 23 Q 35

BOOTH, Mrs. Catherine. Life of; by F. de L. Booth-Tucker. 2 vols. 8vo. Lond., 1892. C 15 R 21, 22

BOOTH, Charles. Life and Labour of the People in London. Vols. 5, 6. 8vo. Lond., 1895. F 10 U 12, 13
The Aged Poor in England and Wales. 8vo. Lond., 1894. F 8 P 29

BOOTH, Edwin. Life and Art of; by W. Winter. 12mo. Lond., 1893. C 19 Q 6
[Plaster Cast of.] [See Hutton, L.—Portraits in Plaster.] A 23 V 13

BOOTH, Prof. Jas. C., AND MORFIT, Campbell. On Recent Improvement in the Chemical Arts. 8vo. Wash., 1852. A 21 U 2

BOOTH, Rev. Wm. General Booth at Home at Hadley Wood; with Portrait. [See Blathwayt, R.—Interviews.] J 10 U 34

BOOTH-TUCKER, F. de L. [See Tucker, F. de L. B.-]

BOOTHBY, Benjamin. Correspondence between the Governor of South Australia and the Secretary of State, relative to Mr. Justice Boothby. Sm. fol. Lond., 1862. MF 3 U 6

BOOTHBY, Guy. A Lost Endeavour. 18mo. Lond., 1895. MJ 3 P 32
The Marriage of Esther: a Torres Straits Sketch. 8vo. Lond., 1895. MJ 3 Q 20
On the Wallaby: or, Through the East and across Australia. Illustrated. 8vo. Lond., 1894. MD 7 S 40

BORDEAUX WINE EXHIBITION, 1882. Official Catalogue of the Wines of New South Wales, forwarded to the Philomatic Society of Bordeaux for the Exhibition of 1882. 8vo. Sydney, 1882. MK 2 R 4

BORGEAUD, Chas. Adoption and Amendment of Constitutions in Europe and America. Translated by Prof. C. D. Hazen. 8vo. Lond., 1895. F 2 V 10
The Rise of Modern Democracy in Old and New England. Translated by Mrs. Birkbeck Hill. 8vo. Lond., 1894. F 5 Q 2

BORLASE, Wm. C. The Age of the Saints. 8vo. Truro, 1893. G 6 S 31

BORNET, E., et GRUNOW, A. Mazœa: Nouveau Genre d'algue de l'ordre des Cryptophycées. 8vo. (n p.n.d.) A 30 U 27

BOSANQUET, Bernard. Aspects of the Social Problem; by various writers. 8vo. Lond., 1895. F 8 U 31
The Social Contract. [See Rousseau, J. J.] F 8 U 42

BOSCAWEN, Wm. St. C. The Bible and the Monuments: the Primitive Hebrew Records in the Light of Modern Research. 8vo. Lond., 1895. G 3 R 18
Mummies of the Priests of Ammon, discovered at Thebes. [See Roy. Soc. of Lit., 2nd series, 16.] E
A Chat with; with Portrait. [See Blathwayt, R.—Interviews.] J 10 U 34

BOSE, Pramatha Nath. History of Hindu Civilization during British Rule. 2 vols. 12mo. Calcutta, 1894.
F 7 V 7, 8

BOSTON CHILDREN'S AID SOCIETY. Report 1891. 8vo. Boston, 1893.
E

BOSTON PUBLIC LIBRARY. Annual Reports of Trustees, 1854, 1856–57, 1860–61, 1866–67, 1869–72, 1875–75, 1877–78, 1880–87, 1889–93. 29 vols. 8vo. Boston, 1854–93.
E

Bulletins, 1890–94. 17 vols. Roy. 8vo. Boston, 1890–94.
Libr.

Hand-book for Readers, containing the Regulations of the Library, with an Account of the Catalogues, &c. 9th ed. 12mo. Boston, 1890.
J 12 S 40

BOSWELL, Chas. S. The Vita Nuova and its author. [See Dante Alighieri.]
J 9 R 29

BOSWELL, Jas. Journal of a Tour to the Hebrides with Samuel Johnson, LL.D. 8vo. Lond. (n.d.)
D 19 R 26

BOTHWELL, James Hepburn, Earl of. [Life of], 1536–78; by G. G. Smith. (Lives of Twelve Bad Men.) 8vo. Lond., 1894.
C 18 T 9

BOTSFORD, Dr. G. W. Development of the Athenian Constitution. (Cornell Studies.) 8vo. Boston, 1893.
F 14 U 10

BOTTONE, S. R. Electric Bells and all about them: a Practical Book for Practical Men. 4th ed. Illustrated. 12mo. Lond., 1892.
A 21 P 35

BOUCHOT, Henri. The Book: its Printers, Illustrators, and Binders, from Gutenberg to the Present Time; with a Treatise on the Art of collecting and describing early printed Books, edited by H. Grevel. Illustrated. Roy. 8vo. Lond., 1890.
B 36 U 2

BOUCICAULT, Dion. [Plaster Cast of.] [See Hutton L.—Portraits in Plaster.]
A 23 V 13

BOUCICAUT, Maréchal. Expéditions du. [See Delaville le Roulx, J.—La France en Orient au XIVe siècle.]
B 26 V 20, 21

BOUGAINVILLE, Baron de. Journal de la Navigation autour du Globe, de la Frégate La Thétis et de la Corvette L'Espérance, pendant les années 1824–26, 2 vols. 4to. Paris, 1837.
MD 2 Q 37, 38

Atlas [to the above]. Fol. Paris, 1837.
MD 5 Q 15

BOUGAINVILLE, Louis A., Comte de. Essai Historique sur la vie et les travaux de Bougainville. [See Pascal, M.]
MD 8 Q 18

Histoire d'un Voyage aux Isles Malouines, 1763–64; avec des Observations sur le Détroit de Magellan, et sur les Patagons. 2 vols 8vo. Paris, 1770.
D 20 S 10, 11

BOULENGER, G. A. The Geckos of New Caledonia. 8vo. Lond., 1883.
MA 3 R 38

BOULGER, Prof. G. S. The Country Month by Month. [See Visgar, Mrs.]
A 29 S 9-11

BOULLENOIS, Frédéric de. Conseils aux Nouveaux Educateurs de Vers à Soie. 3e édition. 8vo. Paris, 1875.
A 18 S 16

BOULNOIS, H. Percy. Construction of Carriageways and Footways. Illustrated. 8vo. Lond, 1895.
A 22 S 9

BOULTBEE, Jas. Wm. Report respecting Artesian Boring. Fol. Sydney, 1891–92.
MF 2 U 46

BOULTON, Samuel B. Preservation of Timber by the use of Antiseptics. 18mo. New York, 1885.
A 22 P 37

BOURBON, Marie C. F. L. de. [See Berry, Duchess of.]

BOURGADE LA DARDYE, Dr. E. de. Paraguay: the Land and the People, Natural Wealth, and Commercial Capabilities. English edition, edited by E. G. Ravenstein. With Map and Illustrations. 8vo. Lond., 1892.
D 15 R 10

BOURGEOIS, Dr. Emile. Neuchatel et la Politique Prussienne en Franche-comté, 1702–13. 8vo. Paris, 1887.
B 31 V 1

BOURGET, Paul. Outre-mer Impressions of America. 8vo. Lond., 1895.
B 1 U 15

BOURGOING, Dr. D. Tragedy of Fotheringay. [See Scott, Hon. Mrs. M.]
B 32 T 16

BOURINOT, Dr. John G. Federal Government in Canada. (Johns Hopkins University Studies, 7.) 8vo. Baltimore, 1889.
B 18 S 7

Local Government in Canada: an Historical Study. (Johns Hopkins University Studies, 5.) 8vo. Baltimore, 1887.
B 18 S 5

Parliamentary Procedure and Practice; with a Review of the Origin, Growth, and Operation of Parliamentary Institutions in the Dominion of Canada. 2nd ed. 8vo. Lond., 1891.
F 14 R 17

BOURKE, Hon. Algernon. Correspondence of J. Jekyll. [See Jekyll, J.]
C 16 S 16

BOURKE, E. M. Little History of New Zealand, progressive from discovery to 1880, for children. 12mo. Melb., 1883.
MB 1 P 17

BOUVIER, J. le. Recovery of Normandy from the English, 1419. [See Collectanea Adamantæa.]
J 18 R 30

BOWDEN, John E. Life and Letters of the Rev. Dr F. W. Faber. 8vo. Lond., 1869.
C 18 P 17

BOWDEN, Thos. A., and HECTOR, Sir Jas. Manual of New Zealand Geography; with Maps and Examination Questions. 12mo. Lond., 1869.
MD 2 W 48

BOWDICH, Mrs. New Vegetarian Dishes. 12mo. Lond., 1892.
A 6 Q 29

BOWEN, Lord. Sketch of. [*See* Smalley, G. W.—Studies of Men.] C 19 R 20

BOWER, Capt. Hamilton. Diary of a Journey across Tibet. Illustrated. 8vo. Lond., 1894. D 17 T 9

BOWIE, Augustus J., jun. Practical Treatise on Hydraulic Mining in California. 5th ed. [with Map and Illustrations]. Roy. 8vo. New York, 1893.
A 24 V 28

BOWIE *versus* WILSON. Report of the Inquiry into the Management of the Yarra Bend Lunatic Asylum, as detailed in the nine days Trial of the action for libel, Bowie v. Wilson. 8vo. Melb., 1862.
MF 2 Q 74

BOWLES, Caroline. [*See* Southey, Mrs. C.]

BOWLEY, Arthur L. Short Account of England's Foreign Trade in the 19th Century. 8vo. Lond., 1893. F 14 Q 27

BOWMAN, Mrs. William. Sermon preached on the Life and Character of; by the Rev. Dr. W. Woolls. 8vo. Sydney, 1885. MG 2 Q 20

BOWRING, Lewin B. Haidar Alí and Tipú Sultán. 12mo. Oxford, 1893. C 13 R 20

BOWRING, W. B. Home Rule in Newfoundland. [*See* Subjects of the Day, 3.] F 7 U 28

BOX, T. H. The Silver Question. [*See* Jamieson, G.]
F 9 T 10

BOYD, A. J. The Earth's History for Boys; or, Geology in Verse. 12mo. Brisb., 1889. MA 2 P 28

Ocean Currents. (Roy. Geograph. Soc. of Australasia, Q. Branch, 6.) 8vo. Brisbane, 1891. ME 20

Reminiscences of the Chincha Islands. (Roy. Geograph. Soc. of South Australasia, Q. Branch, 8.) 8vo. Brisbane, 1893. ME 20

BOYD, Rev. Dr. Andrew K. H. Twenty-five Years of St. Andrews, 1865-90. 2 vols. 8vo. Lond., 1892.
C 16 S 3, 4

BOYD, Lieut.-Col. J. A. Supply Handbook for the Army Service Corps. 8vo. Lond., 1892. A 29 Q 18

BOYD, R. Nelson. Coal Mines Inspection; its History and Results. 8vo. Lond., 1879. A 24 T 23

Coal Pits and Pitmen: A Short History of the Coal Trade and the Legislation Affecting it. 8vo. Lond., 1892. A 24 Q 18

BOYESEN, Hjalmar H. Commentary on the Writings of Henrik Ibsen. 8vo. New York, 1894. J 4 Q 12

Essays on Scandinavian Literature. 8vo. Lond., 1895.
J 9 S 25

BOYLE, Frederick. The Orchid Seekers. [*See* Hussan, A.] D 17 Q 31

BOYLE, Robert. Sketch of. [*See* Thorpe, Dr. T. E.—Historical Chemistry.] C 17 R 2

BOYNE, Wm. Tokens issued in the 17th, 18th, and 19th Centuries, in Yorkshire; also the Seals of all the Corporations in that County. 4to. Headingly, 1858.
A 13 S 51

Trade Tokens issued in the 17th Century in England, Wales, and Ireland. New and revised edition by G. C. Williamson. 2 vols. 8vo. Lond., 1889-91.
A 27 T 5, 6

BOYS' BRIGADE. Annual Report, 1892-93. 8vo. Sydney, 1893. ME 6 S

BRABANT, Arthur B. Colonisation of Indo-China. [*See* Bert, J. Chailley-.] F 14 R 31

BRACKEN, Thos. Behind the Tomb, and other Poems. 12mo. Melb., 1871. MH 1 U 65

Musings in Maoriland; with an Historical Sketch, by Sir R. Stout. 4to. Dunedin, 1890. MH 1 T 14

BRACKETT, Dr. Jeffrey R. The Negro in Maryland: a Study of the Institution of Slavery. (Johns Hopkins University Studies, extra vol. 6.) 8vo. Baltimore, 1889. B 18 T 6

Notes on the Progress of the Colored People of Maryland since the War. (Johns Hopkins University Studies, 8.) 8vo. Baltimore, 1890. B 18 S 8

BRADDON, Sir Edward. Thirty years of Shikar. Illustrated. 8vo. Edinb., 1895. D 17 V 19

BRADFORD, Dr. Thos. L. Life and Letters of Dr. Samuel Hahnemann. Roy. 8vo. Philad., 1895.
C 16 U 10

BRADFORD, Rev. Wm. Sketches of the Country, Character, and Costume, in Portugal and Spain, in 1808 and 1809. (Eng. and Fr.) Fol. Lond., 1812.
D 20 Q 10‡

BRADLAUGH, Charles: a Record of his Life and Work: by his daughter, Hypatia Bradlaugh Bonner. 2 vols. 8vo. Lond., 1894. C 21 R 1, 2

Catalogue of the Library of. 8vo. Lond., 1891.
K 7 R 56

Force or Conciliation in Labour Disputes. [*See* Subjects of the Day, 2.] F 7 U 27

BRADLEE, Rev. Dr. Caleb D. Recollections of a Ministry of forty years, 1854-94. 8vo. Boston, 1895.
G 4 T 15

BRADLEY, A. G. [Life of] Wolfe. 12mo. Lond., 1895. C 21 P 20

BRADLEY, Very Rev. George G. Life of Dean Stanley. [*See* Prothero, R. E.] C 19 R 3, 4

BRADSHAW, J. The Future of North Australia. (Roy. Geogr. Soc. Australasia, Vic. Branch, 9.) 8vo. Melb., 1892. ME 20

Notes on a recent Trip to Prince Regent's River. (Roy. Geogr. Soc. Australasia, Vic. Branch, 9.) 8vo. Melb., 1892. ME 20

BRADSHAW, Dr. John. A Concordance to the Poetical Works of John Milton. Roy. 8vo. Lond., 1894.
K 17 R 30

Sir Thomas Munro and the British Settlement of the Madras Presidency. (Rulers of India.) 8vo. Oxford, 1894.
C 14 P 13

BRADY, Dr. G. Stewardson. Ostracoda, Zoology, 1; Copepoda, Zoology, 8. [See Thomson, Sir C. W., and Murray, Dr. J.—Voyage of H.M.S. Challenger.]
A 6†

BRADY, Hy. Bowman. Foraminifera. [See Thomson, Sir C. W., and Murray, Dr. J.—Voyage of H.M.S. Challenger.]
A 6†

BRADY, Dr. N. Psalms of David. [See Liturgics.]
MG 1 P 54

BRADY, Rev. Dr. Wm. M. Rome and Fenianism: the Pope's anti-Parnellite circular. 8vo. Lond., 1883.
G 15 P 43

BRAHMS, Johannes. Studies in Modern Music. [See Hadow, W. H.]
C 21 Q 15

BRAINNE, C. La Nouvelle-Calédonie, 1774-1854. [With Map.] 12mo. Paris, 1854.
MD 7 T 11

BRAITHWAITE, Dr. Robt. Mosses. [See Taylor, Dr. J. E.—Collecting Natural History Objects.]
A 29 Q 38

BRANDES, Dr. G. Account of. [See Tweedie, Mrs. A.]
D 18 T 15

BRANDRAM, Samuel. Selections from Shakespeare, suitable for Recitation, with an Essay on Elocution. 8vo. Lond, 1893.
J 4 R 2

Selected Pieces in Prose and Verse. 8vo. Lond., 1893.
J 4 R 2

BRANNT, Wm. T. The Manufacture of Vinegar and Acetates, Cider, and Fruit Wines; Preservation of Fruits and Vegetables by Canning and Preserving; Preparation of Fruitbutters, Jellies, Marmalades, Catchups, Pickles, Mustards, &c. 8vo. Philad., 1890.
A 22 T 2

The Metallic Alloys: a Practical Guide for the Manufacture of Alloys, Amalgams, and Solders, used by metal-workers. 8vo. Philad., 1890.
A 24 S 4

Petroleum: its History, Origin, &c. 8vo. Philad., 1895.
A 24 V 31

Practical Scourer and Garment Dyer, and the Manufacture of Soaps and Fluids for cleansing purposes. Illustrated. 8vo. Philad., 1893.
A 25 R 11

Electro-deposition of Metals. [See Langbein, Dr. G.]
A 21 V 13

Raw Materials and Distillation of Alcohol. [See Stammer. Dr. K.]
A 25 Q 39

———, and WAHL, Dr. Wm. H. Techno-Chemical Receipt-book. Illustrated. 8vo. Philad., 1895.
A 21 R 28

BRASSEY, Thomas. Biographical Sketch of. [See Smith, C. B.—Leaders of Modern Industry.]
C 14 P 14

BRASSEY, Thomas, Baron. Papers and Addresses by. Naval and Maritime, 1872-93. 2 vols. 8vo. Lond., 1894.
F 12 P 36, 37

Papers and Addresses: Imperial Federation and Colonisation, from 1890-94. 8vo. Lond., 1895.
F 10 U 2

Papers and Addresses: Work and Wages. 8vo. Lond, 1894.
F 2 V 17

Papers and Addresses: Mercantile Marine and Navigation 8vo. Lond., 1894.
F 2 V 18

Papers and Addresses: Political and Miscellaneous, 1861-94. Arranged and edited by A. H. Loring. 8vo. Lond., 1895.
F 2 V 14

Voyages and Travels, 1862-94. Edited by Capt. S. Eardley-Wilmot. 2 vols. 8vo. Lond., 1895.
D 20 S 8, 9

Yachting. [See Sullivan, Sir E.]
A 24 Q 40, 41

BRASSEY, Thos. Allnutt. [See Naval Annual.]
E

BRASSINGTON, W. S. History of the Art of Bookbinding; with some account of the Books of the Ancients. Sm. fol. Lond., 1894.
A 26 S 22 ‡

BRAYBROOKE, Lord. Notes to Pepys' Diary. [See Pepys, S.]
C 14 V 1-4

BRAYLEY, Edward W. Journal of the Plague Year. [See De Foe, Daniel]
B 28 R 22

BRAZIER, John. Australian Museum. Catalogue of the Marine Shells of Australia and Tasmania. Part 3. Gasteropoda, Murex. 8vo. Syd., 1893.
MA 2 U 46

Trochidæ and other Genera of South Australia, with their synonyms. (Trans. Roy. Soc., S. Australia, 9.) 8vo. Adelaide, 1887.
ME 1 S

BRAZIL. Balanço da Receita e Despeza do Imperio no Exercicio de 1888. Sm. fol. Rio do Janeiro, 1891.
E

Bibliotheca Nacional do Rio de Janeiro, Annaes da, 1886-88. Vols. 14-16. 3 vols. (in 4.) Imp. 8vo. Rio de Janeiro, 1890-93.
E

Regulamento para a Bibliotheca Nacional approvado pelo Decreto 1195 do 28 do Dezembro do 1892. 8vo. Rio de Janeiro, 1893.
J 10 S 23

Camara dos Deputados. Reforma do Ensino secundario e superior. Parecer e Projecto. Sm. fol. Rio de Janeiro, 1892.
G 36 P 10 ‡

Relatorio e Synopse dos Trabalhos da, 1891-92. 3 vols. Sm. fol. Rio de Janeiro, 1892-93.
E

Annaes da, 1890-92. 13 vols. 8vo. Rio de Janeiro, 1891-93.
E

Regimento interno da. 32mo. Rio de Janeiro, 1893.
F 12 S 14

Congresso Nacional; Annaes do Senado Federal, 1891-92. 12 vols. 8vo. Rio de Janeiro, 1891-93.
E

Immigração e Colonisação. Contratos para Introducção e Localisação de Immigrantes. Ob. fol. Rio do Janeiro, 1891.
E

Message adressé au Congrès National par le Maréchal Floriano Peixoto à l'occasion de l'ouverture de la 1ᵉ Session ordinaire de la 2ᵉ Législature. 8vo. Rio de Janeiro, 1894.
F 10 U 20

BRAZIL—*continued.*
Ministro da Fazenda. Relatorio, 1891-92. 3 vols. 8vo. Rio de Janeiro, 1891-92. E
Ministro do Interior. Relatorio, 1891. 8vo. Rio de Janeiro, 1891. E
Ministro da Justiça. Relatorios, 1888 e 1892. Sm. fol. and 8vo. Rio de Janeiro, 1889-92. F
Ministro da Marinha. Relatorios, 1888 e 1892. Sm. fol. and 8vo. Rio de Janeiro, 1889-92. E
Ministro dos Negocios Estrangeiros. Relatorio, 1888. Sm. fol. Rio de Janeiro, 1889. E
Ministro dos Negocios do Imperio. Relatorio, 1888. Sm. fol. Rio de Janeiro, 1889. E
Ministro do Instrucção Publica, Correios e Telegraphos, Relatorios, 1889-92. 5 vols. 8vo. Rio de Janeiro, 1891-92. E
Ministro dos Negocios da Agricultura, Commercio e Obras Publicas, Relatorios, 1888, 1891-92. 4 vols. 8vo., 3 vols. sm. fol. Rio de Janeiro, 1860-92. E
Correio Geral. Relatorio, 1888. Sm. fol. Rio de Janeiro, 1889. E
Orcamento da receita e despeza, 1894. Sm. fol. Rio de Janeiro, 1893. E
Primeiro e Segundo Congresso Brazileiro de Medicina e Cirurgia do Rio de Janeiro. 4 vols. 8vo. Rio de Janeiro, 1889-92. E
Regimento Interno do Senado Federal, e Additamento ao. 12mo. Rio de Janeiro, 1891. E
Relatorio apresentado ao Chefe do Governo Provisorio. 8vo. Rio de Janeiro, 1890. D 18 V 21
Relatorio apresentado ao Vice-Presidente da Republica dos Estados Unidos do Brazil, 1892-93. 6 vols. 8vo. Rio de Janeiro, 1892-93. E
Relatorio do Tribunal de Contas, 1893. 8vo. Rio de Janeiro, 1893. F 9 T 32
Relatorio do Vice-Presidente do Senado Federal para ser apresentado na Sessao ordinaria de 1894. 4to. Rio de Janeiro, 1894. E
Senado Federal. Manual do Senador. 12mo. Rio de Janeiro, 1893. F 12 S 12

BREIL, C. du, Marquis de Rays. Nouvelle-France. [*See* Groote, P. de.] MD 7 S 38

BRENCHLEY, J. May Bloom and Wattle Blossoms. 12mo. Melb., 1876. MH 1 P.61

BRENTANO, Lujo. Hours and Wages in relation to Production. Translated by Mrs. William Arnold. 8vo. Lond., 1894. F 5 Q 1

BRETT, Edwin J. Pictorial and Descriptive Record of the Origin and Development of Arms and Armour. Illustrated. 4to. Lond., 1894. B 5 S 18†

BRETT, Henry. Brett's New Zealand and South Pacific Pilot, with Nautical Almanac for 1887-88. Compiled by Capt. Tilly. 8vo. Auckland, 1886. ME 6 R

BRETT, Reginald B. Footprints of Statesmen during the 18th Century in England. 8vo. Lond., 1892. B 21 R 16

BREWER, Chas. B. Australian Colonies Better Government Act, with Notes. 8vo. Hobart, 1850. MF 2 Q 75

BREWER, R. F. Voice, Speech, and Gesture. [*See* Campbell, Dr. H.] J 8 T 36

BREWERS' EXHIBITION. Fifteenth Annual National Exhibition and Market: Catalogue. 8vo. Lond., 1893. K 7 R 53

BREWERY COMPANIES. A reprint from the *Statist* of a series of articles furnishing full particulars and authentic data concerning all Brewery Companies; by "H.S." 8vo. Lond., 1893. F 9 Q 28

BREWSTER, Sir David. The Home Life of; by Mrs. Gordon. 2nd ed. 8vo. Edinb., 1870. C 13 P 25

BREYTON, A. Mélanges Carolingiens. [*See* Bardot, G.] B 26 V 22

BRIALMONT, Col. A. Hasty Intrenchments. Translated by Lieut. C. A. Empson. With Plates. 8vo. Lond., 1872. A 29 T 23

BRIDGES, Robert. Poetry of. [*See* Dowden, Dr. E.] J 5 S 16

BRIDGES, Capt. W. T. Modern Coast Defence. (United Service Institution, N.S.W., 5.) 8vo. Sydney, 1894. ME

BRIDGMAN, J. B. Hymenoptera. [*See* Taylor, Dr. J. E.—Collecting Natural History Objects.] A 29 Q 38

BRIGGS, Robert. Steam Heating. 18mo. New York, 1888. A 22 P 20

BRIGHAM, Wm. T. Notes on the Volcanic Phenomena of the Hawaiian Islands, with a Description of the Modern Eruptions. 4to. Boston, 1868. MA 9 P 34†

BRIGHT, Chas. Debate on the Divine Origin of Christianity. [*See* Green, Rev. M. W.] MG 1 P 67
The Crows and their "Caws"; a Fable founded on facts. (Pam.) 8vo. Sydney, 1880. MG 1 Q 53

BRIGNOLE, Atilio C. El Derecho Internacional Privado y sus Fundamentos. 8vo. Montevideo, 1894. F 9 R 34

BRINE, Vice-Adm. Lindesay. Travels amongst American Indians: their Ancient Earthworks and Temples; including a Journey to Guatemala, Mexico, and Yucatan, and a Visit to the Ruins of Patinamit, Utatlan, Palenque, and Uxmal. Illustrated 8vo. Lond., 1894. D 15 S 23

BRINTON, Dr. Daniel G., and ANTHONY, Rev. A. S. Lenâpé-English Dictionary. 8vo. Philad., 1888. J 10 U 32

BRISBANE. Views of Brisbane Queensland. Folded 12mo. (n.p.n.d.) MD 8 P 18

BRISSET, George. The Apology of. [*See* Bibliotheca Curiosa.] J 18 Q 15

BRISTOW, Henry Wm. Portrait of. [*See* Ramsay, Sir A. C.—Memoir of.] C 21 R 20

BRITISH ALMANAC AND COMPANION, 1893-95. 3 vols. 12mo. Lond., 1893-95. E

BRITISH AND FOREIGN BIBLE SOCIETY. Report of the Geelong Auxiliary of, 1875. 8vo. Geelong, 1876. ME 0 S

BRITISH ARCHÆOLOGICAL ASSOCIATION. Journal, vols. 47-50. 8vo. Lond., 1891-94. E

BRITISH ASSOCIATION FOR THE ADVANCEMENT OF SCIENCE. Address by Sir H. E. Roscoe, 1887. [*See* Roscoe, Sir H. E.] A 21 S 33
Birmingham Meeting, 1886; Programme of Excursions. 8vo. Birm., 1886. E
Exhibition of Local Products and Industries in Bingley Hall, Birmingham, 1886. Official Catalogue. 12mo. Birm., 1886. K 7 P 7
Index to the Reports and Transactions of the British Association for the Advancement of Science, 1861-90 inclusive. 8vo. Lond., 1893. E
Reports of the 62nd, 63rd, and 64th Meetings, 1892-94. 8vo. Lond., 1893-94. E
Souvenir of the Birmingham Meeting. Sm. 4to. Birm., 1886. A 30 U 38

BRITISH ASTRONOMICAL ASSOCIATION. Journal, vols. 1-3, 1890-93. 8vo. Lond., 1890-93. E

BRITISH AUSTRALASIAN, The, 1892-94. Fol. Lond., 1892-94. E

BRITISH COLUMBIA. The Kootenay District. 8vo. (n.p.n.d.) D 15 R 15

BRITISH DAIRY FARMERS' ASSOCIATION. Journal of, Vol. 9. 8vo. Lond., 1894. E

BRITISH MEDICAL ASSOCIATION, NEW SOUTH WALES BRANCH. Proceedings, Feb.-Dec., 1880. 8vo. Sydney, 1880. ME 7 T
Report of the Annual Meeting, 1891. 12mo. Sydney, 1891. ME 7 T

BRITISH NEW GUINEA. [*See* New Guinea, British.]

BRITISH NORTH AMERICA. [*See* Great Britain and Ireland.]

BRITISH NORTH BORNEO CO. Report, 1883. Sm. 4to. Lond., 1883. E

BRITISH RECORD SOCIETY (with which is incorporated the Index Society). Publications. Index Library, Edited by W. P. W. Phillimore. 11 vols. Roy. 8vo. Lond., 1888-95. E
Abstracts of Gloucestershire Inquisitiones Post Mortem. Part 1. 1-11. Charles I, 1625-36.
Calendar of Chancery Proceedings: Bills and Answers, *temp.* Charles I. Vols. 1-3.
Calendars of Wills and Administrations in the Consistory Court of the Bishop of Lichfield and Coventry, 1516-1652; also those in the "Peculiars" at Lichfield, Birmingham, and Derby, 1529-1652, 1675-1790, 1753-1790.
Calendar of Wills proved in the Consistory Court of the Bishop of Gloucester, 1541-1650; edited by W. P. W. Phillimore and L. L. Duncan.
Calendar of Wills relating to Northampton and Rutland, 1510-1652.
Index Nominum to the Royalist Composition Papers. Vol. 1.
Index to Bills of Privy Signet, commonly called Signet Bills, 1584-1596, 1603-1624; with a Calendar of Writs of Privy Seal, 1601-1603.
Index to Wills proved and Administrations granted in the Court of the Archdeacon of Berks, 1508-1652.
Index to Wills proved in the Prerogative Court of Canterbury, 1363-1558.

BRITTEN, Emma H. Nineteenth Century Miracles; or, Spirits and their Work in every Country of the Earth. 8vo. New York, 1884. G 2 T 26
On the Road; or, the Spiritual Investigator. 12mo. Melb., 1878. MG 1 P 63

BRITTEN, Jas. Flowering Plants and Ferns. [*See* Taylor, Dr. J. E.—Collecting Natural History Objects.] A 29 Q 38

BRITTON, Alexander. History of New South Wales. [*See* New South Wales.] MB 2 S 33

BROADBENT, K. Birds of Central Queensland. (Proc. Roy. Soc., Queensland, 5.) 8vo. Brisbane, 1888. ME 1 T
Birds of the Chinchilla District. (Proc. Roy. Soc., Queensland, 2.) 8vo. Brisbane, 1886. ME 1 T
On the Migrations of Birds at the Cape York Peninsula. (Proc. Roy. Soc., Queensland, 1.) 8vo. Brisbane, 1884. ME 1 T

BROADER BRITAIN. Photographs depicting the Scenery, Cities, and Industries of the Colonies and Dependencies of the Crown, as well as of certain countries which, although not politically a part of the Empire, are by their Language, their Customs, or their History, associated with Great Britain. Ob. imp. 8vo. Chicago, 1895. A 3 R 21 †

BROADHURST, Rev. Thomas. Funeral Orations in praise of Military Men. Translated from the Greek of Thucydides, Plato, and Lysias, by the Rev. T. Broadhurst. 8vo. Bath, 1811. G 1 R 30

BROCK, Robt. Wm. Minawhenua: the Adventures of a party of Tourists amongst a tribe of Maoris discovered in Western Otago, New Zealand. 12mo. Dunedin, 1888. MJ 3 P 18

BROCKETT, John T. Glossary of North Country Words in use. 8vo. Newcastle, 1829. K 14 P 8

BRODHEAD, J. M. N. Slav and Moslem. 8vo. Charleston, South Carolina, 1894. B 31 S 3

BRODRIBB, T. Manual of Health and Temperance; with an Appendix on Infectious Diseases and Ambulance Work; by Dr. J. W. Springthorpe. 12mo. Melb., 1891. MA 3 U 4

BRODRIBB, W. A. Results of Inquiries and Correspondence during the year 1874, in regard to the Wool Trade in London, the Continent, and the Colonies. 8vo. Melb., 1875. MF 4 Q 24

BRODSKY, Maurice. Historical Sketch of the two Melbourne Synagogues. 8vo. Melb., 1877. MG 1 S 1

BROFFERIO, Prof. Angelo. Per lo Spiritismo. 2a. edizione. 8vo. Milano, 1893. G 7 U 22

BROINOWSKI, Gracius J. The Birds of Australia. 6 vols. fol. Melb., 1890-91.* MA 7 Q 16-21‡

BROKEN HILL PROPRIETARY BLOCK 10 CO. Reports and Statement of Accounts, 1892. Sm. 4to. Melb., 1892. ME 7 R

BROKEN HILL PROPRIETARY COMPANY. Reports and Statement of Account, 1892-93. 4to. Melb., 1892-93. ME 7 Q

Barrier Ranges Silver Field, New South Wales. Reports, Schedules, and Statement of Account, for half-year ending 31st May, 1894. 4to. Melb., 1894. ME

BROMFIELD, James. Brittany and the Chase. 12mo. Lond., 1853. A 29 S 15

BRONN, Dr. H. G. Klassen und Ordnungen des Thier-Reichs, wissenschaftlich dangestellt in Wort und Bild. Band 2, Ab. 3. Echinodermen (Stachelhäuten) von Dr. H. Ludwig. Buch 1. Die See Walzen. Band 4, Ab. 1. Vermes. (Mionelminthes, Trichoplax und Trematodes.) Roy. 8vo. Leipzig, 1879-93. E

BRONTË, Charlotte. Life of; by E. C. Gaskell. 8vo. Lond., 1858. C 21 Q 4

BROOK, George. Antipatharia. [See Thomson, Sir C. W., and Murray, Dr. J., Voyage of H.M.S. Challenger.] A 6†

BROOKE, Mrs. Frances. Rosina: an Opera. [See London Stage, 2.] H 2 S 34

BROOKE, Gustavus Vaughan. Life of; by W. J. Lawrence. Roy. 8vo. Belfast, 1892. C 13 V 5

BROOKE, Henry. Gustavus Vasa; or, the Deliverer of his Country: a Tragedy. [See London Stage, 3.] H 2 S 35

BROOKE, Sir Jas. Letter from Borneo; with Notices of the Country and its Inhabitants. 8vo. Lond., 1842. B 33 R 2

Private Letters of, narrating the Events of his Life to 1838. 3 vols. 8vo. Lond., 1853. C 22 P 4-6

BROOKE, Rev. Stopford. The Development of Theology as illustrated in English Poetry, 1780-1830. 12mo. Lond., 1893. G 7 U 2

History of Early English Literature; being the History of English Poetry from its Beginnings to the Accession of King Alfred. 2 vols. Lond., 1892. B 5 T 46, 47

Tennyson: his Art and Relation to Modern Life. 8vo. Lond., 1894. H 5 T 42

BROOKE, Sir Victor, Sportsman and Naturalist: a Memoir; by O. L. Stephen. Illustrated. 8vo. Lond., 1894. C 17 S 15

BROOKER, A. Electrical Engineering. [See Slingo, W.] A 21 R 22

BROOKS, Charles Shirley. The Russians of the South. 12mo. Lond., 1854. D 19 P 8

BROOKS, Chas. W. Early Migrations: Arctic Drift and Ocean Currents illustrated by the discovery on an icefloe off the Coast of Greenland of relics of the American Arctic steamer Jeannette. 8vo. San Francisco, 1884. D 16 T 13

BROOKS, E. J. Constitutional Antiquities of Sparta and Athens. [See Gilbert, Dr. G.] F 9 T 22

BROOKS, Edward. Course of Instruction in Cookery for the Public Schools of Philadelphia. 8vo. Philadelphia, 1893. A 22 R 4

Course of Instruction in Modelling for the Primary and Secondary Schools of Philadelphia. 8vo. Philad., 1892. G 18 S 10

Course of Instruction in Sewing, including Pattern Drafting for the Girls of the Public Schools of Philadelphia. 8vo. Philad., 1893. G 18 R 24

Course of Study in Arithmetic for the Public Schools of Philadelphia. 8vo. Philad., 1892. G 18 R 13

Syllabus of a Course in Pedagogy. 8vo. Philad., 1892. G 18 R 26

BROOKS, J. P. Victoria Spring, Western Australia, revisited. (Roy. Geog. Soc. Australasia, Vic. Branch, 8.) 8vo. Melb., 1891. ME 20

BROOKS, Noah. Statesmen. (Men of Achievement.) 8vo. Lond., 1894. C 16 R 20

BROOKS, Rt. Rev. Phillips. Essays and Addresses. 8vo. Lond., 1894. J 6 S 38

Sketch of; with Portrait. [See Bolton, Sarah K.— Famous Leaders.] C 17 P 27

BROOKS, S. W. Grammarial and Glossarial Similarities of the Languages of New Guinea and Fiji. (Roy. Geog. Soc. of Australasia, Q. Branch, 8.) 8vo. Brisbane, 1893. ME 20

BROOKS, Dr. Wm. K. The Genus Salpa. 2 vols. 4to. Baltimore, 1893. A 15 Q 7, 8 †

Stomatopoda. [See Thomson, Sir C. W., and Murray, Dr. J. Voyage of H.M.S. Challenger, Zoology, 16.] A 6 †

BROOME, Rev. A. Duty of Humanity to Inferior Creatures. [See Primatt, Rev. Dr. H.] G 7 U 36

BROOMFIELD, Fred. J. Ode to Victor Hugo. [See Villeval, A.—Victor Hugo.] MC 1 S 17

BROTIER, G. Taciti Opera. [See Tacitus, C. C.] B 30 T 24-27

BROUGH, Louisa. The Alps. [See Umlauft, Prof. F.] D 18 V 13

BROUGH, Wm. Natural Law of Money. 8vo. New York, 1894. F 8 U 26

BROUGHAM, Henry, Lord. Dialogues on Instinct. 18mo. Lond., 1844. A 28 P 7

Plaster Cast of. [See Hutton, L.—Portraits in Plaster.] A 23 V 13

Sketch of. [See Bagehot, W.—Biographical Studies.] C 22 P 10

BROUGHTON, Thos. Duer. Letters written in a Mahratta Camp during the year 1809, descriptive of the Character, Manners, Domestic Habits, and Religious Ceremonies of the Mahrattas. 8vo. Lond., 1892. D 17 Q 13

BROUGHTON, W. R. Sketch of Port Stephens, New Holland, 1795. Fol. [MS.] (n.p.) 1795. MD 1 P 16 ‡

BROUGHTON, Rt. Rev. Wm. Grant. The Farewell Address of. 8vo. Sydney, 1853. MG 1 S 7

Speech in the Legislative Council, on the Resolutions for Establishing a System of General Education. 8vo. Sydney, 1830. MG 1 S 6

"Take Heed": a Sermon. 12mo. Sydney, 1844. MG 1 P 52

BROUN, Capt. Thos. Manual of the New Zealand Coleoptera. Pts. 5-7. 8vo. Wellington, 1893. MA 2 U 29

BROWER, J. V. Prehistoric Man at the Basin of the Mississippi, and references concerning the succeeding races of humanity. 8vo. St. Paul, Minn., 1895. A 30 U 36

BROWN, Alex. Coffee Planter's Manual; including a Summary of Opinions on Manuring of Coffee Estates. 8vo. Colombo, 1872. A 18 S 32

BROWN, D. Kinnear. Almanac and Guide to New South Wales, 1886. 12mo. Sydney, 1886. ME 6 T

BROWN, Edward. Poultry Fattening. Illustrated. 12mo. Lond., 1895. A 19 P 7

BROWN, G. P. Drainage Channel and Waterway: an effort to secure an effective and harmless method for the disposal of the Sewage of the City of Chicago, and to create a navigable channel between Lake Michigan and the Mississippi River. 8vo. Chicago, 1894. A 22 R 23

BROWN, George A., and HUTSON, B. Does the Bible teach conditional immortality? 8vo. Auckland, 1883. MG 1 S 74

BROWN, Geo. Wm. Baltimore and the 10th of April, 1861: a Study of the War. (Johns Hopkins University Studies, extra vol. 3.) 8vo. Baltimore, 1887. B 18 T 3

BROWN, Glenn. Healthy Foundations for Houses. Illustrated. 18mo. New York, 1885. A 19 P 28

BROWN, Henry Y. L. Catalogue of South Australian Minerals, with the Mines and other localities where found, and brief remarks on the mode of occurrence of some of the principal Metals and Ores. 8vo. Adelaide, 1893. MA 2 U 31

A Record of the Mines of South Australia. 2 vols. 8vo. Adelaide, 1887-90. MA 2 U 62, 63

BROWN, Horatio F. Venice: an Historical Sketch of the Republic. 8vo. Lond., 1893. B 30 T 23

J. A. Symonds: a Biography. Illustrated. 2 vols. 8vo. Lond., 1895. C 16 U 6, 7

BROWN, J. Moray. Stray Sport. 2 vols. 8vo. Edinb., 1893. A 29 R 9, 10

BROWN, Dr. James. The Forester: being Plain and Practical Directions for the Planting, Rearing, and General Management of Forest Trees. 12mo. Lond., 1847. A 18 R 32

Another copy. 5th ed. Roy. 8vo. Edinb., 1882. A 18 U 25

Another copy. 6th ed., edited by Dr. J. Nisbet. 2 vols. roy. 8vo. Edinb., 1894. A 32 T 9, 10

BROWN, John. Barbarossa: a Tragedy. [See London Stage, 2.] H 2 S 34

BROWN, Dr. John. Horæ Subsecivæ. 2nd series. 8vo. Edinb., 1861. J 12 T 2

Recollections of; with a Selection from his Correspondence by Dr. A. Peddie. 8vo. Lond., 1893. C 13 C 28

BROWN, Rev. Dr. John [of Bedford]. [Life of] G. Herbert. (In Masson's Footsteps of the Poets.) 8vo. Lond. (n.d.) J 6 R 43

BROWN, Dr. John C. People of Finland in Archaic Times. 8vo. Lond., 1892. B 31 Q 2

BROWN, John Ednie. Reports on planting Olives and Mulberries on Mallee Lands, and Dates in the Far North; also, Wattle Cultivation generally in the Colony [South Australia]. Sm. fol. Adelaide, 1884. MA 9 P 15 †

Progress Report of State Forest Administration in New South Wales, 1890. Sm. fol. Sydney, 1891. ME

BROWN, N. E. English Botany. [See Sowerby, J.] A 32 U 15

BROWN, P. Hume. Scotland before 1700, from contemporary documents. 8vo. Edinb., 1893. B 31 T 23
John Knox: a Biography. 2 vols. 8vo. Lond., 1895. C 22 R 5, 6

BROWN, R. New Zealand Mosses (*Genus Pottia*). (Trans. N.Z. Inst., 26.) 8vo. Wellington, 1893. ME 2 R
New Zealand Mosses (*Gen. Grimmia and Ortholrichum*). (Trans. N.Z. Inst., 27.) 8vo. Wellington, 1894. ME 2 R

BROWN, Dr. Robert. Our Earth and its Story: a Treatise on Physical Geography. Vols. 2, 3, illustrated. Imp. 8vo. Lond., 1888. A 9 V 28, 29
The Story of Africa and its Explorers. 4 vols. imp. 8vo. Lond., 1892-94. D 15 V 24-27

BROWN, T. Craig-. History of Selkirkshire; or, Chronicles of Ettrick Forest. 2 vols. 4to. Edinb., 1886. B 15 S 2, 3 †

BROWN, Walter Lee. Manual of Assaying Gold, Silver, Copper, and Lead Ores. 2nd ed. 8vo. Chicago, 1886. A 24 Q 16

BROWN UNIVERSITY, Rhode Island. Catalogue of the Officers and Students, 1892, 1893. 8vo. Providence, 1893. E

BROWNE, C. Wade. Overlanding in Australia. 18mo. Melb., 1868. MD 2 W 50

BROWNE, Edward G. A Year amongst the Persians. 8vo. Lond., 1893. D 18 T 8

BROWNE, Rev. Edward Geo. K. History of the Tractarian Movement. 2nd ed. 8vo. Dublin, 1856. G 15 R 25

BROWNE, Rt. Rev. Edward Harold: a Memoir; by Very Rev. G. W. Kitchin. 8vo. Lond., 1895. C 21 R 11

BROWNE, Gordon, illustrator of the Irving Shakespeare. [*See* Shakespeare, William.] H 4 V 1-8

BROWNE, Henry. English-Greek Lexicon. [*See* Fridersdorff, Dr. J. W.] K 14 P 10

BROWNE, Hugh J. The Religion of the Future; or, the Higher Law of Truth and Right. 8vo. Melb., 1883. MG 1 P 85

BROWNE, Dr. Lennox. Anatomy of Vocal Organs. [*See* Miles, A. H.—New Standard Elocutionist.] J 8 T 33
Diphtheria and its associates. Illustrated. 8vo. Lond., 1893. A 33 U 19
—— and BEHNKE, Emil. Voice, Song, and Speech: a practical guide for singers and speakers. 14 ed. 8vo. Lond., 1892. A 13 Q 32

BROWNE, Phyllis. [*See* Diet and Cookery.] A 22 Q 14

BROWNE, Sir Thos. Religio Medici. Edited by Dr. W. A. Greenhill. 12mo. Lond., 1881. G 4 V 12

BROWNE, Thos. Alex. "Rolf Boldrewood." The Crooked Stick; or, Pollie's Probation. 12mo. Lond., 1895. MJ 3 Q 40

BROWNE, Mrs. W. C. Encore. 8vo. Parramatta, 1892. MJ 1 T 30

BROWNING, Mrs. Elizabeth Barrett. Aurora Leigh. 3rd ed. 8vo. Lond., 1857. H 7 Q 24
Life of; by the Lord Bishop of Ripon. [*See* Masson, Prof. D.—In the Footsteps of the Poets.] J 6 R 43
Records of; by Anne Ritchie. 8vo. Lond., 1892. C 16 R 17
Sermon on. [*See* Fletcher, Rev. W. R.] MC 1 S 16
Sketch of the Work of. [*See* Dawson, W. J.—Makers of Modern English.] H 10 S 14

BROWNING, Oscar. The Age of the Condottieri: a short History of Mediæval Italy, from 1409-1530. 8vo. Lond., 1895. B 30 R 9
The Citizen, his Rights and Responsibilities. 12mo. Lond., 1893. F 9 U 50
Guelphs and Ghibellines: a Short History of Mediæval Italy from 1250-1409. 12mo. Lond., 1893. B 16 P 7

BROWNING, Robert. Browning Studies: being Select Papers by Members of the Browning Society. Edited by Dr. E. Berdoe. 8vo. Lond., 1895. J 6 U 14
Essay on. [*See* Bagehot, W.—Literary Studies.] J 9 P 23
How the Browning Society came into being. [*See* Furnivall, F. J.] J 15 S 28
Life of; by W. Sharp. 12mo. Lond., 1894. C 17 P 14
Life of; by R. H. Hutton. [*See* Masson, Prof. D.—In the Footsteps of the Poets.] J 6 R 43
Records of; by Anne Ritchie. 8vo. Lond., 1892. C 16 R 17
Selections from. [*See* Harlin, T.] MJ 1 U 24
Sketch of the Work of. [*See* Dawson, W. J.—Makers of Modern English.] H 10 S 14

BROWNRIGG, Rev. M. B. The British Nation: the Lost Ten Tribes. 8vo. Launceston (n.d.) MG 2 R 19

BRUCE, Alexander. Judging Sheep by Points. 8vo. Sydney, 1890. MA 1 Q 58
The Meat Trade of Australia and its Prospects. Roy. 8vo. Sydney, 1895. MA 3 R 41
Points of Stock and their Relative Value. 8vo. Sydney, 1891. MA 1 Q 58
Report on the Frozen Meat Trade of New Zealand. 8vo. Sydney, 1893. MA 1 Q 58
Stock Breeding and Fattening in New Zealand. 8vo. Sydney, 1893. MA 1 Q 58
Treatment of Sheep for Worms. 8vo. Sydney, 1893. MA 1 Q 58

BRUCE, Rev. Dr. Alexander B. St. Paul's Conception of Christianity. 8vo. Edinb., 1894. G 19 Q 7

BRUCE, J. Hints for the teaching of the accompanying system of Penmanship. Sm. 4to. Lond. (n.d.)
MG 2 Q 44

BRUCE, J. Y. A. Cornish and Bruce v. the Queen. [See Cornish.] MF 4 T 40

BRUCE, Robert. The New Kreuz Polka Winifred. [See Milbourn, S.] MA 7 Q 31 †

BRUNER, Dr. J. Juan. La Substancia Immortal del Organismo Humano. 8vo. Santiago, 1879. G 2 U 9

BRUNER, Lawrence. The more Destructive Locusts of America, North of Mexico. Illustrated. 8vo. Washington, 1893. A 27 U 14

BRÜNNOW, Dr. Francis. Spherical Astronomy. 8vo. Berlin, 1865. A 3 T 39

BRUNO, Capt. A. E. New Caledonia. 8vo. San Francisco, 1882. MD 8 R 41

BRUNO, Giordano. Bruno and his Time. [See Whittaker, T.—Essays.] G 3 R 9

Sketch of. [See Owen, Rev. J.—Skeptics of Italian Renaissance.] G 2 S 33

BRUNOR, Martin. The Practical Electroplater. Illustrated. 8vo. New York, 1894. A 25 T 23

BRUNOT, Ferdinand. La Doctrine de Malherbe, d'après son Commentaire sur Desportes. (Annales de l'Université de Lyon, 1.) Roy. 8vo. Paris, 1891.
J 12 V 2

BRUNT, Henry van. Greek Lines and other Architectural Essays. 8vo. Boston, 1893. A 19 S 1

BRUNTON, Dr. Thos. L. The Bible and Science. Illustrated. 8vo. Lond., 1881. G 2 U 5

BRY, Theodore de. Emblemata Sæcularia: Life and Manners of the 16th Century. Fac-simile of original edition of 1311 by F. Warnecke. 4to. Berlin, 1895.
A 39 P 16 ‡

Emblemata Nobilitatis: Album Amicorum. Reproduced after the original of 1593. Edited by F. Warnecke. 4to. Berlin, 1895. A 39 P 17 ‡

BRYAN, C. W. Modern Framed Structures. [See Johnson, J. B.] A 36 P 5 ‡

BRYAN, E. A. The Mark in Europe and America: a Review of the Discussion on Early Land Tenure. 8vo. Boston, 1893. F 6 T 1

BRYANT, Edwin. What I saw in California, 1846-47; with an Appendix containing Accounts of the Goldmines, Routes, Outfit, &c. 8vo. New York, 1849.
D 15 Q 21

BRYANT, Sophie. Short Studies in Character. (Ethical Library.) 12mo. Lond., 1894. G 16 Q 34

BRYANT, Wm. Cullen. Life and Writings of. [See Curtis, G. W.] F 14 U 3

BRYCE, Dr. A. H.—Trans. [See Arnobius.] G 14 U 19
[See Virgilius Maro, P.] J 11 R 24

BRYCE, Rev. Dr. George. Early Days in Winnepeg. (Hist. and Scientific Soc. of Manitoba.) 8vo. Winnipeg, 1894. B 18 R 7

BRYCE, Jas. The Predictions of Hamilton and De Tocqueville. (Johns Hopkins University Studies, 5.) 8vo. Baltimore, 1887. B 18 S 5

BRYCE v. RUSDEN. [Action for Libel] in the High Court of Justice [England], Queen's Bench Division, March, 1886. 8vo. Lond. (n.d.) MF 3 T 10

BRYDEN, H. Anderson. Gun and Camera in Southern Africa: a Year of Wanderings in Bechuanaland, the Kalahari Desert, and the Lake River Country, Ngamiland, with Notes on Colonisation, Natives, Natural History, and Sport. 8vo. Lond, 1893. D 14 T 17

BRYN MAWR COLLEGE. Program, 1893. 8vo. Philad., 1893. E

BRYSON, Mrs. Mary I. F. C. Roberts, of Tientsin; or, for Christ and China. 8vo. Lond., 1895. C 22 P 19

BUCHAN, Dr. Alexander. Report on Oceanic Circulation. [See Thomson, Sir C. W., and Murray, Dr. J.—Scientific Results of Voyage of H.M.S. Challenger.]
A 6 S †

Report on Atmospheric Circulation. [See Thomson, Sir C. W., and Murray, Dr. J.—Voyage of H.M.S. Challenger.] A 3 †

BUCHANAN, J. Y. Narrative of the Cruise of H.M.S. Challenger. [See Thomson, Sir C. W., and Murray, Dr. J.—Voyage of H.M.S. Challenger.] A 3 †

Specific Gravity of Ocean Water. [See Thomson, Sir C. W., and Murray, Dr. J.—Voyage of H.M.S. Challenger.] A 3 †

BUCHANAN, James. Sketch of. [See Thompson, R. W.—Recollections of Sixteen Presidents.] C 18 T 21, 22

Sketch of. [See Wilson, J. G.—Presidents of the United States.] C 2 V 30

BUCHANAN, N. History of Dogma. [See Harnack, Dr. A.] G 15 R 31

BUCHANAN, Robert Williams. The Wandering Jew: a Christmas Carol. 8vo. Lond., 1893. H 10 Q 27

BUCKALEW, Chas. R. Proportional Representation. 8vo. Philad, 1872. F 12 Q 39

BUCKINGHAM, Duchess of. Glimpses of four Continents: Letters written during a Tour in Australia, New Zealand, and North America, in 1893. Illustrated. 8vo. Lond., 1894. MD 1 R 32

BUCKLAND, Very Rev. Wm. Life and Correspondence of; by Mrs. Gordon. Illustrated. 8vo. Lond., 1894.
C 17 R 16

BUCKLAND, Dr. Francis T. The Acclimatisation of Animals. 8vo. Melb., 1861. MA 2 T 30

BUCKLER, W. Larvæ of the British Butterflies and Moths. Edited by G. T. Porritt. (Ray Soc. Pubs.) 8vo. Lond., 1893-95. E

BUCKLER, W. H. The Origin and History of Contract in Roman Law down to the end of the Republican Period. 8vo. Lond., 1895. F 8 V 1

BUCKLEY, Dr. J. M. Travels in three Continents: Europe, Africa, Asia. Roy. 8vo. New York, 1895. D 20 U 2

BUCKLEY, Robert B. Irrigation Works in India and Egypt. Roy. 8vo. Lond., 1893. A 22 V 15

BUCKMAN, Prof. J. Grasses, &c. [See Taylor, Dr. J. E.—Collecting Natural History Objects.] A 29 Q 38

Natural and Artificial Grasses, their variations in form and quality: a Lecture. (Inst. of Agricult., Lond.) 8vo. Lond., 1884. A 18 R 28

BUDDIVENT, P. Lucien. The Centennial; or Simple Rhymes of an Idle Rhymster. 8vo. Sydney, 1888. MH 1 S 40

BUDGE, Dr. Ernest A. T. W. The Mummy: Egyptian Funeral Archæology. 8vo. Camb., 1893. B 21 T 6

[See Book of the Dead, The.] B S Q 2 †

BUEL, Clarence Clough. Battles and Leaders of the Civil War. [See Johnson, R. U.] B 11 Q 12-15 †

BUEL, J. W. America's Wonderlands. Obl. 8vo. Philad. (n.d.) D 42 S 19 ‡

BUFFEN, F. Forster. Musical Celebrities. 2nd series. 4to. Lond., 1893. C 12 S 14 †

BUFTON, John. The Light of Eden, and other poems. 12mo. Melb., 1890. MH 1 Q 21

BUGBEE, Jas. McKellar. The City Government of Boston. (Johns Hopkins University Studies, 5.) 8vo. Baltimore, 1887. B 18 S 5

BUILDER, The: an Illustrated Weekly Magazine for the Architect, Engineer, Archæologist, Contractor, Sanitary Reformer, and Art-lover. Vols. 63-67. Fol. Lond., 1892-94. E

BUILDING AND ENGINEERING JOURNAL of Australia and New Zealand, July, 1890-Dec., 1893. 14 vols. fol. Sydney, 1890-93. ME

BUILDING NEWS AND ENGINEERING JOURNAL, The. Vols. 63-67. Fol. Lond., 1892-93. E

BULA N'ZAU. [See Bailey, H.]

BULFINCH, Thos. The Age of Fable; or, Beauties of Mythology. 8vo. Boston, 1894. B 36 R 5

Age of Chivalry; or, Legends of King Arthur. 8vo. Boston, 1895. B 36 R 6

BULLEN, Arthur Henry. [See Anacreon.] H 7 U 9

BULLER, Sir Walter Lawry. Illustrations of Darwinism. (Trans. N.Z. Inst., 27.) 8vo. Wellington, 1894. ME 2 R

Notes on the Ornithology of New Zealand. (Trans. N.Z. Inst., 27.) 8vo. Wellington, 1894. ME 2 R

On Birds observed during a Voyage from New Zealand to England. (Trans. N.Z. Inst., 26.) 8vo. Wellington, 1894. ME 2 R

BULLETIN MONUMENTAL, publié sous les auspices de la Société Française d'Archéologie, 1893. 8vo. Paris, 1893. E

BULLETIN, The. 22 vols. fol. Sydney, 1884-95. ME

BULLEY, Agnes Amy, and WHITLEY, Margaret. Women's Work. 12mo. Lond., 1894. F 14 R 23

BULMER, Rev. J. Some Account of the Aborigines of the Lower Murray, Wimmera, Gippsland, and Maneroo. (Roy. Geog. Soc. Australasia, Vic. Branch, 5.) 8vo. Melb., 1888. ME 20 P

BUNBURY, Major W. St. P. Notes on Armour and the Artillery Defence of a Coast Fortress. Roy. 8vo. Sydney, 1888. MA 2 V 36

Notes on Elementary Gunnery. 12mo. Sydney, 1888. MA 2 P 22

BUNCE, Daniel. Language of the Aborigines of Victoria, and other Australian Districts. 2nd ed. 12mo. Geelong, 1859. MK 1 P 17

Australian Manual of Horticulture. 3rd ed. 12mo. Melb., 1851. MA 1 P 79

BUNGENER, L. F. France before the Revolution; or, Priests, Infidels, and Huguenots in the Reign of Louis XV. 2 vols. 8vo. Edinb., 1854. B 26 R 14, 15

BUNKER, E. View of Northern Islands, New South Wales, 1803. Fol. [MS.] MD 1 P 15 ‡

BUNSEN, Christian C. J., Baron von. [Sketch of.] [See Müller, F. Max.—Chips from a German Workshop.] J 0 R 32

BUNSTER, Grosvenor, and THATCHER, Richmond. It Runs in the Blood: a colonial serio-comicality. 12mo. Bathurst, 1872. MJ 1 S 29

BUNYAN, John. A new Pilgrim's Progress, purporting to be given by John Bunyan through an impressional writing medium. 8vo. Melb., 1877. MG 2 R 44

Sketch of; with Portrait. [See Bolton, Sarah K.—Famous Leaders.] C 17 P 27

BUONARROTI, Michael Angelo. [See Michael Angelo Buonarroti.]

BURBIDGE, F. W. The Narcissus, its History and Culture. Roy. 8vo. Lond., 1875. A 4 U 18

BURCH, George J. Manual of Electrical Science. 12mo. Lond., 1893. A 21 Q 38

BÜRDE, Lieut. J. Problems in Applied Tactics. [With Map.] 8vo. Lond., 1894. A 29 T 25

BURDETT, Henry C. Hospitals and Asylums of the World: their Origin, History, Construction, &c.; with Plans of the Chief Medical Institutions accurately drawn to a uniform scale. 5 vols. roy. 8vo., and Atlas, fol. Lond., 1891. A 27 V 7-10, and 32 P 18 ‡

BUREAU DES LONGITUDES, PARIS. Annuaire pour 1895. 18mo. Paris, 1894. E

BUREAU INTERNATIONAL DES POIDS ET MESURES. Travaux et Mémoires du. Tome 10. 4to. Paris, 1894. E

BURGE, Chas. O. Light Railways for New South Wales. (Journal Roy. Soc., N.S.W., 27.) 8vo. Sydney, 1893. ME 1 R

BÜRGER, Gottfried August. Gedichte von. 18mo. Leipzig (n.d.) H 10 U 14

BURGESS, Dr. John W. Political Science and Comparative Constitutional Law. 2 vols. 8vo. Boston, 1893. F 11 U 18, 19

BURGH, Nicholas P. The Slide Valve practically considered. 14th ed. 12mo. Lond., 1890. A 22 Q 37

BURGHERSH, Lady. Letters of, from Germany and France, 1813-14. Lond., 1893. C 13 Q 11

BURGIS, E. Paris to British Trade, how to avert them. 8vo. Lond., 1895. F 8 U 32

BURGOYNE, Lieut.-Gen. John. The Heiress: a Comedy. [See London Stage, 3.] H 2 S 35
Richard Cœur de Lion: an Historical Drama. [See London Stage, 3.] H 2 S 35
The Maid of the Oaks: a Dramatic Entertainment. [See London Stage, 3.] H 2 S 35
Surrender of. [See Curtis, G. W.] F 14 U 3

BURKE, Rt. Hon. Edmund. Answer to his Attack on the French Revolution. [See Paine, T.—Rights of Man.] F 4 P 27
Character of. [See Hazlitt, W.—Winterslow.] J 12 S 33
[Plaster Cast of.] [See Hutton, L.—Portraits in Plaster.] A 23 V 13

BURKE, Sir Bernard (in full John Bernard). Family Romance; or, Episodes in the Domestic Annals of the Aristocracy. 3rd ed. 12mo. Lond. (n.d.) J 8 U 7
Genealogical and Heraldic Dictionary of the Peerage and Baronetage, together with Memoirs of the Privy Councillors and Knights. 3 vols. Roy. 8vo. Lond., 1893-95. E
Genealogical and Heraldic History of the Landed Gentry of Great Britain and Ireland. 8th ed. 2 vols. Roy. 8vo. Lond., 1894. K 10 U 3, 4
Genealogical and Heraldic History of the Colonial Gentry. Vol. 2. Imp. 8vo. Lond., 1895. MK 1 U 27

BURKE, Peter. Romance of the Forum; or, Narratives, Scenes and Anecdotes from Courts of Justice. 8vo. Lond. (n.d.) F 8 U 7

BURKE, Robert O'Hara, and WILLS, W. J. Report of the Commission appointed to enquire into the circumstances connected with the sufferings and death of Burke and Wills, the Victorian Explorers. Sm. fol. Melb., 1862. MD 9 P 11 †

BURKE, Ulick Ralph. History of Spain, from the earliest times to the death of Ferdinand the Catholic. 2 vols. 8vo. Lond., 1895. B 34 R 10, 11

BURKITT F. C. Gospels in Syriac. [See Bensly, Prof. R. L.] G 6 V 24

BURLINGTON VOLUNTARY RELIEF DEPARTMENT. Report, 1892. 8vo. Chicago, 1892. E

BURN, David Will. M. Cantilerose Nugæ. 8vo. Oamaru, 1891. MH 1 S 33

BURN, Robt. Scott. Mechanics and Mechanism: being Elementary Examples of the leading principles of Mechanics. 7th ed. 8vo. Lond., 1892. A 25 T 36

BURNABY, Evelyn. Ride from Land's End to John O'Groats. 12mo. Lond., 1893. D 18 Q 6

BURNE-JONES, Sir E. [See Jones, Sir E. Burne-.]

BURNET, John. Practical Hints on Portrait Painting. 4to. Lond., 1850. A 8 U 35

BURNEY, Frances. [See D'Arblay, Mme. F.]

BURNS, David. Scottish Echoes from New Zealand: Poems. 12mo. Edinb., 1880. MH 1 U 20

BURNS, Sir George. [Biographical Sketch.] [See Smith, G. B.—Leaders of Modern Industry.] C 14 P 14

BURNS, John, the Mind of him; with Portrait. [See Blathwayt, R.—Interviews.] J 10 U 34

BURNS, Robert. Works of. 6 vols. Imp. 8vo. Edinb., 1877-79. J 21 U 1-6
Address on the unveiling of the Statue of, in New York. [See Curtis, G: W.] F 14 U 3
Burns in a new aspect. [See Haliburton, H.—Furth in Field.] B 32 R 5
Burnsiana: a Collection of Literary Odds and Ends relating to Robert Burns. Compiled by J. D. Ross. Vols. 2-4. Sm. 4to. Paisley, 1893-94. J 6 U 30-32
[Outline of his Life and Work]; by T. Carlyle. 12mo. Lond., 1854. C 17 P 18
[Plaster Cast of.] [See Hutton, L.—Portraits in Plaster.] A 23 V 23
Sketch of the Work of. [See Dawson, W. J.—Makers of Modern English.] H 10 S 14

BURNS, PHILP & CO. British New Guinea. 4to. Sydney, 1886. MD 7 U 19

BURR, Aaron. [Plaster Cast of.] [See Hutton, L.—
Portraits in Plaster.] A 23 V 13

BURR, Frederic M. Life and Works of Alexander
Anderson, M.D., the first American Wood Engraver.
Illustrated. Roy. 8vo. New York, 1893. C 19 S 3

BURR, Thos. Chart of Flinders'-Lake and Franklin-
Harbour [South Australia]. Fol. (n.p.) 1840.
MD 3 Q 7 ‡
Remarks on the Geology and Mineralogy of South
Australia. 12mo. Adelaide, 1846. MA 3 U 28

BURRELL, Rev. Dr. David Jas. The Religion of the
Future. 8vo. New York, 1894. G 2 V 41

BURROUGHS, John. Birds and Poets; with other
Papers. 12mo. Boston, 1894. J 16 T 38
Fresh Fields. 12mo. Boston, 1893. J 16 T 35
Indoor Studies. 12mo. Boston, 1894. J 16 T 40
Locusts and Wild Honey. 12mo. Boston, 1895.
J 16 T 33
Pepacton. 12mo. Boston, 1894. J 16 T 41
Riverby. 12mo. Boston, 1894. J 16 T 34
Signs and Seasons. 12mo. Boston, 1895. J 16 T 37
Wake Robin. 12mo. Boston, 1894. J 16 T 36
Winter Sunshine. 12mo. Boston, 1894. J 16 T 39

BURROWS, Prof. Montagu. Commentaries on the
History of England, from the earliest times to 1865.
8vo. Edinb., 1893. B 24 R 3

BURSTON, J. J. The New State School Grammar.
12mo. Melb., 1886. MK 2 P 10

BURTON, Rev. H. St. Luke. [See Expositor's Bible.]
G 19 S 3

BURTON, Isabel, Lady. Life of Captain Sir Richard F.
Burton; by his Wife. 2 vols. 8vo. Lond., 1893.
C 14 U 20, 21

BURTON, Dr. John Hill. History of Scotland, from
Agricola's Invasion to the Examination of the last
Jacobite Insurrection. 8 vols. 12mo. Edinb. (n.d.)
B 32 Q 2-9

BURTON, Sir Richard Francis. Il Pentamerone. [See
Basile, G. B.] J 5 T 31, 32
Plain and Literal Translation of the Arabian Nights'
Entertainments, now intituled the Book of the Thou-
sand Nights and a Night, and Supplemental Nights;
with notes, &c.; by Sir R. F. Burton. 16 vols. 8vo.
Benares [Lond.], 1885-88. Libr.
One Hundred Illustrations to above, from Paintings by
S. L. Wood. 8vo. Lond. (n.d.) Libr.
Life of; by his Wife, Isabel Burton. 2 vols. 8vo.
Lond., 1893. C 14 U 20, 21

BURTON, Robert. The Anatomy of Melancholy. Edited
by Rev. A. R. Shilleto. 3 vols. 8vo. Lond., 1893.
G 19 Q 9-11

BURTON, Prof. W. K. Earthquake in Japan, 1891.
[See Milne, Prof. J.] A 37 P 10 ‡
The Water Supply of Towns and the Construction of
Waterworks; to which is appended a paper on the
effects of Earthquakes on Waterworks, by Prof. J.
Milne, F.R.S. Illustrated. Roy. 8vo. Lond., 1894.
A 22 T 19
[See Ayame-San.] J 4 U 14

BURTON, Sir Wm. W. The Insolvent Law of New
South Wales, with Practical Directions and Forms.
8vo. Sydney, 1842. MF 2 R 54

BUSBY, Jas. Catalogue of Vines in the Botanic Garden,
Sydney, introduced into the Colony of New South
Wales in the year 1832. Sm. 4to. Sydney, 1842.
MA 1 V 76

BUSCH, Dr. Wilhelm. England under the Tudors. Vol.
1. Translated by Alice M. Todd. 8vo. Lond., 1895.
B 21 U 1
1. Henry VII, 1485-1509.

BUSH, Dr. George Gary. History of Higher Education
in Massachusetts. 8vo. Wash., 1891. G 18 R 10

BUSH ET FILS ET MEISSNER, MM. Catalogue
illustré et descriptif des Vignes Américaines. 2ᵉ
édition. Roy. 8vo. Montpellier, 1885. A 36 P 9 ‡

BUSHILL, T. W. Profit-sharing and the Labour Question.
8vo. Lond., 1893. F 6 S 40

BUSHMAN, A. [See Sidney, S. & J.]

BUSHNAN, Dr. John S. Miss Martineau and her Master.
12mo. Lond., 1851. G 9 V 24

BUSK, George. The Polyzoa. [See Thomson, Sir C. W.,
and Murray, Dr. J.—Voyage of H.M.S. Challenger.]
A 6 †

BUSSEY INSTITUTION. Bulletins of, 1874-84. 2
vols. 8vo. Boston, 1874-84. E

BUSTALL & CAMPBELL, Messrs. Steam Communication with England, as it has been, and as it ought to
be. 8vo. Melb., 1862. MF 2 R 47

BUTCHER, Dr. Samuel H. Aristotle's Theory of Poetry
and Fine Art. [See Aristotle's.] J 4 T 25
Life and Works of Demosthenes. [See Demosthenes.]
J 16 P 32

BUTCHERS, Rev. B., and HALEY, J. J. Christian
Baptism: an Authentic Report of Debate. 8vo.
Geelong, 1882. MG 1 S 5

BUTLER, Alfred. The Castaway, &c. 8vo. Melb., 1886.
MG 1 P 86

BUTLER, Alfred Joshua. Churches and Monasteries of
Egypt. [See Abû Sâlih.] G 16 U 20

BUTLER, Arthur John. Life and Work of Dante Alighieri. 8vo. Lond., 1895. C 21 P 9
Count Cavour and Mme. de Circourt. [See Cavour, Conté di] C 14 V 14
Select Essays of Sainte-Beuve. [See Sainte-Beuve, C. A.] J 9 S 10

BUTLER, Chas. Contingent Remainders. [See Fearne, C.] F 7 U 20

BUTLER, Edward A. Our Household Insects: an Account of the Insect-Pests found in Dwelling Houses. 8vo. Lond., 1893. A 28 Q 30

BUTLER, Most Rev. Dr. Jas. Third Catechism. 18mo. Sydney, 1884. MG 2 P 52

BUTLER, Rt. Rev. Joseph. Essay on. [See Bagehot, W.—Literary Studies.] J 9 P 22-24
[Life and Works of Butler]; by the Rev. W. L. Collins. (Philosophical Classics.) 12mo. Edinb., 1881. G 9 V 2
Sketch of. [See Bagehot. W.—Estimates of some Englishmen and Scotchmen.] J 10 V 32

BUTLER, Dr. Nicholas M. The Effect of the War of 1812 upon the Consolidation of the Union. (Johns Hopkins University Studies, 5.) 8vo. Baltimore, 1887. B 18 S 5

BUTLER & BROOKE, Messrs. Butler's Wood's Point and Gippsland General Directory, 1866. Compiled by Henry Young and John Dixon. 8vo. Melb., 1866. ME 6 S

BUTTERS, R. "Old Testament Scriptures": History from Alexandrian Translation to Oxford and Cambridge revision. 8vo. Sydney, 1892. MG 1 R 40

BUTTERWORTH, Arthur R. The Vagliano Case in Australia. Roy. 8vo. Lond., 1894. MF 3 R 57

BUXTON, E. N. Short Stalks; or, Hunting Camps North, South, East, and West. 8vo. Lond., 1892. D 10 S 37

BUXTON, Sydney Chas. Hand-book to Political Questions of the Day, and the arguments on either side. 9th ed. 8vo. Lond., 1892. J 9 T 9

BYERLY, Dr. Wm. E. Elementary Treatise on Fourier's Series, and Spherical, Cylindrical, and Ellipsoidal Harmonics; with applications to problems in Mathematical Physics. 8vo. Boston, 1893. A 25 U 24

BYRNE, Oliver. First Six Books of Euclid. [See Euclides.] A 25 V 24

BYRNE, W. Antiquities of Great Britain. Illustrated in Views of Monasteries, Castles, and Churches now existing, from Drawings made by T. Hearne, with Descriptions in English and French. 2 vols. fol. Lond., 1807. B 2 P 29, 30 ‡

BYRNE, W. E. The Ode of Federation. Sm. 4to. Sydney (n.d.) MH 1 P 74

BYROM, John. Poems of. (Chetham Soc. Pubs) Sm. 4to. Manchester, 1894. E

BYRON, Anna Isabella, Lady. Lady Byron vindicated; by Harriet Beecher Stowe. 12mo. Lond., 1870. C 14 P 85

BYRON, George Gordon, Lord. Poetical Works of. Roy. 8vo. Lond., 1852. H 7 V 32
Tales and Poems. Illustrated. Roy. 8vo. Lond., 1855. H 7 V 9
Selections from the Writings of. New ed. 2 vols. (in 1.) 12mo. Lond., 1857. J 6 P 42
Childe Harold's Pilgrimage: a Remaunt. 18mo. Lond., 1848. H 10 T 4
Childe Harold's Pilgrimage; [with autograph of Lady C. Bacon, "Ianthe," and some notes by Sir Henry Parkes.] 12mo. Lond., 1858. H 10 U 3
The Island; or, Christian and his Comrades. 2nd ed. 8vo. Lond., 1823. MH 1 V 4
Journal of Conversations with the Countess of Blessington. 8vo. Lond, 1893. C 17 T 17
Life of; by Thomas Moore. Roy. 8vo. Lond., 1844. C 12 U 31
Sketch of the Work of. [See Dawson, W. J.—Makers of Modern English.] H 10 S 14

BYRON, Commodore John. Byron's Narrative of the Loss of the *Wager*, with an Account of the great distresses suffered on the Coast of Patagonia, 1740-46. 12mo. Lond., 1832. D 15 P 5

BYSTANDER, A. [See Whitworth, R. P.]

C

C., A. [See Essai de la Langue de Viti.] MK 1 R 48

C.J.S. [See Sketch of Turkish History.] MB 1 R 43

CABLE, Geo. W. Famous Adventures and Prison Escapes of the Civil War. Illustrated. 8vo. Lord., 1894. B 19 V 1

CABOT, J. [See Hakluyt Soc., 8G.] E

CADIER, Léon. Essai sur l'administration du Royaume de Sicile sous Charles I et Charles II d'Anjou. 8vo. Paris, 1891. B 35 R 15

CÆSAR, Caius Julius. Cæsar de Bello Gallico. Books I-III. An interlinear Translation by E. D. Greve. 12mo. Sydney, 1870. MB 1 R 32

———— et HIRTIUS, Aulus. De rebus à C. Julio Cæsare gestis Commentarii, cum C. J. Cæsaris fragmentis. 12mo. Lond., 1772. B 33 P 12

CAFFYN, Dr. S. Mannington. How, when, and what to eat: a Guide to Colonial Diet. 8vo. Melb., 1888. MA 3 T 20

Opals. [See Praed, Mrs. Campbell.—Under the Gum Tree.] MJ 2 T 44

CAIN, Prof. Wm. Maximum Stresses in Framed Bridges. 18mo. New York, 1878. A 22 P 23

Practical Designing of Retaining Walls. 18mo. New York, 1893. A 22 P 21

Theory of Solid and Braced Elastic Arches. 18mo. New York, 1879. A 22 P 20

Voussoir Arches applied to Stone Bridges, &c. 18mo. New York, 1879. A 22 P 19

Theory of Voussoir Arches. 18mo. New York, 1893. A 22 P 22

CAINE, Thos. Hy. Hall. Hall Caine at Home; with Portrait. [See Blathwayt, R.—Interviews.] J 10 U 34

CAINE, Mary E. Mathematical Geography. 8vo. Gympie, 1893. MA 1 T 59

CAIRD, Prof. Edward. The Evolution of Religion. 2nd ed. 2 vols. 8vo. Glasgow, 1894. G 2 U 2, 3

Hegel, Philosopher. 12mo. Edinb., 1880. G 9 V 6

CAIRD, Rev. Dr. John. Introduction to the Philosophy of Religion. 8vo. Glasgow, 1880. G 11 T 13

CAIRNES, Earl. Sketch of. [See Bagehot, W.—Biographical Studies.] C 22 P 10

CAIRNES, Dr. John Elliott. Character and Logical Method of Political Economy. 12mo. Lond., 1888. F 7 V 18

CAIRNS, Rev. Dr. Adam. The Jews, their Fall and Restoration. 8vo. Melb., 1854. MG 1 S 68

CAIRNS, Rev. Dr. John. Life and Letters of; by Rev. Dr. A. R. MacEwen. 8vo. Lond., 1895. C 22 R 1

CAJORI, Prof. F. Teaching and History of Mathematics in the United States. 8vo. Wash., 1890. G 18 R 23

CALDWELL, Geo. S. Is Sir Walter Raleigh the Author of Shakspere's Plays and Sonnets? 8vo. Melb., 1877. MJ 2 S 41

CALDWELL, Major H. Invasion of Canada in 1775. 8vo. Quebec, 1887. B 17 T 14

CALDWELL, Rt. Rev. Dr. Robert. Comparative Grammar of the Dravidian or South-Indian Family of Languages. 2nd ed. 8vo. Lond., 1875. K 12 V 31

CALHOUN, John C. [Plaster Cast of.] [See Hutton, L.—Portraits in Plaster.] A 23 V 13

Sketch of. [See Brooks, N.—Statesmen.] C 16 R 20

CALIFORNIA—STATE MINING BUREAU. Annual Reports of the State Mineralogist, 1885-92. 7 vols. 8vo. Sacramento, 1886-92. E

CALIFORNIA STATE AGRICULTURAL SOCIETY. Transactions, 1884-85, 1888-89. 9 vols. 8vo. Sacramento, 1885-94. E

CALIFORNIA UNIVERSITY. Register, 1892, 1893. 8vo. Berkeley, 1893. E

Reports of the University Agricultural Experiment Stations. [See Hilgard, E. W.] E

CALLCOTT, Dr. John W. Musical Grammar. 3rd ed. 12mo. Lond., 1817. A 23 P 7

CALLISTIA; or, the Prize of Beauty: a Poem. Sm. fol. Lond., 1738 H 39 Q 13 ‡

CALVERT, Albert F. The Aborigines of Western Australia. 12mo. Lond., 1892. MA 1 P 85

Another copy. 12mo. Lond., 1894. MA 3 U 3

The Discovery of Australia. Roy. 8vo. Lond., 1893. MD 3 V 44

The Exploration of Australia. Roy. 8vo. Lond., 1895. MD 7 U 21

The Gold-fields of Western Australia. (From the Pall Mall Budget.) Obl. 12mo. Lond., 1892. MD 1 P 48

The Mineral Resources of Western Australia. 12mo. Lond., 1893. MA 2 P 24

Pearls, their origin and formation. 12mo. Lond., 1892. MA 2 P 33

Sketch Plan and Plates to illustrate Calvert's Exploring Expedition into the Interior of North-western Australia, 1891. Obl. 12mo. Lond, 1892. MD 1 P 48

West Australian Mining Investors' Hand-book. 8vo. Lond., 1894. MA 3 U 14

Western Australia and its Gold-fields. 12mo. Lond., 1893. MD 1 P 21

[See Maps relating to Australia.] MD 7 Q 29†

CALVERT, Mrs. (Caroline Louisa Waring Atkinson.) Gertrude, the Emigrant: a Tale of Colonial Life. 8vo. Sydney, 1857. MJ 1 V 17

CALVIN, John. Institutes of the Christian Religion. Translated by J. Allen. 3rd ed. 2 vols. 8vo. Lond., 1844. G 10 Q 3, 4

Life and Work. [See Bettany, G. T.—Popular History of the Reformation.] G 14 Q 33

CAMBRIAN ARCHÆOLOGICAL ASSOCIATION. Annual Meeting, 1893. Routes of Excursions and Notes of Chief Places of Interest to be visited. 8vo. Lond., 1893. E

Archæologia Cambrensis: Journal of the Cambrian Archæological Association. 5th Series, vols. 9-11. Lond., 1892-94. E

CAMBRIDGE, MASSACHUSETTS. Annual Report of the School Committee, prepared by the Superintendent of Schools, 1892. 8vo. Camb., Mass., 1893. E

CAMBRIDGE PHILOLOGICAL SOCIETY. Transactions, vol 3, 1886-93. 8vo. Lond., 1894. E

CAMBRIDGE UNIVERSITY. Complete Collection of the English Poems which have obtained the Chancellor's Gold Medal in the University of Cambridge. Vol. 2, 1859-93. 12mo. Lond., 1894. H 7 Q 44
Calendars for 1892-95. 3 vols. 12mo. Camb., 1892-94. E

CAMBRIDGE UNIVERSITY OBSERVATORY. Astronomical Observations, 1828-69. 22 vols. 4to. Camb., 1829-80. E

CAMDEN SOCIETY PUBLICATIONS. 4 vols. Sm. 4to. Lond., 1894-95. E
   Camden Miscellany, vol. 9 :—
     Visitation of Churches in the Patronage of St. Paul's Cathedral.
     "The Spousells" of Princess Mary, 1508.
     Original Letters from the Bishops to Privy Council, 1564.
     Papers relating to Thomas Wentworth, 1st Earl of Strafford.
     Hamilton Papers. Addenda.
     Memoirs of Nathaniel, Lord Crewe.
     Journal of Major R. Ferrier, M.P., 1687.
     The Clarke Papers. Edited by C. H. Firth. Vol. 2.
     Expeditions to Prussia and the Holy Land, made by Henry, Earl of Derby, 1390-92. Edited by Lucy T. Smith.
     Visitations of Churches belonging to St. Paul's Cathedral, 1297 and 1458; by the Rev. Dr. W. S. Simpson.

CAMERON, Alexander M. Light as the interpretation of the law of gravity. 8vo. Sydney, 1893. MA 3 T 57
Light phenomena of the atmosphere. 8vo. Walgett, 1886. MA 1 U 64

CAMERON, Sir Chas. A. Agricultural Chemistry. [See Johnston, A. F. W.] A 19 R 30

CAMERON, Rev. Chas. Innes Poems and Hymns. 12mo. Geelong, 1870. MH 1 U 66

CAMERON, Rev. J. My two Servants; or, Incidents in the Earlier Years of my Ministry in Australia. 12mo. Edinb., 1867. MG 2 R 46

CAMERON, Dr. J. B. Sir William Macgregor's Ascent of Mount Owen Stanley. (Roy. Geog. Soc. Australasia, Vic. Branch, 7.) 8-o. Melb., 1889. ME 20 P

CAMERON, K. The Gull; a weekly newspaper published on board the Otago during a four months' voyage from Glasgow to Brisbane. 8vc. Brisbane, 1884. MJ 3 R 16

CAMERON, P. British Phytophagous Hymenoptera. [See Ray Society.] E

CAMERON, Hon. W. E. History of the World's Columbian Exposition. 2nd ed Fol. Chicago, 1893. B 6 S 5

CAMPBELL, A. J. The Gymnorhinæ or Australian Magpies. (Proc. Roy. Soc., Vict., n.s. 7.) 8vo. Melb., 1895. ME 1 P

CAMPBELL, Ada. Christianity v. Freethought. [See Turnbull, Rev. A.] MG 1 R 67

CAMPBELL, Alexander. Letter to the Queensland Investment Sheep Company. 8vo. Sydney, 1866. MF 1 R 42

CAMPBELL, Rev. Colin. Henry George and his remedies analysed. 8vo. Melb., 1895. MF 4 R 26

CAMPBELL, Lieut.-Col. Colin Fred. Letters from Camp to his Relatives during the Siege of Sebastopol. 8vo. Lond., 1894. B 31 R 3

CAMPBELL, Dr. Francis. On the Cultivation of Flax and Hemp. 8vo. Sydney, 1864. MA 1 P 48

CAMPBELL, Fred. A. Some Coral and Volcanic Islands of the Western Pacific; with an Account of the active volcano of Tana. (Roy. Geog. Soc. Australasia, Vic. Branch, 6.) 8vo. Melb., 1885. ME 20 P
Tensile Strength of a few of the Colonial Timbers. (Roy. Soc., Vict., 16.) 8vo. Melb., 1880. ME 1 P
Experiments upon the Hardwoods of Australia. (Roy. Soc., Vict., 19.) 8vo. Melb., 1883. ME 1 P

CAMPBELL, Sir Geo. Memoirs of my Indian Career. Edited by Sir C. E. Bernard. 2 vols. 8vo. Lond., 1893. C 15 P 16, 17

CAMPBELL, H. [See Arnobius.] G 14 U 19

CAMPBELL, Dr. Henry Johnstone. The Cell. [See Hertwig, Dr. O.] A 28 U 12

CAMPBELL, Dr. Hugh, BREWER, R. F., and NEVILLE, Henry. Voice, Speech, and Gesture: a Practical Handbook to the Elocutionary Art; including Essays on Reciting and Recitative by C. Harrison, and on Recitation with Musical Accompaniment by F. Corder. 8vo. Lond., 1895. J 8 T 36

CAMPBELL, Jas. Dykes. Samuel Taylor Coleridge a Narrative of the Events of his Life. 8vo. Lond., 1894. C 19 R 10

CAMPBELL, John, Lord. Lives of the Lord Chancellors and Keepers of the Great Seal of England. 10 vols. 12mo. Lond., 1868. C 19 T 1-10
Lives of the Chief Justices of England, from the Norman Conquest to the Death of Lord Tenterton. 3rd ed. 4 vols. 12mo. Lond., 1874. C 19 T 11-14

CAMPBELL, Rev. John Gregorson. Waifs and Strays of Celtic Tradition : Clan Traditions and Popular Tales of the Western Highlands and Islands. 8vo. Lond., 1895. B 32 T 71

CAMPBELL, Dr. John P. Biological Teaching in the Colleges of the United States. 8vo. Washington, 1891. G 18 R 11

CAMPBELL, Rev. Joseph. The Amateur Photographer's Primer. 12mo. Sydney, 1884. MA 2 P 30
Norfolk Island and its Inhabitants. 8vo. Sydney, 1879. MD 1 Q 39
Physical and Political Geography of Australia, Tasmania, and New Zealand. 12mo. Sydney, 1876. MD 1 P 26
Simple Tests for Minerals; or, every Man his own Analyst. 3rd ed. 12mo. Sydney, 1895. MA 3 U 15

CAMPBELL, Dr. Lewis. Guide to Greek Tragedy for
English readers. 8vo. Lond., 1891. H 9 U 24
Plato's Republic. [*See* Plato.] F 14 V 26-28
Seven Plays of Sophocles. [*See* Sophocles.] H 10 S 10

CAMPBELL, Rev. Peter. [*See* Wasp, The.] MG 1 Q 53

CAMPBELL, Thos. Poetical Books of. Illustrated.
12mo. Lond., 1854. H 10 T 27
Poetical Works of. 8vo. Lond., 1852. H 7 U 34
The Pleasures of Hope, Gertrude of Wyoming, and
other Poems. 18mo. Lond., 1852. H 10 U 4
Life of. 18mo. Lond., 1852. H 10 U 4

CAMPBELL, Walter Scott. Flowering Plants and Ferns
of New South Wales. [*See* Maiden, J. H.]
MA 3 R 40
Report on Sericulture. Fol. Sydney, 1893.
MA 10 T 49 †
Report on Silk Culture. 8vo. Sydney, 1893.*
MA 1 S 31

CAMPBELL, Wm. India in six and Australia in sixteen
days. 8vo. Lond., 1889. MF 4 R 18

CAMUS, N. Terentii Comœdiæ sex. [*See* Terentius, P.]
H 3 S 40

CANADA—*General.*
Manuscripts relating to the early History of. 8vo.
Quebec, 1867-75. B 17 T 13
Mémoires sur le Canada, 1749-60. 8vo. Quebec, 1873.
B 17 T 15
[*See also* Great Britain and Ireland—British North
America.]

CANADA—*Government Departments, Reports, and Publications.*
CONFEDERATION.
Parliamentary Debates on the subject of the Confederation of the British North American Provinces.
Roy. 8vo. Quebec, 1865. F 7 U 26

DEPARTMENT OF AGRICULTURE.
Report of the Dairy Commissioner for the Dominion
of Canada, 1892-93. 8vo. Ottawa, 1894. E
Experimental Farms: Reports, 1893-94. 2 vols. 8vo.
Ottawa, 1894. E
Report of the Minister of Agriculture for the Dominion of Canada, 1893. 8vo. Ottawa, 1894. E
Statistical Year-book of Canada, 1892, 1893. 2 vols.
8vo. Ottawa, 1893-94. E
Western Canada and its great resources. 8vo.
Ottawa, 1893. D 15 V 18

DEPARTMENT OF THE INTERIOR.
Report for 1893. 8vo. Ottawa, 1894. E
Official Handbook of information relating to the
Dominion of Canada. 8vo. Ottawa, 1893.
D 15 R 15
Another copy. 8vo. Ottawa, 1894. D 15 S 21

CANADA—*contd.*
GEOLOGICAL AND NATURAL HISTORY SURVEY.
Reports of, 1885-87, 1892-93. 6 vols. 8vo. Ottawa,
1886-95. E
Mineral Productions of Canada, 1892. [*See* Ingall,
E. D.] E
Catalogue of a stratigraphical collection of Canadian
Rocks; by W. F. Ferrier. 8vo. Ottawa, 1893. E
PATENTS' OFFICE.
The Canadian Patent Office Record and Register of
Copyrights and Trade Marks, 1890-94. 5 vols.
Imp. 8vo. E
Rules and Forms of, 1892. Roy. 8vo. Ottawa, 1892.
F 14 V 14
STATUTES.
An Act respecting the sale of intoxicating liquors and
the issue of licenses therefor. Fol. Lond., 1884.
F 39 U 22 ‡
Intoxicating Liquors Act, 1882-83. 4 vols. 8vo.
(n.p., n.d.) F 7 U 21-24

CANADIAN INSTITUTE. Reports, 1892, 1894: Archæology. 2 vols. 8vo. Toronto, 1893-95. E
Transactions, vol. 4, pt. 1. [*See* Morice, Rev. A. G.]
A 30 V 12

CANAWAY, A. P. Real Property Law; with Notes and
Cases. 8vo. Sydney, 1887. MF 2 R 62

CANDIDUS. [*See* Inglis, C.]

CANDLER, C. Koch's Proposed Cure for Consumption;
with Suggestions on the Prevention of Consumption.
8vo. Melb., 1891. MA 3 S 59

CANDLOT, E. Ciments et Chaux Hydrauliques. Fabrication, Propriétés, Emploi. 8vo. Paris, 1891.
A 25 V 6

CANDOLLE, Alphonse P. de, and Casimer de. Monographiæ Phanerogamarum Prodromi. Vol. 8. Roy.
8vo. Parisiis (n.d.) A 32 T 23

CANEL, A. History of the States-General of Normandy.
[*See* Collectanea Adamantæa.] J 18 R 38

CANNAN, Edwin. History of the Theories of Production
and Distribution in English Political Economy, 1776-
1848. 8vo. Lond., 1893. F 14 S 21

CANNEY, Edward H. The Land of the Dawning. 12mo.
Lond., 1894. MD 7 T 59

CANNING, Charlotte, Countess. Memorial of; by A. J.
C. Hare. 3 vols. 12mo. Lond., 1893.
C 19 Q 23-25

CANNING, Rt. Hon. George. Poetical Works of. 32mo.
Lond, 1848. Libr.

CANOVA, Antonio. [Plaster Cast of.] [*See* Hutton,
L.—Portraits in Plaster.] A 23 V 13
[*See* Elliott, Frances—Roman Gossip.] C 21 Q 10

CANSDELL, C. Stuart-. A new European-Australian Route : Proposals for a new Route which will enable Passengers, Mails, Light Goods and Produce to be carried between London and Sydney in sixteen, and Heavy Goods and Cattle in twenty-three days, combined with a system of Canals, to be used for Transit, Irrigation, and General Water Supply throughout Central Australia. 8vo. Sydney, 1895. MF 4 Q 29

Federation, Colonial and British. 8vo. Sydney, 1891. MF 2 Q 42

CANTERBURY ASSOCIATION. Copy of Correspondence between the Colonial Office and the Canterbury Association since the date of the Charter of Incorporation of that body. Sm. fol. Lond., 1853. MF 9 U 15

CANTERBURY COLLEGE, NEW ZEALAND. Calendars, 1893-95. 12mo. Christchurch, 1893-95. ME 5 S

CANTERBURY COLLEGE PUBLIC LIBRARY. Catalogue of Books in the Circulating Department, 1895. 8vo. Christchurch, 1895. MK 1 T 34

CANTLIE, Jas. Beri-Beri. [See Pekelharing, C. A.] A 33 T 21

CANTON, Wm. [Life of] Tennyson. [See Masson, Prof. D.—Footsteps of the Poets.] J 6 R 43

CAPE OF GOOD HOPE, Notes on, made during an Excursion in that Colony, 1820. 8vo. Lond., 1821. D 14 S 8

CAPEFIGUE, Jean B. H. R. A King's Mistress. [See Bibliotheca Curiosa.] J 18 Q 46

CAPGRAVE, Rev. Dr. J. Life of St. Katherine of Alexandria. [See Early English Text Soc.] E

CAPPER, John. The Three Presidencies of India. Illustrated. 8vo. Lond., 1853. B 29 U 6

CAPPER, Richard. Dramatic Illustrations of Ancient History. 12mo. Melb., 1868. MH 1 P 65

Judith: an Historical Drama. 12mo. Melb., 1867. MH 1 U 69

CARANGARA COPPER-MINING CO. Deed of Settlement and Act of Incorporation. 8vo. Sydney, 1854. MF 4 R 55

CARDEW, J. H. The Australian Municipal Pocket-book of Engineering for the use of Laymen. 12mo. Sydney, 1895. MA 3 P 41

CAREY, Chas. Nicholas. The Australian Miners' Guide. 12mo. Sydney, 1892. MA 2 P 36

CAREY, Henry. Chrononhotonthologos : a Burlesque Opera. [See London Stage, 3.] H 2 S 35

The Dragon of Wantley : a Burlesque Opera. [See London Stage, 2.] H 2 S 34

The Contrivances : a Ballad Opera. [See London Stage, 4.] H 2 S 36

CAREY, Dr. Henry Chas. Manual of Social Science ; being a condensation of the " Principles of Social Science ;" by Kate M'Kean. 8vo. Philad., 1888. F 14 R 11

CARHART, Prof. Daniel. Field-book for Civil Engineers. 12mo. Boston, 1893. A 22 Q 17

CARLISLE, Geo. Wm. Fred. Howard, Seventh Earl of. Lectures and Addresses in aid of Popular Education. 12mo. Lond., 1852. J 12 S 26

CARLISLE INDIAN INDUSTRIAL SCHOOL. Report, 1893. 8vo. Carlisle, Pa., 1893. E

CARLYLE, Thomas. Critical and Miscellaneous Essays. 4 vols. 8vo. Lond., 1887. J 4 R 43—46

The French Revolution : a History. 8vo. Lond., 1888. B 26 R 7

Latter-day Pamphlets. 8vo. Lond., 1858. J 5 R 39

Life of John Sterling. 2nd ed. 8vo. Lond., 1852. C 21 Q 3

Oliver Cromwell's Letters and Speeches ; with Elucidations. 5 vols. (in 1.) 8vo. Lond., 1888. C 21 Q 2

On the Choice of Books : the Inaugural Address of, to the University of Edinburgh ; with a Memoir of the Author. 12mo. Lond., 1866. J 11 T 38

Robert Burns. 12mo. Lond., 1854. C 17 P 18

Translations from Musæus, Tieck, and Richter. 8vo. Lond., 1858. J 5 R 42

Wilhelm Meister's Apprenticeship and Travels. Translated. 2 vols. 8vo. Lond , 1858. J 5 R 40, 41

Goethe and Carlyle. [See Müller, F Max.—Chips from a German Workshop.] J 9 P 31—33

The Humourist as Prophet. [See Lilly, W. S.—Four English Humourists.] J 5 T 30

In Carlyle's Country. [See Burroughs, J.—Fresh Fields.] J 16 T 35

CARMAN, Ezra A. Special Report on Sheep Industry, U.S.A [See Salmon, Dr. D. E.] A 30 U 7

CARMICHAEL, G. E. Jennings. Hospital Children : Sketches of Life and Character in the Children's Hospital, Melbourne. 12mo. Melb., 1891. MA 3 U 8

CARNARVON, Henry J. G. Herbert, Earl of. Deputation to, on the subject of Acts passed in the Colonies for legalizing Marriage with a Deceased Wife's Sister. 8vo. (n.p.n.d.) MF 4 Q 38

CARNEGIE, Andrew. A Chat with ; with Portrait. [See Blathwayt, R.—Interviews.] J 10 U 34

CARNOT, Marie François Sadi, President of France. Sketch of. [See Smalley, G. W.—Studies of Men.] C 19 R 20

CAROLINA, NORTH, AGRICULTURAL EXPERIMENT STATION. Bulletin No. 92. Culture of Orchard Fruits. 8vo. Raleigh, 1893. A 32 R 6

Reports 1880-83, 1890-93. 3 vols. 8vo. Raleigh, 1880-93. E

G

CAROLINA, SOUTH. Hand-book of. 8vo. Richmond, 1893. D 15 T 5

CARPENTER, Edward. From Adam's Peak to Elephanta: Sketches in Ceylon and India. 8vo. Lond., 1892. D 17 V 5

CARPENTER, J. E. The Popular Elocutionist and Reciter. New edition, thoroughly revised, by L. Wagner. 8vo. Lond., 1889. J 4 R 37

CARPENTER, P. Herbert. Crinoidea. [*See* Thompson, Sir C. W., and Murray, Dr. J.—Voyage of H.M.S. *Challenger*.] A 6 †

CARPENTER, Dr. Wm. Benjamin. Specimens of the Genus Orbitolites. [*See* Thomson, Sir C. W., and Murray, Dr. J.—Voyage of H.M.S. *Challenger*, Zoology, 7.] A 6 †

CARPENTER, Rt. Rev. Wm. Boyd. [Life of] Mrs. Browning. [*See* Masson, Prof. D.—In the Footsteps of the Poets.] J G R 43
Lectures on Preaching. 8vo. Lond., 1895. G 3 P 27

CARR, A. B. Three Months in a Workshop. [*See* Göhre, P.] F 6 T 37

CARR, George S. Social Evolution and the Evolution of Socialism. 8vo. Lond., 1895. G 14 Q 31

CARR, Most Rev. Thos. J. Origin of the Church of England: three Lectures. 8vo. Melb., 1893. MG 1 R 39

CARR, Wm. Wilkins. Judicial Interpretation by the United States Courts of the Acts of Congress relating to the Tariff. Roy. 8vo. Philad., 1894. F 14 U 20

CARRASCO Y JELVES, Rosendo. Cristobal Colon. 2a ed. 12mo. Santiago, 1888. H 0 P 17

CARRICK, Robert. New Zealand's Lone Lands. 8vo. Wellington, 1892. MD 8 R 31
Romance of Lake Wakitipu; being Episodes of Early Gold-fields Life in New Zealand; with Itinerant, Statistical, Historical, and other Notes. 8vo. Wellington, 1892. MB 1 R 50

CARROLL, Edward. Principles and Practice of Finance. 8vo. New York, 1895. F 10 U 21

CARRUTHERS, Dr. Robt. Pope's Poetical Works. [*See* Pope, A.] H 2 U 10-13

CARRUTHERS, W. Farm Seeds and their Adulterations: a Lecture. (Inst. of Agricult., Lond.) 8vo. Lond., 1884. A 18 R 28

CARSON, Enoch T. Historical Sketch of the Ancient Accepted Scottish Rite, Northern Masonic Jurisdiction of the United States; also, a Historical Sketch of the Formation of the General Grand Encampment of Knights Templars of the United States in 1816. 8vo. Dayton, 1892. B 17 R 16
Report on Foreign Communications to the Grand Commandery of Knights Templars of Ohio, 1892. 8vo. Dayton, 1892. E

CARSON, Hampton L. The Supreme Court of the United States, its History. 2 vols. sm. 4to. Philad., 1892. B 36 S 17, 18 ‡

CARSTAIRS, R. Human Nature in Rural India. 8vo. Edinb., 1895. D 17 Q 24

CARTAULT, A. La Trière Athénienne: étude d'Archéologie Navale. 8vo. Paris, 1881. B 35 R 22

CARTER, George B. Laws of Wisconsin concerning the Organization and Government of Towns. 8vo. Madison, 1885. F 2 V 8

CARTER, Thos. War Medals of the British Army, and how they were won. Revised, enlarged, and continued by W. H. Long. 8vo. Lond., 1893. B 7 R 17

CARTWRIGHT, John R. Cases decided on the North American Act, 1867, in the Privy Council, the Supreme Court of Canada, and the Provincial Courts. 4 vols. 8vo. Toronto, 1882-92. F 10 U 22-25

CARTWRIGHT, Julia. [*See* Ady, Mrs. Henry.]

CARUS, Dr. Paul. Fundamental Problems. 8vo. Chicago, 1891. G 3 P 30

CARVER, Jonathan, the Explorer of Minnesota. Sketch of. [*See* Greeley, Gen. A. W.—Explorers.] C 17 R 4

CARY, Edward. [Life of] Geo. Wm. Curtis. (Am. Men of Letts.) 12mo. Boston, 1894. C 17 P 24

CARY, Henry. The Common Law Procedure Acts, and the Law of Evidence Amendment Act. 8vo. Sydney, 1868. MF 1 Q 45

CARY, Rev. Henry Francis. Poetical Works of W. Cowper. [*See* Cowper, W.] H 7 V 8

CASANOVA, Jacques. Memoirs of. 12 vols. 8vo. (n.p.) 1894. Libr.

CASEY, Dr. John. Cubic Transformations. (Trans. R.I. Academy—Cunningham Memoirs, 1.) 4to. Dublin (n.d.) E

CASKET OF GEMS, The; by "Mona Marie." 8vo. Ballarat, 1882. MH 1 Q 27

CASSELL & CO. Cassell's Universal Portrait Gallery. 8vo. Lond., 1895. A 23 U 28
Cassell's History of England. Jubilee ed. 8 vols. 8vo. Lond. (n.d.) B 20 V 13-20
New Technical Educator. 6 vols. 8vo. Lond., 1893-95. H 7 U 26-31
Pictorial New Zealand. Illustrated. 8vo. Lond., 1895. MD 7 U 22

CASTANHEDA, Fernão Lopez de. Historia do descobrimento e conquista da India per los Portuguese. 8 vols. (in 5.) sm. fol. Coimbra, 1552-61. D 8 S 2-6 †
The First Booke of the Historie of Discoverie and Conquest of the East Indias enterprised by the Portugales. Now translated into English by M.L. [Nicolas Litchfield.] 12mo. Lond., 1582. Libr.

CASTELLA, F. de. Arguments in favour of Vine Culture. (Victorian Dept. of Agriculture.—Lectures.) 8vo. Melb., 1892. MA 3 V 15
Points requiring consideration by intending planters. (Victorian Dept. of Agriculture.—Lectures.) 8vo. Melb., 1892. MA 3 V 15

CASTLE, Edward W. and Robert. Yachting. [See Sullivan, Sir E.] A 29 Q 41

CASTLE, Egerton. English Book-plates: an illustrated handbook for Students of Ex-Libris. 8vo. Lond., 1892. K 19 Q 9
Schools and Masters of Fence, from the Middle Ages to the end of 18th Century New ed. 12mo. Lond., 1893. A 20 Q 34

CASTLE, Lewis. Flower Gardening for Amateurs in Town, Suburban, and Country Gardens, with a chapter on the Greenhouse. 8vo. Lond., 1888. A 18 R 18
Orchids: their Structure, History, and Culture. 12mo. Lond., 1887. A 20 Q 6

CASTLEMAINE MINING BOARD. Bye-laws, 1864-5. 12mo. Castlemaine, 1864. MF 1 P 60

CASTLEMOATE SILVER-MINING CO. Rules. 8vo. (n.p.) 1889. MF 4 R 35

CASTRACANE, Conte Abate Francesco. Marine Diatomaceæ. [See Thomson, Sir C. W., and Murray, Dr. J.—Voyage of H.M.S. Challenger.] A 6 †

CASWELL, Rev. Alexis. Meteorological Observations made at Providence, R.I. 1831-60. 4to. Wash., 1860. A 15 Q 10 †

CATALOGUE ILLUSTRÉ de l'Exposition Historique de l'Art Belge et du Musée Moderne de Bruxelles, 1830-80. 8vo. Bruxelles, 1880. K 7 T 19

CATCH-A-CATCH. [See Comical Cricket.] MH 1 U 48

CATECHISM on the History of the Presbyterian form of Church Government, with more especial reference to the Church of Scotland. 12mo. Maitland (n.d.) MG 2 R 24

CATHCART, Rev. Dr. Wm. The Ancient British and Irish Churches, including the Life and Labour of St. Patrick. With Maps and Illustrations. Roy. 8vo. Philad., 1894. G 14 Q 27

CATHERINE II, Empress of Russia. Romance of an Empress; from the French of K. Waliszowski. 2 vols. 8vo. Lond., 1894. C 19 R 8, 9
The Story of a Throne; from the French of K. Waliszowski. 2 vols. 8vc. Lond., 1895. C 17 S 13, 14

CATHOLIC CLERGYMAN, A. [See Instruction on the Duty of Prisoners.] MG 2 R 58

CATHOLIC DIRECTORY AND ALMANAC, for the Clergy and Laity in Victoria, 1863. 12mo. Melb. 1863. ME 5 Q

CATHOLIC UNIVERSITY OF AMERICA. Yearbook, 1893, 1894. 8vo. Wash., 1893. E

CATTLEY, Rev. Stephen R. Acts and Monuments of John Foxe. [See Fox, J.] G 16 U 9-16

CATULLUS, Caius Valerius. The Attis of; Translated into English Verse, with Dissertations on the Myth of Attis, on the Origin of Tree-Worship, and on the Galliambic Metre, by Grant Allen. 8vo. Lond., 1892. H 9 Q 21

CAUNT, Ben. [Plaster Cast of.] [See Hutton, L.—Portraits in Plaster.] A 23 V 13

CAUVIN, Dr. Charles. Mémoire sur les Races de l'Océanie. Roy. 8vo. Paris, 1881. MA 3 R 17

CAVAN, Earl of. With the Yacht, Camera, and Cycle in the Mediterranean. 8vo. Lond., 1895. D 18 R 28

CAVE, Henry W. Picturesque Ceylon: Colombo and the Kelani Valley. 4to. Lond., 1893. D 19 V 8
Picturesque Ceylon: Kandy and Poradeniya. 4to. Lond., 1894. D 36 S 23 ‡

CAVENDISH, Capt. A. E. J. Korea and the sacred White Mountain, being a brief Account of a Journey in Korea in 1891; with an Account of an Ascent of the White Mountain by Captain H. E. Goold-Adams. 8vo. Lond., 1894. D 17 U 21

CAVENDISH, Henry. Sketch of. [See Thorpe, Dr. T. E.—Historical Chemistry.] C 17 R 2

CAVENDISH, Thomas. Sketch of. [See Southey, R.—English Seamen.] B 23 S 15

CAVOUR, Camillo Benso, Conté di. Count Cavour and Madame de Circourt: Some unpublished Correspondence. Edited by Count Nigra. Translated by A. J. Butler. 8vo. Lond., 1894. C 14 V 14
[Plaster Cast of.] [See Hutton, L.—Portraits in Plaster.] A 23 V 13

CAWTHORNE, W. A. The Legend of Kuperree; or the Red Kangaroo: an aboriginal tradition of the Poet Lincoln Tribe. 2nd ed. Adelaide (n.d.) MH 1 Q 37

CECIL, Evelyn. Primogeniture: a short History of its Development in various countries, and its practical effects. 8vo. Lond., 1895. F 1 R 5

CECIL, Sir Robert, Earl of Salisbury. Secret Correspondence of, with James VI. [See Colloctanea Adamantea.] J 18 R 28

CENTENARY OF SUNDAY SCHOOLS, 1880. A Memorial of the Celebrations held in London, the Provinces, and the Colonies. 12mo. Lond., 1881. G 7 U 32

CENTENNIAL MAGAZINE, The. August, 1888—Dec., 1889, and July-Sept., 1890. 3 vols. roy. 8vo. Sydney, 1888-90. ME 6 U

CENTENNIAL PORTFOLIO. Views of New South Wales. 40 plates. 4to. Sydney, 1888. MD 3 Q 12 ‡

CENTLIVRE, Mrs. Susannah. A Bold Stroke for a Wife. [*See* London Stage, 1.] H 2 S 33
The Busybody: a Comedy. [*See* London Stage, 2.] H 2 S 34
The Wonder a Woman Keeps a Secret: a Comedy. [*See* London Stage, 2.] H 2 S 34

CENTRAL BROKEN HILL SILVER-MINING CO. Reports and Statements of Accounts, 1891. Sm. 4to. Sydney, 1891. ME 7 R

CENTURY, The; Illustrated Monthly Magazine, N.S. Vols. 1–27. 8vo. New York, 1881–95. E

CERVANTES SAAVEDRA, Miguel de, his Life and Works; by H. E. Watts. 8vo. Lond., 1895. C 13 V 17
Leben und Thaten des scharfsinnigen Edlen Don Quixote von la Mancha. 5 vols. 12mo. Wien, 1818. J 9 P 41–45

CESARESCO, Countess Evelyn M. The Liberation of Italy, 1815–70. 8vo. Lond., 1895. B 30 S 11

CHADWICK, Very Rev. Geo. Alex. Exodus and St. Mark. [*See* Expositor's Bible.] G 19 R and S

CHAILLEY-BERT, J. [*See* Bert, J. Chailley-.]

CHALMERS, D., & Co. The Aberdeen Almanac and Northern Register for 1841. 12mo. Aberdeen, 1841. E

CHALMERS, George. Caledonia: Historical and Topographical Account of North Britain. Vol. 7. 4to. Paisley, 1894. B 31 V 18

CHALMERS, J. A. The Gold Mines of the Rand. [*See* Hatch, F. H.] A 24 V 15

CHALMERS, James. Adventures in New Guinea. 18mo. Lond., 1886. MD 1 P 27
Pioneer Life and Work in New Guinea, 1877–94. 8vo. Lond., 1895. MG 2 Q 46

CHALMERS, Robert. History of Currency in the British Colonies. Roy. 8vo. Lond., 1893. MF 1 S 64
The Jātaka. Vol. 1. [*See* Cowell, Prof. E. B.] G 5 T 20

CHALMERS, Rev. Dr. Thos. Christian Revelation, viewed in connection with Modern Astronomy. 8vo. Edinb. (n.d.) G 2 V 33
Thomas Chalmers, Preacher, Philosopher, and Statesman; by Mrs. Oliphant. 8vo. Lond., 1893. C 13 Q 26
[Plaster Cast of.] [*See* Hutton, L.—Portraits in Plaster.] A 23 V 13

CHAMBERLAIN, Basil Hall. Things Japanese. 8vo. Lond., 1890. B 33 P 2

CHAMBERLAIN, John. Memoirs of; by W. Yates. 8vo. Lond., 1826. C 2 V 31

CHAMBERLAIN, Montague. Popular Ornithology of the United States and Canada. Illustrated. 2 vols. 8vo. Boston, 1891. A 28 U 3, 4

CHAMBERS, C. Haddon. Thumb-nail Sketches of Australian Life. 8vo. New York, 1891. MJ 3 Q 82

CHAMBERS, Edmund K. English Pastorals. 8vo. Lond., 1895. H 9 U 38

CHAMBERS, Wm. and Robt. Chambers's Concise Gazetteer of the World; with Atlas. 2 vols. 8vo. Lond., 1895. D 11 S 18, 19
Chambers's Encyclopædia: a Dictionary of Universal Knowledge. New edition. Vol. 10. Imp. 8vo. Lond., 1892. K 4 T 10

CHAMBERS'S JOURNAL, 1892 and 1894. 2 vols. 8vo. Lond., 1892–94. E

CHAMIER, Geo. Philosopher Dick: Adventures and Contemplations of a New Zealand Shepherd. 8vo. Lond., 1891. MJ 2 P 13

CHAMPION, H. H. The Root of the Matter; being a series of Dialogues on Social Questions. 12mo. Melb., 1895. MF 4 P 18

CHAMPLIN, John D., jun., and APTHORP, Wm. F. Cyclopedia of Music and Musicians. Illustrated. 3 vols. roy. 8vo. New York, 1893. K 18 S 9–11

CHANCELLOR, Richard. Voyage to Muscovy, 1630. [*See* Bibliotheca Curiosa.] J 18 Q 35

CHANNING, Dr. Edward. Town and Country Government in the English Colonies of North America. (Johns Hopkins University Studies, 2.) 8vo. Baltimore, 1884. B 18 S 2
The Narragansett Planters: a Study of Causes. (Johns Hopkins University Studies, 4.) 8vo. Baltimore, 1886. B 18 S 4

CHANSON DE ROLAND, La; Traduction Archaique et Rythmée, accompagnée de notes explicatives par L. Cledat. 8vo. Paris, 1887. H 5 U 40

CHANUTE, O. Progress of Flying Machines. 8vo. New York, 1894. A 25 U 7

CHAP-BOOKS. 2 vols. sm. 4to. Lond., 1885. J 6 P 45, 46
The History of Thomas Hickathrift.
History of the seven Wise Masters of Rome.
Mother Bunch's Closet newly broke open.
History of Patient Grisel, 1619.
History of Sir Richard Whittington.

CHAPMAN, C. M. Digest of Reported Decisions. [*See* Fisher, R. A.] F 12 V 3–9

CHAPMAN, George. Homer's Iliad. [*See* Homer.] H 15 P 11 †

CHAPMAN, Henry S. The New Zealand Portfolio. No. 1—Letter to the Rt. Hon. Lord Stanley, on the Administration of Justice in New Zealand. No. 2— Letter to John Abel Smith on the Advantages which would accrue to English Capitalists from the Establishment of a Loan Company for New Zealand. 8vo. Lond. (n.d.) MF 2 R 45

CHAPPELSMITH, J. Account of a Tornado near New Harmony, Ind., April, 1852, with a Map of the Track. 4to. Wash., 1853. A 15 Q 11 †

CHARBONNET, Mdlle. [See Kellerman, Mme. C-.]

CHARITIES REGISTER AND DIGEST. A Classified Register of Charities, 1895. 8vo. Lond., 1895. E

CHARITY ORGANIZATION SOCIETY. 11th Report of. Sydney, 1889. ME 6 S

CHARLES I, King of England. Life and Reign of. [See Disraeli, I.] B 21 U 7, 8

CHARLES II, King of England. King Charles II's Escape from Worcester. [See Bibliotheca Curiosa.] J 18 Q 2

Charles II and Scotland in 1650. [See Scottish History Society, 17.] E

Conspiracy to assassinate Charles II at the Rye House, 1684. [See Collectanea Adamantæa.] J 18 R 22

Tryal of E. Coleman for conspiring the Death of. [See Collectanea Adamantæa.] J 18 R 37

CHARLES I, Emperor of Germany.—Charlemagne. Life of the Emperor Karl the Great. Translated from Eginhard, by Wm. Glaister. 8vo. Lond., 1877. C 13 P 18

CHARLES V, Emperor of Germany. History of the Reign of. [See Robertson Rev. Dr. W.] B 25 Q 21-23

CHARLES XII, King of Sweden. Histoire de Charles XII. [See Voltaire, F. M. A. de.] B 25 P 8

[Plaster Cast of.] [See Hutton, L.—Portraits in Plaster.] A 23 V 13

CHARLES, Cecil. Costa Rica. [See Biolley, P.] D 12 T 16

CHARLES, R. H. Ethiopic version of the Hebrew Book of Jubilees. (Anecdota Oxoniensia, Semitic series part 8.) Sm. 4to. Oxford, 1895. E

CHARLEY, Sir Wm. T. The Crusade against the Constitution : an Historical Vindication of the House of Lords. 12mo. Lond., 1895. F 8 U 14

CHARTERIS, Col. Francis, Libertine. [Life of]. 1675-1732 ; by A. Vincent. (Lives of Twelve Bad Men.) 8vo. Lond , 1894. C 18 T 6

CHARTERS TOWERS GOLD-FIELD, Queensland its Rise and Progress. 8vc. Lond., 1886. MD 8 Q 42

CHARTIST CIRCULAR, The. Vols. 1 and 2 (in 1 vol.) Fol. Glasgow, 1841-42. E

CHASE, Salmon P. Biographical Sketch of. [See Brooks, N.—Statesmen.] C 16 R 20

CHATEAUBRIAND, François A., Vicomte de. The Genius of Christianity. 8vo. Baltimore, 1884. G 3 P 31

CHATELAIN, Emile. Notice sur les Manuscrits des Poésies do St. Paulin de Nole. 8vo. Paris, 1880. J 7 U 37

CHATHAM, Rt. Hon. Wm. Pitt, Earl of. Character of. [See Hazlitt, W.—Winterslow.] J 12 S 33

CHATWOOD, Arthur B. Photography. [See Johnson, Robt.] A 8 Q 10

CHAUCER, Geoffrey. Complete Works of. Edited by Rev. Dr. W. W. Skeat. Vols. 1-5. 8vo. Oxford, 1894. H 9 S 27-31

CHAUCER SOCIETY. Publications. 11 vols. 8vo. Lond., 1868-92. E
Chronology of Chaucer's Writings ; by Dr. J. Koch.
Essays on Chaucer, parts 5, 6.
Life-Records of Chaucer, part 3.
Observations on the Language of Chaucer's Troilus ; by G. L. Kittredge.
Originals and Analogues of some of Chaucer's Canterbury Tales, parts 4, 5.
The Romaunt of the Rose. Edited by Max Kaluza.
Specimens of all the accessible unprinted MSS. of the Canterbury Tales.
Temporary Preface to the six-text edition of Chaucer's Canterbury Tales, part 1.
Trial-Forewords to my Parallel-text edition of Chaucer's minor Poems ; by F. J. Furnivall.

CHAUVENET, Prof. Wm. Manual of Spherical and Practical Astronomy : embracing the General Problems of Spherical Astronomy, the Special Application to Nautical Astronomy, and the Theory and Use of Fixed and Portable Astronomical Instruments. 2 vols. Roy. 8vo. Philad., 1893. A 31 Q 4, 5

CHEETHAM, Rev. Dr. S. History of the Christian Church during the first six centuries. 12mo. Lond., 1894. G 2 V 8

CHEMICAL INDUSTRY, SOCIETY OF. [See Society of Chemical Industry.]

CHEMICAL SOCIETY, The. Journal of. Vols. 61-36. 8vo. Lond., 1892-94. E

CHENEY, W. T. An Apocalypse of Life. 8vo. Boston, 1893. G 19 Q 5

CHENNELLS, Ellen. Recollections of an Egyptian Princess; by her Egyptian Governess: being a Record of Five Years' Residence at the Court of Ismael Pasha, Khedive. 2 vols. 8vo. Edinb., 1893. D 14 S 10, 11

CHERRY, Andrew. The Soldier's Daughter : a Comedy. [See London Stage, 1.] H 2 S 33

CHESHIRE, Frank R. Bees in relation to Flowering Plants and Fruit Production: a Lecture. (Inst. of Agricult., Lond.) 8vo. Lond., 1884. A 18 R 28

CHESNAYE-DESBOIS, F. A. A. de la. [See Desbois.]

CHESNEY, Gen. Sir George T. The British Empire. [See Roy. Col. Inst., Proc., 25.] E
Indian Polity: a View of the System of Administration in India. 3rd ed. 8vo. Lond., 1894. F 14 U 19

CHESTERFIELD, Phillip Dormer Stanhope, Earl of. Some Advice on Men and Manners. 18mo. Edinb., 1776. G 18 P 23
Life, Character, and Opinions; by A. Hayward. 12mo. Lond., 1854. C 18 P 21
Memoirs of the Life of; by W. Ernst. 8vo. Lond., 1893. C 15 P 13

CHETHAM SOCIETY. Publications. New Series. Vols. 26–33. Sm. 4to. Manchester, 1892–95. E
  26, 31. Materials for the History of the Church of Lancaster; by W. O. Roper. Vols. 1, 2.
  27. Notes on the Churches of Lancashire; by Sir S. R. Glynne.
  28. Lancashire and Cheshire Wills and Inventories, 1572–1696.
  29, 30. Poems of John Byrom.
  32. Notes on the Churches of Cheshire; by Sir S. R. Glynne.
  33. Note-book of the Rev. T. Jolly, 1671–93.
General Index to the Remains, Historical and Literary, Published by the Chetham Society. Vols. 31–114. Sm. 4to. Manchester, 1893. E

CHEVRON, Père Joseph. Les Tonga. [See Monfat, Père A.] MD 7 S 30

CHEWINGS, Dr. C. Notes on Sedimentary Rocks. (Trans. Roy. Soc., S. Australia, 18.) 8vo. Adelaide, 1894. ME 1 S

CHEYNE, Dr. Wm. Watson. Tuberculous Diseases of Bones and Joints. Illustrated. 8vo. Edinb., 1895. A 33 U 16

CHICAGO. Annual Report of the Trade and Commerce of Chicago for 1893. Roy. 8vo. Chicago, 1894. E
Reports of the Fire Marshal to the City Council of the City of Chicago, 1892 and 1894. 2 vols. 8vo. Chicago, 1893–95. E

CHICAGO COLLEGE OF PHARMACY. Announcement of Regular Course, 1893–94. 8vo. Chicago, 1893. E

CHICAGO EXHIBITION, 1893. Amtlicher Katalog der ausstellung des Deutschen Reiches. Roy. 8vo. Leipzig, 1893. K 7 U 4
Board of World's Fair Managers of the State of Montana: Reports. 8vo. Helena, 1892. K 7 U 9
Catálogo de la Seccion Española. 8vo. Madrid, 1893. K 7 S 40
Catálogo Oficial de la Exposicion del Imperio Alemán. Roy. 8vo. Leipzig, 1893. K 7 U 6

CHICAGO EXHIBITION, 1893—contd.
Catalogue of Educational Exhibit of Massachusetts. 8vo. Chicago, 1893. K 7 S 38
Catalogue of the Exhibits of the State of Pennsylvania. Roy. 8vo. Philad., 1893. K 7 U 3
Catalogue of the Russian Section. Roy. 8vo. St. Petersburg, 1893. K 8 R 20
Catalogue of the World's Columbian Exposition, 1893. Roy. 8vo. Sydney, 1893. MK 1 S 34
Christianity Practically Applied. The Discussions of the International Christian Conference held at Chicago, 1893. 8vo. New York, 1894. G G T 28
Classification of the World's Columbian Exposition, Chicago, 1893. 8vo. Chicago, 1891. K 7 S 39
Details of Industrial Specimens exposed at the World's Columbian Exposition by Japan. 8vo. Tokyo, 1893. K 7 T 2
Details of the Weights and Measures by the Bureau of Commerce, Japan. 8vo. Tokyo, 1893. A 23 S 23
Engineering Education; being the Proceedings of Section E of the World's Engineering Congress. 8vo. Columbia, 1894. G 18 R 60
Explanatory Notes on the Exhibits [Astronomical—Japan.] 8vo. Tokio, 1893. A 19 T 33
Exposition Internationale de Chicago. Section Française: Catalogue Officiel. (French and English.) Roy. 8vo. Paris, 1893. K 7 U 2
General Regulations, with Classification of Exhibits, Customs Regulations, &c., also copy of New South Wales Commission. Roy. 8vo. Sydney, 1891. MK 1 S 13
History of the World's Columbian Exposition. [See Cameron, Hon. W. E.] B G 8 5
Hospitals, Dispensaries, and Nursing: Papers and Discussions in the International Congress of Charities, Correction, and Philanthropy. Roy. 8vo. Baltimore, 1894. A 33 U 13
New York and the World's Fair. 8vo. Chicago, 1892. J 2 8 7
Official Catalogue. 8vo. Chicago, 1893. K 7 R 59
Official Catalogue: Exhibition of the German Empire. Roy. 8vo. Leipzig, 1893. K 7 U 5
Official Catalogue issued by the Royal Danish Commission. 8vo. Copenhagen, 1893. K 7 U 32
Official Catalogue of the British Section. 12mo. Lond., 1893. K 7 P 1
Official Catalogue of the British Section. 2nd ed. 8vo. Lond., 1893. K 7 R 54
Official Manual and Minutes of the World's Columbian Commission, 1st–8th Sessions. 2 vols. 8vo. Chicago, 1892–93. K 7 U 21, 22
Proceedings of the International Conference on Aerial Navigation, held in Chicago, August, 1893. 8vo. New York, 1894. A 22 T 9
Proceedings of the International Engineering Congress Division of Marine and Naval Engineering and Naval Architecture. Edited by G. W. Melville. 2 vols. 8vo. New York, 1894. A 22 T 16, 17

CHICAGO EXHIBITION, 1893—*contd.*
Report of the Executive Commissioner for New South Wales. Roy. 8vo. Sydney, 1894. MK 2 R 1
Report of the President of the New South Wales Commission. Fol. Sydney, 1894. MK 3 P 23 †
Some Artists at the Fair: F. D. Millet, W. H. Low, J. A. Mitchell, W. H. Gibson, F. H. Smith. 8vo. New York, 1893. A 23 U 21
The Sunday Problem: its present day aspect, Physiological, Industrial, Social, Political, and Religious— Papers presented at the Congress on Sunday Rest. Chicago, 1893. 8vo. New York, 1893. G 17 Q 49
Trabajos Escolares. 8vo. Buenos Aires, 1893. G 18 R 3
Verzeichniss der in Deutschland erschienenen wissenschaftlichen zeitschriften für die Universitäts-Ausstellung in Chicago, 1893. Roy. 8vo. Berlin, 1893. K 11 R 12
World's Congress of Bankers and Financiers. Roy. 8vo. Chicago, 1893. F 2 T 16
World's Fair Appropriations. 8vo. Chicago, 1893. K 7 T 1
World's Fair Expenditure: United States Report. 8vo. Wash., 1892. K 7 T 7
World's Fair Photographed. [*See* Shepp, J. W. and D. B.] B 15 V 17

CHICHELE or CHICHELEY, Henry, Archbishop of Canterbury. Sketch of. [*See* Fowler, Rev. M.— Notable Archbishops.] C 13 V 12

CHICO STATE NORMAL SCHOOL, California. Catalogue and Circular for year ending June 30, 1893. 8vo. Sacramento, 1893. E

CHILD, Prof. Francis James. English and Scottish Popular Ballads. Parts 5-8. 3 vols. imp. 8vo. Boston, 1888-94. H 1 Y 16-18

CHILD, Jacob T. The Pearl of Asia: Reminiscences of the Court of a Supreme Monarch; or, Five Years in Siam. 8vo. Chicago, 1892. D 17 V 7

CHILD, Lydia Maria. Fact and Fiction: a Collection of Stories. Roy. 8vo. (n.p., n.d.) J 4 U 2

CHILI. Acontecimientos en Chile, 1891. Roy. 8vo. Valparaiso (n.d.) B 17 U 14
Acusacion a los ex-Ministros del Despacho. Roy. 8vo. Santiago, 1893. F 11 V 8
Anuario de la Prensa Chilena, 1886-91. 6 vols. 8vo. Santiago, 1887-92. E
Biblioteca Nacional. Catalogo de los Manuscritos relativos a los antiguos Jesuitas de Chile. Roy 8vo. Santiago, 1891. K 7 U 11
Boletin de las Sesiones Especiales en 1893. Imp. 8vo. Santiago, 1893. E
Constitución Politica de la República de Chile. 8vo. Santiago, 1893. F 9 R 35
Cuenta Jeneral de las Entradas y Gastos Fiscales de la Republica de Chile, 1891. 3 vols. roy. 8vo. Santiago, 1893-94. E

CHILI—*contd.*
Disposiciones Vigentes en Chile sobre Policia Sanitaria y Beneficencia Pública. 8vo. Santiago, 1889. F 14 U 21
Documentos de la Cuenta Jeneral de Entradas y Gastos. 1891. 2 parts (in 1.) Fol. Santiago, 1893. E
Estadistica Comercial de la Republica de Chile, 1893. Roy. 8vo. Valparaiso, 1895. E
Fomento de la Industria Salitrera. 8vo. Santiago, 1889. F 9 T 30
Lei de Organizacion i Atribuciones de los Tribunales. Roy. 8vo. Santiago, 1875. F 3 V 13
Memoria del Superintendente de Aduanas, 1893. 8vo. Santiago, 1893. E
Ministro del Interior. Recopilación de Leyes y Decretos de Interés General, vigentes en 21 de Mayo, 1888. 8vo. Santiago, 1888. E
Sinopsis Estadistica de Chile, 1876-92. 8 parts (in 1.) 8vo. Santiago, 1877-93. E

CHILTON-YOUNG, F. [*See* Young, F. C.-]

CHINIQUY, Rev. Chas. A series of Lectures delivered by, in the Protestant Hall, Sydney. 2nd ed. 8vo. Sydney, 1878. MG 2 Q 26
The Chiniquy Lectures. 35th thousand. 8vo. Melb., 1870. MG 1 R 66
Papal Idolatry. 8vo. Sydney, 1879. MG 2 S 2
The Perversion of Dr. Newman to the Church of Rome. 8vo. Melb. (n.d.) MG 2 Q 26
[*See* Hobart Town Riots.] MG 1 S 25

CHINNER, G. F. 'Twixt Shadow and Shine: a Volume of Poems. 12mo. Adelaide, 1890. MH 1 P 52

CHINNOCK, Rev. E. J. Arrian's Anabasis of Alexander. [*See* Arrian, F.] B 14 P 36

CHIPIEZ Charles. History of Art in Primitive Greece. [*See* Perrot, Prof. G.] A 22 T 16, 17

CHIPS; by "An Old Chum"; or, Australia in the Fifties. 8vo. Lond. (n.d.) MJ 3 P 39

CHISHOLM, James. Medical Hand-book of Life Assurance. [*See* Pollock, Dr. J. E.] A 33 S 6

CHITTY, Joseph. The Practice respecting Amendments of Variances, pending a Trial at *Nisi Prius* or before a Sheriff; and observations upon the necessity for extending liberality in such amendments, or for alterations in allowing several Counts, Pleas, &c. 8vo. Lond. 1835. F 2 V 16

CHOPIN, Frederic François. [Life of]; by C. Willeby. 8vo. Lond., 1892. C 12 Q 49
Sketch of. [*See* Heine, H.—Heine in Art and Letters.] J 11 T 39
Studies in Modern Music. [*See* Hadow, W. H.] C 21 Q 15

CHRIST CHURCH, GEELONG. Historical Sketch of. 8vo. Geelong, 1855. MG 2 Q 27

CHRISTIE, Thos. North. Cinchona Cultivation. 8vo. Colombo, 1883. A 18 S 38

CHRISTISON, J. Breeding and Rearing of Horses. (Proc. Roy. Agricult. Soc. of S. Australia, 1885.) 8vo. Adelaide, 1885. ME 1 S

CHRIST'S COLLEGE LIBRARY. Catalogue, Pt. 1. Sm. 4to. Hobart, 1848. MK 1 P 16

CHRISTY, F. C. Improvement of the Water Communication between Melbourne and Hobson's Bay. 8vo. Melb., 1879. MA 1 V 43

CHRISTY, M. Voyages of Capt. L. Foxe and Capt. T. James in search of a North-west Passage, in 1631–32. (Hakluyt Soc., 88, 89.) 2 vols. 8vo. Lond., 1894. E

CHRONICLES AND MEMORIALS OF GREAT BRITAIN AND IRELAND. [See Great Britain and Ireland.—Chronicles and Memorials.]

CHUBB, P. Select Writings of R. W. Emerson. [See Emerson, R. W.] J 12 S 36

CHURCH, Prof. Arthur Herbert. English Earthenware. 8vo. Lond, 1884. A 23 R 20

English Porcelain. 8vo. Lond., 1885. A 23 R 9

Food: some Account of its Sources, Constituents, and Uses. 8vo. Lond., 1876. A 26 R 16

Josiah Wedgwood. (Portfolio Monograph, 3.) Roy. 8vo. Lond., 1894. E

Precious Stones, considered in their scientific and artistic relations. 8vo. Lond., 1883. A 23 R 31

CHURCH, E. M. Sir Richard Church in Italy and Greece. 8vo. Edinb., 1895. C 10 T 46

CHURCH, Gen. Sir Richard, in Italy and Greece; by E. M. Church. 8vo. Edinb., 1895. C 10 T 46

CHURCH, Very Rev. Richard Wm. Life and Letters of. Edited by his daughter. 8vo. Lond., 1894. C 16 U 4

CHURCH, S. H. Oliver Cromwell: a History. 8vo. New York, 1894. C 16 U 9

CHURCH OF ENGLAND. Diocese of Christchurch. Proceedings of the First Session of the Ninth Synod, 1875. 8vo. Christchurch 1875. ME 6 Q

Diocese of Melbourne. Acts of the Assembly, to which are prefixed the Church Constitution Acts, the Trusts Corporation Act, &c. 8vo. Melb., 1888. MF 2 R 53

Statistics of, 1889. 8vo. Melb., 1890. ME 6 Q

Diocese of Newcastle. Ordinances, Rules, and Resolutions of the Synod, 1880. 8vo. Sydney, 1880. MF 2 Q 46

CHURCH OF ENGLAND—contd.

Diocese of Sydney. Proceedings of the Synod, for filling up the Vacancy of the See, 1882. 8vo. Sydney, 1883. ME 6 Q

Papers read at the Conference, 1885. 8vo. Sydney, 1885. MG 1 S 73

Report of the Church Society for 1892. 8vo. Sydney, 1893. ME 6 Q

Diocese of Tasmania. Digest of Acts and Resolutions passed in the Synod. 8vo. Hobart, 1876.* MF 2 Q 55

Another copy. 8vo. Hobart, 1883. ME 6 Q

Report of the Church Society, 1880. 8vo. Hobart, 1881. ME 6 Q

Official Record of the Proceedings of the Synod, 1883. 8vo. Hobart, 1884. MF 2 Q 56

Year-book of the Church of England in Tasmania, for 1892-93. 2 vols. 8vo. Hobart, 1892-93. ME 6 Q

General Conference and Synod of the Dioceses of Australia and Tasmania, 1872. 12mo. Sydney, 1872. ME 6 Q

CHURCH OF ENGLAND GRAMMAR SCHOOL, MELBOURNE. Liber Melburniensis: the Book of the Church of England Grammar School, Melbourne, its History, Register, and various Memoranda. 8vo. Melb., 1879. MB 2 R 46

CHURCH OF ROME. Second Provincial Council of Australia, 1869. Proceedings. 8vo. Melb., 1869. MG 1 T 31

CHURCH PARTIES: an Essay. 12mo. Lond., 1854. G 4 V 14

CHURCH SENTINEL, The. Vol. 1, 1858-59. Sm. 4to. Sydney, 1858-59. ME 20 S

CHURCHILL, John. [See Marlborough, Duke of.]

CHURCHILL, Lord Randolph. Randolph Spencer Churchill as a Product of his Age: being a Personal and Political Monograph by T. H. S. Escott. 8vo. Lond., 1895. C 19 V 11

Sketch of. [See Smalley, G. W.—Studies of Men.] C 19 R 20

CHURCHMAN'S AUSTRALIAN ALMANAC, 1886. Sm. 4to. Sydney, 1886. ME 4 R

CIBBER, Colley. A Careless Husband: a Comedy. [See London Stage, 3.] H 2 S 35

Love makes a Man; or, the Fop's Fortune: a Comedy. [See London Stage, 3.] H 2 S 35

She would and she would not; or, the Kind Impostor: a Comedy. [See London Stage, 3.] H 2 S 35

The Provoked Husband: a Comedy. [See London Stage, 2.] H 2 S 34

CICERO, Marcus Tullius. Select Letters; with English Introductions, Notes, and Appendices, by A. Watson. (Clar. Press.) 4th ed. 8vo. Oxford, 1891.
C 14 U 24
Speech of, in defence of Cluentius. Translated into English, with an Introduction and Notes, by W. Peterson. 8vo. Lond., 1895. J 9 S 21
Cicero and the Fall of the Roman Republic; by J. L. Strachan-Davidson. 8vo. New York, 1894.
C 16 R 22

CINCINNATI PUBLIC LIBRARY. Bulletin of Books in the various departments of Literature and Science added during 1892 and 1893. 2 vols. imp. 8vo. Cincinnati, 1893-94. Libr.

CIRCOLO ENOFILO ITALIANO. Annuario Generale per la Viticoltura e la Enologia, 1892, 1893. 2 vols. 8vo. Roma, 1892-93. A 30 T 21, 22

CIRCOURT, Mme. de. Correspondence with Cavour. [See Cavour, Conte.] C 14 V 15

CITY NIGHT REFUGE AND SOUP KITCHEN. 20th Report of. 8vo. Sydney, 1887. ME 6 S

CIVIL ENGINEERS, AMERICAN SOCIETY OF. [See American Society of Civil Engineers.]

CIVIL ENGINEERS, INSTITUTION OF. [See Institution of Civil Engineers.]

CIVIL SERVICE. Political Influences, &c.; by "Corvus." Complete ed., with Map. 8vo. Sydney, 1883.
MF 4 R 44

CLAFLIN, Horace B. Sketch of. [See Stoddard, W. O. —Men of Business.] C 16 R 10

CLAMPITT, John W. Echoes from the Rocky Mountains. Illustrated. Roy. 8vo. Lond., 1888. B 17 U 17

CLANCY, Jas. J. The "Castilo" System, and its Operation. [See Subjects of the Day, 3] F 7 U 28

CLAPIN, Adolphus P., and ARNOLD, Richard A. New South Wales Parliamentary Hand-book. 5th ed. 8vo. Sydney, 1894. MF 2 T 52

CLARE, George. The ABC of the Foreign Exchanges. 8vo. Lond., 1893. F 14 Q 10

CLARENCE AND AVONDALE, H.R.H. Duke of: a Memoir; by J. E. Vincent. 12mo. Lond., 1893.
C 10 Q 8

CLARENCE AND NEW ENGLAND S. N. CO. Deed of Settlement and Act of Incorporation of. 8vo. Grafton, 1866. MF 1 R 48

CLARK, Chas. Heber. Out of the Hurly-Burly; or, Life in an Odd Corner; by "Max Adeler." 12mo. Lond. (n.d.) J 12 T 3

CLARK, Charles H. Practical Methods in Microscopy. 12mo. Boston, 1894. A 20 R 22

CLARK, Daniel Kinnear. Manual of Rules, Tables, and Data for Mechanical Engineers, based on the most recent investigations. 6th edition. 8vo. Lond., 1891. A 6 U 23

The Steam Engine: a Treatise on Steam Engines and Boilers. Illustrated. 2 vols. roy. 8vo. Lond., 1890.
A 22 T 20, 21

CLARK, Henry Jas. Iëre, the Land of the Humming Bird; being a Sketch of the Island of Trinidad. 8vo. Trinidad, 1893. D 15 R 14

CLARK, J. H. Field Sports of New South Wales Natives. 4to. Lond., 1813. MA 10 P 8 †

CLARK, J. W. Libraries in the Medieval and Renaissance Periods. (The Rede Lecture, 1894.) 12mo. Cambridge, 1894. J 6 P 24

CLARK, John B., and GIDDINGS, Franklin H. The Modern Distributive Process: Studies of Competition and its Limits, of the Nature and Amount of Profits, and of the Determination of Wages. 8vo. Boston, 1888. F 12 F 2

CLARK, Robt. Golf, a Royal and Ancient Game. 8vo. Lond., 1893. A 29 T 16

CLARK, Capt. Wm. Expedition to the Sources of the Missouri River, 1804-6. [See Coues, E.]
D 16 V 12-15
Sketch of. [See Greeley, Gen. A. W.—Explorers and Travellers.] C 17 R 4

CLARK, Wm. Geo. Review of a Pamphlet entitled "The Present Dangers of the Church of England." [See Religious Pamphlets, 1.] G 9 V 16

CLARK-RUSSELL, W. [See Russell, W. Clark-.]

CLARKE, A. W. On the Mineral Scolecite occurring on Granite, Charters Towers. (Proc. Roy. Soc., Queensland, 4.) 8vo. Brisbane, 1887 ME 1 T
Queensland Minerals. 8vo. Brisbane, 1886.
MA 2 V 63

CLARKE, Col. Alexander Ross. Geodesy. 8vo. Oxford, 1880. A 25 V 22

CLARKE, Alfred. Simple Treatise on Spectacles and Defective Vision. 8vo. Sydney, 1893. MA 2 S 66

CLARKE, Mary C. Instrumentation and Orchestration. [See Berlioz, H.] A 23 V 12

CLARKE, Rev. George. Objections to the Policy of Perpetuating State Aid to Religion in Tasmania. 8vo. Hobart, 1867. MG 1 S 8

CLARKE, Maj. Sir George S. Imperial Defence. [See Labilliere, F. P. De.] F 9 U 47

CLARKE, H. Butler. Spanish Literature: an Elementary Handbook. 8vo. Lond., 1893. B 34 Q 4

CLARKE, Rev. Henry Wm. History of Tithes. 2nd ed. 12mo. Lond., 1894. F 8 U 10

CLARKE, Hyde. On the Yarra Dialect and the Language of Australia in connection with those of the Mozambique and Portuguese Africa. (Roy. Soc., Vict., 10.) 8vo. Melb., 1880. ME 1 P

CLARKE, J. Livingstone. The Bulli Disaster; the *Mignonette* Disaster; Loss of the *Dunbar*. Fol. Sydney (n.d.) MJ 2 P 30 ‡

CLARKE, J. R. Road Map of the Colonies of New South Wales and Queensland. Folded 12mo. (u.p.n.d.) MD 8 P 4

CLARKE, Marcus A. H. The Austral Edition of the Selected Works of, together with a Biography and Monograph of the Deceased Author. Compiled and Edited by H. Mackinnon. 8vo. Melb., 1890. MJ 2 S 14

Goody Two Shoes and Little Boy Blue; or, Sing a Song of Sixpence, Harlequin Hey-diddle-diddle-'em, and the Kingdom of Coins. 12mo. Melb., 1870. MH 1 P 71

'Twixt Shadow and Shine: an Australian Story. 8vo. Melb., 1875. MJ 1 S 12

The Future Australian Race. 8vo. Melb., 1877. MJ 2 S 18

Mystery of Major Molineux, and Human Repetends. 8vo. Melb., 1881. MJ 1 S 30

Twinkle Twinkle Little Star; or, Harlequin Jack Frost. [*See* Strachan, J.] MH 1 U 47

CLARKE, Percy. The Valley Council. 8vo. Lond., 1891. MJ 2 T 45

CLARKE, W. The Clarke Papers. Vol. 2. Edited by C. H. Firth. (Cam. Soc. Pubs.) Sm. 4to. Lond., 1894. E

CLARKE, Dr. W. B. Wreck of The *Favourite*. [*See* Nunn, J.] D 4 S 42

CLARKE, Wm. Water Supply for Sydney. [*See* Manning, J.] MA 2 V 48

CLARKE, Rev. Wm. B. The claims of. 8vo. Sydney, 1860. MA 2 V 55

CLARSON, Wm. The Fruit Garden: a Guide to the Planting and Managing in Victoria of the Chief Fruit-yielding Plants of Temperate Zones. Parts 1, 2. 3rd ed. 12mo. Melb. (n.d.) MA 3 P 48

The Flower Garden and Shrubbery. 5th ed. 12mo. Melb. (n.d.) MA 3 P 49

The Kitchen Garden and Cottagers' Manual. 5th ed. 12mo. Melb. (n.d.) MA 3 P 50

CLASSICAL REVIEW, The. Vols. 6-8. Imp. 8vo. Lond., 1882-94. E

CLAUSON-THUE, W. [*See* Thue, W. C.]

CLAY, Henry. Sketch of. [*See* Brooks, N.—Statesmen.] C 16 R 20

Plaster Cast of. [*See* Hutton, L.—Portraits in Plaster.] A 23 V 13

CLAYTON, Reginald. His Chinese Cook. [*See* Praed, Mrs. R. M.—Under the Gum Tree.] MJ 2 T 44

CLEAVE, A., & Co. Auckland City, Suburban, Provincial, Commercial, Municipal, and General Directory, 1889 and 1894. 2 vols. 8vo. Auckland, 1889-94. ME

New Zealand Bradshaw and A B C Commercial Guide and Trades Directory, 1894. 3 vols. 18mo. Auckland, 1894. ME 4 P

CLÉDAT, Prof. Léon. Role Historique de Bertrand de Born, 1175-1200. [*See* Bertrand de Born.] B 35 R 25

La Chanson de Roland. [*See* Chanson de Roland.] H 5 U 40

CLEGG, Thos. B. Manual of the Trade Disputes Conciliation and Arbitration Act, 1892. Roy. 8vo. Sydney, 1892. MF 1 S 41

CLEMENS, Samuel Langhorne. "Mark Twain." An Interview with; with Portrait. [*See* Blathwayt, R.—Interviews.] J 10 U 34

CLEMENT OF ALEXANDRIA. Writings of. Translated by Rev. W. Wilson. (Ante-Nicene Christ. Lib., 4, 12.) 2 vols. 8vo. Edinb., 1867-69. G 14 U 4, and 12

CLEMENT OF ROME. Recognitions of. Translated by Rev. Dr. T. Smith. (Ante-Nicene Christ. Lib., 3.) 8vo. Edinb., 1867. G 14 U 3

The Clementine Homilies. Translated by Rev. Dr. T. Smith, P. Peterson, and Dr. J. Donaldson. (Ante-Nicene Christ. Lib., 17.) 8vo. Edinb., 1870. G 14 U 17

CLEMENT, Clara Erskine. Naples, the City of Parthenope, and its Environs. Illustrated. 8vo. Lond., 1894. B 30 S 10

The Queen of the Adriatic; or, Venice, Mediæval and Modern. 8vo. London (n.d.) D 18 S 4

CLEOFAS. [*See* Bird in a Golden Cage.] MJ 3 P 8

CLERC, Michel. Les Méteques Athéniens: étude sur la Condition Légale, la Situation Morale, et le Rôle Social, et Economique des Etrangers domiciliés à Athènes. 8vo. Paris, 1893. F 1 R 9

CLERCQ, F. S. A. de. Het Eiland Wiak of Biak, benoorden de Geelvinkbaai. Roy. 8vo. Leiden, 1888. MD 3 V 4

De baai van Wandamèu in het zuidwesten der Geelvinkbaai. Roy. 8vo. (n.p.n.d.) MD 3 V 4

Langs de Zuidkust der Maccluer-golf. Roy. 8vo. (n.p.n.d.) MD 3 V 4

CLERGY, WIDOW, AND ORPHANS' FUND, Melbourne. Fourth Annual Report, 1869. 8vo. Melb., 1870. MG 2 Q 48

CLERK, Dugald. Theory of the Gas Engine. 12mo.
New York, 1891. A 22 P 31

CLERK, Sir John. Life of. [*See* Scottish History Soc., 13.] E

CLERKE, Miss Agnes Mary. The Herschels and Modern Astronomy. 12mo. Lond., 1895. A 19 Q 19

CLEVELAND, Chas. B. Mexico. [*See* Cubas, A. G.] F 14 U 13

CLEVELAND, Grover. Sketch of. [*See* Wilson, J. G — Presidents of the United States.] C 2 V 30
Sketch of. [*See* Brooks, N.—Statesmen.] C 16 R 20

CLIFFORD, Edward. Father Damien: a Journey from Cashmere to Hawaii. 12mo. Lond., 1890.
MC 1 S 10

CLINCH, George, and KERSHAW, S. W. Bygone Surrey. 8vo. Lond., 1895. B 21 T 10

CLIVE, Robert, Lord. Essay on; by Lord Macaulay. [*See* Macaulay, Lord.] MJ 3 P 21
Life of; by Col. G. B. Malleson. (Rulers of India.) 8vo. Oxford, 1893. C 13 P 16

CLOUD, T. C. Catalogue of South Australian Minerals. (Trans. Roy. Soc., S. Australia, 6.) 8vo. Adelaide, 1883. ME 1 S

CLOUD, Mrs. T. C. Drift: a volume of stray verse; by "Lindsay Duncan." 12mo. Adelaide, 1891.
MH 1 Q 34

CLOUGH, Albert L. What an Engineer should know about Electricity; also, the Rules and Requirements of the Underwriters' International Electric Association for the installation of Electric Light and Power. 12mo. Boston, 1894. A 21 P 37

CLOUGH, Arthur Hugh. Essay on. [*See* Bagehot, W.— Literary Studies.] J 9 P 22-24

CLOWES, Alice A. Charles Knight: a sketch. 8vo Lond., 1892. C 15 R 14

CLUTTERBUCK, Dr. Jas. Bennett. Essay on the Nature and Treatment of Australian Diseases, including more especially Dysentery and Fever. 8vo. Melb., 1868
MA 1 V 75

CLYDE, Colin Campbell, Lord. [Life of]; by A. Forbes 8vo. Lond., 1895. C 21 P 8

COATES, Dandeson. The New Zealanders and their Land: the Report of the Select Committee of the House of Commons on New Zealand considered in a letter to Lord Stanley. 3rd ed. 8vo. Lond., 1845.
MB 2 R 57
Coates and the New Zealand Association. [*See* Wakefield, E. G.] MB 2 R 57

COATS, Dr. Joseph. Manual of Pathology. 3rd ed. 8vo. Lond., 1895. A 26 T 22

COBB, James. The Doctor and the Apothecary: a Musical Entertainment. [*See* London Stage, 2.] H 2 S 34
The First Floor: a Farce. [*See* London Stage, 3.]
H 2 S 35
The Haunted Tower: a Comic Opera. [*See* London Stage, 2.] H 2 S 34
Paul and Virginia: a Musical Entertainment. [*See* London Stage, 4.] H 2 S 36
The Siege of Belgrade: a Comic Opera. [*See* London Stage, 4.] H 2 S 36

COBB, Dr. Nathan Augustus. Cold Storage for Apples from the Vegetable Pathologist's Point of View. 8vo. Sydney, 1892. MA 1 Q 32
Dialogue concerning the manner in which a Poisonous Spray does its work preventing Blight. 8vo. Sydney, 1892. MA 1 Q 37
Diseases of the Sugar-cane. Illustrated. 8vo. Sydney, 1893. MA 1 Q 37
Host and Habitat Index of the Australian Fungi. [*See* Cooke, M. C.] MA 1 R 50
Plant Diseases and how to prevent them. 8vo. Sydney, 1892. MA 1 Q 67

COBBE, Miss Frances Power. Life of; by herself. Illustrated. 2 vols. 8vo. Lond., 1894. C 14 S 20, 21

COBBETT, Wm. Sermons. 12mo. Lond., 1822.
G 9 V 14
1. Hypocrisy and Cruelty.
2. Drunkenness.
3. Bribery.
4. Oppression.
5. Unjust Judges.
6. The Sluggard.
7. Murder.
8. Gaming.
9. Public Robbery.
10. The Unnatural Mother.
11. Forbidding Marriage.
12. Parson's Tithes

Sketch of [Thomas] Paine. [*See* Conway, M.D.]
C 8 U 38

COBDEN, Richard. 1793-1853, in three letters. 8vo. Lond., 1853. F 14 T 41
An English Hero; by Frances E. Cooke. 12mo. Lond., 1890. C 21 P 1
Reminiscences of; by Mrs. S. Schwabe. 8vo. Lond., 1895. C 21 T 13
Sketch of. [*See* Bagehot, W.—Biographical Studies.]
C 22 P 10

COBDEN CLUB. Reports of Annual Meetings, 1884-85. 2 vols. 8vo. Lond., 1884-85. F 10 U 6
Annual Dinner. Special Report 1884-85. 2 vols. 8vo. Lond., 1884-85. F 10 U 6

COCHIN, Henri. Œuvres. 6 vols. 4to. Paris, 1771-80.
J 12 V 2-7†

COCKBURN, John. A Journey overland from the Gulf of Honduras to the great South Sea. 8vo. Lond., 1735. D 15 S 29

COCKBURN, Rev. Dr. John. History of Duels. [*See* Collectanea Adamantæa.] J 18 R 36

CODLIN, James. The Transported Smuggler. 12mo. Sydney, 1893.* MH 1 Q 35

CODMAN, John Thos. Brook Farm: Historical and Personal Memoirs. 8vo. Boston, 1894. F 8 U 38

CODRINGTON, Rev. Dr. Robt. Henry. Notes on the Customs of Mota, Banks Islands. (Roy. Soc., Vict., 16.) 8vo. Melb., 1880. ME 1 P
Lecture on the Melanesian Mission. 8vo. (n.p.) 1893. MG 2 S 4
The Melanesians: Studies in their Anthropology and Folk-lore. Illustrated. 8vo. Oxford, 1891. MD 8 R 19

COELLA, Francisco. Nota sobre los planos de las bahias descubiertas en el ano de 1606 an las islas del Espiritu Santo y de Nueva Guinea. (Boletin de la Sociedad Geografica de Madrid, 1878.) 8vo. Madrid, 1878. MD 7 U 20

COFFEY, C. The Devil to Pay: a Ballad Farce. [*See* London Stage, 1.] H 2 S 33

COFFEY, W. H., and ELLES, Herbert L. Supplement to the District Courts Acts, containing Notes of the Reported Cases, Rules, &c. 8vo. Sydney, 1893.* MF 2 Q 6

COGHLAN, Timothy Augustine. New South Wales Statistical Register, 1889-93. [*See* New South Wales.] ME 8 R
Results of a Census of New South Wales, taken on the 5th April, 1891. Sm. 4to. Sydney, 1894. ME
Report on the Census of New South Wales. [*See* New South Wales.] MF 3 U 54
Sheep and Wool in New South Wales. Roy. 8vo. Sydney, 1893. MA 1 P 54
Statistical Account of the Seven Colonies of Australasia. 8vo. Sydney, 1893. ME
Statistical Survey of New South Wales, 1893-94. 8vo. Sydney, 1895. MF 3 T 46
Vital Statistics, 1888. Annual Report from the Government Statistician. Fol. Sydney, 1890. ME
The Wealth and Progress of New South Wales, 1893 and 1894. 2 vols. 8vo. Sydney, 1893-95. ME 5 R

COGLEY, Thos. S. The Law of Strikes, Lockouts, and Labor Organizations. Roy. 8vo. Washington, 1894. F 2 T 17

COHAUSEN, John Henry. Hermippus Redivivus. [*See* Collectanea Adamantæa.] J 18 R 12-14

COHEN, Philip. The Marine Fish and Fisheries of New South Wales, past and present, in their commercial aspect. Roy. 8vo. Sydney, 1892. MA 2 U 41

COLBURN, George. Poems on Mankind and Nature. 8vo. Glasgow, 1891. H 9 U 25

COLE, E. W. Advice of Ten Doctors. Edited by E. W. Cole. 8vo. Melb., 1892. MA 2 P 42
Cyclopædia of Short Prize Essays on the Federation of the Whole World. First series. Edited by E. W. Cole. 8vo. Melb. (n.d.) MF 1 P 70

COLE, Prof. Grenville A. J. The Gypsy Road: a Journey from Krakow to Coblentz. Illustrated. 12mo. Lond., 1894. D 18 Q 10
Open-air Studies: an Introduction to Geology Out-of-doors. Illustrated. 8vo. Lond., 1895. A 24 R 16

COLE, H. S., and MORRIS, Thos. Health Act, Infant Life Protection Act, Margarine Act; with Regulations, Notes of English and Victorian Cases, and Index. 8vo. Melb., 1894. MF 3 T 26

COLE, Timothy, and STILLMAN, Wm. Jas. Old Italian Masters. Imp. 8vo. Lond., 1892. A 8 U 38

COLEBROOKE, Henry Thos. [Sketch of.] [*See* Müller, F. Max.—Chips from a German Workshop, 2.] J 9 R 32

COLEMAN, Edward. Tryal of, for Conspiring the Death of the King [Charles II]. [*See* Collectanea Adamantæa.] J 18 R 37

COLENSO, Rt. Rev. John Wm. Bishop Colenso's Criticisms answered. [*See* Morison, Rev. A.] MG 1 S 31
Moses and Colenso: ten Lectures. [*See* Ewing, Rev. R. K.] MG 2 R 43
Trial of. [*See* Wirgman, Rev. A. T.—Church of England in South Africa.] G 2 V 42

COLENSO, Rev. Wm. Notes and Reminiscences of Early Crossings of Lake Waikaremoana. (Trans. N. Z. Inst., 27.) 8vo. Wellington, 1894. ME 2 R
Phænogams. (Trans. N. Z. Inst., 27.) 8vo. Wellington, 1894. ME 2 R

COLERIDGE, E. P. Tragedies of Sophocles. [*See* Sophocles.] H 2 Q 50

COLERIDGE, Hartley. Essay on. [*See* Bagehot, W.—Literary Studies.] J 9 P 22
Sketch of. [*See* Bagehot, W.—Estimates of some Englishmen and Scotchmen.] J 10 V 32

COLERIDGE, Samuel Taylor. Dramatic Works of. 12mo. Lond., 1852. H 1 Q 43
The Golden Book of Coleridge. 12mo. Lond., 1895. H 10 U 15
Anima Poetæ. Edited by Ernest Hartley Coleridge. 8vo. Lond., 1895. J 10 R 26
Confessions of an Inquiring Spirit. 18mo. Lond., 1886. J 7 P 47
The Rime of the Ancient Mariner. Illustrated. 8vo. Lond., 1857. H 9 Q 10
A Sailor's Fortune. 18mo. Lond., 1886. J 7 P 47
Coleridge as a Poet. [*See* Dowden, Dr. E.] J 5 S 16
Coleridge's Criticism, &c. [*See* Wylie, Laura J.—Evolution of English Criticism.] J 9 S 8

COLERIDGE, Samuel Taylor—*contd.*
Letters of. Edited by E. H. Coleridge. 2 vols. 8vo.
Lond., 1895. J 6 U 39, 40
Narrative of the Events of his L fe; by J. D. Campbell.
8vo. Lond., 1894. C 19 R 10
[Plaster Cast of.] [*See* Hutton, L.—Portraits in Plaster.]
A 23 V 13
Sketch of [*See* Bell, Rev. Dr C. D.—Some of our
English Poets.] C 21 P 11
Sketch of the Work of. [*See* Dawson, W. J.—Makers
of Modern English.] H 10 S 14
Spiritual Philosophy. [*See* Green, J. H.]
G 14 Q 25, 26

COLLECTANEA ADAMANTÆA. 30 vols. 12mo.
Edinb., 1884-88. J 18 R 1-30
Ancient Popular Poetry.
Charitable Remonstrance to the Wives and Maidens of
France touching their dissolute adornments; by Antoine Esteenne.
The Chronicles of London, Henry III to Edward III.
Collection of Epitaphs and Inscriptions.
Conspiracy against James I, commonly called the Gunpowder Treason.
Cottoni Posthuma : divers choice pieces of Sir W. Cotton.
The Devils of Loudun and the Execution of U. Grandier.
An Essay on Gaming; by Jeremy Collier.
The Field of Bloud.
Hermippus Redivivus; by J. H. Cohausen.
Historical Documents illustrative of the Reigns of the Tudors and Stuarts.
History of Amulets; by M. P Blumler.
History of Duels; by the Rev Dr. J. Cockburn.
History of Manon Lescaut and the Chevalier des Grieur;
by the Abbé Prevost.
History of the States-General of Normandy; by A. Canel.
Horrid Conspiracy to assassinate Charles II at the Ryehouse.
Kempes Nine Daies Wonder.
Lucina sine Concubitu; by the Rev. H. Coventry.
Memoirs of Robert Dudley, Earl of Leicester.
Memoirs of the Bastile; from the French of Mr. Linguet.
Papers relating to the first settlement of New York by the Dutch, 1657.
Pathomachia; or, the Battell of Affections.
Quaint Gleanings from Ancient Poetry.
Rare Tracts relating to the state of New York, 1609-15.
The Recovery of Normandy from the English in 1449; by J. le Bouvier.
Secret Correspondence of Sir Robert Cecil with James VI.
The Siege of Lyons.
Tryal of E. Coleman for conspiring the death of the King [Charles II].
Unnatural History of Myths of Ancient Science.
Works of Anacreon and Sappho : by the Earl of Winchelsea.

COLLIE, Prof. George L. The Geology of Conanicut
Island. Roy. 8vo. Beloit, Wis., 1895. A 25 V 2

COLLIER, Adm. Sir George. France, Holland, and the
Netherlands a century ago. 8vo. Lond., 1865.
B 25 S 21

COLLIER, Jeremy. Essay on Gaming. [*See* Collectanea
Adamantæa.] J 18 R 16

COLLIGNON, Maxime. Catalogue des Vases, Peints, au
Musée de la Société Archéologique d'Athènes. 8vo.
Paris, 1877. K 7 T 4
Essai sur les Monuments Grecs et Romains relatifs au
Mythe de Psyché. 8vo. Paris, 1877. B 35 R 18

COLLING, James Kellaway. Art Foliage, for Sculpture
and Decoration. 2nd ed. 4to. Lond., 1878.
A 39 Q 14 ‡
Examples of English Mediæval Foliage and Coloured
Decoration. Illustrated. 4to. Lond., 1874.
A 39 Q 15 ‡

COLLINGRIDGE, George. The Discovery of Australia :
a critical, documentary, and historic investigation
concerning the priority of discovery in Australasia by
Europeans before the arrival of Lieut. James Cook, in
the *Endeavour*, in 177C. 4to. Sydney, 1895.
MD 9 P 5 †
The Fantastic Islands of the Indian Ocean and of
Australasia in the Middle Ages, and their significance
in connection with the early Cartography of Australia.
(Roy. Geog. Soc. Australasia, Vic. Branch, 11.) 8vo.
Melb., 1894. ME 2 Q

COLLINGS, George. Roof Carpentry : Practical Lessons
in the Framing of Wood Roofs. (Weale's series.)
12mo. Lond., 1893. A 17 R 27

COLLINGWOOD, Wm. G. Life and Work of John
Ruskin. 2 vols. 8vo. Lond., 1893. C 11 P 20, 21
Poems of Ruskin. [*See* Ruskin, J.] H 5 V 31, 32

COLLINS, A Keith. Lecture on New Guinea. 8vo.
Sydney, 1867. MD 3 S 46

COLLINS, F. Howard. An Epitome of the Synthetic
Philosophy. 2nd ed. 8vo. Lond., 1890. G 16 S 52

COLLINS, John. Portrait of. [*See* Gammage, R. G.—
Chart st Movement.] F 7 R 24

COLLINS, John Churton. Jonathan Swift : a Biographical and Critical Study. 8vo. Lond., 1893.
C 13 P 22

COLLINS, Wm. Poetical Works of; with Life of the
Author and Critical Observations by Dr. Langhorne.
18mo. Lond., 1815. H 10 U 7
Poetical Works of. 12mo. Lond., 1827. H 7 U 35
Poetical Works of. 18mo. Lond., 1839. H 10 T 28

COLLINS, Rev. Wm. Lucas. Butler, Philosopher. [*See*
Butler, J.] G 9 V 2

COLLINS, Wm. Wilkie. Anecdotes of. [*See* Fitzgerald, P.
—Memoirs.] C 21 R 15

COLLINS-STREET INDEPENDENT CHURCH,
Melbourne. Manual of. 12mo. Melb., 1888.
MG 2 R 25

COLLINSON, John. Rainmaking and Sunshine. 8vo.
Lond , 1894. A 19 Q 30

COLMAN, George. Broad Grins. 8vo. Lond. (n.d.)
H 9 Q 12
Clandestine Marriage : a Comedy. [*See* London Stage, 1.]
H 2 S 33
The Deuce is in him : a Farce. [*See* London Stage, 3.]
H 2 S 33
The Jealous Wife : a Comedy. [*See* London Stage, 1.]
H 2 S 33
Polly Honeycombe : a Dramatic Novel. [*See* London
Stage, 2.] H 2 S 34

COLMAN, George, Junior. Ways and Means: a Comedy.
[*See* London Stage, 3.] H 2 S 35

COLNETT, Capt. James. Plan of the Island Cocos, 1793.
Fol. Lond., 1798. MD 1 P 15 ‡
Chart of the Galapagos, 1793-94. Fol. Lond., 1798.
MD 1 P 15 ‡
Plan of the Islands Felix and Ambrose, 1793. Fol.
Lond., 1798. MD 1 P 15 ‡
Plan of the Islands of Revillagigedo. Fol. Lond.,
1798. MD 1 P 15 ‡

COLOMB, Vice-Adm. Philip Howard. Essays on Naval
Defence. 8vo. Lond., 1893. A 29 Q 30
[*See* Great War of 189-.] J 2 Q 21

COLOMBO MUSEUM. 1st Reports. 8vo. Colombo
(n.d.) A 29 T 31
1. Collection of Lizards.
2. Collection of Batrachia.
3. Collection of Snakes.
4. Collection of Moths.
5. Coins, and List of Minerals.

COLONIAL AND AUSTRALIAN BANKING COMPANIES. Copies of the Charters granted. Sm. fol.
Lond., 1898. MF 3 U 7

COLONIAL CHURCH ATLAS, arranged in Dioceses.
4to. Lond, 1845. G 15 Q 19 †

COLONIAL MILITARY GAZETTE. Vols. 6, 7, 1892-
94. Sm. fol. Sydney, 1892-94. ME 10 T

COLONIAL OFFICE LIST. [*See* Great Britain and
Ireland—Colonial office.]

COLONIAL SUGAR REFINING CO. OF SYDNEY.
Reply to a pamphlet published by, entitled, "Remarks
on the Bill to authorise the Establishment of Bonded
Distilleries and Bonded Sugar Houses." 8vo. Sydney,
1862. MF 4 Q 35

COLORADO.—*State Departments, Reports and Publications.*
ADJUTANT-GENERAL. Report, 1891-92. 8vo. Denver,
1893. E
AGRICULTURAL COLLEGE. Course of Study and Work.
8vo. Fort Collins, 1893. E
Report of Agricultural Experiment Station, 1889. 8vo.
Fort Collins, 1889. E
AGRICULTURAL DEPARTMENT. The Resources, Wealth,
and Industrial Development of Colorado. 8vo.
(n.p.) 1893. D 15 T 20
AUDITOR. Report, 1891-92. 8vo. Colorado Springs,
1892. E
BOARD OF CHARITIES AND CORRECTIONS. Report, 1892.
8vo. Denver, 1893. E
BUREAU OF LABOR STATISTICS. Laws of the State of
Colorado relating to Labor. 8vo. Denver, 1893.
F 14 T 16
ENGINEER. Irrigation Laws and Instructions to Superintendents and Water Commissioners, Colorado.
8vo. Denver, 1893. F 14 T 16

COLORADO—*contd.*
FISH COMMISSION. Game and Fish Laws as amended
by the 9th Session of the General Assembly of the
State of Colorado. 8vo. Denver, 1893. F 14 T 16
GENERAL ASSEMBLY. School Law of the State of. 8vo.
Denver, 1893. G 18 R 12
INSTITUTION FOR THE EDUCATION OF THE DEAF AND
THE BLIND. Proceedings of the 7th National Conference of Superintendents and Principals of Institutions for the Deaf, held at Colorado Institution,
August 7th to 11th, 1892. 8vo. Colorado Springs,
1893. E
Report, 1892. 8vo. Colorado Springs, 1893. E
NORMAL SCHOOL. Annual Catalogue, 1892-1893. 8vo.
Denver, 1893. E
PENITENTIARY. Report, 1892. 8vo. Denver, 1893. E
REFORMATORY. Report, 1892. 8vo. Denver, 1893. E
SCHOOL OF MINES. Catalogue, 1892-93. 8vo. Denver,
1892. E
SECRETARY OF STATE. Report, 1891-92. 8vo. Colorado
Springs, 1893. E
SUPERINTENDENT OF INSURANCE. Report, 1892. 8vo.
Denver, 1893. E
Colorado Insurance Laws. Conditions of Admission
to Colorado for all Companies other than Cooperative or Assessment Life and Casualty. 8vo.
Denver, 1893. E
TREASURER. Report, 1891-92. 8vo. Colorado Springs,
1892. E

COLORADO UNIVERSITY. Summer Bulletin, 1893.
8vo. Denver, 1893. E

COLQUHOUN, Archibald Ross. Matabeleland. [*See*
Roy. Col. Inst., Proc., 25.] E

COLSON, C. Notes on Docks and Dock Construction.
Roy. 8vo. Lond., 1894. A 22 S 32

COLUMBA, St. Vita. [*See* Adamnan.] G 2 U 1

COLUMBAN, St. Life of St. Columban in France. [*See*
Stokes, Margaret.] G 3 R 15

COLUMBIA COLLEGE, NEW YORK. Historical
Sketch and Present Condition. 8vo. New York,
1893. B 20 S 5

COLUMBUS, Christopher. First Letter to Raphael
Sanchez announcing the Discovery of America, facsimile from the copy of the Latin version of 1493 now
in the Boston Public Library; with a new translation.
Fol. Boston, 1891. B 39 P 15 ‡
The Latin Letter of Columbus, printed in 1493, and
announcing the Discovery of America. Reproduced
in fac-simile. Sm. 4to. Lond., 1893. D 15 S 12
The Spanish Letter of Columbus to Luis de Sant' Angel,
dated 15 February, 1493. Reprinted in reduced facsimile, and translated. Sm. 4to. Lond., 1893.
D 15 S 12

COLUMBUS, Christopher—*contd.*
Columbus and his Discovery of America; by H. B. Adams and H. Wood. (Johns Hopkins Univ. Studies, vol. 10.) 8vo. Baltimore, 1892. B 18 S 10
Life and Times of; by A. M. L. P. de Lamartine. [*See* Bibliotheca Curiosa.] J 13 Q 48
Life of; by C. R. Markham 8vo. Lond., 1892. C 13 P 20
Story of the Life of; by F. Candall. [*See* Journal, Inst. of Jamaica, Vol. 2, No. 1.] E 1, 16
Journal of. [*See* Hakluyt Soc., 86.] E
[*See* Isabella I, Queen of Spain.] C 14 S 25
[*See* Ramusio, G. B.—Navigationi et Viaggi.] D 36 T 5-7 ‡

COLVILE, Zélie. Round the Black Man's Garden. 8vo. Edinb., 1893. D 14 S 12

COLVILLE, Col. Sir Henry The Land of the Nile Springs: being chiefly an recount of how we fought Kabarega. 8vo. Lond., 1895. D 14 S 21

COLVIN, Sir Auckland. John Russell Colvin, the last Lieutenant-Governor of the North-west under the Company. 8vo. Oxford 1895. C 21 P 7

COLYMBIA. 12mo. Lond., 1873. MJ 3 Q 26

COMAN, Prof. Katharine, and KENDALL, Elizabeth. The Growth of the English Nation. 8vo. New York, 1894. B 23 S 12

COMBE, Dr. Andrew. Management of Infancy. 8th ed., with Appendix by Dr. J. Coxe. 8vo. Edinb., 1854. A 26 R 20

COMBE, George. Moral Philosophy; or, the Duties of Man. 8vo. Edinb., 1841. G 15 T 24

COMBES, Edward. Report on Technical Education and Manual Training at the Paris Exhibition, 1889, and in Great Britain, France, and the United States. Fol. Sydney, 1891. MG 7 Q 10 †

COMICAL CRICKET in Rhyme and Picture: by "Catch-a-Catch." Obl. 18mo. Melb. (n.d.) MH 1 U 48

COMMENTATORS AND HIEROPHANTS; or, the Honesty of Christian Biblical Interpreters. [*See* Religious Pamphlets, 3.] G 9 V 18

COMMERCIAL BANK OF AUSTRALIA, LTD., Melbourne. Opinions of the City and Country Press. 8vo. Melb., 1866. MF 1 Q 56

COMMODIANUS. Works of. [*See* Tertullianus, Q. S. F.] G 14 U 11-18

COMMONS, John R. Higher Education in Ohio. [*See* Knight, Dr. G. W.] G 18 R 15

COMPARETTI, Domenico. Vergil in the Middle Ages. Translated by E. F. M. Benecke. 8vo. Lond., 1895. J 12 R 3

COMPAYRÉ, Gabriel. Abelard and the Origin and Early History of Universities. 8vo. Lond., 1893. G 18 Q 6

COMPLETE EAST INDIA PILOT, or Oriental Navigator: being a Collection of Charts of the Indian and China Seas, New Holland, the British Isles, and the Cape of Good Hope. 2 vols. fol. Lond., 1799. D 8 P 27, 28 ‡

COMPTON, Herbert. A Particular Account of the European Military Adventures in Hindustan, 178.— 1803. 8vo. Lond., 1893. C 16 R 15

COMSTOCK, Anna B. Manual for Study of Insects. [*See* Comstock, J. H.] A 15 Q 22

COMSTOCK, John Henry. Report upon Cotton Insects. 8vo. Wash., 1879. A 30 U 8

—— and Anna B. Manual for the Study of Insects. Roy. 8vo. Ithaca, N.Y., 1895. A 15 Q 22

COMTE, Auguste. Comte, Mill, and Spencer. [*See* Watson, Dr. J.] G 2 U 14

CONDELL, Claude F. New South Wales. 12mo. (n.p.n d.) MB 1 P 47

CONDER, Edward, jun. Records of the Holy Crafte and Fellowship of Masons; with a Chronicle of the History of the Worshipful Company of Masons of the City of London. Roy. 8vo. Lond., 1894. B 36 U 10

CONGREVE, Wm. The Double Dealer: a Comedy. [*See* London Stage, 4.] H 2 S 36
Love for Love: a Comedy. [*See* London Stage, 3.] H 2 S 35
The Mourning Bride: a Tragedy. [*See* London Stage, 4.] H 2 S 36
The Way of the World: a Comedy. [*See* London Stage, 4.] H 2 S 36

CONIGRAVE, J. Fairfax. The City of Adelaide: Historical Sketch of the Municipality, &c. 8vo. Adelaide, 1871. MB 2 R 51

CONKLING, A. R. City Government in the United States. 12mo. New York, 1894. F 7 V 20

CONN, H. W. Milk Fermentations and their Relations to Dairying. 8vo. Sydney, 1892. MA 1 Q 08

CONNECTICUT.—*State Departments, Reports, and Publications.*
AGRICULTURAL EXPERIMENT STATION. Report, 1879-94. 16 vols. 8vo. New Haven, 1880-95. E
BOARD OF AGRICULTURE. Reports, 1879-94. 16 vols. 8vo. Hartford, 1880-95. E
BOARD OF EDUCATION. School Document, No. 9. Catalogue of Connecticut Educational Exhibit [Chicago Exhibition.] 8vo. (n.p.) 1893. G 18 S 16
NORMAL TRAINING SCHOOL. Catalogue of, 1892, 1893. 8vo. Hartford, 1893. E
Work in Model Schools, First District, Willimantic, Conn., 1893. 8vo. Hartford, 1893. G 18 E 17
STORRS SCHOOL AGRICULTURAL EXPERIMENT STATION. Reports, 1888-94. 7 vols. 8vo. Hartford, 1889-95. E

CONNECTICUT HISTORICAL SOCIETY. Collections of. Vols. 2 and 4. 8vo. Hartford, 1870.   E

CONNELL, J. Aitken. The Difficulties of Evolution. 8vo. Dunedin, 1881.   MA 3 T 28

CONROY, J. M. False, and other Tales. 12mo. Melb., 1872.   MJ 3 P 11

CONSERVATIVE. Settlement of the Country. [*See* Victoria.]   MF 3 Q 83

CONTEMPORARY REVIEW, The. Vols. 62-66. Roy. 8vo. Lond., 1892-04.   E

CONWAY, Moncure Daniel. George Washington and Mount Vernon; a Collection of Washington's unpublished Agricultural and Personal Letters. (Memoirs of Long Island Hist. Soc.) Roy. 8vo. Brooklyn, N.Y., 1889.   C 21 S 16
Life of Thomas Paine; to which is added a sketch of Paine, by Wm. Cobbett. 2 vols. 8vo. New York, 1892.   C 8 U 37, 38
Writings of Thomas Paine. [*See* Paine, T.]   J 6 T 22, 23

CONWAY, Sir Wm. Martin. Climbing and Exploration in the Karakoram-Himalayas. Illustrations and Map. Roy. 8vo. New York, 1894.   D 15 V 15
Climbing and Exploration in the Karakoram-Himalayas. Scientific Reports and Maps. Roy. 8vo. Lond., 1894.   D 18 V 15
The Alps from end to end. Illustrated by A. D. M'Cormick. 8vo. Lond., 1895.   D 18 V 20

CONYBEARE, Fred. C. Aristotle's Categories. [*See* Anecdota Oxoniensia.]   E
Contemplative Life. [*See* Philo Judæus.]   J 5 T 27

COO-E-E: an illustrated Shorthand Magazine of General Literature. Vols. 1 and 2. 12mo. Melb., 1878-80.   ME 15 P

COOK, Albert John. Birds of Michigan. Illustrated. Roy. 8vo. Lansing, 1893.   A 30 U 11

COOK, Dr. Albert S. What is Poetry? [*See* Hunt, Leigh.]   H 9 Q 17

COOK, Mme. Charles. Arguments on Education. 8vo. Sydney, 1876.   MG 1 S 50

COOK, C. J. Bowen. British Locomotives, their history, construction, and modern development. 8vo. Lond., 1893.   A 22 Q 24

COOK, Capt. Jas. Captain Cook's Journal during his voyage round the World, made in H.M. Bark *Endeavour*, 1768-71. Edited by Capt. W. J. L. Wharton. Roy. 8vo. Lond., 1893.   MD 6 P 18 †
Discovery of Australasia, before the arrival of Cook in 1770. [*See* Collingridge, G.—Discovery of Australia.]   MD 9 P 5 †
Life of. 18mo. Dublin, 1820.   MC 1 P 67
Life, Voyages, and Discoveries of. 5th ed. 18mo. Lond., 1855.   MC 1 P 68
Photograph of. [*See* Photographs of New South Wales Scenery, 4.]   MA 45 ‡

COOKE, Rev. A. H. Molluscs. 8vo. Lond., 1895.   A 30 U 19

COOKE, Alfred R. Wellington: the Story of his Life. 12mo. Lond. (n.d.)   C 17 P 13

COOKE, Frances E. An English Hero: the Story of Richard Cobden, written for young people. 12mo. Lond., 1890.   C 21 P 1
Story of Father Damien. 2nd ed. 12mo. Lond., 1890.   MC 1 S 15

COOKE, G. W. China, 1857-58. 8vo. Lond., 1858.   B 16 P 27

COOKE, Dr. Mordecai Cubitt. Hand-book of Australian Fungi; with Host and Habitat Index [by Dr. N. A. Cobb]. 8vo. Lond., 1892.   MA 1 R 50
Hand-book of British Hepaticæ. 12mo. Lond., 1894.   A 20 P 19
Introduction to Freshwater Algæ; with an Enumeration of all the British Species. Illustrated. 8vo. Lond., 1890.   A 20 Q 14
Romance of Low Life amongst Plants: Facts and Phenomena of Cryptogamic Vegetation. 8vo. Lond., 1893.   A 20 S 15

COOKE, S. J. A Letter addressed to the Shareholders and Bondholders of the Geelong and Melbourne Railway Co. 8vo. Lond., 1858.   MF 4 Q 10

COOKE, W. Ernest. Remarks about Weather Forecasting for South Australia. (Trans. Roy. Soc., S. Australia, 8.) 8vo. Adelaide, 1886.   ME 1 S
A few Notes on Jupiter. (Trans. Roy. Soc., S. Australia, 9.) 8vo. Adelaide, 1887.   ME 1 S

COOKE-TAYLOR, R. W. [*See* Taylor, R. W. C-.]

COOLEY, Dr. Le Roy Clark. Laboratory Studies in Elementary Chemistry. 12mo. New York, 1894.   A 21 R 18

COOLGARDIE AND YILGARN GOLD-FIELDS. Map of the Routes of, containing particulars as to Wells, Tanks, and Halting-places on the York-Yilgarn Road. Folded 8vo. Melb. (n.d.)   MD 1 R 34

COOLIDGE, H. D., and McLAUGHLIN, E. A. Commonwealth of Massachusetts. Manual for the use of the General Court, containing the Rules for the two Branches. 12mo. Boston, 1893.   E

COOPER, Dr. C. D. Notes on the Skull of an Aboriginal Australian. (Anthrop. Inst., 23.) 8vo. Lond., 1893.   E

COOPER, Sir Daniel. A Federal British Empire the best Defence of the Mother Country and her Colonies. 8vo. Lond., 1880.   MJ 3 Q 16

COOPER, Dr. J. G. Catalogue of Californian Fossils, parts 2-5. 8vo. Sacramento, 1894.   A 27 T 14

COOPER, James Fenimore. The Centenary of. [*See* Matthews, B.—Books and Play-books.]   J 8 T 34

COOPER, Peter. Sketch of. [*See* Stoddard, W. O.—Men of Business.]   C 16 R 19

COOPER, Thos. The Atonement and other discourses; being a second series of "Plain Pulpit Talk." 12mo. Lond., 1880.   G 7 U 18
    The Bridge of History over the Gulf of Time: a popular view of the historical evidence for the truth of Christianity. 12mo. Lond., 1892.   G 7 U 14
    Evolution, the Stone Book, and the Mosaic Record of Creation. 12mo. Lond., 1884.   G 7 U 13
    God, the Soul, and a Future State. 12mo. Lond., 1892.   G 7 U 19
    Life of, written by himself. 12mo. Lond., 1886.   C 13 P 30
    Old-Fashioned Stories. 8vo. Lond., 1880.   J 4 R 35
    Plain Pulpit Talk. 8vo. Lond., 1886.   G 7 U 17
    Poetical Works of. 2nd edition. 8vo. Lond., 1886.   H 10 Q 25
    Thoughts at Fourscore, and earlier. 8vo. Lond., 1885.   J 4 R 36
    The Verity and Value of the Miracles of Christ. 12mo. Lond., 1887.   G 7 U 15
    The Verity of Christ's Resurrection from the Dead. 12mo. Lond., 1892.   G 7 U 12
    Portrait of. [*See* Gammage, R. G.—Chartist Movement.]   F 7 R 24

COOPER, Walter H. Debate on the Prerogative of Pardon. [*See* Parkes, Sir H.]   MF 4 Q 40

COOPER, The: his Work, and how it is done. 5th ed. 12mo. Lond., 1883.   A 25 P 8

CO-OPERATIVE CONGRESS, 1890, held May, 1890 in the City Hall, Glasgow. 4to. Manchester, 1890.   E

COOTE, Henry Chas. The Practice of the High Court of Admiralty of England. 2nd edition. 8vo. Lond. 1869.   F 9 S 12

COPINGER, Walter Arthur. Law of Copyright in Works of Literature and Art; together with International and Foreign Copyright, with the Statutes relating thereto. 3rd ed. 8vo. Lond., 1893.   F 14 T 20

COPLESTON, Rt. Rev. Reginald S. Buddhism, primitive and present, in Magadha and in Ceylon. 8vo. Lond., 1892.   G 13 P 36

COPLIN, Dr. W. M. L., and BEVAN, Dr. D. A Manual of Practical Hygiene; designed for Sanitary and Health Officers, Practitioners, and Students of Medicine. Illustrated. Roy. 8vo. Philad., 1893.   A 26 V 15

CORA, Prof. G. [*See* Cosmos.]   E

CORBETT, Francis A. The conjugal condition of the people of Victoria considered in relation to the laws of divorce. 8vo. Melb., 1862.   MF 4 Q 13

CORBETT, Miss Maud. Mayfield House. [*See* Knapp, J. H.—The Universities and the Social Problem.]   F 8 U 22

CORBETT, R. Sydney. Universal Mining Code. [*See* Stevens, J.]   K 9 S 12

CORBETT, W. J. Fontenoy: an Historical Poem. 8vo. Melb., 1888.   MH 1 V 5

CORBIAU, Dr. Jean. De l'Acte d'Accusation. 8vo. Bruxelles, 1892.   F 9 R 20

CORBIN, J. The Elizabethan Hamlet: a study of the sources of, and of Shakspere's environments, to show the mad scenes had a comic aspect, now ignored. Sm. 4to. Lond., 1895.   J 5 R 47

CORDEIL, Paul. Origines et Progrès de la Nouvelle-Calédonie. 12mo. Nouméa, 1885.   MD 8 Q 26

CORDELL, H. Queenscliffe: how to see it. 8vo. Queenscliffe, Vic., 1876-77.   MD 1 S 48

CORDER, F. Recitation with Musical Accompaniment. [*See* Campbell, Dr. H.—Voice, Speech, and Gesture.]   J 8 T 36

CORFIELD, Prof. Wm. Henry. Sewerage and Sewage Utilization. 18mo. New York, 1875.   A 22 P 33
    Water and Water Supply. 2nd ed. 18mo. New York, 1890.   A 22 P 36

CORK, J. F. Education in West Virginia. [*See* Morgan, B. S.]   G 13 R 18

CORLETTE, Rev. Dr. J. C. The Final and Sustaining Cause of Creation: a Sermon. 8vo. Hobart, 1892.   MG 2 S 1

CORNELL UNIVERSITY, Register, 1892. 12mo. Ithaca, N.Y., 1892.   E

CORNELL UNIVERSITY AGRICULTURAL EXPERIMENT STATION. Reports, 1892-93. 2 vols. 8vo. Albany, 1893-94.   E

CORNHILL MAGAZINE. New Series, vols. 19-23. 8vo. Lond., 1892-94.   E

CORNISH, C. J. The New Forest. (Portfolio Monograph, 8.) Roy. 8vo. Lond., 1894.   E

CORNISH and BRUCE *v.* The QUEEN. Trial at Bar, 1886. Fol. Melb., 1886.   MF 4 T 40

CORNWALL, Barry. [*See* Proctor, B. W.]

CORROYER, Edouard. Gothic Architecture. Edited by W. Armstrong. 8vo. Lond., 1893.   A 19 R 2

CORSALI, Andrea. [*See* Ramusio, G. B.—Navigation et Viaggi.]   D 36 T 5-7 ‡

CORSON, Dr. Hiram. A Primer of English Verse. 12mo. Boston, 1893.   H 9 Q 16

CORTEZ, M. F. [*See* Ramusio, G. B.—Navigationi et Viaggi.] D 36 T 5-7 ‡

CORVUS. [*See* Civil Service.] MF 4 R 44

COSMOPOLITAN GOLD-MINING CO. Rules and Regulations. 8vo. Sydney (n.d.) MF 4 R 35

COSMOS. Comunicazioni sui Progressi più recenti e notevoli della Geografia é delle Scienze Affini del Prof. G. Cora. Vol. 11, 1892-93. Imp. 8vo. Torino, 1893. E

COSSA, Dr. Luigi. Taxation: its Principles and Methods. Translated by Horace White. 8vo. New York, 1893. F 8 U 21

COSTA, A. F. da. O Ensino Publico Primario na Italia, França, e Belgica. 8vo. Rio de Janeiro, 1893. G 18 R 50

COSTE, F. Derecho Penal. 8vo. Montevideo, 1894. F 9 R 36

COSTER, Frederick. Land System for Victoria. 8vo. Melb., 1857. MF 2 Q 77

COTGRAVE, Randle. Dictionary of the French and English Tongues. Imp. 8vo. Lond., 1632. J 7 V 15

COTTERELL, J. H. Map of the City of Bath. [Folded] 8vo. Bath, 1852. D 18 Q 17

COTTERILL, Rt. Rev. Henry. On the relation between Science and Religion through the principles of Unity, Order, and Causation. 8vo. Lond., 1880. G 15 P 43

COTTERILL, James H. Applied Mechanics: an Elementary General Introduction to the Theory of Structures and Machines. 3rd ed. [illustrated]. 8vo. Lond., 1892. A 25 S 27

COTTON, Chas. Montaigne's Essays. [*See* Montaigne, M. de.] J 8 P 41-46

COTTON, Sir Robert. Posthuma. [*See* Collectanea Adamantæa.] J 18 R 3-6

COUCH, Arthur Thos. Quiller. The Story of the Sea; edited by "Q." Roy. 8vo. Lond., 1895. B 21 V 7

COUCH, M. and L. Quiller. Ancient and Holy Wells of Cornwall. 8vo. Lond., 1894. G 2 U 18

COUES, Dr. Elliott. History of the Expedition under the command of Lewis and Clark to the sources of the Missouri River, thence across the Rocky Mountains and down the Columbia River to the Pacific Ocean, 1804-6; with new Maps and other Illustrations. 4 vols. Roy. 8vo. Lond., 1893. D 16 V 12-15

—— Handbook of Field and General Ornithology: a manual of the structure and classification of birds, with instructions for collecting and preserving specimens. 8vo. Lond., 1890. A 13 T 34

COULSON, W. [*See* Australian Colonies Government Bill]. MF 1 U 25

COUPLAND, W. C.—*Trans.* Personal Recollections. [*See* Siemens, W. von.] C 13 S 23.

COURMONT, J. Propriétés attribuées à Tuberculine [*See* Arloing, S.] A 33 U 24

COURRIER AUSTRALIEN. April—Dec., 1892. Fol. Sydney, 1892. ME

—— Almanach du Courrier Australien, 1895. 8vo. Sydney, 1895. ME 4 U

COURTHOPE, Wm. John. History of English Poetry. Vol. 1. 8vo. Lond., 1895. H 4 V 0

COURTNEY, Dr. Wm. L. Life of J. S. Mill. 12mo. Lond., 1889. C 17 P 19

COURTNEY, Wm. Prideaux. English Whist and English Whist Players. 8vo. Lond., 1894. A 20 T 29

COUSINS, G. From Island to Island in the South Seas. 12mo. Lond., 1893. MD 4 R 42

—— The Story of the South Seas. With Map and Illustrations. Sm. 4to. Lond., 1894. MD 7 S 6

COUSINS, Rev. W. E. Madagascar of to-day: with Map. 12mo. Lond., 1895. B 16 P 22

COUTO, Diogo de. Asia. 15 vols. 12mo. Lisboa, 1778. D 17 P 14-28

—— Asia. [*See* Barros, J. de.] D 17 P 5-13

COUVREUR, E. Sur le Pneumogastrique des Oiseaux. (Annales de l'Université de Lyon, 2.) Roy. 8vo. Paris, 1892. A 27 V 17

COUVREUR, Mme. Jessie Catherine. "Tasma." In her earliest youth. 8vo. Lond., 1891. MJ 1 U 41

—— John Grantley's Conversion. [*See* Praed, Mrs. R. M.—Under the Gum Tree.] MJ 2 T 44

—— The Penance of Portia James. 8vo. Lond., 1891. MJ 1 U 42

—— A Sydney Sovereign, and other Tales. 8vo. Lond., 1890. MJ 1 U 40

—— Uncle Piper, of Piper's Hill: a novel. 8vo. Lond., 1892. MJ 1 U 39

COVEL, Dr. J. Extracts from the Diaries of, 1670-79. (Hakluyt Soc., 87.) 8vo. Lond., 1893. E

COVENTRY, Rev. H. Lucina sine Concubitu. [*See* Collectanea Adamantæa.] J 18 R 15

COWAN, A. M. Flower Gardening. 12mo. Brisb., 1889. MA 1 Q 69

COWAN, E. M., and POWNALL, S. Beaty-. Fast Day and Vegetarian Cookery. 12mo. Lond., 1895. A 22 Q 38

COWARD, W. M. Advantages of Gas for Lighting, Cooking, and Warming. 18mo. Sydney, 1883. MA 2 P 81

COWDEROY, Benjamin. Notes of a Holiday Tour round the World in 1883–84. 8vo. Melb., 1884. MD 8 Q 22

COWELL, Prof. Edward Byles. The Buddha-Karita. [*See* Anecdota Oxoniensia.] E
Buddha Karita of Asvaghosha. [*See* Müller, F. Max—Sacred Books, 49.] G 3 S 36
The Jātaka; or, Stories of Buddha's Former Births. Translated from the Pāli by various hands. Vol. 1, translated by R. Chalmers. Roy. 8vo. Camb., 1895. G 5 T 20

COWIE, Rt. Rev. Wm. G. Notes of a Visit to Norfolk Island, the head of the Melanesian Mission, 1872. 8vo. Auckland, 1872. MB 2 R 59

COWLEY, Mrs. Hannah. The Belle's Stratagem : a Comedy. [*See* London Stage, 2.] H 2 S 34
A Bold Stroke for a Husband : a Comedy. [*See* London Stage, 3.] H 2 S 35
Which is the Man ? a Comedy [*See* London Stage, 2.] H 2 S 34
Who's the Dupe ? a Farce. [*See* London Stage, 1.] H 2 S 33

COWPER, H. Swainson. Through Turkish Arabia : a Journey from the Mediterranean to Bombay by the Euphrates and Tigris Valleys and the Persian Gulf. 8vo. Lond., 1894. D 17 U*15

COWPER, Wm. Poetical Works of. Edited by Rev. H. F. Cary. Illustrated. Roy. 8vo. Lond., 1851. H 7 V 8
Essay on. [*See* Bagehot, W.—Literary Studies.] J 9 P 22–24
Life of ; by Thomas Wright. 8vo. Lond., 1892. C 15 P 9
[Life of] ; by the Rev. Canon Benham. [*See* Masson, Prof. D.—In the Footsteps of the Poets.] J 6 R 43
Sketch of. [*See* Bagehot, W.—Estimates of some Englishmen and Scotchmen.] J 10 V 32
Sketch of. [*See* Bell, Rev. Dr. C. D.—Some of our English Poets.] C 21 P 11

COWPER, Very Rev. Wm. M. Sermon preached on the occasion of the Death of the Rev. G. W. Richardson. [*See* Richardson, Rev. G. W.] MG 2 Q 23
The Christian Training of Children by their Parents : a Sermon, 1852. 8vo. Sydney, 1852. MG 2 S 1
The Lord's Day viewed in three lights : Religious, Moral, and Social. 8vo. Sydney, 1880. MG 2 S 6

COWPERTHWAIT, J. Howard. Money, Silver, and Finance. 2nd ed. 8vo. New York, 1892. F 8 U 23

COX, Frank P. Continuous-current Dynamos and Motors : their Theory, Design, and Testing. 12mo. New York, 1893. A 21 P 30

COX, Harding, and LASCELLES, Hon. Gerald. Coursing and Falconry. (Badminton Library.) 8vo. Lond., 1892. A 17 U 46

COX, Harold. Land Nationalization. 12mo. Lond., 1892. F 14 Q 32

COX, J. Chas. How to do Business ; or, the Royal Road to Success ; also How to Remember, and How to do Figures. 8vo. Sydney (n.d) MJ 3 Q 31

COX, M. E. Cinderella. [*See* Folk Lore Society—Pubs. vol. 3L] E

COX, Rev Dr. Samuel. Ecclesiastes. [*See* Expositor's Bible.] G 19 R 18

COX, Water Gibbons. Artesian Wells as a means of Water Supply. 8vo. Brisbane, 1895. MA 3 S 65

COXE, Dr. Jas. Management of Infancy. [*See* Combe, Dr. J.] A 26 R 20

COXEN, Mrs. C. Notes on the Cyprææ. (Proc. Roy. Soc., Queensland, 10.) 8vo. Brisbane, 1893. ME 1 T

COXHEAD, Mrs. A. Heart Gleanings : a Collection of Poems. 12mo. Ballarat, 1884. MH 1 U 46

CRABB, George. Auswahl vorzüglicher Stellen, aus den besten Deutschen Schriftstellern. 12mo. Lond., 1820. J 9 P 40

CRAIG, Thos. On the Motion of a Solid in a Fluid. 18mo. New York, 1879. A 25 P 33
Wave and Vortex Motion. 18mo. New York, 1879. A 25 P 34

CRAIG-BROWN, T. [*See* Brown, T. Craig-.]

CRAIK, Dr. George Lillie. Bacon : his Writings and Philosophy. 12mo. Lond., 1860. J 12 S 31
English Causes Célèbres ; or, Reports of Remarkable Trials. 12mo. Lond., 1844. F 6 S 42

CRAIK, Henry. English Prose : selections, with critical introcuctions ; edited by Henry Craik. Vols. 1–3. 14th–17th Century. 8vo. Lond , 1893–94. J 6 Q 35-37

CRAMP, W. B. Narrative of a Voyage to India, and a Description of New South Wales. 8vo. Lond., 1823. MD 8 R 26

CRANBROOK, Rev. James. God's Method of Government. [*See* Religious Pamphlets, 1.] G 9 V 16
Tendencies of Modern Religious Thought. [*See* Religious Pamphlets, 1.] G 9 V 16

CRANDALL, C. L. Tables for the Computation of Railway and other Earthwork. Roy. 8vo. New York, 1893. A 22 T 18
The Transition Curve by offsets and deflection angles. 12mo New York, 1893. A 22 Q 21

CRANE, W. J. E. Bookbinding for Amateurs : being descriptions of the various Tools and Appliances required, and minute Instructions for their effective use. Illustrated. 8vo. Lond. (n.d.) A 25 R 9

CRANE, Walter. The Claims of Decorative Art. Sm. 4to. Lond., 1892. A 23 T 17

CRANE, CRANE, & CO. Crane's Universal Directory of Manufacturers and Merchants of the United Kingdom, and Buyers' Guide, with Colonial and Continental Appendix, 1892-93. Imp. 8vo. Fakenham, 1892. E

CRANMER, Most Rev. Thos. Sketch of. [*See* Fowler, Rev. M.—Notable Archbishops.] C 13 V 12

CRANSTOUN, James. Satirical Poems of the Time of the Reformation, Vol. 2. (Scottish Text Society.) 8vo. Edinb., 1893. E

CRAVEN, A. W. Remarks on a proposed improvement in the method of suspending the plummet from theodolites. 8vo. Melb., 1884. MA 3 T 14

CRAVEN, Mme. Augustus. (Pauline de la Ferronnays). Le Père Damien. 12mo. Paris, 1890. MC 1 S 11
Memoir of; by Maria C. Bishop. 2 vols. 8vo. Lond., 1894. C 21 P 3, 4

CRAVEN, H. T. Our Nelly: a Domestic Drama. 18mo. Sydney, 1855. MH 1 U 54

CRAWFORD, Mrs. Emily. Education and Status of Women. [*See* Subjects of the Day, 1.] C 18 S 18

CRAWFORD, Francis Marion. Constantinople. Illustrated by E. L. Weeks. 8vo. Lond., 1895.
D 18 S 12

CRAWFORD, Frazer S. Insect and Fungoid Pests. (Proc. Roy. Agricult. and Horticult. Soc., S. Aust., 1882-84.) 8vo. Adelaide, 1882-84. ME 1 S
Report on the Fusicladiums, the Codlin Moth, and other Fungus and Insect Pests attacking Apple and Pear Trees in South Australia. 8vo. Adelaide, 1886.
MA 2 U 65
The Apricot Disease. (Trans. Roy. Soc., S. Australia, 8.) 8vo. Adelaide, 1886. ME I S

CRAWFORD, Jas. Coutts. The Reform of English Spelling. 12mo. Lond., 1883. J 11 U 27

CRAWFORD, John Martin. Industries of Russia. 2 vols. roy. 8vo. St. Petersburg, 1893. F 3 V 3, 4

CRAWFURD, John. History of the Indian Archipelago; with Maps and Engravings. 3 vols. 8vo. Edinb., 1820. B 33 Q 3-5
Descriptive Dictionary of the Indian Islands and the Adjacent Countries. 8vo. Lond., 1856. D 17 V 21

CRAWFURD, Oswald. A Year of Sport and Natural History. Illustrated. 4to. Lond., 1895.
A 12 U 17 †

CREAK, E. W. Magnetical Results obtained by H.M.S. *Challenger*. [*See* Thomson, Sir C. W., and Murray, Dr. J.—Voyage of H.M.S. *Challenger*.] A 6 †

CREED, Dr. John Mildred. Cremation. 8vo. Sydney, 1890. MA 2 V 49

CREHORE, Dr. Albert C. Alternating Currents. [*See* Bedell, Dr. F.] A 21 V 17

CREIGHTON, Dr. Charles. History of Epidemics in Britain. Vol. 2. 8vo. Camb., 1894. A 26 T 20
2. From the Extinction of Plague to the present time.
Jenner and Vaccination: a strange chapter of Medical History. 8vo. Lond., 1889. A 26 Q 29

CREIGHTON, J. E. Psychology. [*See* Wundt, W.] A 26 V 12.

CREIGHTON, Rt. Rev. Mandell. History of the Papacy during the period of the Reformation. Vol. 5. The German Revolt, 1517-27. 8vo. Lond., 1894.
G 14 T 21

CREPAZ, Adèle. The Emancipation of Women and its probable consequences. 8vo. Lond., 1893.
F 14 Q 37

CRÉPIEUX-JAMIN, J. Handwriting and Expression. Translated and edited by J. H. Schooling. 8vo. Lond., 1892. A 13 R 17

CRESWELL, A. W. Additional Notes on the Lilydale Limestone. (Proceedings Royal Society, Victoria, n.s., 6.) 8vo. Melb., 1894. ME 1 P

CREWE, Nathaniel, Lord. Memoirs of. [*See* Camden Soc. Pubs., 53.] E

CRICHTON, David Alex. The Australasian Fruit Culturist, containing full and complete information about all Useful Fruits. 8vo. Melb., 1893. MA 1 Q 78
Fruit Cultivation. (Victorian Department of Agriculture.—Lectures.) 8vo. Melb., 1892. MA 3 V 15
History, Uses, and Culture of the Orange, and other species of the Citrus Family. 8vo. Melb., 1875.
MA 1 P 71
[*See* Australian Horticultural Magazine.] ME 3 S

CRIMP, W. Santo. Sewage Disposal Works: a Guide to the Construction of Works for the prevention of the pollution by sewage of Rivers and Estuaries. 2nd ed., illustrated. 8vo. Lond., 1894. A 22 S 17

CRIPPS, Wilfred Joseph. College and Corporation Plate: a Handbook to the Reproduction of Silver Plate in the South Kensington Museum. 8vo. Lond., 1881.
A 23 R 27
Old French Plate: its Makers and Marks. 2nd edition. Roy. 8vo. Lond., 1893. A 25 U 4

CRISP, Frederick A. Visitation of England and Wales. [*See* Howard, Dr. J. J.] K 12 U 4 †

CRISPI, Francesco: a Modern Italian Statesmen. [*See* Kingston, W. Beatty.—Men, Cities, and Events.]
C 22 R 4

CRITIC, The, in Church; or, Melbourne Preachers and Preaching. 8vo. Melb., 1872.* MG 1 P 64

CRITICISM, the Restoration of Christianity. [*See* Religious Pamphlets, 3.] G 9 V 18

CRITO. [See Launceston and Western Railway.]
MF 2 Q 58

CROAL, D. O. The Silver Question. [See Jamieson, G.]
F 9 T 19

CROCKETT, S. R. The Stickit Minister and some Common Men. Illustrated. Imp. 8vo. Lond., 1894.
J 8 V 3

CROFTON, Denis. Genesis and Geology. 8vo. Glasgow (n.d.)
G 2 U 4

CROKER, Rt. Hon. John Wilson. History of the Guillotine. 12mo. Lond. 1853.
B 26 P 5

CROKER, W. H. Masonic Lodge of Sorrow: Ceremony in memory of Brother W. A. Croker. 8vo. Melb., 1885.
MG 2 Q 37

CROLY, Rev. Dr. George. Works of A. Pope. [See Pope, A.]
H 0 U 29-32

CROMBIE, Chas. M. Guide to Property Assessment Act, 1879. 8vo. Wellington, 1880.
MF 2 Q 76

CROMBIE, Rev. Frederick. [See Apostolic Fathers.]
G 14 U 1
[See Origen.]
G 14 U 10, 23

CROMBIE, Rev. James M. Lichens. [See Taylor, Dr. J. E.—Collecting Natural History Objects.]
A 29 Q 39

A Monograph of Lichens found in Britain, being a Descriptive Catalogue of the species in the Herbarium of the British Museum. Part 1. 8vo. Lond., 1894.
A 20 S 12

CROMWELL, Oliver. Letters and Speeches; by T. Carlyle. 3 vols. (in 1.) 8vo. Lond., 1888.
C 21 Q 2
[Plaster Cast of.] [See Hutton, L.—Portraits in Plaster.]
A 23 V 18
[Life of.] A History; by S. H. Church. 8vo. New York, 1894.
C 16 U 2

CROOKE, Wm. The Financial Crisis: Suggestions for Financial Reform, and the Removal of the Existing Depression. 8vo. Melb., 1892.
MF 2 Q 30

CROOKES, Wm., F.R.S. Chemical Technology. [See Wagner, R. von.]
A 21 V 10

CROSLAND, Mrs. Newton. Landmarks of a Literary Life. 12mo. Lond., 1893.
C 13 Q 12

CROSS, C. F., BEVAN, E. J., and BEADLE, C. Cellulose: an Outline of the Chemistry of the Structural Elements of Plants. 8vo. Lond., 1895.
A 20 S 17

CROSS, J. C. The Purse; or, the Benevolent Tar: a Musical Entertainment. [See London Stage, 4.]
H 2 S 36

CROSS, J. W. Impressions of Dante and of the New World, with a few words on Bimetallism. 8vo. Edinb., 1893.
J 4 Q 4

CROSS, Mrs. Mary Ann. "George Eliot." Works of. 20 vols. 12mo. Lond. (n.d.)
J 21 P 1-20
Adam Bede. 2 vols.
Daniel Deronda. 3 vols.
Felix Holt. 2 vols.
Impressions of Theophrastus Such.
Jubal, and other Poems.
Middlemarch. 3 vols.
The Mill on the Floss. 2 vols.
Romola. 2 vols.
Scenes of Clerical Life. 2 vols.
Silas Marner; The Lifted Veil; Brother Jacob.
The Spanish Gypsy.

Selections from. [See Harlin, T.]
MJ 1 U 24
Adam Bede. 2 vols. 8vo. Edinb. (n.d.)
J 17 V 1, 2
Felix Holt, the Radical. 2 vols. 8vo. Edinb. (n.d.)
J 17 V 3, 4
Middlemarch. 3 vols. 12mo. Lond. (n.d.)
J 17 V 7-9
Romola. 8vo. Edinb. (n.d.)
J 12 Q 25
Scenes of Clerical Life. 2 vols. 8vo. Edinb. (n.d.)
J 17 V 5, 6
"George Eliot": the Humourist as Poet. [See Lilly, W. S.—Four English Humourists.]
J 5 T 30

CROSSE, Mrs. Andrew. Red Letter Days of my Life. 2 vols. 8vo. Lond., 1892.
C 13 Q 24, 25

CROSSKEY, R. The Soil in relation to Health. [See Miers, H. A.]
A 13 P 4

CROSTON, Jas. History of Lancaster. [See Baines, E.]
B 23 V 12

CROWE, Eyre. With Thackeray in America. 8vo. Lond., 1893.
B 17 R 35

CROWE, Sir Joseph. Reminiscences of thirty-five years of my Life. 8vo. Lond., 1895.
C 22 R 7

CROZET'S Voyage to Tasmania, New Zealand, the Ladrone Islands, and the Philippines in 1771-72. Translated by H. L. Roth; with a brief reference to the Literature of New Zealand. Illustrated. 8vo. Lond., 1891.
MD 8 Q 43

CROZIER, A. A. Cultivated Raspberries of the United States. (Michigan State Agricultural College, Bulletin 3.) 8vo. Michigan, 1894.
A 30 R 26

CRUIKSHANK, George. Dibdin's Sea Songs illustrated. [See Dibdin, C.]
H 7 U 37

CRUISE OF THE WAIRARAPA. 4to. Auckland, 1884.
MD 1 P 20 †

CRULS, L. Instrucções para as Commissões Brazileiras que têm de observar a Passagem de Venus pelo disco do Sol, em 5-6 de Dezembro de 1882. 4to. Rio de Janeiro, 1882.
A 5 P 19 †

CRUMP, M. H. Kentucky Highways: History of the Old and New Systems. 8vo. Wash., 1895.
A 22 V 10

CRUNDEN, Frederick M. The Free Public Library, its uses and value. 8vo. St. Louis, 1893.
J 2 Q 25

CRUTTWELL, Rev. Chas. Thos. Literary History of Early Christianity, including the Fathers and the Chief Heretical Writers of the Ante-Nicene Period. 2 vols. 8vo. Lond., 1893. G 2 Q 34, 35

CRÜWELL, G. A. Letters on Liberia. [See Liberian Coffee in Ceylon.] A 18 P 27

CUBAS, Antonio Garcin. Mexico, its Trade, Industries and Resources. Translated by W. Thompson and C. B. Cleveland. 8vo. Mexico, 1893. F 14 U 13

CUCUEL, Chas., et ALLÈGRE, P. Mélanges Grecs. Œuvres complètes de l'orateur Antiphon (traduction); Une Scène des "Grenouilles" d'Aristophane. 8vo. Paris, 1888. J 7 U 44

CUDMORE, P. Buchanan's Conspiracy, the Nicaragua Canal and Reciprocity. 8vo. New York, 1892. F 8 U 44

CUITT, George. Wanderings and Pencillings amongst Ruins of the Olden Time. Fol. Lond., 1855. B 2 P 27 †

CULCHETH, W. W. Floods on the River Barwon. (Roy. Soc., Vict., 18.) 8vo. Melb., 1882. ME 1 P

The Drainage of Melbourne. (Roy. Soc., Vict., 18.) 8vo. Melb., 1882. ME 1 P

Quantity of Water consumed in Irrigation. (Roy. Soc., Vict., 19.) 8vo. Melb., 1883. ME 1 P

Shingle on the East Coast of New Zealand. (Roy. Soc., Vict., 21.) 8vo. Melb., 1885. ME 1 P

CULLEN, Wm. Practical Treatise on the construction of Horizontal and Vertical Waterwheels. 2nd edition. Sm. 4to. Lond., 1871. A 6 U 25

CULLEY, John L. Theory of the Construction of Helicoidal Oblique Arches. 18mo. New York, 1886. A 22 P 32

CUMBERLAND, Earl of. Sketch of. [See Southey, R, —English Seamen.] B 23 S 15

CUMBERLAND, Richard. The Brothers: a Comedy. [See London Stage, 2.] H 2 S 34

The Carmelite: a Tragedy. [See London Stage, 4.] H 2 S 36

False Impressions: a Comedy. [See London Stage, 4.] H 2 S 36

The Fashionable Lover: a Comedy. [See London Stage, 2.] H 2 S 34

First Love: a Comedy. [See London Stage, 3.] H 2 S 35

The Jew: a Comedy. [See London Stage, 1.] H 2 S 33

The Mysterious Husband: a Tragedy. [See London Stage, 3.] H 2 S 35

The West Indian: a Comedy. [See London Stage, 1.] H 2 S 33

The Wheel of Fortune: a Comedy. [See London Stage, 1.] H 2 S 33

CUMING, E. D. In the Shadow of the Pagoda. 12mo. Lond., 1893. D 14 Q 11

CUMMING, Miss Constance Frederika Gordon. A Lady's Cruise in a French Man-of-war. New ed., illustrated. 8vo. Edinb., 1882. MD 8 Q 38

CUNDALL, Frank. The Story of the Life of Columbus and the Discovery of Jamaica. (Journal of Inst. of Jamaica, Vol. 2, No. 1.) Imp. 8vo. Kingston, Jamaica, 1894. E 1, 16

CUNDALL, Joseph. Brief History of Wood-engraving, from its invention. 8vo. Lond., 1893. A 23 R 42

CUNINGHAM, Granville C. A Scheme for Imperial Federation. 8vo. Lond., 1895. F 8 U 52

CUNNINGHAM, A. Poems and Songs. 18mo. Lond., 1847. H 10 U 2

CUNNINGHAM, Prof. D. J. Anatomy of the Thylacine, Cuscus, and Phascogale; with an Account of the Comparative Anatomy of the Intrinsic Muscles and Nerves of the Mammalia pes. [See Thomson, Sir C. W., and Murray, Dr. J.—Voyage of H.M.S. Challenger. Zoölogy, 5.] A 6 †

Contribution to the Surface Anatomy of the Cerebral Hemispheres; with a Chapter upon Cranio-Cerebral Topography, by Dr. V. Horsley, F.R.S. (Trans. R.I. Academy.—Cunningham Memoirs, 7.) 4to. Dublin, 1892. E

The Lumbar Curve in Man and the Apes. (Trans. R. I. Academy.—Cunningham Memoirs, 2.) 4to. Dublin, 1886. E

Manual of Practical Anatomy. Vols. 1 and 2. 8vo. Edinb., 1893-94. A 26 Q 20, 21

CUNNINGHAM J. T. Organic Evolution. [See Eimer, Prof. G. H. T.] A 13 T 36

CUNNINGHAM, T. J. Blue Book of the State of Wisconsin. 8vo. Madison, 1893. E

CUNNINGHAM, Rev. Dr. Wm., and McARTHUR, Ellen A. Outlines of English Industrial History. 8vo. Camb., 1895. F 2 U 38

CUQ, Edouard. De quelques inscriptions relatives à l'Administration de Dioclétien. 1. L' "Examinator per Italian." 2. Le "Magister Sacrarum Cognitionum." 8vo. Paris, 1881. B 35 R 26

CURLEWIS, H. R. Statutes (England-New South Wales.) [See McIntyre, W. D.] MF 3 P 60

CURNOW, J. Cultivation of the Orange. (Proc. Roy. Agricult. and Horticult. Soc. of S. Australia, 1884.) 8vo. Adelaide, 1884. ME 1 S

CURRAN, E. J. Secrets of Cutting [Tailoring] revealed. 8vo. Sydney, 1895. MA 2 Q 69

CURRAN, Rev. J. Milne. Structure and Composition of a Basalt from Bondi. (Journal Roy. Soc., N.S.W., 28.) 8vo. Sydney, 1894. ME 1 R
Natural Mineral Spring at Bungonia. (Journal Roy. Soc., N.S.W., 28.) 8vo. Sydney, 1894. ME 1 R

CURRAN, Rt. Hon. John Philpot. [Plaster Cast of] [*See* Hutton, L.—Portraits in Plaster.] A 23 V 13

CURRY, J. L. M. The Southern States of the American Union. 8vo. New York, 1895. B 17 Q 14

CURRY, W. T. Rural Water Supply. [*See* Greenwell, A.] A 22 Q 42

CURTICE, Cooper. Animal Parasites of Sheep; to which is added an article on Worms in Sheep, by "A Pastoralist." 8vo. Sydney, 1892. MA 1 S 30

CURTICE, E. Index to *The Times*, the London Morning and Evening Papers, 120 Weeklies, and 31 Provincial Newspapers, July–Sept., 1893. Sm. 4to. Lond., 1893. E

CURTIN, Jeremiah. Hero-tales of Ireland. 8vo. Lond., 1894. J 12 T 36
Tales of the Fairies and the Ghost World, collected from Oral Tradition S.W. Munster. 8vo. Lond., 1895. B 36 Q 7

CURTIS, Geo. Wm. Orations and Addresses of. Edited by C. E. Norton. 3 vols. 8vo. New York, 1894. F 14 U 1-3
1. American Institutions, and the Duties of American Citizens, 1856-91.
2. Reform of the Civil Service of the United States.
3. Historical and Memorial Addresses.

[Life of]; by E. Cary. (Am. Men of Letts.) 12mo. Boston, 1894. C 17 P 24
Sketch of. [*See* Smalley, G. W.—Studies of Men.] C 10 R 20

CURTIS, John. Farm Insects; being the Natural History and Economy of the Insects injurious to the Field Crops of Great Britain and Ireland. Roy 8vo. Lond., 1883. A 18 U 23

CURTIS'S BOTANICAL MAGAZINE, comprising the Plants of the Royal Gardens of Kew and of other Botanical Establishments in Great Britain. 3rd series, vols. 48–50. Roy. 8vo. Lond., 1892-94. E

CURTISS, Rev. Dr. Geo. L. Arminianism in History; or, the Revolt from Predestinationism. 8vo. Cincinnati, 1894. G 17 Q 50

CURTIUS, E., und KAUPERT, J. A. Karten von Attika. 10 parts (in 2 vols.), fol. Berlin, 1881–83. D 15 R 16 †, and D 8 P 30 ‡

CURZON, Hon. George N. Problems of the Far East: Japan, Korea, China. [Maps and Illustrations.] 8vo. Lond., 1894. D 17 T 12

CUST, Lionel. Albert Dürer's Engravings. (Portfolio Monograph, 11.) Roy. 8vo. Lond., 1894. E

CUTHBERT, A. A. Questions on the Holy Scriptures. 8vo. Glasgow, 1893. G 2 Q 29

CUTHBERTSON, W. R. Exploration of the Highlands of South-Eastern British New Guinea. (Roy. Geog. Soc. Australasia, Vic. Branch, 5.) 8vo. Melb., 1887. ME 20 P

CUTTER, Charles. Guide to Hot Springs of Arkansas. 35th ed., illustrated. 8vo. St. Louis, 1893. D 15 P 15

CUTTS, Rev. Dr. Edward L. History of Early Christian Art. (Side-lights of Church History.) 8vo. Lond., 1893. A 23 S 9

CUZENS, Rev. Benjamin. The Footprints of Jesus: a Poem. 12mo. Geelong, 1861. MH 1 P 72

CYPRIAN. Writings of, together with the Writings of Novatian and Minucius Felix, &c. Translated by Rev. Dr. R. E. Wallis. (Ante-Nicene Christ. Lib., 8, 13.) 2 vols. 8vo. Edinb., 1868–69. G 14 U 8, and 13

D

D.M. [*See* Mary, a Tale, and other Poems.] MH 1 S 71

DACOSTA, John. Articles on Legal and Administrative Difficulties in India. [*See Law Magazine and Review*, 1893–94.] E

DADANT, C., and SON. The Hive and Honey Bee. [*See* Langstroth, L. L.] A 18 S 29

DADD, Dr. G. H. American Cattle Doctor: Directions for preserving the health and curing the disease of Oxen, Cattle, Sheep, and Swine. 8vo. New York, 1890. A 18 R 20

DADELSZEN, E. J. von. The New Zealand Official Year-book, 1893-94. 2 vols. 8vo. Wellington, 1893-94. ME 5 S
Report on the Results of a Census of New Zealand, 1891. 8vo. Wellington, 1893. MF 2 Q 59

DAFFORNE, James. Biographical Sketch of C. Stanfield. [*See* Stanfield, C.] A 39 Q 15 ‡

DAFT, Richard. Kings of Cricket: Reminiscences and Anecdotes, with Hints on the Game. 8vo. Bristol, 1893. C 18 P 1

DAHLEN, Heinrich Wm. Die Weinbereitung. 8vo. Braunschweig, 1882. A 18 S 15

DAHLGREN, Rear-Admiral John Adolph. Memoir of; by his widow. 8vo. Boston, 1882. C 19 S 9

DAHLSTROM, Karl P. Hoisting Machinery. [*See* Weisbach, Dr. J.] A 25 S 26

DAILY COMMERCIAL NEWS, April, 1891–June, 1895. 13 vol. fol. Sydney, 1891–92. ME

DAILY TELEGRAPH, The (formerly the Sydney Daily Telegraph). Oct., 1892-Dec., 1895. 9 vols. fol. ME

DAKYNS, H. G. [See Xenophon.] J 11 S 40, 41

DALE, John. Round the World by Doctors' Orders, being a Narrative of a year's Travel in Japan, Ceylon, Australia, China, New Zealand, Canada, the United States, &c. 8vo. Lond., 1894. D 17 T 6

DALE, Lieut. R. Panoramic View of King George's Sound, Swan River. Obl. 8vo. Lond., 1834. MD 8 R 23

DALE, Rev. Dr. Robt. Wm. Christian Doctrine: a series of Discourses. 2nd thousand. 8vo. Lond., 1894. G 13 S 46

DALLAM, T. Diary of, 1599-1600. (Hakluyt Soc., 87.) 8vo. Lond., 1893. E

DALLEY, Rt. Hon. Wm. Bede. Opinions of, from March, 1875, to Jan., 1877. 4 vols. sm. fol. Sydney, 1875-77. MF 4 S 44, 45, 47, 48
Sydney Platforms and European Cabinets: an address to the Catholics of New South Wales on the Education Question. 8vo. Sydney, 1879. MG 1 S 13

DALRYMPLE, Alexander. Collection of Plans of Ports in the East Indies. 4to. Lond., 1775. D 15 R 8 †
Oriental Repertory. 2 vols. 4to. Lond., 1793-1808. D 15 R 6, 7 †
Voyages dans la Mer du Sud, par les Espagnols et les Hollandois. 8vo. Paris, 1774. MD 8 Q 30

DALRYMPLE, D. H., and NELSON, Wallace. For and against Socialism: an epistolary debate. 8vo. Brisbane, 1895. MF 4 R 31

DALRYMPLE, Sir How. at Gibraltar and in Portugal, 1808; by Adm. Sir E. G. Fanshawe. 8vo. Lond., 1895. C 13 V 11

DALTON, Lt.-Col. J. C. Army Book for British Empire. [See Goodenough, Lt.-Gen. W. H.] B 23 T 18

DALTON, John, and the Rise of Modern Chemistry; by Sir H. E. Roscoe. 12mo. Lond., 1895. C 17 P 28

D'ALVIELLA, Count Goblet. The Migration of Symbols. Illustrated. Roy. 8vo. Lond., 1894. B 37 S 2

DAMIEN, Rev. Father Joseph. A Journey from Cashmere to his home in Hawaii; by E. Clifford. 12mo. Lond., 1890. MC 1 S 10
Le Père Damien; par Mme. Augustus Craven. 12mo. Paris, 1890. MC 1 S 11
Life and Letters. Edited by Father Pamphile. 12mo. Lond., 1889. MC 1 S 13
An Open Letter to Rev. Dr. Hyde. [See Stevenson, R. L.] MC 1 S 14
Story of; written for young people by Frances E. Cooke. 2nd ed. 12mo. Lond., 1890. MC 1 S 15

DANTE ALIGHIERI. A Companion to Dante; by G. A. Scartazzini. 8vo. Lond., 1893. C 13 P 21
Impressions of. [See Cross, J. W.] J 4 Q 4
Influence of, on Modern Thought. [See Oelsner, H.] J 12 S 41
Life and Work; by A. J. Butler. 8vo. Lond., 1895. C 21 P 9
Les Manuscrits de Dante. [See Auvray, L.] K 10 S 4
[Plaster Cast of.] [See Hutton, L.—Portraits in Plaster.] A 23 V 13
Readings on Inferno of. [See Vernon, Hon. W. W.] H 9 Q 5, 6
Sketch of. [See Oliphant, Mrs. M.—Makers of Florence.] B 30 Q 20
The Vita Nuova and its author. Translated by C. S. Boswell. 8vo. Lond., 1895. J 9 R 29

DANVERS, Frederick Chas. The Portuguese in India. 2 vols. 8vo. Lond., 1894. B 29 U 4, 5

D'ANVERS, N. [See Bell, Mrs. Nancy R. E.]

DANVERS LUNATIC HOSPITAL, Mass. Report for year ending September, 1892. 8vo. Boston, 1893. E

DAPTO AGRICULTURAL AND HORTICULTURAL SOCIETY. Annual Show, 1882 and 1886. Prize List. 2 vols. 8vo. Kiama, 1891-85. ME 1 S G

D'ARBLAY, Mme. Frances (Frances Burney). Diary and Letters of. Edited by Charlotte Barrett. 4 vols. 8vo. Lond. (n.d.) C 17 R 10-13

D'ARC, Jeanne. Joan of Arc; by Lord R. Gower. 8vo. Lond., 1893. C 16 T 18

DARIUS RITT. [See Uninhabitable House.] MJ 3 P 2

DARLEY, Cecil West. Notes on Drilling and Boring Artesian Wells, as practiced in the United States of America. 8vo. Sydney, 1884. MA 3 R 47

DARLEY, George. The Works of Beaumont and Fletcher. [See Beaumont, F.] H 2 U 26, 27

DARLING, Lieut. Gen. Sir Ralph. Letter to, by J. Hume. [See Hume, J.] MB 2 Q 59

DARLINGTON, T. Edwin Bainbridge: a Memoir. 12mo. Lond., 1887. MC 1 P 52

DARMESTETER, James. Selected Essays of. Translated from the French by Helen B. Jastrow. 8vo. Lond., 1895. J 9 S 26
Sketch of the Work of. [See Ecole Pratique, Annuaire, 1895.] E

DARTNELL, G. E. and GODDARD, Rev. E. H. Glossary of Words used in the County of Wiltshire. (English Dialect Soc.) 8vo. Lond., 1893. E

DARWIN, Charles. Life of; by G. T. Bettany. 12mo. Lond., 1887. C 17 P 19

Darwin and Hegel. [*See* Ritchie, D. G.] G 10 S 30

DARWIN, Erasmus. Zoönomia; or, the Laws of Organic Life. 2 vols. 8vo. Philad., 1818. A 33 S 1, 2

DARWIN, Francis and ACTON, E. Hamilton. Practical Physiology of Plants. Illustrated. Camb., 1894. A 20 Q 13

DASENT, Sir George Webbe. The Orkneyingers' Saga, Saga of Hacon and Magnus [*See* Great Britain and Ireland—Chrons. and Mems.] E

DASENT, J. R. Acts of the Privy Council. [*See* Great Britain and Ireland.] E

DAUDET, Alphonse. Biographical and Critical Study; by R. H. Sherard. Roy. 8vo. Lond., 1894. C 16 U 8

DAVENPORT, Samuel. Some New Industries for South Australia. 12 no. Adelaide, 1864. MA 3 U 6

DAVID, A. J. Notes on Fertilisers and Feeding Stuffs Act, 1893. [*See* Dyer, D.] A 13 Q 46

DAVID, Prof. Tannatt Wm. Edgeworth. Artesian Water in New South Wales and Queensland. (Journal Roy. Soc., N.S.W., 27.) 8vo. Sydney, 1893. ME 1 R

Barytes at Five Dock, Pennant Hills, and Hawkesbury. (Journal Roy. Soc., N.S W., 27.) 8vo. Sydney, 1893. ME 1 R

Occurrence of a Calcareous Sandstone allied to Fontainebleau Sandstone at Rock Lily, near Narrabeen. (Journal Roy. Soc., N.S.W., 27.) 8vo. Sydney, 1893. ME 1 R

———, and PITTMAN, Edward Fisher. Notes on the Cremorne Bore. (Journal Roy. Soc., N.S.W., 27.) 8vo. Sydney, 1893. ME 1 R

———, SMEETH, Wm. F., and WATT, John A. Preliminary note on the occurrence of a Chromite-bearing Rock in the Basalt at the Pennant Hill Quarry, Parramatta. (Journal Roy. Soc., N.S.W., 27.) 8vo. Sydney, 1893. ME 1 R

DAVIDS, Prof. Thos. Wm. Rhys. The Questions of King Milinda. [*See* Müller, F. Max—Sacred Books, 36.] G 3 R 36

DAVIDSON, Dr. George. The Discovery of Humboldt Bay, California. 8vo. San Francisco, 1891. D 13 V 2

Shoaling of the Bar at the Entrance to San Francisco Harbour. 8vo. San Francisco, 1884. A 20 U 4

DAVIDSON, Jas. Leigh Strachan-. Cicero and the Fall of the Roman Republic. 8vo. New York, 1894. C 16 R 22

DAVIDSON, John. Plays by, being an Unhistorical Pastoral; a Romantic Farce; Bruce, a Chronicle Play; Smith, a Tragic Farce; and Scaramouch in Naxos, a Pantomime. 8vo. Lond., 1894. H 2 R 41

DAVIDSON, Thos. Report on the Brachiopoda. [*See* Thomson, Sir C. W., and Murray, Dr. J.—Voyage of H.M.S. *Challenger*.] A 6 †

DAVIDSON, Thos. The Education of the Greek People and it influence on civilization. 12mo. Lond., 1895. G 18 P 27

DAVIE, Oliver. Methods in the Art of Taxidermy. Engravings by Dr. T. Jasper. Roy. 8vo. Columbus, 1894. A 30 V 11

DAVIES, A. C. Fox. Fairbairn's Book of Crests. [*See* Fairbairn, J.] K 10 V 26, 27

DAVIES, Dr. A. M. Hand-book of Hygiene. Illustrated. 12mo. Lond., 1895. A 26 P 17

DAVIES, Arthur. Thoughts on Colonization, with the view of suppressing the Slave Trade; containing proposals for the forming an association to aid and assist the Government in founding a Colony in New Holland directly from the Mother Country. 8vo. Lond., 1850. MF 2 Q 07

DAVIES, Mrs. Christian. Life of. [*See* Dowie, M. M.—Women Adventurers.] C 15 S 24

DAVIES, D. Christopher. Yachting. [*See* Sullivan, Sir E.—Yachting.] A 29 Q 41

DAVIES, John. Act to regulate the sale of Liquors, with explanatory notes. 8vo. Hobart, 1854. MF 2 Q 66

DAVIES BROS. *v.* HENN & CO. Action for Libel tried at Hobart, 1875. 8vo. Hobart, 1875. MF 2 Q 68

DAVIS, C. O. Life and Times of Patuone, the celebrated Ngapuhi Chief. 12mo. Auckland, 1876. MC 1 P 48

DAVIS, Dr. Chas. H. S. The Egyptian Book of the Dead the most ancient and the most important of the extant Religious Texts of Ancient Egypt. 4to. New York, 1894. G 37 Q 10 ‡

DAVIS, George E. Practical Microscopy. 3rd ed., illustrated. 8vo. Lond., 1895. A 30 T 13

DAVIS, Horace. American Constitutions. The Relations of the three Departments as adjusted by a Century. (Johns Hopkins University Studies, 3.) 8vo. Baltimore, 1885. B 18 S 3

DAVIS, Mrs. J. W. Memoirs of Duchesse de Gontaut. [*See* Gontaut, Duchesse de.] C 18 T 12, 13

DAVIS, Sir John Francis. The Chinese: a General Description of China and its Inhabitants. New ed. 12mo. Lond., 1840. D 17 P 4

DAVIS, Dr. John Francis. Seven Years' Civil Service Examinations for second-class Clerkships. Sm. 4to. Lond., 1893. K 9 U 30

DAVIS, John P. The Union Pacific Railway: a Study in Railway Politics, History, and Economics. 8vo. Chicago, 1894.   F 14 S 36

DAVIS, Dr. Jos. Barnard. On the peculiar Crania of the Inhabitants of certain Groups of Islands in the Western Pacific. 4to. Haarlem, 1866.   MA 9 P 32 †

DAVIS, Peter Stevenson. An Analytical Digest of the Cases decided in the Supreme Court of Victoria in 1873. 8vo. Melb., 1874.   MF 1 P 53

DAVIS, Richard Harding. Our English Cousins. Illustrated. 12mo. Lond., 1894.   D 18 T 20

The Rulers of the Mediterranean. 12mo. New York, 1894.   D 18 Q 9

DAVIS, Prof. Wm. M. Elementary Meteorology. Roy. 8vo. Boston, 1894.   A 19 T 15

DAVISON, John. Sketch of. [*See* Newman, Cardinal.—Essays.]   G 1 U 6

DAVITT, Michael. Speech delivered in Defence of the Land League. (*Times*—Parnell Commission.) 8vo. Lond., 1890.   F 7 V 5

DAVY, Dr. John. The Angler and his Friend; or, Piscatory Colloquies and Fishing Excursions. 8vo. Lond., 1855.   A 29 R 18

DAWE, W. C. The Golden Lake; or, a Marvellous History of a Journey through the Great Lone Land of Australia. 12mo. Lond., 1894.   MJ 3 P 24

DAWSON, Sir John Wm. The Canadian Ice Age, being Notes on the Pleistocene Geology of Canada, with especial reference to the Life of the Period and its Climatal Conditions. 8vo. Montreal, 1894.   A 24 R 11

The Meeting-place of Geology and History. 12mo. Lond., 1894.   A 24 Q 26

Some salient points in the Science of the Earth. Illustrated. 8vo. New York, 1894.   A 24 R 12

DAWSON, W. J. The Makers of Modern English: a Popular Hand-book to the Greater Poets of the Century. 8vo. Lond., 1893.   H 10 S 14

The Making of Manhood. 8vo. Lond., 1894.   G 18 R 34

DAWSON, Wm. H. Germany and the Germans. 2 vols. 8vo. Lond., 1894.   D 18 T 12, 13

DAWSON, Dr. Wm. Richard. Pathological Histology. [*See* Weichselbaum, Dr. A.]   A 33 U 9

DAY, Chas. Wm. Hints on Etiquette and the Usages of Society, with a Glance at Bad Habits; by "Agogos." 9th edition. 12mo. Hobart, 1838.   MJ 1 P 2

DAY, S. H. Elections. [*See* Rogers, F. N.]   F 14 R 33

DAY, Wm. The House of the Forest of Lebanon; or, the Proverbs of Solomon: a political commentary, with notes and dissertations. 8vo. Hobart, 1862.   MG 1 T 21

DAYET, Chas. Recherches pour servir à l'histoire de la Peinture et de la Sculpture Chrétiennes en Orient avant le querelle des Iconoclastes. 8vo. Paris, 1879.   A 23 U 8

DAYOT, Armand. Napoléon raconté par l'Image d'après les Sculpteurs, les Graveurs, et les Peintres. Sm. fol. Paris, 1895.   C 15 R 14 †

DAYSPRING AND NEW HEBRIDES MISSION. Reports, 1870-71, 1874, 1877, 1880, 1882-86, 1888-91. 8vo. Melb. and Sydney, 1871-92.   ME 6 S

DEACON, C. W., & Co. Dictionary of Foreign Phrases and Classical Quotations. Edited by R. D. Blackman. 12th ed. 12mo. Lond. (n.d.)   K 12 Q 48

DEAKIN, Hon. Alfred. Irrigated India: an Australian View of India and Ceylon, their Irrigation and Agriculture. 8vo. Lond., 1893.   MA 1 R 40

Temple and Tomb in India. 8vo. Melb., 1893.   MD 5 Q 53

Water Supply and Irrigation. 8vo. Melb., 1886.   MA 3 T 14

DEAN, Dr. Bashford. Fishes, Living and Fossil: an outline of their forms and probable relationships. 8vo. New York, 1895.   A 28 U 14

Physical and Biological Characteristics of the Natural Oyster Grounds of South Carolina. Imp. 8vo. Washington, 1892.   A 12 S 16 †

Report on the European Methods of Oyster-culture. Roy. 8vo. Washington, 1893.   A 13 P 21 †

Report on the Present Method of Oyster-culture in France. Roy. 8vo. Washington, 1892.   A 13 P 20 †

DEASY, J., M.P. Report: Tampering with Letters. [*See* New South Wales.]   MF 4 T 3

DEBATER, The: a Weekly Liberal Newspaper for the free discussion of all subjects. Sm. fol. Sydney, 1882.   ME 18 T

DE BAYE, Baron J. [*See* Baye, Baron J. de.]

DEBRETT, John. Peerage, Barouetage, Knightage, and Companionage, 1893-95. 8vo. Lond., 1893-95.   E

DE BRY, Theodore. [*See* Bry, T. de.]

DECAISNE, J. Botany. [*See* Le Maout, E.]   A 20 V 29

DE CASTELLA, F. [*See* Castella, F. de.]

DE COQUE, John V. Timbers of New South Wales. (Journal Roy. Soc., N.S.W., 28.) 8vo. Sydney, 1894.   ME 1 R

DEEP WATERWAYS CONVENTION. Proceedings of, held at Toronto, 1894. Roy. 8vo. Toronto, 1894.   F 1 T 18

DE FOE, Daniel. A Journal of the Plague Year. Revised ed., by E. W. Brayley; with some Account of the Great Fire in London, by Dr. G. Harvey. 8vo. Lond. (n.d.)   B 23 R 22
Life of, by T. Wright. 8vo. Lond., 1894.   C 18 T 11

DE GONTAUT, Duchesse de. [*See* Gontaut, Duchesse de.]

DE GROOTE, Dr. Paul. Nouvelle France: Colonie libre de Port Breton, Océanie. Œuvre de Colonisation, Agricole, Chrétienne et libre de C. du Breil, Marquis de Rays. 8vo. Paris, 1890.   MD 7 S 38

DEIGHTON, K. [*See* Dryden, J.]   H 10 Q 29

DELABAUME, P. La Nouvelle-Calédonie devant la France. 8vo. Paris, 1886.   MD 7 R 40

DE LA BECHE, Sir Henry T. Portrait of. [*See* Ramsay, A. C.—Memoir of.]   C 21 R 20

DELABORDE, H. François. Chartes de Terre Sainte provenant de l'Abbaye de Notre Dame de Josaphat. 8vo. Paris, 1880.   B 35 R 14
La Chronique en Prose de Guillaume le Breton. [*See* Guillaume le Breton.]   J 7 U 19

DELAMBRE, Jean Bapt. Jos. Histoire de l'Astronomie Ancienne. 2 vols. 4to. Paris, 1817. A 19 V 13, 14
Histoire de l'Astronomie Moderne. 2 vols. 4to. Paris, 1821.   A 19 V 15, 16

DELAND, Margaret. Sketch of; with Portrait. [*See* Blathwayt, R.—Interviews.]   J 10 U 34

DELANO, W. H. Practical Experience of Natural Asphalt and Mineral Bitumen. 8vo. Lond., 1893.   A 22 Q 33

DELAVILLE LE ROULX, Joseph. La France en Orient au XIVe siècle. Expéditions du Maréchal Boucicaut. 8vo. Paris, 1886.   B 26 V 20, 21

DELAWARE COLLEGE AGRICULTURAL EXPERIMENT STATION. Reports, 1890-92. 3 vols. 8vo. Wilmington, 1891-93.   E
Texas Fever. Bulletin, 23. 8vo. Newark, 1894.   A 30 R 9

DE LESSEPS, Ferdinand. [*See* Lesseps, F. de.]

DELESSERT, Eugene. Souvenirs d'un Voyage à Sydney, 1845. 8vo. Paris, 1847.   MD 5 Q 52

DE L'ISLE, G., et BAUCHE, P. Hemisphere Meridional pour voir plus distinctement les Terres Australes. [Folded] 12mo. Paris, 1782.   MD 8 P 23

DE LISSA, Alfred. Companies' Work and Mining Law in New South Wales and Victoria. 8vo. Lond., 1894.   MF 1 P 82
Protection and Federation. 12mo. Sydney, 1890.   MF 4 P 16

DE LONG, George W., and the Siberian Arctic Ocean. [*See* Greeley, Gen. A. W.—Explorers and Travellers.]   C 17 R 4

DELORME, René, "Saint Juirs." The Tavern of the Three Virtues. Translated by D. Vierge; with a Critical Essay on the Art of Vierge by E. Gosse. S n. fol. Lond. (n.d.)   J 15 R 12 †

DEMBO, Dr. J. A. The Jewish Method of Slaughtering compared with other methods from the humanitarian, hygienic, and economic points of view. Roy. 8vo. Lond., 1894.   A 33 U 1

D'EMDEN, H. J. The Parliamentary Guide: a Manual for the Electors of both Houses of the Parliament of Tasmania. 8vo. Hobart, 1893.   MF 2 Q 9

DE MARIA, Isidoro. Páginas Históricas do la República del Uruguay. 8vo. Montevideo, 1892. B 17 R 39
Compendio de la Historia de la República o. del Uruguay. 12mo. Montevideo, 1880.   B 19 P 4
Geografia Elemental de la Republica Oriental del Uruguay. 8vo. Montevideo, 1890.   D 15 S 32

DEMARR, James. Adventures in Australia fifty years ago, 1839-44. 8vo. Lond., 1893.   MD 5 R 39

DEMONAX. [*See* Transformations.]   MJ 2 T 37

DE MORGAN, Sophia Elizabeth. Threescore years and ten: Reminiscences. 8vo. Lond., 1895.   C 22 R 9

DEMOSTHENES. Life and Works of; by Dr. S. H. Butcher. 12mo. Lond., 1895.   J 16 P 32

DE MOUNCEY, Wm. A. Catalogue of the Colonial Secretary's Library. 8vo. Sydney, 1892. MK 1 B 42

DENDY, Prof. Arthur. The Hatching of a Peripatus Egg. (Proceedings of Royal Society, Victoria, n.s., 6.) 8vo. Melb., 1894.   ME 1 P
Monoxonida. [*See* Thomson, Sir C. W., and Murray, Dr. J.—Voyage of H.M.S. *Challenger*.]   A 6 †
A new variety of *Peripatus Novæ-Zelandiæ*, Hutton. (Trans. N.Z. Inst., 27.) 8vo. Wellington, 1894.   ME 2 R
New Zealand Land Nemertine. (Trans. N.Z. Inst., 27.) 8vo. Wellington, 1894.   ME 2 R
New Zealand Land Planarians. (Trans. N.Z. Inst., 27.) 8vo. Wellington, 1894.   ME 2 R
Non-calcareous Sponges collected in the neighbourhood of Port Phillip Heads. (Proc. Roy. Soc., Victoria, n.s., 7.) 8vo. Melb., 1895.   ME 1 P
Note from the Biological Laboratory of the Melbourne University: On a Crayfish with abnormally developed appendages. (Proc. of Roy. Soc., Victoria, n.s., 6.) 8vo. Melb., 1894.   ME 1 P
Notes on some new or little-known Land Planarians from Tasmania and South Australia. (Proceedings Royal Society, Victoria, n.s., 6.) 8vo. Melb., 1894.   ME 1 P

DENDY, Helen. Logic. [See Sigwart, Dr. C.]
G G T 21, 22

DENIEHY, Daniel Henry. Papers on the Reliques of. [See Donohue, F. J.]
MJ 3 S 2

DENIS, A. Océanie : de l'occupation des îles Marquises, et de l'île de Taïti. 8vo. (n.p.n.d.)
MD S R 10

DENISON, Maj.-Gen. Sir Wm. Thos. Two Lectures on Colonisation. 8vo. Richmond, 1870.
MF 3 T 51
Another Copy. (Vic. Pams.) Richmond, 1870.
MJ 3 Q 15

DENNANT, J. Marine Tertiaries of Australia. [See Tate, Prof. R.]
ME 1 S

DENNEY, Rev. J. 2nd Corinthians and Thessalonians. [See Expositor's Bible.]
G 19 S 10, 11, 15

DENNIS, John. The Age of Pope. 12mo. Lond., 1894.
J 11 U 2

Robert Southey : the Story of his Life. 12mo. Lond., 1894.
C 17 P 10

[Life of] Sir W. Scott. [See Masson, Prof. D.—In the Footsteps of the Poets.]
J 6 R 43

DENNISS, E. W. Practical Gas-fitting. [See Edwinson, G.]
A 25 R 10

DENNYS, John. The Secrets of Angling. (Bibliotheca Curiosa.) 12mo. Edinb., 1885.
J 18 Q 28

DENT, John Chas. The last forty years : Canada since the Union of 1841. 2 vols. roy. 8vo. Toronto (n.d.)
B 1 V 19, 20

DENT, Robt. K. The Making of Birmingham. 4to. Birm., 1894.
B 11 Q 16 †

DENTON, Wm. The Deluge in the Light of Modern Science. 12mo. Wellesley, Mass., 1882.
G 9 V 15

DENVER BOARD OF EDUCATION. Report of School District No. 1, 1890, 1893. 2 vols. 8vo. Denver, 1893.
E
Exhibit of the Condition of Music in the Public Schools of Denver. 8vo. Denver, 1893.
A 23 U 23

DEPEW, Chauncey M. Life and Later Speeches of. 8vo. New York, 1894.
C 21 Q 18
Orations and After-dinner Speeches. 8vo. New York, 1890.
J 8 T 31
Sketch of. [See Stoddard, W. O.—Men of Business.]
C 16 R 19

DE QUINCEY, Thomas. Confessions of an English Opium-eater. Roy. 8vo. Lond. (n.d.)
J 4 U 2

DERBY, Edward Henry, 15th Earl of. Speeches and Addresses of. Edited by Sir T. H. Sanderson and E. S. Roscoe. 2 vols. 8vo. Lond., 1894.
F 14 R 19, 20

DERBY, Henry, Earl of. [See Henry IV, King of England.]

DERECHEF, Ralph. The Anarchist Peril. [See Dubois, F.]
F 5 Q 49

DE ROOS, J. D. C. Linkages : the different Forms and Uses of Articulated Links. 18mo. New York, 1870.
A 25 P 35

DE ROS, Georgiana, Lady. Sketch of the Life of; by the Hon. Mrs. J. R. Swinton. 8vo. London, 1893.
C 13 Q 20

DE ROSNY, L. [See Rosny, L. de.]

DESBOIS, Fr. Alex. de la Chenaye. Dictionnaire de la Noblesse, avec Supplément. 15 vols. 4to. Paris, 1770-86.
K 6 R 9-23

DESCARTES, René ; by Prof. J. P. Mahaffy. (Philosophical Classics.) 12mo. Edinb., 1884.
G 9 V 1

DESCEMET, Ch. Inscriptions Doliaires Latines : Marques de Briques relatives à une partie de la Gens Domitia. 8vo. Paris, 1880.
B 35 R 12

DESCHANEL, A. Privat. Elementary Treatise on Natural Philosophy ; by Prof. J. D. Everett, F.R.S. 13th ed. 8vo. Lond., 1894.
A 28 U 10

DESIGNS FOR CHURCH EMBROIDERY ; by "A. R." Letterpress by Alethea Wiel. 4to. Lond., 1894.
A 12 S 17 †

DESPEISSIS, J. Adrian. Hand-book of Horticulture and Viticulture of Western Australia. 8vo. Perth, 1895.
MA 3 W 13

Silos, Ensilage, and Silage. 8vo. Sydney, 1891.
MA 1 Q 68
Mechanical Application of Insecticides. 8vo. Sydney, 1891.
MA 1 Q 66
Sugar-cane Disease on the North Coast. 8vo. Sydney, 1892.
MA 1 Q 67
The Vineyard and the Cellar. 8vo. Sydney, 1892.
MA 1 Q 73

DESSAR, Dr. Leonard A. Home Treatment for Catarrhs and Colds. Illustrated. 12mo. New York, 1894.
A 26 R 10

DES VŒUX, Major C. H. Hints for Rifle Clubs. 12mo. Brisb., 1890.
MA 2 P 54

DEUSSEN, Dr. Paul. Elements of Metaphysics, being a Guide for Lectures and private use. Translated by C. M. Duff, with an appendix "On the Philosophy of the Vedânta in its relations to Occidental Metaphysics." 12mo. Lond., 1894.
G 2 V 7

DEUTSCHEN GEOLOGISCHEN GESELLSCHAFT. Zeitschrift der. Bände 1-45. 8vo. Berlin, 1849-93.
E

DEUTSCHER LANDWIRTHSCHAFTSRATH. Bericht über die Verhandlungen der zwanzigsten Versammlung des Deutschen Landwirthschaftsraths, 1892. 8vo. Berlin, 1892.
E

DENEY, J. Works of Lord Bacon. [See Bacon, Lord.]
G 2 V 32

DEVIL IN SYDNEY, The; or, Barmaids, Baldheads, Mashers, &c.   12mo.   Sydney, 1895.   MF 4 P 35

DE VIS, Chas. W. Apparently new species of *Halmaturus*. (Proc. Roy. Soc., Queensland, 1.) 8vo. Brisbane, 1884.   ME 1 T

Australian ancestry of the Crowned Pigeon of New Guinea. (Proc. Roy. Soc., Queensland, 5.) 8vo. Brisbane, 1886.   ME 1 T

Colluricincia sibila. (Proc. Roy. Soc., Queensland, 5.) 8vo. Brisbane, 1884.   ME 1 T

A conspect of the genus *Heteropus*. (Proc. Roy. Soc., Queensland, 1.) 8vo. Brisbane, 1884.   ME 1 T

Description of a species of *Eleotris* from Rockhampton. (Proc. Roy. Soc., Queensland, 1.) 8vo. Brisbane, 1885.   ME 1 T

Description of new Snakes, with a synopsis of the genus *Hoplocephalus*. (Proc. Roy. Soc., Queensland, 1.) 8vo. Brisbane, 1884.   ME 1 T

Fossil Birds. (Proc. Roy. Soc., Queensland, 6.) 8vo. Brisbane, 1889.   ME 1 T

Further Account of *Prionodura Newtoniana*. (Proc. Roy. Soc., Queensland, 6.) 8vo. Brisb., 1889.   ME 1 T

The Moa in Australia. (Proc. Roy. Soc., Queensland, 1.) 8vo. Brisbane, 1884.   ME 1 T

New Australian Lizards. (Proc. Roy. Soc., Queensland, 1.) 8vo. Brisbane, 1884.   ME 1 T

New Fish from Moreton Bay. (Proc. Roy. Soc., Queensland, 1.) 8vo. Brisbane 1884.   ME 1 T

New species of *Hyla*. (Proc. Roy. Soc., Queensland, 1.) 8vo. Brisbane, 1884.   ME 1 T

New Birds from Herberton. (Proc. Roy. Soc., Queensland, 6.) 8vo. Brisbane, 1889.   ME 1 T

Notes on the Fauna of the Gulf of Carpentaria. (Proc. Roy. Soc., Queensland, 1.) 5vo. Brisb., 1884. ME 1 T

Notice of a Fish apparently undescribed. (Proc. Roy. Soc., Queensland, 2.) 8vo. Brisbane, 1886. ME 1 T

On a bone of an extinct Eagle. (Proc. Roy. Soc., Queensland, 6.) 8vo. Brisbane, 1889.   ME 1 T

On a Fossil Saurian. (Proc. Roy. Soc., Queensland, 2.) 8vo. Brisbane, 1886.   ME 1 T

On a Lizard and three species of Salarias. (Proc. Roy. Soc., Queensland, 1.) 8vo. Brisbane, 1885. ME 1 T

On a new form of the genus *Therapon*. (Proc. Roy. Soc., Queensland, 1.) 8vo. Brisbane, 1884.   ME 1 T

On a Naked-eyed Scink, apparently new. (Proc. Roy. Soc., Queensland, 5.) 8vo. Brisbane, 1889. ME 1 T

On an extinct Monotreme, *Ornithorhynchus Agilis*. (Proc. Roy. Soc., Queensland, 1.) 8vo. Brisb., 1885. ME 1 T

On an extinct Mammal of a genus apparently new. (Proc. Roy. Soc., Queensland, 4.) 8vo. Brisbane, 1887.   ME 1 T

On an extinct genus of Mammals. (Proc. Roy. Soc. Queensland, 5.) 8vo. Brisbane, 1889.   ME 1 T

On Bones and Teeth of a large extinct Lizard. (Proc. Roy. Soc., Queensland, 1.) 8vo. Brisb., 1884. ME 1 T

DE VIS, Chas. W.—*contd*.
On Ceratodus Post-Pliocene. (Proc. Roy. Soc., Queensland, 1.) 8vo. Brisbane, 1884.   ME 1 T

On *Diprotodon Minor—Hux*. (Proc. Roy. Soc., Queensland, 5.) 8vo. Brisbane, 1888.   ME 1 T

On *Megalania* and its allies. (Proc. Roy. Soc., Queensland, 6.) Brisbane, 1889.   ME 1 T

On New Queensland Lizards. (Proc. Roy. Soc., Queensland, 1.) 8vo. Brisbane, 1884.   ME 1 T

On the genera *Nototherium* and *Zygomaturus*. (Proc. Roy. Soc., Queensland, 5.) 8vo. Brisb., 1888. ME 1 T

On the *Phalangistidæ* of the Post-tertiary Period in Queensland. (Proc. Roy. Soc. Queensland, 6.) 8vo. Brisbane, 1889.   ME 1 T

The Ribbon Fish. (Proc. Roy. Soc., Queensland, 8.) 8vo. Brisbane, 1892.   ME 1 T

DE VIT, Dr. V. Totius Latinitatis Lexicon. [*See* Forcellini, A.]   K 3 R 26 †

DEVON, Earl of. Letter to, on the late massacre at Wairau. [*See* Stokes, R.]   MB 2 R 58

DEVONSHIRE, Duke of. Sketch of. [*See* Smalley, G. W.—Studies of Men.]   C 19 R 20

DEVONSHIRE DOMESDAY, The, and Geld Inquest: Extensions, Translations, and Indices. 2 vols. 8vo. Plymouth, 1884-92.   B 21 T 13, 14

DEWAR, D. Gardeners' Dictionary. [*See* Johnson, C. W.]   A 20 T 8

DEWAR, J. Cumming. Voyage of the *Nyanza*, R.N.Y.C.; being a Record of Three Years' Cruise in the Atlantic and Pacific, and her subsequent shipwreck. 8vo. Edinb., 1892.   D 10 S 36

DEWAR, Dr. Jas. On the Application of Sulphurous Acid, to the Prevention, Limitation, and Cure of Contagious Diseases. 8vo. Sydney, 1868. MA 2 S 65

DEWAR, Thos. R. A Ramble round the Globe. Illustrated. 8vo. Lond., 1894.   D 20 Q 13

DE WITT, Henry C. Lucinda and the Queen of the Fairies: an operetta in two acts. 12mo. Sydney, 1892.   MH 1 P 64

DE WULF, Dr. Maurice. La Valeur esthétique de la Moralité dans l'Art. 8vo. Bruxelles, 1892. G 3 R 19

DIAMOND, Arthur. Prince Enterprise. [*See* Lazar, S.] MH 1 Q 28

DIBDIN, Chas. Songs of; with a Memoir, illustrated by G. Cruikshank. 3rd ed. 12mo. Lond., 1850.
H 7 U 37

The Deserter: a Musical Drama. [*See* London Stage, 1.]   H 2 S 33

The Quaker: a Comic Opera. [*See* London Stage, 1.]   H 2 S 33

The Waterman; or, the First of August: a Ballad Opera. [*See* London Stage, 4.]   H 2 S 36

DIBDIN, Charles, jun. The Farmer's Wife: a Comic Opera. [*See* London Stage, 4.] H 2 S 36
The Lord of the Manor: an Opera. [*See* London Stage, 2.] H 2 S 34
My Spouse and I: an Operatical Farce. [*See* London Stage, 4.] H 2 S 36

DIBDIN, J. C., and AYLING, John. Book of the Lifeboat. Sm. 4to. Edinb., 1894. F 14 T 33

DIBDIN, Thos. What Next? a Farce. [*See* London Stage, 4.] H 2 S 36

D'IBERVILLE, Pierre Le Moyne, Sieur, Founder of Louisiana. Sketch of. [*See* Greeley, Gen. A. W.—Explorers and Travellers.] C 17 R 4
Voyage d'Iberville. Journal du Voyage fait par deux Frégates du Roi *La Badine* et *Le Marin*. 8vo. Montreal, 1871. D 14 V 3

DICEY, Edward. The Peasant State: an Account of Bulgaria in 1894. 8vo. Lond., 1894. D 18 U 11

DICK, Rev. Jas. The authority of Christ over the individual, the Church, and the nation. 8vo. Sydney 1893. MG 2 Q 23

DICKENS, Charles. Works of. Illustrated Library Edition. 30 vols. 8vo. Lond., 1874-89. J 21 R 1-30
1. Sketches by Boz.
2, 3. Pickwick Papers.
4. Oliver Twist.
5, 6. Nicholas Nickleby.
7, 8. Old Curiosity Shop.
9. Barnaby Rudge.
10. Barnaby Rudge; Hard Times.
11. American Notes and Letters from Italy.
12, 13. Martin Chuzzlewit.
14, 15. Dombey and Son.
16, 17. David Copperfield.
18, 19. Bleak House.
20. A Child's History of England.
21, 22. Little Dorrit.
23. A Tale of two Cities.
24. Uncommercial Traveller.
25. Great Expectations.
26, 27. Our Mutual Friend.
28, 29. Christmas Stories.
30. Edwin Drood.

Speeches, Literary and Social. 12mo. Lond. (n.d.) J 12 S 10
Anecdotes of. [*See* Fitzgerald, P.—Memoirs.] C 21 R 15, 16
Essay on. [*See* Bagehot, W.—Literary Studies.] J 9 P 23
The Humourist, as Democrat. [*See* Lilly, W. S.—Four English Humourists.] J 5 T 80

DICKENS, Charles, jun. Dictionary of London, 1884: an Unconventional Handbook. 12mo. Lond., 1884. D 18 P 23

DICKENS, Frederick V. Life of Sir Harry Parkes. [*See* Poole, S. L.] C 13 V 9, 10

DICKENSON, Sidney. Art Lectures. 8vo. Sydney, 1889. MA 3 V 39

DICKINS, C. Australasian Bee-keeper's Guide-book for Amateurs. 8vo. Adelaide, 1887. MA 1 U 52

DICKINSON, G. Lowes. Revolution and Reaction in Modern France. 8vo. Lond., 1892. B 26 R 9

DICKINSON, Rev. Jonathan. Familiar Letters to a Gentleman on several important subjects in Religion. 18mo. Lond., 1835. G 9 U 21

DICKINSON, Rev. R. B. Scripture and Science: a Lecture in reply to the Lecture of Mr. Justice Higinbotham on Science and Religion. 8vo. Melb., 1883. MG 2 Q 23

DICKSON, W. K. L. and A. Life and Inventions of T. A. Edison. [*See* Edison, T. A.] C 17 U 18

DICTIONARY of the English and German Languages, compiled from the best authorities. 2 vols. 8vo. Leipsic, 1813. J 5 S 34, 35

DIEHL, Prof. Charles. Etudes sur l'Administration Byzantine dans l'exarchat de Ravenne, 568-751. 8vo. Paris, 1888. B 30 T 90
L'Eglise et les Mosaïques du Couvent de Saint-Luc en Phocide. 8vo. Paris, 1889. B 35 R 27
Excursions in Greece to recently explored sites of classical interest. Translated by Emma R. Perkins. 8vo. Lond., 1893. D 18 R 12

DIET and Cookery for Common Ailments; by "A Fellow of the Royal College of Physicians" and Phyllis Browne. 12mo. Lond., 1894. A 22 Q 44

DIGGINGS, The, the Bush, and Melbourne; or, Reminiscences of Three Years' Wanderings in Victoria. 8vo. Glasgow, 1864. MB 1 R 51

DILKE, Sir Charles W. Against Reformed Upper Houses. [*See* Subjects of the Day, 4.] F 7 U 29
Problems of Greater Britain. 2 vols. 8vo. Lond., 1890. F 3 R 22, 23

DILLON, Prof. E. J. Sceptics of the Old Testament: Job, Koheleth, Agur. 8vo. Lond., 1895. G 15 Q 33

DILLON, Dr. John F. Laws and Jurisprudence of England and America: being a series of Lectures delivered before the Yale University. Roy. 8vo. Lond, 1894. F 12 Q 41

DINGEY, P. S. Machinery Pattern Making. 8vo. New York, 1891. A 25 R 5

DINGLER'S POLYTECHNISCHES JOURNAL. Band 278. 8vo. Stuttgart, 1890. E

DIODORUS SICULUS. [*See* Ramusio, G. B.—Navigationi et Viaggi.] D 36 T 5-7 ‡

DIONYSIUS, the Areopagite. [*See* Westcott, Rt. Rev. B. F.—Religious Thought in the West.] G 2 U 37

DIONYSIUS of Alexandria. Works of. (Ante-Nicene Christ. Lib., 20.) 8vo. Edinb., 1871. G 14 U 20

DISRAELI, Rt. Hon. Benjamin. [See Beaconsfield, Earl of.]

DISRAELI, Isaac. Commentaries on the Life and Reign of Charles I, King of England. 2 vols. 8vo. Lond., 1851. B 21 U 7, 8

DITCHFIELD, P. H. Books fatal to their Authors. 12mo. Lond., 1895. J 10 P 10

DITTMAR, Prof. Wm. Composition of Ocean Water. [See Thomson, Sir C. W., and Murray, Dr. J.—Voyage of H. M. S. *Challenger*.] A 6 †

DIVINITY HALL RECORD, No. 1, December, 1879. 8vo. Brisbane, 1879. ME 15 Q

DIXON, Charles. The Game Birds and Wild Fowls of the British Islands; being a Handbook for the Naturalist and Sportsman. 8vo. Lond., 1893. A 13 T 35

DIXON, D. B. Vade Mecum: a Work of Reference, with a comprehensive Treatise on Electricity by T. G. Grier. 8vo. Chicago, 1893. K 18 P 33

DIXON, John. Wood's Point Directory, 1866. [See Butler and Brooke, Messrs.] ME 6 S

DIXON, Samuel. Notes on the supposed Coal-beds of the Fitzgerald River. (Trans. Roy. Soc., S. Australia' 7.) 8vo. Adelaide, 1885. ME 1 S

Indigenous shrubs of South Australia suitable for cultivation as fodder. (Trans. Roy. Soc., S. Australia, 8.) 8vo. Adelaide, 1886. ME 1 S

DIXON, W. A. Artesian Water in connection with Irrigation. (Journal Roy. Soc., N.S.W., 27.) 8vo. Sydney, 1893. ME 1 R

Tables of Qualitative Analysis. 4th edition. 8vo. Sydney, 1892. MA 1 R 47

Analyses of Soils. [See Mackay, A.] MA 1 P 67

DIXON, W. M. English Poetry, from Blake to Browning. 12mo. Lond., 1894. H 8 Q 47

DIXON, Rev. Wm. Henry. Fasti Eboracenses. Lives of the Archbishops of York. Edited and enlarged by Rev. J. Raine. Vol. 1 (*all published*). 8vo. Lond., 1863. C 16 S 15

DIXON, Wm. Hepworth. Story of Lord Bacon's Life. 12mo. Lond., 1862. C 17 P 11

DOBBIE, A. W. Rough Notes of a Traveller. 2nd series. 8vo. Lond., 1890. MD 1 Q 59

DOBSON, Henry Austin. Eighteenth Century Vignettes. 1st and 2nd series. 8vo. Lond., 1892-94. J 14 T 15, 16

Horace Walpole: a Memoir; with an Appendix of Books printed at the Strawberry Hill Press. Roy. 8vo. Lond., 1890. C 13 V 6

DOCHNAHL, Friedrich Jacob, and RAWALD, Gustav' Der Weinkeller: Praktische Mittheilungen über Weinbau, Obst-und Trauben-Weinbereituug, Kellerwirthschaft und Weinhandel. 2 vols. 8vo. Frankfurt a.m., 1873-76. A 18 S 12, 13

DOCUMENTS and Correspondence connected with the Royal Commission on a Federal Union of the Australian Colonies. 8vo. Melb., 1871. MJ 3 Q 15

DOD, R. P. Peerage, Baronetage, and Knightage of Great Britain and Ireland, 1893-95. 3 vols. 12mo. Lond., 1893-95. E

DODD, George. History of the Indian Revolt, 1856-58. Illustrated. Roy. 8vo. Lond., 1859. B 20 V 3

DODDRIDGE, Rev. Dr. Philip. Life of Col. Jas. Gardiner. 32mo. Halifax, 1851. C 10 P 8

DODGE, Prof. Chas. W. Elementary Practical Biology. 8vo. New York, 1894. A 27 T 20

DODGE, J. R. Reports of the Division of Statistics of the United States Department of Agriculture, 1892. 8vo. Wash., 1893. E

DODS, Rev. Dr. Marcus. Genesis, Gospel of St. John, vols. 1 and 2, and 1st Corinthians. [See Expositor's Bible.] G 10 R and S

Writings of Justin Martyr. [See Justin Martyr.] G 14 U 2

Writings of Theophilus. [See Theophilus.] G 14 U 3

DODSLEY, Robt. The Miller of Mansfield: a Dramatic Entertainment. [See London Stage, 4.] H 2 S 36

DODWELL, E. S. The Carnation: its history, properties, and management; with a descriptive list of the best varieties in cultivation. 3rd edition. 8vo. Lond., 1886. A 18 R 19

DÖLLINGER, Prof. John J. von. Addresses on Historical and Literary Subjects. Translated by Margaret Warre. 8vo. Lond., 1894. B 35 R 8

Conversations of; recorded by Louise von Kobell. 8vo. Lond., 1892. C 18 P 4

DOLMAN, Frederick. Municipalities at Work: the Municipal Policy of Six Great Towns, and its influence on their social welfare. 12mo. Lond., 1895. F 8 U 11

D'OMBRIAN, Rev. Henry H. Roses for Amateurs: a practical guide to the selection and cultivation of the best roses for exhibition or mere pleasure. 8vo. Lond., (n.d.) A 18 R 11

DOMESDAY BOOK. [Fac-simile copy of.] 2 vols. 4to. (n.p.n.d.) B 37 Q 17, 18 ‡

DONALDSON, Prof. Henry H. The Growth of the Brain: a Study of the Nervous System in relation to Education. 12mo. Lond., 1895. A 25 R 23

DONALDSON, Dr. Jas. [See Ante-Nicene Christian Library.] G 14 U 1-24

DONALDSON, Dr. Thos. L. Hand-book of Specifications. Illustrated. 8vo. Lond. (n.d.)   A 19 T 16

DONALDSON, Wm. Principles of Construction and Efficiency of Water-wheels. 8vo. Lond., 1876.   A 22 S 19

DONAN, P. Utah: a Peep into a Mountain-walled Treasury of the Gods. 8vo. Buffalo, N.Y., 1891.   D 15 T 13

DONAT, Lieut. Karl von. Tactical Problems. [See Moltke, Count von.]   A 29 V 22

DONCKER, H. Oosterdeel van Oost Indien. Fol. Amsterdam (n.d.)   D 8 P 34 ‡

DONISTHORPE, Wordsworth. Law in a Free State. 8vo. Lond., 1895.   F 8 U 1

DONKIN, B. A text-book on Gas, Oil, and Air Engines; or, Internal Combustion Motors without Boilers. 8vo. Lond., 1894.   A 22 S 18

DONNE, Dr. John. Poetry of. [See Dowden, Dr. E.]   J 5 S 16
Life of. [See Walton, Izaak.]   C 19 V 6

DONNE, Wm. Bodham. Tacitus. [See Tacitus, C. C.]   B 30 Q 21

DONOHUE, Francis J. Stray Leaves: a Republication of two Literary Papers on the Reliques of the late Henry Kendall and Daniel Henry Deniehy. 8vo. Tamworth, 1883.   MJ 3 S 2

DORAN, Dr. John. Bentley Ballads. [See Bentley Ballads.]   H 7 U 32

DORÉ, Paul Gustave. The Legend of the Wandering Jew: a series of 12 designs. Fol. Lond. (n.d.)   B 41 P 23 ‡

DORMAN, Marcus R. P. From Matter to Mind. 8vo. Lond., 1895.   G 1 R 28

D'ORSEY, Rev. Alex. Jas. Donald. Portuguese Discoveries, Dependencies, and Missions in Asia and Africa. 12mo. Lond., 1893.   B 17 P 25

DOUGAL, F. H., and Co. Index to Advertisements for Next-of-kin, Heirs-at-law, Legatees, &c. 8vo. Lond. (n.d.)   K 10 T 29

DOUGHTY, Henry M. Our Wherry in Wendish Lands: from Friesland, through the Mecklenburg Lakes, to Bohemia. 8vo. Lond., 1893.   D 8 U 39

DOUGLAS, Dr. Chas. John Stuart Mill: a Study of his Philosophy. 12mo. Edinb., 1895.   G 9 V 25

DOUGLAS, James. Canadian Independence, Annexation, and British Imperial Federation. 8vo. New York, 1894.   F 8 U 6

DOUGLAS, James. Bombay and Western India: a Series of Stray Papers. 2 vols. roy. 8vo. Lond., 1893.   B 20 V 8, 9

DOUGLAS, Hon. John. The Islands of Torres Straits. (Roy. Geograph. Soc. of Australasia, Q. Branch, 1.) 8vo. Brisbane, 1896.   ME 20
Sudest and the Louisiade Archipelago. (Roy. Geograph. Soc. of Australasia, Q. Branch, 4.) 8vo. Brisbane, 1889.   ME 20

DOUGLAS, Prof. R. K. Chinese Stories. 8vo. Edinb., 1893.   J 2 Q 22
[Life of] Li Hungchang. 8vo. Lond., 1895.   C 22 P 12

DOUGLASS, Henry M. Change of Mexican Axolotl to an Amblystoma. [See Weismann, Dr. A.]   A 30 R 6

DOVE, Patrick Edward. Elements of Political Science; with an Account of A. Yarranton. 8vo. Edinb., 1854.   F 7 R 28

DOWDEN, Dr. Edward. Introduction to Shakespeare. 8vo. Lond., 1893.   C 13 Q 31
New Studies in Literature. 8vo. Lond., 1895.   J 5 S 16

DOWIE, Ménie Muriel. Women Adventurers: Lives of Madame Velazquez, Hannah Snell, Mary Ann Talbot, and Mrs. Christian Davies; edited by M. M. Dowie. 8vo. Lond., 1893.   C 15 S 24

DOWLING, Edward. Australia and America in 1892: a Contrast. Roy. 8vo. Sydney, 1893.   MF 1 S 62

DOWLING, Dr. F. The Turkish Bath, its use in Health and Disease. 12mo. Melb., 1864.   MA 3 P 57

DOWLING, James P., and M'CAFFREY, Frank. Practical Dairying for Australia. Roy. 8vo. Sydney, 1893.   MA 1 S 43

DOWN, Richard. Second Thoughts: a Collection of Ballads, Poems, and Fugitive Pieces. 12mo. Emerald Hill, 1872.   MH 1 U 50

DOWNES, Dr. A., and BLUNT, T. P. The influence of Light on Bacteria. (Roy. Soc., Vict., 20.) 8vo. Melb., 1884.   ME 1 P

DOWNES, John. Occultations visible in the United States during 1848 and 1851. 2 vols. 4to. Philad. and Wash., 1848-51.   A 15 Q 12, 13 †

DOWNEY, A. J. The Australian Grapegrowers' Manual. 8vo. Melb., 1895.   MA 3 U 24

DOWSE, Dr. Thos. Stretch. Lectures on Massage and Electricity in the Treatment of Diseases. 2nd ed. 8vo. Bristol, 1891.   A 33 S 3

DOWSING, H. J. Griffin's Electrical Engineer's Pricebook. [See Griffin, C., & Co.]   A 21 Q 42

DOZY, Ch. M. Abel Janszoon Tasman. Roy. 8vo. (n.p.n.d.)   MC 1 R 55

DRAGE, Geoffrey. The Unemployed. 12mo. Lond., 1894.   F 9 U 40
The Problem of the Aged Poor. 8vo. Lond., 1895.   F 7 V 40

DRAKE, Sir Francis. Sketch of. [*See* Southey, R.— English Seamen.] B 23 S 15
Sketch of. [*See* Froude, Prof. J. A.—English Seamen.] B 21 U 9
DRAKE DEL CASTILLO, E. Remarques sur la Flore de la Polynésie. 4to. Paris, 1890. MA 10 P 11 †

DRAPER, Prof. John Wm. History of the Intellectual Development of Europe. 2 vols. 12mo. Lond., 1875. G 7 U 34, 35

DRAYTON, Michael. The Battaile of Agincourt; with introduction and notes, by R. Garnett. 8vo. Lond., 1893. H 10 Q 28

DRAYTON, Marian. Ephemeris; or, Leaves from ye Journall of. 12mo. Lond., 1592. G 2 V 38

DREAM OF THE PAST, A or Valerian, a Dramatic Poem; by "Unda." 8vo. Melb., 1874. MH 1 Q 26

DREDGE, James. A Record of the Transportation Exhibits at the World's Columbian Exposition of 1893. 4to. Lond., 1894. A 40 U 1 ‡

DREVAR, George. The Great Sea Serpent and Sperm Whale Conflict. 8vo. Sydney, 1889. MA 3 V 38

DRIVER, Richard. Debate on the Prerogative of Pardon. [*See* Parkes, Sir H.] MF 4 Q 40

DROYSEN, Prof. Johann G. Outline of the Principles of History. Translated by E. B. Andrews. 8vo. Boston, 1893. B 35 Q 9

DRUMMOND, Prof. Henry. The Lowell Lectures on the Ascent of Man. 8vo. Lond., 1894. A 27 T 33
Natural Law in the Spiritual World. 30th ed. 8vo. Lond., 1893. G 10 P 17
A Talk with, on Science and Religion; with Portrait. [*See* Blathwayt, D.—Interviews.] J 10 U 34

DRUMMOND, Wm. Poems of. Edited by W. C. Ward. 2 vols. 12mo. Lond., 1894. H 9 P 15, 16

DRURY, G. Thorn. [Life of] J. Maclaine, "The Gentleman Highwayman," 172—50. (Lives of Twelve Bad Men.) 8vo. Lond., 1894. C 18 T 9
Waller's Poems. [*See* Waller, E.] H 3 P 37

DRYDEN, John. All for Love; or the World well Lost: a Tragedy. [*See* London Stage, 3.] H 2 S 35
Annus Mirabilis, 1666. [*See* Morris, E. E.] MJ 1 S 14
Aureng-zobe, a Tragedy; by John Dryden and Book II of the Chace, a poem; by Wm. Somerville. Edited with Biographical Memoirs and Notes by K. Deighton. 8vo. Lond., 1892. H 10 Q 29
Works of. Illustrated with notes, &c., by Sir W. Scott. Revised by G. Saintsbury. Vols. 15-18. 4 vols. 8vo. Lond., 1892-93. H 4 U 15-18
[*See* Wylie, Laura, J.—Evolution of English Criticism.] J 9 S 8

DRYSDALE, Dr. J. H. Elementary Practical Bacteriology. [*See* Kanthack, Dr. A. A.] A 26 R 11

DUANE, Dr. Alexander. Student's Dictionary of Medicine and the allied Sciences. 8vo. Philad., 1893. K 9 R 16

DUBLIN REVIEW, The. Vols. 111-115. 8vo. Lond., 1892-94. E

DUBLIN UNIVERSITY. Calendar, 1893-95. 3 vols. 12mo. Dublin, 1893-95. E

DU BOIS, Dr. Augustus Jay. Elementary Principles of 1st ed. 2 vols. 8vo. New York, 1894. A 25 U 22, 23
1. Kinematics.
2. Statics.

DUBOIS, Rev. E. My Pocket-book; or, Hints for "A Ryghte Merrie and Conceitede Tour, in Quarto, to be called 'The Stranger in Ireland.'" 12mo. Lond., 1808. D 20 P 4

DUBOIS, Félix. The Anarchist Peril. Translated, edited, and enlarged with a supplementary chapter by R. Derechef. 8vo. Lond., 1894 F 5 Q 49

DUBOIS, Marcel. Les Ligues Étoliennne et Achéenne. 8vo. Paris, 1885. B 35 R 20

DUBOIS, Dr. Raphaël. Anatomie et Physiologie comparées de la Pholade Dactyle: Structure, Locomotion, Tact, Olfaction, etc. (Annales de l'Université de Lyon, 2.) Roy. 8vo. Paris, 1892. A 27 V 16

DU BREUIL, A. Principes Généraux d'Arboriculture: anatomie et physiologie végétales, agents de la végétation-pépinières greffes. 8vo. Paris, 1884. A 18 Q 41

DU CAMP, Maxime. Literary Recollections. 2 vols. 8vo. Lond., 1893. C 16 T 16, 17
[Life of] Théophile Gautier. 8vo. Lond., 1893. C 19 Q 10

DU CHAILLU, Paul Belloni. Sketch of. [*See* Greeney, Gen. A. W.—Explorers and Travellers.] C 17 R 4

DUCHESNE, L'Abbé Louis. De Codicibus MSS. Græcis Pii II in Bibliotheca Alexandrino-Vaticana. 8vo. Paris, 1880. K 7 T 5
Étude sur le Liber Pontificalis. 8vo. Paris, 1877. J 7 U 45

DUCKETT, Sir Geo. Floyd. Visitations and Chapters-General of the Order of Cluni, from 1269-1529. Roy. 8vo. Lond., 1893. G 16 U 1

DUCKWORTH, A. A comparison of populations and rates of mortality in New South Wales and Victoria, in Sydney and Melbourne. Roy. 8vo. Sydney, 1894. MF 3 T 50

DUCKWORTH, W. Laurence Henry. Study of Collection of Crania of Aboriginal Australians in the Cambridge University Museum. (Anthropol. Inst., 23.) 8vo. Lond., 1893. E
Notes on Skulls from Queensland and South Australia. (Anthropol. Inst., 23.) 8vo. Lond., 1893. E

DUDEVANT, Mme. Amandine Lucile Aurre. "George Sand." Letters of a Traveller. Translated by Eliza A. Ashurst. 12mo. Lond., 1847. C 17 P 22
Essay on. [*See* Arnold, M.—Mixed Essays.] J 11 T 25

DUDLEY, B. The Woodman: a Comic Opera. [*See* London Stage, 4.] H 2 S 36

DUDLEY, Mrs. Lucy B. Contribution to the knowledge of the Termites. 8vo. Wellesley Hills, 1893. A 30 T 14

DUDLEY, Robt. Marriage of the Prince of Wales. Illustrated. [*See* Russell, W. H.] U 6 P 3 ‡

DUDLEY, Sir Robt. Life of; by J. T. Leader. Roy. 8vo. Florence, 1895. C 19 U 13

DUFF, C. M. Metaphysics. [*See* Deussen, Dr. P.] G 2 V 7

DUFF, E. Gordon. Information for Pilgrims unto the Holy Land. Edited by E. Gordon Duff. 8vo. Lond., 1893. D 17 T 1
Early Printed Books. 8vo. Lond., 1893. B 14 Q 30

DUFF, J. W., Consul at Gothenburg. Copy of a Letter from, with Statistics [of Crimes and Liquors]. Fol. Lond., 1877. F 30 U 1 ‡

DUFF, Rt. Hon. Sir Mountstuart E. Grant-. Ernest Renan, in Memorian. 8vo. Lond., 1893. C 12 Q 47
Sir Henry Maine : a Brief Memoir of his Life, with some of his Indian Speeches and Minutes. 8vo. Lond., 1892. C 15 R 16

DUFFERIN, Helen, Lady. Songs, Poems, and Verses. Edited, with a Memoir and some Account of the Sheridan Family, by the Marquess of Dufferin and Ava. 8vo. Lond., 1894. H 7 R 28

DUFFERIN AND AVA, Marq. of. Memoir of Helen, Lady Dufferin. [*See* Dufferin, Lady.] H 7 R 28
Yachting. [*See* Sullivan, Sir E.] A 20 Q 41

DUFFIELD, Alex. Jas. Notes on the Inhabitants of New Ireland and its Archipelago, their Fine and Industrial Art, Customs, and Language. (Proc. Roy. Soc., Queensland, 1.) 8vo. Brisbane, 1894. ME 1 T

DUFFUS, R. D. L. The Financial Depression, its cause and remedy. 8vo. Auckland, 1886. MF 4 R 37

DUFFY, Bella. The Tuscan Republics (Florence, Sienna, Pisa, and Lucca) with Genoa. (Story of the Nations.) 8vo. Lond., 1892. B 30 Q 15

DUFFY, Sir Chas. Gavan. Policy of the New Government: a Speech. 8vo. Melb., 1871. MJ 3 Q 15

——— SIGERSON, Dr. George, and HYDE, Dr. Douglas. The Revival of Irish Literature. 12mo. Lond., 1894. J 7 P 45

DUFFY, Frank Gavan, and EAGLESON, J. C. Transfer of Land Act of 1890, with Notes thereon, and a Comparative Table of the whole of the Australasian Land Transfer Acts. 8vo. Melb., 1895. MF 3 T 59

——— and MacHUGH, Alfred. The Insolvency Act, 1890, with Notes, Rules, and Index. 8vo. Melb., 1893. MF 2 R 50

DUFFY, Susan G. The English Abroad. 8vo. Lond., 1894. MD 8 P 1

DUGDALE, Mrs. H. A. Few Hours in a Far-off Age. [On Woman's Rights.] 8vo. Melb., 1883. MF 1 P 71

DUKES, Dr. Clement. Health at School, considered in its Mental, Moral, and Physical Aspects. 3rd ed. 8vo. Lond., 1894. A 26 Q 40

DUMAS, Alexandre. Celebrated Crimes. 8vo. Lond., 1843. J 4 T 24
[Life of] Napoleon. Translated by J. B. Larner. 8vo. New York, 1894. C 17 S 7

DUMAS, G. Sunshine and Showers. 12mo. Melb. (n.d.) MJ 3 P 27

DUMAS, Jean B. A. Sketch of. [*See* Thorpe, Dr. T. E. —Historical Chemistry.] C 17 R 2

DUN, Finlay. Veterinary Medicines, their Actions and Uses. 8th ed. 8vo. Edinb., 1892. A 30 R 19

DUNBAR, Prof. Chas. F. Chapters on the Theory and History of Banking. 8vo. New York, 1894. F 8 U 33

DUNBAR, Wm. Poems of. [*See* Scottish Text Society.] E

DUNBAR, The. A Narrative of the melancholy Wreck of the *Dunbar*, 1857. 8vo. Sydney, 1857. MD 8 R 29

DUNCAN, Edward. Marine Painting [in water-colours]. 4to. Lond. (n.d.) A 8 U 34

DUNCAN, George. Prof. Koch on the Bacteriological Diagnosis of Cholera. [*See* Koch, Prof.] A 33 T 20

DUNCAN, Miss L. J. The Sailor of the Istar; by "El Jady." 8vo. Lond., 1893. MJ 1 T 40

DUNCAN, L. L. Gloucester Wills, 1541-1650. [*See* British Record Society.] E

DUNCAN, Lindsay. [*See* Cloud, Mrs. T. C.]

DUNDERDALE, George. Prairie and Bush. 8vo. Lond., 1891. MD 7 T 38

DUNMORE, Earl of. The Pamirs. 2 vols. 8vo. Lond., 1893. D 14 R 9, 10

DUNN, E. J. Glaciation of the Western Highlands, Tasmania. (Proceedings Royal Society, Victoria, n.s., 6.) 8vo. Melb., 1894. ME 1 P

DUNN, Jacob Piat. The Libraries of Indiana. 8vo. Indianapolis, 1893. J 4 S 28
Slavery Petitions and Papers. 8vo. Indianapolis, 1894. F 11 U 7
Documents relating to the French Settlements on the Wabash. 8vo. Indianapolis, 1894. B 19 R 37

DUNN, Malcolm. Report of the Apple and Pear Congress, held by the Royal Caledonian Horticultural Society, Edinburgh, from 25th to 28th November, 1885. 8vo. Edinb., 1887. A 16 S 27
Horticultural Hand-book. [See Williamson, W.] A 32 R 10

DUNN, Mrs. Sara H. The World's Highway, with some first Impressions whilst journeying along it. 8vo. Lond., 1894. D 20 S 2

DUNNING, Rev. Dr. Albert E. Congregationalists in America, their Origin, Fidity, Growth, and Work. Roy. 8vo. New York, 1894. G 8 U 28

DUNSTAN, B. Occurrence of Triassic Plant Remains in a Shale Bed near Manly. (Journal Roy. Soc., N.S.W., 27.) 8vo. Sydney, 1893. ME 1 R

DUNSTAN, Rev. E. Tremayne. Facts and Fancies of Prior Vaughan and Cardinal Moran. 8vo. Sydney, 1895. MG 1 T 34

DUPLAIS, P., Aine et Jeune. Manufacture and Distillation of Alcoholic Liquors. Translated by Dr. M. McKennie. Illustrated. 5vo. Philad., 1871. A 25 V 23

DUPRÉ, A., and HAKE, H. Wilson. Short Manual of Inorganic Chemistry. 2nd edition. 8vo. Lond., 1892. A 21 R 5

DÜRER, Albrecht. Engravings of; by L. Cust. [See Portfolio Monograph, 11.] E

D'URFEN, Mr. A Commonwealth of Women. [See Bibliotheca Curiosa.] J 18 Q 33

DURHAM, Earl of. [See Great Britain and Ireland—British North America.] F 9 Q 18, F 36 Q 22-24†

DURRANCE, F. J. Brass Casting at Home. [See Edwinson, G.]. A 25 R 10

DURRIEU, Paul. Les Archives Angevines de Naples: Etude sur les registres du Roi Charles I, 1265-85. 8vo. Paris, 1886. B 35 R 10

DURRIEU, Xavier. Present State of Morocco: a Chapter of Mussulman Civilisation. 12mo. Lond., 1854. F 7 V 19

D'URTE, Pierre. Earliest Translation of the Old Testament into the Basque Language. (Anecdota Oxoniensia.) Sm. 4to. Oxford, 1894. E

DURUY, George. Memoirs of Barras. [See Barras, Paul.] C 21 T 15, 16

DUTHIE, J. F. Fodder Grasses of Northern India. [Illustrated.] 2 vols. roy. 8vo. Roorkee, 1888. A 20 V 28

DUTHIE, J. F., and FULLER, J. B. Field and Garden Crops of the North-western Provinces and Oudh. Illustrated. Parts 1 and 2. 4to. Roorkee, 1882. A 12 S 11, 12†

DUTT, Romesh Chunder. Lays of Ancient India: Selections from Indian Poetry rendered into English Verse. 8vo. Lond., 1894. H 5 T 43

DUTTON, Capt. Clarence Edward. Tertiary History of the Grand Cañon District. (U.S. Geol. Survey, 2.) 4to. Wash., 1882. E

DUTTON, Dr. Thos. Food and Drink rationally discussed. 8vo. Lond., 1894. A 26 R 22

DVORÁK, Antonin. Studies in Modern Music. [See Hadow, W. H.] C 21 Q 15

DWYER, Major Francis. Seats and Saddles, Bits and Bitting, Draught and Harness, and the Prevention and Cure of Restiveness in Horses. 4th ed. 12mo. Lond., 1886. A 29 R 20

DWYER, Rev. P. Siege of Londonderry, 1689. [See Walker, Rev. G.] B 29 T 21

DYCE, Rev. Alex., and FORSTER, John. Hand-book of the Dyce and Forster Collections in the South Kensington Museum. 8vo. Lond., 1880. A 23 R 38

DYER, B. Fertilisers and Feeding Stuffs: their Properties and Uses; with full text of the Fertilisers and Feeding Stuffs Act, 1893, the Regulations of the Board of Agriculture, and Notes on the Act by A. J. David. 12mo. Lond., 1894. A 18 Q 46
Some scientific aspects of Cheese-making: a Lecture. (Inst. of Agricult., Lond.) 8vo. Lond., 1884. A 18 R 28

DYER, Dr. Henry. The Evolution of Industry. 8vo. Lond., 1895. F 9 T 23

DYER, Rev. Thos. F. T. Strange Pages from Family Papers. 12mo. Lond., 1895. J 12 T 38

DYKES, Rev. Dr. Jas. Oswald. The Written Word, and other Essays. 12mo. Melb., 1868. MG 1 P 66

E

E., J.W. [See Sketches from Life.] MJ 1 Q 1
E.P.R. [See Romance of the Bush.] MJ 1 P 64
E.W.Y. [See Want of Lucidity.] G 16 S 51

EAGLESON, J. G. Transfer of Land Act of 1890. [See Duffy, F. G.] MF 3 T 59
Liability of Employers: Statutes and Forms. 8vo. Melb., 1895. MF 3 T 54
——— and WASLEY, J. S. Digest of Reported Cases in the Supreme Court, Court of Insolvency, and the Courts of Mines in Victoria, 1885-90. Roy. 8vo. Melb., 1893. MF 1 S 63

EARL, Alfred. Practical Lessons in Physical Measurement. Illustrated. 12mo. Lond., 1894. A 25 P 24

EARLE, J. The Psalter of the Great Bible of 1539: a Landmark in English Literature. 8vo. Lond., 1894. G 13 P 38

EARLE, Rev. John. English Prose, its Elements, History, and Usage. 8vo. Lond., 1890. K 18 R 33

EARLY BALLADS, illustrative of History, Traditions, and Customs. Edited by R. Bell. 12mo. Lond., 1861. H 10 T 32

EARLY ENGLISH TEXT SOCIETY. Publications. 8 vols. Lond., 1874-94. E
   Cursor Mundi (The Cursur o the World): a Northumbrian Poem of the XIVth Century in four versions. Edited by Rev. R. Morris. Vols. 1-3.
   The Earliest English Translation of De Imitatione Christi. Edited by Dr. J. K. Ingram.
   History of the Holy Rood-tree. Edited by A. S. Napier.
   Life of St. Katharine of Alexandria; by Rev. Dr. J. Capgrave.
   Lydgate and Burgh's Secrees of Old Philisoffres: a Version of the "Secreta Secretorum." Edited by R. Steele.
   Romance of Sir Beues of Hamtoun. Edited by Prof. E. Kölbing.

EARLY VENETIAN PRINTING ILLUSTRATED. Sm. fol. Venice, 1895. A 30 T 18 ‡

EARWAKER, John Parsons. The Constables' Account of the Manor of Manchester, 1612-47, and 1743-76. Edited by J. P. Earwaker. 3 vols. Roy. 8vo. Manchester, 1891-92. B 22 V 13-15

EASDOWN, W. R. Editha: a Poetical Tale, founded on certain Kentish Legends. 8vo. Sydney, 1883. MH 1 S 36

EAST, J. J. On a Geological Section from the Head of St. Vincent Gulf Eastward across the Wakefield and Light River Basins. (Trans. Roy. Soc., S. Australia, 8.) 8vo. Adelaide, 1886. ME 1 S

EAST INDIA CO. Register of Letters, &c., of the Governour and Company of Merchants of London trading into the East Indies, 1600-19. Edited by Sir Geo. Birdwood and W. Foster. Roy. 8vo. Lond., 1893. B 29 V 2

EASTER MANŒUVRES of 1885, together with an Account of the Naval Attack on the Heads. 8vo. Sydney, 1885. MA 2 V 59

EATON, Wm. L. Account of the Movement in Massachusetts to close the Rural Schools. 8vo. Boston, 1893. G 18 Q 21

ECCLES, Dr. A. Symons. The Practice of Massage, its Physiological Effects and Therapeutic Uses. 8vo. Lond., 1895. A 26 S 22

ECCLESTON, R. H. Handbook for the Tasmanian Artillery Volunteers. 12mo. Hobart, 1868. MA 2 P 48

ECHO, The. Oct., 1892-July, 1893. 3 vols. fol. Sydney, 1892-93. ME

ECKSTEIN, Ernst. The Art Treasures of Italy. 2 vols. 4to. Lond. (n.d.) A 23 R 23, 24 ‡

ECLECTIC, An. [See Human Life.] MF 4 R 2

ÉCOLE PRATIQUE DES HAUTES ÉTUDES. Annuaire, 1893-95. 8vo. Paris, 1893-95. E

ECONOMIC JOURNAL, The. The Journal of the British Economic Association. Vols. 1-4. 8vo. Lond., 1891-94. E

ECONOMIC REVIEW, The. Vols. 1-4. 8vo. Lond., 1891-94. E

EDDY, Edward Millar G. Report of the Royal Commission appointed to inquire into the charges against E. M. G. Eddy, preferred by W. F. Schey. Fol. Sydney, 1892. MF 2 U 48

EDDY, Dr. Henry Turner. Thermodynamics. 18mo. New York, 1879. A 21 P 17

EDELFELT, E. G. Notes on New Guinea. (Roy. Geograph. Soc. of Australasia, Q. Branch, 2, 3.) 8vo. Brisbane, 1887-89. ME 20
   Customs and Superstitions of New Guinea Natives. (Roy. Geograph. Soc. of Australasia, Q. Branch 7.) 8vo. Brisbane, 1892. ME 20

EDELMAN, Henry. School History of Peter the Great, Czar of Russia. 8vo. Melb., 1871. MB 1 P 20

EDGAR, F. S. Map of the Aboriginal Settlement at Flinders Island, surveyed by the Commandant, G. A. Robinson, and copied by F. S. Edgar. Fol. Hobart, 1838. MD 5 Q 16 ‡

EDGAR, Lieut. Thomas. Chart of the West Falkland Islands, 1786-87. Fol. Lond., 1797. MD 1 P 15 ‡

EDGEWORTH, Maria. Life and Letters of. Edited by A. J. C. Hare. 2 vols. 8vo. Lond., 1894. C 21 P 5, 6

EDINBURGH, H.R.H. Duke of. Record of the Visit of, to Australia. [See Tulk, A. H.] MD 2 P 24, 25 ‡

EDINBURGH AND LEITH P.O. DIRECTORY, 1893-94. 8vo. Edinb., 1894. E

EDINBURGH ARCHITECTURAL ASSOCIATION. Sketch-book, 1875-79. 2 vols. fol. Edinb. (n.d.) A 6 U 3, 4 ‡

EDINBURGH HOSPITAL REPORTS. Vols. 1 and 2. Roy. 8vo. Edinb., 1893-94. E

EDINBURGH PUBLIC LIBRARY. Catalogue of Books added to the Lending Library, 1890-93. 8vo. Edinb., 1893. K 8 R 22
   Catalogue of Books in the Juveniles' Library. 8vo. Edinb., 1893. K 8 R 23

EDINBURGH REVIEW, The: or, Critical Journal. Vol. 176. 8vo. Lond., 1892. E

EDINBURGH UNIVERSITY Calendar, 1892-95.
3 vols. 12mo. Edinb., 1892-94. E

EDISON, Thos. A. Life and Inventions of; by W. K. L.
and A. Dickson. Illustrated. Imp. 8vo. Lond.,
1894. C 17 U 18
Sketch of. [See Hubert, P. G.—Inventors.] C 17 R 3

EDMONDS, H. H. Sydney Nautical Almanac and Postal
Guide, 1893 and 1894. 2 vols. 8vo. Sydney, 1893-94.
ME 6 R

EDMUND, St., of Canterbury. Life of, from original
sources; by Dr. W. Wallace. 8vo. Lond., 1893.
C 16 T 14

EDNIE-BROWN, J. [See Brown, J. Ednie-.]

EDUCATIONAL GAZETTE, The, Literary Companion
and General Review. Vol. 1. Roy. 8vo. Melb.,
1892. ME 8 R

EDWARD I., King of England. [Life of]; by Prof. T.
F. Tout. (Twelve English Statesmen.) 8vo. Lond.,
1893. C 13 Q 30

EDWARDS, C. The Witness of Assyria; or, the Bible
contrasted with the Monuments. 12mo. Lond., 1893.
G 16 R 46

EDWARDS, Dennis, & Co. The Gold Fields of South
Africa. 8vo. Capetown, 1890. A 24 V 11

EDWARDS, Henry. [Plaster Cast of.] [See Hutton, L.—
Portraits in Plaster.] A 23 V 13

EDWARDS, Miss Matilda Barbara Bethan-. France of
To-day; a Survey Comparative and Retrospective.
2 vols. 8vo. Lond., 1894. D 18 R 21, 22

EDWARDS, Rev. Thos. Chas. Hebrews. [See Expositor's
Bible.] G 19 S 17

EDWINSON, George, DENNISS, E. W., and DUR-
RANCE, F. J. Metal Working for Amateurs. Part
1. Brazing and Soldering. Part 2. Practical Gas-
fitting. Part 3. Brass Casting at Home. Illustrated.
8vo. Lond., 1893. A 25 R 10

EDWORDS, Clarence E. Camp-fires of a Naturalist.
12mo. Lond., 1893. D 14 P 2

EELKING, Capt. H. von. The German Allied Troops
in the North American War of Independence, 1776-
83. Translated and abridged by J. G. Rosengarten.
Sm. 4to. Albany, 1893. B 17 R 24

EERELMAN, O. Horses and Dogs. Translated from
the Dutch by Carn Bell. 4to Lond., 1895.
A 40 U 4 ‡

EGAN'S TOWN ST. PATRICK'S SOCIETY. Rules and
By-laws. 8vo. Daylesford, 1869. MF 2 R 55

EGGELING, Julius. Satapatha-Brahmana. [See Müller,
F. Max.—Sacred Books.] G 3 S 36

EGINARD. Life of the Emperor Karl, the Great.
Translated by Wm. Glaister. 8vo. Lond., 1877.
C 13 P 18

EGLESTON, Melville. The Land System of the New
England Colonies. (Johns Hopkins University
Studies, 4.) 8vo. Baltimore, 1886. B 18 S 4

EGLESTON, Dr. Thos. Catalogue of Minerals, with their
Formulas, &c., prepared for the Smithsonian Institution. 8vo. Wash., 1833. A 20 V 17

EGLINTON, Wm. 'Twixt Two Worlds: a Narrative
of Life and Works of; by J. S. Farmer. 4to. Lond.,
1886. C 1 W 7

EGYPT EXPLORATION FUND. Ahnas el Medineh
(Heracleopolis Magna) with Chapters on Mendes, the
Nome of Thoth, and Leontopolis; by Dr. E. Naville.
Illustrated. 4to. Lond., 1894. B 12 T 5 †
Archæological Report, 1892-93. Illustrated. Sm. 4to.
Lond. (n.d.) E
An Atlas of Ancient Egypt. Sm. fol. Lond., 1894.
D 13 P 18 †
Beni Hasan; by P. E. Newberry. 4to. Lond., 1893.
B 12 T 2, 3 †
El Bersheh. Pt. 1. The Tomb of Tehuti Hetep; by
P. E. Newberry. 4to. Lond., 1894. B 2 P 22 †
The Festival Hall of Osorkon II. in the Great Temple
of Bubastis, 1887-89; by Dr. E. Naville. 4to. Lond.,
1892. B 12 T 1 †
The Temple of Deir el Bahari; by Dr. E. Naville. 4to.
Lond., 1894. B 2 P 26 †

EHA. [See Naturalist on the Prowl.] A 28 U 2

EHRICH, L. R. The Question of Silver. 8vo. New
York, 1892. F 8 U 27

EIGENMANN, Dr. Carl H. and Rosa S. A Revision of
the South American *Nematognathi*, or Cat-fishes. 8vo.
San Francisco, 1890. A 30 U 14

EIMER, Prof. G. H. T. Organic Evolution as the result
of the Inheritance of Acquired Characters according
to the Laws of Organic Growth. Translated by J. T.
Cunningham. 8vo. Lond., 1890. A 13 T 36

EISSLER, M. The Cyanide Process for the Extraction of
Gold. 8vo. Lond., 1895. A 24 R 15

ELDER SCIENTIFIC EXPLORING EXPEDITION,
1891-92, Journal of the. 2 vols. 8vo. Adelaide,
1893. MD 8 Q 44, 45

ELECTORS BEWARE; by "Veritas." 8vo. Melb.,
1861. MF 4 Q 22

ELECTRIC UNIVERSE, The. Flashing Thoughts and
Facts from Many Sources; by "Torpedo." 8vo.
Auckland, 1883. MA 1 V 41

ELECTRICAL WORLD, The. Vols. 23, 24, 1894. Fol.
New York, 1894. E

ELGER, Thos. Gwyn. The Moon: a full Description and Map of its Principal Physical Features. Roy. 8vo. Lond., 1895.   A 19 V 23

ELIAS, N. The Tarikh-i-Rashidi; or, Mirza Muhammad Haidar Dughlát: a History of the Moguls of Central Asia. Translated by E. D. Ross. 8vo. Lond., 1895.   B 33 R 1

ELIOT, George. [See Cross, Mrs. M. A.]

ELIZABETH, Queen of England. Catalogue of Portraits [See O'Donoghue, F. M.]   K 11 R 11

ELIZABETH, Saint, of Hungary. Chronicle of the Life of; written in French by the Count de Montalembert; translated by Ambrose Lisle Phillipps. 4to. London, 1839.   C 2 W 24

EL JADY. [See Duncan, Miss L. J.]

ELLERY, Robert L. J. A Description of a new Pendulum Apparatus, with half-seconds Pendulums. (Proceedings Royal Society, Victoria, n.s., 6.) 8vo. Melb., 1894.   ME 1 P

An improved Ombrograph, or self-registering Rain-gauge. (Roy. Soc., Vic., 17.) 8vo. Melb., 1891.   ME 1 P

Monthly Record of Results of Observations in Meteorology, Terrestrial Magnetism, &c., during November, 1872, and April, 1874. 8vo. Melb., 1872-74.   ME 6 Q

The new Chain Test Range at the Melbourne Observatory. (Proceedings, Royal Society, Victoria, n.s., 6.) 8vo. Melb., 1894.   ME 1 P

Notes on the Rainfall Map recently issued by the Government of Victoria. (Roy. Soc., Vict., 20.) 8vo. Melb., 1884.   ME 1 P

Relation between Forest Land and Climate in Victoria. (Roy. Soc., Vict., 16.) 8vo. Melb., 1880.   ME 1 P

Tidal Datum of Hobson's Bay. (Roy. Soc., Vict., 16.) 8vo. Melb., 1880.   ME 1 P

ELLES, Herbert L. Supplement to District Court Acts. [See Coffey, W. H.]   MF 2 Q 6

ELLICOTT, Rt. Rev. Chas. John. New Testament Commentary for English Readers. 6th ed. Imp. 8vo. Lond., 1893.   G 13 V 33

ELLIOT, Frances. Diary of an Idle Woman in Constantinople. 8vo. Lond., 1893.   D 18 R 8
Roman Gossip. 8vo. Lond., 1894.   C 21 Q 10

ELLIOT, Robert Henry. Gold, Sport, and Coffee Planting in Mysore. 8vo. Lond., 1894.   A 29 R 11

ELLIOT, S. F. The Canadian Controversy: its Origin, Nature, and Merits. 2nd ed. 8vo. Lond., 1838.   F 14 R 10

ELLIOTT, Maud Howe. Art and Handicraft in the Woman's Building of the World's Columbian Exposition, Chicago, 1893. Roy. 8vo. Paris, 1893.   A 23 V 9
Sketch of, with Portrait. [See Blathwayt, R.—Interviews.]   J 10 U 34

ELLIOTT, Wm. Australian Gardener. [See Adamson, Wm.]   MA 1 R 53

ELLIS, Lieut.-Col. Alfred Burdon. History of the Gold Coast of West Africa. 8vo. Lond., 1893.   B 10 S 3
The Yoruba-speaking peoples of the Slave Coast of West Africa, their Religion, Manners, Customs, Laws, Language, &c. 8vo. Lond., 1894.   A 18 S 24

ELLIS, Annie R. Sylvestra: Studies of Manners in England, 1700-1800. 2 vols. 12mo. Lond., 1881.   F 7 V 41, 42

ELLIS, Edwin John. Works of William Blake, poetic, symbolic, and critical. [See Blake, Wm.]   J 4 U 11-13

ELLIS, Havelock. Man and Woman: a Study of Human Secondary Sexual Characters. Illustrated. 8vo. Lond., 1894.   A 29 P 3
The Nationalisation of Health. 8vo. Lond., 1892.   A 12 Q 29

ELLIS, J. H. Chess Sparks; or, Short and Bright Games of Chess. 8vo. Lond., 1895.   A 29 T 32

ELLIS, Smith. Preventive for Rust in Wheat. 8vo. Melb., 1890.   MA 3 V 23

ELLIS, Wm. A. Wagner's Prose Works. [See Wagner, R.]   J 4 S 14, 15

ELLISTON, Robt. Wm. Life and Enterprises of; by G. Raymond. Illustrated. 12mo. Lond., 1857.   C 17 P 6

ELLOY, Rev. Mgr. Louis. Le Missionnaire des Samoa; par le Père A. Monfat. 3rd ed. 8vo. Lyon (n.d.)   MC 1 T 19

ELSASSER, Chas. Life of Handel. [See Handel, G. F.]   MC 1 T 20

ELSNER, Dr. F. Raw Materials and Distillation of Alcohol. [See Stammer, Dr. K.]   A 25 Q 39

ELTING, Irving. Dutch Village Communities on the Hudson River. (Johns Hopkins University Studies, 4.) 8vo. Baltimore, 1886.   B 18 S 4

ELTON, Chas. Isaac. Account of Shelley's Visits to France, Switzerland, and Savoy, in 1814 and 1816; with extracts from "The History of a six weeks' Tour," and "Letters descriptive of a sail round the Lake of Geneva and of the Glaciers of Chamouni," first published in 1817. Illustrated. 12mo. Lond., 1894.   D 18 Q 11

—— and Mary Augusta. The Great Book-Collectors. 8vo. London, 1893.   B 14 Q 20

ELTON, O. Danish History of Saxo Grammaticus. [See Folk-lore Society, 33.]   E

ELVIN, Chas. Norton. Handbook of the Orders of Chivalry, War Medals, and Crosses, with their Clasps and Ribbons, and other Decorations. 4to. Lond., 1893.   K 10 T 5

ELWELL, Thos. D. An Official Guide to the National Park of New South Wales. Sm. 4to. Sydney, 1893.
MD 5 R 49

ELWIN, E. F. Bones. [See Taylor, Dr. J. E.—Collecting Natural History Objects.] A 29 Q 35

ELWIN, Rev. Fountain. Sermons preached at the Octagon Chapel Bath. 12mo. Lond., 1842. G 17 Q 5

ELY, Dr. Richard T. The Past and the Present of Political Economy. (Johns Hopkins University Studies, 2.) 8vo. Baltimore, 1884. B 18 S 2

Recent American Socialism : Early American Communism ; Henry George and the Beginnings of Revolutionary Socialism ; International Working Men's Association ; Propaganda of Deed and the Educational Campaign ; Socialistic Labor Party ; Strength of Revolutionary Socialism ; Remedies. (Johns Hopkins University Studies, 3.) 8vo. Baltimore, 1885.
B 18 S 3

ELYARD, Samuel. Explanation of a Portion of the Prophecies relating to the Jews and the Romish Papacy, Roy. 8vo. Nowra, 1887. MG 1 T 29

EMBDEN, Baron Ludwig von. Family Life of Heine. [See Heine, H.] C 16 R 19

EMERSON, Edward Waldo. Emerson in Concord: a Memoir. 8vo. Lond., 1889. C 21 Q 1

EMERSON, Dr. George L, and FLINT, Chas. L. Manual of Agriculture for the School, the Farm, and the Fireside. New Edition, revised by Prof. C. A. Goessmann. 8vo. New York, 1895. A 18 Q 34

EMERSON, Dr. O. F. History of the English Language. 8vo. New York, 1894. J 8 R 12

EMERSON, Ralph Waldo. Select Writings of; with an Introduction by P. Chubb. 12mo. Lond., 1888.
J 12 S 36

Essays and Orations. 8vo. Lond., 1853. J 4 U 1
Natural History of Intellect. 8vo. Lond., 1894.
J 9 S 20

Representative Men : Seven Lectures. 12mo. Lond., 1850. C 17 P 10

Emerson in Concord : a Memoir. 8vo. Lond., 1889.
C 21 Q 1

Life of ; by Dr. R. Garnett. 8vo. Lond., 1888.
C 17 S 17

Sketch of. [See Burroughs, J.—Birds and Poets.]
J 16 T 38

EMERTON, Dr. Ephraim. Mediæval Europe, 814-1300. 8vo. Boston, 1894. B 25 Q 24

EMINENT PERSONS : Biographies reprinted from The Times. Vols. 1-4, 1876-90. 4 vols. 8vo. Lond., 1892-93. C 19 Q 17-20

EMMET, Wm Le Roy. Alternating Current Wiring and Distribution. 12mo. New York, 1894. A 21 P 94

EMMONS, S. F. Geology and Mining Industry of Leadville, Colorado ; with atlas. (U.S. Geol. Survey, 12.) 4to. Wash., 1886. E

EMPLOYERS, SERVANTS, AND REGISTRY OFFICES; or, The Little Wonder ; by a Great Fool : and Both Sides of the Question, by W.M. 12mo. Melb., 1865.
MF 1 F 77

EMPORIA STATE NORMAL SCHOOL, Kansas. Catalogue, 1892, 1893. 8vo. Emporia, 1893. E

EMPSON, Lieut. Chas. A. Hasty Intrenchments. [See Beaumont, Col. A.] A 29 T 23

ENCYCLOPÆDIA BRITANNICA. Supplement to the 9th ed. 4 vols. 4to. Philad., 1885-02. K 2 T 16-19

ENCYKLOPÆDIE DER NATURWISSENSCHAFTEN Abtheilung 2, Theil 3. Handwörterbuch der Chemie ; von Prof. Dr. A. Ladenburg.—Abtheilung 3, The l 1. Handbuch der Physik ; von Prof. Dr. A. Winkelmann. 2 vols. Roy. 8vo. Breslau, 1893-94. E

ENDICOTT ROCK. Report of the Commissioners for the preservation, protection, and appropriate designation of the Endicott Rock [Mass., U.S.] 8vo. Concord, Mass., 1893. D 18 E 13

ENDLICH, F. M. Manual of Qualitative Blowpipe Analysis and Determinative Mineralogy. 8vo. New York, 1892. A 24 U 15

ENGEL, Carl. Musical Instruments. 8vo. Lond., 1875.
A 23 R 20

ENGINEER, The. Vols. 74-78. Fol. Lond., 1892-94.
E

ENGINEERING : an Illustrated Weekly Journal. Vols. 54-58. Fol. Lond., 1892-94. E

ENGINEERING AND MINING JOURNAL. Statistical Supplement. The Mineral Industry its Statistics, Technology, and Trade, in the United States and other countries, from the earliest times to the end of 1893. Edited by R. P. Rothwell. Vols. 1 and 2. Roy. 8vo. New York, 1893-94. E

ENGINEERING ASSOCIATION OF NEW SOUTH WALES. Minutes of Proceedings. Vols. 6 and 7. 2 vols. 8vo. Sydney, 1891-92. ME 1 T

ENGINEERING MAGAZINE, The. Vols. 4, 5, Oct., 1892—Nov., 1893. Vol. 7, Apr.-Sept., 1894. Vol. 9, Apr.-Sept., 1895. Fol. New York, 1893-95. E

ENGINEERING RECORD, The, Building Record, and the Sanitary Engineer. Vols. 26-29. Fol. New York, 1892-94. E

ENGLISH, John. [See Norton, John.]

ENGLISH CHARTIST CIRCULAR, The, and Temperance Record for England and Wales, 1841-42. Fo. London, 1841-42. E

ENGLISH DIALECT SOCIETY. Publications of. 9 vols. 8vo. Lond., 1886-94. E
- Folk-phrases of four Counties ; Gloucester, Stafford, Warwick, Worcestershire ; by G. F. Northall.
- Glossary of the Lancashire Dialect ; by J. H. Nodal and G. Milner.
- Glossary of Words used in the County of Chester ; by R. Holland.
- Glossary of Words used in the County of Northumberland and on Tyneside ; by R. O. Heslop. 2 vols.
- Glossary of Wiltshire Words.
- Northumberland Words ; by Rd. O. Heslop.
- Surrey Words ; by G. L. Gower.
- S.E. Worcestershire Words ; by J. Salisbury.

Reports, 1877, 1884, 1887. 3 vols. 8vo. Manchester, 1877-88. E

ENGLISH FORESTS AND FOREST TREES, Historical, Legendary, and Descriptive. Illustrated. 8vo. Lond., 1853. B 23 T 20

ENGLISH HISTORICAL REVIEW, The. Vols. 7-10. Roy. 8vo. Lond., 1892-95. E

ENGLISH ILLUSTRATED MAGAZINE. Vols. 1-13. Roy. 8vo. Lond., 1883-95. E

ENGLISH MECHANIC AND WORLD OF SCIENCE. Vols. 56-59. Sm. fol. Lond., 1893-94. E

ENGRAVINGS AND WOOD-CUTS BY OLD MASTERS, reproduced in fac-simile and published under the direction of Dr. F. Lippman. 6 vols. fol. Lond., 1889-95. A 41 P 29-34 ‡

ENKO, Dr. P. Sketch of the St. Petersburg Alexander Institution. 8vo. St. Petersburg, 1893. G 18 Q 17

ENLART, C. Origines Françaises de l'Architecture Gothique en Italie. 8vo. Paris, 1894. A 19 V 26

ENRIQUES, R. De Zayas. Los estados unidos Mexicanos sus condiciones naturales y sus elementos de prosperidad. 4to. Mexico, 1893. D 12 U 7 †

ENTOMOLOGIST'S MONTHLY MAGAZINE, The. 2nd Series, vols. 3-5. 8vo. Lond., 1892-94. E

EPICTETUS. [Life of.] [*See* Farrar, Archdeacon F. W.—Seekers after God.] C 21 Q 6

EPILEPTIC AND CRIPPLED, The, Child and Adult: a Report on the Present Condition of these Classes of Afflicted Persons, with Suggestions for their better Education and Employment. (Charity Organisation Series.) 8vo. Lond., 1893. A 12 Q 40

EPISTLE from a Nobleman to a Doctor of Divinity, in answer to a Latin Letter in verse. Sm. fol. Lond., 1733. H 39 Q 13 ‡

EPISTLE from S—r S——o to S——a F——a. Sm. fol. Lond., 1727. H 39 Q 13 ‡

EPISTLE to a Lady who desired the author to make verses on her in the heroick stile. Sm. fol. Dublin, 1734. H 39 Q 13 ‡

EPISTLE to a young Nobleman from his Præceptor. Sm. fol. Lond., 1736. H 39 Q 13 ‡

EPPS, Wm. Land Systems of Australasia. 12mo. Lond., 1894. MF 3 P 5

EQUAL LEGAL STATUS, The, of all Churches in the Australian Colonies: Result of the meeting of the Presbyterian inhabitants of Van Diemen's Land, held in St. Andrew's Church, Hobart Town, on August, 12th, 1846. 8vo. Hobart, 1851. MG 2 Q 25

ERASMUS ROTERDAMUS, Desiderius. Life and Letters of ; by J. A. Froude. 8vo. Lond., 1894. C 18 T 10

ERCILLA I ZUNIGA, Don. A. de. La Araucana de. [*See* König, A.] H 5 U 38

ERICHSEN, Sir John Eric. The Science and Art of Surgery. 10th ed., by Drs. M. Beck and R. Johnson. 2 vols. 8vo. Lond., 1895. A 33 T 25, 26

ERICSSON, John. Sketch of. [*See* Hubert, P. G.—Inventors.] C 17 R 3

ERMAN, Adolf. Life in Ancient Egypt. Translated by Helen Mary Tivard. Illustrated. Roy. 8vo. Lond., 1894. B 27 V 17

ERNEST, J. A. Græcum Lexicon Manuale. [*See* Hederich, B.] J 12 V 1 †

ERNST, W. Memoirs of the Life of Philip Dormer, fourth Earl of Chesterfield. 8vo. Lond., 1893. C 15 P 13

ERRERA, Leo. The Russian Jews, Extermination or Emancipation ? Translated by Bella Löwy. 8vo. Lond., 1894. B 31 T 10

ERSKINE, Hon. J. Journal of, 1683-87. (Scottish History Society, 14.) 8vo. Edinb., 1893. E

ESCOTT, Thos. Hay Sweet. Randolph Spencer Churchill as a Product of his Age. 8vo. Lond., 1895. C 19 V 11

Platform, Press, Politics, and Play: being Pen and Ink Sketches of Contemporary Celebrities from the Tone to the Thames, *via* Avon and Isis. 8vo. Bristol, 1895. C 19 V 5

ESPINASSE, Francis. Life of Ernest Renan. 8vo. Lond., 1895. C 21 T 12

Literary Recollections and Sketches. 8vo. Lond., 1893. C 18 T 3

ESPINOZA, E. Geografía descriptiva de la República de Chile. 8vo. Santiago, 1892. D 15 P 16

ESSAI de Grammaire de la Langue de Viti, d'après les Manuscrits des Missionnaires Maristes Coordonnés ; par. le p. A.C. s.m. 8vo. Paris, 1884. MK 1 R 48

ESSEX, Earl of. The Hearse of the renowned the Rt. Hon. Robert Earl of Essex [*See* Bibliotheca Curiosa.] J 18 Q 39

ESTIENNE, Antoine. Charitable Remonstrance addressed to the Wives and Maidens of France, touching their dissolute adornments. [*See* Collectanea Adamantæa.] J 18 R 32

ETHERIDGE, Robert, jun. An Australian Aboriginal Musical Instrument. (Anthropol. Inst., 23.) 8vo. Lond., 1893. E

Australian and Tasmanian Aborigines. [*See* N. S. Wales Geological Survey, Memoirs.—Palæontology, 8.] ME

The Geology and Palæontology of Queensland and New Guinea. [*See* Jack, R. L.] MA 2 R 46-48

A highly ornate "sword" from the Coburg Peninsula, North Australia. (Anthropol. Inst., 24.) 8vo. Lond., 1894. E

The largest Australian Trilobite hitherto discovered. (Proceedings Royal Society, Victoria, n.s., 6.) 8vo. Melb., 1894. ME 1 P

On a modification of the Australian Aboriginal Weapon, termed the Leonile, Langeel, Bendi, or Buccan. (Anthropol. Inst., 23.) 8vo. Lond., 1893. E

The Mirrn Yong Heaps at N.W. Bend, River Murray. (Trans. Roy. Soc., S. Australia, 17.) 8vo. Adelaide, 1893. ME 1 S

An Operculum from the Lilydale Limestone. (Proceedings Royal Society, Victoria, n.s., 6.) 8vo. Lond., 1894. ME 1 P

Rush Basket from the Northern Territory of South Australia. (Anthropol. Inst., 23.) 8vo. Lond., 1893. E

ETLER, Chas. What is Electricity? 8vo. Melb., 1869. MA 3 S 62

ETTRICK SHEPHERD, The [*See* Hogg, James.]

EUCLIDES. First Six Books of the Elements of Euclid in which coloured diagrams and symbols are used instead of letters; by O. Byrne. 4to. Lond., 1847. A 25 V 24

EUMENES. Life of. [*See* Plutarch.] MC 1 R 45

EURIPIDES. Euripides the Rationalist. [*See* Verrall, Dr. A. W.] G 14 Q 28

Euripides as a Religious Teacher. [*See* Westcott, Rt. Rev. B. F.—Religious Thought in the West.] G 2 U 37

Life and Works of; by J. P. Mahaffy. 12mo. Lond., 1879. J 16 P 37

Phœnissæ. [*See* Trollope, W.] H 3 S 37

EVANS, Arthur J. History of Sicily. [*See* Freeman, Dr. E. A.] B 30 U 11

EVANS, Chas. H. Table of the average ad valorem rates under the tariff of 1883; Mills Bill of 1888; Tariff of 1890; House Bill 4864 as it passed the House and also as amended by the Senate and passed July 2; computed on the basis of the import values of 1890. 8vo. Wash., 1894. F 11 U 5

EVANS, Elwood. The State of Washington. 8vo. Wash., 1893. B 18 R 11

EVANS, G. E. [*See* Antipodean, The.] M E

EVANS, Rev. G. W. D. The Classic and Connoisseur in Italy and Sicily. 3 vols. 8vo. Lond., 1835. D 18 V 6-8

EVANS, Howard. "Noblesse Oblige." Our Old Nobility. 2nd ed. 12mo. Lond. (n.d.) C 17 P 17

EVANS, J. G. Book of Llan Dâv. [*See* Welsh Text Society.] E

EVANS, Maria Millington. Chapters on Greek Dress. 8vo. Lond., 1893. A 23 T 18

EVANS, Richardson. Lord Amherst, &c. [*See* Ritchie, Anne.] C 14 P 26

EVENING HOURS; or, Unpublished Gatherings and Experience of a Lifetime; by "A Freemason." Vol. 2. 12mo. Melb., 1869. MJ 1 P 57

EVENING MAIL, The. Oct., 1881—Aug., 1882. Fol. Melb., 1881-82. M E

EVENING NEWS. Oct., 1882-Dec., 1895. 13 vols. fol. Sydney, 1892-95. ME

EVERETT, Prof. Joseph David. Treatise on Natural Philosophy. [*See* Deschanel, A. P.] A 28 U 10

EVETTS, Basil Thos. A. Churches and Monasteries of Egypt. [*See* Abû Sâlih.] G 16 U 20

New Light on the Bible and the Holy Land; being an Account of some Recent Discoveries in the East. 8vo. Lond., 1892. G 2 S 32

EWALD, Alex. Chas. The Spectator: Selected Essays, with Notes. [*See* Addison, J.] J 12 T 26

EWART, Henry C. [Life of] William Wordsworth. [*See* Masson, Prof. D.—In the Footsteps of the Poets.] J 6 R 43

EWART, Lieut. J. S. Historical Records of the 79th Queen's Own Cameron Highlanders. [*See* Mackenzie, Capt. T. A.] B 22 R 5

EWING, Prof. J. A. The Steam Engine and other Heat Engines. 8vo. Cambridge, 1894. A 22 S 14

EWING, Rev. R. K. [Lecture replying to objections against Phrenology. 12mo. Launceston, 1852. MA 2 F 29

Moses and Colenso: ten Lectures. 8vo. Hobart, 1864. MG 2 R 43

EWING, Rev. T. C. Dr. Vaughan answered by the highest historical authorities. The Ancient Church and Faith of England not Romish, but Apostolic. 8vo. Sydney, 1875. MG 1 S 15

EXAMINATION of some recent writings about immortality. [*See* Religious Pamphlets, 1.] G 9 V 16

EXERCISES on the parallel bars from a medical point of view. 8vo. Milwaukee (n.d.). G 18 R 35
EX-MEMBER of the National Anti-Corn Law League, An. [*See* Our National Duties.] MF 2 Q 78
EXPERIENCED AUSTRALIAN COOK, An. [*See* May, Mrs. Walter.]
EXPERIENCED CHIROPODIST, An. [*See* Art of Preserving the Feet.] A 33 P 2
EXPOSITOR'S BIBLE, The. Edited by Rev. Dr. W. R. Nicoll. 42 vols. 8vo. Lond., 1887-04. G 10 R and S.
Acts of the Apostles; by Rev. Dr. G. T. Stokes.
Chronicles; by Prof. W. H. Bennett.
Colossians; by Rev. D. A. MacLaren.
1 Corinthians; by Rev. Dr. M. Dods.
2 Corinthians; by Rev. J. Denney.
Ecclesiastes; by Rev. Dr. S. Cox.
Ephesians; by Rev. G. G. Findlay.
Esther; by Prof. W. F. Adeney.
Exodus; by Rev. Dr. G. A. Chadwick.
Ezra; by Prof. W. F. Adeney.
Galatians; Rev. G. Findlay.
Genesis; by Rev. Dr. M. Dodds.
Hebrews; by Rev. Dr. T. C. Edwards.
Isaiah, 1-66; by Rev. Dr. G. A. Smith.
Jeremiah; by Rev. C. J. Ball.
Job; by Rev. Dr. R. A. Watson.
Joshua; by Rev. Dr. W. G. Blaikie.
Judges; by Rev. Dr. R. A. Watson.
1 Kings; by Archdeacon Farrar.
2 Kings; by Archdeacon Farrar.
Leviticus; by Rev. S. H. Kellogg.
Nehemiah; by Prof. W. F. Adeney.
Numbers; by Rev. D. R. A. Watson.
Pastoral Epistles; by Rev. Dr. A. Plummer.
Philemon; by Rev. Dr. A. MacLaren.
Philippians; by Rev. Dr. R. Rainy.
Proverbs; by R. F. Horton.
Psalms, 1-150; by Rev. Dr. A. MacLaren.
Revelation; by Rev. Dr. W. Milligan.
Romans; by H. C. G. Moule.
Ruth; by Rev. Dr. R. A. Watson.
St. James; by Rev. Dr. A. Plummer.
St. John, Gospel of; by Rev. Dr. M. Dods.
St. John, Epistle of; by Wm. Alexander, Bishop of Derry.
St. Jude; by Rev. Dr. A. Plummer.
St. Luke; by Rev. H. Burton.
St. Mark; by Rev. Dr. G. A. Chadwick.
St. Matthew; by Rev. Dr. J. M. Gibson.
St. Peter; by Rev. Dr. J. R. Lumby.
1 Samuel; by Rev. Dr. W. G. Blaikie.
2 Samuel; by Rev. Dr. W. G. Blaikie.
Thessalonians; by Rev. J. Denney.

F

F——NA'S ANSWER TO S——NO'S EPISTLE. Sm. fol. London, 1727. H 39 Q 13 ‡
FABER, Rev. Francis Atkinson. Brief Sketch of the Early Life of Rev. Dr. F. W. Faber. 12mo. Lond., 1869. C 18 P 16
FABER, Rev. Dr. Frederick Wm. Life and Letters of; by J. E. Bowden. 2nd ed. 8vo. Lond., 1869. C 18 P 17
Brief Sketch of the Early Life of; by F. A. Faber. 12mo. Lond., 1869. C 18 P 16

FABRE, Paul. La Bibliothèque du Vatican au 15ᵉ Siècle. [*See* Muntz, E.] J 7 U 34
Étude sur le Liber Censuum de l'Église Romaine. (Bibliothèque des Ecoles Françaises d'Athènes et de Rome, 62ᵉ. Fasciculo.) 8vo. Paris, 1892. G 13 P 35
FAIRBAIRN, James. Fairbairn's Book of Crests of the Families of Great Britain and Ireland; revised and brought down to the present date, by A. C. Fox-Davies. 2 vols. 4to. Edinb., 1892. K 10 V 26, 27
FAIRBAIRN, Sir Peter. Sketch of. [*See* Smith, G. B.—Leaders of Modern Industry.] C 14 P 14
FAIRBAIRN, Sir Wm. Sketch of. [*See* Smith, G. B.—Leaders of Modern Industry.] C 14 P 14
FAIRCHILD, D. G. Bordeaux Mixture as a Fungicide. Roy. 8vo. Wash., 1894. A 32 T 13
FAIRHOLT, Frederick Wm. Eccentric and Remarkable Characters. Illustrated. 8vo. Lond., 1853. C 14 P 33
FAITH AND DUTY OF A CHRISTIAN, The. 12mo. Hobart, 1851. MG 1 P 69
FALCONER, J. Queensland Gold Deposits. (Proc. Roy. Soc., Queensland, 1.) 8vo. Brisbane, 1884. ME 1 T
FALKLAND, Lord. Essay on. [*See* Arnold, M.—Mixed Essays.] J 11 T 25
FALLOWS, Rev. Dr. Samuel. Complete Dictionary of Synonyms and Antonyms. 12mo. Lond., 1895. J 9 P 25
FAMILY JO MILLER, The; a Drawing-room Jest-book. 12mo. Lond., 1848. J 7 R 57
FAMOUS PAINTINGS OF THE WORLD; a Collection of Photographic Reproductions of great Modern Masterpieces. Ob. imp. 8vo. New York, 1894. A 3 R 22 †
FANNING, J. T. Practical Treatise on Hydraulic and Water-Supply Engineering. 8vo. New York, 1882. A 22 S 7
FANSHAWE, Adm. Sir E. G. Sir Hew Dalrymple at Gibraltar and in Portugal, 1808. 8vo. Lond., 1895. C 13 V 11
FARADAY, Michael. Sketch of. [*See* Thorpe, Dr. T. E.—Historical Chemistry.] C 17 R 2
FARMER, A. Present Condition of Agriculture in N.S.W. [*See* Agriculture.] MA 1 Q 71
FARMER AND STOCK-BREEDER, The. New Series. Vols. 5-7. Fol. Lond., 1892-94. E
FARMER, John S. 'Twixt Two Worlds: a narrative of the Life and Work of William Eglinton. 4to. Lond., 1886. C 1 W 7

FARMER, John S., and HENLEY, Wm. Ernest. Slang and its Analogues, Past and Present: a Dictionary, Historical and Comparative, of the Heterodox Speech of all Classes of Society for more than 300 years. Vol. 3. Sm. 4to. Lond., 1893. Libr.

FARQUHAR, George. The Beaux' Stratagem: a Comedy. [See London Stage, 2.] H 2 S 34
The Constant Couple; or, a Trip to the Jubilee: a Comedy. [See London Stage, 2.] H 2 S 34
The Inconstant: a Comedy. [See London Stage, 1.] H 2 S 33
The Recruiting Officer: a Comedy. [See London Stage, 1.] H 2 S 33

FARQUHAR, H. New Zealand Echinoderms. (Trans. N.Z. Inst., 27.) 8vo. Wellington, 1894. ME 2 R

FARRAR, Ven. Frederick Wm. 1st and 2nd Kings. [See Expositor's Bible.] G 19 R 9, 10
The Life of Christ as represented in Art. 8vo. Lond., 1894. A 23 U 22
An Interview with, on Poets and Preachers; with Portrait. [See Blathwayt, R.—Interviews.] J 10 U 34
Seekers after God. 8vo. Lond (n.d.) C 21 Q 6

FARRER, Rev. Edmund. The Church Heraldry of Norfolk. 3 vols. 8vo. Norwich, 1887-93.
B 23 T 15-17

FAUCON, Maurice. La Librairie des Papes d'Avignon, 1316-1420. 2 vols. 8vo. Paris, 1886-87.
J 7 U 21, 22

FAVENC, Ernest. The Last of Six: Tales of the Austral Tropics. 8vo. Sydney, 1893. MJ 2 S 47
The Secret of the Australian Desert. 12mo. Lond., 1896. MJ 3 Q 42

FAVILLA NUNES, J. P. Recenseamento do Estado do Rio de Janeiro, 1893. Roy. 8vo. Rio de Janeiro, 1893. E

FAWCETT, Mrs. Millicent G. Life of Her Majesty Queen Victoria. 8vo. Lond. 1895. C 17 P 31

FAWCETT, W. Economic Plants: an Index to Economic Products of the Vegetable Kingdom in Jamaica. 8vo. Jamaica, 1891. A 20 S 16

FAWKES, F. The Works of Anacreon, Sappho, Bion, Moschus and Musæus. Translated from the original Greek. 12mo. Lond., 1760. H 9 U 28

FAXON, Chas. E. Silva of South America. Illustrated. [See Sargent, C. S.] A 40 S 24 ‡

FAXON, Walter. Bibliography of Crustacea. [See Harvard University.—Bulletins of Museum of Comparative Zoology.] A 30 U 37
Descriptions of new species of Cambarus, to which is added a synonymical list of the known species of Cambarus and Astacus. 8vo. (n.p.) 1884. A 30 U 24

FEARNE, Chas. Essay on the Learning of Contingent Remainders and Executory Devises. 9th ed.; by C. Butler. Roy. 8vo. Lond., 1831. F 7 U 20

FEDERAL ASSOCIATION of the Australian Colonies. [See Great Britain and Ireland—Federation.]

FEEBLE-MINDED, The, Child and Adult: a Report on an Investigation of the Physical and Mental Condition of 50,000 School Children. (Charity Organisation Series.) 8vo. Lond., 1893. A 13 P 2

FEILDEN, Henry St. Clair. Short Constitutional History of England. 2nd ed. 12mo. Oxford, 1887.
B 24 Q 7

FEISTMANTEL, Dr. Ottokar. Relations of the Coal and Plant-bearing Beds of Palæozoic and Mesozoic Age in Eastern Australia and Tasmania. [See N. S. Wales Geological Survey, Memoirs.—Palæontology, 3.] ME

FEITH, J. A., en HEERES, J. E. Groningsche Volks-almanak voor het jaar 1893. 8vo. Groningen, 1892.
D 18 R 25

FELIX, M. Minucius. Writings of. (Ante-Nicene Christ. Lib.) 8vo. Edinb., 1869. G 14 U 18

FELKIN, Henry M. and Emmie. Introduction to Herbart's Science and Practice of Education. 8vo Lond., 1895. G 18 P 33

FELLOW OF THE ROYAL COLLEGE OF PHYSI-CIANS, A. [See Diet and Cookery.] A 22 Q 14

FEMALE SCHOOL OF INDUSTRY. [See Sydney Female School of Industry.]

FENN, Chas. The Civil Jurisdiction of the Local Courts of South Australia. 8vo. Adelaide, 1872.
MF 2 R 37

FENNELL, Chas. A. M. The Stanford Dictionary of Anglicised Words and Phrases. 8vo. Camb., 1892.
K 10 U 24

FENTON, F. W. This Side Up: a Hamper of Holiday Fare. 8vo. Melb. (n.d.) MJ 3 Q 5

FENTON, James. Bush Life in Tasmania fifty years ago. 12mo. Lond., 1891. MD 1 Q 36

FENTON, James J. Calculating Slide-rule. (Roy. Soc., Vict., 22.) 8vo. Melb., 1886. ME 1 P
Public Finances, Loans, and Statistics of Australia and Tasmania. 8vo. Melb., 1888. MF 4 Q 15

FENWICK, Lieut. Extracts from my Diary, being the Account of the preparation for, and successful accomplishment of, an attack on Sydney Harbour; by a Russian Naval Captain. 8vo. Sydney, 1883.
MA 1 U 53

FERGUSON, A. M. & John. All about Tobacco, including Practical Instructions for Planting, Cultivation, and Curing of the Leaf. 8vo. Colombo, 1889.
A 18 T 32

Tropical Agriculturalist. [See Tropical Agriculturalist.] E

FERGUSON, C. Sailing Directions for Port Phillip, in the Colony of Victoria, including the Ports of Melbourne and Geelong. 8vo. Melb., 1854.
MD 6 R 24

FERGUSON, Prof. Henry. Essays in American History. 12mo. New York, 1894.
B 18 Q 8

FERGUSON, John. Ceylon in 1893, describing the Progress of the Island since 1803, its present Agricultural and Commercial Enterprises, and its unequalled Attractions to Visitors. Map and Illustrations. 8vo. Lond., 1893.
D 17 R 15
The Ceylon Hand-book and Directory, 1893-94. 8vo. Colombo, 1893.
E
All about Tobacco. [*See* Ferguson, A. M.] A 18 T 32

FERGUSON, R. Swiss Men and Swiss Mountains. 12mo. Lond., 1853.
D 19 P 6

FERGUSON, Richard Saul. History of Westmorland. 8vo. Lond., 1894.
B 22 R 3

FERGUSON, James. History of Architecture in all Countries, from the earliest times to the present day. Edited by R. P. Spiers. 3rd ed. Vols. 1, 2. Roy. 8vo. Lond., 1893.
A 19 T 11, 12
History of Indian and Eastern Architecture. Illustrated. Roy. 8vo. Lond., 1876.
A 19 T 12

FERGUSSON & MITCHELL, Messrs. Tasmanian Scenery. Obl. 8vo. Melb. (n.d.)
MD 4 P 7 †

FERNIQUE, Emmanuel. Inscriptions inédites du Pays des Marses. 8vo. Paris, 1879.
B 35 R 10
Etude sur Préneste ville du Latium. 8vo. Paris, 1880.
B 35 R 9

FERNOW, B. E. Reports of the Chief of the Division of Forestry. [*See* United States—Department of Agriculture.]
E
What is Forestry? 8vo. Wash., 1891.
A 32 R 2

FERREIRA DA SILVA, Dr. Antonio A. A capital do estado do Rio de Janeiro, estudos de Demographia Sanitaria durante 34 annos. 8vo. Rio de Janeiro, 1893.
F 11 U 9

FERRERO, Wm. The Female Offender. [*See* Lombroso, Prof. C.]
F 2 V 5

FERRIER, Dr. David. Forensic Medicine. [*See* Guy, Dr. W. A.]
F 11 U 14

FERRIER, Major R. Journal of, 1687. [*See* Camden Socs. Pubs., 53.]
E

FERRIER, W. F. Catalogue of a Stratigraphical Collection of Canadian Rocks. (Geol. Survey of Canada.) Roy. 8vo. Ottawa, 1893.
E
Another copy, prepared for the World's Columbian Exposition, 1893. Roy. 8vo. Ottawa, 1893.
A 24 U 23

FERRONNAYS, Pauline de la. [*See* Craven, Mrs. Augustus.]
C 21 P 3, 4

FESQUET, A. A. Guide for Coach Painters. [*See* Arlot, M.]
A 25 Q 38

FETHERSTONHAUGH, Cuthbert. The Meat Export Trade. 8vo. Sydney, 1894.
MF 3 Q 86

FEUILLET, Octave. Œuvres Complètes. Théâtre Complet. Tomes 1–4. 8vo. Paris, 1892-93.
J 11 Q 52-55

FEWKES, J. Walter. Bibliography of Acalephs. [*See* Harvard University.—Bulletins of Museum of Comparative Zoology.]
A 30 U 37
On the Development of Agalma. 8vo. Camb., Mass., 1885.
A 30 U 26

FICHTE, Johann Gottleib; by Prof. R. Adamson. (Philosophical Classics.) 12mo. Edinb., 1881.
G 9 V 4

FIDLER, Prof. T. Claxton. Bridge Construction : being a Text-book on the Design and Construction of Bridges in Iron and Steel. 2nd ed., illustrated. 8vo. Lond., 1893.
A 23 S 13

FIELD, Cyrus West. Sketch of. [*See* Stoddard, W. O.—Men of Business.]
C 16 R 19

FIELD, George. Chromatography. [*See* Taylor, J. S.]
A 23 R 39

FIELD, Henry M. The Barbary Coast. Illustrated. 8vo. New York, 1893.
D 14 S 17

FIELD, Marshall. Sketch of. [*See* Stoddard, W. O.—Men of Business.]
C 16 R 19

FIELD, Michael. Stephania : a trialogue. 8vo. Lond., 1892.
H 1 Q 2

FIELD, The, the FARM, the GARDEN: the Country Gentleman's Newspaper. Vols. 80–84. Fol. Lond., 1892-93.
E

FIELDE, Adele M. A Corner of Cathay : Studies from Life among the Chinese. Illustrated. Sm. 4to. New York, 1894.
D 17 Q 20

FIELDEN, J. C. Freetrade *v.* Reciprocity. 8vo. Manchester, 1891.
F 10 U 8

FIELDING, Henry. The Miser : a Comedy. [*See* London Stage, 1.]
H 2 S 33
The Mock Doctor; or, the Dumb Lady Cured. [*See* London Stage, 2.]
H 2 S 34
The Virgin Unmasked : a Musical Farce. [*See* London Stage, 3.]
H 2 S 35

FIENNES, Gerard. Federation of Working Men's Social Clubs : what it is, and what it may be. [*See* Knapp, J. M.—The Universities and the Social Problem.]
F 8 U 22

FIESCHI, Count de. Conspiracy of, against the Republick of Gencua, 1547. [See Bibliotheca Curiosa.]
J 18 Q 34

FIGUIER, Lou s. L'Année Scientifique et Industrielle, 1890-93. 4 vols. 8vo. Paris, 1891-94.   E

FIJNJE VAN SALVERDA, J. G. W. Aërial Navigation. Translated by G. E. Waring. 12mo. New York, 1894.   A 22 Q 16

FILLMORE, Millard. Sketch of. [See Thompson, R. W.—Recollections of Sixteen Presidents.] C 18 T 21, 22
Sketch of. [See Wilson, J. G.—Presidents of the United States.]   C 2 V 30

FILMORE, Lewis. Faust. [See Goethe, J. W. von.]
H 1 S 45

FINANCIAL REFORM ALMANACK, 1893-95: a Vade Mecum for Fiscal Reformers, Free-traders, Politicians, Public Speakers, and Writers. 3 vols. roy. 8vo. Lond., 1893-95.   E

FINCK, Henry T. Lotos Time in Japan. Illustrated. 8vo. Lond., 1895.   D 17 T 18

FINDLAY, Lieut. C. Historical Records of the 79th Queen's Own Cameron Highlanders. [See Mackenzie, Capt. T. A.]   B 22 R 5

FINDLAY, Rev. G. G. Galatians and Ephesians. [See Expositor's Bible.]   G 19 S 11, 12

FINDLAY, Sir George. The Working and Management of an English Railway. 8vo. Lond., 1894. F 8 U 2

FINLAND in the 19th Century; by Finnish Authors. Illustrated by Finnish Artists. 4to., Helsingfors, 1894.   B 40 T 1 ‡

FINLAY, A. K. The Phylloxera: a short treatise on the Vine Destroyer, with a Report upon the Bi-sulphide of Carbon Treatment, by M. Marion. 12mo. Melb., 1880.   MA 1 P 51

FINLEY, Lieut. John P. Certain Climatic Features of the two Dakotas. Illustrated. 4to. Washington, 1893.   A 15 Q 3 †

FINN, Edmund. Der Eggsheriences ov Hans Schwartz. 8vo. Melb., 1878.   MJ 1 Q 49

FINNAMORE, John. Endorby: a tragedy. 8vo. Melb. (n.d.)   MH 1 Q 25
Francesca Vasari: a tragedy. 8vo. Melb., 1865.
MH 1 S 32

FINSCH, Dr. O. Birds collected in Tongatabu, Fiji, New Hebrides, and Tahiti. [See Thomson, Sir C. W., and Murray, Dr. J.—Voyage of H.M.S. Challenger.] A 6 †

FIRESIDE JOURNAL, The, and Oddfellow: a Miscellany of Literature, Amusement, and Romance. Fol. Lond., 1842-43.   E

FIRMINGER, Walter K. Religion. [See Molinari, G. de.]   G 16 Q 40

FIRTH, C. H. The Clarke Papers. [See Camden Society.]
E
Memoirs of Lieut-Gen. E. Ludlow, 1625-72. 2 vols. 8vo. Oxford, 1894.   C 17 S 8, 9
Scotland and the Commonwealth: Letters and Papers relating to the Military Government of Scotland, from 1651-Dec. 1653. (Scottish History Soc., 18.) 8vo. Edinb., 1895.   E

FISCHER, Kuno. Francis Bacon of Verulam: Realistic Philosophy and its Age. 8vo. Lond., 1857.
G 13 S 43

FISCHER, Dr. Paul. Manuel de Conchyliologie et de Paléontologie Conchyliologique, ou Histoire Naturelle des Mollusques vivants et fossiles. [Illustrated.] Roy. 8vo. Paris, 1887.   A 30 U 4

FISHER, Robt. Alex. Digest of the Reported Decisions of the Courts of Common Law, Bankruptcy, Probate, Admiralty, and Divorce, together with a select on from those of the Court of Chancery and Irish Courts, 1756-1883; founded on Fisher's Digest, by John Mews, assisted by C. M. Chapman, H. H. W. Sparham, and A. H. Todd. 7 vols. roy. 8vo. Lond., 1884.
F 12 V 3-9

FISHER'S Drawing-room Scrap-book. [See Norton, Hon. Mrs. C. E. S.]   H 2 V 7, 8

FISKE, John. The Critical Period of American History, 1783-89. 8vo. Lond., 1891.   B 17 Q 15
Cyclopædia of American Biography. [See Appleton & Co.]   C 16 U 1-6
Life and Letters of E. L. Youmans. 8vo. Lond., 1894.
C 16 R 21

FISON, E. Herbert. Flocks and Fleeces; being a concise History of the Sheep and its Wool in all Countries, with a special chapter on the Frozen Mutton Industry. 8vo. Lond., 1894.   MA 2 V 50

FISON, Rev. L. Notes on the Customs of Mota, Banks Islands. (Roy. Soc., Vic., 16.) 8vo. Melb., 1880.
ME 1 P

FITZGERALD, Edward. Letters of, to Fanny Kemble, 1871-83. 8vo. Lond., 1895.   C 19 T 15

FITZGERALD, G. P. President's Address delivered by, at the distribution of prizes, Board of Technical Education, Hobart, Tasmania; also, ceremony in connection with the laying of the foundation-stone of the Hobart Technical School, 1889. 8vo. Hobart, 1889.
MG 2 S 3

FITZGERALD, George Robt. "Fighting Fitzgerald." [Life of], 1748-86: by G. Le G. Norgate. (Lives of Twelve Bad Men.) 8vo. Lond., 1894.   C 18 T 9

FITZGERALD, Mrs. P. F. A Protest against Agnosticism; the Rationale or Philosophy of Belief. 8vo. Lond., 1890.   G 18 Q 2
Treatise on the Principles of Sufficient Reason: a Psychological Theory of Reason. 8vo. Lond., 1887.
G 2 T 28

Supplementary Catalogue—1893-95.

FITZGERALD, Percy H. Henry Irving: a Record of Twenty Years at the Lyceum. 8vo. Lond., 1893.
C 8 P 2
London City Suburbs as they are to-day. 4to. Lond., 1893.
D 19 V 9
Principles of Comedy and Dramatic Effect. 8vo. Lond., 1870.
H 4 U 27
Memoirs of an Author. 2 vols. Roy. 8vo. Lond., 1895.
C 21 R 15, 16
Stonyhurst Memoirs; or, Six Years at School. 8vo. Lond., 1895.
G 18 Q 28
The World's own Book, or the Treasury of à'Kempis. 8vo. Lond., 1895.
J 15 S 25

FITZGERALD, R. D. In Memory of; Poem by Rev. Dr. W. Woolls. 8vo. Sydney, 1892.
MA 1 R 1 ‡

FITZGIBBON, Edmond Gerald. Government by Committees: all Members all Ministers. 8vo. Melb., 1872.
MF 2 T 74
Parliamentary Reform. 8vo. Melb., 1875.
MJ 3 Q 16
Party Government and Suggestions for Better. 8vo. Melb., 1893.
MF 3 Q 82

FITZGIBBON, Col. James. A Veteran of 1812; by Mary A. Fitzgibbon. 8vo. Lond., 1894.
C 18 P 24

FITZMAURICE, Edmond, Lord. Life of Sir W. Petty. 8vo. Lond., 1895.
C 21 S 17

FITZPATRICK, John. The Australian Cricket Record. 1894-95. 12mo. Sydney, 1896.
MA 3 U 25

FITZ-SIMON, James A. Report upon the State of Secondary and Normal Education in the Argentine Republic. 8vo. La Plata, 1893.
G 18 S 15

FITZ-STUBBS, Madeline. The Cicada Gavotte. Fol. Sydney, 1893.
MA 7 Q 31 †

FLAGG, J. B. Life and Letters of Washington Allston. 8vo. Lond., 1893.
C 12 U 30

FLAMMARION, Camille. La Planète Mars, et ses conditions d'habitabilité. Imp. 8vo. Paris, 1892.
A 19 V 17
Popular Astronomy. Translated by J. E. Gore. Illustrated. 8vo. Lond., 1894.
A 19 V 22

FLAXMAN, John. Illustrations of the Odyssey and Iliad of Homer. [See Homer.]
H 9 U 4, 5; H 9 P 13, 14

FLEISCHMANN, Dr. Wilhelm. Das Molkereiwesen. 8vo. Braunschweig, 1876.
A 18 U 15

FLEMING, Prof. J. A. Electric Lamps and Electric Lighting. Illustrated. 8vo. Lond., 1894.
A 21 S 27

FLETCHER, John. Works of. [See Beaumont, F.]
H 2 U 26, 27

FLETCHER, Rev. Joseph H. The Second Century of Australian History and the Christian Principles most likely to influence it. 8vo. Melb., 1888.
MG 2 Q 28

FLETCHER, Joseph J. The Macleay Memorial Volume. [See Linnean Soc. of N.S.W.]
MA 2 Q 1 †

FLETCHER, Price. Hints to New-comers. [See Wright, T.—The Queensland Horticulturist.]
MA 1 P 59

FLETCHER, Dr. Robt. Index Medicus. [See Index Medicus.]
E

FLETCHER, Wm. The Steam Jacket. 2nd ed., illustrated. 12mo. Lond., 1895.
A 22 Q 39

FLETCHER, Rev. Dr. Wm. Works of Lactantius. [See Lactantius.]
G 14 U 21, 22

FLETCHER, Wm. I. Public Libraries in America. Illustrated. 12mo. Lond., 1894.
J 5 P 18
Index to General Literature. Imp. 8vo. Boston, 1893.
Libr.
Index to Periodical Literature. [See Poole, W. F.]
Libr.

FLETCHER, Rev. Wm. Roby. Buddha and Buddhism, with some sketches of the Rock Temples of Damboola and the Ruins of Anuradhapura in Ceylon. 12mo. Adelaide, 1893.
MG 1 P 68
Biographical Sketch of; with Selections from his Lectures, Sermons, &c., by the Rev. J. J. Halley. 12mo. Adelaide, 1895.
MC 1 S 16

FLETCHER, Wm. Y. Bookbinding in France. (Portfolio Monograph, 10.) Roy. 8vo. Lond., 1894.
E

FLEURI, G. From Number to Quaternion. (Journal Roy. Soc., N.S.W., 28.) 8vo. Sydney, 1894.
ME 1 R

FLEURY, Lamé. L'Histoire Moderne, 1434-1763, racontée à la jeunesse. 2 vols. 18mo. Paris, 1875.
B 25 P 6, 7

FLINDERS, Capt. Matthew. Chart of part of the Coast of New South Wales, from Ram Head to Northumberland Isles, 1800. Fol. Lond., 1801.
MD 1 P 15 ‡
Chart of Bass's Strait. Fol. Lond., 1800.
MD 1 P 15 ‡
[Charts of] Port Dalrymple, on the Coast of Van Diemen's Land, Furneaux's Islands, Twofold Bay, on the East Coast of New South Wales. Fol. Lond., 1801.
MD 1 P 15 ‡
Plan of the Settlement of New South Wales. [See Grimes, C.]
MD 1 P 15 ‡

FLINT, Chas. L. Manual of Agriculture. [See Emerson, G. B.]
A 18 Q 34

FLINT, Prof. Robert. Vico. (Philosophical Classics for English Readers.) 8vo. Edinb., 1884.
G 9 V 9
Socialism. 8vo. Lond., 1894.
F 14 U 8

FLINT, Weston. Statistics of Public Libraries in the United States and Canada. 8vo. Wash., 1893.
J 5 T 28

FLORIDA. Report of the Commissioner of Agriculture, 1891-92. 8vo. Tallahassee, 1893.
E

FLORIDA STATE HORTICULTURAL SOCIETY. Proceedings of the sixth Annual Meeting, held at Pensacola, Florida, April, 1893. 8vo. Tallahassee, 1893.
E

FLOWERS of Australia. Fol. (n.p.n.d.) MA 2 P 31 ‡

FLÜGEL, Dr. F. Universal English-German and German-English Dictionary. Second Part. German and English. Imp. 8vo. Brunswick, 1894.
J 7 V 25

FOCK, Dr. Andreas. Introduction to Chemical Crystallography. Translated by W. J. Pope. 8vo. Oxford, 1895.
A 21 R 32

FOELSCHE, Paul. Notes on the Aborigines of North Australia. (Trans. Roc. Soc., S. Australia, 5.) 8vo. Adelaide, 1882.
ME 1 S

FOLK-LORE: a Quarterly Review of Myth, Tradition, Institution, and Custom. Vols. 3-5. 8vo. Lond., 1892-94.
E

FOLK-LORE SOCIETY. Publications, vols 29, 31, 33, 35, and 37. 8vo. Lond., 1892-95.
E
   29, 35. The Denham Tracts. Edited by Dr. J. Hardy. Vol. 1.
   31. Cinderella; with notes &c.; by M. R. Cox.
   33. Saxo Grammaticus.
   37. County Folk-lore, vol. 1. Gloucestershire, Suffolk, Leicestershire, and Rutland.

FOLLOW THE TRACK: an Australian Novel, written by "Twig." 8vo. Melb., 1861.
MJ 3 Q 8

FONTAINE, Wm. M. Older Mesozoic Flora of Virginia. (U.S. Geol. Survey, 6.) 4to. Wash., 1883.
E
The Potomac or Younger Mesozoic Flora. (U.S. Geol. Survey, 15.) 4to. Wash., 1889.
E

FOOTE, Samuel. The Liar: a Farce. [*See* London Stage, 2.]
H 2 S 34
The Mayor of Garratt: a Farce. [*See* London Stage, 1.]
H 2 S 33

FORBES, Archibald. Czar and Sultan: Adventures of a British Lad in the Russo-Turkish War of 1877-78. [Illustrated.] 8vo. Bristol, 1894.
B 31 T 4
Great War of 189—. [*See* Great War of 189—.]
J 2 Q 21
[Life of] Colin Campbell, Lord Clyde. 8vo. Lond., 1895.
C 21 P 8
Memories and Studies of War and Peace. 8vo. Lond., 1895.
B 26 V 17

FORBES, Edward. Portrait of. [*See* Ramsay, Sir A. C.—Memoir of.]
C 21 R 20

FORBES, Dr. Henry O. Hand-book to the Primates. 2 vols. 8vo. Lond., 1894.
A 28 P 24, 25

FORBES, Rt. Rev. Robert. The Lyon in Mourning; or, a Collection of Speeches, Letters, Journals, &c., relative to the affairs of Prince Charles Stuart. Vols. 1, 2. (Scottish History Soc., 20, 21.) 2 vols. 8vo. Edin., 1895.
E

FORBES, W. A. Birds collected at Cape York and the Neighbouring Islands. [*See* Thomson, Sir W. C., and Murray, Dr. J.—Voyage of H.M.S. *Challenger*.—Zoology, 3.]
A 6 †
Anatomy of the Petrels. [*See* Thomson, Sir W. C., and Murray, Dr. J.—Voyage of H.M.S. *Challenger*.—Zoology, 4.]
A 6 †

FORCELLINI, A. Totius Latinitatis Lexicon: Onomasticon opera Dr. V. De Vit. Tomus X. 4to. Prati, 1887.
K 3 R 26 †

FORD, Isaac N. Tropical America. 8vo. Lond., 1893.
D 4 P 32

FORD, R. Thistledown: a Book of Scotch Humour, Character, Folk-lore, Story, and Anecdote. 8vo. Paisley, 1895.
J 9 S 18

FORD, Wm. Wilbraham, and RATHBONE, John. Practical Suggestions as to Instruction in Farming in Canada, and the United States and Tasmania. 14th ed. 8vo. Lond. (n.d.)
MA 1 P 2

FORD, Worthington Chauncey. The American Citizen's Manual. 12mo. New York, 1892.
F 7 V 10

FOREIGN OFFICE LIST, The. [*See* Great Britain and Ireland—Foreign Office.]

FOREMAN PATTERN-MAKER, A. [*See* Helical Gears.]
A 22 Q 23
[*See* Plating and Boiler-making.]
A 25 R 16

FOREST PARK UNIVERSITY FOR WOMEN. [Calendar and Register, 1893.] 8vo. St. Louis, Mo. (n.p.n.d.)
E

FORLONG, Wm. and A. Copies of Papers relative to the claim of [to grants of land]. Sm. fol. Lond., 1837.
MF 3 U 18

FORMAN, Harry Buxton. Letters of John Keats. [*See* Keats, John.]
C 19 V 13

FORNANDER, Abraham. Légendes des Iles Hawaii. [*See* Lesson, Dr. A.]
MB 2 U 2

FORREST, Prof. George W. Selections from Letters, Despatches, and other State Papers in the Foreign Department of the Government of India, 1772-85. 3 vols. sm. fol. Calcutta, 1890.
B 15 R 10-12 ‡
The Indian Mutiny, 1857-58: Selections from Letters, Despatches, and other State Papers preserved in the Military Department of the Government of India, 1857-58; with Maps and Plans. Vol. 1. Roy. 8vo. Calcutta, 1893.
B 29 V 4

FORREST, Sir John. The Kimberley District. [*See* Royal Geographical Society, Victoria, 1885-86.]
ME 20
Notes on Western Australia, with Statistics for 1885. 8vo. Perth, 1886. MD 8 Q 32

FORRESTER, Lieut.-Col. James. The Polite Philosopher. 18mo. Edinb., 1776. G 18 P 23

FORRESTER, Mrs. John. Myrtle: a Novel. 8vo. Melb., 1891. MJ 1 S 48

FORSTER, Henry L. Australian Essays. No. 1 What is man? No. 2. The Soul: what is it? 8vo. Sydney, 1894. MG 2 Q 31

FORSTER, John. Hand-book of the Dyce and Forster Collection. [*See* Dyce, A.] A 23 R 36
Life and Adventures of Oliver Goldsmith. 8vo. Lond., 1848. C 21 R 6

FORSTER, Wm. Australian Federation: a Review of Mr. Forster's Paper "Fallacies of Federation." 8vo. Sydney, 1879. MF 1 Q 37

FORSYTH, Archibald. Free, Fair, and Protected Trade: which is the best for England, New South Wales, and Australia? 8vo. Sydney, 1895. MF 4 R 5

FORTESCUE, Hon. J. W. State Socialism and the Collapse in Australia. (A Policy of Free Exchange.) 8vo. Lond., 1894. F 14 S 26

FORTNIGHTLY REVIEW, The. New Series, vols. 52-56. Roy. 8vo. Lond., 1892-94. E

FORTNUM, Chas. Drury Edward. Bronzes. 8vo. Lond., 1877. A 23 R 17
Maiolica. 8vo. Lond., 1875. A 23 R 24

FORTUNATE MEN: How they made Money and won Renown: a curious Collection of Rich Men's Mottoes and Great Men's Watchwords; their Financial Tests and Secrets, &c. 12mo. Lond., 1875. J 8 Q 48

FORUM, The. Vols. 14-17. Roy. 8vo. New York, 1892-94. E

FOSS, Sam. Walter. Black Country Poems. Illustrated. 8vo. Boston, 1894. H 10 S 9

FOSTER, Clement Le Neve. Text-book of Ore and Stone Mining. Illustrated. 8vo. Lond., 1894. A 24 S 8

FOSTER, Dr. Frank P. An Illustrated Encyclopædic Medical Dictionary. 4 vols. 4to. Lond. (n.d.) K 18 T 16-19

FOSTER, John. Reminiscences of. [*See* Fitzgerald, P.—Memoirs.] C 21 R 15

FOSTER, Joseph. Index Ecclesiasticus; or, Lists of all Ecclesiastical Dignitaries in England and Wales since the Reformation. Roy. 8vo. Oxford, 1890. G 15 T 23
Oxford Men, 1880-92; with a Record of their Schools, Honours, and Degrees. 4to. Lond., 1893. C 17 U 1
Oxford Men and their Colleges. 4to. Lond., 1893. C 17 U 2

FOSTER, L. L. Annual Report of the Agricultural Bureau, Texas, 1887-88. [*See* Texas.] E

FOSTER, Dr. Michael. [*See* Journal of Physiology.] E

FOSTER-MELLIAR, Rev. A. [*See* Melliar, Rev. A. Foster-.]

FOSTER, Wm. Register of Letters, 1600-19. [*See* East India Co.] B 20 V 2

FOSTER, Wm. Eaton. Town Government in Rhode Island. (Johns Hopkins University Studies, 4.) 8vo. Baltimore, 1886. B 18 S 4

FOSTER, Wm. John, and MURRAY, Chas. E. R. Practice of the District Courts of New South Wales. 8vo. Sydney, 1870. MF 1 Q 47

FOULIS, Sir John. Account Book of. (Scottish History Society, 16.) 8vo. Edinb., 1894. E

FOUR GOSPELS, The, as Historical Records. 8vo. Lond., 1895. G 16 U 18

FOURNIER, Prof. Marcel. Les Statuts et Privilèges des Universités Françaises depuis leur Fondation jusqu'en 1789. Tomes 3, 4. 4to. Paris, 1892-94. F 36 V 3, 4 ‡

FOURTH UNION BENEFIT BUILDING AND INVESTMENT SOCIETY. Rules. 8vo. Melb., 1867. MF 4 Q 34

FOWKE, Gerard. Archæologic Investigations in James and Potomac Valleys. 8vo. Wash., 1894. B 17 R 38

FOWLE, Rev. Thos. W. The Boarding-out System as applied to neglected and destitute children; a criticism with reply. 8vo. Melb., 1888. MF 4 R 8

FOWLER, Dr. George R. A Treatise on Appendicitis Illustrated. Roy. 8vo. Philad., 1894. A 33 T 18

FOWLER, Dr. J. J. Adamnani Vita S. Columbae. [*See* Adamnan.] G 2 U 1

FOWLER, J. K. Echoes of Old Country Life, being Recollections of Sport, Politics, and Farming in the Good Old Times. 8vo. Lond., 1892. C 16 S 1

FOWLER, Rev. Montague. Some Notable Archbishops of Canterbury. 8vo. Lond., 1895. C 13 V 12

FOWLER, Rev. Dr. Thos. Progressive Morality; an Essay in Ethics. 8vo. Lond., 1895. G 2 U 44

FOWLER, W. Warde. The City State of the Greeks and Romans. 8vo. Lond, 1893. B 27 Q 9

FOX, Caroline. Memories of Old Friends, 1835–71. 2 vols. 12mo. Lond., 1882. C 22 P 16, 17

FOX, Rt. Hon. Chas. James. Character of [*See* Hazlitt, W.—Winterslow.] J 12 S 33

FOX or FOXE, John. Acts and Monuments of; with a preliminary dissertation by the Rev. G. Townsend; edited by Rev. S. R. Cattley. 8 vols. 8vo. Lond., 1837–41. G 16 U 9–16.

FOX or FOXE, Capt. Luke. Voyage of. [*See* Hakluyt Soc., 58.] E

FOX, T. W. Mechanism of Weaving. 12mo. Lond., 1894. A 25 R 15

FOX, Dr. Tilbury. Atlas of Skin Diseases. 4to. Lond., 1877. A 12 T 16 ‡

FOX, Wm. War in New Zealand. 8vo. Lond., 1860. MB 2 Q 52

FOX, Wm. Johnson. Lectures addressed chiefly to the Working-classes. 4 vols. 8vo. Lond., 1845. J 12 T 31–34

Memorial edition of collected Works. 12 vols. 8vo. Lond., 1865–68. J 11 V 31–42
1. Lectures and Sermons.
2. Christ and Christianity.
3. Miscellaneous Lectures and Sermons.
4. Anti-Corn Law Speeches.
5. Letters on the Corn Laws.
6. Miscellaneous Essays.
7-12. Reports of Lectures.

FOXALL, E. W. The Claims of "Capital," involving an Enquiry into the subjects of Currency and Banking. 12mo. Sydney, 1894. MF 1 P 83

FOXALL, W. S. The Southern District Weather Almanac, Business Guide, and Local Electoral Directory for 1896. 8vo. Goulburn, 1892. ME 1 S

FRÄDERSDORFF, Dr. J. W. Copious Phraseological English-Greek Lexicon. 6th ed. Revised by T. K. Arnold and H. Browne. 8vo. Lond., 1882. K 14 P 10

FRAENKEL, Prof. Carl. Text-book of Bacteriology. 3rd ed. Roy. 8vo. Edinb., 1891. A 26 U 21

FRAGMENTA GENEALOGICA. Vol. 2. Imp. 8vo. Lond., 1894. K 12 S 24 †

FRANCE. Album de Statistique Agricole: résultats généraux de l'enquête décennale de 1882. 8vo. Nancy, 1887. E

Bulletin de l'Administration Pénitentiaire, 1886. 8vo. Melun, 1886. F 11 U 31

Code des Prisons, 1600–1890. 12 vols. 8vo. Paris and Melun, 1845–90. E

Code Pénitentiaire. [*See* France—Code des Prisons.] E

Conseil Supérieur de l'Assistance Publique. 2 vols. 4to. Paris (n.d.) E

FRANCE—*contd.*
Les Conseils Généraux, 1887–93. 8 vols. roy. 8vo. Paris, 1887–94. E

Décret portant Règlement du Service et du Régime des Prisons de Courtes Peines affectées à l'emprisonnement en Commun. 8vo. Melun, 1888. F 11 U 30

Dénombrement de la Population, 1891. 8vo. Paris, 1892. F 11 U 23

Enquête Parlementaire sur le Régime des Etablissements Pénitentiaires. Tomes 1–5, 7, 8. 7 vols. 4to. Versaills, 1873–75. F 12 V 8–15 †

Exposé Général concernant la mise en pratique du système de la Libération Conditionnelle. 8vo. Melun, 1890. F 11 U 28

Lois et Règlements sur l'Enseignement Supérieur, 1789–1889. 4 vols. imp. 8vo. Paris, 1880–89. F 11 V 23–26

Note sur l'application du Système de la Libération Conditionnelle, 1888. 8vo. Melun, 1888. F 11 U 29

Rapport sur l'Application de la Loi de Relégation, 1890–92. 8vo. Melun, 1891–93. F 11 U 31

Rapport sur la Situation Financière et Matérielle des Communes en 1877. 4to. Paris, 1881. E

Rapport sur les Opérations des Sociétés de Secours Mutuels, 1886, 1888–89, 1892. 4 vols. 4to. Melun, 1889–94. E

Rapport sur l'Enseignement Agricole en France. 2 vols. imp. 8vo. Paris, 1894. A 32 U 22, 23

Recueil des Travaux du Comité Consultatif d'Hygiène Publique de France et des Actes Officiels de l'Administration Sanitaire, 1884–1886. 2 vols. 8vo. Paris, 1885–87. E

La Relégation des Récidivistes, 1886–88. 8vo. Melun, 1889. F 11 U 32

Service Vicinal. Compte rendu général des opérations effectuées, 1869–82. 14 vols. 4to. Paris, 1870–71. E

Situation des Recettes et Dépenses des Communes en 1885 et des Emprunts et Dettes au 31 Dec., 1886. 4to. Melun, 1888. E

La Situation Financière des Communes de France et d'Algérie, 1893. 4to. Melun, 1894. E

Sociétés de Secours Mutuels: Statuts-Modèles, Lois et Décrets. 8vo. Melun, 1893. F 2 V 19

Statistique Agricole Annuelle, 1892–93. 2 vols. 8vo. Paris, 1893–94. E

Statistique Agricole de la France. Imp. 8vo. Nancy, 1887. A 32 U 24

Statistique de l'Enseignement Supérieur, 1878, 1888. 2 vols. 4to. Paris, 1878–89. G 12 W 7, 8 †

Statistique de l'Industrie Minérale et des Appareils à Vapeur en France et en Algérie pour l'année 1893. 4to. Paris, 1894. E

Statistique des Etudiants, 1890–93. 4to. Paris, 1893. E

Statistique Pénitentiaire, 1891–92. 2 vols. roy. 8vo. Melun, 1894. E

Statistique Sanitaire des Villes de France et d'Algérie, 1891–92. 2 vols. 8vo. Melun, 1893–94. E

FRANCESCO DA BARBERINO et la Littérature Provençale en Italie au Moyen Age; par A. Thomas. 8vo. Paris, 1883. J 7 U 32

FRANCIS, St., of Assisi. Life of; by P. Sabatier. Translated by Louise Seymour Houghton. 8vo. Lond., 1894. C 14 S 19

FRANCIS, George Wm. The Acclimatisation of Animals and Plants. 8vo. Adelaide, 1862. MA 2 T 30

FRANCIS, Henry. Public Warning on Life Insurance. 4 nos. 8vo. Sydney, 1882. MF 4 R 45
Report upon the Report of the 23rd Annual Meeting of the Australian Mutual Provident Society. 8vo. Sydney, 1872. MF 4 R 45
The Railways and Tramways. (Pam. 2.) 8vo. Sydney, 1885. MF 4 R 42

FRANCIS, J. G. The New Electoral Bill: a Speech. 8vo. Melb., 1873. MJ 3 Q 10

FRANCKLIN, Prof. Thomas. The Earl of Warwick: a Tragedy. [*See* London Stage, 3.] H 2 S 35

FRANKLAND, Dr. Percy Faraday. Agricultural Chemical Analysis. 8vo. Lond., 1889. A 21 P 28
Our Secret Friends and Foes. 12mo. Lond., 1893. A 26 P 7
———— and FRANKLAND, Mrs. P. Micro-Organisms in Water: their Significance, Identification, and Removal; specially designed for the use of those connected with the sanitary aspects of Water-supply. 8vo. Lond., 1894. A 26 V 14

FRANKLIN, Benjamin, and the University of Pennsylvania. [*See* Thorpe, Dr. F. N.] G 18 S 8
Autobiography of. Edited by Prof. J. Sparks. 12mo. Lond., 1850. C 17 P 10
[Plaster Cast of.] [*See* Hutton, L.—Portraits in Plaster.] A 23 V 13
Sketch of. [*See* Hubert, P. G.—Inventors.] C 17 R 3

FRANKLIN, Frederick Augustus. Description of the Upper Ganges Canal and other systems of Irrigation in India. Roy. 8vo. Sydney, 1892. MA 1 V 56

FRANKLIN, Julia. Five Lectures on Shakespeare, by B. Ten Brink. [*See* Ten Brink, B.] J 10 R 28

FRASER, Prof. Alexander Campbell. Berkeley. (Philosophical Classics.) 12mo. Edinb., 1884. G 9 V 3
Locke. (Philosophical Classics.) 12mo. Edinb., 1890. G 9 V 13

FRASER, C. Fruits cultivated in the Botanic Garden, Sydney. 8vo. Sydney, 1828. MA 2 T 31

FRASER, G. W. Beni Hasan, Part 2. Measurement, &c., of the Tombs. [*See* Newberry, P. E.] B 12 T 3 †

FRASER, Dr. John. The Aborigines of New South Wales. Roy. 8vo. Sydney, 1892. MA 1 R 46
An Australian Language. [*See* Threlkeld, L. E.] MK 1 R 49

FRASER, Joseph. Melbourne and Mars: my Mysterious Life on two Planets. 8vo. Melb. (n.d.) MJ 2 T 27

FRASER, Col. Malcolm. Extract from a MS. Journal, relating to the Operations before Quebec in 1759. 8vo. Quebec (n.d.) B 17 T 18

FRASER, Malcolm A. C. Western Australian Year-book for 1892-94. 8vo. Perth, 1893-95. ME 6 S

FRASER, Marie. In Stevenson's Samoa. 12mo. Lond., 1895. MD 8 P 8

FRASER, Simon. [*See* Lovat, Lord.]

FRASER, Sir Wm. Hic et Ubique. 12mo. Lond., 1893. J 4 P 1

FRAZAO, Manoel José P. O Ensino Publico Primario na Ital a, Suissa, Suecia, Belgica, Inglaterra, e França. 8vo. Rio de Janeiro, 1893. G 18 R 51

FREAM, Dr. Wm. The Complete Grazier. [*See* Youatt, W.] A 18 U 18
Farm Crops, their Habits and Requirements: a Lecture. (Inst. of Agricult., Lond.) 8vo. Lond., 1884. A 18 R 28

FREDERIC, Harold. The New Exodus: a Study of Israel in Russia. 8vo. Lond, 1892. B 31 T 3

FREDERICK II, King of Prussia. Illustrations des Œuvres de. [*See* Menzel, A] B 38 Q 8-11 ‡
Plaster Cast of. [*See* Hutton, L.—Portraits in Plaster.] A 23 V 13

FREDERICK III, Emperor of Germany. The Second German Emperor. [*See* Kingston, W. Beatty-.—Men, Cities, and Events.] C 22 R 4

FREDERICK WILLIAM II, King of Prussia. Secret History of the Court of Berlin. [*See* Mirabeau, Count.] B 25 T 19, 20

FREDERICQ, Prof. Paul. The Study of History in England and Scotland. Authorized Translation from the French by Henrietta Leonard. (Johns Hopkins University Studies, 5.) 8vo. Baltimore, 1887. B 18 S 5
The Study of History in Germany and France. Authorized Translation from the French by Henrietta Leonard. (Johns Hopkins University Studies, 8.) 8vo. Baltimore, 1890. B 18 S 8
The Study of History in Holland and Belgium. Authorized Translation from the French by Henrietta Leonard. (Johns Hopkins University Studies, 8.) 8vo. Baltimore, 1890. B 18 S 8

FREE CHURCH NARRATIVE, The: an Account of Negotiations for Union from October, 1853, till April, 1857. 8vo. Melb., 1857. MG 1 S 16

FREELAND, Mary de Witt. The Records of Oxford, Mass.; including Chapters of Nipmuck, Iluguenot, and English History, from 1630; with Manners and Fashions of the Time. Sm. 4to. Albany, New York, 1894.
B 18 R 9

FREEMAN, Prof. Edward Augustus. History of Federal Government in Greece and Italy. 2nd ed. 8vo. Lond., 1893.
B 27 Q 10

History of Sicily, from the Earliest Times. Vol. 4. Edited by A. J. Evans. With Maps and Plate. 8vo. Oxford, 1894.
B 30 U 11

An Introduction to American Institutional History; with an Account of his Visit to Baltimore. by H. B. Adams. (Johns Hopkins University Studies, 1.) 8vo. Baltimore, 1882.
B 18 S 1

Life and Letters of; by the Very Rev. Dean Stephens. 2 vols. 8vo. Lond., 1895.
C 19 V 1, 2

Origin and Growth of the House of Lords. [See Subjects of the Day, 4.]
F 7 U 29

Sicily, Phœnician, Greek, and Roman. (Story of the Nations.) 8vo. Lond., 1892.
B 30 Q 16

Studies of Travel: Greece. 18mo. New York, 1893.
D 18 P 13

Studies of Travel: Italy. 18mo. New York, 1893.
D 18 P 12

FREEMAN'S JOURNAL, The. 1892. 2 vols. fol. Sydney, 1892.
ME

FREEMANTLE, Very Rev. W. F. College Sermons by Rev. Dr. B. Jowett. [*See* Jowett, Rev. Dr. B.]
G 1 U 24

FREEMASON, A. [*See* Evening Hours.]
MJ 1 P 57

FREESE, J. H. Orations of Isocrates. [*See* Isocrates.]
J 16 R 24

FREMONT, John Charles, the Pathfinder. Sketch of. [*See* Greeley, Gen. A. W.—Travellers and Explorers.]
C 17 R 4

FRENCH, C. Hand-book of the Destructive Insects of Victoria. Parts 1 and 2. 2 vols. 8vo. Melb., 1891-93.
MA 3 T 5, 6

FRERE, Sir Henry Bartle Edward. Life and Correspondence of; by John Martineau. 2 vols. 8vo. Lond., 1895.
C 21 R 13, 14

FRERE, J. H. Aristophanes. [*See* Aristophanes.]
H 9 U 23

FRÈRE-ORBAN, Hubert Joseph W. De l'Abus des Boissons Enivrantes. Imp. 8vo. Bruxelles, 1868.
F 11 V 22

FREUDENREICH, Dr. Ed. von. Dairy Bacteriology. 12mo. Lond., 1895.
A 19 P 5

FREYCINET, Capt. Louis. Voyage autour du Monde, exécuté sur les corvettes *l'Uranie* et *la Physicienne*, 1817-20. 10 vols. 4to., and 4 vols. fol. Paris, 1824-44.
MD 8 Q 1-10†, and MD 2 P 19-22‡

FRIAS Ricardo F. Resistencia de Materiales. Imp. 8vo. Santiago, 1886.
A 22 V 12

FRITTS, Charles Edgar. The Watch Adjuster's Manual. Illustrated. 8vo. Lond., 1895.
A 25 T 5

FROGGART, Walter W. Notes on *Brachyseliдæ*. (Trans. Roy. Soc., S. Australia 18.) 8vo. Adelaide, 1894.
ME 1 S

Report on a Beetle destroying Boots and Shoes in Sydney. 8vo. Sydney, 1891.
MA 2 T 32

FROISSART, Sir John. Chronicles of. Translated by Lord Berners, and edited by G. C. Macaulay. 8vo. Lond., 1895.
B 23 S 14

FROM SUAKIM TO THE NILE; with list of the New South Wales Contingent. 12mo. Sydney, 1885
MD 1 P 22

FRONTAURA Y ARANA, José M. Historia del Contvictorio Carolino. 8vo. Santiago, 1889.
B 16 S 23

FROST, C. The Lizards indigenous to Victoria. (Proc. Roy. Soc., Vic., 6.) [*See* Lucas, A. H. S.]
ME 1 P

New Species of Lizards. [*See* Lucas, A. H. S.]
ME 1 P

FROST, Edwin Brant. Astronomical Spectroscopy. [*See* Scheiner, Prof. Dr. J.]
A 19 V 20

FROST, John. Portrait of. [*See* Gammage, R. G.—Chartist Movement.]
A 7 R 24

FROST, T. Secret Societies of the European Revolution, 1776-1876. 2 vols. 8vo. Lond., 1876.
B 25 R 5, 6

FROUDE, Prof. James Anthony. England and her Colonies. 8vo. (n.p.) 1870.
MJ 3 Q 15

English Seamen in the 16th Century. 8vo. Lond., 1895.
B 21 U 9

Life and Letters of Erasmus. 8vo. Lond., 1894.
C 18 T 10

Reminiscences of. [*See* Skelton Dr. J.—Table-talk of Shirley.]
C 19 V 10

Sketch of. [*See* Smalley, G. W.—Studies of Men.]
C 19 R 20

A Talk with; with Portrait. [*See* Blathwayt, R.—Interviews.]
J 10 U 34

FRY, Rev. Dr. Henry Phibbs. Scriptural Evidence of the Apostolic Ministry and Tradition of the Church Catholic. Roy. 8vo. Hobart, 1843.
MG 1 T 19

Sermons on the Nature and Design of Heresy, &c. 12mo. Hobart, 1846.
MG 1 P 57

FRYAR, W. The Temperature of the Earth as exhibited in Mines, with special reference to observations in some of the deepest mines on the Gympie Gold-field. (Proc. Roy. Soc., Queensland, 7.) 8vo. Brisbane, 1891.
ME 1 T

FULL REPORT of the Four Great Trials at Hokitika. James Wilson, alias Murray, for the murder of Mr. George Dobson; George Henry Chamberlaine, for porjury; William de Lacey, for conspiring to rob; and John Carr, for larceny. 12mo. Hokitika (n.d.)   MF 4 P 11

FULLER, Andrews. The Small Fruit Culturist. 8vo. New York, 1891.   A 18 Q 39

FULLER, J. B. Field and Garden Crops of the N.W. Provinces and Oudh. [*See* Duthie, J. F.]   A 12 T 11, 12 †

FULLER, Thos. Essay on the Life and Genius of. [*See* Rogers, H.]   J 12 S 38

FULLERTON, Wm. Architectural Examples in Brick, Stone, Wood, and Iron. 4to. Lond., 1890.   A 12 T 13 †

FULTON, James Alexander. Peach Culture. 8vo. New York, 1892.   A 18 Q 37

FULTON, Robert. Illustrated Book of Pigeons, with Standards for Judging. Edited by Lewis Wright. 4to. Lond. (n.d.)   A 12 T 14 †

FULTON, Robert. Sketch of. [*See* Hubert, P. G.—Inventors.]   C 17 R 3

FUNK, Dr. B. Samoanischen Sprache: Grammatik und Vokabularium. 8vo. Berlin, 1893.   MK 2 Q 1

FUNKE, W. Versuche über das Verdauungsvermögen, &c. [*See* Wolff, Dr. E.]   A 32 T 6

FURMAN, H. Van F. A Manual of Practical Assaying. 8vo. Lond., 1893.   A 24 U 21

FURNAS, R. W. Annual Report of the Nebraska State Board of Agriculture, 1892. 8vo. Lincoln, 1893.   E

FURNEAUX, W. British Butterflies and Moths. Illustrated. 8vo. Lond., 1894.   A 28 U 8

FURNIVALL, Frederick James. How the Browning Society came into being; with some words on the Characteristics and Contrasts of Browning's early and late work. 12mo. Lond., 1884.   J 15 S 28

Temporary Preface to Chaucer's Canterbury Tales, Part 1, and Trial-Forewords to Chaucer's Minor Poems. [*See* Chaucer Society.]   E

Shakspere's England. [*See* New Shakspere Society.]   E

FURSE, Col. George Armand. Information in War: its acquisition and transmission. 8vo. Lond., 1895.   A 29 V 7

FURTWÄNGLER, Adolf. Masterpieces of Greek Sculpture. Edited by E. Sellars. Sm. fol. Lond., 1895.   A 39 R 5 ‡

FUSSELL, J. C. Squatting Directory of New South Wales. Compiled by J. Vann. Roy. 8vo. Sydney, 1865.   ME 4 V

FYFFE, Charles Alan. The Land Question. 8vo. Lond., 1885.   F 2 V 15

G

G.F.W. [*See* Glance of Life.]   H 10 Q 26

G.H. [*See* Lecture on Capital Punishment.]   MF 4 R 9

GADD, W. Lawrence. Soap Manufacture: a practical treatise on the fabrication of hard and soft soaps. 8vo. Lond., 1893.   A 25 P 7

GADEA, Juan. Unidad y Pluralidad de Sucesiones. 8vo. Montevideo, 1894.   F 9 R 31

GAINSBOROUGH, Thomas. [Sketch of]; by Walter Armstrong. [*See* Portfolio, Monograph, 9.]   E

GAISFORD, H. Steam Machinery. [*See* Langmaid, J.]   A 6 S 34

GALE, Albert. Judge's Report on Apiculture. 8vo. Sydney, 1892.   MA 1 Q 60

GALLIENNE, R. Le. [*See* Le Gallienne, R.]

GALLOIS, L. Les Géographes Allemands de la Renaissance. 8vo. Paris, 1890.   D 13 V 1

GALLOWAY, Prof. B. T. Some Practical Results of the Treatment of Plant Diseases. 8vo. Sydney, 1892.   MA 1 Q 67

GALTON, Arthur. Military Art of the Romans, as illustrated by the Wars of Cæsar. (United Service Institution, N.S.W., 5.) 8vo. Sydney, 1894.   ME

GALTON, Francis. Finger Prints. [Illustrated.] 8vo. Lond., 1892.   A 20 V 23

Finger-print Directories. 8vo. Lond., 1895.   F 11 U 1

GALTON, Frank W. Workers on their Industries. 12mo. Lond., 1895.   F 8 U 9

GAMA, Vasco di. [*See* Ramusio, G. B.—Navigationi et Viaggi.]   D 36 T 5–7 ‡

GAMBLE, Eliza Burt. The Evolution of Woman: an inquiry into the dogma of her inferiority to man. 8vo. New York, 1894.   A 27 R 1

GAMGEE, Dr. Arthur. Text-book of the Physiological Chemistry of the Animal Body, including an Account of the Chemical Changes occurring in Disease. 2 vols. 8vo. Lond., 1880-93.   A 26 U 24,25

GAMLIN, Hilda. George Romney and his Art. Illustrated. 8vo. Lond., 1894.   C 17 R 20

GAMMAGE, R. G. History of the Chartist Movement, 1837-54. Illustrated. 8vo. Newcastle-on-Tyne, 1894.   F 7 R 24

GANNETT, Henry. Manual of Topographic Methods. 4to. Wash., 1893.   D 15 S 4 †

GANOT, Prof. Adolphe. Elementary Treatise on Physics, Experimental and Applied. Translated and edited by Dr. E. Atkinson. 14th ed. 8vo. Lond., 1893.
A 29 R 12

GARCELON, G. W. Preparation of the Lemon for Market. 8vo. Sydney, 1892. MA 1 Q 62

GARDEN, The: an Illustrated Weekly Journal of Horticulture in all its branches. Vol. 45. 4to. Lond., 1894. E

GARDENERS' CHRONICLE, The: a Weekly Illustrated Journal of Horticulture and allied subjects. 3rd series. Vols. 12-16. Sm. fol. Lond., 1892-94. E

GARDENERS' MAGAZINE, The, for Amateur Cultivators, Exhibitors of Plants, Flowers, and Fruits, &c. Vols. 35-37. Sm. fol. Lond., 1892-94. E

GARDINER, Col. James. Life of; by Rev. Dr. P. Doddridge. 32mo. Halifax, 1851. C 19 P 8

GARDINER, Dr. Samuel R. History of the Commonwealth and Protectorate, 1849-60. Vol. 1, 1849-51. 8vo. Lond., 1894. B 24 R 13

Letters and Papers illustrating the relations between Charles II and Scotland in 1650. (Scottish Hist. Soc. 17.) 8vo. Edinb., 1894. E

Personal Government of Charles I, 1628-37. 2 vols. 8vo. Lond., 1877. B 24 R 16, 17

GARDNER, Mrs. Alan. Rifle and Spear with the Rajpoots: being the Narrative of a Winter's Travel and Sport in Northern India. Illustrated. Imp. 8vo. Lond., 1895. D 15 P 8 †

GARDNER, Alice. Julian: Philosopher and Emperor, and the last struggles of Paganism against Christianity. 8vo. New York, 1895. C 14 S 23

GARFIELD, President James A. Address on the day of the burial of. [*See* Curtis, G. W.] F 14 U 3

Sketch of. [*See* Brooks, N.—Statesmen.] C 16 R 20

Sketch of. [*See* Wilson, J. G.—Presidents of the United States.] C 2 V 30

GARIBALDI, Giuseppe. [*See* Elliot, Frances—Roman Gossip.] C 21 Q 10

GARNEAU, F. X. History of Canada, from the time of its discovery till the Union Year, 1840-41. Translated by A. Bell. 3 vols. 8vo. Montreal, 1860.
B 16 Q 38-40

GARNETT, Dr. Richard. Life of Ralph Waldo Emerson. 8vo. Lond., 1888. C 17 S 17

GARNIER, Edward. French Pottery. [*See* Gasnault, P.] A 23 R 22

GARNIER, Jules. Mines de Nickel, Cuivre, et Platine du District de Sudbury (Canada). 8vo. Paris, 1891. A 24 V 23

GARNIER, Russell M. Annals of the British Peasantry. 8vo. Lond., 1895. F 9 T 21

History of the English Landed Interest; its Customs, Laws, and Agriculture. (Modern Period.) 8vo. Lond., 1893. F 9 S 30

GARRAN, Hon. Dr. Andrew. Australasia Illustrated. 3 vols. fol. Sydney, 1892. MD 8 Q 13-15 †

GARRETT, E. Isis very much unveiled: being the Story of the Great Mahatma Hoax. 12mo. Lond., 1895. G 2 U 21

GARRETT, Thos. W. The Ecclesiastical Practice, with Standing Rules and Notes thereon. 8vo. Sydney, 1889. MF 1 S 1

———and WALKER, W. A. The Probate Act of 1890, and the Probate Act of 1890 Amendment Act, and the Rules of Court issued thereunder. 8vo. Sydney, 1893. MF 1 S 37

GARRICK, David. [Life of]; by J. Knight. 8vo. Lond., 1894. C 18 T 4

Bon Ton; or, High Life Above Stairs: a Farce. [*See* London Stage, 3.] H 3 S 35

The Chances: a Comedy. [*See* London Stage, 4.] H 2 S 36

The Country Girl: a Comedy (altered from Wycherly.) [*See* London Stage, 1.] H 2 S 33

Cymon: a Dramatic Romance. [*See* London Stage, 3.] H 2 S 35

Every Man in his Humour: a Comedy. [*See* London Stage, 3.] H 2 S 35

The Guardian: a Comedy. [*See* London Stage, 3.] H 2 S 35

The Irish Widow: a Farce. [*See* London Stage, 3.] H 2 S 35

The Lying Valet: a Farce. [*See* London Stage, 1.] H 2 S 33

Miss in her Teens: or, the Medley of Lovers: a Farce. [*See* London Stage, 2.] H 2 S 34

Rule a Wife: a Comedy (altered from Beaumont and Fletcher.) [*See* London Stage, 1.] H 2 S 33

[Plaster Cast of.] [*See* Hutton, L.—Portraits in Plaster.] A 23 V 13

——— and COLMAN, George. Clandestine Marriage: a Comedy. [*See* London Stage, 1] H 2 S 33

GARTENLAUBE, Die. Illustrirtes familienblatt, 1884-85. 2 vols. fol. Leipzig, 1884-85. E

GASCOIGNE, George. Life and Writings of; with three poems hitherto not printed, by F. E. Schelling. 8vo. Boston (n.d.) C 21 R 7

GASKELL, George Edward. The Voyage out: a Poem. 8vo. Geelong, 1856. MH 1 S 71

GASNAULT, Paul, and GARNIER, Edouard. French Pottery. Illustrated. 8vo. Lond., 1884. A 23 R 22

GASQUET, Rev. Dr. Francis Aidan. The Great Pestilence (A.D. 1348-49), now commonly known as the Black Death. 8vo. Lond., 1893. B 23 T 19
First Divorce of Henry VIII. [See Hope, Mrs.] B 24 Q 6

GÄTKE, Heinrich. Heligoland as an Ornithological Observatory: the result of fifty years' experience. Translated by Rudolph Rosenstock. Roy. 8vo. Edinb., 1895. A 30 U 31

GAUDARD, Jules. Foundations. 2nd ed. 18mo. New York, 1891. A 22 P 18

GAUHAROU, Léon. Géographie de la Nouvelle-Calédonie, avec une Carte. 2ᵉ éd. 8vo. Noumea, 1892. MD S Q 27

GAUTIER, Théophile. [Life of]; by Maxime Du Camp. 8vo. Lond., 1893. C 19 Q 10

GAY, John. The Beggars' Opera: an Opera. [See London Stage, 1.] H 2 S 33
Poetical Works of; edited with a Life and Notes by John Underhill. 2 vols. 12mo. Lond., 1893. H 10 P 31, 32

GAY, Wm. Walt Whitman: his relation to Science and Philosophy. [See Whitman, W.] MJ 3 P 37
Walt Whitman, the Poet of Democracy. 8vo. Melb., 1893. MC 1 S 2

GAYLEY, Prof. Charles Mills. Classic Myths in English Literature. 2nd ed. 8vo. Boston, 1894. B 35 Q 8

GAZETTE DES BEAUX-ARTS. 3ᵉ Période, Tomes 8-12. 5 vols. Imp. 8vo. Paris, 1892-94. E

GEARY, J. Mrs. Sloper's Bundle of Holiday Stories. 8vo. Melb., 1876. MJ 2 S 30

GEARY, Nevill. The Law of Marriage and Family Relations: a Manual of Practical Law. 8vo. Lond., 1892. F 5 Q 4

GEDDES, Prof. Patrick. Chapters in Modern Botany. 12mo. Lond., 1893. A 20 P 18

——— and THOMPSON, J. Arthur. The Evolution of Sex. Illustrated. 12mo. Lond. (n.d.) A 28 P 4

GEELONG AND MELBOURNE RAILWAY CO. Reports, 1855-56, 1858. 4 vols. 8vo. Geelong, 1855-58. ME 6 S

GEELONG AND WESTERN DISTRICT AGRICULTURAL AND HORTICULTURAL SOCIETY. Rules and Regulations of the Society, and Annual Reports 1-3. 4 vols. 8vo. Geelong, 1855-58. ME 15 Q

GEELONG CHAMBER OF COMMERCE. Report, 1854. 8vo. Geelong, 1854. ME 15 Q

GEELONG ECLECTIC MAGAZINE, October to December, 1853. (*All published.*) 12mo. Geelong, 1853. ME 3 Q

GEELONG INFIRMARY. Reports of the Committee of Management, 1852-56. 5 vols. 8vo. Geelong, 1853-57. ME 6 S

GEGENBAUR, Prof. C. [*See* Morphologisches Jahrbuch.] E

GEIER, John. Thespis on Trial; or, the Moralitie of Playes considered. (Bibliotheca Curiosa.) 12mo. Edinb., 1887. J 18 Q 45

GEIKIE, Sir Archibald. Memoir of Sir A. C. Ramsay. 8vo. Lond., 1895. C 21 R 20
Text-book of Geology. 3rd ed. 8vo. Lond., 1893. A 24 U 22

GEIKIE, Prof. James. The Great Ice Age and its relation to the Antiquity of Man. 3rd ed., illustrated. 8vo. Lond., 1894. A 24 U 27
Fragments of Earth Lore: sketches and addresses, geological and geographical. Roy. 8vo. Edinb., 1893. A 24 V 19

GEISLER, Capt. Die Oster-Insel: eine Stätte prähistorischer Kultur in der Südsee. 8vo. Berlin, 1893. MB 2 U 24

GELL, Philip L. The Work of Toynbee Hall in East London. [*See* Montague, F. C.] B 18 S 7

GELLIBRAND, J. F. Tracking. 8vo. Hobart, 1868. MG 1 S 22

GEMS of the Granite State. [*See* New Hampshire.] D 15 Q 25

GENEALOGICA CURIOSA. 12mo. Lond., 1885. J 11 P 46
8. The Burning of St. Paul's, 1561.

GENEALOGIST, The: a Quarterly Magazine of Genealogical, Antiquarian, Topographical, and Heraldic Research. Vols. 8-10, n.s. 8vo. Lond., 1892-94 E

GENTH, Frederick A., and KERR, Washington C. Minerals and Mineral Localities of North Carolina. 8vo. Raleigh, 1895. A 24 U 29

GENTLEMAN, F. The Tobacconist: a Farce. [*See* London Stage, 2.] H 2 S 34

GENTLEMAN'S MAGAZINE, The. Vols. 273-275, and 277. 8vo. Lond., 1892-93. E

GEOGHEGAN, J. Some account of Silk in India. Sm. fol. Calcutta, 1872. A 12 R 15 †

GEOGRAPHICAL JOURNAL, The. [*See* Royal Geographical Society.]

GEOGRAPHICAL SOCIETY OF AUSTRALASIA. [*See* Royal Geographical Society of Australasia.]

GEOGRAPHICAL SOCIETY OF THE PACIFIC. Transactions and Proceedings of, January, 1883–July, 1891. 2 vols. 8vo. San Francisco, 1883–91.   E

GEOGRAPHY AND READER. (Burra School.) 8vo. Kooringa, 1891.   MD 1 Q 46

GEOLOGICAL MAGAZINE; or, Monthly Journal of Geology, with which is incorporated "The Geologist." New series, Decade 3, vols. 9 and 10, and Decade 4, vol. 1. 8vo. Lond., 1893–94.   E

GEOLOGICAL SOCIETY OF AUSTRALASIA. Transactions of. Vol. 1, Parts 1–3. Sm. 4to. Melb., 1886–92.   ME 16 S

GEOLOGICAL SOCIETY OF LONDON, The. List of, 1879. 8vo. Lond., 1879.   E

Quarterly Journal of. Vols. 48–50. 8vo. Lond., 1892–94.   E

GEOLOGISCHEN REICHSANSTALT, K.K. [*See* Kaiserlich-Kön. Geol. Reichsanstalt.]

GEOLOGIST, The. [*See* Geological Magazine, The.]

GEORGE, Henry, and the Beginnings of Revolutionary Socialism. [*See* Ely, Dr. R. T.]   B 18 S 3

A Perplexed Philosopher; being an examination of Mr. Herbert Spencer's various utterances on the Land question. 8vo. Lond., 1893   F 14 Q 35

The Land Question: what it is, and how only it can be settled. 8vo. Melb. (n.d.)   MF 4 Q 14

Single Tax Theory as propounded by. [*See* White, Rev. Dr. J. S.]   MF 4 Q 14

His remedies analysed. [*See* Campbell, Rev. C.]   MF 4 R 26

Henry George and his Utopia. [*See* Rennick, C.]   MF 3 R 55

GERARD, Rev. John. Stonyhurst College, 1592–1894. 4to. Belfast, 1894.   B 12 U 8 †

GERMAN LANGUAGE. A series of Progressive Lessons. Sm. 4to. Lond., 1828.   J 7 P 51

GERRALD, J. A Convention the only means of saving us from ruin. 2nd. ed. 8vo. Lond., 1794.   F 9 Q 28

GESCHICHTE DER WISSENSCHAFTEN in Deutschland. Band 22.—Geschichte der Medicinischen Wissenschaften. 8vo. München, 1893.   A 17 V 38

GIBBINGS, Alfred H. Dynamo Attendants and their Dynamos. 8vo. Lond., 1894.   A 21 R 16

GIBBINS, H. de B. British Commerce and Colonies, from Elizabeth to Victoria. 8vo. Lond., 1893.   F 14 Q 47

The Economics of Commerce. 12mo. Lond., 1894.   F 5 Q 10

A Shorter Working Day. [*See* Hadfield, R. A.]   F 14 Q 30

GIBBON, Edward. Essay on. [*See* Bagehot, W.—Literary Studies.]   J 9 P 22–24

Proceedings of the Gibbon Commemoration, 1794–1894. Roy. 8vo. Lond., 1895.   C 19 U 15

[*See* Bagehot, W.—Estimates of some Englishmen and Scotchmen.]   J 10 V 32

GIBBONS, James, Cardinal. The Faith of Our Fathers, being a plain exposition and vindication of the Church founded by our Lord Jesus Christ. 44th ed. 18mo. Baltimore, 1893.   G 19 P 29

GIBBONS, Sydney. Notes on Diet. [Australian Health Soc.) 8vo. Melb., 1879.   MA 3 S 33

GIBBS, Henry Hucks. A Colloquy on Currency. 3rd ed. 8vo. Lond., 1894.   F 2 V 9

GIBBS, Richard. Portrait of. [*See* Ramsay, Sir A. C.—Memoir of.]   C 21 R 20

GIBBS, SHALLARD & CO. Plan of the City of Sydney and Suburbs, with Port Jackson and Soundings. Folded imp. 8vo. Sydney, 1879.   MD 6 V 1

GIBERNE, Miss Agnes. Radiant Suns. Illustrated. 8vo. Lond., 1895.   A 19 S 22

GIBLIN *v.* AIKENHEAD & BUTTON. The libel case, Attorney-General of Tasmania *v. Launceston Examiner.* 8vo. Launceston, 1874.   MF 4 R 51

GIBSON, Andrew. Epidemic Catarrh among Sheep. [*See* Bennett, Dr. G.]   MA 1 P 47

GIBSON, Dr. Frank M. Amateur Telescopist's Handbook. 12mo. New York, 1894.   A 19 Q 21

GIBSON, George Herbert. "Ironbark." Ironbark Chips and Stockwhip Cracks. Illustrated. 8vo. Melb., 1893.   MH 1 V 2

GIBSON, Herbert. History of the Sheep-breeding Industry in the Argentine Republic. 8vo. Buenos Aires, 1893.   A 18 S 11

GIBSON, Rev. Dr. John M. St. Matthew. [*See* Expositor's Bible.]   G 19 S 1

GIBSON, T. Phillips. Medicinal Plants. 8vo. Sydney, 1893.   MA 1 Q 65

GIBSON, Wm. Hamilton. Some Artists at the Fair. [*See* Chicago Exhibition, 1893.]   A 23 U 21

GIDDINGS, T. F. Insurance Laws of Michigan, 1893. 8vo. Lansing, 1893.   E

GIFFORD, John. The complete English Lawyer; or, Every Man his own Lawyer. 8vo. Lond., 1822.   F 7 R 27

GIFFORD, Wm. Baviad and Mæviad: Pasquin *v.* Faulder: Epistle to Peter Pindar; with the Author's Memoir of his own Life. 32mo. Lond., 1858.   Libr.

GILBERT, Dr. The Grandeur of True Manhood. 8vo. Wanganui (n.d.)   MA 2 S 56

GILBERT, E. Address to the Colonists of Van Diemen's Land on the Tea Trade. 8vo. Hobart, 1848.   MA 1 P 77

GILBERT, Grove Karl. Lake Bonneville. (U.S. Geol. Survey, 1.) 4to. Wash., 1890.   E

GILBERT, Dr. Gustav. Constitutional Antiquities of Sparta and Athens. Translated by E. J. Brooks and T. Nicklin. 8vo. Lond., 1895.   F 9 T 22

GILBERT, Dr. John Thos. Documents relating to Ireland, 1795-1804. 4to. Dublin, 1893.   B 29 V 10

Narratives of the Detention, Liberation, and Marriage of Maria Clementina Stuart. [*See* Stuart, Maria Clementina.]   C 19 U 11

GILBERT, Wm. The Inquisitor; or, the Struggle in Ferrara: an Historical Romance. 3 vols. 12mo. Lond., 1870.   J 6 P 17-19

GILBERT, Dr. Wm. On the Loadstone and Magnetic Bodies, and on the Great Magnet, the Earth. Translated by P. Fleury Mottelay. Roy. 8vo. Lond., 1893.   A 21 V 5

GILBERT, Wm. Schwenck. Original Plays. 3rd series. 12mo. Lond., 1895.   H 1 Q 46

GILCHRIST, Rev. Dr. A. Attachment to the House of God: a Sermon preached at the opening of the Union Memorial Church, North Melbourne. 12mo Melb., 1879.   MG 2 R 45

Preparation for Death: a Funeral Sermon preached after the death of Mrs. Isabella Morrison. 8vo. Sydney, 1863.   MG 2 R 45

GILCHRIST, W. J. Hand Book on the Laws relating to Public Health. 8vo. Melb., 1876.   MF 1 P 56

Manual of Borough Law. 4to. Melb., 1870.   MF 3 U 59

Local Government Manual. 4to. Melb., 1875.   MF 3 U 58

GILES, Dr. Arthur E. Moral Pathology. 8vo. Lond., 1895.   G 18 Q 29

GILES, Fayette S. Shadows before, or a Century onward. 8vo. New York, 1893.   F 8 U 15

GILES, P. A Short Manual of Comparative Philology. 8vo. Lond., 1895.   J 11 U 4

GILFILLAN, George. Letters and Journals, with Memoir; by Robert A. and Elizabeth S. Watson. 8vo. Lond., 1892.   C 15 R 9

GILL, Harry P. Elementary Design. 4to. Adelaide, 1892.   MA 2 Q 34†

GILL, W. B. The Yellow Dwarf. [*See* Banks, S. H.]   MH 1 P 53

GILL, Rev. Dr. Wm. Wyatt. From Darkness to Light in Polynesia; with Illustrative Clan Songs. 8vo. Lond., 1894.   MD 1 R 31

GILLIES, Dr. H. Cameron. Theory and Practice of Counter-irritation. 8vo. Lond., 1895.   A 33 U 17

GILLINGHAM, B. Visions in the Isle of Patmos; their symbolical meaning shown in a chronological, consecutive, and harmonious scheme. 8vo. Sebastopol, Vic., 1869.   MG 1 S 18

GILLMORE, Capt. Parker. Leaves from a Sportsman's Diary. 8vo. Lond., 1893.   A 17 T 61

Gun, Rod, and Saddle: A record of personal experiences. 8vo. Lond., 1893.   A 17 T 60

GILMAN, Dr. Daniel Coit. The Johns Hopkins University (1876-91); with Supplementary Notes on University Extension and the University of the Future, by R. G. Moulton. (Johns Hopkins University Studies, 9.) 8vo. Baltimore, 1891.   B 18 S 9

GILMAN, Nicholas S. Socialism and the American Spirit. 8vo. Lond, 1893.   F 14 R 8

GILMORE, Hugh. Sermons by the late, 1889-91. Roy. 8vo. Adelaide, 1892.   MG 1 S 21

GILMOUR, James. Diaries, Letters, and Reports. Edited by R. Lovett. 3rd ed. 8vo. Lond., 1895.   G 15 P 38

More about the Mongols: selected and arranged by R. Lovett. 8vo. Lond., 1893.   D 17 Q 12

GILPIN, Dr. Edwin. Minerals of Nova Scotia. 8vo. Halifax, N.S., 1893.   A 24 S 13

GIOLLA. [*See* Weale, J. C. M.]

GIOTTO, Angiolotto Bondone. Sketch of. [*See* Oliphant, Mrs. M.—Makers of Florence.]   B 30 Q 20

GIPPSLAND LAKES AND RIVERS, Our Guide to the; by "Tanjil." 12mo. Melb., 1886.   MD 1 Q 35

GIPPSLAND SPORTING CASE, The. 8vo. Melb., 1867.   MF 4 Q 20

GIRARD, Maurice. F. Péron, Naturaliste, Voyageur aux Terres Australes. [*See* Péron, F.]   MA 3 R 34

GIRARD, Paul. L'Asclépicion d'Athènes d'après de récentes découvertes. 8vo. Paris, 1881.   B 35 R 23

GIRDLESTONE, Dr. F. M. Under the Floor. [*See* Australian Health Soc., Melb.]   MA 3 S 33

GIRDLESTONE, Rev. Robert Baker. Deuterographs: Duplicate Passages in the Old Testament 8vo. Oxford, 1894.   G 4 Q 36

GIVOVICH, A. El Rigor de la Corneta. Roy. 8vo. Valparaiso, 1887.   J 8 V 24

GLADDEN, Rev. Dr. Washington. Social Problems in the United States. [*See* Subjects of the Day, 2.]
F 7 U 27

GLADSTONE, Rt. Hon. Wm. Ewart. England and her Colonies: a Lecture delivered at Chester, Nov. 12, 1855. 12mo. Melb., 1871.
MJ 3 Q 15

Financial Statements of 1853, 1860-63. 8vo. Lond., 1864.
F 11 U 25

Home Rule for Ireland. [*See* Subjects of the Day, 3.]
F 7 U 28

Odes of Horace. [*See* Horatius Flaccus, Q.]
H 7 U 27

[Life of]; by E. W. E. Russell. (Prime Ministers of Queen Victoria.) 8vo. Lond., 1892.
C 18 P 3

Early Public Life of; by A. F. Robbins. 8vo. Lond., 1894.
C 17 R 17

Sketch of. [*See* Bagehot, W.—Biographical Studies.]
C 22 P 10

A Study from Life; by H W. Lucy. 12mo. Lond., 1895.
C 2 R 37

GLAISHER, Dr. John. Dr. W. Smellie and his Contemporaries: a Contribution to the History of Midwifery in the 18th Century. 8vo. Glasgow, 1894.
C 16 U 3

GLAISTER, Wm. Life of Emperor Karl. [*See* Eginhard.]
C 13 P 18

GLANCE OF LIFE, and other Poems; by "G. W. F." 8vo. Lond., 1892.
H 10 Q 26

GLASGOW POST OFFICE DIRECTORY, 1893-94. 2 vols. 8vo. Glasgow, 1893.
E

GLASS, Chas. E. Miner's Companion for 1857. 2nd ed. 8vo. Castlemaine, Vic., 1857.
MA 3 P 56

Pocket Road Guide to the Gold Fields [of Victoria]. 18mo. Castlemaine, 1858.
MD 1 P 47

GLAVE, E. J. Six Years of Adventure in Congo-Land. Roy. 8vo. Lond., 1893.
D 14 V 5

GLAZEBROOK, R. T. Laws and Properties of Matter. 8vo. Lond., 1893.
A 29 Q 4

GLENELG, Lord. Mr. D. Coates and the New Zealand Association. [*See* Wakefield, E. G.]
MB 2 R 57

GLENNIE, Col. F. Records of 24th Regiment. [*See* Paton, Col. G.]
B 22 R 4

GLIDDON, J. Chart of Coast on East side of St. Vincent's Gulf, South Australia. Fol. Lond. (n.d.)
MD 3 Q 7‡

GLOBE, The. Jan.-March, 1894. 8vo. Chicago, 1894.
F 9 R 37

GLOUCESTER FISHERMEN'S INSTITUTE. First Annual Report. 8vo. Gloucester, Mass., 1893.
E

GLOVER, Chas. W. National Airs. [*See* Moore, Thomas.]
A 23 V 11

GLOVER, John R. Napoleon's Last Voyages. [*See* Napoleon Bonaparte.]
C 22 R 3

GLYDE, Miss Ethel L. Blanchewater to Cooper's Creek. (Roy. Geog. Soc. Australasia, Vic. Branch, G.) 8vo. Melb., 1889.
ME 20 P

GLYNN, P. McM. The Irish State Trials. [*See* Sullivan, A. M.]
MF 4 Q 20

GLYNN, M. S. Victorian Rowing Register and Oarsman's Companion, 1878. 8vo. Melb., 1878.
ME 5 Q

GLYNNE, Sir Stephen Richard. Notes on Churches of Cheshire. [*See* Chetham Soc. Pubs., n.s. 32.]
E

Notes on the Churches of Lancashire. [*See* Chetham Soc. Pubs., n.s., 27.]
E

GNEIST, Dr. Rudolf von. History of the English Parliament through a thousand years, 800-1887. 3rd. ed. 8vo. Lond., 1889.
B 23 S 9

GOADBY, Edwin. The Gothenburg Licensing System. 12mo. Lond., 1895.
F 7 V 25

GODDARD, Rev. E. H. Glossary of Words used in Wiltshire. [*See* Dartnell, G. E.]
E

GODEY, Chas. Tablettes d'un ancien fonctionnaire de la Nouvelle-Calédonie: comprenant la relation du Voyage par les Caps de Bonne-Espérance et Horn; avec Cartes de la route et une Carte de la Nouvelle-Calédonie. 2 vols. 12mo. Paris, 1886.
MD 7 T 35, 36

GODFREY, Edgar James. Literary Curiosities: a Series of Letters to the New South Wales Public Newspapers. 8vo. Sydney, 1882.
MJ 3 Q 4

GODKIN, Lawrence. Legal Medicine. [*See* Hamilton, Dr. A. M.]
F 1 V 5 6

GODMAN, F. Ducane. Persian Ceramic Art. [*See* Wallis, H.]
A 6 P 11 ‡

GOESSMANN, Prof. C. A. Manual of Agriculture. [*See* Emerson, G. B.]
A 18 Q 34

GOETHE, Johann Wolfgang von. Poetische und Prosaische Werke. 2 vols. roy 8vo. Stuttgart, 1854-5.
J 7 V 28, 29

Faust: a Dramatic Poem. Translated by A. Hayward. 7th ed. 12mo. Lond., 1860.
H 1 U 1

Faust; with Critical and Explanatory Notes by Dr. G. G. Zerffi. 8vo. Lond., 1862.
H 1 U 4

Faust: eine Tragödie. 8vo. Stuttgart, 1863.
H 1 U 5

Faust: a Tragedy. Translated by L. Filmore. 12mo. Lond. (n.d.)
H 1 S 45

Faust: a Tragedy; with Notes by Dr. F. Labahn. 8vo. Lond., 1853.
H 2 U 28

Wilhelm Meister's Apprenticeship and Travels. Translated by T. Carlyle. 2 vols. 8vo. Lond., 1858.
J 5 R 40, 41

GOETHE, Johann Wolfgang von—*contd.*
A French Critic on. [*See* Arnold, M.—Mixed Essays.]
  J 11 T 25
Goethe and Carlyle. [*See* Müller, F. Max.—Chips from a German Workshop.]   J 9 R 31-33
Goethe's Wilhelm Meister, &c. [*See* Dowden, Dr. E.]
  J 5 S 16
Goethe; or, the Writer. [*See* Emerson, R. W.—Representative Men.]   C 17 P 10
Goethe reviewed after sixty years; by J. R. Seeley. 12mo. Lond., 1894.   C 19 Q 15

GÖHRE, Paul. Three Months in a Workshop. Translated by A. B. Carr. 8vo. Lond., 1895. F 6 T 37

GOLDEN CLAD GOLD-MINING CO. Memorandum and Articles of Association. 8vo. Sydney (n.d.)
  MF 4 R 35

GOLDEN GATES OF AUSTRALIA, with its Temptations and its Perils; by "An Australian." 8vo. Lond. (n.d.)   MD 7 T 64

GOLD-FIELDS, Ancient and Modern. 8vo. Melb., 1855.   MA 3 S 61

GOLD-FIELDS REMINISCENCES, 1851-84; by "Bonanza." 8vo. Melb., 1884. MA 3 S 58

GOLDSMITH, Oliver. Selections from. [*See* Harlin, T.]
  MJ 1 U 34
Essays. 8vo. Lond., 1853.   J 4 U 1
Goldsmith's Traveller, edited and annotated by C. H. Pearson and Prof. H. A. Strong. 8vo. Melb., 1877.
  MH 1 Q 23
The Good-natured Man: a Comedy. [*See* London Stage, 2.]   H 2 S 34
Letters from a Citizen of the World. 8vo. Lond., 1853.   J 4 U 1
Poetical Works of. 8vo. Lond., 1852. H 7 U 34
She Stoops to Conquer: a Comedy. [*See* London Stage, 1.]   H 2 S 33
She Stoops to Conquer; with Drawings by E. A. Abbey. Fol. New York, 1887.   H 40 T 3 ‡
Life and Adventures of; by J. Forster. 8vo. Lond., 1848.   C 21 R 6
Sketch of. [*See* Bell, Rev. Dr. C. D.—Some of our English Poets.]   C 21 P 11

GOLDSTEIN, J. R. Y. Some new Species of Bryozoa from the Marion Islands, with Notes on Bicellaria Grandis. (Roy. Soc., Vict., 18.) 8vo. Melb., 1882.
  ME 1 P

GOMME, Alice Bertha. Traditional Games of England, Scotland and Ireland, with Tunes, Song-rhymes, and Methods of Playing according to the variants extant and recorded in different parts of the Kingdom. [Illustrated.] Vol. 1. 8vo. Lond., 1894. A 30 T 9

GONCOURT, Edmond and Jules de. [Lives of]; with Letters and Leaves from their Journals. Compiled and translated by M. A. Belloc and M. Shedlock. 2 vols. 8vo. Lond., 1895. C 21 R 3, 4

GONNESSIAT, F. Recherches sur l'Équation Personnelle dans les Observations Astronomiques de Passage. (Annales de l'Univ. de Lyon, 3.) Roy. 8vo. Paris, 1892.   A 19 V 28

GONTAUT, Duchesse de. Memoirs of 1773-1836. Translated from the French, by Mrs. J. W. Davis. 2 vols. 8vo. Lond., 1894.   C 18 T 12, 13

GONZALEZ, J. A. y. Fundamento de la Extradición. 8vo. Montevideo, 1894.   F 9 R 19

GOOD TEMPLARS, Independent Order of. Journals and Proceedings of the Grand Lodge of N.S.W. 8vo. Sydney, 1880.   ME

GOOD WORDS, 1892-94. 3 vols. roy. 8vo. Lond., 1892-94.   E

GOODALE, Dr. George Lincoln. The Wild Flowers of America; with coloured Plates by I. Sprague. 4to. Boston, 1894.   A 15 Q 22 †

GOODCHILD, K. Who are you? A volume of verse; by "Keighley." 12mo. Echuca, 1893. MH 1 P 57

GOODE, George Brown. Classification of the Collection to illustrate the Animal Resources of the United States. 8vo. Wash., 1876.   K 7 U 8

GOODENOUGH, Lt.-Gen. W. H., and DALTON, Lt.-Col. J. C. The Army Book for the British Empire: a Record of the Development and Present Composition of the Military Forces, and their Duties in Peace and War. 8vo. Lond., 1893. B 23 T 18

GOODNOW, Prof. Frank J. Comparative Administrative Law: Analysis of the Administrative Systems, National and Local, of the United States, England, France, and Germany. 2 vols. 8vo. New York, 1893.   F 8 P 33, 34
 1. Organisation.
 2. Legal Regulations.
Municipal Home Rule: a Study in Administration. 8vo. Lond., 1895.   F 8 U 40

GOODWIN, George Augustus. The Land Selector's Guide. 2nd ed. 8vo. Melb., 1873. MF 2 R 41

GOODYEAR, Chas. Sketch of. [*See* Hubert, P. G.—Inventors.]   C 17 R 3

GOODYEAR, Wm. H. Renaissance and Modern Art. 8vo. New York, 1894.   A 23 R 14

GOOLD, Most Rev. James Alipius. Biographical Sketch of; by Jas. F. Hogan. With Portrait. 8vo. Melb., 1886.   MC 1 T 20

GOOLD-ADAMS, Capt H. E. [See Adams, Capt. H. E. G.]

GOOS, Pieter. De Zee-Atlas ofte Water-Weereld, waer in vertoontwerden alle de Zoe-Kusten van het bekonde des Aerd Bodems. Fol. Amsterdam, 1666.
D 8 P 26 ‡

GORDAY, Prof. J. P. Rise and Growth of the Normal School Idea in the United States. 8vo. Wash., 1891.
G 18 R 16

GORDON, Adam Lindsay. Poems: Sea Spray and Smoke Drift—Bush Ballads and Galloping Rhymes—Miscellaneous Poems—Ashtaroth, a dramatic lyric—The Roll of the Kettledrum. 8vo. Melb., 1892.
MH 1 Q 16

A Memoir of the Life of; by J. H. Ross. 8vo. Lond., 1892.
MC 1 Q 29

Reminiscences and unpublished Poems. 4to. Sydney (n.d.)
MH 10 P 10 †

GORDON, Alexander. Freedom of Thought in Matters of Religious Belief, its use and abuse. 8vo. Sydney, 1880.
MG 1 P 71

——— and KNOX, G. Joint Opinion of, re Bishop of Sydney. Sm. fol. Sydney, 1882.
MG 9 P 9 †

——— and STUART, Sir Alexander. Speeches [on Church Property] at the Meeting of the General Conference of the Church of England in New South Wales, April 12-17, 1866. 8vo. Sydney, 1866.
MG 1 S 19

GORDON, Hon. Sir Arthur. The Earl of Aberdeen. (Prime Ministers of Queen Victoria.) 8vo. Lond., 1893.
C 13 P 28

GORDON, Gen. Charles George. Gordon Memorial Statue: an Account of the Gordon Memorial Meeting, at Melbourne, May, 1885. 8vo. Melb., 1885.
MC 1 T 18

Tribute to the Memory of. [See Tucker, Rev. H. F.]
MG 1 R 69

GORDON, E. A. Clear Round: Seeds of Story from other Countries. Illustrated. 8vo. Lond., 1895.
D 20 Q 17

GORDON, George. Amateur's Rose Book. [See Hibberd, S.]
A 32 R 9

GORDON, H. Compendium of Painting. [See Blockx, J.]
A 23 P 4

GORDON, Henry A. Mining and Engineering, and Miners' Guide. Roy. 8vo. Wellington, 1894
MA 3 R 35

GORDON, Jas. Edward Henry. Practical Treatise on Electric Lighting. 8vo. New York, 1891.
A 21 S 21

GORDON, Prof. Joseph C. Notes and Observations upon the Education of the Deaf. Roy. 8vo. Washington, 1892.
G 17 R 27

GORDON, Mrs. Life and Correspondence of Very Rev. Dean Buckland. Illustrated. 8vo. Lond., 1894.
C 17 R 16

GORDON, Mrs. Margaret Maria. The Home Life of Sir David Brewster. 2nd ed. 8vo. Edinb., 1870.
C 13 P 25

GORDON, P. R. The Drover's Guide: a summary of such clauses of various Acts of Parliament as relate to the Passage of Stock in Queensland and New South Wales. 2nd ed. 12mo. Brisb., 1886. MF 2 P 49

GORDON & GOTCH, Messrs. The Australian Hardbook for 1893-95. 3 vols. roy. 8vo. Lond., 1893-95.
ME 13 R

GORE, Rev. Chas. Thoughts on Religion by G. J. Romanes. [See Romanes, G. J.] G 1 U 23

Dissertations on subjects connected with the Incarnation. 8vo. Lond., 1895.
G 3 R 17

GORE, J. Ellard. An Astronomical Glossary. 12mo. Lond., 1893.
A 19 P 24

Popular Astronomy. [See Flammarion, C.] A 19 V 22

The Visible Universe: Chapters on the Origin and Construction of the Heavens. Illustrated. 8vo. Lond., 1893.
A 19 S 23

GORGAS, Dr. Ferdinand J. S. Dentistry. [See Harris, Dr. C. A.]
A 26 V 12

GORST, Rt Hon. Sir John E. Settlements in England and America. [See Knapp, J. M.—The Universities and the Social Problem.]
F 8 U 22

GOSCHEN, Rt. Hon. George Joachim. Theory of the Foreign Exchanges. 10th ed. 8vo. Lond., 1894.
F 14 T 40

GOSMAN, Rev. Alexander. Mr. Justice Higinbotham on the Orthodox Faith. 8vo. Melb., 1887.
MG 2 Q 23

GOSPEL OF THE KINGDOM, The. [See Religious Pamphlets, 1.]
G 9 V 16

GOSSE, Edmund Wm. Letters of Thos. L. Beddoes. [See Beddoes, T. L.]
C 19 P 5

Essay on Georgian Sculpture. [See Nollekens, J.—Nollekens and his Times.]
C 12 R 18

The Jacobean Poets. 12mo. Lond., 1894. C 18 P 0

The Tavern of the Three Virtues. [See Delorme, R.]
J 15 R 13 †

GOSTWICK, Joseph, and HARRISON, Robert. Outlines of German Literature. 2nd ed. 8vo. Lond., 1883.
J 8 Q 43

GOTHAISCHER GENEALOGISCHER HOFKALENDER nebst diplomatisch-statistischen Jahrbuch, 1883-95. 3 vols. 18mo. Gotha, 1893-95. E

GOTHAISCHES GENEALOGISCHES TASCHENBUCH der Gräflichen Häuser, 1803-85. 3 vols. 18mo. Gotha, 1893-94. E

GOTHAISCHES GENEALOGISCHES TASCHEN-BUCH der Freiherrlichen Häuser, 1893-95. 3 vols. 18mo. Gotha, 1893-94. E

GOTO, Seitara. On Diplozoon nipponicum. 8vo. (n.p.n.d.) A 30 V 16

GOUIN, François. The Art of Teaching and Learning Languages. 2nd edition. 8vo. Lond., 1892. K 20 Q 43

GOULD, A. C., "Ralph Greenwood." Modern American Pistols and Revolvers. New ed., illustrated. 8vo. Boston, 1894. A 25 S 4

GOULD, Benjamin Apthorp. Resultados del Observatorio Nacional Argentino en Córdoba. Catálogo General. 4to. Córdoba, 1886. A 14 S 17 †

Uranometria Argentina: Brightness and Position of every fixed star, down to the seventh magnitude, within one hundred degrees of the South Pole. (Spanish and English.) 4to. Buenos Aires, 1879. A 14 S 12 †

Atlas to above. Fol. Buenos Aires, 1877. A 12 P 23 ‡

Zone Catalogue: Mean Positions for 1870 of Stars observed in the Zones at the Argentine National Observatory. 2 vols. 4to. Córdoba, 1884. A 14 S 14, 15 †

GOULD, Dr. E. R. L. Local Government in Pennsylvania. (Johns Hopkins University Studies, 1.) 8vo. Baltimore, 1883. B 18 S 1

The Social Condition of Labour. Johns Hopkins University Studies, 11.) 8vo. Baltimore, 1893. B 18 S 11

Popular Control of the Liquor Traffic. 12mo. Lond., 1894. F 7 V 31

GOULD, Dr. George M. Illustrated Dictionary of Medicine, Biology, and allied Sciences. Roy. 8vo. Lond., 1894. A 33 V 14

GOULD, John. Analytical Index to the Works of, with a Biographical Memoir; by R. B. Sharp. 4to. Lond., 1893. A 12 S 7 †

GOULD, Nat, "Verax." On and off the Turf in Australia. 12mo. Lond., 1895. MA 3 U 26

GOULD, Robert Freke. The History of Freemasonry: its Antiquities, Symbols, Constitutions, Customs, &c. 3 vols. 4to. Lond., 1885-87. B 12 S 2-4 †

GOULD, Rev. S. Baring-. [See Baring-Gould, Rev. S.]

GOUVÊA, Dr. H. de, and LIMA E CASTRO, Dr. J. C. de. O Contracto de Saneamento do Solo do Rio de Janeiro. 8vo. Rio de Janeiro, 1891. A 26 U 22

GOVE, A. Teachers' Hand-book, Denver, 1893. 12mo. Denver, 1893. G 18 P 20

GOVETT, Wm. Romaine. Manuscript Note-book of; including Copies of some Letters written by him, 1835-37. Notes on the Aborigines of New South Wales, and an Account of Govett's Leap, with a description of the scenery on the Blue Mountain Road, forming the basis of Govett's "Sketches of New South Wales," in the *Saturday Magazine*, 1836-37; with extracts on Oil Painting, from "The Compleat Gentleman, by H. Peacham." Sm. 4to. (n.p.) 1828-37. Libr.

GOW, Wm. The Apocalypse unveiled, and a Fight with Death and Slander. 12mo. Perth, 1888. G 17 Q 52

Legends of Strathmore. 12mo. Perth, 1886. J 11 U 28

GOW, Dr. Wm. Marine Insurance. 12mo. Lond., 1895. F 7 V 33

GOWEN, Rev. H. H. The Paradise of the Pacific: Sketches of Hawaiian Scenery and Life. 12mo. Lond., 1892. MD 7 T 56

GOWER, Hon. F. L. Letters of Harriet, Countess Granville. [See Granville, Countess.] C 16 S 18, 19

GOWER, G. L. Glossary of Surrey Words. (Eng. Dialect Soc.) 8vo. Lond., 1893. E

GOWER, Ronald Chas. Sutherland Leveson, Lord. Joan of Arc. 8vo. Lond., 1893. C 16 T 17

GOWER, Wm. H. The Orchid Album. [See Warner, R.] A 14 P 10 †

GOWERS, Dr. Wm. R. Clinical Lectures on Diseases of the Nervous System. 8vo. Lond., 1895. A 13 Q 35

GRAAF, Dr. L. von. Myzostomida. [See Thomson, Sir C. W., and Murray, Dr. J.—Voyage of H.M.S. *Challenger*.] A 6 †

GRACE, Joseph. The End of the World, containing wonderful historical facts. 8vo. Sydney, 1893. MG 1 P 70

GRACE, Dr. W. G. Batting, Bowling, Fielding. 18mo. Bristol (n.d.) A 29 S 16

GRAHAM, Andrew J. Standard or American Phonography. 8vo. New York, 1894. J 12 T 46

GRAHAM, Gabriela C. Santa Teresa; being some Account of her Life and Times, together with some pages from the History of the last great Reform in the Religious Orders. 2 vols. 8vo. Lond., 1894. G 3 R 10, 11

GRAHAM, Dr. J. Hydatid Disease in its Clinical Aspects. 8vo. Edinb., 1891. A 13 Q 34

GRAHAM, Robt. C. The Carved Stones of Islay. 4to. Glasgow, 1895. B 15 P 3 †

GRAHAM, Thos. Sketch of. [See Thorpe, Dr. T. E.—Historical Chemistry.] C 17 R 2

GRAHAM, Dr. Thos. J. On the Diseases of Females, including the Diseases and Management of Pregnancy and Confinement. 6th ed. 8vo. Lond., 1856.
A 33 T 15

GRAMMONT, Count Philibert. Memoirs of; by Count Anthony Hamilton. 4to. Lond., 1793. C 18 U 5

GRAND MAGAZINE OF MAGAZINES, October, 1759. 8vo. Lond., 1759. J 4 U 8

GRANDIER, Urbain. History of the Devils of London. [See Collectanea Adamantæa.] J 18 R 31

GRANDJEAN, J. M. Mélanges de Philologie Indo-Européenne. [See Regnaud P.] J 7 U 40

GRANT, A. J. Greece in the Age of Pericles. 12mo. Lond., 1893. B 16 P 1

GRANT, Rev. Dr. George M. The Religions of the World. 8vo. Lond, 1895. G 1 U 21

GRANT, Gen. Sir Hope. Life of with Selections from his Correspondence. Edited by Col. H. Knollys. With Portraits, and Maps and Plans. 2 vols. 8vo. Edinb., 1894. C 17 R 5, 6

GRANT, M. Forsyth. Scenes in Hawaii ; or, Life in the Sandwich Islands. 12mo. Toronto, 1888. MD 8 P 2

GRANT, Gen. Ulysses S. [Plaster Cast of.] [See Hutton, L.—Portraits in Plaster.] A 23 V 13
Sketch of. [See Wilson, J. G.—Presidents of the United States.] C 2 V 30

GRANVILLE, Harriet, Countess. Letters of, 1810–45. Edited by the Hon. F. L. Gower. 2 vols. 8vo. Lond., 1894. C 16 S 18, 19

GRANVILLE, Lord. Sketch of. [See Smalley, G. W.—Studies of Men.] C 19 R 20

GRAPHIC, The; an illustrated weekly newspaper. Vols. 46-50. Fol. Lond., 1892-94. E

GRASBY, W. Catton. Our Public Schools. 2nd ed. 8vo. Adelaide, 1891. MG 1 S 43

GRATTANN, W. H. Seaweeds. [See Taylor, Dr. J. E. —Collecting Natural History Objects.] A 29 Q 38

GRAU, Rev. Dr. R. F. The Geal of the Human Race ; or, the Development of Civilisation, its Origin and Issue. 8vo. Lond., 1892. G 2 P 33

GRAY, Prof. Andrew. Theory and Practice of Absolute Measurements in Electricity and Magnetism. 2 vols. (in 3). 8vo. Lond., 1883-95. A 21 Q 16-18

———— and MATHEWS, Prof. G. B. Treatise on Bessel Functions and their Applications to Physics. 8vo. Lond., 1895. A 25 U 21

GRAY, Rev. James Cowper. The Sunday School World. 12mo. Lond., 1871. G 2 V 43

GRAY, Dr. John Edward. Supplement to Catalogue of Seals and Whales in the British Museum. 8vo. Lond., 1871. A 27 U 34

GRAY, John M. Life of Sir John Clerk. [See Scottish History Soc., 13.] E

GRAY, Capt. R., the Discoverer of the Columbia River. Sketch of. [See Greeley, Gen. A. W.—Explorers and Travellers.] C 17 R 4

GRAY, Roderick. Tongariro, the Sacred Mountain of the Maori. 12mo. Lond. (n.d.) MG 2 R 51

GRAY, Samuel. Pamphlets on Poultry :—Table Birds, Australian Game, the Plymouth Rock, Egg Producers and Experiments in Egg Production, Soft Food, Fowls on the Farm. 8vo. Sydney, 1893. MA 1 Q 60

GRAY, Thomas. Designs by R. Bentley for six Poems by T. Gray. Fol. Lond., 1765. H 40 T 8 ‡
Poetical Works of. 12mo. Lond., 1863. H 10 T 3
Poetical Works of. 18mo. Lond., 1839. H 10 T 28
Sketch of. [See Bell, Rev. Dr. C. D.—Some of our English Poets.] C 21 P 11

GRAY, Wm. Works of Sir Philip Sidney. [See Sidney, Sir P.] J 2 Q 23

GRAY, Rev. Wm. Presbyterian Church of South Australia, Home and Foreign Missions. 12mo. Adelaide, 1888. MG 2 R 51

GRAYSON, L. Boiler Explosions. 8vo. Adelaide, 1886. MA 2 V 57

GREAT BRITAIN AND IRELAND :—
ARMY LIST. [See WAR OFFICE.]
BRITISH NORTH AMERICA. Report on the Affairs of, from the Earl of Durham. 2 vols. sm. fol. Lond., 1839. F 36 Q 22, 23 ‡
Copies of Extracts of Correspondence relative to the Affairs of. Sm. fol. Lond., 1839. F 36 Q 24 ‡
Report and Despatches of the Earl of Durham. 8vo. Lond., 1839. F 9 T 19
CHRONICLES AND MEMORIALS OF GREAT BRITAIN AND IRELAND. 6 vols. Roy. 8vo. Lond., 1892-94. E
Historians of the Church of York and its Archbishops. Vol. 3, edited by Rev. Dr. J. Raine.
Icelandic Sagas and other Historical Documents relating to the Settlements and Descents of the Norsemen on the British Isles. Vol. 3. The Orkneyingers' Saga. Translated by Sir G. W. Dasent. Vol. 4. The Saga of Hacon, and a Fragment of the Saga of Magnus. Translated by Sir G. W. Dasent.
Cartularium Monasterii de Rameseia. Vol. 3.
Memorials of St. Edmund's Abbey. Vol. 2.
Records of the Parliament holden at Westminster, 28th February, 1305.

GREAT BRITAIN AND IRELAND—*contd.*

CIVIL SERVICE. Report of the Civil Service Inquiry Commission, with Correspondence. Sm. fol. Lond., 1875. E

Report of the Royal Commission appointed to inquire into the Civil Establishments of the different offices of state at home and abroad. 3 vols. sm. fol. Lond., 1887-89. E

Rules and Regulations for Her Majesty's Colonial Service. 8vo. Lond., 1867. F 2 V 7

Rules and Regulations respecting Examinations. Roy. 8vo. Lond., 1894. F 8 T 2

COLONIAL OFFICE. The Colonial Office List, 1893-95, compiled by J. Anderson. 8vo. Lond., 1893-95. E

COLONIAL POSSESSIONS. Annual Colonial Reports, Nos. 35-132, 1889-95. 8vo. Lond., 1892-95. E

Statistical Abstract for the several Colonial and other Possessions of the United Kingdom, 1877-91 and 1878-92. 2 vols. Roy. 8vo. Lond., 1892-93. E

CONTRACT PACKETS. Report of the Committee on. Sm. fol. Lond., 1853. F 39 U 20 ‡

CONVICTS. Copies of Correspondence with the Colonial Office, relative to Convicts who were Holders of Conditional Pardons. Sm. fol. Lond., 1846. MF 3 U 13

Copies of Correspondence with the Governor of Tasmania, connected with the Institution of an Inquiry into the Working of the Convict Department. Sm. fol. Lond., 1856. MF 3 U 14

Return of the Number of Convicts in New South Wales, 1826-28; Expense of the Department of the Superintendent in 1829; and the Number of Applications for Female Convicts as Servants. Sm. fol. Lond., 1832. MF 3 U 11

CO-OPERATION. Reports by Her Majesty's Representatives abroad on the system of Co-operation in Foreign Countries. Roy. 8vo. Lond., 1886. F 1 T 12

ELECTRIC POWERS. Report on Electric Powers (protective clauses). Fol. Lond., 1893. A 39 U 24 ‡

ESTIMATES. Army Estimates, 1893-95. 2 vols. sm. fol. Lond., 1893-94. E

Estimates for Revenue Departments, 1894-95. 2 vols. sm. fol. Lond., 1893-94. E

Estimates for Civil Services, 1894-95. 2 vols. sm. fol. Lond., 1893-94. E

Navy Estimates, 1893-95. 2 vols. sm. fol. Lond., 1893-94. E

FEDERATION. Copy of Correspondence between the Australian Colonists in London and the Colonial Office on the subject of a Federal Association of the Australian Colonies. Sm. fol. Lond., 1857. MF 3 U 19

FOREIGN OFFICE. The Foreign Office List, 1893-95. 8vo. Lond., 1893-95. E

FRIENDLY SOCIETIES. Reports from the Select Committee, 1888 and 1889. 2 vols. sm. fol. Lond., 1888-89. F 36 P 11, 12 ‡

GREAT BRITAIN AND IRELAND—*contd.*

HISTORICAL MSS. COMMISSION. 13th Report and Appendices 2, 4-8; 14th Report, Appendices 1-10; and Calendar of the MSS. of the Marquis of Salisbury, at Hatfield House, Pts. 4 and 5. 18 vols. Roy. 8vo. Lond., 1892-95. E

INDIA OFFICE. The India List, Civil and Military, 1893-95. 3 vols. 8vo. Lond., 1893-95. E

The India Office List, containing an account of the services of officers in the Indian Service, and other information, 1893-95. 3 vols. 8vo. Lond., 1893-95. E

IDENTIFICATION OF CRIMINALS. Report of a Committee to enquire into the best means for identifying habitual Criminals. Sm. fol. Lond., 1894. F 36 T 1 ‡

INTOXICATING LIQUORS. Act for regulating the Sale of Intoxicating Liquors. Imp. 8vo. Lond., 1872. F 11 V 14

Act to amend the Laws relating to the sale and consumption of Intoxicating Liquors. Imp. 8vo. Lond., 1874. F 11 V 15

Beer Dealers' Retail Licences. Imp. 8vo. Lond., 1882. F 11 V 20

Habitual Drunkards Act. Imp. 8vo. Lond., 1879. F 11 V 17

Imposition and Restrictions upon the sale of Intoxicating Liquors in the Colonies, 1872, 1882-83. 3 vols. fol. Lond., 1872-83. MF 4 T 9-11

Index to Report on Sale of Liquors on Sunday Bill. Fol. Lond., 1868. F 39 U 18 ‡

Index to the Report on Sale of Intoxicating Liquors on Sunday (Ireland) Bill. Fol. Lond., 1877. F 39 U 19 ‡

Inland Revenue Act. Imp. 8vo. Lond., 1880. F 11 V 19

Payment of Wages in Public-houses Prohibition Act. Imp. 8vo. Lond., 1883. F 11 V 21

Permissive Prohibitory Liquor: a Bill, 1870-77. 7 vols. fol. Lond., 1870-77. F 39 U 4-10 ‡

Public-houses: Returns, 1875. Fol. Lond., 1875. F 39 U 20 ‡

Publicans' Certificates, Scotland. Imp. 8vo. Lond., 1876. F 11 V 16

Report from Select Committee on Public-houses, Scotland: Evidence, Appendix, and Index. Fol. Lond., 1846. F 39 U 23 ‡

Report of Committee on Intemperance, 1878-79, and Indexes 1877-78. 3 vols. fol. Lond., 1877-79. F 39 U 15-17 ‡

Report of Inspector of Retreats under the Habitual Drunkards Act, 1879. Fol. Lond., 1885. F 39 U 21 ‡

Reports on the Sale of Beer, 1817, 1819, 1855. 4 vols. fol. Lond., 1817-55. F 29 U 11-14 ‡

Spirits Act. Imp. 8vo. Lond., 1880. F 11 V 18

KEW ROYAL GARDENS. Bulletin, 1893. 8vo. Lond., 1893. E

GREAT BRITAIN AND IRELAND—contd.

LABOUR, ROYAL COMMISSION ON. The Employment of Women. Sm. fol. Lond., 1893. F 39 U 25 ‡

Foreign Reports, vol. 2. The Colonies and the Indian Empire, with an Appendix on the Migration of Labour. Sm. fol. Lond., 1893. F 36 Q 26 ‡

MINERAL STATISTICS of the United Kingdom, with the Isle of Man, for 1892-93. 2 vols. sm. fol. Lond., 1893-94. E

MURRAY RIVER. Copies of Despatches from the Governor of South Australia, on the Navigation of the River Murray. Sm. fol. Lond., 1854. MF 3 U 37

NEW SOUTH WALES. Abstract of the Expenditure of the Colonial Revenues of New South Wales, 1825-38, including the Disbursements made both from the Colonial Treasury and by the Colonial Agent-General in London. Sm. fol. Sydney, 1840. MF 4 T 23

Charter establishing Courts of Justice in New South Wales, 1823. 8vo. Sydney, 1875. MF 2 Q 40

Copies or Extracts of a Despatch relative to the Condition of the Licensed Occupiers of Crown Lands in Port Phillip and New South Wales. Sm. Fol. Lond., 1844. MF 3 U 12

Despatch on the Subject of Quit Rents. Sm. Fol. Lond., 1849. MF 3 U 35

Electoral Act, passed by the Legislature of New South Wales, 1858. Sm. fol. Lond., 1859. MF 3 U 17

Instructions relative to the Division of the Territory into Counties, Parishes, and Districts. Sm. fol. Lond., 1853. MF 3 U 33

Papers relating to [Distillation, Convicts, &c., in] His Majesty's Settlements at New South Wales, 1811-14. Sm. fol. Lond., 1816. MF 3 U 26

Returns of the Revenues arising from Crown Lands, in New South Wales, from 1831 to the latest period. Sm. fol. Lond., 1840. *MF 3 U 8

NEW ZEALAND. Copies of Communications relative to an Expedition sent from New South Wales to New Zealand, for the Recovery of British Subjects who had been detained by the Natives. Sm. fol. Lond., 1835. MF 3 U 31

Copies of Correspondence relating to the Political Institutions of [New Zealand]. Sm. fol. Lond., 1852. MF 3 U 34

Correspondence with the Secretary of State relative to New Zealand. Fol. Lond, 1840. MF 4 T 2

Copies of Correspondence relative to the New Zealand Estimates. Sm. fol. Lond., 1843. MF 3 U 27

Copies of Papers relating to the Appointment of, Members to the Upper House of Representatives in New Zealand and the Colonies. Sm. fol. Lond., 1893. MF 3 U 40

Copies of Correspondence relative to an Attack on the British Settlement at the Bay of Islands by the Natives of New Zealand. Sm. fol. Lond., 1845. MF 3 U 28

GREAT BRITAIN AND IRELAND—contd.

NEW ZEALAND—contd.

Copy or Extracts from any recent Despatch from the Governor of New South Wales, respecting Outrages by the Natives in the Bay of Islands. Sm. fol. Lond., 1845. MF 3 U 29

Copy of a Despatch from Governor Sir R. Bourke relative to the Affairs of New Zealand. [Native Troubles at Bay of Islands.] Sm. fol. Lond., 1838. MF 3 U 29

Copies of the Laws and Ordinances passed by the Governor and Council of New Zealand. Sm. fol. Lond., 1844. MF 3 U 22

Copies of Letters from Mr. Shortland and Mr. Busby. [On Natives and New Zealand Co.] Sm. fol. Lond., 1845. MF 3 U 30

NEW ZEALAND COMPANY. Report of the Select Committee on Loan for defraying the debt of the Colony to the New Zealand Company. Sm. fol. Lond., 1857. MF 3 U 22

Copies of Despatches from the Governor, enclosing or having reference to Reports and Awards made by Mr. Spain, Commissioner of Land Claims, upon the Titles to Land of the New Zealand Company. Sm. fol. Lond., 1846. MF 3 U 21

PARLIAMENT. Parliamentary Debates. Vols. 1-59, 3rd series (1830-41) and vols. 6-29, 4th series (1893). Roy. 8vo. Lond., 1831-94. E

PRIVY COUNCIL. [See Public Record Office.]

PUBLIC RECORD OFFICE. List of original Ministers' Accounts preserved in. Pt. 1. Sm. fol. Lond., 1894. E

Acts of the Privy Council. Vols. 1-12, 1542-81; edited by John R. Dasent. Roy. 8vo. Lond., 1890-93. B 38 T 1-12

Rotuli Scaccarii Regum Scotorum—The Exchequer Rolls of Scotland. Vol. 14, 1513-22. Roy. 8vo. Edint., 1893. B 33 U 2

QUEENSLAND. Further Correspondence relating to Polynesian Labour. Sm. fol. Lond., 1893. MF 2 Q 39 †

RECORD COMMISSIONERS' PUBLICATIONS. Annals of Ulster, otherwise Annals of Senat: a Chronicle of Irish Affairs, 431-1131, 1155-1541. Vol. 3, 1370-1541. Edited by Rev. Dr. B. MacCarthy. Imp. 8vo. Dublin, 1895. B 30 V 18

SECONDARY PUNISHMENT. Copies or Extracts of Correspondence between the Secretary of State for the Colonial Departments and the Governors of the Australian Provinces on the subject of Secondary Punishment; also, Copies or Extracts of Correspondence between the Secretaries of State for the Home and Colonial Departments on the subject. Sm. fol. Lond., 1834. MF 4 T 45

SOUTH AUSTRALIAN COLONIZATION COMMISSIONERS. Second and Fourth Annual Reports of, 1837 and 1839. Sm. fol. Lond., 1838-40. MF 3 U 9, 10

GREAT BRITAIN AND IRELAND—*contd.*
STATE TRIALS, Reports of. New Series, vols. 1-3, edited by John Macdonell; vols. 4-6, edited by J. E. P. Wallis. 6 vols. roy. 8vo. Lond., 1888-94.
F 3 T 4-9
STATUTES. The Statutes. 2nd revised ed. Vols. 6 and 8, 1837-42, 1847-52. Roy. 8vo. Lond., 1893-94. E
Chronological Table and Index of the Statutes. 11th edition. 1235-1889. Imp. 8vo. Lond., 1890. E
STEAM COMMUNICATION. Copies of Despatches from the Governors of the Australian Colonies and New Zealand, on Steam Communication. Sm. fol. Lond., 1851. MF 3 U 36
TAHITI. Correspondence relative to the proceedings of the French at Tahiti, 1825-43. Fol. Lond., 1843.
MB 12 P 26 †
TASMANIA. Copies of Despatches and Petitions relating to the Passing and Operation of the Act 5 Vic. c. 3. "To confirm an Act of the Legislature of Van Diemen's Land, for authorizing the Levy of certain Duties of Customs and on Spirits." Sm. fol. Lond., 1845.
MF 3 U 39
Return of the Population, Revenue and Expenditure, Exports and Imports, from the 1st January, 1836. Sm. fol. Lond., 1846. MF 3 U 43
TRANSPORTATION. Copy of a Communication upon the Subject of Transportation; by the Lord Bishop of Tasmania. Sm. fol. Lond., 1847. MF 3 U 40
Copies of Despatches from the Governor of New South Wales, and the Lieutenant-Governor of Van Diemen's Land, relative to Transportation and the Assignment of Convicts. Sm. fol. Lond., 1839. MF 3 U 38
Copy of a Letter from Mr. E. S. Hall, and the Reply thereto, on Transportation and Convict Discipline. Sm. fol. Lond., 1850. MF 3 U 41
Convict Discipline and Transportation, copies of Petitions on, since 1838. Sm. fol. Lond., 1851. MF 3 U 42
Twenty-eighth Report from the Select Committee on Finance, &c.; Police, including Convict Establishments. Sm. fol. Lond., 1810. F 39 U 35 ‡
First Report from the Select Committee appointed to inquire into the execution of the Criminal Law, especially respecting juvenile offenders and transportation. Sm. fol. Lond., 1847. MF 7 Q 28 †
Report from the Select Committee of the House of Lords on an Act to substitute, in certain cases, other punishments in lieu of transportation. Sm. fol. Lond., 1856.
F 39 U 34 ‡
VICTORIA. Copy of the Electoral Law of Victoria passed by the Colonial Legislature, 1856. Sm. fol. Lond., 1857. MF 3 U 16
WAR OFFICE. The Monthly Army List, 1894-95. 8 vols. 12mo. Lond., 1894-95. E
Aidé-Mémoire for the use of Officers of Royal Engineers. Vol. 2. 12mo. Lond., 1889. A 29 P 41
Army Service Corps—Drills and Exercises, 1891. 16mo. Lond., 1891. A 29 P 42
Cavalry Drill. Vols. 1 and 2. 12mo. Lond., 1891.
A 29 P 33, 34

GREAT BRITAIN AND IRELAND—*contd.*
WAR OFFICE—*contd.*
Field Artillery Drills. Vols. 1 and 3. 16mo. Lond., 1889. A 29 P 37, 39
Garrison Artillery Drill. 2 vols. 16mo. Lond., 1891-92.
A 29 P 35, 36
Infantry Drill, 1893. 16mo. Lond., 1893. A 29 P 32
Instruction in Military Engineering. Parts 2, 3, and 5. 3 vols. 8vo. Lond., 1887-90. A 29 T 19-22
Manual of Field Range-finding, 1890. Roy. 8vo. Lond., 1890. A 29 V 15
Manuals for Field Service—Cavalry, Infantry. 8vo. Lond., 1888. A 29 Q 22
Manual for Field Service—Royal Artillery. 8vo. Lond., 1889. A 29 Q 23
Manual for Field Service—Army Service Corps. 8vo. Lond., 1889. A 29 Q 20
Manuals for Field Service—Army Signallers, Army Post Office Corps, Bearer Companies and Field Hospital. 8vo. Lond., 1888. A 29 Q 21
The Queen's Regulations and Orders for the Army, 1892. 8vo. Lond., 1892. A 29 Q 10
Regimental Transport—Saddling and Loading Pack Mules and Camels. 8vo. Lond., 1889. A 29 Q 24
Regulations and Field Service Manual for Mounted Infantry. 8vo. Lond., 1889. A 29 Q 27
Regulations for Army Service Corps Duties, 1889. 8vo. Lond., 1889. A 29 Q 31
Regulations for Army Medical Service, 1890. 8vo. Lond., 1890. A 29 Q 32
Royal Warrant for the Pay, Appointment, Promotion, and Non-effective Pay of the Army, 1892. 8vo. Lond., 1892. A 29 Q 28
Text-book of Fortification and Military Engineering. 2 vols. roy. 8vo. Lond., 1892. A 29 V 19, 20
Treatise on Ammunition, 1892. 5th edition, Roy. 8vo. Lond., 1892. A 29 V 13
Trumpet and Bugle Sounds. 8vo. Lond., 1891.
A 29 Q 33

GREAT EXPLORERS of Africa. Illustrated. 2 vols. roy. 8vo. Lond., 1894. D 15 V 21, 22

GREAT GIPPSLAND RAILWAY, Melbourne to Sale: Outline of Project. 8vo. Melb., 1871. MA 1 V 68

GREAT PROBLEM of Substance and its Attributes, The, involving the relationship and laws of matter and of mind as a phenomena of the World, derived from the absolute. 8vo. Lond., 1895. G 2 U 11

GREAT WAR OF 189—, The: a Forecast; by Rear-Adm. P. Colomb, Col. J. F. Maurice, Capt. F. N. Maude, Archibald Forbes, Charles Lowe, D. C. Murray, and F. Scudamore. 8vo. Lond., 1893. J 2 Q 21

GREELEY, Gen. Adolphus Washington. Explorers and Travellers. (Men of Achievement.) 8vo. Lond., 1894. C 17 R 4

GREEN, Arthur G. Organic Colouring Matters. [*See* Schultz, Dr. G.] A 25 V 8

GREEN, J. L. Rural Industries of England. 8vo. Lond. (n.d.) A 25 S 5

GREEN, Mrs. J. R. Town Life in the 15th Century. 2 vols. 8vo. Lond., 1894. B 22 T 10, 11

GREEN, Joseph Henry. Spiritual Philosophy: founded on the teaching of the late S. T. Coleridge; edited by John Simon. 2 vols. 8vo. Lond., 1865. G 14 Q 25, 26

GREEN, Rev. M. W., and BRIGHT, Chas. The Divine Origin of Christianity: Debate. 8vo. Dunedin, 1879. MG 1 P 67

GREEN, Thos. Hill. Lectures on the Principles of Political Obligation. 8vo. Lond., 1895. F 11 U 3

GREENE, G. A. Italian Lyrists of To-day. 12mo. Lond., 1893. H 8 T 48

GREENE, Dr. Wm. H. Modern Chemistry. [*See* Wurtz, C. A.] A 21 R 34

GREENHILL, Prof. Alfred George. Treatise on Hydrostatics. 12mo. Lond., 1894. A 25 Q 23

GREENHILL, Dr. W. A. Sir T. Browne's Religio Medici. [*See* Browne, Sir T.] G 4 V 12

GREENIDGE, A. H. J. Infamia: its Place in Roman Public and Private Law. 8vo. Oxford, 1894. F 14 S 27

GREENWELL, Allan, and CURRY, W. T. Rural Water Supply: Practical Hand-book on the Supply of Water and Construction of Waterworks for small Country Districts. 8vo. Lond., 1896. A 22 Q 24

GREENWICH ROYAL OBSERVATORY. Astronomical and Magnetical, and Meteorological Observations, 1892. 4to. Lond., 1894. A 13 S 4†

GREENWOOD, F. The Lover's Lexicon: a Hand-book for Novelists, Playwrights Philosophers, &c. 12mo. Lond., 1893. J 8 Q 49

GREG, R. P. Comparative Philology of the Old and New Worlds in Relation to Archaic Speech. Imp. 8vo. Lond., 1893. K 16 U 23

GREGOROVIUS, Fedinand. History of the City of Rome in the Middle Ages; translated by Annie Hamilton. Vols. 1-3. 8vo. Lond., 1894. B 30 R 10-12

GREGORY THAUMATURGUS. Works of; translated by Rev. S. D. F. Salmond. (Ante-Nicene Christ. Lib., 20.) 8vo. Edinb., 1871. G 14 U 20

GREGORY, Hon. Augustus C. The Brisbane River Floods of 1893. (Roy. Geograph. Soc. of Australasia Q. Branch, 8.) 8vo. Brisbane, 1893. M E 20

Notes on the Geographical Conditions of the Catchment Area of the Brisbane River: the Floods and their origin. (Roy. Geograph. Soc. of Australasia, Q. Branch, 8.) 8vo. Brisbane, 1893. M E 20

Observations on occurrence of Gold at Mount Morgan. (Proc. Roy. Soc., Queensland, 1.) 8vo. Brisbane, 1884. M E 1 T

GREGORY, J. W. Jurassic Fauna of Cutch: the Echinoidea of Cutch. [*See* India, Geological Survey, series 9, vol. 2.] E

GREGORY, Sir Wm., formerly M.P., and sometime Governor of Ceylon: an Autobiography. 8vo. Lond., 1894. C 18 T 14

GRENSIDE, Dr. F. C. Dropping after Calving. 8vo. Sydney, 1893. MA 1 Q 53

GRENVILLE, Sir Richard. The last fight of the *Revenge*, and the death of Sir Richard Grenville. [*See* Bibliotheca Curiosa.] J 18 Q 33

GRESSWELL, Dr. D. Astley. Report on the Sanitary Condition of Melbourne. Sm. fol. Melb., 1890. MA 9 Q 14†

GRESWELL, Rev. Wm. Parr. Outlines of British Colonisation. 8vo. Lond., 1893. MB 1 P 21

GREVEL, H. The Book. [*See* Bouchot, H.] B 36 U 9

GREVILLE, Edward. Year-book of Australia, 1893-95. 3 vols. 8vo. Sydney, 1893-95. M E

Legal Year-book of Australasia. 8vo. Sydney, 1893.* M E 6 R

The Year-book of New South Wales for 1888. [MS. List of Governors and several memos. by Sir A. Stephen, Lieut.-Governor of New South Wales.] 8vo. Sydney, 1888. M E

GREVILLE-NUGENT, Hon. Mrs [*See* Nugent, Hon. Mrs. G.]

GREVILLEA: A Quarterly Record of Cryptogamic Botany and its Literature. Vols. 21, 22. 8vo. Lond., 1891-94. E

GREY, E. Travels of P. della Valle in India. [*See* Hakluyt Soc., 84, 85.]

GREY, Sir George. The Irish Land Question : A Reprint of Letters to the *London Daily News* in 1868. 8vo. Auckland, 1889. MF 4 R 46

The Great Pro-Consul. [*See* Rees, W. L.] MJ 1 U 37, 38

GREY, Harold. (T. E. Argles.) Haunted Sydney; by "The Pilgrim." (Pam.) 8vo. Sydney, 1878.
MG 1 Q 53

My Unnatural Life: an Autobiographical Apology. Nos. 1 and 2. 8vo. Sydney, 1878. MJ 2 S 46

The Pilgrim: a Sensational Weekly Pamphlet. 16 Nos. 8vo. Sydney, 1877. MJ 2 S 43

Scenes in Sydney by Day and Night: a series of Social Sketches; by "The Moocher." No. 1. 8vo. Sydney (n.d.) MJ 2 S 45

Ye Prodigal: a Weekly Social and Moral Pamphlet. [5 odd Nos.] 8vo. Sydney, 1879. MJ 2 S 44

GREY, Henry M. Lloyd's Yesterday and To-day. 8vo. Lond., 1893. F 6 U 3

GREY, Dr. Richard. Memoria Technica; or, Method of Artificial Memory, applied to and exemplified in Chronology, History, Geography, Astronomy; also, Jewish, Grecian, and Roman Coins, Weights, Measures, &c.; to which are subjoined Lowe's Mnemonics delineated. New ed. 12mo. Oxford, 1880.
G 19 P 22

GRIER, Thos. G. Treatise on Electricity. [See Dixon, D. B.—Vade Mecum.] K 18 P 33

GRIFFEN, Prof. W. Hall. English Writers. [See Morley, Dr. H] B 21 R 35

GRIFFIN, Chas., & Co. Griffin's Electrical Engineer's Price-book; edited by H. J. Dowsing. 8vo. Lond., 1893. A 21 Q 42

GRIFFIN, Gerald. Poetical Works of. 8vo. Lond., 1851. H 10 T 14

GRIFFIN, John. Memoirs of Capt. James Wilson; containing an account of his enterprise and sufferings in India, his conversion to Christianity, his missionary Voyage to the South Seas, and his Peaceful and Triumphant Death. 2nd ed. 8vo. Lond. (n.d.)
MC 1 R 44

GRIFFIN, R. B., and LITTLE, A. D. Chemistry of Paper-making. Roy. 8vo. New York, 1894.
A 21 V 16

GRIFFIS, Rev. Dr. Wm. Elliott. Corea, the Hermit Nation. 3rd ed. [Map and Illustrations.] 8vo. New York, 1888. B 35 R 4

T. Harris, first American Envoy in Japan. 8vo. Lond., 1895. C 13 V 20

Massachusetts: a typical American Commonwealth. Sm. 4to. Camb., 1893. B 18 R 14

The Religions of Japan. 8vo. Lond., 1895. G 2 U 20

GRIFFITH, F. L. Tomb of Pahori, at El Kab. [See Naville, E.] B 12 T 5 †

GRIFFITH, M. India's Princes: Short Life Sketches of the Native Rulers of India. 4to. Lond., 1894.
C 18 U 1

GRIFFITH, Sir Samuel Walker. The Political Geography of Australia. (Roy. Geograph. Soc. of Australasia, Q. Branch, 6.) 8vo. Brisbane, 1891. ME 20

GRIFFITHS, Arthur. Secrets of the Prison-house; or, Gaol Studies and Sketches. 2 vols. 8vo. Lond., 1894.
F 3 R 19, 20

GRIFFITHS, Dr. A. B. Manual of Bacteriology. 8vo. Lond., 1893. A 26 R 2

GRIFFITHS, George Samuel. Evidences of a Glacial Epoch in Victoria during Post-Miocene Times. (Roy. Soc., Vict., 21.) 8vo. Melb., 1885. ME 1 P

Recent Earth Tremors, and the conditions which they indicate. (Roy. Soc., Vict., 22.) 8vo. Melb., 1886.
ME 1 P

Report of the Antarctic Committee of the Royal Society of Victoria. (Proceedings Royal Society, Victoria, 6; new series.) 8vo. Melb., 1894. ME 1 P

Reports of the Tarawera Outbreak, with objections to some of the conclusions drawn by Dr. Hector. (Roy. Soc., Vict.) 8vo. Melb., 1886. MA 3 S 47

GRIFFITHS, J. Alfred. New Velocity Recorder and its application to Anemom-try and other purposes. (Journal Roy. Soc., N.S.W., 24.) 8vo. Sydney, 1894. ME 1 R

GRIFFITHS, Thos. Propulsion of ships by steam direct from the boiler. 12mo. Solva, 1884. MA 2 P 79

GRIMALDI, Jacques. Recherches sur les Manuscrits Archéologiques de Grimaldi. [See Duchesne, l'Abbé L.—Etude sur le Liber Pontificalis.] J 7 U 45

GRIMES, C., and FLINDERS, Capt. Matthew. Plan of the Settlements of New South Wales. Fol. Lond., 1799. MD 1 P 18 ‡

GRIMES, Samuel. Arrowroot Cultivation and Manufacturing in Queensland. 8vo. Brisb., 1888.
MA 1 Q 69

GRIMM, Rev. George. The Bulwarks of our Faith. 8vo. Sydney, 1893. MG 1 Q 49

The Plenary Inspiration of the Bible: a Defence and Reply. 8vo. Sydney, 1894. MG 1 Q 50

Twelve Lectures on the Immortality of the Soul and the Life Everlasting. 8vo. Sydney, 1892.* MG 1 S 26

GRIMM, Dr. Jacob L. and Wilhelm K. Deutsches Wörterbuch. Band 8. Imp. 8vo. Leipzic, 1893.
K 14 R 25

Kinder und Hausemärchen gesammelt durch die Brüder Grimm. 12mo. Berlin, 1853. J 7 P 50

GRIMSHAW, Robert. A Supplement to "Grimshaw on Saws." Illustrated. Imp. 8vo. Philad., 1882.
A 25 V 7

GRINGO, A. [See Mexico.]

GROOTE, Dr. Paul de. [See De Groote, Dr. P.]

GROSART, Rev. Dr. Alexander Balloch. "Thoughts that Breathe and Words that Burn," from the Writings of Francis Bacon. 18mo. Lond , 1893. J 7 P 46

GROSSET, J. Mélanges de Philologie Indo-Européenne. [See Regnaud, P.] J 7 U 40

GROTIUS, Hugo. Origin of the Native Races of America. (Bibliotheca Curiosa.) 12mo. Edinb., 1884. J 18 Q 3

GROUSSET, René. Etude sur l'Histoire des Sarcophages Chrétiens. 8vo. Paris, 1885. B 35 R 29

GROUVELLE, E. New Genus and five Species of Australian *Nitidulidæ* and *Colydiidæ*. (Trans Roy. Soc., S. Australia, 17.) 8vo. Adelaide, 1893. ME 1 S

GROVE, E. D. Cæsar de Bello Gallico. [See Cæsar, C. J.] MB 1 R 32

GROVES, Chas Edward, and THORP, Wm. Chemical Technology ; or Chemistry in its applications to Arts and Manufactures. Vols. 1, 2. Roy. 8vo. Lond., 1889-95. A 21 V 6, 7
1. Fuel and its Applications ; by F. J. Mills and F. J. Rowan.
2. Lighting.

GROVES, Lieut.-Col. Percy. History of the 42nd Royal Highlanders (the Black Watch), 1729-1893. 4to. Edinb., 1893. B 12 T 9 †

History of the 2nd Dragoons (Royal Scots Greys), 1678-1893. 4to. Edinb., 1893. B 12 T 8 †

History of the 79th Queen's Own Cameron Highlanders, now the First Battalion Queen's Own Cameron Highlanders, 1794-1893. Illustrated. 4to. Edinb., 1893. B 12 T 7 †

GRUBB, Rev. G. C. Mission Tour of. [See Millard, E. C.] MG 1 S 20

GRUBER, Dr. August. Neue Infusorien. 8vo. Freiburg, 1879. A 30 U 27

Kleine Beiträge zu Kenntniss der Protozoen. 8vo. Freiburg (n.d.) A 30 U 27

GRUEL, Léon. Catalogue des Reliures de Style et Objets Artistiques en Cuir Ciselé. 12mo. Paris, 1893. K 7 P 6

GRUNOW, A. Vorläufige Bemerkungen zu einer systematischen Anordnung der Schizonema-und Berkeleya-Arten. 8vo. Berndorf, 1880. A 30 U 27

Ueber die Arten der Gattung Grammatophora mit Bezug auf die Tafeln 53, und 53 B in van Heurck's Synopsis der belgischen Diatomeen. 8vo. (n.p.n.d.) A 30 U 27

Mazæa. [See Bornet, E.] A 30 U 27

GRYE, A. Bouquet de la. Mission de l'Ile Campbell : Mémoires, Rapports et Documents relatifs à l'Observation du Passage de Vénus sur le Soliel, Dec., 1874. 4to. Paris, 1875. MA 3 P 8 †

GSELL, Stéphane. Essai sur le règne de l'Empereur Domitien. 8vo. Paris, 1894. B 35 R 32

GUENON, F. On Milch Cows : a Treatise on the Bovine Species in General ; translated by T. J. Hand. 8vo. New York, 1888. A 18 R 22

GUÉRIN, Léon. Histoire Maritime de France. Nouvelle éd. 6 vols. imp. 8vo. Paris, 1851-62. B 26 V 8-13

Les Navigateurs Français : Histoire des Navigations, Découvertes, et Colonisations Françaises. Illustrated. Roy. 8vo. Paris, 1847. D 18 V 14

GUEST, E Classified List of *Geometrinæ* found round Balharnah : with Notes on Species. (Trans. Roy. Soc., S. Australia, 9.) 8vo. Adelaide, 1887. ME 1 S

List of Diurnal Lepidoptera about Balhannah. (Trans. Roy. Soc., S. Australia, 5.) 8vo. Adelaide, 1882. ME 1 S

Remarks on the nomenclature of some South Australian Butterflies. (Trans. Roy. Soc., S. Australia, 8.) 8vo. Adelaide, 1886. ME 1 S

GUILD, Reuben A. The Librarian's Manual : a Treatise on Bibliography, comprising a select and descriptive list of Bibliographical Works ; to which are added, Sketches of Public Libraries. Sm. 4to. New York, 1858. J 6 U 26

GUILFOYLE, W. R. Fibres from Plants eligible for industrial culture and experiment in Victoria. 8vo. Melb., 1894. MA 3 V 20

GUILLAUME, Ch. Ed. Traité Pratique de la Thermométrie de Précision. 8vo. Paris, 1889. A 21 V 21

GUILLAUME LE BRETON. La Chronique en Prose de ; par H. F. Delaborde. 8vo. Paris, 1881. J 7 U 19

GUILLAUME DE LORRIS. Roman de la Rose. [See Langlois, E.] J 7 U 38

GUIZOT, François Pierre Guillaume. History of Civilisation from the Fall of the Roman Empire to the French Revolution. Translated by Wm. Hazlitt. 3 vols. 8vo. Lond., 1860-93. B 25 P 2-4

Sketch of. [See Bagehot, W.—Biographical Studies.] C 22 P 10

GUMMERE, Dr. Francis B. Hand-book of Poetics for Students of English Verse. 12mo. Boston, 1892. H 9 Q 15

GUN, RIFLE, AND HOUND in East and West ; by "Snaffle." Illustrated. 8vo. Lond., 1894. A 20 V 27

GUNDRY, R. S. China and her Neighbours : France in Indo-China ; Russia and China ; India and Thibet ; 8vo. Lond., 1893. D 17 V 3

China, Present and Past. 8vo. Lond., 1895. B 20 S 9

GÜNTHER, Dr. Albert. Shore Fishes; Deep-sea Fishes ; Pelagic Fishes. [See Thomson, Sir C. W., and Murray, Dr. J.—Voyage of H.M.S. *Challenger*.] A 6 †

GÜNTHER, Rev. W. J. The Church of England in Australia, 1788-1829 : a Lecture. 8vo. Parramatta, 1898. MG 1 S 17

GUTHRIE, F. B. Comparison of American and Australian Maize. 8vo. Sydney, 1893. MA 1 Q 05
Experiments with Babcock's Milk-tester. [*See* McCaffrey, F.] MA 1 Q 68
Supposed Poisonous Plant (Darling Pea). 8vo. Sydney, 1893. MA 1 T 56

GUTTMANN, O. Manufacture of Explosives. 2 vols. 8vo. Lond., 1895. A 25 U 10, 11

GUY, A. F. Electric Light and Power, giving the result of Practical Experience in Central-station Work. Illustrated. 8vo. Lond., 1894. A 21 R 14

GUY, Dr. Wm. A., and FERRIER, Dr. David. Principles of Forensic Medicine. 7th ed., revised by Dr. W. R. Smith, F.R.S. 8vo. Lond., 1895. F 11 U 14

GUYAU, J. M. Education and Heredity : a Study in Sociology. 8vo. Lond., 1891. G 18 Q 5

GUYOT, Yves. Principles of Social Economy. 2nd ed. 8vo. Lond., 1892. F 14 Q 36
The Tyranny of Socialism ; edited by J. H. Levy. 8vo. Lond., 1894. F 9 U 42

GWILLIAM, G. H. Palestinian Version of the Holy Scriptures. [*See* Anecdota Oxoniensia.] E

H

H., G. [*See* Lecture on Capital Punishment.] MF 4 R 9

H.R.H. [*See* McKellar, Campbell.]

H.S. [*See* Brewery Companies.] F 9 Q 28

H., W. [*See* Labour's Rest.] MH 1 U 74

HACON, Earl of Norway. The Saga of. [*See* Great Britain and Ireland—Chrons. and Mems.] E

HADCOCK, A. G. Artillery. [*See* Lloyd, E. W.] A 29 V 21

HADDON, Prof. Alfred C. The Decorative Art of British New Guinea. (Trans. R.I. Academy.—Cunningham Memoirs, 10.) 4to. Dublin, 1894. E
Polyplacophora. [*See* Thomson, Sir C. W., and Murray, Dr. J.—Voyage of H.M.S. *Challenger*.] A 6 †

HADDON, James. Elements of Algebra. 8th ed. 12mo. Lond., 1890. A 25 P 36
Key and Companion to the Rudimentary Algebra. 12mo. Lond., 1859. A 25 P 37

HADFIELD, R. A., and GIBBINS, H. de B. A Shorter Working Day. 8vo. Lond., 1892. F 14 Q 39

HADOW, W. H. Studies in Modern Music. 2nd series. 8vo. Lond., 1895. C 21 Q 15
2nd series.—Frederick Chopin, Antonin Dvorák, Johannes Brahms.

HAECKEL, Dr. Ernst. Die Tiefsee-Medusen der *Challenger*—Reise und der Organismus der Medusen. Band 2. 4to. Jena, 1881. A 40 T 20 ‡
Deep-sea Medusæ ; Radiolaria ; Siphonophoræ ; Deep-sea Keratosa. [*See* Thomson, Sir C. W., and Murray, Dr. J.—Voyage of H.M.S. *Challenger*, Zoology.] A 6 †

HAGA, A. Nederlandsch Nieuw Guinea en de Papoesche eilanden, 1500-1883. 2 vols. 8vo. Batavia, 1884. MB 2 Q 48, 49

HAGAR, C. Die Marshall-Inseln in Erd-und Völkerkunde Handel und Mission ; mit einem Anhang, die Gilbert-Inseln. 8vo. Leipzig, 1886. MD 7 S 13

HAGEN, O. von. Die Forstlichen Verhältnisse Preussens 2 vols. 8vo. Berlin, 1894. A 33 U 25, 26

HAGUE, Arnold. Geology of the Eureka District, Nevada. (U.S. Survey, 20.) 4to. Wash., 1892. E

HAHNEMANN, Dr. S. Life and Letters of ; by Dr. T. L. Bradford. Roy. 8vo Philad., 1895. C 16 U 10

HAIG, Major-Gen. M. R. The Indus Delta Country : a Memoir, chiefly of its ancient Geography and History ; with Maps. Roy. 8vo. Lond., 1894. D 18 V 16

HAILEYBURY COLLEGE, OLD. Memorials of. With Illustrations and Plans. Sm. 4to. Lond., 1894. B 21 U 16

HAKE, C. Napier. Explosives and their power. [*See* Berthelot, M.] A 21 S 14

HAKE, G. Memoirs of Eighty Years. 8vo. Lond., 1892. C 16 T 15

HAKE, H. Wilson. Inorganic Chemistry. [*See* Dupré, A.] A 21 R 5

HAKLUYT SOCIETY. Publications of. Vols. 84-91. 8vo. Lond., 1892-95. E
84, 85. Travels of Pietro Della Valle in India. Edited by E. Grey.
86. Journal of Christopher Columbus, 1492-93 ; and Documents relating to the Voyages of J. Cabot and G. C. Real.
87. Early Voyages and Travels in the Levant ; by T. Dallam and Dr. J. Covel.
88, 89. The Voyages of Capt. Luke Foxe and Capt. Thomas James.
90. Letters of Amerigo Vespucci and other Documents illustrative of his career.
91. Narratives of the Voyages of Pedro Sarmiento de Gamboa to the Straits of Magellan ; translated by C. R. Markham, F.R.S.

HALE, Col. L. What to observe, and how to report it. 6th edition. 16mo. Lond., 1883. A 29 P 31

HALE, Sir Matthew. On the Knowledge of Christ Crucified, and other Divine contemplations. 8vo. Glasgow, 1858.   G 2 U 42

HALEVY, K. Mythology. Fol. Philad. (n.d.)   B 44 Q 11 ‡

HALFER, Josof. The Progress of the Marbling Art. 8vo. New York, 1894.   A 23 U 26

HALFORD, Prof. George Britton. Not like man, bimanous and biped, nor yet quadrumanous, but cheiropodus. 8vo. Melb., 1863.   MA 1 R 44

Thoughts, Observations, and Experiments on the Action of Snake Venom on the Blood. 8vo. Melb., 1894.   MA 3 T 11

HALIBURTON Hugh. [Life of] James Thomson. [See Masson, Prof. D.—In the Footsteps of the Poets.]   J G R 43

Furth in Field: a Volume of Essays on the Life, Language, and Literature of Old Scotland. 8vo. Lond., 1894.   B 32 R 5

HALL, Capt. Basil. The Lieutenant and Commander: being autobiographical sketches. 18mo. Lond., 1862.   D 20 P 3

Voyage to Corea and the Island of Loo-Choo. New ed. 12mo. Lond., 1820.   D 17 P 30

HALL, Capt. Chas. Francis, and the North Pole. [See Greeley, Gen. A. W.—Explorers and Travellers.]   C 17 R 4

HALL, Edgar, and STOKES, Henry G. Asbestos. (Proc. Roy. Soc., Queensland, 8.) 8vo. Brisbane, 1892.   ME 1 T

HALL, Edward Smith. Transportation and Convict Discipline. [See Great Britain and Ireland.] MF 3 U 41

HALL, Dr. Edward Swarbreck. Who translated the Bible? or, Biblical Memoranda concerning the Holy Scriptures, showing the part taken by the Catholic Church in their translation and dissemination. 12mo. Hobart, 1875.   MG 2 R 39

HALL, Frederic. History of San José and Surroundings, with Biographical Sketches of Early Settlers; with Map and Illustrations. 8vo. San Francisco, 1871.   B 10 S 21

HALL, Dr. John R. Clark. A Concise Anglo-Saxon Dictionary. Sm. 4to. Lond., 1894.   K 14 P 35

HALL, Kate Emily. Attempted Murder of. [See Hall, T.]   MF 1 S 47

HALL, Rupert. The Universal Telegraphic Abbreviation and Confidential Correspondence Guide for business and private purposes. Roy. 8vo. Sydney (n.d.)   MF 3 R 63

HALL, T., and HOUSTON, Margaret G. Report and Narrative of the Trial of, charged with attempting to murder Kate Emily Hall. Roy. 8vo. Christchurch, 1886.   MF 1 S 47

HALL, Thos. Bartlett. The Infringement of Patents for Inventions, not Designs; with sole reference to the opinions of the Supreme Court of the United States. Roy. 8vo. Cincinnati, 1893.   F 2 T 15

HALL, Thos. Sergeant. The Geology of Castlemaine, Victoria. (Proc. Roy. Soc., Victoria, n.s., 7.) 8vo. Melb., 1895.   ME 1 P

——— and PRITCHARD, G. B. Notes on the Eocene Strata of the Bellarine Peninsula; with brief reference to other deposits. (Proceedings, Royal Society, Victoria, n.s., 6.) 8vo. Melb, 1894.   ME 1 P

The Older Tertiaries of Maude, with an indication of the sequences of the Eocene Rocks of Victoria. (Proc. Roy. Soc., Victoria, n.s., 7.) 8vo. Melb., 1895.   ME 1 P

HALL, Wm. Edward. Treatise on the Foreign Powers and Jurisdiction of the British Crown. 8vo. Oxford, 1894.   F 8 P 30

HALL'S DIRECTORY OF NEW SOUTH WALES, 1895. 8vo. Sydney, 1895.   ME

HALLE, Ernst von. Trusts or Industrial Combinations and Coalitions in the United States. 8vo. New York, 1895.   F 7 V 22

HALLEY, Rev. J. John. Biographical Sketch of Rev. Wm. Roby Fletcher. 12mo. Adelaide, 1895.   MC 1 S 16

HALLIBURTON, Prof. W. D. The Essentials of Chemical Physiology. 8vo. Lond., 1893.   A 12 S 25

HALLIWELL-PHILLIPS, James Orchard. Letters of the Kings of England. 2 vols. 12mo. Lond., 1846.   B 10 P 2, 3

List of Works illustrative of the Life and Writings of Shakespeare, printed 1850-66. 8vo. Lond., 1837.   K 19 Q 13

HALLORAN, Henry. Jubilee Ode. Sm. 4to. Sydney, 1886.   MH 1 S 4

HAMANN, Dr. Otto. Beiträge zur Histologie der Echinodermen. 8vo. Leipzig (n.d.)   A 30 U 27

Studien über Coelenteraten. 8vo. Jena (n.d.) A 30 U 27

HAMERTON, Philip Gilbert. Drawing and Engraving: a brief Exposition of Technical Principles and Practice. Illustrated. 8vo. Lond., 1892.   A 23 U 24

Human Intercourse. 12mo. Lond., 1886. J G R 32

Man in Art: Studies in Religious and Historical Art, Portrait, and Genre. 4to. Lond., 1892.   A 8 U 40

Rembrandt's Etchings. (Portfolio, Monograph, 1.) Roy. 8vo. Lond., 1894.   E

HAMILTON, Dr. Allan M., and GODKIN, Lawrence. A System of Legal Medicine. Vols. 1 and 2. Roy. 8vo. New York, 1894.   F 1 V 5, 6

HAMILTON, Annie. City of Rome in the Middle Ages. [See Gregorovius, F.]   B 30 R 10 11

HAMILTON, Anthony, Count. Memoirs of Count Philibert Grammont. 4to. Lond., 1793. C 18 U 5

HAMILTON, Augustus. Materials for a Bibliography of the *Dinornithidæ*, usually called Moas. (Trans. N.Z. Inst., 26.) 8vo. Wellington, 1893. ME 2 R
Notes on a Visit to Macquarie Island. (Trans. N.Z. Inst., 27.) 8vo. Wellington, 1894. ME 2 R

HAMILTON, Prof. David James. A Text-book of Pathology. Vol. 2, Parts 1 and 2. 1 vol. (in 2). 8vo. Lond., 1894. A 26 U 11, 12

HAMILTON, General Douglas. Records of Sport in Southern India, 1844-70. 4to. Lond., 1892. A 15 R 10

HAMILTON, Edward B. Manual of the Law and Practice of Banking in Australia and New Zealand. 8vo. Melb., 1890. MF 1 P 54

HAMILTON, Rt. Rev. Dr. Hugh. Four Introductory Lectures in Natural Philosophy. 8vo. Dublin, 1774. A 29 R 34

HAMILTON, Janet. Poems, Sketches, and Essays. 8vo. Glasgow, 1885. H 9 Q 13

HAMILTON, Peter J. Rambles in Historic Lands: Travels in Belgium, Germany, Switzerland, Italy, France, and England. Illustrated. 8vo. New York, 1893. D 18 R 24

HAMILTON, Capt. Thos. Men and Manners in America. New ed. 12mo. Edinb., 1843. D 15 P 7

HAMILTON, Rev. W. Practical Discourses, intended for circulation in the interior of New South Wales. Roy. 8vo. Sydney, 1843. MG 1 T 18

HAMILTON, Walter. French Book-Plates. 8vo. Lond., 1892. K 19 Q 10

HAMILTON, Sir Wm.; by Prof. J. Veitch. (Philosophical Classics.) 12mo. Edinb., 1882. G 9 V 5

HAMLET, Wm. Mogford. Cement Analyses. (Journal Roy. Soc., N.S.W., 28.) 8vo. Sydney, 1894. ME 1 R
Handbook of Sydney; for the use of the Members of the Australasian Association for the Advancement of Science. 12mo. Sydney, 1888. MA 1 P 73

HAMLEY, Gen. Sir Edward Bruce. Life of; by A. I. Shand. 2 vols. 8vo. Edinb., 1895. C 13 V 15, 16

HAMMARSTEN, Prof. Olof. Text-book of Physiological Chemistry; translated by John A. Mandell. Roy. 8vo. New York, 1893. A 33 T 6

HAMMOND, Basil E. The Political Institutions of the Ancient Greeks. 8vo. Lond., 1895. F 1 R 6

HAMMOND, John. Poetical Works of; with Biographical Sketch. 18mo. Lond., 1818. H 10 U 7

HANBURY, Ada. Advanced Studies of Flower Painting in Water Colours. 4to. Lond. (n.d.) A 8 U 33

HANCE, Edward M. Elementary Education in England. [*See* Subjects of the Day, 1.] G 18 S 18

HANCOCK, Anson Uriel. History of Chile. (Latin-American Republics.) [With Maps and illustrations.] 8vo. Chicago, 1893. B 16 S 24

HANCOCK, Gen. Winfield Scott. [Life of]; by Gen. Francis A. Walker. 8vo. New York, 1894. C 14 S 24

HAND, Thos. J. Milch Cows. [*See* Guenon, F.] A 18 R 22

HANDEL, George Frederic. Life of: a Sketch compiled by C. Elsasser. 8vo. Melb. (n.d.) MC 1 T 20

HANDY, Major M. P. Vistas of the Fair : a Portfolio of familiar Views of the World's Columbian Exposition. Fol. Chicago, 1893. D 1 P 18 ‡

HANDYSIDE, Dr. F. D. Portrait of. [*See* Lowe, Dr. J.—Medical Missions.] G 3 P 25

HANNA, Geo. B. Ores of North Carolina. [*See* Kerr, W. C.] A 24 V 27

HANNAFORD, Samuel. Sea and River-side Rambles in Victoria. 12mo. Geelong, 1860. MA 2 P 34

HANNAY, James. Characters and Criticisms : a Book of Miscellanies. 12mo. Edinb., 1865. J 11 T 27

HANNEN, James C. Digest of Admiralty Law. [*See* Pritchard, W. T.] F 8 T 18, 19

HANS BREITMANN. [*See* Leland, C. G.]

HANSARD, T. C. Parliamentary Debates. [*See* Great Britain.] E

HANSEN, Dr. G. Armauer, and LOOFT, Dr. Carl. Leprosy, in its clinical and pathological aspects. Translated by Dr. Norman Walker. 8vo. Bristol, 1895. A 33 S 13

HANSON, Sir Richard Davies. Science and Theology. [*See* Religious Pamphlets, 2.] G 9 V 17

HANSON, Wm. Geographical Encyclopædia of New South Wales. Roy. 8vo. Sydney, 1892. MK 1 S 21

HAPGOOD, Isabel Florence. The Epic Songs of Russia. 8vo. New York, 1885. H 9 T 3
Russian Rambles. 8vo. Lond., 1895. B 31 R 5

HARASZTHY, A. Grape Culture, Wines, and Winemaking. Illustrated. 8vo. New York, 1862. A 18 V 28

HARCOURT, Sir Wm. Geo. Granville Venables Vernon-. Sketch of. [*See* Smalley, G. W.—Studies of Men.] C 19 R 20

HARCUS, Wm. Hand-book for Emigrants proceeding to South Australia. 8vo. Lond., 1873. MD 2 Q 58

HARDING, Hor. George Rogers. The Acts and Orders relating to Joint Stock Companies. 8vo. Brisb., 1877. MF 2 R 49
Acts and Orders relating to Joint Stock Companies. 2 vols. 8vo. Brisbane, 1887-95. MF 3 T 60, 61
——— and MACPHERSON, Hon. P. The Acts and Rules Relating to Insolvercy. 8vo. Brisb., 1887. MF 2 R 30

HARDING, J. D. Lessons on Art. 10th ed. Imp. 8vo. Lond., 1880. A 8 U 36
Principles and Practice of Art. Fol. Lond., 1845. A 38 Q 13 ‡

HARDING, Rev. John. Letter to a Member of the Committee of the Church Pastoral-Aid Society, in reference to certain Animadversions upon that Society recently published by the Rev. Dr. Molesworth. 12mo. Lond., 1841. G 4 V 14

HARDINGHAM, George G. M. The Adumbration of Inventions. 8vo. Lond., 1893. F 12 P 30
Patents for Inventions, and How to Procure them. 8vo. Lond., 1891. F 12 P 31

HARDWICKE, Mrs. Poems. 12mo. Melb., 1894. MH 1 U 40

HARDWICKE'S SCIENCE GOSSIP. Vols. 28-30. Roy. 8vo. Lond., 1892-94. E

HARDY, Dr. J. The Denham Tracts. [*See* Folk-lore Society—Pubs. vol. 29.] E

HARDY, Thomas. A Chat with; with Portrait. [*See* Blathwayt, R.—Interviews.] J 10 U 3½
[Criticism of his Works]; by Annie MacDonnell. 18mo. Lond., 1894. J 7 P 30
Art of. [*See* Johnson, L.] J 6 S 37

HARDY, W. J. Book-plates. 8vo. Lond., 1893. K 19 Q 8

HARE, Augustus John Cuthbert. The Gurneys of Earlham. 2 vols. 8vo. Lond., 1895. C 19 V 7, 8
Life and Letters of Maria Edgeworth. 2 vols. 8vo. Lond., 1894. C 21 P 5, 6
The Story of Two Noble Lives, being Memorials of Charlotte, Countess Canning, and Louisa, Marchioness of Waterford. 3 vols. 12mo. Lond., 1893. C 19 Q 23-25

HARE, Rt. Rev. Francis. Difficulties which attend the Study of the Scriptures. [*See* Religious Pamphlets.] G 9 V 15

HARE, Dr. Hobart Amory. A System of Practical Therapeutics. 3 vols. Roy. 8vo. Edin., 1892. A 27 V 4-6

HARE, Julius Charles and Augustus Wm. Guesses at Truth. 5th ed. 8vo. Lond., 1859. G 11 P 42

HARE, Dr. Robert. Experimental Investigations of the Spirit Manifestations. Roy. 8vo. New York, 1855. G 6 T 20

HARGRAVE, John Fletcher. Introductory Lecture on General Jurisprudence. 8vo. Sydney, 1860. MF 2 Q 33

HARGRAVE, Lawrence. Flying Machine Motors and Cellular Kites. (Journal, Roy. Soc., N.S.W., 27.) 8vo. Sydney, 1893. ME 1 R

HARGRAVES, Edward Hammond. Address on the subject of the Gold Discovery of February 12, 1851. 8vo. Sydney, 1882. MF 2 Q 32

HARIOT, Thomas. Narrative of the First English Plantation of Virginia. Sm. 4to. Lond., 1893. B 17 R 22

HARKER, Alfred. Petrology for Students. 8vo. Lond., 1895. A 24 Q 29

HARLEIAN SOCIETY. Publications. Vols. 33-39, and Registers—vols. 17-20. 10 vols. Imp. 8vo. Lond., 1891-95. E
33, 34. Allegations for Marriage Licences issued by the Vicar-General of the Archbishop of Canterbury, 1660-79.
35, 36. Hampshire Allegations for Marriage Licences, 1689-1837.
37-39. Familiæ Minorum Gentium, diligentia J. Hunter. Registers—vols. 17, 19, 20. Register of Christeninges, Marriages, and Burialles in Parish of St. James, Clarkenwell. Vols. 4-6—Burials, 1551-1754.
Registers—vol. 18. Registers and Monumental Inscriptions of Charterhouse Chapel.

HARLIN, Thomas. Milton's Comus; to which are added ten Essays from *The Spectator*. Prepared with Notes for Matriculation Examination, Melbourne University. 8vo. Lond., 1890. MJ 2 T 28
Selections from Goldsmith, Wordsworth, and Macaulay, with notes. 8vo. Melb., 1885. MJ 1 U 34
Selections from Lord Macaulay, Robert Browning, George Eliot, and James Russell Lowell, with notes. 8vo. Melb., 1891. MJ 1 U 24

HARNACK, Dr. Adolph. History of Dogma; translated from the German by N. Buchanan. Vol. 1. 8vo. Lond., 1894. G 15 R 31

HARNEY, George J. Portrait of. [*See* Gammage, R. G.—Chartist Movement.] F 7 P 24

HAROLD, J. Judge's Report on English Fruit Orchards. 8vo. Sydney, 1892. MA 1 Q 64

HARPER, Andrew. State Schools and Religion: The Canadian System. 8vo. Melb. (n.d.) MG 1 S 23

HARPER, Charles G. The Brighton Road: Old Times and New on a Classic Highway. 8vo. Lond., 1892. D 18 S 5
From Paddington to Penzance. 8vo. Lond., 1893. D 14 S 5
Revolted Woman; Past, Present, and to Come. 8vo. Lond., 1894. F 14 U 5

HARPER, Rev. Francis Whaley. What is the Meaning of the Ornaments Rubric? 2nd ed. 8vo. Lond., 1879. G 1 R 33

HARPER'S CYCLOPÆDIA of United States History. [*See* Lossing, Dr. B. J.] B 17 U 11, 12

HARPER'S MAGAZINE. The Story of; with Portraits of the Harper Brothers. [*See* Blathwayt, R.—Interviews.] J 10 U 34

HARPER'S NEW MONTHLY MAGAZINE. Dec., 1877-Nov., 1890, and June, 1892-May, 1895. 12 vols. Roy. 8vo. New York, 1878-80. E

HARRINGTON, Rose M. Rousseau's Social Contract. [*See* Rousseau, J. J.] F 5 Q 15

HARRIS, Dr. Chapin A. Principles and Practice of Dentistry. 12th ed., edited by Dr. F. J. S. Gorgas. Illustrated. Roy.8vo. Manchester, 1885. A 26 V 12

HARRIS, Charles H. Variation of the Compass in South Australia. (Trans. Roy. Soc., S. Australia, 7.) 8vo. Adelaide, 1885. ME 1 S

HARRIS, James Rendel. Gospels in Syriac. [*See* Bensly, Prof. R. L.*] G 6 V 24

HARRIS, John. Fac-simile of Map of Terra Australis from Harris's "Voyages and Travels." Folded 4to. Melb., 1886. MD 8 R 22

HARRIS, Joseph. On the Pig: Breeding, rearing, management, and improvement. 8vo. New York, A 18 R 23

HARRIS, Townsend. First American Envoy in Japan; by W. E. Griffis. 8vo. Lond., 1895. C 13 V 20

HARRIS, Walter B. A Journey through the Yemen. 8vo. Edinb., 1893. D 14 S 6

HARRIS, Wm. T. A. Bronson Alcott, his Life and Philosophy. [*See* Sanborn, F. B.] C 13 P 26, 27

HARRISON, Benjamin. Sketch of. [*See* Wilson, J. G.—Presidents of the United States.] C 2 V 30
President Harrison at Home; with Portrait. [*See* Blathwayt, R.—Interviews.] J 10 U 34

HARRISON, Clifford. Chapter on Elocution. [*See* Miles, A. H.—New Standard Elocutionist.] J 8 T 33
Reciting. [*See* Campbell, Dr. H.—Voice, Speech, and Gesture.] J 8 T 36

HARRISON, Frederic. Annals of an Old Manor House, Sutton-place, Guildford. 4to. Lond., 1893. B 6 V 32
The Meaning of History, and other Historical Pieces. 8vo. Lond., 1894. B 35 R 5

HARRISON, George. Culpable Compulsion [Vaccination]; a condemnation by competent authorities. 8vo. Hobart, 1889. MA 2 S 67

HARRISON, J. E., and MacCOLL, D. S. Greek Vase Paintings. Illustrated. 4to. Lond., 1894. A 6 P 2 ‡

HARRISON, Robt. Outlines of German Literature. [*See* Gostwick, J.] J 8 Q 43

HARRISON, William. England in Shakspere's Youth. [*See* New Shakspere Society.—Shakspere's England.] E

HARRISON, Wm. H. Biographical Sketch of. [*See* Thompson, R. W.—Recollections of Sixteen Presidents.] C 18 T 21
Sketch of. [*See* Wilson, J. G.—Presidents of the United States.] C 2 V 30

HARRISON, Wilmot. Memorable Paris Houses. 12mo. Lond., 1893. B 14 P 3

HARRISSE, Henry. Americus Vespuccius. [*See* Vespucci, A.] C 13 V 14

HARROP, Joseph. Monograph on Flavoring Extracts; with Essences, Syrups, and Colorings, also Formulas for their preparation. 12mo. Columbus, Ohio, 1891. A 22 Q 15

HART, Dr. Albert Bushnell. Practical Essays on American Government. 12mo. Lond., 1893. F 5 Q 6
Studies in American Education. 8vo. New York, 1895. G 18 P 31

HART, Dr. Ernest. The Truth about Vaccination; being a Report on Vaccination as a Branch of Preventive Medicine. 8vo. Lond., 1895. A 33 S 11

HART, Mrs. Ernest. Diet in Sickness and in Health. 8vo. Lond., 1895. A 26 T 7

HART, Francis. Miner's Hand-book and Invertor's Guide to Western Australia; with Maps and Illustrations. 8vo. Melb., 1894. MA 3 T 25
Western Australia in 1893. 8vo. Lond., 1893. MD 4 U 9

HART, Lieut.-Gen. H. G. The New Annual Army List for 1894-95. 2 vols. 8vo. Lond., 1894-95. E

HART, J. Hinchley. Cacao. 8vo. Trinidad, 1892. A 18 S 35

HART, T. S. Notes on the Trawling Expedition off Lake Entrance. (Proceedings Royal Society, Victoria, 6, new series.) 8vo. Melb., 1894. ME 1 P

HART, Thos. Poems. 12mo. (n.p.n.d.) MH 1 Q 30

HARTIG, Prof. R. Text-book of the Diseases of Trees; translated by Prof. W. Somerville; revised and edited by Prof. H. M. Ward, F.R.S. 8vo. Lond., 1895. A 18 V 31

HARTLAND, Edwin Sidney. English Fairy and other Folk Tales. 12mo. Lond., 1890. J 11 Q 7
Legend of Perseus. Vols. 1, 2. 8vo. Lond., 1894-95. B 36 P 6, 7

HARTLAUB, Dr. Clemens. Entstehung der Sexualzellen bei Obelia. 8vo. Leipzig, 1884. A 30 U 27

HARTLEY, L. L. Catalogue of the Library of. Compiled by J. C. Anderson. Part I. 8vo. Lond., 1885.
K 7 U 33

HARTZER, Rev. Fernand. Cinq Ans parmi les Sauvages de la Nouvelle-Bretagne ot de la Nouvelle-Guinée. 8vo. Issoudun, 1858.
MG 2 Q 32

HARVARD UNIVERSITY. Bulletins of the Museum of Comparative Zoology. 8vo. Camb., Mass., 1882-84.
A 30 U 37

   9, No. 6. Bibliography of Crustacea; by W. Faxon.
   10, No. 2. Bibliography of Echinodermata; by A. Agassiz.
   11, N 10. Bibliography of Acalephos; by J. W. Fewkes.

Bulletin of the Museum of Comparative Zoology. Vols. 23 and 25. Roy. 8vo. Camb. Mass., 1892-94.
E

Catalogue, 1892-93. 8vo. Camb., Mass., 1892.
E

Die Abteilung für Deutsche Litteratur und Philologie an der Harvard Universität. 8vo. Camb., Mass., 1893.
G 18 Q 27

Harvard Law School. Sm. 4to. Camb., Mass., 1893. E

Harvard Studies in Classical Philology. 4 vols. 8vo. Boston, 1890-93.
J G U 24-27

Instruction and Equipment in the Department of Geology, 1893. 8vo. Camb., Mass., 1893.
G 18 R 48

List of Students, 1892-93; Circular of the Graduate School, 1892-94; Announcement of the Department of French, 1893-94; Announcement of the Department of German, 1893-94; Announcement of the Department of Zoology, 1893-94; Courses in History, Government and Law, and Economics, 1893-94; Announcement of the Departments of Classical Philology and Indo-Iranian Languages, 1893-94; Courses of Instruction in the Divinity School; Announcement of the Department of Music, 1893-94; Opportunities provided for Religious Worship, Instruction, and Fellowship. 8vo. Camb., Mass., 1892-94.
G 18 R 49

The Medical School of Harvard University. 8vo. Camb., Mass., 1893.
G 18 R 40

Report of the Curator of the Museum of Comparative Zoology, 1886-87. 8vo. Camb., Mass., 1897.
E

Report of the Trustees of the Museum of Comparative Zoology, 1870. 8vo. Bostor, 1871.
E

HARVARD UNIVERSITY ASTRONOMICAL OBSERVATORY. Annals of. 7 vols. 4to. Camb., Mass., 1884-95.

   Vol. 14, pts. 1, 2. Observations with the Meridian Photometer, 1879-82.
   Vol. 23, pt. 1. Discussion of observations made with the Meridian Photometer, 1882-88.
   Vol. 24. Results of observations made with the Meridian Photometer, 1882-88.
   Vol. 26, pt. 1. Preparation and Discussion of the Draper Catalogue.
   Vol. 27. The Draper Catalogue of Stellar Spectra.
   Vols. 32, pt. 1. Investigations in Astronomical Photography.

[Description of.] Roy. 8vo. Camb., Mass. (n.d.)
A 19 U 28

[List of] Publications and Photographic Illustrations issued by. 8vo. Camb., Mass., 1893.
K 7 U 32

Report of the Director, 1894. 8vo. Camb., Mass., 1894.
E

Q

HARVEN, Emile de. Mission Commerciale en Nouvelle-Zélande. 8vo. Bruxelles, 1887.
MF 3 T 44

HARVEY, F. J. The Teacher's Manual of Physical Exercises. Ob. 18mo. Lond., 1894.
G 18 P 18

HARVEY, Dr. Gideon. Great Fire in London, 1666.
[See De Foe, Daniel—Journal of the Plague Year.]
B 23 R 22

HARVEY, Rev. Dr. Moses. Newfoundland as it is in 1894: a Hand-book and Tourists' Guide. With Map. 12mo. Lond., 1894.
D 11 S 9

HARVEY, R. W. Handy Register of Mining Companies.
[See Trickett, O.]
MF 10 S

HARVEY, Dr. Wm. Henry. Seaside Book; being an Introduction to the Natural History of the British Coasts. 4th ed. 12mo. Lond., 1857.
A 29 P 8

HASLAM, John. A Glimpse of Australian Life: Facts and Experiences. 12mo. Sydney, 1890. MD 1 P 30

House Sanitation. (Trans. Roy. Soc., S. Australia, 6.) 8vo. Adelaide, 1883.
ME 1 S

HASLUCK, Paul N. Woodworker's Handybook of Manual Instruction. Illustrated. 12mo. Lond., 1894.
A 25 P 39

HASSALL, A. Louis XIV and the zenith of the French Monarchy. 8vo. New York, 1895.
C 21 P 19

HASSALL Rev. Thomas. Funeral Sermon on Death of.
[See King, Rev. R. L.]
MG 1 S 11

HASSINGER, John A. Catalogue of the Hawaiian Exhibits at the Exposition Universelle, Paris, 1889. 8vo. Honolulu, 1889.
MK 1 T 18

HASTIE, Rev. Thos. A Voice from the Bush: Sermons, 8vo. Edinb., 1877.
MG 1 P 73

HASTINGS, Francis Rawdon-, Marquess of. [Life of]; by Major J. Ross. (Rulers of India.) 8vo. Oxford, 1893.
C 13 P 17

HASTINGS, Rev. Fred. This Life; or, Great Questions affecting Man's Present State. 12mo. Adelaide, 1891.
MG 1 P 74

HASTINGS, Warren. Life of; by Col. G. B. Malleson. 8vo. Lond., 1894.
C 16 U 5

Private Life of; by Sir C. Lawson. 8vo. Lond., 1895.
C 22 R 8

HASWELL, George H. The Maister: a Century of Tyneside Life, being the Life of Thomas Haswell. Illustrated. 8vo. Lond., 1895.
C 22 R 2

HASWELL, Thomas. Life of. [See Haswell, G. H.]
C 22 R 2

HATCH, Frederick H., and CHALMERS, J. A. The Gold Mines of the Rand: being a Description of the Mining Industry of Witwatersrand, South African Republic. Roy. 8vo. Lond., 1895.
A 24 V 15

HATTON, Richard G. Figure Drawing and Composition. 8vo. Lond., 1895. A 23 U 27

HAUG, H. Auch ein Kulturbild. 12mo. Gotha, 1894. G 2 U 41

HAUGHTON, Rev. Dr. Samuel. New Researches on Sunheat, Terrestrial Radiation, &c. (Trans. R.I. Academy.—Cunningham Memoirs, 3.) 4to. Dublin, 1886. E

HAUPT, Prof. Lewis M. Manual of Engineering Specifications and Contracts. 2nd edition. 8vo. Philad., 1881. A 22 S 22

HAUSSOULLIER, Bernard. La Vie Municipale en Attique. 8ro. Paris, 1884. F 1 R 8

HAUVETTE-BESNAULT, Am. Les Stratèges Athéniens. 8vo. Paris, 1885. B 28 U 9

HAVENS, B. F. Indiana at the World's Columbian Exposition, 1893. 8vo. Chicago, 1893. K 7 U 7

HAWAIIAN ALMANAC AND ANNUAL, 1893-95. 3 vols. 8vo. Honolulu, 1892-95. ME 3 S

HAWEIS, Rev. Hugh Reginald. Rev. H. R. Haweis at Home; with Portrait. [*See* Blathwayt, R.—Interviews.] J 10 U 34
Sir Morell Mackenzie, Physician and Operator : a Memoir. 8vo. Lond., 1883. C 16 R 11
My Musical Life. 3rd ed. 8vo. Lond., 1891. C 18 P 2

HAWKER, Col. Peter. The Diary of, 1802-53. 2 vols. 8vo. Lond., 1893. C 15 P 1, 2

HAWKESBURY AGRICULTURAL COLLEGE AND EXPERIMENTAL FARM. Prospectus, Regulations, Reports, &c., 1892-94. 8vo. Sydney, 1893-95. ME 7 S

HAWKESWORTH, Alfred. Illustrations of types of Wool; with Notes on their Formation, Qualities, &c. With coloured plates depicting ninety-two different Wools. 8vo. Sydney, 1892. MA 1 S 47
Raw Wools, and Specimens to illustrate the uses of Wool. Roy. 8vo. Sydney, 1892*. MA 1 S 35

HAWKINS, C. C., and WALLIS, F. The Dynamo; its Theory, Design, and Manufacture. 8ro. Lond., 1893. A 21 P 21

HAWKINS, E. J. The Fitzdolphus Papers. 12mo., Melb., 1878. MJ 1 Q 51

HAWKINS, H. S. Elementary Exercises in Algebra. 8vo. Sydney, 1850. MA 1 U 61

HAWKINS, Dr. Herbert P. On Diseases of the Vermiform Appendix; with a consideration of the Symptoms and Treatment of the resulting forms of Peritonitis. 8vo. Lond., 1895. A 33 T 23

HAWKINS, Sir John. Sketch of. [*See* Froude, Prof. J. A.—English Seamen.] B 21 U 9
Sketch of. [*See* Southey, R.—English Seamen.] B 23 S 15

HAWKINS, S. The *Wagga Express* Riverine Directory, 1887, 1893-95. 4 vols. 12mo. Wagga, 1887-95. ME 6 T

HAWTHORNE, Nathaniel. Mosses from an Old Manse. 12mo. Lond., 1894. J 12 S 8

HAWTREY, Rev. Montague J. G. An Earnest Address to New Zealand Colonists with reference to their intercourse with the Native Inhabitants. 12mo. Lond., 1840. MB 1 P 33
Justice to New Zealand, Honour to England. 12mo. Lond, 1861. G 4 V 14

HAY, Prof. George W. Catechism of Practical Agriculture. 8vo. Hobart, 1856. MA 1 Q 75

HAY, John. Abraham Lincoln. [*See* Lincoln, A.] F 8 T 25, 26

HAY, Robt. Geology and Mineral Resources of Kansas, 1891-92. 8vo. Topeka, 1893. A 24 U 24

HAYCRAFT, Dr. John B. Darwinism and Race Progress. 8vo. Lond., 1895. A 28 P 17

HAYDON, Benjamin Robt. [Plaster Cast of] [*See* Hutton, L.—Portraits in Plaster.] A 23 V 13

HAYES, Alice M. The Horsewoman : a Practical Guide to Side-saddle Riding. 8vo. Lond., 1893. A 29 R 8

HAYES, Dr. Isaac I., and the Open Polar Sea. [*See* Greeley, Gen. A. W.—Explorers and Travellers.] C 17 R 4

HAYES, Rutherford B. Sketch of. [*See* Wilson, J. G.—Presidents of the United States.] C 2 V 30

HAYNES, Capt. Alfred E. Man-hunting in the Desert, being a Narrative of the Palmer Search-Expedition (1882-83); with an Introduction by W. Besant. [Illustrated.] Roy. 8vo. Lond., 1894. D 14 V 14

HAYNES, G. H. The State of Maine in 1893. Ob. 12mo. New York, 1893. D 15 P 10

HAYNES, Dr. George H. Representation and Suffrage in Massachusetts, 1620-91. (Johns Hopkins Univ. Studies, 12.) Roy. 8vo. Baltimore, 1894. B 18 S 12

HAYNES, John. Popular Election of United States Senators. (Johns Hopkins University Studies, 11.) 8vo. Baltimore, 1893. B 18 S 11

HAYS, Rev. Dr. George P. Presbyterians : a popular Narrative of their origin, progress, doctrines, and achievements. Roy. 8vo. New York, 1892. G 6 T 27

HAYTER, Henry H. General Report of the Census of Victoria, 1891. 4to. Melb., 1893. ME
Hand-book to the Colony of Victoria. 8vo. Melb., 1884. MD 8 Q 29
Victorian Year-book. [*See* Victoria.] ME

HAYWARD, Abraham. Faust. [*See* Goethe, J. W. von.] H 1 U 1
Life, Character, and Opinions of Lord Chesterfield. 12mo. Lond., 1854. C 18 P 21
Life and Times of G. Selwyn. 12mo. Lond., 1854. C 18 P 21

HAYWOOD, Howard. Colonists' Advertiser and Visitors' Guide to Tasmania. 8vo. Latrobe, 1888. MD 5 Q 54

HAZELL'S ANNUAL for 1893-95: a Cyclopædic Record of Men and Topics of the Day. 3 vols. 8vo. Lond., 1893-95. E

HAZEN, Allen. The Filtration of Public Water-supplies. 8vo. New York, 1895. A 22 S 8

HAZEN, Prof. Chas. D. Constitutions in Europe and America. [*See* Borgeaud, C.] F 2 V 10

HAZLITT, Wm. Guizot's History of Civilisation. [*See* Guizot, F. P. G.] B 25 P 2-4
Lectures on the English Poets. 3rd ed. 12mo. Lond., 1841. J 12 S 34
Liber Amoris; or, the New Pygmalion: with an Introduction by R. Le Gallienne. 12mo. Lond., 1893. J 4 P 11
Another Copy with additional matter now printed for the first time from the original manuscripts. Sm. 4to. Privately printed, 1894. J 4 U 3
The Round Table [Essays.] 18mo. Lond., 1869. J 7 P 49
Selected Essays. [*See* Morris, E. E.] MJ 1 S 11
Table-Talk; or, Original Essays on Men and Manners. 2nd ed. 2 vols. 8vo. Lond., 1824. J 2 Q 15, 16
Winterslow: Essays and Characters written there. 12mo. Lond., 1850. J 12 S 33

HAZLITT, Wm. Carew. Coinage of the European Continent. 8vo. Lond., 1893. A 27 T 4
Montaigne's Essays. [*See* Montaigne, M. E. de.] J 8 P 41-46

HEAD, N. Mabel: a Tale of Filial Love. 12mo. Lond., 1894. MH 1 U 61

HEADLAM, A. C. Ecclesiastical Site in Isauria. [*See* Society for the Promotion of Hellenic Studies.] E

HEADLEY, F. W. The Structure and Life of Birds, Illustrated. 8vo. Lond., 1895. A 28 U 13

HEALEY, Daniel. The Cornstalk, his Habits and Habitat; by "Whaks Li Kell." 12mo. Sydney, 1893. MJ 1 S 33

HEARN, Lafcadio. Glimpses of Unfamiliar Japan. 2 vols. 8vo. Lond., 1894. D 17 R 16, 17
Out of the East: Reveries and Studies in New Japan. 12mo. Boston, 1895. B 35 Q 10

HEARN, Prof. Wm. Edward. Payment by Results in Primary Education. 8vo. Melb., 1872. MG 2 Q 30

HEARNE, Thos. Antiquities of Great Britain. [*See* Byrne, W.] B 2 P 29, 30 ‡

HEARTWELL, Henry. The Castle of Sorrento: a Musical Entertainment. [*See* London Stage, 4.] H 2 S 36

HEATH, H. A. Special Report on Sheep, U.S.A. [*See* Salmon, Dr. D. E.] A 30 U 7

HEATH, Richard. The English Peasant: Studies, Historical, Local, and Biographic. 8vo. Lond., 1893. F 14 Q 43

HEATH, Dr. Richard. Deafness, its Causes and Cure. 2nd ed. 12mo. Geelong, 1859. MA 2 P 41

HEATHER, J. F. Mathematical Instruments: their Construction, Adjustment, Testing, and Use, comprising Drawing, Measuring, Optical, Surveying, and Astronomical Instruments. Illustrated. 3 vols. (in 1). 12mo. Lond., 1888-92. A 25 P 38

HEAVISIDE, Oliver. Electrical Papers. 2 vols. 8vo. Lond., 1892. A 21 S 18, 19
Electro-magnetic Theory. Vol. I. 8vo. Lond., 1893. A 21 T 17

HEBER, Rt. Rev. Reginald, Poet and Chief Missionary to the East, 1783-1826; by Dr. G. Smith. 8vo. Lond., 1895. C 13 V 31

HECKETHORN, Chas. Wm. The Secret Societies of all Ages and Countries. 2 vols. 12mo. Lond, 1875. B 35 P 22, 23

HECTOR, Sir James. Catalogue of the Colonial Museum, Wellington. 12mo. Wellington, 1870. MA 2 V 20
Meteorological Report, 1868: together with Abstract of all Meteorological Returns for New Zealand prior to that date. Roy. 8vo. Wellington, 1869. ME
New Zealand Geography. [*See* Bowden, T. A.] MD 2 W 18
Phormium Tenax as a Fibrous Plant; edited by [Sir] J. Hector. Roy. 8vo. Wellington, 1872. MA 1 U 28
3rd, 8th, 17th, and 27th Annual Reports on the Colonial Museum and Laboratory. Roy. 8vo. Wellington, 1868-93. ME
Geological Survey of New Zealand. Reports of Geological Explorations during 1870-74, 1876-77, and 1881. 5 vols. roy. 8vo. Wellington, 1871-82. ME
Index to Reports of the Geological Survey of New Zealand, 1866-85 inclusive. Roy. 8vo. Wellington, 1887. ME
On the anatomy of flight of certain birds. (Trans. N.Z. Inst. 27.) 8vo. Wellington, 1894. ME 2 R
Tarawera Eruption. [*See* Griffiths, G. S.] MA 3 S 47

HEDERICH, Benjamin. Græcum Lexicon Manuale, primum a B. Hederico institutum; dein auctum cura J. A. Ernesti; auctum A. T. Morell, Thesauri Græcæ Poeseos autore. 4to. Lond., 1790.   J 12 V 1†

HEDGER-WALLACE, R. [*See* Wallace, R. H.]

HEDLEY, Chas. List of Land Shells recorded from Queensland. (Proc. Roy. Soc., Queensland, 5.) 8vo. Brisbane, 1888.   ME 1 T
Ancitia Graffei and its allies. (Proc. Roy. Soc., Queensland, 5.) 8vo. Brisbane, 1889.   ME 1 T
Uses of some Queensland Plants. (Proc. Roy. Soc., Queensland, 5.) 8vo. Brisbane, 1888.   ME 1 T
Description of a new Slug, with notes on other Terrestrial Mollusca. (Proc. Roy. Soc., Queensland, 5.) 8vo. Brisbane, 1888.   ME 1 T
Notes on Queensland Land-shells. (Proc. Roy. Soc., Queensland, 6.) 8vo. Brisbane, 1888.   ME 1 T
Anatomical Notes on the *Helicidæ*. (Proc. Roy. Soc., Queensland, 6.) 8vo. Brisbane, 1889.   ME 1 T
On a Molluscan Genus new to, and another forgotten, from Australia. (Proc. Roy. Soc., Victoria, n. s., 7.) 8vo. Melb., 1895.   ME 1 P

HEDLEY, Harry W. At the Wickets: New South Wales *versus* Victoria. 12mo. Melb., 1888.   MA 3 U 11

HEERES, J. E. Groningsche Volksalmanak, 1893. [*See* Feith, J. A.]   D 18 R 25

HEGEL, Georg Wm. Friedrich. Lectures on the History of Philosophy. Vol. 1. 8vo. Lond., 1892.   G 12 Q 29
Hegel; by Prof. E. Caird. (Philosophical Classics.) 12mo. Edinb., 1886.   G 9 V 6
Philosophical Study of. [*See* Ritchie, D. G.] G 10 S 30

HEIDEN, Dr. Eduard. Lehrbuch der Düngerlehre. 2 vols. 8vo. Hannover, 1879-87.   A 18 S 30, 31

HEINE, Heinrich. Works of. Vols. 1-8. 8vo. Lond., 1891-93.   J 8 R 34-41
  1. Florentine Nights; Memoirs of Herr von Schnabelewopski; the Rabbi of Bacharach; and Shakespeare's Maidens and Women.
  2, 3. Pictures of Travel.
  4. The Salon; or Letters on Art, Music, Popular Life and Politics.
  5, 6. Germany.
  7, 8. French Affairs.
The Family Life of. Edited by Baron L. von Embden. 8vo. Lond., 1893.   C 16 R 10
Heine in Art and Letters; translated with a Prefatory Note, by Elizabeth A. Sharp. 12mo. Lond. (n.d.)   J 11 T 39
Heine on Shakespeare: a Translation of his Notes on Shakespeare Heroines; by Ida Benecke. 8vo. Lond., 1895.   J 10 R 27

HEINRICH, G. A. Histoire de la Littérature Allemande. 3 vols. 8vo. Paris, 1889-91.   J 7 U 41-43

HELICAL GEARS. A Practical Treatise; by "A Foreman Pattern-maker." 12mo. Lond., 1893.   A 22 Q 23

HELLENIC STUDIES. Society for the Promotion of. [*See* Society for the Promotion of Hellenic Studies.]

HELLER, Robert, his Doings. 12mo. Melb. (n.d.)   MJ 3 P 26

HELLMUTH COLLEGE, London, Ontario, Canada. [Calendar and Register, 1893, 1894.] 8vo. (n.p. n.d.)   E

HELM, E. The Joint Standard: a plain Exposition of Monetary Principles and of the Monetary Controversy. 12mo. Lond., 1894.   F 9 U 46

HEMSLEY, Wm. B. Report on the present state of knowledge of various Insular Floras; Report on the Botany of the Bermudas and various other Islands of the Atlantic and Southern Oceans; Report on the Botany of Juan Fernandez, the South-eastern Molluccas, and the Admiralty Isles. [*See* Thomson, Sir C. W. and Murray, Dr. J.—Voyage of H.M.S. *Challenger*.]   A 6†

HENDERSON, Dr. Ebenezer. Annals of Dunfermline and Vicinity, 1069-1878. 4to. Glasgow, 1879.   B 24 V 7

HENDERSON, Ernest F. Select Historical Documents of the Middle Ages; translated and edited by E. F. Henderson. 8vo. Lond., 1892.   B 25 P 5

HENDERSON, George G. Increase in the Produce of the Soil. [*See* Wagner, Prof. P.]   A 29 T 5

HENDERSON, Prof. J. R. Anomura. [*See* Thompson, Sir C. W., and Murray, Dr. J.—Voyage of H.M.S. *Challenger*.]   A 6†

HENDERSON, W. J. Story of Music. 12mo. New York, 1893.   A 23 Q 48

HENDRIX COLLEGE. Annual Catalogue, 1893. 8vo. Conway, Ark., 1893.   E

HENLEY, William Ernest. Slang and its Analogues. [*See* Farmer, J. S.]   Libr.
———— and WHIBLEY, C. A Book of English Prose Character and Incident, 1387-1649. 8vo. Lond., 1894.   J 5 P 17

HENN & CO. Action for Libel. [*See* Davies Bros.]   MF 2 Q 66

HENNELL, C. C. Christian Theism. 8vo. Lond., 1853.   G 19 P 32

HENNESSEY, J. D. The Dis-Honourable. 8vo. Sydney, 1895.   MJ 3 Q 29

HENNESSY, Capt. J. M. A few Months' Experience in New Guinea. (Roy. Geograph. Soc. of Australasia, Q. Branch, 1.) 8vo. Brisbane, 1886. ME 20
Report of a Trip to the Western Part of the South Coast of British New Guinea. (Roy. Geograph. Soc. of Australasia, Q. Branch, 3.) 8vo. Brisbane, 1889. ME 20
Notes made in the Fly River, British New Guinea. (Roy. Geograph. Soc. of Australasia, Q. Branch, 5.) 8vo. Brisbane, 1890. ME 20

HENNESSY, Sir John Pope. Colonial Home Rule. [See Subjects of the Day, 3.] F 7 U 28

HENRICUS. [See Ignorant Learned.] MJ 2 S 9
[See Masonic Signs.] MJ 2 S 8

HENRIETTA, Princess. Life of; by Julia Cartwright. 8vo. Lond., 1894. C 15 P 6

HENRIQUEZ, Camilo. [Vida de]; par M. L. Amunátegui. 2 vols. 8vo. Santiago, 1889. C 21 T 4, 5

HENRY IV, King of England. Expeditions to Prussia and the Holy Land made by Henry, Earl of Derby. (Camden Society Pubs.) sm. 4to. Lond., 1894. E

HENRY IV, King of France. [Plaster Cast of.] [See Hutton, L.—Portraits in Plaster.] A 23 V 13
Henry of Navarre and the Religious Wars; by E. T. Blair. Roy. 8vo. Philad., 1895. B 26 V 14

HENRY VIII, King of England. First Divorce of. [See Hope, Mrs.] B 24 Q 6

HENRY, Prof. Joseph. Eulogy on Prof. A. D. Bache. 8vo. Wash., 1872. C 19 S 5

HENRY, T. Shekleton. Spookland: Spirit Materialisation, and Hints and Illustrations as to the possibility of artificially producing the same. 8vo. Sydney, 1894 MG 2 Q 35

HENRY, William. Swimming. [See Sinclair, A.] A 17 U 47

HENRY ANCRUM: a Tale of the Last New Zealand War. 2 vols. 12mo. Lond., 1872. MJ 1 T 50, 51

HENSLOW, Rev. George. The Origin of Plant Structures by self-adaption to the environment. 8vo. Lond., 1895. A 20 Q 19

HEPBURN, James. [See Bothwell, Earl of.]

HEPBURN, Rev. James D. Twenty Years in Khama's Country, and Pioneering among the Batauana of Lake Ngami. 8vo. Lond., 1895. G 3 P 34

HERALD VICTORIA ALMANAC for 1854. 8vo. Melb., 1854. ME 4 U

HERBART, Johann Friedrich. Introduction to Herbart's Science and Practice of Education. [See Felkin, H. M. and E.] G 18 P 33

HERBERT, George. Life of. [See Walton, Izaak.] C 19 V 6
Life of. 8vo. Lond., 1893. C 15 P 5
Life of; by the Rev. Dr. J. Brown. [See Masson, Prof. D.—In the Footsteps of the Poets.] J 6 R 43
Poetical Works of. Illustrated. 8vo. Lond., 1856. H 5 U 25

HERBERT, William V. Defence of Plevna, 1877. 8vo. Lond., 1895. B 31 T 8

HERBERT-PERCY, Major A. [See Percy, Major. A.H.]

HERDMAN, Prof. W. A. Tunicata. [See Thomson, Sir C. W., and Murray, Dr. J.—Voyage of H.M.S. Challenger, Zoölogy.] A 6 †

HEREFORDSHIRE POMONA, The, containing Colored Figures and Descriptions of the most esteemed kinds of Apples and Pears. 2 vols. 4to. Hereford, 1876-85. A 6 P 6, 7 ‡

HERFORD, Dr. Charles Harold. Ibsen's "Brand." [See Ibsen, H.] H 4 P 38

HERNDON, William H., and WEIK, Jesse W. Abraham Lincoln: the True Story of a Great Life. 2 vols. 8vo. Lond., 1893. C 13 P 36, 37

HERNSHEIM, Franz. Beitrag zur Sprache der Marshall-Inseln. 12mo. Leipzig, 1880. MK 2 Q 4

HERODOTUS. Textus J. Schweighæuseri. [Greek Text and Latin Notes.] 4 vols. 8vo. Glasguæ, 1818. B 28 U 3-6
Dictionarium Ionicum Græco-Latinum, quod indicem in omnes Herodoti libros continet. [See Portus, E.] B 28 U 7

HERON-ALLEN. [See Allen, E. H..]

HERRERA, Antonio de. Descripcion de las Indias Occidentales. 5 vols. sm. fol. Madrid, 1725-26. B 36 T 8-12 ‡

HERRESHOFF, Lewis. Yachting. [See Sullivan, Sir E.] A 29 Q 41

HERRICK, C. L. The Mammals of Minnesota. Roy. 8vo. Minneapolis, 1892. A 13 T 39

HERRMANN, Prof. Gustav. Hoisting Machinery. [See Weisbach, Dr. J.] A 25 t 26

HERSCHEL, Caroline L. The Herschels and Modern Astronomy. [See Clerke, Agnes M.] A 19 Q 19

HERSCHEL, Sir Friedrich Wilhelm. The Herschels and Modern Astronomy. [See Clerke, Agnes M.] A 19 Q 19

HERSCHEL, Sir John F. W. The Herschels and Modern Astronomy. [See Clerke, Agnes M.] A 19 Q 19

HERSCHELL, Dr. George. Indigestion: an Introduction to the Study of the Diseases of the Stomach. 2nd ed. 12mo. Lond., 1895. A 26 R 8

HERTWIG, Dr. Oscar. The Cell: Outlines of General Anatomy and Physiology; edited by Dr. H. J. Campbell. 8vo. Lond., 1895. A 28 U 12
Text-book of the Embryology of Man and Mammals. 8vo. Lond., 1892. A 13 T 38

HERTWIG, Prof. Richard. Actiniaria. [*See* Thomson, Sir C. W., and Murray, Dr. J.—Voyage of H.M.S. *Challenger*—Zoölogy, 6.] A 6 †

HERTZ, Dr. Heinrich. Electric Waves, being Researches on the Propagation of Electric Action with finite velocity through space. Authorised English translation by D. E. Jones. 8vo. Lond., 1893. A 21 T 21

HERVEY, Rev. James. Meditations and Contemplations. New ed. 12mo. Lond. (n.d.) G 4 V 11

HERVEY, Lord. Poetical Works of, with Biographical Sketch. 18mo. Lond., 1818. H 10 U 7

HESLOP, R. O. Northumberland Words. (Eng. Dialect Soc. Pubs.) 2 vols. 8vo. Lond., 1893-94. E

HESSELL, Rev. William. The Connexional Financial Economy of Wesleyan Methodism. 8vo. Lond., 1856. G 1 R 34

HETHERINGTON, Henry. Portrait of. [*See* Gammage, R. G.—Chartist Movement.] F 7 R 24

HETLEY, Mme. Ch., et RAOUL, E. Fleurs Sauvages et Bois Précieux de la Nouvelle-Zélande. 4to. Lond., 1889. MA 9 Q 2 †

HEUCHER, M. J. H. Magic Plants. [*See* Bibliotheca Curiosa.] J 18 Q 36

HEWINS, Eben Newell. American Book-plates. [*See* Allen, C. D.] J 8 U 6

HEWISON, Rev. James King. The Isle of Bute in the Olden Time. Vol. 1. Roy. 8vo. Edinb., 1893. B 13 S 21

HEWITT, J. F. The Ruling Races of Pre-historic Times in India, South-western Asia, and Southern Europe. 2 vols. 8vo. Lond., 1894-95. A 30 Q 6, 7

HEYSINGER, Dr. I. W. Source and Mode of Solar Energy throughout the Universe. Illustrated. 8vo. Philad., 1895. A 19 S 21

HEYWOOD, Thomas. Love's Mistress; or, the Queen's Masque. [*See* Bibliotheca Curiosa.] J 18 Q 40

HIBBERD, Rev. F. Baptismal Regeneration the Corollary of the Prayer-book, and the Teaching of the Church Clergy. 8vo. Sydney, 1874. MG 2 Q 24

HIBBERD, Shirley. The Amateur's Greenhouse and Conservatory. New ed., revised by T. W. Sanders. Illustrated. 12mo. Lond., 1894. A 18 P 10
The Amateur's Rose Book. New ed., by G. Gordon. Illustrated. 8vo. Lond., 1894. A 32 R 9
Familiar Garden Flowers. [*See* Humle, F. E.] A 20 Q 7-11

HICKS, R. D. Politics of Aristotle. [*See* Susemihl, Prof. F.] F 7 R 30

HICKSON, Dr. J. B. Medical Reform: Homœopathy vindicated as a Necessary and Scientific Reform in Medical Practice. 8vo. Melb., 1856. MA 1 V 71

HICKSON, J. C. Notes on Travels from Pacific to Atlantic. 12mo. Parramatta, 1894. MD 7 T 65

HICKSON, Robt. R. P. Sewage Purification and Disposal. Roy. 8vo. Sydney, 1895. MA 2 U 59

HICKSON, Dr. Sydney J. The Fauna of the Deep Sea. 12mo. Lond., 1894. A 27 Q 22

HIDALGO, Dr. Wenceslao. Medicina Domestica de la Infancia. 2nd ed. 8vo. Santiago, 1885. A 33 T 24

HIGGINS, C. A. The Land of Sunshine. Illustrated. 12mo. Chicago, 1892. D 15 P 12

HIGGINS, J. Frederick. Sewage Matters: their treatment and application. 8vo. Melb., 1868. MA 1 V 44

HIGGINSON, Thos. W. Atlantic Essays. 12mo. New York, 1894. J 12 T 39

HIGHLAND AND AGRICULTURAL SOCIETY OF SCOTLAND. Transactions, 1829-94, and Indexes, 1799-1888. 47 vols. 8vo. Edinb., 1829-94 E

HIGINBOTHAM, George. Science and Religion; or, the Relations of Modern Science with the Christian Churches. 8vo. Melb., 1883. MG 1 S 24
Speech addressed to the Electors of the District of Brighton. 8vo. Brighton, 1865. MJ 3 Q 15
Mr. Justice Higinbotham on the Orthodox Faith. [*See* Gosman, Rev. A.] MG 2 Q 23
Memoir of; by E. E. Morris. 8vo. Lond., 1895. MC 1 T 22
[*See* Dickinson, Rev. R. B.—Scripture and Science.] MG 2 Q 23

HIGINBOTHAM & ROBINSON, Messrs. Yachting and Excursion Map of Port Phillip and the surrounding Country, Melbourne, and Suburbs. Folded 8vo. Melb. (n.d.) MD 8 R 40

HILARION. [*See* McKellar, Campbell.]

HILDEBRAND, Dr. Hans. Industrial Arts of Scandinavia in the Pagan Time. 8vo. Lond., 1883. A 23 R 33

HILGARD, Prof. Eugene W. Reports on the Agricultural Experiment Stations of the University of California, 1888-94. 4 vols. 8vo. Sacramento, 1890-94. E
Reports of Examinations of Waters, Water Supply, and related Subjects, 1886-89. 8vo. Sacramento, 1889. A 18 V 21
Alkali Lands: Irrigation and Drainage in their Mutual relations. 8vo. Sacramento, 1892. A 18 V 22

HILGARD, Prof. Eugene W.—*contd*.
Reports of Experiments in Methods of Fermentation and related subjects, 1886-87. 8vo. Sacramento, 1888.   A 18 V 29

University of California, College of Agriculture Experiment Station. Report of the Viticultural Work during the seasons 1887-89, with data regarding the Vintage of 1890. Part 1. Red Wine Grapes. Part 2. Record of Work in the Viticultural Laboratory for the season 1887-89; by L. Paparelli. Part 3. Preservative and Remedial Processes applied to Wines of Warm Countries. 8vo. Sacramento, 1892.   E

HILL, Aaron. Zara: a Tragedy. [*See* London Stage, 4.]   H 2 S 36

HILL, A. Fraser. The Land and Wealth of New South Wales. 8vo. Sydney, 1894.   MF 1 Q 62

HILL, Mrs. Birkbeck. Rise of Modern Democracy. [*See* Borgeaud, C.]   F 5 Q 2

HILL, Constance. Autobiography of Frederic Hill. [*See* Hill, F.]   C 19 R 17

HILL, Frederic. An Autobiography of fifty years in Times of Reform; edited by his daughter, Constance Hill. 8vo. Lond., 1893   C 19 R 17

HILL, Dr. George Birkbeck. Harvard College; by an Oxonian. 8vo. New York, 1894.   B 19 Q 13

HILL, Georgiana. History of English Dress, from the Saxon period to the present time. 2 vols. 8vo. Lond., 1893.   A 23 T 12

HILL, Rev. J. Hamlyn. Diatessaron of Tatian. [*See* Tatian.]   G 13 P 44

HILL, Rev. James. The Attitude of the Church to Modern Life and Thought. 8vo. Sydney, 1886.   MG 1 R 74

HILL, Rev. Pascoe G. Fifty days on board a Slave Vessel in the Mozambique Channel, 1843. 12mo. Lond., 1844.   D 14 P 7

HILL, Hon. Richard, and THORNTON, Hon. George. Notes on the Aborigines of New South Wales. Roy. 8vo. Sydney, 1892.   MA 1 R 45

HILL, Robt. T. Clay Materials of the United States. 8vo. Wash., 1893.   A 20 V 16

HILL, S. P. Letter to the Members of the Congregational or Independent Church, under the pastoral care of the Rev. Dr. R. Ross. 8vo. Sydney, 1846.   MG 2 S 16

HILL, Thos. Padmore. The Young Speaker: a Series of Short Selections in Prose and Verse. 12mo. Melb., 1867.   MJ 3 P 6

HILL, W. H. F. Entomogenous Fungi of Victoria. [*See* Royal Soc., Vic., Proc., n.s. 7.]   ME 1 P

HILL, Walter. Botanic Gardens, Brisbane: Collection of Economic and other Plants. Brisb., 1880.   MA 1 T 60

———— and THOZET, M. Specimens of Queensland Woods. 8vo. (n.p. n.d.)   MA 2 T 31

HILLER, H Croft. Rhythmic Heredity: Matter a property of energy. 8vo. Lond., 1894.   G 1 U 2

HILLHOUSE HIGH SCHOOL, New Haven, Conn. Catalogue, 1892. 8vo. New Haven, 1892.   E

HIMMELSTJERNA, H. von Samson. [*See* Samson-Himmelstierna.]

HINDE, Dr. George J., and HOLMES, W. H. On the Sponge-remains in the Lower Tertiary Strata near Oamaru, New Zealand. [*See* Linnean Society, London, Journal 24.]   E

HINDS, Allen B. The Making of the England of Elizabeth. 8vo. Lond., 1895.   B 23 S 13

HINDS, Rt Rev. Samuel. A Reply to the Question, "Shall I seek Ordination in the Church of England?" [*See* Religious Pamphlets, 1.]   G 9 V 16

Reply to the Question, "Apart from Supernatural Revolation, what is man's prospect of living after death?" [*See* Religious Pamphlets, 1.]   G 9 V 16

Reply to the Question, "What have we to rely on, if we cannot rely on the Bible?" [*See* Religious Pamphlets, 1.]   G 9 V 16

HINE, Edward. Forty-seven Identifications of the British Nation with the Lost Ten Tribes of Israel. 8vo. Lond. (n.d.)   G 4 P 20

HINKINS, John T. Life amongst the Native Race [Victoria]. Sm. 4to. Melb., 1884.   MA 3 S 36

HINKSON, H. A. Dublin Verses; by Members of Trinity College. Sm. 4to. London 1895.   H 10 R 20

HINTON, A. Horsley. Hand-book of Illustration. 8vo. Lond. (n.d.)   A 23 T 21

HIORNS, Arthur H. Metal Colouring and Bronzing. 12mo. Lond., 1892.   A 25 P 6

HIPPOLYTUS, St. Writings of. Fragments of Writings of 3rd Century; translated by Rev. S. D. F. Salmond. (Ante-Nicene Christ. Lib., 9.) Edinb., 1869.   G 14 U 9

The Refutation of all Heresies; with Fragments from his Commentaries on various Books of Scripture. Translated by Rev. J. H. MacMahon and Rev. S. D. F. Salmond. (Ante-Nicene Christ. Lib., 6.) 8vo. Edinb. 1868.   G 14 U 6

HIROI, Isami. Plate-Girder Construction. 12mo. New York, 1893.   A 22 P 17

HIRSCH, Max. The Fiscal Superstition. 12mo. Melb., 1895.   MF 4 P 17

HIRSCHFELD, Dr. Eugen. Prevalence of Cancer in Australasia. (Proc. Roy. Soc., Queensland, 10) 8vo. Brisbane, 1893. ME 1 T

HIRST, Prof. Barton Cooke. Systems of Obstetrics ; by American Authors. 2 vols. roy. 8vo. Edinb., 1888-89. A 33 U 5, 6

—————— and PIERSOL, Prof. George A. Human Monstrosities. Illustrated. Fol. Edinb. and Lond., 1892-93. A G P 4 ‡

HIRST, Edith H. Round the Camp Fire, and other Australian Poems. 12mo. Lond. (n.d.) MH 1 U 41

HISLOP, Rev. Alexander. The two Babylons, or the Papal worship proved to be the worship of Nimrod and his wife. Illustrated. 8vo. Lond. (n.d.) G 4 P 27

HISLOP, Dr. John. History of the Knox Church, Dunedin. 8vo. Dunedin, 1892. MG 2 S 5

HISSEY, James John. Through ten English Counties. Illustrated. 8vo. Lond., 1894. D 18 U 13

HISTOIRE LITTÉRAIRE DE LA FRANCE. Tome 31. 4to. Paris, 1893. B 11 S 11 †

HISTORIC CHURCHES OF AMERICA, their Romance and their History ; with full letter text. Fol. Philad. (n.d.) B 44 Q 10 ‡

HISTORICAL MSS. COMMISSION. [See Great Britain and Ireland.]

HISTORICAL REPRINTS. 2 vols. 12mo. Edinb., 1885-86. J 10 P 42, 43
1. Political Creed of a Tory Malecontent.
Duke Hamilton's conditions for surrendering himself.
A Remonstrance ; or, the Declaration of the Lords and Commons, 1642.
A Letter from the Rt. Hon. Ferdinando Lord Fairfax, to His Excellency Robert Earle of Essex.
No Blinde Guides, in answer to a seditions pamphlet of J. Milton's.
Affairs of Scotland in 1680.
News from Dublin in Ireland.
The Rye House Plot.
The Impostor painted in his own colours.
The Reign of William the Conqueror.
2. Genealogy of the Kings of Britain, from Brutus to the Death of Alfred.
Four original Documents relating to the marriage of Henry VIII to Anne of Cleves.
Instructions of Henry VIII for the general visitation of the Monasteries and Nunneries.
Four curious Documents.
Two important State Papers, 1569.
Earl of Heroford's Expedition against Scotland, 1544.
Exact and certaine newes from the Siege at Yorke.
Answer to second manifesto of the Pretender's eldest son.

HISTORY OF MUSIC ; with Methods employed in the New Haven Public Schools. Obl. 12mo. New Haven, Conn., 1893. A 23 P 5

HITCHCOCK, Chas. Henry. Geology of New Hampshire, 3 vols. imp. 8vo., and 1 vol. atlas fol. Concord, 1878. A 12 S 9-11 †

HITCHCOCK, Rev. Dr. Edward. The Religion of Geology and its connected Sciences. 8vo. Glasgow (n.d.) A 24 Q 23

HITCHCOCK, Harvey R. An English-Hawaiian Dictionary. 12mo. San Francisco, 1887. MJ 2 T 47

HITTELL, John S. History of the Mental Growth of Mankind in Ancient Times. 4 vols. 8vo. New York, 1893. A 30 Q 1-4
1. Savagism.
2. Heathen Barbarism.
3. Judea and Greece.
4. Rome and Early Christianity.

Physical and Commercial Geography of Western Washington. Imp. 8vo. (n.p.) 1890. D 15 V 23

HITTELL, Theodore H. History of California. 2 vols 8vo. San Francisco, 1885. B 17 T 11, 12

HOADLY, Dr. Benjamin. The Suspicious Husband : a Comedy. [See London Stage, 2.] H 2 S 34

HOARE, Benjamin. Some Comments on Crime : Irish Catholics and Criminal Statistics. 12mo. Melb., 1888. MF 4 P 5

HOARE, Chas. The Slide-rule, and how to use it. 6th ed. 8vo. Lond., 1890. A 25 S 22

HOARE, E. Wallis. Manual of Veterinary Therapeutics and Pharmacology. 12mo. Lond., 1895. A 33 P 6

HOBART. The Right of the Inhabitants of Hobart Town to an Independent Supply of Pure Water. Roy. 8vo. Hobart (n.d.) MF 1 S 54

HOBART TOWN CHAMBER OF COMMERCE. Rules. 8vo. Hobart, 1874. ME 6 Q

HOBART TOWN RIOTS. Full Account of the, in connection with Pastor Chiniquy's Lectures, together with correspondence from Rev. H. E. M. Watson, suppressed by the *Lyttelton Times*. 8vo. Dunedin, 1879. MG 1 S 25

HOBBES, R. G. Reminiscences of 70 years' Life, Travel, and Adventure ; Military and Civil ; Scientific and Literary. Vol. 1. Soldiering in India. 8vo. Lond., 1893. D 14 T 13

HOBBES, Thos., by Prof. G. C. Robertson. (Philosophical Classics.) 12mo. Edinb., 1886. G 9 V 8

HOBHOUSE, L. T. The Labour Movement. 8vo. Lond., 1893. F 14 Q 38

HOBSON, J. A. Co-operative Labour upon the Land. 8vo. Lond., 1895. F 8 U 45

The Evolution of Modern Capitalism : a Study of Machine Production. 8vo. Lond., 1894. F 9 U 43

HOCKINGS, Albert John. The Flower Garden in Queensland. 12mo. Brisb., 1875. MA 1 P 74

Queensland Garden Manual. 3rd. ed. 12mo. Brisb., 1888. MA 1 P 75

HODDER, Edwin. The History of South Australia. 2 vols. 8vo. Lond., 1893.   MB 1 R 44, 45
[Life of] John Macgregor, "Rob Roy." Illustrated. 8vo. Lond., 1894.   C 15 P 18

HODGE, Frederick Webb. List of Publications of the Bureau of Ethnology, with Index to Authors and Subjects. Roy. 8vo. Wash., 1894.   A 30 U 17

HODGKIN, Dr. Thos. Italy and her Invaders. Vols. 5, 6. 8vo. Oxford, 1895   B 11 S 13, 14
    5. The Lombard Invasion, 553-600.
    6. The Lombard Kingdom, 600-744.

HODGSON, J. The Destiny of the World: an Enquiry concerning the teaching of Scripture relative to the punishment of those who neglect the great salvation. 8vo. Sydney, 1874.   MG 2 S 1

HOEK, Dr. P. P. C. Pyenogonida; Cirripedia. [See Thomson, Sir C. W., and Murray, Dr. J.—Voyage of H.M.S. Challenger.]   A 6 †

HOERNING, Charles Ad. Causes and Cures of our growing Distress. 12mo. Sydney, 1893.   MF 1 P 81

HOFFMAN, Prof. Frank Sargent. The Sphere of the State; or, the People as a Body Politic. 8vo. New York, 1894.   F 14 R 20

HOFFMAN, Dr. Walter Jas. The Beginnings of Writing. 8vo. Lond., 1895.   A 23 R 41

HOFFMANN, G. Christian. Catalogue of Section One of the Geological Survey, Canada, embracing the Systematic Collection of Minerals and Rocks and Specimens, illustrative of Structural Geology. Roy. 8vo. Ottawa, 1893.   A 24 U 17

HOFMAN, Prof. H. O. The Metallurgy of Lead and the Desilverization of Base Bullion. 2nd ed. Roy. 8vo. New York, 1893.   A 24 V 21

HOGAN, Jas. F. Biographical Sketch of the late Most Rev. J. A. Goold; with Portrait. 8vo. Melb, 1886.   MC 1 T 20
The Convict King; being the Life and Adventures of Jorgen Jorgenson. 12mo. Hobart, 1893. MC 1 P 58
Life of Robert Lowe, Viscount Sherbrooke, 8vo. Lond., 1893.   MC 1 P 53

HOGG, E. G. Geological Notes. [See Officer, G.]   ME 1 P

HOGG, James. "The Ettrick Shepherd." Songs and Ballads. 12mo. Glasgow, 1852.   H 10 T 24
The Queen's Wake: a Legendary Poem. 32mo. Lond., 1841.   H 10 T 30

HÖHNEL, Lieut. Ludwig von. Discovery of Lakes Rudolf and Stefanie: a Narrative of Count Samuel Teleki's Exploring and Hunting Expedition in Eastern Equatorial Africa in 1887 and 1888; translated by Nancy Bell (N. D'Anvers). 2 vols. roy. 8vo. Lond., 1894.   D 14 V 11, 12

HOKOR. [See Rusden, H. K.]

HOLCOMB, Dr. Wm. P. Pennsylvania Boroughs. (Johns Hopkins University Studies, 4.) 8vo. Baltimore, 1886   B 18 S 4

HOLCOMBE, Chester. The Real Chinaman. Illustrated. 8vo. Lond., 1895.   B 33 Q 2

HOLCROFT, Thos. Deaf and Dumb; or, the Orphan Protected: an Historical Drama. [See London Stage, 1.]   H 2 S 34
The Deserted Daughter: a Comedy. [See London Stage, C.]   H 2 S 35
Duplicity: a Comedy, [See London Stage, 4.] H 2 S 33
The Follies of a Day: a Comedy [See London Stage, 2.]   H 2 S 34
He's Much to Blame: a Comedy [See London Stage, 4.]   H 2 S 35
The Road to Ruin: a Comedy. [See London Stage, 1.]   H 2 S 33
The School for Arrogance: a Comedy. [See London Stage, 4.]   H 2 S 36
Seduction: a Comedy. [See London Stage, 4.] H 2 S 36

HOLDEN, Dr. Edwin S. The Mogul Emperors of Hindustan, 1398-1707. 8vo. Lond., 1895.   B 29 T 6

HOLDEN, Frances Gillam. Trained Nursing. 12mo. Sydney, 1882.   MA 2 P 78

HOLE, Very Rev. Samuel Reynolds. Book about Roses; how to grow and show them. 12th ed. 12mo. Lond., 1892.   A 18 R 12
The Memories of Dean Hole. 8vo. Lond., 1892.   C 8 Q 14
More Memories: being Thoughts about England spoken in America. 8vo. Lond., 1894.   F 14 U 4

HOLE, Wm. Auld Licht Idylls. Illustrated. [See Barrie, J. M.]   J 2 U 26

HOLLAND, Philemon. Plutarch's Romane Questions. [See Plutarch.]   B 30 Q 18

HOLLAND, Robt. Glossary of Words used in the County of Chester. (Eng. Dialect Soc., 16.) 8vo. Lond., 1886.   E

HOLLANDER, J. H. The Cincinnatti Southern Railway: a Study in Municipal Activity. (Johns Hopkins Univ. Studies, 12.) Roy. 8vo. Baltimore, 1894. B 18 S 12

HOLM, Adolph. History of Greece, from its commencement to the close of the independence of the Greek Nation; translated from the German. Vol. 1. 8vo. Lond., 1894.   B 27 S 21

HOLMAN, J. G. Abroad and at Home: a Comic Opera. [See London Stage, 4.]   H 2 S 36
The Votary of Wealth: a Comedy. [See London Stage, 4.]   H 2 S 36

HOLMES, James. [Life of]; by A. T. Story. 8vo. Lond., 1894. C 21 R 17

HOLMES, Oliver Wendell. At my Fireside; with Portrait. [See Blathwayt, R.—Interviews.] J 10 U 34
[Life of]; by W. Jerrold. 12mo. Lond., 1893. C 10 P 4
Sketch of. [See Noble, J. Ashcroft.—Impressions and Memories.] J 10 Q 10
Sketch of. [See Smalley, G. W.—Studies of Men.] C 19 R 20

HOLMES, Dr. P. Writings of Tertullian. [See Tertullianus, Q. S. F.] G 11 U and 14 U

HOLMES, Wm. Henry. An Ancient Quarry in Indian Territory. Roy. 8vo. Wash., 1894. A 30 U 18

HOLMES, W. M. Sponge-remains, New Zealand. [See Hinde, Dr. G. L.] E

HOLROYD, Arthur Todd. Prickly Comfrey; its History, Cultivation, &c. 8vo. Sydney, 1876. MA 1 Q 54

HOLT, Thos. Two Speeches on Education in New South Wales. 8vo. Sydney, 1857. MG 1 R 10
The Water Supply of the City of Sydney. 8vo. Sydney (n.d.) MA 3 T 31

HOLUB, Emil. The Zambesi Region. [See Great Explorers.] D 15 V 21, 22

HOLYOAKE, George Jacob. Co-operation and Socialism. [See Subjects of the Day, 2.] F 7 U 27
History of the Rockdale Pioneers. 12mo. Lond., 1893. F 14 Q 28
Public Speaking and Debate. 8vo. Lond. (n.d.) J 4 P 34
Sixty Years of an Agitator's Life. 2 vols. 8vo. Lond., 1892. C 14 T 24, 25

HOMBRON, J. B. Australie et Papouasie : Comparaison de la côte de la Nouvelle-Hollande et de la côte de la Nouvelle-Guinée ; des races noires qui les habitent. 8vo. (n.p.) 1846. MD 8 Q 31
Malaisie. Les Montagnes d'Amboine. Des Races Malaise et Polynésiennes. 8vo. (n.p.n.d.) MA 3 R 39

HOME, Hon. Henry. [See Kames, Lord.]

HOME AND TRAINING SCHOOL FOR NURSES FOR THE SICK, SYDNEY. 5th and 6th Annual Reports. 12mo. Sydney, 1887-89. ME 5 Q

HOME VISITING AND RELIEF SOCIETY. 26th and 27th Annual Reports. 12mo. Sydney, 1888-89. ME 5 Q

HOMER. Homer and the Epic. [See Lang, A.] J 4 Q 36
Iliad, Book 1. (Greek Text.) Melb., 1876. MH 1 U 36
Iliad of Homer. Translated by A. Pope, and illustrated by J. Flaxman. 2 vols. 8vo. Lond., 1853. H 9 U 4, 5
The Iliad of. Translated by A. Pope; with Notes by the Rev. J. T. Watson. Illustrated with Flaxman's Designs. 12mo. Lond., 1866. H 9 P 14
Iliad. Translated by G. Chapman. Illustrated. 4to. Lond., 1887. H 15 P 11 †
The Odyssey of. Translated by A. Pope; with Notes by the Rev. J. S. Watson. Illustrated with Flaxman's Designs. 12mo. Lond., 1866. H 9 P 13

HOMOLLE, Théophile. Les Archives de l'intendance sacrée à Délos, 315-166 B.C. 8vo. Paris, 1887. G 16 U 24

HONE, Wm. Some Account of the Conversion from Atheism to Christianity of. 12mo. Lond., 1817. G 4 V 14

HONEY, W. R. Glaucus : a drama. 8vo. Hobart, 1870. MH 1 Q 20

HONORE, Carlos. Loi du Rayonnement Solaire et ses Principales Conséquences. Imp. 8vo. Montevideo, 1894. A 30 V 17
Polaires Thermiques du Soleil. Imp. 8vo. Montevideo, 1895. A 30 V 17

HOOD, J. T. Manual of the Law and Practice of Trade Marks Registration in Victoria. 8vo. Melb., 1892. MF 3 T 42

HOOD, Thomas. Poems of Wit and Humour. 8th ed. 2mo. Lond., 1858. H 10 T 23
Whims and Oddities in Prose and Verse. 12mo. Lond., 1857. J 11 Q 2
Sketch of the work of. [See Dawson, W. J.—Makers of Modern English.] H 10 S 14

HOOD, Thomas. [Son of the preceding.] Practical Guide to English Versification 4th ed. 12mo. Lond., 1892. H 10 T 17
Pen and Pencil Pictures. 2nd ed. 8vo. Lond., 1857. J 8 U 5

HOOD, Thomas Cockburn. Observations and Suggestions regarding the Pacific Region in the Past and Present. Lond., 1850. MA 1 S 27

HOOK, Rev. Dr. Walter F. Hear the Church : a Sermon. 12mo. 5th ed. Lond., 1838. G 4 V 14
Another Copy. 12mo. Sydney, 1839. MG 2 R 56

HOOKER, Sir Joseph Dalton. Botany. [See Le Maout, E.] A 20 V 20
On the Cedars of Lebanon, &c. 8vo. Lond., 1862. MA 2 T 31

HOOKER, Richard. Life of. [See Walton, Izaak.] C 19 V 6

HOOKER, Sir Wm. Jackson, and BAKER, John G. Synopsis Filicum; or, a Synopsis of all known Ferns. 2nd ed. 8vo. Lond., 1883.   A 20 T 13

HOOPER, Miss M. S. Synopsis of the History of Geography. (Roy. Geog. Soc. Australasia, Vic. Branch, 7.) 8vo. Melb., 1889.   ME 20

HOOPER, Miss S. H. Paris International Geographical Congress. (Roy. Geog. Soc. Australasia, Vic. Branch, 7.) 8vo. Melb., 1889.   ME 20

HOOPER, Wynnard. The Influence of State Borrowing on Commercial Crises. (A Policy of Free Exchange.) 8vo. Lond., 1894.   F 14 S 26

HOOS, Conrad. The New Zealand Practical Agriculturist. 8vo. Dunedin, 1882.   MA 1 P 55

HOPE, Mrs. The First Divorce of Henry VIII, as told in the State Papers. Edited by Rev. F. A. Gasquet. 8vo. Lond., 1894.   B 24 Q 6

HOPE, I. [See Bromfield, James.]

HOPE, Robt. C. The Legendary Lore of the Holy Wells of England. 8vo. Lond., 1893.   B 21 T 16

HOPKINS, F. R. C. The Australian Ladies' Annual. 4to. Melb., 1878.   MJ 2 S 40
Confessions of a Cynic. 12mo. Echuca, 1882.   MG 1 P 76

HOPKINS, George M. Experimental Science; Elementary, Practical, and Experimental Physics. Illustrated. Roy. 8vo. New York, 1890.   A 29 V 26

HOPKINS, Manley. A Manual of Marine Insurance. 8vo. Lond., 1867.   F 7 R 21

HOPKINS, Matthew, Witchfinder. [Life of]; by J. O Jones. (Lives of Twelve Bad Men.) 8vo. Lond., 1894.   C 18 T 9

HOPKINS, Prof. W. J. Telephone Lines and their Properties. 8vo. Lond., 1893.   A 5 R 44

HOPKINSON, Dr. Joseph. Dynamo Machinery and allied subjects. 12mo. New York, 1893.   A 21 R 28

HORACE MANN SCHOOL. Brief Circular of Information. 8vo. New York, 1893.   E

HORATIUS FLACCUS, Quintus. Odes of. Translated by W. E. Gladstone. 8vo. Lond., 1894.   H 7 U 27
[Works of] translated. [See Lytton, Lord.]   H 9 U 1

HORDEN, Rt. Rev. J. Indians and Eskimo. [See Batty, Beatrice.]   D 15 Q 20

HORDER, W. Garrett. The Hymn Lover: an Account of the Rise and Growth of English Hymnody. 8vo. Lond., 1889.   G 8 S 35

HORE, Capt. Edward C. How I went to Lake Tanganyika. (Roy. Geog. Soc. Australasia, Vic. Branch, 8.) 8vo. Melb., 1891.   ME 20

HORN, H. Yacht Racing in 1893. [See Sullivan, Sir E.]   A 29 Q 41

HORNBROOK RAGGED SCHOOL ASSOCIATION. Seventh Annual Report. 8vo. Melb. (n.d.)   MG 2 Q 48

HORNE, Herbert P. The Binding of Books: an Essay in the History of Gold-tooled Bindings. 8vo. Lond., 1894.   A 25 P 9

HORNE, Richard Henry Hengist. Ballad Romances. 12mo. Lond. (n.d.)   H 3 P 40
Bible Tragedies: John the Baptist; or, the Valour of the Soul.—Rahman, the Apocryphal Book of Job's Wife.—Judas Iscariot, a mystery 8vo. Lond. (n.d.)   H 1 Q 8
Cosmo de' Medici: an Historical Tragedy, and other Poems. 8vo. Lond., 1875.   H 2 S 32
The Dreamer and the Worker: a Story of the Present Time. 2 vols. 8vo. Lond., 1852.   J 6 P 22, 23
Exposition of the False Medium and Barriers excluding Men of Genius from the public. 12mo. Lond., 1833.   J 6 Q 39
The Good-natured Bear, &c. 12mo. Lond. (n.d.)   J 6 P 29
The Great Peace-maker: a sub-marine dialogue. 12mo. Lond., 1871.   H 8 Q 34
Gregory VII: a Tragedy. 2nd ed. 8vo. Lond., 1840.   H 2 T 30
Laura Dibalzo; or, the Patriot Martyrs: a Tragedy. 12mo. Lond., 1880.   H 8 R 30
New Spirit of the Age. 2 vols. 12mo. Lond., 1844.   C 13 Q 15, 16
Orion: an Epic Poem. 12mo. Lond., 1872.   H 8 Q 44
The Poor Artist; or, Seven Eye-sights and One Object. 2nd edition. 12mo. Lond., 1871.   J 6 P 21
Spirit of Peers and People: a National tragi-comedy. 8vo. Lond., 1834.   H 1 Q 4

HORNE, Thos. Hartwell. Introduction to the Study of Bibliography, to which is prefixed a Memoir on the Public Libraries of the Antients. Illustrated 2 vols. 8vo Lond., 1814.   K 17 R 25, 26

HORSBURGH, E. L. S. Waterloo: a Narrative and a Criticism. 8vo. Lond., 1895.   B 23 S 8

HORSLEY, Dr. Victor A. H. Chapter upon Cranio-Cerebral Topography. [See Royal Irish Academy.— Cunningham Memoirs, 2.]   E

HORT, Rev. Dr. Fenton J. A. Prolegomena to St. Paul's Epistles to the Romans and the Ephesians. 8vo. Lond., 1895.   G 1 U 20

HORTENSE, Queen. [See Elliot, Frances — Roman Gossip.]   C 21 Q 10

HORTICULTURAL MAGAZINE AND GARDENERS' AND AMATEURS' CALENDAR. Parts 31 and 33, July and Sept., 1866. 8vo. Sydney, 1866.   ME 3 R

HORTICULTURAL SOCIETY OF NEW SOUTH WALES. 2nd and 3rd Annual Reports. 8vo. Sydney, 1888–89. ME 6 S
Grand Autumn Show of Fruit, Plants, and Flowers, 1889. Prize Schedule. 8vo. Sydney, 1889. ME 6 S
Schedule of Prizes for the Spring Rose Show, 1890. 8vo. Sydney, 1890. ME 6 S
Schedule of Prizes for the Autumn Chrysanthemum Show, 1891. 8vo. Sydney, 1891. ME 6 S
Official Catalogue, Autumn Exhibition and Flower and Fruit Show, 1890. 8vo. Sydney, 1890. ME 6 S

HORTICULTURAL SOCIETY OF SYDNEY. Transactions of. [*See Horticultural Magazine*.] ME 8 S

HORTICULTURAL SOCIETY OF VICTORIA. Report for 1884. 8vo. Melb., 1884. ME 6 S
List of Fruits grown at the Gardens, Richmond Park. 8vo. Melb., 1884. MA 1 P 60

HORTON, R. F. Proverbs. [*See* Expositor's Bible.] G 19 R 17

HOSKING, Rev. John. God's Aristocracy in Rags, and Stray Thoughts for Spare Moments. 8vo. Ballarat, 1887. MG 1 P 75

HOSMER, Prof. Jas. Kendall. Samuel Adams, the Man of the Town-Meeting. (Johns Hopkins University Studies, 2.) 8vo. Baltimore, 1884. B 18 S 2

HOTHAM, Sir Charles. Copy of Despatch [Report on Financial State of Victoria on the Proclamation of the New Constitution.] Sm. fol. Lond., 1856. MF 3 U 20

HOTTEN, John C. History of Signboards. [*See* Larwood, J.] B 35 Q 4

HOUDIN, Jean E. R-. Memoirs of; written by himself. 3rd ed. 12mo. Lond., 1860. C 21 P 2

HOUFE, Chas. A. The Question of the Houses. 12mo. Lond., 1895. F 12 S 8

HOUGHTON, Louise Seymour. Life of St. Francis of Assisi. [*See* Sabatier, P.] C 14 S 19

HOUGHTON, Robert, Lord. Stray Verses, 1889–90. 2nd ed. 12mo. Lond., 1893. H 8 P 45

HOUSMAN, Laurence. Essay on Blake. [*See* Blake, Wm.] H 10 P 30

HOUSTON, Prof. Edwin J. Electric Transmission of Intelligence, and other advanced Primers of Electricity. 12mo. New York, 1893. A 21 P 29
Electrical Measurements and other advanced primers of Electricity. 8vo. New York, 1893. A 21 P 31
Electricity and Magnetism. 12mo. New York, 1893. A 21 R 26
Electricity 100 years ago and to-day. 12mo. New York, 1894. A 21 R 25
Dictionary of Electrical Words, Terms, and Phrases. Roy. 8vo. New York, 1894. A 21 V 19

HOUSTON, Mrs. M. C. A Woman's Memories of World-known Men. 3rd ed. 8vo. Lond., 1883. C 21 Q 7

HOUSTON, Margaret G. Trial of. [*See* Hall, T.] MF 1 S 47

HOUTMAN, Frederick. Gebleven op de *Abrioolhos*. [*See* Polsaert, F. — Ongeluckige Voyagie van 't schip *Batavia*.] D 20 R 6

HOVELL, Joseph. Practical Manager's Slide-rule Companion. 12mo. Dundee, 1886. A 25 P 23

HOVELL, Capt. Wm. H., and HUME, Henry. Journal of Discovery to Port Phillip, New South Wales, in 1824 and 25. [Reprint.] (Roy. Geog. Soc. Australasia, Vic. Branch, 11.) 8vo. Melb., 1894. ME 20

HOW, Wm. Field. Treatment of Manufactured Iron and Steel for Constructional Purposes. (Journal Roy. Soc., N.S.W., 27.) 8vo. Sydney, 1893. ME 1 R

HOW to relieve the Poor of Edinburgh and other great cities without increasing pauperism. 8vo. Melb., 1868. MG 2 Q 48

HOWARD, B. Douglas. Life with Trans-Siberian Savages. 8vo. Lond., 1893. D 17 Q 30

HOWARD, Dr. G. S. New Royal Encyclopædia and Cyclopædia or Dictionary of Arts and Sciences. 3 vols. fol. Lond., 1788. K 6 P 8-10 ‡

HOWARD, Lord George. Sketch of. [*See* Southey, R. —English Seamen.] B 29 S 15

HOWARD, Prof. George E. An Introduction to the Local Constitutional History of the United States. (Johns Hopkins University Studies, extra vol. 4.) 8vo. Baltimore, 1889. B 18 T 4

HOWARD, John Eliot. Examination of the Belfast Address of the British Association, 1874, from a scientific point of view. 8vo. Lond., 1875. A 20 T 33

HOWARD, Dr. Joseph J. [*See* Miscellanea Genealogica.] E

—— and CRISP, Frederick A. Visitation of England and Wales. Vol. 2. Sm. fol. Lond., 1894. K 13 T 6 †

HOWARD, Maj.-Gen. Oliver O. [Life of] Isabella of Castile. Illustrated. 8vo. New York, 1894. C 14 S 25

HOWARD ASSOCIATION. Pamphlets issued by. 8vo. Lond. (n.d.) F 11 U 35

HOWCHIN, Walter. Fossil Foraminifera from the Government Boring at Hergott, with General Remarks on the Section, and on other forms of Microzoa observed therein. (Trans. Roy. Soc., S. Australia, 8.) 8vo. Adelaide, 1886. ME 1 S
Tarkaninna and Mirrabuckinna Borings. (Trans. Roy. Soc., S. Australia, 17.) 8vo. Adelaide, 1893. ME 1 S

HOWE, E. G. Systematic Science Teaching. 12mo. New York, 1895. G 17 Q 48

HOWE, Elias. Sketch of. [*See* Hubert, P. G.—Inventors.] C 17 R 3

HOWE, H. M. The Metallurgy of Steel. Vol. 1. 3rd ed. 4to. New York, 1894. A 38 P 21 ‡

HOWE, Joseph. A Letter to the Rt Hon. C. B. Adderley, M.P., on the Relations of England with her Colonies. 8vo. Lond., 1868. MJ 3 Q 15

HOWE, Mrs. Julia Ward. Interview, with Portrait. [*See* Blathwayt, R.—Interviews.] J 10 U 34

HOWE, W. W. Plan of the Town and Suburbs of Melbourne. Fol. Melb., 1843. MD 3 Q 7 ‡

HOWE, Wm. W. Municipal History of New Orleans. (Johns Hopkins University Studies, 7.) Baltimore, 1889. B 18 S 7

HOWELL, Andrew. The General Statutes of the State of Michigan to 1890. 3 vols roy. 8vo. Chicago, 1882-90. F 7 U 2-4

HOWELL, H. Spencer. An Island Paradise, and Reminiscences of Travel. 8vo. Toronto, 1892. MD 5 S 24

HOWELLS, Wm. D. A Talk with; with Portrait. [*See* Blathwayt, R.—Interviews.] J 10 U 34

HOWITT, A. W. The Diorites and Granites of Swift's Creek and their contact zones, with Notes on the Auriferous Deposits. (Roy. Soc., Vic., 16.) 8vo. Melb., 1880. ME 1 P

Notes on the Diabase Rocks of the Buchan District. (Roy. Soc., Vict., 18.) 8vo. Melb., 1882. ME 1 P

The Rocks of Noyang. (Roy. Soc., Vict., 20.) 8vo. Melb., 1884. ME 1 P

Sedimentary, Metamorphic, and Igneous Rocks of Enany, (Roy. Soc., Vict., 22.) Melb., 1886. ME 1 P

The Rocks of Noyang. 8vo. Melb., 1883. MA 3 S 46

HOWLEY, Most Rev. Wm. Sketch of. [*See* Fowler, Rev. M.—Notable Archbishops.] C 13 V 12

HOWORTH, Sir Henry H. The Glacial Nightmare and Flood: a second appeal to common sense, from the extravagance of some recent Geology. 2 vols. 8vo. Lond, 1893. A 24 T 16, 17

HOYLE, Wm. Evans. Cephalopoda. [*See* Thomson, Sir C. W., and Murray, Dr. J.—Voyage of H.M.S. Challenger.] A 6 †

HUBERT, Philip G. Inventors. (Men of Achievement.) 8vo. Lond., 1894. C 17 R 3

HUBRECHT, Prof. A. A. W. Nemertea. [*See* Thomson, C. W., and Murray, Dr. J.—Voyage of H.M.S. Challenger.—Zoology.] A 6 †

HUDSON, W. H. Idle Days in Patagonia. 8vo. Lond., 1893. D 4 P 53

The Naturalist in La Plata. 8vo. Lond., 1895. A 28 V 20

HUDSON, Wm. Henry. Introduction to the Philosophy of Herbert Spencer. 8vo. Lond., 1895. G 2 U 8

HUFELAND, C. W. Art of Prolonging Life; edited by E. Wilson, F.R.S. 12mo. Lond., 1853. A 26 P 10

HUGGINS, Samuel. The Course and Current of Architecture: being an Historical Account of the Origin, successive and simultaneous Developments, Relations, Periods, and Characteristics of its various known styles. 8vo. Lond., 1863. A 19 R 3

HUGHAN, F. M. Ambition: a sarcastic Poem. 8vo. Geelong, 1855. MH 1 S 71

HUGHES, D. A. Statement of facts respecting negotiation and agreement for lease of wharf premises between the Government and D. A. Hughes. 8vo. Melb., 1854. MF 4 Q 19

HUGHES, Herbert W. Text-book of Coal-mining, for the use of colliery managers and others. 8vo. Lond., 1892. A 24 T 19

HUGHES, John [1677-1720]. The Siege of Damascus: a Tragedy. [*See* London Stage, 3.] H 2 S 35

HUGHES, John. Ceylon Coffee Soils and Manures. 8vo. Lond., 1879. A 18 S 37

HUGHSON, Shirley C. The Carolina Pirates and Colonial Commerce, 1670-1740. (Johns Hopkins Univ. Studies, 12.) Roy. 8vo. Baltimore, 1894. B 18 S 12

HUGO, Victor Marie, Vicomte. Napoleon the Little. 12mo. Lond., 1852. C 17 P 12

Notre-Dame de Paris. Imp. 8vo. Paris (n.d.) J 7 V 13

A Biographical Sketch; by A. Villemal. With an Ode to Victor Hugo, by F. J. Broomfield. 12mo. Sydney, 1895. MC 1 S 17

HUISH, Marcus Bourne. The Year's Art, 1893-95: a concise Epitome of all matters relating to the Arts of Painting, Sculpture, and Architecture. 3 vols. 8vo. Lond., 1893-95. E

HULL, A. A. Queensland, as it was and as it is. (Roy. Geograph. Soc. of Australasia, Q. Branch, 1.) 8vo. Brisbane, 1886. ME 20

HULL, Prof. Edward. Volcanoes, Past and Present. 8vo. Lond., 1892. A 24 Q 21

HULL, Hugh M. The Statute Index, Tasmania, 1877. Sm. fol. Hobart, 1877. ME

The Statute Index, Tasmania, 1880. Sm. fol. Hobart, 1880. ME

HULL, Nora. Official Records of the Centennial: Bath, Stouben County, New York, June, 1893. 8vo. Bath, N.Y., 1893.   B 20 S 6

HUMAN LIFE: an Inquiry touching the duty of the State in relation to pauper children; by "An Eclectic." 8vo. Sydney, 1877.   MF 4 R 2

HULME, F. Edward. The Birth and Development of Ornament. 8vo. Lond., 1893.   A 23 Q 38

———— and HIBBERD, Shirley. Familiar Garden Flowers. 1st—5th Series. 5 vols. 8vo. Lond. (n.d.)   A 20 Q 7-11

HUME, David. An Enquiry concerning the Human Understanding, and an Enquiry concerning the Principles of Morals. Reprinted from the posthumous edition of 1777, and edited by L. A. Selby-Bigge. 12mo. Oxford, 1894.   G 16 Q 41

Life and Philosophy of. [*See* Huxley, Prof.—Essays, 6.]   J 11 P 40

HUME, Fergus W. Professor Brankel's Secret: a psychological study. 12mo. Melb. (n.d.)   MJ 1 Q 52

HUME, Henry. Journal of Discovery, &c. [*See* Hovell, W. H.*]   ME 2 Q

HUME, Joseph. Letter to Lieut.-Gen. R. Darling, late Governor of New South Wales. 8vo. Lond., 1832.   MB 2 Q 53

HUMES of Polwarth, The. [*See* Warrender, M.]   C 17 S 6

HUMPHREY, James E. Botanical Microtechnique. [*See* Zimmermann, Dr. A.]   A 20 T 11

HUMPHREYS, H. Morin-. Boot and Saddle: Bits of South African Life in Bush and Barracks. 12mo. Melb., 1875.   MD 8 P 26

HUNT, Gaillard. The Department of State of the United States: its History and Functions. 8vo. Washington, 1893.   F 3 R 15

HUNT, Henry Ambrose. Essay on Southerly Busters. (Journal Roy. Soc. N.S.W., 28.) 8vo. Sydney, 1894.   ME 1 R

HUNT, John. Life of; by G. S. Rowe. 12mo. Lond., 1860   MC 1 P 46

HUNT, James Henry Leigh. An Answer to the Question, What is Poetry? including Remarks on Versification. Edited by Prof. A. S. Cook. 12mo. Boston, 1893.   H 9 Q 17

Poetical Works of. 12mo. Lond., 1860.   H 10 T 33

A Tale for a Chimney Corner, and other Essays. 12mo. Lond. (n.d.)   J 16 T 32

HUNT, Dr. Thos. Sterry. A New Basis for Chemistry: a Chemical Philosophy. 4th ed. 8vo. New York, 1892.   A 21 P 34

Systematic Mineralogy based on a National Classification. 2nd ed. 8vo. New York, 1892.   A 24 V 16

HUNTER, Dr. Chas. D. What kills our Babies? 8vo. Melb., 1878.   MA 2 S 68

Another Copy. [*See* Australian Health Society.]   MA 3 S 33

HUNTER, George. Journal of an Expedition from Kappa Kappa to the Heads of the Kemp Welch River. (Roy. Geograph. Soc. of Australasia, Q. Branch, 2.) 8vo. Brisbane, 1887.   ME 20

HUNTER, Rev. Dr. Henry. Sacred Biography: a Course of Lectures on the principal characters mentioned in the Old Testament, and on the principal events in the life of Jesus Christ. 8vo. Edinb., 1841.   G 3 R 4

HUNTER, John. Life of; by Dr. G. R. Mather. Sm. 4to. Glasgow, 1893.   C 13 S 25

HUNTER, Jos. Familiæ Minorum Gentium. [*See* Harleian Soc. Pubs., 37, 38.]   E

HUNTER, Dr. Wm. [Life of]; by Dr. G. R. Mather. Sm. 4to. Glasgow, 1893.   C 13 S 25

HUNTER, Sir Wm. Wilson. Ancient Civilization and Modern Education in India. [*See* Subjects of the Day, 1.]   G 18 S 18

Bengal MS. Records: a selected list of 14,136 letters in the Board of Revenue, Calcutta, 1782-1807. 4 vols. 8vo. Lond., 1894.   F 14 S 29-32

Brief History of the Indian Peoples. 20th ed. 8vo. Oxford, 1893.   B 29 Q 21

The Indian Empire; its peoples, history, and products. 3rd ed. 8vo. Lond., 1893.   D 17 V 1

Orissa. 2 vols. 8vo. Lond., 1872.   B 29 U 8, 9

HURST, Dr. C. Herbert. Practical Zoology. [*See* Marshall, Dr. A. M.]   A 28 P 31

HURST, George H. Painters' Colours, Oils and Varnishes: a practical manual. 8vo. Lond., 1892.   A 25 R 7

HURST, J. The Chinese Question in Australia. 8vo. Sydney, 1880.   MF 4 R 36

Objects and Intentions of the Mutual Trade Protection Association of South Australia. 12mo. Adelaide, 1879.   MF 4 P 19

HUSMANN, George. American Grape-growing and Wine-making. 8vo. New York, 1892.   A 18 Q 36

Grape Culture and Wine-making in California. 8vo. San Francisco, 1888.   A 18 R 40

HUSON, T. Round about Helvellyn. 24 Plates. Sm. 4to. Lond., 1895.   D 42 S 18 ‡

HUSS, George Martin. Rational Building. [*See* Viollet-le-Duc, E. E.]   A 19 V 24

HUSS, John. [*See* Bettany, G. T.—Popular History of the Reformation.]   G 14 Q 33

HUSTON, Judge H. Right of Appropriation and the Colorado system of Laws in regard to Irrigation. 18mo. Denver, 1893.   F 12 S 7

HUTCHINSON, G. W. Caldwell. Some Hints on Learning to Draw. Roy. 8vo. Lond., 1893.   A 8 U 32

HUTCHINSON, Rev. H. N. Extinct Monsters: a popular account of some of the larger forms of ancient animal life. 8vo. Lond., 1892.   A 24 S 5

HUTCHINSON, Dr. Thos. Jos. Narrative of the Niger, Tshadda, and Binuë Exploration. 12mo. Lond., 1855.   D 14 P 12

HUTSON, B. Does the Bible teach conditional immortality? [See Brown, G. A.]   MG 1 S 74

HUTTON, A. W. Young's Tour in Ireland. [See Young, A.]   D 18 P 10, 11

HUTTON, Capt. Frederick W. On the axial skeleton in the *Dinornithidæ*. (Trans. N.Z. Inst., 27.) 8vo. Wellington, 1894.   ME 2 R
Report on the Geology of the Thames Gold-field. 8vo. Wellington, 1867.   MA 2 Q 61

HUTTON, Laurence. Portraits in Plaster. Roy. 8vo. New York, 1894.   A 23 V 13

HUTTON, Richard Holt. Criticisms on Contemporary Thought and Thinkers, selected from the *Spectator*. 2 vols. 12mo. Lond., 1894.   J 6 P 33, 34
[Life of] Robert Browning. [See Masson, Prof. D.—In the Footsteps of the Poets.]   J 6 R 43

HUTTON, Wm. Life of. Sm. 4to. Lond, 1841.   C 17 P 15

HUTTON, Rev. Wm. Holden. The Household of Sir Thomas More. [See More, Sir T.]   C 19 V 15
[Life of] the Marquess Wellesley, K.G. (Rulers of India.) 8vo. Oxford, 1893.   C 13 P 14

HUXLEY, Rt. Hon. Prof. Thos. Henry. Collected Essays. 9 vols. 12mo. Lond., 1894   J 11 P 35-43
   1. Method and Result.
   2. Darwiniana.
   3. Science and Education.
   4. Science and Hebrew Tradition.
   5. Science and Christian Tradition.
   6. Hume: with helps to the Study of Berkeley.
   7. Man's Place in Nature and other Anthropological Essays.
   8. Discourses, Biological and Geological.
   9. Evolution and Ethics.
Correspondence with. [See Youmans, E. L.]   C 16 R 21
Essay on Owen's position in Anatomical Science. [See Owen, Sir Richard—Life of.]   C 21 Q 16, 17
Evolution and Ethics. (Romanes Lecture, 1893.) 8vo. Lond., 1893   G 2 Q 32
Social Diseases, and Worse Remedies. 12mo. Lond. 1891.   F 7 V 15

HUXLEY, Rt. Hon. Prof. Thos. Henry, and PELSENEER, Prof. P. Report on the Specimen of the Genus Spirula collected by H.M.S. *Challenger*. [See Thomson, Sir C. W.—Scientific Results of Voyage of H.M.S. *Challenger*.]   A G 8 †

HUYSHE, Wentworth. The Liberation of Bulgaria: War Notes in 1877. Illustrated. 8vo. Lond., 1894.   B 25 T 15

HYACINTHE, Rev. Father. [See Loyson, Rev. H.]

HYATT Prof. Alpheus. Genera of Fossil Cephalopoda. 8vo. (n.p.n.d.)   A 20 T 17

HYDE, Rev. Dr. C. M. Father Damien: an open Letter to Rev. Dr. Hyde from R. L. Stevenson. [See Stevenson, R. L.]   MC 1 S 14

HYDE, Dr. Douglas. Revival of Irish Literature. [See Duffy, Sir C. G.]   J 7 P 45
The Story of Early Gaelic Literature. 18mo. Lond., 1895.   J 16 T 42

HYDE, Prof. Edward Wyllys. Skew Arches. 18mo. New York, 1875.   A 22 P 16

HYDE, Dr. James Nevins. Practical Treatise on Diseases of the Skin. 2nd ed. Roy. 8vo. Philad., 1888.   A 33 T 7

HYDE, Rev. Dr. Wm. De Witt Outlines of Social Theology. 8vo. New York, 1895.   G 15 R 29

HYMAN, Coleman P. Account of the Coins, Coinages, and Currency of Australasia. Roy. 8vo. Sydney, 1893.*   MA 2 Q 32
Catalogue of Coins, Coinages, and Currency of Australasia, with Specimens of Medals. Roy. 8vo. Sydney, 1893.   MA 2 Q 34

HYNDMAN, Frederick Arthur. Vindication of the English Constitution. [See Beaconsfield, Earl of.]   F 7 V 30

HYSLOP, Dr. T. B. Mental Physiology, especially in its relations to Mental Disorders. 8vo. Lond., 1895.   G 3 R 13

I

IBBETSON, Sir H. S. Copies of further Letters on the Gothenburg Licensing System. Fol. Lond., 1877.   F 30 U 2 ‡
Copies of Report of the Municipality of Stockholm, relating to the Gothenburg Scheme. Fol. Lond., 1877.   F 30 U 3 ‡

IBBETSON, John Holt. Specimens of Eccentric Circular Turning. 3rd ed. 8vo. Lond., 1851.   A 25 S 2

IBERVILLE, P. le M., Sieur d'. [See D'Iberville, P. le M.]

IBIS, The; a quarterly journal of Ornithology. 6th Series. Vols. 4-6. 8vo. Lond., 1892-94.   E

IBSEN, Henrik. Brand: a Dramatic Poem. Translated, with an Introduction and Notes, by Dr. C. H. Herford. 8vo. Lond. 1894.   H 4 P 38
Account of. [*See* Tweedie, Mrs. A.]   D 18 T 15
Commentary on the Writings of. [*See* Boyesen, H. H.]   J 4 Q 12

ICERYA PURCHASI, The, and its cure (*Vedalia cardinalis*). 8vo. Wellington, 1891.   MA 3 R 44

ICONOCLAST. [*See* New South Wales Municipal Assoc.]

IDAHO. Gem of the Mountains [a Hand-book.] 4to. St. Paul, Minn., 1893.   D 12 U 6 †
Description of Resources. 12mo. St. Louis, 1893.   D 15 Q 23
Southern Idaho: a few Words about a Fertile Land. 12mo. Seattle, 1893.   A 18 P 11

IDDINGS, Joseph P. Rock-making Minerals. [*See* Rosenbusch, H.]   A 24 A 29

IDELL, F. E. Chimneys and Chimney Draught. [*See* Armstrong, R.]   A 19 P 4

IGNORAMI LAMENTATIO super Legis Communis, translationum ex Latino in Anglicum. Sm. fol. Lond., 1736.   H 30 Q 13 ‡

IGNORANT LEARNED: proving that Theology, Mythology, Astronomy, and Free Masonry are Sciences unknown to our modern scholars; by "Henricus." 8vo. Lond., 1863.   MJ 2 S 9

ILLIDGE, T. On *Ceratodus Fosteri*. (Proc. Roy. Soc., Queensland, 10.) 8vo. Brisbane, 1893.   ME 1 T

ILLINGWORTH, J. R. Personality, Human and Divine. (Bampton Lectures, 1894.) 8vo. Lond., 1894.   G 5 R 32

ILLINOIS—*State Departments, Reports, and Publications*. Board of Trade. 35th Annual Report. 8vo. Chicago, 1893.   E
Geological Survey. Vol. 8.—Geology and Palæontology. Text and Plates. 2 vols. Imp. 8vo. Springfield, 1890.   E
Institution for the Education of the Blind. Brief History, 1849-93. 8vo. Chicago, 1893.   G 18 R 41

ILLINOIS UNIVERSITY. Report of the Board of Trustees, 1894. 8vo. Springfield, Ill., 1894.   E

ILLUSTRATED AMERICAN, The. Jan.–June, 1894. 4to. New York, 1894.   E

ILLUSTRATED BOOK OF SCOTTISH SONGS. 8vo. Lond. (n.d.)   H 9 U 6

ILLUSTRATED LONDON NEWS. Vols. 101-106. Fol. Lond., 1892-95.   E

ILLUSTRATED SYDNEY NEWS ALMANAC for 1869. 8vo. Sydney, 1869.   ME 4 U

IMAGINARY DIALOGUES IN CAMBRIDGE. 12mo. Lond., 1866.   MJ 1 S 47

IMBERT DE SAINT-AMAND, Arthur Léon, Baron. The Revolution of 1848. 8vo. Lond., 1895.   B 26 S 9
The Court of Louis XIV. (Women of Versailles.) 12mo. Lond., 1893.   B 17 Q 12
The Court of Louis XV. (Women of Versailles.) 12mo. Lond., 1894.   B 17 Q 11
The Duchess of Berry and the Revolution of 1830. 8vo. Lond., 1893.   C 19 Q 14
The Duchess of Berry and the Court of Louis XVIII. 8vo. Lond., 1892.   C 19 Q 12
The Duchess of Berry and the Court of Charles X. 8vo. Lond., 1893.   C 19 Q 13
Last Years of Louis XV. (Women of Versailles.) 12mo. Lond., 1894.   B 26 Q 28
Women of the Valois Court. 8vo. Lond., 1893.   C 19 Q 11

IMPERIAL AND ASIATIC QUARTERLY REVIEW, The. 2nd Series, vols. 4-8. 8vo. Woking, 1892-94.   E

IMPERIAL DICTIONARY OF UNIVERSAL BIOGRAPHY: a series of original Memoirs of Distinguished Men of all Ages and all Nations. Edited by Dr. J. F. Waller. 14 vols. imp. 8vo. Lond. (n.d.)   C 21 U 1-14

IMPERIAL FEDERATION. Report of the Conference held July 29, 1884. 8vo. Lond., 1884.   F 10 U 7

IMPERIAL FEDERATION LEAGUE. Report of the adjourned Conference and of the first meeting of the League, held Nov. 18, 1884. 8vo. Lond., 1884.   F 10 U 7
Information for the use of Branches. 8vo. Lond., 1884.   F 10 U 7
Victorian Branch. Report of Public Meeting held in the Town Hall, Melbourne, 5th June, 1885. 8vo. Melb., 1885.   MF 2 R 38

IMPERIAL INSTITUTE. Year-book of, 1893 and 1894, and Supplement for 1895. 3 vols. roy. 8vo. Lond. 1893-95.   E

INABA, Masamaro. Development of the suprarenal bodies in the mouse. 8vo. (n.p.n.d.)   A 30 V 17

INCHBALD, Mrs. Elizabeth. Animal Magnetism: a Farce. [*See* London Stage, 4.]   H 2 S 36
The Child of Nature: a Drama. [*See* London Stage, 2.]   H 2 S 34
Every One has his Fault: a Comedy. [*See* London Stage, 2.]   H 2 S 34
Lover's Vows: a Play. [*See* London Stage, 3.]   H 2 S 35
The Midnight Hour: a Petite Comedy. [*See* London Stage, 1.]   H 2 S 33
Such Things are: a Play. [*See* London Stage, 1.]   H 2 S 33
The Wedding Day: a Farce. [*See* London Stage, 2.]   H 2 S 34
Wives as they were, and Maids as they are; a Comedy. [*See* London Stage, 2.]   H 2 S 34

INDEPENDENT ORDER OF GOOD TEMPLARS, N.S.W. Journal of the seventh Annual Session of the Grand Lodge of, held April, 1880. 8vo. Sydney, 1880. ME 8 Q

INDEX LIBRARY, The. [See British Record Society.] E

INDEX LIBRORUM PROHIBITORUM sanctissimi Domini nostri Leonis XIII Pont. Max. 12mo. Roma, 1895. K 7 P 5

INDEX MEDICUS: a monthly classified record of the Current Medical Literature of the World. Vols. 14-16. Imp. 8vo. Boston, 1892-94. E

INDEX SOCIETY. [See British Record Society.]

INDIA—*General*. Pascaert van t'Ooster gedeelte van Oost Indien van C. Comorin tot Japan.. Fol. (n p.n.d.) D 8 P 34 ‡

INDIA—*Government Departments, Reports, and Publications*.

GEOLOGICAL SURVEY. Palæontologia Indica; being figures and descriptions of the organic remains procured during the progress of the Geological Survey of India. Ser. 9, vol. 2, pt. 1; Ser. 10 vol. 4, pts. 1-3; Ser. 13, vol. 4, pt. 1, and Index. 6 parts. Fol. Calcutta, 1886-93. E

    Ser. 9, vol. 2, pt. 1. Jurassic Fauna of Cutch ; the Echinoidea of Cutch ; by G. W. Gregory.
    Ser. 10, vol. 4, pts. 1-3. Indian Tertiary and Post-Tertiary Vertebrata ; Siwalik Mammalia, the Fauna of Karnul Caves, Eocene Chelonia from the Salt Range ; by R. Lydekker.
    Ser. 13, vol. 4, pt. 1. Salt Range Fossils : Geological Results ; by Dr. W. Waagen.
    Index to the Genera and Species described in the Palæontologia Indica up to 1891 ; by W. Theobald.

Records of the Geological Survey. Vols. 25-27. 3 vols. Roy. 8vo. Calcutta, 1892-94. E

Contents and Index of the First Twenty Volumes of the Records. Imp. 8vo. Calcutta, 1892. E

METEOROLOGICAL DEPARTMENT Reports on the Administration of, 1876-77. 2 vols. sm. fol. Calcutta, 1876-77. E

INDIA LIST, The. [See Great Britain and Ireland—India Office.] E

INDIA OFFICE LIST, The [See Great Britain and Ireland—India Office.] E

INDIAN ANTIQUARY, The. Vols. 21-23. 4to. Bombay, 1892-94. E

INDIANA. Report of the Superintendent of Public Instruction, 1891-92. 8vo. Indianapolis, 1893. E

INDUSTRIAL BLIND INSTITUTION, Sydney. 5th, 8th, and 10th Reports. 8vo. Sydney, 1886-91. ME 6 S

INDUSTRIAL SCHOOLS, The : an exposure and appeal; by "Bohemian." 12mo. Richmond, Vic. (n.d.) MF 1 P 73

INDUSTRIES AND IRON: a Journal for the Engineering, Electrical, Chemical, and Metallurgical Trades. Vols. 15-17. 4to. Lond., 1893-94. E

INFERNAL PARLIAMENT, The. Opening of, for 1867. 8vo. Ballarat, 1867. MJ 3 Q 3

INGALL, E. D. Summary of the Mineral Productions of Canada, 1892. (Geol. Survey Dept.) 8vo. Ottawa, 1893. E

INGEGNERIA CIVILE, L', e le Arti Industriali, 1892-94. 3 vols. 4to. Torino, 1892-94. E

INGHAM, Rt. Rev. E. G. Sierra Leone after a hundred years. Illustrated. 8vo. Lond., 1894. D 14 R 13

INGLE, Edward. Parish Institutions of Maryland ; with Illustrations from Parish Records. (Johns Hopkins University Studies, 1.) 8vo. Baltimore, 1883. B 18 S 1

Local Institutions of Virginia. (Johns Hopkins University Studies, 3.) 8vo. Baltimore, 1883. B 18 S 3

The Negro in the District of Columbia. (Johns Hopkins University Studies, 11.) 8vo. Baltimore, 1893. B 18 S 11

INGLIS, Charles, "Candidus." Plain Truth, addressed to the Inhabitants of America ; containing remarks on a late Pamphlet intitled "Common Sense." 8vo. Dublin, 1776. F 4 P 6

INGLIS, James, "Maori." The Humour of the Scot. 12mo. Edinb., 1894. MJ 2 T 54

Oor ain Folk, being Memories of Manse Life in the Mearns and a Crack aboot auld times. 8vo. Edinb., 1894. MJ 2 T 55

Hindoo Juggling and Christian Credulity. [See Mediums and their Dupes.] MG 2 Q 36

Recent Economic Developments of Australian Enterprise. [See Roy. Col. Inst., Proc., 25.] E

INGLIS, Rev. John. The New Hebrides Mission and the Polynesian Labour Traffic. 8vo. Lond. (n.d.) MG 2 Q 34

INGONYAMA. [See Robertson, —.]

INGRAM, Rev. A. F. Winnington. Working-men's Clubs. [See Knapp, J. M.—The Universities and the Social Problem.] F 8 U 22

INGRAM, Dr. John Kells. De Imitatione Christi. [See Early English Text Society.]

History of Slavery and Serfdom. 8vo. Lond., 1895. F 7 V 24

INNES, A. D. Britain and her Rivals in the 18th Century, 1713-1789. 8vo. Lond., 1895. B 22 R 13

INNES, Lieut.-Gen. McLeod. Lucknow and Oude in the Mutiny. 8vo. Lond., 1895. B 29 U 7

INNES, Robt. T. A. List of probably New Double Stars. 8vo. Lond., 1895. A 19 R 24
Secular Perturbations of the Earth, arising from the action of Venus. 8vo. Lond., 1893. A 19 R 24.
Secular Perturbations of the Earth's Orbit by Mars. 8vo. Lond., 1893. A 19 R 24
Note on the Secular Perturbations of the Earth by Mars. 8vo. Lond., 1893. A 19 R 24
Tables to facilitate the application of Gauss's method of computing secular variations. 8vo. Lond., 1893. A 19 R 24

INQUIRY at the Yarra Bend Asylum. 8vo. Richmond (Vict.) 1859. MA 3 T 30

INSECT LIFE: devoted to the Economy and Life-habits of Insects, especially in their relations to Agriculture. Vols. 1-5. 8vo. Wash., 1888-93. E

INSTITUTE OF ACTUARIES. Journal of, January, 1889. 8vo. Lond., 1889. E

INSTITUTE OF AGRICULTURE, LONDON. Lectures on Agricultural Science, and other Proceedings of the Institute of Agriculture, South Kensington, London, 1883-84. 8vo. Lond., 1884. A 18 R 28

INSTITUTE OF JAMAICA. Journal of. Vol. 2, Nos. 1 and 2. 8vo. Kingston, Jam., 1894-95. E

INSTITUTION OF CIVIL ENGINEERS. Catalogue of the Library. A-Pa. 3 vols. 8vo. Lond., 1895. K 7 T 8-10
Minutes of Proceedings. Vols. 101-122. 8vo. Lond., 1890-95. E

INSTITUTION OF MECHANICAL ENGINEERS. Proceedings, 1892-93. 2 vols. 8vo. Lond., 1892-93. E

INSTITUTION OF MINING AND METALLURGY, LONDON. Transactions. Vol. 1, pts. 1 and 2; vol. 3, pt. 3. 8vo. Lond., 1893-95. E

INSTITUTUL METEOROLOGIC AL ROMANIEI. Analele Institutului Meteorologic al Romaniei. Tom. 6, 7, Anul 1890-91. 4to. Bucuresti, 1893. E

INSTRUCTION on the Duty of Prisoners, by "A Catholic Clergyman." 12mo. Sydney, 1839. MG 2 R 53

INSTRUCTIONS NAUTIQUES sur les côtes Est et N.E. d'Australie (de Sydney au Detroit de Torrès), la mer du Corail, la côte Sud-est de la Nouvelle-Guinée, et l'Archipel de la Louisiade. 8vo. Paris, 1889. MD 7 R 52

INSTRUCTIONS to Surgeon-Superintendents of Queensland Ships. 8vo. Lond., 1860. MF 3 T 48

INTERCOLONIAL MEDICAL CONGRESS OF AUSTRALASIA. Transactions of the Third Session, held in Sydney, 1892. Roy. 8vo. Sydney, 1893. ME 1 T

INTERNATIONAL CLINICS: a Quarterly of Clinical Lectures. 14 vols. roy. 8vo. Edinb., 1891-95. A 31 R 1-14

INTERNATIONAL CONFERENCE FOR EXCHANGES, held at Brussels, 1883, Translation of Papers relating to. Roy. 8vo. Sydney, 1893. MF 1 S 46

INTERNATIONAL CONGRESS OF CHARITIES, &c. Hospitals, &c. [See Chicago Exhib., 1893.] A 33 U 13

INTERNATIONAL ENGINEERING CONGRESS, CHICAGO, 1893. [See American Society of Civil Engineers, July to December, 1893.] E

INTERNATIONAL MARITIME CONGRESS, London, 1893. General Report, and Minutes of Proceedings. Sec. 1—Harbours and Breakwaters; Sec. 2—Docks; Sec. 3—Shipbuilding and Marine Engineering; Sec. 4—Lighthouses, Buoys, Fog-signals, &c. Roy. 8vo. Lond., 1893. A 22 V 19

INWARDS, Richard. Weather Lore; a Collection of Proverbs, Sayings, and Rules concerning the Weather. 8vo. Lond., 1893. A 19 T 20

IOWA—General. Blue Grass Region of Iowa. 8vo. Chicago, 1893. D 15 T 5
Hand-book of. 8vo. Dubuque, 1893. D 15 T 12

IOWA—State Departments, Reports, and Publications.
LEGISLATURE. Constitution of Iowa. 12mo. Des Moines, 1880. F 7 V 36
Legislative Documents, 1892. 6 vols. 8vo. Des Moines, 1892. E
Iowa Official Register, 1894. 8vo. Des Moines, 1894. F 4 U 40

LIBRARY. Catalogue of the State Library, compiled by Mrs. Mary H. Miller, State Librarian. 8vo. Des Moines, 1889. K 7 T 6
Reports of the State Librarian, 1889-93. 2 vols. 8vo. Des Moines, 1891-93. E

IOWA ACADEMY OF SCIENCES. Proceedings of, 1893. Vol. 1, Part 4. 8vo. Des Moines, 1894. E

IOWA HISTORICAL RECORD, published quarterly by the State Historical Society, 1894-95. Roy. 8vo. Iowa, 1894-95. E

IOWA STATE HORTICULTURAL SOCIETY. Report for 1893. 8vo. Des Moines, 1894. E

IRELAN, W. California State Mining Bureau; Reports, State Mineralogist, 1887-89, 1894. 4 vols. 8vo. Sacramento, 1888-94. E

IRENÆUS, Sanctus. Writings of. Translated by Rev. Dr. A. Roberts and Rev. W. H. Rambaut. (Ante-Nicene Christ. Lib., 5, 9.) 2 vols. 8vo. Edinb., 1868-69. G 14 U 5, and 9

IRENICUM, An. 8vo. Sydney, 1885. MG 1 T 13

IRISH LOYAL AND PATRIOTIC UNION. Publications issued during 1890. 8vo. Dublin, 1890.
F 4 P 25

IRON. Vols. 40 and 41. Fol. Lond., 1892. E

IRONBARK. [*See* Gibson, G. H.]

IRONSIDE, Frederick James. Australasian Cricketing Hand-book. 12mo. Sydney, 1880. MA 3 P 64
World of Cricket. 12mo. Sydney, 1895. MA 3 U 23

IRONSIDE, Rev. Samuel. New Zealand and its Aborigines: a Lecture. 12mo. Sydney, 1863.
MD 7 T 63

IRVINE, Hans W. H. The Australian Wine Trade. 8vo. Sydney, 1893. MA 1 Q 73
Report on the Australian Wine Trade. 8vo. Melb. (n.d.) MA 3 T 9
Report on the Australian Wine Trade. 8vo. Melb. (n.d.) MA 3 V 24

IRVING, Henry. The Drama: Addresses. 12mo. Lond., 1893. J 4 P 27
[Life of]: a Record of Twenty Years at the Lyceum; by P. Fitzgerald. 8vo. Lond., 1893. C 8 P 2
Irving Shakespeare. [*See* Shakespeare, William.]
H 4 V 1-8

IRVING, Joseph. Supplement to the Annals of our Time, from July 22, 1878, to the Jubilee, June 20, 1887. 8vo. Lond., 1889. B 21 T 27

IRVING, Washington. Beauties of. Illustrated. 18mo. Lond., 1835. J 7 P 48

IRWIN, D. Hastings. War Medals and Decorations issued to the British Military and Naval Forces, 1588-1889. 8vo. Lond., 1890. B 23 R 18

ISABELLA I, Queen of Spain. [Life of] Isabella of Castile; by Maj.-Gen. O. O. Howard. Illustrated. 8vo. New York, 1894. C 14 S 25

ISOCRATES. Manuscrit de. [*See* Martin, A.] J 7 U 20
Orations of. Translated by J. H. Freese. Vol. 1. 12mo. Lond., 1894. J 16 R 24

ISRAEL'S WANDERINGS: a connected account, tracing the Lost Tribes of Israel into the British Isles. 3rd ed. Illustrated. 8vo. Lond., 1892. G 19 Q 6

IVAN THE TERRIBLE. Life and Times; by A. Pember. 8vo. Lond., 1895. C 21 P 10

IYENAGA, Dr. Toyokichi. The Constitutional Development of Japan, 1853-81. (Johns Hopkins University Studies, 9.) 8vo. Baltimore, 1891. B 18 S 9

J

J.K.M. [*See* Mary Ira, The.] MD 1 Q 32

J.S.S. [*See* Shearston, J. S.]

J.W.E. [*See* Sketches from Life.] MJ 1 Q 1

JACK, Robt. Logan. Artesian Water in the Western Interior of Queensland. 8vo. Brisbane, 1895.
MA 2 V 53
——— and ETHERIDGE Robt., jun. Geology and Palæontology of Queensland and New Guinea. 3 vols. sm. 4to. Brisbane, 1892. MA 2 R 46-48

JACKMAN, Isaac. All the World's a Stage: a Farce. [*See* London Stage, 1.] H 2 S 33
Hero and Leander: an Operatic Burletta. [*See* London Stage, 3.] H 2 S 35

JACKSON, Dr. Sermon preached by Dr. Jackson, 1881. 8vo. Sydney, 1881. MG 1 R 76

JACKSON, Andrew. Sketch of. [*See* Thompson, R. W. —Recollections of Sixteen Presidents.] C 18 T 21, 22
Sketch of. [*See* Wilson J. C.—Presidents of the United States.] C 2 V 30

JACKSON, Benjamin Daydon. Index Kewensis: an Enumeration of the Genera and Species of Flowering Plants. Parts 1-3. 3 vols. 4to. Oxford, 1893-94.
A 14 S 5-7 †

JACKSON, Cyril. Children's Country Holidays Fund and the Settlements. [*See* Knapp, J. M.—The Universities and the Social Problem.] F 8 U 22

JACKSON, Frank G. Theory and Practice of Design: an advanced Text-book on Decorative Art. Illustrated. 8vo. Lond., 1894. A 23 T 20

JACKSON, Frederick George. The Great Frozen Land: Narrative of a Winter Journey across the Tundras and a Sojourn among the Samoyads. Illustrated. Edited by A. Montefiore. 8vo. Lond., 1895.
D 18 V 19
Polar Gleams. [*See* Peel, H.] D 16 T 11

JACKSON, Dr. H. W. Contagious Diseases Acts as measures of reform. 8vo. Sydney, 1882. MF 4 R 43

JACKSON, Jas. Tableaux de diverses Vitesses, exprimées en mètres par seconde. 8vo. Nice, 1893. A 25 T 24

JACKSON, John. Theory and Practice of Handwriting. 8vo. Lond., 1893. G 17 R 29

JACKSON, John Dettmer Dodds. Sir Roger Tichborne Revealed! The Discovery of Sir Roger Charles Doughty Tichborne, *alias* Edward Caleb Souper, Secretary to Lady Ogle, and his Confederates. 8vo. Sydney, 1885. MF 2 R 39

JACKSON, Luis. The Industrial West, its advantages and destiny. 8vo. Chicago, 1890. D 15 T 5

JACKSON, Thos. G. Wadham College, Oxford, its Foundation, Architecture, and History. 4to. Oxford, 1893. B 6 V 33
Architecture. [*See* Shaw, R.N.] A 3 P 41

JACOB, Col. S. S. Jeypore Portfolio of Architecture. Details. Part 7. String and Band Patterns. Fol Lond., 1894. A 31 R 15 ‡

JACOB, Capt. Wm. Memoir on the Practicability of Establishing a Permanent Communication across the River Derwent by means of a Pontoon Bridge. 12mo. Hobart, 1832. MA 2 P 35

JACOBI, Chas. Thos. Some Notes on Books and Printing: a Guide for Authors and Others. 8vo. Lond., 1892. A 25 T 2

JACOBI, Hermann. Gaina Sûtras. Part 2. 8vo. Oxford, 1895. G 3 S 33
2. The Uttarâdhyana Sûtra. The Sûtrakritânga Sûtra.

JACOBI, Joseph. Enquiry into the sources of the History of the Jews in Spain. 8vo. Lond., 1894. MB 2 R 54
The Jews of Angevin England. 18mo. Lond., 1893. B 26 P 9
Studies in Biblical Archæology. 8vo. Lond., 1894. G 17 Q 44
Tennyson and "In Memoriam": An Appreciation and a Study. 12mo. Lond., 1892. J 4 P 8

JACOBI, Dr. Mary Putnam-. Common Sense applied to Woman Suffrage. 12mo. New York, 1894. F 14 R 28

JACOLLIOT, Louis. La Vérité sur Taïti. 8vo. Paris, 1869. MB 2 R 52

JAGO, Wm. Inorganic Chemistry, Theoretical and Practical: a Manual for Students in advanced classes. 4th ed. 8vo. Lond., 1893. A 21 P 33

JAHRESBERICHT über der Fortschritte der Anatomie und Physiologie. Bände 19, 20. 8vo. Leipzig, 1891–93. E

JAMAICA. Jamaica in 1895: a Handbook of Information for Intending Settlers and others. [With Map.] 8vo. Kingston, Jamaica, 1892. D 17 T 20
Handbook of Jamaica, 1893-95. 3 vols. 8vo. Lond., 1893-95. E

JAMES I, King of Aragon. Life and Times of; by F. D. Swift. 8vo. Oxford, 1894. C 10 S 20

JAMES I, King of England. Counter Blast to Tobacco. [*See* Bibliotheca Curiosa.] J 18 Q 7
Conspiracy against James I, 1603. [*See* Collectanea Adamantæa.] J 18 R 19
Secret Correspondence of Sir Robert Cecil with James VI, King of Scotland. [*See* Collectanea Adamantæa.] J 18 R 28

JAMES, G. P. R. The Convict: a Tale. 12mo. Lond., 1851. MJ 1 P 59
Life and Times of Louis XIV. 2 vols. 8vo. Lond., 1851. B 26 R 12, 13

JAMES, Dr. J. A. English Institutions and the American Indian. (Johns Hopkins University Studies, 12.) Roy. 8vo. Baltimore, 1894. B 18 S 12

JAMES, Capt. Thos. Voyage of. [*See* Christy, M.— Hakluyt Soc., 88, 89.] E

JAMESON, Dr. J. Franklin. An Introduction to the Study of the Constitutional and Political History of the States. (Johns Hopkins University Studies, 4.) 8vo. Baltimore, 1886. B 18 S 4

JAMESON, Mrs. Sketches in Canada and Rambles among the Red Men. 12mo. Lond., 1852. D 15 P 8

JAMIESON, G. The Silver Question: injury to British Trade and Manufactures; together with other papers on the same subject by T. H. Box and D. O. Croal. 8vo. Lond., 1895. F 9 T 10

JAMIESON, Dr. James. Diseases which should be prevented. [*See* Australian Health Soc., Melb.] MA 3 S 33
Another copy: 8vo. Melb., 1879. MA 3 T 20
Summer Diseases: Sunstroke. [*See* Australian Health Soc., Melb.] MA 3 S 33
How to feed Infants: a Manual of Diet and Digestion; with Remarks on Infant Mortality. 12mo. Melb., 1871. MA 3 P 63
Influence of Light on Bacteria. (Roy. Soc., Vict., 19, 20.) 8vo. Melb., 1883-84. ME 1 P

JANVIER, Thos A. In Old New York. Illustrated. 12mo. New York, 1894. B 15 Q 24

JAPAN. Chambers of Commerce in the Empire of Japan. 8vo. Tokyo, 1893. F 3 R 14
Descriptive Catalogue of the Agricultural Products, exhibited in the World's Columbian Exposition. 8vo. Tokio, 1893. K 7 T 3
General View of Commerce and Industry in the Empire of Japan. With Maps. 12mo. Tōkyō, 1893. F 7 V 4

JAPAN SOCIETY, LONDON. Transactions and Proceedings of. Vols. 1, 2. 8vo. Lond., 1893-95. E

JAQUES, Mary J. Texan Ranch Life; with three months through Mexico in a "Prairie Schooner." [Illustrated.] Roy. 8vo. Lond., 1894. D 15 V 16

JAQUET, John Blockley. Geology of the Broken Hill Lode and Barrier Ranges Mineral Field, New South Wales. (Memoirs of the Geological Survey of N.S.W., 5.) 4to. Sydney, 1894. ME

JARRETT, F. C. The Mercantile Navy List of Australia and New Zealand. 8vo. Sydney, 1871. MK 1 R 47

JARVIE, Rev. A. Milne. In Memoriam : [a] Sermon in Reference to the death Rev. Dr. Lang. [See Lang, Rev. Dr. J. D.] MG 2 S 8

JASPER, Dr. Theodore. Taxidermy. [See Davie, O.]
A 30 V 11

JASTROW, Helen B. Selected Essays of J. Darmesteter. [See Darmesteter, J.] J 9 S 26

JAUSSEN, Tepano. L'Ile de Paques. 8vo. Paris, 1893.
MB 2 R 53

JAVA. Review of the Administration, Value, and State of Java as it was, as it is, and as it may be. 8vo. Lond., 1816. B 33 Q 6

Sketches, Civil and Military, of the Island of Java and its immediate dependencies: comprising interesting details of Batavia, and authentic particulars of the celebrated poison-tree. Illustrated with Map, Plan, and Chart. 8vo. Lond., 1812. D 17 T 16

JAY, Rev. O. Shelters. [See Knapp, J. M.—The Universities and the Social Problem.] F 8 U 22

JEAFFRESON, John Cordy. A Book of Recollections. 2 vols. 12mo. Lond., 1894. C 13 Q 13, 14
Victoria, Queen and Empress. 2 vols. 8vo. Lond., 1893. C 15 R 12, 13

JEANNENEY, A. La Nouvelle-Calédonie, Agricole, Nature, Minéralogique et Géologique du Sol. 12mo. Paris, 1894. MF 2 P 77

JEANS, James S. Trusts, Pools, and Corners, as affecting Commerce and Industry. 12mo. Lond., 1894.
F 9 U 44

JEBB, John Gladwyn. A Strange Career: Life and Adventures of; by his Widow. 8vo. Edinb., 1894.
C 17 R 18

JEBB, Dr. Richard C. The Growth and Influence of Classical Greek Poetry. 12mo. Lond , 1893.
J 10 P 41
Sophocles. [See Sophocles.] H 1 S 27

JEFFERIES, Richard. A Study; by H. S. Salt. 12mo. Lond., 1894. C 19 P 3
Thoughts from the Writings of ; by H. S. H. Waylen. 12mo. Lond., 1893. J 8 U 10

JEFFERSON, Thos. Writings of. Edited by P. L. Ford, 1760–97. 5 vols. roy. 8vo. New York, 1892–95. J 4 U 16-20
Sketch of. [See Wilson, J. G.—Presidents of the United States.] C 2 V 30
Sketch of. [See Thompson. R. W.—Recollections of Sixteen Presidents.] C 18 T 21, 22

JEFFRAY, R. J. Address delivered at the Annual Meeting of the Melbourne Chamber of Commerce held on the 10th May, 1876, and containing comments on the Revenue and Expenditure of Victoria. 8vo. Melb., 1876. MJ 3 Q 16

JEFFREY, Francis, Lord. Contributions to the *Edinburgh Review*. 8vo. Lond., 1853. J 10 U 29
Contributions to the *Edinburgh Review*. 8vo. Lond., 1854. J 12 U 8

JEFFREYS, George, Lord. [Life of], 1648–89 ; by W. A. C. Archbold. (Lives of Twelve Bad Men.) 8vo. Lond., 1894. C 18 T 9

JEFFREYS, Archdeacon J. Intoxicating Stimulants ; their Primary and Secondary Effects upon the Human System. 12mo. Melb., 1860. MA 3 P 52

JEKYLL, Joseph. Correspondence of, with his sister-in-law, Lady Gertrude Sloane Stanley, 1818–38. Edited by the Hon. A. Bourke. 8vo. Lond., 1894.
C 16 S 16

JENAISCHE ZEITSCHRIFT FÜR NATURWISSENCHAFT. Bände, 27, 28. 8vo. Jena, 1892-94. E

JENKINS, Dr. E. H. The Farmer's Annual Hand-book for 1883. [See Armsby, Dr. E. P.] A 18 P 7

—— and WINTON, A. L. Compilation of Analyses of American Feeding Stuffs. Roy. 8vo. Washington, 1892. A 32 T 11

JENKINS, R. L. Universal Education : a Lecture. 8vo. Sydney, 1860. MG 1 R 21

JENKINS, Wm. Stitt. The Lost Children. 8vo. Geelong, 1864. MH 1 S 69

JENKS, Prof. Edward. History of the Australasian Colonies, from their foundation to the year 1893. 8vo. Camb., 1893. MB 2 P 56
An Outline of English Local Government. 12mo. Lond., 1894. F 8 U 13

JENKS, T. The Century World's Fair Book for Boys and Girls: being the Adventures of Harry and Philip with their tutor, Mr. Douglass, at the World's Columbian Exposition. Illustrated. 4to. New York, 1893.
J 4 U 15

JENNER, Dr. Edward. Jenner and Vaccination : a strange chapter of Medical History ; by Dr. C. Creighton. 8vo. Lond., 1889. A 26 Q 29

JENNINGS, Rev W. The Confucian Analects. 12mo. Lond., 1895. G 3 P 26

JENSEN, F. Liisberg. The Strawberry, its History and Cultivation. 8vo. Sydney, 1892. MA 1 Q 32

JENVEY, H. W. Practical Telegraphy : a Guide for the use of Officers of the Victorian Post and Telegraph Department. Vol. 1. 8vo. Melb., 1891. MA 3 W 14

JEPHCOTT, Sydney. The Secrets of the South : Australian Poems. 12mo. Lond. (n.d.) MH 1 U 39

JEPHSON, Robert. Braganza; a Tragedy. [*See* London Stage, 4.] H 2 S 36
Count of Narbonne: a Tragedy. [*See* London Stage, 3.] H 2 S 35
The Law of Lombardy: a Tragedy. [*See* London Stage, 4.] H 2 S 36
Two Strings to your Bow; a Farce. [*See* London Stage, 3.] H 2 S 35

JERNINGHAM, Frederick. Steam Communication with the Cape of Good Hope, Australia, and New Zealand suggested as the means of promoting Emigration to those Colonies. 8vo. Lond., 1848. MF 3 T 45

JEROME, Armand. Australian Boys and Girls: an Illustrated Annual of Stories by Australian Writers. No. 1. Sm. 4to. Sydney, 1895. MJ 1 V 18
A Counterblast to Spookland; or, Glimpses of the Marvellous. Illustrated. 8vo. Sydney, 1895. MG 2 Q 53

JERROLD, Douglas. The Catspaw: a Comedy. 12mo. Lond., 1850. H 3 P 51
Hand-book of Swindling, and other Papers. 12mo. Lond. (n.d.) J 11 T 26
The Wit and Opinions of. 12mo. Lond., 1859. J 11 T 42

JERROLD, Walter. [Life of] Oliver Wendell Holmes. 12mo. Lond., 1893. C 19 P 4

JERSEY, Countess of. Eric, Prince of Lorlonia; or, the Valley of Wishes: a Fairy Tale of the days of chivalry. 8vo. Lond., 1895. J 8 S 31
Maurice; or, the Red Jar: a Tale of Magic and Adventure for Boys and Girls. Illustrated. 8vo. Lond., 1894. J 6 S 36

JERVOIS, Sir William F. D. Anniversary Address of the President of the New Zealand Institute, Sir W. F. D. Jervois. Roy. 8vo. Wellington, 1883. MA 2 U 57

JESPERSEN, Dr. O. Progress in Language, with special reference to English. 8vo. Lond., 1894. J 11 T 12

JESSE, Edward. Windsor Castle. [*See* Ritchie, L.] B 21 U 12

JESSOPP, Rev. Dr. Augustus. Studies by a Recluse, in Cloister, Town, and Country. 8vo. Lond., 1893. B 23 R 15

JEUNE, Lady. Ladies at Work. [*See* Ladies at Work.] F 9 T 2½
Lesser Questions. 4th ed. 12mo. Lond., 1895. J 12 T 40

JEVONS, Frank Byron. Plutarch's Romane Questions. [*See* Plutarch.] B 30 Q 18

JEVONS, William. Claims of Christianity to the character of a Divine relevation considered. [*See* Religious Pamphlets, 3.] G 9 V 18
The Book of Common Prayer examined in the light of the present age. [*See* Religious Pamphlets, 3.] G 9 V 18
The Prayer Book adapted to the age. [*See* Religious Pamphlets, 3.] G 9 V 18

JEWETT, Charles Coffin. Notices of Public Libraries in the United States of America. 8vo. Wash., 1851. J 6 T 30

JEWISH WOMEN'S CONGRESS, CHICAGO, 1893. Papers of. 8vo. Philad., 1894. G 2 T 29

JEWITT, Llewellyn F. W. The Wedgwoods: being a Life of Josiah Wedgwood; with Notices of his Works and their Productions, Memoirs of the Wedgwood and other Families, and a History of the early Potteries of Staffordshire. Illustrated. 8vo. Lond., 1865. C 21 S 13

JOAN OF ARC. [*See* D'Arc, Jeanne.]

JOANNA I, Queen of Naples, Sicily, and Jerusalem: an Essay on Her Times; by St. Clair Baddeley. 8vo. Lond., 1893. C 16 T 13

JOBSON, Dr. David Wemyss. Hand-book for Bathers; or, Hints on the various kinds of Baths. 12mo. Melb. (n.d.) MA 3 P 51
Metrical Version of the Sermon on the Mount. 8vo. Melb., 1864. MH 1 S 35

JOCELYN, Major Julian R. J. Notes on Electricity, for the use of the Garrison Artillery. 12mo. Lond., 1891. A 20 Q 26

JOCHIM, John W. Official Directory and Legislative Manual of the State of Michigan for 1893-94. 8vo. Lansing, 1893. E
Township Officers' Guide, Michigan. 8vo. Lansing, 1893. F 1 T 17

JOFFILY, Dr. Ireneo. Notas sobre a Parahyba. 8vo. Rio de Janeiro, 1822. D 15 V 8

JOHNS HOPKINS' UNIVERSITY. Register, 1892, 1893. 8vo. Baltimore, 1893. E

JOHNS HOPKINS' UNIVERSITY STUDIES in Historical and Political Science. Vol. 1-12, and extra vols. 1-5. Roy. 8vo. Baltimore, 1883-94. B 18 S 1-12, B 18 T 1-5

JOHNSON, Andrew. Sketch of. [*See* Wilson, J. G.— Presidents of the United States.] C 2 V 30

JOHNSON, C. The Rifle, and how to use it. 12mo. Sydney, 1888. MA 2 P 56

JOHNSON, Cuthbert W. Gardeners' Dictionary. New ed., revised by C. H. Wright and D. Dewar. 8vo. Lond., 1894. A 20 T 8

JOHNSON, J. A. Dairying. (Proc. Roy. Agricult. and Horticult. Soc., S. Australia, 1884.) 8vo. Adelaide, 1884. ME 1 S

JOHNSON, J. B., BRYAN, C. W., & TURNEAURE, F. E. The Theory and Practice of Modern Framed Structures. 4to. New York, 1893. A 36 P 5‡

JOHNSON, J. C. F. An Austral Christmas. 8vo. Melb., 1888. MJ 1 R 31

JOHNSON, James C. Introduction of the Study of Music into the Public Schools of America. 8vo. Chicago, 1893.   A 23 R 13

JOHNSON, John. Old Maryland Manors; with the Records of a Court Leet and a Court Baron. (Johns Hopkins University Studies, 1.) 8vo. Baltimore, 1883.   B 18 S 1

Rudimentary Society among Boys. (Johns Hopkins University Studies, 2.) 8vo. Baltimore, 1884.   B 18 S 2

JOHNSON, Lionel. The Art of Thomas Hardy. 8vo. Lond., 1894.   J G S 37

JOHNSON, Miss Nora. Questions on Australian and General Geography, with other useful facts for Junior Classes in Schools. 12th ed. 12mo. Sydney, 1894.   MD 8 P 16

JOHNSON, R. U., and BUEL, C. C. Battles and Leaders of the Civil War. 4 vols. imp. 8vo. New York, 1887-88.   B 11 Q 12-15 †

JOHNSON, R. W. The Making of the Tyne; a Record of 50 Years' Progress. Sm. 4to. Lond., 1895.   B 21 V 6

JOHNSON, Dr. Raymond. Surgery. [See Erichsen, Sir J. E.]   A 33 T 25, 26

JOHNSON, Rev. Richard. Address to the Inhabitants of the Colonies established in New South Wales and Norfolk Island. 12mo. Lond., 1794.   MG 1 P 58

JOHNSON, Robert, and CHATWOOD, Arthur B. Photography, Artistic and Scientific. Illustrated. 8vo. Lond., 1895.   A S Q 40

JOHNSON, Dr. Samuel. Tour to the Hebrides with. [See Boswell, J.]   D 18 R 26
[Plaster Cast of.] [See Hutton, L.—Portraits in Plaster.]   A 23 V 13
London : a Poem. Sm. fol. Lond., 1738.   H 39 Q 13 ‡
Poems of, to which is prefixed a Life of the Author. 18mo. Lond., 1820.   H 10 U 7
The Rambler. 18th ed. 3 vols. 8vo. Lond., 1820.   J 4 S 25-27
The Wisdom of the Rambler, Adventurer, and Idler. 12mo. Lond., 1848.   J 11 T 41

JONHSON, Prof. Samuel Wm. How Crops Grow. 8vo. New York, 1893.   A 18 Q 24
How Crops Feed. 8vo. New York, 1892.   A 18 Q 23

JOHNSON, Sün. The Self-educator. [Chinese-English.] 8vo. Sydney, 1892.   MJ 3 P 38

JOHNSON, T. The Culture of the Rose. 12mo. Melb., 1866.   MA 1 P 84

JOHNSON, Dr. Alexander The Genesis of a New England State (Connecticut). Johns Hopkins University Studies, 1.) 8vo. Baltimore, 1883.   B 18 S 1

JOHNSTON, Alexander W. Strikes, Labour Question, and other economic difficulties. 8vo. Lond., 1895.   F 8 U 20

JOHNSTON, Governor. Speech on American Affairs. [See Bibliotheca Curiosa.]   J 18 Q 25

JOHNSTON, J. F. W. Elements of Agricultural Chemistry. From the edition of Sir C. A. Cameron, by Prof. C. M. Aikman. 17th ed. 8vo. Edinb, 1894.   A 18 R 30

JOHNSTON, Dr. James. Reality versus Romance in South Central Africa. 8vo. Lond., 1893.   D 14 V 3

JOHNSTON, R. M. Hand-book of Tasmania for 1892. Roy 8vo. Hobart, 1894.   ME
Tasmanian Official Record, 1892. Roy. 8vo. Hobart, 1892.   ME

JOHNSTON, Rev. Samuel Fulton, Missionary on Tanna (New Hebrides). Memoir of; by Rev. G. Patterson. 8vo. Philad., 1864.   MC 1 S 4

JOHNSTON, W. and A. K. Atlas of Physical Geography. Imp. 8vo. Edinb., 1892.   A 15 S 12 †
New Map of the Crimea. 8vo. Edinb., 1854.   D 12 T 18
New Plan of Edinburgh, Leith, and Portobello; with index. Folded 8vo. Edinb. (n.d.)   D 12 T 17
Portable Wall Map of New Zealand. Folded 4to. Edinb., 1864.   MD 9 P 4 †

JOHNSTON, Wm. Agriculture. The Art of Farming adapted to the Colonies. 8vo. Sydney, 1873.   MA 1 R 43

JOHNSTONE, Chev. A Dialogue in Hades : a Parallel of Military Errors during the Campaign of 1759, in Canada. 8vo. Quebec, 1867.   B 17 R 12
The Campaign of 1760 in Canada. 8vo. Quebec, 1887.   B 17 R 13

JOHNSTONE, C. L. The Historical Families of Dunfrieshire and the Border Wars. 2nd edition. 8vo. Dumfries, 1889.   B 31 Q 14

JOHNSTONE, Rev. James. King Haco's Expedition against Scotland, 1263. [See Bibliotheca Curiosa.]   J 18 Q 13

JOINVILLE, F. F. P. L. M. d'Orleans, Prince de. Memoirs of. 8vo. Lond., 1895.   C 18 T 20

JOLIET, Louis, Re-discoverer of the Mississippi. Sketch of. [See Greeley, Gen. A. W.—Explorers.]   C 17 R 4

JOLLY, Rev. T. Note-book of. (Chetham Soc. Pubs., 33.) Sm. 4to. Manchester, 1894.   E

JOLLY, Wm. Ruskin on Education : some needed but neglected Elements; restated by W. Jolly. 12mo. Lond., 1894.   G 17 Q 46

JOLY, Charles. Note sur les Eucalyptus Geants de l'Australie. 8vo. Paris, 1885.   MA 2 V 58

JONES, Alex. J. Sketch of Wm. M. Springer. [*See* Springer, W. M.] F 4 P 24

JONES, Benjamin. Co-operative Production. 2 vols. 8vo. Oxford, 1894. F 12 P 39, 39

JONES, D. E. Electric Waves. [*See* Hertz, Dr. H.] A 21 T 21

JONES, Sir E. Burne-. Sketch of. [*See* Smalley, G. W. —Studies of Men.] C 19 R 20

JONES, Ernest. Portrait of. [*See* Gammage, R. G.— Chartist Movement.] F 7 R 24

JONES, Frederic. Labour Town: an Address. 8vo. Sydney, 1891. MF 4 R 2

JONES, H. I. Shilling Almanack and Directory for 1877. 8vo. Wanganui, 1877. ME 1 S

JONES, Dr. H. Lewis. Medical Electricity. Illustrated. 12mo. Lond., 1895. A 21 R 31

JONES, H. Stuart. Select Passages from Ancient Writers, illustrative of the History of Greek Sculpture. 8vo. Lond., 1895. A 23 S 10

JONES, Henry. The Earl of Essex: a Tragedy. [*See* London Stage, 3.] H 2 S 35

JONES, Henry. The New Valuations; or, the case of the South Australian Squatters fairly stated. 8vo. Melb., 1894. MF 4 R 14

JONES, Henry Arthur. The Renascence of the English Drama. 8vo. Lond., 1895. H 9 U 22

JONES, Inigo, and Wren. [*See* Loftie, W. J.] A 19 V 6

JONES, J. O. [Life of] M. Hopkins, Witchfinder, died 1647. (Lives of Twelve Bad Men.) 8vo. Lond., 1894. C 18 T 9

JONES, John. Hand-book of the Jones Collection in the South Kensington Museum. 8vo. Lond., 1883. A 23 R 23

JONES, Richard. Peasant Rents. 8vo. New York, 1895. F 7 V 39

JONES, W. A. Notes on the Crepuscula Glimmer, or the Red Glow. (Trans. Roy. Soc., S. Australia, 7.) 8vo. Adelaide, 1885. ME 1 S

JONSON, Ben. [Dramatic Works of.] Vols. 1–3. (Best Plays of the Old Dramatists.) 8vo. Lond., 1893–94. H 1 Q 40–42

Poetical Works. Edited by R. Bell. 12mo. Lond., 1856. H 10 T 1

JÖRGENSEN, Alfred. Micro-organisms and Fermentation. Translated by Dr. A. K. Miller and E. A. Lennholm. Illustrated. 8vo. Lond., 1893. A 28 U 9

JORGENSON, Jorgen. The Convict King; being the Life and Adventures of. Retold by J. F. Hogan. 12mo. Hobart, 1893. MC 1 P 58

JOSEPH, Alfred. A Bendigonian Abroad, being Sketches of Travel. 12mo. Melb., 1892. MD 8 P 6

JOSEPH, R. E. Electric Fire Alarms. (Roy. Soc., Vict. 18.) 8vo. Melb., 1882. ME 1 P

Electric Lighting. (Roy. Soc., Vic., 19, 20.) 8vo. Melb., 1883–84. ME 1 P

Incandescent Lamps for Surgical and Microscopical purposes. (Roy. Soc., Vict., 20.) 8vo. Melb., 1884. ME 1 P

Induction Currents Balance and Sonometer. (Roy. Soc., Vict. 16.) 8vo. Melb., 1880. ME 1 P

Recent Improvements in Electric Lighting. (Roy. Soc. Vic , 17.) 8vo. Melb., 1881. ME 1 P

JOSEPHINE, Empress of France. Historical and Secret Memoirs of; by Mdlle. M. A. Le Norman. 2 vols. 8vo. Lond., 1895. B 20 V 15, 16

JOUËT, Rev. Père Victor. La Société des Missionnaires Sacré-Cœur dans les Vicariats Apostoliques de la Mélanésie et de la Micronésie. Roy. 8vo. Issoudun, 1887. MG 1 U 3

JOUBERT, Jules. Shavings and Scrapes. 12mo. Dunedin, 1890. MJ 3 Q 36

JOURNAL ASIATIQUE. 8ᵉ Série. Tomes 19 et 20, et N.S. tomes 1–3. 8vo. Paris, 1892–94. E

JOURNAL DES ÉCONOMISTES. 5ᵉ Série. Tomes 11–20. Roy. 8vo. Paris, 1892–94. E

JOURNAL OF AGRICULTURE (formerly *The Quarterly Journal of Agriculture*), 1828–63. 26 vols. 8vo. Edinb., 1829–63. E

JOURNAL OF EDUCATION, 1872, July 1873, Feb., Aug., Oct., Dec., 1875, April 1878. 4 vols. 8vo. Lond., 1872–78. E

JOURNAL OF INDIAN ART. Vol. 5, 1894. Fol. Lond., 1894. E

JOURNAL OF PATHOLOGY AND BACTERIOLOGY. Edited by Dr. G. S. Woodhead. Vol. 1. Roy. 8vo. Edinb., 1893. A 31 P 5

JOURNAL OF PHYSIOLOGY. Edited by Dr. M. Foster. 16 vols. roy. 8vo. Lond., 1878–79. E

JOWETT, Rev. Prof. Benjamin, Master of Balliol. College Sermons. Edited by the Very Rev. W. H. Fremantle. 8vo. Lond., 1895. G 1 U 24

Passages from Plato for English Readers. 2 vols. 8vo. Oxford, 1895. G 3 P 35, 36

Plato's Republic [*See* Plato.] F 14 V 26–28

[Life of]; by the Hon. L. A. Tollemache. 8vo. Lond., 1895. C 19 V 14

JOYCE, Herbert. History of the Post Office, from its establishment down to 1836. 8vo. Lond., 1893.
B 16 S 4

JUDD, Prof. John W. Microchemical Analysis. [See Behrens, Prof. H.]
A 21 P 26

JUDSON, Dr. H. P. Europe in the 19th Century. 8vo. New York, 1894.
B 23 S 11

JUGLAR, Clement. Brief History of Panics and their periodical occurrence in the United States. Englished and edited with an Introductory Essay setting forth the indications of approaching panics by De C. W. Thom. 8vo. New York, 1893.
F 14 R 9

JUKES, Joseph Beete. Portrait of. [See Ramsay, Sir A. C.—Memoir of.]
C 21 B 20

JULIAN, C. St. Essay on the Future Land Policy of New South Wales. 8vo. Sydney, 1870.
MF 4 Q 30

JULIANUS, Flavius Claudius. Julian, Philosopher and Emperor, and the last struggle of Paganism against Christianity. 8vo. New York, 1895.
C 14 S 23

JULIUS, Dr. P. Organic Colouring Matters. [See Schultz, Dr. G.]
A 25 V 8

JULLIAN, Camille. Les Transformations Politiques de l'Italie sous les Empereurs Romains, 43 B.C.-330 A.D. 8vo. Paris, 1884.
B 35 R 11

JULLIEN, Emile. Histoire de L. Munatius Plancus, le Fondateur de Lyon. (Annales de l'Université de Lyon, 5.) Roy. 8vo. Paris, 1892.
C 16 U 12

JUNOR, C. Mental and Material Existence. 8vo. Lond., 1885.
MG 2 S 14

Thoughts and Theories. 8vo. Lond., 1885. MF 4 R 61

JUSSERAND, J. J. Piers Plowman (W. Langland): a Contribution to the History of English Mysticism. Translated from the French by "M.E.R." Illustrated. Lond., 1894.
J 9 T 27

JUST, Thos. C. Leading Facts connected with Federation. [With Bibliography.] Sm. fcl. Hobart, 1891.
MF 3 U 45

Tasmania! A Description of the Island of Tasmania and its Resources. 8vo. Sydney 1879.
MD 5 R 44

Official Handbook of Tasmania. 3rd edition. 8vo. Hobart, 1897.
MD 5 S 48

JUSTIN MARTYR. Writings of. Translated by Rev. M. Dods, Rev. G. Reith, and Rev. B. P. Pratten. (Ante-Nicene Christ. Lib., 2.) 8vo. Edinb., 1867.
G 14 U 2

JUVENALIS, Decimus Junius. Satyræ. 8vo. Amst., 1684.
H 9 U 34

K

KADEN, Woldemar. Italia. [See Stieler, C.] D 37 P 23 ‡

KAISERLICH-KONIGLICHEN GEOLOGISCHEN REICHSANSTALT, Jahrbuch der. Bände 40-44, 1890-94. Roy. 8vo. Wien, 1891-95. E
Verhandlungen der, 1892-94. 3 vols. roy. 8vo. Wien, 1892-94. E

KAISERLICHEN AKADEMIE DER WISSENSCHAFTEN, WIEN. Sitzungsberichte der. Mathematisch-naturwissenschaftliche Classe. Bände 1-102 102 vols. (in 210). 8vo. Wien, 1848-93. E

KALUZA, Max. The Romaunt of the Rose. [See Chaucer Society Pubs.] E

KAMBOOLA and other Tales; by "Voyageur." 12mo. Sydney, 1891.
MJ 3 Q 38

KAMES, Hon. H. Home, Lord. The Gentleman Farmer: being an attempt to improve Agriculture by subjecting it to the test of rational principles, to which is added, a Supplement containing an account of the present state of Agriculture, and of the improvements recently introduced. 6th ed. 8vo. Edinb., 1815. A 18 S 28

KANDT, Dr. Moritz. Ueber die Entwickelung Australischen Eisenbahnpolitik. 8vo. Berlin, 1894.
MF 2 T 54

KANE, Dr Elisha Kent. Tidal Observations in the Arctic Seas. 4to. Wash., 1860. A 15 Q 15 †
Sketch of. [See Greeley Gen. A. W.—Explorers and Travellers] C 17 R 4

KANSAS—General. Columbian History of Education in Kansas. Illustrated. 8vo. Topeka, 1893. G 18 S 1

KANSAS—State Departments, Reports and Publications.
AGRICULTURAL COLLEGE. Experiment Station Report, 1894. 8vo. Manhattan, 1895. E
BOARD OF AGRICULTURE. World's Fair Report. 8vo. Topeka, 1893. A 30 R 3

KANSAS CITY PUBLIC SCHOOLS. Report, 1891, 1892. 8vo. Kansas City, 1892. E

KANSAS STATE HISTORICAL SOCIETY. Biennial Report of the Board of Directors, 1892-94; also, Proceedings of the Meeting, 1893. 8vo. Topeka, 1893. E

KANSAS STATE HORTICULTURAL SOCIETY. Proceedings. Vol. 17, 1887-88. 8vo. Topeka, 1889. E

KANSAS UNIVERSITY. [History and Description of, 1866-93.] Ob. 18mo. Topeka, 1893. D 15 P 14

KANTHACK, Dr. A. A. and DRYSDALE, Dr. J. H. Course of Elementary Practical Bacteriology. 12mo. Lond., 1895. A 26 R 11

KAPOSI, Dr. Moriz. Pathology and Treatment of Diseases of the Skin. Roy. 8vo. Lond., 1895.
A 33 U 22

KAPP, Gisbert. Dynamos, Alternators, and Transformers. 8vo. Lond., 1893.
A 21 P 20

KARL, Emperor. [*See* Charles I, Emperor of Germany.]

KÁROLY, K. Guide to the Paintings of Florence. 12mo. Lond., 1893.
A 7 P 38

Raphael's Madonnas and other Pictures; with a Life of Raphael. Sm. fol. Lond., 1894.
A 36 S 16 ‡

KAUFMANN, Johann Heinrich. Gedichte briefe und tageblatter. 12mo. Frankfurt, 1821.
H 10 U 9

KAUFMANN, Rev. Moritz. Charles Kingsley, Christian Socialist and Social Reformer. 8vo. Lond., 1892.
C 13 P 24

Pre-scientific Socialism. [*See* Subjects of the Day, 2.]
F 7 U 27

Scientific Socialism. [*See* Subjects of the Day, 2.]
F 7 U 27

Socialism and Modern Thought. 12mo. Lond., 1895.
F 7 V 43

KAUPERT, J. A. Karten von Attika. [*See* Curtius, E.]
D 15 R 16 †, and D 8 P 30 ‡

KAVANAGH, Mrs. M. Fruit-Preserving. Melb. (n.d.)
MA 3 T 9

KAYSER, Prof. E. Text-book of Comparative Geology. 8vo. Lond., 1893.
A 24 T 18

KEAN, Edmund. [Plaster Cast of.] [*See* Hutton, L.— Portraits in Plaster.]
A 23 V 13

KEANE, Prof. Augustus H. Africa. Vol. 1. North Africa. (Stanford's Compendium of Geography and Travels.) Maps and Illustrations. 8vo. Lond., 1895.
D 14 R 14

KEATE, George. Account of the Pelew Islands, composed from the Journals of Capt. H. Wilson, 1783. 4th ed. 8vo. Lond., 1789.
MD 8 Q 37

Relation des Iles Pelew, composée sur les journaux et les communications du Capitaine Henri Wilson. 2 vols. 8vo. Paris, 1788.
MD 8 Q 35, 36

KEATING, Dr. John M. Cyclopædia of the Diseases of Children, Medical and Surgical. 4 vols roy. 8vo. Edinb., 1889-90.
A 27 V 11-14

KEATS, John. Poetical Works of. Roy. 8vo. (n.p.n.d.)
J 4 U 2

The Eve of St. Agnes. Illustrated. 8vo. Lond., 1856.
H 9 U 2

The Letters of John Keats. Edited by H. B. Forman. 8vo. Lond., 1895.
C 19 V 13

[Plaster Cast of.] [*See* Hutton, L.—Portraits in Plaster.]
A 23 V 13

Sketch of the Work of. [*See* Dawson, W. J.—Makers of Modern English.]
H 10 S 14

KEBBEL, Thos. Edward. Conservative Estimate of the House of Lords. [*See* Subjects of the Day, 4.]
F 7 U 29

KEBLE, Rev. John. The Christian Year: Thoughts in Verse. 18mo. Oxford, 1829.
H 10 P 29

John Keble: a Biography; by Walter Lock. 8vo. Lond., 1893.
C 13 P 23

Sketch of. [*See* Newman, Cardinal.—Essays, 2.]
G 1 U 6

KECHT, J. S. Verbesserter praktischer Weinbau in Gärten und auf Weinbergen. 8vo. Leip. (n d.)
A 18 Q 42

KEELER, Chas. A. Evolution of the Colors of North American Land Birds. Roy. 8vo. San Franc., 1893.
A 15 R 11

KEELY, John Worrell, and his Discoveries: Aerial Navigation; by Mrs. Bloomfield Moore. 8vo. Lond., 1893.
A 29 T 17

KEENE, Henry George. Oriental Biographical Dictionary. [*See* Beale, T. W.]
C 18 T 2

History of India. Vols. 1 and 2. 12mo. Lond., 1893.
B 29 V 15, 16

KEIGHLEY. [*See* Goodchild, K.]

KEITH, Rev. Dr. Alexander. Evidence of the truth of the Christian Religion derived from the literal fulfilment of prophecy. 30th ed. 8vo. Edinb., 1848.
G 15 S 21

KELLER, Dr. C. Mittheilungen über Medusen. 8vo. Geneva, 1884.
A 30 T 15

KELLER, Dr. Harry F. Modern Chemistry. [*See* Wurtz, C. A.]
A 21 R 84

KELLERMAN, Mme. Charbonnet-. Principles of the Method Le Couppey [How to play the Pianoforte]. 12mo. Melb., 1880.
MA 3 P 43

KELLEY, Sir Edward, Necromancer. [Life of], 1555-95; by A. F. Pollard. (Lives of Twelve Bad Men.) 8vo. Lond., 1894.
C 18 T

KELLOGG, Rev. Dr. Samuel H. Leviticus. [*See* Expositor's Bible.]
G 19 R 3

KELLY & CO. Post Office London Directory, 1894-95. 4 vols. imp. 8vo. Lond., 1894-95.
E

KELLY, Edmond. Evolution and Effort, and their relation to Religion and Politics. 8vo. Lond., 1895.
G 1 U 26

KELLY, Edward, Bushranger. [Life of], 1855-80; by J. W. Allen. (Lives of Twelve Bad Men.) 8vo. Lond., 1894.
C 18 T 9

KELLY, Hugh. The School for Wives: a Comedy. [*See* London Stage, 4.]
H 2 S 36

KELLY, J. Report on the Prospects of Trade with India. [*See* Rowe, S. H.]
MF 4 R 3

KELLY, Rev. Wm. Aleilat; or the Challenge: a Drama in three acts. 12mo. Dubl n, 1870. MH 1 U 47

KELTIE, John Scott. History of the Scottish Highlands, Highland Clans, and Highland Regiments. 2 vols. imp. 8vo. Edinb., 1885. B 31 V 10, 11
The Partition of Africa; with maps. 8vo. Lond., 1893. B 16 R 10
Another Copy. 8vo. Lond., 1895. B 16 R 12

KELVIN, Baron. Popular Lectures and Addresses. 3 vols. 12mo. Lond., 1889-94. A 29 R 1-3
[*For earlier works see Thomson, Sir Wm., in earlier catalogues.*]

———— and TAIT, Prof. P. G. Treatise on Natural Philosophy. 2 vols. 8vo. Cambridge, 1890.
A 30 T 7, 8

KEMBLE, Fanny. Letters of Edward Fitzgerald to, 1871-83. 8vo. Lond., 1895. C 19 T 15

KEMBLE, John Philip. Lodoiska: a Melo-dramatic Opera. [*See* London Stage, 2.] H 2 S 34
The Panel: a Comedy. [*See* London Stage, 4.] H 2 S 36

KEMP, George Meikle. Biographical Sketch of; by T. Bonnar. 8vo. Edinb., 1892. C 21 R 5

KEMP, Dr. T. Lindley. Indications of Instinct. 12mo. Lond., 1854. A 28 P 6
Natural History of Creation. 12mo. Lond., 1852. A 26 P 12

KEMP, Wilfred. The Practical Plasterer. (Weale's Series.) 12mo. Lond., 1893. A 17 R 26

KEMP, William. Nine Daies Wonder. [*See* Collectanea Adamantæa.] J 18 R 2

KEMPE, Harry Robt. Engineers' Year-book of Formulæ, Rules, Tables, Data, and Memoranda in Civil, Mechanical, Electrical, Marine, and Mine Engineering, 1895. 8vo. Lond., 1895. E

KEMPIS, Thos. à. The Imitation of Christ. A fac-simile Reproduction of the 1st edition, 1471-72; with an Introduction by Canon W. J. K. Little. Sm. fol. Lond., 1893. G 5 U 25
The World's Own Book. [*See* Fitzgerald, P.] J 15 S 25

KENDALL, Elizabeth. Growth of the English Nation. [*See* Coman, Katherine.] B 23 S 12

KENDALL, Henry. Papers on the Reliques of the late Henry Kendall and Daniel Henry Denieby. [*See* Donohue, F. J.] MJ 3 S 2

KENDALL, J. D. The Iron Ores of Great Britain and Ireland. 8vo. Lond., 1893. A 24 S 8

KENNEDY, Dr. John. Instrumental Music. 8vo. Sydney, 1883. MA 2 V 56

KENNEL CLUB CALENDAR AND STUD BOOK. Vols 19-21. 8vo. Lond., 1892-94. E

KENT, Wm. Mechanical Engineer's Pocket-book. 12mo. New York, 1895. A 22 P 7
The Strength of Materials. 18mo New York, 1890. A 22 P 15

KENT, Wm. Saville-. The Great Barrier Reef of Australia, its products and potentialities. 4to. Lond., 1893.* MA 7 Q 13†
Preliminary Observations on a Natural History Collection. (Proc. Roy. Soc., Queens and, 6.) 8vo. Brisbane, 1889. ME 1 T
Notes on the Embryology of the Australian Rock Oyster. (Proc. Roy. Soc., Queensland, 7.) 8vo. Brisbane, 1891. ME 1 T
Description of a new species of true Barramundi, *Osteoglossum Jardinii*, from North Queensland. (Proc. Roy. Soc., Queensland, 8.) 8vo. Brisbane, 1892. ME 1 T

KENT ARCHÆOLOGICAL SOCIETY. Archæologa Cantiana: being Transactions of the Kent Archæological Society. Vols. 20, 21 Roy. 8vo. Lond., 1893-95 E

KENTUCKY. Facts and Figures to show how Lexington, Kentucky, maintains her Matchless Supremacy. Obl. 12mo. Lexington, 1893. D 15 P 13
Report of the Inspector of Mines, 1892. 8vo. Frankfort, 1892. E

KENTUCKY STATE COLLEGE. A. and M. College, Lexington, 1893, 1894. 8vo. Lexington, 1893. E

KEOPUOLANI, Queen of the Sandwich Islands. Memoir of, and other Tracts. 18mo. Lond., 1825. MG 2 P 34

KERN, H. De Fidjitaal vergeleken met hare verwanten in Indonisië en Polynesië. 4to. (n.p.n.d.) MJ 1 V 13

KERN DELTA, The. Location, Resources, Attractions, and Development of the Kern Delta, California. 8vo. Bakersfield, Cal, 1893. D 16 V 11

KERNER VON MARILAUN, Prof. Anton. Natural History of Plants. From the German, by Dr. F. W. Oliver. Vol. 1. Imp. 8vo. Lond., 1894. A 22 V 2

KERNOT, Prof. Wm. Chas. Best form for a Balance Beam. (Roy. Soc., Vict., 17, and n.s., vol. 7.) 8vo. Melb., 1881-95. ME 1 P
Experiments on Model Girders. 8vo. Melb., 1882. MA 3 S 49
Floods on the River Barwon. (Roy. Soc., Vict., 13.) 8vo. Melb., 1883. ME 1 P
Notes on small Motors. (Roy. Soc., Vict., 16.) 8vo. Melb., 1890. ME 1 P
The Tay Bridge. (Roy. Soc., Vict., 17.) 8vo. Melb., 1881. ME 1 P

KERR, Dr. Norman Shanks. Inebriety or Narcomania, its Etiology, Pathology, Treatment, and Jurisprudence. 3rd ed. 8vo. New York, 1894. F 10 U 3

KERR, Walter M. Through Zambesi. [*See* Great Explorers.] D 15 V 21, 22

KERR, Prof. Washington C. Minerals and Mineral Localities of North Carolina. [*See* Genth, F. A.] A 24 U 29

———— and HANNA, George B. Ores of North Carolina. (Geo. Survey of North Carolina.) Roy. 8vo. Raleigh, 1888. A 24 V 27

KERSHAW, S. Wayland. Bygone Surrey. [*See* Clinch, G.] B 21 T 10

KESWICK, and its Neighbourhood: a Hand-book for the use of Visitors. 12mo. Windermere, 1852. D 18 P 26

KETTLEWELL, Rev. John Life and Times of, with Details of the History of the Nonjurors. 8vo. Lond., 1895. C 19 V 17

KEULEN, Joannes van. Nieuwe Pascaert van Oost Indien. Fol. Amsterdam, 1680. D 8 P 34 ‡

KEVIN, John W. Poetic Selections for the use of Schools. 12mo. Sydney, 1894. MH 1 U 63

KEW, Harry Wallis. The Dispersal of Shells. 12mo. Lond., 1893. A 27 P 24

KEW ROYAL GARDENS. [*See* Great Britain and Ireland.]

KEYS, J. Contribution to the Flora of Mount Perry. (Proc. Roy. Soc., Queensland, 1.) 8vo. Brisbane, 1885. ME 1 T

KEYSER, Leander S. In Bird Land. 8vo. Chicago, 1894. A 27 P 23

KHAME, African Chief. [*See* Lloyd, Rev. E.—Three Great African Chiefs.] B 1 P 21

KIDD, Benjamin. Social Evolution. 8vo. Lond., 1894. F 14 T 18

KIDDLE, Hugh Chas. Small Whirlwinds. (Journal Roy. Soc., N.S.W., 27.) 8vo. Sydney, 1893. ME 1 R

KIEPERT, Heinrich. Formæ orbis antiqui. Part 1. Fol. Berlin, 1894. D 8 P 24 ‡

KIERSTED, Wynkoop. Prevailing Theories and Practices relating to Sewage Disposal. 12mo. New York, 1894. A 22 Q 41

KILBORNE, F. L. Texas Fever. [*See* Smith, Dr. T.] A 30 R 4

KILGOUR, Martin H., SWAN, H., and BIGGS, C. H. W. Electrical Distribution: its Theory and Practice. 12mo. Lond., 1893. A 21 Q 39

KILLEN, Rev. Dr. Wm. D. The Ecclesiastical History of Ireland from the earliest period to the present times. 2 vols. 8vo. Lond., 1875. G 15 S 22, 23

KILLWORTH, Rev. Arthur. The Federation of Australasia. 8vo. Sydney, 1892. MF 2 R 46

Papers on the Christian Life. 12mo. Sydney, 1892. MG 1 P 87

KIMBER, Diana C. Text-book of Anatomy and Physiology for Nurses. 8vo. New York, 1895. A 33 T 22

KING, Lieut.-Col. Cooper. [Life of] George Washington. 8vo. Lond., 1894. C 17 R 19

KING, F. H. The Soil, its Nature, Relations, and Fundamental Principles of Management. 12mo. New York, 1895. A 19 P 6

KING, Georgina. The Palæozoic Carboniferous Formation in New South Wales and the occurrence of our Mineral Wealth. 12mo. Sydney, 1895. MA 3 U 30

KING, Harriet E. H. Cardinal Manning. [*See* Manning, Cardinal.] G 9 U 26

KING, John Chas. Acts of Council relating to the Corporations of Melbourne and Geelong; with Bye-laws and Market Regulations of the City Council of Melbourne. 8vo. Melb., 1850. MF 3 T 33

KING, Rev. Joseph. In Memoriam, a Veteran Missionary of the London Missionary Society, the late Rev. A. W. Murray; a Sermon. 8vo. Sydney, 1892. MG 2 Q 29

Ten Decades: the Australian Centenary Story of the London Missionary Society. 12mo. Lond., 1895. MG 2 R 58

KING, Moses. Hand-book of New York City; an Outline History and Description of the American Metropolis. 2nd ed., illustrated. 8vo. Boston, 1893. D 15 R 9

KING, Capt. Philip Gidley. Description of Norfolk Island. [*See* Philip, Capt. A.—Extracts of Letters.] MC 9 P 1 †

KING, Rev. Robt. L. Farewell: a Sermon preached at Broughton Chapel, Moore College. 12mo. Sydney, 1878. MG 2 R 31

The Path of the Just: a funeral sermon preached on the occasion of the death of the Rev. Thos. Hassall. 8vo. Sydney, 1868. MG 1 S 11

Letter addressed to the Jews in Sydney. 12mo. Sydney, 1877. MG 1 P 55

Farewell Sermon, preached in St. Philip's Church, Sydney, June 10th, 1855; also a Sermon preached in the Temporary Church, Parramatta, June 17th, 1855. 8vo. Sydney, 1855. MG 1 S 12

Plea for the Baptism of Infants. 8vo. Sydney, 1867. MG 1 S 10

Guide to the Study of the Prophecies which relate to "The Kingdom and Coming of our Lord Jesus Christ." 8vo. Sydney, 1854. MG 1 S 9

KING, Rufus. Life and Correspondence of. Edited by his grandson. Vols. 1 and 2, 1755-05. Roy. 8vo. New York, 1894. C 16 U 14, 15

KING, Thos. Lovers' Quarrels; or, Like Master Like Man: an Interlude. [See London Stage, 3.] H 2 S 35

KING, The! The KING! VIVE LE ROI! Seventh pamphlet of the second manifestation and personal reign on earth of the Lord Jesus Christ in flesh. 12mo. Melb., 1889. MG 2 R 23

KINGLAKE, Alexander Wm. Eothen. New ed. 12mo. Lond., 1851. D 20 Q 15

KINGLAKE, Edward. The Australian at Home: Notes and Anecdotes of Life at the Antipodes, including Useful Hints to those intending to settle in Australia. 12mo. Lond. (n.d.) MD 7 T 37

KING'S COLLEGE, London Calendars for 1892-93 and 1893-04. 2 vols. 12mo. Lond., 1892-93. E

KING'S SCHOOL MAGAZINE. Nos. 1-9, June, 1887- Oct., 1889. 8vo. Sydney 1887-89. ME 15 Q

KINGSBURY, J. J. The Financial Position of the Colonies in relation to Banking. 8vo. Brisbane, 1894. MF 4 R 20

KINGSFORD, C. L. The Crusades. [See Archer, T. A.] B 36 Q 5

KINGSFORD, Wm. History of Canada. Vols. 6, 7, 1776-1807. 8vo. Toronto, 1893-94. B 17 R 6, 7

KINGSLEY, Rev. Charles. Selections from some of the Writings of. 8vo. Lond., 1873. J 11 S 6

Glaucus; or, the Wonders of the Shore. 12mo. Camb., 1855. A 28 P 14

[Life of]; by Rev. M. Kaufmann. 8vo. Lond., 1892. C 13 P 24

Sketch of. [See Muller, F. Max.—Chips from a German Workshop.] J 9 R 32

Sketch of; with Portrait. [See Bolton, Sarah K.— Famous Leaders.] C 17 P 27

KINGSTON, Alfred. Hertfordshire during the Great Civil War and the Long Parliament. Sm. 4to. Lond., 1894. B 21 U 14

KINGSTON, Wm. Beatty-. Men, Cities, and Events. 8vo. Lond., 1895. C 22 R 4

KINLOCH, George Ritchie The Ballad Book. [See Bibliotheca Curiosa.] J 18 Q 22

KINNAIRD, D. The Merchant of Bruges; or, Beggar's Bush: a Play. [See London Stage, 4.] H 2 S 36

KINNS, Rev. Dr. Samuel. Moses and Geology; or, the Harmony of the Bible with Science. Revised ed. 8vo. Lond., 1895. G 3 R 16

KIPLING, Rudyard. Barrack-Room Ballads and other verses. 5th ed. 8vo. Lond, 1893. H 10 Q 24

Departmental Ditties and other Verses. 7th ed. 12mo. Calcutta, 1892. H 8 T 53

KIRBY, Capt. J. Narrative of a Voyage from Melbourne to the Gulf of Carpentaria. 12mo. Melb., 1862. MD 1 P 28

KIRBY, Wm. Cultivation of the Soil in Ancient and Modern Times. 8vo. Melb., 1862. MA 1 Q 55

KIRBY, Wm. F. A Hand-book to the Order Lepidoptera. Part 1.—Butterflies. 8vo. Lond., 1894. A 27 S 23

The Hero of Esthonia, and other Studies in the Romantic Literature of that country. With a Map of Esthonia. 2 vols. 8vo. Lond., 1895. B 35 R 6, 7

KIRCHNER, E., & Co. Saw-mill and Wood-working Machinery. Illustrated. 4to. Leipzig, 1893. A 12 T 6 †

KIRK, H. B. A Knowledge of the New Zealand Sponges. (Trans. N.Z. Inst., 27.) 8vo. Wellington, 1894. ME 2 R

KIRK, John Foster. History of the Reign of Ferdinand and Isabella. [See Prescott, W. H.] B 34 Q 8-10

History of the Conquest of Mexico. [See Prescott, W. H.] B 19 Q 8-10

History of the Conquest of Peru. [See Prescott, W. H.] B 19 Q 11, 12

History of the Reign of Philip II. [See Prescott, W. H.] B 34 Q 5-7

KIRK, Rev. Robt. The Secret Commonwealth of Elves, Fauns, and Fairies. Comment by A. Lang. 12mo. Lond., 1893. B 37 P 6

KIRK, T. Preparation and Preservation of Botanical Specimens. (Trans. N.Z. Inst., 27.) 8vo. Wellington, 1894. ME 2 R

———, BALFOUR, J. M., and WARD, Capt. E. W. Report on the Durability of New Zealand Timber in Constructive Works, &c. Roy. 8vo. Wellington, 1875. MA 1 V 59

KIRKMAN, Rev. Thos. Penyngton. Church Cursing and Atheism. [See Religious Pamphlets, 2.] G 9 V 17

Orthodoxy from the Hebrew point of view. 12mo. Lond. (n.d.) G 9 V 34

Church Cursing and Disestablishment. 12mo. Warrington, 1874. G 9 V 34

KIRKPATRICK, T. S. G. Simple Rules for the discrimination of Gems. 18mo. Lond., 1895. A 24 R 17

KISKINOUYE, K. On the Development of Araneina. 8vo. (n.p.n.d.) A 30 V 17

KISSACK, A. H. The Savo Megapode. (Proc. Roy. Soc., Queensland, 1.) 8vo. Brisbane, 1885. ME 1 T

KITCHIN, Very Rev. Geo. Wm. Memoir of Bishop E. H Browne. 8vo. Lond., 1895. C 21 R 11

KITTREDGE, G. L. Language of Chaucer's Troilus. [See Chaucer Soc. Pubs.] E

KLEIN, Augusta. Among the Gods: Scenes of India, with Legends by the way. Illustrated. 8vo. Edinb., 1895.
G 1 P 28

KLOSSOVSKY, A. Distribution annuelle des orages à la surface du globe terrestre. 4to. Odessa, 1894.
A 15 Q 18 †

Organisation de l'étude Climatérique Spéciale de la Russie et Problèmes de la Météorologie agricole. 4to. Odessa, 1894.
A 15 Q 18 †

KNAGGS, Dr. Henry. Butterflies and Moths. [See Taylor, Dr. J. E.—Notes on Collecting.] A 29 Q 38

KNAGGS, R. C., & Co. Newcastle Nautical Almanac, Directory, and Guide to the Port of Newcastle, with Sailing Directions for Torres Straits for 1893-95. 3 vols. 8vo. Newcastle, 1892-94.
ME 3 S

KNAGGS, Dr. Samuel Thos. An analysis of the mechanism producing flexion of the Human Fingers. 8vo. Sydney, 1875.
MA 1 U 59

Dr. De Lion, Clairvoyant: Confessions of a Vagabond Life in Australia. 12mo. Sydney, 1895.
MJ 3 P 30

Recreations of an Australian Surgeon. 8vo. Sydney, 1888.
MA 3 T 55

Some Observations on Medical Ethics. 8vo. Sydney, 1890.
MA 3 T 20

Slade and the Spirits. Spiritualism considered as an infectious mental disease. [See Mediums and their Dupes.]
MG 2 Q 36

KNAPP, John M. The Universities and the Social Problem; an Account of the University Settlements in East London. 8vo. Lond., 1895.
F 8 U 22

KNAUFF, T. C. Athletics for Physical Culture. 12mo. New York, 1894.
G 18 Q 16

KNEASS, Strickland L. Practice and Theory of the Injector. 8vo. New York, 1894.
A 25 U 9

KNECHT, Dr. Edmund, RAWSON, Christopher, and LOEWENTHAL, Dr. Richard. Manual of Dyeing. 3 vols. 8vo. Lond., 1893.
A 11 R 28-30

KNEIPP, Rev. Sebastian. Thus shall thou live: Hints and Advice for the Healthy and the Sick on a simple rational mode of Life and a natural method of cure. Translated from 19th German ed. 8vo. Lond., 1894.
A 26 Q 32

KNIES, Dr. Max. Relations of Diseases of the Eye to General Diseases. Edited by Dr. Henry D. Noyes. Roy. 8vo. New York, 1895.
A 33 U 10

KNIGHT & VON RIEBEN, Messrs. *Barrier Miner* Business Directory, 1892. 8vo. Broken Hill, 1892.
ME 10 S

KNIGHT, C. Description of a new species of *Parmelia* from Victoria. (Proc. Roy. Soc., Queensland, 1.) 8vo. Brisbane, 1884.
ME 1 T

KNIGHT, Charles. Shadows of the Old Booksellers. 8vo. Lond., 1865.
C 21 Q 13

Works of Shakespeare. Imp. ed. [See Shakespeare, William.]
H 40 T 7, 8 ‡

Sketch of. [See Smith, G. B.—Leaders of Modern Industry.]
C 14 P 14

A Sketch; by Alice A. Clowes. 8vo. Lond., 1892
C 15 R 14

KNIGHT, Edward Frederick. The Cruise of the *Falcon*: a Voyage to South America in a 30-ton yacht. 6th ed. Illustrated. 12mo. Lond. (n.d.)
D 15 Q 27

Where Three Empires Meet: a narrative of recent travel in Kashmir, Western Tibet, Gilgit, and the adjoining Countries. 8vo. Lond., 1893.
D 17 V 4

Yachting. [See Sullivan, Sir E.]
A 29 Q 40

KNIGHT, George H. Patent-office Manual, including the Law and Practice of Cases in the U.S. Patent Office. Roy. 8vo. Boston, 1894.
F 4 R 13

KNIGHT, Dr. Geo. W., and COMMONS, John R. History of Higher Education in Ohio. 8vo. Wash., 1891.
G 18 R 15

KNIGHT, J. J. In the Early Days: History and Incident of Pioneer Queensland. With Dictionary of Dates in chronological order. Illustrated. 8vo. Brisbane, 1895.
MB 2 P 57

KNIGHT, Joseph. Crystallized or Glacéd Fruits. 8vo. Melb. (n.d.)
MA 3 T 9

The Castor Oil Plant. 8vo. Melb. (n.d.)
MA 3 T 9

Cultivation of Flax and its after treatment. 8vo. Melb. (n.d.)
MA 3 T 9

KNIGHT, Joseph. Theatrical Notes. 8vo. Lond., 1893.
J 2 T 28

[Life of] David Garrick. 8vo. Lond., 1894.
C 18 T 4

KNIGHT, Thos. The Honest Thieves: a Farce. [See London Stage, 1.]
H 2 S 33

KNIGHT, Prof. Wm. The Philosophy of the Beautiful. 2 vols. 8vo. Lond., 1891-93.
G 7 U 24, 25

KNIGHT, Wm. Henry. Western Australia, its history, progress, condition, and prospects. 8vo. Perth, 1870.
MD 4 Q 22

KNIGHTON, Dr. Wm. Sporting Literature of Ancient Greece and Rome. [See Roy. Soc. of Lit., 2nd series, 16.]
E

KNIGHTS TEMPLARS OF MASSACHUSETTS AND RHODE ISLAND. Proceedings, 1892. 8vo. Central Falls, 1892.
G 14 T 24

KNIGHTS TEMPLARS OF OREGON. Proceedings of the Sixth Annual Conclave, 1892. 8vo. Eugene, 1892.
G 14 T 29

KNOLLYS, Col. Henry. Life of Gen. Sir H. Grant, with Selections from his Correspondence; with Portraits, Maps, and Plans. 2 vols. 8vo. Edinb., 1894.
C 17 R 5, 6

KNOWLEDGE. Vols. 14–16. 4to. Lond., 1891–93.
E

KNOWLES, James Sheridan. The Elocutionist: Pieces in prose and verse, with principles of elocution. 26th ed. 8vo. Lond. (n.d.)
J 4 R 3

KNOX, E. F. V. The Irish Parliament of the Past. [*See* Subjects of the Day, 3.]
F 7 U 28

KNOX, G. Opinion *re* Bishop of Sydney. [*See* Gordon, A.]
MG 9 P 9 †

KNOX, John. A Biography; by ?. H. Brown. 2 vols. 8vo. Lond., 1895.
C 22 R 5, 6

[Life of]; by Florence A. MacCunn. 8vo. Lond., 1895.
C 19 V 4

The Scottish Reformation. [*See* Bettany, G. T.—Popular History of the Reformation.]
G 14 Q 33

KOBELL, Louise von. Conversations of Dr. Döllinger. 8vo. Lond., 1892.
C 18 P 4

KOCH, C. F. Courage, Independence, Presence of Mind, and a Cheerful Disposition as a result of Gymnastic Exercise. 8vo. Milwaukee (n.d.)
G 18 R 35

KOCH, G. Die Indo-Australische Lepidopteren-Fauna. 8vo. Leipzig, 1865.
MA 2 U 66

KOCH, Dr. J. Chronology of Chaucer's Writings. [*See* Chaucer Society Pubs.]
E

KOCH, Prof. Robert. Bacteriological Diagnosis of Cholera, Waterfiltration and Cholera, and the Cholera in Germany during the Winter of 1892–93. Translated by G. Duncan. 8vo. Edinb., 1894.
A 33 T 20

Treatment of Tubercular Disease. [*See* Springthorpe, Dr. J. W.]
MA 3 S 32

Proposed Cure for Consumption. [*See* Candler, C.]
MA 3 S 53

Propriétés attribuées à la Tuberculine. [*See* Arloing, Dr. S.]
A 33 U 24

KOETAIMI O TONGA. Nos. 1 and 2. 4to. Nukualofa, 1882.
ME 9 Q 29 †

KÖLBING, Prof. E. Romance of Sir Beues of Hamtoun. [*See* Early English Text Society.]
E

KÖLLIKER, Prof. Albert von. Pennatulida. [*See* Thomson, Sir C. W., and Murray, Dr. J.—Voyage of H.M.S. *Challenger*.]
A 6 †

KONGELIGT NORDISK OLDSKRIFT-SELSKAB. Aarbøger for Nordisk Oldkyndighed og Historie, 1892–93. 2 vols. 8vo. Kjöbenhavn, 1892–93.
E

KÖNIG, Abraham. La Araucana de Ercilla. Roy. 8vo. Santiago, 1888.
H 5 U 38

KONINCK, L. G. de. Faune du Calcaire Carbonifère de Belgique. [*See* Musée Royal d'Histoire Natural de Belgique, Annales du.]
A 6 V and W ‡

KONINKLIJKE ACADEMIE DER SCHOONE KUNSTEN VAN ANTWERPEN, 1892–93. Jaarlijksch Versing en plechtige prijsuitdeeling. 8vo. Anvers, 1894.
E

KOPP, Hermann. Sketch of. [*See* Thorpe, Dr. T. E.—Historical Chemistry.]
C 17 R 2

KOSMOS. [*See* Ruin of the Turf.]
MJ 1 Q 22

KOSSUTH, Louis. Authentic Life of His Excellency. 8vo. Lond., 1851.
C 14 R 15

Memoirs of my Exile. 8vo. Lond., 1880.
C 13 V 13

KOTTMAN, Dr. G. The Scrch Cane Disease. 8vo. Sydney, 1893.
MA 1 Q 67

The Sugar Cane Disease. 8vo. Sydney, 1893.
MA 1 Q 67

KOVALEVSKY, Sonya. A Biography; by Anna C. Leffler, Duchess of Cajanello, and Sisters Rajevsky: being an Account of her Life; by Sonya Kovalevsky. Illustrated. 8vo. Lond., 1895.
C 19 S 8

KOWALSKI, Henri. Festal Lyric, composed and dedicated to His Holiness Leo XIII. [Music.] Fol. Sydney, 1893.
MA 7 Q 31 †

KREUZHAGE, C. Versuche über das Verdauungsvermögen &c. [*See* Wolff, Dr. E.]
A 32 T 6

KUENEN Dr. A. Three Notices of the Speaker's Commentary. [*See* Religious Pamphlets, 2.]
G 9 V 17

KUZ. [*See* Trial Four, The.]
MJ 3 Q 37

L

LABILLIÈRE, Francis Pe er de. British Federalism, its rise and progress. 8vo. Lond. 1893.
F 12 P 12

The Constitutions of the Australian Colonies. 8vo. Lond., 1872.
MJ 3 Q 16

Federal Britain; or, Unity and Federation of the Empire; with Chapter on Imperial Defence, by Major Sir G. S. Clarke. 8vo. Lond., 1894.
F 9 U 47

LABOUR LEAGUE OF SOUTH AUSTRALIA, Rules for the Government of. 12mo. Adelaide, 1877.
MF 1 P 80

LABOUR TROUBLES and the result of Co-operative Associations in the year 1000; by "A Railway Porter." 12mo. Sydney, 1892.
MF 1 P 66

LABOUR'S REST; an Ode to the day commonly called Sunday; by "W.H." 12mo. Melb., 1871.
MH 1 U 74

LACOUPERIE, A. E. J. B. Terrien de. [*See* Terrien de Lacouperie, A. E. J. B.]

LACOUR, Pierre. Manufacture of Liquors, Wines, and Cordials, without the aid of distillation; also, the Manufacture of Effervescing Beverages and Syrups, Vinegar, and Bitters. Prepared and arranged expressly for the trade. 8vo. New York (n.d.)   A 25 Q 37

LACRETELLE, Chas. Histoire de France pendant le 18ᵉ siècle. 6 vols. 8vo. Paris, 1844.   B 26 S 3-8

LACTANTIUS. Works of. Translated by Rev. Dr. W. Fletcher. (Ante-Nicene Christ. Lib., 21, 22.) 2 vols. 8vo. Edinb., 1871.   G 14 U 21, 22

LADENBURG, Dr. A. Handwörterbuch der Chemie. (Encyklo. der Naturwissenschaften.) Bände 11, 12. Roy. 8vo. Breslau, 1893-94.   E

LADIES AT WORK. Papers on paid employment for ladies; by experts in the several branches. With an Introduction by Lady Jeune. 8vo. Lond., 1893.   F 9 T 24

LADIES' GUIDE TO ARCHERY; by "A late member of a Toxopholite Club in London." 12mo. Melb., 1859.   MA 3 P 39

LADY, A. Seven Years Residence at the Mauritius. [*See* Mauritius.]   D 17 Q 29

LAFARGUE, H. The Study of Languages. 8vo. Melb., 1857.   MK 2 P 11

LAFAYE, Georges. Histoire du culte des Divinités d'Alexandrie: Sérapis, Isis, Harpocrate et Anubis. 8vo. Paris, 1884.   G 16 U 22

LA FAYETTE, Marquis de. In the American Revolution. [*See* Tower, Dr. C.]   B 20 V 7, 8

LAFOND, G. Des Iles Marquises et des Colonies de la France. Roy. 8vo. Paris, 1844.   MD 6 U 18

LAGRANGE, Joseph Louis, Comte de. Œuvres de. Tome 14. 4to. Paris, 1892.   A 32 U 14

LAING, Dr. David. Early Metrical Tables. 12mo. Edinb., 1826.   H 7 U 38

LAING, Robt. M. The Algæ of New Zealand. (Trans. N.Z. Inst., 27.) 8vo. Wellington, 1894.   ME 2 R

LAMARTINE, Alfonse M. L. P. de. History of the Constituent Assembly, 1789-90. 4 vols. (in 2). 12mo. Lond., 1858.   B 8 P 35, 36
Memoirs of my Youth. 12mo. Lond., 1850.   C 17 P 7
The Wanderer and his Home, being a continuation of "Memoirs of my Youth." 12mo. Lond, 1851.   C 17 P 7

LAMB, Charles. Eliana: being the hitherto uncollected Writings of. 12mo. Lond., 1867.   J 11 T 16
The Adventures of Ulysses, to which is added Mrs. Leicester's School; or, the history of several young ladies, related by themselves. Roy. 8vo. Lond., 1841.   J 4 U 2
The Essays of Elia. 1st and 2nd series. Roy. 8vo. Lond., 1840.   J 4 U 2
Memoirs of; by Sir T. N. Talfourd. 8vo. Lond., 1892.   C 13 P 33

LAMB, Prof. H. Cause of the Luminosity of Flame. (Trans. Roy. Soc., S. Australia, 8.) 8vo. Adelaide, 1886.   ME 1 S

LAMB, John. Practical Hints for Agriculturists on Remedies for Rust in Wheat, Phylloxera in Vines, the Codlin Moth in Apples, the Feeding of Cattle, How to grow Beetroot. 8vo. Melb., 1893.   MA 3 W 17

LAMB, Samuel. Tobacco: Cultivation in Queensland. 8vo. Brisb., 1890-92.   MA 1 Q 69
Tobacco Growing in New South Wales. 8vo. Sydney, 1893.   MA 1 Q 65

———— and SUTHERLAND, George Frederick. Report on the Tobacco-growing Industry in the Tumut District. 8vo. Sydney, 1893.   MA 1 Q 65

LAMBROS, Prof. S. P. Catalogue of the Greek Manuscripts on Mount Athos. Vol. I. 4to. Camb., 1895.   K 12 T 19 †

LAMING, Jas. Steam Communication with Australia. (*Bound with Waghorn on Emigration*.) 8vo. Lond., 1856.   MF 2 Q 83

LANCE, Mrs. Jack Hanmer's sad story. [*See* Praed, Mrs. Campbell.—Under the Gum Tree.]   MJ 2 T 44

LANCET, The: a Journal of British and Foreign Medicine, Surgery, Obstetrics, Physiology, Chemistry, Pharmacology, Public Health and News. July, 1892–June, 1895. 6 vols. Imp. 8vo. Lond., 1895.   E

LANCIANI, Prof. Rodolfo. Pagan and Christian Rome. Roy. 8vo. Lond., 1892.   B 30 U 17
Roman Antiquities. [*See* Ramsay, W.]   B 30 S 12

LAND NATIONALISATION LEAGUE OF NEW SOUTH WALES. Manifesto and Rules of. 8vo. Sydney (n.d.)   MF 2 Q 39

LAND QUESTION, The. 8vo. Sydney, 1873.   MF 4 P 22

LAND REFORM LEAGUE. Tracts, Nos. 1 and 2. 8vo. Melb., 1870-71.   MF 2 Q 51, 52

LANDAU, Dr. Wilhelm. Reisen in Asien, Australien, und Amerika. 8vo. Berlin, 1889.   D 20 Q 12

LANDMANN, Col. Universal Gazetteer; or, Geographical Dictionary of the World. 8vo. Lond., 1835.   D 12 T 19

LANDON, Letitia Elizabeth. Poetical Works of. 2 vols. 12mo. Lond., 1850. H 7 U 29, 30

LANDOR, A. H. Savage. Alone with the Hairy Ainu; or, 3,800 miles on a pack saddle in Yezo and a Cruise to the Kurile Islands. 8vo. Lond., 1893. D 14 T 6
Corea or Cho-Sen, the Land of the Morning Calm. Illustrated. 8vo. Lond., 1895. D 17 V 17

LANDSCAPE SCENERY, illustrating Sydney, Parramatta, Richmond, Maitland, Windsor, and Port Jackson. Obl. 8vo. Sydney, 1855. MD 4 P 8 †

LANDSCAPE WONDERS of the Western World. 12mo. Chicago, 1883. D 15 P 18

LANE, Edward Wm. The Arabian Nights' Entertainments. [See Arabian Nights'.] J 5 S 33-35

LANE-POOLE, Stanley. [See Poole, S. L.]

LANG, Dr. Andrew. Ban and Arriere Ban: a Rally of Fugitive Rhymes. 2nd ed. 12mo. Lond., 1894. H 10 U 16
Cock Lane and Common Sense. 12mo. Lond., 1894. G 2 V 39
Homer and the Epic. 8vo. Lond., 1893. J 4 Q 36
St. Andrews. 8vo. Lond., 1893. B 31 U 11
Secret Commonwealth of Elves, Fauns, and Fairies. [See Kirk, Rev. R.] B 37 P 6
Sketch of. [See Matthews, B—Books and Playbooks.] J 8 T 34

LANG, Rev. Dr. John Dunmore. In Memoriam: Two Sermons, preached by Rev. A. M. Jarvie and Rev. P. F. Mackenzie. 8vo. Sydney, 1878. MG 2 S 8
St. Andrews; or, the Presbyterian College, and how it has fallen into its present anomalous and discreditable condition. 8vo. Sydney, 1872. MG 1 S 33

LANG, Dr. William. The Methodical Examination of the Eye: being pt. 1 of a Guide to the Practice of Ophthalmology for Students and Practitioners. 8vo. Lond., 1895. A 26 Q 37

LANGBEIN, Dr. George. Complete Treatise on the Electro-deposition of Metals, as well as Descriptions of the Electric Elements, Dynamo-electric Machines, Thermo-piles, and of the Materials and Processes used in every department of the art; with additions by W. T. Brannt. 2nd ed. Illustrated. Roy. 8vo. Philad., 1894. A 21 V 13

LANGHORNE, Rev. Dr. John. Poetical Works of W. Collins. [See Collins, W.] H 10 U 7

LANGHORNE, Rev. W. H. Reminiscences connected chiefly with Inveresk and Musselburgh, and Sketches of Family Histories. 8vo. Edinb., 1893. B 22 T 9

LANGLAND, William. Piers Plowman. [See Jusserand, J. J.] J 9 T 27
Vision of Piers the Plowman; with Introduction by Kate M. Warren. 12mo. Lond., 1895. J 11 T 43

LANGLOIS, Ernest. Origines et Sources du Roman de la Rose. 8vo. Paris, 1891. J 7 U 33

LANGMAID, J., and GAISFORD, H. Elementary Lessons in Steam Machinery and the Marine Steam Engine, with a short description of the construction of a Battleship. 8vo. Lond., 1893. A 6 S 34

LANGSTROTH, Lorenzo Lorain. The Hive and Honey Bee. Revised, enlarged, and completed by C. Dadart and Son. Illustrated. 8vo. Hamilton, Ill., 1890. A 18 S 29

LANKESTER, Dr. Edwin. On Food. 12mo. Lond., 1861. A 26 Q 36

LANSDELL, Rev. Dr. Henry. Chinese Central Asia: a Ride to Little Tibet. 2 vols. 8vo. Lond., 1893. D 14 T 9, 10

LARA, Horacio. Crónica de la Araucania. 2 vols. 8vo. Santiago, 1888-89. B 16 S 18, 19

LARMINIE, William. West Irish Folk-tales and Romances. (The Camden Library.) 8vo. Lond., 1893. J 9 S 40

LARNED, J. N. History for ready reference, with numerous Historical Maps from original studies. Vols. 1-4. Imp. 8vo. Springfield, Mass., 1894. K 18 T 21-24

LARNER, John B. [Life of] Napoleon. [See Napoleon Bonaparte.] C 17 S 7

LARRAIN ZAÑARTU, J. J. El Ciudadano y el Gobierno. Nueva lei del Rejimen interior de Enero 22 de 1886 concordada y comparada con todos los codigos i leyes del estado. 8vo. Santiago, 1886. F 9 T 31

LARWOOD, Jacob, and HOTTEN, John Camden. The History of Signboards, from the Earliest Times to the Present Day. 8vo. Lond., 1866. B 35 Q 4

LASCELLES, Hon. Gerald. Falconry. [See Cox, Harding.] A 17 U 46

LASLETT, Thomas. Timber and Timber Trees, Native and Foreign. 2nd ed. Revised by Dr. H. M. Ward. 12mo. Lond., 1894. A 20 T 10

LASSALLE, Ferdinand, as a Social Reformer; by E. Bernstein. 8vo. Lond., 1893. C 13 P 32

LASTARRIA, J. V. Proyecto de Código Rural para la Republican de Chile. 8vo. Santiago, 1878. F 14 U 22
Recuerdos Literarios: Datos para la Historia Literaria de la América Española i del Progreso Intelectual en Chile. 8vo. Santiago, 1885. J 5 S 29

LATHAM, Baldwin. Sanitary Engineering: a Guide to the Construction of Works of Sewerage and House Drainage. 2nd ed. 8vo. Lond., 1878. A 22 T 29

Supplementary Catalogue—1893-95.

LATIMER, Elizabeth W. Russia and Turkey in the 19th Century. 8vo. Chicago, 1893. B 31 S 2

LATORRE, Enrique C. Estudio sobre la Lei de Matrimonio Civil. Roy. 8vo. Santiago, 1887. F 7 U 14

LAUD, Rt. Rev. William, Archbishop of Canterbury. Life and Times of; by Rev. C. H. Simpkinson. 8vo. Lond., 1894. C 21 Q 19
Life of; by "A Romish Recusant." 8vo. Lond., 1894. C 16 S 21
Sketch of. [*See* Fowler, Rev. M.—Notable Archbishops.] C 13 V 12

LAUER, Paul E. Church and State in New England. (Johns Hopkins University Studies, 10.) 8vo. Baltimore, 1892. B 18 S 10

LAUGHTON, Prof. John Knox. [Life of] Nelson. 12mo. Lond., 1895. C 22 P 14
State Papers relating to the Defeat of the Spanish Armada, 1588. (Navy Record Soc., 1.) 8vo. Lond., 1894. E

LAUNCESTON AND WESTERN RAILWAY, no Loss to the Country: Promoters *v.* Antagonists; by "Crito." 8vo. Launceston, 1872. MF 2 Q 58

LAURIE, A. P. Facts about Processes, Pigments, and Vehicles: a Manual for Art Students. 12mo. Lond., 1895. A 23 Q 40

LAURIE, Henry. Conservatism and Democracy. 8vo. Melb., 1808. MF 2 T 75

LAURIE, Dr. Joseph. Homœopathic Domestic Medicine. 12mo. Lond., 1842. A 26 P 11
The Homœopathic Domestic Medicine. 27th edition. 8vo. Lond., 1885. A 26 S 8

LAURIE, R. H. Map of New Zealand. Folded 18mo. Lond., 1845. MD 2 W 53

LAURIE, Prof. Simon Somerville. Historical Survey of pre-Christian Education. 8vo. Lond., 1895. G 15 R 30

LAUTERER, Dr. Joseph. Gums of *Eucalypts* and *Angophoras*. (Proc. Roy. Soc., Queensland, 8.) 8vo. Brisbane, 1891. ME 1 T
Leprosy in the North of Europe and its contagious character. (Proc. Roy. Soc., Queensland, 10.) 8vo. Brisbane, 1893. ME 1 T
Queensland Scorpions. (Proc. Roy. Soc., Queensland, 10.) 8vo. Brisbane, 1893. ME 1 T

LAUZUN, Duc de, and the Court of Louis XV. From the French of G. Maugras. 8vo. Lond., 1895. C 21 S 20

LAVALETTE, Count, Adjutant and Private Secretary to Napoleon, and Postmaster-General under the Empire. Memoirs of. 8vo. Lond., 1894. C 17 R 14

LAVAQUI, M. S. Principios del Derecho. [*See* Seneuil, J. G. C.] F 0 T 28

LAVOISIER, Antoine L. Sketch of. [*See* Thorpe, Dr. T. E.—Historical Chemistry.] C 17 R 2

LAW INSTITUTE OF NEW SOUTH WALES. Rules. 8vo. Sydney (n.d.) MF 4 Q 37

LAW MAGAZINE AND LAW REVIEW. 4th series, vols. 17-19. 3 vols. 8vo. Lond., 1892-94. E

LAW REPORTS OF GREAT BRITAIN AND IRELAND. Admiralty and Ecclesiastical Cases. Vols. 1-4, 1865-75. Roy. 8vo. Lond., 1867-75. E
Chancery Appeal Division Cases, 1865-95. 58 vols. Roy. 8vo. Lond., 1866-95. E
Common Pleas Division Cases, 1865-80. 15 vols. Roy. 8vo. Lond., 1866-80. E
Crown Cases Reserved. Vols. 1, 2, 1865-75. Roy 8vo. Lond., 1872-75. E
Current Index of Cases, 1893. Roy. 8vo. Lond., 1893. E
Digest of Cases, 1865-90. 3 vols. Roy. 8vo. Lond., 1892. E
English and Irish Appeal Cases. Vols. 1-7, 1866-75. Roy. 8vo. Lond., 1866-75. E
Equity Cases. Vols. 1-20, 1865-75. Roy. 8vo. Lond., 1866-75. E
Exchequer Cases, 1865-80. 15 vols. Roy. 8vo. Lond., 1866-80. E
Privy Council Appeals, Vols. 1-6, 1865-75; and Appeal Cases before House of Lords, Judicial Committee of the Privy Council, and Peerage Cases, 1875-94. 25 vols. Roy. 8vo. Lond., 1866-94. E
Probate and Divorce Cases, Vols. 1-3, 1865-75; and Probate Division Cases, 1875-94. 22 vols. Roy. 8vo. Lond., 1865-94. E
Public General Statutes, 1866-94. 29 vols. Roy. 8vo. Lond., 1866-94. E
Queen's Bench Division Cases, 1865-95. 44 vols. Roy. 8vo. Lond., 1866-95. E
Scotch and Divorce Appeal Cases, Vols. 1, 2; 1865-75. Roy. 8vo. Lond., 1869-75. E
The Weekly Notes: being Notes of Cases heard and determined by the House of Lords, the Court of Appeal, the Chancery, Queen's Bench, and Probate, Divorce, and Admiralty Divisions of the High Court of Justice and Cases in Bankruptcy, 1893 and 1894. 2 vols. Sm. 4to. Lond., 1893-94. E

LAWRENCE, John Laird Mair, Lord. [Life of]; by Sir Charles Aitchison. (Rulers of India.) 8vo. Oxford, 1892. C 13 P 15

LAWRENCE, Sir Thos. [Plaster Cast of.] [*See* Hutton, L.—Portraits in Plaster.] A 23 V 13

LAWRENCE, W. J. Life of Gustavus Vaughan Brooke, tragedian. Roy. 8vo. Belfast, 1892. C 13 V 5

LAWRENCE, Walter R. The Valley of Kashmir. Illustrated. Roy. 8vo. Lond., 1895. D 19 V 23

LAWSON, Sir Charles. Private Life of Warren Hastings. 8vo. Lond., 1895. C 22 R 8

LAYARD, George Somes. Tennyson and his Pre-Raphaelite Illustrators. 8vo. Lond., 1894. A 23 T 19

LAYMAN, A. [See Thoughts on Religion.] G 19 P 34

LAZAR, Samuel, and DIAMOND, Arthur. Prince Enterprise; or Harlequin Ogre and the Kangaroo, Cockatoo, and 'Possum-too; Extravaganza and Pantomime. 12mo. Adelaide, 1874. MH 1 Q 28

LAZARUS, Henry. The English Revolution of the 20th Century: a Prospective History. 8vo. Lond., 1894. J 6 T 26

LEA, Dr. A. Sheridan. The Chemical Basis of the Animal Body. 8vo. Lond., 1892. A 26 T 15

LEACH, Sir George. The American Cup Races, 1893. [See Sullivan, Sir E.—Yachting, 2.] A 29 Q 41

LEADER, John Temple. Life of Sir Robt. Dudley. Roy. 8vo. Florence, 1895. C 19 U 13

LEAF, Dr. Walter. A Modern Priestess of Isis. [See Solovyoff, V. S.] G 2 U 12

LEANE, Caroline Agnes, (Agnes Neale.) Shadows and Sunbeams. 18mo. Adelaide, 1893. MH 1 U 49

LEASK, A. Ritchie. Breakdowns at Sea, and how to repair them. Illustrated. 12mo. Lond., 1894. A 22 P 39

Refrigerating Machinery. Illustrated. 8vo. Lond., 1895. A 25 R 17

LEAVITT, T. W. H. The Jubilee History of Tasmania. 2 vols. 4to. Melb., 1887. MB 1 U 18, 19

LEBAHN, Dr. Falck. Faust. [See Goethe, J. W. von.] H 2 U 28

LE CARON, Major Henry, (Thomas Beach). Twenty-five Years in the Secret Service: the Recollections of a Spy. 8vo. Lond., 1892. C 16 R 18

LE COINTE, Abbé. Conspiracy of the Norman Barons against William the Bastard. [See Bibliotheca Curiosa.] J 18 Q 43

LECONTE, Dr. John L. List of the Coleoptera of North America. Part 1. 8vo. Wash., 1863. A 27 U 18

New Species of North American Coleoptera. Part 1. 8vo. Wash., 1866. A 30 R 7

LECTURE on Capital Punishment; by "G.H." 8vo. Orange, 1871. MF 4 R 9

LÉCRIVAIN, Chas. A. Le Sénat Romain depuis Dioclétien à Rome et à Constantinople. 8vo. Paris, 1888. F 1 R 7

LEE, Miss Harriet. The Chapter of Accidents: a Comedy. [See London Stage, 2.] H 2 S 34

LEE, Nathaniel. Alexander the Great: a Tragedy. [See London Stage, 1.] H 2 S 33

LEE, Rawdon B. History and Description of the Modern Dogs of Great Britain and Ireland. (Non-sporting Division.) 8vo. Lond., 1894. A 28 U 1

LEE, General Robt. E., of the Confederate Army. [Life of]; by F. Lee. 8vo. Lond., 1895. C 21 Q 12

LEE, S. Dictionary of National Biography. [See Stephen, L.] C 11 R

LEE, Susan P. Memoirs of W. N. Pendleton, D.D., and Brig.-Gen., Confederate States of America. Roy. 8vo. Philad., 1893. C 18 U 3

LEECH, H. J. The Life of Mr. Gladstone, told by himself in Speeches and Public Letters. 12mo. Lond., 1894. C 14 Q 29

LEES, Rev. Dr. Jas. Cameron. St. Giles', Edinburgh, Church, College, and Cathedral, from the earliest times to the present day. [Illustrated.] 4to. Edinb., 1889. B 32 V 9

LEE-WARNER, W. [See Warner, W. L.]

LE FANU, W. R. Seventy Years of Irish Life: being Anecdotes and Reminiscences. 8vo. Lond., 1893. J 10 S 22

LEFÈVRE, A. Race and Language. 12mo. Lond., 1894. K 19 P 17

LEFFLER, Anna C., Duchess of Cajanello. Sonya Kovalevsky: a Biography. 8vo. Lond., 1895. C 19 S 8

LE GALLIENNE, Richard. Prose Fancies. 12mo. Lond., 1894. J 6 Q 40

Religion of a Literary Man. 12mo. Lond., 1893. G 16 R 44

Liber Amoris. [See Hazlitt, W.] J 4 U 3 and J 4 P 11

LEGGE, Alfred O. Sunny Manitoba: its peoples and its industries. 8vo. Lond., 1893. D 3 T 34

LEGGE, Hugh. The Repton Club. [See Knapp, J. M. —The Universities and the Social Problem.] F 8 U 22

LEGGE, Rev. J. Lawlessness and Lust; or, Absalom and Ammon: a Sermon. 8vo. Melb., 1870. MG 1 R 68

LEGGE, Prof. James. Chinese Classics; with Translation and Notes. Vols. 1-5 (in 8) roy. 8vo. Hongkong, 1861-72. J 6 V 15-22

LEGOUVÉ, Ernest. Sixty Years of Recollections; translated, with notes, by A. D. Vandam. 2 vols. 8vo. Lond., 1893. C 16 R 13, 14

LEHMANN, Prof. K. B. Methods of Practical Hygiene. 2 vols. 8vo. Lond., 1893.   A 26 T 13, 14

LEHMANN, R. An Artist's Reminiscences. 8vo. Lond., 1894.   D 19 U 2

LEIBNITZ, Gottfried Wilhelm; by J. T. Merz. (Philosophical Classics.) 12mo. Edinb., 1884.   G 9 V 7

LEICESTER, Robert Dudley, Earl of. Memoirs of. [*See* Collectanea Adamantæa.]   J 18 R 25

LEICESTER, Simon de Montfort, Earl of. Life of, with special reference to the Parliamentary History of his Time; by G. W. Prothero. 8vo. Lond., 1877.   C 22 P 15

LEIGHTON, Rev. W. A. A Guide, Descriptive and Historical, through the town of Shrewsbury. 4th ed. 18mo. Shrewsbury (n.d.)   D 18 P 25

LEIPZIGER STUDIEN ZUR CLASSISCHEN PHILOLOGIE. Bände, 14-16. 8vo. Leip., 1893-94.   E

LEITCH, Richard P. Course of Water-colour Painting. 11th edition. Obl. 8vo. Lond. (n.d.)   A 23 Q 31
Course of Sepia Painting. 1st and 2nd series. Obl. 8vo. Lond. (u.d.)   A 23 Q 32
Course of Painting in Neutral Tint. 3rd edition. Obl. 8vo. Lond. (n.d.)   A 23 Q 33

LELAND, Chas. Godfrey, "Hanns Breitmann." Memoirs. 2 vols. 8vo. Lond., 1893.   C 15 P 3, 4
Etruscan Roman Remains in Popular Tradition. Imp. 8vo. Lond., 1892.   B 30 V 13
Hans Breitmann's Party, with other Ballads. 12mo. Melb., 1869.   MH 1 U 75
Hans Breitmann in Politics. 12mo. Lond., 1869.   H 10 U 17
Hans Breitmann's Ballads. 8vo. Lond. (n.d.)   H 9 U 36

LELAND STANFORD JUNIOR UNIVERSITY. Register for 1892-93, 1894-95. 2 vols. 8vo. Palo Alto, 1893-95.   E

LELONG, B. M. The Olive in California. 8vo. Sacramento, 1889.   A 18 V 27

LE MAIRE, Jakob. Speculum orientalis occidentalisque Indiæ Navigationum. [*See* Speculum.]   MD 8 P 9
Voyage to the Canaries, Cape Verd, and the Coast of Africa, 1682. [*See* Bibliotheca Curiosa.]   J 18 Q 47

LEMAÎTRE, Jules. Sketch of. [*See* Matthews, B.—Books and Playbooks.]   J 8 T 34

LE MAOUT, E., and DECAISNE, J. General System of Botany. Translated by Mrs. Hooker and arranged by J. D. Hooker. 2nd thousand. Sm. 4to. Lond., 1876.   A 20 V 29

LE MOYNE, Pierre. [*See* D'Iberville, Sieur.]

LENDENFELD, Dr. R. von. Australische Reise; mit Illustrationen. Roy. 8vo. Innsbruck, 1892.   MD 7 U 17
Der Tasman-Gletscher und seine Umrandung. (Ergänzungsheft 75 zu Petermann's Mittheilungen.) 4to. Gotha, 1884.   E

LENDON, Dr. Alfred A. Hydatid Disease. [*See* Thomas, Dr. J. D.]   MA 2 Q 66

LENNHOLM, E. A. Micro-organisms and Fermentation. [*See* Jörgensen, A.]   A 28 U 9

LE NORMAN, Mdlle. M. A. Historical and Secret Memoirs of the Empress Josephine. 2 vols. 8vo. Lond., 1895.   B 26 V 15, 16

LENTZNER, Dr. Karl. Dictionary of the Slang-English of Australia, and of some Mixed Languages. Roy. 8vo. Halle, 1892.   MK 1 S 22

LEO XIII, Pope. His Life and Letters; edited and compiled by Rev. J. F. Talbot. Roy 8vo. Boston, 1886.   C 12 V 16
Sketch of. [*See* Elliot, Frances.—Roman Gossip.]   C 21 Q 10
Sketch of. [*See* Kingston, W. Beatty.—Men, Cities, and Events.]   C 24 R 4

LEONARD, Major Arthur G. The Camel, its Uses and Management. 8vo. Lond., 1894.   A 27 T 22

LEONARD, E. A. Some Remarks upon the Cardwell District. (Roy. Geograph. Soc. of Australasia. Q. Branch, 3.) 8vo. Brisbane, 1888.   ME 20

LEONARD, Henrietta. Frederica's Study of History. [*See* Fredericq, Prof. P.]   B 18 S 5 and 8

LEONARD, Isabella S. The Power of Grace; or, Memorials of Harriett Mosely. 12mo. Sydney, 1886.   MC 1 P 49

LEONCAVALLO, Ruggiero. Sketch of. [*See* Streatfield, R. A.—Masters of Italian Music.]   C 22 P 18

LEOPARDI, Giacomo. [Plaster Cast of.] [*See* Hutton, L.—Portraits in Plaster.]   A 23 V 13

LEPSIUS, Prof. Carl R. [Sketch of.] [*See* Muller, F. Max.—Chips from a German Workshop.]   J 9 R 31-33

LERMOLIEFF, Ivan. [*See* Morelli, G.]

LEROY-BEAULIEU, A. [*See* Beaulieu, A. Leroy.]

LE SAGE, Alain René. Histoire de Gil Blas de Santillane. Roy. 8vo. Paris, 1855.   J 2 U 27

LESLIE, Chas. Robt. Hand-book for Young Painters. 3rd ed., illustrated. 8vo. Lond., 1887.   A 23 Q 47

LESLIE, Fred. Recollections of; by W. T. Vincent. 2 vols. 8vo. Lond., 1894.   C 19 R 11, 12

LESLIE, Robt. C. A Waterbiography. Illustrated. 8vo. Lond., 1894.   C 18 T 8

LE SOUEF, D. Australian Birds Eggs and Nests collected at Bloomfield, Queensland. (Proc. Roy. Soc., Victoria, n.s. 7.) 8vo. Melb. 1895.   ME 1 P

LESQUEREUX, L. Flora of the Dakota Group. (U.S. Geol. Survey, 17.) 4to. Wash., 1891.   E

LESSEPS, Ferdinand, Comte de. The Great Frenchman. [See Kingston, W. Beatty-.—Men, Cities, and Events.]   C 22 R 4
Life and Enterprises of; by G. B. Smith. 8vo. Lond., 1893.   C 13 P 29

LESSING, Gotthold Ephraim. Fabeln. 18mo. Stuttgart, 1871.   J 9 P 35
Sketch of. [See Lowell, J. R.]   J 6 P 10

LESSING, O. Architectural Ornaments in Berlin. [100 Plates.] Fol. Lond., 1880.   A 6 S 4 ‡

LESSON, Dr. Pierre Adolphe. Légendes des Iles Hawaii, tirées de Fornander et commentées avec une réponse à M. de Quatrefages. Roy. 8vo. Niort, 1884.   MB 2 U 2

LESTER, A. Trial of. [See Parramatta River Murders.]   MG 1 Q 53

LESTER, Miss Mary, "Maria Soltera." A Lady's Ride across Spanish Honduras. Illustrated. 8vo. Edinb., 1884.   D 15 R 13

LETHABY, W. R., and SWAINSON, Harold. The Church of Sancta Sophia, Constantinople: a Study of Byzantine Building. Imp. 8vo. Lond., 1894.   A 19 V 19

LETHBRIDGE, Sir Roper. The Golden Book of India: a Genealogical and Biographical Dictionary of the Ruling Princes, Chiefs, Nobles, &c. Roy. 8vo. Lond., 1893.   C 12 V 18

LETOURNEAU, Ch. Property, its Origin and Development. 8vo. Lond., 1892.   F 14 Q 42

LETTER, A, from a lady to her husband abroad. Sm. fol. Lond., 1728.   H 39 Q 13 ‡

LEVERMORE, Dr. Chas. H. The Town and City Government of New Haven. (Johns Hopkins University Studies, 4.) 8vo. Baltimore 1886.   B 18 S 4
The Republic of New Haven: a History of Municipal Evolution. (Johns Hopkins University Studies, extra vol. 1.) 8vo. Baltimore, 1886.   B 18 T 1

LEVEY, G. C. Korte beschrijving der Kolonie Victoria. 8vo. Melb. (n.d.)   MF 3 R 53

LEVI, Sylvain. La Science des Religions et les Religions de l'Inde. 8vo. Paris, 1892.   G 13 P 34

LEVY, Arthur. The Private Life of Napoleon; from the French, by L. S. Simeon. 2 vols. 8vo. Lond., 1894.   C 19 R 15, 16

LEVY, J. H. Tyranny of Socialism. [See Guyot, Y.]   F 9 U 42

LEWES, Dr. L. The Women of Shakespeare. Translated from the German by Helen Zimmern. 8vo. Lond., 1894.   J 6 T 5

LEWIS, Dr. Dio. Chastity; or, Our Secret Sins. 8vo. New York, 1894.   Libr.

LEWIS, E. A. M. Templars in Cyprus. [See Werner, F. L. Z]   H 2 Q 51

LEWIS, Sir George C. Essay on the Government of Dependencies. Edited, with an Introduction, by C. P. Lucas. 8vo. Oxford, 1891.   F 8 P 31
Sketch of. [See Bagehot, W.—Biographical Studies.]   C 22 P 10

LEWIS, Matthew Gregory. The Castle Spectre: a Dramatic Romance. [See London Stage, 1.]   H 2 S 33

LEWIS, Capt. Meriwether. Expedition to the Sources of the Missouri River, 1804-6. [See Coues, E.]   D 16 V 12-15
Sketch of. [See Greeley, Gen. A. W.—Explorers and Travellers.]   C 17 R 4

LEWIS, Prof. Thos. Hayter. Byzantine Sculptures. [See Naville, E.]   B 12 T 5 †

LEWKOWITSCH, Dr. J. Chemical Analysis of Oils, Fats, and Waxes. [See Benedikt, Prof. Dr. R.]   A 21 U 3

LEY, Rev. Wm. Clement. Cloudland: a Study on the Structure and Character of Clouds. Illustrated. 8vo. Lond., 1894.   A 19 U 20

LIBRAIRIE FRANCAISE, Catalogue de la. Tome 12, 1886-90. Roy. 8vo. Paris, 1892.   Libr.

LIBRARY, The: a Magazine of Bibliography and Literature. Vols. 4-6. 8vo. Lond., 1893-94.   E

LIBRARY ASSOCIATION OF THE UNITED KINGDOM Report of the Proceedings of the Meeting held September, 1893. 8vo. Lond., 1895.   E
Library Association Year-book, 1895 8vo. Lond., 1895.   E

LIBRARY JOURNAL; chiefly devoted to Library Economy and Bibliography. Vols. 17, 18. 4to. New York, 1892-93.   E

LIBER MELBURNIENSIS. [See Church of England Grammar School, Melbourne.]   MB 2 R 46

LIBERIAN COFFEE IN CEYLON. History of the Progress of the Cultivation up to 1878; with Letters on Liberia, by G. A. Crüwell. 12mo. Colombo, 1878.   A 18 P 27

LIDDON, Rev. Dr. Henry Parry. Life of Edward Bouverie Pusey. Vols. 1-3. 8vo. Lond., 1893-94.   C 16 S 5-7

Supplementary Catalogue—1893-95.

LIEBIG, Justus von; his Life and Work, 1803-73. 12mo. Lond., 1895. A 21 R 33

LIGHT, Col. W. Survey of the Coast on the East side of St. Vincent's Gulf. Fol. Lond. (n.d.) MD 5 Q 16 ‡

[Plan of] the District of Adelaide, South Australia. Fol. Lond., 1839. MD 5 Q 16‡

LIGHT OF EGYPT; or the Science of the Soul and the Stars. 8vo. Lond., 1889. G 2 P 31

LIGHTNING TIMBER CALCULATOR, for round or square logs, exhibiting at one view the superficial contents. Sm. 4to. Sydney, 1885. MA 2 P 82

LIGUORI, Saint Alfonso Maria di. Theologia Moralis. 2 vols. 8vo. Augustæ Taurinorum, 1874. G 3 R 2, 3

LI HUNGCHANG. [Life of]; by Prof. R. K. Douglas. 8vo. Lond., 1895. C 22 P 12

LILLIE, Arthur. Madame Blavatsky and her Theosophy. 12mo. Lond., 1895. G 2 U 13

LILLIE, Rev. John. Advantages of Science: a Lecture. 8vo. Hobart, 1839. MA 3 T 27

LILLO, George. Arden of Feversham: an Historical Tragedy. [*See* London Stage. 2.] H 2 S 34

Fatal Curiosity: a Tragedy. [*See* London Stage, 3.] H 2 S 35

LILLY, Arnold. On some curious effects of Lightning at Gabo Island. (Roy. Soc., Vict., 17.) 8vo. Melb., 1881. ME 1 P

LILLY, Wm Samuel. The Claims of Christianity. 8vo. Lond., 1894. G 12 Q 39

Four English Humourists of the 19th Century. 8vo. Lond., 1895. J 5 T 30

The Great Enigma. 8vo. Lond., 1892. G 2 Q 20

LIMA E CASTRO, Dr. J. C. de. Saneamento do Rio de Janeiro. [*See* Gouvêa, Dr. H. de.] A 26 U 22

LINCOLN, Abraham. Complete Works, comprising his Speeches, Letters, State Papers, and Miscellaneous Writings. Edited by J. G. Nicolay and J. Hay. 2 vols. 8vo. New York, 1894. F 8 T 25, 26

The True Story of a Great Life; by Wm. H. Herndon and J. W. Weik. 2 vols. 8vo. Lond., 1893. C 13 P 36, 37

[Life of]; by J. T. Morse, jun. (American Statesmen.) 2 vols. 12mo. Boston, 1893. C 13 P 34, 35

[Plaster Cast of.] [*See* Hutton, E.—Portraits in Plaster.] A 23 V 13

Sketch of. [*See* Brooks, N.—Statesmen.] C 16 R 20

Sketch of. [*See* Thompson, R. W.—Recollections of Sixteen Presidents.] C 18 T 21, 22

Sketch of. [*See* Wilson, J. G.—Presidents of the United States.] C 2 V 30

LINCOLNSHIRE NOTES AND QUERIES: a Quarterly Journal. Illustrated. Vol. 3. 8vo. Horncastle, 1894. E

LINDON, E. B. Catalogue of such Minerals as are at present known in Queensland, with their principal associations and places of occurrence. (Proc. Roy. Soc., Queensland, 4.) 8vo. Brisbane, 1887. ME 1 T

LINDSAY, David. Brief Notes on the Aborigines met with by the Elder Expedition of 1891-92. (Roy. Geog. Soc. Australasia, Vic. Branch, 11.) 8vo. Melb., 1894. ME 20

LINDSAY, W. M. The Latin Language: an Historical Account of Latin Sounds, Stems, and Flexions. 8vo. Oxford, 1894. K 14 P 25

LINDT, J. W. Ascent of the Tanna Volcano, and a Tour through the New Hebrides Group. (Roy. Geog. Soc. Australasia, Vic. Branch, 8.) 8vo. Melb., 1891. ME 20

The Fire Ordeal at Bega, Fiji Islands. (Roy. Geog. Soc. Australasia, Vic. Branch, 11.) 8vo. Melb., 1894. ME 20

Notes on Modern Photography. 12mo. Melb., 1888. MA 2 P 32

Reminiscences of Travel in British New Guinea. (Roy. Geog. Soc. Australasia, Vic. Branch, 9.) 8vo. Melb., 1892. ME 20

LINEHAM, Ray S. The Street of Human Habitations. Illustrated. 12mo. Lond., 1894. A 19 Q 7

LINEHAM, Wilfred J. A Text-book of Mechanical Engineering. 8vo. Lond., 1894. A 22 S 12

LINGUET, Simon Nicolas Henri. Memoirs of the Bastille. [*See* Collectanea Adamantæa.] J 18 R 7-9

LINNEAN SOCIETY, LONDON. Journal of. Zoology. Vol. 24. 8vo. Lond, 1894. E

Journal of. Botany. Vol. 29. 8vo. Lond., 1893. E

List of, 1881. 8vo. Lond., 1881. E

Transactions of. 2nd Series. Botany. Vol. 4, pt. 2. 4to. Lond., 1894. E

Transactions of. 2nd Series. Zoology. Vol. 5. 4to. Lond., 1888-94. E

LINNEAN SOCIETY OF NEW SOUTH WALES. Act of Incorporation, Rules, List of Members, &c., 1893. 8vo. Sydney, 1893. MF 2 R 1

Catalogue of, 1886. 8vo. Sydney, 1886. MK 1 T 36

The Macleay Memorial Volume, edited by J. J. Fletcher. 4to. Sydney, 1893. MA 2 Q 1 †

Proceedings. 2nd series. Vols. 7-9. 8vo. Sydney, 1893-94. ME 2 Q

Record of Proceedings, October 31st, 1885. 8vo. Sydney, 1885. ME 2 Q

Rules, with List of Members and Catalogue of the Library, 1882. 8vo. Sydney, 1882. ME 2 Q

Rules and List of Members, 1885. 8vo. Sydney, 1885. ME 2 Q

LINNELL, John. Life of; by A. T. Story. 2 vols. 8vo. Lond., 1892.   C 15 R 19, 20

LINSTOW, Dr. O. von. Entozea. [See Thomson, Sir C. W., and Murray, Dr. J.—Voyage of H.M.S. *Challenger*.]   A 6 †

LINTON, Wm. Jas. European Republicans: Recollections of Mazzini and his Friends. 8vo. Lond., 1892.   C 12 S 33
— Memories. 8vo. Lond., 1895.   C 21 S 18

LION, J. C. Concerning the Method of Teaching Gymnastics in our Gymnastic Schools. 8vo. Milwaukee (n.d.)   G 18 R 35
— Why is the German System of Gymnastics entitled to recognition. 8vo. Milwaukee (n.d.)   G 18 R 35

LIPPINCOTT'S MONTHLY MAGAZINE. Vol. 53, Jan.–June, 1894. 8vo. Philad., 1894.   E

LIPPMANN, Dr. F. Engravings by Old Masters. [See Engravings.]   A 41 P 29–34 ‡

LIRA, José B. Proyecto de Código de Enjuiciamiento Criminal. 8vo. Santiago, 1888.   F 7 U 16

LISTER, John. Cotton Manufacture. Illustrated. 8vo. Lond., 1894.   A 25 S 3

LISZT, Abbé Franz. The Abbé Liszt. [See Kingston, W. Beatty-.—Men, Cities, and Events.]   C 22 R 4
— Sketch of. [See Heine, H.—Heine in Art and Letters.]   J 11 T 39

LITCHFIELD, Nicolas. Historic of Discoverie and Conquest of the East Indias by the Portugales. [See Castanheda, F. L. de.]   Libr.

LITERARISCHES CENTRALBLATT für Deutschland, 1892-94. 3 vols. 4to. Leipzig, 1892-94.   E

LITERARY AND HISTORICAL SOCIETY OF QUEBEC. Fifth Series of Historical Documents; published under the auspices of the Literary and Historical Society of Quebec. 8vo. Quebec, 1877.   B 16 S 5
— Index of the Lectures, Papers, and Historical Documents published by the Literary and Historical Society of Quebec, 1829-91. 8vo. Quebec, 1891.   E
— Manuscripts published under the auspices of the Literary and Historical Society of Quebec.—Trade and Shipping 1793. 8vo. Quebec, 1889.   B 16 S 2
— Transactions of the Literary and Historical Society of Quebec. Sessions of 1864-92. 14 parts. 8vo. Quebec, 1865-92.   E

LITERARY CHÂTELAINE, The. 12mo. Launceston, 1858.   MJ 1 Q 50

LITHGOW, Dr. R. A. Douglas. Early English Alliterative Poetry. [See Roy. Soc. of Lit., 2nd series, 16.]   E

LITTLE, A. D. Chemistry of Paper-making. [See Griffin, R. B.]   A 21 V 16

LITTLE, Rev. Wm. John Knox. Introduction to the Imitation of Christ. [See Kempis, T. à.]   G 5 U 28

LITTLE ROCK PUBLIC SCHOOLS. Report of, for year ending June, 1895. 8vo. Little Rock, Arkansas, 1892.   E

LITTLE SNOW WHITE, or Harlequin King Kokahoop; or, the Damsel who never saw a Glass. 12mo. Sydney, 1875.   MH 1 U 70

LITTLEDALE, Prof. Harold. Essays on Lord Tennyson's "Idylls of the King." 8vo. Lond., 1893.   J 4 Q 35
— The two Noble Kinsmen. [See New Shakspere Society.]   E

LITURGIES. The Book of Common Prayer and Administration of the Sacraments, and other Rites and Ceremonies of the Church of England. Sm. 4to. Lond., 1630.   G 13 T 49
— Liturgies and other Documents of the Ante-Nicene Period; translated by W. Macdonald, G. R. Merry, and Dr. Donaldson. (Ante-Nicene Christ. Lib., 24.) 8vo. Edinb., 1872.   G 14 U 24
— Psalter of the Great Bible of 1539: a Landmark in English Literature; edited by Prof. J. Earle. 8vo. Lond., 1894.   G 13 P 38
— Select Portions of the Psalms of David, according to the version of Dr. N. Brady and N. Tate; to which are added Hymns. 12mo. Sydney, 1853.   MG 1 P 54
— Whole Booke of Psalmes. Sm. 4to. Lond., 1637.   G 13 T 49

LIVERMORE, E. P. Prospectus of the Land League. 8vo. Rockhampton, 1865.   MF 3 R 35

LIVERPOOL GEOGRAPHICAL SOCIETY. Report of the Council, 1894. 8vo. Liverpool, 1895.   E

LIVERSIDGE, Prof. Archibald. Australasian and other Stone Implements. (Journal Roy. Soc., N.S.W., 28.) 8vo. Sydney, 1894.   ME 1 R
— Boleite, Nantokite, Kerargyrite, and Cuprite from Broken Hill. (Journal Roy. Soc., N.S.W., 28.) 8vo. Sydney, 1894.   ME 1 R
— Gold in the Hawkesbury Rocks. (Journal Roy. Soc., N.S.W., 28.) 8vo. Sydney, 1894.   ME 1 R
— On the Origin of Moss Gold. On the condition of Gold in Quartz and Calcite Veins. On the Origin of Gold Nuggets. On the Crystallization of Gold in Hexagonal Forms. Gold Moiré-Métallique. A Combination Laboratory Lamp, Retort, and Filter Stand. 8vo. Sydney, 1893.   MA 2 Q 50
— Reports on certain Museums for Technology, Science, and Art. Fol. Sydney, 1880.   MG 10 P 14 †

LIVING AGE, The: a Journal devoted to Social, Political and Religious Comment, Criticism, and Controversy. Sm. 4to. Sydney, 1879.   ME 17 T

LIVING ENGLISH POETS. 8vo. Lond., 1893.
H 8 Q 45

LIVINGSTONE, Rev. Dr. David. Missionary Travels and Researches in South Africa. Roy. 8vo. Lond., 1857.
D 14 V 16
Sketch of his Work. [*See* Great Explorers.]
D 15 V 21, 22
The Crossers of Africa. [*See* Brown, Dr. R.—Story of Africa.]
D 15 V 24–26

LIVIUS, Titus. La Langue et la Grammaire de Tite-Live. [*See* Riemann, O.]
J 7 U 33

LLOYD, Rev. E. Three Great African Chiefs: Khame, Sebele, and Bathoeng. 8vo. Lond., 1895.
B 1 P 21

LLOYD, E. W., and HADCOCK, A. G. Artillery: its Progress and Present Position. Roy. 8vo. Portsmouth, 1893.
A 29 V 21

LLOYD, Henry Demarest. Wealth against Commonwealth. 8vo. New York, 1894.
F 10 U 4

LLOYD, Wm. Watkyss. On the Central Groups of the Eastern Frieze of the Parthenon. [*See* Roy. Soc. of Lit., 2nd series, 16.]
E

LOBO, Americo. Poemas de Longfellow. [*See* Longfellow, H. W.]
H 10 Q 23

LOCK, Chas. G. Warnford. Economic Mining. 8vo. Lond., 1895.
A 24 T 24

LOCK, Walter. John Keble: a Biography. 8vo. Lond., 1893.
C 13 P 23

LOCKE, James. Analytical Chemistry. [*See* Menschutkin, M.]
A 21 U 5

LOCKE, John; by Prof. A. C. Fraser. (Philosophical Classics.) 12mo. Edinb., 1890.
G 9 V 13
The Reasonableness of Christianity. 8vo. Lond., 1859.
J 4 U 1

LOCKEYEAR, J. R. "Mr. Bunyip;" or, Mary Somerville's Ramble. 8vo. Melb., 1891.
MJ 3 P 28

LOCKHART, Chas. Draft Act and Regulations for the erection of Dams on the Billabong. 8vo. Deniliquin, 1859.
MF 3 R 34

LOCKHART, J. H. Stewart. A Manual of Chinese Quotations, being a Translation of the Ch'êng Yü K'ao. 8vo. Hongkong, 1893.
K 14 Q 38

LOCKWOOD, C., & Son. Catalogue of Scientific and Technical Books. 8vo. Lond., 1893.
K 7 R 57

LOCKWOOD, Edward. Early Days of Marlborough College; or, Public School Life between 40 and 50 years ago; to which is added, a Glimpse at Old Haileybury, Patna during the Mutiny, a Sketch of the Natural History of the Riviera, and Life in an Oxfordshire Village. Illustrated. Sm. 4to. Lond., 1893.
B 23 S 10

LOCKYER, Joseph Norman. The Dawn of Astronomy: a Study of the Temple-Worship and Mythology of the Ancient Egyptians. 8vo. Lond., 1894.
A 19 U 24

LODD, Prof. G. T. Psychology, Descriptive, and Explanatory. Roy. 8vo. New York, 1894.
G 15 S 18

LODGE, Edmund. The Peerage and Baronetage of the British Empire, 1893–94. 2 vols. Roy. 8vo. Lond., 1893–94.
E

LODGE, James Lee. Coffee, history, growth, &c. 12mo. Birm., 1894.
A 19 R 4

LODGE, Rev. Samuel. Scrivelsby, the Home of the Champions. Roy. 8vo. Horneastle, 1893.
B 21 V 19

LOEWENTHAL, Dr. Richard. Dyeing. [*See* Knecht, E.]
A 11 R 28–30

LOFTIE, Rev. Wm. John. Inigo Jones and Wren'; or, the Rise and Decline of Modern Architecture in England. 4to. Lond., 1893.
A 19 V G

LOFTUS, Rt. Hon. Augustus Wm. Frederick Spencer, Baron. Diplomatic Reminiscences of, 1862–79. 2 vols. 8vo. Lond., 1894.
C 14 V 17, 18

LOGAN, Alexander. Lays o' Hame an' Country. 12mo. Edinb. (n.d.)
H 7 U 40

LOGAN, Wm. E. Portrait of. [*See* Ramsay, Sir A. C.—Memoir of.]
C 21 R 20

LOGIC of the Sabbath Controversy. 8vo. Melb., 1883.
MG 1 T 32

LOGIER, J. B. Logier's System of Science of Music, Harmony, and Practical Composition. 4to. Lond. (n.d.)
A 7 V 25

LOMBROSO, Prof. Cæsar, and FERRERO, Wm. The Female Offender; with an Introduction by W. Douglas Morrison. Illustrated. 8vo. Lond., 1895.
F 2 V 5

LONDON, Chronicles of: Henry III to Edward III. [*See* Collectanea Adamantæa.]
J 18 R 18

LONDON INTERNATIONAL EXHIBITION OF MINING AND METALLURGY, 1890. Report of the Executive Commissioner of New South Wales. Roy. 8vo. Sydney, 1891.
MA 2 Q 59

LONDON STAGE, The. A Collection of the most reputed Tragedies, Comedies, Operas, Melo-dramas, Farces, and Interludes. 4 vols. 8vo. Lond. (n.d.)
H 2 S 33–36

1. Adopted Child, The : a Musical Drama ; by S. Birch.
Alexander the Great ; a Tragedy ; by N. Lee.
All the World 's a Stage : a Farce ; by I. Jackman.
Beggars' Opera, The : an Opera ; by J. Gay.
Bold Stroke for a Husband : a Comedy ; by Mrs. Centlivre.
Castle Spectre, The : a Dramatic Romance ; by M. G. Lewis.
Citizen, The : a Farce ; by A. Murphy.
Clandestine Marriage, The : a Comedy ; by G. Colman and D. Garrick.
Country Girl, The : a Comedy ; by D. Garrick.
Critic, The : or, a Tragedy Rehearsed : a Dramatic Piece ; by R. B. Sheridan.

LONDON STAGE, The—*contd.*

Deaf and Dumb; or, The Orphan Protected: an Historical Drama; by T. Holcroft.
Deserter, The: a Musical Drama; by C. Dibdin.
Devil to Pay, The; or, The Wives Metamorphosed: a Ballad Farce; by C. Coffey.
Duenna, The: a Comic Opera; by R. B. Sheridan.
Gamester, The: a Tragedy; by E. Moore.
High Life Below Stairs: a Farce; by Rev. J. Townley.
Honest Thieves, The: a Farce; by T. Knight.
Hypocrite, The: a Comedy; by I. Bickerstaff.
Inconstant, The: a Comedy; by George Farquhar.
Jealous Wife, The: a Comedy; by G. Colman.
Jew, The: a Comedy; by R. Cumberland.
Lionel and Clarissa: an Opera; by I. Bickerstaff.
Love in a Village: an Opera; by I. Bickerstaff.
Lying Valet, The: a Farce; by D. Garrick.
Maid of the Mill, The: an Opera; by I. Bickerstaff.
Man of the World, The: a Comedy; by C. Macklin.
Mayor of Garratt, The: a Farce; by S. Foote.
Midas: a Burletta; by K. O'Hara.
Midnight Hour, The: a Petite Comedy; by Mrs. Inchbald
Miser, The: a Comedy; by H. Fielding.
Padlock, The: a Comic Opera; by I. Bickerstaff.
Pizarro: a Tragedy; by R. B. Sheridan.
Quaker, The: a Comic Opera; by C. Dibdin.
Recruiting Officer, The: a Comedy; by G. Farquhar.
Revenge, The: a Tragedy; by E. Young.
Rivals, The: a Comedy; by R. B. Sheridan.
Road to Ruin, The: a Comedy; by T. Holcroft.
Rule a Wife and have a Wife: a Comedy; by D. Garrick.
She Stoops to Conquer: a Comedy; by O. Goldsmith.
Soldier's Daughter, The: a Comedy; by A. Cherry.
Such Things are: a Play; by Mrs. Inchbald.
Three Weeks after Marriage: a Comedy; by A. Murphy
Way to keep him, The: a Comedy; by A. Murphy.
West Indian, The: a Comedy; by R. Cumberland.
Whool of Fortune, The: a Comedy; by R. Cumberland.
Who's the Dupe: a Farce; by Mrs. Cowley.

2. All in the Wrong: a Comedy; by A. Murphy.
Arden of Feversham: an Historical Tragedy; by G. Lillo.
Barbarossa: a Tragedy; by J. Brown.
Beaux' Stratagem, The: a Comedy; by G. Farquhar.
Belle's Stratagem, The: a Comedy; by Mrs. Cowley.
Brothers, The: a Comedy; by R. Cumberland.
Busybody, The: a Comedy; by Mrs. Centlivre.
Cato: a Tragedy; by J. Addison.
Chapter of Accidents, The: a Comedy; by Miss Lee.
Child of Nature: a Drama; by Mrs. Inchbald.
Comus: a Masque, altered from Milton.
Conscious Lovers, The: a Comedy; by Sir R. Steele.
Constant Couple, The; or a Trip to the Jubilee: a Comedy; by G. Farquhar.
Cross Purposes: a Farce; by Mr. O'Brien.
Doctor and the Apothecary, The: a Musical Entertainment; by J. Cobb.
Dragon of Wantley, The: a Burlesque Opera; by H. Carey.
Duke of Milan, The: a Tragedy; by P. Massinger.
Everyone has his Fault; a Comedy; by Mrs. Inchbald.
Fair Penitent, The: a Tragedy; by A. Rowe.
Fashionable Lover, The: a Comedy; by R. Cumberland.
Follies of a Day, The: a Comedy; by T. Holcroft.
Fortune's Frolic: a Farce; by J. T. Allingham.
Good-natured Man, The: a Comedy; by Dr. Goldsmith.
Haunted Tower, The: a Comic Opera; by J. Cobb.
Isabella; or, the Fatal Marriage: a Tragedy; by T. Southern.
Know your own Mind; a Comedy; by A. Murphy.
Liar, The: a Farce; by S. Foote.
Lord of the Manor, The: an Opera; by C. Dibdin, jun.
Lodoiska: a Melo-dramatic Opera; by J. P. Kemble.
Miss in her Teens; or, the Medley of Lovers: a Farce; by D. Garrick.
Mock Doctor, The; or, the Dumb Lady Cured; by H. Fielding.
New Way to Pay Old Debts, A: a Comedy; by P. Massinger.
Oroonoko: a Tragedy; by T. Southern.

Orphan of China, The: a Tragedy; by A. Murphy.
Polly Honeycombe: a Dramatic Novel; by G. Colman, the Elder.
Provoked Husband, The; or, a Journey to London: a Comedy; by Vanbrugh and Cibber.
Rosina: an Opera; by Mrs. Brooke.
Suspicious Husband, The: a Comedy; by Dr. Hoadly.
Trip to Scarborough, A: a Comedy; by R. B. Sheridan.
Tobacconist, The: a Farce; by F. Gentleman.
Wedding Day, The: a Farce; by Mrs. Inchbald.
Which is the Man?: a Comedy; by Mrs. Cowley.
Wives as they were, and Maids as they are: a Comedy; by Mrs. Inchbald.
Wonder a Woman keeps a Secret, The: a Comedy; by Mrs. Centlivre.

3. All for Love; or, the World Well Lost: a Tragedy; by J. Dryden.
Better Late than Never: a Comedy; by M. P. Andrews.
Bold Stroke for a Husband, A: a Comedy; by Mrs. Cowley.
Bon Ton; or, High Life Above Stairs: a Farce; by D. Garrick.
Careless Husband, The: a Comedy; by C. Cibber.
Chrononhotonthologos: a Burlesque Opera; by H. Carey.
Confederacy, The: a Comedy; by Sir J. Vanbrugh.
Count of Narbonne: a Tragedy; by R. Jephson.
Cymon: a Dramatic Romance; by D. Garrick.
Deaf Lover, The: a Farce; by F. Pilon.
Deserted Daughter: a Comedy; by T. Holcroft.
Dence is in Him, The: a Farce; by G. Colman, the Elder.
Earl of Essex, The: a Tragedy; by H. Jones.
Earl of Warwick, The: a Tragedy; by Dr. T. Franklin.
Every Man in his Humour: a Comedy; by D. Garrick.
Fatal Curiosity: a Tragedy; by G. Lillo.
First Floor, The: a Farce; by J. Cobb.
First Love: a Comedy; by R. Cumberland.
Foundling, The: a Comedy; by E. Moore.
Giovanni in London; or, the Libertine Reclaimed: an Operatic Extravaganza; by W. T. Moncrieff.
Grecian Daughter, The: a Tragedy; by A. Murphy.
Guardian, The: a Comedy; by D. Garrick.
Gustavus Vasa; or, the Deliverer of his Country: a Tragedy; by H. Brooke.
He would be a Soldier: a Comedy; by F. Pilon.
Heiress, The: a Comedy; by Gen. Burgoyne.
Hero and Leander: an Operatic Burletta; by I. Jackman.
Irish Widow, The: a Farce; by D. Garrick.
Lady Jane Grey: a Tragedy; by N. Rowe.
Love à la Mode: a Farce; by C. Macklin.
Love for Love: a Comedy; by W. Congreve.
Love makes a Man; or, the Fop's Fortune: a Comedy; by C. Cibber.
Lovers' Quarrels; or, Like Master Like Man: an Interlude; by T. King.
Lovers' Vows: a Play; by Mrs. Inchbald.
Maid of the Oaks, The: a Dramatic Entertainment; by J. Burgoyne.
Monsieur Tonson: a Farce; by W. T. Moncrieff.
Mysterious Husband: a Tragedy; by R. Cumberland.
Orphan, The; or, the Unhappy Marriage: a Tragedy; by T. Otway.
Provoked Wife, The: a Comedy; by Sir J. Vanbrugh.
Recruiting Sergeant, The: a Musical Entertainment; by I. Bickerstaff.
Richard Cœur De Lion: an Historical Romance; by Gen. Burgoyne.
Roman Father, The: a Tragedy; by W. Whitehead.
She would and She would not; or, the Kind Imposter: a Comedy; by C. Cibber.
Siege of Damascus, The: a Tragedy; by J. Hughes.
Stranger, The: a Drama; by B. Thompson.
Sultan, The; or, a Peep into the Seraglio: a Farce; by I. Bickerstaff.
Tamerlane: a Tragedy; by N. Rowe.
Tender Husband, The; or, the Accomplished Fools: a Comedy; by Sir R. Steele.
Two Misers, The: a Musical Entertainment; by K. O'Hara.
Two Strings to your Bow: a Farce; by R. Jephson.

LONDON STAGE, The—*contd.*
   Virgin Unmasked, The : a Musical Farce ; by H. Fielding.
   Ways and Means : a Comedy ; by G. Colman, the Younger.
4. Abroad and at Home : a Comic Opera ; by J. G. Holman.
   Animal Magnetism : a Farce ; by Mrs. Inchbald.
   Appearance is against Them : a Farce.
   Bashful Man, The : a Comic Drama ; by W. T. Moncrieff.
   Braganza : a Tragedy ; by R. Jephson.
   Carmelite, The : a Tragedy ; by R. Cumberland.
   Castle of Sorrento : a Musical Entertainment ; by Henry Heartwell.
   Chances, The : a Comedy ; by D. Garrick.
   Cheats of Scapin, The : a Comedy ; by T. Otway.
   Contrivances, The : a Ballad Opera ; by H. Carey.
   Curfew, The : a Play ; by J. Tobin.
   Distrest Mother, The : a Tragedy ; by A. Philips.
   Double Dealer, The : a Comedy ; by W. Congreve.
   Duplicity : a Comedy ; by T. Holcroft.
   Edward the Black Prince ; or, the Battle of Poictiers : an Historical Tragedy ; by W. Shirley.
   False Impressions : a Comedy ; by R. Cumberland.
   Farmer's Wife, The : a Comic Opera ; by Charles Dibdin, jun.
   He's Much to Blame : a Comedy ; by T. Holcroft.
   Law of Lombardy, The : a Tragedy ; by R. Jephson.
   Mahomet, the Imposter : a Tragedy ; by the Rev. Mr. Miller.
   Merchant of Bruges, The ; or, Beggar's Bush : a Play ; by D. Kinnaird.
   Miller of Mansfield, The : a Dramatic Entertainment ; by R. Dodsley.
   Mogul Tale, The ; or, the Descent of the Balloon : a Farce.
   Mourning Bride : a Tragedy ; by W. Congreve.
   My Spouse and I : an Operatic Farce ; by C. Dibdin, jun.
   Panel, The : a Comedy ; by J. P. Kemble.
   Paul and Virginia : a Musical Entertainment ; by J. Cobb.
   Purse, The ; or, the Benevolent Tar : a Musical Entertainment ; by J. C. Cross.
   Register Office, The : a Farce ; by J. Reed.
   Romp, The : a Comic Opera ; by I. Bickerstaff.
   School for Arrogance : a Comedy ; by T. Holcroft.
   School for Wives, The : a Comedy ; by H. Kelly.
   Seduction : a Comedy ; by T. Holcroft.
   Siege of Belgrade, The : a Comic Opera ; by J. Cobb.
   Tancred and Sigismunda : a Tragedy ; by J. Thomson.
   Thomas and Sally ; or, the Sailor's Return : a Musical Entertainment.
   Votary of Wealth, The : a Comedy ; by J. G. Holman.
   Waterman, The ; or, the First of August : a Ballad Opera ; by C. Dibdin.
   Way of the World, The : a Comedy ; by W. Congreve.
   What Next ? a Farce ; by T. Dibdin.
   Woodman, The : a Comic Opera ; by B. Dudley.
   Zara : a Tragedy ; by Aaron Hill.

LONDON UNIVERSITY. Calendar, 1893-96. 3 vols. 8vo. Lond., 1893-95.   E

LONG, James. Dairy-farming : a Lecture. (Inst. of Agricult., Lond.) 8vo. Lond., 1884.   A 18 R 28
   Handbook for Farmers and Small Holders. 8vo. Lond., 1892.   A 18 R 24

LONG, W. H. War Medals. [*See* Carter, T.]   B 7 R 17

LONGFELLOW, Henry Wadsworth. Poetical Works of. 12mo. Lond., 1851.   H 10 T 9
   Prose Works. 12mo. Lond., 1851.   J 12 S 24
   Poemas Norte-Americanos de ; [translated into Spanish by Americo Lobo]. 8vo. Rio de Janeiro, 1887.   H 10 Q 23
   Hyperion : a Romance. Illustrated. 8vo. Lond., 1853.   J 7 S 9

LONGFORD, John Walter. The Black Book : Under Lock and Key—Darlinghurst Gaol in 1849 and 1894. 8vo. Sydney, 1894.   MF 4 R 58

LONGLEY, Rt. Rev. Chas. Thos. (Archbishop of Canterbury). Life of. [*See* Fowler, Rev. M.—Notable Archbishops.]   C 13 V 12

LONGMAN, C. J., and WALROND, Col. H. Archery. Illustrated. 8vo. Lond., 1894.   A 29 R 17

LONGMAN'S MAGAZINE. Vols. 4, 13-26. 8vo. Lond., 1884-95.   E

LONGMORE, Surg.-Gen. Sir Thos. Gunshot Injuries : their History, Characteristic Features, Complications, and General Treatment. 2nd ed., illustrated. 8vo. Lond., 1895.   A 33 S 9

LOOFT, Dr. Carl. Leprosy. [*See* Hansen, Dr. G. A.]   A 33 S 13

LOOMIS, Prof. Elias. Elements of Astronomy. 8vo. New York, 1889.   A 3 S 40

LOPEZ, Thome. [*See* Ramusio, G. B.—Navigationi et Viaggi.]   D 36 T 5-7 ‡

LORD, R. P. G., and RUSH, J. and W. The Veterinary Vade Mecum. 8vo. Lond., 1875.   A 18 S 40

LORING, Arthur H. Political and Miscellaneous Papers and Addresses of Lord Brassey. [*See* Brassey, Lord.]   F 2 V 14

LORTET, L., et VIALLETON, L. Etude sur le Bilharzia Haematobia et la Bilharziose. 8vo. Paris, 1894.   A 33 U 23

LOSSING, Dr. Benson John. Harpers' Popular Cyclopædia of United States History, from the Aboriginal Period. Revised ed., illustrated. 2 vols. imp. 8vo. New York, 1893.   B 17 U 11, 12

LOTTO, Lorenzo. An Essay in Art Criticism ; by B. Berenson. 8vo. New York, 1895.   C 21 R 12

LOTZE, Hermann. Mikrokosmus : Ideen zur Naturgeschichte und Geschichte der Menschheit. 3 vols. 8vo. Leipzig, 1884-88.   G 15 P 23-25

LOUGHRAN, Edward Booth. 'Neath Austral Skies : Poems. 8vo. Melb., 1894.   MH 1 U 21

LOUIS XIV, King of France. Life and Times of ; by G. P. R. James. 2 vols. 8vo. Lond., 1851.   B 20 R 12, 13
   Louis XIV and the zenith of the French Monarchy ; by A. Hassall. 8vo. New York, 1895.   B 16 R 19

LOUIS, Henry. Hand-book of Gold Milling. 8vo. Lond., 1894.   A 24 Q 22

LOUISE, of Prussia. [Plaster Cast of.] [*See* Hutton, L.—Portraits in Plaster.]   A 23 V 13

LOUISIANA. [A Hand-book.] 8vo. New Orleans, 1888. D 15 T 18

South-west Louisiana. [A Hand-book.] 8vo. Chicago, 1893. D 15 T 18

Some late words about. 8vo. New Orleans, 1891. D 15 T 18

LOVAT, Simon Fraser, Lord. Life of, 1667-1747; by J. W. Allen. (Lives of Twelve Bad Men.) 8vo. Lond., 1894. C 18 T 9

LOVE, E. F. J. Observations with Kater's Invariable Pendulums, Sydney, 1894; with an Appendix on the stability of the Pendulum Stand. (Proc. Roy. Soc., Victoria, n.s. vol. 7.) 8vo. Melb., 1895. ME 1 P

Report of the Gravity Survey Committee of the Royal Society of Victoria. (Proceedings Roy. Soc., Victoria, n.s. vol. 6.) 8vo. Melb., 1894. ME 1 P

Value of Gravity at the Sydney Observatory. (Journal Roy. Soc., N.S.W., 28.) 8vo. Sydney, 1894. ME 1 R

LOVELESS, George. The Victims of Whiggery; being a statement of the Persecutions experienced by the Dorchester Labourers; also, Reflections upon the present system of Transportation, with an account of Van Dieman's Land. 8vo. Lond., 1837. MF 2 P 48

LOVETT, Richard. Diaries, Letters, and Reports of James Gilmour. 3rd ed. 8vo. Lond., 1895. G 15 P 38

LOVETT, Wm. Portrait of. [See Gammage, R. G.— Chartist Movement.] F 7 R 24

LOW, Lieut. Chas. Rathbone. History of the Indian Navy, 1613-1863. 2 vols. 8vo. Lond., 1877. B 29 T 4, 5

LOW, Sampson, & Co. English Catalogue of Books for 1892-94. 3 vols. roy. 8vo. Lond., 1893-95. Libr.

English Catalogue of Books. Index of Subjects. Vol. 4, 1881-89. Roy. 8vo. Lond., 1893. Libr.

LOW, Will H. Some Artists at the Fair. [See Chicago Exhibition, 1893.] A 23 U 21

LOWE, Charles. Great War of '89-. [See Great War of 189-.] J 2 Q 21

[Life of] Alexander III of Russia. 8vo. Lond., 1895. C 21 P 12

[Life of] Prince Bismarck. 12mo. Lond., 1895. C 21 P 17

LOWE, Edward Joseph. Fern-growing: Fifty Years' Experience in Crossing and Cultivation. Illustrated. Imp. 8vo. Lond., 1895. A 22 V 1

LOWE, Dr. John. Medical Missions, their place and power. 8vo. Edinb., 1895. G 3 P 25

LOWE, Rt. Hon. Robt. [See Sherbrooke, Viscount.]

LOWE, Solomon. Mnemonics delineated. [See Grey, Dr. R.] G 19 P 22

LOWE-WARREN, J. [See Warren, J. L.]

LOWELL, James Russell. A Conversation with; with Portrait. [See Blathwayt, R.—Interviews.] J 10 U 34

Address on. [See Curtis, G. W.] F 14 U 3

The English Poets; Lessing; Rousseau: Essays. 12mo. Lond., 1888. J 6 P 10

Letters of. Edited by C. E. Norton. 2 vols. 8vo. New York, 1894. C 17 S 11, 12

The Old English Dramatists. 8vo. Lond., 1894. C 13 P 19

Recollections and Appreciations of; by F. H. Underwood. 12mo. Lond., 1893. C 13 Q 23

Selections from. [See Harlin, T.] MJ 1 U 24

LOWELL, Percival. Occult Japan. 8vo. Boston, 1895. G 3 P 28

LOWER, Oswald B. New Australian Heterocera. (Trans. Roy. Soc., S. Australia, 17, 18.) 8vo. Adelaide, 1894-95. ME 1 S

New Australian Lepidoptera. (Trans. Roy. Soc., S. Australia, 17.) 8vo. Adelaide, 1893. ME 1 S

On Australian Rhopalocera. (Trans. Roy. Soc., S. Australia, 18.) 8vo. Adelaide, 1894. ME 1 S

South Australian Rhopalocera. (Trans. Roy. Soc., S. Australia, 17.) 8vo. Adelaide, 1893. ME 1 S

LOWRY, Rev. S. C. The Work of the Holy Spirit. 12mo. Lond., 1895. G 3 P 38

LOWTH, G. T. Around the Kremlin; or, Pictures of Life in Moscow. 8vo. Lond., 1868. D 19 R 1

LÖWY, Bella. The Russian Jews. [See Errera, L.] B 31 T 10

LOYAU, George E. Notable South Australians; or, Colonists, past and present. 12mo. Adelaide, 1885. MC 1 P 56

LOYSON, Rev. Charles. Peace: an Address; by the "Rev. Father Hyacinthe." 8vo. Lond., 1870. F 12 P 13

LUBBOCK, Gertrude. Some Poor Relief Questions. 8vo. Lond., 1895. F 8 U 51

LUBBOCK, Rt. Hon. Sir John. The Beauties of Nature and the Wonders of the World we live in. 8vo. Lond., 1892. A 16 P 10

The Use of Life. 12mo. Lond., 1894. G 18 P 14

LUCANUS, Marcus Annæus. Pharsalia; sive De Bello Civili, libri decem. 18mo. Lond. 1815. H 10 U 5

LUCAS, A. H. S., and FROST, C. The Lizards indigenous to Victoria. (Proceedings Royal Society, Victoria, r.s., 6.) 8vo. Lond., 1894. ME 1 P

New species of Lizards from Central Australia. (Proc. Roy. Soc., Vict., n.s., 7.) 8vo. Melb., 1895. ME 1 P

LUCAS, Chas. Prestwood. Essay on the Government of Dependencies. [*See* Lewis, Sir G. C.] F 8 P 31
Historical Geography of the British Colonies. Vol. 3. 8vo. Oxford, 1894. D 11 S 15

LUCAS, John. Paper and Letters upon the Sydney Water Supply. Sm. 4to. Sydney, 1876. MA 3 V 32

LUCAS, R. B. On the British Standards. (Trans. Roy. Soc., S. Australia, 9.) 8vo. Adelaide, 1887. ME 1 S

LUCAS, Samuel. Biography and Criticism. 12mo. Lond., 1860. J 12 S 7
Eminent Men and Popular Books. New ed. 12mo. Lond., 1860. J 12 S 25
The Sandwich Islands: a Prize Poem. 12mo. Oxford, 1841. MH 1 U 67

LUCAS, Dr. Thos. P. My Hospital Campaign; or, Reasons against prescribing indiscriminately alcoholic beverages for the sick. 8vo. Melb., 1888. MA 3 T 18
New species of Queensland Butterflies. (Proc. Roy. Soc., Queensland, 6.) 8vo. Brisbane, 1889. ME 1 T
Six new species of *Rhopalocera*. (Proc. Roy. Soc. Queensland, 6, 7.) 8vo. Brisbane, 1889-91. ME 1 T
On thirty-four new species of Australian *Lepidoptera*. (Proc. Roy. Soc., Queensland, 8.) 8vo. Brisbane, 1892. ME 1 T

LUCY, Henry W. Diary of the Salisbury Parliament, 1886-92. 8vo. Lond., 1892. B 7 Q 35
W. E. Gladstone, a Study from Life. Lond., 1895. C 2 R 37

LUDLOW, Lieut.-Gen. Edmund. Memoirs of, 1625-72. Edited by C. H. Firth. 2 vols. 8vo. Oxford, 1894. C 17 S 8, 9

LUDWIG, Dr. H. Echinodermen. [*See* Bronn, Dr. G. H.—Their-Reichs, Band 2, Ab. 3.] E

LUFF, Dr. Arthur P. Text-book of Forensic Medicine and Toxicology. 2 vols. 8vo. Lond., 1895. F 2 V 12, 13

LUFFMANN, C. Bogue. A Vagabond in Spain. 8vo. 1895. D 18 R 27

LUGARD, Capt. Frederick D. Rise of our East African Empire: Early Efforts in Nyasaland and Uganda. 2 vols. 8vo. Edinb., 1893. D 14 T 7, 8

LUKIS, Rev. Wm. C. Account of Church Bells; with some notices of Wiltshire Bells and Bell-founders. 8vo. Lond., 1857. B 21 T 15

LUMBY, Rev. Dr. Joseph R. St. Peter. [*See* Expositor's Bible.] G 19 R and S

LUMMIS, Chas. F. The Land of Poco Tiempo. 8vo. Lond., 1893. D 14 T 4
The Man who married the Moon, and other Pueblo Indian Folk-stories. 8vo. New York, 1894. J 10 R 2
The Spanish Pioneers. Illustrated. 8vo. Chicago, 1893. B 18 Q 7

LUMMIS-PATERSON, G. W. [*See* Paterson, G. W. Lummis-.]

LUPLAU, Wm. The Sebastopol Plateau, being a section of the Ballarat Gold-field proper. 8vo. Ballarat, 1887. MA 2 V 51

LURCY, Capt. Gabriel Lafond de. Quelques Semaines dans l'Archipel de Samoa, les Iles des Navigateurs de Lapeyrouse. 8vo. Paris, 1845. MD 8 R 18

LURZ, Dr. Albin. Aphorisms of Electricity in Medical Science. 8vo. Melb., 1886. MA 3 S 42
On combined Electric and Rubbing Treatment (Massage) in Nervous, Rheumatic, and Joint Affections. 8vo. Melb., 1889. MA 2 S 61

LUSITANIA LUCIFER, The: an Illustrated Journal, written on board the s.s. *Lusitania* while on her passage from London to Melbourne, 1878-79. 8vo. Melb., 1879. MJ 3 Q 13

LUTHER Martin, his History to the Diet of Worms. [*See* Bettany, G. T.—Popular History of the Reformation.] G 14 Q 33
Address on. [*See* Brooks, Rt. Rev. P.] J 6 S 38

LUTWYCHE, Alfred J. P. Narrative of the Wreck of the *Meridian* on the Island of Amsterdam. 12mo. Sydney, 1854. MD 2 W 26

LYALL, Sir Alfred Comyns. The Rise of the British Dominion in India. 8vo. Lond., 1893. B 29 Q 10

LYDE, Lionel W. Commercial Geography of the British Empire. 12mo. Lond., 1894. D 14 P 4

LYDEKKER, Richard. Hand-book to the Carnivora. Part 1. Cats, Civets, and Mungooses. 8vo. Lond. (n.d.) A 28 P 27
Hand-book to the Marsupialia and Monotremata. (Allen's Naturalist's Library.) 8vo. Lond., 1894. MA 3 U 1
Indian Tertiary and Post-Tertiary Vertebrata; Siwalik Mammalia; the Fauna of the Karnul Caves; Eocene Chelonia from the Salt Range. [*See* India, Geological Survey, ser. 10, vol. 4.] E
The Royal Natural History. Vols. 1-4. Illustrated. Roy. 8vo. Lond., 1893-95. A 28 V 21-24

LYELL, Sir Charles, and Modern Geology; by Dr. T. G. Bonney. 12mo. Lond., 1895. C 19 V 9
Principles of Geology. 9th ed., illustrated. 8vo. Lond., 1853. A 20 T 15

LYMAN, Dr. Henry Munson. Artificial Anæsthesia and Anæsthetics. 8vo. Lond., 1883. A 26 T 16

LYMAN, Theodore. Ophiuroidea. [*See* Thomson, Sir C. W., and Murray, Dr. J.—Voyage of H.M.S. *Challenger*—Zoology, 5.] A 6 †

LYNCH, Arthur. A Koran of Love, the Caliph, and other Poems. 32mo. Lond. (n.d.) H 10 T 18

LYNCH, Rev. Monsignor J. T. Letters on the Education Bill of New South Wales, 1880. 8vo. Sydney, 1880.   MG 2 S 3

LYNDHURST, Lord. Sketch of. [*See* Bagehot, W.—Biographical Studies.]   C 22 P 10

LYNN, Wm. T. Remarkable Comets. 12mo. Lond., 1893.   A 19 P 27

Brief Lessons in Astronomy. 16mo. Lond., 1892.   A 19 P 26

LYONS, Joseph A. The American Elocutionist and Dramatic Reader. 7th edition. 8vo. Philad. (n.d.)   J 4 R 4

LYSIAS. Funeral Orations in Praise of Military Men. [*See* Broadhurst, Rev. T.]   G 1 R 30

LYSONS, Gen. Sir Daniel. The Crimean War from first to last. 8vo. Lond., 1895.   B 31 S 4

LYTTELTON, Hon. Alfred. The Law of Trade Combinations. (A Policy of Free Exchange.) 8vo. Lond., 1894.   F 14 S 26

LYTTON, Sir Edward G. E. L. Bulwer, Baron. Works of; Schiller and Horace translated. 8vo. Lond., 1875.   H 9 U 1

Criticisms of the Works of. [*See* Senior, N. W.—Essays on Fiction.]   J 6 S 40

M

M., A. [*See* Ayame-San.]   J 4 U 14

M., D. [*See* Mary: a Tale, &c.]   MH 1 S 71

M.E.R. [*See* Jusserand, J. J.]

M., J. K. [*See* Mary Ira, The.]   MD 1 Q 32

M., W. [*See* Employers, Servants, and Registry Offices.]   MF 1 P 77

MACALISTER, Capt. Norman. Historical Memoir relative to Prince of Wales Island. Sm. 4to. Lond., 1803.   MD 6 V 2

McALPINE, Prof. A. N. Best Forage Plants. [*See* Stebler, Dr. F. G.]   A 36 T 4 ‡

McALPINE, D. Report on Rust in Wheat experiments, 1892-93. 8vo. Melb., 1894.   MA 1 U 56

Systematic arrangement of Australian Fungi, together with host-index and list of works on the subject. 4to. Melb., 1895.   MA 2 R 45

Australian Fungi. (Proc. Roy. Soc., Victoria, n.s., 7.) 8vo. Melb., 1895.   ME 1 P

—— and HILL, W. H. F. Entomogenous Fungi of Victoria. (Proc. Roy. Soc., Vict., n.s., 7.) 8vo. Melb., 1895.   ME 1 P

McALPINE, D., and McALPINE, A. N. Biological Atlas; a Guide to the Practical Study of Plants and Animals; with accompanying Text, containing Arrangement and Explanation, Equivalent Terms, Glossary, and Classification. 4to. Edinb., 1881.   A 5 R 21 †

—— and TEPPER, J. G. O. New Australian Stonemaking Fungus. (Proc. Roy. Soc., Victoria, n.s., 7) 8vo. Melb., 1895.   ME 1 P

MacARTHUR, Dr. A. Biography of the English Language. 8vo. Washington, 1883.   J 8 T 28

McARTHUR, Ellen A. Outlines of English Industrial History. [*See* Cunningham, Rev. Dr. W.]   F 2 U 78

MACARTNEY, Very Rev. Hussey Burgh. Education in Victoria for the Future: a Lecture delivered at the Mechanics' Institute on the 1st Oct., 1860. 8vo. Melb., 1860.   MJ 3 Q 5

State Aid to Religion and Education. 8vo. Melb., 1836.   MG 2 Q 22

MACARTNEY, Wm Ellison. A Plea for the Union. [*See* Subjects of the Day, 3.]   F 7 U 28

MACAULAY, Thos. Babington, Lord. Essay on Lord Clive; with Notes &c., by J. M. Taylor. 12mo. Sydney, 1865.   MJ 3 P 21

Lays of Ancient Rome; with Ivry and the Armada. New ed. 12mo. Lond., 1860   H 9 Q 18

Anecdotes of his Life and Literary Labours; with some Account of his early and unknown Writings. 12mo. Lond., 1860.   C 17 P 8

Essay on. [*See* Bagehot, W.—Literary Studies.]   J 0 P 22-24

Sketch of. [*See* Bagehot, W.—Estimates of some Englishmen and Scotchmen.]   J 10 V 32

Selections from. [*See* Harlin, T.]   MJ 1 U 24

McCAFFREY, Frank. The Chemistry of Cheese-making. 8vo. Sydney, 1892.   MA 1 Q 68

Cheese-making. 8vo. Sydney, 1892.   MA 1 Q 68

Practical Dairying. [*See* Dowling, J. P.]   MA 1 S 43

—— and GUTHRIE, F. B. Experiments with Babcock's Milk-tester. 8vo. Sydney, 1893.   MA 1 Q 68

MacCALLUM, Prof. Mungo W. Tennyson's Idylls of the King and Arthurian Story from the 16th Century. 12mo. Glasgow, 1894.   H 8 Q 29

McCANDLISH, John M. Scotland's Free Church. [*See* Ryley, G. B.]   G 13 P 37

MacCARTHY, Rev. Dr. B. Annals of Ulster. [*See* Great Britain and Ireland.—Record Commissioners' Publications.]   B 30 V 18

MacCARTHY, Rev. E. F. M. Western State Education. [*See* Subjects of the Day, 1.]   G 18 S 18

Notes on Education in Canada and Australia. [*See* Subjects of the Day, 1.]   G 18 S 18

McCARTHY, Justin. Irish Statesmen and Self-Government. [*See* Subjects of the Day, 3.] F 7 U 28

MacCARTHY, Major R. H. Defence of North-western Provinces of India. [*See* United Service Inst.] MA 2 V 38

MacCARTIE, Justin Charles. The Darleys of Dingo Dingo; a modern Australian Story. 8vo. Lond., 1895. MJ 3 Q 27

McCARTHY, L. P. The Statistician and Economist, 1893-94. 2 vols. 8vo. San Francisco, 1893-94. E

M'CAW, M. Cheese-making: being a Practical Explanation of the Cheddar System. 8vo. Melb., 1871. MA 3 S 60

M'CAY, Rev. A. R. Boyd. Marriage with a Deceased Wife's Sister scripturally unlawful. 8vo. Melb., 1874. MF 2 Q 38

McCLELLAN, Dr. George. Regional Anatomy in its relation to Medicine and Surgery. 2 vols. sm. 4to. Edinb., 1891-92. A 12 T 17, 18 †

McCLELLAND, James. Social Science and Social Schemes. 8vo. Lond., 1894. F 14 R 21

McCLINTOCK, Sir Francis Leopold. Meteorological Observations in the Arctic Seas, 1857-59. 4to. Wash., 1861. A 15 Q 16 †

McCLURE, M. L. Dawn of Civilization. [*See* Maspero, G.] B 17 U 15

McCLURE'S MAGAZINE. Vols. 2-6. 8vo. New York, 1893-96. E

MacCOLL, D. S. Greek Vase Paintings. [*See* Harrison, J. E.] A 6 P 2 ‡

McCOOK, Rev. Dr. Henry Christopher. Tenants of an Old Farm: Leaves from the Note-book of a Natualist. 6th ed., Illustrated. 8vo. Lond., 1891. A 27 Q 42

McCONNELL, Primrose. Note-book of Agricultural Facts and Figures for Farmers and Farm Students. 5th ed. 18mo. Lond., 1894. A 18 P 8

McCORMACK, Thos. J. Mechanics. [*See* Mach, Dr. E.] A 25 S 24

M'CORMICK, A. D. The Alps from end to end. [*See* Conway, Sir W. M.] D 18 V 20

McCORMICK, Cyrus Hall. Sketch of. [*See* Hubert, P. G.—Inventors.] C 17 R 3

McCORMICK, P. D. A Temperance Tale for Boys. 12mo. Sydney, 1894. MJ 3 P 9

MACCRACKAN, W. D. Rise of the Swiss Republic: a History. 8vo. Boston, 1892. B 25 T 13

Swiss Solutions of American Problems. 8vo. Boston, 1894. F 8 U 37

McCREATH, Andrew S. Mineral Wealth of Virginia. 8vo. Harrisburgh, Pa., 1884. A 24 U 32

M'CRIE, Rev. Charles Greig. The Public Worship of Presbyterian Scotland, historically treated. 8vo. Edinb., 1892. G 2 Q 33

McCULLOCH, Rev. C. The Outlook. (Divinity Hall Record.) 8vo. Brisbane, 1879. ME 15 Q

Religion and Science. (Divinity Hall Record.) 8vo. Brisbane, 1879. ME 15 Q

McCULLOCH, Sir James. The Ministerial Policy. 8vo. Melb., 1877. MJ 3 Q 16

McCULLOCH, J. R. London in 1850-51. 12mo. Lond., 1851. D 10 P 5

McCULLOCH, R. W. Coffee-growing, and its preparation for Market. 8vo. Brisbane, 1893. MA 1 Q 69

Sericulture. 8vo. Brisbane, 1893. MA 1 Q 63

M'CULLOUCH, John. [Plaster Cast of.] [*See* Hutton, L.—Portraits in Plaster.] A 23 V 13

MACCUNN, Florence A. [Life of] John Knox. 8vo. Lond., 1895. C 19 V 4

MACCUNN, Prof. John. Ethics of Citizenship. 12mo. Glasgow, 1894. F 6 T 38

McCURDY, Dr. James Frederick. History, Prophecy, and the Monuments. Vol. 1, to the Downfall of Samaria. 8vo. New York, 1894. B 27 V 18

M'CURE, John Bunyan. My Log-book; or, a Voyage from Australia to England in 1867 in the *Great Britain*. (Pam.) 8vo. Sydney, 1867. MG 1 Q 53

McDERMOTT, P. L. British East Africa or Ibea: a History of the Formation and work of the Imperial British East Africa Company. 8vo. Lond., 1893. B 16 R 9

MACDONALD, A. Abnormal Man. [*See* United States Bureau of Educat.] F 14 T 15

MACDONALD, A. C. Adelaide to Blanchewater. (Roy. Geog. Soc. Australasia, Vic. Branch, 6.) 8vo. Melb., 1889. ME 20

Notes on the Early Discovery of Australia. (Roy. Geog. Soc. Australasia, Vic. Branch, 1885-86.) 8vo. Melb., 1886. ME 20

MACDONALD, A. Fraser-. Our Ocean Railways; or, the Rise, Progress, and Development of Ocean Steam Navigation. 8vo. Lond., 1893. A 19 R 1

MACDONALD, Rev. Alexander Hugh. A paper on Santo, New Hebrides. (Roy. Geog. Soc. Australasia, Vic. Branch, 9.) 8vo. Melb., 1891. ME 20

MACDONALD, Rev. D. Asiatic Origin of the Oceanic Languages: Etymological Dictionary of the Language of Efate (New Hebrides). 8vo. Melb., 1894.
MK 2 Q 2
The Historical and Commercial Aspects of the New Hebrides. (Roy. Geog. Soc. Australasia, Vic. Branch, 6.) 8vo. Melb., 1889. ME 20
The Labour Traffic *versus* Christianity in the South Sea Islands. 12mo. Melb., 1878. MG 2 R 37
The Oceanic Languages Shemitic: a Discovery. (Roy. Soc. Vict., 19.) 8vo. Melb., 1883. ME 1 P

MACDONALD, Capt. D. Narrative of the Early Life and Services of. 3rd. ed. 8vo. Weymouth (n.d.)
C 15 P 19

McDONALD, Donald. Sweet-scented Flowers and Fragrant Leaves. Illustrated. 8vo. Lond., 1895.
A 20 Q 15

MACDONALD, J. M. Mineralogy. (Divinity Hall Record.) 8vo. Brisbane, 1879. ME 15 Q

MACDONALD, Rev. J. Middleton. Thunderbolt: an Australian Story. 8vo. Lond. (n.d.) MJ 2 T 40

M'DONALD, Rev. John. Pamphlet on "The Paraphrases." 8vo. Sydney, 1887. MG 1 R 75

MACDONALD, Rt. Hon. Sir John Alexander. Memoirs of; by J. Pope. 2 vols. roy. 8vo. Lond., 1894.
C 21 S 14, 15

MACDONALD, John Graham. Journal of, on an Expedition from Port Denison to the Gulf of Carpontaria and back. 12mo. Brisbane, 1865. MD 2 P 3

MACDONALD, W. Liturgies, &c., of the Ante-Nicene Period. [*See* Liturgies.] G 14 U 24

MACDONALD, W. A. Science and Ethics. 12mo. Lond., 1895. F 8 U 8

MacDONELL, Annie. [Criticism of the Works of] Thomas Hardy. 12mo. Lond., 1894. J 7 P 30

MACDONELL, John. State Trials. [*See* Great Britain and Ireland.] F 3 T 4-9

MACDONNELL, Rev. G. A. Knights and Kings of Chess. 12mo. Lond., 1894. A 29 S 13

M'DOUALL, Dr. Peter Murray. Portrait of. [*See* Gammage, R. G.—Chartist Movement.] F 7 R 24

McDOUGALL, Mrs. Harriett. Letters from Sarawak an Account of the Manners, Customs, and Religion of the Inhabitants of Borneo. 12mo. Lond., 1854.
D 17 P 29

MACE, Mrs. Thrift and Social Intercourse. [*See* Knapp, J. M.—The Universities and the Social Problem.]
F 8 U 22

MACEDO, Dr. Joaquim Teixeira de. O Ensino Normal Primario na Prussia. 8vo. Rio de Janeiro, 1875.
G 17 R 26
Breves Apontamentos para o Estado das Questões relativas as Ensino Normal Primario. 8vo. Rio de Janeiro, 1876. G 17 R 28

MACEWEN, Rev. Dr. Alexander R. Life and Letters of Rev. Dr. John Cairns. 8vo. Lond., 1895. C 22 R 1

MACFADDEN, C. K., and RAY, W. D. Dynamo Electric Machinery. 18mo. Chicago, 1894. A 21 P 45

McFALL, Capt. Crawford. With the Zhob Field Force, 1890. Illustrated. 8vo. Lond., 1895. D 18 V 18

McFARLANE, Rev. Dr. Samuel. Among the Cannibals of New Guinea. 12mo. Lond., 1888. MD 7 T 61

MACFARLANE, W., & CO. Illustrated Catalogue of Castings. 6th ed. 2 vols. fol. Glasgow (n d.)
A 29 Q 17, 18 ‡

McFERRAN, James. Royal Yachts and English Yacht Clubs. [*See* Sullivan, Sir E.—Yachting.] A 29 Q 41

MACFIE, Matthew. Cardinal Dogmas of Calvinism. [*See* Religious Pamphlets, 1.] G 9 V 16

MACFIE, R. A. Colonial Questions pressing for immediate solution in the interest of the Nation and the Empire. 8vo. Lond., 1871. MF 4 Q 8

MACGAHAN, Januarius A. The Turkish Atrocities in Bulgaria. 8vo. Lond., 1876. B 25 R 12

MACGEORGE, G. W. Ways and Works in India: being an Account of the Public Works in that country from the earliest times to the present day; with Map and Illustrations. 8vo. Lond., 1894. A 22 R 24

McGILLIVRAY, M. The Commerce of New Hebrides—Planting and Trading. (Roy. Geog. Soc. Australasia, Vic. Branch, 9.) 8vo. Melb., 1891. ME 20

MacGILLIVRAY, Dr. P. H. Australian species of Amathia. (Proc. Roy. Soc., Vict., n.s., vol. 7.) 8vo. Melb., 1895. ME 1 P
On two new genera of Polyzoa. (Roy. Soc., Vict., 17–22.) 6 parts. 8vo. Melb., 1881–86. ME 1 P
On some new species of Catenicella and Dictyopora; and on Urceolipora, a new genus of Polyzoa. (Roy. Soc., Vict., 17.) 8vo. Melb., 1881. ME 1 P
Notes on the Reproduction of the Ornithorhynchus. (Roy. Soc., Vict., 21.) 8vo. Melb., 1885. ME 1 P

MACGREGOR, Dr. John. Toil and Travel; being a true story of roving and ranging when on a voyage homeward bound round the world. 8vo. Lond., 1892.
D 10 S 35

MACGREGOR, John, "Rob Roy." [Life of]; by E. Hodder. Illustrated. 8vo. Lond., 1894. C 15 P 18

MacGREGOR, Samuel. Observations on extinct Volcanoes. (Proc. Roy. Soc., Queensland, 10.) 8vo. Brisbane, 1893. ME 1 T

MACGREGOR, Sir Wm. Handbook of Information for Intending Settlers in British New Guinea, 8vo. Brisb., 1892. MD 5 R 46

MACH, E. Handbuch der Weinbaues, &c. [See Babo, A. von.] A 18 U 16, 17

MACH, Dr. Ernst. The Science of Mechanics. Translated from the 2nd German edition by T. J. McCormack. Illustrated. 8vo. Chicago, 1893. A 25 S 24

MacHUGH, Alfred. Bills of Sale. 8vo. Melb., 1895. MF 3 T 53
Insolvency Act, 1890. [See Duffy, F. G.] MF 2 R 50

McILVAIN, Rev. J. Wm. Early Presbyterianism in Maryland. (Johns Hopkins University Studies, 8.) 8vo. Baltimore, 1890. B 18 S 8

McILWAINE, Dr. Henry R. Struggle of Protestant Dissenters for Religious Toleration in Virginia. (Johns Hopkins Univ. Studies, 12.) Roy. 8vo. Baltimore, 1894. B 18 S 12

MacINNES, Rev. George. The Death of the Verbal Theory and the Unveiling of Christ; or, the Bible a "Sufficient Witness" to the "Self-evidencing Christ." 8vo. Sydney, 1894. MG 1 Q 48

M'INTOSH, Prof. Wm. C. Annelida Polychæta; Cephalodiscus Dodecalophus; Phoronis Buskii, n. sp. [See Thomson, Sir C. W., and Murray, Dr. J.—Voyage of H.M.S. Challenger.] A 6 †

McINTYRE, A. G. The Plebiscite historically considered. 8vo. Melb., 1880. MF 4 R 41

MACINTYRE, Maj.-Gen. Donald. Hindu-Koh: Wanderings and Wild Sport on and beyond the Himalayas. Illustrated. Roy. 8vo. Edinb., 1889. D 17 V 14

McINTYRE, Rev. Wm. Faith, its Nature and the Warrant and Motive to exercise it. 18mo. Sydney, 1869. MG 2 P 51
Union of the Presbyterian Church of Eastern Australia in erecting a Presbyterian College within the University of Sydney. 12mo. Sydney, 1857. MG 1 R 24
The Heathenism of Popery proved and illustrated: a Lecture. 8vo. Maitland, 1860. MG 1 R 23

McINTYRE, Wm. D. Legal Tables, Memoranda, and Precedents. 32mo. Sydney, 1893. Libr.

————, and CURLEWIS, H. R. Statutes (England–New South Wales), Comparative Tables. 8vo. Sydney, 1894. MF 3 P 60

MacIVOR, Clarence. The History and Development of Sheep Farming. 8vo. Sydney, 1893.* MA 1 R 37

MACKAIL, John Wm. Latin Literature. 8vo. Lond., 1895. J 12 Q 19

MACKAY, A. H. Report on the Public Schools of Nova Scotia, 1892. 8vo. Halifax, 1893. E

MACKAY, Angus. Bee-keeping as a business in Australia. Illustrated. 8vo. Sydney, 1895. MA 3 U 17
Grazing, Farm, and Garden Soils of New South Wales; with quantitative analyses, by W. A. Dixon. 12mo. Sydney, 1888. MA 1 P 07
Steam; its Properties and Uses. (Divinity Hall Record.) 8vo. Brisbane, 1879. ME 15 Q

MACKAY, Dr. C. The Mormons or Latter Day Saints; with Memoirs of the Life and Death of Joseph Smith, the "American Mahomet." 8vo. Lond., 1852. G 15 P 28
Poetical Works of. 12mo. Lond., 1857. H 10 T 7

MACKAY, Capt. John. Discovery of the Pioneer River, and Early Settlement of Mackay, Queensland. (Roy. Geograph. Soc. of Australasia, Q. Branch, 3.) 8vo. Brisbane, 1898. ME 20 P
Tucopia. (Roy. Geograph. Soc. of Australasia, Q. Branch.) 8vo. Brisbane, 1887. ME 20 P

MACKAY, M. Speech in the Synod of Eastern Australia, relative to the erection of a Presbyterian College in connection with the University of Sydney. 8vo. Sydney, 1857. MG 1 R 25

MACKAY, Robt. Wm. The Eternal Gospel. [See Religious Pamphlets, 1.] G 9 V 16

MACKAY, Thos. Manual of Grasses and Forage Plants useful to New Zealand. Pt. 1. Roy. 8vo. Wellington, 1887. MA 1 S 40

MACKAY, Thos. A Policy of Free Exchange: Essays by various writers on the economical and social aspects of free exchange and kindred subjects. 8vo. Lond., 1894. F 14 S 26
The Interest of the Working Class in Free Exchange. (A Policy of Free Exchange.) 8vo. Lond., 1894. F 14 S 26

M'KEAN, James. Act to amend the Law relating to Divorce and Matrimonial Causes. 8vo. Melb., 1861. MF 4 R 13
Real Property Act of Victoria, 1862. 8vo. Melb., 1862. MF 4 Q 13

M'KEAN, Kate. Social Science. [See Carey, Dr. H. C.] F 14 R 11

M'KEAN, Rev. Thos. S. Memoirs of; by Rev. Joseph A. Miller. 12mo. Lond., 1847. MC 1 P 47

McKELLAR, Campbell, "Hilarior." Greece, her Hopes and Troubles. 8vo. Glasgow 1895.   M B 2 P 55
Griffin Rinsky, and other Tales. 12mo. Lond., 1892.   MJ 2 T 48
A Jersey Witch. 12mo. Lond., 1892.   MJ 2 T 50
Lothair's Children. 12mo. Lond., 1890.   MJ 2 T 51
The Old Stradivari, and other Dramatic Sketches. 8vo. Lond., 1894.   MH 1 V 1
Prince Maurice of Statland; by "H.R.H." 12mo. Lond., 1890.   MJ 2 T 49

MACKELLAR, Dr. Charles Kinnaird. Federal Quarantine. 8vo. Sydney, 1893.   MA 2 S 60

M'KENDRICK, Prof. John Gray, and SNODGRASS, Wm. Physiology of the Senses. 8vo. Lond., 1893.   A 26 Q 14

McKENNIE, Dr. M. Alcoholic Liquors. [See Duplais, P.]   A 25 V 23

McKENZIE, Fred. A. Sober by Act of Parliament. 12mo. Lond., 1894.   F 7 V 2

MACKENZIE, John S. Introduction to Social Philosophy. 8vo. Glasgow, 1890.   F 14 T 42

MACKENZIE, Sir Morell. Physician and Operator: a Memoir; by Rev. H. R. Haweis. 8vo. Lond., 1893.   C 16 R 11

MACKENZIE, Rev. P. Falconer. In Memoriam of John Dunmore Lang. [See Lang, Rev. Dr. J. D.]   MG 2 S 8

MACKENZIE, Capt. T. A., EWART, Lieut. J. S., and FINDLAY, Lieut. C. Historical Records of the 79th Queen's Own Cameron Highlanders. [Illustrated.] 8vo. Lond., 1887.   B 22 R 5

MACKILLOP, Rev. Donald. Aboriginal Tribes of the Daly River. (Trans. Roy. Soc., S. Australia, 17.) 8vo. Adelaide, 1893.   ME 1 P

MACKIN, Charles T. Constitutional Origin of Nervous Disorders. 12mo. Melb., 1875.   MA 2 P 60

MACKINLAY, Major G. Text-book of Gunnery, 1887. Roy. 8vo. Lond., 1887.   A 29 V 16
Gunnery Tables. Roy. 8vo. Lond., 1887.   A 29 V 17

MACKINLAY, James M. Folk-lore of Scottish Lochs and Springs. 8vo. Glasgow, 1893.   B 32 T 8

McKINNEY, Hugh Griffen. Irrigation. (Dept. of Agriculture, N.S.W., The National Prize Competition, 1892.—Report of the Judge.) 8vo. Sydney, 1893.   MA 1 Q 64
Progress and Position of Irrigation in New South Wales. (Journal Roy. Soc., N.S.W., 27.) 8vo. Sydney, 1893.   ME 1 R
———, and WARD, F. W. Report on utilisation of the River Darling. Fol. Sydney, 1893.   MA 10 P 50 †

MACKINNON, Hamilton. Selected Works of Marcus Clarke. [See Clarke, M.]   MJ 2 S 14

MACKINTOSH, Sir James. Miscellaneous Works of. 2nd ed. 8vo. Lond., 1851.   J 6 T 4

MACKINTOSH, Mary. Catholic Socialism. [See Nitti, F. S.]   F 11 U 17

MACKINTOSH, Rev. Dr. Wm. The Natural History of the Christian Religion: being a study of the doctrine of Jesus as developed from Judaism and converted into dogma. 8vo. Glasgow, 1894.   G 13 P 40

MACKLIN, Charles. Love à la Mode: a Farce. [See London Stage, 3.]   H 2 S 35
The Man of the World: a Comedy. [See London Stage, 1.]   H 2 S 33

M'KONOCHIE, Captain. [See Maconochie, Capt. A.]

MACLACHLAN, David. Law of Marine Insurance. [See Arnould, J.]   F 6 V 28, 29

MACLAINE, Rev. Dr. A. Ecclesiastical History. [See Mosheim, Rev. Dr. J. L.]   G 4 P 28–33

MACLAINE, James. "The Gentleman Highwayman." [Life of,] 1724–50; by G. T. Drury. (Lives of Twelve Bad Men.) 8vo. Lond., 1894.   C 18 T 9

MACLAREN, Rev. Albert A. A Visit to the North-East Coast of British New Guinea. (Roy. Geog. Soc. Australas., Vic. Branch, 9.) 8vo. Melb., 1891.   ME 20

MacLAREN, Rev. Dr. Alexander. Psalms, 1-150, Colossians and Philemon. [See Expositor's Bible.]   G 10 R and S

MACLAREN, Archibald. The Fairy Family: a series of Ballads and Metrical Tales illustrating the Fairy Mythology of Europe. 8vo. Lond., 1857.   H 9 U 3

MACLAREN, Archibald. Physical Education. Illustrated. 8vo. Oxford, 1895.   G 18 Q 26

McLAUGHLIN, A. C. History of Higher Education in Michigan. 8vo. Wash., 1891.   G 18 R 45

McLAUGHLIN, E. A. Manual for the use of the General Court, Massachusetts. [See Coolidge, H. D.]   E

MacLAURIN, Dr. Henry Norman. Report on Sanitary Legislation and Administration in England. 4to. Sydney, 1893.   MF 2 S 35

MACLAY, Edgar Stanton. History of the United States Navy, 1775-1894. [Illustrated.] 2 vols. 8vo. Lond., 1894.   B 19 S 19, 20

MACLEAN, C. W. An improved Grab Crane. (Roy. Soc., Vic., 19.) 8vo. Melb., 1883.   ME 1 P

MACLEAY, Sir Wm. Description of Twenty New Species of Australian Coleoptera. 8vo. Sydney, 1862.
MA 2 T 33

The Macleay Memorial Volume. [*See* Linnean Society of N.S.W.] MA 2 Q 1 †

McLEOD, Anne C. [*See* Wilson, Anne C.]

MacLEOD, Henry Dunning. Bi-metalism. 8vo. Lond., 1894. F 10 Q 27

The Science of Economics and its relation to Free Exchange and Socialism. (A Policy of Free Exchange.) 8vo. Lond., 1894. F 14 S 26

Theory of Credit. 2nd ed. Vols. 1 and 2, part 1. 2 vols. 8vo. Lond., 1893-94. F 8 S 30, 31

M'LEOD, Dr. John. Voyage of H.M.S. *Alceste* along the Coast of Corea to the Island of Lewchew, with an Account of her subsequent shipwreck. 2nd ed. 8vo. Lond., 1818. D 17 T 19

McLEOD, Thos. Tables of Towns. 12mo. Brisb., 1890. MD 1 Q 40

MACLISE, Daniel. Maclise Portrait Gallery. [*See* Bates, W.] C 17 R 21

MacMAHON, Maj.-Gen. Alexander Ruxton. Far Cathay and Farther India. 8vo. Lond., 1893. D 17 U 16

MacMAHON, Rev. J. H. Refutation of all Heresies. [*See* Hippolytus, St.] G 14 U 6

McMASTER, John Bach. Bridge and Tunnel Centres. 18mo. New York, 1892. A 22 P 13

High Masonry Dams. 18mo. New York, 1876. A 22 P 14

History of the People of the United States, from the Revolution to the Civil War. Vol. 1-3. 8vo. New York, 1891-93. B 18 R 1-3

MACMILLAN, Prof. Michael. The Globe Trotter in India 200 years ago and other Indian Studies. 8vo. Lond., 1895. B 29 Q 20

McMILLAN, Robt. The Woolly Festival: a Record of the Sydney Stud Sheep Sales, July, 1895. 8vo. Sydney, 1895. MA 3 T 58

M'MILLAN, Thomas. Cultivation and Management of the Melon, Cucumber, Gourd, and Vegetable Marrow. 12mo. Melb. (n.d.) MA 1 P 66

Rule's Economical Gardening for Cottagers; being concise Rules for cultivating useful Culinary Vegetables. 8vo. Melb., 1859. MA 3 S 55

MACMILLAN'S MAGAZINE. Vols. 66-72. 8vo. Lond., 1892-95. E

MACNAB, Wm. Explosives. [*See* Berthelot, M.] A 21 S 14

McNABB, Dr. D. Diseases in the New Hebrides. (Anthropol. Inst., 23.) 8vo. Lond., 1893. E

MACNABB, J. D. The Image of War. [*See* Newland, Surg.-Capt. A. G. E.] D 12 S 15 †

McNEILL, J. Report of Inspector of Coal-mines, Colorado, 1889-90. 8vo. Denver, 1890. E

McNEILL, Dr. Roger. Prevention of Epidemics, and the Construction and Management of Isolation Hospitals. Illustrated. 8vo. Lond., 1894. A 33 T 17

M'NEILL, Rev. John. Australasian Addresses. 8vo. Melb., 1894. MG 2 Q 29

"Off the Line"; the Life Story of. With Portrait. 12mo. Sydney, 1894. MC 1 S 9

MACONOCHIE, Capt. Alexander. Report on the State of Prison Discipline in Van Diemen's Land, &c. Sm. fol. Lond., 1838. MF 3 U 23

Summary View of the Statistics and existing Commerce of the principal Shores of the Pacific Ocean. 8vo. Lond., 1818. MF 3 T 27

MACPHAIL, Myles. National Directory of Tasmania, 1867-68. 8vo. Hobart, 1867. ME 12 U

MACPHERSON, Rev. H. A. Vertebrate Fauna of Lakeland, including Cumberland and Westmorland with Lancashire north of the Sands. 8vo. Edinb., 1893. A 13 T 37

MACPHERSON, Rev. H. A., and others. The Partridge. Natural History; by Rev. H. A. Macpherson. Shooting; by A. J. Stuart-Wortley. Cookery; by G. Saintsbury. Illustrated. 12mo. Lond., 1894. A 28 Q 29

The Grouse. Natural History; by Rev. H. A. Macpherson. Shooting; by A. J. Stuart-Wortley. Cookery; by G. Saintsbury. Illustrated. 12mo. Lond., 1894. A 29 Q 43

MACPHERSON, James. Life and Letters of; by Bailey Saunders. 8vo. Lond., 1894. C 14 V 19

McPHERSON, Dr. J. H. T. History of Liberia. (Johns Hopkins University Studies, 9.) 8vo. Baltimore, 1891. B 18 S 9

MACPHERSON, T. A. Sketch of the Southern Districts of South Australia. Fol. Adelaide, 1838. MD 5 Q 16 ‡

MacRITCHIE, David. Fians, Fairies, and Picts. 8vo. Lond., 1893. B 17 R 14

Scottish Gypsies under the Stewarts. 8vo. Edinb., 1894. B 32 T 15

The Testimony of Tradition. Illustrated. 8vo. Lond., 1890. B 34 T 14

MACVICAR, Dr. M. Principles of Education. 12mo. Boston, 1894. G 18 P 16

MACY, Prof. Jesse. Institutional Beginnings in a Western State. (Johns Hopkins University Studies, 2.) 8vo. Baltimore, 1884. B 18 S 2

MADAN, Falconer. Books in Manuscript. 8vo. Lond., 1893. B 14 Q 42

Summary Catalogue of Western MSS. in the Bodleian Library at Oxford. Vol. 3. 8vo. Oxford, 1895. K 7 U 25

MADDEN, Dr. Richard Robert Life and Martyrdom of G. Savonarola, illustrative of the History of Church and State Connexion. 2nd ed. 2 vols. 8vo. Lond., 1854. C 14 V 20, 21

MADDEN, Dr. Thomas More. Clinical Gynæcology; being a Hand-book of Diseases peculiar to Women. Illustrated. Roy. 8vo. Philad., 1893. A 26 V 16

MADDOCK, Wm. Illustrated Guide to Sydney, comprising Description of the City and its Institutions, with which is incorporated the Tourists' Hand-book, and Description of the Resources of New South Wales. 12mo. Sydney, 1892. MD 3 P 45

MADISON, James. Sketch of. [See Thompson, R. W.—Recollections of Sixteen Presidents.] C 18 T 21, 22

Sketch of. [See Wilson, J. G.—Presidents of the United States.] C 2 V 30

MADRAS GOVERNMENT OBSERVATORY. Results of Observations of the Fixed Stars, made with the Meridian Circle at the Government Observatory, Madras, 1862-87. 8 vols. sm. 4to. Fort St. George, Madras, 1887-91. E

MADRAS PRESIDENCY. Manual of the Administration of. 3 vols. sm. fol. Madras, 1885-93. D 39 U 31-33 ‡

Report of the Administration of, 1891-94. 3 vols. sm. fol. Madras, 1892-94. E

Report on Public Instruction, 1891-94. 3 vols. sm. fol. Madras, 1892-94. E

Report of the Lunatic Asylums in the Madras Presidency, 1879-87. 5 vols. sm. fol. Fort St. George, 1880-88. E

Reports of the Madras Government Lying-in Hospital, 1879-80. 2 vols. sm. fol. Fort St. George, 1880-81. E

Manual of Standing Information, 1893. Sm. fol. Madras 1893. E

MAFFEI, Giovanni Pietro. Historiarum Indicarum Libri, XVI. Fol. Florentiæ, 1588. B 6 P 1 ‡

MAGALHAES Domingos Jose Goncalves de. Confederação los Tamoyos: Poema. 4to. Rio de Janiero, 1856. H 5 V 33

MAGAZINE OF AMERICAN HISTORY. Vols. 28, 29. Sm. 4to. New York, 1892-93. L

MAGILL, Wm E. Laws of the State of Michigan relating to Fire and Marine Insurance Companies in force July, 1891. 8vo. Lansing, 1891. F 1 T 15

MAGINN, Dr. W. Shakespeare Papers; Pictures Grave and Gay. 12mo. Lond., 1859. J 11 T 20

MAGNARD, Francis. Sketch of. [See Smalley, G. W.—Studies of Men.] C 19 R 20

MAGNUS, Sir Philip. Technical Instruction; and Payment on Results. [See Subjects of the Day, 1.] G 18 S 18

MAGNUSSON, Arn. Saga of Magnus. [See Great Britain and Ireland.—Chrons. and Mems.] E

MAGNUSSON, Eirikr. Stories of the Kings of Norway. [See Snorro Sturleson.] J 14 Q 29, 30

MAGUIRE, John Francis. Father Matthew: a Biography. 8vo. New York, 1871. C 21 Q 9

MAHAFFY, Prof. John Pentland. Descartes, Philosopher. [See Descartes, R.] G 6 V 1

Euripides. [See Euripides.] J 16 P 37

The Flinders Petrie Papyri; with Transcriptions, Commentaries, and Index. (Trans. R.I. Academy.—Cunningham Memoirs, 8, 9.) 2 vols. 4to. Dublin, 1891-93. E

MAHAN, Capt. Alfred Thayer. Influence of Sea Power upon the French Revolution and Empire, 1793-1812. 2 vols. 8vo. Lond., 1892. B 8 U 3 4

MAHON, Hugh. The Land League: a Narrative of four years of Irish agitation. 8vo. Melb., 1883. MF 4 Q 45

MAHON, John. Butter and Cheese Making. 8vo. Brsb., 1893. MA 1 Q 69

MAIDEN, Joseph Henry. Notes on the Commercial Timbers of New South Wales. 8vo. Sydney, 1895. MA 2 U 60

Notes on the Resins of two species of *Araucaria*. (Proc. Roy. Soc., Queensland, 7.) 8vo. Brisbane, 1891. ME 1 T

On the Oleo-Resin of *Canarium Mulleri.* (Proc. Roy. Soc., Queensland, 8.) 8vo. Brisbane, 1892. ME 1 T

——— and CAMPBELL, Walter Scott. The Flowering Plants and Ferns of New South Wales. Parts 1-3. Sm. 4to. Sydney, 1895. MA 3 R 49

MAIDMENT, James. A North Countrie Garland. [See Bibliotheca Curiosa.] J 18 Q 5

New Books of Old Ballads. [See Bibliotheca Curiosa.] J 18 Q 14

MAIL, The. Jan., 1892—June, 1893. 3 vols. fol. Lond., 1892-93. E

MAIN, G. M. The Newspaper Press of Auckland [New Zealand]. 8vo. Auckland, 1894. MB 2 U 20

MAIN, Rev. Robert. Practical and Spherical Astronomy, for the use chiefly of Students in the Universities. 8vo. Camb., 1863. A 20 U 7

MAINE, Sir Henry James Sumner. A brief Memoir of his life; by the Rt. Hon. Sir M. E. Grant Duff; with some of his Indian Speeches and Minutes. 8vo. Lond., 1892.   C 15 R 16

MAINE DE BIRAN, F. P. G. Science et Psychologie; nouvelles œuvres inédites de Maine de Biran par A. Bertrand. 8vo. Paris, 1887.   G 10 U 27

MAINE STATE COLLEGE AGRICULT. EXP. STATION. Annual Reports, 1888–91. 4 vols. 8vo. Augusta and Bangor, 1889–92.   E

MAISEY, Gen. F. C. Sánchi and its Remains. 4to. Lond., 1892.   B 23 R 9 ‡

MAISTRE, Count Xavier de. Journey round my Room, and a Nocturnal Expedition Round my Room. Roy. 8vo. Lond. (n.d.)   J 4 U 2
Journey round my Room. [See Bibliotheca Curiosa.]   J 18 Q 20
Nocturnal Expedition round my Room. [See Bibliotheca Curiosa.]   J 18 Q 21

MAITLAND, Edward. How to complete the Reformation. [See Religious Pamphlets, 1.]   G 9 V 16

MAITLAND, Dr. Frederick Wm. History of English Law. [See Pollock, Sir F.]   F 3 V 9, 10

MAITLAND, Wm. The Coming Industrial Struggle. (A Policy of Free Exchange.) 8vo. Lond., 1894.   F 14 S 26

MAJERONI, Giulia. A Living Statue: a novel. 8vo. Lond., 1893.*   MJ 1 U 35

MAKOWER, Felix. The Constitutional History and Constitution of the Church of England. 8vo. Lond., 1895.   G 14 Q 34

MALABARI, Behramji M. The Indian Eye on English Life; or, Rambles of an Indian Reformer. 2nd ed. 12mo. Lond., 1893.   D 17 T 11

MALDEN, Henry Elliot. Rights and Duties of the English Citizen. 8vo. Lond., 1894.   F 8 U 18

MALHERBE, François de. La Doctrine de. [See Brunot, F.]   J 12 V 2

MALIBRAN, Maria. [Plaster Cast of.] [See Hutton, L.—Portraits in Plaster.]   A 23 V 13

MALLESON, Col. George Bruce. History of Afghanistan, to the Outbreak of the War of 1878. 8vo. Lond., 1878.   B 20 S 4
[Life of] Lord Clive. (Rulers of India.) 8vo. Oxford, 1893.   C 13 P 16
Life of Warren Hastings. 8vo. Lond., 1894.   C 16 U 5
The Refounding of the German Empire, 1818–71. 8vo. Lond., 1893.   B 9 R 5

MALLET, Bernard. The Principle of Progression in Taxation. (A Policy of Free Exchange.) 8vo. Lond., 1894.   F 14 S 26

MALLET, Chas. Edward. The French Revolution. 8vo. 1893.   B 8 P 38

MALLET DU PAN, Jacques. The British Mercury; or historical and critical views of the events of the present times. 5 vols. 8vo. Lond., 1798–1800.   F 0 T 11–15

MALLOCH, Christian A. Natural Value. [See Wieser, F. von.]   F 0 T 10

MALLOCK, Wm. Hurrell. Labour and the Popular Welfare. 8vo. Lond., 1893.   F 9 U 48
Letters, &c., of Edward Adolphus Seymour, Twelfth Duke of Somerset. [See Somerset, Duke of.]   C 13 S 24
Studies of Contemporary Superstition. 8vo. Lond., 1895.   G 3 P 21

MALTHUS, Rev. Thos. Robt. Parallel Chapters from the 1st and 2nd editions of an Essay on the Principle of Population. 12mo. New York, 1895.   F 7 V 32
Essay on. [See Bagehot, W.—Economic Studies.]   F 7 V 35

MAN OF TASTE, The: an Epistle. Sm. fol. Lond., 1733.   H 39 Q 13 ‡

MANAKAU NEW ZEALAND COMPANY; Correspondence relating to. Sm. fol. Lond., 1845.   MF 3 U 24

MANCHESTER NATIONAL SOCIETY FOR WOMEN'S SUFFRAGE. Annual Reports of the Executive Committee, 1880–82. 2 vols. 8vo. Manchester, 1880–82.   E

MANCHESTER QUARTERLY, The: a Journal of Literature and Art. Vols. 11–13. 8vo. Manchester, 1892–94.   E

MANDELL, John A. Physiological Chemistry. [See Hammarsten, O.]   A 33 T 6

MANGIN, Arthur. Voyage à la Nouvelle-Calédonie, suivi de les Bêtes criminelles au moyen âge. 8vo. Paris, 1883.   MD 7 S 41

MANITOBA. 200 millionen Acker zu Ansiedlungszwecken in Manitoba. 8vo. (n.p.) 1893.   D 15 R 15

MANITOBA HISTORICAL AND SCIENTIFIC SOCIETY. Transactions, Nos. 45–47. 3 vols. 8vo. Winnipeg, 1894.   B 18 R 6-8
45. The Old Crow Wing Trail; by Hon. J. Schultz.
46. Early Days in Winnipeg; by Dr. G. Bryce.
47. A Forgotten Northern Fortress; by Hon. J. Schultz.

MANN, Dr. Matthew Darbyshire. A System of Gynæcology; by American Authors. 2 vols. roy. 8vo. Edinb., 1887–88.   A 33 U 7, 8

MANNING, Miss Anne. [*See* Rathbone, Mrs.]

MANNING, Henry Edward, Cardinal; a Character Sketch, or Foreshadowings. Edited by E. H. King. 12mo. Lond., 1895.   G 9 V 26

Personal Reminiscences of; with Portrait. [*See* Blathwayt, R.—Interviews.]   J 10 U 34

MANNING, James. Review on the Report of Wm. Clarke on the question of Water Supply for Sydney. 8vo. Sydney, 1877.   MA 2 V 48

MANSEL, Very Rev. Henry Longueville. Metaphysics; or, the Philosophy of Consciousness. 8vo. Edinb., 1860.   G 15 P 32

MANSERGH, James. Report on the Sewerage and Sewage Disposal of the proposed Melbourne Metropolitan District. Fol. Melb., 1890.   MA 2 Q 42 †

MANSFIELD, Robert Blachford. Log of the *Water Lily* during two cruises, 1851-52, on the Rhine, Neckar, Main, Moselle, Danube, and other streams of Germany. 3rd ed. 8vo. Lond., 1854.   D 20 Q 16

MANTELL, Dr. Gideon Algernon. Thoughts on a Pebble; or, a First Lesson in Geology. Sm. 4to. Lond., 1849.   A 24 P 16

MAORI. [*See* Inglis, Jas.]

MAPLESTONE, C. M. Observations on some living Polyzoa. (Roy. Soc., Vict., 18.) 8vo. Melb., 1882.   ME 1 P

MAPS relating to Australia. Five Reproductions by A. F. Calvert. Sm. 4to. Lond. (n.d.)   MD 7 Q 29 †

MARAT, Jean Paul. [Plaster Cast of.] [*See* Hutton, L. —Portraits in Plaster.]   A 23 V 13

MARBLE, Albert P. Sanitary Conditions for Schoolhouses. 8vo. Washington, 1891.   A 19 T 32

MARCH, Dr. Francis Andrew. The Spelling Reform. 8vo. Wash., 1893.   J 5 T 29

MARCHMONT and the Humes of Polwarth. [*See* Warrender, M.]   C 17 S 6

MAREY, Etienne Jules. Movement; translated by E. Pritchard. 8vo. Lond., 1895.   A 20 R 31

MARGARET DE VALOIS, Queen of Navarre. Memoirs of, containing the Secret History of the Court of France, 1565-82. 8vo. Lond., 1895.   B 26 V 18

MARGAROT, Maurice. Trial of Maurice Margarot, Delegate from London to the British Convention, at Edinburgh, on the 13th and 14th January, 1794, for sedition. 8vo. Edinb., 1794.   F 14 R 14

MARGESSON, Lady Isabel. Hand-book to the Study of Natural History, for the use of Beginners. 8vo. Lond., 1894.   A 28 P 5

MARILLIER, L. La Survivance de l'Ame et l'Idée de Justice chez les Peuples non civilisés. 8vo. Paris, 1894.   G 16 U 28

MARIN, Aylic. [*See* Petit, Edouard.]

MARION, M. Bi-sulphide of Carbon Treatment of the Phylloxera. [*See* Finlay, A. K.]   MA 1 P 51

MARITIME NOTES AND QUERIES. Vol. 8. 4to. Lond., 1892.   E

MARK LANE EXPRESS, The, and Agricultural Journal, 1892-94. 3 vols. fol. Lond., 1892-94.   E

MARK TWAIN. [*See* Clemens, S. L.]

MARKHAM, Clements Robert. Life of Christopher Columbus. 8vo. Lond., 1892.   C 13 P 20

Major J. Rennell and the rise of Modern Geography. 8vo. Lond., 1895.   C 17 P 20

Narratives of the Voyages of Pedro Sarmiento de Gamboa. [*See* Sarmiento, P.]   E

MARKS, Edward Lloyd. New and economical method for the scientific production of some acids. (Roy. Soc., Vict., 17.) 8vo. Melb., 1881.   ME 1 P

MARKS, Henry Stacy. Pen and Pencil Sketches. 2 vols. 8vo. Lond., 1894.   C 18 T 16, 17

MARLBOROUGH, John Churchill, Duke of. Life of, to the accession of Queen Anne; by General Viscount Wolseley. 2 vols. 8vo. Lond., 1894.   C 14 V 15, 16

MARQUIS, D. Views around Brisbane. [*See* Wright, G. P.]   MD 3 Q 11 ‡

MARRIOTT, H. P. F. Facts about Pompei, its Masons' Marks, Town Walls, Houses, and Portraits. Illustrated. 4to. Lond. (n d.)   B 36 T 17 ‡

MARRYAT, Frank. Mountains and Molehills; or, Recollections of a burnt Journal. Illustrated. 8vo. Lond., 1855.   D 15 U 5

MARSDEN, Kate. Or Sledge and Horseback to outcast Siberian Lepers. 8vo. Lond., 1893.   D 17 U 17

MARSH, M. H. Letter to the Colonists of Queensland. 8vo. Salisbury, 1859.   MB 2 Q 52

MARSH, Dr. Othniel Chas. Dinocerata: a Monograph of an extinct order of Gigantic Mammals. (U.S. Geol. Survey, 10.) 4to. Wash., 1886.   E

MARSHALL, Dr. Arthur Milnes. Biological Lectures and Addresses. Edited by Dr. C. F. Marshall. 8vo. Lond., 1894.   A 27 R 24

Lectures on the Darwinian Theory. Illustrated. 8vo. Lond., 1894.   A 30 U 6

———— and HURST, Dr. C. Herbert. A Junior Course of Practical Zoology. 4th ed. 8vo. Lond., 1895.   A 28 P 31

MARSHALL, Dr. C. F. Biological Lectures. [*See* Marshall, Dr. A. M.] A 27 R 24

MARSHALL, Frances and Hugh. Old English Embroidery; its Technique and Symbolism. Imp. 8vo. Lond., 1894. A 22 V 13

MARSHALL, Frank A. The Irving Shakespeare. [*See* Shakepeare, William.] H 4 V 1-8

MARSHALL, Henry. Depression and Superstition. 8vo. Adelaide, 1886. MF 4 R 50
Gold and Mining. 8vo. Adelaide, 1885. MA 2 V 62

MARSHALL, Henry Rutgers. Æsthetic Principles. 8vo. New York, 1895. G 3 P 28

MARSHALL, Hugh. Old English Embroidery. [*See* Marshall, Frances.] A 22 V 13

MARSHALL, Prof. John. Description of the Human Body, its structure and functions; with plates. 4th edition. 1 vol. 4to; 1 vol. fol. Lond., 1882.
A 37 Q 5, 6 ‡

MARSHALL, John. Reply to the Misrepresentations which have been put forth respecting Female Emigration to Australia. 2nd edition. 8vo. Lond., 1882. MF 1 P 52

MARSON, Charles L. Fnery Stories. 12mo. Adelaide (n.d.) MJ 1 P 63

MARSTON, John W. The Patrician's Daughter: a Tragedy in five acts. 2nd ed. 8vo. Lond., 1842.
H 10 S 8

MARSTON, R. B. Walton and some Earlier Writers on Fish and Fishing. 12mo. Lond., 1894. J 6 P 35

MARTELLI, A. The Silkworm and its Food. 12mo. Melb., 1863. MA 1 P 68

MARTENS, Frederick. Observations made in Groenland. [*See* Narbrough, Sir J.] MD 5 P 23

MARTHA, Jules. Les Sacerdoces Athéniens. 8vo. Paris, 1882. G 16 U 23

MARTIN, Albert. Les Cavaliers Athéniens. 8vo. Paris, 1886. B 35 R 19
Le Manuscrit d'Isocrate Urbinas III de la Vaticane. 8vo. Paris, 1881. J 7 U 20
Les Scolies du Manuscrit d'Aristophane à Ravenne. 8vo. Paris, 1882. J 7 U 18

MARTIN, Arthur Patchett. Bush Bandits. [*See* Praed, Mrs. Campbell.—Under the Gum Tree.] MJ 2 T 44
Life and Letters of the Rt. Hon. Robert Lowe, Viscount Sherbrooke. 2 vols. 8vo. Lond., 1893.
MC 1 R 46, 47
True Stories from Australasian History. 12mo. Lond., 1893. MB 1 Q 34

MARTIN, George H. Brief Historical Sketch of the Massachusetts Public School Systems. 8vo. Boston, 1893. G 18 Q 20

MARTIN, Mrs. H. Patchett. A Night in a Custom-house. [*See* Praed, Mrs. Campbell.—Under the Gum Tree.]
MJ 2 T 44

MARTIN, Dr. K. Die Fossilien von Java. 4to. Leiden, 1891. A 40 T 16 ‡

MARTIN, Robt. Montgomery. History of Southern Africa, the Cape of Good Hope, Mauritius, Seychelles, &c. 12mo. Lond., 1836. B 16 P 6
History of the British Possessions in the Indian and Atlantic Oceans. 12mo. Lond., 1837. B 16 P 5
History of the West Indies. 2 vols. 12mo. Lond., 1836.
B 18 P 3, 4
History of the British Possessions in the Mediterranean. 12mo. Lond., 1837. B 25 P 9
History of Nova Scotia, Cape Breton, the Sable Islands, New Brunswick, Prince Edward Island, the Bermudas, Newfoundland, &c. 12mo. Lond., 1837. B 18 P 6
History, Statistics, and Geography of Upper and Lower Canada. 12mo. Lond., 1838. B 18 P 5
History of the Possessions of the Hon. East India Co. 2 vols. 12mo. Lond., 1837. B 29 P 1, 2

MARTIN, Dr. Sidney. Functional and Organic Diseases of the Stomach. Illustrated. 8vo. Edinb., 1895.
A 12 T 83

MARTIN, Sir Theodore. Madonna Pia: a Tragedy, and three other Dramas. 12mo. Edinb., 1894. H 4 R 38

MARTIN, Thomas Commerford. Inventions, Researches, and Writings of Nikola Tesla; with special reference to his work in Polyphase Currents and High Potential Lighting. 2nd ed. 8vo. New York, 1894.
A 21 V 14

MARTIN, Sir Wm. England and the New Zealanders. Part 1. 12mo. Bishops' Auckland, 1847. MF 4 P 20

MARTIN, Lieut.-Col. Wm. G. Wood-. Pagan Ireland: an Archæological Sketch; a Hand-book of Irish Pre-Christian Antiquities. Illustrated. 8vo. Lond., 1895. B 29 R 10

MARTINEAU, Miss Harriet. Life in the Sick Room. 3rd ed. 12mo. Lond., 1849. A 33 P 3
Society in America. 3 vols. 8vo. Lond., 1837.
F 14 R 34-36
Miss Martineau and her Master. [*See* Bushnan, Dr. J.S.]
G 9 V 24

MARTINEAU, Rev. Dr. James. A Study of Spinoza. 8vo. Lond., 1895. G 3 P 32
The Rationale of Religious Enquiry; or, the Question stated of Reason, the Bible, and the Church. 4th ed. 8vo. Lond., 1853. G 15 P 35

MARTINEAU, John. Life and Correspondence of Sir Bartle Frere. 2 vols. 8vo. Lond., 1895. C 21 R 13, 14

MARVIN, Arthur Tappan. The Olive, its Culture in Theory and Practice. Illustrated. Roy. 8vo. San Francisco, 1889.   A 18 V 25

MARVIN, Prof. C. F. Barometers and the Measurement of Atmospheric Pressure. Roy. 8vo. Wash., 1894.   A 31 Q 2

MARWICK, John G. Spare Moments in Australia. 8vo. Sydney, 1877.   MJ 3 Q 32

MARY: a Tale, and other Poems; by "D.M." 8vo. Kilmore, 1872.   MH 1 S 71

MARY IRA, The; being the Narrative Journal of a Yachting Expedition from Auckland to the South Sea Islands; by J.K.M. 8vo. Lond., 1867.   MD 1 Q 32

MARY STUART, Queen of Scots. Tragedy of Fotheringay. [*See* Scott, Hon. Mrs. M.]   B 32 T 16
Life of; by J. Skelton. 4to. Lond., 1893.   C 1 W 8

MARY TUDOR, Queen of France, Daughter of Henry VII of England. "The Spousells" of. [*See* Camden Soc. Pubs., 53.]   E

MARYBOROUGH (Q.) CHAMBER OF COMMERCE. Annual Report and Proceedings of, 1883. 8vo. Maryborough, 1883.   ME 6 S

MARYLAND, its Resources, Industries, and Institutions. 4to. Baltimore, 1893.   F 2 T 21

MARZIALS, Frank T. Life of Thackeray. [*See* Merivale, H.]   C 14 P 31

MASCAGNI, Pietro. Sketch of. [*See* Streatfeild, R. A. — Masters of Italian Music.]   C 22 P 13

MASKELL, Alfred. Russian Art, and Art Objects in Russia. 8vo. Lond., 1884.   A 23 R 32

MASKELL, Wm. Ivories, Ancient and Mediæval. 8vo. Lond., 1875.   A 23 R 30

MASKELL, W. M. Further Coccid Notes, &c. (Trans. N.Z. Inst., 27.) 8vo. Wellington, 1894.   ME 2 R
History of the Warfare against Insect Pests. (Trans. N.Z. Inst., 27.) 8vo. Wellington, 1894.   ME 2 R
Synoptical List of Coccidæ reported from Australasia and the Pacific Islands, up to Dec. 1894. (Trans. N.Z. Inst., 27.) 8vo. Wellington, 1894.   ME 2 R

MASKELYNE, John Nevil. "Sharps and Flats": a complete revelation of the Secrets of Cheating at Games of Chance and Skill. 8vo. Lond., 1894.   A 29 Q 37

MASKELYNE, Prof. Mervin H. N. Story. Crystallography: a Treatment on the Morphology of Crystals. 8vo. Oxford, 1895.   A 25 S 21

MASON, George Champlin. Life and Works of Gilbert Stuart. Imp. 8vo. New York 1879.   C 15 P 1 †

MASON, Rev. George H. Life with the Zulus of Natal, South Africa. 8vo. Lond., 1855.   D 14 P 10

MASON, Sir Josiah. [Biographical Sketch.] [*See* Smith, G. B.—Leaders of Modern Industry.]   C 14 P 14

MASON, Dr. Otis T. Educational Aspect of the United States National Museum. (Johns Hopkins University Studies, 8.) 8vo. Baltimore, 1890.   B 18 S 8
Origins of Inventions. Illustrated. 8vo. Lond., 1895.   A 25 Q 20
Woman's Share in Primitive Culture. Illustrated. 8vo. Lond., 1895.   F 2 U 37

MASON, Walter G. The Australian Picture Pleasure Book. 4to. Sydney, 1857.   MD 10 P 9 †

MASONIC BOARD OF BENEVOLENCE, Canterbury, New Zealand. Rules and Regulations. 12mo. Christchurch, N.Z., 1883.   MG 2 T 18

MASONIC SIGNS AND SYMBOLS: by "Henricus." 8vo. Sydney (n.d.)*   MJ 2 S 8

MASPERO, Prof. Gaston. Dawn of Civilization: Egypt and Chaldæa. Edited by A. H. Sayce, and translated by M. L. McClure. Illustrated. Imp. 8vo. Lond., 1894.   B 17 U 15

MASSACHUSETTS—*State Departments, Reports and Publications.*

ADJUTANT-GENERAL. Report, 1892. 8vo. Boston, 1893.   E

ALMSHOUSE at Tewksbury. Report, 1892. 8vo. Boston, 1893.   E

ATTORNEY-GENERAL. Report for the year ending January, 1893. 8vo. Boston, 1893.   E

AUDITOR OF ACCOUNTS. Report, 1892. 8vo. Boston, 1893.   E

BOARD OF AGRICULTURE. Report, 1892. 8vo. Boston, 1893.   E
Comparative Statistics concerning the Agriculture of Massachusetts. 8vo. Chicago, 1893.   A 30 Q 5

BOARD OF ARBITRATION. Report, 1892. 8vo. Boston, 1893.   E

BOARD OF COMMISSIONERS OF PRISONS. Report, 1892. 8vo. Boston, 1893.   E

BOARD OF COMMISSIONERS OF SAVINGS BANKS. Report, 1892. 2 vols. 8vo. Boston, 1893.   E
Supplementary Report relating to Unclaimed Deposits, 1892. 8vo. Boston, 1893.   E

BOARD OF EDUCATION. Report, 1891-92. 8vo. Boston, 1893.   E

BOARD OF GAS AND ELECTRIC LIGHT COMMISSIONERS. Report, 1893. 8vo. Boston, 1893.   E

BOARD OF HARBOR AND LAND COMMISSIONERS. Report, 1892. 8vo. Boston, 1893.   E

MASSACHUSETTS—*contd.*

BOARD OF HEALTH. Experimental Investigations upon the Purification of Sewage by Filtration and Chemical Precipitation, and upon the Intermittent Filtration of Water, 1888–90. Roy. 8vo. Boston, 1890. E

BOARD OF LUNACY AND CHARITY. Report, 1892. 8vo. Boston, 1893. E

Massachusetts' Care of Dependent and Delinquent Children. 8vo. Boston, 1893. F 14 U 16

BOARD OF RAILROAD COMMISSIONERS Report, 1892. 8vo. Boston, 1893. E

BOARD OF REGISTRATION IN DENTISTRY. Report, 1892. 8vo. Boston, 1893. E

BOARD OF REGISTRATION IN PHARMACY. Report, 1892. 8vo. Boston, 1893. E

BUREAU OF STATISTICS OF LABOR. Annual Statistics of Manufactures, 1892–93. 2 vols. 8vo. Boston, 1893–94. E

Reports, 1892–93. 2 vols. 8vo. Boston, 1893–94. E

Analysis and Index of all Reports issued by Bureaus of Labor Statistics. 8vo. Washington, 1893. E

CHIEF OF DISTRICT POLICE. Report, 1892. 8vo. Boston, 1893. E

COMMISSIONER OF FOREIGN MORTGAGE CORPORATIONS. Report, 1892. 8vo. Boston, 1893. E

COMMISSIONERS ON INLAND FISHERIES AND GAME. Report, 1892. 8vo. Boston, 1893. E

FARM AT BRIDGEWATER. Report, 1892. 8vo. Boston, 1893. E

FREE PUBLIC LIBRARY COMMISSION. Reports, 1892–93. 2 vols. 8vo. Boston, 1892–93. E

GENERAL COURT. Abstract of Certificates of Corporation for 1892. 8vo. Boston, 1893. E

Acts and Resolves, 1892, 1893. 2 vols. roy. 8vo. Boston, 1892–93. E

[Consolidated] Public Statutes of the Commonwealth of Massachusetts to 1882. Roy. 8vo. Boston, 1882. F 3 V 6

Statutes relating to Public Instruction. 8vo. Boston, 1892. F 14 U 14

GENERAL SUPERINTENDENT OF PRISONS. Report relating to Prison Labor, 1892. 8vo. Boston, 1893. E

INSURANCE COMMISSIONER. Report, 1892. 8vo. Boston, 1893. E

LIBRARY. Report, 1892. 8vo. Boston, 1893. E

PRIMARY AND REFORM SCHOOLS. Report, 1892. 8vo. Boston, 1893. E

SCHOOL FOR THE FEEBLE-MINDED at Waltham. Report, 1892. 8vo. Boston, 1893. E

SECRETARY OF STATE. Report, 1892. 8vo. Boston, 1893. E

TREASURER AND RECEIVER-GENERAL. Report, 1892. 8vo. Boston, 1893. E

MASSACHUSETTS AGRICULTURAL COLLEGE. Report for 1892. 8vo. Boston, 1893. E

MASSACHUSETTS HOSPITAL FOR DIPSO-MANIACS AND INEBRIATES. Report, March, 1893. 8vo. Boston, 1893. E

MASSACHUSETTS INSTITUTE OF TECHNOLOGY. [Lists of Officers and Courses of Instruction in the different Schools.] 8vo. Boston, 1892–93. E

MASSEY, Gerald. The Ballad of Babe Christabel ; with other Lyrical Poems. 5th ed. 12mo. Lond., 1855. H 10 T 2

MASSINA, A. H., & CO. Guide to Melbourne, with Map of the City. 12mo. Melb., 1886. MD 1 P 24

Weather Almanac and General Guide and Hand-book for Victoria for 1894. 8vo. Melb., 1894. ME 4 U

MASSINGER, Philip. The Duke of Milan : a Tragedy. [*See* London Stage, 2.] H 2 S 34

A New Way to pay Old Debts : a Comedy. [*See* London Stage, 2.] H 2 S 34

MASSON, Prof. David. British Novelists and their Styles. 8vo. Camb., 1859. J 12 Q 1

Edinburgh Sketches and Memories. 8vo. Lond., 1892. B 34 U 18

In the Footsteps of the Poets ; by Prof. D. Masson and others. Illustrated. 8vo. Lond. (n.d.) J 6 R 43
 1. Milton ; by Prof. D. Masson.
 2. Herbert ; by Rev. Dr. J. Brown.
 3. Cowper ; by the Rev. Canon Benham.
 4. Thomson ; by Hugh Haliburton.
 5. Wordsworth ; by H. C. Ewart.
 6. Scott ; by J. Dennis.
 7. Mrs. Browning ; by the Lord Bishop of Ripon.
 8. Robert Browning ; by R. H. Hutton.
 9. Tennyson ; by W. Canton.

Life of John Milton. Index vol. 8vo. Lond., 1894. C 8 R 38*

MASSON, Frédéric. Napoleon and the Fair Sex. 8vo. Lond., 1894. C 17 S 10

MATHER, Dr. George R. Two Great Scotsmen, the Brothers W. and J. Hunter. Sm. 4to. Glasgow, 1893. C 13 S 25

MATHER, Helen. One Summer in Hawaii. Illustrated. 8vo. New York, 1891. MD 8 P 3

MATHESON, A. Scott. The Church and Social Problems. 2nd ed. 8vo. Edinb., 1894. F 14 R 38

MATHESON, Ewing. Works in Iron. Bridge and Roof Structures. 2nd ed. Roy. 8vo. Lond., 1877. A 22 T 22

MATHESON, Rev. John William, Missionary on Tanna (New Hebrides). Memoirs of ; by Rev. G. Patterson. 8vo. Philad., 1864. MC 1 S 4

MATHESON, Mrs. Mary J., Missionary on Tanna (New Hebrides). Memoirs of ; by Rev. G. Patterson. 8vo. Philad., 1864. MC 1 S 4

MATHEW, Rev. John. Cave Paintings of Australia. (Anthropol. Inst., 23.) 8vo. Lond., 1893. E

MATHEW, Father Theobald. A Biography; by J. F. Maguire. 8vo. New York, 1871. C 21 Q 9

MATHEWS, Prof. G. B. Bessel Functions and Physics. [See Gray, Prof. A.] A 25 U 21

MATHEWS, R. H. Aboriginal Bora held at Gundabloui in 1894. (Journal Roy. Soc., N.S.W., 28.) 8vo. Sydney, 1894. ME 1 R

Aboriginal Rock Paintings and Carvings in New South Wales. (Proc. Roy. Soc., Victoria, n.s., 7.) 8vo. Melb., 1895. ME 1 P

The Bora; or, Initiation Ceremonies of the Kamilaroi Tribe. (Anthropol. Inst., 24.) 8vo. Lond., 1894. E

Rock Paintings near Singleton. (Journal Roy. Soc., N.S.W., 27.) 8vo. Sydney, 1893. ME 1 R

Stone Implements used by the Aborigines of New South Wales. (Journal Roy. Soc., N.S.W., 28.) 8vo. Sydney, 1894. ME 1 R

MATIVET, M., "Mouchoir." La Nouvelle Cythère [Tahiti]. 12mo. Paris, 1888. MD 7 T 10

MATRIMONIAL CHRONICLE, July, 1879–April, 1880. Sm. 4to. Tumut, N.S.W., 1879-80. ME 19 R

MATSON, Henry. References for Literary Workers; with Introductions to Topics and Questions for Debate. 8vo. Chicago, 1892. K 19 Q 11

MATSON, Sarah Ann. St. George and the Dragon. 2nd ed. 8vo. Lond., 1893. B 22 Q 29

MATTHEW, St. Oracles ascribed to, by Papias. [See Papias.] G 10 Q 60

MATTHEWS, D. Report of the Echuca Aboriginal Mission School, Murray River, New South Wales 8vo. Echuca, 1879. ME 15 Q

MATTHEWS, James Brander. Books and Play-books; Essays on Literature and the Drama. 8vo. Lond., 1895. J 8 T 34

Pen and Ink. 12mo. New York, 1894. J 11 P 44

MAUD, Constance. Wagner's Heroes. 8vo. Lond., 1895. H 10 S 15

MAUDE, Col. Francis Cornwallis. Five Years in Madagascar; with Notes on the Military Situation. 8vo. Lond., 1895. B 1 P 22

Memories of the Mutiny; with which is incorporated the personal Narrative of J. W. Sherer. 2 vols. 8vo. Lond., 1894. B 29 U 2, 3

MAUDE, Capt. F. N. Great War of 189–. [See Great War of 189–.] J 2 Q 21

MAUGHAN, Wm. Chas. Roseneath, Past and Present. Sm. 4to. Paisley, 1893. B 31 U 10

MAUGRAS, G. Duc de Lauzun and the Court of Louis XV. 8vo. Lond., 1895. B 34 R 8

MAURICE, Col. John Frederick. Great War of 189–. [See Great War of 189–.] J 2 Q 21

MAURITIUS. Account of the Island of Mauritius and its dependencies. 8vo. Lond., 1842. D 17 V 30

Recollections of Seven Years' Residence at the Mauritius, or Isle of France; by "A Lady." 12mo. Lond., 1830. D 17 Q 29

MAX ADELER. [See Clark, C. H.]

MAX O'RELL. [See Blouet, Paul.]

MAXWELL, Rev. Andrew. Christ's Headship. 8vo. Sydney, 1855. MG 2 S 1

Review of Recent Proceedings in the Free Presbyterian Synod respecting Letters on Union. 8vo. Melb., 1869. MG 1 S 32

MAXWELL, Sir Herbert. Life and Times of the Rt. Hon. W. H. Smith. 2 vols. 8vo. Edinb., 1893. C 19 R 1 2

Post Meridian: Afternoon Essays. 8vo. Edinb., 1895. J 7 S 11

Scottish Land-names, their Origin and Meaning. 8vo. Edinb., 1894. K 12 Q 47

MAXWELL, James Clerk. Matter and Motion. 18mo. New York, 1892. A 29 P 30

MAY, Dr. S. P. Catalogue of School Appliances, Pupils' Work, &c., exhibited by the Education Department of Ontario, Canada, at the World's Columbian Exposition, 1893. 8vo. Toronto, 1893. K 8 R 26

MAY, Mrs. Walter. The Economic Housewife's and Beekeeper's Guide to Cookery; by "An Experienced Australian Cook." 18mo. West Maitland, 1894. MA 3 U 31

MAY, W. J. Greenhouse Management for Amateurs. 2rd ed. 8vo. Lond. (n.d.) A 19 R 16

MAYCOCK, W. Perren. Electric Lighting and Power Distribution: an Elementary Manual. Illustrated. 12mo. Lond., 1894. A 21 R 15

MAYER, Gertrude Townshend. Women of Letters. 2 vols. 8vo. Lond., 1894. C 18 F 14

MAYES, Chas. The Australian Builders' Price-book. 8vo. Melb., 1891. MA 3 U 16

MAYET, Prof. P. Agricultural Insurance in organic connection with Savings Banks, Land Credit, and the Commutation of Debts. 8vo. Lond., 1893. F 4 G 33

MAYHEW, Henry, and BINNY, J. Criminal Prisons of London and Scenes of Prison Life. Roy. 8vo. Lond., 1862. F 6 V 20

MAYO, Rev. Amory Dwight. Southern Women in the recent Educational Movement in the South. 8vo. Wash., 1892. G 18 R 21

MAYOUX, Mdlle. A. Recherches sur la Production et la Localisation du Tannin, chez les Fruits Comestibles fournis par la Famille des Pomacées. 8vo. Paris, 1894. A 30 R 24

———— Recherches sur la Valeur Morphologique des Appendices Superstaminaux de la Fleur des Aristoloches. (Annales de l'Université de Lyon, 2.) Roy. 8vo. Paris, 1892. A 20 V 30

MAZZINI, Giuseppe. Scritti. Vols. 16–18.—Politica. 12mo. Roma, 1888-91. F 4 U 17, 18
Recollections of. [See Linton, W. J.] C 12 S 33

MECHANICAL ENGINEERS, American Society of. [See American Society of Mechanical Engineers.]

MECHANICAL ENGINEERS, Institution of. [See Institution of Mechanical Engineers.]

MEDICAL ANNUAL, The, and Practitioner's Index, 1895. 8vo. Bristol, 1894. E

MEDICAL REGISTER, The. 1894 and 1895. 2 vols. roy. 8vo. Lond., 1894-95. E

MEDINA, J. T. Ensayo acerca de una Mapoteca Chilena. 8vo. Santiago, 1889. K 7 P 8

MEDIUMS and their Dupes. 8vo. Sydney, 1879. MG 2 Q 36

MEDIUMS and their Dupes: a complete exposure of the Chicaneries of Professional Mediums, and explanation of so-called Spiritual Phenomena. 8vo. Sydney, 1879. MG 2 Q 36
1. The World of Dupes; by "The Vagabond."
2. Slade and the Spirits; by Samuel T. Knaggs, M.D.
3. Another Seance with Slade; by T. T. Wilton.
4. Hindoo Juggling and Christian Credulity; by "Maori."
5. Spiritualism considered as an Infectious Mental Disease; by Samuel T. Knaggs, M.D.
6. The Spirits at Albury.

MEECH, W. W. Quince Culture. 12mo. New York, 1888. A 18 Q 36

MEEHAN, Wm. E. Fish, Fishing, and Fisheries of Pennsylvania. 8vo. Harrisburg, 1893. A 30 R 1

MEESTER DE RAVESTEIN, E. de. Musée Royal d'Antiquités et d'Armures, Bruxelles. Musée de Ravestein. 12mo. Bruxelles, 1884. K 7 P 9

MEGGY, Percy R. From Sydney to Silverton. 8vo. Sydney, 1895. MD 5 R 43

MEIKLE, Robt. The Fencer's Manual: a practical treatise on Small Sword Exercises. 8vo. Melb., 1859. MA 2 V 28

MEISSNER, M. Catalogue des Vignes Américaines. [See Bush et Fils et Meissner.] A 36 P 9 ‡

MELANESIAN MISSION. Report and Accounts for 1891. 8vo. Auckland, 1892. ME 6 S

MELBOURNE. Melbourne as it is and as it ought to be; with Remarks on Street Architecture generally. 8vo. Melb., 1850. MA 3 T 15
Melbourne Building Act. An Act for regulating Buildings and Party Walls, and for preventing mischief by fire in the City of Melbourne, 1849. 8vo. Melb., 1849. MF 4 Q 18
Pen and Pencil in Collins-street; by "Wayfarer." 8vo. Melb. (n.d.) MH 1 S 63

MELBOURNE AND HOBSON'S BAY UNITED RAILWAY COMPANY. 17th Report. 8vo. Melb., 1873. MF 2 R 44

MELBOURNE EXHIBITION, 1866. Guide to the Intercolonial Exhibition of 1866. 8vo. Melb., 1866. MK 2 Q 5

MELBOURNE GENERAL CEMETERY. Rules and Regulations of. 8vo. Melb., 1860. MF 4 Q 17

MELBOURNE GUIDE-BOOK; with Pictorial Map of the City and Bird's-eye Views of the Streets. 8vo. Melb. (n.d.) MD 8 P 27

MELBOURNE HARBOR TRUST COMMISSIONERS. Regulations of, 1878. 8vo. Melb., 1878. MF 3 P 30

MELBOURNE INDUSTRIAL AND TECHNOLOGICAL MUSEUM. [See Victoria—Public Library, Museums, and National Gallery.]

MELBOURNE OBSERVATORY. Astronomical Observations, 1861–84. 7 vols. 8vo. Melb., 1869-88. ME 16 R
First and Second Melbourne General Catalogues of Stars, reduced from Observations extending from 1863-87. 2 vols. 4to. Melb., 1874-89. MA 9 P 28, 29 †

MELBOURNE PUBLIC LIBRARY, MUSEUMS, AND NATIONAL GALLERY. [See Victoria.]

MELBOURNE UNIVERSITY. Calendar, 1858–77, 1881-82, 1891-96. 25 vols. 12mo. Melb., 1858-91. ME 5 S
Calendar of Ormond College, 1886. 12mo. Melb., 1886. ME 5 T
Examination Papers, 1876. 12mo. Melb., 1876. ME 5 T
Proceedings on laying the Foundation Stone of the Wilson Hall by the Hon. Sir Samuel Wilson, October, 1879. Roy. 8vo. Melb., 1879. MB 2 S 31

MELLIAR, Rev. A. Foster-. Book of the Rose. Illustrated. 8vo. Lond., 1894. A 32 R 12

MELSHEIMER, Dr. Fredrich Ernst. Catalogue of the described Coleoptera of the United States. Roy. 8vo. Washington, 1853. A 27 U 10

MELVILLE, Dr. A. G. The Dodo and its kindred. [*See* Strickland, H. E.] A 15 R 9 †

MELVILLE, Herman. Typee ; or a Narrative of a Four Months' Residence among the Natives of a valley of the Marquesas Islands. 8vo. Lond., 1861.
MD 4 R 46

Omoo ; a Narrative of Adventures in the South Seas : a Sequel to " Typee." 8vo. Lond., 1861.
MD 4 R 47

MENDELEEFF, Dmitri Ivanovitsh. The Principles of Chemistry. 2 vols. roy. 8vo. Lond., 1891.
A 21 T 14, 15

Sketch of. [*See* Thorpe, Dr. T. E.—Historical Chemistry.]
C 17 R 2

MENDELSSOHN-BARTHOLDY, Felix. An Improvisation by. [*See* Kingston, W. Beatty.—Men, Cities, and Events.] C 22 R 4

Plaster Cast of. [*See* Hutton, L.—Portraits in Plaster.]
A 23 V 13

Selected Letters of. Edited by W. F. Alexander. 12mo. Lond., 1894.
C 19 P 6

MÉNEVAL, Baron Claude François de. Memoirs to serve for the History of Napoleon I, 1802-15. Translated by R. H. Sherard. 3 vols. 8vo. Lond., 1894.
C 17 R 7-9

MENNELL, Philip. Dictionary of Australasian Biography, 1855-92. 8vo. Lond., 1892. MC 1 Q 27

The Coming Colony : Practical Notes on Western Australia. 8vo. Lond., 1892. MD 5 Q 40

MENSCHUTKIN, Prof. N. Analytical Chemistry; translated from the German by J. Lock. 8vo. Lond., 1895. A 21 U 5

MENZEL, A. Illustrations des Œuvres de Frédéric-le-Grand. 4 vols. 4to. Berlin, 1882. B 38 Q 8-11 ‡

MENZIES, Rev. Dr. Allan. History of Religion. 8vo. Lond., 1895. G 3 P 24

MERCANTILE NAVY LIST AND MARITIME DIRECTORY for 1893. 8vo. Lond., 1893. E

MERCATOR'S TELEGRAPHIC POCKET CODE 12mo. Lond., 1886. K 7 P 8

MERCER, Rev. Dr. P. Once a Month. [*See* Once a Month.] ME 7 Q

MERCHANT, C. E. Manual of Mining on Geological Principles. 8vo. Melb. 1867. MA 3 T 12

MERCIER, Dr. Chas. Lunatic Asylums, their Organization and Management. Roy. 8vo. Lond., 1894.
A 19 V 3

MERCIER, Louis Sébastien. L'An deux mille quatre cent quarante. 12mo. Lond., 1772. F 12 P 32

MEREDITH, George. Ballads and Poems of Tragic Life. 12mo. Lond., 1894. H 9 Q

Poems and Lyrics of the Joy of Earth. 12mo. Lond., 1891. H 9 Q 3

Poems : The Empty Purse. 12mo Lond., 1892.
H 9 Q 13

Meredith in his Poems. [*See* Dowden, Dr. E.] J 5 S 13

MEREDITH, Mrs. Louisa A. Grandmamma's Versebook for Young Australia. 12mo. Hobart, 1878.
MH 1 Q 24

Waratah Rhymes for Young Australia. 4to. Lond., 1891. MH 1 T 11

MÉREJKOWSKY, C. de. Développement de la Méduse Obelia. 8vo. Paris, 1883. A 30 U 27

Zoonérythrine et autres pigments animaux. 8vo. Paris, 1883. A 30 U 27

MÉRIMÉE, Prosper. Sketch of. [*See* Pater, N.—Miscellaneous Studies.] J 7 S 10

MERIVALE, Herman. Historical Studies. 8vo. Lond., 1865. B 25 T 14

———— and MARZIALS, Frank T. Life of W. M. Thackeray. 8vo. Lond., 1891. C 14 P 31

MERIWETHER, Lee. Afloat and Ashore on the Mediterranean. 8vo. Lond., 1892. D 18 Q 8

MERRALL, Edwin. An unknown portion of Victoria. (Roy. Geog. Soc. Australasia, Vic. Branch, 5.) 8vo. Melb., 1888. ME 20

MERRIAM, Dr. Clinton H. Monographic revision of the Pocket Gophers. 8vo. Wash., 1895. A 30 U 30

MERRIAM, George S. Noah Porter : a Memorial by Friends. 8vo. Lond., 1893. C 14 S 17

MERRIAM, Dr. Lucius Salisbury Higher Education in Tennessee. 8vo. Wash., 1893. G 18 R 38

MERRILL, Chas. A. Supplement to the Public Statutes of the Commonwealth of Massachusetts, 1882-88. Roy. 8vo. Boston, 1890. F 3 7

MERRIMAN, Prof. Mansfield. Text-book of Retaining-walls and Masonry Dams. Roy. 8vo. New York, 1892. A 22 S 21

MERRUAU, Paul. Les Convicts en Australie, 1851-52. 8vo. Paris, 1853. MD 1 P 46

MERLY, George Row. *Trans.*—Liturgies. [*See* Liturgies.] G 14 U 24

MERRY ENGLAND. Vols. 19-23. 8vo. Lond., 1892-94. E

MERZ, Dr. H. Bilder-Atlas zur Weltgeschichte. [*See* Weisser, Prof. L.] B 6 S 6 ‡

MERZ, John Theodore. Leibniz, Philosopher. [*See* Leibnitz, G. W.] G 9 V 7

MESSER, Dr. A. B. An Enquiry into the reputed poisonous nature of the arrows of the South Sea Islanders. Roy. 8vo. (n.p.) 1876. MA 3 R 36

MESTON, Archibald. Geographic History of Queensland. 8vo. Brisbane, 1895. MB 2 Q 55
On the Australian Cassowary. (Proc. Roy. Soc., Queensland, 10.) 8vo. Brisbane, 1893. ME 1 T
Queensland Railway and Tourists' Guide. 8vo. Brisb., 1892. MD 5 R 40

METCALFE, G. Australian Zoölogy. 12mo. Sydney, 1895. MA 3 U 21

METHODIUS. Writings of, and several Fragments. (Ante-Nicene Christ. Lib., 14.) 8vo. Edinb., 1869. G 14 U 14

METROPOLITAN STREET TRAMWAYS. Explanatory Statement of the advantages of Street Tramways as applied to the traffic of the Metropolis. 8vo. Lond., 1869. A 22 R 21

MEURISSE, Mdlle. The difficulties of the "Couacrit de 1813" removed. 12mo. Melb., 1875. MJ 3 P 33

MEWS, John. Digest of all the Reported Decisions of the Superior Courts, 1884-88, inclusive. Roy. 8vo. Lond., 1889. F 12 V 10
Digest of Reported Decisions. [*See* Fisher, R. A.] F 12 V 3-9
———, and TODD, A. H. Annual Digest of all the Reported Decisions of the Superior Courts, 1889-92. Roy. 8vo. Lond., 1890-93. F 12 V 11

MEXICO. Ley Minera y ley de Impuesto á la Minería con sus respectivos reglamentos. 8vo. Mexico, 1893. F 3 R 21
Through the Land of the Aztecs; or Life and Travel in Mexico; by "A Gringo." 8vo. Lond., 1892. D 4 P 51

MEYER, A. B. Uber die Färbung der Nestjungen von Eclectus. 8vo. Leipzig, 1882. A 30 U 27

MEYER, Prof. Franz Sales. Handbook of Ornament. 8vo. Lond., 1893. A 23 T 15

MEYER, Dr. Kuno. Aislinge Meic Conglinne: The Vision of MacConglinne: a Middle-Irish Wonder Tale. (Irish and English.) 8vo. Lond., 1892. B 29 R 13
The Voyage of Bran, son of Febal, to the Land of the Living; an old Irish Saga now first edited, with Translations, Notes, and Glossary, by Kuno Meyer; with an Essay upon the Irish Vision of the happy otherworld and the Celtic doctrine of re-birth, by Alfred Nutt. 8vo. Lond., 1895. B 36 P 9

MEYERBEER, J. Sketch of. [*See* Heine, H.—Heine in Art and Letters.] J 11 T 39

MEYNELL, Alice. The Rhythm of Life, and other Essays. 12mo. Lond., 1893. J 4 P 26
Poems. 12mo. Lond., 1893. H 3 P 38

MEYRICK, E. List of South Australian Micro-Lepidoptera. (Trans. Roy. Soc., S. Australia, 7.) 8vo. Adelaide, 1885. ME 1 S
Hand-book of British Lepidoptera. 8vo. Lond., 1895. A 27 S 20

MIALL, Prof. Louis C. The Natural History of Insects. 8vo. Lond., 1895. A 28 P 32

MICHAEL, W. H. Official Congressional Directory for the use of the United States Congress. 8vo. Wash., 1891. E

MICHAEL ANGELO BUONARROTI. Life of; by J. A. Symonds. 2 vols. 8vo. Lond., 1893. C 16 T 19, 20
Life of. [*See* Emerson, R. W.—Natural History of Intellect.] J 9 S 20
Sketch of. [*See* Oliphant, Mrs. M. O. W.—Makers of Florence.] B 30 Q 20

MICHAEL APOSTOLIUS. Lettres inédites de Michel Apostolis; par H. Noiret. 8vo. Paris, 1889. J 7 U 36

MICHIGAN—*General*—
Early History of Michigan; with Biographies of State Officers, Members of Congress, Judges and Legislators. 8vo. Lansing, 1888. C 21 R 9
Michigan and its Resources. 8vo. Lansing, 1893. D 15 T 14

MICHIGAN—*State Departments, Reports, and Publications*—
AGRICULTURAL COLLEGE—EXPERIMENT STATION. Horticultural Department. Bulletin III. 8vo. Lansing, 1894. A 30 R 26
 3. The Cultivated Raspberries of the United States; by A. A. Crozier.
Horticultural Department Bulletins, 103-106. Fruit Growing. 8vo. Lansing, 1894. A 32 R 1
AUDITOR-GENERAL. Report, 1894. 8vo. Lansing, 1895. E
Tax Law of the State, 1893. 8vo. Lansing, 1893. F 1 T 14
BOARD OF AGRICULTURE. Reports of the Secretary, 1872, 1879, 1881-94. 15 vols. 8vo. Lansing, 1873-94. E
BOARD OF FISH COMMISSIONERS. Report, 1892-94. 8vo. Lansing, 1895. E
BOARD OF HEALTH. Reports, 1881-91. 11 vols. roy. 8vo. Lansing, 1882-94. E
BUREAU OF LABOR AND INDUSTRIAL STATISTICS. Reports, 1889 and 1891. 2 vols. 8vo. Lansing, 1890-92. E
COMMISSIONER OF THE BANKING DEPARTMENT. Reports, 1889, 1891, 1892. 3 vols. roy. 8vo. Lansing, 1890-93. E

MICHIGAN—*contd.*
COMMISSIONER OF INSURANCE. Report, 1894. 2 vols. 8vo. Lansing, 1895. E

COMMISSIONER OF MINERAL STATISTICS. Michigan Mines and Mineral Statistics. Report for 1893; by J. B. Knight. 8vo. Lansing, 1895. E

DAIRY AND FOOD COMMISSIONER. Report, 1894. 8vo. Lansing, 1894. E

HORTICULTURAL SOCIETY. Reports, 1886-88, 1890-91, 1893. 6 vols. roy. 8vo. Lansing, 1887-94. E

LEGISLATURE. Acts of the Legislature, 1857, 1859, 1861, 1862, 1865, 1867, 1866-74, 1877, 1879, 1881-83, 1885, 1887, 1889, 1891, 1893. 36 vols. 8vo. Detroit and Lansing, 1857-93. E

LIBRARY. Report, 1892-94. 8vo. Lansing, 1894. E

NORMAL SCHOOL; its plan and purpose, and an outline of its work. 8vo. Grand Rapids (n.d.) G 18 P 21

POMOLOGICAL SOCIETY. Reports, 1878 and 1880. 2 vols. roy. 8vo. Lansing, 1879-81. E

SALT INSPECTOR. Report, 1894. 8vo. Lansing, 1895. E

SECRETARY OF STATE. Annual Report relating to Farms and Farm Products, 1892-94. 2 vols. 8vo. Lansing, 1894. E

Census of the State of Michigan, 1884. 2 vols. roy. 8vo. Lansing, 1886. E

Official Directory and Legislative Manual of the State of Michigan, 1895-96. 8vo. Lansing, 1895. E

Reports relating to Births, Marriages, and Deaths, 1881-91, 1893. 12 vols. roy. 8vo. Lansing, 1884-95. E

MICHIGAN DAIRYMEN'S ASSOCIATION. Annual Reports, 1892-93. 8vo. Lansing, 1893. E

MICHIGAN PIONEER AND HISTORICAL SOCIETY. Collections and Researches made by. Vols. 1-20, 23. Roy. 8vo. Lansing, 1877-95. E

MICHIGAN UNIVERSITY. Calendar for 1892-93. 12mo. Ann Arbor, Mich., 1893. E

MIDDLETON, Prof. John Henry. The Remains of Ancient Rome. 2 vols. 8vo. Lond., 1892. B 20 T 28, 29

MIDDLETON, T. B. Irish Clubs. [*See* Sullivan, Sir E. —Yachting.] A 29 Q 41

MIDGLEY, Alfred. Helen Young, and other Poems. 12mo. Toowoomba, Q., 1873. MH 1 U 76

MIERS, Edward J. Brachyura. [*See* Thomson, Sir C. W., and Murray, Dr. J.—Voyage of H.M.S. *Challenger.*] A 6 †

MIERS, H. A., and CROSSKEY, F. The Soil in Relation to Health. 8vo. Lond., 1893. A 13 P 4

MIKKELSEN, Dr. Michael A. Bishop Hill Colony: a Religious Communistic Settlement in Henry County, Illinois. (Johns Hopkins University Studies, 10.) 8vo. Baltimore, 1892. B 18 S 10

MILAN, Bona Sforza, Duchess of. Miniatures and Borders from the Book of Hours of. 4to. Lond., 1894. A 22 V 14

MILBOURN, S. The New Kreuz Polka Winifred. Words by R. Bruce. Fol. Adelaide (n.d.) MA 7 Q 31 †

MILES, Alfred H. The Aldine Speaker: an Encyclopædia of Poetic and Dramatic Literature. 4to. Lond. (n.d.) J G U 1

New Standard Elocutionist, comprising Anatomy of the Vocal Organs by L. Browne, and a Chapter on the Art of Elocution by C. Harrison. 8vo. Lond., 1895. J 8 T 33

Poets and Poetry of the Century. 12mo. Lond. (n.d.) H 10 T 19

MILES, L. Roger-. [*See* Roger-Miles, L.]

MILES, Dr. Manly. Silos, Ensilage, and Silage: a Practical Treatise on the Ensilage of Fodder Corn. 12mo. New York, 1892. A 18 Q 40

Stock-breeding: a Treatise on the Application of the Laws of Development and Heredity to the Improvement and Breeding of Domestic Animals. 8vo. New York, 1893. A 18 T 17

MILES, W. J. Modern Practical Farriery; a Complete Guide to all that relates to the Horse. 8vo. Lond. (n.d.) A 5 P 15 †

MILL, Dr. Hugh Robt. The Realm of Nature: an Outline of Physiography. Illustrated. 12mo. Lond., 1891. A 24 Q 27

MILL, John Stuart. Considerations on Representative Government. 8vo. Lond., 1861. F 8 R 1

Utilitarianism. 12th ed. 8vo. Lond., 1895. F 11 U 11

A Study of his Philosophy; by Dr. C. Douglas. 12mo. Edinb., 1895. G 9 V 25

Life of; by W. L. Courtney. 12mo. Lond., 1889. C 17 P 19

Comte, Mill, and Spencer. [*See* Watson, Dr. J.] G 2 U 14

MILLAR, J. Educational System of the Province of Ontario, Canada. 8vo. Toronto, 1893. G 18 S 3

MILLAR, Wm. J. Modern Steam Practice. [*See* Winton, J. G.] A 22 T 14

MILLARD, Edward C. The Same Lord: an Account of the Mission Tour of the Rev. George C. Grubb in Australia, Tasmania, and New Zealand. 8vo. Lond., 1893. MG 1 S 20

MILLARD, G. W. Appendix to Williams' Law of Real Property for the use of New South Wales. 8vo. Sydney, 1894. MF 3 T 28

MILLENNIUS. [*See* Zahel, C. P.]

MILLER, Dr. Alexander F. Micro-organisms and Fermentation. [*See* Jörgensen, A.] A 28 U 9

MILLER, Rev. E. K. Reminiscences of forty-seven years' Clerical Life in South Australia. 12mo. Adelaide, 1895. MG 2 R 36

MILLER, Ellen, and WHITING, Margaret Christine. Wild Flowers of the North-eastern States. 4to. New York, 1895. A 15 S 1 †

MILLER, George. The Prison System of New South Wales. Roy. 8vo. Sydney, 1893. MF 1 S 48

MILLER, Rev. James. Mahomet, the Imposter: a Tragedy. [See London Stage, 4.] H 2 S 36

MILLER, Rev. Joseph A. Memoir of the Rev. Thomas S. M'Kean, Missionary at Tahiti. 12mo. Lond., 1847. MC 1 P 47

MILLER, Mrs. Mary H. Catalogue of the State Library of Iowa. [See Iowa.] K 7 T 6

MILLER, Thomas. History of the Anglo-Saxons from the earliest period to the Norman Conquest. 8vo. Lond., 1848. B 23 R 21
Picturesque Sketches of London Past and Present. 8vo. Lond. (n.d.) D 19 Q 30

MILLET, Francis Davis. Some Artists at the Fair. [See Chicago Exhibition, 1893.] A 23 U 21

MILLIGAN, Rev. Dr. William. Revelation. [See Expositor's Bible.] G 19 S 21

MILLS, Dr. Edmund J. Fuel. [See Groves, C. E.] A 21 V 6

MILLS, H. E. Australasian Federal Pastoral Directory, 1893. 4to. Sydney, 1893.* ME

MILLS, John. On the right state of the Heart. 8vo. Parramatta, 1887. MG 2 R 31

MILN, Louise J. When we were Strolling Players in the East. Illustrated. 8vo. Lond., 1895. D 17 V 18

MILNE, Prof. John. Effects of Earthquakes on Waterworks. [See Burton, W. K.—Water Supply.] A 22 T 19
The Miner's Handbook: Mineral Deposits, Mining Operations, Ore Dressing, &c. 16mo. Lond., 1893. A 24 P 11
———— and BURTON, Prof. W. K. The Great Earthquake in Japan, 1891. 2nd edition. Obl. imp. 8vo. Yokohama, 1892. A 37 P 10‡

MILNER, Alfred. England in Egypt. 8vo. Lond., 1892. F 8 P 23

MILNER, George. Glossary of the Lancashire Dialect. [See Nodal, J. H.] J 2 T 19

MILNER, Rev. Thomas. Astronomy and Scripture; or, some illustrations of that science, and of the solar, lunar, stellar, and terrestrial phenomena of Holy Writ. 12mo. Lond., 1843. G 9 V 27

MILNES, Alfred. When Doctors disagree: a Vision of Vaccine. 12mo. Lond., 1886. A 26 R 19

MILTON, John. English Prose Writings of. Edited by Prof. Henry Morley. 8vo. Lond., 1889. J 8 T 30
The Poetical Works of. 12mo. Lond., 1853. H 7 U 31
Prose Works of. 5 vols. 12mo. Lond., 1889-94. J 6 P 37-41
1. Defence of the People of England. Second Defence of the People of England. Eikonoklastes.
2. Tenure of Kings and Magistrates. Areopagitica. Tracts on the Commonwealth. Observations on Ormond's Peace. Letters of State. Brief Notes on Dr. Griffith's Sermon. Of Reformation in England. Of Prelatical Episcopacy. The Reason of Church Government urged against Prelacy. Of True Religion, Heresy, Schism, Toleration. Of Civil Power in Ecclesiastical Causes.
3. The Likeliest Means to remove Hirelings out of the Church. Animadversions upon the Remonstrants' Defence against Smectymnuus. Apology for Smectymnuus. The Doctrine and Discipline of Divorce. The Judgment of Martin Bucer concerning Divorce. Tetrachordon. Colasterion. Tractate on Education. Declaration for the election of John III., King of Poland. Familiar Letters.
4. Treatise on Christian Doctrine.
5. Treatise on Christian Doctrine. History of Britain. History of Moscovia. Accedence Commenced Grammar [Latin.] Index to the five volumes.

L'Allegro. Illustrated. 12mo. Lond., 1859. H 9 U 14
The Fall of Satan: Selections from Milton's Paradise Lost, Books V. and VI. Edited, with notes, by A. B. Piddington. 12mo. Sydney, 1893.* MH 1 P 62
Lycidas, analysed, with notes, by W. Powning. 4th edition. 12mo. Melb., 1873. MH 1 Q 22
Paradise Lost: Selections from Books V. and VI., with notes by G. Thornton. 12mo. Sydney, 1893. MH 1 P 37
Comus. [See Harlin, T.] MJ 2 T 28
Comus: a Masque (altered from Milton). [See London Stage, 2.] H 2 S 34
Concordance to Works of. [See Bradshaw, Dr. J.] K 17 R 30
Essay on. [See Bagehot, W.—Literary Studies.] J 9 P 22-24
A French Critic on. [See Arnold, M.—Mixed Essays.] J 11 T 25
Life of; by Prof. D. Masson. Index vol. 8vo. Lond., 1894. C 8 R 38*
[Life of]; by Prof. D. Masson. [See Masson, Prof. D.— In the Footsteps of the Poets.] J 6 R 43
[Life of.] [See Emerson, R. W.—Natural History of Intellect.] J 9 S 20
Milton as an Educator. [See Brooks, Rt. Rev. P.] J 6 S 38
Milton's Poetry. [See Seeley, Sir J. R.—Lectures and Essays.] J 9 S 24

MILTON, Mrs. Mary. The Maiden and Married Life of Mary Powell, afterwards Mistress Milton. 3rd ed. 8vo. Lond. (n.d.) C 21 Q 5

MILWAUKEE. Rules and Regulations for Normal School for Teachers of Gymnastics. 8vo. Milwaukee (n.d.) G 18 R 35

MIND: a quarterly review of Psychology and Philosophy. New Series, vols. 1–3. 8vo Lond., 1892–94. E

MINGAYE, John C. H. Notes and Analysis of a Metallic Meteorite from Moonbi, New South Wales. (Journal Roy. Soc., N.S.W., 27.) 8vo. Sydney, 1893. ME 1 R

MINING AND METALLURGY, INSTITUTION OF. [*See* Institution of Mining and Metallurgy.]

MINING ENGINEERS, American Institute of. [*See* American Institute of Mining Engineers.]

MINING MANUAL for 1893 and 1894. 2 vols. 8vo. Lond., 1892–93. E

MINNEAPOLIS. Trade and Commerce, 1892. 8vo. Minneapolis, 1892. E

MINNESOTA. GEOLOGICAL AND NATURAL HISTORY SURVEY. Reports, 1884–85, 1891. 3 vols. 8vo. St. Paul and Minneapolis, 1885–93. E

MINNESOTA HISTORICAL SOCIETY. Collections of. Vols. 1–7. 8vo. St. Paul, 1872–93. E

Report of, 1895. 8vo. St. Paul, 1895. E

MINNESOTA UNIVERSITY. Agricultural Experiment Station, 1893, Annual Report. 8vo. Minneapolis, 1894. E

Catalogue for the year 1892, 1893, and Announcement for 1893, 1894. 8vo. Minneapolis, 1893. E

School of Mining and Metallurgy. Obl. 18mo. Minneapolis, 1893. G 18 P 24

MINTO, John. Special Report on the Sheep Industry of the United States. [*See* Salmon, Dr. D. E.] A 30 U 7

MINTO, Prof. William. Logic, inductive and deductive 8vo. Lond., 1893. G 7 U 20

Autobiographical Notes of William Bell Scott. [*See* Scott, W. B.] C 14 U 22, 23

MINUCIUS FELIX. [*See* Felix, M. M.]

MIRABEAU, Honoré Gabriel Riquetti, Comte de. Secret History of the Court of Berlin; or the Character of the King of Prussia, his Ministers, Mistresses, Generals, and the Royal Family of Prussia. 2 vols. 8vo. Lond., 1895. B 25 T 19, 20

[Plaster Cast of.] [*See* Hutton, L.—Portraits in Plaster.] A 23 V 13

MIRROR, The. Vol. 1, 1888–89. Sm. fol. Sydney, 1888–89. ME 16 T

MISCELLANEA GENEALOGICA ET HERALDICA. Edited by Dr. J. J. Howard. Illustrated. Vols. 4, 5. 2nd series. Roy. 8vo. Lond., 1892–94. E

MISKIN, W. H. Further Notes on Australian *Sphingidæ*. (Proc. Roy. Soc., Queensland, 8.) 8vo. Brisbane, 1892. ME 1 T

New Species of Australian *Hesmeridæ*. (Proc. Roy. Soc., Queensland, 6.) 8vo. Brisbane, 1889. ME 1 T

New species of Australian *Micro-Lepidoptera*. (Proc. Roy. Soc., Queensland, 8.) 8vo. Brisbane, 1892. ME 1 T

Notes on some undescribed Australian *Lepidoptera*, (Proc. Roy. Soc., Queensland 6.) 8vo. Brisbane, 1889. ME 1 T

Revision of the Australian species of *Terias*, with description of some new species. (Proc. Roy. Soc., Queensland, 6.) 8vo. Brisbane, 1889. ME 1 T

Revision of the Australian *Sphingidæ*. (Proc. Roy. Soc., Queensland, 8.) 8vo. Brisbane, 1891. ME 1 T

The Upper South Johnstone River. (Roy. Geographical Soc. of Australasia, Queensland Branch, 1.) 8vo. Brisbane, 1886. ME 20

MISSING FRIENDS; being the Adventures of a Danish Emigrant in Queensland, 1871–80. 8vo. Lond., 1892. MD 5 R 41

MISSION to the Working-men of Paris. Report, 1879. 8vo. Sunderland, 1880. G 2 P 40

MISSOURI. Missouri at the World's Fair. Imp. 8vo. St. Louis, 1893. D 19 V 20

Public Schools Report for year ending June, 1892. Roy. 8vo. Jefferson City, 1893. E

School Laws of, 1891–93. Roy 8vo. Jefferson City, 1893. F 2 T 19

MISSOURI UNIVERSITY. Catalogue, 1892–93. 8vo. Jefferson City, 1893. E

MITCHELL, Dr. Hubbard Winslow. The Evolution of Life; or, Causes of change in Animal Forms: a Study in Biology. Illustrated. 8vo New York, 1891. A 27 Q 44

MITCHELL, J. A. Some Artists at the Fair. [*See* Chicago Exhibition 1893.] A 23 U 21

MITCHELL, O. M. The Orbs of Heaven; or, the Planetary and Stellar Worlds. 8vo. Lond., 1851. A 19 R 23

MITCHELL, Lieut.-Col. Sir Thomas L. The Australian Geography, with the Shores of the Pacific and those of the Indian Ocean. 12mo. Sydney, 1851. MD 1 I 25

MITCHELL, W. Forbes-. Reminiscences of the Great Mutiny, 1857–59, including the Relief, Siege, and Capture of Lucknow, and the Campaigns in Rohilcand and Oude. 8vo. Lond., 1893. B 20 R 1

MITFORD, E. R. Pasquin: the Pastoral Advocate. [*See* Pasquin.] ME

MITRE, Gen. B. The Emancipation of South America; being a condensed translation, by Wm. Pilling, of "The History of San Martin," by General Don B. Mitre. 8vo. Lond., 1893. B 17 E 30

MITSUKURI, Prof. K. On the Fœtal Membranes of Chelonia. 8vo. (n.p.n.d.)   A 30 V 16

MITTEN, William. Australian Mosses. (Rev. Soc., Victoria, 19.) 8vo. Melb., 1883.   ME 1 P

MIVART, St. George. Types of Animal Life. 8vo. Lond., 1893.   A 28 Q 31

MIYOSHI, M. Notes on the irritability of the Stigma. 8vo. (n.p.n.d.)   A 30 V 17

MODERA, J. Verhaal van eene Reize naar en langs de Zuid-Westkust van Nieuw-Guinea, 1828. 8vo. Haarlem, 1830.   MD 7 S 12

MOELLER, Dr. Wilhelm. History of the Christian Church, A.D. 1–600. 8vo. Lond., 1892.   G 6 Q 35

History of the Christian Church in the Middle Ages. 8vo. Lond., 1893.   G 13 P 33

MOFFETT, S. E. Suggestions on Government. 8vo. Chicago, 1894.   F 8 U 40

MOFFETT, S. L. Population of the Towns and Municipalities of the seven Colonies of Australasia, 1894. Sm. 4to. Sydney, 1894.   ME

MOFFITT, Dr. A. Papers on Typhoid. 8vo. Sydney, 1883.   MA 1 U 54

MOGUL TALE, The; or, the Descent of the Balloon: a Farce. [*See* London Stage, 4.]   H 2 S 36

MOHL, Prof. Julius. [Sketch of.] [*See* Müller, F. Max.—Chips from a German Workshop.]   J 9 R 32

MOHR, Edward. The Region South of the Zambesi. [*See* Great Explorers.]   D 15 V 21, 22

MOHR, Dr. Frodr. Der Weinbau und die Weinbereitungskunde. 8vo. Braunschweig, 1865.   A 18 S 14

MOIR, Dr. George. Magic and Witchcraft. 12mo. Lond., 1852.   G 18 P 25

MOLESCHOTT, Jac. Untersuchungen zur Naturlehre des Menschen und der Thiere. Band 12. Drittes und viertes heft. 8vo. Giessen, 1880.   A 30 V 10

MOLESWORTH, Rev. Dr. J. E. N. Letter to the Lord Bishop of Chester upon certain symptoms of sectarian designs in the Pastoral Aid Society; and upon the Catholic, Comprehensive, and Church Regulations of the Society for promoting the employment of additional curates in populous places. 12mo. Lond., 1840.

Letter in reference to Rev. Dr. Molesworth's Animadversions. [*See* Harding, Rev. J.]   G 4 V 14

MOLINARI, G. de. Religion. (Philosophy at Home Series.) Translated from the second (enlarged) edition by W. K. Firminger. 12mo. Lond., 1894.   G 16 Q 40

MOLINIER, Emile. Le Trésor de la Basilique de Saint Marc à Venise. Roy. 8vo. Venise, 1888.   A 19 V 18

MOLL, G. Verhandeling over eenige vroegere zontogton der Nederlanders. 8vo. Amsterdam, 1825.   MD 8 R 39

MOLLOY, Dr. C. H. Accidents and Emergencies: what to do till the Doctor comes; with Hints on Nursing. Illustrated. 12mo. Melb. (n.d.)   MA 3 P 63

MOLLOY, Rev. Dr. Gerald. Gleanings in Science: a Series of Popular Lectures on Scientific Subjects. 8vo. New York, 1894.   A 21 R 19

MOLONEY, Dr. Joseph A. With Captain Stairs to Katanga. 8vo. Lond., 1893.   D 14 P 8

MOLTKE, Field-Marshall Hellmuth, Count von. A Biographical and Critical Study; by W. O'C. Morris. 8vo. Lond., 1893.   C 13 S 10

Essays, Speeches, and Memoirs of. 2 vols. 8vo. Lond., 1893.   J 10 S 26, 27

Tactical Problems, from 1858–82; translated by Lieut. K. von Donat: with Plans and Maps. Roy. 8vo. Lond., 1894.   A 29 V 22

MOMERIE, Rev. Dr. Alfred Williams. Agnosticism: Sermons preached 1883–84. 4th ed. 12mo. Edinb., 1891.   G 19 P 25

The Basis of Religion. 3rd ed. 8vo. Edinb., 1890.   G 19 P 36

Inspiration, and other Sermons. 2nd ed. 8vo. Edinb., 1890.   G 19 P 35

Origin of Evil, and other Sermons. 7th ed. 12mo. Edinb., 1891.   G 19 P 27

The Religion of the Future and other Essays. 12mo. Edinb., 1893.   G 19 P 28

MONA MARIE. [*See* Casket of Gems, The.]   MH 1 Q 27

MONCHOISY. [*See* Mativet, M.]

MONCRIEFF, W. T. The Bashful Man: a Comic Drama. [*See* London Stage, 4.]   H 2 S 36

Giovanni in London; or, the Libertine Reclaimed. [*See* London Stage, 3.]   H 2 S 35

Monsieur Tonson: a Farce. [*See* London Stage, 3.]   H 2 S 35

MONDE DRAMATIQUE, Le. Revue des Spectacles Anciens et Modernes. Roy. 8vo. Paris, 1835.   H 5 V 34

MONEY, C. L. Knocking about in New Zealand. 12mo. Melb., 1871.   MD 8 P 20

MONEY: how the Banks make it scarce and dear; the Remedy, the Banks and their stability; by "Sigma." 8vo. Melb., 1871.   MF 2 Q 45

MONFAT, Père A. Dix années en Mélanésie: étude historique et religieuse. 8vo. Lyon, 1891.
MG 2 Q 13

Mgr. L. Elloy, le Missionnaire des Samoa. 3ᵉ éd. 8vo. Lyon (n.d.)
MC 1 T 10

Les Samoa ou Archipel des Navigateurs; étude historique et religieuse. 8vo. Lyon, 1890. MD 8 R 15

Les Tonga ou Archipel des amis et le Père Joseph Chevron. 2ᵉ éd. [Illustrated.] 8vo. Lyon, 1893.
MD 7 S 30

MONRO, David Binning. Modes of Ancient Greek Music. 8vo. Oxford, 1894. A 23 U 20

MONROE, James. Sketch of. [*See* Wilson, J. G.—Presidents of the United States.] C 2 V 30

Sketch of. [*See* Thompson, R. W.—Recollections of Sixteen Presidents.] C 18 T 21, 22

MONTAGU, Basil. Works of Francis Bacon, with Life. [*See* Bacon, Francis.] J 9 V 26-28

MONTAGU, Mary Wortley, Lady. Letters from the Levant during the Embassy to Constantinople, 1716-18. 12mo. Lond., 1838. D 19 P 9

Essay on. [*See* Bagehot, W.—Literary Studies.]
J 9 P 22-24

MONTAGUE, Francis Chas. Arnold Toynbee; with an Account of the Work of Toynbee Hall in East London, by P. L. Gell; also an Account of the Neighbourhood Guild in New York, by C. B. Stover. (Johns Hopkins University Studies, 7.) 8vo. Baltimore, 1889.
B 18 S 7

The Old Poor-law and the New Socialism; or, Pauperism and Taxation. 12mo. Lond., 1886. F 7 V 45

MONTAGUE, Major-Gen. Wm. Edward. Military Topography. 8vo. Edinb., 1883. A 29 Q 29

MONTAIGNE, Michel Eyquem de; or, the Sceptic. [*See* Emerson, R.W.—Representative Men.] C 17 P 10

The Essays of. Translated by C. Cotton, and edited by W. C. Hazlitt. 3 vols. 12mo. Lond., 1892.
J 8 P 44-46

MONTALEMBERT, Charles Forbes, Comte de. Chronicle of the Life of St. Elizabeth of Hungary, Duchess of Thuringia. Translated by Ambrose Lislo Philipps. 4to. Lond., 1839. C 2 W 24

MONTANA.—*General*. History, Resources, Possibilities. 12mo. Butte, Mont., 1893. D 15 P 11

MONTANA.—*State Departments and Publications*.

ADJUTANT-GENERAL. Report, 1891-92. 8vo. Helena, 1892. E

ATTORNEY-GENERAL. Reports, 1890-92. 8vo. Helena, 1892. E

AUDITOR. Reports, 1892-93. 2 vols. 8vo. Helena, 1892-94. E

BOARD OF EQUALISATION. Reports, 1891-92. 8vo. Helena, 1892. E

MONTANA—*contd*.

BOARD OF LAND COMMISSIONERS. Report, 1892. 8vo. Helena, 1892. E

BOARD OF MEDICAL EXAMINERS. Report, 1892. 8vo. Helena, 1892. E

BOARD OF PARDONS. Reports, 1891-92. 8vo. Helena, 1892. E

BOARD OF STATE PRISON COMMISSIONERS. Report, 1891-92. 8vo. Helena, 1892. E

BOARD OF STOCK COMMISSIONERS and the Recorder of Marks and Brands. Reports, 1892. 8vo. Helena, 1893. E

BOILER INSPECTOR. Report, 1891-92. 8vo. Helena, 1892. E

BUREAU OF AGRICULTURE, LABOR AND INDUSTRY. Information relating to the State of Montana. 12mo. Helena, 1893. D 15 P 11

LAND AGENT. Reports, 1891-92. 8vo. Helena, 1892. E

SECRETARY OF STATE. Report, 1891-92. 8vo. Helena, 1892. E

SUPERINTENDENT OF PUBLIC INSTRUCTION. Report, 1892. 8vo. Helena, 1893. E

TREASURER. Report, 1892-93. 2 vols. 8vo. Helena, 1892-94. E

MONTBARD, Georges. Among the Moors: Sketches of Oriental Life. Roy. 8vo. Lond., 1894. D 14 V 13

The Land of the Sphinx. Illustrated. Roy. 8vo. Lond., 1894. D 14 V 15

MONTEAGUDO, Don J. de Mendoza. Las Guerras de Chile: Poema Historico. 8vo. Santiago, 1888.
H 9 U 20

MONTEFIORE, Arthur. *Editor*.—The Great Frozen Land. [*See* Jackson, F. G.] D 18 V 19

MONTEFIORE, C. G. Lectures on the Origin and Growth of Religion, as illustrated by the Religion of the Ancient Hebrews. (Hibbert Lectures, 1892.) 8vo. Lond., 1892. G 2 Q 31

MONTEFIORE, Eliezer Levi. Art Criticism. 8vo. Sydney, 1880. MA 1 U 62

MONTEFIORE, J. A. A few words upon the Finance of New South Wales. 8vo. Sydney, 1856. MF 4 R 48

MONTERO Y VIDAL, J. El Archipielago Filipino y las Islas Marianas, Carolinas y Palaos. 8vo. Madrid, 1886. D 17 R 21

MONTFORT, Simon de. [*See* Leicester, Earl of.]

MONTGOMERY, E. E. M. The Tohunga, and Incidents of Maori Life: Poetry. Sm. 4to. Wanganui, 1892.
MH 1 S 41

The Land of the Moa: a poem. Sm. 4to. Wanganui (n.d.) MH 1 S 42

The Story of Hinemoa. Sm. 4to. Wanganui (n.d.)
MH 1 S 43

2 A

MONTGOMERY, Rt. Rev. Henry Hutchinson. Aborigines of Tasmania—photos. L. 4to. (n.p.n.d.)
MA 1 R 18 ‡
Views in Melanesia—58 photos. Obl. 8vo. (n.p.n.d.)
MD 4 P 21 †
Views in Norfolk Island and Bass' Straits—60 photos. Obl. 8vo. (n.p.n.d.) MD 4 P 20 †

MONTGOMERY, James. The Pelican Islands, and other Poems. 12mo. Lond., 1827. MH 1 U 59

MONTH, The: a Catholic Magazine and Review. Vols. 76–82. 8vo. Lond., 1892-94. E

MONTOYA, Antonio R. de. Gramatica y Diccionarios de la Lengua Tupí ó Guaraní. 8vo. Viena, 1876.
K 14 P 1

MONTPELLIER UNIVERSITY. Cartulaire de l'Université de Montpellier. Tome I, 1181-1400. 4to. Montpellier, 1890. G 15 S 9 †

MONTREAL. Account of the Schools controlled by the Roman Catholic Board of School Commissioners of the City of Montreal. 8vo. Montreal, 1893.
G 18 R 32
Histoire du Montreal, 1640-72. (Publié sous la direction de la Société Littéraire et Historique de Québec.) Roy. 8vo. Montreal, 1871. B 16 V 2

MONTROSE, James, Marquis of. Memoirs of, 1639-50; by the Rt. Rev. G. Wishart. Translated by the Rev. A. D. Murdoch and H. F. M. Simpson. Sm. 4to. Lond., 1893. B 31 V 9

MONTT, Luis. Poesias. 12mo. Santiago, 1882.
H 9 P 18

MOOCHER, The. [*See* Grey, H.]

MOODIE, Duncan Campbell Francis. History of the Battles and Adventures of the British, the Boers, and the Zulus, in Southern Africa, 1495-1879; also a short sketch of South Australia. 8vo. Adelaide, 1879. MB 1 P 22

MOON, Miss A. C. Preservation of the Teeth. [*See* Australian Health Soc., Melb.] MA 3 S 33

MOONEN, L. Australian Wines. 8vo. Melb., 1883.
MA 1 U 60

MOOR, C. G. Analysis of Food and Drugs. [*See* Pearmain, T. H.] A 26 P 19

MOOR, Lieut. H., and BALLARD, Capt. V. V. New General Chart of the Moluccas and Eastern Islands. Fol. Lond., 1801. D 1 S 18 ‡

MOORE, A. W. Sodor and Man. (Diocesan Histories.) 12mo. Lond., 1893. G 18 P 5

MOORE, Mrs. Bloomfield. Keely and his Discoveries: Aerial Navigation. 8vo. Lond., 1893. A 20 T 17

MOORE, Chas. Plants with their habitats, discovered to be indigenous to this colony since the publication of the Hand-book of the Flora of New South Wales. (Journal Roy. Soc., N.S.W., 27.) 8vo. Sydney, 1893.
ME 1 R
————, and BETCHE, Ernst. Handbook of the Flora of New South Wales. 8vo. Sydney, 1893.*
MA 1 T 63

MOORE, Cunninghame Wilson. A Practical Guide for Prospectors, Explorers, and Miners. 8vo. Lond., 1893. A 24 T 14

MOORE, Edward. The Foundling: a Comedy. [*See* London Stage, 3.] H 2 S 35
The Gamester: a Tragedy. [*See* London Stage, 1.]
H 2 S 33

MOORE, George, Merchant and Philanthropist; by Dr. S. Smiles. Roy. 8vo. Lond., 1878. C 21 S 12

MOORE, Harold E. Back to the Land. 8vo. Lond., 1893. F 14 Q 34

MOORE, J. J. Australian Almanac and Country Directory, 1890-94. 5 vols. 12mo. Sydney, 1890-94.
ME 4 S

MOORE, Joseph West. The American Congress, 1774-1895. 8vo. Lond., 1895. B 17 R 36

MOORE, T. B. Western Tasmania. (Roy. Geograph. Soc. of Australasia, Q. Branch, 1.) 8vo. Brisbane, 1886. ME 20

MOORE, Thomas. The Epicurean: a Tale. 8vo. Lond., 1850. J 11 U 16
History of Ireland, from the earliest Kings of that Realm down to its last Chief. 4 vols. 12mo. Lond. (n.d.) B 20 P 14-17
Irish Melodies. New ed. 12mo. Lond., 1848.
H 10 T 6
National Airs; with words by Thos. Moore. Edited by C. W. Glover. Sm. 4to. Lond., 1860. A 29 V 11
Life of Lord Byron. Roy. 8vo. Lond., 1844. C 12 U 31
[Plaster Cast of.] [*See* Hutton, L.—Portraits in Plaster.] A 23 V 13

MOORE, Thos., F.L.S. Gardener's Assistant. [*See* Thompson, R.] A 32 T 4

MOORE, Rev. Wm. Handbook of the Fijian Language. 12mo. Hobart, 1866. MK 1 P 43

MOOREHEAD, Warren K. Primitive Man in Ohio. 8vo. New York, 1892. A 18 S 20

MOORHOUSE, Rt. Rev. James. Address of, to the Church of England Assembly, Melbourne, September, 1885. 8vo. Melb., 1885. MG 2 Q 38
The Galatian Lapse: six lectures. 8vo. Melb., 1885.
MG 1 S 34

MOORS, H. On the Sea-coll as a possible source of danger in torpedo experiments. (Roy. Soc., Vict., 18.) 8vo. Melb., 1882. ME 1 P

MORA, José Joaquin de. Apuntes Biográficos; por M. L. Amunátegui. 8vo. Santiago, 1888. C 21 T 6

MORALEDA I MONTERO, José de. Esporaciones Jeograficas e Hidrograficas. 8vo. Santiago, 1888. D 15 T 24

MORAN, Most Rev. Patrick Francis, Cardinal. The Analecta of David Rothe, Bishop of Ossory. 12mo. Dublin, 1884. G 7 U 33

The Civilization of Ireland before the Anglo-Norman Invasion. 8vo. Sydney, 1885 MB 2 R 60

History of the Catholic Church in Australasia. Sm. 4to. Sydney, 1895. MG 1 U 5

Letters on the Anglican Reformation, and other Papers. 12mo. Sydney, 1895. MG 2 R 50

The Mission Field of the 19th Century. 8vo. Sydney, 1895. MG 2 Q 45

Occasional Papers. 12mo. Dublin, 1890. MG 2 R 5

Pastoral Letter of, to the Clergy and Faithful of the Diocese on the Perpetuity of the Church. 8vo. Sydney, 1895. MG 2 Q 45

The Reunion of Christendom. 8vo. Sydney, 1895. MG 2 Q 45

Spicilegium Ossoriense: being a Collection of original Letters and Papers illustrative of the History of the Irish Church from the Reformation to 1800. 3 vols. roy. 8vo. Dublin, 1874-84. G 16 U 2-4

MORANDI, Luigi. Prose e Poesie Italiane. 8vo. Castello, 1892. J G P 9

MORE, Hannah. Sacred Dramas. New ed. 18mo. Edinb. (n.d.) H 3 U 15

MORE, Sir Thomas. The Household of; by Miss Annie Manning. 4th ed. 12mo. Lond., 1860. C 17 P 5

The Household of; with an Introduction by the Rev. W. H. Hutton. 8vo. Lond., 1896. C 10 V 16

Utopia; or, the Happy Republic; to which is added the New Atlantis, by Lord Bacon; with an Analysis of Plato's Republic, by J. A. St John. 12mo. Lond., 1852. F 15 Q 7

MOREL, E. Graving Docks in Hobson's Bay. 8vo. Melb., 1863. MA 1 V 54

MORELL, A. T. Græcum Lexicon Manuale. [See Hederich, B.] J 12 V 1 †

MORELLI, Giovanni. "Ivan Lermolieff." Italian Painters: Critical Studies of their Works. (The Galleries of Munich and Dresden.) 8vo. Lond., 1893. A 28 T 11

MORETON, S. H. Milford Sound and the Scenery of the Middle Island of New Zealand. 8vo. Invercargill, 1882. MD 8 R 28

MORFILL, Wm. Richard. Poland. (Story of the Nations.) 8vo. Lond., 1893. B 25 R 3

MORFIT, Campbell. Improvements in the Chemical Arts. [See Booth, Prof. J. C.] A 21 U 2

MORGAN, Benj. S., and CORK, J. F. Columbian History of Education in West Virginia. 8vo. Charleston, 1893. G 18 R 18

MORGAN, C. L. An Introduction to Comparative Psychology. 8vo. Lond., 1894. G 19 P 30

MORGAN, Dr. Cosby W. Citizenship: an Address. 8vo. Newcastle, 1887. MF 3 T 56

MORGAN Edwin Denison. Sketch of. [See Stoddard, W. O.—Men of Business.] C 16 R 19

MORGAN, George O. Settlers in Australia: a Prize Poem. 12mo. Oxford, 1846. MH 1 Q 20

MORHANGE, Salvador. Etude sur l'Australie, 1862-69. 12mo. Bruxelles, 1869. MD 7 T 9

MORIARTY, G. P. Dean Swift and his Writings. 8vo. Lond., 1893. C 16 R 9

The Paris Law Courts: Sketches of Men and Manners. Roy. 8vo. Lond., 1894. F 14 V 2

MORIARTY, James. Arbitration Act, 1892, with the Rules of 24th March, 1893. 8vo. Sydney, 1893.* MF 2 R 31

MORICE, Rev. A. G. Notes Archæological, Industrial, and Sociological on the Western Dénés, with Ethnographical Sketch of same. (Trans. Canadian Inst., March, 1894.) Roy. 8vo. Toronto, 1894. A 30 V 12

MORIN-HUMPHREYS, H. [See Humphreys, H. M.]

MORISON, Rev. A. Bishop Colenso's Criticisms on the Pentateuch and the Book of Joshua answered. 2nd ed. 8vo. Melb., 1863. MG 1 S 31

MORISON G. S. The Memphis Bridge. Fol. New York, 1894. A 8 Q 13 ‡

MORISON James Augustus Cotter. The Service of Man: an Essay towards the Religon of the Future. 3rd ed. 8vo. Lond., 1888. G 15 P 31

MORLAND, George. [Life of] George Morland, painter, 1763-1804; by R. Richardson. 8vo. Lond., 1895. C 16 U 11

MORLEY, Dr. H. Forster. Watts' Chemistry, vol. 4. [See Watts, H.] K 9 R 8

MORLEY, Prof. Henry. English Writers: an attempt towards a History of English Literature. Vols. 9-11. 8vo. Lond., 1892-95. B 21 R 33-35
  9. Spenser and his Time.
 10. Shakespeare and his Time under Elizabeth.
 11. Shakespeare and his Time under James I. Completed by Prof. W. H. Griffin.
English Prose Writings of John Milton. [See Milton, John.] J 8 T 30
Swift's Tale of a Tub, and other Writings. [See Swift, Rev. J.] C 18 U 2

MORMONISM. 12mo. Lond., 1854. G 2 V 40

MORPHOLOGISCHES JAHRBUCH, eine Zeitschrift für Anatomie und Entwickelungsgeschichte, herausgegeben von C. Gegenbaur. Bände 19-21, und Namen—und Sachregister, bände 1-20. 8vo. Leipzig, 1893-95. E

MORRIS, Dr. Beverley R. British Game Birds and Wild Fowl. 4th ed., by W. B. Tegetmeir. Illustrated. 2 vols. imp. 8vo. Lond., 1895. A 30 V 6, 7

MORRIS, D. Campaign of 1879 against Coffee Leaf Disease (*Hemileia Vastatrix*). 12mo. Colombo, 1879. A 18 P 9

MORRIS, Prof. Edward Ellis. Dryden's Annus Mirabilis, 1666; an historical poem; together with Hazlitt's Selected Essays; with notes and other help for students, by E. E. Morris. 8vo. Melb., 1882. MJ 1 S 11
Memoir of George Higinbotham, an Australian Politician and Chief Justice of Victoria. 8vo. Lond., 1895. MC 1 T 22

MORRIS, G. S. Convicts and Colonies: Thoughts on Transportation and Colonization with reference to the Islands and Mainland of Northern Australia. 8vo. Lond., 1853. MF 3 T 50

MORRIS, J. Advance Japan: a Nation thoroughly in earnest. 8vo. Lond., 1895. B 33 Q 7

MORRIS, Lewis. Poetical Works of. 5 vols. 12mo. Lond., 1889-92. H 9 P 1-5
A Vision of Saints. 12mo. Lond., 1890. H 9 P 6

MORRIS, R. Anna. Physical Education in the Public Schools: an eclectic system of Exercises, including the Delsartean principles of execution and expression. Illustrated. 8vo. New York, 1892. G 17 R 30

MORRIS, Rev. Dr. Richard. Cursor Mundi. [See Early English Text Society.] E

MORRIS, Thos. Health Act [Victoria]. [See Cole, H. S.] MF 3 T 26

MORRIS, Wm. Sketch of. [See Dawson, W. J.—Makers of Modern English.] H 10 S 14
Stories of the Kings of Norway. [See Snorro Sturleson.] J 14 Q 29, 30
————, and BAX, Ernest Belfort. Socialism, its Growth and Outcome. 12mo. Lond., 1893. F 14 Q 29

MORRIS, Wm. O'Connor. Memoirs and Thoughts of a Life. 8vo. Lond., 1895. C 21 S 19
Moltke: a Biographical and Critical Study. 8vo. Lond., 1893. C 13 S 19

MORRISON, Dr. G. E. An Australian in China. Illustrated. 8vo. Lond., 1895. MD 8 R 32

MORRISON, Miss Isabella. Preparation for Death: a Funeral Sermon after the death of; by the Rev. Dr. A. Gilchrist, 1863. 8vo. Sydney, 1863. MG 2 R 45

MORRISON, J. *Trans.*—Russia under Alexander III. [See Samson-Himmelstierna, H. von.] B 31 T 2

MORRISON, Samuel. New South Wales Public School Arithmetic for Third Class. 12mo. Sydney, 1895. MA 3 U 29

MORRISON, W. Douglas. Introduction to "The Female Offender." [See Lombroso, Prof. C.] F 2 V 5

MORROW, John T., and REID, Thorburn. Arithmetic of Magnetism and Electricity. 12mo. Lynn, Mass., 1893. A 21 P 98

MORROW, Dr. Prince A. A System of Genito-urinary Diseases: Syphilology and Dermatology. Vol. I, Parts 1 and 2. Roy. 8vo. Edinb., 1893. A 26 V 17, 18

MORSE, John Torrey. [Life of] Abraham Lincoln. (American Statesmen.) 2 vols. 12mo. Boston, 1893. C 13 P 34, 35

MORSE, Samuel F. B. Sketch of. [See Hubert, P. G.—Inventors.] C 17 R 3

MORSHEAD, Edmund Doidge A. The Ajax and Electra of Sophocles. [See Sophocles.] H 9 U 39

MORTIMER, John. Cotton-spinning: the Story of the Spindle. Illustrated. 8vo. Manchester, 1895. A 25 T 4

MORTLOCK, J. Sketch of the New Caroline Islands, and Sketch of Hunter's Islands. Sm. fol. Lond., 1796. MD 1 P 15 ‡

MORTON, Alexander. Handbook for the use of the Members of the Australasian Association for the Advancement of Science. Hobart meeting, 1892. 12mo. Hobart, 1891. MA 1 P 72

MORTON, John. The Hobart Coffee Palace Visitors' Guide to Hobart and Suburbs. 8vo. Hobart, 1891. MD 5 Q 49
The Launceston Coffee Palace Visitors' Guide to Launceston and Suburbs. 8vo. Launceston (n.d.) MD 5 S 49

MORTON, John Chalmers. Cyclopedia of Agriculture, Practical and Scientific, in which the Theory, the Art, and the Business of Farming are thoroughly and practically treated by upwards of fifty of the most eminent practical and scientific men of the day. Illustrated. 2 vols. roy. 8vo. Lond., 1875. A 18 V 19, 20

MORTON, Levi Parsons. Sketch of. [See Stoddard, W. O.—Men of Business.] C 16 R 19

MOSCHUS. Works of. [See Fawkes, F.] H 6 U 28

MOSELY, Harriett. The Power of Grace; or, Memorials of Harriett Mosely; by Isabella S. Leonard. 12mo. Sydney, 1886. MC 1 P 49

MOSELEY, Prof. H. N. Narrative of the Cruise of H.M.S. "*Challenger*." [See Thomson, Sir C. W., and Murray, Dr. J.—Report on the Scientific Results of the Voyage of H.M.S. "*Challenger*."] A 6 †

Hydroid, Alcyonarian, and Madreporanian Corals. [See Thomson, Sir C. W., and Murray, Dr. J.—Voyage of H.M.S. "*Challenger*."] A 6 †

MOSES, Dr. Alfred J., and PARSONS, Prof. Chas. L. Elements of Mineralogy, Crystallography, and Blowpipe Analysis, from a practical standpoint. 8vo. New York, 1895. A 24 V 34

MOSES, Prof. Bernard. The Establishment of Municipal Government in San Francisco. (Johns Hopkins University Studies, 7.) 8vo. Baltimore, 1889. B 18 S 7

MOSES, Dr. Henry. Sketches of India. 8vo. Lond., 1850. D 17 R 19

MOSHEIM, Rev. Dr. Johann Lorentz von. An Ecclesiastical History, Ancient and Modern. Translated by the Rev. Dr. A. Maclaine. 6 vols. 8vo. Lond., 1826. G 4 P 28-33

MOSLEY, M. New Zealand Illustrated Annual. [See New Zealand Illustrated Annual.] MJ 3 S 4

MOSSMAN, Samuel F. Railways in Victoria : a safe, sound, cheap, and expeditious system for their construction. 8vo. Melb., 1857. MA 1 V 55

MOTTELAY, P. Fleury. Trans.—On the Loadstone, &c. [See Gilbert, Wm.] A 21 V 5

MOULE, Rev. Handley Car Glyn. Romans. [See Expositor's Bible.] G 19 S 8

MOULTON, Louise C. Arthur O'Shaughnessy, his Life and Work, with Selections from his Poems. 12mo. Lond., 1894. C 14 P 32

MOULTON, Dr. Richard Green. Four Years of Novel Reading. 8vo. Lond., 1895. J 12 Q 8

Notes on University Extension. [See Gilman, Dr. D. C.] B 18 S 9

MOUNCEY, Wm. A. de. [See De Mouncey, W. A.]

MOUNT MORGAN GOLD-MINING COMPANY. Report of the Extraordinary General Meeting, held on Dec. 23, 1890. 12mo. Rockhampton, 1890. ME 5 Q

MOUNTAIN, A. C. The City Railway Extension. Sm. fol. Sydney, 1880. MA 9 P 6 †

Hyde Park Destruction. Sm. fol. Sydney, 1889. MA 9 P 6 −

MOUZÉ, Major. Traité de Fortification Souterraine suivi de quatre Mémoires sur les Mines. Sm. 4to. Paris, 1804. A 30 V 3

MOXOM, P. S. The Aim of Life : Plain Talks to Young Men and Women. 2nd ed. 8vo. Boston, 1894. G 18 Q 14

MUDDOCK, J. E. For Valour, the Victoria Cross : a record of the brave and noble deeds for which Her Majesty has bestowed the Victoria Cross. 8vo. Lond., 1895. B 23 S 17

MUDIE, J. An Historical and Critical Account of a grand series of National Medals. 4to. Lond., 1820. A 11 Q 3 †

MUELLER, Dr. A. On Snake Poison, its action and its antidote. Roy. 8vo. Sydney, 1893.* MA 2 S 71

MUELLER, Sir Ferdinand von, Baron. Account of some New Australian Plants. 8vo. Melb., 1857. MA 2 T 81

Additions to Lists of Timber Trees, &c., eligible for Victorian Culture. 8vo. Melb., 1872. MA 2 T 81

Additions to the Extra-Tropical Flora of South Australia. (Trans. Rcy. Soc., S. Australia, 9.) 8vo. Adelaide, 1887. ME 1 S

Dendrobium cincinnatum, Sp. Nov. (Proc. Roy. Soc., Queensland, 1.) 8vo. Brisbane, 1884. ME 1 T

Description and Illustrations of the Myoporinous Plants of Australia. Vol. 2. 4to. Melb., 1886. MA 9 P 21 †

=. Lithograms.

Description of a new Tilliaceous Tree from N.E. Australia. (Proc. Roy. Soc., Queensland, 2.) 8vo. Brisbare, 1886. ME 1 T

Descriptive Notes on Papuan Plants, parts 6-9. 8vo. Melb., 1885-90. MA 1 V 2

Diagnoses of a new genus of Verbenaceæ from Arnheim Land. (Trans. Rcy. Soc., S. Australia, 6.) 8vo. Adelaide, 1883. ME 1 S

Diagnoses of some New Plants from South Australia (Trans. Roy. Soc., S. Australia, 6.) 8vo. Adelaide, 1883. ME 1 S

Forest Culture in its relation to Industrial Pursuits. 8vo. Melb., 1871. MA 3 S 35

Geological Survey of Victoria.—Observations on New Vegetable Fossils of the Auriferous Drifts. 1st and 2nd Decade. Roy. 8vo. Melb., 1874-83. ME

Iconography of Australian Salsolaceous Plants. Decades 1-9. 4to. Melb., 1889-91. MA 8 Q 2 †

Iconography of Candolleaceous Plants. 1st decade. 4to. Melb., 1892. MA 9 P 17 †

On a new Acanthaceous Plant from Arnheim Land. (Trans. Roy. Soc., S. Australia, 5.) 8vo. Adelaide, 1882. ME 1 S

MUELLER, Sir Ferdinand von, Baron—*contd.*
On the Advancement of the Natural Sciences through Ministers of the Christian Church. 8vo. Melb., 1877.
MG 1 S 60
Second Systematic Census of Australian Plants, with Chronologic, Literary, and Geographic Annotations. Part 1. Vasculares. Obl. 8vo. Melb., 1889. MA 1 R 58
Select extra-tropical Plants readily eligible for Industrial Culture or Naturalisation. 8th ed. 8vo. Melb., 1891.
MA 3 T 24
Suggestions on the Maintenance, Creation, and Enrichment of Forests. 12mo. Melb., 1879. MA 3 U 6

————, and TATE, Prof. R. On a new Dilleniaceous Plant from Arnheim Land. (Trans. Roy. Soc., S. Australia, 5.) 8vo. Adelaide, 1882. ME 1 S
On a new Rhamnaceous Plant from South Australia. (Trans. Roy. Soc., S. Australia, 5.) 8vo. Adelaide, 1882. ME 1 S

MUENCH, H. Physical Culture: a National Want. 8vo. Milwaukee, 1890. G 18 R 35

MUIR, John. The Mountains of California. 8vo. Lond., 1894. D 15 R 12

MUIR, Dr. John. [Sketch of.] [*See* Müller, F. Max.— Chips from a German Workshop.] J 9 R 31-33

MUIR, Matthew M. P. The Chemistry of Fire. 12mo. Lond., 1893. A 21 P 18
Watts' Chemistry. [*See* Watts, H.] K 9 R 8

MULHALL, Michael G. and E. T. Hand-book of the River Plate, comprising the Argentine Republic, Uruguay, and Paraguay. 6th ed. 12mo. Buenos Ayres, 1892. D 4 P 50

MÜLLENHOFF, Dr. Karl. Die Ortsbewegungen der Tiere. 4to. Berlin, 1885. A 30 V 10
Die Grösse der Flugflächen. 8vo. Bonn, 1884. A 30 U 27

MÜLLER, Prof. F. Max. Chips from a German Workshop. New ed. 3 vols. 8vo. Lond., 1894.
J 9 R 31-33
India, what can it teach us? 8vo. Lond., 1883.
J 2 Q 28
Sacred Books of the East. Vols. 36, 41, 45, 49. 8vo. Oxford, 1891-95. G 20 S 2, 7, 11, 15
36. The Questions of King Milinda; translated from the Pâli by T. W. R. Davids. Part 2.
41. Satapatha-Brâhmana; translated by Julius Eggeling. Part 3.
45. Gaina Sûtras; translated by H. Jacobi. Part 2.
49. Buddhist Mahâyâna Texts. Part 1. The Buddha-Karita of Asvaghosha; translated by Prof. E. B. Cowell.
Theosophy; or Psychological Religion. (The Gifford Lectures, 1892.) 8vo. Lond., 1893. G 19 P 18
Three Lectures on the Vedanta Philosophy, delivered at the Royal Institution, 1894. 8vo. Lond., 1894.
G 13 P 39

MÜLLER, Wilhelm. [Sketch of.] [*See* Müller, F. Max. —Chips from a German Workshop.] J 9 R 32

MULLINS, Dr. George Lane. Epidemic Diseases and their Prevention in the Eastern Suburbs of Sydney. Sm. 4to. Sydney, 1895. MA 3 R 55
Notes on Hydatid Disease in New South Wales. Sm. 4to. Sydney, 1895. MA 3 R 55
Notes on Phthisis in New South Wales and other Australasian Colonies. Sm. 4to. Sydney, 1895. MA 3 R 55

MUMMERY, A. F. My Climbs in the Alps and Caucasus. Illustrated. Imp. 8vo. Lond., 1895. D 19 V 22

MUN, Thos. England's Treasure by Forraign Trade. 12mo. New York, 1895. F 7 V 38

MUNATIUS PLANCUS, L. [*See* Plancus, L. Munatius.]

MUNICIPAL ASSOCIATION OF NEW SOUTH WALES. Proceedings at Fourth, Seventh, Eighth, and Ninth Sessions. 4 vols. 12mo. Sydney, 1886-91.
ME 6 R

MUNRO, Colin. Fern Vale; or, the Queensland Squatter. 3 vols. 8vo. Lond., 1862. MJ 3 Q 21-23

MUNRO, Sir Thos., and the British Settlement of the Madras Presidency. (Rulers of India.) 8vo. Oxford, 1894. C 14 P 13

MUNROE, Kirk. The White Conquerors of Mexico: a Tale of Toltec and Aztec. Illustrated. 12mo. Lond., 1894. J 4 R 39

MÜNTZ, Eugène. Les Arts à la Cour des Papes pendant le XVe et le XVIe Siècle, 1417-1521. 3 vols. 8vo. Paris, 1878-82. A 23 U 30-32

————, et FABRE, Paul. La Bibliothèque du Vatican au 15e Siècle. 8vo. Paris, 1877. J 7 U 34

MURCHISON, Sir Roderick Impey. Portrait of. [*See* Ramsay, Sir A. C.—Memoir of.] C 21 R 20

MURDOCH, Rev. Alexander D. Memoirs of Montrose. [*See* Montrose, Marquis of.] B 31 V 9

MURDOCH, W. G. Burn. Edinburgh to the Antarctic: an Artist's Notes during the Dundee Antarctic Expedition of 1892-1893. 8vo. Lond., 1894.
D 16 T 12

MURDOCK, A. From Australia to Japan. 8vo. Lond., 1892. MJ 2 T 24

MURPHY, Arthur. All in the Wrong: a Comedy. [*See* London Stage, 2.] H 2 S 34
The Citizen: a Farce. [*See* London Stage, 1.]
H 2 S 33
The Grecian Daughter: a Tragedy. [*See* London Stage, 3.] H 2 S 35
Know your own Mind: a Comedy. [*See* London Stage, 2.] H 2 S 34
The Orphan of China: a Tragedy. [*See* London Stage, 2.] H 2 S 34
Three Weeks after Marriage: a Comedy. [*See* London Stage, 1.] H 2 S 33
The way to keep him: a Comedy. [*See* London Stage, 1.] H 2 S 33

MURPHY, G. Read. History of Federation. 8vo. Melb., 1894.   MF 3 T 47

MURPHY, Dr. Shirley F. Hygiene and Public Health. [*See* Stevenson, Dr. T.]   A 33 U 2-4
Our Homes, and how to make them healthy. Edited by S. F. Murphy. Roy. 8vo. Lond., 1883.   A 3 P 2

MURRAY AND OVENS DISTRICT DIRECTORY for 1892-93. 12mo. Albury, 1892.   ME 10 S

MURRAY, Rev. A. W. In Memoriam: a Veteran Missionary of the London Missionary Society: Sermon preached by Rev. Joseph King, July, 1892. 8vo. Sydney, 1892.   MG 2 Q 29

MURRAY, Andrew. Economic Entomology: Aptera. 8vo. Lond., 1876.   A 28 P 22

MURRAY, Chas. E. R. Practice of District Courts, N.S.W. [*See* Foster, W. J.]   MF 1 Q 47

MURRAY, Dr. David. Japan. 8vo. Lond., 1894.   D 17 R 14

MURRAY, David Christie. Great War of 189—. [*See* Great War of 189—.]   J 2 Q 21

MURRAY, George. Introduction to the Study of Seaweeds. 12mo. Lond., 1895.   A 27 P 22

MURRAY, Rt. Rev. Dr. James. Pastoral Letter to the Catholic Clergy and Laity of the Diocese of Maitland, on Catholic Education and the Public Schools Act of New South Wales. 8vo. W. Maitland, 1868.   MG 1 R 22

MURRAY, Dr. James A. H. New English Dictionary on Historical Principles. Consignificant—Crouching, D—Dee, Dep-Dev, Everybody—Fee, Fee-Fei. 5 parts. 4to. Oxford, 1888-95.   K 20 V

MURRAY, John. Hand-book of Rome and its Environs. 15th ed. 12mo. Lond., 1894.   D 12 S 15
Hand-book for Travellers in Constantinople, Brûsa, and the Troad. 12mo. Lond., 1893.   D 12 S 8
Hand-book for Travellers in Denmark, with Schleswig and Holstein, and Iceland. 6th edition. 12mo. Lond., 1893.   D 12 S 6
Hand-book for Travellers in New Zealand; by F. W. Pennefather. 12mo. Lond., 1893.   MD 4 R 46
Hand-book for Travellers in Scotland. 6th ed., with Maps and Plans. 12mo. Edinb., 1894.   D 12 S 14

MURRAY, Dr. John. How to Live in Tropical Africa: a Guide to Tropical Hygiene. The Malarial Problem: Cause, Prevention, and Cure. Illustrated. 8vo. Lond., 1895.   A 26 R 6

MURRAY, John, F.R.S.E. Scientific Results of Voyage of H.M.S. *Challenger*, 1872-76. [*See* Thomson, Sir C. W.]   A G S
Summary of the Scientific Results obtained at the Sounding, Dredging, and Trawling Stations of H.M.S. *Challenger*. [*See* Thomson, Sir C. W.—Scientific Results of Voyage of H.M.S. *Challenger*.]   A G S †

MURRAY, John, F.R.S.E., and RENARD, A. Volcanic Ashes and Cosmic Dust and their Distribution in Deep Sea Deposits. 8vo. Edinb., 1877.   A 20 T 16
Nomenclature, Origin, and Distribution of Deep Sea Deposits. 8vo. Edinb., 1877.   A 20 T 16

MURRAY, Lieut. John. Charts of Bass's Strait. Fol. Lond., 1803.   MD 1 P 16 ‡

MURRAY, Dr. John O'Kane. The Prose and Poetry of Ireland. 10th ed. 8vo. New York, 1882.   J 6 U 2

MURRAY, K. L. Corrosion and Incrustation in Steam Boilers. 8vo. Melb., 1885.   MA 3 S 63

MURRAY, Pembroke L. Volunteer Act, Regulations, Orders of Dress, Standing Orders, and General Orders of Permanent Series. 3rd edition. 12mo. Sydney, 1892.   MA 2 P 51

MURRAY, T. Douglas, and WHITE, A. Silva. Sir Samuel Baker: a Memoir. 8vo. Lond., 1895.   C 21 T 10

MURRAY, Rev. Thos. Boyle. Pitcairn: the Island, &c.; to which is added, a short Notice of Norfolk Island. 12mo. Lond., 1885.   MB 2 P 52

MUSÆUS [Greek Poet]. Works of. [*See* Fawkes, F.]   H 9 U 28

MUSÆUS, Johann Carl August. Translations of Works of. [*See* Carlyle, T.]   J 5 R 42

MUSEUM FLORENTINUM: Statua Antique Deorum et Virorum illustrium. Fol. Florentia, 1734.   A 1 S 1. †

MUSÉE ROYAL D'HISTOIRE NATURELLE DE BELGIQUE. Annales du. 24 vols. fol. Bruxelles, 1878-86.   A 6 V and W ‡
Description des Ossements Fossiles des environs d'Anvers; par P. J. Van Beneden.
Faune du Calcaire Carbonifère de Belgique; par L. G. de Koninck.
Conchyliologie des Terrains Tertiaires de la Belgique; par P. H. Nyst.
Bulletin du, 1882-86. 4 vols. 8vo. Bruxelles, 1882-86.   E

MUSKETT, C. Australasian Almanac, 1877. 8vo. Melb., 1877.   ME 3 S

MUSKETT, Dr. Philip E. Art of Living in Australia. 8vo. Lond., 1893.   MA 1 V 59
An Australian Appeal; the evil—the cause—the remedy. 8vo. Sydney, 1892.   MA 2 S 63
Prescribing and Treatment in Diseases of Infants and Children. 3rd ed. 18mo. Edinb., 1894.   MA 3 P 31

MUSSON, Chas. T. Book-keeping for Farmers and Orchardists. 8vo. Sydney, 1893.   MA 1 G 62

MUTUAL LIFE ASSOCIATION OF AUSTRALASIA. Proceedings at Annual General Meeting, 1877. 8vo. Sydney, 1877.   ME 3 P

MY NOTE-BOOK. Vol. 3, January-June, 1858. 4to. Melb., 1858.   MJ 1 V 2*

MYERS, Francis. Botany Bay, Past and Present. Sm. 4to. Sydney, 1885.   MD 7 U 1
Irrigation; or, the New Australia. 8vo. Melb., 1891.   MA 1 U 66

MYLNE, Rev. Dr. A. Elementary Treatise on Astronomy. 2nd ed. 8vo. Edinb., 1819.   A 20 U 1

MYSTERIES OF MELBOURNE LIFE, a story; by the author of "Scripopolis." Roy. 8vo. Melb., 1873.   MJ 2 S 30

N

NABER, H. A. Standard Methods in Physics and Electricity criticised, and a test for electric Motors proposed. 8vo. Lond., 1894.   A 21 S 28

NADEN, Miss Constance C. W. Complete Poetical Works of. 8vo. Lond., 1894.   H 9 Q 9

NADIRIAN, The. Vol. 1, 1894. Sm. 4to. Brisbane, 1894.   ME 15 Q

NAIRNE, Rev. Alexander Kyd. Flowering Plants of Western India. 12mo. Lond., 1894.   A 20 P 20

NAIRNE, Caroline, Baroness, the Scottish Songstress; by her great grand-niece, M. S. Simpson. 8vo. Edinb., 1894.   C 17 Q 14

NANGLE, James. Notes on Bricks and Brick-making in and around Sydney. 8vo. Sydney, 1894.   MA 3 U 12

NANSEN, Dr. Fridjof. Eskimo Life. 8vo. Lond., 1893.   D 14 T 11
Account of. [*See* Tweedie, Mrs. A.—Winter Jaunt to Norway.]   D 18 T 15

NANSON, Prof. E. J. Proportional Representation. (Roy. Soc., Vict., 17, 19.) 8vo. Melb., 1881-83.   ME 1 P

NAPIER, A. S. History of the Holy Rood-tree: a 12th Century Version of the Cross Legend; with Notes on the Orthography of the Ormulum and a Middle English Compassio Mariæ. (Early English Text Society, Original Series, 103.) 8vo. Lond., 1894.   E

NAPIER, George G. Homes and Haunts of Alfred, Lord Tennyson. 8vo. Glasgow, 1892.   C 15 P 11

NAPOLEON I., Emperor of the French. An Aide-de-camp of. [*See* Ségur, Gen. Count de.]   B 25 S 20
Decline and Fall of; by Viscount Wolseley. Illustrated. 12mo. Lond., 1895.   B 26 R 10
[Life of]; by A. Dumas; translated by J. B. Larner. 8vo. New York, 1894.   C 17 S 7

NAPOLEON I., Emperor of the French—*contd.*
Memoirs to serve for the History of, from 1802-15; by Baron C. F. de Méneval; translated by R. H. Sherard. 3 vols. 8vo. Lond., 1894.   C 17 R 7-9
Napoleon and the Fair Sex; translated from the French of Frédéric Masson. 8vo. Lond., 1894.   C 17 S 10
Napoleon Bonaparte; or, the Man of the World. [*See* Emerson, R. W.—Representative Men.]   C 17 P 10
Napoléon raconté par l'Image d'apres les Sculpteurs, les Graveurs, et les Peintres. Sm. fol. Paris, 1895.   C 15 R 14†
Napoleon's last Voyages; being the Diaries of Admiral Sir T. Ussher and J. R. Glover. Illustrated. 8vo. Lond., 1895.   C 22 R 3
[Plaster Cast of.] [*See* Hutton, L.—Portraits in Plaster.]   A 23 V 13
The Private Life of Napoleon; by A. Levy. From the French of S. L. Simeon. 2 vols. 8vo. Lond., 1894.   C 19 R 15, 16
Sketch of; with Portrait. [*See* Bolton, Sarah K.—Famous Leaders.]   C 17 P 27

NAPOLEON III. Napoleon the Little; by Victor Hugo. 12mo. Lond., 1852.   C 17 P 12
[Plaster Cast of.] [*See* Hutton, L.—Portraits in Plaster.]   A 23 V 13

NARBROUGH, Sir J. Account of Several Late Voyages and Discoveries: 1, Sir John Narbrough's Voyage to the South Sea; 2, Capt. J. Tasman's Discoveries on the Coast of the South Terra Incognita; 3, Capt. J. Wood's Attempt to Discover a North-East Passage to China; 4, F. Marten's Observations made in Greenland and other Northern Countries. 8vo. Lond., 1711.   MD 5 P 23

NARES, Sir George S. Scientific Results of Voyage of H.M.S. *Challenger*, 1872-76. [*See* Thomson, Sir C. W.]   A 6 S†

NASH, George V. American Ginseng, its Commercial History, Protection, and Cultivation. 8vo. Wash., 1896.   A 30 U 32

NASMITH, John W. The Slide Rule, its Principles and Application. 8vo. Manchester (n.d.)   A 25 R 24

NASON, Frank L. Report on the Iron Ores of Missouri. (Geological Survey of Missouri.) 8vo. Jefferson City, 1892.   A 0 U 35

NATIONAL ACADEMY OF SCIENCES. Memoirs of. Vol. 5. 4to. Wash., 1891.   E

NATIONAL AGRICULTURAL SOCIETY OF VICTORIA. Second Annual Spring Exhibition: Catalogue of Exhibits. 8vo. Melb., 1872.   MK 1 R 41

NATIONAL AUSTRALASIAN CONVENTION. Banquet to Members. Menu Card. 8vo. Sydney, 1891.   MA 1 V 37

NATIONAL CYCLOPÆDIA OF AMERICAN BIOGRAPHY, being the History of the United States; [with Portraits of all distinguished characters.] 5 vols. imp. 8vo. New York, 1894.   C 18 U G-10

NATIONAL EDUCATION: a Series of Letters in Defence of the National System; by the Teachers of the National Schools of Sydney. 8vo. Sydney, 1857.   MG 1 R 18

NATIONAL GALLERY, VICTORIA. [*See* Victoria, Public Library, Museums, and National Gallery.]

NATIONAL REVIEW, The. Vols. 15-24. Roy. 8vo. Lond., 1890-95.   E

NATIONAL RIFLE ASSOCIATION. Proceedings of, 1882-93. 12 vols. 8vo. Lond. 1882-93.   E

NATIONAL TEMPERANCE SOCIETY, NEW YORK. Report, 1892. 8vo. New York, 1892.   E

NATURALIST ON THE PROWL, A; or, in the Jungle; by "Eha." Illustrated. 8vo. Lond., 1894.   A 28 U 2

NATURE: a Weekly Illustrated Journal of Science. Vols. 46-50. 4to. Lond., 1892-94.   E

NAUTICAL ALMANAC, The, and Astronomical Ephemeris for 1896-98. 3 vols. roy. 8vo. Lond., 1893-94.   E

NAUTICAL MAGAZINE, The, and Journal of the Royal Naval Reserve. Vols. 61-63. 8vo. Lond., 1892-94.   E

NAVAL ANNUAL, The. Edited by T. A. Brassey. 3 vols. roy. 8vo. Portsmouth, 1893-95.   E

NAVILLE, Dr. Edouard. Ahnas el Medineh (Heracleopolis Magna), with Chapters on Mendes, the Nome of Thoth, and Leontopolis; appendix on Byzantine Sculptures; by Prof. T. H. Lewis; the Tomb of Paheri, at El Kab; by J. J. Tylor and F. L. Griffith. (Egypt Exploration Fund.) [Illustrated.] 4to. Lond., 1894.   B 12 T 5†

The Festival Hall of Osorkon II. in the Great Temple of Bubastis, 1887-89. (Egypt Exploration Fund.) 4to. Lond., 1892.   B 12 T 1†

The Temple of Deir el Bahari, its Plan, its Founders, and its Explorers. (Egypt Exploration Fund.) 4to. Lond., 1894.   B 2 P 26†

NAVY RECORD SOCIETY. Publications of. 8vo. Lond., 1894.   E
    1, 2. Defeat of the Spanish Armada; edited by Prof. J. K. Laughton.

NAYLER, B. S. Commonsense Observations on the existence of rules regarding the English Language; followed by, Pronunciation made Easy. 8vo. Melb., 1869.   MK 1 Q 36

NEALE, Agnes. [*See* Leane, Caroline Agnes.]

NEBRASKA. Information concerning. 12mo. St. Louis, 1893.   D 15 Q 23
Resources Advantages, and Development. 12mo. Omaha, Neb., 1893.   D 15 P 11
Great Opportunities for Farmers and Investors in. 12mo. Chicago, 1893.   D 15 Q 23

NEBRASKA—STATE BOARD OF AGRICULTURE. Report, 1892. 8vo. Lincoln, 1892.   E

NEBRASKA UNIVERSITY. Reports of the University Agricultural Experiment Station, 1888-93. 6 vols. 8vo. Lincoln, 1889-94.   E

NEEDHAM, John, son. Lecture on Writing. 12mo. Melb. (n.d.)   MG 2 R 21

NEIL, Rev. James. Pictured Palestine. Illustrated. 8vo. New York (n.d.)   D 16 V 9

NEILD, Dr. James Edward. Address delivered at the Annual Meeting of the Victorian Branch of the British Medical Association, 1882. 8vo. Melb., 1882.   MA 1 V 72
On the Advantages of Burning the Dead. 8vo. Melb, 1873.   MA 2 S 62

NELSON, Adm. Horatio, Viscount, Duke of Bronté. [Life of]; by J. K. Laughton. 12mo. Lond., 1895.   C 22 P 14
Sketch of; with Portrait. [*See* Belton, Sarah K.—Famous Leaders.]   C 17 P 27

NELSON, O. N. History of the Scandinavians and successful Scandinavians in the United States. Vol. 1, parts 1 and 2. 8vo. Minneapolis, 1893.   B 25 R 7

NELSON, Wallace. For and against Socialism. [*See* Dalrymple, D. H.]   MF 4 R 31

NEREVY, J. F. The Silkworm. 8vo. Melb. (n d.)   MA 3 S 56
The Torrent of the French Revolutions; or, a Guide to the reading of the History of France from 1789-1873, with Chronological and Genealogical Maps of the different Dynasties. 2 vols. 8vo. Melb., 1873.   MB 2 R 61, 62

NERNST, Dr. Walter, and PALMER Dr. Chas. Skeele. Theoretical Chemistry. Illustrated. 8vo. Lond., 1895.   A 21 U 1

NETTLESHIP, Henry. Lectures and Essays. 2 vols. 8vo. Oxford, 1885-95.   J 10 R 40, 41

NETTLETON, C. Photo-Views of Victoria. [60 Photographs.] 4to. Melb. (n.d.)   MA 9 P 13†

NEUES JAHRBUCH für Mineralogie, Geologie, und Palæontologie, 1890-94. 95 vols. 8vo. Heidelberg and Stuttgart, 1830-94.   E

NEVADA AGRICULTURAL EXPERIMENT STATION. Reports, 1889, 1891-93. 4 vols. 8vo. Carson City and Reno, 1889-94.   E

NEVADA STATE UNIVERSITY. Report, 1890. 8vo. Reno, 1891.   E

NEVILLE, Henry. Voice, Speech, and Gesture. [See Campbell, Dr. H.]   J 8 T 36

NEW BOOK OF SPORTS. 12mo. Lond., 1885.   A 29 R 30

NEW BRUNSWICK. Report on Agriculture, for the Province of New Brunswick, for 1893. Fredericton, 1894.   E

NEW CHUM'S ADVICE to Public Speakers and Public Readers. 8vo. Melb. (n.d.)   MJ 3 Q 11

NEW FEDERATION MOVEMENT, The, from the Corowa Conference, 1893, to the A. N. A. Conference, 1894. 8vo. Bendigo, 1894.   MF 2 T 56

NEW GUINEA, British. Reports on, 1888-94. 4 vols. sm. fol. Sydney, Brisbane, and Melb., 1882-94.   ME

NEW HAMPSHIRE—*State Departments, Reports, and Publications.*

ADJUTANT-GENERAL. Reports for 1866 and 1868. 3 vols. 8vo. Concord, &c., 1866-68.   E

BOARD OF AGRICULTURE. Gems of the Granite State. Obl. 8vo. Concord (n.d.)   D 15 Q 25

BOARD OF LIBRARY COMMISSIONERS. Report, 1892. 8vo. Concord, 1892.   E

FORESTRY COMMISSION. Second Report. 8vo Concord, 1893.   E

GENERAL COURT. Annual [Departmental] Reports, 1890-92. 9 vols. 8vo. Manchester and Concord, 1891-93.   E

 Adjutant-General, Reports, 1890-1892.
 Asylum for the Insane, Reports, 1890-1892.
 Bank Commissioners, Reports, 1890-1892.
 Board of Agriculture, Reports, 1890-1892.
 Board of Equalization, Reports, 1891, 1892.
 Board of Health, Reports, 1890-1892.
 Commissioners of Lunacy, Reports, 1890-1892.
 Fish Commissioners, Reports, 1890-1892.
 Forestry Commissioners, Report of, 1890.
 Industrial School, Reports, 1890-1892.
 Insurance Commissioner, Reports, 1890-1892.
 Normal School, Reports, 1890-1892.
 Railroad Commissioners, Reports, 1890-1892.
 State Librarian, Reports, 1890-1892.
 State Prison, Reports, 1890-1892.
 State Treasurer, Reports, 1890-1892.
 Superintendent of Public Instruction, Reports, 1890-1892.
 Vital Statistics, Reports, 1890-92.

LIBRARY. Reports of the State Librarian, 1892-94. 2 vols. 8vo. Concord, 1892-94.   E

NEW HAMPSHIRE—*contd.*

PROVINCIAL, TOWN, AND STATE PAPERS; edited by Albert S. Batchellor. Vols. 2-20. Manchester, &c., 1868-91.   E

Journals of the Senate and House of Representatives, Special Session, December, 1890, and January Session, 1891. 2 vols. 8vo. Manchester, 1891.   E

Laws of the State of New Hampshire, 1891, 1893. 2 vols. roy. 8vo. Concord, 1891-93.   E

Public Statutes of New Hampshire. Roy. 8vo. Manchester, 1891.   E

SECRETARY OF STATE. Manual for the General Court, 1891 and 1893. 2 vols. 8vo. Concord, 1891-93.   E

SOLDIERS' HOME. Report for 1891-92. 8vo. Concord, 1893.   E

SUPREME COURT. Reports, 1888-89. Vol. 65. 8vo. Concord, 1891.   E

NEW HEBRIDES. Description of. 8vo. Lond., 1846.   MD 8 R 30

NEW JERSEY—*State Departments, Reports, and Publications.*

AGRICULTURAL EXPERIMENT STATION. Reports, 1884, 1887-92, and 1894. 7 vols. 8vo. Trenton, 1885-95.   E

BOARD OF EDUCATION. Report, 1892, part 1. 8vo. Trenton, 1893.   E

NEW MEXICO. Mineral and other Resources of Sierra County. [See Robin, G. E.]   D 15 T 19

Colfax County, its resources and opportunities. 8vo. Denver, 1893.   D 15 T 19

NEW MONTHLY MAGAZINE, The. Part 3, 1842, 1843, 1844. 3 vols. 8vo. Lond., 1842-44.   E

NEW REVIEW, The. Vols. 7-13. 8vo. Lond., 1892-95.   E

NEW SHAKSPERE SOCIETY. Publications. 5 vols. 8vo. Lond., 1881-89.   E

 Plays: The Two Noble Kinsmen, edited by H. Littledale.
 Shakspere's England: Harrison's Description of England in Shakspere's youth. Edited by F. J. Furnival.
 Transactions, 1887-92.

NEW SOUTH WALES—*General.*

District Maps, compiled by Messrs. Higinbotham and Robinson. Fol. Sydney, 1882-87.   MD 1 P 13 ‡

 Ashfield.
 Balmain.
 Bourke.
 Burwood.
 Canterbury.
 Clarence, New England, and Macleay River Districts.
 Cook's River and George's River.
 Hunter's Hill.
 North Shore.
 Pennant Hills Districts.
 Petersham.
 St. Leonards.
 St. Peters to Liverpool.

Historical Records of New South Wales. Vols. 1-3. 1762-1799. 8vo. Sydney, 1892-95.   MB 2 T 20-23

Facsimiles of Charts to accompany Vol. 1; pt. 1 [of the above]. 4to. Sydney, 1893.   MB 8 P 6 †

NEW SOUTH WALES—*General—contd.*

History of New South Wales, from the Records. Vol. 2, by A. Britton; edited by F. M. Bladen. 8vo. Sydney, 1894.   MB 2 S 33
    2. Phillip and Grose, 1789-1794.

Map of New South Wales, showing Roads, Gold, Tin, and Copper Districts, Distances, &c. Folded 12mo. Sydney, 1871.   MD 2 W 53

New South Wales, its Past, Present, and Future Condition. 12mo. Lond., 1839.   MB 1 P 48

Papers respecting New South Wales [relating to Police and Gaol Establishments, Discovery and Occupation of the Colony, and Immigration]. Sm. fol. Sydney, 1841.   MF 3 U 48

Photographs of the Heads of the People during the Governorship of Sir W. T. Denison, 1855-61. Fol. [Framed.]   Libr.

Photographs of Scenery, Views, &c. 8 vols. fol. Sydney, 1895.   MA 45 ‡

Religious Wants of New South Wales. 8vo. Lond., 1840.   MG 1 S 36

NEW SOUTH WALES—*Government Departments, Reports, and Publications.*

ACTS OF PARLIAMENT. [See STATUTES.]

AGRICULTURE.

Agricultural Gazette of New South Wales. Vols. 1-4. Roy. 8vo. Sydney, 1890-94.   ME 9 R

Annual Report of Department of Agriculture, 1891. Sm. fol. Sydney, 1892.   ME

Bulletin of the Conference of Delegates of Agricultural Societies, 1895. 8vo. Sydney, 1895.   MA 1 S 48

Bulletin of the Proceedings of the Conference of Vine and Fruit-growers, 1895. 8vo. Sydney, 1895.   MA 1 S 49

Hawkesbury Agricultural College and Experimental Farm. Prospectus, Regulations, Reports, &c. 8vo. Sydney, 1892-94.   ME 6 S

Report from the Select Committee on Disease in Fruit Trees. Sm. fol. Sydney, 1866.   MA 2 Q 31 †

Pamphlets on Commercial Crops. 8vo. Sydney, 1892-93.   MA 1 Q 65
    The Cultivation of the Australian Nut.
    Sorghum.
    Report on the Tobacco-growing Industry in the Tumut District ; by S. Lamb and G. F. Sutherland.
    Cultivation and Extraction of the Fibre from Sisal Hemp Plant.
    Flower-farming for Perfumes and Medicines.
    The Cultivation of the Black or Green Wattle ; by F. Turner. 3rd edition.
    The Cultivation and Uses of the Bael or Bengal Quince.
    Comparison of American and Australian Maize ; by F. B. Guthrie.
    Report on Maize Crop grown at Hawkesbury Agricultural College Farm.
    Cultivation and Uses of the Thousand-Headed Kale.
    Cultivation and Uses of the "Catjang-Bean" or "Cow-pea."
    Tobacco as a Farmer's Crop in N.S.W. ; by G. F. Sutherland.
    Olive Culture ; by J. L. Thompson.
    The Cultivation of Rape : The advantage of alternate Crops ; by J. L. Thompson.
    Medicinal Plants [Dandelion, Squill, Jalap, Dill] ; by T. Phillips-Gibson.
    Tan Substances—Cañaigré.
    Olive Culture and the Manufacture of Olive Oil.
    Flower-farming for Perfumes.
    Report on the Yield of Maize, April, 1893.

NEW SOUTH WALES—*contd.*

AGRICULTURE—*contd.*

Pamphlets. Reports on Condition of Growing Crops, Nos. 1-7. Oct. 1892—Apl., 1893. 8vo. Sydney, 1892-93.   MA 1 Q 59

Pamphlets. Report of Conference of Delegates from Agricultural Societies, March, 1891. 8vo. Sydney, 1891.   MA 1 Q 70

Pamphlets on Dairying. 8vo. Sydney, 1892-93.   MA 1 Q 68
    Cheese-making ; by F. McCaffrey.
    Silos, Ensilage, and Silage ; by J. A. Despeissis.
    The Chemistry of Cheese-making ; by F. McCaffrey.
    Milk Fermentations and their Relations to Dairying ; by H. W. Conn.
    How to increase the percentage of Butter-fat in Milk ; by H. C. L. Anderson.
    Economical Silage Stack.
    The Milking Machine at Bodalla.
    Cheese-making by small farmers.

Pamphlets on Fruit-growing. 8vo. Sydney, 1890-93.   MA 1 Q 62
    Temperatures for Fruit Export.
    Cold Storage of Fruit.
    Cold Storage for Apples, from the Vegetable Pathologist's Point of View ; by N. A. Cobb.
    Prune-growing and Curing ; by A. H. Benson.
    The Strawberry ; Its History and Cultivation ; by F. L. Jensen.
    Grafting.
    On Budding ; by F. Turner.
    Canning and Preserving Fruits ; by Prof. E. M. Shelton.
    The English Market for New South Wales Fruit : Report by F. W. Ward.
    Book-keeping for Farmers and Orchardists ; by C. T. Musson.
    Curl-leaf in Peach, Nectarine, and other Stone Fruits.
    Spraying Fruit-trees.
    Preparation of the Lemon for Market ; by G. W. Garcelon.
    Report of Conference of Fruit-growers and Vine-growers, Oct., 1890.
    Report of Conference of Fruit-growers, Feb., 1891.

Pamphlets on Insects injurious to Fruit-trees and Farm Crops. 8vo. Sydney, 1890-93.   MA 1 Q 66
    The Codling Moth, its Life-history and Habits ; by A. S. Olliff.
    Directions for Collecting, Packing, and Forwarding Specimens of Insects, Plants, Fungi, and Soils. 3rd edition.
    Insect Pests : the Maize Moth ; by A. S. Olliff.
    How and When to Spray for Codling Moth and Aphides on Fruit-trees ; by A. H. Benson.
    Woolly Aphis or American Blight ; by A. S. Olliff.
    The Bronzy Orange Bug ; by A. S. Olliff.
    Principal Insect and Fungus Pests, on Fruit and Fruit-trees, found in New South Wales, with a few well-known and tested remedies ; by A. H. Benson.
    Report on a visit to the Clarence River District for the purpose of ascertaining the nature and extent of Insect Ravages in the Sugar-cane Crops ; by A. S. Olliff.
    Entomological Notes ; by A. S. Olliff. Two little known Scale-insects affecting Fruit-trees. The Banded Pumpkin Beetle and Two-spotted Monolepta. The Cabbage Moth in the New Hebrides. The Potato Moth destroying Tobacco at Tamworth. Suggestions for Observations and Experiments : Life-history of the Potato Moth and its Ravages. The Migratory Locust in Egypt.
    The Use of Paris Green as an Insecticide ; by A. H. Benson.
    The Hessian Fly.
    Quotations for the various mixtures recommended for the treatment of Insect Pests and Plant Diseases.
    Mechanical application of Insecticides ; by J. A. Despeissis

NEW SOUTH WALES—contd.
AGRICULTURE—contd.
Pamphlets on Live Stock. 8vo. Sydney, 1891-93.
MA 1 Q 58
The Pig, its Breeding, Management, and Commercial Value; by J. L. Thompson.
Pig Raising and Pork Making; by Prof. E. M. Shelton.
The Clydesdale Horse; by J. L. Thompson.
The Frozen Mutton Industry; by A. B. Suttor.
Stock Breeding and Fattening in New Zealand; by A. Bruce.
Report on the Frozen Meat Trade of New Zealand; by A. Bruce.
Dropping after Calving; by Dr. F. C. Grenside.
The Treatment of Sheep for Worms; by A. Bruce.
Breeding Sheep for the Frozen Mutton Industry; by A. B. Suttor.
Judging Sheep by Points; by A. Bruce.
The Points of Stock and their Relative Values; by A. Bruce.
Description and Explanation of System of Sheep Ear-marks in N.S.W. since 1878.
Explanation of System of Horse and Cattle Brands in New South Wales.

Pamphlets on Manures and Fertilisers. 8vo. Sydney, 1890-93.
MA 1 Q 61
Farmers' Guide to Manuring; by A. N. Pearson.
Orchard Manures; by H. C. L. Anderson.
Analyses and Values of Commercial Fertilisers.
How are Nitrogen and Phosphoric Acid to be obtained in the cheapest way? by Prof. P. Wagner.
Dried Blood as a Manure; by H. C. L. Anderson.

Pamphlets on Plant Diseases, Fungi, &c. 8vo. Sydney, 1892-93.
MA 1 Q 67
Some Practical Results of the Treatment of Plant Diseases; by Prof. B. T. Galloway.
Plant Diseases and How to Prevent them; by N. A. Cobb.
Arrowing and its Relation to the present Disorder in the Sugar-cane; by E. de P. O'Kelly.
The Sorch Cane Disease; by Dr. G. Kottman.
The Sugar-cane Disease; by Dr. G. Kottman.
Sugar-cane Disease on the North Coast; by J. A. Despeissis.
Dialogue concerning the manner in which a Poisonous Spray does its work in preventing or checking Blight; by N. A. Cobb.
Smut in Oats and Wheat; Jensen or Hot-water Treatment.
Rust in Wheat.
Plant Diseases and their Remedies—Diseases of the Sugar-cane; by N. A. Cobb.

Pamphlets on Supposed Poisonous Plants. 8vo. Sydney, 1893.
MA 1 T 56
Supposed Poisonous Plant [Darling-pea, Indigo, Cranky-pen]; by F. B. Guthrie and F. Turner.
The Zamia Palm and its Relation to the Disease known as Rickets in Cattle; by F. Turner.

Pamphlets on Poultry and Bees. 8vo. Sydney, 1893.
MA 1 Q 60
Plants visited by Bees.
Heredity in Bees.
Poultry—Fowls on the Farm.
Poultry—Soft Foods.
Poultry—Egg-producers and Experiments in Egg-production.
Poultry—Table Breeds; by S. Gray.
Poultry—The Australian Game; by S. Gray.
Poultry—The Plymouth Rock.
Judge's Report on Apiculture; by A. Gale.

Pamphlets.—Reports on Orchards, Farms, &c. 8vo. Sydney, 1892-93.
MA 1 Q 64
Citrus Orchards—Vineyards and Wine Cellars.
Irrigation : Report by H. G. M'Kinney.
The Western Districts; by A. B. Suttor.
Clearing Land by the aid of a Team of Bullocks.
Judge's Report on English Fruit Orchards; by J. Harold.
Mixed Farms.
National Prizes for District Agricultural Shows, 1892.

NEW SOUTH WALES—contd.
AGRICULTURE—contd.
Pamphlets on the Vineyard and Cellar. 8vo. Sydney, 1892-93.
MA 1 Q 73
The Vineyard and the Cellar; by J. A. Despeissis.
Remarks on the sending and judging of Wine Samples in connection with the competition for National Prizes and cognate matters; by P. F. Adams.
The Australian Wine Trade; by H. W. Irvine.

Rust in Wheat. Report of Proceedings of Conference held in Sydney, June, 1891. Sm. fol. Sydney, 1891.
MA 7 Q 32 †

AUDITOR-GENERAL. Public Accounts, 1893. Sm. fol. Sydney, 1894. ME

BARQUE ELLEN INQUIRY BOARD. Report. Sm. fol. Sydney, 1891. MF 4 U 1

BILLS. [See STATUTES.]

BOARD FOR THE PROTECTION OF THE ABORIGINES. Report, 1891. Sm. fol. Sydney, 1892. ME

BLUE BOOK. [See PUBLIC SERVICE.]

BOARD OF HEALTH. Publications. Fol. Sydney, 1883-92.
MA 7 Q 30 †
Directions for Restoring the Apparently Drowned.
Australian Maritime Quarantine; by J. A. Thompson.
A District Hospital, its Construction and Cost; by J. A. Thompson.
Record of the Sanitary State of New South Wales; by J. A. Thompson.
Directions for Collection and Transmission of Samples of Water for Chemical Examination.
Report on Sanitary Condition of Public Schools in Sydney and Suburbs.
Quarantine Station, North Head, Report on, 1883.
Report upon the late Epidemic of Small-pox, 1881-82.
The late case of the M. M. S.S. Oceanien.
Quarantining of the S.S. Preussen.
Recent Importation of Small-pox by the S.S. Oroya.
Vessels arriving at, and leaving, Ports of New South Wales : Return, 1891-92.
Comparative View of the Mortality of the different Colonies.
The Luctometer : directions for using.
Dairies' Supervision Act, Administration of, 1887-89.
Treatment of Typhoid Fever at the Coast Hospital.
Report upon the Outbreak of Typhoid Fever in Leichhardt, due to Polluted Milk, 1886.
Typhoid Fever in Sydney and Suburbs, 1876-88.
Report upon the Outbreak of Typhoid Fever in Newtown and Macdonaldtown, 1889.
Report on an Outbreak of Fever at Balranald, caused by Polluted Water, 1889.
Report on Outbreak of Typhoid Fever at Waverley and Randwick, 1890.
Returns : Number of Persons suffering from Typhoid Fever, 1888.
Leprosy in the Australian Colonies. Report, 1890.
Leprosy in New South Wales. Report, 1891.
Bovine Tuberculosis, in the South Coast District, 1890.
Eureka Patent Sanitary Burning Works, Newcastle, Report on, 1889.
Papers relating to the Collection and Disposal of Night-soil in Unsewered Municipal Districts.
Report on Deposit of Garbage in Redfern on Site for Building Purposes.
Epidemic of Influenza. Reports, 1890-91.
Maintenance of Sick Paupers : Reports on Votes for 1887-89.
Government Laboratory : Reports, 1890-91.
Coast Hospital, Little Bay : Report, 1884.
Rabbit Destruction.
Vaccination : Report, 1882.
Views of Board of Health in regard to Compulsory Vaccination.

[Parliamentary] Report upon Management of the Quarantine Station, North Head, and the Hulk Far-away. Fol. Sydney, 1882. MA 10 P 15 †

NEW SOUTH WALES—*contd.*
BOARD OF TECHNICAL EDUCATION. [*See* PUBLIC INSTRUCTION.]
CHARITIES AND CHARITABLE INSTITUTIONS. Department of Charitable Institutions. Report, 1890. Sm. fol. Sydney, 1891. ME
Public Charities, Second Report of the Commission on. Sm. fol. Sydney, 1874. MF 4 T 49
State Children's Relief Department. Reports, 1884-87, 1890 and 1894. 2 vols. Sm. fol. Sydney, 1884-94. ME
CIVIL SERVICE. [*See* PUBLIC SERVICE.]
COLLIERIES. Report on Working of Collieries. Sm. fol. Sydney, 1894. MA 3 P 23 †
COLONIAL CONFERENCE, OTTAWA. Report on. Sm. fol. Sydney, 1894. MF 4 U 5
COSTA RICA PACKET Case. Sm. fol. Sydney, 1894. MF 4 U 4
COUNCIL OF EDUCATION. [*See* PUBLIC INSTRUCTION.]
CROWN LANDS. [*See* LANDS.]
CUSTOMS. Customs Handbook to May, 1893. 8vo. Sydney, 1893. MF 4 S 08
DEFENCE FORCES. Description and Drill of the Maxim Automatic Rifle-Calibre Machine Gun, 1892. 8vo. Sydney, 1892. MA 2 V 34
Description and Drill of the 80-pr. R.M.L. Converted Gun of 5 tons. 8vo. Sydney, 1892. MA 2 V 34
Drill for 6-inch Breech-loading Gun on Casemate Carriage and Slide. 32mo. Sydney 1892. MA 2 P 53
Drill for 6-inch Breech-Loading Gun on H.P. Mounting 32mo. Sydney, 1892. MA 2 P 53
Drill for Nordenfelt 45-inch 5-Barrelled Gun mounted on Travelling Carriage with Limber. 32mo. Sydney, 1892. MA 2 P 53
Gun Drill. 32mo. Sydney, 1891. MA 2 P 53
Handbook for "40-pounder" Rifled Breech-Loading Armstrong Gun. 8vo. Sydney, 1872. MA 2 V 34
Handbook of 10-inch 18-ton R.M.L. Gun—Land Service. 8vo. Sydney, 1892. MA 2 V 34
Handbook for Watkin's Field Range-Finder (Artillery and Infantry). 18mo. Sydney, 1892. MA 2 P 53
Instructions for 6-inch Rifle Breech-Loading Armstrong Gun and Casemate Carriage and Platform. 8vo. Sydney, 1891. MA 2 V 34
Instructions for 6-inch Rifle Breech-Loading Armstrong Gun and Hydro-pneumatic Disappearing Carriage 8vo. Sydney, 1891. MA 2 V 34
Instructions for 8-inch Rifled Breech-Loading Armstrong Gun with Hydro-pneumatic Disappearing Carriage. 8vo. Sydney, 1891. MA 2 V 34
Instructions for use of, and Drill with, 10-inch Rifled Muzzle-Loading Armstrong Gun of 25 tons weight. 8vo. Sydney, 1890. MA 2 V 34
Manual or Drill for 6-inch and 8-inch B.L. Guns on Hydro-pneumatic Disappearing Carriages. 12mo. Sydney, 1890. MA 2 P 53

NEW SOUTH WALES—*contd.*
DEFENCE FORCES—*contd.*
Nordenfeldt Quick-firing and Machine Guns; Instructions and Drill. 8vo Sydney, 1891. MA 2 V 34
80-pr. R.M.L. Gun on Traversing Slide, and 9-inch and 10-inch R.M.L. Guns in Casemate or open Batteries. 18mo. Sydney, 1893. MA 2 P 53
Report of Royal Commission appointed to enquire into the Military Service of New South Wales, 1892. Fol. Sydney, 1892. MF 4 T 4
Report of the Royal Commission on Defence Works, 1890. Sm. fol. Sydney, 1891. MA 10 P 58 +
Standing Orders and Regulations for the New South Wales Commissariat and Transport Corps. 8vo. Sydney, 1891. MA 2 V 35
Watkin's Depression Range-Finder: Depression and Instructions for Use 8vo. Sydney, 1891. MA 2 V 34
DISTRICT COURTS. Annual Returns under the District Courts Act of 1858. Sm. fol. Sydney, 1891. ME
EDUCATION. [*See* PUBLIC INSTRUCTION.]
ELECTORAL ROLLS, 1893-95. 8 vols. Sm. fol. Sydney, 1893-95. ME
ESTIMATES. [*See* FINANCE.]
EXHIBITIONS. Centennial International Exhibition, Melbourne, 1888. Report of the President of the New South Wales Commission. 8vo. Sydney, 1890. MF 2 Q 35
International Exhibition of Mining and Metallurgy, London, 1890. Report. sm. fol. Sydney, 1891. MK 10 P 53 †
New Zealand and South Seas Exhibition, 1889-90. Report. Sm. fol. Sydney, 1891. MK 10 P 54 †
World's Columbian Exposition, Chicago, 1893. Report of the Executive Commissioner for New South Wales to. Sm. fol. Sydney, 1894. MK 9 Q 5 †
FINANCE. Estimates, 1891-95. 3 vols. fol. Sydney, 1890-94. ME
Estimates of Expenditure, 1894, as passed. Sm. fol. Sydney, 1894. ME
Schedule to the Military and Naval Estimates, 1894. Sm fol. Sydney, 1894. ME
Financial Statement, 1891. Speeches. Roy. 8vo. Sydney, 1891. MF 1 S 40
Report on the Creation, Inscription, and Issue of Stock, 1892. Sm. fol. Sydney, 1892. ME
Speeches in Parliament on the Inscribed Stock Bill. Roy. 8vo. Sydney, 1893. MF 1 S 45
FIRE BRIGADES' BOARD. Reports, 1891 and 1893. 2 vols. sm. fol. Sydney, 1882-94. ME
FISHERIES of the Colony, 1891. Sm. fol. Sydney, 1892. ME
FORESTRY. State Forest Administration. Annual Progress Report for 1892. sm. fol. Sydney, 1893. ME
FRIENDLY SOCIETIES. Friendly Societies Act Inquiry Commission, Report, 1883. Fol. Sydney, 1883. MF 4 T 30

NEW SOUTH WALES—contd.

GEOLOGICAL SURVEY. Memoirs of the Geological Survey. Geology, No. 5. Geology of the Broken Hill Lode and Barrier Ranges Mineral Field, New South Wales: with Maps, Plates, and Sections by J. B. Jaequet. 4to. Sydney, 1894. ME

Memoirs of the Geological Survey. Palæontology. No. 3. Geological and Palæontological relations of the Coal and Plant-bearing beds of Palæozoic and Mesozoic Age in Eastern Australia and Tasmania, with special reference to the Fossil Flora; by Dr. O. Feistmantel. 4to. Sydney, 1890. ME

Memoirs of the Geological Survey. Palæontology, No. 8. Contributions to a Catalogue of Works, Reports, and Papers on the Anthropology, Ethnology, and Geological History of the Australian and Tasmanian Aborigines; by R. Etheridge, jun. Parts 1-3. 4to. Sydney, 1890-95. ME

Memoirs of the Geological Survey. Palæontology, No. 9. The Fossil Fishes of the Talbragar Beds; by A. S. Woodward. 4to. Sydney, 1895. ME

Records of the Geological Survey. Vols. 3, 4. Sm. 4to. Sydney, 1892-95. ME 15 T

GOLD DISCOVERY. Report on Claims of W. Tom, J. Tom, and J. H. A. Lister as the First Discoverers of Gold in Australia. Sm. fol. Sydney, 1890. MA 3 P 57 †

GOVERNMENT GAZETTE, 1892-95. 24 vols. sm. fol. Sydney, 1892-95. ME

HARBOURS AND RIVERS. Report on Dredging. Sm. fol. Sydney, 1891. MA 9 P 24 †

INSANE. Report of the Inspector-General of the Insane, 1890. Fol. Sydney, 1891. ME

JUSTICE. Handbook for 1892. 8vo. Sydney, 1892. MF 2 Q 78

LANDS. Cases determined in the Land Appeal Court. Vol. 1, pt. 7 and Index, and vols. 2-4. Roy. 8vo. Sydney, 1893-95. ME 6 U

Conditional Purchases of J. Smith, J. M. D. Sullivan, and A. Campbell, Land District of Lismore. Sm. fol. Sydney, 1890. MF 4 U 3

Handbook of the Crown Lands Acts. Roy. 8vo. Sydney, 1890. MF 1 S 50

List of Crown Lands that may be selected at the upset price, in terms of section 25 of the Lands Act Further Amendment Act of 1880, Nos. 1 and 2, 1882. 2 vols. sm. fol. Sydney, 1882 MF 4 T 41, 42

List of Pastoral Leases, 1895-96. 8vo. Sydney, 1895. ME 3 R

List of Runs; showing the Rents for the year 1884, payable on or before 31st December, 1883. 8vo. Sydney, 1883. MF 5 R 64

Measured Lands open to Conditional Purchase and Conditional Lease, and Special Areas in the Eastern and Central Divisions. Sm. 4to. Sydney, 1891. MF 2 Q 43

Measured Lands open to Conditional Purchase within Special Areas. Sm. 4to. Sydney, 1893. MF 2 Q 44

Proclaimed Gold-fields in the Colony, also the reserves from conditional purchase on account of gold. 8vo. Sydney, 1878. MA 2 V 62

NEW SOUTH WALES—contd.

LANDS—contd.

Report of Inquiry into the state of the Public Lands. Fol. Sydney, 1883. MF 4 T 15

Reports of the Department of Lands, 1888-89, 1891-93. 2 vols. fol. Sydney, 1890-94. ME

Synopsis of subjects relating to Crown Lands, compiled from Sydney Gazettes from 1803-32. 8vo. Sydney, 1893. MF 3 R 65

Report on the Resumption of Land, Woolloomooloo Bay, 1895. Sm. fol. Sydney, 1895. MF 4 T 43

LEGISLATIVE ASSEMBLY. Report upon the Proposed Standing Orders. Sm. fol. Sydney, 1888. MF 4 U 8

Standing Rules and Orders, 1894. 8vo. Sydney, 1894. MF 4 R 38

Votes and Proceedings of, 1891-95. 32 vols. sm. fol. Sydney, 1892-93. ME

LEAD-POISONING AT BROKEN HILL. Prevalence and Prevention of Lead-poisoning at Broken Hill Silverlead Mines. Sm. fol. Sydney, 1893. MA 10 P 45 †

LEGISLATIVE COUNCIL. Journal of, 1856-74, 1892-95. 42 vols. sm. fol. Sydney, 1856-95. ME

MINES. Annual Reports, 1882-84, 1891-94. 7 vols. sm. fol. Sydney, 1883-95. ME

Extracts from the Annual Report for 1892. Roy. 8vo. Sydney, 1893. MA 2 Q 58

NOXIOUS TRADES. Report of the Noxious and Offensive Trades Inquiry Commission. Sm. fol. Sydney, 1889. MA 9 Q 8 †

PARLIAMENTARY DEBATES, 1892-95. Vols. 59-78. Roy. 8vo. Sydney, 1892-95. ME

PARLIAMENTARY STANDING COMMITTEE ON PUBLIC WORKS. General Reports, 1890-92 and 1894. 4 vols. sm. fol. Sydney, 1890-94. E

PATENTS. Index to Letters of Registration of Inventions, 1854-87. Roy. 8vo. Sydney, 1891. ME 6 U

Index to Letters Patent, 1887-91. Roy. 8vo. Sydney, 1892-93. ME 6 U

Name Index of Applicants for Certificates of Provisional Protection and Letters Patent, 1887-88. Roy. 8vo. Sydney, 1889. ME 6 U

POLICE. Report on W. Stafford, ex-mounted Sergeant of Police. Sm. fol. Sydney, 1893. MF 4 T 17

Rules for the Government and Discipline of the Police Force. 8vo. Sydney, 1877. MF 4 R 29

POST AND TELEGRAPHS. Map showing Roads and Postal Stations, prepared for the use of the Post Office Department. Folded 12mo. Sydney, 1871. MD 2 W 39

Post and Telegraph Conference. Reports of Proceedings of the Conferences, 1890, 1892, 1894. 3 vols. sm. fol. Sydney, 1890-94. ME

Report of Commission on alleged tampering with letters of J. Deasy, M.P. Sm. fol. Sydney, 1889. MF 4 T 3

Reports of the Postmaster-General, 1891, 1893. 2 vols. fol. Sydney, 1892-93. ME

Supplementary Catalogue—1893-95. 199

NEW SOUTH WALES—*contd.*

PUBLIC INSTRUCTION. Board of Technical Education. The Sydney Technical College and Suburban and Provincial Technical Schools. 8vo. Sydney, 1888.
 MG 2 S 3

Board of Technical Education: Report for 1885; and Calendars of Sydney Technical College for 1887, 1889. 2 vols. 8vo. Sydney, 1886-88. ME 6 Q

Common School System of the United States and Canada. Sm. fol. Sydney, 1338. MG 3 P 21 †

Council of Education. Reports upon the Condition of the Public Schools, and of the Certified Denominational Schools, 1870. Roy. 8vo. Sydney, 1871.
 ME 6 Q

Education Regulations framed under the Public Instruction Act of 1880. Sm. fol. Sydney, 1891.
 MG 10 P 55 †

Proposed College for the Training of Teachers of Public Schools. Sm. fol. Sydney, 1891. MA 10 P 29 †

The Public Instruction Act of 1880, and Regulations. Roy. 8vo. Sydney, 1893. MG 1 T 17

Public Schools. Reading Books. 15 vols. 12mo. Glasgow, London, and Sydney (n.d.) MG 2 T 1-15

Regulations for the establishment and conduct of National Schools in New South Wales. 8vo. Sydney, 1853. ME 2 S 3

Reports of the Minister for Public Instruction, 1889-91. 3 vols. sm. fol. Sydney, 1890-92. ME

Reports of the Minister of Public Instruction upon the Condition of Public Schools, 1893-94. 2 vols. roy. 8vo. Sydney, 1894-95. ME

Sydney Technical College: Annual Meeting for presentation of prizes and certificates. 8vo. Sydney, 1889.
 ME 6 Q

Technical Education Branch: Calendars, 1889, 1892, and 1893. 3 vols. roy. 8vo. Sydney, 1892. ME 6 Q

Regulations and Directions to be attended to in making application to the Commissioners of National Education for aid towards the building of School-houses, or for the support of Schools. 8vo. Sydney, 1849.
 MG 2 S 13

[*See also under* Sydney Mechanics' School of Arts.]

PUBLIC LIBRARY. Report from the Trustees of the Sydney Free Public Library, 1892. Sm. fol. Sydney, 1893. ME

PUBLIC SERVICE. Blue Book, 1890-94. 5 vols. sm. fol. Sydney, 1891-95. ME

Civil Service Board. Report, 1893. Sm. fol. Sydney, 1894. ME

Civil Service Commission. Report, 1895. Sm. fol. Sydney, 1895. MF 4 T 21

Public Service Inquiry Commission. Report. Sm. fol. Sydney, 1890. MF 4 U 2

NEW SOUTH WALES—*contd.*

PUBLIC WORKS. Annual Reports, 1892-94. 2 vols. sm. fol. Sydney, 1893-94. ME

Preliminary Catalogue of the Library of the Department of Public Works. Roy. 8vo. Sydney, 1894.
 MK 1 T 1

Proposed Bridge over the Hunter River at Jerry's Plains. Sm. fol. Sydney, 1890. MA 9 Q 11 †

Proposed Bridge to connect Bullock Island with the mainland at Newcastle. Sm. fol. Sydney, 1890.
 MA 10 P 30 †

Proposed Hospital Building, Macquarie-street. Sm. fol. Sydney, 1891. MA 10 P 28 †

Proposed Improvements at Darling Island. Sm. fol. Sydney, 1892. MA 10 P 34 †

Proposed Lunatic Asylum at Kenmore, near Goulburn. Sm. fol. Sydney, 1892. MA 10 P 35 †

Report relating to the proposed Removal of the Pyrmont and Glebe Island Bridges. Sm. fo. Sydney, 1894.
 MA 9 Q 6 †

Report, together with Minutes of Evidence and Appendix, relating to the proposed Dredge and Plant for Sydney Harbour. Sm. fol. Sydney, 1890. MF 2 U 44

RABBITS. Royal Commission of Inquiry into Schemes for Extermination of Rabbits in Australasia. Progress Report, &c. Sm. fol. Sydney, 1890. MF 2 U 27

RAILWAYS AND TRAMWAYS. Act to make better provision for the Management of the Government Railways and Tramways. 8vo. Sydney, 1892. MF 1 S 53

Inquiry into the alleged defectiveness and unsuitability of the Baldwin Locomotives, 1892. Sm. fol. Sydney, 1892. MA 10 P 37 †

Peat's Ferry Railway Accident, Report. Sm. fol. Sydney, 1888. MF 4 U 9

Proposed Deviation to avoid the Lithgow Zigzag. Sm. fol. Sydney, 1894. MA 3 P 22 †

Proposed Extension of Kiama-Nowra Railway into the town of Nowra. Sm. fol. Sydney, 1891. MA 7 Q 33 †

Proposed Railway Extensions, Report on. Sm. fol. Sydney, 1891. MA 9 Q 10 †

Proposed Railway from Culcairn to Corowa. Sm. fol. Sydney, 1889. MA 10 P 18 †

Proposed Railway from Eden to Bega. Sm. fol. Sydney, 1892. MA 10 P 20 †

Proposed Railway from Glen Innes to Inverell, Second Report. Sm. fol. Sydney, 1893. MA 10 P 23 †

Proposed Railway from Goulburn to Crookwell. Sm. fol. Sydney, 1880. MA 10 P 19 †

Proposed Railway from Grafton to Lismore. Sm. fol. Sydney, 1892. MA 10 P 21 †

Proposed Railway from Jerilderie to Berrigan, Report. Sm. fol. Sydney, 1895. MA 10 P 56 †

Proposed Railway from Jerilderie to Deniliquin. Sm. fol. Sydney, 1895. MA 10 P 55 †

Proposed Railway from Marrickville to Burwood Road. Sm. fol. Sydney, 1890. MA 10 P 25 †

NEW SOUTH WALES—*contd.*
RAILWAYS AND TRAMWAYS—*contd.*
Proposed Railway from Narrabri to Moree. Sm. fol. Sydney, 1894. MA 3 P 24
Proposed Railway to connect North Shore Railway with Port Jackson at Milson's Point, Reports. Sm. fol. Sydney, 1890. MA 10 P 24 †
Railway Bridges Inquiry Commission. Sm. fol. Sydney, 1886. MA 10 P 26 †
Report of the Royal Commission appointed to inquire into the Charges against E. M. G. Eddy, preferred by W. F. Schey, M.L.A. Sm. fol. Sydney, 1892. MF 2 U 48
Reports of the Commissioners, 1890-94. 3 vols. sm. fol. Sydney, 1890-94. ME
REGISTRAR-GENERAL. Report of the Royal Commission appointed to inquire into the working of the Deeds and Search Branch, 1893. Sm. fol. Sydney, 1894. MF 4 T 47
Report on Registration of Births, Deaths, and Marriages. Sm. fol. Sydney, 1886. MF 4 U 6
SAVINGS BANK. Post Office Savings Bank—National Bank. Sm. fol. Sydney, 1893. MF 4 T 19
SEWERAGE. Proposed Sewerage Works at Cottage Creek. Sm. fol. Sydney, 1892. MA 10 P 36 †
Proposed Sewerage Works for Parramatta. Sm. fol. Sydney, 1892. MA 10 P 48 †
Second Report relating to the proposed Sewerage Works for Parramatta. Sm. fol. Sydney, 1894. MA 9 Q 30 †
Proposed Storm-water Sewer discharging into Johnston's Bay. Sm. fol. Sydney, 1892. MA 10 P 47 †
Report, together with Minutes of Evidence, relating to the proposed Reticulation of the Western Suburbs Drainage Scheme. Sm. fol. Sydney, 1890. MF 2 U 42
STATISTICS. General Report on the eleventh Census of New South Wales; by T. A. Coghlan. Sm. 4to. Sydney, 1894. MF 3 U 54
Results of a Census of New South Wales, taken on 5th April, 1891. Part 3—Conjugal Condition. Part 4—Religions of the People. Part 5—Birthplaces. Part 6—Sickness and Infirmity. Industrial Returns—Fire and Marine Insurance, Life Assurance, Investment and Finance Companies receiving Deposits. 4to. Sydney, 1893. ME
The Statistician's Report on the Eleventh Census of New South Wales; 1st Instalment. 4to. Sydney, 1893. ME
Statistical Register, 1889-93; by T. A. Coghlan. 5 vols. roy. 8vo. Sydney, 1890-94. ME S R
Statistics of the Seven Colonies of Australasia, 1861-94. 8vo. Sydney, 1895. MF 4 R 57
STATUTES AND BILLS. An Act for the speedy recovery of the possession of Tenements, to which is added the amended Court of Requests Act. (Pam.) 8vo. Sydney, 1853. MG 1 Q 53
An Act to consolidate the Laws relating to Medical Practitioners, 1871. 8vo. Sydney, 1872. MF 4 R 56
An Act to provide for Trial by Jury. 8vo. Sydney (n.d.) MF 3 R 60

NEW SOUTH WALES—*contd.*
STATUTES AND BILLS—*contd.*
Acts and Ordinances of New South Wales, 1844-50. 5 vols. sm. 4to. Sydney, 1844-50. ME
A Bill to consolidate and amend the Laws relating to the Corporation of the City of Sydney. Sm. fol. Sydney, 1877. MF 4 T 5
Commons Regulation Act of 1873. Commons Regulation Act Amendment Act of 1886, with Regulations. Roy. 8vo. Sydney, 1892. MF 1 S 51
Crown Lands Act of 1889. Sm. fol. Sydney, 1889. MF 4 T 6
Improvement (Sydney). An Act to make better provision for the construction of the Buildings, and for the safety and health of the inhabitants within the City of Sydney. (Pam.) 8vo. Sydney, 1879. MG 1 Q 53
Land Boilers' Inspection Bill. Sm. fol. Sydney, 1893. MA 10 P 51 †
Law of Evidence Acts. 8vo. Sydney, 1873. MF 4 R 40
Menindie Irrigation Bill. Sm. fol. Sydney, 1893. MF 4 T 22
Metropolitan Water and Sewerage Act; Metropolitan Water and Sewerage Act Amendment Acts. Roy. 8vo. Sydney, 1892. MF 1 S 52
Mining on Private Lands Act, 1894. 8vo. Sydney, 1894. MF 3 R 61
Municipalities Acts. Roy. 8vo. Sydney, 1892. MF 1 S 49
Rabbit Act of 1890, with Regulations. Roy. 8vo. Sydney, 1891. MF 1 S 55
Statutes, 1892-95. Sm. fol. Sydney, 1892-95. ME
Sydney Electric Lighting Bill, Report on. Sm. fol. Sydney, 1891. MA 10 P 59 †
STOCK AND BRANDS. Quarantine Regulations for Stock and Outbreak of Scab in Sheep. Sm. fol. Sydney, 1884. MA 10 P 16 †
Report of the Meeting of the Chief Inspectors of Stock, 1891. Sm. fol. Sydney, 1891. MA 9 Q 7 †
Report of the Stock and Brands Branch, 1891. Sm. fol. Sydney, 1892. ME
Sheep Brands and Marks Directory for 1891. Sm. fol. Sydney, 1892. ME
SUPREME COURT. Rules and Orders of the Supreme Court of New South Wales, for the District of Port Phillip. 8vo. Melb., 1841. MF 2 Q 71
In Equity: Consolidated Standing Rules of 29 June, 1883. Roy. 8vo. Sydney, 1883. MF 1 S 60
TECHNOLOGICAL, INDUSTRIAL, AND SANITARY MUSEUM. Reports, 1883-86, 1888-90. Sm. fol. Sydney, 1883-90. ME
THEATRES. Report of Commission on. Sm. fol. Sydney, 1887. ME
WATER CONSERVATION. Locking of the River Darling: Reports, Plans, &c. Sm. fol. Sydney, 1890. MA 9 Q 3 ‡
Royal Commission—Conservation of Water. 3 vols. sm. fol. Sydney, 1885. MA 10 P 31-33 †

NEW SOUTH WALES—*cont'd.*

WATER SUPPLY. Board of Water Supply and Sewerage. Reports, 1889-91, 1893. 2 vols. sm. fol. Sydney, 1890-94. ME

Broken Hill and District Water Supply Co.: Correspondence respecting. Sm. fol. Sydney, 1891.
MA 10 P 42 †

Broken Hill Water Supply Act Amendment Bill, Report on. Sm. fol. Sydney, 1892. MF 4 U 7

Proposed Reservoir at Centennial Park for Sydney Water Supply. Report. Sm. fol. Sydney, 1892.
MA 9 Q 9 †

Proposed second pipe-line from Walka to Buttai, for Hunter River District Water Supply. Sm. fol. Sydney, 1892. MA 10 P 41 †

Proposed Water Supply for Armidale. Sm. fol. Sydney, 1892. MA 10 P 38 †

Proposed Water Supply for Lithgow. Sm. fol. Sydney, 1392. MA 10 P 40 †

Proposed Water Supply for Tamworth. Sm. fol. Sydney, 1892. MA 10 P 39 †

Proposed Water Supply for Wollongong and surrounding districts. Sm. fol. Sydney, 1892. MA 10 P 43 †

Proposed Waterworks for the Town of Junee. Sm. fol. Sydney, 1893. MA 10 P 44 †

Report, together with Minutes of Evidence, Appendices, and Plans, relating to the proposed Offices for Board of Water Supply and Sewerage. Sm. fol. Sydney, 1890. MF 2 U 43

Report, together with Minutes of Evidence and Plan, relating to the proposed Extension of Sydney Water Supply to Southern Suburbs—Hurstville and Rockdale. Sm. fol. Sydney, 1890. MF 2 U 45

WEIGHTS AND MEASURES. Report, 1893. Sm. fol. Sydney, 1893. MF 4 T 13

WOOD PAVEMENT BOARD, Report. Sm. fol. Sydney, 1884. MA 2 Q 33 †

NEW SOUTH WALES ABORIGINES PROTECTION ASSOCIATION. Report, 1881. Sm. fol. Sydney 1881. MF

Our Black Brethren, their Past, Present, and Future being the Annual Report for 1891. 8vo. Sydney, 1892. ME 15 Q

NEW SOUTH WALES AUXILIARY BIBLE SOCIETY. The Jubilee Memorial, 1867. 8vo. Sydney, 1867. MG 2 S 1.

Sixty-second and Sixty-third Reports, 1878-79. 2 vols. 8vo. Sydney, 1879-80. ME 6 S

NEW SOUTH WALES BANKRUPTCY, COMPANY, AND PROBATE CASES. Vols. 3-5. Sm. 4to. Sydney, 1893-95. ME 7 R

NEW SOUTH WALES CREMATION, FUNERAL, AND SANITARY REFORM REVIEW. June, 1890. 8vo. Sydney, 1890. ME 3 S

NEW SOUTH WALES EDUCATIONAL GAZETTE, June, 1891-May, 1894. 3 vols. 4to. Sydney, 1891-94. ME

NEW SOUTH WALES INSTITUTION FOR THE DEAF AND DUMB AND THE BLIND, Reports, 1861-66, 1868, 1875-82, 1884-94. 17 vols. 8vo Sydney, 1864-94. ME 6 S

NEW SOUTH WALES LAW ALMANAC, for 1881, 1883, 1891, 1893-94. 5 vols. 18mo. Sydney, 1891.
ME

NEW SOUTH WALES LAW REPORTS. Vols. 13-15, 8vo Sydney, 1892-94. ME 21

NEW SOUTH WALES MEDICAL GAZETTE. Vol. 5. 8vo. Sydney, 1375. ME 7 T

NEW SOUTH WALES MUNICIPAL ASSOCIATION; by 'Iconoclast.' Sm. 4to. Redfern, 1892.
MF 2 Q 41

NEW SOUTH WALES MUNICIPAL DIRECTORY AND LOCAL GOVERNMENT BLUE BOOK, 1893-94. 12mo. Sydney, 1893. ME G T

NEW SOUTH WALES NAVAL BRIGADE WIDOWS AND ORPHANS PROVIDENT SOCIETY. Rules and Regulations. 12mo. Sydney, 1893. MF 1 P 72

NEW SOUTH WALES POLITICAL ASSOCIATION FOR THE SUPPRESSION OF INTEMPERANCE. Report for 1868. 12mo. Sydney, 1869. ME 15 P

NEW SOUTH WALES RELIGIOUS TRACT AND BOOK SOCIETY. Report for 1862. 8vo. Sydney, 1862. ME 6 S

NEW SOUTH WALES RIFLE ASSOCIATION. Reports, 1884-93. 8vo. Sydney, 1885-94. ME

NEW SOUTH WALES SOCIETY FOR THE PREVENTION OF CRUELTY TO CHILDREN. Fifth Annual Report, 1894. 12mo. Sydney, 1894.
ME 6 R

NEW SOUTH WALES WEEKLY NOTES. Vols. 9-11. Sm. 4to. Sydney, 1893-95. ME 7 R

NEW SYDENHAM SOCIETY. Report, 1893. 8vo. Lond., 1893. E

NEW YEAR'S DAY ON THE MOUNTAIN: a Tasmanian Christmas Book. 8vo. Hobart (n.d.)
MJ 1 S 10

NEW YEAR'S GIFT, A: Miscellaneous Poems; by "A Tasmanian." 12mo. Hobart, 1865. MH 1 R 62

Supplementary Catalogue—1893-95.

NEW YORK.—*State Departments, Reports, and Publications.*
AGRICULTURAL EXPERIMENT STATION. Reports of the Board of Control, 1885, 1887-88, 1890-93. 7 vols. 8vo. Albany, N.Y., 1886-94.　　　E
BOARD OF HEALTH. Reports for 1883-85, 1888-93. 11 vols. roy. 8vo. Albany, 1888-93.　　　E
BUREAU OF STATISTICS OF LABOR. Report, 1892. 2 vols. 8vo. Albany, 1893.　　　E
MUSEUM. Annual Report, 1893. 8vo. Albany, 1894.　E
NORMAL AND TRAINING SCHOOL. Circular. 8vo. New York, 1893.　　　E

NEW YORK CATHOLIC SUMMER SCHOOL. Official Prospectus. Roy. 8vo. New York, 1893.　G 18 S 7

NEW YORK UNIVERSITY. Catalogue and Announcements, 1892, 1893. 12mo. New York, 1892.　E

NEW YORK UNIVERSITY SCHOOL OF PEDAGOGY. Catalogue and Circular, 1893, 1894. 8vo. New York, 1893.　　　E

NEW ZEALAND.—*General.*
Descriptive Guide to Lakes Wakatipu and Wanaka, and the Southern Alps of Otago. 12mo. Dunedin, 1884.　MD 7 T 62
Domestic Scenes in New Zealand. 16mo. Lond., 1845.　MD 1 P 80
New Zealand: a Lecture; by "A Young Missionary." 8vo. Lond., 1840.　MD 5 S 51
New Zealand Tourists' Vade Mecum. 3rd ed. 12mo. Dunedin, 1885.　MD 1 P 38
New Zealand War of 1860; an inquiry into its origin and justice, together with some remarks on the land question in relation to the Natives. 8vo. Lond., 1861.　MB 1 R 41
Notes of a Tour through various parts of New Zealand, including a Visit to the Hot Springs; by "A German Lady." 8vo. Sydney, 1877.　MD 3 S 50
Plain Facts relating to the late War in New Zealand. 8vo. Auckland, 1847.　MB 1 Q 47

NEW ZEALAND.—*Government Departments, Reports, and Publications.*
ACTS. [*See* STATUTES.]
BLUE-BOOK, 1890. Sm. fol. Wellington, 1891.　ME
BUREAU OF INDUSTRIES. Report. Sm. fol. Wellington, 1892.　　　ME
CENSUS. Results of a Census of the Colony of New Zealand, 1886, pts. 1-3; and 1891. 3 vols. sm. fol. Wellington, 1887, 1891-92.　　　ME
CIVIL SERVICE. Act to reform the Civil Service, 1886. 4to. Wellington, 1886.　MF 3 U 66
Act to amend the Civil Service Reform Act, 1886. 4to. Wellington, 1887.　MF 3 U 65

NEW ZEALAND—*contd.*
COLONIAL MUSEUM. Reports on the Colonial Museum and Laboratory, 1879-88. 7 vols. 8vo. Wellington, 1880-89.　　　ME 16 Q
Meteorological Reports, 1883 and 1885; including Returns for 1881-84, and averages for previous years. 2 vols. 8vo. Wellington, 1884-86.　ME 16 Q
LANDS. Crown Lands Guides. Nos. 13, 14. 2 vols. sm. fol. Wellington, 1894.　　　ME
Department of Lands and Survey. Reports, 1891, 1894. Sm. fol. Wellington, 1891-94.　　　ME
Particulars respecting the Native Lands in the Colony. Sm. fol. Wellington, 1891.　MF 4 U 12
Surveys of New Zealand: Report, 1890-91. Sm. fol. Wellington, 1894.　　　ME
CUSTOMS. Customs, October, 1893. 8vo. Wellington, 1894.　MF 4 R 32
EDUCATION. Report of the Minister of Education, 1891. Sm. fol. Wellington, 1892.　ME
Report of the Education Commission, 1893. 8vo. Christchurch, 1894.　MG 1 S 20
ESTIMATES. [*See* FINANCE.]
FINANCE. Appropriations chargeable on the Consolidated Fund and other Accounts, March, 1895. Sm. fol. Wellington, 1895.　　　ME
Correspondence relating to the 3½ per cent. loan, 1891. Sm. fol. Wellington, 1891.　MF 4 U 11
Financial Statements, 1891, 1894. 2 vols. sm. fol. Wellington, 1891-95.　　　ME
Public Accounts, 1889-91. 2 vols. sm. fol. Wellington, 1890-91.　　　ME
Public Accounts Committee, 1892. Sm. fol. Wellington, 1892.　MF 4 T 14
FRIENDLY SOCIETIES. Friendly Societies. Sm. fol. Wellington, 1894.　　　ME
HARBOUR AND QUARANTINE REGULATIONS for the Ports of New Zealand. 12mo. Wellington, 1868.　MF 1 P 68
HOSPITALS. Dunedin Hospital Commission. Sm. fol. Wellington, 1891.　MA 2 Q 12 †
Report on Hospitals and Charitable Institutions in the Colony. Sm. fol. Wellington, 1892.　MA 0 Q 12 †
MARINE DEPARTMENT: Report, 1891-92. Sm. fol. Wellington, 1892.　　　ME
MINES. General and special rules for Coalmines under the Coalmines Act, 1891. Roy. 8vo. Wellington, 1891.　MA 3 R 62
Goldfields, Roads, Water-races, and other Works in connection with Mining. Sm. fol. Wellington, 1891.　ME
The Mines Statement; by the Hon. R. J. Seddon; and Report on the Goldfields of New Zealand. Sm. fol. Wellington, 1893.　　　ME
Mining Machinery and Treatment of Ores in Australian Colonies. Sm. fol. Wellington, 1889.　MA 2 Q 32 †

NEW ZEALAND—*contd.*
MINES—*contd.*
Papers and Reports relating to Minerals and Mining. Sm. fol. Wellington, 1894. ME
Report of the Commissioners upon the Grey Valley Coal-mines. Sm. fol. Wellington, 1891. MA 2 Q 5 †
Report on Coal-mines of New Zealand, 1891. Sm. fol. Wellington, 1892. ME
Reports on the Mining Industry in New Zealand, 1890-92. 3 vols. sm. fol. Wellington, 1890-92. ME

NATIVE AFFAIRS. Report on Middle Island Native Claims. Sm fol. Wellington, 1891. MF 4 U 14
Report on the Claims of Natives to Wairarapa Lakes and adjacent lands. Sm. fol. Wellington, 1891. MF 4 U 16

PARLIAMENTARY DEBATES. Vols. 64, 65, 71–74, 83–86. 10 vols. 8vo. Wellington, 1889-94. ME

PATENTS, DESIGNS, AND TRADE-MARKS. Sm. fol. Wellington, 1894. ME

POST AND TELEGRAPHS. Papers on the Ocean Mail Services. Sm. fol. Wellington, 1892. MF 4 U 17
Report of the Department, 1891. Sm. fol. Wellington, 1891. ME
Report of the Postal and Telegraph Conference, 1894. Sm. fol. Wellington, 1894. MF 4 T 1

PUBLIC WORKS. Public Works Statement, 1892. Sm fol. Wellington, 1893. ME

RAILWAYS. North Island Main Trunk Railway Committee. Sm fol. Wellington, 1892. MA 2 Q 6 †
Railway Works under the Co-öperative System. Sm. fol. Wellington, 1892. MF 4 U 10
Report on Working Railways, 1891, 1894. 2 vols. sm. fol. Wellington, 1891-94. ME

REPRESENTATION COMMISSION. Report of. Sm. fol. Wellington, 1892. MF 4 U 15

STATISTICS. Report on the Statistics of New Zealand, 1889-90. 2 vols. 8vo. Wellington, 1891. ME
Statistics of the Colony, 1891 and 1893. 2 vols. sm. fol. Wellington, 1892-94. ME

STATUTES. Coal Mines Act of 1891. 4to. Wellington, 1892. MF 3 U 53
The Labour Laws of New Zealand. 8vo. Wellington, 1894. MF 4 R 21
Mining Act of 1891. 4to. Wellington, 1892. MF 3 U 52
Ordinances of New Munster, 1839, and of the Province of Nelson, 1853-63; to which are added, the Imperial Acts relating to the Constitution of New Zealand. 8vo. Nelson, 1864. MF 3 T 30

STOCK AND BRANDS. Annual Sheep Returns, 1891-93. 3 vols. sm. fol. Wellington, 1891-93. ME

NEW ZEALAND ALMANAC, COMMERCIAL HAND BOOK, AND DIRECTORY, 1888 and 1889. 2 vols. 8vo. Auckland, 1888-89. ME 1 S

NEW ZEALAND CO. Copies of Despatches from the Governor, enclosing or having reference to Reports and Awards made by Mr. Spain, Commissioner of Land Claims, upon the Titles, to Land of the New Zealand Company. Sm. fol. Lond., 1846. MF 3 U 21
Reports of the Directors of, 1844-45. 2 vols 8vo. Lond., 1844-45. ME 15 J
Report of the Select Committee on Loan for Defraying the Debt of the Colony to the New Zealand Company. Sm. fol. Lond., 1857. MF 3 U 22

NEW ZEALAND ILLUSTRATED ANNUAL, 1881. 8vo. Christchurch, 1881. MJ 3 S 4

NEW ZEALAND INSTITUTE. Anniversary Address of the President, 1883. [*See* Jervois, Sir W. F. D.] MA 2 U 57
Transactions and Proceedings of. Vols. 25, 26. 8vo. Wellington, 1893-94. ME 2 R

NEW ZEALAND LOAN AND MERCANTILE AGENCY CO. Annual Review of the Victorian Wool and Grain Markets, 1892-93. 8vo. Melb., 1893. MF 1 S 31

NEW ZEALAND UNIVERSITY. Calendar, 1875, 1877. 2 vols. 8vo. Christchurch, 1875-77. ME 5 U
Minutes of Proceedings of the Session of the Senate of the University of New Zealand 1876-77. 2 vols. 4 o. Christchurch, 1876-77. ME

NEWBERRY, John S. Fossil Fishes and Fossil Plants of the Triassic Rocks of New Jersey and the Connecticut Valley. (U.S. Geol. Survey, 14.) 4to. Wash., 1888. E
Palæozoic Fishes of North America. (U.S. Geol. Survey, 16.) 4to. Wash., 1889. E

NEWBERRY, Percy E. Beni Hasan, Parts 1 and 2, with Appendix, Plans, and Measurements of the Tombs; by G. W. Fraser. (Egypt Exploration Fund.) Illustrated. 2 vols. 4to. Lond., 1893. B 12 T 2, 3 †
El Bersheh. Part 1. The Tomb of Tehuti Hotep. (Egypt Exploration Fund.) 4to. Lond., 1894. B 2 P 22 †

NEWBERY, J. Cosmo. Notes on the Dressing of Tin Ore. 8vo. Melb., 1883. MA 3 S 45
Some new localities for Minerals in Victoria. (Roy. Soc., Vict., 16.) 8vo. Melb., 1880. ME 1 P
Dressing of Tin Ore. (Roy. Soc., Vict., 20.) 8vo. Melb., 1884. ME 1 P
The Examination of Waters. (Roy. Soc., Vict., 22.) 8vo. Melb., 1886. ME 1 P

NEWCOMB, Prof. Simon. Astronomical Papers prepared for the use of the American Ephemeris and Nautical Almanac. Vols. 2 and 3. 4to. Washington, 1891. E
Observations of the Transit of Venus, December 8-9, 1874. 4to. Washington, 1890. A 39 Q 17 ‡
Principles of Political Economy. 8vo. New York, 1885. F 10 Q 28

NEWELL, Rev. E. J. History of the Welsh Church to the Dissolution of the Monasteries. 8vo. Lond., 1895.
G 15 S 28

NEWINGTONIAN, The, Nos. 5-9, 11, 12, 23, 39, 40-42 8vo. Sydney, 1885-94.
ME 15 Q

NEWLAND, Surg.-Capt. A. G. E. The Image of War; or, Service on the Chin Hills; with an Introductory Historical Note by J. D. Macnabb. Illustrated. 4to. Calcutta, 1894.
D 12 S 15 †

NEWLAND, S. Paving the Way: a Romance of the Australian Bush. 12mo. Lond., 1893.
MJ 1 U 33

NEWMAN, Edward. Illustrated Natural History of British Butterflies and Moths. Roy. 8vo. Lond., 1884.
A 30 V 13

NEWMAN, Prof. Francis Wm. Against Hero-making in Religion. [*See* Religious Phamphlets, 2.]
G 9 V 17
Ancient Sacrifice. [*See* Religious Pamphlets, 2.] G 9 V 17
Causes of Atheism. [*See* Religious Pamphlets, 2.]
G 9 V 17
The Controversy about Prayer. [*See* Religious Pamphlets, 2.]
G 9 V 17
Defective Morality of the New Testament. [*See* Religious Pamphlets, 2.]
G 9 V 17
Phases of Faith; or, Passages from the History of my Creed. 2nd ed. 8vo. Lond., 1853.
G 19 P 29
Relations of Theism to Pantheism and on the Galla Religion. [*See* Religious Pamphlets, 2.] G 9 V 17
Religious Weakness of Protestantism. [*See* Religious Pamphlets, 2.]
G 9 V 17
The true Temptation of Jesus. [*See* Religious Pamphlets, 2.]
G 9 V 17

NEWMAN, G. M. The Northern Territory and its Gold-fields. 8vo. Adelaide, 1875.
MA 2 V 62

NEWMAN, John Henry, Cardinal. Discussions and Arguments on various subjects. 8vo. Lond., 1878.
G 1 U 8
Essays: Critical and Historical. 2 vols. 8vo. Lond., 1877.
G 1 U 5, 6
Essays on Biblical and on Ecclesiastical Miracles. 8vo. Lond., 1875.
G 1 U 7
Fifteen Sermons preached before the University of Oxford. 8vo. Lond., 1872.
G 1 U 10
History of my Religious Opinions. 8vo. Lond., 1865.
G 15 P 33
Loss and Gain. 8vo. Lond., 1876.
G 1 U 9
Parochial and Plain Sermons. Vols. 2-5, 7, 8. 6 vols. 8vo. Lond., 1873-78.
G 1 U 13-16, 18, 19
Sermons bearing on Subjects of the Day. 8vo. Lond., 1879.
G 1 U 11
The Via Media of the Anglican Church. 2 vols. 8vo. Lond., 1877.
G 1 U 3, 4
Verses on various occasions. 8vo. Lond., 1889.
H 9 U 35
Sketch of. [*See* Smalley, G. W.—Studies of Men.]
C 19 R 20

NEWSHOLME, Dr. Arthur. Treatise on Public Health [*See* Palmberg, Dr. A.]
A 33 T 19

NEWTON, Sir Isaac. [Plaster Cast of.] [*See* Hutton, L. —Portraits in Plaster.]
A 23 V 13

NICHOL, Prof. John. Life and Philosophy of Francis Bacon. [*See* Bacon, Francis.]
G 9 V 11, 12

NICHOLAS, Wm. The Coolgardie Gold-fields, Western Australia. Illustrated. 8vo. Melb., 1895.
MD 8 P 17
New System of Winding in Deep Mining Shafts. 8vo. Melb., 1884.
MA 3 T 19

NICHOLLS, Dr. H. A. Alford. Text-book of Tropical Agriculture. 12mo. Lond., 1892.
A 18 Q 33

NICHOLS, Prof. Edward L. Laboratory Manual of Physics and Applied Electricity. Vol. 1. Junior Course in General Physics. Vol. 2. Senior Course and Outlines of Advanced Work. 8vo. New York, 1894.
A 21 S 25, 26

NICHOLS, George Robt. Trial of. [*See* Parramatta River Murders.]
MG 1 Q 53

NICHOLS, Thos. Handy-book of the British Museum for Every-day Readers. 8vo. Lond., 1870.
K 7 S 43

NICHOLS, Wm. Ripley. Publications of the Massachusetts Institute of Technology, 1862-93. 8vo. Boston, 1893.
K 7 S 37

NICHOLSON, George. Illustrated Dictionary of Gardening. 4 vols. roy. 8vo. Lond. (n.d.)
K 11 R 13-16

NICHOLSON, Gilbert. Notes on a visit to North Hullabor Plains. (Roy. Geog. Soc. Australasia, Vic. Branch, 9.) 8vo. Melb., 1892.
ME 20

NICHOLSON, John H. Hubert, and other Poems. 12mo. Brisb., 1871.
MH 1 P 56

NICHOLSON, Dr. Joseph Shield. Historical Progress and Ideal Socialism. 8vo. Lond., 1894. F 8 U 49
Principles of Political Economy. Vol. 1. 8vo. Lond., 1893.
F 8 Q 34

NICHOLSON, Renton. The Lord Chief Baron Nicholson: an Autobiography. 12mo. Lond. (n.d.)
C 17 P 29

NICKLIN, T. *Trans.*—Constitutional Antiquities of Sparta and Athens. [*See* Gilbert, Dr. G.]
F 9 T 22

NICOL, John. Life and Adventures of. 12mo. Edinb., 1822*.
MC 1 P 50

NICOLAY, John George. Abraham Lincoln. [*See* Lincoln, A.]
F 8 T 25, 26

NICOLL, Rev. Dr. Wm. Robertson. Expositor's Bible. [*See* Expositor's Bible.]
G 19 R and S

NICOLLS, C. F. Rise and Progress of Quartz Mining at Clunes. 12mo. Ballarat, 1889. MA 3 P 55

NICOLSON, Rev. Dr. Wm. Review of the Rev. Dr. Guthrie's Letter on the Organ Question. 8vo. Sydney, 1883. MG 1 R 71

NIEBUHR, Bartho-d Georg. [Sketch of.] [See Müller, F. Max.—Chips from a German Workshop.] J 9 R 32

NIELSEN, A. E. The Vortices Demonstration of Nature; or, the Philosophy of Obscurant Astronomy. 8vo. Melb., 1882. MA 1 T 62

NIETNER, J. The Coffee Tree and its Enemies; being Observations on the Natural History of the Enemies of the Coffee Tree in Ceylon. 8vo. Colombo, 1880. A 18 S 34

NINETEENTH CENTURY, The. Vols. 32–36. Roy. 8vo. Lond., 1892–94. E

NISBET, Hume. A Face at the Window. [See Praed, Mrs. Campbell.—Under the Gum Tree.] MJ 2 T 44
The Savage Queen: a Romance of the Natives of Van Diemen's Land. 12mo. Lond., 1892. MJ 3 P 16

NISBET, Dr. John. British Forest Trees and their Sylvicultural Characteristics and Treatment. 8vo. Lond., 1893. A 18 Q 22
The Forester. [See Brown, Dr. J.] A 32 T 9, 10
Studies in Forestry: being a short Course of Lectures on the Principles of Sylviculture. 12mo. Oxford, 1894. A 18 R 33

NISH, Rev. James. Is Marriage with a Deceased Wife's Sister forbidden in Scripture? 8vo. Melb., 1873. MG 2 Q 23

NISSER, Pedro. The Patent Gunpowder invented by Pedro Nisser. 8vo. Melb., 1865. MA 2 P 46

NITTI, Prof. Francesco S. Catholic Socialism. Translated by Mary Mackintosh. 8vo. Lond., 1895. F 11 U 17
Population and the Social System. 12mo. Lond., 1894. F 11 P 72

NIVEN, F. W., & Co. Niven's Guide Book and Souvenir of Ballarat. 12mo. Ballarat, 1885. MD 1 Q 49

NIXON, Rt. Rev. Francis Russell. Aborigines of Tasmania. 4to. Hobart (n.d.) MA 45 ‡

NOBLE, James Ashcroft. Impressions and Memories. 8vo. Lond., 1895. D 14 S 9
The Sonnet in England, and other Essays. 12mo. Lond., 1893. J 6 P 8

NOBLE, John. Illustrated Official Handbook of the Cape and South Africa. 8vo. Lond., 1893. D 14 S 9

NOBLESSE OBLIGE. [See Evans, H.]

NODAL, John H., and MILNER, George. Glossary of the Lancashire Dialect. 8vo. Manchester, 1875. J 2 T 10

NOEHDEN, Dr. G. H. Grammar of the German Language. 8vo. Lond., 1843. J 9 P 29

NOICE, C S. Trades Directory of City and Suburbs, 1893–95. 3 vols. 8vo. Sydney, 1893–95. ME

NOIRET, Hippolyte. Lettres inedites de Michel Apostolis. [See Michael Apostolius.] J 7 U 36

NOLASCO, José Antonio. Recopilacion de Leyes, Decretos, Reglamentos, órdenes i circulares de carácter jeneral que se refieren especialmente a la Guardia Nacional de Chile. Roy. 8vo. Santiago, 1890. F 7 U 19

NOLLEKENS, Joseph, and his times; by J. T. Smith; edited, with Essay on Georgian Sculpture, by E. Gosse. 8vo. Lond., 1895. C 21 R 18

NORDAU, Max. Conventional Lies of our Civilization. 8vo. Lond., 1895. F 11 U 13
Paradoxes. 8vo. Chicago, 1896. F 6 S 41

NORGATE, G. Le G. [Life of] G. R. Fitzgerald, "Fighting Fitzgerald," 1748–96. (Lives of Twelve Bad Men.) 8vo. Lond., 1894. C 18 T 9

NORMAN Henry. Peoples and Politics of the Far East: Travels and Studies in the British, French, Spanish, and Portuguese Colonies, Siberia, China, Japan, Korea, Siam, and Malaya. Illustrated. 8vo. Lond., 1895. D 18 V 17

NORMAN Philip. London Signs and Inscriptions. 8vo. Lond., 1893. B 24 R 4

NORTH, Rev. A. Some Chapters of Baptist History. 12mo. Dunedin, 1894. MG 2 R 49

NORTH, Alfred John. Description of Eggs of three species of South Australian Parrakeets. [See Ibis, The, 1894.] E

NORTH, Marianne. Some further Recollections of a Happy Life, 1859–69. 8vo. Lond., 1893. D 20 R 3

NORTH AMERICAN REVIEW. Vols. 155–160. 8vo. New York, 1893–95. E

NORTH BRITISH AGRICULTURIST, 1892–94. 3 vols. fol. Edinb., 1892–94. E

NORTH CAROLINA.—State Departments, Reports, and Publications.
AGRICULTURAL EXPERIMENT STATION. North Carolina Weather during 1894. 8vo. Raleigh, 1895. E
Report of the Meteorological Division, 1892. 8vo. Raleigh, 1893. E
Work during 1894. 8vo. Raleigh, 1895. E

NORTH TERRIBLE DICK SILVER-MINING CO. Memorandum and Articles of Association. 8vo. Sydney (n.d.) MF 4 R 35

NORTH-WESTERN UNIVERSITY, Chicago. Catalogue, 1892, 1893. 8vo. Chicago, 1892. E

NORTHALL, G. F. Folk-phrases of Gloucestershire, Staffordshire, Warwickshire, Worcestershire. (Eng. Dial. Soc. Pubs.) 8vo. Lond., 1894. E

NORTHAMPTON LUNATIC HOSPITAL, Mass. Report for year ending September, 1893. 8vo. Boston, 1893. E

NORTHERN AGRICULTURAL ASSOCIATION, SINGLETON, N.S.W. Members' Pamphlet, 1881-82, 1884-85, 1895. 5 vols. 8vo. Singleton, 1881-95. ME 9 P

NORTON, A. Tuberculosis. (Proc. Roy. Soc., Queensland, 10.) 8vo. Brisbane, 1893. ME 1 T

NORTON, Chas. Eliot. Orations and Addresses of G. W. Curtis. [See Curtis, G. W.] F 14 U 1-3
Letters of J. R. Lowell. 2 vols. 8vo. New York, 1894. C 17 S 11, 12

NORTON, Hon. Mrs. Caroline E. S. Fisher's Drawing-room Scrap-book, 1847-48. 2 vols. sm. to. Lond., 1847-48. H 2 V 7, 8

NORTON, John. Reid, the Wriggler; or, the False Prophet of Freetrade tried and convicted on his Professions, Promises, and Performances; by "John English." 8vo. Sydney, 1895. MF 4 R 52

NORWAY. The Fisheries of Norway and their Products. 8vo. Chicago (n.d.) A 30 R 2

NOTES AND QUERIES: a Medium of Intercommunication for Literary Men, General Readers, &c. 8th series. Vols. 2-6. Sm. 4to. Lond., 1892-94. E

NOTTAGE, Charles G. In search of a Climate. Roy. 8vo. Lond., 1894. MD 6 U 21

NOVA SCOTIA. Education: a Conspectus of the Public Free School System. 8vo. Halifax, 1893. G 18 S 4

NOVATIAN. Writings of. (Ante-Nicene Christian Library.) 8vo. Edinb., 1869. G 14 U 13

NOVY, Dr. Frederick G. Directions for Laboratory Work in Bacteriology. Roy. 8vo. Ann Arbor, Mich., 1894. A 27 U 20

NOYES, Rev. Dr. George R. Collection of Theological Essays from various Authors. 2nd ed. 8vo. Boston, 1857. G 8 S 34

NOYES, Dr. Henry D. Diseases of the Eye. [*See* Knies, Dr. M.] A 33 U 10

NUGENT, Hon. Mrs. Greville-. A Land of Mosques and Marabouts. 8vo. Lond., 1894. D 14 S 13

NUMBER ONE. [*See* Tynan, P. J. P.]

NUMISMATIC AND ANTIQUARIAN SOCIEY OF PHILADELPHIA. Report of the Proceedings of, 1880-81. 2 vols. 8vo. Phi!ad., 1881-82. E

NUNN, John. Narrative of the Wreck of the *Favorite* on the Island of Desolation: an Historical Account of the Island, and its Whale and Seal Fisheries. Edited by Dr. W. B. Clarke. 8vo. Lond., 1850. D 4 S 42

NUTT, Alfred. The Irish Vision of the Happy Otherworld. [*See* Meyer, Kuno.—The Voyage of Bran.] B 36 P 9

NYST, P. H. Conchyliologie des Terrains Tertiaires de la Belgique. [*See* Musée Royal d'Histoire Naturelle de Belgique, Annales du.] A 6 V and W †

O

OAHSPE: a new Bible in the words of Jehovah and his angel ambassadors. Sm. 4to. Boston, 1891. G 1 T 20
Selections from. 4to. (n.p.n.d.) G 1 T 21

OATES, John. The Teaching of Tennyson. 8vo. Lond. (n.d.) J S T 35

OATES, Rev. Dr. Titus. [Life of], 1649-1705; by T. Seccombe. (Lives of Twelve Bad Men.) 8vo. Lond., 1894. C 18 T 9
An Exact Discovery of the Mystery of Iniquity as it is now practised among the Jesuits. [*See* Bibliotheca Curiosa.] J 18 Q 32

OBALSKI, J. Mines and Minerals of the Province of Quebec. Roy. 8vo. (n.p.n.d.) A 24 V 16

O'BRIEN, Mr. Cross Purposes: a Farce. [*See* London Stage, 2.] H 2 S 34

O'BRIEN, James Bronterre. Portrait of. [*See* Gammage, R. G.—Chartist Movement.] F 7 R 24

O'BRIEN, R. Barry. The Autobiography of Theobald Wolfe Tone, 1763-98; edited, with an introduction, by R. B. O'Brien. 2 vols. roy. 8vo. Lond., 1893. C 19 S 1, 2

OBSERVATORY, The: a Monthly Review of Astronomy. Vols. 1-17, 1877-94. 8vo. Lond., 1878-94. E

OCEAN CAVERN, The: a tale of the Tonga Isles, in three cantos. 8vo. Lond., 1819. MH 1 S 39

O'CONNOR, Feargus. Portrait of. [*See* Gammage, R. G.—Chartist Movement.] F 7 R 24

O'CONNOR, Richard Edward. Digest of Criminal and Magistrates' Cases. [*See* Watkins, J. L.] MF 1 Q 61

O'CONNOR, Thos. Power. Irish Representation in the Imperial Parliament. [*See* Subjects of the Day, 3.] F 7 U 28

ODE to His Royal Highness on his Birthday. Sm. fol. Lond., 1730. H 30 Q 13 ‡

O'DONNELL, Capt. H. Historical Records of the 14th Regiment, now the Prince of Wales's Own (West Yorkshire Regiment), from its formation in 1685 to 1892. [Illustrated.] 8vo. Devonport, 1893. B 22 R 7

O'DONOGHUE D. J. Humour of Ireland. 8vo. Lond., 1894. J 9 S 28

O'DONOGHUE, Freeman M. Descriptive and Classified Catalogue of Portraits of Queen Elizabeth. Roy. 8vo. Lond., 1894. K 11 R 11

OELSNER, H. Influence of Dante on Modern Thought. 12mo. Lond., 1895. J 12 S 41

OFFICER, Graham. Further Note on the Glacial Deposits of Bacchus Marsh. (Proceedings Royal Society, Victoria, n.s., 6.) 8vo. Melb., 1894. ME 1 P

—— BALFOUR, L., and HOGG, E. G. Geological Notes on the Country between Strahan and Lake St. Clair, Tasmania. (Proc. Roy. Soc., Vict., n.s., 7.) 8vo. Melb., 1895 ME 1 P

OFFORD, Joseph, jun. Recent Discoveries in Classical Literature. [*See* Roy. Soc. of Lit., 2nd series, 16.] E
Recent Discoveries in Patristic Literature. [*See* Roy Soc. of Lit., 2nd series, 16.] E

OGG, Rev. C. The Institution. (Divinity Hall Record.) 8vo. Brisbane, 1879. ME 15 Q

OGILBY, J. Douglas. Catalogue of Australian Mammals (Australian Museum.) Roy. 8vo. Sydney, 1892. MA 2 U 42
Edible Fishes and Crustaceans of New South Wales. Roy. 8vo. Sydney, 1893. MA 2 U 42

OGLE, Arthur The Marquis d'Argenson: a Study in Criticism; being the Stanhope Essay, Oxford, 1893. 12mo. Lond., 1893. C 19 Q 16

O'GORMAN, Edith. [*See* Auffray, Mrs.]

O'HARA, John Bernard. Songs of the South. 2nd Series. 8vo. Lond., 1895. MH 1 V 3

O'HARA, Kane. Midas: a Burletta. [*See* London Stage, 1.] H 2 S 33
Tom Thumb: a Burlesque Opera. [*See* London Stage, 1.] H 2 S 34
The Two Misers: a Musical Entertainment. [*See* London Stage, 3.] H 2 S 35

O'HARA, P. K. The Maid of Millewa: an Australian Poem. 12mo. Melb., 1878. MH 1 U 23

O'HEA, Wm. Joseph. The Introduction of New Rural Industries into Victoria, and the Utilisation of Juvenile Labor at the disposal of the State. 8vo. Melb., 1871. MA 1 Q 57

OHIO AGRICULTURAL EXPERIMENT STATION. Bulletin of, for May, 1890. 8vo. Columbus, 1890. E
Reports for 1889, 1890. 2 vols. 8vo. Columbus, 1889-91. E

OHIO STATE UNIVERSITY. Catalogue for 1892, 1893. 8vo. Columbus, 1893. E

OHM, George Simon. Scientific Work of. [*See* Smithsonian Institution.—Report, 1891.] E

OHRWALDER, Rev. Joseph. Ten Years' Captivity in the Mahdi's Camp, 1882-92; from the original manuscripts of Father Joseph Ohrwalder, by Major F. R. Wingate. 2nd ed. 8vo. Lond., 1892. D 14 T 20

OKA, A. Observations on Fresh-water Polyzoa. 8vo. (n.p.n.d.) A 30 V 17

O'KELLY, E. de P. Arrowing and its Relation to Disorder in Sugar-cane. 8vo. Sydney, 1893. MA 1 Q 67

OLD COLONIST, An. [*See* Battle of the Yarra.] MJ 1 P 60

OLD HOUSEKEEPER, An. [*See* Australian Housewives' Manual.] MA 3 P 60

OLD ROAD AND NEW ROADS. 12mo. Lond., 1832. J 10 T 31

OLD SALT, An. [*See* Situation, The.] MF 3 Q 84

OLDEN, Rev. Charles. Immorality, its fascinating temptations, its awful consequences, and the way to avoid it. 8vo. Sydney, 1885. MG 1 S 73

OLESON, Prof. W. B. Picturesque Hawaii. [*See* Stevens, Hon. J. L.] MB 2 Q 4 †

OLDHAM, Thos. Portrait of. [*See* Ramsay, Sir A. C.— Memoir of.] C 21 R 20

OLIN, W. M. Polls, Property, Taxes, &c., Massachusetts, May 1, 1892. 8vo. Boston, 1893. E
Number of Polls, Voters, and Persons who voted, Massachusetts, 1892. 8vo. Boston, 1893. E

OLIPHANT, Mrs. Margaret O. W. The Makers of Florence: Dante, Giotto, Savonarola, and their City. 8vo. Lond., 1892. B 30 Q 20
Historical Sketches of the Reign of Queen Anne. 8vo. Lond., 1894. B 36 Q 6
Thomas Chalmers, Preacher, Philosopher, and Statesman. 8vo. Lond., 1893. C 13 Q 26

OLIVE CULTURE, reprinted from *S. A. Advertiser.* 8vo. Adelaide, 1877. MA 1 P 70

OLIVER, Dr. Chas. A. The Comparative Action of Sulphate of Daturia and of Sulphate of Hyoscyamia upon the Iris and Ciliary Muscle. 8vo. Philad., 1882. A 26 U 20

Description of a Revolving Astigmatic Disk. 8vo. Philad., 1883. A 26 U 20

A New Series of Berlin Wools for the scientific detection of subnormal Color-perception (Color-blindness). 8vo. Philad., 1886. A 26 U 20

Third Annual Report of the Ophthalmological Department of the State Hospital at Norristown, Pa., for 1858. 8vo. Philad., 1888. A 26 U 20

OLIVER, Dr. Daniel. Illustrations of the principal natural orders of the Vegetable Kingdom, prepared for the Science and Art Department of the Council of Education. Imp. 8vo. Lond., 1893. A 31 P 1

OLIVER, Dr. F. W. Natural History of Plants. [*See* Kerner von Marilaun, A.*]* A 22 V 2

OLIVER, John. Milk, Cheese, and Butter: a Practical Hand-book on their Properties and the Processes of their Production, including a Chapter on Cream and the methods of its separation from Milk. Illustrated. 8vo. Lond., 1894. A 18 R 34

OLIVER & BOYD. Edinburgh Almanac and National Repository, 1893-95. 3 vols. 12mo. Edinb., 1893-95. E

OLLIFF, Arthur Sidney. The Codlin Moth, its Life-history and Habits. 8vo. Sydney, 1892. MA 1 Q 66

Insect Pests: The Maize Moth. 8vo. Sydney, 1890. MA 1 Q 66

Woolly Aphis; or, American Blight. 8vo. Sydney, 1892. MA 1 Q 66

Entomological Notes: Bronzy Orange Bug; Two little-known Insects affecting Fruit Trees; Potato Moth, Migratory Locust, &c. 8vo. Sydney, 1892. MA 1 Q 66

Report on a Visit to the Clarence River District for the purpose of ascertaining the nature and extent of Insect Ravages in the sugar-cane crops. 8vo. Sydney, 1893. MA 1 Q 66

OMAN, Chas. Europe, 476-918. (Periods of European History, Period 1.) 12mo. Lond., 1893. B 25 Q 13

ON EITHER SIDE OF THE RED SEA; with Illustrations of the Granite Ranges of the Eastern Desert of Egypt and Sinai. 8vo. Lond., 1895. D 14 S 20

ON POETRY; a Rhapsody. Sm. fol. Dublin, 1733. H 39 Q 13‡

ONCE A MONTH: a Magazine of Australasia; conducted by Rev. Dr. P. Mercer. Vols. 1-4, 1884-86. 8vo. Melb., 1884-86. ME 7 Q

ONE OF THEM. [*See* Seven Rovers.] MD 5 R 47

ONGANIA, Ferd. Streets and Canals in Venice. L. fol. Venezia, 1893. D 34 Q 13‡

La Basilica di San Marco in Venezia. Fol. Venezia, 1881. A 40 R 18 †

ONSLOW, Earl of. State Socialism and Labour Government in Antipodean Britain. [*See* Roy. Col. Inst., Proc., 25.] E

Yachting in New Zealand. [*See* Sullivan, Sir E.—Yachting.] A 29 Q 41

ONTARIO.—*State Departments, Reports, and Publications.*

AGRICULTURAL COLLEGE AND EXPERIMENTAL FARM. Report 1889-93. 4 vols. roy. 8vo. Toronto, 1890-94. E

AGRICULTURE AND ARTS ASSOCIATION. Report, 1892. 8vo. Toronto, 1893. E

BUREAU OF INDUSTRIES. Reports, 1890, 1891. 2 vols. roy. 8vo. Toronto, 1891-92. E

BUREAU OF MINES. Report, 1891. 8vo. Toronto, 1892. E

Catalogue of the Mineral Exhibit of the Province of Ontario. [Chicago Exhibition, 1893.] Roy. 8vo. Toronto, 1893. K 7 U 10

Report of Royal Commission on the Mineral Resources of Ontario, and Measures for their Development. Roy. 8vo. Toronto, 1890. A 24 V 30

COMMISSION ON THE DEHORNING OF CATTLE. Report. 8vo. Toronto, 1892. A 32 T 15

DAIRYMEN'S AND CREAMERIES' ASSOCIATIONS. Reports, 1892. 8vo. Toronto, 1893. E

DEPARTMENT OF AGRICULTURE. Report, 1892. Roy. 8vo. Toronto, 1893. E

EDUCATION DEPARTMENT. Acts relating to the Education Department: Public and High Schools and Truancy. Roy. 8vo. Toronto, 1891. F 2 T 20

Examination Papers. 8vo. Toronto, 1893. G 18 R 44

Regulations and Correspondence relating to French and German Schools in the Province of Ontario. 8vo. Toronto, 1889. G 18 S 2

FRUITGROWERS' ASSOCIATION. Reports, 1885-87, 1889-91. 6 vols. 8vo. Toronto, 1886-92. E

INSTITUTION FOR THE EDUCATION OF THE DEAF AND DUMB. Report, 1892. Roy. 8vo. Toronto, 1893. E

VETERINARY COLLEGE. Annual Announcement, 1893-94. 8vo. Toronto, 1893. E

OPPERT, Dr. Gustav. On the Original Inhabitants of Bharatavarsa, or India. 8vo. Lond., 1893. A 18 S 21

ORANGE FREE LAND CO. Memorandum and Articles of Association. 8vo. Sydney (n.d.)
MF 4 R 35

ORANGE INSTITUTION OF N.S.W. Laws and Regulations of. (Pam.) 8vo. Sydney, 1868.
MG 1 Q 35

ORDISH, T. Fairman. Early London Theatres. 8vo. Lond., 1894.
H 1 S 30

OREGON—*General*. Resources of the State of. 8vo. Salem, 1893.
D 15 T 17

Resources of Eastern Oregon. 8vo. Salem, 1892.
D 15 R 15

Arbor Day, 1891. 8vo. Salem, 1891.
G 18 R 31.

OREGON—STATE BOARD OF HORTICULTURE. First and Second Biennial Reports, 1891 and 1892. 2 vols. 8vo. Portland, 1891-93.
E

Bulletin No. 8. 8vo. Portland, 1894.
A 32 R 7

O'REILLY, John Boyle. [Plaster Cast of.] [*See* Hutton, L.—Portraits in Plaster.]
A 23 V 13

O'RELL, Max. [*See* Blouet, P.]

ORFORD, Earl of. [*See* Walpole, Horace.]

ORIGEN. Beginnings of Christian Philosophy. [*See* Westcott, Rt. Rev. B. F.—Religious Thought in the West.]
G 2 U 37

Writings of; translated by Rev. F. Crombie. (Ante-Nicene Christ. Lib., 10, 23.) 2 vols. 8vo. Edinb., 1869.
G 14 U 10, and 23,

ORLEANS, Prince Henri d' Around Tonkin and Siam. 8vo. Lond., 1894
D 14 T 12

ORMEROD, Eleanor A. Letter from. (Proc. Roy. Agricult. and Horticult. Soc., S. Aust., 1882). 8vo. Adelaide, 1882.
ME 1 S

A Manual of Injurious Insects, with Methods of Prevention and Remedy for their attacks to Food Crops, Forest Trees, and Fruit. 8vo. Lond., 1890.
A 27 T 24

Report of Observations of Injurious Insects and Common Farm Pests, 1892, 1894. 2 vols. roy. 8vo. Lond., 1893-95.
E

OSBORN, Dr. Henry Fairfield. From the Greeks to Darwin: an Outline of the Development of the Evolution Idea. 8vo. New York, 1894.
A 30 U 5

OSBORN, Prof. Henry Stafford. The Prospector's Field-Book and Guide. 8vo. Philad., 1892.
A 24 Q 17

OSBORNE, W. H. Digest of the Questions set by the Boards of Examiners for Barristers and Solicitors, 1887. 12mo. Brisbane, 1888.
MK 1 P 44

2 D

OSBOURNE, L. The Ebb-tide. [*See* Stevenson, R. L.]
MJ 3 Q 34

The Wrong Box. [*See* Stevenson, R. L.]
J 12 R 31

O'SHANASSY, Sir John. Primary Education in Victoria: Speeches by, together with his Amending Bill and the Imperial Act recently passed upon the same question with reference to intermediate education in Ireland. 2nd ed. 8vo. Melb., 1878.
MG 2 Q 30

O'SHAUGHNESSY, Arthur; his Life and Work; with Selections from his Poems, by Louise C. Moulton. 12mo. Lond, 1894.
C 14 P 32

OSMOND, Sophie. Dulgabeena: an Australian Story. 12mo. Melb., 1894.
MJ 3 P 20

OSTROGORSKI, M. The Rights of Women: a Comparative Study in History and Legislation. 12mo. Lond, 1893.
F 14 Q 30

OSTWALD, Prof. Wilhelm. Manual of Physico-Chemical Measurements. Translated by Dr. J. Walker. 8vo. Lond., 1894.
A 29 V 25

O'SULLIVAN, Edward W. Social, Industrial, Political, and Co-operative Associations, etc., in New South Wales. Roy. 8vo. Sydney, 1892.
MF 1 S 42

OSWEGO NORMAL SCHOOL. [History of.] 8vo. Washington, 1891.
G 18 R 27

OTAGO. The Province of Otago, in New Zealand: its Progress, Present Condition, Resources, and Prospects. 8vo. Dunedin, 1869.
MD 8 R 33

OTAHEITEAN ISLANDS. History of; with an Account of the Society, the Friendly Islands, and the Marquesas; with an Historical Sketch of the Sandwich Islands. 12mo. Edinb., 1800.
MB 1 P 46

OTKEN, Dr. Charles H. The Ills of the South, or related causes hostile to the general prosperity of the Southern People. 8vo. New York, 1894.
F 14 R 27

OTTAWA EXPERIMENTAL FARMS. Reports of Director, Entomologist and Botanist, Chemist, Horticulturalist, Poultry Manager, &c., 1887-93. 7 vols. 8vo. Ottawa, 1888-94.
E

OTTERSON, H. Index to Principal Resolutions passed by, and Motions negatived, withdrawn, and lapsed in the House of Representatives, 1854-92. 12mo. Wellington, 1892.
MF 1 P 78

OTWAY, Thos. The Cheats of Scapin: a Comedy. [*See* London Stage, 4.]
H 2 S 36

The Orphan; or, the Unhappy Marriage: a Tragedy. [*See* London Stage, 3.]
H 2 S 35

OUIDA. [*See* Ramé, L. de la.]

OUR ALMA MATER: a School Journal edited by the Students of St. Ignatius' College, Riverview, 1886-97, 1890, 1893-95. 7 vols. 8vo. Sydney, 1886-95.
ME 15 Q

OUR CELEBRITIES; an Art Annual of Australian Favourites. No. 1. 4to. Sydney, 1895. ME 19 R

OUR COAL AND OUR COAL PITS: the People in them and the Scenes around them. 12mo. Lond., 1853. A 24 P 14

OUR NATIONAL DUTIES in relation to Population, Protection, and Legislation; by "An Ex-member of the National Anti-Corn Law League." 8vo. Melb., 1864. MF 4 R 5

OVALLE, F. O., and ACUNA, R. A. Recopilación de Leyes Constitucionales y Administrativas. Roy. 8vo. Santiago, 1893. F 7 U 17

OVERLAND MONTHLY. 2nd Series, vols. 19-25. 8vo. San Francisco, 1892-95. E

OVIDIUS NASO, Publius. Opera. 3 vols. 8vo. Argentorati, 1807. H 10 R 21-23

OWEN, J. A. [See Visgar, Mrs. H.]

OWEN, Rev. John. The Skeptics of the French Renaissance. 8vo. Lond., 1893. G 4 P 25
The Skeptics of the Italian Renaissance. 8vo. Lond., 1893. G 2 S 33

OWEN, Rev. John W. Some Australian Sermons. 8vo. Lond., 1892. MG 2 Q 15
What the Colonies need: a Plea for a National Church of Australasia. 8vo. Adelaide, 1886. MG 1 S 76

OWEN, Mary A. Old Rabbit, the Voodoo, and other Sorcerers. 8vo. Lond., 1893. J 4 P 14

OWEN, Sir Richard. A Talk with; with Portrait. [See Blathwayt, R.—Interviews.] J 10 U 34
Life of; by Rev. R. Owen. Also an Essay ou Owen's position in Anatomical Science; by Rt. Hon. T. H. Huxley, F.R.S. 2 vols. 8vo. Lond., 1894. C 21 Q 16, 17

OWEN, T. C. Cinchona Planter's Manual. 8vo. Colombo, 1881. A 18 S 36
Tea Planter's Manual. 8vo. Colombo, 1886. A 18 S 33

OXENFORD, John. Trans.—Francis Bacon of Verulam. [See Bacon, Francis.] G 13 S 43

OXFORD UNIVERSITY. Oxford Honours, 1220-1894. 12mo. Oxford, 1894. B 23 Q 16
Calendar, 1893-95. 3 vols. 12mo. Oxford, 1892-94. E

P

PACIFIC ISLAND TRADING CO. Memorandum and Articles of Association of. 8vo. Melb., 1867.
MF 1 Q 31

PACKARD, Dr. Alpheus Spring. Guide to the Study of Insects, and a Treatise on those injurious and beneficial to Crops, for the use of Colleges, Farm-schools, and Agriculturists. 9th ed. Illustrated. Roy. 8vo. New York, 1889. A 30 U 3
The Hessian Fly: its Ravages, Habits, Enemies, and means of preventing its increase. [Map and Illustrations.] 8vo. Washington, 1880. A 32 T 1
Report on the Rocky Mountain Locust and other Insects now injuring or likely to injure Field and Garden Crops. Illustrated. 8vo. Washington, 1877. A 27 U 16
Insects injurious to Forest and Shade Trees. Illustrated. 8vo. Washington, 1881. A 27 U 15

PAGE, David. Geology for General Readers. 8vo. Edinb., 1866. A 20 Q 16
Rudiments of Geology. 12mo. Edinb., 1851.
A 24 P 15
The Past and Present Life of the Globe. 12mo. Edinb., 1861. A 24 R 13

PAGE, Jesse. Among the Maoris; or, Daybreak in New Zealand. 8vo. Lond. (n.d.) MG 2 R 41

PAGE, John Lloyd W. The Rivers of Devon, from Source to Sea. 8vo. Lond., 1893. D 18 R 11

PAGÈS, Léon. Fac-simile reprint of Bibliographie Japonaise. [See Wonckstern, F. von.] J 8 V 23

PAGÈS, Pierre M. F., Vicomte de. Voyages autour du Monde, et vers les Deux Poles, par Terre et par Mer. 1767-76. 2 vols. 8vo. Paris, 1782. MD 8 Q 40, 41

PAIN, A. Queensland Statutes. [See Queensland.]
MF 3 S 24-28

PAINE, Thomas. Writings of, 1774-92. Collected and edited by M. D. Conway. Vols. 1-3. 8vo. New York, 1894-95. J 6 T 22-24
The Age of Reason; being an Investigation of True and Fabulous Theology. 8vo. Paris, 1794. G 2 P 28
Common Sense. 8vo. Philad., 1776. F 4 P 26
A Letter addressed to the Abbé Raynal on the Affairs of North America, in which the Mistakes in the Abbé's Account of the Revolution of America are corrected, and cleared up. 8vo. Dublin, 1782. B 19 V 2
Rights of Man; being an Answer to Mr. Burke's Attack on the French Revolution. 8vo. Dublin, 1791-92.
F 4 P 27
Life of; by Moncure D. Conway: to which is added a sketch of Paine, by Wm. Cobbett. 2 vols. 8vo. New York, 1892. C 8 U 37, 38
[Plaster Cast of.] [See Hutton, L.—Portraits in Plaster.] A 23 V 13

PAINE, Rev. Dr. Timothy O. Solomon's Temple and Capitol Ark of the Flood, and Tabernacle or the Holy Houses. 4to. Lond., 1886. B 40 U 2 ‡

PALAZ, Dr. A. Treatise on Industrial Photometry; with special application to Electric Lighting; translated by G. W. and M. R. Patterson. Roy. 8vo. New York, 1894. A 21 V 15

PALÆOGRAPHICAL SOCIETY. Facsimiles of Ancient Manuscripts, &c. 2nd series, pt. 9. Folio. Lond., 1892. E

PALAEONTOGRAPHICA. Bände 39, 40. 4to. Stuttgart, 1892-93. E

PALÉONTOLOGIE FRANÇAISE. Description des Fossiles de la France. Livraisons, 10, 13, 19, 29-33. 8 vols. 8vo. Paris, 1873-84. E

PALESTINE EXPLORATION FUND. Index to the Quarterly Statement, 1869-92 inclusive. 8vo. Lond., 1893. E

Quarterly Statement for 1892-94. 3 vols. 8vo. Lond., 1892-94. E

PALGRAVE, R. H. Inglis. Dictionary of Political Economy. Vol 1. A-E. 8vo. Lond., 1894. F 7 S 27

PALL MALL MAGAZINE. Vols. 3-6, May, 1894-Aug., 1895. 8vo. Lond., 1894-95. E

PALMBERG, Dr. Albert. Treatise on Public Health and its application in different European countries; translated by Dr. A. Newsholme. Illustrated. 2nd ed. 8vo. Lond., 1895. A 33 T 19

PALMER, Dr. Chas. Skeele. Theoretical Chemistry. [*See* Nernst, Dr. W.] A 21 U 1

PALMER, E. Bovine Pleuro-Pneumonia in Queensland. (Proc. Roy. Soc., Queensland, 4.) 8vo. Brisbane, 1887. ME 1 T

Hot Springs and Mud Eruptions of the Lower Flinders River. (Proc. Roy. Soc. Queensland, 1.) 8vo. Brisbane, 1884. ME 1 T

Notes on a great Visitation of Rats in the North and North-western Plain Country of Queensland. (Proc. Roy. Soc., Queensland, 2.) 8vo. Brisbane, 1886. ME 1 T

PALMER, Prof. Edward Henry. Search-Expedition. [*See* Haynes, Capt. A. E.] D 14 V 14

PALMER, John R. National Credit, how to use it. 8vo. Sydney, 1895. MF 4 Q 46

PALMER, Julius A. Memories of Hawaii and Hawaiian Correspondence. 8vo. Boston, 1894. MB 2 U 21

PALMER, Ray. Book of Praise, from the Best English Hymn Writers. 12mo. Lond., 1862. H 10 T 5

PALMER, Samuel. Index to *The Times* Newspaper, 1892-93, 1892-94. 8 vols. sm. 4to. Lond., 1892-94. E

PALMER, Thos. Derivations of Words selected from English Text prescribed for Matriculation Examination, 1891-2. 12mo. Melb., 1891. MJ 3 P 20

PALMERSTON, Henry John Temple, Third Viscount. [Plaster Cast of.] [*See* Hutton, L.—Portraits in Plaster.] A 23 V 13

Sketch of. [*See* Bagehot, W.—Biographical Studies.] C 22 P 10

Life of; by L. C. Sanders. 12mo. Lond. (n.d.) C 17 P 32

PAMPHILE, Father. Life and Letters of Father Damien. 12mo. Lond., 1889. MC 1 S 13

PAOLI, Cesare. Collezione Fiorentina di Facsimili Paleografici Greci e Latini. [*See* Vitelli, G.] J 41 P 24-27 ‡

PAPAL DOMINATION, embracing the present claims of the Papacy, the famed syllabus of intolerant dogmas, the proceedings of the late Vatican Council, and the culmination of apostacy in the assumed infallibility, with the repressive measures needed in Australia to check a revived energy to secure the universal supremacy. 8vo. Sydney, 1879. MG 2 S 15

PAPARELLI, L. Report of Viticultural Laboratory Work [Cal.] 1887-89. [*See* Hilgard, Prof. E. W.—Univ. of California, College of Agriculture, Experiment Station.] E

PAPIAS, Bishop of Hierapolis. The Oracles ascribed to Mathew by; a Contribution to the Criticism of the New Testament; with Appendix on the Authorship of the De Vita Contemplativa, Date of the Crucifixion, and Date of the Martyrdom of Polycarp. 8vo. Lond., 1894. G 10 P 52

PARIS ILLUSTRÉ. Nouveau Guide des Voyageurs, avec 18 plans. 12mo. Paris (n.d.) D 18 P 27

PARIS SALON. Catalogue illustré, 1893-94. 2 vols. 8vo. Paris, 1893-94. E

The Salon, 1892 and 1894: Plates, Photogravures, and Etchings; with Text in English by H. Bacon. 2 vols. fol. Paris, 1894. E 1 R 56

PARK, Mungo. Seekers after Timbuctoo. [*See* Brown, Dr. R.—Story of Africa.] D 15 V 24-26

PARKE, Dr. Thos. Heazle. Guide to Health in Africa, with notes on the country and its inhabitants. 8vo. Lond., 1893. A 12 P 46

PARKER, E. H. A Thousand Years of the Tartars. 8vo. Lond., 1895. B 35 R 3

PARKER, E. R. A Plain Book for Plain People, and a Warning to the Churches. 8vo. Melb., 1894. MG 2 Q 30

PARKER, Francis Wayland. Talks on Pedagogics. 8vo. New York, 1894.
G 18 Q 25

PARKER, J. Thermodynamics treated with Elementary Mathematics, and containing applications to Animal and Vegetable Life, Tidal Friction, and Electricity. 8vo. Lond., 1894.
A 21 R 9

PARKER, J. A. Destruction of Rabbits and other noxious animals. 8vo. Sydney, 1885.
MA 1 U 51

PARKER, Rev. Dr. Joseph. An Interview with; with Portrait. [*See* Blathwayt, R.—Interviews.]
J 10 U 34

PARKER, Leonard F. Higher Education in Iowa. Roy. 8vo. Wash., 1893.
G 18 S 11

Teachers in Iowa before 1858. 8vo. Iowa City, 1894.
B 17 R 34

PARKER, Matthew, Archbishop of Canterbury. Sketch of. [*See* Fowler, Rev. M.—Notable Archbishops.]
C 13 V 12

PARKER, Theodore. Theism, Atheism, and the Popular Theology: Sermons. 8vo. Lond., 1853.
G 15 P 34

PARKER, Wm. Kitchen. On the Morphology of the Duck and Auk Tribe. (Trans. R.I. Academy.—Cunningham Memoirs, 6.) 4to. Dublin, 1890.
E

Development of the Green Turtle. [*See* Thomson, Sir C. W., and Murray, Dr. J.—Voyage of H.M.S. *Challenger.*]
A 6 †

PARKES, Sir Harry. Life of, sometime Her Majesty's Minister to China and Japan; by S. Lane-Poole and F. V. Dickens. With a Portrait and Maps. 2 vols. 8vo. Lond., 1894.
C 13 V 9, 10

PARKES, Sir Henry. Debate on the Prerogative of Pardon, as involved in the release of Gardiner and other prisoners: Speeches by the Hon. Sir Henry Parkes, Hon. G. W. Allen, and Messrs. B. Driver, J. Stewart, and W. H. Cooper. 8vo. Sydney, 1874.
MF 4 Q 40

The English Press on the Policy of the Parkes Administration. 8vo. Sydney, 1874.
MF 4 Q 41

Fifty Years in the Making of Australian History. 2 vols. roy. 8vo. Lond., 1875*
MB 1 T 35, 36

Irish Immigration. (Pam.) 8vo. Sydney, 1869.
MG 1 Q 53

The English Press on the Policy of the Parkes Administration. (Pam.) 8vo. Sydney, 1873.
MG 1 Q 53

Public Education: a Speech. 8ro. Sydney, 1866.
MG 1 R 26

Sonnets, and other Verse. 12mo. Lond., 1895.
MH 1 U 60

PARKES, Varney. Many funny absurdities in the labours of a patriotic Parliamentary Committee. 12mo. Sydney, 1895.
MF 4 P 21

PARKHURST, C. D. Dynamo and Motor-building for Amateurs; with Working Drawings. 12mo. New York, 1893.
A 21 P 27

PARKIN, Dr. George R. The Great Dominion: Studies of Canada; with Maps. 12mo. Lond., 1895.
D 15 Q 26

PARKINSON, John. The Equity Practice Procedure Act, 1880, with Rules and Regulations. Roy. 8vo. Sydney, 1880.
MF 1 S 66

PARMENTIER, Prof. Paul. Histologie comparée des Ebénacées dans ses rapports avec la Morphologie et l'Histoire généalogique de ces Plantes. (Annales de l'Université de Lyon, 6.) Roy. 8vo. Paris, 1892.
A 20 V 18

PARNELL, Col. the Hon. Arthur. British Policy from social, home, and imperial points of view. 12mo. Lond., 1895.
F 12 S 9

PARNELL, Chas. Stuart. Sketch of. [*See* Smalley, G W.—Studies of Men.]
C 19 R 20

PARRAMATTA RIVER MURDERS. Exciting Trial of Nichols and Lester, the notorious Parramatta River murderers. (Pam.) 8vo. Sydney, 1872.
MG 1 Q 53

PARRY, Chas. Hubert Hastings. The Art of Music. 8vo. Lond., 1893.
A 23 T 14

PARRY, Rev. Edward. Memoirs of Rear-Admiral Sir W. Edward Parry. 3rd edition. 12mo. Lond., 1867.
MC 1 P 57

PARRY, Oswald H. Six months in a Syrian Monastery. 8vo. Lond., 1895.
G 15 S 27

PARRY, Sir W. Edward. Memoirs of; by tho Rev. E. Parry. 3rd ed. 12mo. Lond., 1867.
MC 1 P 57

PARSONS, Prof. Chas. L. Elements of Mineralogy. [*See* Moses, Dr. A. J.]
A 24 V 34

PARSONS, Harold G. A Hand-book to Western Australia and its Gold-fields: being a Guide to the Resources (Agricultural, Mineral, and Miscellaneous) of the Colony; and a Collection of Hints to the intending Immigrant. 12mo. Lond., 1894.
MD 5 Q 48

PARSONS, Samuel, Jr. Landscape Gardening. Roy. 8vo. New York, 1891.
A 18 V 9

PARSONS, Dr. Theophilus. Treatise on the Law of Marine Insurance and Average. 2 vols. roy. 8vo. Boston, 1868.
F 3 V 11, 12

PARSONS, Thos. Fifth Letter to the Duke of Buckingham. 8vo. Melb., 1868.
MJ 3 Q 15

PARTHENON, The, 1889-91. 3 vols. sm. 4to. Sydney, 1889-91.
ME 20 S

PARTRIDGE, Wm. Ordway. Art for America. 12mo. Boston, 1894.
A 23 Q 46

PARVIN, Hon. Theodore S. Early Bar of Iowa. 8vo. Iowa City, 1894.
B 17 R 34

PASCAL, Blaiso Sketch of. [See Pater, W.—Miscellaneous Studies.] J 7 S 10

PASCAL, M. Essai Historique sur la vie et les travaux de Bougainville, suivi de la relation de son Voyage autour du Monde. 8vo. Marseille, 1831. MD 8 Q 18

PASCO, Crawford. Proposed Antarctic Exploration. (Roy. Geog. Soc. Australasia, Vic Branch, 8.) 8vo. Melb., 1891. ME 20

PASQUIER, Chancellor. Memoirs of: a History of my Time; edited by the Duc D'Audiffret-Pasquier, and translated by C. E. Roche. Vos. 1-3. 8vo. Lond., 1893-94. C 14 S 14-16

PASQUIN: the Pastoral, Mineral, and Agricultural Advocate; edited by E. R. Mitford. Vols. 1-3, 1867-69. 4to. Lond., 1892. ME 7 Q

PASTIME: a Weekly Journal of Cricket and Sports generally. Vol. 1, No. 1, January, 1883. Sm. 4to. Sydney, 1885. ME 7 P

PASTOR, Dr. Ludwig. History of the Popes from the close of the Middle Ages; edited by F. I. Antrobus. 8vo. Lond., 1891. G 15 S 24, 25

PASTORIUS, Franz Daniel. Literary Work of. [See Seidensticker, O.] K 17 R 29

PATCHETT-MARTIN, II. A. [See Martin, II. A. P.]

PATER, Walter Horatio. Greek Studies: a series of Essays. 8vo. Lond., 1895. J 8 T 32

Plato and Platonism: a series of lectures. 8vo. Lond., 1893. G 2 P 36

Marius, the Epicurean: his Sensations and Ideas. 2 vols. 8vo. Lond., 1892. G 15 P 36, 37

Miscellaneous Studies. 8vc. Lond., 1895. J 7 S 10

PATERSON, A. B. The Man from Snowy River, and other Verses. 8vo. Sydney, 1895. MH 1 U 62

PATERSON, C. W. Lummis-. The Management of Dynamos. 12mo. Lond., 1895. A 5 S 18

PATERSON, R. S. Flowers and Insects. (Divinity Hall Record.) 8vo. Brisbane, 1879. ME 15 Q

PATON, Col. G., GLENNIE, Col. F., and SYMONS, Col. W. P. Historical Records of the 24th Regiment, from its formation in 1689. [Illustrated.] 8vo. Lond., 1892. B 22 R 4

PATON, James. British History and Papal Claims. 2 vols. 8vo. Lond., 1893. B 23 T 10, 11

PATON, Maggie Whitecross. Letters and Sketches from the New Hebrides. 8vo. Lond., 1894. MD 8 Q 16

PATRICK, St. Life and Labour of. [See Cathcart, Rev. W.] G 14 Q 27

PATRIOTIC SENTIMENTS on the Chinese and Polynesian Questions; by "A Future Legislator and probable Premier." 8vo. Sydney, 1884. MF 4 R 36

PATTEN, Dr. Simon Nelson. The Premises of Political Economy. 8vo. Philad., 1885. F 6 T 21

Theory of Dynamic Economics. Roy. 8vo. Philad., 1892. F 14 U 18

PATTERSON, Rev. George. Memoirs of Rev. S. F. Johnston, Rev. J. W. Matheson, and Mrs. Mary J. Matheson, Missionaries on Tanna (New Hebrides). 8vc. Philad., 1864. MC 1 S 4

PATTERSON, George W. and Merib R. Trans.— Industrial Photometry. [See Palaz, Dr. A.] A 21 V 15

PATTESON, Rt. Rev. John Coleridge. Lecture on the Melanesian Mission. 8vo. (n.p.) 1863. MG 2 S 4

Sketch of. [See Müller, F. Max.—Chips from a German Workshop.] J 9 R 31-33

Sketches of the Life of, in Melanesia. 12mo. Lond., 1883. MC 1 S 3

PATTON, Dr. Jacob Harris. Natural Resources of the United States. 8vo. New York, 1894. F 10 Q 29

PATTON, W. M. Practical Treatise on Foundations. 5th ed., illustrated. Roy. 8vo. New York, 1893. A 19 V 7

PATUONE, the Celebrated Ngapuhi Chief. Life and Times of; by C. O. Davis. 12mo. Auckland, 1875. MC 1 P 43

PAUL, Wm. The Rose Garden. 9th edition. Imp. 8vo. Lond., 1888. A 5 Q 29

Observations on the Cultivation of Roses in Pots, including the Autobiography of a Pot-Rose. 7th edition. 12mo. Lond. (n.d.) A 18 R 13

PAULIN DE NOLE, St. Notices sur les Manuscrits les Poésies de; par E. Chatelain. 8vo. Paris, 1880. J 7 U 37

PAULSEN, Prof. Friedrich. The German Universities, their Character and Historical Development; translated by E. D. Perry. 8vo. New York, 1895. G 18 Q 23

PAULUS, Edward. Italia. [See Stieler, C.] D 37 P 23 ‡

PAYNE, Edward J. History of European Colonies; with Maps. 18mo. Lond., 1889. F 12 S 10

PAZIG, Christianus. A Treatise of Magic Incantations. (Bibliotheca Curiosa.) 12mo. Edinb., 1886. J 18 Q 37

PEABODY, Prof. Andrew Preston. The Scientific Education of Mechanics and Artizans. 8vo. Wash., 1873. G 18 R 43

PEABODY, Dr. George L. Supplement to Ziemssen's Cyclopædia of the Practice of Medicine. Roy. 8vo. New York, 1881. K 9 Q 21

PEACHAM, Henry. Oil Painting: Extracts from "The Compleat Gentleman." [*See* Govett, W. R.] Libr.

PEAKE, R. B. IIB: a Dramatic Caricature. 8vo. Lond. (n.d.) H 4 P 40

PEARMAN, T. H., and MOOR, C. G. Aids to the Analysis of Food and Drugs. 12mo. Lond., 1895.
A 26 P 19

PEARSON, A. N. Complete List of Manures, with current values and prices in the Melbourne Market. 8vo. Melb., 1894. MA 3 T 9
Cultivation of Sugar Beet. 8vo. Melb., 1893.
MA 3 T 9
The Farmer's Guide to Manuring. 8vo. Melb., 1888.
MA 3 T 9
Another Copy. (From *New South Wales Agricultural Gazette*.) 8vo. Sydney, 1890. MA 1 Q 61
The Future of Australian Agriculture. 8vo. Melb. (n.d.) MA 3 T 9
Soils and their Cultivation. (Vict. Dept. of Agricult.—Lectures.) 8vo. Melb., 1892. MA 3 V 15

PEARSON, Charles Henry. Brief Statement of the Constitutional Question in Victoria. 8vo. Melb. (n.d.) MJ 3 Q 16
National Life and Character: a forecast. 8vo. Lond., 1893. F 6 U 27
Goldsmith's Traveller. [*See* Goldsmith, O.] MH 1 Q 23
Report on the state of Public Education in Victoria, and suggestions as to the best means of improving it. Roy. 8vo. Melb., 1878. MG 1 T 36

PEARSON, Prof. Karl. History of the Theory of Elasticity, &c. [*See* Todhunter, Dr. I.] A 11 U 21-23

PEARY, Josephine Diebitsch. My Arctic Journal; with an Account of the Great White Journey across Greenland, by R. E. Peary. 8vo. Lond., 1893.
D 16 S 3

PEARY, Robert E. The Great White Journey across Greenland. [*See* Peary, J. D.] D 16 S 3

PEASE, Alfred E. Biskra and the Oases and Desert of the Zibans. 12mo. Lond., 1893. D 14 P 14

PEDDIE, Dr. Alexander. Recollections of Dr. John Brown. 12mo. Lond., 1893. C 13 Q 28

PEEL, Rt. Hon. Arthur Wellesley, Speaker of the House of Commons. Decisions of, on Points of Order, Rules of Debate, and the General Practice of the House, 1884-90. 3 vols. 12mo. Adelaide, 1887-92.
MF 4 P 29-31

PEEL, Helen. Polar Gleams: an Account of a Voyage on the Yacht *Blencathra*; with Contributions by Capt. J. Wiggins and F. G. Jackson. Illustrated. 8 vo. Lond., 1894. D 16 T 11

PEEL, Sir Robt. Sketch of. [*See* Bagehot, W.—Estimates of some Englishmen and Scotchmen.]
J 10 V 32
Sketch of. [*See* Bagehot, W.—Biographical Studies.]
C 22 P 10

PEKELHARING, Prof. C. A., and WINKLER, C. Beri-Beri: Researches concerning its Nature and Cause, and the Means of its Arrest; translated by J. Cantlie. Illustrated. 8vo. Edinb., 1893.
A 33 T 21

PELSAERT, François. Ongeluckige Voyagie van't schip *Batavia*, na Oost-Indien: Uyt-gevaren onder de E. François Pelsaert. Gebleven op de *Abriolhos* van F. Houtman, 1628-29. Sm. 4to. Utrecht, 1649.
D 20 R 6

PELSENEER, Prof. Paul. Pteropoda; Anatomy of the Deep-sea Mollusca. Specimen of the Genus Spirula. [*See* Thomson, Sir C. W., and Murray, Dr. J.—Voyage of H.M.S. *Challenger*.] A 6 †

PEMBER, Austen. Ivna the Terrible, his Life and Times. 12mo. Lond., 1895. C 21 P 10

PEMBER, G. H. Earth's Earliest Ages and their connection with Modern Spiritualism and Theosophy. 8vo. Lond., 1894. G 15 P 39

PEMBERTON, T. Edgar. Life and Writings of T. W. Robertson. 8vo. Lond., 1893. C 13 R 15

PEMBROKE, Earl of. Conservative Reform of the House of Lords. [*See* Subjects of the Day, 4.]
F 7 U 29
Yacht's Sailing Boats. [*See* Sullivan, Sir F.—Yachting.]
A 29 Q 40

PENDLETON, J. Our Railways, their Origin, Development, Incident, and Romance. [Illustrated.] 2 vols. 8vo. Lond., 1894. A 22 S 15, 16

PENDLETON, Rev. Dr. Wm. Nelson. Memoirs of; by Susan P. Lee. Roy. 8vo. Philad., 1893. C 18 U 3

PENLEY, Aaron. Sketching from Nature in Water Colours. Fol. Lond. (n.d.) A 22 P 19‡

PENNEFATHER, Dr. F. W. Hand-book for Travellers in New Zealand. (Murray's Hand-book.) 12mo. Lond., 1893. MD 4 R 45

PENNELL, Elizabeth Robins. To Gipsyland. 12mo. 1893. D 14 P 5

PENNELL, Joseph. English Cathedrals. [*See* Rensselaer, Mrs. S. van.] A 2 U 36

PENNSYLVANIA.—*General*. Statement of Work done by Women in Instruction, Reform, Philanthropy, and Missions during one year in Pennsylvania. 8vo. Harrisburg, 1893. F 14 U 23

PENNSYLVANIA.—*State Departments, Reports, and Publications.*

ADJUTANT-GENERAL. Annual Report, 1891. Roy. 8vo. Harrisburg, 1892. E

AUDITOR-GENERAL. Report of the Finances, 1891. Roy. 8vo. Harrisburg, 1892. E

Reports of the several Banks and Savings Institutions and Banks organized under the Free Banking Laws. 8vo. Harrisburg, 1892. E

BOARD OF AGRICULTURE. Reports of State Board of Agriculture, State Agricultural Society, State Dairymen's Association, State Horticultural Association, and the State College, for 1893. Roy. 8vo. Harrisburg, 1893. E

BOARD OF COMMISSIONERS OF PUBLIC CHARITIES. 22nd Annual Report. Roy. 8vo. Harrisburg, 1892. E

BOARD OF HEALTH. 7th Annual Report. Roy. 8vo. Harrisburg, 1892. E

COMMISSIONERS OF FISHERIES Report, 1889-91. Roy. 8vo. Harrisburg, 1892. E

DEPARTMENT OF INTERNAL AFFAIRS. Annual Report, 1891. 4 vols. roy. 8vo. Harrisburg, 1892. E
  Pt. 1. Land Office, State Weather Service, Vital Statistics.
  Pt. 2. Assessments, Taxes.
  Pt. 3. Industrial Statistics
  Pt. 4. Railroad, Canal, Navigation, Telegraph, and Telephone Companies.
  Pt. 5. Reports of Inspectors of Mines.

STATE COLLEGE. Annual Report for 1892. Part 1. Department of Instruction. Part 2. Agricultural Experiment Station. [Illustrated.] Roy. 8vo. Harrisburg, 1893. E

Agricultural Experiment Station. Reports, 1891-94. 2 vols. roy. 8vo. Harrisburg, 1892-95. E

STATE LIBRARIAN. Report, 1891. Roy. 8vo. Harrisburg, 1892. E

SUPERINTENDENT OF PUBLIC INSTRUCTION. Report, 1891. Roy. 8vo. Harrisburg, 1892. E

TREASURER. Report of, 1891. Roy. 8vo. Harrisburg, 1892. E

PENNSYLVANIA UNIVERSITY. Catalogue and Announcements, 1692-93 8vo. Philad., 1893. E

The Courses in Civil Engineering, 1892-93, and Rights of Graduates. 12mo. Philad., 1893. E

Catalogue and Announcement, Department of Veterinary Medicine, 1892-94. 8vo. Philad, 1893. E

PENNY, Isabel B. God's Way of Healing. 18mo. Melb. (n.d.) MG 2 P 50

PENNY MAGAZINE, The, 1832-38. Imp. 8vo. Lond. 1832-38. F

PENNY READINGS, both what they unfortunately now are in Melbourne and its vicinity, and what they ought to be—namely, Institutions for elevating the unlettered masses. 8vo. Melb., 1866. MJ 3 Q 2½

PENROSE, Lieut.-Col. Modern Infantry Fire. [*See* United Service List.] MA 2 V 38

PENROSE, Boies. The City Government of Philadelphia. [*See* Allinson, E. P.] B 18 S 5
Philadelphia, 1681-1887. [*See* Allinson, E. P.] B 18 T 2

PEPPIN, T. S. The Clubs of the Club and Institute Union. [*See* Knapp, J. M.—The Universities and the Social Problem.] F 8 U 22

PEPYS Samuel. Diary of; with Lord Braybrooke's Notes. Edited by H. B. Wheatley. Vols. 1-6. 8vo. Lond., 1893-95. C 14 V 1-6

PERCY, Major A. Herbert-. Visit to Bashan and Argob. 8vo. Lond., 1895. D 17 S 12

PERIAM, Jonathan. The Pictorial Home and Farm Manual. 4to. Sydney, 1885.* MA 1 S 28

PERICLES and the Golden Age of Athens. [*See* Abbott, E.] B 27 Q 8

PERKINS, Arthur J. Vine-pruning, its Theory and Practice. 8vo. Adelaide, 1895. MA 1 S 30

PERKINS, Edward T. Na Motu; or Reef-Rovings in the South Seas: a Narrative of Adventures at the Hawaiian, Georgian, and Society Islands. 8vo. New York, 1854. MD 5 S 47

PERKINS, Emma R. *Trans.*—Excursions in Greece. [*See* Diehl, Prof. C.] D 18 R 12

PERKINS, Frederic Beecher. The Best Reading: Hints on the selection of Books; on the formation of Libraries, public and private; on Courses of Reading, &c.; with a classified Bibliography for easy reference. 8vo. New York, 1877. K 7 R 58

PERKINS, J. Scheme of Taxation for Tasmania, in lieu of Customs' and other Duties. 12mo. Hobart, 1872. MF 1 Q 43

PERKINS FAMILY, History of. [*See* Sharp, A. M.] B 21 V 21

PERKINS INSTITUTION, Boston, Massachusetts. Report of the Trustees of the Perkins Institution and Massachusetts School for the Blind, 1892. 8vo. Boston, 1893. E

PERL, Henry. Venezia; from the German, by Mrs. A. Bell. 4to. Lond., 1894. D 42 U 1. ‡

PERON, François Aug. Naturaliste, Voyageur aux Terres Australes, sa vie appréciation de ses Travaux analysés raisonnée de ses recherches sur les Animaux vertébrés et invertébrés, par M. Girard. 8vo. Paris, 1857. MA 3 R 34

PERPETUAL TRUSTEE, EXECUTOR, and AGENCY CO. Memorandum and Articles of Association. 8vo. Sydney (n.d.) MF 4 R 35

PERROT, Prof. Georges, and CHIPIEZ, Chas. History of Art in Primitive Greece. 2 vols. roy. 8vo. Lond., 1894. A 22 V 16, 17

PERRY, Rev. Dr. Chas. The Doctrine of the Lord's Supper, as taught in Holy Scripture and by the Church of England. 12mo. Lond., 1884. G 2 V 40
Science and the Bible. 8vo. Melb., 1869. MG 2 Q 40

PERRY, Prof. Edward D. *Trans.*—German Universities. [*See* Paulsen, F.] G 18 Q 23

PERRY, J. Tavenor. Chronology of Mediæval and Renaissance Architecture. 8vo. Lond., 1893. A 3 P 3

PERRY, Sampson. An Historical Sketch of the French Revolution. 2 vols. 8vo. Lond., 1796. B 8 U 1, 2

PERRY'S MANUFACTURERS' AND MERCHANTS' DIRECTORY of Great Britain and Ireland, and Continental, Colonial, and American Mercantile Guide, 1893 and 1894. 2 vols. imp. 8vo. Lond., 1893-94. E

PERSIUS FLACCUS, Aulus. Satyræ. 8vo. Amst., 1684. H 0 U 34

PETER, St. L'Evangile de Pierre. [*See* Sabatier, A.] G 12 P 20

PETER, Bishop of Alexandria. Writings of. (Ante-Nicene Christ. Lib., 14.) 8vo. Edinb., 1869. G 11 U 14

PETER THE GREAT, Emperor of Russia. Histoire de Russie sous Pierre le Grand. [*See* Voltaire, F. M. A. de.—Histoire de Charles XII.] B 20 P 8
School History of; by H. Edelman. 8vo. Melb., 1871. MB 1 P 20

PETERMANN, Dr. A. Mitteilungen aus Justus Perthes' geographischer Anstalt, 31, 32, 35-39, ergänzungsbands 16-18, 22, 23. Ergänzungsheft Nr. 113. 13 vols. 4to. and imp. 8vo. Gotha, 1884-94. E

PETERS, Dr. Edward. Modern American Methods of Copper Smelting. 5th ed. 8vo. New York, 1892. A 24 V 20
Another copy. 6th ed. Roy. 8vo. New York, 1894. A 21 V 12

PETERSILIE, Dr. A. Die Volks- und die Mittelschulen im preussischen Staate, 1891. [*See* Schneider, Dr. K.] G 12 U 2 †

PETERSON, P. Clementine Homilies. [*See* Clement of Rome.] G 14 U 17

PETERSON, Dr. W. *Trans.*—Speech of Cicero in Defence of Cluentius. [*See* Cicero, M. T.] J 9 S 21

PETIT, Edouard. "Aylie Marin." En Océanie. 18mo. Paris, 1888. MD 2 W 52

PETRIE, Prof. George. Church and State in Early Maryland. (Johns Hopkins University Studies, 10.) 8vo. Baltimore, 1892. B 18 S 10

PETRIE, Prof. W. M. Flinders. Coptic Manuscripts brought from the Fayyum. 4to. Lond., 1893. G 5 U 27
Egyptian Decorative Art. 8vo. Lond., 1895. A 23 R 43
Egyptian Tales; translated from the Papyri. 1st and 2nd series. Illustrated. 2 vols. 8vo. Lond., 1895. B 16 R 14, 15
History of Egypt, from the earliest times to the 16th Dynasty. Vol. 1. 8vo. Lond., 1894. B 21 R 3
Tell el Amarna. 4to. Lond., 1894. B 14 S 4 †

PETTIT, James S. Modern Reproductive Graphic Processes. 18mo. New York, 1894. A 23 P 3

PETTY, Sir William. Life of, 1623-87; by Lord Edmond Fitzmaurice. 8vo. Lond., 1895. C 21 S 17

PFEFFER, D. Revivals: are they in accordance with the "revealed purpose" of the great and glorious Majesty of the Heaven to mankind? (Pam.) 8vo. Warrnambool (n.d.) MG 1 Q 53

PFEIL, Major Richard Graf von. Experiences of a Russian Officer in the Russian Service, during the Turkish War of 1877-78. 8vo. Lond., 1893. D 18 R 9

PHÆDRUS. Extracts from, for the use of the Lower Forms in the Sydney Grammar School. 12mo. Sydney, 1863. MH 1 P 67

PHARMACEUTICAL SOCIETY OF GREAT BRITAIN. Pharmaceutical Journal and Transactions. 3rd series. Vols. 22-25. Roy. 8vo. Lond., 1892-95. E

PHELPS, William Walter. Sketch of. [*See* Smalley, G. W.—Studies of Men.] C 10 R 20

PHILIP, G., and SON. County Maps [England]. 42 vols. Folded 18mo. Lond. (n.d.) D 12 P 16-57

Bedford.	Middlesex.
Berks.	Monmouth.
Buckingham.	Norfolk.
Cambridge.	Northampton.
Cheshire.	Northumberland.
Cornwall.	Nottingham.
Cumberland.	Oxford.
Derby.	Shropshire.
Devon.	Somerset.
Dorset.	Stafford.
Durham.	Suffolk.
Essex.	Surrey.
Gloucester.	Sussex.
Hampshire.	Warwick.
Hereford.	Westmoreland.
Hertford.	Wiltshire.
Huntingdon.	Worcester.
Kent.	Yorkshire, N.W.
Lancashire.	Yorkshire, N.E.
Leicester and Rutland.	Yorkshire, S.W.
Lincoln.	Yorkshire, S.E.

Map of the English Lakes. Folded 18mo. Lond. (n.d.) D 12 P 58

Map of the Isle of Man, with its Railways. Folded 18mo. Lond. (n.d.) D 12 P 59

Supplementary Catalogue—1893-95. 217

PHILIP, G., and SON—*contd.*
Map of the Isle of Wight. Folded 18mo. Lond. (n.d.)
D 12 P 60

Map of the Channel Islands. Folded 18mo. Lond.
(n.d.) D 12 P 61

Maps of North and South Wales. 2 vols. Folded 18mo. Lond. (n.d.) D 12 P 62, 63

PHILIPS, Ambrose. The Distrest Mother: a Tragedy. [*See* London Stage, 4.] H 2 S 36

PHILIPS, Nathaniel George. Views in Lancashire and Cheshire of Old Halls and Castles. Imp. 4to. Lond., 1893. D 22 P 18 ‡

PHILLIMORE, Sir Robert Joseph. The Ecclesiastical Law of the Church of England. 2 vols. 8vo. Lond., 1873. F 10 T 22, 23

PHILLIMORE, William P. W. Index Library. [*See* British Record Society.] E

PHILLIP, Capt. Arthur. Extracts of Letters from, to Lord Sydney; to which is annexed a Description of Norfolk Island, by Philip Gidley King, and an Account of Expenses incurred in transporting Convicts to New South Wales. 4to. Lond., 1791. MC 9 P 1 †

PHILLIPPS, Ambrose Lisle. *Trans.*—Life of St. Elizabeth of Hungary. [*See* Mouzclembert, Comte de.]
C 2 W 24

PHILLIPPS-WOLLEY, C. [*See* Wolley, C. P.]

PHILLIPS, Claude. [Life of] Sir Joshua Reynolds. 8vo. Lond., 1894. C 14 S 13
Frederick Walker and his Works. (Portfolio Monograph, 6.) Roy. 8vo. Lond., 1894. E

PHILLIPS, J. Enciclopedia Comercial, 1888. Fol. Valparaiso, 1888. K 40 T 18 ‡

PHILLIPS, Major J. Scott. A Paper on some curious and original discoveries concerning the Re-settlement of the Seed of Abraham in Syria and Arabia. 12mo. Dunedin, 1877. MG 1 P 78

PHILLIPS, Maberley. History of Banks, Bankers, and Banking in Northumberland, Durham, and North Yorkshire, 1755-1894. Roy. 8vo. Lond., 1894. F 3 V 5

PHILLIPS, Maurice. The Teaching of the Vedas; what light does it throw on the origin and development of Religion? 8vo. Lond., 1895. G 2 U 10

PHILLIPS, Robt. E. One Thousand Patent Facts. 8vo. Lond. (n.d.) F 8 U 16

PHILLIPS, Wendell. Eulogy on. [*See* Curtis, G. W.]
F 14 U 3
Sketch of; with portrait. [*See* Bolton, Sarah K.—Famous Leaders.] C 17 P 27

2 E

PHILO JUDÆUS. Contemplative Life; or, the Fourth Book of the Treatise concerning Virtues. Edited by F. C. Conybeare. 8vo. Oxford, 1895. J 5 T 27

PHILOLCGICAL MUSEUM, The. 2 vols. 8vo. Camb., 1832-33. J 6 T 28, 29

PHILOLCGICAL SOCIETY. Transactions, 1891-94. 8vo. Lond., 1894. E

PHILOSOPHICAL MAGAZINE AND JOURNAL OF SCIENCE, The London, Edinburgh, and Dublin. 5th Scries. Vols. 34-39. 8vo. Lond., 1892-95. E

PHIPSON, Evacustes A. How to establish Australia's Prosperity. 8vo. Sydney, 1884. MF 1 Q 32

PHONETIC JOURNAL, The. Vols. 51-53. Sm. 4to. Lond., 1892-94. E

PHOSPHO-GUANO: Scientific and Practical Proofs of its Value and Importance as a Permanent Fertiliser. 8vo. Hobart, 1894. MA 1 P 56

PHOTOGRAM, The. Vol. 1, 1894. 8vo. Lond., 1894. E

PHYLLOXERA and other Diseases of the Grape-vine. 8vo. Wellington, 1881. MA 1 U 67

PHYSICIAN, A. [*See* Seventy Years of Life in the Victor an Era.] MD 1 Q 34

PICK, Dr. Edward. On Memory, and the rational means of improving it. 2nd ed. 12mo. Lond., 1862.
G 9 P 51

PICKARD, Dr. J. L. Early Clergy of Iowa. 8vo. Iowa City, 1894. B 17 R 34

PICKERING, Wm. Henry. Investigations in Astronomical Photography. (Harvard University Astronomical Observatory, Annals, 32, pt. 1.) 4to. Camb., 1895. E

PICTON, Sir James A. A Biography; by his son, J. Allanson Picton. 8vo. Lond., 1891. C 15 P 15

PICTORIAL HAND-BOOK OF LONDON. Illustrated. 12mo. Lond., 1854. D 18 Q 14

PICTURESQUE TASMANIA. [Photographs.] Sm. fol. Hobart (n.d.) MD 9 P 2 †

PIDDINGTON, Albert Bathurst. The Fall of Satan. [*See* Milton, J.] MH 1 P 62

PIDDINGTON, Wm. Richman. Manhood Suffrage: Report of the Speech delivered in the Legislative Assembly on 30th July, 1858. 8vo. Sydney, 1858.
MF 1 Q 33

PIDGEON, Henry. Memorials of Shrewsbury. 2nd. ed. 8vo. Shrewsbury, 1851 B 23 S 16

PIERCE, Franklin. Sketch of. [*See* Thompson, R. W.—Recollections of Sixteen Presidents.] C 18 T 21, 22
Sketch of. [*See* Wilson, J. G.—Presidents of the United States.] C 2 V 30

PIERS PLOWMAN. [*See* Jusserand, J. J.] J 9 T 27

PIERSOL, Dr. George A. Human Monstrosities. [*See* Hirst, Dr. B. C.] A 6 P 4 ‡

PIERSON, Rev. Dr. Arthur T. The New Acts of the Apostles; or, the Marvels of Modern Missions, with Map showing Religions of the World. 8vo. Lond., 1894. G 17 Q 47

PIESSE, Chas. Henry. Art of Perfumery, and the Methods of obtaining the Odours of Plants, the Growth and General Flower Farm System of raising Fragrant Herbs. 5th ed. 8vo. Lond., 1891. A 11 R 27

PIETSCH, L. Contemporary German Art at the Centenary Festival of the Royal Academy of Arts, Berlin; translated by N. D'Anvers. 2 vols. 8vo. Lond., 1888. A 33 Q 18, 19 ‡

PIGGOTT, F. T. Music and Musical Instruments of Japan. 4to. Lond., 1893. A 8 U 37

PIKE, G. Herbert. Digest of all Cases determined in the Land Appeal Court of New South Wales, 1890-94. Roy. 8vo. Sydney, 1895. MF 3 R 69

PIKE, Luke Owen. Constitutional History of the House of Lords. Roy. 8vo. Lond, 1894. F 12 R 30

PIKE, Zebulon M., Explorer of the Sources of the Mississippi and Arkansas Rivers. Sketch of. [*See* Greeley, Gen. A. W.—Explorers.] C 17 R 14

PILCHER, Chas. E. Common Law Procedure Acts, 1853-57, and other statutes and enactments relating to the practice of the Supreme Court of New South Wales in its Common Law Jurisdiction. 2nd ed., compiled and arranged by F. J. Smith. 8vo. Sydney, 1895. MF 3 T 56

PILGRIM, The. [*See* Grey, H.]

PILLARS, Rev. James. Short Religious Services for Sunday Schools and the Home Circle. 8vo. Sydney, 1869. MG 1 P 77

PILLING, Wm. Emancipation of South America. [*See* Mitre, Gen. B.] B 17 R 30

PILON, Frederick. The Deaf Lover: a Farce. [*See* London Stage, 3.] H 2 S 35
He would be a Soldier: a Comedy. [*See* London Stage, 3.] H 2 S 35

PILSBRY, Prof. Henry A. Manual of Conchology. [*See* Tryon, G. W.] A 32 P-Q

PINE BLUFF COLORED INDUSTRIAL INSTITUTE, Ark. Catalogue of. 8vo. Arkansas, 1893. G 18 R 30

PINERO, A. W. The Amazons: a Farcial Romance. 18mo. Lond., 1895. H 10 V 11
The Cabinet Minister: a Farce. 18mo. Lond., 1892. H 10 V 1
Dandy Dick: a Farce. 18mo. Lond., 1893 H 10 V 2
The Hobby Horse: a Comedy. 18mo. Lond., 1892. H 10 V 3
Lady Bountiful: a Play. 18mo. Lond., 1891. H 10 V 4
The Magistrate: a Farce. 18mo. Lond., 1892. H 10 V 5
The Profligate: a Play. 18mo. Lond., 1892. H 10 V 6
The Schoolmistress. 18mo. Lond., 1894. H 10 V 9
The Second Mrs. Tanqueray. 12mo. Lond., 1895. H 10 V 10
Sweet Lavender: a Drama. 12mo. Lond., 1893. H 10 V 7
The Times: a Comedy. 18mo. Lond., 1891. H 10 V 8
The Weaker Sex: a Comedy. 18mo. Lond., 1894. H 10 V 13

PINK, J. A Plea for the Hybridisation of Plants. (Proc. Roy. Soc., Queensland, 1.) 8vo. Brisbane, 1885. ME 1 T

PINKERTON, John. Modern Geography: a Description of Empires, States, and Colonies; with the Oceans, Seas, and Isles in all parts of the World. 2 vols. 4to. Lond., 1802. D 15 P 6, 7 †

PINSON, H. The Contrast; or, Our Saviour and St. Paul, St. Peter, St. James, St. John, and St. Jude. 8vo. Durban, 1884-85. G 15 P 45
Good News. 8vo. Durban, 1886. G 1 R 35
Fraud and Falsity: attempted Destruction of the Scriptures by Priests. 8vo. Pietermaritzburg, 1889-90. G 15 P 44

PINTO, Major Alexandre de Serpa. Between Angola and the Zambesi. [*See* Great Explorers.] D 15 V 21, 22

PIONEER, A. [*See* Reminiscences of Australian Early Life.] MD 1 Q 33

PIONEER, The: a Weekly Newspaper published on board the s.s. *Queen of the Thames*. 8vo. Melb., 1871. MJ 3 Q 17

PIRANI, Frederic Joy. Method of measuring the resistance of a Battery. (Roy. Soc., Vic., 18.) 8vo. Melb., 1882. ME 1 P

PIRRIE, Wm. Technical Dictionary (English-French and French-English) of Sea Terms, Phrases, and Words in the English and French Languages for the use of Seamen, Engineers, and others. 12mo. Lond., 1895. A 19 P 23

PISSIS, A. Geografía Fisica de la República de Chile, 2 vols. 8vo. and fol. Paris, 1875. A 24 S.16, and 2 P 31 ‡

PITMAN, Isaac. Complete Phonographic Instructor. Revised ed. 12mo. New York, 1894. K 20 P 19

PITT, Christopher. Poetical Works of. 18mo. Edinb., 1782. H 10 P 28

PITT, Rt. Hon. William. Character of. [See Hazlitt, W.—Winterslow.] J 12 S 33
Sketch of. [See Bagehot, W.—Biographical Studies.] C 22 P 10

PITTMAN, Edward Fisher. Occurrence of a new Mineral at Broken Hill. (Journal Roy. Soc., N.S.W., 27) 8vo. Sydney, 1893. ME 1 R
Notes on the Cremorne Bore. [See David, Prof. T. W. E.] ME 1 R

PIUS II. De Codicibus MSS. Græcis Pii II in Bibliotheca Alexandrino-Vaticana. [See Duchesne, L.] K 7 T 5

PIUS IX. The Great Aggregate Meeting held in the Cathedral Church, Dublin, 1867, to sympathise with His Holiness. 8vo. Hobart, 1868. MG 1 S 28
Sketch of. [See Elliot, Frances—Roman Gossip.] C 21 Q 10
[Plaster Cast of.] [See Hutton, L.—Portraits in Plaster.] A 23 V 13
A Roman Pontiff. [See Kingston, W. Beatty-.—Men Cities, and Events.] C 22 R 4

PIZARRO, Francisco. Viaggi. [See Ramusio, G. B.—Navigationi et Viaggi.] D 36 T 5-7 ‡

PIZEY, S. V. Flax Culture: an appeal for its adoption in South Australia. (Proc. Roy. Agricult. and Horticult. Soc., S Aust., 1882.) 8vo. Adelaide, 1882. ME 1 S

PLANCUS, L. Munatius. Histoire de; par E. Jullien. (Annales de l'Université de Lyon.) Roy. 8vo. Paris, 1892. C 16 U 12

PLARR, Victor G. Men and Women of the Time. 14th ed. 8vo. Lond., 1895. C 21 T 14

PLATING AND BOILER-MAKING; by "A Foreman Pattern-maker." Illustrated. 8vo. Lond., 1895. A 25 R 16

PLATNER, Prof. S. B. Selections from Pliny. [See Plinius Secundus, C.] J 11 P 45

PLATO. The Parmenides of Plato; with Introduction by W. W. Waddell. 4to. Glasgow, 1894. J 15 Q 21 †
Republic. The Greek Text, edited by Prof. B. Jowett and Prof. L. Campbell. 3 vols. 8vo. Oxford, 1894. F 14 V 26-28
Funeral Orations in Praise of Military Men. [See Broadhurst, Rev. T.]
Myths of. [See Westcott, Rt. Rev. B. F.—Religious Thought in the West.] G 2 U 37
Passages from Plato for English Readers. [See Jowett. Prof. B.] G 3 P 35, 36
Plato; or, the Philosopher. [See Emerson, R. W.—Representative Men.] C 17 P 10
Platonism. [See Strong, T. B.] G 4 V 15
Republic of. Analysis; by J. A. St. John. [See More Sir, T.—Utopia.] F 15 Q 7
Plato and Platonism. [See Pater, W.] G 2 P 36

PLAUTUS, Marcus Accius. Comœdiæ; ad præstantium librorum fidem recensuit, versus ordinavit, difficiliora interpretatus est C. H. Weise. 2 vols. 8vo. Quedlnburgi, 1847-48. H 3 S 38, 39

PLEA FOR SEPARATION, A; or, the Freedom and Independence of Australia. 8vo. Melb., 1888. MF 4 R 10

PLINIUS SECUNDUS, C. Selections from Pliny; by Prof. S. B. Platner. 12mo. Boston, 1895. J 11 P 45

PLUMMER, Rev. Dr. Alfred. Pastoral Epistles, St. James and St. Jude. [See Expositor's Bible.] G 19 R and S

PLUNKETT, John Hubert. The Magistrate's Pocket Book. 12mo. Sydney, 1859. MF 1 P 59

PLUTARCH. Plutarch's Lives of Sertorius, Eumenes, Agesilaus, and Pompey; reprinted from Langhorne's Translation. 8vo. Sydney, 1868. MC 1 R 45
Plutarch's Romane Questions; translated by P. Holland, and edited by F. B. Jevons. 8vo. Lond., 1892. B 30 Q 18

PLYMLEY, Peter. [See Smith, Rev. S.]

POCHET, Leon. Steam Injectors, their Theory and Use. 18mo. New York, 1900. A 22 P 11

POCOCK, Frank. Death of. [See Great Explorers.] D 15 V 22

PODMORE, Frank. Apparitions and Thought-transference: an Examination of the Evidence for Telepathy. Illustrated. 8vo. Lond., 1894. G 17 Q 45

POE, Edgar Allen. Tales of Mystery, Imagination, and Humour; and Poems. 12mo. Lond. (n.d.) J 11 U 26
Works of, newly collected and edited by E. C. Stedman and G. E. Woodberry. Vols. 1 and 2. 8vo. Lord., 1895. J 14 R 1, 2

POISSON, J. Recherches sur les Casuarina et en particulier sur ceux de la Nouvelle-Calédonie. 4to. Paris (n.d.) MA 10 P 12 †

POLE, S. The Queensland Turf Guide and Racing Calendar for 1891-92. 12mo. Brisb., 1892. ME C T

POLE, Dr. Wm. Evolution of Whist. 12mo. Lord., 1895. A 29 S 17

POLÉJAEFF, Dr. N. Über das Sperma und Spermatogenese bei Sycandraraphanus Haeckel. 8vo. Wein, 1882. A 30 U 37
Keratosa; Calcarea. [See Thomson, Sir C. W., and Murray, Dr. J.—Voyage of H.M.S. Challenger Zoology, 8.] A 3 †

POLETAÏEW, Nicolas. Speicheldrüsen bei den Odonaten. 8vo. St. Petersburg, 1879. A 30 U 27
Du développement des muscles d'ailes chez les Odonates. 8vo. St. Petersburg, 1879. A 30 U 27

POLITICAL SCIENCE QUARTERLY. Vols. 7-9, 8vo. New York, 1892-94. E

POLK, James Knox. Sketch of. [*See* Wilson, J.G.—Presidents of the United States.] C 2 V 30
Sketch of. [*See* Thompson, R. W.—Recollections of Sixteen Presidents.] C 18 T 21, 22

POLLARD, A. F. [Life of] Sir E. Kelley, Necromancer, 1555–95. (Lives of Twelve Bad Men.) 8vo. Lond., 1894. C 18 T 9

POLLARD, Alfred Wm. Early Illustrated Books: a History of the Decoration and Illustration of Books in the 15th and 16th Centuries. 12mo. Lond., 1893. B 17 Q 9
Italian Book Illustrations. (Portfolio Monograph, 12.) Roy. 8vo. Lond., 1894. E

POLLEN, John Hungerford. Ancient and Modern Furniture and Woodwork. 8vo. Lond., 1875 A 23 R 25
Gold and Silversmith's Work. 8vo. Lond., 1879. A 23 R 18

POLLOCK, Sir Frederick, and MAITLAND, Prof. Frederic Wm. History of English Law before the time of Edward I. 2 vols. roy. 8vo. Camb., 1895. F 3 V 9, 10

POLLOCK, Dr. James Edward, and CHISHOLM, James. Medical Handbook of Life Assurance. 4th ed. 8vo. Lond., 1895. A 33 S 6

POLLOK, Robert. The Course of Time: a Poem. 22nd ed. 12mo. Edinb., 1858. H 10 T 31

POLO, Marco. Viaggi. [*See* Ramusio, G. B.—Navigationi et Viaggi.] D 36 T 5–7 ‡

POLYNESIA. Progress of the Gospel in Polynesia (Southern Group), Georgian, Society, and Harvey Islands. 18mo. Edinb., 1831. MG 2 R 30

POLYNESIAN SOCIETY, Journal of. Vols. 1–3. 8vo. Wellington, 1892–94. ME 6 S

POMFRET, Rev. John. Poems upon several occasions, with Life of the Author. 18mo. Lond., 1810. H 10 U 7

POMPEIUS, Cneius. Life of. [*See* Plutarch.] MC 1 R 45

POOLE, Mrs. Hester M. Fruits, and how to use them. 8vo. New York, 1890. A 22 Q 12

POOLE, Stanley Lane-. Aurangzib. (Rulers of India.) 8vo. Oxford, 1893. C 13 P 11
Cairo: Sketches of its History, Monuments, and Social Life. 8vo. Lond., 1893. D 14 T 18
The Mohammadan Dynasties. 8vo. Lond., 1894. B 35 P 21
Social Life in Egypt: a Description of the Country and its People. 4to. Lond., 1884. D 12 R 21 †

———— and DICKENS, Frederick V. Life of Sir Harry Parkes, sometime Her Majesty's Minister to China and Japan; with a Portrait and Maps. 2 vols. 8vo. Lond., 1894. C 13 V 9, 10

POOLE, Dr. William Frederick. Poole's Index to Periodical Literature; the Second Supplement, 1887–92, by W. I. Fletcher. Imp. 8vo. Lond., 1893. Libr.
The University Library and the University Curriculum. 12mo. Chicago, 1894. G 18 P 12

POORE, Dr. George Vivian. Essays on Rural Hygiene. 8vo. Lond., 1893. A 26 R 14

POPE, Alexander. Works of. 6 vols. 12mo. Lond., 1764. J 8 U 34–39
Works of; with Commentaries and Notes by Mr. Warburton. 9 vols. 8vo. Lond., 1751. J 9 T 28–36
Works of; with a Memoir of the Author, Notes, and Critical Notices on each Poem by the Rev. Dr. G. Croly. 4 vols. 12mo. Lond., 1835. H 9 U 29–32
Poetical Works of; edited by R. Carruthers. 4 vols. 8vo. Lond., 1853. H 9 U 10–13
The Female Dunces; inscribed to Mr. Pope. Sm. fol. Lond., 1733. H 30 Q 13 ‡
State Dunces; inscribed to Mr. Pope. Sm. fol. Lond., 1733. H 30 Q 13 ‡
An Epistle to, occasioned by Theobald's Shakespear and Bentley's Milton. Sm. fol. Lond., 1733. H 39 Q 13 ‡
The Odyssey and Iliad of Homer. [*See* Homer.] H 9 P 13, 14; H 9 U 4, 5

POPE, Joseph. Memoirs of the Rt. Hon. Sir John Alexander MacDonald. 2 vols. 8vo. Lond., 1894. C 24 S 14, 15

POPE, Rev. Wm. Burt. The Abiding Word: a Sermon. 8vo. Lond. (n.d.) G 15 P 43

POPE, Wm. J. *Trans*—Chemical Crystallography. [*See* Fock, Prof. A.] A 21 R 82

POPOWSKI, Josef. The Rival Powers in Central Asia; or, the Struggle between England and Russia in the East. 8vo. Lond., 1893. F 8 S 6

POPULAR ENCYCLOPEDIA; or, Conversations Lexicon. 7 vols. roy. 8vo. Glasgow, 1850. K 7 U 14–20

POPULAR ENCYCLOPEDIA: a General Dictionary of Arts, Sciences, Literature, Biography, and History; edited by C. Annandale. 14 vols. roy. 8vo. Illustrated. Lond., 1892. K 4 T 11–24

POPULAR SCIENCE MONTHLY. Vols. 41–46. Roy. 8vo. New York, 1892–95. E

PORRITT, Edward. The Englishman at Home, his responsibilities and privileges. 8vo. Lond., 1893. F 14 R 12

PORRITT, G. T. Larvæ of British Butterflies and Moths. [*See* Buckler, W.] E

PORT ARTHUR. Regulations for the Pauper and Invalid Depôt for Males. 8vo. Hobart, 1876. MF 2 Q 79

PORTAL, Sir Gerald. The British Mission to Uganda in 1893; edited by Rennell Rodd; with the Diary of the late Capt. R. Portal. Illustrated. 8vo. Lond., 1894. D 14 S 19

PORTAL, Capt. Raymond. Diary of. [See Portal, Sir G.] D 14 S 19

PORTER, D. A. Minerals and Mineral Localities in the Northern Districts of New South Wales. (Journal Roy. Soc., N.S.W., 28.) 8vo. Sydney, 1894. ME 1 R

PORTER, J. Hampden. Wild Beasts: a Study of the Characters and Habits of the Elephant, Lion, Leopard, Panther, Jaguar, Tiger, Puma, Wolf, and Grizzly Bear. Illustrated. 8vo. New York, 1894.
A 27 S 21

PORTER, John Addison. The City of Washington, its Origin and Administration. (Johns Hopkins University Studies, 3.) 8vo. Baltimore, 1885.
B 18 S 3

PORTER, Noah: a Memorial by Friends; edited by G. S. Merriam. 8vo. Lond., 1893. C 14 S 17

PORTFOLIO, The: an Artistic Periodical, 1892-93; edited by P. G. Hammerton. Roy. 4to. Lond., 1892-93. E

Monographs, Nos. 1-12, 1894. Roy. 8vo. Lond., 1894. E
1. Rembrandt's Etchings; by P. G. Hamerton.
2. Malta and the Knights Hospitallers; by W. K. Bedford.
3. Josiah Wedgwood; by Professor Church.
4. Jules Bastien-Lepage; by Julia Cartwright (Mrs. Henry Ady).
5. Dante Gabriel Rossetti; by F. G. Stephens.
6. Frederick Walker and his Works; by Claude Phillips.
7. Fair Women in Painting and Poetry; by Wm. Sharp.
8. The New Forest; by C. J. Cornish.
9. Thomas Gainsborough; by Walter Armstrong.
10. Bookbinding in France; by Wm. Y. Fletcher.
11. Albert Dürer's Engravings; by Lionel Cust.
12. Italian Book Illustrations; by A. W. Pollard.

PORTLAND. [See Whist Table, The.] A 29 T 28

PORTUS, Æmilius. Dictionarium Ionicum Græco-Latinum, quod indicem in omnes Herodoti libros continet. 8vo. Oxonii, 1810. B 28 U 7

POSSE, Baron Nils. The Special Kinesiology of Educational Gymnastics. Illustrated. Sm. 4to. Boston, 1894. G 15 S 19

POTT, August Friedrich. Sketch of. [See Müller, F. Max.—Chips from a German Workshop.] J 9 R 32

POTTER, Beatrice. The Co-operative Movement in Great Britain. New ed. 12mo Lond., 1893. F 7 V 12

POTTER, M. C. An Elementary Text-book of Agricultural Botany. 12mo. Lond., 1893. A 19 P 1

POTTER, Rev. Robt. *Trans.*—Tragedies of Æschylus. [See Æschylus.] H 2 T 27

POTTER, Rev. Robt. Two Essays on the Coming of Christ. 1. The Spiritual Body. 2. Forever with the Lord. 8vo. Melb., 1866. MG 2 Q 23
An Examination of Secularism. 8vo. Melb., 1883.
MG 1 S 69

POTTIE, John. The Science of Scripture. 12mo. Sydney (n.d.) MG 2 R 23

POTTIER, Edmond. Études sur les Lécythes Blancs Attiques a Représentations Funéraires. 8vo. Paris, 1883. B 35 R 28

———— et REINACH, Salomon. La Nécropole de Myrina. 2 vols. 4to. Paris, 1887. B 15 R 2, 3 †

POUZET, P. Mélanges Carolingiens. [See Bardot, G.]
B 26 V 32

POWELL, Arthur. Practical Printing. [See Southward, J.] A 24 Q 14, 15

POWELL, Rev. Baden. Autobiography of F. Arago. [See Arago, F.] C 17 P 16

POWELL, B. F. S. Baden-. In Savage Isles and Settled Lands, Malaysia, Australasia, and Polynesia, 1888-91. 8vo. Lond., 1892. MD 5 S 23

POWELL, Frederick York. Saxo Grammaticus. [See Folk-lore Soc., 33.] E

POWELL, Dr. John Wesley. Seventh-Twelfth Annual Reports of the Bureau of Ethnology. [See U.S.—Bureau of Ethnology.] E

POWELL, Mary. [See Milton, Mrs. Mary.]

POWELL, Maurice. Elections. [See Rogers, F. N.]
F 14 R 32

POWELL, Lieut.-Col. Wm. H. The Army Office-'s Examiner; containing questions and answers on all subjects prescribed for an officer's examination; together with Rules to guide Boards of Examination. 8vo. New York, 1894. A 20 R 21

POWER, T. P. The Footballer: an Annual Record of Football in Victoria and the Australian Colonies. 8vo. Melb., 1875-76. ME 5 Q

POWERS, Hiram [Plaster Cast of.] [See Hutton, L.—Portraits in Plaster.] A 23 V 13

POWERS, Stephen. The American Merino, for Wool and Mutton. 8vo. New York, 1887. A 18 R 21

POWNALL, S. Beaty-. Fast Day and Vegetarian Cookery. [See Cowan, E. M.] A 22 Q 38

POWNING, Wm. Lycidas. [See Milton, J.]
MH 1 Q 22

POYNTING, Prof. J. H. The Mean Density of the Earth. (Adams Prize Essay, 1893.) Illustrated. 8vo. Lond., 1894. A 24 S 11

POYSER, Arthur Wm. Magnetism and Electricity; a Manual for Students in advanced classes. 12mo. Lond., 1892. A 21 R 10

PRAED, Mrs. R. M. (Campbell.) Under the Gum Tree: Australian Bush Stories; edited by Mrs. H. P. Martin. 12mo. Lond., 1890. MJ 2 T 44
   1. A Disturbed Christmas; by Mrs. Campbell Praed.
   2. Broken Billy; by H. B. Marriott Watson.
   3. John Grantley's Conversion; by "Tasma."
   4. A Night in a Custom-house; by Mrs. Patchett Martin.
   5. A Face at the Window; by Hume Nisbet.
   6. Jack Hammer's Sad Story; by Mrs. Lance.
   7. Opals; by Dr. M. Caffyn.
   8. His Chinese Cook; by R. Clayton.
   9. Old Shilling's Bush Wedding; by Mrs. Campbell Praed.
  10. Jerry, and a Close Shave; by E. S. Rawson.
  11. Interviewed by a Bushranger; by R. Richardson.
  12. Bush Bandits; by A. Patchett Martin.

PRAIRIE FARMER, The: a Weekly Journal for the Farm, Garden, and Rural Home. 3 vols. fol. Chicago, 1892–94. E

PRAT, Arturo. La Apoteósis de; por J. A. Rosales. 8vo. Santiago, 1888. C 21 T 9

PRATT INSTITUTE, Brooklyn, N.Y. Hand-book of Information, 1892, 1893. 8vo. New York, 1893. E
Catalogue, 1893–94. 8vo. New York, 1893. E

PRATTEN, Rev. B. P. *Trans.*—Writings of Justin Martyr. [*See* Justin Martyr.] G 14 U 2
Trans.—Writings of Tatian. [*See* Tatian.] G 14 U 3

PREECE, Wm. Henry, and STUBBS, Arthur J. Manual of Telephony. 8vo. Lond., 1893. A 21 P 22

PRESBYTERIAN CALENDAR of Australasia for 1894. 8vo. Melb., 1894. ME

PRESBYTERIAN CHURCH, Victoria. Proceedings of the General Assembly, 1866. Roy. 8vo. Melb., 1866. MG 2 T 16
Business of General Assembly, 1866. 8vo. Melb., 1866. MG 1 S 30
Rules and Forms of Procedure in the Courts and Congregations of. 12mo. Melb., 1877. MG 2 R 24

PRESBYTERIAN CHURCHES OF AUSTRALIA AND TASMANIA. Proceedings of the Fourth Conference. June, 1883. Roy. 8vo. Melb., 1883. MG 1 T 15

PRESCOTT, Wm. H. History of the Reign of Ferdinand and Isabella the Catholic; edited by J. F. Kirk. 3 vols. 12mo. Philad. (n.d.) B 34 Q 8–10
History of the Conquest of Mexico; edited by J. F. Kirk. 3 vols. 12mo. Philad. (n.d.) B 19 Q 8–10
History of the Conquest of Peru; edited by J. F. Kirk. 2 vols. 12mo. Philad. (n.d.) B 19 Q 11, 12
History of the Reign of the Emperor Charles V. [*See* Robertson, Rev. Dr. W.] B 25 Q 21–23
Life of; by G. Ticknor. 12mo. Philad. (n.d.) C 18 P 22
Biographical and Critical Miscellanies. 12mo. Philad. (n.d.) J 12 Q 2
History of the Reign of Philip II, King of Spain; edited by J. F. Kirk. 3 vols. 12mo. Philad. (n.d.) B 34 Q 5–7

PRESSEY, George Shaddack. Teeth in Australia. 4to Melb., 1893.* MA 2 R 36

PRIEST, Rev. C. Letters on the Home Work of Wesleyan Methodism, its Sustentation and Extension. 8vo. Lond., 1836. G 1 R 31

PRESTON, Prof. Thomas. The Theory of Heat. 8vo. Lond., 1894. A 21 S 20

PRESTWICH, Prof. Joseph. Collected Papers on some controverted questions of Geology. 8vo. Lond., 1895. A 24 U 34
On certain phenomena belonging to the close of the last geological period, and on their bearing upon the tradition of the flood. 8vo. Lond., 1895. A 24 U 35

PREVOST, Antoine F. History of Manon Lescaut and the Chevalier des Grieur. [*See* Collectanea Adamantaea.] J 18 R 26

PRICE, J. S. Early History of the Suez Canal. 8vo. Lond. (n.d.) B 24 R 12

PRICE, W. R. Mesmerism, its use and abuse. 8vo. Melb., 1888. MA 2 S 73

PRICE, Wm. Arthur. Treatise on the Measurement of Electrical Resistance. 8vo. Oxford, 1894. A 21 S 23

PRICE WARUNG. [*See* Astley, Wm.]

PRIDEAUX, Frederick. Precedents in Conveyancing; with Dissertations on its Law and Practice. 15th ed., by J. Whitcombe. 2 vols. 8vo. Lond., 1893. F 8 T 23, 24

PRIDEAUX, S. T. An Historical Sketch of Bookbinding. 8vo. Lond., 1893. A 25 Q 16

PRIEST OF THE LIVING TEMPLE, A. [*See* Spiritual Bombshell, The.] MG 1 S 41

PRIEST, The; the Publican; and the Strange Woman. 8vo. Geelong, 1867. MF 4 Q 9

PRIESTLEY, Herbert. Bankrupts' Accounts, New South Wales. 8vo. Sydney, 1894. MF 3 T 55

PRIESTLEY, Dr. Joseph. Sketch of. [*See* Thorpe, Dr. T. E.—Historical Chemistry.] C 17 R 2

PRIMATT, Rev. Dr. Humphrey. Duty of Humanity to Inferior Creatures; by Rev. A. Broome. 12mo. Lond., 1831. G 7 U 36

PRINCE, Thos. History of New England in the form of Annals. [*See* Bibliotheca Curiosa.] J 18 Q 50

PRINCE ALFRED HOSPITAL, Sydney. Reports, 1887–89. 8vo. Sydney, 1888–90. ME 6 S

PRINCESS, The: a Drama of Woman's Future; adapted from Tennyson's Princess. 8vo. Melb., 1876. MH 1 S 68

PRING, Ratcliffe. Criminal Statutes in force in the Colony of Queensland. Roy. 8vo. Brisbane 1863. MF 3 R 54

PRINSEP, Augustus. Illustrations to Prinsep's Journal of a Voyage from Calcutta to Van Diemen's Land, 1820-30. 4to. Lond., 1833   MD 10 P 13 †

PRIOR, W. D. Races and their Culture. 3rd edition. 8vo. Lond., 1892.   A 18 R 14

PRITCHARD, Eric. Trans.—Movement. [See Marey, E. J.]   A 29 R 31

PRITCHARD, G. B. Eocene Strata of the Bellarine Peninsula. (Roy. Soc. Vic., n.s., 6.) 8vo. Melb., 1894.   ME 1 P
—— Occurrence of Fossil Bones at Werribee. (Proc. Roy. Soc., Vict., n.s., 7.) 8vo. Melb., 1895.   ME 1 P
—— Palæontology of the older Tertiary of Victoria. Lamellibranchs. (Proc. Roy. Soc. Vict., n.s., 7.) 8vo. Melb., 1895.   ME 1 P
—— Lancefield Graptolites. (Proc. Roy. Soc., Vict, n.s., 7.) 8vo. Melb., 1895.   ME 1 P
—— Older Tertiaries of Maude. (Roy. Soc. Vict., n.s., 7.) 8vo. Melb., 1895.   ME 1 P

PRITCHETT, R. T. Yachting. [See Sullivan, Sir E.]   A 29 Q 40, 41

PRITCHARD, W. Tarn, and HARNEN, James C. Digest of Admiralty and Maritime Law; including cases on Average, Carriage of Goods, and Marine Insurance. 3rd ed. 2 vols. roy 8vo. Lond., 1887.   F 8 T 18, 19

PROBYN, John Webb. L'Italia, dalla Caduta di Napoleone I all'anno 1892. 8vo. Firenze, 1892.   B 30 Q 17

PROCTER, Adelaide Anne. Legends and Lyrics. Vol. 2. 12mo. Lond., 1892.   H 10 V 15
Legends and Lyrics. 8vo. Lond., 1895.   H 9 U 87

PROCTER, Bryan Waller, "Barry Cornwall." Dramatic Scenes, with other Poems. Illustrated. 8vo. Lond., 1857.   H 4 R 30
Memoir of Shakespeare. [See Shakespeare, Wm.—Works of.]   H 2 V 1-3

PROCTOR, Richard A. Lectures on Astronomy: Comets and Meteors—Life in other Worlds than ours—Star Depths. (3 parts). 8vo. Sydney, 1880.   MA 1 Q 56

—— and RANYARD, A. C. Old and New Astronomy. Imp. 8vo. Lond., 1892.   A 3 U 34

PROCTECTION AGAIN. Reprinted from the Financial Reformer. 8vo. Liverpool, 1881.   F 10 U 8

PROTESTANT WATCHMAN. The Apostate of the Age reproving Sin. [See Apostate of the Age.]   MG 1 S 78

PROTHERO, George Walter. The Life of Simon de Montfort, Earl of Leicester. 8vo. Lond., 1877.   C 22 P 13
—— Select Statutes and other Constitutional Documents illustrative of the Reigns of Elizabeth and James I. 8vo. Oxford, 1894.   F 4 T 14

PROTHERO, Richard E., and BRADLEY, Very Rev. George G. Life and Correspondence of Arthur P. Stanley, late Dean of Westminster. Illustrated. 2 vols. 8vo. Lond., 1893.   C 19 R 3, 4

PROWSE, D. W. A History of Newfoundland, from the English, Colonial, and Foreign Records. Roy. 8vo. Lond., 1895.   B 17 V 16

PSALMS, The: God's Book of Praise has He authorised a Supplement? 8vo. Sydney, 1890.   MG 2 S 9

PSALTER, The. [See Liturgies.]

PSYCHICAL RESEARCH, Society for. [See Society for Psychical Research.]   E

PTOLEMY, Claude. Supplement to Ptolemy's Description of the Earth. [See Wytfliet, C.]   D 19 V 16

PUBLIC OPINION, 1892-93. 4 vols. sm. fol. Lond., 1892-93.   E

PUBLICANS' QUESTION, The; by "Traveller." 8vo. Sydney (n.d.)   MF 4 R 23

PUCCINI, Giacomo. Sketch of. [See Streatfeild, R. A.—Masters of Italian Music.]   C 22 P 13

PUFENDORFF, Esaias The Druids. [See Bibliotheca Curiosa.]   J 18 Q 41

PUGH'S QUEENSLAND ALMANAC, Law Calendar, Directory, and Coast Guide, for 1869, 1870, and 1895. 3 vols. 12mo. Brisb., 1869-95.   ME 4 P

PULLEN, Rev. Henry Wm. Hand-book of Ancient Roman Marbles. 12mo. Lond., 1894.   A 23 P 6
—— Modern Christianity, a Civilized Heathenism. 12mo. Salisbury, 1873.   G 9 V 19

PULLING, A. The Law Reports: Index to Orders in Council, &c., published in the *London Gazette*, 1830-83. Imp. 8vo. Lond., 1885.   K 11 R 9

PULLMAN, George Mortimer. Sketch of. [See Stoddard, W. O.—Men of Business.]   C 16 R 19

—— and WICKES, T. H. The Strike at Pullman. 8vo. (n.p.n.d.)   F 10 Q 31

PULSFORD, Edward. Free-trade and Protection: an answer to Mr. Forsythe's pamphlet. 8vo. Sydney, 1885.   MF 4 R 40
—— The Rise, Progress, and Present Position of Trade and Commerce in New South Wales. Roy. 8vo. Sydney, 1892.   MF 1 S 43
—— Special Record of the Proceedings of Geographical Society of Australasia, in fitting out and starting the Exploratory Expedition to New Guinea. 8vo. Sydney, 1885.   MD 5 R 48

PUNCH; or, the London Charivari. Vols. 103-108. 4to. ' Lond., 1892-95. E

PURCELL, H. B. Aborigines of Australasia. (Roy. Geog. Soc., Vic. Branch, 11.) 8vo. Melb., 1894.
ME 20

PURCHAS, A. Book of Reference to Map of the Settled Districts around Melbourne, Victoria. 8vo. Melb., 1853.
MD 8 P 22

PURDUE UNIVERSITY, Lafayette, Indiana. Register, 1892-94. 8vo. Indianapolis, 1893. E

PURVES, James L. A Young Australian's Log; being the Narrative of a Voyage from Melbourne to London, in *The Pacific*, 1855. 12mo. Lond., 1856.
MD 1 P 33

PUSEY, Rev. Dr. Edward Bouverie. Life of; by Rev. Dr. Henry P. Liddon. Vols. 1-3. 8vo. Lond., 1893-94.
C 16 S 5-7

PUTNAM, George Haven. Authors and the Public in Ancient Times. 8vo. New York, 1894.
J 8 R 18

PUTNAM, Ruth. William the Silent. 2 vols. 8vo. New York, 1895.
C 22 P 6, 7

PUTNAM-JACOBI, Dr. Mary. [See Jacobi, Dr. Mary P..]

PYCROFT, Rev. James. Ways and Words of Men of Letters. 8vo. Lond., 1861.
J 9 S 38

PYKE, Vincent. Gold-miners' Guide: a handy book of Mining Law. 8vo. Wellington, 1892. MF 4 R 34

Q

Q. [*See* Couch, A. T. Quiller-.]

QUAIFE, Dr. Barzillai. The Intellectual Sciences. Vol. 1, Mental Philosophy or Psychology, and Metaphysical Science. Vol. 2, Moral Philosophy and Logic. 2 vols. 8vo. Sydney, 1872. MG 1 P 79, 80

QUARTERLY JOURNAL OF MICROSCOPICAL SCIENCE. New Series, vols. 33 and 36. Roy. 8vo. Lond., 1892-94. E

QUARTERLY REVIEW. Vols. 174-180. 8vo. Lond., 1892-95. E

QUATREFAGES, Armand de. The Pygmies; translated by F. Starr. Illustrated. 8vo. Lond., 1895.
A 19 Q 5

Légendes des Iles Hawaii. [*See* Losson, Dr. P. A.]
MB 2 U 2

QUEBEC. Commissioner of Railways. Report for the year 1881-82. 8vo. Quebec, 1882. E

QUEENSLAND—*General*. The Colony of Queensland: with the New Land Act and Extracts from the Immigration Bill of 1869. 8vo. Lond., 1870. MD 1 P 42

The Queensland Guide, for the use of Farmers, Fruit-growers, Vignerons, and others. 8vo. Brisb., 1888.
MD 5 Q 37

The latest political device for partitioning Queensland among Southern land sharks and squatting rings. 8vo. Brisbane, 1883. MF 4 R 4

Prospects of the Land League. 8vo. Rockhampton (n.d.) MF 4 Q 30

Queensland, Australia: its Territory, Climate, and Products, Agricultural, Pastoral, and Mineral; with Emigration Regulations. 8vo. Lond. (n.d.) MD 8 R 38

QUEENSLAND.—*Government Departments, Reports, and Publications.*

ACTS. [*See* Statutes.]

AGRICULTURE. Annual Report for 1892-93 Sm fol. Brisb., 1893. E

Bulletin 3, 2nd series. Manures. [*See* Shelton, E. M.]
MA 3 S 54

Botany abridged. [*See* Bailey, F. M.] MA 1 T 55
Notes for Amateur Fruit-growers. [*See* Bailey, F. M.]
MA 1 T 55

Gumming of Cane. [*See* Tryon, H.] MA 1 T 55

Pamphlets on Commercial Crops, Dairying &c. 8vo. Brisbane, 1889-93. MA 1 Q 69
 Rice-growing and its Preparation for Market.
 Recent Experiments made at the American Agricultural Experiment Stations; edited by E. M. Shelton.
 Tobacco, its Cultivation in Northern Queensland; by S. Lamb.
 Guide to the Culture of Broom Corn.
 Wheat-growing in Queensland; by E. M. Shelton.
 Tobacco, its Cultivation in Southern Queensland; by S. Lamb.
 Tree-planting for Shade and Ornament; by E. M. Shelton.
 Sugar-planting in Queensland.
 Coffee-growing and its Preparation for Market; by R. W. McCulloch.
 Cultivation of Maize; by E. M. Shelton.
 Our Stock Foods, and how to use them; by E. M. Shelton.
 Pig Raising and Pork Making; by E. M. Shelton ; with an appendix on Ham and Bacon Curing; by W. Watson.
 Establishment of Creameries; Insecticides; Manures and their Preservation; Ramie Culture; Clarifying re-agent in Sugar-making; and Potato Trials; by E. M. Shelton.
 Cheese-making Simplified.
 Suggestions for Building a Cool Dairy.
 Butter and Cheese-making, including the Canadian System of Cheese-making; by J. Mahon.
 Canning and otherwise Preserving Fruits for the Home and Market; by E. M. Shelton.
 Cultivation of Wheat in Queensland; by E. M. Shelton.
 Arrowroot Cultivation and Manufacturing in Queensland; by S. Grimes.
 Flower Gardening; by A. M. Cowan.

Pamphlets on Botany. 8vo. Brisbane, 1890-93.
MA 1 T 55
 Official Guide to the Museum of Economic Botany; by F. M. Bailey.
 Contributions to the Flora of Queensland; by F. M. Bailey. Bulletins, Oct., 1890; March, May, Dec., 1891; May, 1892; Jan., Feb., Dec., 1893.
 Companion for the Queensland Student of Plant Life; by F. M. Bailey.

QUEENSLAND—*contd.*
AGRICULTURE—*contd.*
Pamphlets. Reports of Conferences. 8vo. Brisbane, 1891-93. . . . . MA 1 Q 74
   Report of Agricultural Conferences held at Maryborough, Rockhampton, and Bundaberg.
   Report of Agricultural Conferences held at Beenleigh, Bundaberg, Rockhampton, and Mackay.
Pamphlet on Sericulture. 8vo. Brisb., 1893. . . . MA 1 Q 63
   Sericulture ; or, Silkworms and how to rear them ; by R. W. McCulloch.
BLUE BOOK. [*See* Civil Service.]
CIVIL SERVICE. Index to List of Officers. Sm. fol. Brisbane, 1894. . . . . MF 3 Q 14 ‡
Blue Book for 1894. Sm. fol. Brisb., 1895. . . . ME
FRIENDLY SOCIETIES. Report of the Registrar, 1888-89, 1892. 2 vols. sm. fol. Brisbane, 1890-93. . . . ME
Friendly Societies, Building Societies, and Trade Unions, 1887. Sm. fol. Brisbane, 1887. . . . ME
POLYNESIAN LABOUR, Further Correspondence relating to. [*See* Great Britain and Ireland—Queensland.] MF 2 Q 39 †
STATISTICS of the Colony of Queensland, 1893. Sm. fol. Brisbane, 1894. . . . . ME
STATUTES. The Queensland Statutes ; edited by A. Pain and J. L. Woolcock. 5 vols. roy. 8vo. Brisb., 1889. MF 3 S 24-28
Acts and Regulations relating to Waste Lands. 8vo. Brisb., 1861. . . . . MF 2 Q 81
Acts of the Parliament of Queensland, 55°, 56°, 58°, Vic., and a Selection of Acts of the Imperial Parliament, 55°-56° Vic. 7 vols. roy. 8vo. Brisbane, 1890-95. ME
Merchant Shipping Act, 1891. Sm. fol. Brisbane, 1895. . . . . MF 4 U 19
Patents, Designs, and Trade Marks Acts, 1884-90. 4to. Brisb., 1884-90. . . . . MF 3 U 61
WATER SUPPLY. Report of the Hydraulic Engineer, 1891-92. Sm. fol. Brisb., 1893. . . . MA 3 Q 39 †

QUEENSLAND POST OFFICE DIRECTORY, 1895-96. 8vo. Brisb., 1895. . . . . ME

QUELCH, John J. Reef Corals. [*See* Thomson, Sir C. W., and Murray. Dr. J.—Voyage of the H.M.S. *Challenger*, Zoology, 16.] . . . . A 6 †

QUESNAY, F. Tableau Œconomique (fac-simile of 1758 edition). 4to. Lond., 1894. . . . . F 39 Q 20 ‡

QUESTIONS OF THE DAY : a series of Papers on, the Revised New Testament, Modern Objections to Christianity, Everlasting Punishment, Parochial Missions, Sympathy as a Power in Church Work. 8vo. Sydney, 1882. . . . . MG 1 S 38

QUICK, Dr. John. History of Land Tenure in the Colony of Victoria. 8vo. Sandhurst, 1883. . . . MF 4 Q 14

QUILLER-COUCH. [*See* Couch.]

QUILTER, Harry. Preferences in Art, Life, and Literature. Imp. 8vo. Lond., 1892. . . . A 8 U 39

QUIROS, Capt. Pedro Fernandez de. Historia del descubrimiento de las Regiones Australes ; publicada por Don J. Zaragoza. 3 vols. 8vo. Madrid, 1876-82. MB 2 R 47-49
Jornada y Nuevo Descubrimiento. [*See* Torquemada, F. J. de.] . . . . B 36 T 13 ‡

R

R., A. [*See* Designs for Church Embroidery.] A 12 S 17 †

R., E. P. [*See* Romance of the Bush.] . . . MJ 1 P 34

RABBENO, Prof. Ugo. The American Commercial Policy. 8vo. Lond., 1895. . . . . F 11 U 12

RABELAIS, Dr. François. The Five Books and Minor Writings, together with Letters and Documents illustrating his life ; a new translation with notes, by W. F. Smith. 2 vols. roy. 8vo. Lond., 1893. J 4 T 3, 4
Works of. Translated by Sir T. Urquhart. 2 vols. 8vo. Lond., 1864. . . . . J 11 U 5, 6

RADET, G. La Lydie et le Monde Grec au temps des Mermnades. (Bibliothèque des Ecoles Françaises d'Athenes et de Rome, 63ᵉ Fascicule.) 8vo. Paris, 1893. . . . . B 27 U 10

RADFORD, Lewis B. Thomas of London before his Consecration. (Camb. Hist. Essays, 7.) 8vo. Camb., 1894. . . . . C 18 P 18

RAE, John. Eight Hours for Work. 8vo. Lond., 1894. F 5 C 9
Life of Adam Smith. 8vo. Lond., 1895. . . . C 21 T 2

RAE, W. F. Egypt To-day : the first to the third Khedive. 8vo. Lond., 1892. . . . . . B 21 T 7

RAFFLES, Sir Thos. Stamford. History of Java ; with Maps and Plates. 2 vols. 4to. Lond., 1817. B 36 S 19, 20 ‡

RAFTER, George W. Mechanics of Ventilation. 18mo. New York, 1878. . . . . A 22 P 10

—— and BAKER, M. N. Sewage Disposal in the United States. [Illustrated.] Imp. 8vo. New York, 1894. . . . . A 22 V 18

RAGOZIN, Mme. Zénaïde A. The Empire of the Tsars. [*See* Beaulieu, A. Leroy-.] . . . . . B 31 T 5, 6
Vedic India, as embodied principally in the Rig-Veda. 8vo. Lond., 1895. . . . . B 29 R 4

RAILWAY PORTER, A. [*See* Labour Troubles.]
MF 1 P 66

RAINE, Rev. Dr. James. Historians of the Church of York. [*See* Great Britain and Ireland—Chrons. and Mems.] E

York. (Historic Towns.) 8vo. Lond, 1893.
B 22 Q 27
Fasti Eboracenses. [*See* Dixon, Rev. W. H.] C 16 S 15

RAINY, Rev. Dr. Robt. Philippians. [*See* Expositor's Bible.]
G 19 S 13

RAKE, Chas. Silos and Ensilage. (Proc. Roy. Agricult. and Horticult. Soc., S. Aust., 1884.) 8vo. Adelaide, 1884.
ME 1 S

RALEIGH, Sir Walter. Is Raleigh the Author of Shakspere's Plays. [*See* Caldwell, G. S.] MJ 2 S 41

RALEIGH, Prof. Walter. The English Novel; being a short Sketch of its History from the earliest times to the appearance of Waverley. 12mo. Lond., 1894.
J 5 P 9

[Life of] R. L. Stevenson. 8vo. Lond., 1895.
C 19 V 16

RALPH, T. S. Bacteria in Living Plants. (Roy. Soc., Vict., 20.) 8vo. Melb., 1884.
ME 1 P

RALPH GREENWOOD. [*See* Gould, A. C.]

RALSTON, A. G. Divorce Law, with all the Acts and Rules now in force relating to Marriage, Divorce, and all matters Matrimonial. 8vo. Sydney, 1893.*
MF 2 R 35

RAM, Gilbert S. The Incandescent Lamp and its Manufacture. 8vo. Lond., 1893.
A 21 S 13

RAMAGE, B. James. Local Government and Free Schools in South Carolina. (Johns Hopkins University Studies, 1.) 8vo. Baltimore, 1883.
B 18 S 1

RAMBAUT, Rev. W. H. *Trans.*—Writings of Irenæus. [*See* Irenæus, St.]
G 14 U 5 & 9

RAMÉ, Louise de la, "Ouida." Views and Opinions. 8vo. Lond., 1895.
J 9 R 22

RAMOS, Don Melchor José. [Vida de] ; por M. L. Amunátegui. 8vo. Santiago, 1889.
C 21 T 3

RAMSAY, Allan. The Gentle Shepherd: a Pastoral Comedy. 18mo. Edinb., 1851.
H 10 U 1

RAMSAY, Sir Andrew Crombie. Memoir of ; by Sir A. Geikie; with Portrait. 8vo. Lond., 1895.
C 21 R 20

RAMSAY, Dr. Edward Pierson. Catalogue of the Australian Birds in the Australian Museum. Part 4. *Picariæ*, Sub-order *Halcyones*. 8vo. Sydney, 1894.
MA 1 S 26

Fisheries Exhibition, London, 1883: Catalogue of the Exhibits in the New South Wales Court. 8vo. Lond., 1883.
MK 2 R 3

RAMSAY, John. *Trans.*—Trans-Pacific Cable. [*See* Trans-Pacific Cable.]
MF 1 R 54

RAMSAY, Prof. W. M. The Church in the Roman Empire, before A.D. 170. 8vo. Lond., 1893.
G 2 S 34

RAMSAY, Prof. Wm. Manual of Roman Antiquities; revised by Prof. R. Lanciani (University of Rome). 15th ed. 8vo. Lond., 1894.
B 30 S 12

RAMSAY, Wm. G. Useful Information for Practical Men. 12mo. Wilmington, Del., 1893.
A 22 Q 20

RAMSDEN, Lady G. Letters, &c., of the 12th Duke of Somerset. [*See* Somerset, Duke of.]
C 13 S 24

RAMUSIO, Giovanni Battista. Navigationi et Viaggi. 3 vols. sm. fol. Venetia, 1556–83.
D 36 T 5–7 ‡

RAND, Addison C. The Use of Compressed Air. Illustrated. Obl. 12mo. New York, 1894.
A 29 S 12

RANDALL, C. D. Fourth International Prison Congress, St. Petersburg, Russia. 8vo. Wash., 1891.
F 14 U 17

RANDALL, Dr. Daniel Richard. A Puritan Colony at Annapolis, in Maryland. (Johns Hopkins University Studies, 4.) 8vo. Baltimore, 1886.
B 18 S 4

Coöperation in Maryland and the South. (Johns Hopkins University Studies, 6.) 8vo. Baltimore, 1888.
B 18 S 6

RANKEN, George. Windabyne: a Record of By-gone Times in Australia. 8vo. Lond., 1895.
MJ 3 Q 33

RANKIN, Daniel J. The Zambesi Basin and Nyassaland. 8vo. Lond., 1893.
D 14 R 11

RANNIE, Douglas. New Ireland. (Roy. Geograph. Soc. of Australasia, Q. Branch, 3.) 8vo. Brisbane, 1889.
ME 20 P

The Torres Group: the Natives and their Ways. (Roy. Geograph. Soc. of Australasia, Q. Branch, 5.) 8vo. Brisbane, 1890.
ME 20 P

Notes on the New Hebrides. (Roy. Geograph. Soc. of Australasia, Q. Branch, 6.) 8vo. Brisbane, 1891.
ME 20 P

Among the South-east Solomons. (Roy. Geograph. Soc. of Australasia, Q. Branch, 6.) 8vo. Brisbane, 1891.
ME 20 P

RANYARD, A. C. Old and New Astronomy. [*See* Proctor, R. A.]
A 3 U 34

RAOUL, E. Fleurs Sauvages et Bois Precieux de la Nouvelle-Zélande. [*See* Hetley, Mme. C.]
MA 9 Q 2 †

RAPHAEL SANZIO, or SANTI, DA URBINO. Raphael's Madonnas and other great Pictures, reproduced from the original Paintings; with a Life of Raphael and an Account of his Chief Works; by Karl Károly. Sm. fol. Lond., 1894.
A 36 S 16 ‡

Sketch of. [*See* Pater, W.—Miscellaneous Studies.]
J 7 S 10

RATHBONE, Mrs. (Anne Manning.) The Colloquies of Edward Osborne, Citizen and Cloth-maker of London. 3rd ed. 12mo. Lond., 1890. J 16 T 30

The Household of Sir Thomas More. 4th ed. 12mo. Lond., 1860. C 17 P 5

RATHBONE, John. Farming in Canada. [*See* Ford, W. W.] MA 1 P 2

RATTE, A. Felix. Hints for collecting Geological and Mineralogical Specimens. 1st and 2nd eds. 8vo. Sydney, 1886-87. MA 2 V 66

RAVAILLAC, Francis. Trial of, for the Murder of King Henry the Great. [*See* Bibliotheca Curiosa.] J 18 Q 23

RAVENSTEIN, E. G. Paraguay. [*See* Bourgade la Dardye, Dr.] D 15 R 10

RAWLE, Edwin John. Annals of the Ancient Royal Forest of Exmoor. 4to. Taunton, 1893. B 23 V 13

RAWLINGS, Thos. Confederation of the British North American Provinces. Roy. 8vo. Lond., 1865. F 7 U 1

RAWLINSON, Prof. George. Parthia. (Story of the Nations.) 8vo. Lond., 1893. B 20 R 1

RAWLINSON, Thos. E. Notes on the Discovery of some Keys in the Shore Formation of Corio Bay, near Geelong. (Roy. Soc. of V c.) 8vo. Melb, 1874. MA 3 S 41

RAWNSLEY, Rev. Hardwicke Drummond. Literary Associations of the English Lakes. 2 vols. 12mo. Glasgow, 1894. D 18 Q 12, 13

RAWSON, Christopher. Dyeing. [*See* Knecht, E.] A 11 R 28-30

RAWSON, E. S. Jerry, and a Close Shave. [*See* Praed, Mrs. Campbell.—Under the Gum Tree.] MJ 2 T 44

RAY, Sidney H. Language of the New Hebrides. (Journal Roy Soc., N.S.W., 27.) 8vo. Sydney, 1893. ME 1 R

Languages of British New Guinea (Anthropol. Inst., 24.) 8vo. Lond., 1894. E

RAY, W. D. Dynamo Electric Machinery. [*See* Mac-Fadden, C. K.] A 21 P 45

RAY SOCIETY. Publications of. Vols. 4-6. 8vo. Lond., 1893-95. E
4. Monograph of British Phytophagous Hymenoptera (Cynipidæ, and Appendix), by P. Cameron.
5, 6. Larvæ of British Butterflies and Moths; by W. Buckler.

RAYLEIGH, (John Wm. Strutt), Baron. Theory of Sound, vol. 1. 2nd ed. Roy. 8vo. Lond., 1894. A 21 T 28

RAYMOND, G. Life and Enterprises of R. W. Elliston, Comedian. Illustrated. 12mo. Lond., 1857. C 17 P 6

RAYMOND, Prof. George Lansing. Art in Theory: an Introduction to the Study of Comparative Æsthetics. 8vo. New York, 1894. A 23 R 12

RAYNAL, F. E. Les Naufragés ou vingt mois sur un Récif des Iles Auckland. Illustré. Imp. 8vo. Paris, 1870. MD 6 U 26

RAYNAL, Wm. Thomas, Abbé. Letter on the Affairs of North America. [*See* Paine, T.] B 19 V 2

REAGAN, H. C., jun. Locomotive Mechanism and Engineering. 1st ed. 8vo. New York, 1894. A 22 Q 34

REAL, G. C. Documents relating to Voyages of. [*See* Hakluyt Soc., 86.] E

RECHABITES, INDEPENDENT ORDER OF. Jubilee Celebration. Proceedings of the First Intercolonial Convention, held at Melbourne, 1855. 12mo. Melb., 1886. MG 1 P 72

RECKENZAUN, Anthony. Electric Traction on Railways and Tramways. 8vo. Lond, 1892 A 5 S 34

RECLUS, Jean Jacques Elisée. Nouvelle Géographie Universelle : la Terre et les Hommes. Tome 19. Imp. 8vc. Paris, 1894. D 10 V 19

Primitive Folk : Studies in Comparative Ethnology. 8vo. Lond. (n.d.) A 18 R 27

RECORDS OF THE PAST, being English Translations of the Ancient Monuments of Egypt and Western Asia. New Series. Vol. 6. Edited by Prof. A. H. Sayce. 8vo. Lond., 1892. B 21 Q 19

REDGRAVE, Chas. A. H. Guide to the Police Acts of New South Wales : comprising a collection of Cases relating thereto ; with a General Index of Offences thereunder. Roy. 8vo. Sydney, 1895. MF 3 R 66

REDGRAVE, Gilbert R. Calcareous Cements, their Nature and Uses. 12mo. Lond., 1895. A 19 S 2

REDGRAVE, Richard. Manual of Design. 8vo. Lond., 1876. A 23 R 26

—— and REDGRAVE, Samuel. A Century of Painters of the English School. 8vo. Lond., 1890. A 23 E 7

REDWOOD, Boverton. Petrolum, its Production and Use. 18mo. New York, 1887. A 24 P 13

REDWOOD, Iltyd I. Ammonia Refrigeration. 18mo. New York, 1895. A 18 P 24

REED, Elizabeth A. Persian Literature, ancient and modern. 8vo. Chicago, 1893. B 20 E 2

REED, F. R. C. Branchiopods (Fossil). 8vo. Lond.,
1805. A 30 U 19

REED, Dr. Henry. Lectures on the British Poets. 8vo.
Lond., 1859. J 12 T 35

REED, J. E. Gallery of Contemporary Art. [*See* Silvestre, A.] A G 8 8, 9 ‡

REED, Joseph. The Register Office: a Farce. [*See* London Stage, 4.] H 2 S 36

REES, Rowland. Customs Comparative Duties of the Australasian Colonies and Fiji, 1890-91. Sm. fol. (n.p.n.d.) MF 9 P 27 †

REES, W. L. Sir Gilbert Leigh; or Pages from the History of an Eventful Life; with an Appendix—the Great Pro-Consul. 2 vols. 12mo. Lond., 1878. MJ 1 U 37, 38

REEVE, Edward. Railway Guide of New South Wales. 4to. Sydney, 1879. MD 5 V 44

REEVE, Wybert. From Life: selected, and re-published by request, from *The Australasian* and other journals. 8vo. Lond., 1891. MH 1 U 42

REEVES, Dr. Chas. Evans. On the Cure of Fluke in Sheep; with Observations on Fluke in Man. 8vo. Melb., 1878. MA 3 T 17

REEVES, Edward. Homeward Bound after Thirty Years; a Colonist's Impressions of New Zealand, Australia, Tangier, and Spain. Illustrated, 8vo. Lond., 1892. MD 5 R 42

REEVES, Dr. Jesse Siddall. International Beginnings of the Congo Free State. (Johns Hopkins Univ. Studies, 12.) Roy. 8vo. Baltimore, 1894. B 18 8 12

REFORM CLUB LIBRARY, NEW YORK. Catalogue, 1892. 8vo. New York, 1892. K 7 S 42

REFUGE, The, Melbourne. Thirteenth Annual Report. 8vo. Melb., 1870. MG 2 Q 48

RÉGAMEY, Félix. Japan in Art and Industry, with a Glance at Japanese Manners and Customs. 8vo. Lond., 1893. A 25 R 8

REGISTER OF AUSTRALIAN AND NEW ZEALAND SHIPPING, 1874-80, 1882-84. 7 vols. 8vo. Melb., 1874-83. ME 6 R

REGNAUD, Paul, GROSSET, J., et GRANDJEAN, J. M. Mélanges de Philologie Indo-Européenne. 8vo. Paris, 1888. J 7 U 40

REGO, Dr. J. P. Memoria Historica das Epidemias da Febre Amarello e Cholera-morbo que têm reinado en Brazil. 8vo. Rio de Janeiro, 1873. A 26 U 23

REID, A. Vox Clamantium: the Gospel of the People; by Writers, Preachers, and Workers. 8vo. Lond., 1894. F 14 T 19

REID, Surg.-Lieut.-Col. A. Scott. Chin-Lushai Land. With Maps. 8vo. Calcutta, 1893. D 17 T 7

REID, Andrew. The New Party, described by some of its members. 8vo. Lond., 1894. F 14 T 17

REID, J. Arbuckle. The Australian Reader: Selections from Leading Journals on Memorable Historic Events. Roy. 8vo. Melb., 1882. MB 1 U 17

REID, S. J. [Life of] Lord John Russell. 8vo. Lond., 1895. C 21 P 21

REID, Thorburn. Arithmetic of Magnetism and Electricity. [*See* Morrow, J. T.] A 21 P 38

REID, William Fergusson. Draft of Measure for the Alienation, Settlement, and Utilisation of Crown Lands in the Australian Colonies, in 10 clauses. 8vo. Sydney, 1884. MF 4 R 46

The First of Days. 8vo. Ipswich, Q., 1881. MH 1 V 7

REIGNS of the Kings and Queens of England; put into Rhyme by "A Tasmanian Lady." 8vo. Hobart, 1867. MH 1 S 34

REINACH, Salomon. La Necropole de Myrina. [*See* Pottier, E.] B 15 R 2, 3 †

REITH, Rev. G. *Trans.*—Writings of Justin Martyr. [*See* Justin Martyr.] G 14 U 2

REIZEN IN MIDDEN-SUMATRA, 1877-79. 6 vols. (in 11). Imp. 8vo. and fol. Leiden, 1881. D 12 V 16-24 †, and G U 4, 5 ‡

RELIGION. On Religion; by "A Former Elder in a Scotch Church." [*See* Religious Pamphlets, 3.] G 9 V 18

RELIGIOUS PAMPHLETS. 3 vols. 12mo. Ramsgate and Lond., 1864-74. G 9 V 16-18

1. Reply to the Question, "Shall I seek Ordination in the Church of England?" by Bishop Hinds.
Reply to the Question, "Apart from Supernatural Revelation, what is man's prospect of living after death?" by Bishop Hinds.
Reply to the Question, "What have we to rely on, if we cannot rely on the Bible?" by Bishop Hinds.
Difficulties which attend the study of the Scriptures; by Bishop Hare.
The Opinions of Prof. D. F. Strauss.
The Eternal Gospel; by Rev. R. W. Mackay.
Basis of a New Reformation.
How to complete the Reformation; by E. Maitland.
Spiritual Pantheism.
The Gospel of the Kingdom.
Examination of some recent Writings about Immortality.
Necessity of Free Inquiry and Plain Speaking.
Review of a Pamphlet entitled, "The Present Dangers of the Church of England;" by W. G. Clark.
Cardinal Doctrines of Calvinism; by M. Macfie.
Tendencies of Modern Religious Thought; by Rev. J. Cranbrook.
The Story of the Garden of Eden; by W. Stone.
God's Method of Government; by Rev. J. Cranbrook.

RELIGIOUS PAMPHLETS—*contd.*

2. The true Temptation of Jesus ; Religious Weakness of Protestantism ; Defective Morality of the New Testament ; Against Hero-making in Religion ; the Controversy about Prayer ; Causes of Atheism ; Relations of Theism to Pantheism, and on the Galla Religion ; Ancient Sacrifices ; by Prof. F. W. Newman.
Sacred History as a Branch of Elementary Education.
Science and Theology ; by R. D. Hanson.
Three Notices of the Speaker's Commentary ; by Dr. A. Kuenen.
Church Cursing and Atheism : by Rev. T. P. Kirkman.
A Critical Catechism ; by T. L. Strange.
3. The Book of Common Prayer ; by W. Jevons.
Church of England Catechism examined ; by J. Bentham.
Physical Resurrection of Jesus ; by T. Scott.
Commentators and Hierophants.
The Christian Society ; by T. Scott.
Claims of Christianity to the Character of a Divine Revelation considered ; by W. Jevons.
On Religion.
Criticism the Restoration of Christianity.

RELIGIOUS TRACT SOCIETY OF VICTORIA.
10th, 12th, 13th, 18th, 20th Annual Reports. 8vo. Melb., 1866–76. ME 6 Q

REMARKABLE MAPS of the 15th, 16th, and 17th Centuries, reproduced in their original size. Fol. Amsterdam, 1894. D 8 P 22 ‡
1. The Bodel Nyenhuis Collection at Leyden.

REMBRANDT VAN RYN, Hermanzoon. Etchings.
[See Portfolio Monograph, 1.] E

REMFRY & REMFRY, Messrs. Patents and their relation to the wants of India. 8vo. Calcutta, 1881. F 7 V 37

REMINGTON, Prof. Joseph Price. Dispensatory of the United States. [See Wood, Dr. G. B.] A 26 V 13

REMINISCENCES of Australian Early Life; by "A Pioneer." 8vo. Lond., 1893. MD 1 Q 33

REMSEN, Daniel S. Primary Elections: a study of methods for improving the basis of party organisation. 12mo. New York, 1894. F 5 Q 8

RENAN, Ernest. Averroës et l'Averroïsme, essai historique. 4ᵉ éd. 8vo. Paris, 1882. G 12 U 2
L'Avenir de la Science. 7ᵉ éd. 8vo. Paris, 1890. G 12 U 10
Le Cantique des Cantiques, traduit de l'Hébreu, avec une étude sur le plan, l'âge et le caractère du poëme. 6ᵉ éd. 8vo. Paris, 1891. G 12 U 4
Conférences d'Angleterre. Rome et le Christianisme, Marc-Aurèle. 3ᵉ éd. 8vo. Paris, 1880. G 12 U 1
Dialogues et Fragments Philosophiques. 3ᵉ éd. 8vo. Paris, 1886. G 12 U 11
Discours et Conférences. 2ᵉ éd. 8vo. Paris, 1887. G 12 U 12
Drames Philosophiques. 8vo. Paris, 1888. G 12 U 3
L'Ecclésiaste, traduit de l'Hébreu, avec une étude sur l'âge et le caractère du livre. 3ᵉ éd. 8vo. Paris, 1890. G 12 U 5

RENAN, Ernest—*contd.*
Essais de Morale et de Critique. 4ᵉ éd. 8vo. Paris, 1889. G 12 U 13
Études d'Histoire Religieuse. 7ᵉ éd. 8vo. Paris, 1880. G 12 U 7
Feuilles Détachées, faisant suite aux Souvenirs d'Enfance et de Jeunesse. 8vo. Paris, 1892. C 2 V 6
Histoire des Origines du Christianisme. 8 vols. 8vo. Paris, 1873–91. G 12 U 16–23
Vie de Jésus. 20ᵉ éd.
Les Apôtres. 12ᵉ éd.
Saint Paul. 12ᵉ éd.
L'Antechrist. 3ᵉ éd.
Les Évangiles. 3ᵉ éd.
L'Église Chrétienne. 4ᵉ éd.
Marc Aurèle et la Fin du Monde Antique. 6ᵉ éd.
Index Général.
Histoire du Peuple d'Israël. Tomes 1–5. 8vo. Paris, 1887–93. G 12 U 24–28
Le Livre de Job, traduit de l'Hébreu, avec une étude sur l'âge et le caractère du poëme. 4ᵉ éd. 8vo. Paris, 1882. G 12 U 6
Mélanges d'Histoire et de Voyages. 8vo. Paris, 1890. G 12 U 9
Nouvelles Études d'Histoire Religieuse. 16ᵉ éd. 8vo. Paris, 1884. G 12 U 8
Questions contemporaines. 3ᵉ éd. 8vo. Paris, 1870. G 12 U 14
Recollections of my Youth. 2nd ed. 8vo. Lond., 1892. C 12 Q 48
La Réforme intellectuelle et morale. 4ᵉ éd. 8vo. Paris, 1875. G 12 U 15
Souvenirs d'Enfance et de Jeunesse. 8vo. Paris, 1883. C 2 V 5
Studies of Religious History. 8vo. Lond., 1893. G 12 U 31
The Book of Job, translated from the Hebrew, with a study of the plan, the age, and the character of the poem. 8vo. Lond. (n.d.) G 12 U 29
The Song of Songs, translated from the Hebrew, with a study of the plan, the age, and the character of the poem. 8vo. Lond. (n.d.) G 12 U 30
Ernest Renan (in memoriam) ; by the Rt. Hon. Sir M. E. G. Duff. 8vo. Lond., 1893. C 12 Q 47
Life of; by F. Espinasse. 8vo. Lond., 1895. C 21 T 12
[Sketch of.] [See Darmesteter, J.—Selected Essays.] J 6 S 26

RENARD, A. Volcanic Ashes and Cosmic Dust. [See Murray, J.] A 20 T 16
Deep Sea Deposits. [See Murray, J.] A 20 T 16
Deep Sea Deposits. [See Thomson, Sir C. W., and Murray, Dr. J.—Voyage of H.M.S. *Challenger*.] A 6 †
Rock Specimens collected on Oceanic Islands. [See Thomson, Sir C. W., and Murray, Dr. J.—Voyage of H.M.S. *Challenger*.] A 6 †

RENDLE, Dr. R. Notes on Snake-bite: what to do, including the use of strychnin. 8vo. Brisbane, 1892. MA 3 V 43

RENEY, Wm. A Narrative of the Shipwreck of the *Corsair* in the month of January, 1835, on an unknown reef near the Kingsmill Islands in the South Pacific Ocean. 12mo. Lond., 1836. MD 7 T 60

RENNELL, Major James, and the rise of Modern English Geography; by C. R. Markham. 8vo. Lond., 1895.
C 17 P 30

RENNICK, Chas. Henry George and his Utopia: a Lecture delivered at Melbourne, October, 1890. Roy. 8vo. Melb., 1890. MF 3 R 55

RENNIE, Edward Alexander. Outline of the History of St. George's Church, Sydney. 8vo. Sydney, 1881.
MG 1 S 77

RENNIE, Prof. Dr. Edward Henry. Colouring Matter from *Lomatia Ilicifolia* and *Lomatia Longifolia*. 8vo. Adelaide, 1895. MA 2 T 72
Poisoning by Tinned Fish. (Trans. Roy. Soc., S. Australia, D.) 8vo. Adelaide, 1887. ME 1 S

———— and TURNER, E. F. Poisonous Constituents of *Stephania hernandifolia*. (Trans. Roy. Soc., S. Australia, 17.) 8vo. Adelaide, 1892. ME 1 S

RENNIE, Rev. James. Insect Architecture. New ed. 8vo. Lond., 1857. A 29 P 9

RENNIE, John and George. [Biographical Sketches.] [*See* Smith, G. B.—Leaders of Modern Industry.]
C 14 P 14

RENOUARD, Ant. Aug. Bibliographical Sketch of the Aldine Press at Venice, 1494–1597. 12mo. Edinb., 1889. J 18 Q 40

RENSSELAER, Mrs. Schuyler van. English Cathedrals: illustrated by J. Pennell. Imp. 8vo. Lond., 1892.
A 2 U 36

RENSSELAER POLYTECHNIC INSTITUTE. Handbook of Information. Courses in Civil Engineering and Natural Science. 8vo. Troy, N.Y., 1893. E
Annual Register, 1893. Register of Graduates, 1876–92. 8vo. Troy, N.Z., 1893. E
Records of Work of Graduates. 8vo. (n.p.n.d.) E

RENTON, Wm. Outlines of English Literature. 8vo. Lond., 1893. B 23 Q 14

RENWICK, Dr. Arthur. The Realm of Knowledge and the Realm of Faith: a lecture. 8vo. Sydney, 1882.
MG 1 S 37

REPPLIER, Agnes. Books and Men. 12mo. Lond., 1893. J 6 Q 33
Essays in Idleness. 12mo. Lond., 1893. J 6 Q 34

REQUENA, M. del C. Validez de los Actos de disposicion de Heredero Aparente respecto de tercero de buena fé. 8vo. Montevideo, 1894. F 9 R 33

RESEARCH. [*See* Beilby, J. W.]

REULEAUX, F. The Constructor: a Hand-book of Machine Design; translated by H. H. Suplee. 4to. Philad., 1893. A 12 U 1 †

REUNERT, Theodore. Diamonds and Gold in South Africa. 8vo. Lond., 1893. A 24 S 2

RE-UNION OF CHRISTENDOM, The. 4to. Sydney, 1893. MG 9 P 16 †

REVELATIONS OF COMMON SENSE, The; by "Antipodes." 12mo. Lond., 1884. G 10 P 23

REVIEW OF REVIEWS. Vols. 6–8, 10. 4to. Lond., 1892–94. E
Australasian edition. Vols. I, 3, 4. 4to. Lond., 1892–94.
ME 6 U
Annual Index of Periodicals and Photographs for 1890–92. 4 vols. sm. 4to. Lond., 1891–93. E
Two and two make four; being the Review of Reviews Annual, 1893. [*See* Stead, W. T.]

REVILL, Alfred. American Plumbing. Illustrated. 8vo. New York, 1894. A 25 R 13

REVISTA DE DERECHO Y JURISPRUDENCIA. 4 vols. 8vo. Montevideo, 1887–90. E

REVUE DES DEUX MONDES. Vols. 112–129. 8vo. Paris, 1892–95. E
Table. Troisième Période, 1886–93. Roy. 8vo. Paris, 1893. E

REVUE DES QUESTIONS HISTORIQUES. Tomes 52–56. Roy. 8vo. Paris, 1892–94. E

REVUE D'ETHNOGRAPHIE. Tomes 1–8. Roy. 8vo. Paris, 1882–89. E

REYER, Prof. Edward. Die Euganeen: Bau und Geschichte eines Vulcanes. 8vo. Wien, 1877.
A 24 U 18
Beitrag zur Fysik der Eruptionen und der Eruptiv-Gesteine. 8vo. Wien, 1877. A 24 T 15
Die Culturentwicklung Australiens. 8vo. Berlin, 1894.
MG 1 T 35
Granit und Schiefer von Schlackenwald. Roy. 8vo. Wien, 1880. A 24 V 22
Entwicklung und Organisation der Volksbibliotheken. Roy. 8vo. Leipzig, 1893. J 7 U 28

REYNOLDS, Sir Joshua. [Life of]; by C. Phillips. 8vo. Lond., 1894. C 14 S 13

REYNOLDS, Dr. J. Russell. A System of Medicine. 3rd ed. 5 vols. 8vo. Lond, 1876–79. A 33 T 1–5

RHEAD, E. L. Metallurgy: an Elementary Text-book. 8vo. Lond., 1895. A 24 Q 24

RHEES, Wm. John. Catalogue of Publications of the Smithsonian Institution, 1846-82. 8vo. Wash., 1882. E

RHO, Dr. Filippo. Le Isole della Società e gl' indigeni della Polinesie. Roy. 8vo. Roma, 1889. MD 5 V 45

RHODE ISLAND--*State Departments, Reports, and Publications.*

AGRICULTURAL EXPERIMENT STATION. Reports, 1892-93. 2 vols. 8vo. Providence, 1892-93. E

COLLEGE OF AGRICULTURE AND MECHANIC ARTS. Report of the Corporation, 1895. 8vo. Providence, 1895. E

RHODES, J. F. History of the United States, from the compromise of 1850. 3 vols. 8vo. Lond., 1893-95. B 17 R 25-27

RHYS, Prof. John. Book of Llan Dâv. [*See* Welsh Text Society.] E

RIAÑO, Juan F. Industrial Arts in Spain. 8vo. Lond., 1879. A 23 R 34

RICARDO, David. Sketch of. [*See* Bagehot, W.—Economic Studies.] F 7 V 35

RICE, Dr. Wm. North. Twenty-five years of Scientific Progress, and other Essays. 12mo. New York, 1894. A 29 S 18

RICHARD LE POITEVIN. Notice sur divers Manuscrits de la Bibliothèque Vaticane: Richard le Poitevin; par E. Berger. 8vo. Paris, 1879. J 7 U 35

RICHARDS, T. H. Hattou-. Travels with the Hon. Sir William MacGregor, K.C.M.G., Administrator of British New Guinea. (Roy. Geog. Soc. Australasia, Vic. Branch, 8.) 8vo. Melb., 1891. ME 20

RICHARDS, Col. W. H. Text-book of Military Topography. Roy. 8vo. Lond., 1888. A 29 V 14

RICHARDSON, Rev. George Walter. Two Sermons preached in St. Marks Church, Darling Point, January, 1864, on the occasion of the Death of the Rev. G. W. Richardson; by the Very Rev. W. M. Cowper and the Rev. W. H. Walsh. 8vo. Sydney, 1864. MG 2 Q 23

RICHARDSON, Sir John, Description of Australian Fish. 4to. Lond., 1841. MA 2 Q 2 †

RICHARDSON, John. How it can be done; or, Constructive Socialism. 8vo. Lond., 1895. F 8 U 10

RICHARDSON, Major Sir John L. C. Employment of Females and Children in Factories and Workshops. 8vo. Dunedin, 1881. MF 4 R 39

RICHARDSON, M. T. Practical Blacksmithing. Vols. 1-4. 8vo. New York, 1889-91. A 25 R 1-4

RICHARDSON, R. Interviewed by a Bushranger. [*See* Pratt, Mrs. Campbell.—Under the Gum Tree.] MJ 2 T 44

RICHARDSON, Ralph Ireland in 1880; with an Agricultural Map of Ireland. Sm. 4to. Lond., 1881. F 2 V 11

[Life of] G. Morland, Painter, 1763-1804. 8vo. Lond., 1895. C 16 U 11

RICHARDSON, Wm. Analysis and Illustration of some of Shakespeare's Remarkable Characters. 2nd ed. 18mo. Lond., 1774. J 11 U 35

RICHE, Dr. A. Etude Stratigraphique sur le Jurassique Intérieur du Jura Méridional. 8vo. Paris, 1893. A 25 V 9

RICHMOND, W. D. Colour and Colour-printing as applied to Lithography. 3rd ed. 12mo. Lond. (n.d.) A 25 Q 34

RICHTER, Eugene. Pictures of the Socialistic Future. 8vo. Lond., 1893. F 14 Q 44

RICHTER, H. E. How may we preserve our youth? 8vo. Milwaukee (n.d.) G 18 R 35

RICHTER, Jean Paul F. Translations of Works of. [*See* Carlyle, T.] J 5 R 42

RICKS, George, and VAUGHAN, Joseph. Hand and Eye Training: Designing with Coloured Papers. Roy. 8vo. Lond., 1894. G 18 S 14

Hand and Eye Training: Modelling in Cardboard. Roy. 8vo. Lond., 1894. G 18 S 13

Hand and Eye Training: Colour-work. Roy. 8vo. Lond., 1895. G 18 S 12

RIDEAL, Dr. Samuel. Disinfection and Disinfectants; together with an Account of the Chemical Substances used as Antiseptics and Preservatives. 8vo. Lond., 1895. A 33 U 18

RIDGE, G. H. Experience of the Barque *W. H. Besse* in the Java Earthquake, 1883. (Roy. Soc., Vict., 21.) 8vo. Melb., 1885. ME 1 P

RIDLEY, Stuart O. Monaxonida. [*See* Thomson, Sir C. W., and Murray, Dr. J.—Voyage of H.M.S. *Challenger*.] A 6 †

RIDPATH, Dr. John Clark. Royal Photograph Gallery. Sm 4to. Philad., 1893. A 15 P 10 †

RIEMANN, Othon. Etudes sur la Langue et la Grammaire de Tite Live. 8vo. Paris, 1879. J 7 U 33

Recherches Archéologiques sur les Iles Ioniennes. 8vo. Paris, 1879-80. B 35 R 21

RIGGS Dr. Stephen Return. Dakota Grammar, Texts, and Ethnography. 4to. Wash, 1893. J 15 S 6 †

RILEY, Dr. Charles Valentine. Cotton Worm and the Boll Worm. [*See* U.S. Entomological Commission, 4th Report.] E
    The Cotton Worm: Summary of its Natural History, with an Account of its Enemies, and the best means of controlling it. [Illustrated.] 8vo. Wash., 1880.
A 32 T 2
    Destructive Locusts: a popular consideration of a few of the more injurious Locusts [or "Grasshoppers"] of the United States, together with the best means of destroying them. [Illustrated.] 8vo. Wash., 1891.
A 27 U 14
    General Index and Supplement to the Nine Reports on the Insects of Missouri. 8vo. Wash., 1881.
A 27 U 13
    Potato Pests: being an illustrated Account of the Colorado Potato-beetle and the other Insect foes of the Potato in North America; with suggestions for their repression and methods for their destruction. 8vo. New York, 1876. A 18 Q 46
    Reports on the damage by Destructive Locusts during the Season of 1891. 8vo. Wash., 1892. A 27 U 14
    United States Department of Agriculture: Division of Entomology. Practical Work of the Division. 8vo. Wash., 1894. A 32 T 12

RINGROSE, R. C. Establishment of a Geological Survey in Queensland. (Proc. Roy. Soc., Queensland, 2.) 8vo. Brisbane, 1886. ME 1 T

RIPLEY, Rev. George. Brook Farm. [*See* Codman, J. T.] F 8 U 38

RITCHIE, Anne. Records of Tennyson, Ruskin, and Browning. 8vo. Lond., 1892. C 16 R 17

RITCHIE, Anne (Thackeray), and EVANS, Richardson. Lord Amherst and the British advance eastwards to Burma. (Rulers of India.) 12mo. Oxford, 1894.
C 14 P 20

RITCHIE, Daniel. The Voice of our Exiles; or, Stray Leaves from a Convict Ship. 12mo. Edinb., 1854.
MG 1 P 61

RITCHIE, Prof. David G. Darwin and Hegel, with other Philosophical Studies. 8vo. Lond., 1893. G 15 S 26
    Natural Rights: a Criticism on some Political and Ethical Conceptions. Roy. 8vo. Lond., 1895.
F 14 U 12

RITCHIE, Leitch. Travelling Sketches on the Sea-coast of France. Illustrated. 8vo. Lond., 1834.
D 18 R 29
    Scott and Scotland. Illustrated. 8vo. Lond., 1835.
B 32 R 6
    Windsor Castle and its Environs, including Eton College. 2nd ed., with additions by E. Jesse. Illustrated. 8vo. Lond., 1848. B 21 U 12

RIVERINE DISTRICT. Independence of the Riverine District of Australia. 8vo. Deniliquin, 1863.
MF 4 R 6

RIVERINE QUESTION, The: Speeches in the Legislative Assembly of New South Wales. 8vo. Melb., 1864. MF 2 Q 82

RIVIÈRE, Jules. My Musical Life and Recollections. 8vo. Lond., 1893. C 12 Q 46

ROACH, John. Sketch of. [*See* Stoddard, W. O.—Men of Business.] C 16 R 19

ROB ROY. [*See* Macgregor, J.]

ROBBINS, Alfred Farthing. Early Public Life of W. E. Gladstone. 8vo. Lond., 1894. C 17 R 17

ROBERT I., King of Scotland. [Plaster Cast of.] [*See* Hutton L.—Portraits in Plaster.] A 23 V 13

ROBERT-HOUDIN, J. E. [*See* Houdin, J. E. R.]

ROBERTS, Rev. Dr. Alexander. [*See* Ante-Nicene Christian Library.] G 14 U 1-24

ROBERTS, Fred. C., of Tientsin; or, for Christ and China; by Mrs. Bryson. 8vo. Lond., 1895.
C 22 P 10

ROBERTS, General Lord Frederick Sleigh. The Rise of Wellington. 12mo. Lond., 1895. C 5 P 22
    Addiscombe. [*See* Vibart, Col. H. M.] B 21 U 15

ROBERTS, Dr. Isaac. Photographs of Stars, Star-clusters, and Nebulæ. 4to. Lond., 1893. A 14 S 10†

ROBERTS, Marshall Owen. Sketch of. [*See* Stoddard, W. O.—Men of Business.] C 16 R 19

ROBERTS, R. D. The Earth's History: an introduction to modern geology. 8vo. Lond., 1893. A 24 Q 19

ROBERTS, Dr. Richard L. Illustrated Lectures on Ambulance Work. 4th ed. 12mo. Lond., 1895.
A 26 R 9

ROBERTS, Robert. Lectures on the Religious Errors of the Times. 1. The Bible, what it is, and how to interpret it. (Pam.) 8vo. Sydney (n.d.)
MG 1 Q 53

ROBERTS, W. Printers' Marks: a Chapter in the History of Typography. 8vo. Lond., 1893.
B 17 Q 10

ROBERTS, Prof. W. Rhys. The Ancient Bœotians: their Character and Culture, and their Reputation. 8vo. Camb., 1895. B 28 U 8

ROBERTS, W. S. de L. Testing of Cement. (Journal Roy. Soc., N.S.W., 28.) 8vo. Sydney, 1894. ME 1 R

ROBERTS-AUSTEN, W. C. [*See* Austen, W. C. R.]

ROBERTSON, —. The Parson and the Pedlar: a dialogue in verse, &c.; by "Ingonyama." 12mo. (n.p.) 1879. MH 1 P 58

ROBERTSON, A. Bohring Sea Award and Regulations. [See Law Magazine and Review, 1893-94.] E

ROBERTSON, Dr. Alexander. Colloquia Anatomica, Physiologica, atque Chem ca, quæstionibus et responsis; ad usum ingenuæ juventutis accommodata. 12mo. Edinb., 1810. A 26 P 18

ROBERTSON, Rev. Alexander. Fra Paola Sarpi, the greatest of the Venetians. 8vo. Lond., 1893. C 22 P 18

ROBERTSON, Rev. Andrew. Essays on various subjects. 12mo. Melb., 1874. MJ 1 P 61

ROBERTSON, Andrew. Nuggets in the Devil's Punchbowl, and other Australian Tales. 12mo. Lond., 1894. MJ 2 T 52

ROBERTSON, Eric S. The Children of the Poets: an Anthology from English and American Writers of Three Centuries. 18mo. Lond., 1886. H 10 T 10

ROBERTSON, Prof. George Croom. Hobbes, Philosopher. [See Hobbes, T.] G 9 V 8

ROBERTSON, George Wm. The South Australian Protestant Emigration Community. 8vo. Lond. 1837. MB 2 R 08

ROBERTSON, John A. Chatham Islands. (Roy. Geograph. Soc. of Australasia, Q. Branch, 5.) 8vo Brisbane, 1890. ME 20

ROBERTSON, John M. The Eight Hours' Question. 8vo. Lond, 1893. F 14 Q 43
Thomson's Poems, &c. [See Thomson, Jas.] H 10 Q 22

ROBERTSON, T. W. Life and Writings of; by T. E Pemberton. 8vo. Lond, 1893. C 15 R 18

ROBERTSON, Rev. Dr. Wm History of the Reign of the Emperor Charles V; with an Account of his Life after his abdication, by W. H. Prescott. 3 vols. 12mo. Phi ad. (n.d.) B 25 Q 21-23

ROBESPIERRE, Maximilien M. I. de. [Plaster Cast of.] [See Hutton, L.—Portraits in Plaster.] A 23 V 13

ROBIN, C. E. A Scribbler's Scrap Book. 8vo. Sydney, 1893. MJ 1 S 51

ROBIN, George E. Minera and other Resources of Sierra County, New Mexico. 8vo. St. Louis, 1893. D 15 T 19

ROBINET, Edouard. Mar el pratique d'Analyse des Vins. 5' éc. 12mo. Paris, 1888. A 18 Q 43

ROBINS, Edward, jun. Echoes of the Play-house: Reminiscences of some past glories of the English Stage. 8vo. New York, 1895. H 10 S 12

ROBINSON, A Mary F. The End of the Middle Ages. 8vo. Lond, 1889. B 30 U 20

ROBINSON, Commander Chas. N. The British Fleet: the Growth, Achievements, the Duties of the Navy of the Empire. Illustrated. 8vo. Lond., 1894. B 23 R 19

ROBINSON, Edward Forbes. The Early History of Coffee Houses in England; with some account of the first use of Coffee and a Bibliography of the subject. 8vo. Lond., 1893. B 22 Q 28

ROBINSON, G. A. Aboriginal Settlement at Flinder's Island. [See Edgar, F. S.] MD 3 Q 7 ‡

ROBINSON, H. A. Manual of Instructions to Crop Correspondents. 8vo. Wash., 1895. A 30 U 33

ROBINSON, Henry Crabb. Essay on. [See Bagehot, W.—Literary Studies.] J 9 P 24

ROBINSON, Rt. Hon. Sir Hercules G. R. Speech on Border Treaties and Australian Federation, delivered at a Banquet at Albury on the 31st October, 1876. 8vo. Melb., 1876. MJ 3 Q 16
A Speech on Culture and Education, delivered at the University of Sydney, 24th June, 1876. 8vo. Melb., 1876. MJ 3 Q 16

ROBINSON, John Robert. The Last Earls of Barrymore, 1769-1824. 8vo. Lond., 1894. C 10 U 47

ROBINSON, Vincent J. Eastern Carpets. Second series. Folio. Lond., 1893. A 1 P 21†

ROBINSON, Mrs. W. Zermatt and the Valley of the Vièrge. [See Yung, Emile.] D 36 T 2‡

ROBINSON, Wm. The English Flower Garden: Design, Arrangement, and Plans. Illustrated. 4th ed. 8vo. Lond., 1895. A 30 R 23

ROCCA, Comte I. Lettres à. [See Alberoni, J. M.] C 16 U 13

ROCHAS, Dr. Victor de. La Nouvelle Calédonie et ses Habitants. 8vo. Paris, 1862. MD 7 T 5

ROCHE, C. E. Trans.—Memoirs of Chancellor Pasquier. [See Pasquier, Chancellor.] C 14 S 14-16
Memoirs of Barras. [See Barras, Paul.] C 21 T 15, 16

ROCHER, Charles A. W. The Tasmanian Criminal Law Consolidation and Amendment Acts of the 27th Victoria, with notes, observations, and decisions. 8:o. Hobart, 1864. MF 1 Q 43
Analysis of the Criminal Law of England as applicable to this Colony [Tasmania]. 12mo. Hobart, 1839. MF 1 P 74
Analysis of the Criminal Law of Van Diemen's Land. 8vo. Launceston, 1848. MF 1 Q 59

ROCHESTER, Earl of. Some Political Satires of the 17th Century. [See Bibliotheca Curiosa.] J 18 Q 43

ROCHESTER, NEW YORK Public Schools of. 18mo. Rochester, N.Y., 1893 G 18 P 19

ROCHESTER UNIVERSITY, N.Y. Annual Catalogue, 1892, 1893. 8vo. Rochester, 1892. E

ROCHFORT, J. Adventures of a Surveyor in New Zealand and the Australian Gold Diggings. 8vo. Lond., 1853. MD 8 P 13

ROCK, Very Rev. Dr. Daniel. Textile Fabrics. 8vo. Lond., 1876. A 23 R 28

ROCK, Gilbert. Colonists; illustrating gold-fields and city Life in Australia, 1851-70. 12mo. Dunedin, 1888*. MJ 1 Q 28

— By Passion Driven: a Story of a Wasted Life. 12mo. Dunedin, N.Z., 1888. MJ 2 T 26

ROCKWELL, Julius E. Shorthand Instruction and Practice [U.S.] 8vo. Washington, 1893. G 18 R 19

RODD, Rennell. *Editor.*—British Mission to Uganda. [*See* Portal, Sir G.] D 14 S 19

RODET, A. Propriétés attribuées à la Tuberculine. [*See* Arloing, Dr. S.] A 33 U 24

RODGER, Ella H. B. Aberdeen Doctors, at Home and Abroad: the narrative of a medical school. 8vo. Edinb., 1893. C 15 R 10

RODRIGUES, J. Barbosa. Plantas Novas cultivadas no Jardim Botanico do Rio de Janeiro. [Parts 1-3.] Imp. 8vo. Rio de Janeiro, 1891-93. A 1 Q 18†

— Vocabulario Indigena cóm a orthographia correcta. Imp. 8vo. Rio de Janeiro, 1893. J 2 U 14

RODWAY, James. Handbook of British Guiana. 8vo. Georgetown, 1893. D 4 P 54

— History of British Guiana, from 1668 to the present time. Vol. 3. 8vo. Georgetown, Demerara, 1894. B 1 U 26

— In the Guiana Forest. Illustrated. 8vo. Lond., 1894. D 15 S 27

ROGERS, Alexander. The Land Revenue of Bombay. 2 vols. 8vo. Lond., 1892. F 4 Q 31, 32

ROGERS, Clara Kathleen. The Philosophy of Singing. 8vo. Lond., 1893. A 23 R 9

ROGERS, F. N. Elections. Part 1. Registration, 15th ed.; by M. Po ell. Part 2. Elections and Petitions, 16th ed.; by S. H. Day. 2 vols. 8vo. Lond., 1890-92. F 14 R 32, 33

ROGERS, Fairman. The Magnetism of Iron Vessels, with a short Treatise on Terrestrial Magnetism. 18mo. New York, 1877. A 22 P 12

ROGERS, Frederick. Specifications for Practical Architecture: a Guide to the Architect, Engineer, Surveyor, and Builder. 2nd ed. 8vo. Lond., 1886. A 19 U 22

ROGERS, Henry. Essay on the Life and Genius of Thos. Fuller; with Selections from his Writings. 12mo. Lond., 1856. J 12 S 38

ROGERS, Prof. James E. Thorold. The British Citizen, his Rights and Privileges. 12mo. Lond., 1886. F 6 T 39

— Socialism and Land. [*See* Subjects of the Day, 2.] F 7 U 27

— Socialism and Labour. [*See* Subjects of the Day, 2.] F 7 U 27

— Work and Wages; being a popular edition (abridged) of Six Centuries of Work and Wages. 12mo. Lond. (n.d.) F 7 V 11

ROGERS, Walter Thos. Manual of Bibliography: being an Introduction to the knowledge of Books, Library Management, and the Art of Cataloguing. New ed., illustrated. 8vo. Lond., 1891. J 6 S 34

ROGERSON, Col. Wm. Historical Records of the 53rd (Shropshire L. I.) from the formation of the Regiment in 1755, down to 1889. [Illustrated.] 8vo. Lond., 1890. B 22 R 6

ROGGEVEEN, A. Paskaerte beschreven door A. Roggeveen. Fol. Amsterdam (n.d.) D 8 P 34‡
[*See* Moll, G.—Verhandeling.] MD 8 R 39

ROLF BOLDREWOOD. [*See* Browne, T. A.]

ROLFE, A. J. A Sheaf of Sonnets. 8vo. Maitland, 1892. MH 1 Q 39

ROMANCE OF THE BUSH, A; by "E. P. R." 12mo. Edinb., 1855. MJ 1 P 64

ROMANES, Dr. George John. An Examination of Weismannism. 8vo. Lond., 1893. A 28 Q 35

— Darwin and after Darwin. Vol. 2. 8vo. Lond., 1895. G 1 U 28

— Thoughts on Religion; edited by the Rev. C. Gore. 8vo. Lond., 1895. G 1 U 23

— Mind and Motion, and Monism. 12mo. Lond., 1895. G 2 U 43

ROMANES LECTURE, 1893. Evolution and Ethics. [*See* Huxley, Prof. T. H.] A 27 T 19

ROMILLY, Hugh Hastings. New Guinea. (Roy. Geograph. Soc. of Australasia, Q. Branch, 1.) 8vo. Brisb., 1886.) ME 20

ROMISH RECUSANT, A. [*See* Laud, Archbishop.]

ROMNEY, George, and his Art; by Hilda Gamlin. Illustrated. 8vo. Lond., 1894. C 17 R 20

RONNER, Henriette. The Painter of Cat Life and Cat Character; by M. H. Spielmann. Illustrated. 4to. Lond., 1892. A 40 U 3 ‡

ROOS, J. D. C. de. [*See* De Roos, J. D. C.]

ROPER, Mary W. L. Agnes Goldthwaite, and other Poems. Sm. 4to. Sydney, 1883. MH 1 U 77

ROPER, W. O. History of the Church of Lancaster. [See Chetham Soc. Pubs., n.s., 31.] E

ROPES, John Codman. The Story of the Civil War, 1861-65. Part 1. Roy. 8vo. New York, 1894. B 17 R 31

RORER, Mrs. S. T. Canning and Preserving. 12mo. Philad., 1887. A 22 Q 13

ROSA, S. A. The Coming Terror; or, the Australian Revolution: a Romance of the 20th Century. 8vo. Sydney, 1894. MJ 1 S 39

ROSALES, J. A. La Apoteósis de Arturo Prat. 8vo. Santiago, 1888. C 21 T 9
La Cañidilla de Santiago su Historia i sus Tradiciones, 1541-1887. 8vo. Santiago, 1887. B 16 S 17

ROSALES, V. Perez. Ensayo sobre Chile. 8vo. Santiago, 1859. D 15 T 16

ROSCOE, E. S. Speeches of the Earl of Derby. [See Derby, 15th Earl of.] F 14 R 19, 20

ROSCOE, Sir Henry E. Address by Sir H. E. Roscoe, President of the British Association for the Advancement of Science, 1887. 8vo. Lond., 1887. A 21 S 33
John Dalton and the Rise of Modern Chemistry. 12mo. Lond., 1895. C 17 P 28

ROSE, J. H. The Revolutionary and Napoleonic Era, 1789-1815. 8vo. Camb., 1894. B 26 R 6

ROSE, Joshua. Complete Practical Machinist. 19th ed. 8vo. Philad., 1893. A 22 R 22
Modern Machine-shop Practice. Illustrated. 2 vols. 4to. Lond. (n.d.) A 15 R 4, 5 †
Modern Steam Engines. Illustrated. 4to. Philad., 1893. A 14 S 1†

ROSE, T. Kirke. Metallurgy of Gold. Illustrated. 8vo. Lond., 1894. A 24 S 10

ROSEBERY, Earl of. Sketch of. [See Smalley, G. W.—Studies of Men.] C 19 R 20
Speeches delivered at a dinner given in honour of, Sydney, 1883. [See Barton, E.] MF 3 T 57

ROSENBUSCH, H. Microscopical Physiography of the Rock-making Minerals; translated by J. P. Iddings. Illustrated. 3rd ed. Roy. 8vo. New York, 1893. A 24 V 29

ROSENGARTEN, Joseph George. Trans.—The German Allied Troops in the North American War of Independence. [See Eelking, Captain M. von.] B 17 R 24

ROSENSTOCK, Rudolph. Heligoland as an Ornithological Observatory. [See Gätke, H.] A 30 U 31

ROSNEY, Léon de. Education des Vers à soie au Japon. [See Sira-Kawa.] A 18 S 17

ROSS, E. Denison. Trans.—The Tarikh-i-Rashidi. [See Elias, N.] B 33 R 1

ROSS, F. Ruined Abbeys of Britain. 2 vols. 4to. Lond. (n.d.) B 40 T 4, 5 ‡

ROSS, Major J. [Life of] Marquess of Hastings. (Rulers of India.) 8vo. Oxford, 1893. C 13 P 17

ROSS, J. H. Memoir of the Life of Adam Lindsay Gordon, the "Laureate of the Centaure." 8vo. Lond., 1892. MC 1 Q 29

ROSS, James. The Van Diemen's Land Anniversary and Hobart Town Almanack, 1831. 18mo. Hobart, 1831. ME 4 P

ROSS, John D. Burnsiana: a Collection of Literary Odds and Ends relating to Robert Burns. Vols. 2-4. Sm. 4to. Paisley, 1893-94. J 6 U 30-32

ROSS, M. Aorangi; or the Heart of the Southern Alps, New Zealand. 8vo. Wellington, 1892. MD 8 R 25

ROSS, Martin. In the Vine Country. [See Somerville E. Œ.] D 9 P 13

ROSS, Rev. Dr. R. Letter to the Members of the Congregational or Independent Church under the pastoral care of; by S. P. Hill. [See Hill, S. P.] MG 2 S 10

ROSS, Hon. R. D. Wine and Brandy. (Proc. Roy. Agricult. and Horticult. Soc., S. Aust., 1882.) 8vo. Adelaide, 1882. ME 1 S
Scrub Land Cultivation in South Australia. (Proc. Roy. Agricult. and Horticult. Soc., S. Aust., 1882.) 8vo. Adelaide, 1882. ME 1 S

ROSS, W. J. C. Geology of Limekilns, Bathurst District. (Journal Roy. Soc., N.S W., 28.) 8vo. Sydney, 1894. ME 1 R

ROSSETTI, Dante Gabriel. [Plaster Cast of.] [See Hutton, L.—Portraits in Plaster.] A 23 V 13
Reminiscences of. [See Skelton, Dr. J.—Table-talk of Shirley.] C 19 V 10
[Sketch of]; by F. G. Stephens. [See Portfolio Monograph, 5.] E
Rossetti and the Pre-Raphaelite Movement. [See Wood, E.] A 23 R 10

ROSSINI, Gioacchino A. Sketch of. [See Heine, H.—Heine in Art and Letters.] J 11 T 39
Sketch of. [See Elliot, Frances—Roman Gossip.] C 21 Q 10

ROTH, H. L. Crozet's Voyage to Tasmania. [See Crozet's.] MD S Q 43

ROTHE, R:. Rev. David. The Analecta of; edited by Bishop Patrick F. Moran. 12mo. Dublin, 1884. G 7 U 33

ROTHWELL, Richard P. Gold and Silver. Extract from Report on Mineral Industries in the United States at the eleventh Census, 1890. 4to. Washington, 1890. F 12 R 16 †

The Mineral Industry. [See *Engineering and Mining Journal.*] E

Universal Bimetallism and an International Monetary Clearing House, together with a Record of the World's Money, Statistics of Gold and Silver, &c. Roy. 8vo. New York, 1893. F 8 T 20

ROUND, J. H. Feudal England; Historical Studies on the 11th and 12th Centuries. 8vo. Lond., 1895. B 21 U 19

ROUNTHWAITE, H. M. Marine Engineering Rules and Tables. [See Seaton, A. E.] A 22 P 9

ROUSSEAU, Jean Jacques. Sketch of. [See Lowell, J. R.] J 6 P 10

The Social Contract; or, Principles of Political Right; translated by H. J. Tozer and B. Bosanquet. 8vo. Lond., 1895. F 8 U 42

The Social Contract; or, the Principles of Political Rights; translated by Rose M. Harrington; with Introduction and Notes by E. L. Walter. 12mo. New York, 1893. F 5 Q 15

ROUTH, Edward John. Treatise on Analytical Statics. Vol. 2. 8vo. Camb., 1892. A 25 T 27

ROUTLEDGE, R. The Telegraph. [See Tennant, A. L.] A 21 R 20

ROWAN, F. J. Fuel. [See Groves, C.E.] A 21 V 6, 7

ROWAN, W. R. Cheap Railways for Country Districts; with a Description of the Gribskor Branch Line in Denmark; translated from the Danish by F. C. Rowan. Roy. 8vo. Melb., 1881. MA 3 R 27

ROWBOTHAM, John Frederick. The Troubadours and Courts of Love. Illustrated. 8vo. Lond., 1895. H 9 U 16

ROWCROFT, Chas. Perils and Adventures of Mr. William Thornley, one of the pioneer settlers of Van Diemen's Land, 1817-30. 12mo. Hobart (n.d.) MJ 1 Q 47

ROWE, George S. Life of John Hunt, Missionary. 12mo. Lond., 1860. MC 1 P 46

ROWE, Nicholas. The Fair Penitent: a Tragedy. [See London Stage, 2.] H 2 S 34

Tamerlane: a Tragedy. [See London Stage, 3.] H 2 S 35

Lady Jana Grey: a Tragedy. [See London Stage, 3.] H 2 S 35

ROWE, S. H., and KELLY, J. Report on the prospects of Trade with India, China, Japan, &c., in Dairy and other Victorian Products and Manufactures. 8vo. Melb., 1895. MF 4 R 3

ROWNTREE, Joshua. The Opium Habit in the East: a Study of the Evidence given to the Royal Commission on Opium, 1893-94. 8vo. Lond., 1895. A 33 S 12

ROYAL ACADEMY PICTURES, 1893-94. 2 vols. 4to. Lond., 1893-94. E

ROYAL AGRICULTURAL AND HORTICULTURAL SOCIETY OF SOUTH AUSTRALIA. Proceedings, 1882-85. 4 vols. 8vo. Adelaide, 1882-85. ME 1 S

ROYAL AGRICULTURAL SOCIETY OF ENGLAND. Journal. 3rd series. Vols. 3-5. 8vo. Lond., 1892-94. E

ROYAL AGRICULTURAL SOCIETY OF NEW SOUTH WALES. Schedules of Prizes, Metropolitan Shows, 1889-92. 8vo. Sydney, 1889-92. ME 3 R

Journal of Agricultural Society of N.S.W., 1872. Sm. fol. Sydney, 1872. ME 17 S

ROYAL ASIATIC SOCIETY OF GREAT BRITAIN AND IRELAND. Journal for 1892-94. 3 vols. 8vo. Lond., 1892-94. E

CHINA BRANCH. Journal for 1890-91. Vol. 25 (n.s.) 8vo. Shanghai, 1893. E

STRAITS BRANCH. Journal. Nos. 23-26. 2 vols. 8vo. Singapore, 1891-94. E

ROYAL CALEDONIAN HORTICULTURAL SOCIETY. Apple and Pear Congress, 1885. [See Dunn, M.] A 18 S 27

ROYAL COLLEGE OF PHYSICIANS, LONDON. Catalogue of the Fellows, Licentiates, and Extra-Licentiates, 1858. 8vo. Lond., 1858. E

ROYAL COLLEGE OF SCIENCE, LONDON. Prospectus of 1894-95. 8vo. Lond., 1894. G 18 R 42

ROYAL COLONIAL INSTITUTE. List of Fellows, 1884. E

Proceedings. Vols. 22-26. 5 vols. 8vo. Lond., 1891-95. E

Proceedings at the Banquet to celebrate the Completion of the Telegraphic Communication with the Australian Colonies. 8vo. Lond., 1872. MF 2 Q 5

ROYAL GARDENS, KEW. [See Great Britain and Ireland.]

ROYAL GEOGRAPHICAL SOCIETY. The Geographical Journal, including the Proceedings of the Royal Geographical Society. Vols. 1-4. Roy. 8vo. Lond., 1892-94. E

Proceedings and Monthly Record of Geography. New series. Vol. 14. Roy. 8vo. Lond., 1892. E

Supplementary Papers. Vol. 3. Roy. 8vo. Lond., 1893. E

ROYAL GEOGRAPHICAL SOCIETY OF AUSTRALASIA. Instructions issued by, for the guidance of the New Guinea Exploration Expedition, 1885. 8vo. Sydney, 1885. MD 8 R 37

QUEENSLAND BRANCH. Proceedings. Vols. 1-9. 8vo. Brisb., 1886-93. ME

SOUTH AUSTRALIAN BRANCH. Proceedings. Vols. 1 and 2. 8vo. Adelaide, 1886-90. ME 20

VICTORIAN BRANCH. Proceedings of 7th Ordinary Meeting, 1885-86. Melb., 1886. ME 20
Proceedings at the Annual Meeting, January, 1888 8vo. Melb., 1888. ME 20
Transactions and Proceedings. Vols. 5-11. 7 vols. 8vo. Melb., 1888-94. ME 20

ROYAL HORTICULTURAL SOCIETY OF VICTORIA. Reports, 1888-89. 8vo. Melb., 1888-89. ME 6 S

ROYAL HUMANE SOCIETY OF AUSTRALASIA. Annual Reports, 1884 and 1895, and Instructions for Restoring Persons apparently drowned; also for the Treatment of Snake-bites, and in cases of Sunstroke, Choking, &c. 8vo. Melb., 1884-95. ME 6 S

ROYAL INSTITUTE OF BRITISH ARCHITECTS. Kalendar of, 1893-95. 2 vols. 8vo. Lond., 1893-95. E
Transactions, vol. 3, new series. 4to. Lond., 1892. E

ROYAL IRISH ACADEMY. Transactions. Vols. 22-28, 1810-86. 6 vols. (in 7). 4to. Dublin, 1880. E
Transactions. Irish Manuscript series. Vol. 1. 4to. Dublin, 1880. E
Part I. On the Calendar of Oengus; by Dr. W. Stokes.
The Cunningham Memoirs. Vols. 1-10. 8 vols. 4to. Dublin, 1886-94. E

ROYAL KALENDAR, The, and Court and City Register for England, Scotland, Ireland, and the Colonies, for 1893. 12mo. Lond., 1893. E

ROYAL SOCIETY, LONDON. Catalogue of Scientific Papers, from 1800-83. 10 vols. 4to. Lond., 1867-94. K 19 V 6-15
General Index to the Philosophical Transactions, from vol. 1 to vol. 120, 1665-1830. 3 vols. 4to. Lond., 1787-1838 E
Instructions for the use of the Magnetic and Meteorological Observatories, and for the Magnetic Surveys. 8vo. Lond., 1842. A 20 U 2
Philosophical Transactions. Vols. 183-185. 5 vols. 4to. Lond., 1893-95. E
Proceedings, vols. 51-56. 8vo. Lond., 1892-94. E
Report of the Committee of Physics, including Meteorology, on the objects of scientific inquiry in those sciences. 8vo. Lond., 1840. A 20 U 3

ROYAL SOCIETY OF LITERATURE. Transactions. 2nd series. Vols. 13-16. 8vo. Lond., 1883-93. E

ROYAL SOCIETY OF NEW SOUTH WALES. Journal and Proceedings. Vols. 26-28. 8vo. Sydney, 1893-94. ME 1 R

ROYAL SOCIETY OF QUEENSLAND. Proceedings of. Vols. 1, 2, 4-10. 9 vols. 8vo. Brisbane, 1881-94. ME . T

ROYAL SOCIETY OF SOUTH AUSTRALIA. Transactions, Proceedings, and Report, vols. 5-9, 1881-86; and Transactions, vols. 15-18, 1892-94. 7 vols. 8vo. Adelaide, 1882-94. ME 1 S

ROYAL SOCIETY OF TASMANIA. Monthly Notices of Papers and Proceedings, Sept., 1865, and March-August, 1875. 8vo. Hobart, 1865-75. ME . Q
Papers and Proceedings for January, 1855, 1883, 1892-93. 4 vols. 8vo Hobart, 1855-94. ME . Q
Report for 1883. 8vo. Hobart, 1884. ME . Q

ROYAL SOCIETY OF VICTORIA. Proceedings. New series, vols. 5-7. 8vo. Melb., 1893-95. ME 1 P
Progress Reports and Final Report of the Exploration Committee of the Royal Society of Victoria, 1863. Sm. fol. Melb., 1863. MD 9 P 3 †
Transactions and Proceedings. Vols. 16-22, 1880-86. 8vo. Melb., 1880-86. ME 1 P

ROYAL SYDNEY YACHT SQUADRON. Laws and Regulations. 12mo. Sydney, 1863. MF 1 P 75

RUÆUS, C. Virgili Maronis Opera. [See Virgilius Maro, P.] H 9 U 33

RUBERY, Frederick. A charming variety of Poems upon charming subjects. 12mo. Parramatta, 1894. MH 1 U 53

RUCKER, Prof. A. W. Magnetic susceptibilities of specimens of Australian Basalts. (Journal Roy. Soc. N.S.W., 28.) 8vo. Sydney, 1894. ME 1 R

RUDALL, Dr. Summer Diseases: Ophthalmia. [See Australian Health Soc., Melb.] MA 3 S 38

RUDALL, James T. Trans.—Lathology, &c., of Mental Diseases. [See Schrooder van der Kolk, J. L. C.] MA 2 U 58
Railway and Marine Signals, and the necessity of accurate testing of the sight of signal and look-out men. (Roy. Soc., Vict., 29.) 8vo. Melb., 1883. ME 1 P

RUDGE, Edward. Description of Seven New Species of Plants from New Holland. 4to. Lond., 1805. MA 1 U 41

RUIN OF THE TURF IN VICTORIA; by "Kosmos." 12mo. Melb., 1870. MJ 1 Q 22

RULE, J. J. Economical Gardening. [See McMillan, T.] MA 3 S 56

RÜMKER, Dr. Chas. Stargard. Observations for determining the absolute length of the Pendulum vibrating seconds at Parramatta, according to Borda's method. 4to. Lond., 1828. MA 2 R 44
Note-book of Astronomical Observations (1822-25) made at Parramatta Observatory. (*Manuscript.*) Libr.

RURAL AUSTRALIAN, The. Vols. 9-11 and new series vols. 1-3. 6 vols. 4to. Sydney, 1884-91. ME 19 S

RUSDEN, George Wm. Bryce v. Rusden. [*See* Bryce v. Rusden.] MF 3 T 40
Moyarra: an Australian Legend; by "Yittadairn." 8vo. Lond., 1891. MH 1 U 33

RUSDEN, H. K. Cremation and Burial in relation to Death Certification. (Trans. Roy. Soc., Victoria, n.s. 7.) 8vo. Melb., 1893. ME 1 P
Essay on Suicide; by "Hokor." 8vo. Melb. (n.d.) MF 4 R 2
The Subjection of Women; by "Hokor." 8vo. Melb., 1876. MF 2 T 77

RUSH, J. and W. Veterinary Vade Mecum. [*See* Lord, R. P. G.] A 18 S 40

RUSKIN, John. The Harbours of England. Illustrated. 8vo. Orpington, 1895. A 23 R 40
Poems of: collected and edited by W. G. Collingwood. 2 vols. 4to. Orpington, 1891. H 5 V 31, 32
Poetry of Architecture; or, the Architecture of the Nations of Europe considered in its association with Natural Scenery and National Character. Illustrated. 4to. Orpington, 1893. A 12 Q 17 †
Verona, and other Lectures. Illustrated. Roy. 8vo. Orpington, 1894. A 23 U 18
Life and Work of; by W. G. Collingwood. 2 vols. 8vo. Lond., 1893. C 11 P 20, 21
Records of: by Annie Ritchie. 8vo. Lond., 1892. C 16 R 17
Ruskin on Education. [*See* Jolly, W.] G 17 Q 46
Work of. [*See* Waldstein, C.] J 6 P 36

RUSSAN, Ashmore, and BOYLE, Frederick. The Orchid Seekers: a story of adventure in Borneo. Illustrated. 8vo. Lond., 1893. D 17 Q 31

RUSSELL, George W. E. [Life of] the Rt. Hon. W. E. Gladstone. (Prime Ministers of Queen Victoria.) 8vo. Lond., 1892. C 18 P 3

RUSSELL, Henry Chamberlaine. Chart of Circumpolar Stars. (Journal Roy. Soc., N.S.W., 28.) 8vo. Sydney, 1894. ME 1 R
Current Papers. (Journal Roy. Soc., N.S.W., 28.) 8vo. Sydney, 1894. ME 1 R
Diagram of Isothermal Lines of New South Wales. Roy. 8vo. Sydney, 1893. MA 1 U 40
Hail-storms. 8vo. Sydney, 1892. MA 1 T 61

RUSSELL, Henry Chamberlaine —*contd.*
Map of the average Rainfall in New South Wales. (Journal Roy. Soc., N.S.W., 28.) 8vo. Sydney, 1894. ME 1 R
Meteor of June 27th, 1894. (Journal Roy. Soc., N.S.W., 28.) 8vo. Sydney, 1894. ME 1 R
On Meteorite No. 2 from Gilgoin Station. (Journal Roy. Soc., N.S.W., 27.) 8vo. Sydney, 1893. ME 1 R
Moving Anticyclones in the Southern Hemisphere. Roy. 8vo. Lond., 1893. MA 1 U 39
Observations of the Transit of Venus, 1874, made at Stations in New South Wales. 4to. Sydney, 1892.* MA 1 U 42
Pictorial Rain Maps. (Journal Roy. Soc., N.S.W., 27.) 8vo. Sydney, 1893. ME 1 R
Recent Measures of Double Stars made at Sydney. 4to. Kiel, 1894. MA 9 P 33 †
Results of Astronomical Observations made at the Sydney Observatory, 1879-81. Roy. 8vo. Sydney, 1893. ME 6 Q
Results of Meteorological Observations made in New South Wales, 1890. Roy. 8vo. Sydney, 1892.* ME 6 Q
Results of Rain, River, and Evaporation Observations made in New South Wales, 1891-93. 3 vols. roy. 8vo. Sydney, 1893-94. ME

RUSSELL, I. C. Geological History of Lake Lahontan, a quaternary lake of north-western Nevada. (U.S. Geol. Survey, 11.) 4to. Wash., 1885. E

RUSSELL, Rt. Hon. John, Earl. Letters to, on Gold in Australia. [*See* Thomas, F. S.] MF 2 T 52
[Life of]; by S. J. Reid. 8vo. Lond., 1895. C 21 P 21
Speech on Colonial Policy, 1850. 8vo. Lond., 1850. MF 4 R 28

RUSSELL, John, R.A. [Life and Works of]; by G. C. Williamson. Imp. 8vo. Lond., 1894. C 17 U 19

RUSSELL, Rt. Rev. Dr. Michael. Polynesia; or, an Historical Account of the principal Islands in the South Sea, including New Zealand. 2nd ed. 12mo. Edinb., 1843. MD 2 W 54

RUSSELL, Percy. Guide to British and American Novels, being a comprehensive Manual of all forms of popular fiction in Great Britain, Australasia, and America, from its commencement down to 1893. 8vo. Lond., 1894. J 9 Q 8

RUSSELL, T. Baron. Current Americanisms. 16mo. Lond., 1893. K 16 P 42

RUSSELL, Thos. Meteorology: Weather and methods of forecasting, description of Meteorological Instruments and River Flood Predictions in the United States. 8vo. New York, 1895. A 31 Q 1

RUSSELL, Wm. Clark-. Sailors' Language; a Collection of Sea-terms and their Definitions. 12mo. Lond., 1883. A 19 Q 20
How he writes his Novels; with Portrait. [*See* Blathwayt, R.—Interviews.] J 10 U 34

RUSSELL, Dr. Wm. Howard. Great War with Russia, 1854-55. 8vo. Lond., 1895. B 31 R 4

A Memorial of the Marriage of H.R.H. Albert Edward Prince of Wales and H.R.H. Alexandra, Princess of Denmark. Illustrated by R. Dudley. Fol. Lond. (n.d.) C 6 P 3 ‡

RUSSIA. The Industries of Russia. 4 vols. roy. 8vo. St. Petersburg, 1893. A 25 V 10-13

The Russian Ministry of Public Education at the World's Columbian Exposition. Roy. 8vo. St. Petersburg, 1893. G 18 S 5

RUST IN WHEAT. [See under each Colony.] MA 7 Q 32 †

RUTGERS COLLEGE. Catalogue of the Officers and Students of Rutgers College, New Brunswick, N.J., 1892, 1893. 8vo. New Brunswick, 1892. E

RUTHERFORD, E. Magnetization of Iron by high-frequency discharges. (Trans. N.Z. Inst., 27.) 8vo. Wellington, 1894. ME 2 R

RUTHERFORD, Wm. Hamilton. Penthus: an Australian Dramatic Tragic Tale. 8vo. Melb., 1887. MH 1 S 38

RÜTIMING, H. L. E. The Bills of Exchange Act of 1884; with explanatory notes and index. Sm. 4to. Brisb., 1884. MF 1 Q 44

RYAN, Dr. James P. Small-pox and Vaccination. [See Australian Health Society, Melb.] MA 3 S 33

RYAN, John Tighe. Reminiscences of Australia. 8vo. Sydney, 1895. MB 2 Q 51

The Antipodean. [See Antipodean, The.] ME

RYE, F. C. Beetles. [See Taylor, Dr. J. E.—Collecting Natural History Objects.] A 29 Q 38

RYLEY, George Buchanan, and McCANDLISH, John M. Scotland's Free Church. Sm. 4to. Lond., 1893 G 13 P 37

S

S., C. J. [See Sketch of Turkish History.] MB 1 R 43

S., J. S. [See Shearston, J. S.]

SABATIER, A. L'Evangile de Pierre et les Evangiles Canoniques. 8vo. Paris, 1893. G 12 P 29

SABATIER, Paul. Life of St. Francis of Assisi; translated by Louise Seymour Houghton. 8vo. Lond., 1894. C 14 S 19

SACH, A. J. Carbon. (Divinity Hall Record.) 8vo. Brisbane, 1879. ME 15 Q

SACHS, Dr. B. Treatise on the Nervous Diseases of Children, for Physicians and Students. Roy. 8vo. Lond., 1895. A 33 U 21

SACHTLEBEN, William Lewis. Across Asia on a Bicycle. [See Allen, J. G.] D 17 Q 26

SACRED HISTORY as a Branch of Elementary Education. [See Religious Pamphlets, 2.] G 9 V 17

SADLER, Mrs. S. H. Infant Feeding by Artificial Means. Illustrated. 12mo. Lond., 1895. A 33 L 4

SADTLER, Prof. Samuel Philip. Dispensatory of the United States. [See Wood, Dr. G. B.] A 26 V 13

Hand-book of Industrial Organic Chemistry. 2nd ed. 8vo. Philad., 1895. A 21 V 20

—— and TRIMBLE, Prof. Henry. A Text-book of Chemistry, intended for the use of Pharmaceutical and Medical Students. 8vo. Philad., 1895. A 33 U 15

SAFAR NAMEH. Persian Pictures; a Book of Travel. 8vo. Lond., 1894. D 17 Q 21

SAINT-AMAND, I. de [See Imbert de Saint-Amand.]

ST. ANDREW'S CATHEDRAL, SYDNEY. Handbook of, with Subjects of the Windows, &c. 8vo. Sydney, 1868. MB 1 R 39

Service for the Consecration of, on St. Andrew's Day, 30th November, 1868. Sm. 4to. Sydney, 1868. MG 1 S 35

Short Account of. 8vo. Sydney, 1866. MA 3 S 66

SAINT-FOIX, Le Comte de. La République Orientale de l'Uruguay. 12mo. Paris, 1892. D 15 P 17

ST. GEORGE GOLD-MINING CO. Memorandum and Articles of Association. 8vo. Sydney, 1889. MF 4 R 35

ST. JAMES'S PARISH. Report of the Churchwardens and of the Parochial Committee, 1870. 8vo. Melb., 1870. MG 2 Q 48

ST. JOHN, J. A. Analysis of Plato's Republic. [See More, Sir T.—Utopia.] F 15 Q 7

ST. JOHN, Lieut.-Col. J. H. H. Pakeha Rambles through Maori Lands. 8vo. Wellington, 1873. MD 8 P 23

ST. JOHN, NEW BRUNSWICK. Reports of the Accounts of the Corporation of the City of St. John, 1894, and Reports of City Officials with sundry Accounts. 8vo. St. John, N.B., 1895. E

ST. JOHN'S, DARLINGHURST, PAROCHIAL ASSOCIATION. 18th-19th Annual Reports. 8vo. Sydney, 1888-89. ME 6 Q

SAINT-JUIRS. [See Delorme, R.]

ST. LOUIS, U.S.A. Report of the Board of Public Schools, for the year ending June, 1892. 8vo. St. Louis, 1893. E

ST. MARY'S CATHEDRAL, HOBART. Tower of. 8vo. Hobart, 1861. MA 1 R 42

ST. MARY'S HOSPITAL MEDICAL SCHOOL. Sessions, 1889-95; with Regulations for preliminary Examinations. 3 vols. 8vo. Lond., 1889-94. E

ST. MARY'S YEAR-BOOK and Calendar, 1884. 8vo. St. Mary's, South Creek, 1884. ME 4 U

SAINT MAUR, Harry. A Railway Mystery. 8vo. Lond., 1891. MJ 3 P 17

ST. PAUL, MINNESOTA. Some of her Attractions. Obl. 32mo. St. Paul, 1893. D 15 P 9

ST. PAUL'S COLLEGE, SYDNEY. Calendar for 1859. 8vo. Sydney, 1859. ME 5 Q

SAINT PIERRE, J. H. Bernardin de. Paul et Virginie : Edited by E. J. Trechmann. 12mo. Sydney, 1894. MJ 1 Q 2

Voyage to the Isle of France, the Isle of Bourbon, and the Cape of Good Hope. 8vo. Lond., 1800. D 19 R 2

[Life of]; by A. Barine. (Great French Writers). 8vo. Lond., 1893. C 19 Q 9

ST. THOMAS'S CHURCH, BALMAIN. Easter Meeting, 1889. 8vo. Sydney, 1889. ME 6 S

SAINTE-BEUVE, Charles A. Select Essays, chiefly bearing on English Literature; translated by A. J. Butler. 8vo. Lond. (n.d.) J 9 S 10

SAINTSBURY, George E. B. Cookery of the Grouse. [See Macpherson, Rev. H. A.] A 29 Q 43
Cookery of the Partridge. [See Macpherson, Rev. H. A.] A 28 Q 29
Dryden's Works. [See Dryden, J.] H 4 U 15-18

SALA, George Augustus. Things I have seen and People I have known. 2 vols. 12mo. Lond., 1894. C 14 P 29, 30

SALA'S JOURNAL, a Weekly Magazine. Vol. 1. 4to. Lond., 1892. E

SALIS, A. de. La Correction des Torrents en Suisse. 4to. Berne, 1892. A 36 P 8 ‡

SALISBURY, J. A Glossary of Words and Phrases used in South-east Worcestershire, together with some of the Sayings, Customs, Superstitions, Charms, &c., common in that district. 8vo. Lond., 1893. K 12 U 32
South-eastern Worcestershire Words. (Eng. Dial. Soc. Pubs.) 8vo. Lond., 1894. E

SALMON, Charles Spencer. Caribbean Confederation; with a Map; a Plan for the Union of the Fifteen British West Indian Colonies. 12mo. Lond. (n.d.) F 7 V 9

SALMON, Dr. D. E. Investigations concerning Bovine Tuberculosis, with special reference to Diagnosis and Prevention. 8vo. Wash., 1894. A 33 U 12
Special Report on the History and Present Condition of the Sheep Industry of the United States; prepared under the direction of Dr. Salmon, by E. A. Carman, H. A. Heath, and J. Minto. (U.S. Dept. of Agricult., Bureau of Animal Industry.) 8vo. Washington, 1892. A 30 U 7

SALMOND, Rev. Stewart D. F. Writings of St. Hippolytus. [See Hippolytus.] G 14 U 9
Refutation of all Heresies. [See Hippolytus.] G 14 U 9
Writings of Gregory Thaumaturgus. [See Gregory Thaumaturgus.] G 14 U 20

SALMOND, Prof. Wm. The Reign of Grace: a Discussion on the question of the possibility of Salvation for all Men. 12mo. Dunedin, 1888. MD 1 P 59

SALOMONS, Sir D. Electric Light Installations. Vol. 3. 7th ed., illustrated. 8vo. Lond., 1894. A 21 P 42
3. Application.

SALT, Harris Shirley. Richard Jefferies : a Study. 12mo. Lond., 1894. C 10 P 3

SALTER, John W. Portrait of. [See Ramsay, Sir A. C. —Memoir of.] C 21 R 20

SALVADORI, Tommaso. Aggiunte alla Ornitologia della Papuasia e delle Molucche. Sm. fol. Torino, 1889-91. MA 10 P 7 †
Birds collected in Ternate, Amboyna, Banda, the Ki Islands, and the Arrou Islands. [See Thomson, Sir C. W., and Murray, Dr. J.—Voyage of H.M.S. Challenger.] A 6 †

SALVIN, Osbert. Procellariidæ. [See Thomson, Sir C. W., and Murray, Dr. J.—Voyage of H.M.S. Challenger.] A 6 †

SAMSON-HIMMELSTIERNA, H. von. Russia under Alexander III and in the preceding period ; translated by J. Morrison. 8vo. Lond., 1893. B 31 T 2

SAMUELI, Mrs. H. J. Household Cookery Book. 8vo. Sydney, 1894. MA 1 V 34
The Ladies Home Companion. Illustrated. 12mo. Sydney, 1894. MA 3 U 10

SAMUELS, L. A. Origin of the Bendigo (Victoria) Saddle Reefs, and the Cause of their Golden Wealth. Illustrated. 8vo. Bendigo, 1893. MA 3 S 13

SAMUELSON, J. German and French Labour Movements. [See Subjects of the Day, 2.] F 7 U 27
The Lords and the Labourers. [See Subjects of the Day, 4.] F 7 U 29

SANATORIUM FOR HEBREW CHILDREN. Report, 1893. 8vo. New York, 1893. E

SANBORN, Franklin Benjamin. Familiar Letters of Henry D. Thoreau. 8vo. Boston, 1893. C 19 V 3

———— and HARRIS, Wm. T. A. Bronson Alcott: his Life and Philosophy. 2 vols. 8vo. Lond., 1893.
C 13 P 26, 27

SANCHEZ, R. Fac-simile of Letter from Columbus to. [See Columbus, C.] B 30 P 15 ‡

SANCROFT, Most Rev. Wm. Sketch of. [See Fowler, Rev. M.—Notable Archbishops.] C 13 V 12

SAND, George. [See Dudevant, Mme. A. L. A.]

SANDEMAN, Fraser. Angling Travels in Norway. Illustrated. 8vo. Lond., 1895. A 30 T 10

SANDEMAN, Sir Robt., his Life and Work on the Indian Frontier; by Dr. T. H. Thornton. 8vo. Lond., 1895. C 19 S 7

SANDER, Frederick. Reichenbachia: Orchids illustrated and described. 2 vols. fol. Lond., 1888-90.
A 45 P 1, 2 ‡
Reichenbachia. 2nd ser., vols 1 and 2. Fol. Lond., 1892-94. A 45 P 3, 4 ‡

SANDERS, Lloyd Chas. Life of Viscount Palmerston. 12mo. Sydney (n.d.) C 17 P 32

SANDERS, T. W. Amateur's Greenhouse and Conservatory. [See Hibberd, S.] A 18 P 10

SANDERSON, Dr. Robert. Life of. [See Walton, Izaak.]
C 19 V 6

SANDERSON, Sir T. H. Speeches of the Earl of Derby. [See Derby, 15th Earl of.] F 14 R 19, 20

SANDOW, Eugene. Physical Training: a Study in the perfect type of the human form. Compiled and edited by G. M. Adam. Illustrated. Roy. 8vo. Lond., 1894. A 29 U 32

SANDS, John. Landscape Scenery illustrating Sydney, Parramatta, Richmond, Newcastle, Windsor, and Port Jackson, New South Wales. Obl. 12mo. Sydney, (n.d.) MD 8 P 12
Sydney and Suburban Directory, 1893-95. 3 vols. 8vo. Sydney, 1893-95. ME

SANDS & KENNY. Melbourne Directory, 1854, 1858-74, 1877-92. 33 vols. roy. 8vo. Melb., 1854-92.
ME 11

SANDS & McDOUGALL. Melbourne and Suburban Directory, for 1894. 8vo. Melb., 1894. ME
South Australian Directory, 1894-95. 2 vols. 8vo. Adelaide, 1894-95. ME

SANDYS, Dr. John E. Aristotle's Constitution of Athens. [See Aristoteles.] F 4 P 23

SANFORD, Prof. E. Some Observations upon the Conductivity of a Copper Wire in various Dielectrics. 8vo. Palo Alto, 1892. A 21 T 16

SANFUENTES, Don Salvador. Apuntes Biográficos; por M. L. Amunátegui. 8vo. Santiago, 1892.
C 21 T 8

SANGERMANO, Father Vincentius. The Burmese Empire a hundred years ago. 8vo. Westminster, 1893. B 17 R 15

SANTLEY, Charles. Student and Singer: Reminiscences. 3rd ed. 8vo. Lond., 1892. C 8 P 1

SANZ, Pedro Mártir. El Beato Sanz y Compañeros Mártires del Orden de Predicatores. [See Arias, Rev. E. F.] G 3 R 20

SAPPER, Dr. C. Grundzüge der physikalischen Geographie von Guatemala. (Dr. A. Petermann's Mitteilungen, ergänzungsheft, Nr. 113.) Imp. 8vo. Gotha, 1894. E

SAPPHO. Works of. [See Fawkes, F.] H 9 U 28

SARCEY, Francisque. Recollections of Middle Life. 8vo. Lond., 1893. C 15 R 11
Sketch of. [See Matthews, B.—Books and Play-books.] J 8 T 3 ‡

SARGENT, Chas. Sprague. The Silva of North America. Vols. 5-7. Illustrated by C. E. Faxon. 4to. Boston, 1893-95. A 40 S 22-24 ‡

SARGENT, Epes. Communications from another World. 12mo. Melb., 1869. MG 1 P 81

SARMIENTO, Pedro. Narratives of the Voyages of Pedro Sarmiento de Gamboa to the Straits of Magellan. (Hakluyt Soc., 91.) 8vo. Lond., 1895. E

SARPI, Fra Paola, the greatest of the Venetians; by the Rev. A. Robertson. 8vo. Lond., 1893. C 22 P 18

SARS, Prof. G. O. Crustacea of Norway. Imp. 8vo. Kristiania, 1890-94. A 12 U 20 †
Schizopoda; Cumacea; Phylloearida. [See Thomson, Sir C. W., and Murray Dr. J.—Voyage of H.M.S. Challenger.] A 6 †

SATIRIST, The; in imitation of the fourth satire of the first book of Horace. Sm. fol. Lond., 1733.
H 30 Q 13 ‡

SATO, Dr. Shosuke. History of the Land Question in the United States. (Johns Hopkins University Studies, 4.) 8vo. Baltimore, 1886. B 18 S 4

SATURDAY REVIEW. Vols. 74-78. sm. fol. Lond., 1892-94. E

SAUNDERS, Bailey. Life and Letters of James Macpherson. 8vo. Lond., 1894. C 14 V 19

2 H

SAUNDERS, Howard. Laridae. [See Thomson, Sir C. W., and Murray, Dr. J.—Voyage of H.M.S. Challenger.] A 6 †

SAUNDERS, Trelawny. Geographical Account of the Survey of Western Palestine. 8vo. Lond., 1882.
D 14 T 22

SAUSSURE, T. de. Recherches chimiques sur la Végétation. 8vo. Paris, 1804. A 18 S 19

SAUVIN, G. Un Royaume Polynésien: Iles Hawaï. 12mo. Paris, 1893. MD 7 T 7

SAVILLE-KENT, W. [See Kent, W. Saville-.]

SAVONAROLA, Fra, Girolamo Maria Francesco Matteo. Life and Martyrdom of, illustrative of the History of Church and State connexion; by R. R. Madden. 2nd ed. 2 vols. 8vo. Lond., 1854. C 14 V 20, 21
Sketch of. [See Bettany, G. T.—Popular History of the Reformation.] G 14 Q 33
Sketch of. [See Oliphant, Mrs. M.—Makers of Florence.] B 30 Q 20

SAWER, J. Ch. Odorographia: a Natural History of Raw Materials and Drugs used in the Perfume Industry, including the Aromatics used in flavouring. 2nd series (illustrated). 8vo. Lond., 1894.
A 21 S 24

SAXO GRAMMATICUS. The First Nine Books of the Danish History of; translated by O. Elton; with some considerations on Saxo's Sources, Historical Methods, and Folk-lore, by F. Y. Powell. (Folk-lore Soc., 33.) 8vo. Lond., 1894. E

SAYCE, Prof. Archibald Henry. Dawn of Civilization. [See Maspero, G.] B 17 U 15
The "Higher Criticism" and the Verdict of the Monuments. 8vo. Lond., 1894. G 8 R 27
Principles of Comparative Philology. 4th edition. 8vo. Lond., 1892. K 11 U 25
Records of the Past. [See Records.] B 21 Q 19

SCAIFE, Dr. W. B. Seminary Notes on recent Historical Literature. [See Adams, Dr. H. B.] B 18 S 8

SCARLETT, Hon. Peter Campbell. South America and the Pacific: comprising a Journey across the Pampas and the Andes, from Buenos Ayres to Valparaiso, Lima, and Panama. 2 vols. 8vo. Lond., 1838.
D 15 S 30, 31

SCARTAZZINI, G. A. A Companion to Dante. 8vo. Lond., 1893. C 13 P 21

SCHAFF, Rev. Dr. Philip. Religious Encyclopædia; or, Dictionary of Biblical, Historical, Doctrinal, and Practical Theology. 3 vols. imp. 8vo. Edinb., 1883-84. G 15 P 17-19 ‡

SCHÄFFLE, Dr. A. The Theory and Policy of Labour Protection. 12mo. Lond., 1893. F 14 Q 48

SCHAUERMANN, François Louis. Theory and Analysis of Ornament, applied to the work of Elementary and Technical Schools. 8vo. Lond., 1892. A 23 T 16

SCHAW, Major-Gen. The last Glacial Epoch. (Trans. N.Z. Inst., 27.) 8vo. Wellington, 1894. ME 2 R
On some peculiar cases of the reflection of light. (Trans. N.Z. Inst., 27.) 8vo. Wellington, 1894. ME 2 R

SCHEELE, Carl Wilhelm. Sketch of. [See Thorpe, Dr. T. E.—Historical Chemistry.] C 17 R 2

SCHEINER, Prof. Dr. J. A Treatise on Astronomical Spectroscopy; being a Translation of Die Spectral Analyse der Gestirne; translated and enlarged by Prof. E. B. Frost. 8vo. Boston, 1894. A 19 V 20

SCHELL, A. von. The Tactics of Field Artillery. 8vo. Lond., 1887. A 29 Q 25

SCHELLING, Prof. Felix E. Life and Writings of George Gascoign. 8vo. Boston (n.d.) C 21 R 7

SCHERER, Edmond. Sketch of. [See Dowden, Dr. E.]
J 5 S 10

SCHEY, Wm. Francis. Charges against E. M. G. Eddy. [See New South Wales.] MF 2 U 48

SCHIAPARELLI, E. Una Tomba Egiziana Inedita della VI* Dinastia. 4to. Roma, 1893. B 12 S 8 †

SCHILLER, Johann Christoph Friedrich von. Sammtliche Werke. 10 vols. 8vo. Stuttgart, 1814. J 10 T 33-42
[Plaster Cast of.] [See Hutton, L.—Portraits in Plaster.]
A 23 V 13
Sketch of. [See Müller, F. Max.—Chips from a German Workshop.] J 9 R 31-33
Works of, translated. [See Lytton, Lord.] H 9 U 1

SCHIVENOR, Harry. History of the Iron Trade. New ed. 8vo. Lond., 1854. F 14 T 30

SCHLEIERMACHER, Friedrich. On Religion: Speeches to its Cultured Despisers. 8vo. Lond., 1893.
G 2 P 37

SCHLICH, Dr. Wm. Manual of Forestry. Vols. 3, 4. 8vo. Lond., 1895. A 32 R 15, 16

SCHLOSSER, F. C. History of the 18th Century, and of the 19th till the Overthrow of the French Empire. 8 vols. 8vo. Lond., 1843-52. B 25 S 12-19

SCHMIDT, Dr. Adolf. Atlas der Diatomaceenkunde. 2 vols. fol. Leipzig, 1876-90. A 40 T 13, 14 ‡

SCHMIDT, Maj.-Gen. Carl von. Instructions for the Training, Employment, and Leading of Cavalry. Roy. 8vo. Lond. (n.d.) A 29 V 18

SCHMIDT, J. S. Hermann. English Extracts for German Prose, with General Instructions, Annotations, and a Dictionary of Words required. 12mo. Brisb., 1885.
MK 1 P 57
Guide through the Difficulties of the German Declensions. 2nd ed. 12mo. Brisb., 1889. MK 1 P 45

SCHMITZ, L. Dora. The Buchholtz Family. [*See* Stinde, J.] J 9 Q 45

SCHNEIDER, Dr. K., und PETERSILIE, Dr. A. Die Volkssund die Mittelschule sowie die sonstigen niederen Schulen im preussischen Staate im Jahre 1891. 4to. Berlin, 1893. G 12 U 2 †

SCHOENHOF, Jacob. The Economy of High Wages. 8vo. New York, 1893. F 8 U 4

SCHOFIELD, E. Report of Grand Annual Committee of the Manchester Unity of Oddfellows Friendly Societies in New South Wales. 8vo. Sydney, 1893 ME 9 F

SCHOOLING, John H. *Trans.*—Handwriting and Expression. [*See* Crépieux-Jamin, J.] A 18 R 17

SCHOPENHAUER, Arthur. Life of; by W. Wallace 12mo. Lond., 1890. C 18 P 20

SCHORLEMMER, Dr. Carl. Rise and Development of Organic Chemistry. Revised edition, by Prof. A Smithells. 8vo. Lond., 1894. A 21 R 13

SCHÖTTGEN, Chr. Novum Lexicon Græco-Latinum in Novum Testamentum. 8vo. Lipsiæ, 1790. J 15 S 31

SCHREIBER, Th. Atlas of Classical Antiquities, edited by Prof. W. C. F. Anderson. Obl. imp. 8vo. Lond. 1895. B 7 R 8 ‡

SCHREINER, Alfred. La Nouvelle-Calédonie depuis sa Découverte, 1774, jusqu'à nos jours. 8vo. Paris 1882. MB 2 P 58

SCHROEDER VAN DER KOLK, J. L. C. Pathology and Therapeutics of Mental Diseases; translated from the German by J. T. Rudall. 8vo. Melb., 1869. MA 2 U 58

SCHRÖTER, Dr. C. Best Forage Plants. [*See* Stebler Dr. F. G.] A 36 T 4 ‡

SCHUBERT, E. Raw Materials and Distillation of Alcohol. [*See* Stammer, Dr. K.] A 25 Q 39

SCHUERMANS, H. Catalogue des Collections de Grès-Cérames. (Musée Roya. d'Antiquités et d'Armures, Bruxelles.) 12mo. Bruxelles, 1883. K 7 P 2

SCHULENBURG, A. C. Graf v. d. Grammatik der Sprache von Murray Islan L. 8vo. Leipzig (n.d.) MK 1 T 14

SCHULTZ, Dr. G., & JULIUS, Dr. P. Systematic Survey of the Organic Colouring Matters; translated by A. G. Green. Imp. 8vo. Lond., 1894. A 25 V 8

SCHULTZ, Hon. J. A Forgotten Northern Fortress [For. Prince of Wales, Hudson's Bay]. (Hist. and Scientific Soc. of Manitoba.) 8vo Winnipeg, 1894. B 18 R 6

The Old Crow Wing Trail. (Hist. and Scientific Society of Manitoba.) 8vo. Winnipeg, 1894. B 18 R 8

SCHULZE, Dr. F. E. Hexactinellida. [*See* Thomson, Sir C. W., and Murray, Dr. J.—Voyage of H.M.S. *Challenger*.] A 6 †

SCHULZE-GAEVERNITZ, Dr G. von. Social Peace: a Study of the Trade Union Movement in England; translated by C. M. Wicksteed. 8vo. Lond., 1893. F 14 Q 49

SCHWAAB, Ernest F. The Secrets of Canning : a complete Exposition of the Theory and Art of the Canning Industry. 8vo. Baltimore, 1890. A 25 R 12

SCHWABE, Mrs. Salis. Reminiscences of Richard Cobden. 8vo. Lond., 1895. C 21 T 13

SCHWANER, Dr. C. A. L. M. Borneo. 2 vols. imp. 8vo. Amsterdam, 1853-54. D 19 V 26, 27

SCHWEITZER, Paul. Mineral Waters of Missouri. 8vo. Jefferson City, 1892. A 9 U 36

SCIENCE GOSSIP (*Hardwicke's*). [*See* Hardwicke's Science Gossip.] E

SCIENTIFIC AMERICAN, The. Vols. 67-71. Fol. New York, 1892-94. E

SUPPLEMENT. Vols. 34-38. Fol New York, 1892-94. E

ARCHITECTS AND BUILDERS' EDITION. Vols. 13-18. Fol. New York, 1892-94. E

SCLATER, P. L. Birds collected during the Voyage of H.M.S. *Challenger*. [*See* Thomson, Sir C. W., and Murray, Dr. J.—Voyage of H.M.S. *Challenger*.] A 3 †

SCOLLARD, Clinton. On Sunny Shores. Illustrated. 8vo. New York, 1893. D 20 Q 14

SCORESBY, Rev. Dr. Wm. Life of; by R. E. Scoresby-Jackson. 8vo. Lond., 1861. C 22 P 3

SCOTCH COLLEGE, MELBOURNE. Annual Report, 1870. 8vo. Melb., 1870. ME 1 Q

SCOTLAND. [*See* Great Britain and Ireland.]

SCOTS' CHURCH CASE. 8vo. Melb, 1884. MG 2 Q 18

SCOTT, A. W. Australian Lepidoptera, with their Transformations. Fol. Sydney, 1893. MA 1 R 3 ‡

SCOTT, Prof. Austin. The Influence of the Proprietors in founding the State of New Jersey. (Johns Hopkins University Studies, 3.) 8vo. Baltimore, 1885. B 18 S 8

SCOTT, Mrs. David. Pearl and Willie: a Tale; by "Spray." 12mo. Sydney, 1880. MJ 1 P 65

SCOTT, George. Acts relating to District Court, Queensland. [*See* Woolcock, J. L.] MF 1 S 44

SCOTT, H. J. South Australia in 1887-8. 8vo. Adelaide, 1888. MD 5 S 35

SCOTT, John. How to become Quick at Figures. 8vo. Melb., 1892. MA 2 P 45

SCOTT, Dr. John H. Macquarie Island. (Trans. N.Z. Inst., 15.) 8vo. Wellington, 1883. ME 2 R
Osteology of the Aborigines of New Zealand and of the Chatham Islands. (Trans. N.Z. Inst., 26.) 8vo. Wellington, 1894. ME 2 R

SCOTT, Leader. [See Baxter, Mrs. Lucy E.]

SCOTT, Hon. Mrs. Maxwell. The Tragedy of Fotheringay, founded on the Journal of D. Bourgoing, Physician to Mary Queen of Scots, and on unpublished MS. documents. 8vo. Lond., 1895. B 32 T 16

SCOTT, Rev. Thos. The Force of Truth. 8vo. Lond., 1798. G 1 Q 15

SCOTT, Thos. English Life of Jesus. 8vo. Lond., 1872. G 10 P 37
Everlasting Punishment. 12mo. Lond., 1873. G 2 V 35
Tactics and Defeat of the Christian Evidence Society. [See Religious Pamphlets, 3.] G 9 V 18
Challenge to the Members of the Christian Evidence Society. [See Religious Pamphlets, 3.] G 9 V 18
The Physical Resurrection of Jesus in its bearing on the truth of Christianity. [See Religious Pamphlets, 3.] G 9 V 18

SCOTT, Sir Walter. Poetical Works of. Roy. 8vo. Edinb., 1844. H 4 U 22
Familiar Letters of. 2 vols. 8vo. Edinb., 1894. C 19 R 5, 6
Criticisms of the Works of. [See Senior, N. W.—Essays on Fiction] J 6 S 40
Essay an. [See Bagehot, W.—Literary Studies.] J 9 P 22-24
[Life of]; by J. Dennis. [See Mason, Prof. D.] J 6 R 43
Notes to Dryden's Works. [See Dryden, J.] H 4 U 15-18
[Plaster Cast of.] [See Hutton, L.—Portraits in Plaster.] A 23 V 13
Sketch of the Work of. [See Dawson, W. J.—Makers of Modern English.] H 10 S 14
Sketch of. [See Bell, Rev. Dr. C. D.—Some of our English Poets.] C 21 P 11

SCOTT, Wm. B. Autobiographical Notes of; edited by W. Minto. 2 vols. 8vo. Lond., 1892. C 14 U 22, 23

SCOTTISH HISTORY SOCIETY. Publications. Vols. 12-18, 20, 21. 8vo. Edinb., 1892-95. E
12. Court Book of the Barony of Urie, 1604-1747; edited by Rev. D. G. Barron.
13. Memoirs of the Life of Sir John Clerk of Penicuik; edited by J. M. Gray.
14. Erskine of Carnock's Journal, 1683-87.
15. Miscellany.
16. Account Book of Sir J, Foulis, of Ravelston, 1671-1707.
17. Charles II and Scotland in 1650.
18. Scotland and its Commonwealth; edited by C. H. Firth.
20, 21. The Lyon in Mourning, vols. 1 and 2; by Bishop Forbes.

SCOTTISH REVIEW, The. Vols. 3-7, and 15-24. 8vo. Paisley, 1883-94. E

SCOTTISH TEXT SOCIETY. Publications. 2 vols. 8vo. Edinb., 1893. E
Poems of Wm. Dunbar. Vol. 3; edited by J. Small.
Satirical Poems of the Time of the Reformation; edited by J. Cranstoun. Vol. 2.

SCOULAR, Gavin. Past Climatic Changes, with special reference to the occurrence of a Glacial Period in Australia. (Trans. Roy. Soc., S. Australia, 8.) 8vo. Adelaide, 1886. ME 1 S
Geology of the neighbourhood of Gawler. (Trans. Roy. Soc., S. Australia, 5.) 8vo. Adelaide, 1882. ME 1 S
Notes relating to the Geology between the Burra and Farina. (Trans. Roy. Soc., S. Australia, 5.) 8vo. Adelaide, 1882. ME 1 S
Geology of the Southern and Western Parts of the Lake Eyre basin. (Trans. Roy. Soc., S. Australia, 9.) 8vo. Adelaide, 1887. ME 1 S

SCOULLER, John. Practical Book-keeping. 8vo. Melb., 1880. MA 2 P 44
Spiritualism: what and whence it came? 8vo. Melb., 1895. MG 2 R 42

SCOVIL, Elizabeth R. The Care of Children. Revised. ed. 12mo. Philad., 1895. A 26 P 15

SCRIBNER'S MAGAZINE. Vols. 1-17. 8vo. New York, 1887-95. E

SCRYMGOUR'S SIXPENNY GUIDE TO ADELAIDE; edited by D. Gall. 12mo. Adelaide, 1887. MD 1 P 20

SCUDAMORE, Frank. [See Great War of 189-.] J 2 Q 21

SEA SPRAY, The. [See Bloomfield, Capt. H.] MJ 3 Q 7

SEALY, H. B. A Key to the Stamp Act, being a Digest of Stamp Duties payable in New Zealand. 12mo. Napier, 1872. MF 4 P 4

SEAMAN, Susie. Thoughts by the Way. 8vo. Auckland, 1884. MH 1 Q 38

SEARIGHT, Wm. In Memoriam. Sm. 4to. Richmond (Ind.), 1893. C 19 Q 1

SEASONABLE REPROOF; a satire in the manner of Horace. Sm. fol. Lond., 1735. H 30 Q 13 ‡

SEATON, A. E., & ROUNTHWAITE, H. M. A Pocketbook of Marine Engineering Rules and Tables, for the use of Marine Engineers, Naval Architects, Designers, Draughtsmen, Superintendents, &c. 12mo. Lond., 1894. A 22 P 9

SEBELE, African Chief. Sketch of. [See Lloyd, Rev. E.—Three Great African Chiefs.] B 1 P 21

SECCOMBE, Thos. *Editor*—Lives of twelve Bad Men: Original Studies of Eminent Scoundrels, by various hands. [Illustrated.] 8vo. Lond., 1894. C 18 T 9

SECRET MEMOIRS of the Court of St. Petersburg. 8vo. Lond., 1895. B 31 U 1

SEDDING, John D. Art and Handicraft. 8vo. Lond., 1893. A 19 T 8

SEDDON, Col. Henry Cooper Builders' Work and the Building Trades. [Illustrated.] Roy. 8vo. Lond., 1889. A 19 U 21

SEDGWICK, Major Gen. John. Oration delivered at the Dedication of Statue of. [*See* Curtis, G. W.] F 14 U 3

SEE, John. Financial Statements, 1891 and 1892. 2 vols. 8vo. Sydney, 1891-02. MF 1 Q 57, 58

SEEBOHM, Hugh E. Structure of Greek Tribal Society. 8vo. Lond., 1895. F 11 U 16

SEEBOHM, Dr. F. The Tribal System in Wales; being part of an inquiry into the Structure and Methods of Tribal Society. 8vo. Lond., 1895. F 11 U 10

SEEGER & GUERNSEY, Messrs. Cyclopædia of the Manufactures and Products of the United States. Roy. 8vo. New York, 1894. E

SEELEY, Sir John Robt. Lectures and Essays. 12mo. Lond., 1895. J 0 S 24

Goethe reviewed after sixty years. 12mo. Lond., 1894. C 19 Q 15

SÉGUR, Gen. Count de. An Aide-de-camp of Napoleon: Memoirs of, 1800-12. 8vo. Lond., 1895. B 25 S 20

SEIDENSTICKER, Oswald. The first century of German Printing in America, 1728-1830; preceded by a Notice of the Literary Work of F. D. Pastorius. 8vo. Philad., 1893. K 17 R 29

SEISMOLOGICAL JOURNAL OF JAPAN. (*Formerly Transactions of the Seismological Society of Japan.*) Vols. 16-19. 8vo. Tokyo and Yokohama, 1892-93. E

SEISMOLOGICAL SOCIETY OF JAPAN. [*See Seismological Journal of Japan.*]

SELBY-BIGGE, L. A. [*See* Bigge, L. A. S.]

SELENKA, Dr. Emil. Gephyrea. [*See* Thomson, Sir C. W., and Murray, Dr. J.—Voyage of H.M.S. *Challenger*.] A 6 †

SELL, Henry. Telegraphic Code. 8vo. Lond. (n.d.) K 9 S 8

SELLARS, E. Greek Sculpture. [*See* Furtwängler, A.] A 30 R 5 ‡

SELOUS, Frederick Courtney. Travel and Adventure in South-east Africa. Roy. 8vo. Lond., 1893. D 14 V 6

SELWYN, Dr. Alfred Richard Cecil. Colonial and Indian Exhibition, 1886; Descriptive Catalogue of a Collection of the Economic Minerals of Canada. 8vo. Lond., 1886. K 8 R 21

Portrait of. [*See* Ramsay, Sir A. C.—Memoir of.] C 21 R 20

—— and ULRICH, George H. F. Notes sur la Géographie Physique, la Geologie, et la Mineralogie de Victoria. 8vo. Melb., 1866. MA 2 V 30

SELWYN, G. Life and Times of; by A. Hayward. 12mo. Lond., 1854. C 18 P 21

SELWYN, Rt. Rev. George Augustus. Sermon preached, June, 1856. 8vo. Sydney, 1856. MG 1 R 72

SELWYN, Rt. Rev. John Richardson. The Islands of the Western Pacific. [*See* Roy. Col. Inst., Proc., 25.] E

SEMON, Dr. Richard. Zoologische Forschungsreisen in Australien und dem Malayischen Archipel. Band 1. 4to. Jena, 1893. MA 9 P 3 ‡ †

SEMPER, Dr. Carl. Reisen im Archipel der Philippinen. Zweiter theil. Wissenschaftliche Resultate. Dritter band. Landmollusken. 4to. Wiesbaden, 1894. A 9 Q 7 †

SEMPERS, F. W. Manures: how to make and how to use them. 3rd ed. 12mo. Ph lad., 1894. A 18 R 13

SENECA, Lucius Annæus. Tragœdiæ. 12mo. Lond., 1823. H 10 U 6

[Life of.] [*See* Farrar, Archdeacon F. W.—Seekers after God.] C 21 Q 6

SENEUIL, J. G. Courcelle. Estudio de los Principios del Derecho ó preparación para el estudio del Derecho. Obra traducida y armonizada con la lejislación Chilena por M. S. Lavaqui. Roy. 8vo. Santiago, 1887. F 9 T 28

SENIOR, Col. Criticism of the Works of. [*See* Senior, N. W.—Essays on Fiction.] J 6 S 10

SENIOR, Nassau W. Essays on Fiction. 8vo. Lond., 1864. J 6 S 10

Historical and Philosophical Essays. 2 vols. 8vo. Lond., 1865. J 8 U 1 2

SERRURE, Raymond. Catalogue de la Collection de Poids et de Mesures. (Musée Royal d'Antiquités et d'Armures, Bruxelles.) 12mo. Bruxelles, 1883. K 7 F 4

SERTORIUS, Q. [Life of.] [*See* Plutarch] MC 1 R 15

SERVICE, James. Federation of Australasia. Roy. 8vo. Melb., 1884. MF 1 S 58

SETH, Prof. James. Study of Ethical Principles. 8vo. Ed nb., 1894. G 12 Q 11

SETH-SMITH, C. E. [*See* Smith, C. E. S-.]

SEVEN ROVERS, The: a Rollicking Record of Pleasure, Privation, and Peril, afloat and ashore ; by "One of Them." 8vo. Hobart, 1884. MD 5 R 47

SEVENTY YEARS OF LIFE IN THE VICTORIAN ERA, embracing a Travelling Record in Australia, New Zealand, and America, &c.; by "A Physician." 8vo. Lond., 1863. MD 1 Q 34

SEWALL, May W. World's Congress of Representative Women. Roy. 8vo. Chicago, 1894. F 7 R 20

SEWARD, Theodore F. The School of Life: Divine Providence in the Light of Modern Science. 8vo. New York, 1895. G 19 Q 8

SEWARD, Wm. Henry. Sketch of. [See Brooks, N.—Statesmen.] C 16 R 20

SEWEL, Wm. History of the Christian People called Quakers. Roy. 8vo. Philad. (n.d.) G 2 T 25

SEXTON, Prof. A. Humboldt. An Elementary Text-book of Metallurgy. Illustrated. 8vo. Lond., 1865. A 24 R 14

SEYMOUR, Edward Adolphus. [See Somerset, Duke of.]

SHAKESPEAR, R. H. Lighting Country Towns by Electricity or Gas. 8vo. Melb., 1883. MA 3 S 62

SHAKESPEARE, William. Works of; with a memoir by Barry Cornwall. Illustrated. 3 vols imp. 8vo. Lond., 1840. H 2 V 1-3

Works of; edited by Henry Irving and F. A. Marshall. Illustrated by G. Browne. 8 vols. sm. 4to. Lond., 1887-90. H 4 V 1-8

Works of. Imp. edition; edited by C. Knight. Illustrated. 2 vols. fol. Lond. (n.d.) H 40 T 7, 8 ‡

The Bankside Shakespeare, vols. 19, 20, 22. Second and Third Parts of Henry VI; The Comedie of Errors. 8vo. New York, 1892-94. H 9 R 19-22

Heine on Shakespeare; translated by Ida Benecke. 8vo. Lond., 1895. J 10 R 27

Plays of. Edited by H. Staunton. 3 vols. Imp. 8vo. Lond., 1858-60. H 2 V 4-6

Poems of. 18mo. Lond., 1843. H 10 T 13

Selections from, with an Essay on Elocution; by S. Brandram. 8vo. Lond., 1893. J 4 R 2

Shakespearian Anthology; comprising the Choicest Passages and entire scenes. 12mo. Lond., 1830. H 7 U 36

Books on Shakespeare; by S. Timmins. [See Timmins, S.] J 15 S 30

Concordance to the Works of. [See Bartlett, J.] K 17 S 21

The Elizabethan Hamlet. [See Corbin, J.] J 5 R 47

Essay on. [See Bagehot, W.—Literary Studies.] J 9 P 22-24

Five Lectures on. [See Ten Brink, B.] J 10 R 28

Introduction to. [See Dowden, E.] C 18 Q 31

SHAKESPEARE, William—contd.
Is Sir Walter Raleigh the author of Shakespere's Plays? [See Caldwell, C. S.] MJ 2 S 41

List of Works illustrative of the Life of. [See Halliwell, J. O.] K 9 S 16

Papers on, by Douglas Jerrold. [See Jerrold, D.] J 11 T 26

[Plaster Cast of.] [See Hutton, L.—Portraits in Plaster.] A 23 V 13

Shakespeare and his Time under Elizabeth. [See Morley, Henry.] B 21 R 34

Shakespeare in Romance and Reality. [See Thomson, Wm.] MJ 2 S 40

Shakspeare; or, the Poet. [See Emerson, R. W.—Representative Men.] C 17 P 10

Sketch of. [See Bagehot, W.—Estimates of some Englishmen and Scotchmen.] J 10 R 32

A Study of; by A. C. Swinburne. [See Swinburne, A. C.] J 12 R 6

Women of Shakespeare. [See Lewes, Dr. L.] J 6 T 5

SHAKSPERE SOCIETY, NEW. [See New Shakspere Society.]

SHALER, Prof. Nathaniel S. Sea and Land: Features of Coasts and Oceans; with special reference to the Life of Man. Illustrated. 8vo. Lond., 1895. A 30 U 9

The United States of America. Illustrated. 2 vols. Roy. 8vo. New York, 1894. B 20 V 5, 6

SHANAHAN, Patrick. The Exile: a Poem. 8vo. Melb., 1869. MH 1 S 37

SHAND, Alexander Innes. Life of Gen. Sir E. B. Hamley. 2 vols. 8vo. Edinb., 1895. C 13 V 15, 16

SHARP, A. Mary. History of Ufton Court, in the County of Berks, and of the Perkins Family. Roy. 8vo. Lond., 1892. B 21 V 21

SHARP, Elizabeth A. Heine in Art and Letters. [See Heine, H.] J 11 T 39

SHARP, Wm. Life of Robert Browning. 12mo. Lond., 1890. C 17 P 14

Fair Women in Painting and Poetry. (Portfolio Monograph, 7.) Roy. 8vo. Lond., 1894. E

SHARPE, Chas. K. Ballad Book. [See Bibliotheca Curiosa.] J 18 Q 1

SHARPE, Dr. Richard Bowdler. Analytical Index to the Works of the late John Gould, F.R.S., with a Biographical Memoir. 4to. Lond., 1893. A 12 8 7 †

———— and WYATT, Claude W. A Monograph of the Hirundinidæ or Family of Swallows. Illustrated. 2 vols. 4to. Lond., 1885-94. A 13 P 22, 23 †

SHARPE, Dr. Reginald Robinson. London and the Kingdom: a History. Vols. 1 and 2. 8vo. Lond., 1894. B 24 R 5, 6

SHAW, Dr. Albert. Local Self-Government in Illinois. (Johns Hopkins University Studies, I.) 8vo. Baltimore, 1883. B 18 S 1
Co-operation in the Northwest. (Johns Hopkins University Studies, 6.) 8vo. Baltimore, 1888. B 18 S 6
Municipal Government in Great Britain. 8vo. New York, 1895. F 10 Q 30

SHAW, Miss Flora L. The Australian Outlook. [See Roy. Col. Inst., Proc., 25.] E
Letters from Queensland; by "The Times" Special Correspondent." 12mo. Lond., 1893. MD 1 Q 31

SHAW, John. Concise History of New South Wales, from the Earliest Times to the Winning of Responsible Government. 8vo. Parramatta, 1883. MB 1 R 42

SHAW, R. Norman, and JACKSON, T. G. Architecture, a Profession or an Art; thirteen short essays on the qualifications and training of architects. 8vo. Lond., 1892. A 3 P 4

SHAW, Thos. Practical Treatise on Sheep-breeding and Wool-growing. 8vo. Sydney, 1890. MA 2 V 67

SHAW, Capt. Vero-Kemball. Illustrated Book of the Dog; with an Appendix on Canine Medicine and Surgery, by W. G. Stables. 4to. Lond., 1890. A 5 P 16 †

SHAW, W. A. History of Currency 1252-1894. 8vo. Lond. (n.d.) F 7 R 23

SHEARSTON, J. S. H.M.S. *Calliope*: an account of the visit to Apia, Samoa; compiled by J. S. S. Obl. 12mo. Sydney, 1889. MB 1 P 18

SHEDLOCK, M. Lives of E. and J. de Goncourt. [See Goncourt, E. and J. de] C 21 R 3, 4

SHEEHY, Father Joseph Aloysius. In Memoriam. 8vo. Hobart, 1892. MC 1 R 42

SHEEP HUSBANDRY for small Wool-growers; by "Waupmelta." 8vo. Adelaide, 1885. MA 2 V 67

SHEHADI, B. The Confession of Pontius Pilate; translated from the Arabic, by B. Shehadi. 12mo. Sydney, 1893. MG 1 P 60

SHELDON, Prof. J. P. Dairy Management: a Lecture. (Inst. of Agricult., Lond.) 8vo. Lond., 1894. A 18 R 28

SHELDON, M. French—. Sultan to Sultan: Adventures among the Masai and other Tribes of East Africa. Sm. 4to. Lond., 1892. D 14 V 7

SHELLEY, A. C. British and Colonial Union. Conference of Delegates from the various Chambers of Commerce of the British Colonies and Possessions on the subject of British and Inter-Colonial Tariffs, held at the Westminster Palace Hotel, 24th Feb., 20th March, 5th April, 1891. 8vo. Lond., 1891. MJ 3 Q 16

SHELLEY, Percy Bysshe. Account of Visits to France, &c. [See Elton, C. I.] D 18 Q 11
Essay on. [See Bagehot, W.—Literary Studies.] J 9 P 22-24
Sketch of. [See Bagehot, W.—Estimates of some Englishmen and Scotchmen.] J 10 V 32
Sketch of the Work of. [See Dawson, W. J.—Makers of Modern English.] H 10 S 14
Sketch of the Works of. [See Rainé, L. de la.] J 9 R 22
Study of. [See Todhunter, J.] H 3 P 50

SHELLSHEAR, Walter. Light Railways. 8vo. Sydney, 1883. MA 2 T 69

SHELTON, E. M. Canning and otherwise Preserving Fruits for the home and market. 8vo. Brisb., 1891. MA 1 Q 69
The Cultivation of Maize, with facts and suggestions as to its utilisation. 8vo. Brisb., 1890. MA 1 Q 69
The Cultivation of Wheat in Queensland. 8vo. Brisb., 1893. MA 1 Q 69
The Establishment of Creameries; Insecticides; Manures and their preservation; Ramio Culture; Clarifying Re-agent in Sugar-making; and Potato Trials. 8vo. Brisb., 1892. MA 1 Q 69
Manures: their Management and Use; with special reference to Queensland Conditions. (Bulletin 3, 2nd series, Department of Agriculture, Queensland.) 8vo. Brisbane, 1894. MA 3 S 54
Our Stock-foods and how to use them. 8vo. Brisb., 1893. MA 1 Q 69
Pig-raising and Pork-making. 8vo. Brisb., 1891. MA 1 Q 69
Recent Experiments made at the American Agricultural Experiment Stations. 8vo. Brisb., 1891. MA 1 Q 69
Tree-planting for Shade and Ornament. 8vo. Brisb., 1892. MA 1 Q 69
Wheat-growing in Queensland. 8vo. Brisb., 1892. MA 1 Q 69

SHENSTONE, W. A. Justus von Liebig, his Life and Work, 1803-73. 12mo. Lond., 1895. A 21 R 33

SHEPP, James W. and Daniel B. World's Fair Photographed. Obl. 8vo. Chicago, 1893. D 15 V 17

SHEPPARD, Rev. Edgar. Memorials of St. James's Palace. 2 vols. 8vo. Lond., 1894 B 21 U 10, 11

SHERARD, Robert Harborough. Alphonse Daudet: a Biographical and Critical Study. Roy. 8vo. Lond., 1894. C 16 U 8
Emile Zola: a Biographical and Critical Study. 8vo. Lond., 1893. C 19 R 18
Memoirs to serve for the History of Napoleon I. [See Napoleon Bonaparte.] C 17 R 7-9
Chin-Chin. [See Tcheng-ki-Tong.] D 17 Q 24

SHERATON, T. The Cabinet-maker and Upholsterer's Drawing-book. Illustrated. 4to. Lond., 1802. A 15 Q 20 †

SHERBROOKE, Robert Lowe, Viscount. [Life of]: by
  J. F. Hogan. 8vo. Lond., 1893. MC 1 P 53
Life and Letters of; by A. P. Martin. 2 vols. 8vo.
  Lond., 1893. MC 1 R 46, 47
Sketch of. [See Bagehot, W.—Biographical Studies.]
  C 22 P 10
Speeches and Letters on Reform. 1st ed. 12mo. Lond.,
  1867. F 5 Q 13
Speeches and Letters on Reform. 2nd. ed. 8vo. Lond.,
  1837. F 9 U 5
Wentworth's Reply to, on New South Wales Constitution Bill. [See Wentworth, W. C.] MF 3 T 52

SHERER, John W. Narrative of the Mutiny. [See
  Maude, Col. F. C.] B 29 U 2, 3

SHERIDAN FAMILY, Some Account of [See Dufferin,
  Lady.] H 7 R 28

SHERIDAN, Rt. Hon. Richard Brinsley Butler. The
  Critic; or, a Tragedy Rehearsed: a Dramatic Piece.
  [See London Stage, 1.] H 2 S 33
The Duenna: a Comic Opera. [See London Stage, 1.]
  H 2 S 33
The Rivals: a Comedy. [See London Stage, 1.] H 2 S 33
A Trip to Scarborough: a Comedy. [See London Stage,
  2.] H 2 S 34
Pizarro: a Tragedy. [See London Stage, 1.] H 2 S 33
[Plaster Cast of.] [See Hutton, L.—Portraits in
  Plaster.] A 23 V 13

SHERMAN, Prof. L. A. Analytics of Literature: a
  Manual for the Study of English Prose and Verse.
  8vo. Boston, 1893. J 8 Q 42

SHERMAN, General William T. Correspondence between,
  and Senator Sherman, 1837-91. [See Thorndike,
  Rachel S.] C 18 T 15
[Plaster Cast of.] [See Hutton, L.—Portraits in Plaster.]
  A 23 V 13
Sketch of; with Portrait. [See Bolton, Sarah K.—
  Famous Leaders.] C 17 P 27

SHERRARD, James E. Illustrated Official Hand-book to
  the Aquarium, Picture Galleries, and Museum Collections under the control of the Exhibition Trustees.
  8vo. Melb., 1894. MA 2 Q 51

SHERWIN, William. Epidemic Catarrh in Sheep. [See
  Bennett, Dr. G.] MA 1 P 47

SHIELD, William. Principles and Practice of Harbour
  Construction. Illustrated. Roy. 8vo. Lond., 1895.
  A 22 T 10

SHIELDS, G. O. American Book of the Dog: the Origin,
  Development, special Characteristics, Utility, Breeding,
  Training, Points of Judging, Diseases, and Kennel
  Management of all Breeds of Dogs. 8vo. Chicago,
  1891. A 27 U 17

SHIELS, William. Speech on the motion to condemn the
  action of the Trustees of the Public Library, Museum,
  and Picture Gallery, in opening a portion of those
  institutions on Sundays. Roy. 8vo. Melb., 1883.
  MF 3 R 37

SILILETTO, Rev. Arthur R. Editor—Burton's Anatomy
  of Melancholy. [See Burton, R.] G 10 T 38-40

SHINN, Charles Howard. Land Laws of Mining Districts.
  (Johns Hopkins University Studies, 2.) 8vo. Baltimore,
  1884. B 18 S 2
Coöperation on the Pacific Coast. (Johns Hopkins
  University Studies, 6.) 8vo. Baltimore, 1888. B 18 S 6

SHIPLEY, A. E. Branchiopods (Recent). 8vo. Lond.,
  1895. A 30 U 19

SHIPLEY, Lieut. Conway. Sketches in the Pacific. 4to.
  Lond., 1851. MD 2 P 28‡

SHIPPING GAZETTE, The, and Sydney General Trade
  List, 1858-59. Fol. Sydney, 1858-59. ME 8 T

SHIPPING GUIDE, The, 1891-92. 4 vols. Fol.
  Sydney, 1891-92. M E

SHIRLEY, John. Additions to the Lichen Flora of
  Queensland. (Proc. Roy. Soc., Queensland, 5.) 8vo.
  Brisbane, 1888. ME 1 T
Lichen Flora of Queensland, with Description of Species.
  (Proc. Roy. Soc., Queensland, 6.) 8vo. Brisbane,
  1889. ME 1 T
Lichens from Warwick and Neighbourhood. (Proc.
  Roy. Soc., Queensland, 8.) 8vo. Brisbane, 1892.
  ME 1 T
Native Grape Vines of America and Australia. (Proc.
  Roy. Soc., Queensland, 8.) 8vo. Brisbane, 1892.
  ME 1 T
Review of recent Botanical Work in Australia. (Proc.
  Roy. Soc., Queensland, 9.) 8vo. Brisbane, 1893.
  ME 1 T
Some Victorian Lichens. (Proc. Roy. Soc., Queensland,
  10.) 8vo. Brisbane, 1893. ME 1 T

SHIRLEY, William. Edward the Black Prince: an
  Historical Tragedy. [See London Stage, 4.] H 2 S 36

SHIRREFF, Patrick. Improvement of the Cereals and
  an Essay on the Wheat-fly. 12mo. Edinb., 1873.
  A 18 R 38

SHOLL, Martin. Handy Book to Tasmanian Mining and
  General Investment, 1882-83. 8vo. Launceston,
  1882. MF 2 R 52
Handy Book to Tasmanian Mines and Mining, 1881.
  8vo. Launceston, 1881. MA 2 Q 55

SHORTLAND, F. Port Phillip (Charts.) [See Symonds,
  Lieut. T.] MD 5 Q 16‡

SHUCKBURGH, Evelyn S. History of Rome, 753-30 B.C.;
  with Maps and Plans. 8vo. Lond., 1894. B 30 Q 19

SHUMWAY, Henry L. Hand-book on Tuberculosis among Cattle, with considerations of the relation of the Disease to the health and life of the Human Family, and of the facts concerning the use of Tuberculin as a Diagnostic Test. 12mo Lond., 1895. A 12 P 48

SHUTTLEWORTH, Rev. Prof. Henry C. At Home; with Portrait. [See Blathwayt, R.—Interviews.]
J 10 U 34

SIDDONS, Mrs. Sarah. Memoirs of; by J. Boaden. 12mo. Lond., 1893. C 19 Q 2
[Plaster Cast of.] [See Hutton, L.—Portraits in Plaster.]
A 23 V 13

SIDNEY, Sir Philip. Miscellaneous Works of; with a Life of the Author, by William Gray. 8vo. Lond., 1893. J 2 Q 23
[Life of]; by Anna M. Stoddart. Sm. 4to. Edinb., 1894. C 18 T 19

SIDNEY, Samuel. The Book of the Horse. New edition. 4to. Lond., 1893. A 5 P 20 †

SIDNEY, Samuel and John. Sidney's Australian Handbook. How to Settle and Succeed in Australia; by "A Bushman." 18mo. Lond., 1848. MD 1 P 31

SIEMENS, Sir Charles William. [Biographical Sketch.] [See Smith, G. B.—Leaders of Modern Industry.]
C 14 P 14

SIEMENS, Dr. Werner von. Personal Recollections; translated by W. C. Coupland. 8vo. Lond., 1893.
C 13 S 23
Scientific and Technical Papers. Vol. 2. 8vo. Lond., 1895. A 21 S 11

SIENRA, Jorge. Derecho Comercial de los Comerciantes. 8vo. Montevideo, 1894. F 9 R 30

SIGERSON, Dr. George. Revival of Irish Literature. [See Duffy, Sir C. G.] J 7 P 45

SIGHTS AND SCENES in England and Wales. Illustrated. Obl. roy. 8vo. Lond. [1895.] A 8 Q 21 †

SIGMA. [See Money.] MF 2 Q 45

SIGOURNEY, Mrs. Lydia Huntley. Poetical Works of. 18mo. Lond., 1851. H 10 T 11

SIGWART, Dr. Christoph. Logic; translated by Helen Dendy. 2nd ed. 2 vols. 8vo. Lond., 1895.
G 6 T 21, 22

SILVESTRE, Armand. Gallery of Contemporary Art; edited by J. E. Reed. 2 vols. fol. Philad., 1884-88.
A G S 8, 9 ‡

SIMCOX, E. J. Primitive Civilizations; or, Outlines of the History of Ownership in Archaic Communities. 2 vols. 8vo. Lond., 1894. F 14 T 31, 32

SIMEON, Stephen Louis. Napoleon Bonaparte. [See Levy, A.] C 19 R 15, 16

SIMMONDS, J. H. Plants seen in Flower by Field Naturalists on Excursion to Peechey's Scrub. (Proc. Roy. Soc., Queensland, 5.) 8vo. Brisb., 1888.
ME 1 T

SIMMONDS, Thos. C. Art of Modelling in Clay and Wax. Illustrated. 12mo. Lond., 1892. A 23 Q 44

SIMON, John. Editor.—Spiritual Philosophy. [See Green, J. H.] G 14 Q 25, 26

SIMON, Menno. The Amish Mennonites. [See Wick, B. L.] G 14 Q 29

SIMONDS, A. B. American Songs: a Collection of representative American Poems. 8vo. New York, 1894.
H 7 U 11

SIMONDS, Dr. W. E. Introduction to the Study of English Fiction. 12mo. Lond., 1895. J 8 Q 44

SIMONSEN, H. C. Goldmining in the Witwatersrand, S. Africa. [See Abraham, F.] A 24 S 12

SIMPKINSON, Rev. C. H. Life and Times of William Laud, Archbishop of Canterbury. 8vo. Lond., 1894.
C 21 Q 19

SIMPSON, G. Exploration of South-Western Australia. Account of a Trip from York to Hampton Plains. (Roy. Geog. Soc. Australasia, Vic. Branch, 8.) 8vo. Melb., 1891. ME 20

SIMPSON, H. F. Morland. Memoirs of Montrose. [See Montrose, Marquis of.] B 31 V 9

SIMPSON, J. The Wild Rabbit in a new aspect; or, Rabbit-warrens that pay. 12mo. Edinb., 1893.
A 28 P 16

SIMPSON, Margaret S. [Life of] Caroline, Baroness Nairne. [See Nairne, Caroline Baroness.] C 17 Q 24

SIMPSON, Wm. The Seat of War in the East. 4 vols. fol. Lond., 1855. B 11 P 24-27 ‡

SIMPSON, Rev. Dr. Wm. Sparrow. St. Paul's Cathedral and Old City Life. 8vo. Lond., 1894. B 22 U 21
Visitations of Churches belonging to St. Paul's Cathedral, 1297 and 1458. (Camden Soc. Pubs., 55, n.s.) Sm. 4to. Lond., 1895. E

SINCLAIR, Archibald and Henry Wm. Swimming. (Badminton Library.) 8vo. Lond., 1893. A 17 U 47

SINCLAIR, Arthur. In Tropical Lands: Recent Travels to the sources of the Amazon, West Indian Islands, and Ceylon. Illustrated. 8vo Edinb., 1895.
D 20 S 7

SINCLAIR, George. Hortus Gramineus Woburnensis; or, an Account of the Results of Experiments on the Produce and Nutritive Qualities of different Grasses 5 ed., illustrated. 8vo. Lond. 1869. A 20 S 18

SINCLAIR, James M. Report on the Hog-raising and Pork-packing Industry in the United States, and on the Live Stock and Frozen Meat Exportation of the Argentine Republic. 8vo. Melb., 1895. MA 3 V 28
— Preservation of Fruit for Shipment. 8vo. Melb., 1895. MA 3 V 29
— Report on Wheat Production in the United States, Canada, and the Argentine Republic; also the Handling and Shipment of Grain in the United States. 8vo. Melb., 1895. MA 3 V 21

SINGLETON, Dr. John. Alcohol as a Medicine. 12mo. Melb. (n.d.) MA 3 U 13
— Narrative of Incidents in the Eventful Life of a Physician. 8vo. Melb., 1891. MC 1 R 41

SIRA-KAWA DE SENDAÏ. Traité de l'Education des Vers à Soie au Japon; traduit par L. De Rosny. 8vo. Paris, 1868. A 18 S 17

SISCA, Dr. N. Chronic Indigestion, Biliousness, and Management of Children. 12mo. Ballarat, 1889. MA 2 P 40

SITUATION, The. Peace or War? by "An Old Salt." 8vo. Brisbane, 1878. MF 3 Q 84

SKAMP, R. B. The Wool Trade, its History and Growth in Australia and Tasmania. 8vo. Melb. (n.d.) MF 4 R 17

SKEAT, Rev. Dr. Walter Wm. *Editor.*—Chaucer's Works. [*See* Chaucer, G.] H 9 S 27-31

SKELTON, Dr. John. Table Talk of Shirley: Reminiscences of, and Letters from Froude, Thackeray, Disraeli, Browning, Rossetti, Kingsley, Baynes, Huxley, Tyndall, and others. 8vo. Edinb., 1895. C 10 V 10
— [Life of] Mary Stuart. 4to. Lond., 1893. C 1 W 8

SKETCH of Turkish History, A; by "C.J.S." 8vo. Hobart, 1877. MB 1 R 43

SKETCHES from Life; or, Charmed to Death; by "J. W. E." 8vo. Melb., 1877. MJ 1 Q 1

SKETCHES of Life in the Bush; or, Ten Years in the Interior. 12mo. Sydney, 1872. MB 1 P 51

SKINNER, W. R. The Mining Manual for 1895; containing full particulars of Mining Companies, together with a List of Mining Directors. 8vo. Lond., 1894. E

SLADEN, Douglas W. B. On the Cars and off: being the Journal of a Pilgrimage from Halifax to Vancouver's Island. Illustrated. Roy. 8vo. Lond., 1895. D 15 T 22
— The Japs at Home. 8vo. Lond., 1892. D 17 T 2

SLADEN, W. Percy. Asteroidea. [*See* Thomson, Sir C. W., and Murray, Dr. J.—Voyage of H.M.S. *Challenger*] A 6 †

SLANG DICTIONARY. Etymological, Historical, and Anecdotal. 8vo. Lond., 1889. K 12 P 43

SLATER, John Herbert. Early Editions: a Bibliographical Survey of the Works of some popular modern Authors. 8vo. Lond., 1894. K 19 S 29

SLEEMAN, Lucy. Adventures in Mashonaland. [*See* Blennerhassett, R.] D 14 S 7

SLEEMAN, Maj.-Gen. Sir Wm. Henry. Rambles and Recollections of an Indian Official. 2 vols. 12mo. Westm., 1893. D 14 Q 13, 14

SLINGO, W., and BROOKER, A. Electrical Engineering for Electric Light Artisans and Students. New ed., illustrated. 12mo. Lond., 1895. A 21 R 22

SLOANE, T. O'Conor. The Standard Electrical Dictionary. 8vo. Lond., 1893. A 21 P 19

SLOANE, Prof. Wm. Milligan. The French War and the Revolution. 8vo. Lond., 1893. B 17 P 33

SMALL, Dr. Albion Woodbury. The Beginnings of American Nationality: the Constitutional Relations between the Continental Congress and the Colonies and States from 1774-89. (Johns Hopkins University Studies, 8.) 8vo. Baltimore, 1890. B 18 S 8

SMALL, Annie H. Suwarta, and other Sketches of Indian Life. 12mo. Lond, 1894. J 7 P 44

SMALL, Evan W. The Earth: Introduction to the Study of Inorganic Nature. 12mo. Lond., 1894. A 29 R 16

SMALL, J. K. Monograph of the North American Species of the genus *Polygonum*. 4to. Lancaster, Pa., 1895. A 15 Q 2 †

SMALL, Dr. John. Poems of Dunbar. [*See* Scottish Text Soc.] E

SMALLEY, Geo. W. Studies of Men. 8vo. Lond., 1895. C 10 R 20

SMART, Dr. W. *Editor.*—Natural Value. ·[*See* Wieser, F. von.] F 9 T 10

SMEDLEY, A. M. Nara Hodu: Sketches in Japan. 8vo. Sydney, 1884. MD 4 T 46

SMEETH, Wm. Frederick. Perlitic Pitchstone from the Tweed River, with some remarks on the so-called Perlitic Structure in Quartz. (Journal Roy. Soc. N.S.W., 28.) 8vo. Sydney, 1894. ME 1 R
— Chromite-bearing Rock. [*See* David, Prof.] ME 1 R

SMELLIE, Dr. Wm., and his Contemporaries: a Contribution to the History of Midwifery in the 18th Century; by Dr. J. Glaisher. 8vo. Glasgow, 1894. C 10 U 3

SMILES, Dr. Samuel. George Moore, Merchant and Philanthropist. Roy. 8vo. Lond., 1878. C 21 S 12
Josiah Wedgwood, his Personal History. 12mo. Lond., 1894. C 17 P 21

SMILLIE, J. Descriptive Australia and Federal Guide. 8vo. Adelaide, 1890. MD 1 Q 43
Original Poems. 8vo. Adelaide, 1890. MH 1 Q 31

SMITH, Dr. A. On Ventilation. 8vo. Melb., 1875. MA 2 S 60

SMITH, Adam, and our Modern Economy. [See Bagehot, W.—Economic Studies.] F 7 V 35
Sketch of. [See Bagehot, W.—Biographical Studies.] C 22 P 10
Life of; by J. Rae. 8vo. Lond., 1895. C 21 T 2
Select Chapters and Passages from "The Wealth of Nations." 12mo. New York, 1895. F 7 V 26

SMITH, Albert. The Ballet Girl: her Natural History. 18mo. Sydney, 1895. MH 1 U 73
Gavarni in London: Sketches of Life and Character. Roy. 8vo. Lond., 1849. D 19 V 19

SMITH, Rev. Alex. C. Kanaka Labour Question, with special reference to Missionary Efforts in the Plantations of Queensland. 8vo Brisbane, 1892. MG 2 Q 51

SMITH, Rev. Alfred Chas. The Autobiography of an old Passport: chiefly relating how we accomplished many Driving Tours with our own English horses over the roads of Western Europe, before the time of railways. Illustrated. Roy. 8vo. Lond., 1893. D 20 U 4

SMITH, Arthur H. Chinese Characteristics. 8vo. Lond., 1895. B 33 Q 8

SMITH, Benjamin E. Cyclopædia of Names. 4to. Lond., 1894. K 15 R 1 †

SMITH, Bruce. Free-trade and Liberal Associations, their true province. 8vo. Sydney, 1889. MF 4 Q 27
Strikes and their cure. 8vo. Sydney, 1888. MF 4 Q 27

SMITH, C. McKay. Capital Labour, and Taxation; some pleas for common sense. 8vo. Sydney, 1894. MF 4 R 16
Free-trade and its influence on national prosperity. 8vo. Townsville, 1888. MF 4 R 49
Trade Depression and wasted resources; with some remarks on popular Government in New South Wales. 8vo. Sydney, 1887. MF 4 R 50
The Taxation of Property. 8vo. Sydney, 1888. MF 4 R 48

SMITH, Sir C. Euan. Mission to Fez. [See Bonsal, S.] D 14 P 9

SMITH, C. E. Seth-. Corinthian Deep-sea Cruising. [See Sullivan, Sir E.—Yachting.] A 29 Q 40

SMITH, C. M. The Rejected Gifts: a Commercial Drama. 12mo. Townsville, 1888. MH 1 U 72.

SMITH Edgar A. Lamellibranchiata; Heteropoda. [See Thomson, Sir C. W., and Murray, Dr. J.—Voyage of H.M.S. Challenger.] A 6 †

SMITH Veterinary-Captain F. Manual of Veterinary Physiology. 2nd ed. 8vo. Lond., 1895. A 30 R 22

SMITH, Francis Gould. The Australian Protectionist. 8vo. Melb., 1887. MF 1 Q 56

SMITH, Francis Hopkinson. Some Artists at the Fair. [See Chicago Exhibition, 1893.] A 23 U 21

SMITH, Frank J. Common Law Procedure Acts, New South Wales. [See Pilcher, C. E.] MF 3 T 68

SMITH, G. Gregory. [Life of] J. Hepburn, Earl of Bothwell, 1530-78. (Lives of Twelve Bad Men.) 8vo. Lond., 1894. C 18 T 9

SMITH Dr. George. The Conversion of India, from Pantænus to the Present Time, A.D. 193-1893. 8vo. Lord., 1893. B 8 R 26
Bishop Heber, Poet and Chief Missionary to the East, 1783-1826. 8vo. Lond., 1895. C 13 V 31

SMITH. Prof. Goldwin. Essays on Questions of the Day, Political and Social. 8vo. New York, 1893. F 14 R 7
Essays on Questions of the Day. 2nd ed. 8vo. New York, 1894. F 14 R 26
Lectures on Modern History. 8vo. Oxford, 1861. B 37 S 3
Oxford and her Colleges; a View from Radcliffe Library. 18mo. Lond., 1894. B 24 P 9
The United States: an Outline of Political History, 1492-1871. 8vo. Lond., 1893. B 17 R 21

SMITH Rev. Dr. George Adam. Historical Geography of the Holy Land. With Maps. 8vo. Lond., 1894. D 17 T 8
Isaiah, 1-66. [See Expositor's Bible.] G 19 R 19, 20

SMITH, George Barnett. History of the English Parliament, together with an Account of the Parliaments of Scotland and Ireland. 2 vols. roy. 8vo. Lond., 1892. B 23 T 13, 14
Life and Enterprises of Ferdinand de Lesseps. 8vo. Lond., 1893. C 13 P 29
Leaders of Modern Industry: Biographical Sketches. 8vo Lond., 1894. C 14 P 14
Women of Renown: 19th Century Studies. 8vo. Lord., 1893. C 19 Q 3

SMITH, Sir Jas. Edward. Account of two new Genera of Plants from New South Wales. 4to. Lond., 1793. MA 1 U 17

SMITH, Henry G. Occurrence of Evansite in Tasmania. (Journal Roy. Soc., N.S.W., 27.) 8vo. Sydney, 1893. ME 1 R
Almandine Garnets from the Hawkesbury Sandstone at Sydney. (Journal Roy. Soc., N.S.W., 28.) 8vo. Sydney, 1894. ME 1 R

SMITH, Dr. J. B. Catalogue, Bibliographical and Synonymical, of the species of Moths of the Lepidopterous superfamily *Noctuidæ* found in Boreal America. 8vo. Wash., 1893. A 30 U 13

SMITH, James. From Melbourne to Melrose. 8vo. Melb., 1888. MD 7 T 43
The Nervous System, its use and abuse. 8vo. Melb., 1881. MA 1 V 09
Presidential Address delivered at the inauguration of the Kalizoic Society of Victoria. 12mo. Melb., 1884. MG 2 R 31

SMITH, Rev. Jas. E. "Shepherd" Smith, the Universalist: the Story of a Mind; by W. A. Smith. 8vo. Lond., 1892. C 13 P 31

SMITH, Dr. James Walter. Handy-book on the Law concerning Owner, Builder, and Architect. 8vo. Sydney, 1894. MF 3 P 50

SMITH, Joseph. "The American Mahomet." Biographical Sketches of, and his Progenitors for many generations; by Lucy Smith. 12mo. Plano, 1880. C 13 P 8
Memoirs of; by Chas. Mackay. 8vo. 3rd ed. Lond., 1852. G 15 P 28

SMITH, Joseph, jun. *Trans.*--The Book of Mormon. [*See* Book of Mormon.] G 13 V 31

SMITH, John Thomas. Nollekens and his Times. [*See* Nollekens, J.] C 21 R 18
Streets of London; with Anecdotes of their more celebrated residents. New ed. 8vo. Lond., 1854. B 23 Q 15

SMITH, Dr. Louis L. Means of Prolonging Life and avoiding Diseases. 12mo. Melb., 1864. MA 3 P 40
Discoveries in the Nature and Treatment of Gout, 12mo. Melb., 1878. MA 3 U 13

SMITH, Lucy. Biographical Sketches of Joseph Smith, the Prophet, and his Progenitors for many generations. 12mo. Plano, 1880. C 13 P 8

SMITH, Lucy T. Expeditions to the Holy Land. [*See* Camden Soc. Pubs.] E

SMITH, Dr. Nathan D. Meteorological Observations made near Washington, Ark., 1840–59. 4to. Wash., 1860. A 15 Q 14 †

SMITH, Dr. P. W. Bassett-. Aborigines of North-west Australia. (Anthropol. Inst., 23.) 8vo. Lond., 1893. E

SMITH, Percy C. Irrigation for Queensland. 8vo. Brisb., 1889. MA 1 R 41

SMITH, Philip. History of the World from the Earliest Records to the Present Time. 3 vols. 8vo. Lond., 1864. B 37 S 4–6

SMITH, R. A. H. Bickford-. Greece under King George. 8vo. Lond., 1893. F 6 V 26

SMITH, R. Murray. The Finances and Public Debt of the Colony of Victoria. 8vo. Lond., 1882. MJ 3 Q 16

SMITH, Robt. H. Forty-three Graphic Tables or Diagrams for the Conversion of Measurements in different units. 4to. Lond., 1895. A 8 Q 1 †

SMITH, Sir Robt. Murdoch. Persian Art. 8vo. Lond., 1876. A 23 R 21

SMITH, Rev. Sydney. Works of. New ed. 8vo. Lond., 1854. J 8 T 29
Elementary Sketches of Moral Philosophy. 12mo. Lond., 1854. G 6 V 22
Letters of "Peter Plymley," Essays, and Speeches. 12mo. Lond., 1852. J 7 R 58
Wit and Wisdom of. 2nd ed. 8vo. Lond., 1860. J 6 S 41
A Visit to. [*See* Kingston, W. Beatty-.—Men, Cities, and Events.] C 22 R 4

SMITH, T. A. Life Assurance, its Practical and Moral Value, and how to get business. 12mo. Sydney, 1895. MF 4 P 33

SMITH, Dr. Theobald, and KILBORNE, F. L. Nature, Causation, and Prevention of Texas or Southern Cattle Fever. 8vo. Washington, 1893. A 30 R 4

SMITH, Rev. Dr. Thos. The Clementine Homilies. [*See* Clement of Rome.] G 14 U 17
The Clementine Recognitions. [*See* Clement of Rome.] G 14 U 3

SMITH, Dr. Sir Wm. Classical Dictionary of Greek and Roman Biography, Mythology, and Geography; revised and in part rewritten by G. E. Marindin. 8vo. Lond., 1894. K 7 Q 33

SMITH, W. Anderson. "Shepherd" Smith, the Universalist: the Story of a Mind; being a Life of the Rev. Jas. E. Smith. 8vo. Lond., 1892. C 13 P 31

SMITH, W. F. *Trans.*—Rabelais. [*See* Rabelais, F.] J 4 T 3, 4

SMITH, W. P. Haskett. Climbing in the British Isles. 1. England. Illustrated. 18mo. Lond, 1894. A 29 P 44

SMITH, Rev. Wm. A Synopsis of the British Diatomaceæ; with Plates by T. West. 2 vols. roy. 8vo. Lond., 1853–56. A 30 V 14, 15

SMITH, Rt. Hon. Wm. Henry. Life and Times of; by Sir H. Maxwell. 2 vols. 8vo. Lond., 1893.
C 19 R 1, 2

SMITH, Wm. Henry, & SON. Plan of Liverpool; by J. Bartholomew; with Index. Folded 12mo. Lond. (n.d.)
D 12 P 15

Plan of London; with Index. Folded 12mo. Lond. (n.d.)
D 19 P 7

Plan of Manchester; by J. Bartholomew; with Index. Folded 12mo. Lond. (n.d.)
D 12 P 14

SMITH, Dr. Wm. R., F.R.S. Forensic Medicine. [See Guy, Dr. W. A.]
F 11 U 14

SMITH, Dr. Wm. Robertson. Lectures on the Religion of the Semites. 1st series. The Fundamental Institutions. New ed. 8vo. Lond., 1894.
G 15 S 20

The Old Testament in the Jewish Church: Lectures on Biblical Criticism. 8vo. Ed nb., 1881.
G 15 P 27

The Prophets of Israel and their place in History to the close of the 8th Century B.C. 8vo. Edinb., 1882.
G 15 P 26

SMITH, Worthington G. Fungi. [See Taylor, Dr. J. E.—Collecting Natural History Objects.]
A 29 Q 38

Man, the Primeval Savage: his Habits and Relics, from the Hilltops of Bedfurshire to Blackwall. 8vo. Lond., 1894.
A 18 S 23

The two Mildews of Corn: a Lecture. (Inst. of Agricult., Lond.) 8vo. Lond., 1884.
A 18 R 28

SMITHELLS, Prof. Arthur. Organic Chemistry. [See Schorlemmer, Dr. C.]
A 21 R 13

SMITHSON, David J. Elocution and the Dramatic Art. 8vo. Lond., 1889.
J 4 R 38

SMITHSONIAN INSTITUTION. Catalogue of Publications of Societies and of other Periodical Works in the Library, 1856. 8vo. Wash., 1850.
K 7 U 13

Directory of Officers, Collaborators, Employes, &c., of the Smithsonian Institution, National Museum, Geological Survey, and Fish Commission. 8vo. Wash., 1882.
E

Index to Papers on Anthropology, published by the Smithsonian Institution, 1877-78. 8vo. Wash., 1881.
E

List of Foreign Correspondents 1862 and 1882. 2 vols. 8vo. Wash., 1862 and 1882.
E

List of the Institutions, Libraries, Colleges, and other establishments in the United States in correspondence with the Smithsonian Institution. 8vo. Wash., 1872.
E

List of the Principal Scientific and Literary Institutions in the United States, 1879. 8vo. Washington, 1879.
E

SMITHSONIAN INSTITUTION—*contd.*
Meteorological Stations and Observers of the Smithsonian Institution in North America and adjacent Islands, 1810-68. 8vo. Wash., 1869.
E

Publications of Learned Societies and Periodicals in the Library. Part 1. 4to. Wash., 1855.
K 15 Q 17 †

Report of Prof. S. F. Baird, Secretary of the Smithsonian Institution, for 1879. 8vo. Wash., 1880.
E

Reports of the Board, 1891-93. 3 vols. 8vo. Wash., 1893-94.
E

Bureau of Ethnology. [See U.S.—Bureau of Ethnology.]

National Museum. [See United States.—National Museum.]

SMYTH, F. L. Victoria, Legislative Assembly, Standing Orders and Rules. 8vo. Melb., 1871.
MF 1 P 58

SMYTH, Dr. Herbert Weir. The Sounds and Inflections of the Greek Dialects: Ionic. 8vo. Oxford, 1894.
J 6 U 9

SMYTH, Robt. Brough. Geological Survey of Victoria. [See Victoria.]

SMYTH, Sir Warrington Wilkinson. Portrait of. [See Ramsay, Sir A. C.—Memoir of.]
C 21 R 20

SMYTHIES, Capt. R. H. Raymond. Historical Records of the 40th (2nd Somersetshire) Regiment, now 1st Batallion the Prince of Wales's Volunteers, from its formation in 1717, to 1893. 8vo. Devonport, 1894.
B 22 S 5

SNAFFLE. [See Gun, Rifle, and Hound.]
A 29 V 27

SNELL, Albion T. Electric Motive Power. 8vo. Lond., 1894.
A 21 S 29

SNELL, Hannah. Life of. [See Dowie, M. M.—Women Adventurers.]
C 15 S 24

SNODGRASS, William. Physiology of the Senses. [See M'Kendrick, Prof. J. G.]
A 26 Q 14

SNORRO STURLESON. Stories of the Kings of Norway, called the Round World; done into English by W. Morris and E. Magnússon. Vols. 1, 2. (The Saga Library, vols. 3, 4.) 8vo. Lond., 1893-94.
J 14 Q 29, 30

SNOW, Prof. Marshall S. The City Government of St. Louis. (Johns Hopkins University Studies, 5.) 8vo. Baltimore, 1887.
B 18 S 5

SNOWY RIVER. Road Map to. Folio (folded). (n.p. n.d.)
MD 4 P 6 †

SOCIALITIES, 1887. 4to. Sydney, 1887.
MJ 1 V 10

SOCIEDAD DE FOMENTO FABRIL. Boletin de la, 1884-93. 10 vols. imp. 8vo. Santiago, 1884-93.
E

SOCIEDAD GEOGRAFICA DE MADRID. Boletin de la. Tomo 4, Num. 1, 1878. Roy. 8vo. Madrid, 1878.
MD 7 U 20

SOCIEDAD NACIONAL DE MINERIA. Boletin de Mineria. Vols. 1–5. 4to. Santiago, 1888–93. E

SOCIETA ITALIANA DI SCIENZE NATURALI. Atti della, 1890–92. Vols. 33, 34. 8vo. Milano, 1890–92. E

SOCIÉTÉ DE GÉOGRAPHIE. Bulletin de la. 7° sér., tomes 13–15. 8vo. Paris, 1892–94. E
Compte Rendu des Séances de la Société de Géographie et de la Commission Centrale, 1892–93. 2 vols. 8vo. Paris, 1892–93. E

SOCIÉTÉ ROYALE DES ANTIQUAIRES DU NORD. [See Kongeligt Nordisk Oldskrift Selskab.]

SOCIETY. Vols. 4–6, 1887–88. 3 vols. fol. Sydney, 1887–88. ME 16 T

SOCIETY FOR PSYCHICAL RESEARCH. Proceedings. Vols. 8–10. 8vo. Lond., 1892–94. E

SOCIETY FOR THE ASSISTANCE OF PERSONS OF EDUCATION IN DISTRESSED CIRCUMSTANCES. First Annual Report. 8vo. Melb., 1869. MG 2 Q 48

SOCIETY FOR THE PROMOTION OF HELLENIC STUDIES. Journal, vols. 13, 14. Imp. 8vo. Lond., 1893–94. E
Supplementary Paper, No. 1. Ecclesiastical Sites in Isauria; by A. C. Headlam. Fol. Lond., 1893. E
Supplementary Papers. No. 1. Excavations at Megalopolis, 1890–91. Fol. Lond., 1892. E

SOCIETY FOR THE RELIEF OF DESTITUTE CHILDREN, Randwick. 36th–38th Annual Reports. 8vo. Parramatta and Sydney, 1888–90. ME 6 S

SOCIETY OF ANTIQUARIES OF LONDON. Archæologia; or, Miscellaneous Tracts relating to Antiquity. Vols. 53, 54. 4to. Lond., 1893–94. E

SOCIETY OF BIBLICAL ARCHÆOLOGY. Transactions. Vol. 9. 8vo. Lond., 1893. E

SOCIETY OF CHEMICAL INDUSTRY, Journal of. Vols. 10–12. 4to. Lond., 1891–93. E

SOLLAS, Prof. William J. Tetractinellida. [See Thomson, Sir C. W., and Murray, Dr. J.—Voyage of H.M.S. Challenger.] A 6 †

SOLLY, Henry. "These Eighty Years"; or, the Story of an Unfinished Life. 2 vols. 12mo. Lond., 1893. C 19 Q 4, 5

SOLLY, R. H. Elementary Introduction to Mineralogy. 8vo. Lond., 1894. A 24 U 28

SOLOMON, D. L. Northern Territory Times Almanac and Directory, 1887. 8vo. Palmerston, S.A., 1887. ME 4 U

SOLOMON, V. L. Guide to Western Australia and its Goldfields, 1894; with Map of Goldfields, &c. 8vo. Adelaide, 1894. MD 7 S 1

SOLON, M. L. The Ancient Art Stoneware of the Low Countries and Germany. 2 vols. 4to. Lond., 1892. A 38 Q 14, 15 ‡

SOLOVYOFF, Vsevolod S. A Modern Priestess of Isis; translated by Dr. W. Leaf. 8vo. Lond., 1895. G 2 U 12

SOLTERA, Maria. [See Lester, Miss Mary.]

SOME MINOR ARTS as practised in England. Fol. Lond., 1894. A 32 P 20 ‡

SOMERSET, Edward Adolphus Seymour, 12th Duke of. Letters, Remains, and Memoirs of; by W. H. Mallock and Lady G. Ramsden. 8vo. Lond., 1893. C 13 S 24
Christian Theology and Modern Scepticism. 8vo. Lond., 1872. G 15 P 30

SOMERSET, H. Somers. The Land of the Muskeg. Illustrated. 8vo. Lond., 1895. D 15 T 25

SOMERVILE, William. Book II of the Chace. [See Dryden, J.] H 10 Q 29

SOMERVILLE, F. Œ., and ROSS, Martin. In the Vine Country. 8vo. Lond., 1893. D 9 P 13

SOMERVILLE, Mary. Physical Geography. 4th ed. 8vo. Lond., 1858. A 29 R 19

SOMERVILLE, Prof. William. Diseases of Trees. [See Hartig, Prof. R.] A 18 V 31

SONS OF TEMPERANCE, Victoria Grand Division, Friendly Society. Rules. 8vo. Geelong, 1869. MF 1 P 57

SOPHOCLES. The Plays and Fragments; with Critical Notes, Commentary, and Translation in English Prose by Dr. R. C. Jebb. Part 6. 8vo. Camb., 1894. H 9 T 22
The Seven Plays of; by Dr. L. Campbell. 8vo. Lond., 1883. H 10 S 10
The Tragedies of; translated into English Prose from the Text of Jebb by E. P. Coleridge. 12mo. Lond., 1893. H 2 Q 50
The Ajax and Electra of; translated by E. D. A. Morehead. 8vo. Lond., 1895. H 9 U 39
Œdipus Tyrannus, Œdipus Coloneus, et Antigone. [See Trollope, W.] H 3 S 37

SORAUER, Dr. Paul. Popular Treatise on the Physiology of Plants, for the use of Gardeners; translated by Prof. F. E. Weiss. Illustrated. 8vo. Lond., 1895. A 20 T 2

SOTHEBY, W. Oberon. [See Wieland, C. M. von.] H 10 T 26

SOUDAN. Map shewing Routes between Suakim, Khartoum and Dongola, in the Soudan, with Diagrams of the Seat of War. Folded roy. 8vo. Sydney, 1885.
MD 6 U 1

SOUTH AFRICA. The Gold-fields of. [*See* Edwards and Co.] A 24 V 11

SOUTH AFRICAN PHILOSOPHICAL SOCIETY. Transactions of, 1881-85. 3-o. Cape Town, 1884-85. E

SOUTH AUSTRALIA.—*General*.
Photographic Views. 2 vols. 4to. (n.p.n.d.)
MA 3 P 17, 18 ‡
Sketch of South Australia, 1880; with maps and statistical diagrams. 8vo. Adelaide, 1880. MD 8 Q 34
South Australia: its history, progress, and present condition. 8vo. Lond., 1848. MD 8 Q 25

SOUTH AUSTRALIA.—*Government Departments, Reports, and Publications.*

ACTS. [*See* STATUTES.]

AGRICULTURAL BUREAU. Reports, 1890-94. 5 vols. sm. fol. Adelaide, 1890-94. ME
First to Sixth Congress held in Adelaide, 1890-94. 6 vols. 4to. Adelaide, 1890-94. ME
Conference of Northern Branches, held at Gladstone, 1893. 4to. Adelaide, 1893. ME
Proceedings of Conferences of Branches held at Mount Gambier, Gladstone, Quorn, Kadina, and Strathalbyn. 4to. Adelaide, 1894. ME
Rust in Wheat. Report of Proceedings of Conference held in Adelaide, March, 1892. Sm. fol. Adelaide, 1892. MA 7 Q 32 †

BOTANIC GARDEN AND GOVERNMENT PLANTATIONS. Reports, 1880-89. Sm. fol. Adelaide, 1881-90. ME

EDUCATION. Acts and Regulations. 8vo. Adelaide, 1892. MG 2 Q 40

FINANCE. The State Advances Bill: Speech of the Treasurer, to which is appended a copy of the Bill. 8vo. Adelaide, 1895. MF 1 S 71

HOUSE OF ASSEMBLY. Standing Rules and Orders. 12mo. Adelaide, 1887. MF 4 P 28

LEGISLATIVE COUNCIL. Standing Rules and Orders. 12mo. Adelaide, 1878. MF 4 P 27

MARINE BOARD. By-laws and Regulations of. 8vo. Adelaide, 1883. MF 4 Q 25

MURRAY RIVER. [*See* Great Britain and Ireland.]

OBSERVATORY. [*See* Adelaide Observatory.]

PARLIAMENT, Proceedings of, 1892-94. 8 vols. sm. fol. Adelaide, 1893-95. ME

PUBLIC LIBRARY, MUSEUM, AND ART GALLERY. Reports, 1889-90. Sm. fol. Adelaide, 1890. ME

SCHOOL OF MINES AND INDUSTRIES AND TECHNOLOGICAL MUSEUM. Annual Report, 1889. 8vo. Adelaide, 1890. ME 15 Q

STATUTES. Acts of the Parliament, 1892-94. 3 vols. 4to. Adelaide, 1893-95. ME

SOUTH AUSTRALIAN INSTITUTE. Reports, 1879-84. 5 vols. sm. 4to. and fol. Adelaide, 1880-84.
ME 15 Q

SOUTH AUSTRALIAN LAND NATIONALIZATION SOCIETY. The Manifesto of. 2nd edition. 8vo. Adelaide, 1884. MF 2 Q 57

SOUTH AUSTRALIAN NEWS, 1841-45. 8vo. Lond., 1841-45. ME 15 Q

SOUTH END INDUSTRIAL SCHOOL, ROXBURY. Report for 1892. 8vo. Roxbury, Mass., 1893. E

SOUTH KENSINGTON MUSEUM. Conferences held in connection with the Special Loan Collection of Scientific Apparatus, 1876. Chemistry, Biology, Physical Geography, Geology Mineralogy, Meteorology, Physics, and Mechanics. 2 vols. 8vo. Lond. (n.d.) A 29 R 26, 27
Examples of the Works of Art in the Museum, and of the Decorations of the Building. Fol. Lond., 1880.
A 39 R 6 ‡
Hand-book to the Special Loan Collection of Scientific Apparatus, 1876. 8vo. Lond (n.d.) A 29 R 28

SOUTH-WEST and New Mexico for Phthisis, Weak Lungs, Asthma, Bronchitis, &c. 8vo. Chicago, 1892. D 15 S 18

SOUTHAM, A. D. Electrical Engineering as a Profession: how to enter t, and Guide to the Engineering Profession. Illustrated. 8vo. Lond., 1895.
A 21 R 21

SOUTHERN, Thos. Isabella; or, the Fatal Mariage: a Tragedy. [*See* London Stage, 2.] H 2 S 34
Oroonoko: a Tragedy [*See* London Stage, 2.] H 2 S 34

SOUTHERN PROVINCES ALMANAC, Directory, Diary, and Year-book, for 1887. 12mo. Christchurch, 1886. ME 12 Q

SOUTHERN TASMANIAN FOOTBALL ASSOCIATION. 8th Annual Report. 12mo. Hobart, 1887.
ME 5 Q

SOUTHEY, Mrs. C., (Caroline Bowles). The Birthday: a Poem in three parts, to which are added Occasional Verses. 12mo. Edinb., 1836 H 10 T 21

SOUTHEY, Robert. Poetical Works of. New ed. Roy. 8ve. Lond., 1853. H 4 U 23
English Seamen: Howard, Clifford, Hawkins, Drake, Cavendish. 8vo. Lond., 1895. B 23 S 15
A Love Story; edited by Rev. J. W. Warter. 12mo. Lond., 1853. J 12 T 15
Thalaba the Destroyer. 12mo. Lond., 1853. H 10 U 8
Story of his Life written in his Letters; edited by J. Dennis. 12mo. Lond., 1894. C 17 P 20
Life of H. K. White. [*See* White, H. K.—Poetical Works.] H 10 T 25
Sketch of the Work of. [*See* Dawson, W. J.—Makers of Modern English.] H 10 S 14

SOUTHEY, Thos. Observations addressed to the Woolgrowers of Australia and Tasmania respecting improvements in the breed of Sheep. 8vo. Lond., 1830.   MA 2 V 67

SOUTHWARD, John. Practical Printing: a Hand-book of the Art of Typography. 4th ed., by A. Powell. 2 vols. 8vo. Lond., 1892.   A 25 Q 14, 15
Artistic Printing. 8vo. Lond., 1892.   A 25 Q 13

SOUTHWELL, T. Birds' Eggs. [See Taylor, Dr. J. E.—Collecting Natural History Objects.]   A 29 Q 88

SOUTTER, W. Geographical Distribution of Plants. (Roy. Geograph. Soc. of Australasia, Q. Branch, 4.) 8vo. Brisbane, 1889.   ME 20

SOUVESTRE, Emile. An Attic Philosopher in Paris. 12mo. Lond., 1853.   J 12 S 32

SOWERBY, James. English Botany. Supplement to the third edition, vols. 1–4; by N. E. Brown. Imp. 8vo. Lond., 1892.   A 32 U 15

SOWERBY, Wm. Thorough Cultivation. 12mo. Lond., 1893.   A 32 R 11

SPACKMAN, W. H. Trout in New Zealand: where to go and how to catch them. 8vo. Wellington, 1892.   MA 3 T 56

SPALDING, Prof. Fred P. Notes on the Testing and Use of Hydraulic Cement. 12mo. Ithaca, N.Y., 1893.   A 25 P 11

SPALDING, Thos. Alfred. The House of Lords: a Retrospect and a Forecast. 8vo. Lond., 1894.   F 14 S 23

SPANTON, J. Humphrey. Science and Art Drawing: complete Geometrical Course. 8vo. Lond., 1895.   A 23 U 29

SPARHAM, H. H. W. Digest of Reported Decisions. [See Fisher, R. A.]   F 12 V 3–9

SPARKES, W. E. How to shade from models. 3rd ed. Illustrated. 8vo. Lond., 1892.   A 23 R 10

SPARKS, Prof. Jared. Autobiography of Benjamin Franklin. 12mo. Lond., 1850.   C 17 P 10

SPAULDING, Rev. Solomon. The "Manuscript Found"; or, "Manuscript Story" of the late Rev. S. Spaulding. 12mo. Lamoni (Ia.), 1885.   G 8 P 37

SPECTATOR, The: a Weekly Review of Politics, Literature, Theology, and Art. Vols. 60–73. Sm. fol. Lond.,·1892–94.   E

SPECTRUM, The: an Australian Journal of Science, 1891. 4to. Sydney, 1891.   ME 10 R

SPECULUM orientalis occidentalisque Indiæ navigationum; quarum una G. à Spilbergen classis cum potestate Præfecti. altera J. le Maire auspiciis imperioque directa, annis 1614–18. Obl. 12mo. Lugd. Bat., 1619.   MD 8 P 9

SPEECH of Man and Holy Writ. 8vo. Lond., 1894.   J 9 P 12

SPENCE, Miss Charlotte H. The Laws we live under. 12mo. Adelaide, 1880.   MF 4 P 26

SPENCE, Very Rev. Henry Donald Maurice. Cloister Life in the Days of Cœur de Lion. Imp. 8vo. Lond., 1892.   B 21 V 22
The Dean of Gloucester at Home: with Portrait. [See Blathwayt, R.—Interviews.]   J 10 U 31

SPENCE, Joseph. Crito; or, a Dialogue on Beauty; by Sir Harry Beaumont. (Bibliotheca Curiosa.) 12mo. Edinb., 1885.   J 18 Q 27

SPENCER, Prof. Baldwin. New species of Marsupials from Central Australia. (Proc. Roy. Soc., Vict., 7.) 8vo. Melb., 1895.   ME 1 P
Peripatus insignis in Tasmania. (Proc. Roy. Soc., Vict., 7.) 8vo. Melb., 1895.   ME 1 P
Tasmanian Earthworms. (Proc. Roy. Soc., Vict., 7.) 8vo. Melb., 1895.   ME 4 P

SPENCER, David E. Local Government in Wisconsin. (Johns Hopkins University Studies, 8.) 8vo. Baltimore, 1890.   B 18 S 8

SPENCER, Herbert. Principles of Ethics. Vol. I. 8vo. Lond., 1892.   G 19 Q 12
The Right to the use of the Earth. 8vo. Melb., 1872.   MF 2 Q 50
Comte, Mill, and Spencer. [See Watson, Dr. J.]   G 2 U 14
Correspondence with. [See Youmans, E. L.]   C 16 R 21
A Perplexed Philosopher. [See George, H.]   F 14 Q 35
Philosophy of. [See Hudson, W. H.]   G 2 U 8

SPENER, Philipp Jacob. [Life of]; by Rev. F. F. Walrond. 12mo. Lond., 1893.   C 13 P 0

SPENSER, Edmund, and his time. [See Morley, Prof. H.]   B 21 R 33

SPICER, Rev. E. On a sense of Hearing in Ants. (Proc. Roy. Soc., Queensland, 1.) 8vo. Brisb., 1884.   ME 1 T

SPIELMANN, M. H. Henriette Ronner, the Painter of Cat Life and Cat Character. [See Ronner, H.]   A 40 U 3 ‡

SPIERS, R. Phené. Orders of Architecture: Greek, Roman, Italian. Fol. Lond., 1890.   A 6 U 1 ‡
History of Architecture. [See Fergusson, J.]   A 10 T 11, 12

SPIERS, Prof. V. J. T. History of Literature of France in Synoptic Tables. 8vo. Lond., 1894.   B 26 R 8

SPILBERGEN, Georg van. Speculum orientalis occidentalis quæ Indiæ navigationum. [See Speculum.]   MD 8 P 9

SPINOZA, Benedict de. A Study of; by the Rev. Dr. J. Martineau. 8vo. Lond., 1895.   G 8 P 32

SPIRITUAL BOMBSHELL, The; or, Popery and Protestantism exhibited in their relation to Judaism, Christianity, and each other; by "A Priest of the Living Temple." 8vo. Hobart, 1871. MG 1 S 41

SPIRITUAL PANTHEISM; by "F.H.J." [See Religious Pamphlets, 1.] G 9 V 16

SPON, Ernest. Water Supply: the Present Practice of Sinking and Boring Wells; with Geological Considerations and Examples of Wells executed. 2nd ed. 8vo. Lond., 1885. A 22 Q 19

SPRAGUE, Isaac. Wild Flowers of America. [See Goodale, Dr. G. L.] A 15 Q 22 †

SPRAY. [See Scott, Mrs. David.]

SPRINGALL, Percy W. A Trip through the Hot Lake District, New Zealand. (Roy. Geogr. Soc. of Australasia, Q. Branch, 3.) 8vo. Brisbane, 1889. ME 20

SPRINGER, Wm. M. Tariff Reform, the Paramount issue; with a Sketch of the Author, by A. J. Jones. 8vo. New York, 1892. F 4 P 24

SPRINGTHORPE, Dr. J. W. Manual of Infectious Diseases and Ambulance Work. [See Brodribb, T.—Manual of Health.] MA 3 U 4
Report on Koch's Treatment of Tubercular Disease. 8vo. Melb., 1891. MA 3 S 52

SPRY, Frank P. Victorian Butterflies. [See Anderson, E.] MA 3 S 15

SPURGEON, Rev. Charles Haddon. Personal Reminiscences of; by Rev. W. Williams. 8vo. Lond., 1895. C 19 V 12
Sketch of; with Portrait. [See Bolton, Sarah K.—Famous Leaders.] C 17 P 27
Sketch of. [See Smalley, G. W.—Studies of Men.] C 19 R 20

SPURR, J. Edward. Iron-bearing Rocks of the Mesabi Range, Minnesota. 8vo. Minneapolis, 1894. A 24 V 33

SPYBEY, F. G. Annual Register of Nottingham County Cricket Matches, 1880-86. 7 vols. 12mo. Nottingham, 1880-86. E

SPYERS, T. G. The Labour Question : an Epitome of the Evidence and the Report of the Royal Commission on Labour. 12mo. Lond., 1894. F 4 T 15

SQUAREY, Chas. Popular Treatise on Agricultural Chemistry. 8vo. Philad., 1842. A 21 Q 28

SQUATTERS' DIRECTORY, containing a list of all occupants of Crown Lands in the intermediate and unsettled districts of Port Phillip, the names, estimated area, and grazing capabilities of their respective runs. 8vo. Melb., 1849. ME 11 S

2 κ

SQUIRE, Dr. J. Edward. Hygienic Prevention of Consumption. 8vo. Lond., 1893. A 26 Q 45

SQUIRE, Peter. Companion to the latest edition of the British Pharmacopœia. 8vo. Lond., 1894. A 33 S 8

STABLES, Dr. Wm. Gordon. Canine Medicine and Surgery. [See Shaw, V.] A 5 P 16 †

STACK, Frederick Rice. Views in the Province of Auckland, New Zealand. Fol. Lond. (n.d.) MD 5 Q 14 ‡

STAFFORD, Wm. Report on. [See New South Wales, Police.] MF 4 T 17

STAIRS, Capt. W. G. With Capt. Stairs to Katanga. [See Moloney, J. A.] D 14 P 8

STALEY, Rt. Rev. Thos. Nettleship. Five Years' Church Work in the Kingdom of Hawaii. 8vo. Lond., 1868. MG 1 P 83

STAMBULOFF, Stepan. [Life of]; by A. H. Beaman. 8vo. Lond., 1895. C 22 P 11

STAMMER, Dr. K., EISNER, Dr. F., and SCHUBERT, E. Treatise on the Raw Materials and the Distillation and Rectification of Alcohol, and the Preparation of Alcoholic Liquors, Liqueurs, Cordials, and Bitters; translated by W. T. Brannt. Illustrated. 12mo. Philad., 1885. A 25 Q 39

STANDARD DICTIONARY of the English Language. 2 vols. 4to. New York, 1895. K 20 V 30, 31

STANFIELD, Clarkson. Pictures by; with a Biographical Sketch of the Painter, by J. Dafforne. 4to. Lond. (n.d.) A 39 Q 16 ‡

STANFORD, Edward. Australasia. [See Wallace, Dr. A. R.] MD 8 Q 23, 24
Compendium of Geography : Africa. [See Keane, A. H.—Africa.] D 14 R 14
Library Map of London and Suburbs. Folded 8vo. Lond. (n.d.) Libr.

STANFORD, Leland. Sketch of. [See Stoddard, W. O.—Men of Business.] C 16 R 19

STANLEY, Very Rev. Dr. Arthur Penrhyn. The Life and Correspondence of A. P. Stanley, D.D., late Dean of Westminster; by R. E. Prothero, with the cooperation and sanction of the Very Rev. G. G. Bradley, Dean of Westminster. 2 vols. 8vo. Lond., 1893. C 19 R 3, 4
Essay on. [See Brooks, Rt. Rev P.] J 6 S 38
Selection from the Writings of; edited by Rev. A. S. Aglen. 8vo. Lond., 1894. G 15 P 20
Sermons and Essays on the Apostolic Age. 8vo. Lond. (n.d.) G 11 P 43

STANLEY, Rt. Hon. Edward John, Lord. The People's Day. [See Arthur, W.] G 15 P 43

Supplementary Catalogue—1893-95.

STANLEY, Lady Gertrude Sloane. Correspondence with Jos. Jekyll. [*See* Jekyll, J.] C 16 S 16

STANLEY, Henry Morton, and the Congo Free State. [*See* Greeley, Gen. A. W.—Explorers and Travellers.] C 17 R 4
  My Dark Companions and their Strange Stories. 8vo. Lond., 1893. B 16 R 8
  My Early Travels and Adventures in America and Asia. Illustrated. 2 vols. 8vo. Lond., 1895. D 17 Q 27, 28
  Livingstone and Stanley on Lake Tanganika. [*See* Great Explorers.] D 15 V 21, 22
  Sketch of. [*See* Brown, Dr. R.—Story of Africa.] D 15 V 24-26

STANLEY, Hiram M. Studies in the Evolutionary Psychology of Feeling. 8vo. Lond., 1895. G 3 R 12

STANLEY, Thos. *Trans.*—Anacreon. [*See* Anacreon.] H 7 U 9

STANNARD, Mrs. Arthur, "John Strange Winter." Mrs. A. Stannard at Home; with Portrait. [*See* Blathwayt, R.—Interviews.] J 10 U 34

STAPF, Dr. O. Flora of Mount Kinabalu, in North Borneo. [*See* Trans. Linnean Soc., Lond., 4, pt. 2.] E

STAREREN, T. L. M. van. Mijne Reisontmoetingen op den Grooten Oceaan. 8vo. Dordrecht, 1843. MD 8 Q 11

STARK, Gen. John. The Statue erected by the Senate of New Hampshire in honor of: a Sketch of its inception, erection, and dedication. Sm. 4to. Manchester, N.H., 1890. C 19 S 4

STARR, Frederick. *Trans.*—The Pygmies. [*See* Quatrefages, A. de.] A 19 Q 5

STATE EDUCATION FOR THE PEOPLE in America, Europe, India, and Australia; with Papers on the Education of Women, Technical Instruction, and Payment by Results. Roy. 8vo. Syracuse, N.Y., 1895. G 15 T 22

STATE TRIALS,. Reports of. [*See* Great Britain and Ireland.]

STATESMAN'S YEAR-BOOK, The: Statistical and Historical Annual of the States of the World for 1893-95. 3 vols. 12mo. Lond., 1893-95. E

STATHAM, H. Heathcote. Architecture for general readers. 8vo. Lond., 1895. A 20 U 6

STATISTICAL SOCIETY OF LONDON. Journal of, 1838-92. Vols. 1-55, with Indexes and Jubilee vol. 8vo. Lond., 1839-92. E

STAUNTON, Howard. The Chess-player's Hand-book. 8vo. Lond., 1890. A 17 U 8
  The Plays of Shakespeare. [*See* Shakespeare, W.] H 2 V 4-6

STEAD, Richard. Bygone Kent. 8vo. Canterbury, 1892. D 5 T 45

STEAD, Wm. Thos. An Interview with, on the Church of the Future; with Portrait. [*See* Blathwayt, R.—Interviews.] J 10 U 34
  If Christ came to Chicago: a Plea for the union of all who love in the service of all who suffer. 8vo. Lond., 1894. F 5 Q 14
  Two and two make four: being the Review of Reviews Annual, 1893. Sm. 4to. Lond., 1893. E
  [*See* Review of Reviews.] E

STEAM TO AUSTRALIA AND NEW ZEALAND: a Collection of Letters. 8vo. Lond., 1850. MF 4 Q 21

STEANE, G. R. B. Notes on Hydrology. (Roy. Soc., Vic., 20.) 8vo. Melb., 1894. ME 1 P

STEBBING, Rev. Thos. R. R. History of Crustacea—Recent Malacostraca. 8vo. Lond., 1893. A 28 Q 36
  Amphipoda. [*See* Thomson, Sir C. W., and Murray, Dr. J.—Voyage of H.M.S. *Challenger*.] A 6 †

STEBLER, Dr. F. G., and SCHRÖTER, Dr. C. The best Forage Plants fully described and figured; translated by Prof. A. N. McAlpine. Illustrated. 4to. Lond., 1889. A 36 T 4 ‡

STECHER, Wm. A. German System of Physical Education. 8vo. Milwaukee (n.d.) G 18 R 35

STEDMAN, Edmund Clarence. Works of Edgar Allen Poe. [*See* Poe, E. A.] J 14 R 1, 2

STEELE, Sir Richard. [Plays of.] Edited by G. A. Aitken. 12mo. Lond., 1894. H 3 P 40
  The Conscious Lovers: a Comedy. [*See* London Stage, 2.] H 2 S 34
  The Tender Husband; or, the Accomplished Fools: a Comedy. [*See* London Stage, 3.] H 2 S 35
  The Spectator. [*See* Addison, J.] J 12 T 26

STEELE, Robert. Mediæval Lore: an Epitome of the Science, Geography, Animal and Plant Lore, and Myth of the Middle Ages; being the classified gleanings from the Encyclopedia of Bartholomew Anglicus. Roy. 8vo. Lond., 1893. A 30 T 6
  Secrees of old Philisoffres. [*See* Early English Text Society.] E

STEELE, W. Huey. A new Thermo-electric Phenomenon. (Proceedings Royal Society, Victoria, n.s. 6.) 8vo. Melb., 1894. ME 1 P

STEINER, Dr. Bernard C. History of Education in Connecticut. 8vo. Wash., 1893. G 18 R 37
  History of University Education in Maryland. (Johns Hopkins University Studies, 9.) 8vo. Baltimore, 1891. B 18 S 9
  History of Slavery in Connecticut. (Johns Hopkins University Studies, 11.) 8vo. Baltimore, 1893. B 18 S 11
  History of Education in Maryland. 8vo. Wash., 1894. G 18 R 40

STENHOUSE, Andrew. Anatomy of the Pig-Fish (*Agriopus leucopæcilus*). (Trans. N.Z. Inst., 26.) 8vo. Wellington, 1894. ME 2 R

STEPHEN, Sir Alfred. Addresses to Sir A. Stephen in Tasmania and New South Wales, 1830 and 1873. 8vo. Sydney, 1874. MC 1 Q 26

Divorce Extension Bill Speeches. 8vo. Sydney, 1886. MF 4 R 59

Introduction to the law Reform Commissioners' Report on Criminal Law Consolidation. 8vo. Sydney, 1876. MF 4 R 30

Matrimonial Causes Acts and Divorce Law: Letters on the Indissolubility Question and transfer of the divorcing power from Parliament. 8vo. Sydney, 1887. MF 4 R 60

St. Mary's Public School, South Creek; Address on opening. 8vo. Sydney, 1878. MG 2 Q 30

Speech of, at the dinner given to him on his departure for Europe. 8vo. Sydney, 1881. MJ 3 Q 30

Supreme Court Practice: the Rules of Court and Enactments affecting Actions and other Proceedings at Law, 1856. 8vo. Sydney, 1856. MF 1 Q 45

STEPHEN, Sir George. Insolvency Abuses exposed by. 8vo. Melb., 1868. MF 4 R 1

STEPHEN, Harold W. H. Our Exhibition Annual, consisting of Tales, Sketches, Poetry, &c. 8vo. Sydney, 1878. MJ 3 S 1

STEPHEN, Sir Jas. Fitzjames. Essays; by "A Barrister." 8vo. Lond., 1832. J G 8 39

Horæ Sabbaticæ; reprint or articles contributed to *The Saturday Review*. 1st—3rd series. 3 vols. 12mo. Lond., 1892. G 16 Q 35-37

Life of; by his brother. 8vo. Lond., 1895. C 19 S 6

STEPHEN, Leslie. An Agnostic's Apology, and other essays. 8vo. Lond., 1893. G 2 P 35

Hours in a Library. New edition. 3 vols. 8vo. Lond., 1892. J 4 P 5-7

——— and LEE, Sidney. Dictionary of National Biography. Vols. 32-41. Roy. 8vo. Lond., 1893-95. C 11 R

STEPHEN, M. H. Supplement to the Supreme Court Practice, with Acts of Council, and Notes of Cases. 8vo. Sydney, 1851. MF 2 R 51

STEPHEN, Oscar Leslie. Sir Victor Brooke, Sportsman and Naturalist; a Memoir. Illustrated. 8vo. Lond., 1894. C 17 S 15

STEPHENS, A. G. A Queenslander's Travel Notes. 12mo. Sydney, 1894. MD 7 T 4

Why Queensland wants Separation. 8vo. Townsville (n.d.) MF 4 R 50

STEPHENS, Frederic George. Dante Gabriel Rossetti. (Portfolio Monograph, 5). Roy. 8vo. Lond., 1894. E

STEPHENS, Jas. Brunton. The Godelphin Arabian: the Story of a Horse. 18mo. Brisbane, 1894. MH 1 U 57

STEPHENS, Rev. Joseph Rayner. Portrait of. [*See* Gammage, R. G.—Chartist Movement*.*] F 7 R 24

STEPHENS, H. Morse. Albuquerque. (Rulers of India.) 8vo. Oxford, 1892. C 13 P 12

STEPHENS, Very Rev. W. R. W. Life and Letters of Dr. E. A. Freeman. 2 vols. 8vo. Lond., 1895. C 19 V 1, 2

STEPHENS, W. Walker. Life and Times of A. R. J. Turgot. 8vo. Lond., 1895. C 21 T 11

STEPHENSON, Dr. Andrew. Public Lands and Agrarian Laws of the Roman Republic. (Johns Hopkins University Studies, 9.) 8vo. Baltimore, 1891. B 18 S 9

STEPHENSON, George. Sketch of. [*See* Smith, G. B.—Leaders of Modern Industry.] C 14 P 14

STEPHENSON, Robert. Sketch of. [*See* Smith, G. B.—Leaders of Modern Industry.] C 14 P 14

STEPNIAK, Sergius Dragamanoff. Nihilism as it is; being Stepniak's pamphlets translated by E. L. Voynich, and Felix Volkhovsky's claims of the Russian Liberals; with an Introduction by Dr. R. S. Watson. 8vo. Lond., 1895. F 8 U 34

Socialism and Nihilism in Russia. [*See* Subjects of the Day, 2] F 7 U 27

STERLING, John. Life of; by Thomas Carlyle. 2nd ed. 8vo. Lond., 1852. C 21 Q 3

STERNBERG, Dr. George Miller. Manual of Bacteriology. Illustrated. 8vo. New York, 1893. A 26 V 9

STERNE, Laurence. Essay on. [*See* Bagehot, W.—Literary Studies.] J 9 P 22-24

STEVENS, Dr. C. Ellis. Sources of the Constitution of the United States. 8vo. New York, 1894. F 14 R 22

STEVENS, Chas. John. The Barrier Silver and Tin Mines in 1888. 8vo. Adelaide, 1888. MA 2 U 64

STEVENS, Jas. Engineering Telegraph Code. [*See* Blackburn, A. H.] K 9 S 11

——— and CORBETT, E. Sydney. Universal Mining Code for the use of Mining Companies, Mining Engineers, Merchants, &c. Sm. 4to. Lond., 1894. K 9 S 12

STEVENS, Hon. John L., and OLESON, Prof. W. B. Picturesque Hawaii. Obl. imp. 8vo. (n.p.n.d.) MB 2 Q 4 †

STEVENS, W. B. Handbook of Freemasonry. 12mo. Brisbane, 1868. MJ 1 P 41

STEVENSON, Robt. Louis. Father Damien: an open Letter to Rev. Dr. Hyde. 12mo. Lond., 1890.
MC 1 S 14
Island Nights Entertainments, consisting of the Beach of Falesá, the Bottle Imp, the Isle of Voices. 8vo. Lond., 1893.* MJ 2 S 15
[Life of]; by. W. Raleigh. 8vo. Lond., 1895. C 19 V 16
Sketch of. [See Matthews, B.—Books and Play-books.] J 8 T 34
The Merry Men, and other Tales and Fables. 4th ed. 8vo. Lond., 1894. J 12 R 26
The Suicide Club and the Rajah's Diamond. 8vo. Lond., 1894. J 12 R 27
Kidnapped. 8vo. Lond., 1895. J 12 R 28
Catriona. 8vo. Lond., 1895. J 12 R 29
The Dynamiter. 8vo. Lond., 1895. J 12 R 30
The Black Arrow. 8vo. Lond., 1895. J 12 R 32
The Master of Ballantrae. 8vo. Lond., 1895. J 12 R 33
Strange Case of Dr. Jekyll and Mr. Hyde. 8vo. Lond., 1895. J 12 R 34
An Inland Voyage. 12mo. Lond., 1895. J 12 R 35
Travels with a Donkey in the Cevennes. 12mo. Lond., 1895. J 12 R 36

—————— and OSBOURNE, Lloyd. The Ebb-Tide. 8vo. Lond., 1894. MJ 3 Q 34
The Wrong Box. 8vo. Lond., 1893. J 12 R 31

STEVENSON, Dr. Thos., and MURPHY, Dr. Shirley F. Treatise on Hygiene and Public Health. 3 vols. roy. 8vo. Lond., 1892-94. A 33 U 2-4

STEWART, A. P. Hand-book for Bank Clerks. 12mo. Sydney, 1887. MF 4 P 34

STEWART, Rev. Dr. Alexander. Handbook of Christian Evidences. 8vo. Lond., 1895. G 1 U 22

STEWART, Alexander T. Sketch of. [See Stoddard, W. O.—Men of Business.] C 16 R 19

STEWART, Dr. G. N. Manual of Physiology. Illustrated. 8vo. Lond., 1895. A 26 T 21

STEWART, Henry. Irrigation for the Farm, Garden, and Orchard. 8vo. New York, 1892. A 18 Q 44

STEWART, Hubert. Poems and Plays. 12mo. Melb., 1894. MH 1 U 38

STEWART, Hon. John. Debate on the Prerogative of Pardon. [See Parkes, Sir H.] MF 4 Q 40

STEWART, Prof. Wm. University of Glasgow, old and new, illustrated with views and portraits. 4to. Glasgow, 1894. B 4 P 5 ‡

STIELER, Carl, PAULUS, Edward, and KADEN, Woldemar. Italia: Viaggio pittoresco dall' Alpi all' Etna. 4a. edizione. Fol. Milano, 1890. D 37 P 23 ‡

STILLE, Dr. Chas. Janeway. Maj.-Gen. A. Wayne and the Pennsylvania Line in the Continental Army. [See Wayne, Maj.-Gen. A.] C 18 U 2

STILLMAN, Wm. Jas. Old Italian Masters. [See Cole, T.] A 8 U 38

STINDE, J. The Buchholtz Family: Sketches of Berlin Life; translated by L. Dora Schmitz. Part 1. 5th ed. 12mo. Lond., 1890. J 9 Q 45

STIRLING, Dr. E. C. Note on the Osteology of *Notoryctes typhlops*. (Trans. Roy. Soc., S. Australia, 18.) 8vo. Adelaide, 1894. ME 1 S

STIRLING, James. On the Caves perforating Marble Deposits, Limestone Creek. (Roy. Soc., Vict., 20.) 8vo. Melb., 1884. ME 1 P
Cryptogamia of the Australian Alps. (Roy. Soc., Vict., 22.) 8vo. Melb., 1886. ME 1 P
Evidences of Glaciation in the Australian Alps. (Roy. Soc., Vict., 22.) 8vo. Melb., 1886. ME 1 P
Notes on a Geological Sketch-section through the Australian Alps. (Trans. Roy. Soc., S. Australia, 7.) 8vo. Adelaide, 1886. ME 1 S
Phanerogamia of the Mitta Mitta Source Basin and their Habitats. (Roy. Soc., Vict., 19, 21.) 8vo. Melb., 1883-85. ME 1 P
The Physical Features of the Australian Alps. (Roy. Soc., Vict., 18.) Melb., 1882. ME 1 P
Physiography of Mount Hotham and surroundings, embracing Notes on the Physical Features, Geology, Botany, Meteorology, &c. (Roy. Geog. Soc. Australasia, Vic. Branch, 8.) 8vo. Melb., 1890. ME 2 Q
Proteaceæ of the Victorian Alps. (Trans. Roy. Soc., S. Australia, 6.) 8vo. Adelaide, 1883. ME 1 S
The Victorian Coal-fields. Sm. fol. Melb., 1893. MA 9 Q 21 †

STIRTON, Dr. James. Additions to the Lichen Flora of Queensland. (Roy. Soc., Vict., 17.) 8vo. Melb., 1881. ME 1 P

STOCK EXCHANGE OF NEW SOUTH WALES. Memorandum and Articles of Association. 8vo. Sydney, 1890. MF 1 Q 53

STOCKDALE, Harry. The Legend of the Marble Man. 8vo. Sydney, 1889. MA 3 Q 35

STOCKHOLM, The Technical School of. 8vo. Stockholm, 1893. G 18 Q 19

STOCKTON, Francis Richard; with Portrait. [See Blathwayt, R.—Interviews.] J 10 U 34

STOCKWELL, G. S. The Republic of Liberia. 12mo. New York, 1868. B 17 P 34

STOCQUELER, Joachim Hayward. Familiar History of the British Army, including a Description of the Volunteer Movement. Sm. 4to. Lond., 1871. B 21 V 20

STODDARD, Anna M. John Stuart Blackie: a Biography. 2 vols. 8vo. Edinb., 1895.   C 13 V 18, 19

STODDARD, Chas. Augustus. Beyond the Rockies: a Spring Journey in California. Illustrated. 8vo. Lond., 1894.   D 15 R 11
Spanish Cities, with Glimpses of Gibraltar and Tangier. 8vo. Lond., 1892.   D 18 R 10

STODDARD, Chas. Warren. South Sea Idyls. 12mo. New York, 1892.   MJ 3 P 25

STODDARD, John L. Glimpses of the World: a portfolio of the marvellous works of God and man. 4to. Chicago, 1894.   A 8 Q 25 †
Portfolio of Photographs of famous Scenes, Cities, and Paintings. Obl. imp. 8vo. Chicago (n.d.)   A 7 R 18 ‡

STODDARD, Wm. Osborn. Men of Business. (Men of Achievement.) 8vo. Lond., 1894.   C 16 R 19

STODDART, Anna M. [Life of] Sir Philip Sidney. Sm. 4to. Edinb., 1894.   C 18 T 19

STOKES, Anson Phelps. Joint-metallism. 8vo. New York, 1894.   F 14 T 38

STOKES, Rev. Dr. George Thos. Acts of the Apostles, vols. 1 and 2. [See Expositor's Bible.]   G 19 S 6, 7

STOKES, H. G. On the occurrence of a Green Mineral in the Schists of Adelaide-street, Brisbane. (Pro. Roy. Soc., Queensland, 10.) 8vo. Brisbane, 1894.   ME 1 T
Asbestos. [See Hall, E.—Proc. Roy. Soc., Queensland, 8.]   ME 1 T

STOKES, Margaret. Three Months in the Forest of France: a Pilgrimage in search of vestiges of the Irish Saints in France. Illustrated. Sm. 4to. Lond., 1895.   G 3 R 15

STOKES, R. Letter to the Rt. Hon. the Earl of Devon, on the late massacre at Wairau. 8vo. Lond., 1844.   MB 2 R 58

STOKES, Dr. Whitley. On the Calendar of Oengus. (Trans. R I. Academy.—Irish MS., series I.) 4to. Dublin, 1880.   E

STOKVIS, A. M. H. J. Manuel d'Histoire, de Généalogie, et de Chronolgie de tous les Etats du Globe. Tomes 2, 3. Imp. 8vo. Leide, 1889-93.   B 15 U 15, 16

STOLBERG, John S., and STUART, Charles Edward. The Costume of the Clans, with observations on the literature, arts, manufactures, and commerce of the Highlands and Western Isles during the Middle Ages. Fol. Edinb., 1845.   A 34 Q 14‡

STONE, Edward James. Catalogue of 12,441 stars for the epoch 1880; from observations made at the Royal Observatory, Cape of Good Hope, 1871-79. 4to. Lond., 1881.   A 12 Q 19†

STONE, G. F. Annual Report of the Trade and Commerce of Chicago, 1894. 8vo. Chicago, 1895.   E

STONE, John. Otago and Southland Directory and New Zealand Annual, 1893-95. 3 vols. 8vo. Dunedin, 1893-95.   ME 12 S
Wellington, Hawke's Bay, and Taranaki Directory and New Zealand Annual, 1892-93. 1895-96. 2 vols. 8vo. Dunedin, 1892-95.   ME 12 S

STONE, R. Wide Tires: Laws of certain States relating to their use, and other pertinent information. 8vo. Wash., 1895.   F 11 U 4

STONE, William. The Story of the Garden of Eden. [See Religious Pamphlets, 1.]   G 9 V 16

STONE, William Leete. Ballads and Poems relating to the Burgoyne Campaign. Sm. 4to. Albany (N.Y.), 1893.   H 9 T 7

STOPES, Charlotte Carmichael. British Freewomen: their Historical Privilege. 12mo. Lond., 1894.   F 14 R 18

STOPS, Frederick. Statutes of Tasmania. [See Tasmania.]   MF 3 S 29

STORER, Prof. Francis Humphreys. Agriculture in some of its relations with Chemistry. 2 vols. 8vo. 4th ed. New York, 1892.   A 19 S 25, 26

STORRS, Rev. Dr. Richard Salter. Bernard of Clairvaux: the Times, the Man, and his Work. 8vo. Lond., 1892.   C 15 P 14

STORRS SCHOOL AGRICULTURAL EXPERIMENT STATION. [See Connecticut.]

STORY, Alfred T. James Holmes and John Varley. 8vo. Lond., 1894.   C 21 R 17
William Blake: his Life, Character, and Genius. 12mo. Lond., 1893.   C 14 P 12
Life of John Linnell. 2 vols. 8vo. Lond., 1892.   C 15 R 19, 20

STORY-MASKELYNE, Prof. N. [See Maskelyne, Prof. N. Story-.]

STORY OF THE SEA, The. [See Couch, A. T. Q.]   B 21 V 7

STOUGHTON, Rev. Dr. John. Recollections of a Long Life. 8vo. Lond., 1894.   C 17 E 1

STOUT, Sir Robert. Historical Sketch of New Zealand. [See Bracken, T.]   MH 1 T 14
Public Education in New Zealand: a Speech. 8vo. Wellington, 1885.   MG 2 Q 30

STOVER, Charles B. Account of the Neighbourhood Guild in New York. [See Montague, F. C.] B 18 S 7

STOW, J. P. Voyage of the Forlorn Hope, 1865. Roy. 8vo. Melb., 1894.   MD 7 U 18

STOWE, Mrs. Harriet Beecher. Criticisms of the Works of. [*See* Senior, N. W.—Essays on Fiction.] J 6 S 40
Lady Byron vindicated: a History of the Byron Controversy. 12mo. Lond., 1870. C 14 P 35

STRACHAN, Captain John. Exploration in New Guinea. (Roy. Geograph. Soc. of Australasia, Queensland Branch, 1.) 8vo. Brisbane, 1886. ME 20

STRACHAN, John. Twinkle, twinkle little star; or, Harlequin Jack Frost, Little Tom Tucker, and the Old Woman that lived in a Shoe: a grand comic Christmas Pantomime, localized by Marcus Clarke. 12mo. Melb. (n.d.) MH 1 U 47

STRACHAN-DAVIDSON, J. L. [*See* Davidson, J. L. S.]

STRACHEY, St. Loe. National Workshops. (A Policy of Free Exchange.) 8vo. Lond., 1894. F 14 S 26

STRACK, Prof. H. Ziegelbauwerke des Mittelalters und der Renaissance in Italien. Fol. Berlin, 1889. A 34 P 17‡

STRAFFORD, Thomas Wentworth, 1st Earl of. Papers relating to. [*See* Camden Soc. Pubs., 53.] E

STRAHAN, Dr. S. A. K. Suicide and Insanity: a Physiological and Sociological Study. 8vo. Lond., 1893. F 14 R 30

STRAND MAGAZINE, The. Vols. 1-8. 8vo. Lond., 1891-94. E

STRANGE, Maj.-Gen. The Maxim Gun. [*See* United Service Inst.] MA 2 V 38

STRANGE, Thomas L. Clerical Integrity. 12mo. Ramsgate (n.d.) G 2 V 34
Critical Catechism. [*See* Religious Pamphlets, 2.] G D V 17

STRANGEWAYS, T. Veterinary Anatomy. 4th ed., revised by I. Vaughan. 8vo. Edinb., 1892. A 30 R 25

STRATHEDEN AND CAMPBELL, William F., Lord. The Eastern Question: Speeches delivered in the House of Lords, 1871-91. 8vo. Lond., 1894. F 14 U 11

STRATON, Charles R. *Trans.*—Alternating Generations. [*See* Adler, Dr. H.] A 27 Q 41

STRAUS, Oscar S. Roger Williams, the Pioneer of Religious Liberty. 8vo. Lond., 1894. C 17 R 15

STRAUSS, Prof. David F. Opinions of. [*See* Religious Pamphlets, 1.] G 9 V 16

STREAMS OF LIFE to refresh the weary and impart vitality to all. 8vo. Sydney, 1875. MG 1 P 84

STREATFEILD, E. C. Charterhouse, Old and New. [*See* Wilmot, E. P. E] B 36 T 24

STREATFEILD, R. W. Masters of Italian Music. 8vo. Lond., 1895. C 22 P 13

STREET, J. C. The Hidden Way across the Threshold; or, the Mystery which hath been hidden for ages and from generations. Illustrated. 8vo. Lond., 1889. G 14 Q 24

STREETER, Edwin Wm. Precious Stones and Gems. Illustrated. 5th ed. 8vo. Lond., 1892. A 24 S 14

STREETER, G. Skelton. The Northern Shan States. (Roy. Geog. Soc. Australasia, Vic. Branch, 6.) 8vo. Melb., 1880. ME 20

STREIT, F. W. Charte von Australien. 8vo. Nürnberg, 1817. D 8 P 34 †

STRETTON, W. G. Aboriginal Tribes of the Gulf of Carpentaria. (Trans. Roy. Soc., S. Australia, 17.) 8vo. Adelaide, 1893. ME 1 S

STRICKLAND, Hugh Edwin, and MELVILLE, Dr. A. G. The Dodo and its kindred; or, the History, Affinities, and Osteology of the Dodo, Solotaire, and other extinct birds of the Islands Mauritius, Rodriguez, and Bourbon. 4to. Lond., 1848. A 15 R 9 †

STROMBERG, Wm. Steam-user's Guide and Instructor. 18mo. St. Louis, 1894. A 22 P 8

STRONG, Rev. Chas. The Thirst for Gold: a sermon. 12mo. Melb., 1885. MG 1 P 82
Unsectarian Services for use in Schools and Families, and Children's Churches. 8vo. Melb., 1881. MG 2 R 20

STRONG, Capt. Henry Wm. Manual of Drill, for the use of the Public Schools in New South Wales, 1878. 18mo. Sydney, 1878. MA 2 P 49

STRONG, Prof. Herbert Augustus. Address to the Students attending the Classical Lectures at the Melbourne University. 8vo. Melb., 1879. MG 2 Q 17
Goldsmith's Traveller. [*See* Goldsmith, O.] MH 1 Q 23

STRONG, Dr. James. The Exhaustive Concordance of the Bible. 4to. Lond., 1894. K 18 T 20

STRONG, James C. Wah-kee-nah and her People: the curious Customs, Traditions, and Legends of the North American Indians. 8vo. New York, 1893. A 18 R 31

STRONG, Thos. B. Platonism. 12mo. Lond. (n.d.) G 4 V 15

STUART, Sir Alexander. Speech on Church Property. [*See* Gordon, A.] MG 1 S 10

STUART, Chas. Edward. The Costume of the Clans. [*See* Stolberg, J. S.] A 34 Q 14 ‡

STUART, Gilbert. Life and Works of; by G. C. Mason. Imp. 8vo. New York, 1879. C 15 P 1 †

STUART, Maria Clementina. Narratives of the Detention, Liberation, and Marriage of; edited by Dr. J. T. Gilbert. Sm. 4to. Dublin, 1894. C 19 U 11

STUART, Mary, Queen of Scotland. [*See* Mary Stuart.]

STUART, Prof. Thos. Peter Anderson. Green-producing Chromogenic Micro-organisms in Wool. (Journal Roy. Soc., N.S.W., 28.) 8vo. Sydney, 1894.
ME 1 R

Testimonials in favour of Candidate for the chair of Anatomy and Physiology in Sydney University. 8vo. Edinb. (n.d.)
MC 1 R 43

Report on the Koch Method of treating Tuberculosis. Roy. 8vo. Sydney, 1891.
MA 2 S 70

STUART-CANSDELL, C. [See Cansdell, C. Stuart-.]

STUBBS, Arthur J. Telegraphy. [See Preece, W. H.]
A 21 P 22

STUBBS, Dr. John Wm. History of the University of Dublin, from its foundation to the end of the 18th Century. 8vo. Dublin, 1889.
B 29 T 10

STUDER, Jacob H. Birds of North America, drawn and coloured from Nature. 4to. New York, 1888.
A 40 T 9 ‡

STUDER, Prof. T. Alcyonaria. [See Thomson, Sir C. W., and Murray, Dr. J.—Voyage of H.M.S. Challenger.]
A 6 †

STURLESON, S. [See Suorre Sturleson.]

STURMEY, Henry. Handbook to the Optical Lantern. [See Welford, W. D.]
A 29 T 24

SUÁREZ, José Bernardo. Lecciones elementales de Derecho Constitucional Chileno. 12mo. Santiago, 1882.
F 12 S 13

Rasgos Biográficos de Niños Célebres. 8vo. Valparaiso, 1885.
C 21 P 16

SUBJECTS OF THE DAY: a Quarterly Review of Current Topics. 4 vols. 8vo. (All published.) Lond., 1890-91.
G 18 S 18, and F 7 U 27-29

1 State Education for the People:—
Ancient Civilization and Modern Education in India; by Sir W. W. Hunter.
Elementary Education in England; by E. M. Hance.
State Education in Scotland; National Education in Ireland; English and Continental Systems of Elementary Education compared; Western State Education—The United States and English Systems compared; by Rev. E. F. M. MacCarthy.
Notes on Education in Canada and Australia; by Rev. E. F. M. Maccarthy.
Note on Commercial Education; Education and Status of Women; by Mrs. Emily Crawford.
Technical Education and Payment on Results; by Sir Philip Magnus.
New Code for 1890.

2. Socialism, Labour, and Capital:—
Pre-scientific Socialism; by Rev. M. Kaufmann.
Scientific Socialism; by Rev. M. Kaufmann.
Socialism and Land; by Prof. J. E. Thorold Rogers.
Socialism and Labour; by Prof. J. E. Thorold Rogers.
Co-operation and Socialism; by G. T. Holyoake.
Trade Unions, their Policy and Social Work; Force or Conciliation in Labour Disputes; by Chas. Bradlaugh.
Socialism and Nihilism in Russia; by S. D. Stepniak.
German and French Labour Movements; by J. Samuelson.
Social Problems in the United States; by Rev. W. Gladden.

SUBJECTS OF THE DAY—contd.
3. The Government of Ireland:—
Home Rule in Ireland: an Appeal to the Tory Householder; by the Rt. Hon. W. E. Gladstone.
A Plea for the Union; by W. E. Macartney.
The Irish Parliament of the Past; by E. F. V. Knox.
Irish Representation in the Imperial Parliament; by T. P. O'Connor.
Irish Statesmen and Self-Government; by Justin McCarthy.
The Irish Land Question: a Word on Land and Labour; the "Castle" System and its Operations; by J. J. Clancy.
Relations of Austria and Hungary; by Prof. A. Vambery.
Home Rule in Newfoundland: a Parallel; by W. B. Bowring.
Colonial Home Rule; by Sir John Pope Hennessy.

4. The House of Lords and other Upper Houses:—
Origin and Growth of the House of Lords; by E. A. Freeman.
Expansion and Influence of the House; other Houses of Lords and Upper Houses; the Lords on themselves; Conservative Reform of the House of Lords; by the Earl of Pembroke.
The Lords as Landlords; by Arthur Arnold.
Conservative Estimate of the House of Lords; by T. E. Kebbel.
Against Reformed Upper Houses; by Sir Chas. W. Dilke.
The Lords and the Labourers; by J. Samuelson.

SUE, Eugene. Le Juif Errant. 10 vols. 18mo. Paris, 1845.
J 15 Q 47-56

Arthur. 4 vols. 18mo. Paris, 1845.
J 15 Q 57-60

Deux Histoires, 1772-1810. 2 vols. 18mo. Paris, 1843.
J 15 Q 61, 62

Paula Monti. 2 vols. 18mo. Paris, 1845.
J 15 Q 63, 64

Deleytar. 18mo. Paris, 1846.
J 15 Q 65

Thérèse Dunoyer. 2 vols. 18mo. Paris, 1846.
J 15 Q 66, 67

SUFFIELD, Rev. Robt. Rudolph. The Resurrection: a Sermon. 12mo. Lond. (n.d.)
G 2 V 27

SUGAR JOURNAL, The, and Tropical Cultivator, Oct., 1892-Dec., 1893. Sm. 4to. Mackay, Q., 1892-93.
ME 7 P

SULLIVAN, A. M. The Irish State Trials, 1844 and 1883. Speech of A. M. Sullivan; with Introduction by P. McM. Glynn. 8vo. Melb., 1884.
MF 4 Q 50

SULLIVAN, Sir Edward, and others. Yachting. (Badminton Lib.) Illustrated. 2 vols. 8vo. Lond., 1894.
A 29 Q 40, 41

SUMNER, Chas. Eulogy on. [See Curtis, G. W.]
F 15 U 3

[Plaster Cast of.] [See Hutton, L.—Portraits in Plaster.]
A 23 V 13

Sketch of. [See Brooks, N.—Statesmen.]
C 16 R 20

SUMNER, Most Rev. John Bird. Sketch of. [See Fowler, Rev. M.—Notable Archbishops.]
C 13 V 12

SUMNER, Prof. Wm. Graham. Lectures on the History of Protection in the United States. 8vo. New York, 1883.
F L T 16

SUNDAY STORY-TELLER, The. Nos. 1-6, July-August, 1889. 4to. Sydney, 1889.
ME 20 R

SUPLEE, H. H. The Constructor. [*See* Reuleaux, F.]
A 12 U 1 †

SURFACE HILL GOLD-CRUSHING CO. Memorandum and Articles of Association. 8vo. Sydney (n.d.)
MF 4 R 35

SURVEYOR, The. Journal of the Institute of Surveyors New South Wales; with Diagrams. Vols. 3–7. 8vo. Sydney, 1890–94.
ME 8 R

SUSEMIHL, Prof. Franz, and HICKS, R. D. Politics of Aristotle. [Greek Text.] Books 1–5. 8vo. Lond., 1894.
F 7 R 30

SUTCLIFFE, George Wm. Steam Power and Mill Work: Principles and Modern Practice. 8vo. Lond., 1895.
A 25 Q 19

SUTER, Henry. New Zealand Land and Fresh Water Mollusca. (Trans. N.Z. Inst., 26.) 8vo. Wellington, 1894.
ME 2 R

SUTHERLAND, Alexander. A Bad Smell. [*See* Australian Health Soc., Melb.]
MA 3 S 33

―――― Method of calculating the increment in the value of land. (Roy. Soc., Vict., 16.) 8vo. Melb., 1880.
ME 1 P

―――― Some Quantitative Laws of Incubation and Gestation. (Proc. Roy. Soc., Victoria, n.s. 7.) 8vo. Melb., 1895.
ME 1 P

―――― and SUTHERLAND, George. History of Australia and New Zealand from 1606–1890. 12mo. Lond., 1894.
MB 1 P 23

SUTHERLAND, C. L. Horses, Asses, Zebras, and Mules. [*See* Tegetmeier, W. B.]
A 30 R 14

SUTHERLAND, Rev. George. Contributions toward an exposition of the Genesis and D.V. the extinction of a new light called "Georgius Sidus" in the Free Presbyterian Church of Victoria. 8vo. Melb., 1884.
MG 2 S 1

SUTHERLAND, George. South Australian Vinegrower's Manual. 8vo. Adelaide, 1892.
MA 3 S 14

SUTHERLAND, George Frederick. Tobacco as a farmer's crop for New South Wales. Roy. 8vo. Sydney, 1894.
MA 3 R 48

―――― Tobacco as a Farmer's Crop. 8vo. Sydney, 1893.
MA 1 Q 65

―――― Tobacco-growing in Tumut District. [*See* Lamb, S.]
MA 1 Q 65

SUTHERLAND, W. G., FOURNISS, W., SOEDER, L., and PEARCE, W. J. Stencils and Stencilling. Fol. Manchester (n.d.)
A 39 R 7 ‡

SUTTON, H. New form of Secondary Cell for Electrical Storage. (Roy. Soc., Vict., 18.) 8vo. Melb., 1882.
ME 1 P

SUTTON, J. Bland. Evolution and Disease. 8vo. Lond., 1890.
A 28 Q 33

SUTTOR, Albert Bruce. The Frozen Mutton Industry. 8vo. Sydney, 1892.
MA 1 Q 58

―――― Breeding Sheep for Frozen Mutton Industry. 8vo. Sydney, 1893.
MA 1 Q 58

―――― Report on the Western Districts. 8vo. Sydney, 1893.
MA 1 Q 64

SUTTOR, Wm. Henry. Artesian Bores on Bunda Station, Queensland. (Journal Roy. Soc., N.S.W., 27.) 8vo. Sydney, 1893.
ME 1 R

SWAINSON, Harold. The Church of Sancta Sophia. [*See* Lethaby, W. R.]
A 19 V 19

SWAN, H. Electrical Distribution. [*See* Kilgour, M. H.]
A 21 Q 30

SWAN, R. M. W. Orientation of Temples. [*See* Bent, J. T.]
D 14 T 19

SWANK, James Moore. Statistics of the American and Foreign Iron Trades for 1892. Annual Statistical Report of the American Iron and Steel Association. 8vo. Philad., 1893.
E

SWANWICK, Sidney. The Premier's fairplay; or, how Cairns got the railway. 8vo. Brisbane, 1886.
MF 4 R 50

SWANZY, Dr. Henry R. Hand-book of the Diseases of the Eye and their Treatment. 5th ed. Illustrated. 8vo. Lond., 1895.
A 26 R 7

SWAYNE, Capt. H. G. C. Seventeen Trips through Somaliland; a Record of Exploration and Big Game Shooting, 1885–93. 8vo. Lond., 1895.
D 14 V 18

SWEDENBORG, Emanuel; or, the Mystic. [*See* Emerson, R. W.—Representative Men.]
C 17 P 10

SWETTENHAM, Frank A. Malay Sketches. 8vo. Lond., 1895.
B 33 P 1

SWIFT, F. Darwin. Life and Times of James I, King of Aragon. 8vo. Oxford, 1894.
C 16 S 20

SWIFT, Dr. H. Diphtheritic Paralysis; with special reference to the prognosis. 8vo. Adelaide, 1889.
MA 2 S 64

SWIFT, Rev. Jonathan. The Tale of a Tub, and other Works; edited by Henry Morley. 8vo. Lond., 1889.
J 8 T 1

―――― Verses on the death of, written by himself. Sm. fol. Lond., 1739.
H 39 Q 13 ‡

―――― Dean Swift and his writings; by G. P. Moriarty. 8vo. Lond., 1893.
C 16 R 9

―――― Jonathan Swift; a biographical and critical study; by J. C. Collins. 8vo. Lond., 1893.
C 13 P 22

―――― [Plaster Cast of.] [*See* Hutton, L.—Portraits in Plaster.]
A 23 V 13

SWINBURNE, Algernon Charles. Astrophel, and other Poems. 8vo. Lond., 1894. H 9 Q 4
Studies in Prose and Poetry. 8vo. Lond., 1894. J G 8 35
A Study of Shakespeare. 8vo. Lond., 1895. J 12 R 6
Sketch of the Work of. [*See* Dawson, W. J.—Makers of Modern English.] H 10 S 14

SWINBURNE, Henry. The Courts of Europe at the close of the last Century. 2 vols. 8vo. Lond., 1895. B 22 S 22, 23

SWINBURNE, James, and WORDINGHAM, C. H. The Measurement of Electric Currents. Electrical Measuring Instruments; by J. Swinburne. Meters for Electrical Energy; by C. H. Wordingham. 18mo. New York, 1893. A 21 P 23

SWINEY, Col. G. C. Historical Records of the 32nd Cornwall Light Infantry, 1702–1892. 8vo. Lond., 1893. B 22 R 8

SWINTON, Hon. Mrs. J. R. Sketch of the Life of Georgiana, Lady De Ros. 8vo. Lond., 1893. C 13 Q 29

SWITZERLAND. Beiträge zur Geologischen Karte der Schweiz. Vols. 1–20, 22, 23 24, parts 1, 2, 4, 27, 31, and Atlas. 27 vols. 4to. and fol. Neuenburg and Bern, 1859–91. A 31 U, and 8 P 21 ‡

SWYNNERTON, Rev. Charles. Indian Night's Entertainment; or, Folk-tales from the Upper Indus. Roy. 8vo. Lond., 1892. J 2 T 2

SYDNEY, Lord. Extracts of Letters from A. Phillip, Governor of New South Wales. [*See* Phillip, Capt. A.] MC 0 P 1 †

SYDNEY, William Connor. Social Life in England, 1660–1690. 8vo. Lond., 1892. B 23 R 16

SYDNEY. Of the Defenceless State of Sydney. 8vo. Sydney, 1862. MJ 2 S 35

SYDNEY ALLIANCE ASSURANCE CO. Deed of Settlement. 8vo. Sydney, 1839. MF 4 Q 12

SYDNEY BETHEL UNION. Annual Reports, 1853 and 1892. 8vo. Sydney, 1854 and 1893. ME 6 Q

SYDNEY CHAMBER OF COMMERCE. Reports, 1871 and 1880. 8vo. Sydney, 1871–81. ME 6 Q
Rules and Constitution. 2 vols. 8vo. Sydney, 1851–59. MF 4 Q 43

SYDNEY CHRISTMAS ANNUAL for 1884. 8vo. Sydney, 1884. MJ 3 S 3

SYDNEY CITY MISSION. 26th, 27th, 32nd, 33rd Annual Reports. 8vo. Sydney, 1888–95. ME 6 S

SYDNEY COLLEGE. Deed of Association of the Sydney College. 8vo. Sydney, 1841. MG 2 S 12

SYDNEY DAILY TELEGRAPH. [*See* Daily Telegraph.]

SYDNEY DIOCESAN DIRECTORY, 1893–95. 3 vols. 12mo. Sydney, 1893–95. ME 6 Q

SYDNEY FEMALE REFUGE SOCIETY. Reports for 1864, 1876, 1878, 1887, 1888. 5 vols. 8vo. Sydney, 1853–89. ME 6 S

SYDNEY FEMALE SCHOOL OF INDUSTRY. 61st Report of. 18mo. Sydney, 1889. ME 3 Q

SYDNEY FOUNDLING HOSPITAL. 2nd Annual Report. 8vo. Sydney, 1876. ME 6 S

SYDNEY FUN: a Humourous, Quizzical, and Satirical Journal. Vol. 2, 1881. Sm. 4to. Sydney, 1881. ME 10 T

SYDNEY HOSPITAL (formerly Sydney Infirmary and Dispensary). 35th, 43rd, 44th, 50th Annual Reports. 8vo. Sydney, 1888–95. ME 6 S
Correspondence with reference to the Grant of Land on which the Sydney Infirmary is built, and to the Erection of a Permanent Modern Hospital, 1878. 8vo. Sydney, 1878. MF 4 Q 30

SYDNEY HOSPITAL FOR SICK CHILDREN. Rules. 8vo. Sydney, 1878. MA 3 V 31

SYDNEY INFIRMARY AND DISPENSARY. [*See* Sydney Hospital.]

SYDNEY INTERNATIONAL EXHIBITION, 1879. Regulations and Classification. Sm. 4to. Sydney, 1879. MK 1 U 28

SYDNEY MAIL, The. July, 1892–Dec., 1895. 15 vols. fcl. Sydney, 1892–95. ME

SYDNEY MECHANICS' SCHOOL OF ARTS. Report from the Committee of the Technical College at the Sydney Mechanics' School of Arts (to the Hon. the Minister for Public Instruction of N.S.W.), 1881. Sm. fol. Sydney, 1881. MG 0 P 25 †

SYDNEY MORNING HERALD. Sept., 1892–Dec., 1895. 19 vols. fol. Sydney, 1892–95. ME
The Centennial Supplement to, together with Reports of the Principal Events in connection with the Celebration of the Centenary of Australian Settlement. 4to. Sydney, 1888. MB 2 U 14

SYDNEY PROGRESSIVE LYCEUM. Replies to Questions. 8vo. Sydney, 1887. MG 2 R 38

SYDNEY QUARTERLY MAGAZINE, Oct., 1883, Jan. and April, 1884, Dec., 1885, March, June, Dec., 1886, March, 1890–Dec., 1891. 6 vols. 8vo. Sydney, 1883–91. ME 3 R

SYDNEY REVIEW, The, August, 1889. 8vo. Sydney, 1889. ME 3 Q

SYDNEY SOCIETY OF THE NEW CHURCH.
Annual Report, 1892. 12mo. Sydney, 1892. ME 6 R
Constitution and Rules. 12mo. Sydney, 1894.
MG 2 R 25

SYDNEY UNIVERSITY. Calendars, 1893–95. 8vo. Sydney, 1893. ME 5 S
Catalogue of Books in the Library. 8vo. Sydney, 1885. MK 1 R 32
Manual of Public Examinations, 1871, 1694, 1895. 3 vols. 8vo. Sydney, 1872–94. ME 5 S
Rules and Regulations of the Sydney University Union. 18mo. Sydney, 1889. MG 2 R 12

SYDNEY WOOL AND PRODUCE JOURNAL, 1892. Fol. Sydney, 1892. ME

SYDENHAM SOCIETY, New. [See New Sydenham Society.]

SYKES, F. W. The Mount Morgan Gold Mine, Queensland: Mines, Works, and Treatment. 4to. Sydney, 1893. MA 2 Q 57

SYKES, John F. J. Public Health Problems. 8vo. Lond., 1892. A 13 P 5

SYLVESTER, Dr. James Joseph. Laws of Verse. 12mo. Lond., 1870. H 9 Q 14

SYMES, J. E. The French Revolution, 1789–95. 12mo. Lond., 1892. B 26 R 11

SYMONDS, John Addington. A Biography, compiled from his papers by Horatio F. Brown. Illustrated. 2 vols. 8vo. Lond., 1895. C 16 U 6, 7
Giovanni Boccaccio as Man and Author. 8vo. Lond., 1895. C 18 T 18
In the Key of Blue, and other Essays. 8vo. Lond., 1893. J 4 P 15
Life of Michelangelo Buonarroti. 2 vols. 8vo. Lond., 1893. C 16 T 19, 20
Studies of the Greek Poets. 3rd ed. 2 vols. 8vo. Lond., 1883. H 7 U 7, 8
Walt Whitman: a Study. 8vo. Lond., 1893. C 11 S 8

SYMONDS, Margaret. Days spent on a Doge's Farm. 8vo. Lond., 1893. D 14 T 14

SYMONDS, Lieut. T., and SHORTLAND, F. Chart of Port Phillip. Fol. Sydney, 1836. MD 5 Q 16 ‡
The Shoals at the Entrance of Port Phillip. Fol. Sydney, 1836. MD 5 Q 16 ‡

SYMONS, John C. Financial Economy of the Wesleyan Methodist Church. 8vo. Melb., 1876. MG 1 R 70

SYMONS, Col. W. P. Records of 24th Regiment. [See Paton, Col. G.] B 24 R 4

T

TABLES OF INTEREST, Simple and Compound, at 4 and 5 per cent. per annum. 8vo. Sydney, 1893.
MA 2 Q 56

TACITUS, Caius Cornelius. Opera; emendavit G. Brotier. 4 vols. 8vo. Lond., 1823. B 30 T 24–27
Opera. 3 vols. 32mo. Lond., 1817. B 30 P 9–11
Tacitus; by W. B. Donne. 12mo. Edinb., 1873.
B 30 Q 21

TACOMA CITY SCHOOLS. Report of the Board of Education, 1892, 1893. 8vo. Tacoma, Wash., 1893. E

TAHITI. [See Great Britain and Ireland.—Tahiti.]

TAINE, Dr. Hyppolite Adolphe. Les Origines de la France Contemporaine. Le Régime Moderne. Tome 2. 8vo. Paris, 1894. B 26 U 22
The Modern Régime; translated by J. Durand. 2 vols. roy. 8vo. Lond., 1891–94. B 27 T 3, 4

TAIT, Most Rev. Archibald Campbell. Sketch of. [See Fowler, Rev. M.—Notable Archbishops.] C 13 V 12

TAIT, Rev. Jas. Mind in Matter: an Argument on Theism. 3rd ed. 8vo. Lond., 1893. MA 2 Q 56

TAIT, Prof. Peter Guthrie. Dynamics. 8vo. Lond., 1895. A 23 R 23
Sketch of Thermodynamics. 2nd ed. 8vo. Edinb., 1877. A 24 R 7
Physical Properties of Fresh Water and of Sea Water. [See Thomson, Sir C. W., and Murray, Dr. J.—Voyage of H.M.S. Challenger.] A 6 †
Treatise on Natural Philosophy. [See Kelvin, Baron.]
A 30 T 7, 8

TALBOT, Rev. James F. Pope Leo XIII, his Life and Letters. Roy. 8vo. Boston, 1886. C 12 V 16

TALBOT, Miss M. St. Margaret's House, Bethnal Green. [See Knapp, J. M.—The Universities and the Social Problem.] F 8 U 22

TALBOT, Mary Anne. Life of. [See Dowie, M. M.—Women Adventurers.] C 15 S 24

TALBOT, T. The New Guido to the Lakes and Hot Springs, and a Month in Hot Water. 8vo. Auckland, 1892. MD 5 R 45

TALFOURD, Sir Thos. Noon. Dramatic Works of. 11th ed. 12mo. Lond., 1852. H 1 Q 44
Memoirs of Charles Lamb. 8vo. Lond., 1892.
C 13 P 33

TALLEYRAND-PERIGORD, Chas. Maurice de, Prince de Benevento. Life of; by Lady Blennerhassett. 2 vols. 8vo. Lond., 1894. C 17 S 18, 19

TALMAGE, Rev. Dr. Thos. de Witt. America's greatest Preacher; Sketches of the Life and Ministry of; with Portrait. 12mo. Melb., 1894.   MC 1 S 9

Great Sermon on the Bible. 8vo. Sydney, 1894.   MG 2 Q 29

TANAKA, Nobujiro. A new species of Hymenomycetous Fungus injurious to the Mulberry Tree. 8vo. (n.p.n.d.)   A 30 V 16

TANJIL. [See Gippsland Lakes.]   MD 1 Q 35

TANNER, Prof. Henry. Variations in the Quality of Food: a Lecture. (Inst. of Agricult., Lond.) 8vo. Lond., 1884.   A 18 R 28

TARNER, George Edward. A Future Roman Empire: a possible result and solution of some modern political and economic problems. 8vo. Lond., 1895.   F 2 V 4

TARR, Ralph S. Economic Geology of the United States; with briefer mention of Foreign Mineral Products. 8vo. New York, 1894.   A 24 S 6

TARRING, C. J. Chapters on the Law relating to the Colonies. 2nd ed. 8vo. Lond., 1893.   MF 2 R 43

TASMA. [See Couvreur, Mme. J. C.]

TASMAN, Abel Jansz; doer C. M. Dozy. Roy. 8vo. (n.p.n.d.)   MC 1 R 54

Discoveries on the Coast of South Terra Incognita. [See Narbrough, Sir J.]   MD 5 P 23

[See Moll, G.—Verhandeling.]   MD 8 R 36

TASMANIA.—General. A Simple Abstract of the Geography and History of Tasmania. 8vo. Launc. 1871.*   MD 1 Q 44

TASMANIA.—Government Departments, Reports, and Publications.

ACTS. [See Statutes.]

BOARD OF HEALTH. Instructions, Regulations, and Model By-laws for the guidance of local Boards of Health and others. 8vo. Hobart, 1886.   MA 1 U 63

CENSUS. [See Statistics.]

EMIGRATION. Information for Intending Emigrants. 8vo. Lond., 1877.   MF 1 Q 49

EXHIBITIONS. Tasmanian International Exhibition, 1891–92. Official Record. Roy. 8vo. Launceston, 1893.   MK 1 S 20

Tasmanian Juvenile and Industrial Exhibition, 1893. Official Catalogues of Exhibits and Awards. 8vo. Hobart, 1893.   MK 1 R 3

GAZETTE. Hobart Gazette. Vol. 84. Sm. fol. Hobart, 1895.   ME

LANDS. Crown Lands Guide, 1885 and 1887. 2 vols. 8vo. Hobart, 1885–87.   ME 8 P

MARINE BOARD. Rules and Regulations of the Port of Hobart Town. 8vo. Hobart, 1863.   MF 2 Q 47

Rules and Regulations of the Port of Hobart. 8vo. Hobart, 1882.   MF 2 Q 48

TASMANIA—contd.

PARLIAMENT. Journals and Papers of Parliament, 1892. Vols. 25, 26. Sm. fol. Hobart, 1893.   ME

Journals of the Legislative Council, 1893. 3 vols. fol. Hobart, 1893.   ME

POLLING LIST, Hobart, 1866. Sm. fol. Hobart 1866.   MF 3 U 44

STATISTICS. Census, 1891. Parts 1–8. Sm. fol. Hobart, 1893.   ME

Progress of the Colony, 1871–80. Sm. fol. Hobart, 1882.   ME

Statistics of the Colony, 1891, 1892. 2 vols. sm. fol. Hobart, 1892–93.   ME

Statistics of Van Diemen's Land, 1824–47. 5 vols. (in 1) sm. fol. Hobart, 1839–48.   MF 9 P 12 †

STATUTES. The Acts of the Parliament of Tasmania. Vols. 9 (pt. 2), 10, 11. Sm. fol. Hobart, 1889–95.   ME

Act to provide for the Establishment of a Legislative Council, the Division of the Colony of Van Diemen's Land into Electoral Districts and the Election of Members to serve in such Legislative Council. 8vo. Launceston, 1851.   MF 1 Q 50

Statutes of Tasmania, from 7th George 4th (1826) to 46th Victoria (1888). Alphabetically arranged, with Notes, by F. Stops. 5 vols. roy. 8vo. Hobart, 1883–90.   MF 3 S 29–33

[See also Great Britain and Ireland—Tasmania.]

TASMANIAN, A. [See New Year's Gift.]   MH 1 R 62

TASMANIAN CLUB. Rules. 12mo. Hobart, 1873.   MF 1 P 63

TASMANIAN COURSING CLUB. Rules and Regulations. 18mo. Hobart, 1877.   MA 2 V 33

TASMANIAN JOCKEY CLUB. Rules and Regulations. 12mo. Hobart, 1859.   MA 2 V 32

TASMANIAN LITERARY AND DEBATING SOCIETIES' UNION. The Literary Competitor, 1889. 8vo. Hobart, 1889.   ME 5 Q

TASMANIAN MAIN LINE RAILWAY. Rules and Regulations for Guidance of Officers and Servants, and the Conduct of Traffic. 12mo. Hobart, 1876   MF 1 P 65

Rules and Regulations to be observed by Enginemen, Firemen, Guards, &c., during the Construction of the Railway. 18mo. Hobart (n.d.)   MF 1 P 64

Rules for Passenger, Parcel, Live Stock, and Merchandise Traffic; also Rates of Freight, 1889. 8vo. Hobart, 1889.   MF 2 Q 62

TASMANIAN PERMANENT EXECUTORS AND TRUSTEES ASSOCIATION Trustees and Executors Associations, their objects and advantages. 8vo. Launceston, 1889.   MF 2 Q 65

TASMANIAN STEAM NAVIGATION CO. Deed of Co-partnership. 8vo. Hobart, 1852. MF 2 Q 61
Guide for Visitors to Tasmania. 8vo. Hobart, 1860. MD 1 Q 37

TASMAN'S PENINSULA. Sketch of Tasman's Peninsula. 8vo. Hobart, 1878. MD 6 R 30

TASSO, Torquato. [Plaster Cast of.] [*See* Hutton, L.—Portraits in Plaster.] A 23 V 13

TATE, N. Psalms. [*See* Bibles, &c.] MG 1 P 54

TATE, Prof. Ralph. Additions to the Flora of Extra-Tropical South Australia. (Trans. Roy. Soc., S. Australia, 7, 8.) 8vo. Adelaide, 1885-86. ME 1 S

Additions to the Flora of South Australia. (Trans. Roy. Soc., S. Australia, 5, 6.) 8vo. Adelaide, 1882-83. ME 1 S

The Botany of Kangaroo Island; with Historical Sketch of its Discovery and Settlement, and Notes on its Geology. (Trans. Roy. Soc., S. Australia, 6.) 8vo. Adelaide, 1883. ME 1 S

Diagnoses of new species of Miocene Fossils from South Australia. (Trans. Roy. Soc., S. Australia, 5.) 8vo. Adelaide, 1882. ME 1 S

Diagnoses of some new Plants from South Australia. [*See* Mueller, Baron F. von.] ME 1 S

Gastropoda of the Old Tertiary of Australia. (Trans. Roy. Soc. S. Australia, 17.) 8vo. Adelaide, 1893. ME 1 S

The Lamellibranchs of the Older Tertiary of Australia. (Trans. Roy. Soc., S. Australia, 8, 9.) 8vo. Adelaide, 1886-87. ME 1 S

Land and Freshwater Mollusca of Tropical South Australia. (Trans. Roy. Soc., S. Australia, 5.) 8vo. Adelaide, 1882. ME 1 S

Land and Freshwater Shells. [*See* Taylor, Dr. J. E.—Collecting Natural History Objects.] A 29 Q 38

List of Plants unrecorded for Southern Eyre Peninsula. (Trans. Roy. Soc., S. Australia, 6.) 8vo. Adelaide, 1883. ME 1 S

List of Recent Echini of South Australia. (Trans. Roy. Soc., S. Australia, 5.) 8vo. Adelaide, 1882. ME 1 S

List of some Plants inhabiting the North-eastern part of the Lake Torrens Basin. (Trans. Roy. Soc., S. Australia, 6.) 8vo. Adelaide, 1883. ME 1 S

List of unrecorded Plants and new localities for rare Plants in the South-east. (Trans. Roy. Soc., S. Australia, 6.) 8vo. Adelaide, 1883. ME 1 S

New Land-shells from Central Australia. (Trans. Roy. Soc., S. Australia, 18.) 8vo. Adelaide, 1894. ME 1 S

New species of Australian Marine Gastropoda. (Trans. Roy. Soc., S. Australia, 17.) 8vo. Adelaide, 1893. ME 1 S

New species of South Australian Plant. (Trans. Roy. Soc., S. Australia, 7.) 8vo. Adelaide, 1885. ME 1 S

TATE, Prof. Ralph—*contd.*
New species of *Squilla* from South Australia. (Trans. Roy. Soc., S. Australia, 6.) 8vo. Adelaide, 1883. ME 1 S

Notes on the Geological and Physical Features of the Basin of the Lower Murray River. (Trans. Roy. Soc., S. Australia, 7.) 8vo. Adelaide, 1885. ME 1 S

Notes on the Tertiary Strata beneath Adelaide. (Trans. Roy. Soc. S. Australia, 5.) 8vo. Adelaide, 1882. ME 1 S

On a new Dilleniaceous Plant from Arnheim Land. [*See* Mueller, Baron F. von.] ME 1 S

On a new Rhamnaceous Plant from South Australia. [*See* Mueller, Baron F. von.] ME 1 S

On a Winter Flowering State of *Hypoxis pusilla*. (Trans. Roy. Soc., S. Australia, 5.) 8vo. Adelaide, 1882. ME 1 S

Organic Remains of Osseous Clays at Lake Callabonna. (Trans. Roy. Soc., S. Australia, 18.) 8vo. Adelaide, 1894. ME 1 S

Post-Miocene Climate in South Australia. (Trans. Roy. Soc., S. Australia, 9.) 8vo. Adelaide, 1886. ME 1 S

The Pteropods of the Older Tertiary of Australia. (Trans. Roy. Soc., S. Australia, 9.) 8vo. Adelaide, 1887. ME 1 S

Revision of the Recent Lamellibranch and Palliobranch Mollusca of South Australia. (Trans. Roy. Soc., S. Australia, 9.) 8vo. Adelaide, 1887. ME 1 S

The Scaphopods of the Older Tertiary of Australia. (Trans. Roy. Soc., S. Australia, 9.) 8vo. Adelaide, 1887. ME 1 S

South Australian Marine Gastropoda. (Trans. Roy. Soc., S. Australia, 17.) 8vo. Adelaide, 1893. ME 1 S

Supplemental Notes on the Palliobranchs of the Older Tertiary of Australia, and a Description of a new species of Rhynchonella. (Trans. Roy. Soc., S. Australia, 8.) 8vo. Adelaide, 1886. ME 1 S

Unrecorded Genera of the Older Tertiary Fauna of Australia. (Journal, Roy. Soc. of N.S.W., 27). 8vo. Sydney, 1893. ME 1 R

Zidora in Australian Waters. (Trans. Roy. Soc., S. Australia, 18.) 8vo. Adelaide, 1894. ME 1 S

———— and DENNANT, J. Correlation of Marine Tertiaries of Australia. (Trans. Roy. Soc., S. Australia, 17.) 8vo. Adelaide, 1893. ME 1 S

TATIAN. Earliest Life of Christ ever compiled from the four Gospels; being the Diatessaron of Tatian, by the Rev. J. H. Hill. 8vo. Edinb., 1894. G 13 P 44

Writings of; translated by Rev. B. P. Pratten. (Ante-Nicene Christ. Lib., 3.) 8vo. Edinb., 1867. G 14 U 3

TAUNTON LUNATIC HOSPITAL, Mass. Report for year ending September, 1892. 8vo. Boston, 1893. E

TAUSSIG, Dr. Frank Wm. Tariff History of the United States. 8vo. New York, 1893. F 8 U 25

TAYLER, Frederick. Studies in Animal Painting. 2nd edition. Obl. 8vo. Lond., 1885. A 23 Q 36

TAYLOR, Alfred J. Additional Notes on Capital Punishment. 12mo. Hobart, 1878. MF 1 Q 67

Clouds and Sunshine : a Drama. 8vo. Hobart, 1880. MH 1 Q 32

Notes on Tasmanian Mosses. 8vo. Hobart, 1886. MA 2 V 60

TAYLOR, D. W. Resistance of Ships and Screw Propulsion. 8vo. Lond., 1893. A 19 T 9

TAYLOR, Fennings. Are Legislatures Parliaments ? 12mo. Montreal, 1879. F 8 U 41

TAYLOR, George. The Indications of the Creator ; or, the Natural Evidences of Final Cause. 8vo. Glasgow (n.d.) G 2 U 4

TAYLOR, Henry D. International Statistical Uniformity. (Roy. Soc., Vict., 22.) 8vo. Melb., 1886. ME 1 P

TAYLOR, J. Scott. Field's Chromatography : a Treatise on Colours and Pigments for the use of Artists. 12mo. Lond., 1885. A 23 R 39

TAYLOR, Dr. John Ellor. Notes on Collecting and Preserving Natural History Objects. 8vo. Lond., 1876. A 29 Q 38

The Playtime Naturalist. Illustrated. 8vo. Lond., 1889. A 27 R 2

TAYLOR, John Michael. Chief Events and Dates of English History. 32mo. Sydney, 1895. MB 1 P 10

Euclid, Books 1 and 2. 32mo. Sydney, 1895. MA 2 P 85

Geography. 32mo. Sydney, 1895. MD 1 P 68

Grammar and Derivation Book. 32mo. Sydney, 1895 MJ 3 P 30

History of Australia for the use of Junior Pupils. 32mo. Sydney, 1895. MB 1 P 50

Spelling-books for Pupils using the Second, Third, and Fourth Australian Reader. 32mo. Sydney, 1895. MJ 3 P 34

Table Book and Mental Arithmetic for the use of Pupils in Public Schools. 32mo. Sydney, 1894. MA 2 P 83

Macaulay's Essay on Lord Clive. [See Macaulay, Lord.] MJ 3 P 21

TAYLOR, Norman. Geology of the West Tamar District, Tasmania. (Roy. Soc., Vict., 16.) 8vo. Melb., 1880. ME 1 P

TAYLOR, R. Whately Cooke-. The Factory System and the Factory Acts. 8vo. Lond., 1894. F 9 U 45

TAYLOR, Dr. W. F. Disposal of Sewage. (Proc. Roy. Soc., Queensland, 10.) 8vo. Brisbane, 1893. ME 1 T

TAYLOR, Dr. W. Cooke. Natural History of Society in Barbarous and Civilized States. 2 vols. 12mo. Lond., 1840. F 7 V 13, 14

TAYLOR, Zachary. Sketch of. [See Wilson, J. G.— Presidents of the United States.] C 2 V 30

Sketch of. [See Thompson, R. W.—Recollections of Sixteen Presidents.] C 18 T 21, 22

TCHENG-KI-TONG. Chin-Chin ; or, the Chinaman at Home ; translated by R. H. Sherard. 8vo. Lond., 1895. D 17 Q 22

TEACHERS' COLLEGE, NEW YORK. Announcement of Instruction in Pedagogy offered to Candidates. 8vo. New York, 1893. E

TEBB, Wm. The Public Health : Leprosy and Vaccination. 8vo. Lond., 1891. A 33 S 4

TEBBUTT, John. History and Description of Mr. Tebbutt's Observatory, Windsor, New South Wales. 8vo. Sydney, 1887 MA 1 Q 76

Observations and Orbit-elements of Comet Gale, 1894. (Journal Roy. Soc., N.S.W., 28.) 8vo. Sydney, 1894. ME 1 R

On the Comet in the Constellation Andromeda. 8vo. Sydney, 1892. MA 1 T 57

On the probability of extraordinarily high Spring Tides about the December Solstice of 1893. (Roy. Soc., N.S.W., 1893.) 8vo. Sydney, 1893. ME 1 R

Reports of Mr Tebbutt's Observatory, Windsor, New South Wales, 1889-90, 1892-94. 8vo. Sydney, 1889-95. ME C R

Results of Meteorological Observations made at the Observatory, Windsor, N.S.W., 1882-85. Sm. fol. Parramatta, 1886. ME 16 P

Results of Observations of Comet VI (Brooks) 1892, at Windsor, New South Wales. (Roy. Soc. of N.S.W., 27.) 8vo. Sydney, 1893. ME 1 R

Results of Observations of Wolf's Comet (II) 1891, Swift's Comet (I) 1892, and Winnecke's Periodical Comet, 1892, at Windsor, New South Wales. 8vo. Sydney, 1892. MA 1 T 58

TEGETMEIER, Wm. Bernhard. British Game Birds and Wild Fowl. [See Morris, Dr. B. R.] A 30 V 6, 7

—— and SUTHERLAND, C. L. Horses, Asses, Zebras, Mules, and Mule-breeding. 8vo. Lond., 1895. A 30 R 14

TEITKINS, W. H. The hitherto unexplored West Central Australia. (Roy. Geog. Soc. Australasia, Vic. Branch, 8.) 8vo. Melb., 1890. ME 20

TEIXEIRA, Mucio. Novos Ideaes, 1877-79. 2a. edição. 18mo. Rio de Janeiro, 1891. H 10 P 27

Celages, poesias. Roy. 8vo. Caracas, 1889. H 7 T 37

Poesias e Poemas, 1886-87. 2a. edição. 8vo. Rio de Janeiro, 1888. H 7 T 36

TELEKI, Count Samuel. Expedition in Eastern Equatorial Africa. [See Höhnel, Lieut. L. von.] D 14 V 11, 12

TEMMINCK, C. J. Verhandelingen over de Natuurlijke Geschiedenis der Nederlandsche overzeesche bezittingen. 5 vols. fol. Leiden, 1839–44. D G S 10–14 ‡

TEMPLE, A. G. Masterpieces of Art: Reproductions of Pictures. 4to. Lond., 1894. A 14 S 13 †

TEMPLE, Sir Richard. Life in Parliament, being the Experience of a Member of the House of Commons from 1886–92 inclusive. 12mo. Lond., 1893.
B 17 Q 13

[Life of] James Thomason. (Rulers of India.) 8vo. Oxford, 1893. C 13 P 13

TEN BRINK, Bernhard. Five Lectures on Shakespeare; translated by Julian Franklin. 12mo. Lond., 1895.
J 10 R 28

History of English Literature. Vols. 1 and 2. 12mo. Lond., 1883–93. B 3 P 22, 23

TENCH, Cap. Watkin. Complete Account of the Settlement at Port Jackson. 4to. Lond., 1793.
MD 3 P 14 †

TENISON-WOODS, Rev. Julian Edmund. List of the Scientific Writings of. 8vo. (n.p.n.d.) MK 1 T 36

On the Genus Amathia of Lamouroux, with a description of a new species. (Roy. Soc., Vict., 16.) 8vo. Melb., 1880. ME 1 P

The Hodgkinson Gold-field, Northern Queensland. (Roy. Soc., Vict., 17.) 8vo. Melb., 1881. ME 1 P

On some new Marine Mollusca. (Roy. Soc., Vict., 17.) 8vo. Melb., 1881. ME 1 P

Physical Description of the Island of Tasmania. (Roy. Soc., Vict., 19.) 8vo. Melb., 1883. ME 1 P

TENNESSEE—AGRICULTURAL EXPERIMENT STATION. Reports, 1888–93. 8vo. Knoxville, 1889–93. F.

TENNYSON, Alfred, Baron. Works of. 8vo. Lond., 1894. H 9 Q 11

The Death of Œnone, Akbar's Dream, and other poems. 12mo. Lond., 1892. H 8 T 46

Records of; by Anne Ritchie. 8vo. Lond., 1892.
C 16 R 17

Study of his Life and Work; by A. Waugh. 8vo. Lond., 1892. C 15 P 10

Tennyson: his Art and Relation to Modern Life; by S. A. Brooke. 8vo. Lond., 1894. H 5 T 42

Biographical Sketch of. [See Fletcher, Rev. W. R.]
MC 1 S 16

Essay on. [See Bagehot, W.—Literary Studies.]
J 9 P 22–24

Home and Haunts of. [See Napier, G. G.] C 15 P 11

[Life of]; by W. Canton. [See Masson, Prof. D.—In the Footsteps of the Poets.] J 6 R 43

The Princess: adapted from Tennyson's Princess. [See Princess, The.] MH 1 S 66

TENNYSON, Alfred, Baron—contd.
Sketch of. [See Smalley, G. W.—Studies of Men.]
C 19 R 20

Sketch of the Work of. [See Dawson, W. J.—Makers of Modern English.] H 13 S 14

The Teaching of Tennyson; by J. Oates. [See Oates, J.] J 8 T 35

Tennyson and "In Memoriam." [See Jacobs, J.]
J 4 P 8

———— and TENNYSON, Frederick. Poems; by "Two Brothers." 12mo. Lond., 1893. H S T 47

TEPPER, J. G. O. A beautiful and rare Beetle. (Trans. Roy. Soc., S. Australia, 7.) 8vo. Adelaide, 1883.
ME 1 S

The Blattariæ of Australia and Polynesia. 8vo. Adelaide, 1893. MA 2 T 34

Blattariæ of Australia and Polynesia. (Trans. Roy. Soc., S. Australia, 17, 18.) 8vo. Adelaide, 1893–94.
ME 1 S

Botanical Notes relating to South Australia. (Trans. Roy. Soc., S. Australia, 6.) 8vo. Adelaide, 1883.
ME 1 S

Flora of Roebuck Bay, Western Australia. (Trans. Roy. Soc., S. Australia, 17.) 8vo. Adelaide, 1893.
ME 1 S

Habits of some South Australian Ants. (Trans. Roy. Soc., S. Australia, 5.) 8vo. Adelaide, 1882. ME 1 S

List of named Insects in the South Australian Museum, Adelaide. Sm. 4to. Adelaide, 1891–92. MA 2 U 45

New Parasite of the Black Scale. (Trans. Roy. Soc., S. Australia, 17.) 8vo. Adelaide, 1893. ME 1 S

New rare South Australian Lepidoptera. (Trans. Roy. Soc., S. Australia, 5.) 8vo. Adelaide, 1882. ME 1 S

Notes on some South Australian Lizards. (Trans. Roy. Soc., S. Australia, 5.) 8vo. Adelaide, 1882. ME 1 S

Plants of Kangaroo Island. (Trans. Roy. Soc., S. Australia, 7.) 8vo. Adelaide, 1885. ME 1 S

Additions to the Flora of Kangaroo Island. (Trans. Roy. Soc., S. Australia, 9.) 8vo. Adelaide, 1887.
ME 1 S

A rare and curious Hemipterous Insect. (Trans. Roy. Soc., S. Australia, 7.) 8vo. Adelaide, 1885. ME 1 S

South Australian Brachyscelid Galls. (Trans. Roy. Soc., S. Australia, 17.) 8vo. Adelaide, 1893. ME 1 S

Stone-making Fungus. [See McAlpine, D.] ME 1 S

TERENTIUS AFER, Publius. Comœdiæ sex; interpretatione et notis illustravit N. Camus. 8vo. Lond., 1829. H 3 S 40

TERESA, St., her Life and Times. [See Graham, G. C.]
G 3 R 10, 11

TERM REPORTS, The. Decisions of the Supreme Court of New South Wales. Sm. 4to. Sydney, 1881–89.
ME 21 S

TERNANT, A. L. The Telegraph; translated from the French by R. Routledge. Illustrated. 12mo. Lond., 1895.   A 21 R 20

TERQUEM, E. Exposition de la Libraire Française. [Chicago, 1893.] Roy. 8vo. Chicago, 1893.   K 7 U 1

TERRIEN DE LACOUPERIE, A. E. J. B. Beginnings of Writing in Central and Eastern Asia; or, Notes on 450 embryo Writings and Scripts. 8vo. Lond., 1894.   J 10 T 1
The Oldest Book of the Chinese: The Yh-King, and its Authors. Vol. 1. 8vo. Lond., 1892.   K 14 P 11

TERRY, W. H. The Lyceum Leader. 3rd edition. 12mo. Melb., 1884.   MG 1 P 62

TERTULLIANUS, Quintus Septimus Florens. The Five Books of, against Marcion; translated by Dr. P. Holmes. (Ante-Nicene Christ. Lib., 7.) 8vo. Edinb., 1868.   G 14 U 7
Writings of; with the extant Works of Victorinus and Commodianus; translated by Dr. P. Holmes. (Ante-Nicene Christ. Lib., 11, 15, 18) 3 vols. 8vo. Edinb., 1869-70.   G 14 U 11, 15, and 18

TESLA, Nikola. Inventions, &c. [See Martin, T. C.]   A 21 V 14

TEXAS, Report on the climatic conditions of. 4to. Wash., 1892.   A 15 Q 3 †

TEXAS AGRICULTURAL BUREAU. Annual Report, 1887-88; by L. L. Foster. 8vo. Austin, 1889.   E

THACKERAY, Chas. The Amateur Fisherman's Guide. 12mo. Sydney, 1895.   MA 3 U 22

THACKERAY, Wm. Makepeace. Works of. 26 vols. 8vo. Lond., 1883-86.   J 21 Q 1-26
  1. Vanity Fair. 2 vols.
  2. Pendennis. 2 vols.
  3. Esmond.
  4. The Newcomes. 2 vols.
  5. The Virginians. 2 vols.
  6. The Adventures of Philip. 2 vols.
  7. History of Samuel Titmarsh and the Great Hoggarty Diamond.
  8. Christmas Books.
  9. The Book of Snobs.
  10. Burlesques.
  11. Paris Sketch-book.
  12. Memoirs of C. J. Yellowplush.
  13. Irish Sketch-book.
  14. Memoirs of Barry Lindon.
  15. Catherine.
  16. Ballads, and the Rose and the Ring.
  17. Roundabout Papers, and the Second Funeral of Napoleon.
  18. The Four Georges.
  19. Lovel the Widower; the Wolves and the Lamb; Denis Duval.
  20. Miscellaneous Essays, Sketches, and Reviews.
  21. Contributions to Punch.

THACKERAY, Wm. Makepeace—contd.
Roundabout Papers. 12mo. Lond., 1887.   J 11 P 21
Criticisms of the Works of. [See Senior, N. W.—Essay on Fiction.]   J 6 S 40
Essay on. [See Bagehot, W.—Literary Studies.]   J 9 P 22-24
The Humourist as Philosopher. [See Lilly, W. S.—Four English Humourists.]   J 5 T 30
Life of; by H. Merivale and F. T. Marzials. 8vo. Lond., 1891.   C 14 P 31
[Plaster Cast of.] [See Hutton, L.—Portraits in Plaster.]   A 23 V 13
Reminiscences of. [See Skelton, Dr. J.—Table-talk of Shirley.]   C 19 V 10
With Thackeray in America. [See Crowe, E.]   B 17 R 35

THACKER'S INDIAN DIRECTORY, 1893. 8vo. Calcutta, 1893.   E

THALASSA. Yachting. [See Sullivan, Sir E.—Yachting.]   A 20 Q 40, 41

THAMES MINER'S GUIDE, The; with maps. 8vo. Auckland, 1868.   MA 3 T 26

THAMIN, Raymond. St. Ambroise et la Morale Chrétienne au 4ᵉ Siècle. 8vo. Paris, 1895.   G 16 U 29

THATCHER, Chas. R. Thatcher's Colonial Songster. Parts 1 and 2. 12mo. Melb., 1857.   MH 1 U 43
Invercargill Minstrel. 8vo. Invercargill (n.d.)   MH 1 S 67

THATCHER, Richard. Mr. Newcome in Search of a Cattle Station. 12mo. Melb., 1868.   MJ 3 P 12
It runs in the Blood. [See Bunster, G.]   MJ 1 S 29

THAYER, W. Roscoe. Historical Sketch of Harvard University. Imp. 8vo. Cambridge, Mass., 1890.   B 18 V 9

THEAL, George McCall. History of South Africa, 1486-1872. 5 vols. 8vo. Lond. 1888-93.   B 16 S 26-29
South Africa: Cape Colony, Natal, Orange Free State, South African Republic, and all other Territories South of the Zambesi. [Illustrated.] 8vo. Lond., 1894.   B 16 P 24

THEATRE, The: a monthly review of the drama, music, and of fine arts. 1st series, pts. 1-12, 2nd series, pts. 1, 2. 8vo. Melb., 1889-90.   ME 6 R

THEEL, Hjalmar. Holothurioidea. [See Thomson, Sir C. W., and Murray, Dr. J.—Voyage of H.M.S. Challenger.]   A 6 †

THEOBALD, R. M. Bacon, the Poet: Indications of Bacon's Mind in the Shakespearean Poems. [See Roy. Soc. of Lit., 2nd series, 16.]   E

THEOBALD, W. [See India—Geological Survey.] E

THEODORE, Archbishop of Canterdury, 669-690. Sketch of. [See Fowler, Rev. M.—Notable Archbishops.]
C 13 V 12

THEOLOGICAL REVIEW, The: a Journal of Religious Thought and Life. Vols. 3-9. 8vo. Lond., 1866-72.
G 19 Q 15-21

THEOPHILUS. Writings of; translated by Rev. Marcus Dods. (Ante-Nicene Christ. Lib., 3.) 8vo. Edinb., 1867.
G 14 U 3

THERRY, Sir Roger. Reminiscences of Thirty Years' Residence in New South Wales and Victoria, with a Supplementary Chapter on Transportation and the Ticket-of-leave System. 8vo. Lond., 1863.
MB 1 R 40

THIÉBAUT DE BERNEAUD, A. Nouveau Manuel complet du Vigneron. 18mo. Paris, 1873. A 18 P 6

THIÉRY, Gaston. Australie. Roy. 8vo. Bruxelles, 1890.
MD 7 U 15

THOM, A., & CO. Official Directory of the United Kingdom of Great Britain and Ireland, 1893-94. 2 vols. roy. 8vo. Dublin, 1893-94.
E

THOM, De Courcy W. History of Panics. [See Juglar, C.]
F 14 R 9

THOMAS, Antoine. Francesco da Barberino et la Littérature Provençale en Italie au Moyen Age. 8vo. Paris, 1883.
J 7 U 32

Nouvelles Recherces sur l'Entrée de Spagne, Chanson de Geste Franco-Italienne. 8vo. Paris, 1882. J 7 U 23

THOMAS, Charles Ap. Reminiscences of Sailor-Boy Life. 12mo. Gravesend, 1892. C 13 Q 27

THOMAS, Dr. Cyrus. The Chinch-bug, its History, Characters, and Habits, and the means of destroying it or counteracting its injuries. [Map and Illustrations.] 8vo. Washington, 1879. A 32 T 3

THOMAS, F. S. Three Letters addressed to Lord John Russell upon the subject of Gold in Australia. 8vo. Lond., 1852.
MF 2 T 52

THOMAS, H. Guide to Recreations and Calendar for 1874. 12mo. Melb., 1874. MA 2 V 37

THOMAS, J. W. Spiritual Law in the Natural World. 8vo. Lond., 1894.
G 12 Q 40

THOMAS, Dr. John Davies. Hydatid Disease in Australia. (Trans. Roy. Soc., S. Australia, 6.) 8vo. Adelaide, 1893.
ME 1 S

Hydatid Disease, vol. 2. A Collection of Papers on Hydatid Disease, edited and arranged by Dr. A. A. Lendon. 8vo. Sydney, 1894. MA 2 Q 66

THOMAS, Mrs. Julia Martha. Trial of Catherine Webster for the Murder of, at Richmond, England. [See Webster, Catherine.]
MF 4 R 11

THOMAS, Julian, "The Vagabond." South Sea Massacres. 8vo. Sydney, 1881.
MF 1 R 52

Victoria en 1889. Roy. 8vo. Melb., 1889. MB 2 U 22
The World of Dupes. [See Mediums and their Dupes.]
MG 2 Q 36

THOMAS AND SALLY; or, the Sailor's Return: a Musical Entertainment. [See London Stage, 4.]
H 2 S 36

THOMASON, Jas. [Life of]; by Sir R. Temple. (Rulers of India.) 8vo. Oxford, 1893. C 13 P 13

THOMPSON, Benjamin. The Stranger: a Drama. [See London Stage, 3.]
H 2 S 35

THOMPSON, Dr. Edward Maunde. Handbook of Greek and Latin Palæography. 8vo. Lond., 1893. K 14 P 9

THOMPSON, H. A. Notes on the Management of Mining Companies. 12mo. Melb., 1867. MA 3 U 5

THOMPSON, Herbert M. The Theory of Wages and its Application to the Eight Hours Question and other Labour Problems. 12mo. Lond., 1892. F 14 Q 50

THOMPSON, John Low. Olive Culture. 8vo. Sydney, 1891.
MA 1 Q 65
The Pig: its Breeding, Management, and Commercial Value. 8vo. Sydney, 1891. MA 1 Q 58
The Clydesdale Horse. 8vo. Sydney, 1892. MA 1 Q 58
The Cultivation of Rape. 8vo. Sydney, 1893.
MA 1 Q 65
Silos and Ensilage. 8vo. Melb. (n.d.) MA 3 T 9

THOMPSON, Lindsay George. History of the Fisheries of New South Wales. Roy. 8vo. Sydney, 1893.
MA 2 U 43

THOMPSON, Richard W. Recollections of Sixteen Presidents, from Washington to Lincoln. 2 vols. 8vo. Indianapolis, 1894.
C 18 T 21, 22

THOMPSON, Robert. The Gardener's Assistant. New ed., by T. Moore. Illustrated. Roy. 8vo. Lond., 1890.
A 32 T 4

THOMPSON, Prof. Silvanus Phillips. Dynamo-Electric Machinery. 4th edition. 8vo. Lond., 1892. A 21 S 16

THOMPSON, W. Mexico. [See Cubas, A. G.] F 14 U 13

THOMPSON, W. J. Notes on Coffee and its culture in Fiji. 8vo. Levuka (n.d.) MA 1 U 58

THOMSON, B. H. The Kalou-Vu (Ancestor-gods) of the Fijians. (Anthropol. Inst., 24.) 8vo. Lond., 1894.
E

THOMSON, Basil. The Diversions of a Prime Minister [Rev. S. W. Baker.] 8vo. Edinb., 1894. MB 2 R 50
South Sea Yarns. 12mo. Edinb., 1894. MD 7 T 8

THOMSON, Sir C. Wyville, and MURRAY, Dr. John. Report on the Scientific Results of the Voyage of H.M.S. *Challenger* during the years 1872-76, under the Command of Captain (Sir) George S. Nares and the late Captain Frank T. Thomson; prepared under the Superintendence of Sir C. Wyville Thompson and Dr. John Murray. 50 vols. 4to. Lond., 1880-95.
A 6 †

CONTENTS.

Narrative of the Cruise; with a General Account of the Scientific Results of the Expedition; by Staff-Commander T. H. Tizard, Prof. H. N. Moseley, J. Y. Buchanan, and Dr. John Murray. Vol. i., in 2 parts. 1885.

Narrative. Magnetical and Meteorological Results. Vol. ii. 1882.

Botany. Vols. i. and ii. 1885-86.

VOL. I.
1. Report on Present State of Knowledge of various Insular Floras; by William B. Hemsley.
2. Report on the Botany of the Bermudas and various other Islands of the Atlantic and Southern Oceans; by William B. Hemsley.
3. Report on the Botany of Juan Fernandez, the South-Eastern Moluccas, and the Admiralty Islands; by William B. Hemsley.

VOL. II.
Report on the Marine Diatomaceæ; by Conte Abate Francesco Castracane.

Report on Deep-Sea Deposits, based on Specimens collected during the Voyage; by Dr. John Murray and the Rev. Dr. A. F. Renard. 1891.

Physics and Chemistry. Vols. i. and ii. 1884-89.

VOL. I.
1. Report on Researches into the Composition of Ocean Water; by Prof. William Dittmar.
2. Report on the Specific Gravity of Samples of Ocean Water; by J. Y. Buchanan.
3. Report on the Deep-Sea Temperature Observations of Ocean Water taken by the Officers of the Expedition.

VOL. II.
1. Report on some of the Physical Properties of Fresh Water and of Sea Water; by Prof. P. G. Tait.
2. Report on Atmospheric Circulation; by Dr. Alexander Buchan.
3. Report on the Magnetical Results obtained by H.M.S. *Challenger*; by Staff-Commander E. W. Creak.
4. Report on the Rock Specimens collected on Oceanic Islands; by Prof. A. Renard.

Zoology. Vol. i.-xxxii. 1880-89.

VOL. I.
1. General Introduction to the Zoological Series of Reports; by Sir C. Wyville Thomson.
2. Report on the Brachiopoda; by Thomas Davidson.
3. Report on the Pennatulida; by Prof. Albert v. Kölliker.
4. Report on the Ostracoda; by Dr. G. Stewardson Brady.
5. Report on the Bones of Cetacea; by William Turner.
6. Report on the Development of the Green Turtle; by William K. Parker.
7. Report on Shore Fishes; by Dr. Albert Günther.

2 M

THOMSON and MURRAY—*contd.*
Zoology—*contd.*

VOL. II.
1. Report on certain Hydroid, Alcyonarian, and Madreporarian Corals; by H. N. Moseley.
2. Report on the Birds collected during the Voyage; by P. L. Sclater.
 (*a*) On the Birds collected in the Philippine Islands; by the Marquis of Tweeddale.
 (*b*) On the Birds collected in the Admiralty Islands; by P. L. Sclater.
 (*c*) On the Birds collected in Tongatabu, Fiji, New Hebrides, and Tahiti; by Dr. O. Finsch.
 (*d*) On the Birds collected in Ternate, Amboyna, Banda, the Ki Islands and the Arrou Islands; by T. Salvadori.
 (*e*) On the Birds collected at Cape York and on the neighbouring Islands; by W. A. Forbes.
 (*f*) On the Birds collected in the Sandwich Islands; by P. L. Sclater.
 (*g*) On the Birds collected in Antarctic America; by P. L. Sclater.
 (*h*) On the Birds collected on the Atlantic Islands and Kerguelen Island, &c.; by P. L. Sclater.
 (*i*) On the Steganopodes and Impennes collected during the Expedition; by P. L. Sclater.
 (*k*) On the Laridæ collected during the Expedition; by Howard Saunders.
 (*l*) On the Procellariidæ collected during the Expedition; by Osbert Salvin.

VOL. III.
1. Report on the Echinoidea; by Alexander Agassiz.
2. Report on the Pycnogonida; by Dr. P. P. C. Hoek.

VOL. IV.
1. Report on the Anatomy of the Petrels; by W. A. Forbes.
2. Report on the Deep-Sea Medusæ; by Prof. Ernst Haeckel.
3. Report on the Holothurioidea; by Hjalmar Theel.

VOL. V.
1. Report on the Ophiuroidea; by Theodore Lyman.
2. Some points in the Anatomy of the Thylacine, Cuscus, and Phascogale; with an Account of the Comparative Anatomy of the Intrinsic Muscles and Nerves of the Mammalia pes; by Dr. D. J. Cunningham.

VOL. VI.
1. Report on the Actiniaria. Part I; by Prof. Richard Hertwig.
2. Report on the Tunicata. Part I., Ascidia simplices; by Prof. W. A. Herdman.

VOL. VII.
1. Report on the Anatomy of the Spheniscidæ; by Dr. Morrison Watson.
2. Report on the Pelagic Hemiptera; by Dr. F. Buchanan White.
3. Report on the Hydroida. Part I., Plumularidæ; by G. J. Allman.
4. Report on the Specimens of the Genus Orbitolites; by Dr. W. B. Carpenter.

VOL. VIII.
1. Report on the Copepoda; by Dr. G. Stewardson Brady.
2. Report on the Cirripedia; by Dr. P. P. C. Hoek.
3. Report on the Cirripedia; by Dr. P. P. C. Hoek.

VOL. IX. (2 Parts.)
Report on the Foraminifera; by H. B. Brady.

THOMSON and MURRAY—*contd.*
Zoology—*contd.*

Vol. X.
1. Report on the Nudibranchiata ; by Dr. Rudolph Bergh.
2. Report on the Myzostomida ; by Dr. L. von Graaf.
3. Report on the Cirripedia. Anatomical part ; by Dr. P. P. C. Hoek.
4. Report on the Human Skeletons—The Crania ; by Prof. William Turner.
. Report on the Polyzoa. Part I., The Cheilostomata ; by George Busk.

Vol. XI.
1. Report on the Keratosa ; by N. Polójneff.
2. Report on the Crinoidea. Part I., The Stalked Crinoids; by P. Herbert Carpenter.
3. Report on the Isopoda, the genus Serolis ; by Frank E. Beddard.

Vol. XII.
Report on the Annelida Polychæta ; by Prof. William C. M'Intosh.

Vol. XIII.
. Report on the Lamellibranchiata ; by Edgar A. Smith.
2. Report on the Gephyrea ; by Dr. Emil Selenka.
3. Report on the Schizopoda ; by Prof. G. O. Sars.

Vol. XIV.
1. Report on the Tunicata ; by Prof. W. A. Herdman. Part II., Ascidiæ compositæ.
2. Report on the Holothurioidea ; by Hjalmar Théel.

Vol. XV.
1. Report on the Marsepinadæ ; by Dr. Rudolph Bergh.
2. Report on the Scaphopoda and Gasteropoda ; by the Rev. Robert Boog Watson.
3. Report on the Polyplacophora ; by Prof. Alfred C. Haddon.

Vol. XVI.
1. Report on the Cephalopoda ; by W. E. Hoyle.
2. Report on the Stomatopoda ; by Prof. W. K. Brooks.
3. Report on the Reef Corals ; by J. J. Quelch.
4. Report on the Human Crania and other bones of the Skeletons collected during the Voyage. Part II ; by Sir William Turner.

Vol. XVII.
1. Report on the Isopoda ; by Frank E. Beddard.
2. Report on the Brachyura ; by Edward J. Miers.
3. Report on the Polyzoa. Part II ; by George Busk.

Vol. XVIII. (3 Parts).
1. Report on the Radiolaria ; by Prof. Ernst Haeckel. Part I., Introduction and Porulosa ; Part II., Osculosa and Plates.

Vol. XIX.
1. Report on the Nemerten ; by Prof. A. A. W. Hubrecht.
2. Report on the Cumacea ; by Prof. G. O. Sars.
3. Report on the Phyllocarida ; by Prof. G. O. Sars.
4. Report on the Pteropoda. Part I ; by Dr. Paul Pelseneer.

Vol. XX.
1. Report on the Monaxonida ; by Stuart O. Ridley and Arthur Dendy.
2. Report on the Myzostomida (Supplement) ; by Dr. L. von Graaf.
3. Report on Cephalodiscus Dodecalophus, a new type of the Polyzoa procured on the Voyage ; by Prof. W. C. M'Intosh.

Vol. XXI. (2 Parts).
Report on the Hexactinellida ; by Dr. F. E. Schulze.

Vol. XXII.
Report on Deep-Sea Fishes ; by Dr. Albert Günther.

THOMSON and MURRAY—*contd.*
Zoology—*contd.*

Vol. XXIII.
1 Report on the Pteropoda. Part II., The Thecosomata. Part III., Anatomy ; by Dr. Paul Pelseneer.
2. Report on the Hydroida. Part II., The Tubularinæ, Corymorphinæ, Campanularinæ, Sertularinæ, and Thalamophora ; by Prof. G. J. Allman.
3. Report on the Entozoa ; by Dr. O. von Linstow.
4. Report on the Heteropoda ; by Edgar A. Smith.

Vol. XXIV. (2 Parts).
Report on the Crustacea Macrura ; by G. Spence Bate.

Vol. XXV.
Report on the Tetractinellida ; by Prof. W. J. Sollas.

Vol. XXVI.
1. Report on the Crinoidea. Part II., The Comatulæ ; by Dr. P. H. Carpenter.
2. Report on the Seals collected during the Voyage ; by Sir William Turner.
3. Report on the Actiniaria. Part II ; by Prof. Richard Hertwig.

Vol. XXVII.
1. Report on the Anomura ; by Prof. J. R. Henderson.
2. Report on the Anatomy of the Deep-Sea Mollusca ; by Prof. Paul Pelseneer.
3. Report on Phoronis Buskii, n. sp. ; by Prof. W. C. M'Intosh.
4. Report on the Tunicata. Part III ; by Prof. W. A. Herdman.

Vol. XXVIII.
Report on the Siphonophoræ ; by Dr. Ernst Haeckel.

Vol. XXIX. (3 Parts).
Report on the Amphipoda ; by the Rev. Thomas R. R. Stebbing.

Vol. XXX. (2 Parts).
Report on the Asteroidea ; by W. Percy Sladen.

Vol. XXXI.
1. Report on the Alcyonaria ; by Prof. E. P. Wright and Prof. T. Studer.
2. Report on the Pelagic Fishes ; by Dr. Albert Günther.
3. Supplementary Report on the Polyzoa ; by Arthur W. Waters.

Vol. XXXII.
1. Report on the Antipatharia ; by George Brook.
2. Supplementary Report on the Alcyonaria ; by Prof. T. Studer.
3. Report on the Deep-Sea Keratosa ; by Prof. Ernst Haeckel.

Summary of the Scientific Results. 2 parts. 1895.
1. Editorial Notes, with List of the Memoirs making up the *Challenger* Report.
2. Summary of the Scientific Results obtained at the Sounding, Dredging, and Trawling Stations ; by Dr. John Murray.
3. Report on the Specimen of the Genus Spirula ; by the Rt. Hon. T. H. Huxley, and Prof. Paul Pelseneer.
4. Report on Oceanic Circulation ; by Dr. Alexander Buchan.

THOMSON, G. M. On the occurrence of two species of Cumacea in New Zealand. [*See* Linnean Society, London, Journal, 24.] E

THOMSON, H. C. The Chitral Campaign. 8vo. Lond., 1895. B 10 U 38

THOMSON, J. Arthur. Outlines of Zoology. 2nd ed., illustrated. 12mo. Edinb., 1895.   A 28 P 26
Evolution of Sex. [See Geddes, Prof. P.]   A 28 P 4

THOMSON, Prof. J. J. Elements of the Mathematical Theory of Electricity and Magnetism. 8vo. Camb., 1893.   A 21 R 35
Notes on Recent Researches in Electricity and Magnetism. 8vo. Oxford, 1893.   A 21 S 17

THOMSON, J. P. British New Guinea. 8vo. Lond., 1892.   MD 5 T 43
Macuata, the North-west Coast of Vanua Levu, Fiji, from Droketi River, to Cape Udu, and around the Cape to Wainunu, Natewa Bay. (Roy. Geograph. Soc. of Australasia, Q. Branch, 1.) 8vo. Brisbane, 1886.   ME 20
The Rewa River (Fiji): its Tributaries and District. (Roy. Geograph. Soc. of Australasia, Q. Branch, 2.) 8vo. Brisbane, 1887.   ME 20
Report upon the preliminary examination of a hill (supposed to be subsiding) in the Redbank Plains District. (Roy. Geograph. Soc. of Australasia, Q. Branch, 2.) 8vo. Brisbane, 1887.   ME 20
The Importance of the teaching of Geography in the School. (Roy. Geograph. Soc. of Australasia, Q. Branch, 3.) 8vo. Brisbane, 1888.   ME 20
Sir W. MacGregor's Ascent of Mount Victoria, and Explorations of the Owen Stanley Range, British New Guinea. (Roy. Geograph. Soc. of Australasia, Q. Branch, 5.) 8vo. Brisbane, 1889.   ME 20
Notes on Brisbane River Floods. (Roy. Geograph. Soc of Australasia, Q. Branch, 5.) 8vo. Brisbane, 1890.   ME 20
Sir W. MacGregor's Upper Fly River Exploration, British New Guinea. (Roy. Geograph. Soc. of Australasia, Q. Branch, 5.) 8vo. Brisbane, 1890.   ME 20
On the North-east Coast of British New Guinea, and some of the adjacent Islands. (Roy. Geograph. Soc. of Australasia, Q. Branch, 6.) 8vo. Brisbane. 1891.   ME 20
Universal Time Measurement. (Roy. Geograph. Soc. of Australasia, Q. Branch, 7.) 8vo. Brisbane, 1892.   ME 20
Practical Suggestions to Travellers. (Roy. Geograph. Soc. of Australasia, Q. Branch, 7.) 8vo. Brisbane, 1892.   ME 20
The "Melanesian Plateau"; Notes on Mr. C. Hedley's Paper. (Roy. Geograph. Soc. of Australasia, Q. Branch, 8.) 8vo. Brisbane, 1893.   ME 20

THOMSON, James, ("B.V.") Poems, Essays, and Fragments: edited by J. M. Robertson. 8vo. Lond, 1892.   H 10 Q 22

THOMSON, James. The Poet of the Seasons. [See Haliburton, H.—Furth in Field.]   B 32 R 5
The Seasons, and Castle of Indolence. 32mo. Lond., 1835.   H 10 T 29
Sketch of; by Hugh Haliburton. [See Masson, Prof. D.—In the Footsteps of the Poets.]   J G R 43
Tancred and Sigismunda: a Tragedy. [See London Stage, 4.]   H 2 S 36

THOMSON, James. The Australian in India. 8vo Melb., 1889.   MD 8 Q 19

THOMSON, Prof. John Miller. Chemistry. [See Bloxam, C. L.]   A 21 U 4

THOMSON, Dr. Robert Dundas. British Annual, and Epitome of the Progress of Science, for 1838. 18mo. Lond., 1838.   F

THOMSON, T. Poetical Works of. 2nd ed. 12mo. Lond., 1850.   H 10 T 8

THOMSON, Rev. Thos. History of the Scottish People from the Earliest Times. 6 vols. roy. 8vo. Lond. (n.l.)   B 12 V 12-17

THOMSON, Wm. The Germ Origin of Tubercle. 8vo. Melb., 1882.   MA 3 T 12
William Shakespeare in Romance and Reality. 8vo. Melb, 1881.   MJ 2 S 49

THOMSON, Sir Wm. [See Kelvin, Baron.]

THOMSON, Capt. Wm. Campbell The Gulf of Carpentaria. (Roy. Geograph. Soc. of Australasia, Q. Branch, 6.) 8vo. Brisbane, 1889.   ME 20
The "Stone Age" in Australasia. (Roy. Geograph. Soc. of Australasia, Q. Branch, 8.) 8vo. Brisbane, 1893.   ME 20
History of North-east Coast of Australia. (Roy. Geograph. Soc. of Australasia, Q. Branch, 2.) Brisbane, 1887.   ME 20

THORBURN, Col. Wm. Stewart. Guide to the Coins of Great Britain and Ireland. 2nd. ed. 8vo. Lond, 1892.   A 27 Q 2

THOREAU, Herbert David. [Collected Works of.] 10 vols. 12mo. Boston (n.d.)   J G R 33-42
1. Walden.
2. On the Concord and Merrimac Rivers.
3. Excursions.
4. The Maine Woods.
5. Cape Cod.
6. Familiar Letters.
7. A Yankee in Canada.
8. Early Spring in Massachusetts.
9. Summer.
10. Winter.

Walden. 12mo. Lond. (n.d.)   J 9 F 26
Familiar Letters of; edited by F. B. Sanborn. 8vo. Boston, 1895.   C 19 V 3
Sketch of; by J. Burroughs. [See Burroughs, J.—Indoor Studies.]   J 16 T 14

THORN, Major Wm. Memoir of the Conquest of Java. 4to. Lond., 1815.   B 15 Q 5 †

THORNBURN, S. S. Asiatic Neighbours. With Maps. 8vo. Edinb., 1894.   F 14 U 9

THORNBURY, George Walter. Cross Country. 3vo. Lond., 1861.   D 19 Q 31

THORNDIKE, Rachel Sherman. The Sherman Letters: Correspondence between General and Senator Sherman, 1837–91. 8vo. Lond., 1894. C 18 T 15

THORNTON, G. Notes to Paradise Lost. [*See* Milton, J.] MH 1 P 37

THORNTON, Hon. George. Aborigines of N.S.W. [*See* Hill, Hon. R.] MA 1 R 45

THORNTON, Dr. James Howard. Memories of seven Campaigns: a record of thirty-five years' service in the Indian Medical Department in India, China, Egypt, and the Sudan. Illustrated. Roy. 8vo. Lond., 1895. B 21 V 8

THORNTON, John. Advanced Physiography. With Maps and Illustrations. New ed. 8vo. Lond., 1893. A 19 Q 23

Human Physiology. Illustrated. 8vo. Lond., 1894. A 26 Q 31

THORNTON, Dr. Thos. Henry. Col. Sir Robt. Sandeman: his Life and Work on our Indian Frontier. 8vo. Lond., 1885. C 19 S 7

THORPE, Wm. Chemical Technology. [*See* Groves, C. E.] A 21 V 6, 7

THORPE, Dr. Francis Newton. Benjamin Franklin and the University of Pennsylvania. 8vo. Wash., 1893. G 18 S 8

THORPE, Mary and Charlotte. London Church Staves, with some Notes on their surroundings. Roy. 8vo. Lond., 1895. G 5 U 30

THORPE, Prof. Thos. Edward. Dictionary of Applied Chemistry. Vol. 3. Roy. 8vo. Lond., 1893. K 9 R 13

Essays in Historical Chemistry. 8vo. Lond., 1894. C 17 R 2

THORPE, Dr. V. Gunson. *Rotifera* found in the Ponds of the Gardens of the Acclimatisation Society, Brisbane. (Proc. Roy. Soc., Queensland, 4.) 8vo. 1897. ME 1 T

List of Queensland *Rotifera*. (Proc. Roy. Soc., Queensland, 6.) 8vo. Brisbane, 1889. ME 1 T

THOU, Jacques Auguste de. Conspiracy against James I, 1605. [*See* Collectanea Adamantœ.] J 18 R 10

THOUGHTS ON RELIGION AND THE BIBLE; by "A Layman." 2nd ed. 12mo. Lond., 1865. G 19 P 34

THOYTS, E. E. How to decipher and Study Old Documents; being a Guide to the Reading of Ancient Manuscripts. 8vo. Lond., 1893. B 14 Q 17

THOZET, A. Roots, Tubers, Bulbs, and Fruits used as Vegetable Food by the Aboriginals of North Queensland. 8vo. Rockhampton, 1866. MA 1 U 63

THOZET, M. Specimens of Queensland Woods. [*See* Hill, W.] MA 2 T 31

THRELFALL, Mrs. Evelyn. Starlight Songs. 12mo. Lond., 1895. MH 1 U 56

THRELFALL, Prof. Richard. Approximate method of finding the forces acting in magnetic circuits. (Journal Roy. Soc., N.S.W., 27.) 8vo. Sydney, 1893. ME 1 R

THRELKELD, Lancelot Edward. An Australian Language, as spoken by the Awabakal, the People of Awaba or Lake Macquarie; being an Account of their Language, Traditions, and Customs. Re-arranged, &c., by Dr. J. Fraser. 8vo. Sydney, 1892. MK 1 R 49

THRING, Henry, Baron. Practical Legislation; or, the Composition and Language of Acts of Parliament. Roy. 8vo. Lond., 1878. F 14 V 25

THRUM, Thos. G. [*See* Hawaiian Almanac.] ME 3 U

THUCYDIDES. Funeral Orations in praise of Military Men. [*See* Broadhurst, Rev. T.] G 1 R 30

Historia. 2 vols. 18mo. Oxonii, 1864. B 27 P 4, 5

THUDICHUM, Dr. John Louis Wm. The Spirit of Cookery. 8vo. Lond., 1895. A 22 Q 40

THUE, W. Clausen. A B C Universal Commercial Electric Telegraphic Code. 4th ed. 8vo. Lond., 1893. K 9 S 17

THWING, Rev. Dr. Chas. Franklin. The College Woman. 12mo. New York, 1894. G 18 P 26

THYNNE, R. The Story of Australian Exploration. Illustrated. 8vo. Lond., 1894. MD 8 P 17

TICHBORNE, Sir Roger, Revealed! [*See* Jackson, J. D. D.] MF 2 R 39

TICHBORNE TRIAL, The. The Summing-up of the Lord Chief Justice of England, together with the Addresses of the Judges, the Verdict, and the Sentence. 8vo. Lond., 1874. F 9 P 20

TICKNOR, George. Life of W. H. Prescott. 12mo. Philad. (n.d.) C 18 P 22

TIECK, Ludwig. Translations of Works of. [*See* Carlyle, T.] J 5 R 42

TIFFANY, Chas. Louis. Sketch of. [*See* Stoddard, W. O.—Men of Business.] C 16 R 10

TILDEN, Samuel J. Sketch of. [*See* Brooks, N.—Statesmen.] C 16 R 20

TIMBS, John. School Days of Eminent Men. Illustrated. 12mo. Lond., 1858. G 18 P 17

TIME OF THE END, The; or, Historical Facts and Passing Events identified with Scripture Prophecies; by "Victorian." 8vo. Melb., 1870. MG 2 Q 31

TIMES. The weekly edition, 1892-94. 3 vols. fol. Lond., 1892-94. E
Index to *The Times* Newspaper, 1833 and 1894. 2 vols. sm. 4to. Lond. 1894. E
Annual Summaries reprinted from *The Times*. Vols. 1 and 2, 1851-92. 8vo. Lond., 1893. E

TIMES-PARNELL COMMISSION. Speech by M. Davitt. [*See* Davitt, M.] F 7 V 5

TIMMINS, Samuel. Books on Shakespeare. 8vo. Lond. (n.d.) J 15 S 30

TISCHENDORF, L. F. Constantin de. Novum Testamentum Græcæ. [*See* Bibles and Testaments.] G 14 R 17

TISSOT, V., et AMÉRO, C. Aux Antipodes: Terres et Peuplades peu connues de l'Oceanie. 8vo. Lond. (n.d.) MD 5 V 50

TIT-BITS. Vols. 22-26. 4to. Lond., 1892-94. E

TITCHENER, E. B. Psychology. [*See* Wundt, W.] A 26 V 12

TIVARD, Helen Mary. Life in Ancient Egypt. [*See* Erman, A.] B 27 V 17

TIZARD, T. H. Narrative of the Cruise of H.M.S. *Challenger*. [*See* Thomson, Sir C. W., and Murray, Dr J.—Report on the Scientific Results of the Voyage of H.M.S. *Challenger*.] A 6 S †

TOBACCO CULTURE. Practical Details, from the Selection and Preparation of Seed and Soil to Harvesting, Curing, and Marketing the Crop. 8vo. New York (n.d.) A 32 T 14

TOBIN, John. The Curfew: a Play. [*See* London Stage, 4.] H 2 S 30

TODD, A. H. Digest of Reported Decisions. [*See* Fisher, R. A.] F 12 V 3-9

TODD, Alice M. England under the Tudors. [*See* Busch, Dr. W.] B 21 U 1

TODD, Dr. Alpheus. Parliamentary Government in the British Colonies. 2nd ed. 8vo. Lond., 1884. F 9 Q 27

TODD, Sir Charles. Meteorological Observations, Adelaide, 1876-90. [*See* Adelaide Observatory.] ME

TODHUNTER, Dr. Isaac. Key to Plane Trigonometry for the use of Colleges and Schools. 12mo. Lond., 1893. A 25 Q 24
History of the Theory of Elasticity and of the Strength of Materials, from Galileo to the Present Time; edited by Prof. K. Pearson. 2 vols. (in 3.) 8vo. Camb., 1886-93. A 11 U 21-23

TODHUNTER, John. A Study of Shelley. 12mo. Lond., 1880. H 3 P 50

TOLEDO PUBLIC SCHOOLS. Report, 1891. 8vo. Toledo, Ohio, 1891. E

TOLLEMACHE, Hon. Lionel Arthur. [*Life of*] Benjamin Jowett, Master of Baliol. 8vo. Lond., 1893. C 19 V 14

TOLMAN, Dr. Wm. Howe. History of Higher Education in Rhode Island. 8vo. Wash., 1894. G 18 R 39
Municipal Reform Movements in the United States. 8vo. New York, 1895. F 8 U 35

TOLSTOI, Count Leo. The Four Gospels harmonised and translated. 12mo. Lond., 1895. G 3 P 22
Recollections of Count Leo Tolstoy; by C. A. Behrs. 8vo. Lond., 1893. C 16 R 16

TOM CRINGLE. [*See* Walker, W. B.]

TOMKINSON, J. *Editor*—Diary of a Cavalry Officer. [*See* Tomkinson, Lieut.-Col. W.] B 29 U 1

TOMKINSON, Lieut.-Col. W. Diary of a Cavalry Officer in the Peninsular and Waterloo Campaigns, 1809-15. [With Maps.] Edited by J. Tomkinson. 8vo. Lond., 1894. B 29 U 1

TOMLINE, Rt. Rev. George. Introduction to the Study of the Bible; being the first volume of the Elements of Christian Theology. 19th ed. 12mo. Lond., 1849. G 7 U 37

TOMPKINS, Edward S. D. Through David's Realm. Illustrated. 8vo. Lond., 1890. D 17 R 20

TONE, Theobald Wolfe. Autobiography of, 1763-98; edited, with an Introduction, by R. B. O'Brien. 2 vols. roy. 8vo. Lond., 1893. C 19 S 1, 2
Life of; edited by his son, W. T. W. Tone. 2 vols. 8vo. Washington, 1826. C 15 P 7, 8

TONER, J. M. *Editor*—Journal of Col. George Washington. [*See* Washington, G.] B 17 R 23

TONGAN AFFAIRS. Letters and Correspondence re Tongan Affairs and the request of H.M. King George for Tonga to be made an independent district. 8vo. Sydney, 1880. MG 2 Q 51

TONKIN, W. J. K. Gaffer Green. 12mo. Sydney, 1895. MJ 3 Q 30

TORO, B. Recopilación de Leyes y circulares concernientes al Ejército. Roy. 8vo. Santiago, 1888. F 7 U 18

TORONTO UNIVERSITY. Extracts from the Calendar of, 1892, 1893. 12mo. Toronto, 1892. E
Report of the Standing Committee on the Faculty of Medicine on the Subject of Hospital facilities, 1892. 8vo. Toronto, 1892. A 30 U 28
Revenues and Requirements. 8vo. Toronto, 1891. E
Senate Rules of Procedure, and Curriculum: Faculty of Arts, 1891-95, Faculty of Law, 1891-95, Department of Pharmacy, 1892. 8vo. Toronto (n.d.) E

TORPEDO. [*See* Electric Universe, The.] MA 1 V 41

TORQUEMADA, F. J. de. Monarchia Indiana. 3 vols. sm. fol Madrid, 1723. B 36 T 13-15 ‡

TORR, Cecil. Ancient Ships. Illustrated. 8vo. Lond., 1894. A 19 T 30

TORRENS, W. M. History of Cabinets, from the union with Scotland to the acquisition of Canada and Bengal. 2 vols. 8vo. Lond., 1894. B 22 R 1, 2

TORRENS, Wm. McCullagh. Twenty years in Parliament. 8vo. Lond., 1893. C 16 S 2

TOTTEN, Chas. Adiel Lewis. Joshua's Long Day and the Dial of Ahaz: a scientific vindication and a midnight cry. 12mo. New Haven, Conn., 1891. G 9 V 29

The Secret of History, how Empire took its Westward way; the King's Daughters or the flight of David's line, being the sequel to Tea Tephi. 12mo. New Haven, Conn., 1891. G 9 V 30

The Hope of History, the Millennium: Letters and Lectures upon Prophetic Topics. 12mo. New Haven, Conn., 1892. G 9 V 31

The Riddle of History: a chronological itinerary through the period of the Judges, together with other Biblco-Literary Excursus. 12mo. New Haven, Conn., 1892. G 9 V 32

The Answer of History: Objections to the Isrealitish origin of our race. 12mo. New Haven, Conn., 1893. G 9 V 33

TOTTENHAM, Major-General. An Address on Imperial Federation. 12mo. Hobart, 1887. MF 4 P 23

Imperial Federation. 12mo. Hobart, 1887. MF 4 P 23

TOULMIN, Camilla. Lays and Legends illustrative of English Life. Sm. 4to. Lond., 1845. J 15 V 6

TOURRIER, T. John. Pamphlet on Music Teaching and Learning, Pianoforte, and Singing. 8vo. Melb., (n.d.) MG 2 Q 30

TOURS, B. The Violin. 4to. Lond. (n.d.) A 12 S 12 †

TOUT, Prof. T. F. [Life of] Edward the First. (Twelve English Statesmen.) 8vo. Lond., 1893. C 13 Q 30

TOWER, Dr. Charlemagne. The Marquis de La Fayette in the American Revolution; with some account of the attitude of France toward the War of Independence. 2 vols. roy. 8vo. Philad., 1895. B 20 V 7, 8

TOWERS, E. The Land of Sunshine and Gold. 12mo. Lond., 1890. MD 7 T 55

TOWN AND COUNTRY JOURNAL, The. 1892-94. 9 vols. fol. Sydney, 1892-94. ME

TOWNESEND, Col. Richard. An Officer of the Long Parliament and his Descendants; being some account of the Life and Times of Col. Richard Townesend, and a Chronicle of his Family. 8vo. Lond., 1892. C 15 R 18

TOWNLEY, Rev. James. High Life Below Stairs: a Farce. [*See* London Stage, 1.] H 2 S 33

TOWNSEND, Rev. George. Acts and Monuments of John Foxe. [*See* Foxe, J.] G 16 U 9-16

TOYNBEE, Arnold. [Life of]; by F. C. Montague. (Johns Hopkins University Studies, 7.) 8vo. Baltimore, 1889. B 18 S 7

TOZER, Henry J. *Trans.*—The Social Contract. [*See* Rousseau, J. J.] F 8 U 42

TRAILL, Dr. Henry Duff. Social England: a Record of the Progress of the People in Religion, Laws, Learning, Arts, Industry, &c., from the Earliest Times to the Present Day; by various writers; edited by H. D. Traill. Vols. 1-4. 8vo. Lond., 1893-95. B 17 R 17-20

Capitals of the World. [*See* Bell, Mrs. N. R. E] D 9 V 11, 12

TRAIN, George Francis. Commentary on the Letters and Reports of, on the subject of the Port dues of Port Phillip. 8vo. Williamstown, 1855. MF 4 Q 19

TRALL, Dr. Russell Thatcher. Digestion and Dyspepsia. Illustrated. 8vo. New York, 1892. A 33 P 1

TRANSFORMATIONS; or, Scenes and Seances: a Sequel to "Scripopolis," being raps from the spirit of "Demonax." 12mo. Melb., 1873. MJ 2 T 37

TRANSMITTER, The, published in the interests of the Electric Telegraph Society, June, 1893, to May, 1894. Sm. 4to. Sydney, 1893-94. ME 20 S

TRANS-PACIFIC CABLE, The. Extracts from the *Courrier Australien*, of Sydney; translated by J. Ramsay. 8vo. Sydney, 1893. MF 1 R 54

TRAPP, Rev. J. Popery truly stated, and briefly confuted. 8vo. Lond., 1726. G 15 P 42

TREAT, Mary. Injurious Insects of the Farm and Garden, with a chapter on Beneficial Insects. 8vo. New York, 1892. A 27 Q 23

TRECHMANN, Emil J. *Editor*—Paul et Virginie. [*See* Saint-Pierre, B. de.] MJ 1 Q 2

TREGARTHEN, Greville P. Australian Commonwealth. (Story of the Nations.) 8vo. Lond., 1893. MB 1 Q 35

Sketch of the Progress and Resources of New South Wales. Roy. 8vo. Sydney, 1893. MF 1 S 59

TRENCH, Most Rev. Richard C. The Story of Justin Martyr and other Poems. 4th ed. 12mo. Lond., 1857. H 10 T 20

TRENT, Prof. Wm. P. English Culture in Virginia: a Study of the Gilmer Letters and an Account of the English Professors obtained by Jefferson for the University of Virginia. (Johns Hopkins University Studies, 7.) 8vo. Baltimore, 1889. B 18 S 7

TREVERT, Edward. Electrical Measurements for Amateurs. Illustrated. 12mo. Lynn, Mass, 1894.
A 21 P 43

How to Build Dynamo-Electric Machinery. Illustrated. 8vo. Lynn, Mass, 1894. A 21 S 3C

TREVOR-BATTYE, A. [See Battye, A. Trevor-.]

TRIAL FOUR, The; by "KLE." 12mo. Melb., 1873.
MJ 3 Q 37

TRICKETT, O., and HARVEY, R. W. Handy Register of Mining Companies. 8vo. Sydney, 1888. ME 10 S

TRIMBLE, Dr. Henry. The Tannins: History, Preparation, Properties, Methods of Estimation, and Uses of the Vegetable Astringents. Vol. 2. 8vo. Philad., 1894. A 32 A 22

Text-book of Chemistry. [See Sadtler, Dr. S. P.]
A 33 U 15

TRINITY MEDICAL COLLEGE, Toronto. Annual Announcement, 1892, 1893. 8vo. Toronto, 1892. E

TRISTRAM, Rev. Dr. Henry Baker. Eastern Customs in Bible Lands. 8vo. Lond , 1894. F 8 U 3

Rambles in Japan. 8vo. Lond., 1895. D 17 U 23

TROLLOPE, Rev. Wm. Pertalogia Græca. 8vo. Lond., 1825. H 3 S 27
1. Sophoclis Œdipus Tyrannus.
2. Sophoclis Œdipus Coloneus.
3. Sophoclis Antigone.
4. Euripidis Phœnissæ.
5. Æschyli Septem Contra Thebas.

TROPICAL AGRICULTURIST: a Monthly Record of Information for Planters of Coffee, Tea, Cocoa Cinchona, India-rubber, Sugar, Tobacco, Cardamoms. Palms, Rice, and other products suited for cultivation in the Tropics; compiled by A. M. and J. Ferguson 12 vols. sm. 4to. Colombo, 1882-94. E

TROTTER, Capt. Lionel James. The Earl of Auckland. (Rulers of India.) 8vo. Oxford, 1893. C 13 P 10

TRUMAN, E. E. P. The Wooing: Song. Sm. fol Sydney, 1893. MA 7 Q 31 ‡

Thine Eyes have Gazed in Mine, Dear One: Song Sm. fol. Sydney, 1893. MA 7 Q 31 ‡

TRUMBULL, Rev. Dr. Henry Clay. Studies in Oriental Social Life. 8vo. Lond., 1895. F 2 V 1

The Sunday-school: its Origin, Mission, Methods, and Auxiliaries. 8vo. Philad., 1893. G 15 P 40

TRUMBULL, M. M. The Free Trade Struggle in England. 2nd ed. 8vo. Chicago, 1892. F 5 Q 5

Wheelbarrow Articles and Discussions on the Labor Question. 12mo. Chicago, 1890. F 8 U 48

TRYON, George Washington, jun. Manual of Conchology, structural and systematic; continuation by H. A. Pilsbry. Vols. 14, 15. 8vo. Philad., 1892-93.
A 32 P 14, 15

Manual of Conchology, second series, continued by H. A. Pilsbry. Vols. 8, 9 8vo. Philad., 1892-94.
A 32 Q 8, 9

TRYON, Henry. Gumming of Cane. 8vo. Brisbane, 1895. MA 1 T 55

The Sea Scum and its Nature. (Proc. Roy. Soc., Queensland, 1.) 8vo. Brisbane, 1885. ME 1 T

On an undescribed class of Rock Drawings of Aborigines in Queensland. (Proc. Roy. Soc., Queensland, 1.) 8vo. Brisbane, 1884. ME 1 T

Notes on Queensland Ants. (Proc. Roy. Soc., Queensland, 2.) 8vo. Brisbane, 1886. ME 1 T

On *Peripatus* and its occurrence in Australia. (Proc. Roy. Soc., Queensland, 4.) 8vo. Brisbane, 1887.
ME 1 T

On an *Acarus* associated with a diseased condition in the Banana. (Proc. Roy. Soc., Queensland, 4.) 8vo. Brisbane, 1887. ME 1 T

Braula cœca—a Bee Parasite. (Proc. Roy. Soc., Queensland, 4.) 8vo. Brisbane, 1887. ME 1 T

Judicial Entomology, and on an unrecorded habit of White Ants. (Proc. Roy. Soc., Queensland, 4.) 8vo. Brisbane, 1887. ME 1 T

TSUNASHIRO, W. Mining Industry of Japan, 1867-92. 4tc. Tokyo, 1893. A 12 U 19 †

TUCKER, F. de L. Booth. Life of Catherine Booth, the Mother of the Salvation Army. 2 vols. 8vo. Lond., 1892. C 16 R 21, 22

TUCKER, Dr. G. A. Treatise on Psychology, Insanity, and Medicine. 8vo. Sydney, 1872. MG 2 Q 33

TUCKER, Rev. Horace F. A Tribute to the Memory of General Gordon: a Sermon. 8vo. Melb., 1885.
MG 1 R 69

TUCKWELL, Gertrude M. The State and its Children. 12mo. Lond., 1894. F 5 Q 12

TUER, Andrew W. The Book of Delightful and Strange Designs; being One Hundred Facsimile Illustrations of the Art of the Japanese Stencil-cutter. (English, German, and French.) Obl. 8vo. Lond., 1892.
A 23 E 8

TUFTS COLLEGE, MEDFORD. Catalogue of, 1892, 1893. 8vo. Camb., Mass., 1893. E

TUKE, Dr. D. H. Dictionary of Psychological Medicine. 2 vols. roy. 8vo. Lond., 1892. A 26 V 7, 8

TULK, A. H. Record of the Visit of H.R.H. the Duke of Edinburgh to Australia: illustrated by Engravings and Anecdotes, extracted from the Contemporary Australian Press. 2 vols. fol. Melb., 1868.
MD 2 P 24, 25 ‡

TULLY, W. A. Short Account of the Measurement of the Base Line in connection with the Trigonometrical Survey of Queensland. (Proc. Roy. Soc., Queensland, 2.) 8vo. Brisbane, 1886. ME 1 T

TUPPER, Sir Charles. Canada in relation to the unity of the Empire. [*See* Roy. Col. Inst., Proc., 25.] E

TUPPER, Charles Lewis. Our Indian Protectorate : an Introduction to the Study of the Relations between the British Government and its Indian Feudatories. Roy. 8vo. Lond., 1893. F 12 R 19

TURGOT, A. R. J. Life and Times of; edited by W. W. Stephens. 8vo Lond., 1895. C 21 T 11

TURNBULL, Rev. A. Christianity v. Freethought : Reply to Ada Campbell. 8vo. Adelaide, 1884. MG 1 R 67

TURNBULL, Dr. Laurence. Artificial Anæsthesia. Illustrated. 8vo. Philad., 1890. A 33 P 5

TURNEAURE, F. E. Modern Framed Structures. [*See* Johnson, J. B.] A 36 P 5 ‡

TURNER, Dr. A. J. Australian Micro-Lepidoptera. (Trans. Roy. Soc., S. Australia, 18.) 8vo. Adelaide, 1894. ME 1 S

TURNER, Charles. Australian Stories. [*See* Australian Stories.] MJ 3 R 9

TURNER, Dr. Duncan. Notes on the Treatment of Typhoid Fever. 8vo. Melb., 1883. MA 3 T 21

TURNER, E. F. *Stephania hernandifolia.* [*See* Rennie, Dr. E. H.] ME 1 S

TURNER, Fred. Australian Grasses. Vol. 1. 8vo. Sydney, 1895. MA 1 S 51
Cultivation of the Black or Green Wattle. 3rd ed. Sydney, 1892. MA 1 Q 65
On budding. 8vo. Sydney, 1892. MA 1 Q 62
The Zamia Palm and its Relation to Rickets in Cattle. 8vo. Sydney, 1893. MA 1 T 56
Supposed Poisonous Plant : Darling Pea. [*See* Guthrie, F. B.] MA 1 T 56

TURNER, Dr. Frederick Jackson. The Character and Influence of the Indian Trade in Wisconsin. (Johns Hopkins University Studies, 9.) 8vo. Baltimore, 1891. B 18 S 9

TURNER, Rev. Dr. George. O le tusi Numera ma le tusi Keomoteri : Arithmetic and Geometry in the Samoan Dialect. 12mo. Lond., 1882. MA 3 U 27

TURNER, Rt. Rev. James Francis. Address delivered at Armidale, at the Opening of the First Session of the Second Synod of the Diocese of Grafton and Armidale. 8vo. Sydney, 1876. MG 1 S 40

TURNER, Joseph Mallord Wm. [Plaster Cast of.] [*See* Hutton, L.—Portraits in Plaster.] A 23 V 13

TURNER, Sharon. History of the Anglo-Saxons. 7th ed. 3 vols. 8vo. Lond., 1852. B 24 R 9-11

TURNER, Thomas. Metallurgy of Iron and Steel. 8vo. Lond., 1895. A 24 U 34

TURNER, Sir William. Bones of Cetacea; Human Skeletons; Seals. [*See* Thomson, Sir C. W., and Murray, Dr. J.—Voyage of H.M.S. *Challenger.*] A 6 †

TURNER AND HENDERSON, Messrs. Index Map of New South Wales. 8vo. Sydney, 1894. MD 1 Q 38

TURRI, George G. The Cyanide Process and the Cyanide Patents. 8vo. Melb., 1895. MF 2 S 49

TWEEDDALE, Marquis of. Birds collected in the Phillippine Islands. [*See* Thomson, Sir C. W., and Murray, Dr. J.—Voyage of H.M.S. *Challenger.*] A 6 †

TWEEDIE, Mrs. Alec. A Winter Jaunt to Norway; with Accounts of Nansen, Ibsen, Björnson, Brandes, and many others. 8vo. Lond., 1894. D 18 T 15

TWEEDIE, Maj.-Gen. W. The Arabian Horse, his Country and People. Illustrated. 4to. Edinb., 1894. A 36 T 3 ‡

TWICE ROUND THE BLOCK ; or, a Visit to the Auction Rooms of Sydney in 1877. (Pam.) 8vo. Sydney, 1877. MG 1 Q 53

TWIG. [*See* Follow the Track.] MJ 3 Q 8

TWINING, Thomas. Travels in America 100 years ago. 18mo. New York, 1894. D 15 P 6

TWO BROTHERS. [*See* Tennyson, A. and F.]

TWO LETTERS on Rationalism and Christianity ; by "A Layman." 8vo. Melb., 1873. MG 2 Q 23

TYACKE, Mrs. R. H. How I shot my Bears; or, Two Years' Tent Life in Kullu and Laboul. 8vo. Lond., 1893. D 17 Q 14

TYERMAN, John. Freethought vindicated ; or, Infidel Christianity *versus* Honest Unbelief. 12mo. Sydney, 1880. MG 2 R 47

TYLER, John. Sketch of. [*See* Thompson, R. W.—Recollections of Sixteen Presidents.] C 18 T 21, 22
Sketch of. [*See* Wilson, J. G.—President of the United States.] C 2 V 30

TYLER, Rev. Dr. Moses Coit. History of American Literature, 1607-1765. 2 vols. 8vo. Lond., 1879. J 16 U 16, 17

TYLOR, Dr. Edward Burnett. The Tasmanians as representatives of Palæolithic Man. (Anthropol. Inst., 23.) 8vo. Lond., 1893. E
On the occurrence of ground stone implements of Australian type in Tasmania. (Anthropol. Inst., 24.) 8vo. Lond., 1894. E

TYLOR, J. J. Tomb of Paher at El Kab. [See Naville, E.] B 12 T 5 †

TYNAN, Patrick J. P., "Number One." The Irish National Invincibles and their Times. 8vo. Lond., 1894. B 29 U 14

TYNDALL, Prof. John. Correspondence with. [See Youmans, E. L.] C 16 R 21
Heat, a Mode of Motion. 9th ed. 12mo. Lond., 1892. A 21 R 8
Reminiscences of. [See Skelton, Dr. J.—Table-talk of Shirley.] C 19 V 10
Sketch of. [See Smalley, G. W.—Studies of Men.] C 19 R 20

TYROL. Generalkarte der gefursteten grafschaft Tyrol. Folded 8vo. Innsbruck (n.d.) D 20 U 3

TYRRELL, Prof. Robt. Y. Latin Poetry. 8vo. Lond., 1895. J 12 T 42

TYSON, Dr. Edward. A Philological Essay concerning the Pigmies of the Ancients; edited by Dr. C. A. Windle. 12mo. Lond., 1894. A 18 R 42

U

ULRICH, George H. F. La Géographie, la Géologie &c., de Victoria. [See Selwyn, A. R. C.] MA 2 V 30

UGARTE, Dr. J. Hijiene de la Infancia. 12mo. Santiago, 1887. A 26 R 21

ULLATHORNE, Most Rev. Wm. Bernard. The Autobiography of. Roy. 8vo. Lond., 1891. MC 1 R 50

UMLAUFT, Prof. F. The Alps; translated by Louisa Brough. Illustrated. Fcy. 8vo. Lond., 1889. D 18 V 13

UNDA. [See Dream of the Past.] MH 1 Q 26

UNDERHILL, B. S. Rapid Phonography. 12mo. New York, 1891. K 20 Q 44

UNDERHILL, Dr. Edward Bean. Tragedy of Morant Bay; a Narrative of the Disturbances in Jamaica, 1865. 8vo Lond., 1895 B 16 R 13

UNDERHILL, John. Editor.—Poems of J. Gay. [See Gay, J.] H 10 P 31, 32

UNDERWOOD, Dr. Francis Henry. Builders of American Literature Biographical Sketches of American Authors born previous to 1826. 1st series. 8vo. Lond., 1893. C 18 P 11
The Poet and the Man: Recollections and Appreciations of J. R. Lowell. 12mo. Lond., 1893. C 13 Q 23

UNINHABITABLE HOUSE NEAR SYDNEY, The, and other amusing Stories; by "Darius Ritt." 12mo. Sydney (n.d.) MJ 3 P 2

UNION CLUB, Sydney. Rules. 12mo. Sydney, 1868. MF 3 P 33
Another copy. 12mo. Sydney, 1890. MF 3 P 35
Report for 1875, Rules, and List of Members. 12mo. Sydney, 1875. MF 3 P 34

UNITED SERVICE INSTITUTION OF NEW SOUTH WALES. Journal and Proceedings. Vols. 1–5. 8vo. Sydney, 1890–94. ME 6 R
Lectures: Defence of the north-western Provinces of India; by Major MacCarthy.—Modern Infantry Fire; by Lieut.-Col. Penrose.—The Clothing of the Soldier as suitable to the Climate; by Surgeon-Major Williams.—The Maxim Gun; by Maj.-Gen. Strange.—Organisation and Equipment of Harbour Defences; by Lieut.-Col. F. B. Boddam. 8vo. Sydney, 1880–91. MA 2 V 38

UNITED SERVICE MAGAZINE. New Series, vols. 5–10. Roy. 8vo. Lond., 1892–95. E

UNITED STATES.—General. A new Empire: The Fox Butte Country of Nebraska, the Black Hills Region of South Dakota, Sheridan and Johnson Counties, Wyoming; a description of their resources and attractions. 8vo. Omaha, 1893. D 15 Q 23
Summer Homes on the line of the Lake, Shore, and Michigan Railway. 8vo. Chicago, 1893. D 15 T 5

UNITED STATES.—Government Departments, Reports, and Publications.
ATTORNEY-GENERAL. Report, 1891. 8vo. Washington, 1891. E
BUREAU OF AMERICAN REPUBLICS. Bolivia. 8vo. Washington, 1892. D 15 S 8
Coal and Petroleum in Colombia Commercial Information. 8vo. Washington, 1893. A 24 T 20
Coffee in America. Methods of Production and Facilities for successful Cultivation in Mexico, the Central American States, Brazil and other South American Countries, and the West Indies. 8vo. Washington, 1893. A 18 S 18
Colombia. 8vo. Washington, 1893. D 18 T 10
Commercial Directory of Latin America. 8vo. Washington, 1892. E
Commercial Information concerning the American Republics and Colonies, 1891. 8vo. Washington, 1892. F 14 E 18
Guatemala. 8vo. Washington, 1892. D 18 T 11
Haiti. 8vo. Washington, 1892. D 15 S 10
Hand-book of the American Republics, 1893. 8vo. Washington, 1893. D 15 S 11
How the Latin American Markets may be reached by the Manufacturers of the United States. 8vo. Washington (n.d.) F 14 K 14
Minerals and Resources of North-eastern Nicaragua, Nitrate Deposits in Colombia, Manganese Mines in Colombia, Education in Uruguay. 2. Coffee Industry in Haiti, Guatemala, and Mexico, Industrial Progress in Guatemala, Railroad Development. 3. Commercial Information. 8vo. Washington, 1893. A 24 T 20
Uruguay. 8vo. Washington, 1892. D 15 S 9
Venezuela. 8vo. Washington 1892. D 18 T 9

UNITED STATES— *contd*.
BUREAU OF EDUCATION. Abnormal Man: being Essays on Education and Crime and related subjects; with digests of Literature and a Bibliography, by A. Macdonald. 8vo. Wash., 1893. F 14 T 15
Catalog of "A. L. A." Library 5,000 volumes for a popular Library, selected by the American Library Association and shown at the World's Columbian Exposition. 8vo. Washington, 1893. K 7 R 00
Public Libraries in: their History, Condition, and Management. Special Report. Part 1. Illustrated. Roy. 8vo. Washington, 1876. J 4 S 22
Reports of the Commissioner of Education, 1889-92. 4 vols. 8vo. Washington, 1893. E
Report on Legal Education. 8vo. Washington, 1893. G 18 R 14
Statistics of Public Libraries in U. States and Canada. [*See* Flint, W.] J 5 T 28
BUREAU OF EQUIPMENT. The Pacific Coasters' Nautical Almanac for 1895. Roy. 8vo. Washington, 1894. E
BUREAU OF ETHNOLOGY. 7th-12th Annual Reports, 1885-91. 5 vols. imp. 8vo. Washington, 1891-94. E
BUREAU OF LABOR. 7th Annual Report, 1891. Cost of Production: the Textiles and Glass. 2 vols. 8vo. Washington, 1892. E
8th Annual Report, 1892. Industrial Education. 8vo. Washington, 1893. E
9th Annual Report, 1893. Building and Loan Associations. 8vo. Washington, 1894. E
2nd Special Report. Labour Laws of various States, Territories, and the District of Columbia. 8vo. Washington, 1892. E
3rd Special Report. Analysis and Index to all Reports issued by Bureaus of Labor Statistics in the United States prior to November 1, 1892. 8vo. Washington, 1893. E
4th Special Report. The Phosphate Industry of the United States. 8vo. Washington, 1893. E
5th Special Report. The Gothenburg System of Liquor Traffic. 8vo. Washington, 1893. E
BUREAU OF NAVIGATION—NAVY DEPARTMENT. Flags of Maritime Nations from the most authentic sources. 5th ed. 4to. Wash., 1882. K 10 V 28
BUREAU OF NAVIGATION—TREASURY DEPARTMENT. List of Merchant Vessels of the United States, 1894. Sm. 4to. Wash., 1894. E
BUREAU OF ORDNANCE. Description of Modern Gun Mounts in the United States Navy. 8vo. Wash., 1894. A 28 V 28
BUREAU OF THE MINT. Report of the Director of the Mint upon the production of Precious Metals during 1892. 8vo. Washington, 1893. E
BUREAU OF STATISTICS. Papers relating to the Foreign Relations of the United States. 8vo. Wash., 1894. E

UNITED STATES—*contd*.
CENSUS OFFICE. Compendium of the eleventh Census, 1890. 2 vols. imp. 8vo. Wash., 1892-94. E
Report of Wealth, Debt, and Taxation at the Census, 1890. Part 1. Public Debt. 4to. Wash., 1892. F 15 P 12 †
CIVIL SERVICE COMMISSION. Report for 1890-91. 8vo. Wash., 1891. E
COAST AND GEODETIC SURVEY. Reports, 1891, 1892. 8vo. Wash., 1892-94. E
Catalogue of Charts and other Publications, 1894. 4to. Wash., 1894. K 15 S 7 †
COMMISSION ON FISH AND FISHERIES. Reports, 1871-91. 17 vols. 8vo. Wash., 1873-93. E
Bulletins, vols. 1-13, 1881-93. 7 vols. 8vo. and 6 vols. imp. 8vo. Wash., 1882-94. E
COMMISSIONER OF RAILROADS. Report, 1892-93. (Report of Secretary of the Interior, 1892-93.) 2 vols. 8vo. Wash., 1893. E
COMPTROLLER OF THE CURRENCY. Reports, 1891-93. 3 vols. 8vo. Washington, 1891-93. E
CONGRÈS GÉOLOGIQUE INTERNATIONAL. Compte Rendu, 1891. Imp. 8vo. Wash., 1893. A 15 Q 4 †
CONSULAR REPORTS. Nos. 6, 7, 9, 12-19, 21, 22, 24-28, 32, 33, 41½, 42, 43, 47, 50, 53½, 57, 58. 28 vols. 8vo. Wash., 1881-85. E
Reports from the Consuls of the United States. Vols. 39-46. 8vo. Washington, 1892-94. E
Index to vols. 32-41. 8vo. Wash., 1894. E
Special Reports. Vols. 5, 7-11. 8vo. Washington, 1891-94.
5. Canals and Irrigation in Foreign Countries.
7. The Slave Trade in Foreign Countries—Tariffs of Foreign Countries.
8. Fire and Building Regulations in Foreign Countries.
9. Australasian Sheep and Wool—Vagrancy and Public Charities in Foreign Countries.
10. Lead and Zinc Mining and Markets for American Flour.
11. American Lumber in Foreign Markets.
DEPARTMENT OF AGRICULTURE. Album of Agricultural Statistics of the United States. 4to. Wash., 1891. A 15 R 15 †
Annual Convention of the Association of American Colleges and Experiment Stations, 1893. 8vo. Wash., 1894. E
Bureau of Animal Industry. Special Report on Sheep. [*See* Salmon, Dr. D. E.] A 30 U 7
Catalogue of the Exhibit of Economic Entomology at Chicago, 1893. 8vo. Wash., 1893. A 30 U 20
Entomological Commission, First Annual Report. The Rocky Mountain Locust. With Maps and Illustrations. Roy. 8vo. Washington, 1878. E
Entomological Commission, Second Report. Rocky Mountain Locust and the Western Cricket, and treating of the best means of subduing the Locust in its permanent breeding grounds in pursuance of appropriations made by Congress. With Maps and Illustrations. Roy. 8vo. Washington, 1880. E

UNITED STATES—*contd.*
DEPARTMENT OF AGRICULTURE—*contd.*
Entomological Commission, Third Report. Rocky Mountain Locust, Western Cricket, Army Worm, Canker Worms, and the Hessian Fly; with Descriptions of Larvæ of Injurious Forest Insects, Embryological Development of the Locust and other Insects, and on the systematic position of the Orthoptern in relation to other orders of Insects. With Maps and Illustrations. Roy. 8vo. Washington, 1883. E

Entomological Commission, Fourth Report. The Cotton Worm; with Chapters on the Boll Worm; by Dr. C. V. Riley. With Maps and Illustrations. Roy. 8vo. Washington, 1885. E

Experiment Station Record, vols. 3, 4, 1891–93. 2 vols. Roy. 8vo. Wash., 1892–93. E

Forestry Division. Bulletin Nos. 6 and 8. Timber Physics. Parts 1 and 2. Progress Report. Results of Investigations on Long-leaf Pine (*Pinus palustris*); under the Direction of B. E. Fernow. 4to. Wash., 1893. E

Forestry Division, Bulletin 7: Forest Influences. 8vo. 8vo. Wash., 1893. A 10 T 17

Hand-book of Experiment Station Work: Digest of the Publications of the Agricultural Experiment Stations in the United States. 8vo. Wash., 1893. A 18 V 30

Lists of Agricultural Experiment Stations and Agricultural Schools and Colleges in the United States. 8vo. Wash., 1894. G 18 S 0

Proceedings of the National Road Conference, 1894. 8vo. Wash., 1894. A 20 U 5

Proceedings of the Virginia Good Roads Convention, 1894. 8vo. Wash., 1895. A 22 V 11

Reports of the Chief of the Division of Forestry, 1890–92; by B. E. Fernow. 3 vols. 8vo. Wash., 1891–93. E

Reports of Observations and Experiments in the Practical Work of the Division of Entomological. 8vo. Wash., 1892. A 30 U 21

Report of the Secretary of Agriculture, 1892, 1893. 2 vols. 8vo. Wash., 1893–94. E

Report on the Forest Conditions of the Rocky Mountains. 2nd ed. 8vo. Wash., 1880. A 30 R 15

The What and Why of Agricultural Experiment Stations. 8vo. Wash., 1889. A 30 R 10

The World's Markets for American Products: Great Britain and Ireland. 8vo. Wash., 1895. F 1 T 21

DEPARTMENT OF THE INTERIOR. Register of, containing list of persons employed in the Department appointed by the President or by the Secretary of the Interior. 8vo. Wash., 1894. E

DEPARTMENT OF THE NAVY. Instructions for observing the Transit of Venus, December, 1874. 4to. Wash., 1874. A 30 Q 17 ‡

Notes on the year's naval progress, 1894. 8vo. Wash., 1894. A 30 U 20

Register of the Commissioned and Warrant Officers of the Navy of the United States and of the Marine Corps to 1895. 8vo. Wash., 1895. E

UNITED STATES—*contd.*
DEPARTMENT OF THE POST OFFICE. Report of the Postmaster-General for 1891. 8vo. Wash., 1891. E

DEPARTMENT OF THE TREASURY. Report of the Commissioner of Internal Revenue, 1891. 8vo. Wash., 1891. E

Report of the Secretary of the Treasury on the state of the Finances, 1890–91. 2 vols. 8vo. Wash., 1891–92. E

Internal Revenue Laws in force, August, 1894. 8vo. Wash. 1894. F 11 U 22

DEPARTMENT OF WAR. Military Information Division. Notes and Statistics of Organization, Armament, and Military Progress in American and European Armies. 4to. Wash., 1894. A 30 V 9

Official Army Register for 1893. 8vo. Wash., 1894. E

Report of the Secretary for War. 3 vols. 8vo. Wash., 1892. E

GENERAL LAND OFFICE. Decisions of the Department of the Interior and General Land Office in Cases relating to the Public Lands, 1894. 8vo. Wash., 1895. E

Report of the Commissioner, 1893–93. (Report of Secretary of the Interior, 1892–93.) 2 vols. 8vo. Wash., 1893. E

GEOLOGICAL SURVEY. Bulletins 66–86. 5 vols. 8vo. Wash., 1892. E

Mineral Resources of the United States, 1893. 8vo. Wash., 1894. E

Monographs. Vols. 1, 2, 6, 8–18, 20, 23. 17 vols. 4to. Wellington, 1880–94. E

1. Lake Bonneville; by G. K. Gilbert.
2. Tertiary History of the Grand Cañon District; by C. E. Dutton.
6. Older Mesozoic Flora of Virginia; by W. M. Fontaine.
8. Palæontology of Eureka District, U.S.; by C. D. Walcott.
9. Brachiopoda and Lamellibranchiata of the Raritan Clays and Greensand Marls of New Jersey; by R. P. Whitfield.
10. Dinocerata: a Monograph of an extinct order of Gigantic Mammals; by O. C. Marsh.
11. Geological History of Lake Lahontan, Nevada; by I. C. Russell.
12. Geology and Mining Industry of Leadville, Colorado; with Atlas; by S. F. Emmons.
13. Geology of Quicksilver Deposits of the Pacific Slope; by G. F. Becker.
14. Fossil Fishes and Fossil Plants of the Triassic Rocks of New Jersey and the Connecticut Valley; by J. S. Newberry.
15. The Potomac or Younger Mesozoic Flora; by W. M. Fontaine.
16. The Palæozoic Fishes of N. America; by J. S. Newberry.
17. The Flora of the Dakota Group; by L. Lesquereux.
18. Gasteropoda and Cephalopoda of the Raritan Clays and Greensand Marls of New Jersey; by R. P. Whitfield.
20. Geology of the Eureka District, Nevada; by A. Hague.
23. Geology of the Green Mountains in Massachusetts.

Report of the United States Geological Survey to the Secretary of the Interior, 1889–90. Part 1. Geology. Part 2 Irrigation. 2 vols. imp. 8vo. Washington, 1893. E

Report of the Director, 1891–92. (Report of the Secretary of the Interior, 1892.) 3 vols. imp. 8vo. Wash., 1892. E

UNITED STATES—*contd.*
GOVERNMENT HOSPITAL FOR THE INSANE. Report of the Board, 1892–93. (Report of Secretary of the Interior, 1892–93.) 2 vols. 8vo. Wash., 1893. E

HYDROGRAPHIC OFFICE. Contributions to Terrestrial Magnetism: the Variation of the Compass. Roy. 8vo. Wash., 1894. A 19 V 21

Results of the survey for the purpose of determining the practicability of laying a telegraphic cable between the United States and the Hawaiian Islands. 4to. Wash., 1892. A 15 Q 3 †

Sailing Directions for Lake Superior, St. Mary's River, and Straits of Mackinac. 8vo. Wash., 1894. A 19 V 25

LIFE-SAVING SERVICE. Report of operations, 1893. 8vo. Wash., 1894. E

LIGHTHOUSE BOARD. Report, 1893–94. 8vo. Washington, 1894. A 19 V 27

MINE INSPECTOR OF THE INDIAN TERRITORY, Report, 1894. 8vo. Wash., 1894. E

NATIONAL MUSEUM. Report of the Assistant Director, 1881. 8vo. Wash., 1883. E

Reports for 1890–92. 3 vols. 8vo. Washington, 1891–93. E

Report of the Building Commission and the Architects. 8vo. Wash., 1881. E

OFFICE OF INDIAN AFFAIRS. Report of the Commissioner, 1893. (Report of Secretary of the Interior, 1892–93.) 2 vols. 8vo. Wash., 1893. E

Report of the Secretary of the Interior on Indian Affairs. Vol. 2. 8vo. Wash., 1890. E

PATENTS. Alphabetical Lists of Patentees and Inventions, April–Sept., 1894. 2 vols. imp. 8vo. Wash., 1894. E

Catalogue of the Library of the United States Patent Office. Fol. Wash., 1878. K 30 R 8 ‡

Catalogue of additions to the Library of the United States Patent Office, to May, 1883. Fol. Wash., 1883. K 30 R 9 ‡

Celebration of the Beginning of the Second Century of the American Patent System. 8vo. Washington, 1891. F 6 V 27

Decisions, 1893. 8vo. Wash., 1894. F 7 R 25

Official Gazette. Vols. 58–69. Imp. 8vo. Washington, 1892–94. E

Patent Laws, revised to December, 1889. 8vo. (n.p.n.d.) F 8 T 22

Reports of the Commissioner of Patents, 1892–93. 2 vols. imp. 8vo. Wash., 1893. E

Rules and Practice in the United States Patent Office, revised to April, 1892. (n.p.n.d.) F 8 T 22

Statutes concerning the Protection and Registration of Trademarks. 8vo. (n.p.) 1892. F 8 T 22

PENSION OFFICE. Laws of the United States governing the granting of Army and Navy Pensions. 8vo. Wash., 1894. F 6 R 26

Reports of the Commissioner, 1883, 1892–93. (Report of Secretary of the Interior, 1892–93.) 3 vols. 8vo. Wash., 1883, 1893. E

UNITED STATES—*contd.*
SURGEON-GENERAL'S OFFICE. Alphabetical List of Abbreviations of Titles of Medical Periodicals employed in the Index catalogue of the Library of the Surgeon-General's Office, United States Army, from vol. 1–16. Imp. 8vo. Wash., 1895. K 16 Q 2 †

Index-Catalogue of the Library of. Vols. 13–15. Imp. 8vo. Washington, 1892–94. K 16 P 13–15 †

UPTON, Prof. Chas. B. Lectures on the Bases of Religious Belief. (Hibbert Lectures, 1893.) 8vo. Lond., 1894. G 19 Q 1

URIARTE, Carlos M. Derecho Comercial del Concordato. 8vo. Montevideo, 1894. F 9 R 32

URQUHART, F. C. Camp Canzonettes; being Rhymes of the Bush and other things. 12mo. Brisb., 1891. MH 1 U 87

URQUHART, John W. Electric Ship-lighting. 8vo. Lond., 1892. A 21 Q 41

URQUHART, Sir Thos. Works of F. Rabelais. [*See* Rabelais, F.] J 11 U 5, 6

URUGUAY. Anuario Demográfico de la República Oriental del Uruguay, año 3, 1892. Imp. 8vo. Montevideo, 1893. E

Anuario Estadístico de la República Oriental del Uruguay, 1891–92. 2 vols. imp. 8vo. Montevideo, 1892–93. E

Código Civil de la República Oriental del Uruguay. Imp. 8vo. Montevideo, 1893. F 11 V 5

Estadística Agrícola de la República O. del Uruguay, 1892–93. 2 vols. imp. 8vo. Montevideo, 1893. E

Estadística Escolar de la República Oriental del Uruguay, 1893. Sm. 4to. Montevideo, 1894. G 18 S 17

Informe, 1892; presentado á los Señor Inspector Nacional por el Inspector de Instruccion Primaria de Artigas, Canelones, Cerro-Largo, Colonia, Durazno, Florida, Flores, Maldonado, Minas, Paysandú, Rio Negro, Rivera, Rocha, Salto, San Jose, Soriano, Tacuarembo, Trienta y Tres. 17 parts (in 1) imp. 8vo. Montevideo, 1893. E

Leyes, Decretos, y Reglamentos vigentes, con arreglo á la edición oficial del Código Civil. 8vo. Montevideo, 1893. F 7 V 14

Memoria Correspondiente á los años 1890 y 1891, por el Inspector Nacional de I. Primaria. Imp. 8vo. Montevideo, 1892. E

Memoria del Ministerio de Hacienda, 1892–93. Imp. 8vo. Montevideo, 1894. E

Memoria por la Junta de Sanidad de Montevideo, 1893. Imp. 8vo. Montevideo, 1894. E

Memoria por el Ministro de Fomento, comprende el ejercicio de 1891–92. Imp. 8vo. Montevideo, 1892. E

Memoria por el Ministro de Gobierno, 1893. Imp. 8vo. Montevideo, 1894. E

URUGUAY—*contd.*
The Oriental Republic of Uruguay; Geography, Rural Industries, &c. 8vo. Montevideo, 1893. D 15 V 18

Revista del Archivo General Administrativo ó Collección de Documentos para serva al estudio de la Historia de la República Oriental del Uruguay. 4 vols. 8vo. Montevideo, 1885-91. B 16 V 13-16

USHER, Dr. J. E. Alcoholism and its Treatment. 12mo. Lond., 1892. A 26 Q 25

Personal Reminiscences of the Great Eruption of Krakatoa, Java. (Roy. Geog. Soc. Australasia, Vic. Branch, G.) 8vo. Melb., 1888. ME 20

USSHER, Adm. Sir Thos. Napoleon's Last Voyages. [*See* Napoleon Bonaparte.] C 22 R 3

UTAH—AGRICULTURAL COLLEGE. Report of Experiment Station, 1893. 8vo. Salt Lake City, 1894. E

UZANNE, Octave. The Book-hunter in Paris: Studies among the Bookstalls and the Quays. 8vo. Lond., 1893. D 14 V 4

The Mirror of the World. Imp. 8vo. Lond., 1890. J 2 U 12

V

VACCINATION. Some Leading Arguments against Compulsory Vaccination. 8vo. Lond., 1887. A 26 S 22

VAGABOND, The. [*See* Thomas, Julian.]

VAGGIOLI, Rev. Felice. Storia della Nuova Zelanda. Vol. 1. 8vo. Parma, 1891. MD 8 Q 12

VALENZUELA, Luis A. Manual Juridico del Matrimonio, con arreglo a las nuevas leyes. 12mo. Santiago, 1884. F 12 S 17

VALENZUELA, R. del R. La Batalla de Huamachuco. 12mo. Santiago, 1885. B 16 P 23

VALICOURT, E. de. Nerveau Manuel Complet du Tourneur. Imp. 8vo. Paris, 1872. A 11 V 24

VALLE, Pietro della. Travels in India. [*See* Hakluyt Soc. 84, 85.] E

VALLÉE, Léon. Essai d'une Bibliographie de la Nouvelle-Calédonie et Dépendances. 12mo. Paris, 1883. MK 2 Q 3

VALPY, Rev. Edward. The New Testament [in Greek]. [*See* Bibles and Testaments.] G 3 R 5-7

VAMBERY, Prof. Arminius. The Relations of Austria and Hungary. [*See* Subjects of the Day, 3.] F 7 U 28

VANBRUGH, Sir John. Plays written by. 2 vols. 12mo. Lond., 1776. H 1 U 2, 3

The Confederacy: a Comedy. [*See* London Stage, 3.] H 2 S 35

The Provoked Wife: a Comedy. [*See* London Stage, 5.] H 2 S 35

——— and CIBBER, Colley. The Provoked Husband; or, a Journey to London: a Comedy. [*See* London Stage, 2.] H 2 S 34

VAN BUREN, Martin. Sketch of. [*See* Wilson, J. G.—Presidents of the United States.] C 2 V 30

Sketch of. [*See* Thompson, R. W.—Recollections of Sixteen Presidents.] C 18 T 21, 22

VANCOUVER, Capt. George. Charts showing the S.W. Coast of New Holland, the Coast of N.W. America, and the Sandwich Islands; with the tracks of H.M. Sloop *Discovery* and Armed Tender *Chatham*, 1791-94. Fol. Lond., 1793. MD 1 P 1 ‡

VANCOUVER ISLAND. [Information] relating to. 4tc. Winnipeg, 1893. D 12 U 5 †

VANDAM, Albert D. French Men and French Manners; with an Introduction: Paris and its Inhabitants. 8vo. Lond., 1895. B 9 P 18

My Paris Note-book. 8vo. Lond., 1894. B 26 T 27

Notes, &c., to Sixty Years of Recollections. [*See* Legouvé, E.] C 16 R 13, 14

VANDENHOFF, George. Leaves from an Actor's Notebook. 12mo. Lond., 1860. C 11 P 31

VANDERBILT, Cornelius. Sketch of. [*See* Stoddard, W. O.—Men of Business.] C 16 R 19

VAN DE VELDE, Clement. The Sugar-beet Industry. 8vo. Melb., 1895. MA 3 V 30

The Sugar-beet Industry. 8vo. Sydney, 1895. MA 3 R 57

VAN DE VELDE, Mme. M. S. French Fiction of To-day. 2 vols. 8vo. Lond., 1891. J 6 R, 2

VAN HEURCK, Prof. Henri. The Microscope: its Construction and Management. Illustrated. Imp. 8vo. Lond., 1893. A 12 S 6 †

VANINI, Julius Cæsar. Sketch of. [*See* Owen, Rev. J.—Skeptics of the Italian Renaissance.] G 2 S 33

VAN LIEW, Dr. C. C. Physiological Psychology. [*See* Z chen, Dr. T.] G 2 U 6

VANN, J. Squatting Directory of N.S.W. [*See* Fussell, J C.] ME

VAN NOSTRAND'S EOLECTIC ENGINEERING MAGAZINE. Vols. 1-35. Roy. 8vo. New York, 1869-86. E

VAN OSS, S. F. Stock Exchange Values: a Decade of Finance, 1885-95. 8vo. Lond., 1895.　F 11 V 13

VANSITTART, Mrs. Henrietta. History of the Lowe-Vansittart Propeller. 8vo. Lond., 1882.　A 25 S 6

VARIGNY, Dr. Henry de. Experimental Evolution. (Nature Series.) 8vo. Lond., 1892.　A 28 Q 32

VARLEY, Henry. The Impeachment of Gambling. 8vo. Melb., 1890.　MF 4 R 2

VARLEY, John. [Life of]; by A. T. Story. 8vo. Lond., 1894.　C 21 R 17

VASON, George. An Authentic Narrative of Four Year's Residence at Tongataboo. 8vo. Lond., 1810.　MD 5 S 53

VASSAR COLLEGE, POUGHKEEPSIE, N.Y. Annual Catalogue of the Officers and Students, 1892, 1893. 8vo. Poughkeepsie, 1892.　E

VAUGHAN, I. Strangeways' Veterinary Anatomy. [See Strangeways, T.]　A 30 R 25

VAUGHAN, Joseph. Hand and Eye Training. [See Ricks, G.]　G 18 S 12-15

VAUGHAN, Robt. Alfred. Hours with the Mystics: a Contribution to the History of Religious Opinions. 2 vols. 12mo. Lond., 1856.　G 19 P 38, 39

VAUGHAN, Most Rev. Roger Wm. Bede. Archbishop Vaughan's Attack on the Protestant Church. [See Beg, Rev. Dr. W.]　MG 2 S 2

Higher Education. Inaugural Address at St. John's College, within the University of Sydney. 8vo. Sydney, 1875.　MF 1 R 27

Hidden Springs; or, Perils of the Future, and how to meet them. (Pam.) 8vo. Sydney, 1876.　MG 1 Q 53

Dr. Vaughan Answered. [See Ewing, Rev. T. C.]　MG 1 S 15

VAUX, Rev. Jas. Edward. Church Folk-lore: a Record of some Post-Reformation Usages in the English Church, now mostly obsolete. 8vo. Lond., 1894.　G 4 S 36

VEGA, Georg. Thesaurus Logarithmorum completus. Fol. Lipsiæ, 1794.　A 39 R 11 ‡

VEITCH, Prof. John. Dualism and Monism, and other Essays. 12mo. Edinb., 1895.　F 7 V 39

Hamilton, Philosopher. 12mo. Edinb., 1882.　G 9 V 5

VELASCO, Fanor. Nociones de Filosofia Natural. 12mo. Santiago, 1887.　A 20 R 29

VELAZQUEZ, Madame. Life of. [See Dowie, M. M.—Woman Adventurers.]　C 15 S 24

VENABLES, H. Outline of the Geography of Victoria. 5th edition. 12mo. Melb., 1871.　MD 1 P 44

Syallabus of Parsing and Analysis, prescribed by the University of Melbourne for the Pass Examination at Matriculation. 8vo. Melb., 1887.　MK 1 R 34

VERA, R. Prontuario de Enjuiciamiento Criminal. Roy. 8vo. Santiago, 1884.　F 9 T 20

VERAX. [See Gould, Nat.]

VERDI, Giuseppe. Sketch of. [See Streatfeild, R. A.—Masters of Italian Music.]　C 22 P 13

VERITAS. [See Electors beware.]　MF 4 Q 22

VERMONT STATE AGRICULTURAL EXPERIMENT STATION. Reports, 1887, 1889, 1891. 3 vols. 8vo. Rutland, 1888-92.　E

VERNON, Hon. Wm. Warren. Readings on the Inferno of Dante, chiefly based on the Commentary of Benvenuto da Imola. 2 vols. 8vo. Lond., 1894.　H 9 Q 5, 6

VERRALL, Dr. Arthur Woollgar. Euripides, the Rationalist: a Study in the History of Art and Religion. 8vo. Camb., 1895.　G 14 Q 28

VESPUCCI, Amerigo. Americus Vespuccius: a Critical and Documentary Review of two recent English books concerning that Navigator; by H. Harrisse. 8vo. Lond., 1895.　C 13 V 14

The first Four Voyages of. Reprinted in Facsimile, and Translated. Sm. 4to. Lond., 1893.　D 15 S 13

Letters of. (Hakluyt Soc. Pubs.) 8vo. Lond., 1894.　E

[See Ramusio, G. B.—Navigationi et Viaggi.]　D 36 T 5-7 ‡

VETERINARIAN, The. Vols. 65, 66. 8vo. Lond., 1892-93.　E

VETH, P. J. Borneo's Wester-Afdeeling. 2 vols. roy. 8vo. Zaltbommel, 1854-56.　D 19 V 24, 25

VEYRIES, A. Les Figures Criophores dans l'art Grec, l'art Greco-Romain et l'art Chrétien. 8vo. Paris, 1884.　B 35 R 30

VIALLETON, L. Bilharzia Hæmatobia. [See Lortet, L.]　A 83 U 23

VIBART, Col. Henry M. Addiscombe, its Heroes and Men of Note; introduction by Lord Roberts. With Illustrations and Plans. Sm. 4to. Lond. 1894.　B 21 U 15

VICKERMAN, Chas. Woollen Spinning: a Text-book for Students in Technical Schools and Colleges, and for skilful Practical Men in Woollen Mills. 12mo. Lond., 1894.　A 25 Q 17

VICO, G.; by R. Flint. (Philosophical Classics.) 12mo. Edinb., 1884. G 0 V 0

VICKERS, Anna. Voyage en Australie et en Nouvelle-Zélande. Roy. 8vo. Paris. 1893. MD 7 U 10

VICTIM OF CIRCUMSTANTIAL EVIDENCE: a Sensational Story; by "An Australian Colonist." 8vo. Sydney, 1893. MJ 1 R 43

VICTOR EMMANUEL, King of Italy. Interview with. [See Kingston, W. Beatty.—Men, Cities, and Events.] C 22 R 4

Sketch of. [See Elliot, Frances—Roman Gossip.] C 21 Q 10

VICTORIA, Her Majesty the Queen. Her Life and Jubilee; by T. Archer. 4 vols. sm. 4to. Lond., 1888. C 9 V 1-4

Victoria, Queen and Empress; by J. C. Jeaffreson. 2 vols. 8vo. Lond., 1893. C 15 R 12, 13

Life of H.M. Queen Victoria; by Millicent G. Fawcett. 8vo. Lond., 1895. C 17 P 31

VICTORIA—*General*.

The Future of Victoria; by "Acorn." 8vo. Melb., (n.d.) MF 2 P 47

Opinions of the Municipalities of Victoria on the proposed introduction of a Tires Act. 8vo. Geelong, 1876. MF 2 T 73

Photographs of Scenery, Buildings, &c. Fol. (n.p.) 1895. MA 45 ‡

The Settlement of the Country. An Inquiry: Is Public Immigration sound economy and equitable legislation? by "Conservative." 8vo. Melb., 1857. MF 3 Q 83

Victoria Illustrated. Second Series. Obl. 8vo. Melb., 1862. MD 4 P 0 †

Victoria: its History, Resources, and Prospects: an Exhibition Memorial, 1888-89. 12mo. Melb., 1888. MA 1 P 69

VICTORIA — *Government Departments, Reports, and Publications*.

ABORIGINES. Report of the Board for the Protection of the Aborigines, 1894. Sm. fol. Melb., 1894. ME

Report of the Select Committee on the Aborigines. Sm. fol. Melb., 1860. MA 2 P 10 †

AGRICULTURE. Bulletins, 1888. 2 vols. 8vo. Melb., 1888. MA 3 T 59, 60

Bulletin No. 12. Report of the Department of Agriculture for the year 1889-90. 8vo. Melb., 1891. ME 6 S

Course of Lectures delivered by officers of the Department of Agriculture, 1891, in the Working-men's College, Melbourne. 8vo. Melb., 1892. MA 3 T 0

Fruit Trees, &c., recommended for Cultivation as suitable for Marketing, Canning, Drying, Exporting, &c. 8vo. Melb., 1894. MA 3 V 17

VICTORIA—*contd.*

AGRICULTURE—*contd.*

Guides to Growers. Nos. 8-14. 8vo. Melb. (n.d.) MA 3 T 0
  8. Fruit Preserving.
  9. Crystallized or Glaced Fruits
  10. Cultivation of Sugar Beet.
  11. Process of Drying Fruits.
  12. List of Manures, values and prices.
  13. Castor Oil Plant
  14. Cultivation of Flax and its after treatment.

Guides to Growers. Nos. 15-22. 8vo. Melb., 1894-95. MA 3 V 3
  15. Spraying for Fungus Diseases.
  16. Canary Seed : its Cultivation.
  17. Fruit Exportation.
  18. Onion Disease.
  19. Perfume Industry.
  20. Broom Corn.
  21. Spraying for Fungus Diseases.
  22. Muscatel Industry.

Illustrated Description of Thistles, &c., included within the provisions of the Thistle Act of 1890. 8vo. Melb., 1893. MA 3 V 19

List of Fruit Trees, &c., grown at the Royal Horticultural Gardens, Richmond Park, Burnley, 1893. 8vo. Melb., 1893. MA 1 U 56

Monthly Lectures delivered at School of Horticulture by various specialists, during 1892-93. 8vo. Melb., 1893. MA 1 U 56

Poultry-breeding and Management for the English Markets. 8vo. Melb., 1894. MA 3 V 14

Proceedings of Conference of Horticultural Societies and Fruit-growers' Associations. 8vo. Melb., 1894. MA 1 U 56

Proceedings of Conference of Representatives of Fruit-growers' Associations. 8vo. Melb., 1895. MA 3 V 16

Proceedings of Conference of Vine-growers' Associations. 8vo. Melb., 1854. MA 3 V 18

Rust in Wheat: Minutes of Proceedings of Conference [held in Melbourne], March, 1890. 8vo. Melb., 1890. MA 7 Q 32 †

School of Horticulture, Royal Horticultural Gardens, Richmond. 8vo. Melb. (n.d.) MA 1 U 56

Shipping Regulations, 1894-95. 8vo. Melb., 1894. MF 4 P 25

Third Annual Report of the Secretary for Agriculture, 1875. 8vo. Melb. 1875. ME 1 Q

BOARD OF HEALTH. Reports, 1862-64. Sm. fol. Melb., 1864-65. MA 3 Q 48 †

Report, 1890-91. Sm. fol. Melb., 1891. ME

CHARITIES. Reports of Charitable Institutions, 1890, 1892-93. 2 vols. sm. fol. Melb., 1890-93. ME

CIVIL SERVICE. [See PUBLIC SERVICE.]

COAL-FIELDS. Royal Commission on Coal: Final Report. Sm. fol. Melb., 1891. MA 12 P 25 †

CONSTITUTION. Debate in the Legislative Council of the Colony on the second reading of the New Constitution Bill. 8vo. Melb., 1854. MF 2 T 72

VICTORIA—*contd.*

COUNCIL OF AGRICULTURAL EDUCATION. Prospectus and Regulations of the Agricultural Colleges, with Syllabus of Instruction. 8vo. Melb., 1894. MG 2 S 7

Reports, 1884–89. 2 vols. 8vo. Melb., 1887-89. ME 6 S

COURTS OF VICE-ADMIRALTY. Rules and Regulations to be observed in the Courts of Vice-Admiralty abroad; also an Appendix containing Forms of Actions, Pleadings, Instruments, Decrees, and other incidents in the progress of a cause; together with a Table of Fees to be taken in the Vice-Admiralty Courts of Victoria and New South Wales. 8vo. Melb., 1850.
MF 3 R 68

DEFENCE. Council of Defence, 1890. Sm. fol. Melb., 1890. ME

Service of Ordnance. 8vo. Melb., 1866. MA 2 P 50

DUFFY GOVERNMENT. Papers connected with the resignation of the Duffy Government. Sm. fol. Melb., 1872.
MF 4 U 22

EDUCATION. [*See* PUBLIC INSTRUCTION.]

EXHIBITIONS. Victorian Exhibition, 1861. Report on Class 3: Indigenous Vegetable Substances. 8vo. Melb., 1862. MA 2 V 52

EXPLOSIVES. Report of the Inspector of Explosives, 1893. Sm. fol. Melb., 1894. ME

FISCAL SYSTEM BOARD. Evidence taken by Board appointed to inquire into the effect of the Fiscal System. Sm. fol. Melb., 1894. ME

Reports of the Board appointed to inquire into the Fiscal System of Victoria upon Industry and Production, upon the Employment of the People, upon the Condition and Extension of Agriculture, Mining, and other Producing Interests, and upon Exports and Imports. Sm. fol. Melb., 1894-95. MF 9 P 2 †

FINANCE. Appropriation Bill, 1893. Sm. 4to. Melb., 1893. MF 4 U 21

Estimates, 1892, 1894, 1895. 3 vols. sm. fol. Melb., 1891-94. ME

The Treasurer's Statement of the Receipts and Expenditure, 1893-94. 2 vols. sm. fol. Melb., 1893-94. ME

FISHING INDUSTRY. Final Report upon the Fishing Industry of Victoria. Sm. fol. Melb., 1892.
MA 10 P 52 †

FRIENDLY SOCIETIES. Reports, 1888-92. 3 vols. sm. fol. Melb., 1890-94. ME

Friendly Societies Act, 1877. Regulations. 12mo. Melb., 1878. MF 1 P 76

GEOLOGICAL SURVEY OF. Progress Reports. Nos. 1 and 2, by R. Brough Smyth; and No. 5. 3 vols. imp. 8vo. Melb., 1877-78. ME 7 R

Report of Progress, Nos. 6 and 7. 2 vols. 8vo. Melb., 1880-84. MA 2 R 14, 14 *

Progress Report, 8. Sm. fol. Melb., 1894.
MA 9 U 26 †

VICTORIA—*contd.*

GOLD-FIELDS. Acts of Parliament, Bye-laws, and Orders in Council relating to the Gold-fields. 8vo. Melb., 1862. MF 3 R 67

Acts, Orders in Council, and Notices relating to the Gold-fields. Roy. 8vo. Melb., 1860. MF 3 R 46

Acts, Orders-in-Council, Notices, and Mining Board Bye-laws relating to the Gold-fields. Sm. 4to. Melb., 1868. MF 4 U 27

Claims of H. Frencham as Discoverer of the Bendigo Gold-fields. Sm. fol. Melb., 1890. MA 9 Q 16 †

Gold-fields of Victoria, 1884. 2 vols. sm. fol. Melb., 1884. ME

Guide to the Gold-fields of Victoria, with a map. 12mo. Melb., 1855. MD 1 P 32

GOLD-MINING. Report of the Royal Commission on Gold-mining. Sm. fol. Melb., 1891. MA 9 Q 20 †

GOVERNMENT GAZETTE, 1851-66, 1869-73, 1891-94. 56 vols. sm. fol. Melb., 1890. ME

HOSPITALS FOR THE INSANE. Report on the Hospitals for the Insane, 1881. Sm. fol. Melb., 1883.
MF 4 U 26

INDUSTRIAL AND REFORMATORY SCHOOLS. Department for Neglected Children and Reformatory Schools. Report. Sm. fol. Melb., 1891. ME

Report of, 1881. Sm. fol. Melb., 1883. MF 4 U 28

Report of the Inspector of Charitable Institutions, 1891. Sm. fol. Melb., 1891. ME

Report on Industrial Schools and Sanitary Station. Sm. fol. Melb., 1872. MG 9 Q 18†

INTERCOLONIAL CONFERENCE, 1873. Report. Sm. fol. Melb., 1873. MF 4 T 20

LANDS. Lists of Government Towns, Townships, and Villages, Parishes, and Counties in the Colony of Victoria. Sm. fol. Melb., 1873. MD 9 Q 32 †

Regulations and Public Notices in force on 4th July, 1877. 8vo. Melb., 1877. MF 1 Q 48

Settlement under the 42nd Clause of the Amending Land Act, 1865. 8vo. Melb., 1869. MF 4 Q 14

LIFE ASSURANCE. The Life Assurance Companies Act, 1873. Summaries of Statements for the year 1874 to 1884 inclusive, made by Companies transacting Life Assurance business in Victoria. Sm. fol. Melb., 1890. MF 3 Q 47 †

LOCAL GOVERNMENT. Local Government Legislation. Sm. fol. Melb., 1873. MF 4 T 19

MINES. Annual Reports of the Secretary for Mines, 1887-88, 1890-93. 7 vols. sm. fol. Melb., 1889-94. ME

Report of the Mining Managers' Certificate Board. Sm. fol. Melb., 1890. MA 9 Q 17 †

Reports and Statistics of the Mining Department for the quarters ended 30th September, 1890, and 31st March, 1891. 2 vols. sm. fol. Melb., 1890-91. ME

VICTORIA—contd.
PARLIAMENT. Parliamentary Debates, 1894-95. Vols. 74-76. 3 vols. roy. 8vo. Melb., 1894-95. ME
Standing Rules and Orders relating to Public Business, &c., Legislative Council. 12mo. Melb., 1884.
MF 1 P 60
Votes and Proceedings of the Legislative Council, 1891-95. 16 vols. sm. fol. Melb., 1891-95. ME

PATENTS. Abstracts of Specifications of Patents, 1854-66. 2 vols. 4to. Melb., 1872-76. ME
Patents and Patentees: Index, 1854-77. 12 vols. 4to. Melb., 1868-81. ME
Patents and Patentees. Vols. 24, 25. Indexes for 1889-90. 2 vols. sm. 4to. Melb., 1894. ME

PENAL ESTABLISHMENTS AND GAOLS. Report of the Inspector-General, 1890. Sm. fol. Melb., 1891. ME

POSTAL SERVICE AND TELEGRAPHS. Reports of the Post Office and Telegraph Departments, 1889, 1892, 1894. 3 vols. Sm. fo . Melb., 1890-95. ME
Report of the Proceedings of the Postal and Telegraph Conference, 1882. Sm. fol. Melb., 1893.
MF 3 Q 50 †

PRIVILEGE. Report from the Select Committee on Privilege. Sm. fol. Melb., 1869. MF 4 T 46
Papers relating to. Sm. fol. Melb., 1869. MF 4 T 46
Report of the Arguments of Counsel and of the Judgment and Order of the Privy Council in the Case of the Speaker of the Legislative Assembly of Victoria versus Hugh Glass. Sm. fol Melb., 1871.
MF 4 T 46

PUBLIC INSTRUCTION. Education Regulations. Sm. fol. Melb., 1890. MG 9 Q 13 †
Reports of the Minister, 1889-94. 3 vols. sm. fol. Melb., 1890-94. ME

PUBLIC LIBRARY, MUSEUMS, AND NATIONAL GALLERY. Reports, 1892, 1893. Sm. fol. Melb., 1893-94. ME
Illustrated Catalogue of the National Gallery. 8vo. Melb., 1894. MK 1 T 29
Descriptive Catalogue of the Specimens of Rocks of Victoria in the Industrial and Technological Museum, Melbourne. 8vo. Melb., 1894. MA 3 T 29
Descriptive Catalogue of the Specimens in the Museum, illustrating the Economic Woods of Victoria. 8vo. Melb., 1894. MA 2 V 65

PUBLIC SERVICE. Act and Regulations relating to the Public Service of Victoria. 4 o. Melb., 1891.
MF 3 U 56
Alterations and Regulations. Sm. fol. Melb., 1891.
MF 4 T 44
Blue Books, 1888-91. 4 vols. sm. fol. Melb., 1889-92. ME
Reports of the Public Service Board. 2 vols. sm. 4to. Melb., 1890-94. ME
Report of Royal Commission on the Civil Service. Sm. fol. Melb., 1873. MF 4 U 20

2 O

VICTORIA—contd.
RAILWAYS. Hawthorn Railway Accident. Sm. fol. Melb., 1883. MF 4 U 28
Parliamentary Standing Committee on Railways. First and third General Reports. 2 vols. sm. fol. Melb., 1894-95. ME
Proposed Railways from Korumburra to Coal-Creek, Strzelecki, and Jumbunna Coal-mines. Sm. fol. Melb., 1891. MA 2 Q 40 †
Reports of the Victorian Railway Commissioners, 1891, 1894. 2 vols. sm. fol. Melb., 1891-94. ME
Report on Proposed Railway from Newmarket to Keilor Road. Sm. fol. Melb., 1891. MA 9 Q 15 †
Report upon Free Railway Passes. Sm. fol. Melb., 1891. MF 4 U 25

REGISTRAR-GENERAL. Instructions for the Guidance of Clergymen relative to the Celebration and Registration of Marriages. 8vo. Melb., 1876. MF 2 T 76

SANITATION. Sanitary Condition of Melbourne. 3 vols. sm. fo . Melb , 1889-90. MA 12 Q 44-46 †

SAVINGS BANKS. Report. 1891-92. 2 vols. sm. fol. Melb., 1891-92. ME

SETTLEMENT OF THE MALLEE COUNTRY. Report. Sm. fol. Melb., 1891. MF 4 U 26

STATISTICS. Australasian Statistics, 1890. Sm. fol. Melb., 1892. ME
General Report of the Census of Victoria, taken on the 5th April, 1891, containing also References to the Results of Censuses taken at the same date in the other Australasian Colonies. Sm. fol. Melb , 1893. ME
Statistical Register of the Colony of Victoria, pts. 5-8, 1881. Sm. fol. Melb., 1883. MF 4 U 28
Statistical Register of the Colony of Victoria, 1882, pts. 3, 4, 6-9; 1890, pts. 2-7; and 1891-1893. 7 vols. sm. fol., Melb., 1890-94. ME
Victorian Year-book, 1892-94. 5 vols. 8vo. Melb., 1892-95. ME 3 T

STATUTES. Acts and Ordinances of Victoria, 1851-58; and Acts of Parliament of Victoria 1858-66. 14 vols. Sm. fo . Melb., 1852-66. ME
Acts of Parliament, 56-58 Vic., 1892-95; also an Index to Sessional vols. for 1890-95. 4 vols. sm. 4to. Melb., 1893-95. ME
An Act to provide for establishment of Colleges of Agriculture, 1884. Sm. 4to. Melb., 1884. MF 3 U 64
County Court Act, 1890. Sm. fol. Melb., 1890. MF 4 T 7
Copy of the Electoral Law of Victoria passed by the Colonial Legislature, 1856. Sm. fol. Lond., 1857.
MF 3 U 16
Insolvency Act, 1890. 4to. Melb., 1890. MF 3 U 57
Insolvency Act, 1890, Rules of Court. Sm. fol. Melb., 1891. MF 4 U 28
Justices of the Peace Statute, 1865. 12mo. Melb., 1865. MF 1 P 62
The Land Acts 1890 and 1891, and Wattles Act 1890, with amended regulations thereunder; also, the regulations relating to unlocked swing gates. 8vo. Melb., 1893. MF 4 Q 28

VICTORIA—*contd.*
STATUTES—*contd.*
Police Offences Statute, 1865. 12mo. Melb., 1865.
MF 1 P 79
The Public and Private Acts [Consolidated]. 7 vols. imp. 8vo. Melb., 1890. MF 3 S 17–23
The Selector's Hand-book: The Land Act, 1869; Land Act, 1878; New Regulations for both Acts, Fencing Act; Impounding Act, &c. 8vo. Melb., 1879.
MF 3 P 31
SUPREME COURT. Rules of, under the Judicature Act, 1883. 8vo. Melb., 1894. MF 3 U 55
Supreme Court Act, 1890, Rules of Court. Sm. fol. Melb., 1890. MF 4 U 21
TARIFF COMMISSION. Royal Commission on the Tariff: Minutes of Evidence. 15 parts. Sm. fol. Melb., 1881–82. MF 4 T 24–38
1. Hats and Caps.
2. Wearing Apparel.
3. Woollen Mills.
4. Ladies' and Children's Clothing, Millinery, Silks, Laces, Rufflings, &c., Hosiery, Umbrellas, Jute Goods, Cordage, &c.
5. Boots and Shoes and Leather.
6. Saddlery, Harness, and Leatherware.
7. Mining.
8. Agricultural and Pastoral Industries and Products.
9. Other Agricultural Industries.
10. Stock Tax.
11. Manufactures of Metals, Agricultural Implements, Machinery, Hardware, Explosives, &c.
12. Coachbuilding, &c.
13. Glassware and Earthenware; also, Wrought Marble, Bricks, &c.
14. Furniture, Brushware, Woodenware, Casks, &c.; also, Timber, Doors, &c.
15. Stationery, Printing, Photography, &c.

TRADE AND CUSTOMS. Import, Export, Transhipment, and Shipping Returns, 1891. Sm. fol. Melb., 1892.
MF 4 T 18
Import, Export, and Shipping Returns: a General Summary, 1893. Sm. fol. Melb., 1894. ME
Tariff of Victoria, alphabetically arranged and revised to 28th Feb., 1891. 8vo. Melb., 1891. MF 3 T 37
TRADES UNIONS. Report, 1892. Sm. fol. Melb., 1893. ME

VEGETABLE PRODUCTS. Facts from the Evidence taken by the Commission: 1. Ensilage. 2. Perfume Plants and Essential Oils. 8vo. Melb., 1889–90.
MA 3 V 34
Hand-book on Viticulture. (Roy. Com. on Vegetable Products.) 8vo. Melb., 1891. MA 3 S 12
Royal Commission on Vegetable Products. Reports 1–10. 2 vols. 8vo. Melb., 1886–94. MA 3 T 62, 63

WATER SUPPLY. Irrigation Reports. Sm. fol. Melb., 1886. ME
Royal Commission on Water Supply: Further Progress Report. Sm. fol. Melb., 1895. MA 9 P 30 †
Victorian Water Supply: Reports, 1889, 1891. 2 vols. sm. fol. Melb., 1889–91. ME

YARRA FLOODS. Reports of the Yarra Floods Board. Sm. fol. Melb., 1892. MA 2 Q 41 †

VICTORIA AND TASMANIA WESLEYAN METHODIST CHURCH. Minutes of Conversations between the Ministers at the Annual Conferences, 1874, 1876–93. 19 vols. 8vo. Melb., 1874–93. ME 15 Q

VICTORIA AUXILIARY BIBLE SOCIETY. Annual Report, 1870. 8vo. Melb., 1870. MG 2 Q 48

VICTORIA INSTITUTE. Journal of Transactions of. Vols. 16, 17, 20–22, 25, 26. 7 vols. 8vo. Lond., 1883–93. E

VICTORIA INSURANCE CO. Memorandum and Articles of Association. 8vo. Melb., 1879.
MF 4 Q 36

VICTORIA LAND INVESTMENT SOCIETY. Rules of. 8vo. Melb. (n.d.) MF 4 Q 11

VICTORIA LAW ALMANAC for 1894. 12mo. Melb., 1894. ME 4 T

VICTORIA UNIVERSITY, Toronto, Canada. Calendar, 1892, 1893. 8vo. Toronto, 1892. E

VICTORIAN. [*See* Time of the End, The.] MG 2 Q 21

VICTORIAN AGRICULTURAL AND HORTICULTURAL GAZETTE. Vols. 1–4, 1857–60. 4to. Geelong, 1858–60. ME 8 T

VICTORIAN ALLIANCE ANNUAL and Temperance Year-book, 1893. 8vo. Melb., 1893. ME 4 U

VICTORIAN AMATEUR TURF CLUB. Regulations, Bye-laws, Rules of the Club, &c. 2nd ed. 12mo. Melb., 1877. MA 2 V 31

VICTORIAN CHAMBER OF COMMERCE. Report for 1886. 8vo. Melb., 1886. ME 15 Q

VICTORIAN DEAF AND DUMB INSTITUTION. Report for 1868. 8vo. Melb., 1868. MG 2 Q 48

VICTORIAN ENGINEERS' ASSOCIATION. Rules and Bye-laws. 8vo. Melb., 1884. ME 15 Q

VICTORIAN MEDICAL SOCIETY. Australian Medical Journal. [*See* Australian Medical Journal.]
ME 9 S–T

VICTORIAN MINER'S MANUAL, The; by "Aurifera." 12mo. Melb. (n.d.) MA 2 P 38

VICTORIAN NATURALIST, The. Vols. 1–11. 8vo. Melb., 1884–95. ME 6 P

VICTORIAN REVIEW, The. Nos. 26, 31–61, and vol. 11. Roy. 8vo. Melb., 1881–85. ME 18 R

VICTORINUS. Works of. (Anti-Nicene Christian Library.) 8vo. Edinb., 1870. G 14 U 18

VICUÑA, C. Morla. Miguel Luis Amunátegui, 1828-88. 8vo. Paris (n.d.) C 21 T 1

VIERGE, Daniel. Illustrations to "The Tavern of the Three Virtues." [See Delorme, R.] J 15 R 13 †

VIGILANT. [See Australian Sporting Celebrities.] MC 1 T 21

VILLEROY and BOCH. [Pottery and Glass Works.] Obl. 12mo. Berlin, 1893. A 23 P 12

VILLEVAL, A. Victor Hugo: a Biographical Study. 12mo. Sydney, 1895. MC 1 S 17

VILLIERS, Frederic, at Home; with Portrait. [See Blathwayt, R.—Interviews.] J 10 U 34

VILMORIN-ANDRIEUX et Cie, Messrs. Meilleurs Blés: Description et Culture des principales variétés de Froments. 4to. Paris, 1880. A 14 S 3 †

VINCENT, Arthur. [Life of] Col. F. Charteris, Libertine, 1675-1732. (Lives of Twelve Bad Men.) 8vo. Lond., 1894. C 18 T 9

[Life of] J. Wild, Thief-taker, 1682-1725. (Lives of Twelve Bad Men.) 8vo. Lond., 1824. C 18 T 9

VINCENT, Frank. Actual Africa; or, the Coming Continent. Illustrated. 8vo. Lond., 1894. D 14 V 17

VINCENT, Col. H. British Interests in Brazil, &c. [See Vincent, Mrs.—China to Peru.] D 15 Q 19

VINCENT, Mrs. H. China to Peru over the Andes: a Journey through South America; with Reports and Letters on British Interests in Brazil, Argentina, Chili, Peru, Panama, and Venezuela, by Col. H. Vincent. With Map and Illustrations. 12mo. Lond., 1894. D 15 Q 19

VINCENT, Henry. Portrait of. [See Gammage, R. G. —Chartist Movement.] F 7 R 24

VINCENT, Dr. J. M. Seminary Notes on Recent Historical Literature. [See Adams, Dr. H. B.] B 18 S 8

VINCENT, James Edmund. His Royal Highness Duke of Clarence and Avondale: a Memoir. 12mo. Lond, 1893. C 19 Q 8

VINCENT, Rev. Dr. John H. The American Sunday Schools. 12mo. Lond., 1887. G 18 Q 22

VINCENT, R. Harry. The Elements of Hypnotism. The Induction of Hypnosis its Phenomena, its Dangers, and Value. 8vo. Lond, 1893. A 26 Q 26

VINCENT, W. T. Recollections of Fred Leslie. 2 vols. 8vo. Lond., 1894. C 19 R 11, 12

VINES, Prof. Sydney Howard. Students' Text-book of Botany. Illustrated. 8vo. Lond., 1895. A 20 T 14

VINKEROY, E. van. Catalogue des Armes et Armures. (Musée Royal d'Antiquités et d'Armures, Bruxelles.) 12mo. Bruxelles, 1885. K 7 P 10

VIOLLET-LE-DUC, Eugène Emmanuel. Rational Building; being a Translation of the article "Construction," in the Dictionnaire Raisonné de l'Architecture Française, by G. M. Huss. Illustrated. 8vo. New York, 1895. A 19 V 24

VIRGILIUS MARO, Publius. Opera, interpretatione et Notis illustravit C. Ruæus. 8vo. Lond., 1707. H 9 U 33

Works of Virgil, translated by Dr. A. H. Bryce. 12mo. Lond., 1894. J 11 R 24

Vergil in the Middle Ages. [See Comparetti, D.] J 12 R 3

VIRGINIA—General. Hand-book of. (1.) 8vo. Richmond, 1893. D 15 T 15

A Hand-book. (2.) 8vo. Richmond, Va., 1893. D 15 T 15

The Mountain State, Resources of. 8vo. Charleston, 1893. D 15 T 15

VIRGINIA—Board of Agriculture. Reports, 1893, 1894. 2 vols. Richmond, 1893-94. E

VISGAR, Mrs. H., and BOULGER, Prof. G. S. The Country Month by Month, April-December; by J. A. Owen (Mrs. H. Visgar) and Prof. G. S. Boulger. 3 vols. 12mo. Lond., 1894. A 29 S 9 10

VITELLI, Girolamo, e PAOLI, Cesare. Collezione Fiorentina di Facsimili Paleografici Greci e Latini. 4 vols. fol. Firenze, 1884-89. J 41 P 24-27 ‡

VIZETELLY, Henry. Glances Back through 70 years: Autobiographical and other Reminiscences. 2 vols. 8vo. Lond., 1893. C 19 R 13 14

VOELCKER, J. A. Report on the Improvement of Indian Agriculture. 8vo. Lond., 1893. A 18 U 24

VOGDES, A. W. Bibliography of the Palæozoic Crustacea, 1698-1892; to which is added a Catalogue of North American species. 8vo. San Francisco, 1893. A 30 U 10

VOGEL, Sir Julius. The Finances of New Zealand. 8vo. Paris, 1875. MJ 3 Q 16

VOICE OF WARNING, A, and Instruction to the People; or, an Introduction to the Faith and Doctrine of the Church of Jesus Christ of Latter Day Saints. Revised. Also, an Analysis of Isaiah 29. 12mo. Lamoni (Io.), 1880. G 16 Q 33

VOLCANIC GOLD and other Tales, Sketches, &c. 8vo. Melb. (n.d.) MJ 3 Q 19

VOLKHOVSKY, Felix. Claims of the Russian Liberals. [See Stepniak, S.—Nihilism as it is.] P 8 U 34

VOLKSBILDUNGS-VEREIN. Bericht über die Vereins-Thätigkeit, 1890. 8vo. Wien, 1891. E

VOLTAIRE, François Marie Arouet de. Histoire de Charles XII, et Histoire de Russie sous Pierre le Grand. 8vo. Paris, 1845. B 25 P 8
Voltaire's Visit to England. [*See* Ballantyne, A.] C 14 S 26

VOLUNTEER SERVICE GAZETTE. Vols. 33–35. Fol. Lond., 1892–94. E

VORZANDER, C. The Australia Waltz. Fol. Sydney, 1893. MA 7 Q 31 †

VOYAGEUR. Kamboola, and other Tales. [*See* Kamboola.] MJ 3 Q 38

VOYNICH, E. L. The Humour of Russia. Illustrated. 8vo. Lond., 1895. J 9 S 20
Nihilism as it is. [*See* Stepniak, S. P.] F 8 U 34

VOYSEY, Rev. Charles. The Liberal Clergy. 12mo. Ramsgate, 1868. G 2 V 40

VRIESE, W. H. de. Illustrations d'Orchidées des Indes Orientales Néerlandaises, ou choix de plantes nouvelles et peu connues de la famille des Orchidées. Fol. La Haye, 1854. [A 20 P 22 ‡

W

W., G. F. [*See* Glance of Life.] H 10 Q 26

W. M. [*See* Employers, Servants, and Registry Offices.] MF 1 P 77

WAAGEN, Dr. W. Salt Range Fossils: Geological Results. [*See* India, Geological Survey, ser. 13, vol. 4.] · E

WACE, Rev. Dr. Henry. Christianity and Agnosticism. 8vo. Edinb., 1895. G 1 P 9

WADDELL, L. Austine. The Buddhism of Tibet, or Lamaism, with its mystic cults, symbolism and mythology, and in its relation to Indian Buddhism. Illustrated. 8vo. Lond., 1895. G 5 R 31

WADDELL, Rev. Peter Hately. The Parsifal of Wagner. [*See* Wagner, Richard.] H 1 S 29

WADDELL, W. W. The Parmenides of Plato after the paging of the Clarke MS. 4to. Glasgow, 1894. J 15 Q 21 †

WADDIE, Charles. Dunbar, the King's Advocate: A tragic episode in the Reformation. 2nd ed. 8vo. Edinb., 1893. H 1 Q 1

WADE, Chas. G. The Married Women's Property Act, 1893, containing an Introduction and Notes upon the Statute; also References to the Corresponding Acts in England and Victoria. 8vo. Sydney, 1894. MF 1 R 58

WADE, James A. History of St. Mary's Abbey, Melrose, the Monastery of Old Melrose, and the Town and Parish of Melrose. 8vo. Edinb., 1861. B 32 R 4

WADE, John. British History, chronologically arranged. 8vo. Lond., 1839. B 23 T 12

WAGENKNECHT, B. The Rainfall at Brisbane and its periodicity. (Proc. Roy. Soc., Queensland, 2.) 8vo. Brisbane, 1896. ME 1 T

WAGHORN, Lieut. Thos. Waghorn on Emigration to Australia. 8vo. Lond. (n.d.) MF 2 Q 83

WAGNER, Leopold. Manners, Customs, and Observances; their Origin and Signification. 12mo. Lond., 1895. F 8 U 12
The Popular Elocutionist. [*See* Carpenter, J. E.] J 4 R 37

WAGNER, Prof. Paul. How are Nitrogen and Phosphoric Acid to be obtained in the cheapest way? 8vo. Sydney, 1892. MA 1 Q 61
Increase in the Production of the Soil through the rational use of Nitrogenous Manures; translated by G. G. Henderson. 8vo. Lond., 1888. A 32 T 5

WAGNER, Richard. The Parsifal of; by Rev. P. H. Waddell. 8vo. Edinb., 1894. H 1 S 29
Prose Works: translated by W. A. Ellis. Vols. 1 and 2. 8vo. Lond., 1892–93. J 4 S 14, 15
  1. The Art Work of the Future; Wieland the Smith, a dramatic sketch; Art and Climate; A Communication to my Friends.
  2. Opera and Drama.
Wagner's Heroes. [*See* Maud, Constance.] H 10 S 15

WAGNER, Rudolf von. Manual of Chemical Technology; translated by W. Crookes, F.R.S. Illustrated. Roy. 8vo. Lond., 1892. A 21 V 10

WÄGNER, Dr. W. Asgard and the Gods: the Tales and Traditions of our Northern Ancestors, forming a complete manual of Norse Mythology. 4th edition. 8vo. Lond., 1886. B 15 Q 6

WAH-KEE-NAH and her People [N.A. Indians]. [*See* Strong, J. C.] A 18 R 31

WAHL, Dr. W. H. Techno-Chemical Receipt-book. [*See* Brannt, W. T.] A 21 R 23

WAINEWRIGHT, Thos. G., Poisoner. [Life of], 1794–1852; by A. A. Allen. (Lives of Twelve Bad Men.) 8vo. Lond., 1894. C 18 T 9

WAIRARAPA WILDERNESS, The, in which will be found the Wanderings on the Second Cruise of the S.S. *Wairarapa*, from Auckland to the South Sea Islands and back. 8vo. Auckland, 1884. MD 6 U 22

WAITE, Arthur Edward. The Occult Sciences: a Compendium of Transcendental Doctrine and Experiment, embracing an Account of Magical Practices, of Secret Sciences in connection with Magic, of the Professors of Magical Arts, and of modern Spiritualism, Mesmerism, and Theosophy. 8vo. Lond., 1891. G 8 S 33

WAKE, Charles Staniland. Chapters on Man, with the Outlines of a Science of Comparative Psychology. 12mo. Lond., 1868. A 18 T 33

Memoirs of the International Congress of Anthropology. Roy. 8vo. Chicago, 1894 A 18 V 20

WAKEFIELD, E. New Zealand Illustrated: the Story of New Zealand and Descriptions of its Cities and Towns. Fo. Wanganui, 1889. MD 1 Q 9 ‡

WAKEFIELD, Edward Gibbon. Mr. D. Coates and the New Zealand Association; in a letter to Lord Glenelg. 8vo. Lond. 1837. MB 2 R 57

WAKEHAM, Henry Offley. Europe, 1598-1715. Period 5. 12mo. Lond., 1894. B 25 S 17

WAKELING, G. The Oxford Church Movement. 8vo. Lond., 1895. G 3 R 14

WALCH, Garnet. Australasia: an Intercolonial Christmas Annual. 8vo. Melb., 1878. MJ 2 P 19

The Australian Birthday-book and Record of Memorable Events, both in the Old World and the New. 12mo. Melb., 1887. MK 2 P 13

Dyk Whyttyagtonne and hys wonderfulle Catte: Christmas pantomime. 4to Melb., 1881. MH 1 T 12

A Glass of Champagne: the Story of the King of Wines, with a description of its preparation, mode of storage, &c. 8vo. Melb., 1885. MA 1 P 58

Hey-diddle-diddle: an orginal pantomime. 12mo. Melb., 1876. MH 1 P 66

Illustrated Australian Annual. 8vo. Melb., 1882. MJ 3 R 8

The Victorian Jubilee Book 8vo. Melb., 1887. MJ 3 Q 18

WALCH, J., and Sons. Tasmanian Guide Book. 12mo. Hobart, 1874. MD 1 P 39

Handbook of Garden and Greenhouse Culture in Tasmania. 12mo. Hobart, 1870. MA 1 P 65

WALCOTT, Chas. D. Palæontology of Eureka District. (U.S. Geol. Survey, 8.) 4to. Wash., 1884. E

WALDO, Dr. Frank. Modern Meteorology. 8vo. Lond., 1893. A 19 Q 24

WALDSTEIN, C. Work of John Ruskin: its influence upon Modern Thought and Life. 8vo. Camb., 1894. J 6 P 36

WALDUCK, W. W. Constitutionalism in Victoria. 8vo. Melb., 1873 MJ 3 Q 16

WALFORD, Edward. The County Families of the United Kingdom, 1893-95. 3 vols. roy. 8vo. Lond., 1893-95. E

The Windsor Peerage, 1893-95. 3 vols. 12mo. Lond., 1893-95. E

WALISZEWSKI, K. The Story of a Throne: Catherine II of Russia. 2 vols. 8vo. Lond., 1895. C 17 S 13, 14

The Romance of an Empress, Catherine II of Russia. 2 vols. 8vo. Lond., 1894. C 19 R 8, 9

WALKER, Alexander. Trans.—Apocryphal Gospels, &c. [See Apocryphal Gospels.] G 14 U 16

WALKER, Alexander. Beauty: illustrated by an Analysis and Classification of Beauty in Woman. Roy. 8vo. Lond., 1852. A 33 U 14

WALKER, Gen. Sir C. P. Beauchamp. Days of a Soldier's Life: being Letters written during Active Service in the Crimean, Chinese, Austro-Prussian (1866), and Franco-German (1870-71) Wars. 8vo. Lond., 1894. C 21 R 19

WALKER, Gen. F. A. [Life of] Gen. W. S. Hancock. 8vo. New York, 1894. C 14 S 24

WALKER, Dr. Francis A. The Making of the Nation, 1783-1817. 8vo. Lond., 1895. B 19 Q 14

WALKER, Frederick. Practical Dynamo-building for Amateurs. How to Wind for any Output. 12mo. New York, 1890. A 21 P 24

WALKER, Frederick, and his Works; by C. Phillips. [See Portfolio Monograph, 6.] E

WALKER, G. W. Address to the Prisoner Population. [See Backhouse, J.] MG 1 Q 51

WALKER, Rev. George. The Siege of Londonderry, 1689; edited by Rev. P. Dwyer. Sm. 4to. Lond., 1893. B 29 T 21

WALKER, Prof. Hugh. Three Centuries of Scottish Literature. 2 vols. 8vo. Glasgow, 1893. B 31 Q 15, 16

WALKER, J. B. The Deportation of the Norfolk Islanders to the Derwent in 1808. 8vo. Hobart, 1895. MB 2 Q 56

WALKER, J. T. Some Remarks on Australasian Banks and on Banking as a factor in the progress of Australasia. 8vo. Melb., 1888. MF 4 R 47

WALKER, Dr. James. Trans.—Physico-Chemical Measurements. [See Ostwald, Prof. W.] A 29 V 25

WALKER, Louisa. Varied Occupations in Weaving. 12mo. Lond., 1895. A 25 Q 18

WALKER, Dr. Norman. Leprosy. [See Hansen, Dr. G. A.] A 33 S 13

WALKER, Rev. Dr. Norman Lockhart. Chapters from the History of the Free Church of Scotland. 8vo. Edinb., 1895. G 11 T 31

WALKER, R., & Co. Tasmanian Cookery Guide. 12mo. Hobart (n.d.) MA 1 P 32

WALKER, T. Letters on the Land Laws. 8vo. Sydney, 1884. MF 4 R 46

WALKER, Thomas. Orthodoxy Unmasked; or, Clerical Arguments Refuted. 8vo. Melb., 1882. MG 1 S 39

WALKER, Dr. Thos. Alfred. Manual of Public International Law. 8vo. Camb., 1895. F 11 U 2
The Science of International Law. 8vo. Lond., 1893. F 8 R 2

WALKER, W. A. The Probate Act of 1890. [See Garrett, T. W.] MF 1 S 37

WALKER, W. B. Australian Sand-bar Harbours and Rivers; with Hints on the Sea Defences of Melbourne, by "Tom Cringle." 8vo. Melb., 1866. MA 3 S 43

WALKER, Wm. History of the Hawkesbury Benevolent Society. 8vo. Sydney, 1887. MF 2 R 42
Reminiscences of a Fifty Years' Residence at Windsor. 12mo. Sydney, 1890. MC 1 P 55

WALLACE, Alexander. Report on the Culture of the Japanese Silkworm in England, in 1867-68. 8vo. Colchester, 1869. MA 2 T 31

WALLACE, Dr. Alfred Russell. Australasia. (Stanford's Compendium of Geography and Travel.) Maps and Illustrations. 2 vols. 8vo. Lond., 1893-94. MD 8 Q 23, 24
Land Nationalisation: its necessity and its aims. 8vo. Lond., 1892. F 14 Q 33

WALLACE, Edwin R. Descriptive Guide to the Adirondacks. 8vo. Syracuse, N.Y., 1894. D 15 Q 22

WALLACE, R. H. A farmer's Soil. (Vict. Depart. of Agricult.—Lectures.) 8vo. Melb., 1892. MA 3 V 15
What is Scientific Agriculture? 8vo. Melb. (n.d.) MA 3 V 22

WALLACE, Robert L. The Canary Book: containing full directions for the Breeding, Rearing, and Management of Canaries and Canary Mules; Cage-making, &c. 3rd ed., illustrated. 8vo. Lond., 1893. A 27 S 24

WALLACE, Dr. Wilfrid. Life of St. Edmund of Canterbury, from original sources. 8vo. Lond., 1893. C 16 T 14

WALLACE, Prof. Wm. Life of A. Schopenhauer. 12mo. Lond., 1890. C 18 P 20

WALLER, Edmund. Poems of; edited by G. T. Drury. 12mo. Lond., 1893. H 3 P 37
Poetical Works of; edited by R. Bell. 12mo. Lond., 1854. H 10 T 22

WALLER, Dr. J. P. [See Imperial Dictionary of Universal Biography.] C 21 U 1-14

WALLIHAN, A. C. and Mrs. Hoofs, Claws, and Antlers of the Rocky Mountains, by the Camera: Photograpic reproductions of Wild Game from Life. 4to. Denver, Col., 1894. A 15 Q 6 †

WALLIS, F. The Dynamo. [See Hawkins, C. C.] A 21 P 21

WALLIS, Henry. Persian Ceramic Art belonging to Mr. F. Ducane Godman, F.R.S.; with examples of other collections. Fol. Lond., 1891. A 6 P 11 ‡

WALLIS, J. E. P. Reports of State Trials. [See State Trials.] F 3 T 4-9

WALLIS, Rev. Dr. Robt. E. Trans.—Writings of Cyprian. [See Cyprian.] G 14 U 8, 13

WALLMANN, H. F. Pseudomorphism in Minerals. (Proc. Roy. Soc., Queensland, 1.) 8vo. Brisb., 1884. ME 1 T

WALMSLEY, Dr. Francis H. Outlines of Insanity. 8vo. Lond., 1892. G 15 R 26

WALMSLEY, R. Mullineux. The Electric Current; how produced and how used. Illustrated. 8vo. Lond., 1894. A 21 R 17
Electricity in the service of Man. [See Wormell, R.] A 21 V 11

WALPOLE, Horace, 4th Earl of Orford. Letters of Horace Walpole, Earl of Orford; edited by P. Cunningham. 9 vols. 8vo. Lond., 1880. C 19 S 10-19
Horace Walpole: a Memoir; with an Appendix of Books printed at the Strawberry Hills Press; by Austin Dobson. Roy. 8vo. Lond., 1890. C 13 V 6

WALPOLE, Spencer. The Land of Home Rule; an Essay on the History and Constitution of the Isle of Man. 8vo. Lond., 1893. B 23 R 17

WALROND, Rev. F. F. [Life of] Philipp Jacob Spener. 12mo. Lond., 1893. C 13 P 9

WALROND, Col. H. Archery. [See Longman, C. J.] A 29 R 17

WALSH, Rev. Wm. Horatio. Sermon preached on the occasion of the Death of the Rev. G. W. Richardson. [See Richardson, Rev. G. W.] MG 2 Q 23

WALSH, Wm. Shepard. Hand-book of Literary Curiosities. 8vo. Lond., 1893. J 4 Q 2

WALTER, E. L. Notes to "The Social Contract." [See Rousseau, J. J.] F 5 Q 15

WALTER, John. Sketch of. [See Smalley, G. W.—Studies of Men.] C 19 R 20

WALTERS, Rev. George. The Criminal's Ascension; or, From the Gallows to the "Golden Streets." 8vo. Sydney, 1892. MG 2 Q 20
Joseph of Canaan. 8vo. Sydney, 1895. MH 1 V 3

WALTON, George A. Sketch of the Teachers' Training Schools and Classes of Massachusetts. 8vo. Boston, 1893. G 18 Q 18

WALTON, Izaak. Lives of Dr. J. Donne, Sir H. Wotton, R. Hooker, G. Herbert, and Dr. R. Sanderson. 8vo. Lond., 1895. C 10 V 6

WANDERER, A. [See All the Earth Round.] H 9 U 41

WANLISS, T. D. The War in Europe of 1870-71 : with an Enquiry into its Probable Consequences. 12mo. Ballarat, 1871. MB 1 P 10

WANOSTROCHT, N. Recueil Choisi de Traits Historiques et de Contes Moraux. 12mo. Lond., 1839. J 11 T 40

WANT OF LUCIDITY ; or, a Warning Neglected ; by "E. W. Y." 8vo. Lond., 1893. G 16 S 51

WAR CRY, The. Aug., 1891–July, 1892. 2 vols. fol. Sydney, 1891-92. MF

WAR IN THE CRIMEA : a series of Letters from officers, non-commissioned officers, and privates engaged in the Siege of Sevastopol, containing full details of the Battles of Alma, Balaklava, and Inkermann. 8vo. Sydney, 1855. MB 2 Q 54

WARBURTON, Rt. Rev. Dr. Works of A. Pope. [See Pope, A.] J 9 T 28-36

WARD, Chas. J. Jamaica at Chicago : an Account descriptive of the Colony of Jamaica ; with Historical and other Appendices. Roy. 8vo. New York, 1893. D 11 V 13

WARD, C. Osborne. Equilibrat on of Human Aptitudes and Powers of Adaptation. 8vo. Washington, 1895. F 2 U 30

WARD, Captain Edward W. Durability of New Zealand Timber. [See Kirk, T.] MA 1 V 58

WARD, [F. W. The English Market for New South Wales Fruit. 8vo. Sydney, 1892. MA 1 Q 62
The English Market for Australian Fruit. 8vo. Melb., 1891. MA 3 V 36
Utilisation of the River Darling. [See McKinney, H. G.] MA 10 P 50 †

WARD, Prof. H. Marshall. Diseases of Trees. [See Hartig, Prof. R.] A 18 V 31
Timber and Timber Trees. [See Laslett, T.] A 20 T 10

WARD, Harriet. The Cape and the Kaffirs. 3rd ed. ; with Map. 12mo. Lond., 1851. D 14 P 11

WARD, Mrs. Humphrey. Sketch of. [See Smalley, G. W.—Studies of Men.] C 19 R 20

WARD, L. F. The Psychic Factors of Civilisation. 8vo. Boston, 1893. G 5 R 30

WARD, R. Supplejack : a Romance of Maoriland. 12mo. Lond., 1894. MJ 1 P 35

WARD, Wilfred. William George Ward and the Catholic Revival. 8vo. Lond., 1893. C 15 R 17

WARD, Wm. C. Poems of W. Drummond. [See Drummond, W.] H 9 P 15, 16

WARD, Wm. G., and the Catholic Revival ; by Wilfred Ward. 8vo. Lond., 1893. C 15 R 17

WARDROP, Marjory. Georgian Folk Tales. (Grimm Lib. 1.) 12mo. Lond., 1894. B 36 P 5

WARHAM, Most Rev. Wm., Archbishop of Canterbury. Sketch of. [See Fowler, Rev. M.—Notable Archbishops.] C 13 V 12

WARING, George Edwin, jun. Aërial Navigation. [See Fijnje van Salverda, J. G. W.] A 22 Q 16
Modern Methods of Sewage Disposal for Towns, Public Institutions, and isolated Houses. 8vo. New York, 1894. A 22 Q 35
Sanitary Condition of City and Country Dwelling-houses. 18mo. New York, 1877. A 22 P 34

WARINGTON, Robert. On some of the changes which nitrogenous matter undergoes within the soil : a Lecture. (Inst. of Agricult., Lond.) 8vo. Lond., 1884. A 18 R 28

WARN, E. H. The Sheet Metal Worker's Instructor, for Zinc, Sheet-iron, Copper, and Tin-plate Workers, and Others ; containing a Selection of Geometrical Problems. Roy. 8vo. Philad., 1890. A 10 U 8

WARNECKE, F. Emblemata Nobilitatis. [See De Bry, T.] A 30 P 17 ‡
Emblemata Sæcularia. [See De Bry, T.] A 30 P 16 ‡

WARNER, Dr. Amos Griswold. American Charities : a Study in Philanthropy and Economics. 8vo. New York, 1894. F 8 U 39
Three Phases of Coöperation in the West. (Johns Hopkins University Studies, 6.) 8vo. Baltimore, 1888. B 18 S 6

WARNER, Robt., WILLIAMS, Henry, and GOWER, Wm. Hugh. The Orchid Album, comprising Coloured Figures and Descriptions of New, Rare, and Beautiful Orchidaceous Plants. Vol. 10. 4to. Lond., 1893. A 14 P 10 †

WARNER, W. Lee-. The Protected Princess of India. 8vo. Lond., 1894. F 8 P 32

WARR, George C. W. The Greek Epic. 12mo. Lond., 1895. J 6 P 43

WARRE, Margaret. Addresses by Rev. Dr. Döllinger. [See Döllinger, Rev. Dr.] B 35 R 8

WARREN, J. Lowe-. Sussex Tokens issued during the 17th, 18th, and 19th Centuries by the Corporations, Guilds, Overseers of the Poor, Taverns, Tradesmen, &c. ; with an Historical Introduction by the Rev. F. H. Arnold. 8vo. Lond., 1888. A 27 Q 45

WARREN, Kate M. Langland's Vision of Piers the Plowman. [See Langland, W.] J 11 T 43

WARREN, Dr. Samuel. Passages from the Diary of a late Physician. 2 vols. 12mo. Edinb., 1844.
J 11 P 17, 18

WARREN, Prof. Wm. H. Australian Timbers. Roy. 8vo. Sydney, 1892.
MA 1 S 39

WARRENDER, Margaret. Marchmont and the Humes of Polwarth. Roy. 8vo. Edinb., 1894.
C 17 S 6

WARTER, Rev. J. W. A Love Story. [*See* Southey, R.]
J 12 T 15

WASHINGTON, George. Early Sketches of; by W. S. Baker. 8vo. Philad., 1894.
C 21 R 10

George Washington and Mount Vernon: a Collection of Washington's unpublished Agricultural and Personal Letters. (Memoir of the Long Island Hist. Soc.) Roy. 8vo. Brooklyn, N.Y., 1889.
C 21 S 16

Journal of Colonel George Washington, sent across the Alleghany Mountains, in 1754, to build Forts; edited by J. M. Toner. Sm. 4to. Albany, 1893.
B 17 R 23

[Life of]; by Lieut.-Col. C. King. 8vo. Lond., 1894.
C 17 R 19

Maxims of Washington. Compiled for use in Schools, Libraries, and all American Homes. 12mo. New York, 1894.
J 12 S 39

Memorial Arch. [*See* Curtis, G. W.]
F 14 U 3

[Plaster Cast of.] [*See* Hutton, L.—Portraits in Plaster.]
A 23 V 13

Sketch of. [*See* Thompson, R. W.—Recollections of Sixteen Presidents.]
C 18 T 21, 22

Sketch of. [*See* Wilson, J. G.—Presidents of the United States.]
C 2 V 30

Unveiling of the Statue of. [*See* Curtis, G. W.]
F 14 U 3

WASHINGTON NATIONAL MUSEUM. Report of the Building Commission and of the Architects, 1882. 8vo. Wash., 1883.
E

WASLEY, J. S. Digest of Cases, Supreme Court, Victoria. [*See* Eagleson, J. G.]
MF 1 S 63

WASP, The. Edited by Rev. P. Campbell. (Pam.) 8vo. Sydney, 1878.
MG 1 Q 53

WATERFORD, Louisa, Marchioness of. Memorials of; by A. J. C. Hare. 3 vols. 12mo. Lond., 1893.
C 19 Q 23-25

WATERHOUSE, Rev. Joseph. The King and the People of Fiji. 8vo. Lond., 1866.
MB 2 P 54

WATERS, Arthur W. Polyzoa. [*See* Thomson, Sir C. W., and Murray, Dr. J.—Voyage of H.M.S. Challenger.]
A 6 †

WATKIN, Dr. E. I. Official Charge to Young Ministers. 12mo. Melb., 1886.
MG 2 T 17

WATKINS, G. Notes on the Aboriginals of Stradbrooke and Moreton Islands. (Proc. Roy. Soc., Queensland, 8.) 8vo. Brisbane, 1891.
ME 1 T

WATKINS, John Leo, and O'CONNOR, Richard Edward. A Digest of Criminal and Magistrates' Cases decided in New South Wales from 1840-81. 8vo. Sydney, 1882.
MF 1 Q 61

WATKINS, Rev. Oscar D. Holy Matrimony: a Treatise on the Divine Laws of Marriage. 8vo. Lond., 1895.
G 16 U 19

WATMUFF, F. Australian Almanacs, 1879, 1880, 1888, 1891. 4 vols. 8vo. Melb., 1879-91.
ME 4 U

WATSON, Rev. Albert. Cicero's Select Letters. [*See* Cicero, M. T.]
C 14 U 24

WATSON, G. L. Evolution of the Modern Racing Yacht. [*See* Sullivan, Sir E.—Yachting.]
A 29 Q 40

WATSON, H. B. Marriott. Broken Billy. [*See* Praed, Mrs. Campbell.—Under the Gum Tree.]
MJ 2 T 44

WATSON, Rev. H. E. M. [*See* Hobart Town Riots.]
MG 1 S 25

WATSON, Dr. John. Comte, Mill, and Spencer: an Outline of Philosophy. 12mo. Glasgow, 1895.
G 2 U 14

Hedonistic Theories, from Aristippus to Spencer. 8vo. Glasgow, 1895.
G 1 U 25

WATSON, John. *Editor*—Ornithology in relation to Agriculture and Horticulture; by various writers. 8vo. Lond., 1893.
A 27 Q 24

WATSON, Dr. John Forbes. The Imperial Museum for India and the Colonies. 8vo. Lond., 1876.
A 30 U 35

WATSON, Rev. John Selby. Odyssey and Iliad of Homer. [*See* Homer.]
H 9 P 13, 14

WATSON, Dr. Morrison. Anatomy of the Spheniscidæ. [*See* Thomson, Sir C. W., and Murray, Dr. J.—Voyage of H.M.S. *Challenger*, Zoology, 7.]
A 6 †

WATSON, Rev. Dr. R. A. Numbers, Judges, Ruth, and Job. [*See* Expositor's Bible.]
G 19 R and S

WATSON, R. A. and Elizabeth S. George Gilfillan: Letters and Journal, with Memoir. 8vo. Lond., 1892.
C 15 R 9

WATSON, Dr. R. Spence. Introduction to "Nihilism as it is." [*See* Stepniak, S. P.]
F 8 U 31

WATSON, Rev. Robt. Boog. Scaphopoda and Gasteropoda. [*See* Thomson, Sir C. W., and Murray, Dr. J.—Voyage of H.M.S. *Challenger*, Zoology, 15.]
A 6 †

WATSON, S. J. The Powers of Canadian Parliaments. 8vo. Toronto, 1889.
F 14 Q 41

WATSON, Dr. W. Early Medical Practitioners, Iowa. 8vo. Iowa City, 1894.
B 17 R 34

WATSON, W. Ham and Bacon Curing. 8vo. Brisb., 1891.
MA 1 Q 69

WATSON, W., and BEAN, W. Orchids: their Culture and Management; with descriptions of all the kinds in general cultivation. 8vo. Lond., 1890. A 20 S 10
Another copy. 2nd ed. 8vo. Lond., 1895. A 4 U 11

WATSON, Wm. Excursions in Criticism. 8vo. Lond. 1893. J 4 P 13
Odes and other Poems. 12mo. Lond., 1894. H 8 Q 32
Poems. 12mo. Lond., 1893. H 3 P 39

WATT, Prof. George. A Dictionary of the Economic Products of India. 6 vols (in 9) roy. 8vo. Calcutta. 1889-93. A 18 V 10-18

WATT, J. A. Chromite-bear ng Rock. [See David, Prof.] ME 1 E

WATTLE BLOSSOMS AND WILD FLOWERS, gathered by the way. 12mo. Melb. 1886. MH 1 U 54

WATTS, Henry. Dictionary of Chemistry. Vol 4, with Addenda; revised by M. M. P. Muir, and Dr. H. F. Morley. 8vo. Lond., 1894. K 9 R 8

WATTS, Henry Edward. Miguel de Cervantes: his Life and Works. 8vo. Lond., 1895. C 13 V 17

WATTS, W. L. Gas and Petroleum yielding Formations of the Central Valley, California. 8vo. Sacramento, 1894. A 24 T 24

WAUGH, Arthur. Alfred, Lord Tennyson: a Study of his Life and Work. 8vo. Lond., 1892. C 15 P 10

WAUGH, James Wm. The Stranger's Guide to Sydney. 12mo. Sydney, 1861. MD 1 P 44

WAUPMELTA. [See Sheep Husbandry.] MA 2 V 67

WAWN, Wm. T. The South Sea Islanders and the Queensland Labour Trade: a Record of Voyages and Experiences in the Western Pacific, from 1875-91. Roy. 8vo. Lond., 1893. MD 6 U 23

WAYFARER. Pen and Pencil in Collins-street. [See Melbourne.] MH 1 S 63

WAYLEN, H. S. H. Thoughts from the Writings of R. Jefferies. [See Jefferies R.] J S U 10

WAYNE, Maj.-Gen. Anthony, and the Pennsylvania Line in the Continental Army by C. J. Stillé. Imp. 8vo. Philad., 1893. C 18 U 2

WEALE, J. C. M. The Common-sense of Life Insurance: a Review, Historical and Critical, of the various Life Insurance Offices in New Zealand; by "Giolla." 8vo. Wellington, 1889. MF 4 P 54

WEALE, J. C. W. A Colony of Lunatics; a review of Dr. Tucker's pamphlet on the Gheel Lunatic Asylum. Sm. 4to. Sydney, 1884 MA 1 U 57

WEATHERILL and CO. Queensland Post Office Directory, with which is incorporated the Post Office Directory of Brisbane, and Country Guide. 8vo. Brisbane, 1893. ME

WEBB, Dr. Henry J Advanced Agriculture. 12mo. Lond., 1894. A 32 R 8

WEBB, Sidney. What Socialism Means; a Call to the Unconverted. (Reprint.) 8vo. Sydney, 1893. MF 2 Q 03

—— and WEBB Beatrice. History of Trade Unionism. 8vo. Lond., 1894. F 10 T 24

WEBB, Rev. Thos. Wm. Celestial Objects for the Common Telescopes. 5th ed. 2 vols. 12mo. Lond., 1893. A 19 Q 17, 18

WEBBE, Edward. His Travailes, 1590. [See Bibliotheca Curiosa.] J 18 Q 26

WEBSTER, A., & Co. Webster's Royal Red Book or Court and Fashionable Register, 1893-95. 5 vols. 12mo. Lond., 1893-95. E

WEBSTER, Catherine. Trial and Execution of, for the Murder of Mrs. Thomas, at Richmond, England, together with her romantic false statement and final full confession. 8vo. Melb., 1878. MF 4 R 11

WEBSTER, Daniel. Plaster Cast of. [See Hutton, L.— Portraits in Plaster.] A 23 V 13
Sketch of. [See Brooks, N.—Statesmen.] C 16 R 20

WEBSTER, Noah. Webster's International Dictionary of the English Language. 4to. Springfield, 1892. K 10 U 25

WEDDELL, Capt. James. Voyage towards the South Pole, 1822-24, containing an Examination of the Antarctic Sea to the 74th degree of latitude, and a Visit to Tierra Del Fuego. 2nd ed. 8vo. Lond., 1827. D 17 T 17

WEDDERBURN, A. J. Pharmacy and Drug Laws of the several States and Territories. Roy. 8vo. Wash., 1894. F 1 T 19
Report on the extent and character of Food and Drug Adulteration. 8vo. Wash., 1894. A 33 U 11

WEDGWOOD, Josiah: his Personal History; by Dr. S. Smiles. 12mo. Lond., 1894. C 17 P 21
Life of; with Notices of his Works; by L. Jewitt. Illustrated. 8vo. Lond., 1865. C 21 S 13
Sketch of; by Prof. Church. [See Porfolio, Monograph. 3] E
Sketch of. [See Smith, G. B.—Leaders of Modern Industry.] C 14 P 14

WEDMORE, Frederick. Pastorals of France. Renunciations. 12mo. Lond., 1893. J 5 P 48

WEEDEN, Wm. B. Indian Money as a Factor in New England Civilization. (Johns Hopkins University Studies, 2.) 8vo. Baltimore, 1884. B 18 S 2

WEEKLY NOTES, The. [See Law Reports of Great Britain and Ireland.] E

WEEKS, Edward L. Constantinople. [See Crawford, F. Marion.] D 18 S 12

WEEKS, Prof. Stephen B. Religious Development in the Province of North Carolina. (Johns Hopkins University Studies, 10.) 8vo. Baltimore, 1892. B 18 T 10

Church and State in North Carolina. (John Hopkins University Studies, 11.) 8vo. Baltimore, 1893. B 19 S 11

WEICHSELBAUM, Dr. A. Elements of Pathological Histology; translated by Dr. W. R. Dawson. Illustrated. Roy. 8vo. Lond., 1895. A 33 U 9

WEIK, Jesse W. Abraham Lincoln. [See Herndon, W. H.] C 13 P 36, 37

WEISBACH, Dr. J., and HERMANN, Prof. Gustav. Mechanics of Hoisting Machinery, including Accumulators, Excavators, and Pile-drivers: a Text-book for Technical Schools and a Guide for Practical Engineers. Authorised Translation from the 2nd German edition by K. P. Dahlstrom. Illustrated. 8vo. Lond., 1893. A 25 S 26

WEISE, C. H. Plauti Comœdiæ. [See Plautus, M. A.] H 3 S 38, 39

WEISMANN, Prof. August. The Germ-Plasm: a Theory of Heredity. 8vo. Lond., 1893. A 28 Q 34

Effect of External Influences upon Development. (Romanes Lecture, 1894.) 8vo. Lond., 1894. A 27 U 22

On the Change of the Mexican Axolotl to an Amblystoma; translated by H. M. Douglass. 8vo. Wash., 1878. A 30 R 6

WEISS, Prof. F. E. Trans.—Physiology of Plants. [See Sorauer, Dr. P.] A 20 T 12

WEISSER, Prof. L., and MERZ, Dr. H. Bilder-Atlas zur Weltgeschichte. 4to. Stuttgart, 1882. B 0 8 6 ‡

WELBY, Horace. Mysteries of Life, Death, and Futurity; Illustrated from the best and latest authorities. 12mo. Lond., 1861. G 7 U 30

WELCH, C. History of the Tower Bridge and of other Bridges under the Thames. Illustrated. 4to. Lond., 1894. B 36 T 16 ‡

WELFORD, Walter D., and STURMEY, Henry. The "Indispensable Hand-book" to the Optical Lantern: a complete Cyclopædia on the subject of Optical Lanterns, Slides, and accessory apparatus. Illustrated. 8vo. Lond., 1888. A 20 T 24

WELLESLEY, Richard Colley, Marquess of. [Life of]; by Rev. W. H. Hutton. (Rulers of India.) 8vo. Oxford, 1893. C 13 P 14

WELLINGTON, Arthur Wellesley, Duke of. The rise of Wellington; by Gen. Lord Roberts. 12mo. Lond., 1895. C 5 P 22

Story of his Life; by A. R. Cooke. 12mo. Lond. (n.d.) C 17 P 13

WELLS, Wm. Henry. Geographical Dictionary, or Gazetteer of the Australian Colonies. (Original Manuscript.) 4to. Sydney, 1847. Libr.

Plan of the Road between Gundagai and Port Phillip. Fol. (n.p.) 1839. MD 5 Q 16 ‡

Map of the County of Cumberland, in the Colony of New South Wales. Folded 8vo. Sydney, 1840. MD 8 R 27

WELLS, Rev. Wm. P. Official Charge to young Ministers. 12mo. Melb., 1888. MG 2 T 17

WELSH TEXT SOCIETY. The Text of the Llan Dâv, reproduced from the Gwysaney Manuscript, by J. G. Evans and Prof. J. Rhys. Roy. 8vo. Oxford, 1894. E

WENCKSTERN, F. von. A Bibliography of the Japanese Empire, 1859–93, in European Languages, to which is added a fac-simile reprint of Leon Pagès' Bibliographie Japonaise. Roy. 8vo. Leiden, 1895. J 8 V 23

WENTWORTH, Paul. Amos Thorne, and other Poems. 12mo. Melb., 1870. MH 1 P 50

WENTWORTH, Thomas, 1st Earl of Strafford. [See Strafford, Earl of.]

WENTWORTH, William Charles. Reply to Robert Lowe's speech on motion made to bring in a Bill to confer a Constitution on New South Wales. 8vo. Lond. (n.d.) MF 3 T 52

WERNE, Ferdinand. African Wanderings. 12mo. Lond., 1852. D 20 Q 15

WESLEYAN MISSIONARY SOCIETY. Instructions to the Rev. G. Piercy, W. R. Beach, and J. Cox, appointed to commence a Mission in China. 8vo. Lond., 1853. G 9 S 21

WESSLAU, O. E. Free-trade and Protection. 8vo. Lond., 1883. F 10 U 8

WEST, Henry J. To the Members of the Australian Mutual Provident Society. 8vo. Sydney (n.d.) MF 4 R 45

WEST, John. Dried Fruits. (Vict. Dept. of Agriculture.—Lectures.) 8vo. Melb., 1892. MA 3 V 15

Irrigation Development in Western America. (Vict. Dept. of Agricult.—Lectures.) 8vo. Melb., 1892. MA 3 V 15

Process of Drying Fruits. 8vo. Melb. (n.d.) MA 3 V 15

WEST, Rev. John. The Hope of Life Eternal: a Sermon 8vo. Launceston, 1850. MG 2 Q 52

WEST, T. British Diatomaceæ. [See Smith, Rev. W.] A 28 V 24, 25

WEST VIRGINIA UNIVERSITY. Catalogue of, 1892, 1893. 8vo. Charleston, _893. E

WESTBOROUGH INSANE HOSPITAL, Mass. Report for year ending September, 1892. 8vo. Boston, 1893. E

WESTBURY, F. A. "Atha." Talbot Fane, Bachelor: a Tale of thrilling interest, founded on fact. 8vo. Adelaide, 1887. MJ 1 V 16

WESTCOTT, Rt. Rev. Brooke Foss. The Bible in the Church. 18mo. Lond., 1893. G 2 U 40
Christus Consummator. 12mo. Lond., 1890. G 2 U 29
Epistle of St. John, Greek Text. 12mo. Lond., 1892. G 14 R 18
Epistle to the Hebrews, Greek Text. 12mo. Lond., 1892. G 14 R 19
Essays in the History of Religious Thought in the West. 12mo. Lond., 1891. G 2 U 37
From Strength to Strength. 12mo. Lond., 1890. G 2 U 33
Gifts for Ministry. 12mo. Camb., 1889. G 2 U 38
Gospel of the Resurrection. 12mo. Lond., 1891. G 2 U 25
The Historic Faith. 12mo. Lond., 1893. G 2 U 34
History of the Canon of the New Testament. 12mo. Lond., 1889. G 2 U 30
Incarnation and Common Life. 12mo. Lond., 1893. G 2 U 35
Introduction to the Study of the Gospels. 12mo. Lond., 1888. G 2 U 24
New Testament in the original Greek. 12mo. Lond., 1882. G 2 U 23
New Testament in the original Text. 12mo. Lond., 1890. G 2 U 22
Religious Office of the Universities. 12mo. Lond., 1873. G 2 U 31
Revelation of the Father. 12mo. Lond.,1887. G 2 U 26
Revelation of the Risen Lord. 12mo. Lond., 1887. G 2 U 27
Social Aspects of Christianity. 12mo. Lond., 1888. G 2 U 32
Some Thoughts from the Ordinal. 12mo. Lond., 1884. G 2 U 39
Thoughts on Revelation and Life. 12mo. Lond., 1887. G 2 U 36
Victory of the Cross. 12mo. Lond., 1889. G 2 U 28

WESTCOTT, W. Wynn. Numbers: their Occult Power and Mystic Virtue. Roy. 8vo. Lond., 1890. A 24 V 24

WESTERN AUSTRALIA.—*General.* The New Country to the Northward. 8vo. Perth, 1840. MD 5 S 26

WESTERN AUSTRALIA — *Government Departments, Reports, and Publications.*
Acts. [*See* Statutes.]
Civil Service. Blue Books, 1880-92, 1894. 14 vols. sm. fol. Perth, 1881-95. ME
Lands. Map of Western Australia, showing Electoral Districts, 1884. (Mounted on Rollers.) Perth, 1893. Map Room
Map of Western Australia. (Mounted on Rollers.) Perth, 1894. Map Room
Statutes. Acts of the Parliament of Western Australia passed in 1894. Sm. 4to. Perth, 1894. ME

WESTLAKE, Prof. John. Chapters on the Principles of International Law. Cambridge, 1894. F 2 T 18

WESTMINISTER REVIEW, The. Vols. 139-143. 8vo. Lond., 1892-95. E

WESTON, Jessie. Ko Méri; or a Cycle of Cathay a Story of New Zealand Life. 8vo. Lond., 1890. MJ 2 T 25

WEYMOUTH, F. Marten. Drum Armatures and Commutators. 8vo. Lond., 1893. A 21 S 15

WHALESLI KELL. [*See* Healey D.]

WHARTON, Dr. Francis. The Revolutionary Diplomatic Correspondence of the United States. Vols. 2-6. 8vo. Wash., 1889. B 10 V 4-8

WHARTON, Dr. Henry R. Minor Surgery and Bandaging. 8vo. Philad., 1893. A 26 S 21

WHARTON, Capt. Wm. John Lewis. Captain Cook's Journal. [*See* Cook, Capt. Jas.] MD 6 P 13 †

WHATELY, Most Rev Richard. Bacon's Essays annotated. [*See* Bacon, Lord.] J 6 T 3
Miscellaneous Remairs from the Commonplace Book of. 8vo. Lond., 1864. J 6 R 10

WHEATLEY, Henry Benjamin. Literary Blunders a Chapter in the History of Human Error. 12mo. Lond., 1893. J 6 T 7
Pepys' Diary. [*See* Pepys, S.] C 14 V 1-6

WHEELBARROW. [*See* Trumbull, Gen. M. M.]

WHEELER, Daniel. Memoirs of the Life and Labours of the late Daniel Wheeler, a Minister of the Society of Friends. 8vo. Lond., 1852. MG 2 Q 47

WHEELER, Everett P. Real Bi-metallism; or, True Coin *versus* False Coin. 8vo. New York, 1895. F 8 U 50

WHEELER, Olin D. Indianland and Wonderland. Roy. 8vo. St. Paul, 1894. D 15 V 20
Six Thousand Miles through Wonderland: being a description of the Marvellous Region traversed by the Northern Pacific Railroad. 4to. St. Paul, 1893. D 15 V 9

WHEELER; Stephen. [Life of] the Ameer Abdur Rahman. 12mo. Lond., 1895. C 22 P 9

WHEELER, W. F. Catalogue of the Library of the Historical Society of Montana. Roy. 8vo. Helena, Mont., 1892. K 7 S 41

WHEELER, W. H. Tidal Rivers: their Hydraulics, Improvements, Navigation. Roy. 8vo. Lond., 1893. A 22 T 13

WHETMAN, Wm. Cecil Dampier. Solution and Electrolysis. 12mo. Camb., 1895. A 21 R 30

WHIBLEY, Chas. English Prose Character. [See Henley, W. E.] J 5 P 17

WHICHCOTE, Benjamin. Sketch of. [See Westcott, Rt. Rev. B. F.—Religious Thought in the West.] G 2 U 37

WHIPPLE, Leander Edmund. The Philosophy of Mental Healing: a Practical Exposition of Natural Restorative Power. 8vo. New York, 1893. G 1 R 10

WHISHAW, Fred. J. Out of Doors in Tsarland: a Record of the Seeings and Doings of a Wanderer in Russia. 8vo. Lond., 1893. D 18 Q 7

WHIST TABLE, The : a Treasury of Notes on the Royal Game; edited by "Portland." 8vo. Lond. (n.d.) A 20 T 28

WHITAKER, Joseph. Almanac for 1893-95. 3 vols. 8vo. Lond., 1893-95. E

WHITAKER, Rev. Thos. Dunham. History of the original Parish of Whalley, and Honor of Clitheroe, in the Counties of Lancaster and York, to which is subjoined an account of the Parish of Cartwell. 3rd ed. Fol. Lond., 1818. B 37 Q 9 ‡
History and Antiquities of the Deanery of Craven, in the County of York. 2nd ed. Fol. Lond., 1812. B 37 Q 8 ‡

WHITCOMB, Seldon L. Chronological Outlines of American Literature. 8vo. New York, 1894. J 9 R 30

WHITCOMBE, C. D. Descriptive and Historical Handbook to the Auckland Art Gallery and Mackelvie Collection. 12mo. Auckland, 1888. MA 2 P 31

WHITCOMBE, J. Conveyancing. [See Prideaux, F.] F 8 T 23, 24

WHITE, A. S. Sir S. Baker. [See Murray, T. D.] C 21 T 10

WHITE, Andrew Dickson. European Schools of History and Politics. (Johns Hopkins University Studies, 5.) 8vo. Baltimore, 1887. B 18 S 5

WHITE, Archer M. Treatise on the Constitution and Government of Solicitors: their Rights and Duties. 8vo. Lond., 1894. F 14 T 21

WHITE, Arnold, and his Work. [See Blathwayt, R.—Interviews.] J 10 U 34
The English Democracy: its Promises and Perils. 8vo. Lond., 1894. F 14 S 28

WHITE, Charles. Early Australian History: the Story of Australian Bushranging. 8 vols. 12mo. Bathurst, 1891-93. MB 1 P 36-42

WHITE, E. J. Observations of the Outer Satellite of Mars. (Roy. Soc., Vict., 10.) 8vo. Melb., 1880. ME 1 P
On the Performance of some Timekeepers. (Roy. Soc., Vict., 10.) 8vo. Melb., 1883. ME 1 P

WHITE, Dr. Emerson E. Promotions and Examinations in Graded Schools. 8vo. Washington, 1891. G 18 R 28

WHITE, Dr. F. Buchanan. Pelagic Hemiptera. [See Thomson, Sir C. W., and Murray, Dr. J.—Voyage of H.M.S. Challenger—Zoology, 7.] A 6 †

WHITE, Gleeson. Editor—Book-Song: an Anthology of Poems of Books and Bookmen from Modern Authors. 18mo. Lond., 1893. H 8 R 43
Practical Designing. 8vo. Lond., 1893. A 23 Q 30

WHITE, Henry A. Tales of Crimes and Criminals in Australia. 8vo. Lond., 1894. MJ 2 T 46

WHITE, Henry Kirke. Poetical Works and Remains of; with Life by R. Southey. Illustrated. 12mo. Lond., 1852. H 10 T 25

WHITE, Horace. Taxation. [See Cossa, Dr. L.] F 8 U 21

WHITE, Rev. Dr. James S. Lectures on the Eastern Question. 8vo. Singleton, 1877. MF 4 Q 26
Free-trade: a Lecture. 8vo. Singleton, 1882. MF 4 R 19
The "Single Tax" Theory as propounded by Henry George, reviewed. 8vo. Singleton, 1890. MF 4 Q 14
The Land Tax and the reason in justification considered. 12mo. Maitland (n.d.) MF 4 P 5
Lecture on Education, National, Secular, Compulsory, and Free. 8vo. West Maitland, 1875. MG 2 Q 30
War: Should a Christian Nation engage in it? 8vo. Singleton, 1885. MG 2 Q 29
Address delivered at the General Assembly of the Presbyterian Church of New South Wales. 12mo. Sydney, 1892. MG 2 R 31

WHITE, John. Ancient History of the Maori. Vol. 6. 8vo. Wellington, 1890. MB 1 S 37

WHITE, Rev. Joseph Blanco. Observations on Heresy and Orthodoxy. 8vo. Lond., 1835. G 15 Q 32

WHITE, T. Charters. The Microscope, and how to use it: a Hand-book for Beginners. New ed., illustrated. 8vo. Lond., 1893. A 29 Q 39

WHITE, Taylor. On the Bird Moa and its aliases. (Trans. N.Z. Inst., 27) 8vo. Wellington, 1894. ME 2 R

The Kea (*Nestor notabilis*). [Trans. N.Z. Inst., 27.) 8vo. Wellington, 1894. ME 2 R

Rats of New Zealand. (Trans N.Z. Inst., 27.) 8vo. Wellington, 1894. ME 2 R

WHITE, W. Truth illustrated by Great Authors: a Dictionary of nearly four thousand aids to reflection. 12mo. Lond, 1859. K 19 P 18

WHITEAVES, J. F. Contributions to Canadian Palæontology. Vol. 1, pt. 4. Royal 8vo. Ottawa, 1892. E

WHITEHEAD, Paul. Manners: a satire. Sm. fol. Lond., 1739. H 39 Q 13 ‡

WHITEHEAD, Thos. Virginia: a Hand-book giving its History, Climate, and Mineral Wealth, its Educational, Agricultural, and Industrial Advantages. 8vo. Richmond, Va, 1893. D 15 T 11

WHITEHEAD, Wm. The Roman Father: a Tragedy. [*See* London Stage, 3.] H 2 S 35

WHITE'S CLUB. The History of White's, with the Betting book, 1743-1878, and a List of Members, 1736-1892. 2 vols. 4to. Lond, 1892. B 6 V 27, 28

WHITFIELD, Lewis. The Practice in Divorce, New South Wales. 8vo. Sydney, 1893.* MF 2 R 38

WHITFIELD, R. P. Brachiopoda and Lamellibranchiata of the Raritan Clays and Greensand Marls of New Jersey. (U.S. Geol. Survey, 9.) 4to. Wash., 1885. E

Gasteropoda and Cephalopoda of the Raritan Clays and Greensand Marls of New Jersey. (U.S. Geol., Survey, 18.) 4to. Wash., 1892. E

Mollusca and Crustacea of the Miocene Formations of New Jersey. 4to. Wash., 1894. A 15 S 5 †

WHITING, Margaret Christine. Wild Flowers of the North-eastern States. [*See* Miller, Ellen.] A 15 S 1 †

WHITLEY, Margaret. Women's Work. [*See* Bulley, A. Amy.] F 14 R 23

WHITMAN, C. M. American Orators and Oratory. Roy 8vo. Chicago, 1884. C 12 V 17

WHITMAN, C. O Development of some Pelagic Fish Eggs. [*See* Agassiz, A.] A 30 U 25

WHITMAN, E. A. The Cambridge Idea in Temperance Reform and Massachusett Laws for dealing with Drunkenness. 8vo. Boston (n.d.) F 14 U 15

WHITMAN, Walt. Complete Prose Works. 8vo. Philad., 1892. J 10 U 31

Leaves of Grass. 8vo. Philad., 1894. H 9 T 4

His Relation to Science and Philosophy; by W. Gay. 12mo. Melb., 1895. MJ 3 P 37

[Sketch of]; by W. Gay. 8vo. Melb., 1893. MC 1 S 2

Walt. Whitman: a Study; by J. A. Symonds. 8vo. Lond., 1893. C 11 S 8

WHITMEE, Rev. S. J. Missionary Cruise in the South Pacific. 8vo. Sydney, 1871. MD 8 Q 21

WHITNEY, Caspar W. A Sporting Pilgrimage. Illustrated. 8vo. Lond., 1895. A 30 T 12

WHITNEY. Eli. Sketch of. [*See* Hubert, P. G.—Inventors.] C 17 R 3

WHITNEY, Dr. Josiah Dwight. The Yosemite Guidebook: a description of the Yosemite Valley and the adjacent region of the Sierra Nevada, and of the big trees of California. Illustrated. 8vo. Wash, 1870. D 15 U 6

WHITTAKER, Thos. Essays and Notices; Philosophical and Psychological. 8vo. Lond., 1895. G 3 R 9

WHITTELL, Dr. H. T. Notes of the Dissection of a Compound Ascidian found in St. Vincent's Gulf. (Trans. Roy. Soc., S. Australia, 6.) 8vo. Adelaide, 1883. ME 1 S

WHITTOCK, Nathaniel. The New Picture of London, Westminster, and the Metropolitan Boroughs. 12mo. Lond., 1836. D 18 P 20

WHITWORTH, Robt. Percy. Spargles and Sawdust. 8vo. Melb. (n.d.) MJ 3 R 5

Lost and Found: a Romance. Roy 8vo. Melb., 1873. MJ 3 R 6

Melbourne Medical Morals and British Critical Opinion; by "A Bystander." 8vo. Melb., 1877. MA 1 V 70

Velvet and Rags: a Series of Australian Theatrical Stories. 8vo. Melb. (n.d.) MJ 2 S 38

Cobb's Box. 8vo. Melb., 1875. MJ 2 S 37

Bailliere's Queensland, South Australian, and Tasmanian Gazetteers. [*See* Bailliere, F. F.] MD 5 S 54-57

WHOLE BOOKE OF PSALMES. [*See* Liturgics.] G 13 T 40

WICK, B. L. The Amish Mennonites: a Sketch of their Origin, and of their Settlement in Iowa; with their Creed. 8vo. Iowa, 1894. G 14 Q 29

WICKES, T. A. The Strike at Pullman. [*See* Pullman, G. M.] F 10 Q 31

WICKSON, Prof. Edward J. The California Fruits and How to Grow Them. 2nd edition. 8vo. San Francisco, 1891. A 18 U 19

WICKSTEED, C. M. *Trans.*—Social Peace. [*See* Schulze-Gaevernitz, Dr. G. von] F 14 Q 49

WICKSTEED, Richard John. The Elector's Political Catechism. 8vo. Ottawa, 1895. F 11 U 6

WICLIF or WYCLIFFE, John. Sketch of. [*See* Bettany, G. T. —Popular History of the Reformation.] G 14 Q 33

WIEDERSHEIM, Dr. R. The Structure of Man: an Index to his Past History; translated by H. and M. Bernard. Illustrated. 8vo. Lond., 1895. A 33 U 20

WIEL, Alethea. Venice. 8vo. Lond., 1894. B 30 R 8
[*See* Designs for Church Embroidery.] A 12 S 17 †

WIELAND, Christopher M. von. Oberon : a Poem; translated by W. Sotheby. 12mo. Lond., 1844.
H 10 T 26
Oberon. 12mo. Leipzig, 1819. H 9 U 40

WIESER, Friedrich von. Natural Value ; edited, with Analysis, by W. Smart, and translated by C. A. Malloch. 8vo. Lond., 1893. F 9 T 10

WIGG, E. S., & SON. Traveller's Guide to Western Australia, accompanied by latest Maps and Plans and a Directory of Mining Companies. 8vo. Perth, 1894.
MD 7 8 2

WIGG, Henry C. The Custom-house Hand-book of Victoria ; being the Merchants' and Importers' Guide to the business of the Customs, Ports and Harbours, and Shipping Departments. 12mo. Melb., 1869.
MF 4 P 6

WIGGINS, Capt. Joseph. Polar Gleams. [*See* Peel, H.] D 16 T 11

WIGHT, George. Queensland : the Field for British Labour and Enterprise, and the Source of England's Cotton Supply. 3rd ed. 8vo. Lond., 1863.
MD 5 Q 55

WIGRAM, Capt. J. S. New Dial for indicating Ranges in Coast Defence. (United Service Institution, N.S.W., 5.) 8vo. Sydney, 1894. ME

WILBERFORCE, Reginald G. An Unrecorded Chapter of the Indian Mutiny. Illustrated. 8vo. Lond., 1894. B 29 R 3

WILD, C. J. On the Mosses and Hepatics of the Synopsis, Queensland Flora, and its Supplements. (Proc. Roy. Soc., Queensland, 5.) 8vo. Brisb., 1888. ME 1 T
Bryological Notes. (Proc. Roy. Soc., Queensland, 6.) 8vo. Brisbane, 1889. ME 1 T

WILD, Jonathan. [Life of], 1682-1725; by A. Vincent. (Lives of Twelve Bad Men.) 8vo. Lond., 1894.
C 18 T 9

WILDE, Oscar F. O'F. W. A Woman of no Importance : a Drama. 8vo. Lond., 1894. H 1 S 28

WILEY, Harvey. Principles and Practice of Agricultural Analysis. Vol. 1. Roy. 8vo. Easton, Pa., 1894.
A 30 R 16
Report of the Association of Official Agricultural Chemists, 1894. [*See* Association of Official Agricultural Chemists.] E

WILEY, Wm. H. & Sara K. The Yosemite, Alaska, and the Yellowstone. 4to. Lond., 1893. D 12 S 5†

WILHELM, Dr. Lewis W. Local Institutions of Maryland. 1. The Land System. 2. The Hundred. 3. The County. 4. The Town. (Johns Hopkins University Studies, 3.) 8vo. Baltimore, 1885. B 18 S 3

WILKES, Adm. Charles. Narrative of the United States Exploring Expedition, 1838-42. 2 vols. 8vo. Lond., 1852. MD S P 24, 25
Sketch of. [*See* Greeley, Gen. A. W.—Explorers and and Travellers.] C 17 R 4

WILKIE, Sir David. The Wilkie Gallery. 4to. Lond. (n.d.) A 40 T 2 ‡

WILKINS, Wm. Agriculture in New South Wales. Roy. 8vo. Sydney, 1893. MA 1 S 34

WILKINSON, Spenser. The Brain of an Army : a Popular Account of the German General Staff. 8vo. Lond., 1895. A 29 R 32

WILKINSON, W. P. Preliminary Survey of Eucalyptus Oils of Victoria. (Proceedings Royal Society, Victoria, 6 ; new series.) 8vo. Melb., 1894. ME 1 P
Sugar Strength and Acidity of Victorian Musts, with reference to the Alcoholic Strength of Victorian Wines. (Proc. Roy. Soc. Vict., n s. 7.) 8vo. Melb., 1895. ME 1 P

WILKINSON, Wm. Hattam and Frederick Bushby. The Australian Magistrate. 6th ed. 8vo. Sydney, 1894.
MF 1 Q 60

WILKS, Mark. Tahiti : a Review of the Origin, Character, and Progress of French Roman Catholic efforts for the destruction of English Protestant Missions in the South Seas. 8vo. Lond., 1844. MG 2 Q 16

WILKS, Dr. Samuel, and BETTANY, George T. Biographical History of Guy's Hospital. 8vo. Lond., 1892. C 15 P 12

WILLARD, Frances E. My Happy Half-Century : Autobiography of an American Woman. 12mo. Lond., 1894. C 18 P 23

WILLARD, X. A. Practical Butter-book. Illustrated. 12mo. New York (n.d.) A 18 R 44
Practical Dairy Husbandry. Illustrated. Roy. 8vo. New York, 1871. A 30 R 8

WILLEBY, Charles. [Life of] Frederic François Chopin. 8vo. Lond., 1892. C 12 Q 49

WILLEY, Arthur. Amphioxus and the Ancestry of the Vertebrates. 8vo. New York, 1894. A 27 U 21

WILLIAM I, King of England. Conspiracy of the Norman Barons against William the Bastard, 1157. [See Bibliotheca Curiosa.] J 18 Q 43

WILLIAM II, King of Germany. Sketch of. [See Smalley, G. W.—Studies of Men.] C 19 R 20

WILLIAM THE SILENT, Prince of Orange. The Moderate Man of the 16th Century: the Story of his Life, as told from his own Letters, from those of his friends and enemies, and from Official Documents; by Ruth Putman. 2 vols. 8vo. New York, 1895.
C 22 P 6, 7

WILLIAMS, Rev. A. Lukyn. Some Guiding Principles in the Revision of the New Testament; or, the Authorised Version, how it was compared with the most ancient authorities. 12mo. Sydney, 1881.
MG 2 R 54

WILLIAMS, B. The Commodore Perry Express, and Black Ball Ocean Advertiser. Sm. 4to. Melb., 1857.
MJ 1 V 15

WILLIAMS, Benjamin Samuel. Choice Stove and Greenhouse Flowering Plants. 3rd edition. 8vo. Lond., 1883. A 20 R 4

Choice Stove and Greenhouse Ornamental-leaved Plants. 2nd edition. 8vo. Lond. 1875. A 20 R 3

WILLIAMS, Chas. H. Law of Real Property; Appendix. [See Millard, G. W.] MF 3 T 28

WILLIAMS, Edward H., jun. Action of Coal Dust. [See Atkinson, J. J.] A 24 P 12

WILLIAMS, Hamilton. Britain's Naval Power: a short History of the Growth of the British Navy from the Earliest Times to Trafalgar. 8vo. Lond., 1894.
B 23 R 20

The Steam Navy of England, Past, Present, and Future. 8vo. Lond., 1893. A 22 S 20

WILLIAMS, Henry. The Orchid Album. [See Warner, R.] A 14 P 10 †

WILLIAMS, Prof. Henry Shaler. Correlation Papers: Devonian and Carboniferous. 8vo. Wash., 1891.
A 24 V 32

WILLIAMS, Capt. J. Some Remarks on the Island of Espiritu Santo, New Hebrides Group. (Roy. Geogr. Soc. of Australasia, Q. Branch, 1.) 8vo. Brisbane, 1892. ME 20

WILLIAMS, J. Fletcher. History of the City of Saint Paul, and of the County of Ramsey, Minnesota. 8vo. Saint Paul, 1876. B 19 T 14

WILLIAMS, Montagu. Round London, down East and up West. 8vo. Lond., 1892. D 18 T 14

WILLIAMS, Roger, the Pioneer of Religious Liberty; by O. S. Straus. 8vo. Lond, 1894. C 17 R 15

WILLIAMS, Dr. Samuel Wells. The Chinese Commercial Guide with an Appendix of Sailing Directions. 6th edition. 8vo. Hong Kong, 1863. F 9 T 16

WILLIAMS, Thos. Memoir of James Wood. 8vo. Geelong, 1883. MC 1 P 54

Triumph in Suffering: Memorials of Elizabeth Ann Bennett. 2nd ed. 8vo. Ballarat, 1879. MC 1 S 12

WILLIAMS, Rev. W. Personal Reminiscences of Charles Haddon Spurgeon. 8vo. Lond, 1895. C 19 V 12

WILLIAMS, W. H. A Holiday Medley of Tales, Sketches, Poetry, Facetiae, Games, &c. 8vo. Melb. (n.d.)
MJ 3 E 4

WILLIAMS, Capt. W. H. Uganda. [See Roy. Col. Inst., Proc., 25.] E

WILLIAMS. Prof. Wm. Principles and Practice of Veterinary Medicine. 7th ed., illustrated. 8vo. Edinb., 1893. A 30 R 20

Principles and Practice of Veterinary Surgery. 8th ed. Edinb., 1893. A 30 R 21

WILLIAMS, Wm. Secondary Punishments discussed. 8vo. Lond., 1833. MF 2 Q 84

WILLIAMS, Dr. Wm. Klapp. The Communes of Lombardy from the 6th to the 10th Century: an Investigation of the Causes which led to the Development of of Municipal Unity among the Lombard Communes. (Johns Hopkins University Studies, 9.) 8vo. Baltimore, 1891. B 18 8 9

WILLIAMS, Lieut.-Col. Wm. Daniel Campbell. On the Organization, Equipment, and Training of a Federated Medical Service. (United Service Institution, N.S.W., 5.) 8vo. Sydney, 1894. ME

The Clothing of the Soldier. [See United Service Inst.]
MA 2 V 68

WILLIAMSON, George C. [Life and Works of] J. Russell. Imp. 8vo. Lond., 1894. C 17 U 19

WILLIAMSON, George C. Trade Tokens. [See Boyne, Wm.] A 27 T 5, 6

WILLIAMSON, Wm. Horticultural Hand-book and Exhibitors' Guide. New ed. revised by M. Dunn. 8vo. Edinb., 1895. A 32 R 10

WILLS, Dr. Francis. Treatise on Mental Derangement. 2nd ed., revised. 8vo. Lond., 1843. A 26 E 4

WILLS, Nathaniel Parker. Hurry-graphs; or, Sketches of Scenery, Celebrities, and Society. 12mo. Lond, 1851. C 19 T 10

Life Here and There; or, Sketches of Society and Adventure at Far-a-part Times and Places. 12mo. Lond, 1850. J 11 U 26

People I have met: or, Pictures of Society and People of Mark. 12mo. Lond., 1850. J 11 U 25

WILLOUGHBY, W. W. and W. F. Government and Administration of the United States. (Johns Hopkins University Studies, 9.) 8vo. Baltimore, 1891.
B 18 S 9

WILLS, Dr. Chas. James. Behind an Eastern Veil: Experience of a lady of the inner life of ladies of the upper classes in Persia. 8vo. Edinb., 1894.
D 17 T 13

WILLS, Wm. John. Report on the Sufferings and Death of. [See Burke, R. O'H.] MD 9 P 11 †

WILLSHIRE, W. H. The Aborigines of Central Australia. 8vo. Adelaide, 1891. MA 3 V 42

WILMOT, Hon. A. Story of the expansion of Southern Africa. 8vo. Lond., 1894. B 16 R 11

WILMOT, E. P. E., and STREATFIELD, E.C. Charterhouse, Old and New. 8vo. Lond, 1895. B 36 T 24

WILSON, A. J. Glossary of Colloquial Slang and Technical Terms in use on the Stock Exchange and Money Market. 12mo. Lond., 1895. J 12 S 42

WILSON, Anne C. (A. C. McLeod). After Five Years in India; or, Life and Work in a Punjaub District. 8vo. Lond., 1895. D 17 R 18

WILSON, Sir Chas. Wm. Picturesque Palestine, Sinai, and Egypt; edited by Col. Sir W. C. Wilson. 4 vols. 4to. Lond., 1884. D 12 R 17-20 †

WILSON, D. The Dairying Industry. (Vict. Dept. of Agricult.—Lectures.) 8vo. Melb., 1892. MA 3 V 15

A homely chat about Dairying. 12mo. Melb., 1888.
MA 3 T 9

The Dairy Industry. 8vo. Melb., 1890. MA 3 V 27

Dairying Industry in Victoria. 8vo. Melb., 1894.
MA 3 V 27

WILSON, Edward. [See Bowie v. Wilson.] MF 2 Q 74

WILSON, Dr. Edward Livingstone. Cyclopædic Photography: a complete Hand-book arranged in Cyclopædic form. 8vo. New York, 1894. A 23 U 8

WILSON, Erasmus. Art of Prolonging Life. [See Hufeland, C. W.] A 26 P 10

WILSON, Rev. F. R. M. Notes on Lichens in New South Wales. (Proc. Roy. Soc., Queensland, 6.) 8vo. Brisbane, 1889. ME 1 T

Notes on a remarkable Lichen Growth in connection with a new species of Sticta. (Proc. Roy. Soc., Queensland, 7.) 8vo. Brisbane, 1891. ME 1 T

WILSON, Frank T. Minnesota Educational Exhibit for the World's Columbian Exposition. Obl. 8vo. Stillwater, Minn., 1893. G 18 P 22

WILSON, Dr. George. Electricity and the Electric Telegraph: together with the Chemistry of the Stars: an Argument touching the Stars and their Inhabitants. 12mo. Lond., 1852. A 21 P 39

WILSON, George R. Drunkenness. 8vo. Lond., 1893.
A 13 P 3

WILSON, H. D. South Australia. [See Woods, J. D.]
MB 1 Q 48

WILSON, Capt. Henry. Pelew Islands. [See Keate, G.]
MD 8 Q 35-37

WILSON, Herbert M. Manual of Irrigation Engineering. Roy. 8vo. New York, 1893. A 6 U 24

WILSON, Capt. James. First and Second Missionary Voyage to the South Sea Islands, 1796-98, in the ship Duff. (Universal Navigator and Modern Tourist.) 12mo. Lond., 1805. MD 8 P 14

Memoirs of; containing an account of his Enterprises and Sufferings in India, his Conversion to Christianity, his Missionary Voyage to the South Seas, and his Death; by J. Griffin. 2nd ed. 8vo. Lond. (n.d.)
MC 1 R 44

WILSON, Rt. Hon. James. Sketch of. [See Bagehot, W.—Literary Studies.] J 9 P 24

WILSON, James Grant. Cyclopædia of American Biography. [See Appleton & Co.] C 16 U 1-6

The Presidents of the United States, 1789-1894. Illustrated. 8vo. Lond., 1896. C 2 V 30

The World's Largest Libraries. 12mo. New York, 1894. J 11 R 1

WILSON, Capt. John Alexander. Sketches of Ancient Maori Life and History. 8vo. Auckland, 1894.
MA 3 R 39

The modus operandi, or Judgment without Trial; or, how I lost my Judgeship. 8vo. Auckland, 1884.
MF 4 P 22

WILSON, J. B. Dredging Stations at and near Port Phillip Heads. (Proc. Roy. Soc. Victoria, n.s. 7.) 8vo. Melb., 1895. ME 1 P

WILSON, J. J. Practical Treatise on Flax Culture, explaining the whole system and methods. 8vo. Melb., 1895. MA 3 W 12

WILSON, Rev. J. P. From the City of the Plain to the City of the Grey; with poetical allusions to the Scenery of the country 'twixt the Malvern and the Grey. 8vo. Christchurch, N.Z., 1875. MD 8 Q 16

WILSON, Mrs. R. In the Land of the Tui: 'My Journal in New Zealand. Map and Illustrations. 12mo. Lond., 1894. MD 7 T 6

WILSON, Sir Samuel. Proceedings on laying the Foundation Stone of the Wilson Hall, Melbourne University, October, 1879. [See Melbourne University.] MB 2 S 31

WILSON, Rev. W. Trans.—Writings of Clement. [See Clement of Alexandria.] G 14 U 4 and 12

WILSON, W. H. The Pacific Route: Brisbane to New York. 8vo. Brisbane (n.d.) MD 8 R 35

WILSON, Wm. Poems. 2nd ed. 12mo. Poughkeepsie, 1875. H 8 R 42

WILTON, C. E. Jubilee Poems. 8vo. Sydney, 1887. MH 1 V 6

WILTON, H. B. The Somatic Conjurer: a Treatise on Natural and Scientific Magic. 12mo. Melb., 1870. MA 3 U 7

WILTON, T. T. Another Seance with Slade. [See Mediums and their Dupes.] MG 2 Q 36

WIMPOLE, F. Visitors' Guide to Melbourne. 12mo. Melb., 1881. MD 1 P 40

WINCHELL, Dr. Alexander. Walks and Talks in the Geological Field. 8vo. New York, 1894. A 24 S 15

WINDEYER. Sir Wm. Charles. Address to the Electors of the University of Sydney, 1876. 8vo. Sydney, 1876. MF 4 Q 32

Ex parte Collins: a Judgment by Sir W. C. Windeyer, senior puisne Judge, New South Wales. 8vo. Sydney, 1889. MF 4 Q 42

Address delivered before the University Union. 8vo. Sydney, 1895. MG 2 S 10

WINDLE, Dr. C. A. Essay concerning the Pigmies of the Ancients. [*See* Tyson, Dr. E.] A 18 R 42

WINES, Dr. Frederick H. Punishment and Reformation: an Historical Sketch of the Rise of the Penitentiary System. 8vo. Lond., 1895. F 8 U 18

WINGATE, Major F. R. Ten Years' Captivity in the Madhi's Camp. [*See* Ohrwalder, Father J.] D 14 T 20

WINKELMANN, Prof. Dr. A. Handbuch der Physik. (Encyklo. der Naturwissenschaften.) Zweiter Band. Erste Abtheilung. Roy. 8vo. Breslau, 1894. E

WINKLER, C. Beri-Beri. *See* Pekelharing, C. A.] A 33 T 21

WINSLOW, A. Preliminary Report on the Coal Deposits of Missouri. Illustrated. Roy. 8vo. Jefferson City, 1891. A 9 U 34

Geology and Mineral Products of Missouri. Imp. 8vo. St. Louis, 1893. A 24 V 14

WINSLOW, Lieut. F. Report on the Waters of North Carolina, with reference to their possibilities for Oyster Culture. 8vo. Raleigh, 1886. A 28 U 5

WINSOR, Justin. Geographical Discovery in the Interior of North America in its historical relations, 1534-1700. 8vo. Lond., 1894. D 15 S 22

The Kohl Collection of Maps relating to America. Roy. 8vo. Camb., Mass., 1886. D 15 V 10

The Struggle in America between England and France, 1697-1763. 8vo. Lond. 1895. B 18 R 15

WINTER, John Strange. [*See* Stannard, Mrs. A.]

WINTER, Wm. Life and Art of Edwin Booth. 12mo. Lond., 1893. C 19 Q 6

WINTER & CO. The Irish-Australian Almanac and Directory, 1884, 1885, and 1887. 12mo. Melb., 1885-87. ME 3 T

WINTHROP, Robt. Chas. Sketch of. [*See* Smalley, O. W.—Studies of Men.] C 19 R 20

WINTON, A. L. Compilation of Analyses of American Feeding Stuffs. [*See* Jenkins Dr. E. H.] A 32 T 11

WINTON, John G., and MILLAR, W. J. Modern Steam Practice and Engineering. Illustrated. 8vo. Lond., 1884. A 22 T 14

WIRGMAN, Rev. Augustus Theodore. The Church and the Civil Power. 12mo. Lond., 1893. G 8 P 38

History of the Church of England in South Africa. 12mo. Lond., 1895. G 2 V 42

WISCONSIN—*State Departments, Reports, and Publications—*

LEGISLATURE. Laws of, 1878-93. 18 vols. 8vo. Madison, 1878-93. E

Revised Statutes. Roy. 8vo. Madison, 1878. F 11 V 9

LIBRARY. Subject-Index to the Law Books in; by J. R. Berryman, State Librarian. Roy. 8vo. Madison, 1892. K 8 R 21

WISCONSIN ACADEMY OF SCIENCE. Transactions. Vol. 9. Roy. 8vo. Madison, 1893. E

WISCONSIN STATE HISTORICAL SOCIETY. Collections of. Vols. 1-4, 6-12. 8vo. Madison, 1855-92. E

List of Books by Wisconsin authors exhibited at the World's Columbian Exposition, 1893. 8vo. Madison, 1893. K 7 Q 29

Proceedings of, at its meeting, held December, 1894. 8vo. Madison, 1895. E

WISCONSIN UNIVERSITY AGRICULTURAL EXPERIMENT STATION. Reports, 1884-93. 7 vols. roy. 8vo. Madison, 1884-93. E

WISE, Bernhard Ringrose. The Influence of Free-trade on Wages; or, why working-men should be Free-traders. 8vo. Sydney, 1884. MF 4 R 40

An Australian appeal to the English Democracy. 8vo. Sydney, 1885. MF 4 R 50

The Labour Question; or, Social Revolt and its Causes. 8vo. Sydney, 1890. MF 1 S 66

The Position of the Liberal Party. 8vo. Sydney, 1888. MF 2 Q 64

WISE, H., & Co. The New South Wales Post Office Commercial Directory for 1894-95. Roy. 8vo. Sydney, 1894. ME
New Zealand Post Office Directory, 1894-95. Roy 8vo. Dunedin, 1894. ME
Queensland Official Directory, 1894-95. Roy. 8vo. Brisbane, 1894. ME
South Australia Post Office Commercial Directory, 1895-96. Roy. 8vo. Adelaide, 1895. ME
Tasmania Post Office Directory, 1894-95. Roy. 8vo. Hobart, 1894. ME
Victoria Post Office Directory, 1893-94, 1895-96. 2 vols. roy. 8vo. Melb., 1893-95. ME
Western Australia Post Office Directory, 1895-96. Roy. 8vo. Perth, 1895. ME

WISEMAN, Comm. Sir W. Catalogue of Curiosities from the South Sea Islands. 8vo. Sydney, 1865.
MA 1 R 40

WISHART, Rt. Rev. George. Memoirs of Montrose. [*See* Montrose, Marquis of.] B 31 V 9

WIT, F. de. Magnum Mare del Zur cum Insula California. Fol. Amsterdam (n.d.) D 8 P 94 ‡

WITHERBY, Harry F. Forest Birds, their haunts and habits. 12mo. Lond., 1894. A 28 P 15

WITHIRINGTON, W. R. The Solomon Islands. (Roy. Geograph. Soc. of Australasia, Q. Branch, 3.) 8vo. Brisbane, 1888. ME 20

WITSEN, N. Noord en Oost Tartaryen; beholzende eene beschryving van verscheidene Tartersche en nabuurige Gewesten in de Noorder en Oostelykste deelen van Aziën en Europa. 2 vols. fol. Amsterdam, 1785.
D 30 R 12, 13 ‡

WÖHLER, Friedrich. Sketch of. [Thorpe, Dr. T. E.— Historical Chemistry.] C 17 R 2

WOLFE, Gen. James. [Life of]; by A. G. Bradley. 12mo. Lond., 1895. C 21 P 20

WOLFF, Dr. Emil. Aschen-Analysen von landwirthschaftlichen Producten, Fabrik-Abfällen und wildwachsenden Pflanzen. 4to. Berlin, 1871. A 15 Q 10 ‡

Die Ernährung der Landwirthschaftlichen Nutzthiere. Kritische Zusammenstellung. Roy. 8vo. Berlin, 1876. A 18 U 26

Die landwirthschaftlich-chemische Versuchsstation Hohenheim, 1866-70. Roy. 8vo. Berlin, 1871.
A 32 T 7

Die rationelle fütterung der landwirthschaftlichen Nutztiere. 8vo. Berlin, 1894. A 18 R 44

Grundlagen für die rationelle Fütterung des Pferdes. Roy. 8vo. Berlin, 1886. A 32 T 8

Kurze Anleitung zur Qualitativ-chemischen Untersuchung anorganischer Stoffe. 8vo. Berlin, 1867.
A 21 S 22

WOLFF, Dr. Emil—*contd.*
Praktische Düngerlehre mit einer Einleitung über die allgemeinen Nährstoffe der Pflanzen und die Eigenschaften des Kulturbodens. Gemeinverständlicher Leitfaden der Agrikultur-Chemie. 8vo. Berlin, 1892.
A 18 R 36

Zusammensetzung der Asche aller land und forstwirthschaftlich wichtigen Stoffe. 8vo. Stuttgart, 1865.
A 18 R 41

——— FUNKE, W., and KREUZHAGE, C. Versuche über das Verdauungsvermögen verschiedener Schafrassen für Erhaltungsfutter und Mastfutter. Roy. 8vo. Berlin, 1872. A 32 T 6

WOLFF, H. W. People's Banks: a Record of Social and Economic Success. 8vo. Lond., 1893. F 14 S 25

WOLFF, Sir Henry Drummond. Some Notes of the Past, 1870-91. 8vo. Lond., 1893. B 8 P 37

WOLL, Prof. F. W. Agricultural Calendar for 1895. 12mo. New York, 1895. A 18 P 13
Dairy Calendar for 1895. 12mo. New York, 1895.
A 18 P 12

WOLLASTON, H. N. P. Victoria: the Customs Handbook and Merchants' and Importers' Guide. Roy. 8vo. Melb., 1887. MF 1 S 57

WOLLE, Rev. Francis. Desmids of the United States and List of American Pediastrums. Illustrated. Roy. 8vo. Bethlehem, Pa., 1884. A 30 U 10

WOLLEY, Clive Phillipps-. Big Game Shooting. 2 vols. 8vo. Lond., 1894. A 29 Q 35, 36

WOLSELEY, Gen. Sir G. J., Viscount. Decline and Fall of Napoleon. 8vo. Lond., 1895. B 26 R 10
Life of John Churchill, Duke of Marlborough, to the accession of Queen Anne. 2 vols. 8vo. Lond., 1894.
C 14 V 15, 16

WOLVERTON, Lord. Five Months' Sport in Somali Land. 8vo. Lond., 1894. D 14 T 21

WOMANHOOD SUFFRAGE LEAGUE OF NEW SOUTH WALES. Report, 1893. 12mo. Sydney, 1893. ME 5 Q

WOMAN'S SUFFRAGE JOURNAL, The. June-Sept. 1891. Sm. 4to. Sydney, 1891. ME 18 Q

WOMEN'S CO-OPERATIVE SILK GROWING AND INDUSTRIAL ASSOCIATION, N.S.W., its Objects and Plans. 12mo. Sydney, 1894. MA 3 P 47

WOMEN'S SUFFRAGE JOURNAL, January, 1878-December, 1879. Sm. 4to. Manchester, 1878-79 E

WOOD, Miss Catherine E. Narrative of Sittings with the late Miss C. E. Wood, at Sydney. 12mo. Sydney, 1885. MG 2 R 48

WOOD, Catherine Jane. Hand-book for the Nursing of Sick Children; with a few Hints on their Management. 12mo. Lond., 1889. A 26 P 8

WOOD, De Volson. Theory of Turbines. Roy. 8vo. New York, 1895. A 22 T 12

WOOD, Esther. Dante Rossetti and the Pre-Raphaelite Movement. 8vo. Lond., 1894. A 23 R 10

WOOD, Gen. Sir Evelyn. The Crimea in 1854 and 1894. 8vo. Lond., 1895. B 12 U 34

WOOD, George. Rhymes to suit the Times: £10,000; or, Pity the Sorrows of a Poor Old Man. Sm. 4to. Sydney (n.d.) MJ 2 P 30 ‡

WOOD, Dr. George B., and BACHE, Dr. Franklin. Dispensatory of the United States of America. 17th ed., revised by Dr. H. C. Wood, Prof. J. P. Remington, and Prof. S. P. Sadtler. 8vo. Philad., 1894. A 26 V 13

WOOD, Dr. Henry. Columbus and his Discovery of America. [See Adams, Dr. E. B.] B 18 S 10

WOOD, Henry. Political Economy of Natural Law. 12mo. Boston, 1894. F 7 V 6

WOOD, Mrs. Henry. Memorials of; by her son. 8vo. Lond., 1894. C 21 Q 8

WOOD, Dr. Horatio C. Dispensatory of the United States. [See Wood, Dr. G. B.] A 26 V 13

WOOD, Rev. James. Dictionary of Quotations from Ancient and Modern, English and Foreign Sources. 8vo. Lond., 1893. K 20 T 3

WOOD, Jas. Memoir of; by T. Williams. 8vo. Geelong, 1889. MC 1 P 54

WOOD, Capt. John. Attempt to Discover a North-east Passage to China. [See Narbrough, Sir J.] MD 5 P 23

WOOD, John. Hardy Perennials and Old-fashioned Garden Flowers. 8vo. Lond., 1884. A 18 R 15

WOOD, John Dennistoun. On the Benefit to the Colonies of being Members of the British Empire. 8vo. Melb., 1876 MJ 3 Q 16

WOOD, Samuel. The Forcing Garden; or, How to Grow Early Fruits, Flowers, and Vegetables. 8vo. Lond., 1881. A 18 R 17

WOOD, Stanley L. One Hundred Illustrations to Capt. Sir Richard Burton's translation of the Arabian Nights. 8vo. Lond. (n.d.) Libr.

WOOD, Wallace. Editor.—Ideals of Life: a Symposium on the Coming Man, by Men of Science, Men of Letters, Men of Action, and Eminent Women. Illustrated. 8vo. New York, 1892. J 6 T 27

WOODARD, Capt. David. The Narrative of, and four seamen, who lost their ship while in a boat at sea, and surrendered themselves up to the Malays, in the Island of Celebes. 8vo. Lond., 1804. D 17 T 15

WOODBERRY, George Edward. Works of Edgar Allen Poe. [See Poe, E. A.] J 14 R 1, 2.

WOODBURN, Dr. James Albert. Causes of the American Revolution. (Johns Hopkins University Studies, 10.) 8vo. Baltimore, 1892. B 18 S 10

Higher Education in Indiana. 8vo Wash., 1891. G 18 R 22

WOODCOCK, C. A. J. The C.P.S. Manual: a plain Guide to the duties of the Clerk of Petty Sessions in Queensland. 12mo. Brisb., 1883. MF 1 P 55

WOODHEAD, Dr. German Sims. Bacteria and their Products. 8vo. Lond., 1891. A 26 R 3
[See Journal of Pathology.] E

WOOD-MARTIN, W. G. [See Martin, W. G. Wood-.]

WOODS, H. Southdown Sheep: their History, Breeding, and Management; a Lecture. (Inst. of Agricult., Lond.) 8vo. Lond., 1884. A 18 R 28

Ensilage: its influence upon British Agriculture: a Lecture. (Inst. of Agricult., Lond.) 8vo. Lond., 1884. A 18 R 28

WOODS, J. D. The Province of South Australia; with a Sketch of the Northern Territory, by H. D. Wilson. 8vo. Adelaide, 1894. MB 1 Q 48

WOODS, Wm. J. A Visit to Victoria. 12mo. Lond., 1886. MD 5 Q 17

WOODWARD, A. S. Fossil Fishes of the Talbragar Beds. [See N. S. Wales Geol. Survey, Memoirs, Palæontology, 9.] ME

WOODWARD, Dr. George Paul Minchin. New South Wales Railways: Ambulance Handbook. 2nd ed. 12mo. Sydney, 1892. MA 2 P 55

WOODWARD, Harry P. Mining Hand-book to the Colony of Western Australia. Ray. 8vo. Perth, 1894. MA 3 R 33

WOOLCOCK, John L. Queensland: Divisional Boards Acts; being the Acts relating to Local Government outside the Boundaries of Municipalities. Roy. 8vo. Brisb., 1888. MF 1 S 44

Queensland Statutes. [See Queensland.]

———— and SCOTT, George. Acts and Rules relating to the District Court, Queensland. 8vo. Brisb., 1892 MF 1 S 63

WOOLCOTT and CLARKE'S Map of the city of Sydney, 1854. 12mo. Sydney, 1854. MD 1 P 43

WOOLLS, Rev. Dr. Wm. In Memory of R. D. Fitzgerald. [Poem.] 8vo. Sydney, 1892. MA 1 R 1 ‡
Sermon on the Centenary of the Colony. 12mo. Sydney, 1888. 12mo. MG 2 R 52
Sermon preached on the Life and Character of Mrs. William Bowman. [*See* Bowman, Mrs. William.] MG 2 Q 20

WOOLNER, Thos. My Beautiful Lady. 12mo. Lond., 1864. H 10 T 16

WOOLNOUGH, Rev. G. British Possession and Settlement in South-eastern New Guinea. (Roy. Geograph. Soc. of Australasia, Q. Branch, 2.) 8vo. Brisb., 1887. ME

WORCESTER, Dr. A. Training Schools for Nurses in small cities. 8vo. Boston, 1893. A 33 T 16

—— and ATKINSON, W. Small Hospitals: Establishment and Maintenance, and Suggestions for Hospital Architecture. 8vo. New York, 1894. A 19 Q 4

WORDINGHAM, C. H. Measurement of Electric Currents. [*See* Swinburne, J.] A 21 P 23

WORDSWORTH, Rt. Rev. Christopher. Annals of My Life, 1847-56. 8vo. Lond., 1893. C 17 T 13
On the Duration and Degrees of future Rewards and Punishments. 12mo. West Maitland, 1878. MG 2 R 55

WORDSWORTH, Wm. Poems of. New ed. Roy. 8vo. Lond., 1854. H 5 U 11
Essay on. [*See* Bagehot, W.—Literary Studies.] J 9 P 22-24
In Wordsworth's Country. [*See* Burroughs, J.—Fresh Fields.] J 16 T 35
[Life of]; by H. C. Ewart. [*See* Masson, Prof. D.—Footsteps of the Poets.] J 6 R 43
Plaster Cast of. [*See* Hutton, L.—Portraits in Plaster.] A 23 V 13
Selections from. [*See* Harlin, T.] MJ 1 U 34
Sketch of the Work of. [*See* Dawson, W. J.—Makers of Modern English.] H 10 S 14
Sketch of. [*See* Bell, Rev. Dr. C. D.—Some of our English Poets.] C 21 P 11

WORK: the Illustrated Weekly Journal for Mechanics. Vol. 9, January-July, 1895. Fol. Lond., 1895. E

WORMELL, Richard. Electricity in the service of Man; revised by R. M. Walmsley. Illustrated. Roy. 8vo. Lond., 1893. A 21 V 11

WORSAAE, Jens Jakob Asmussen. Industrial Arts of Denmark, from the earliest times to the Danish Conquest of England. 8vo. Lond., 1882. A 23 R 35

WORSFOLD, W. Basil. South Africa. 8vo. Lond., 1895. B 1 P 20
Visit to Java, with an Account of the Founding of Singapore. 8vo. Lond., 1893. D 17 V 6

WORSNOP, Thos. Pre-historic Arts of the Aborigines of Australia. 8vo. Adelaide, 1887. MA 3 V 37

WORTHINGTON, T. Locke. The Dwellings of the Poor and Weekly Wage-earners in and around Towns. 12mo. Lond., 1893. A 19 P 2

WORTHINGTON LECTURES, The: being a Course of Study of Bible Interpretations as taught by the Students of Truth. Vol. 1. 8vo. Christchurch, N.Z., 1894. MG 2 R 26

WORTLEY, A. J. Stuart-. Shooting the Partridge. [*See* Macpherson, Rev. H. A.] A 28 Q 20
Shooting the Grouse. [*See* Macpherson, Rev. H. A.] A 23 Q 43

WOTTON, Sir Henry. Life of. [*See* Walton, Izaak] C 19 V 6

WRAGGE, Clement L. A Brief Account of the Work and Aims of the Chief Weather Bureau, Brisbane. (Roy. Geograph. Soc. of Australasia, Q. Branch, 7.) 8vo. Brisbane, 1892. ME 20
Remarks on the Red Glow. (Trans. Roy. Soc. S. Australia, 7.) 8vo. Adelaide, 1885. ME 1 S
Scientific Observations made during the Voyage of the *Maranoa* from London to Adelaide, 1883. (Trans. Roy. Soc., S. Australia, 9.) 8vo. Adelaide, 1887. ME 1 S

WRAY, Miss F. H. The Importance of Geographical Study. (Roy. Geog. Soc. Australasia, Vic. Branch, 6.) 8vo. Melb., 1888. ME 20

WRECK OF THE DUNBAR: a Narrative of. (Pam.) 8vo. Sydney, 1857. MG 1 Q 53

WREN, Sir Christopher. Inigo Jones and Wren. [*See* Loftie, W. J.] A 19 V 6

WRENCH, Matilda. Visits to Female Prisoners at Home and Abroad. 12mo. Lond., 1852. MF 1 P 61

WRIGHT, A. Elements of Agriculture: being facts necessary to make farming successful. 8vo. Hobart, 1857. MA 1 U 5

WRIGHT, C. H. Gardeners' Dictionary. [*See* Johnson, C. W.] A 20 T 8

WRIGHT, Carroll Davidson. Phosphate Industry. [*See* United States.—Bur. of Labor.] E
The Slums of Baltimore, Chicago, New York, and Philadelphia. 8vo. Wash., 1894. F 9 T 20

WRIGHT, Dr. Chas. Romley Alder. Animal and Vegetable Fixed Oils, Fats, Butters, and Waxes: their Preparation and Properties. 8vo. Lond., 1894. A 25 S 1

WRIGHT, Claude Falls. Outline of the Principles of Modern Theosophy. 12mo. Boston, 1894. G 3 P 20

WRIGHT, Prof. Edward P. Alcyonaria. [*See* Thomson, Sir C. W., and Murray, Dr. J.—Voyage of H.M.S. *Challenger*.] A 6 †

WRIGHT, G. Australian and American Commercial Directory and Gazetteer, 1881-82. Roy. 8vo. New York, 1881. ME 6 Q
Australia, India, China, and Japan Trade Directory and Gazetteer, 1893-94. Roy. 8vo. New York, 1894. E

WRIGHT, G. P., and MARQUIS, D. Views around Brisbane. Fol. Brisbane, 1877. MD 3 Q 11 ‡

WRIGHT, Prof. George Frederick. Man and the Glacial Period. 8vo. Lond., 1892. A 24 Q 20

WRIGHT, John. The Fruitgrower's Guide. 3 vols. 4to. Lond., 1892-94. A 5 R 22-24 †

WRIGHT, Lewis. Book of Pigeons. [See Fulton, R.] A 12 T 14 †
WRIGHT, Mark R. Heat. 8vo. Lond., 1893. A 21 P 32

WRIGHT, Theodore. The Queensland Horticulturist and Gardener's Guide; also, Hints to New-Comers, by P. Fletcher. 8vo. Brisb., 1886. MA 1 P 59

WRIGHT, Thos. Life of Daniel Defoe. 8vo. Lond., 1894. C 18 T 11
Life of William Cowper. 8vo. Lond., 1892. C 15 P 9

WRIGHT, Thos., M.A., &c. Political Songs of England: John to Edward II. [See Bibliotheca Curiosa.] J 18 Q 8-11

WRIGHT, Dr. Wm. Account of Palmyra and Zenobia. 8vo. Lond., 1895. D 17 S 11
The Brontës in Ireland; or, Facts stranger than Fiction. 8vo. Lond., 1893. C 19 Q 7
Short History of Syriac Literature. 8vo. Lond., 1894. B 36 P 4

WRIGHTSON, Prof. John. Conditions influencing Land Drainage: a Lecture. (Inst. of Agricult., Lond.) 8vo. Lond., 1884. A 18 R 23

WRIGHTSON, Richard Heber. History of Modern Italy, from the First French Revolution to 1850. 8vo. Lond., 1855. B 30 Q 14

WRIXON, Henry John. Self-Government in Victoria, its present condition and the questions it has to deal with. 8vo. Melb., 1876. MJ 3 Q 13

WULF, Dr. Maurice de. [See De Wulf, Dr. M.]

WUNDT, Wilhelm. Human and Animal Psychology; translated from the German by J. E. Creighton and E. B. Titchener. 8vo. Lond., 1894. A 26 V 12
Philosophische Studien. Bände 1-10. Roy. 8vo. Leip., 1888-94. G 6 T 1-D

WURTZ, Chas. Adolphe. Elements of Modern Chemistry. 5th American ed., revised by Dr. W. H. Greene and Dr. H. F. Keller. 8vo. Philad., 1895. A 21 R 34

WYATT, C. W. Monograph of the *Hirundinidæ*. [See Sharpe, Dr. R. B.] A 13 P 22, 23†

WYATT, Francis. The Phosphates of America: with Practical Treatises on the Manufacture of Sulphuric Acid, Acid Phosphate, Phosphoric Acid, and Concentrated Super-phosphates, and Selected Methods of Chemical Analysis. 3rd ed. 8vo. New York, 1892. A 18 U 22

WYCHERLEY, William. Plays. 8vo. Lond., 1735. H 3 U 17

WYCLIF, John. [See Wiclif, John.]

WYLIE, Rev. Dr. James Aiken. Disruption Worthies: a Memorial of 1843; with an Historical Sketch of the Free Church of Scotland from 1843 down to the present time. 2 vols. sm. 4to. Edinb., 1881. G 13 V 34, 35

WYLIE, James Hamilton. History of England under Henry IV. Vol. 2. 1405-1406. 12mo. Lond., 1894. B 16 P 9

WYLIE, Laura J. Studies in the Evolution of English Criticism. 12mo. Boston, 1894. J 0 8 8

WYOMING. Wyoming Central Association. 8vo. New York, 1893. D 15 T 5

WYOMING AGRICULTURAL COLLEGE AND EXPERIMENT STATION. Reports, 1891, 1892. 8vo. Laramie, 1892-93. E
Bulletins, 1-8. (*Bound with Wyoming University Annual Report*, 1892.) 8vo. Laramie, 1892. E
  1. On the Organization and Work of the Station.
  2. Plant Lice.
  3. Sugar Beet in Wyoming.
  4. Meteorology, 1891.
Bulletins, 5-10. (*Bound with Wyoming Agric. College Report*, 1892.) 8vo. Laramie, 1893. E
  5. Best Varieties and Breeds for Wyoming.
  6. Soils of the Agricultural Experiment Farms.
  7. Insecticides.
  8. Irrigation and Duty of Water.
  9. Sugar Beets in 1892.
  10. Meteorology for 1892.
Bulletins, 11-16. 8vo. Laramie, 1893. E
  11. Crop Report for 1892.
  12. Ground Squirrels (Gophers).
  13. The Feeding and Management of Cattle.
  14. Geology of the Wyoming Experiment Farms, and Notes on the Mineral Resources of the State.
  15. The Winter-killing of Trees and Shrubs.
  16. Grasses and Forage Plants.

WYOMING UNIVERSITY. First Annual Report, 1892. 8vo. (n.p. n.d.) E
Catalogue for 1891-92, and Announcement for 1892-93. (*Bound with Wyoming University, 1st Report.*) 8vo. Laramie, 1892. E

WYON, Alfred Benjamin and Allen. The Great Seals of England. Fol. Lond, 1887. B 39 Q 12‡

WYTFLIET, C. Descriptionis Ptolemaicæ avgmentvm siue Occidentis notitia, breui commentario illustrata, et hac secunda editione magna sui parte aucta. [With 18 Maps.] Sm. fol. Lovanii, 1599. D 19 V 16

X

XENOPHON. Anabasis, Book 2. (Greek Text.) 12mo. Melb., 1870.   M II 1 U 36
   Opera, Græce et Latine, ex editionibus Schneideri et Zeunii. Accedit Index Latinus. 10 vols. 12mo. Edinb., 1811.   J 11 U 36–45
   Works of; translated by H. G. Dakyns. Vols. 1 and 2. 8vo. Lond., 1890–02.   J 11 S 40, 41

Y

Y., E. W. [*See* Want of Lucidity.]   G 16 S 51

YACHT-RACING CALENDAR AND REVIEW for 1892–93. 8vo. Lond., 1893.   E

YALE UNIVERSITY. Catalogue of, 1893–95. 2 vols. 8vo. New Haven, 1893–95.   E
   Report for the year ending 1894. 8vo. New Haven, 1895.   E
   Report of the Sheffield Scientific School, 1891–93. 8vo. New Haven, 1893.   E

YALWALL VICTORY GOLD-MINING CO. Rules. 8vo. (n.p.) 1889.   MF 4 R 35

YARRANTON, Andrew. Account of. [*See* Dove, P. E.—Political Science.]   F 7 R 28

YARRINGTON, Rev. W. H. H. Approximate Chronology of the Life of our Lord Jesus Christ. 8vo. West Maitland, 1893.   MG 1 S 46
   Australian Verses. 12mo. Melb., 1892.   M II 1 U 51

YATES, Wm. Memoirs of John Chamberlain, late Missionary in India. 8vo. Lond., 1826.   C 2 V 31

YEAR-BOOK OF PHARMACY; comprising Abstracts of Papers relating to Pharmacy, Materia Medica, and Chemistry, contributed to British and Foreign Journals; with the Transactions of the British Pharmaceutical Conference, 1874–94. 21 vols. 8vo. Lond., 1874–94.   E

YEAR-BOOK OF SCIENCE: edited for 1892, by Prof. T. G. Bonney. 8vo. Lond., 1893.   E

YEAR-BOOK OF SCIENTIFIC AND LEARNED SOCIETIES OF GREAT BRITAIN AND IRELAND; comprising lists of the papers read during 1893–95. 3 vols. 8vo. Lond., 1893–95.   E

YEATS, Wm. Butler. A Book of Irish Verse. 8vo. Lond., 1895.   II 9 U 17
   The Celtic Twilight: Men and Women, Dhouls and Faeries. 18mo. Lond., 1893.   J 7 P 43
   Works of Wm. Blake. [*See* Blake, W.]   J 4 U 11–13

YELLAND, Wm. Henry. Essay on Horses. Roy. 8vo. Prahran, 1886.   MA 3 R 37

YELLOW-BOOK, The: an Illustrated Quarterly. Vols. 1–7. Sm. 4to. Lond., 1894–95.   E

YEO, Prof. Isaac Burney. Food, in Health and Disease. 5th thousand. 12mo. Lond., 1893.   A 26 P 9
   Manual of Medical Treatment, or Clinical Therapeutics. 2 vols. 8vo. Lond., 1893.   A 13 Q 30, 31

YEO, John. Steam and the Marine Steam Engine. 8vo. Lond., 1894.   A 22 S 10

YITTADAIRN. [*See* Rusden, G. W.]

YONGE, Charles Duke. An English-Greek Lexicon. 4to. Lond., 1883.   K 16 T 29

YOUMANS, Edward Livingston. Life and Letters of, comprising Correspondence with Spencer, Huxley, Tyndall, and others; by J. Fiske. 8vo. Lond., 1894.   C 16 R 21
   Sketch of his Life; by J. Fiske. 8vo. New York, 1894.   C 21 Q 11

YOUNG, Arthur. Tour in Ireland, 1776–79; edited by A. W. Hutton. 2 vols. 12mo. Lond., 1892.   D 18 P 10, 11

YOUNG, Edward. Poetical Works of. 12mo. Lond., 1853.   H 7 U 28
   The Revenge: a Tragedy. [*See* London Stage, 1.]   H 2 S 33

YOUNG, F. Chilton-. Home Carpentry for Handy Men. 8vo. Lond., 1895.   A 25 U 12

YOUNG, Frederick. England and her Colonies at the Paris Exhibition. 8vo. Lond., 1878.   MJ 3 Q 10

YOUNG, Henry. Wood's Point Directory. [*See* Butler and Brooke, Messrs.]   ME

YOUNG, William. Killed by Vaccination. 2nd ed. 12mo. Lond., 1887.   A 26 Q 28

YOUNG AUSTRALIA: the Official Organ of the Imperial Federation League in Australia. Vol. 4, 1890. Sm. fol. Melb., 1890.   ME

YOUNG MISSIONARY, A. [*See* New Zealand.]

YOUNGHUSBAND, Capt. George John. On Short Leave to Japan. 8vo. Lond., 1894.   D 17 Q 16

YOUATT, William. The Complete Grazier and Farmers' and Cattle-breeders' Assistant. 13th ed. Re-written, &c., by William Fream. Roy. 8vo. Lond., 1893.   A 18 U 18

YUILLE, W. C. [*See* Australian Stud Book.]   MA 1 R 33–36

YUNG, Emile. Zermatt and the Valley of the Vièges; translated by Mrs. W. Robinson. 4to. Genova, 1894.   D 36 T 2 ‡

Z

ZAHEL, C. P. Fin de Siècle Economics: a complete solution of the Social Problem; by "Millennius." 8vo. Sydney, 1894. MF 4 R 50

ZAHNER, Robert. Transmission of Power by Compressed Air. 2nd ed. 18mo. New York, 1890. A 21 P 25

ZARAGOZA, J. Descubrimientos de los espanoles en el mar del Sur y en las costas de la Nueva Guinea. (Boletin de la Sociedad Geografica de Madrid.) Roy. 8vo. Madrid, 1878. MD 7 U 20

Regiones Austriales. [See Quiros, P. F. de.] MB 2 R 47-49

ZEALANDIA: a Monthly Magazine of New Zealand Literature; by New Zealand Authors. Christmas 1889. 8vo. Dunedin, 1889. ME 3 S

ZEITSCHRIFT FÜR ETHNOLOGIE. Organ der Berliner Gesellschaft für Anthropologie, Ethnologie, und Ungeschichte. Bände 1-26. 26 vols. (in 34). 8vo. Berlin, 1868-94. E

General Register zu. (Bände 1-22.) 8vo. Berlin, 1891. E

Supplement, 1892. Fol. Berlin, 1892. E

ZEITSCHRIFT FÜR WISSENSCHAFLICHE ZOOLOGIE. Bände 54-58. 8vo. Leip., 1892-94. E

ZENOBIA. Palmyra and Zenobia. [See Wright, Dr. W.] D 17 S 11

ZERFFI, Dr. G. O. Faust. [See Goethe, J. W. von.] H 1 U 4

ZIEHEN, Dr. Theodor. Physiological Psychology; translated by Dr. C. C. Van Liew and Dr. O. W. Beyer. 2nd ed. 8vo. Lond., 1895. G 2 U 3

ZIEMSSEN, Dr. Hugo W. von. Cyclopædia of the Practice of Medicine. Vol. 20. General Index. Roy. 8vo. New York, 1881. K 9 Q 23

Supplement to Cyclopædia of Medicine. [See Peabody, Dr. G. L] K 9 Q 24

Hand-book of Diseases of the skin. Illustrated. 4to. New York, 1885. A 26 V 10

Hand-book of General Therapeutics. 7 vols. 8vo. Lond., 1885-87. A 33 T 8-14

ZIMMERMANN, Dr. A. Botanical Microtechnique; translated by J. C. Humphrey. 8vo. New York, 1893. A 20 T 11

ZIMMERN, Helen. Holland. [See Amicis, E. de.] B 25 R 10, 11

Women of Shakespeare. [See Lewes, Dr. L.] J 6 T 5

ZITTEL, Prof. Karl A. Palæozoologie. (Handbuch der Palæontologie.) Bände 1-4. Roy. 8vo. München, 1876-93. A 30 P

ZIWET, Prof. A. Elementary Treatise on Theoretical Mechanics. Parts 1 and 2. 2 vols. 8vo. New York, 1893. A 25 U 5, 6

Part 1. Kinematics.
Part 2. Introduction to Dynamics; Statics.

ZOLA, Emile. A Biographical and Critical Study; by R. H Sherard. 8vo. Lond., 1893. C 19 R 18

ZOOLOGICAL RECORD, The; being Records of Zoological Literature for 1892-93. 2 vols. 8vo. Lond., 1893-94. E

ZOOLOGICAL SOCIETY OF NEW SOUTH WALES. 9th and 10th Annual Reports. 8vo. Sydney, 1888-89. ME 6 S

ZOOLOGICAL SOCIETY OF LONDON. Proceedings, 1892-94. 2 vols. 8vo. Lond., 1892-94. E

Transactions, Vol 13, pts. 4-9. 4to. Lond., 1892-94. E

ZOOLOGISCHE STATION ZU NEAPEL. Fauna und Flora des Golfes von Neapel. Monographie 2-12, 16-21. 4to. Leipzig, 1880-94. E

2. Fierasfer.
3. Pantopoda.
4. Corallina.
5. Die Chaetognathen.
6. Caprelliden.
7. Die Cystoscireen.
8. Bangiaceen.
9. Die Actinien.
10. Doliolum.
11. Die Polycladen.
12. Cryptonemiaceen.
16. Pelagische Copepoden, mit Atlas.
20. Grammarini, con Atlante.
21. Ostracoden.

ZOOLOGISCHER JAHRESBERICHT für 1891-93. Roy. 8vo. Berlin 1893-94. E

ZOTTI, R. Orlando Furioso di Ariosto. [See Ariosto, L.] H 10 U 10-13

ZWINGLI, U., and the Early Swiss Reformers. [See Lottany, G. T.—Popular History of the Reformation.] G 14 Q 33

www.ingramcontent.com/pod-product-compliance
Lightning Source LLC
Chambersburg PA
CBHW022044230426
43672CB00008B/1067